W9-BLM-040

Relationship Section

Rotated Alphabetical Terms Section

Term Clusters Section

Margin Index: To use, bend pages of book backward and follow margin index to pages with black edge markers.

THESAURUS

of Psychological Index Terms

30th Anniversary
1974–2004

TENTH EDITION

Lisa A. Gallagher, *Editor*

BENEDICTINE UNIVERSITY LIBRARY
IN THE KINDLON HALL OF LEARNING
5700 COLLEGE ROAD
LISLE, IL 60532-0900

American Psychological Association
Washington, DC

150.5
T413
2005

Copyright © 2005 by the American Psychological Association. All rights reserved. Except as permitted under the United States Copyright Act of 1976, no part of this publication may be reproduced or distributed in any form or by any means, or stored in a database or retrieval system, without the prior written permission of the publisher.

Published by
American Psychological Association
750 First Street, NE
Washington, DC 20002
www.apa.org

To order
APA Order Department
P.O. Box 92984
Washington, DC 20090-2984
Tel: (800) 374-2721; Direct: (202) 336-5510
Fax: (202) 336-5502; TDD/TTY: (202) 336-6123
Online: www.apa.org/books/
E-mail: order@apa.org

In the U.K., Europe, Africa, and the Middle East, copies may be ordered from
American Psychological Association
3 Henrietta Street
Covent Garden, London
WC2E 8LU England

Typeset by PageCentre, Inc., Tempe, AZ

Printer: Automated Graphics Systems, Inc., White Plains, MD
Cover Designer: Naylor Design, Washington, DC

Library of Congress Cataloging-in-Publication Data

Thesaurus of psychological index terms / Lisa A. Gallagher, editor. — 10th ed.
    p. cm.
  Includes bibliographical references.
  ISBN 1–59147–121–4 (alk. paper)
  1. Subject headings—Psychology. I. Gallagher, Lisa A. II. American Psychological Association.

Z695.1.P7T48 2005
025.4'915—dc22   2004010022

British Library Cataloguing-in-Publication Data
A CIP record is available from the British Library.

Printed in the United States of America
Tenth Edition

Table of Contents

Preface

The Tenth Edition of the *Thesaurus of Psychological Index Terms*® marks three decades of dynamic growth for the American Psychological Association, for PsycINFO®, and for the Thesaurus. From the first publication of Roget's thesaurus in 1852, thesauri have been used as a popular research tool to help readers understand the relationship of terminology and identify commonly used terms. The *Thesaurus of Psychological Index Terms*, first published in 1974, has an influential role in research because it reflects the most current trends found in the behavioral and social science literature. The Thesaurus can help authenticate the use of terms as they become accepted nomenclature. This reference is the backbone of any research in psychology because it provides a rich source of concepts that can be used for the most precise search in the PsycINFO or PsycARTICLES® electronic databases.

This edition was developed in conjunction with a team of experts who come from many perspectives within the vast field of psychology. This group collaborated with our editor to update the "language of psychology" as it appears today in the scholarly literature. The *Thesaurus* also links recently added controlled vocabulary with a historical note that helps the researcher navigate the literature to the source of the original concept. The historical links make the *Thesaurus* a more powerful tool to identify word hierarchies that are extremely helpful in the research process.

We encourage your use of the Tenth Edition of the *Thesaurus of Psychological Index Terms* as a multi-disciplinary research and teaching tool for students in psychology, social science, and communications.

Best wishes in all of your research endeavors!

Gary R. VandenBos, PhD
Publisher, American Psychological Association

History of the *Thesaurus*

Psychology has multiple roots in the older disciplines of philosophy, medicine, education, and physics. As a result, the vocabulary of the psychological literature is characterized by considerable diversity. As the field of psychology has grown, each new generation of psychologists has added to the vocabulary in attempting to describe their studies and perceptions of behavioral processes. This uncontrolled evolution of the psychological vocabulary has contributed to complex literature search and retrieval problems.

In response to these problems, the American Psychological Association developed the first edition of the *Thesaurus of Psychological Index Terms* in 1974. This controlled vocabulary was designed to provide a means of structuring the subject matter of psychology and to serve as an efficient indexing and retrieval tool. Since the publication of the first edition, the PsycINFO indexing staff has charted trends and newly emerging areas of interest reflected in the psychological literature as a way of updating and revising the *Thesaurus*. The present edition of the *Thesaurus* represents a concerted effort to provide a more valuable tool for researchers, practitioners, information science providers, students, and others interested in the field of psychology.

First Edition (1974)

Term selection was the first step in the development of the 1974 edition. The 800 index terms used by *Psychological Abstracts* (PA) prior to 1973 and a list of the frequencies of the occurrence of single words in titles and abstracts in PA over a 5-year period were taken as the starting points. In addition, phrases and terms were obtained from key-word-in-context (KWIC) lists produced from 10,000 titles of journal articles, books, separates, and dissertations. Inclusion/exclusion rules were developed, with a resulting list of about 3,000 potential terms reviewed by subject matter specialists for final selection. These terms were arranged to express interrelationships, including use, used for, broader, narrower, and related categories.

Second Edition (1977)

The first revision of the *Thesaurus*, which included 204 new terms, was published in 1977. Some 180 never-used terms from the original *Thesaurus* were deleted, and a rotated alphabetical term section was added to make it faster and easier to find index terms.

Third Edition (1982)

The second revision of the *Thesaurus*, which included 240 new terms, was published in 1982. The most significant change introduced in the third edition was the development of scope notes or definitions for more than 1,300 terms. In addition, superscript dates were added to all terms to indicate the date of inclusion in the *Thesaurus* vocabulary.

Fourth Edition (1985)

The third revision of the *Thesaurus* included 247 new terms and 162 new and revised scope notes. Posting notes (PN) were added to each index term to indicate the number of times the terms had been used for indexing. Also, each postable index term was given a unique five-digit subject code (SC) that can be used in online searching as an alternative to entering the term text.

Fifth Edition (1988)

An important change occurred during the fourth revision—the incorporation of all nonpostable terms into the Rotated Alphabetical Terms Section. These terms appeared in nonbold italic print and were marked with a star (★). More than 250 postable terms and 100 nonpostable terms were added to the vocabulary. In addition, more than 100 new scope notes were added and more than 75 scopes notes were revised. Because the *Thesaurus* had been in use for many years, an extensive hierarchy reconstruction project was begun with the intention of continuing the process for development of future editions.

Sixth Edition (1991)

The sixth revision of the *Thesaurus* included the addition of 200 new postable terms and 100 new nonpostable terms. More than 50 scope notes were rewritten and 120 new scope notes were added to the vocabulary. In a continuing effort to make the *Thesaurus* more useful, the Relationship Section was enhanced by the addition of down arrows (↓) in each main term's hierarchy next to narrower and related terms that also have narrower terms. Term Clusters were developed to present a collection of index terms based on conceptual similarity to assist users unfamiliar with the *Thesaurus* vocabulary. As in earlier editions, revision of existing hierarchical relationships continued.

Seventh Edition (1994)

The 20-year anniversary edition of the *Thesaurus* was marked with many changes to the Relationship Section. Approximately 220 new postable terms and 115 new nonpostable terms were added and nearly 110 new scope notes were added to the existing 1,970 scope notes. These included scope notes for terms new to the seventh edition as well as terms from previous editions. Revision of almost 2,000 hierarchies also occurred to increase their accuracy and to ensure consistent relationships. The hierarchies for array terms, conceptually broad terms identified with a slash (/), were reconstructed for the first time since the inception of the *Thesaurus* and the slash was removed. Posting notes were updated to indicate how many times each postable term was used to index a record through June 1993. A new "Neuropsychology and Neurology" cluster was added to the Term Clusters Section complete with 7 subclusters. Finally, the Rotated Alphabetical Terms section was completely revised so that nonpostable terms appeared for the first time with their "Use" reference.

Eighth Edition (1997)

The seventh revision of the *Thesaurus* included the addition of 254 new postable terms and 191 new nonpostable terms. More than 200 term hierarchies were revised, and 115 new scope notes were added. The 2,026 existing scope notes were reviewed for clarity, and more than 225 of these were revised or rewritten. In addition, close to 60 terms changed from a postable to a nonpostable status and were referred to a synonymous term or a term of broader scope. Finally, all index terms that contained the word "handicapped" (e.g., Multiply Handicapped) were reviewed and changed to "disabled" (e.g., Multiply Disabled) to reflect the changing terminology in the literature.

Ninth Edition (2001)

The ninth revision of the *Thesaurus* included the addition of 100 new postable terms and 50 nonpostable terms. More than 375 hierarchies were revised, 13 new scope notes were added, and more than 155 scope notes were revised to improve clarity. In addition, approximately 10 terms changed from a nonpostable to postable status, and 26 terms changed from a postable to nonpostable status, with reference to a synonymous term or a term of broader scope. With the 1998 advent of the Population/Location, Age Group, and Form/Content Type document identifier fields, 213 terms with content areas overlapping those fields were deleted from the *Thesaurus* entirely. In an effort to use language that is consistent with that used by the general public, to expand terms that had historically been truncated (due to former system constraints), and to correct spelling errors from previous *Thesaurus* editions, 16 terms received spelling or format modifications. A Computer Cluster and its 8 Subclusters were added to the Term Clusters Section, and the Geographic Cluster and its Subclusters were deleted. Lastly, because of insufficient usage or overlap with other terminology, 25 terms were removed from the *Thesaurus* altogether.

Development of the Tenth Edition (2004)

NEW TERMS

The 30-year anniversary of the *Thesaurus* included many important changes. Since the publication of the ninth edition, 200 new postable index terms have been added to the tenth edition. The new terms represent concepts and terminology expressed in the psychological and behavioral literature as well as the literature found in areas related to psychology, for example education, medicine, and sociology. In addition, new terminology was developed for classical psychological concepts requiring appropriate controlled vocabulary. These additions bring the total number of postable index terms to 5,437, nonpostable to 2,449, and the total number of terms to 7,886.

In determining whether terms should be included, staff considered (a) the frequency of the term's occurrence in the psychological literature, (b) the term's potential usefulness in providing access to a concept, (c) the term's relationship to or overlap with existing *Thesaurus* terminology, (d) user feedback, and (e) lack of potential application problems by indexing staff. Every term has been researched extensively and integrated into the hierarchies in the Relationship Section. The Rotated Alphabetical Terms Section has been updated with the new terms as well. See Tables 1–6 on pages xi–xvi for a listing of all new postable index terms, nonpostable index terms, and other significant term changes occurring in this edition.

OTHER CHANGES

Term Hierarchies

Extensive revision of hierarchical relationships occurred during the development of this edition. Hierarchies were examined to ensure accuracy, completeness, and consistency. In a continuation of our efforts to examine hierarchical structures with each edition, over 37 hierarchies were revised to minimize any misleading and redundant relationships as well as to maintain a coherent and cohesive vocabulary structure.

Scope Notes

To the existing 2,213 scope notes, 13 new scope notes (SNs) were added. Scope notes were added to terms with ambiguous meanings, terms that need to be differentiated from existing terms, or terms with restricted indexing usage. In addition, 39 scope notes were also rewritten or revised to improve clarity, to broaden or restrict the term's range of application, or to accommodate new 2004 terms.

Historical Notes

This new *Thesaurus* feature provides information about changes to a term, the range of years a term was in use, and instructions for searching. In past editions, a term's historical information was captured in the scope note, but with the addition of the historical note (HN), the scope note will be used primarily for definitions of terms. Nearly 680 historical notes were added to the *Thesaurus*.

Nonpostable Terminology

In an effort to provide additional entry points into the *Thesaurus* vocabulary and to direct users more efficiently to terms "not used" for indexing, 123 new nonpostable terms were added to this edition. See Table 2 on page xii for a complete list of these terms.

Posting Notes

Primarily as an aid to psychologists, researchers, librarians, and students, each postable index term in the Relationship Section appears with a posting note (PN) reference indicating how many times that index term has been used in the indexing process at the time of this publication. These posting notes are based on accumulations of term usage through March 2004.

Retrospective Indexing Project

In an effort to provide users with the most comprehensive search results, records from the past 10 years were retrospectively indexed (re-indexed) with new tenth edition terms. The number of posting notes for these terms reflect the number of records re-indexed. In past editions, index terms with posting notes (PN) = 0 were new terms that were added to the *Thesaurus*. These terms had 0 postings because they had not been used in the indexing process as of the publication date and had not accumulated any postings. More than 17,200 PsycINFO records were re-indexed with new terms for this edition. The posting note number for new terms indicates how many PsycINFO records were re-indexed.

Change in Term Status

Terms with very low postings, obsolete and out-of-date terms, and terms that have undergone change in usage in the field of psychology were identified for a change in status during this revision. In this edition, 23 terms changed from a nonpostable to a postable status, 23 terms changed from a postable to nonpostable status, and 11 nonpostable terms changed to a different postable counterpart. See Table 3 on page xiii for a full listing of these changes.

Discontinued and Deleted Terms That Were Removed and Replaced

In a continuing effort to increase precision, to decrease overlap and the inconsistent use of terms, and to reflect current terminology, 23 terms were changed from postable to nonpostable status. Although these discontinued terms appear in the *Thesaurus* as nonpostable and are no longer used in indexing, each term is accompanied by a historical note designating the period during which it was used. For these 23 discontinued terms, records once containing such terms were replaced with their appropriate postable counterparts; the nonpostable terms were then removed from the records. One term was deleted from the *Thesaurus* entirely and all records containing it were replaced with a new postable term. Table 6 on page xvi contains a list of these discontinued terms and of the postable terms that replaced them.

Deleted Terms

Because of insufficient usage or overlap with other terminology, 30 terms were removed from the *Thesaurus* entirely. Of these 30 deleted terms, 20 were outdated and insufficiently used test names. These terms were deleted and removed from all records containing them and mapped to the Tests/Measures field. Five of the deleted terms were nonpostable, and one deleted term was removed from all records containing it and replaced with a new postable term. See Table 5 on page xv for a list of all the deleted terms.

Changes to Spelling or Text of Terms

In an effort to use language that is consistent with that used by the field of psychology and to expand terms that have historically been truncated (because of former system constraints), 19 terms received spelling or format modifications. See Table 4 on page xiv for a listing of these changes.

Table 1: New Postable Terms (200)

Abnormal Psychology
Activism
Activity Theory
Acute Stress Disorder
Adrenergic Receptors
After School Programs
Ageism
Aggressive Driving Behavior
Amygdala
Animal Learning
Anterograde Amnesia
Antioxidants
Apolipoproteins
Assisted Living
Behavioral Economics
Bioethics
Broca's Area
Bullying
Cannibalism
Case Based Reasoning
Child Labor
Children of Alcoholics
Cholinergic Receptors
Chronic Stress
Chunking
Class Size
Classical Test Theory
Classroom Management
Clinical Trials
Cloning
Cognitive Appraisal
Cognitive Impairment
Cognitive Science
Community Involvement
Computer Mediated Communication
Conditioned Fear
Conjoined Twins
Conspecifics
Continuum of Care
Crack Cocaine
Criminal Behavior
Criminal Rehabilitation
Cross Cultural Counseling
Culture Bound Syndromes
Cytokines
Debriefing (Psychological)
Decision Theory
Disease Transmission
Distance Education
Diversity in the Workplace
Downsizing
Drug Augmentation
Drug Self Administration
Dual Relationships
Dysphagia
Eating Behavior
Emotional Intelligence
Evidence Based Practice
Evil
Evolutionary Psychology
Falls
Family Conflict
Family Intervention
Family Systems Theory
First Experiences
Flunitrazepam
Fuzzy Logic

Gene Expression
Genetic Testing
Genome
Globalization
Grounded Theory
Groupware
Harm Reduction
Hate Crimes
Heuristics
High School Education
Hoarding Behavior
Homemakers
Homogeneity of Variance
Human Body
Human Capital
Human Resource Management
Humanistic Psychotherapy
Humanities
Hypericum Perforatum
Identity Formation
Immunologic Factors
Implicit Learning
Implicit Memory
Improvisation
Industrial and Organizational
    Psychology
Inflammation
Integrative Psychotherapy
Intelligent Tutoring Systems
Interpersonal Relationships
Intervention
Juvenile Justice
Knowledge Engineering
Learning Environment
Legal Confession
Leptin
Litigation
Logistic Regression
Machine Learning
Mental Models
Middle School Teachers
Middle Schools
Mimicry (Biology)
Modernization
Native Language
Natural Killer Cells
Nefazodone
Neurodegenerative Diseases
Neuroimaging
Neuropeptide Y
Neurotoxicity
Neurotransmission
Nitric Oxide
Olanzapine
Online Therapy
Organizational Learning
Osteopathic Medicine
Panic Attack
Parental Death
Parenting Style
Phonological Awareness
Polymorphism
Polypharmacy
Polysomnography
Popular Culture
Positive Psychology
Premenstrual Dysphoric Disorder

Procedural Justice
Prodrome
Professional Networking
Professionalism
Psychodynamic Psychotherapy
Psychological Contracts
Public Service Announcements
Purging (Eating Disorders)
Qualitative Research
Quantitative Methods
Quantitative Trait Loci
Quasi Experimental Methods
Quetiapine
Rational Emotive Behavior Therapy
Rebelliousness
Relationship Quality
Religious Fundamentalism
Response Inhibition
Retrograde Amnesia
Rhyme
Risk Assessment
Safe Sex
Same Sex Education
School Based Intervention
School Violence
Self Criticism
Self Regulated Learning
Self Regulation
Serial Homicide
Sexual Attraction
Sexual Partners
Sikhism
Sleep
Silence
Skepticism
Social Capital
Social Dilemma
Social Loafing
Social Support
Solution Focused Therapy
Soul
Source Monitoring
South Asian Cultural Groups
Southeast Asian Cultural Groups
Sports (Attitudes Toward)
Striatum
Subtypes (Disorders)
Supply and Demand
Synesthesia
Systems Design
Tardiness
Teasing
Telecommuting
Telemedicine
Thought Suppression
Tourism
Transcranial Magnetic Stimulation
Transformational Leadership
Utility Theory
Venlafaxine
Verbal Abuse
Violent Crime
Visual Attention
Volunteers
Williams Syndrome
Workaholism
Workers' Compensation Insurance

Table 2: New Nonpostable (NP) Terms (123)

Acetylcholine Receptors NP to Cholinergic Receptors
Adrenaline Receptors NP to Adrenergic Receptors
Adrenoceptors NP to Adrenergic Receptors
Adult Children of Alcoholics NP to Children of Alcoholics
Alcoholic Offspring NP to Children of Alcoholics
Ambidexterity NP to Handedness
Anger Management NP to Anger Control
Attrition (Experimental) NP to Experimental Attrition
Autism Spectrum Disorders NP to Pervasive Developmental
    Disorders
Bias Crimes NP to Hate Crimes
Biodata NP to Biographical Data
Brain Development NP to Neural Development
Business Networking NP to Professional Networking
Celebrity NP to Fame
Charismatic Leadership NP to Transformational Leadership
Child Abduction NP to Kidnapping
Child Maltreatment NP to Child Abuse
Cholinoceptors NP to Cholinergic Receptors
Citizen Participation NP to Community Involvement
Civic Behavior NP to Community Involvement
Cognitive Deficits NP to Cognitive Impairment
Cognitive Dysfunction NP to Cognitive Impairment
Computer Based Training NP to Computer Assisted Instruction
Computer Supported Cooperative Work NP to Groupware
Confession (Legal) NP to Legal Confession
Content Validity NP to Test Validity
Continuity of Care NP to Continuum of Care
Contracts (Psychological) NP to Psychological Contracts
Convergent Validity NP to Test Validity
Criminality NP to Criminal Behavior
Criterion Related Validity NP to Test Validity
Critical Incident Stress Debriefing NP to Debriefing
    (Psychological)
Culture Specific Syndromes NP to Culture Bound Syndromes
Cybercounseling NP to Online Therapy
Discriminant Validity NP to Test Validity
Distance Learning NP to Distance Education
Drama Therapy NP to Psychodrama
Eating Habits NP to Eating Behavior
Educational Intervention NP to School Based Intervention
Electronic Mail NP to Computer Mediated Communication
Email NP to Computer Mediated Communication
E-Therapy NP to Online Therapy
Ethnicity NP to Ethnic Identity
Etiopathogenesis NP to Etiology
Event Related Potentials NP to Evoked Potentials
Evidence Based Medicine NP to Evidence Based Practice
Experimental Setting NP to Research Setting
Family Dynamics NP to Family Relations
Family Environment NP to Home Environment
Family Systems Model NP to Family Systems Theory
Female Homosexuality NP to Lesbianism
Field Experiment NP to Observation Methods
First Language NP to Native Language
Galantamine NP to Galanthamine
Genetic Screening NP to Genetic Testing
Glutamate NP to Glutamic Acid
Guns NP to Firearms
Human Computer Interface NP to Human Computer Interaction
Human Genome NP to Genome
Inclusion (Educational) NP to Mainstreaming (Educational)
Internet Counseling NP to Online Therapy
Job Stress NP to Occupational Stress

Lateness NP to Tardiness
Lawsuits NP to Litigation
Learning Organizations NP to Organizational Learning
Life Course NP to Life Span
Life Transitions NP to Life Changes
Light Therapy NP to Phototherapy
Mass Culture NP to Popular Culture
Measurement Error NP to Error of Measurement
Medical Ethics NP to Bioethics
Muscarinic Receptors NP to Cholinergic Receptors
Neostriatum NP to Striatum
Neural Transmission NP to Neurotransmission
Nicotinic Receptors NP to Cholinergic Receptors
Offspring of Alcoholics NP to Children of Alcoholics
Organizational Culture NP to Organizational Climate
Osteopathy NP to Osteopathic Medicine
Pedagogy NP to Teaching
Personal Relationships NP to Interpersonal Relationships
Phonemic Awareness NP to Phonological Awareness
Physical Activity NP to Motor Processes
Postnatal Depression NP to Postpartum Depression
Psyche NP to Mind
Psychoanalytically Oriented Psychotherapy NP to
    Psychodynamic Psychotherapy
Psychological Debriefing NP to Debriefing (Psychological)
Psychostimulant Drugs NP to CNS Stimulating Drugs
Puerperal Depression NP to Postpartum Depression
Puerperal Psychosis NP to Postpartum Psychosis
Qualitative Methods NP to Qualitative Research
Quantitative Research NP to Quantitative Method
Receptors (Adrenergic) NP to Adrenergic Receptors
Receptors (Cholinergic) NP to Cholinergic Receptors
Recycling NP to Conservation (Ecological Behavior)
Repetitive Transcranial Magnetic Stimulation NP to Transcranial
    Magnetic Stimulation
Road Rage NP to Aggressive Driving Behavior
Rohypnol NP to Flunitrazepam
Saint John's Wort NP to Hypericum Perforatum
Self Administration (Drugs) NP to Drug Self Administration
Self Injurious Behavior NP to Self Destructive Behavior
Serial Murder NP to Serial Homicide
Sex Role Stereotyping NP to Sex Role Attitudes
Single Sex Education NP to Same Sex Education
Sleep Monitoring NP to Polysomnography
Social Anxiety Disorder NP to Social Phobia
Social Competence NP to Social Skills
South East Asian Cultural Groups NP to Southeast Asian
    Cultural Groups
Sportsmanship NP to Sports (Attitudes Toward)
Sportspersonship NP to Sports (Attitudes Toward)
St. John's Wort NP to Hypericum Perforatum
Synaptic Transmission NP to Neurotransmission
Telehealth NP to Telemedicine
Teletherapy NP to Online Therapy
Usability (Systems) NP to Human Factors Engineering
Ventral Striatum NP to Basal Ganglia
Visual Impairment NP to Vision Disorders
Volunteerism NP to Volunteers
Web Based Mental Health Services NP to Online Therapy
Work Addiction NP to Workaholism
Work at Home NP to Telecommuting
Work Stress NP to Occupational Stress
Workforce Diversity NP to Diversity in the Workplace
Workplace Diversity NP to Diversity in the Workplace

Table 3: Change in Status Terms (57)

The following terms changed from postable to nonpostable status. Consult the Relationship Section for the appropriate "Use" term.

Activist Movements
Amaurotic Familial Idiocy
Amygdaloid Body
Cultural Assimilation
Experiment Volunteers
Feeding Practices
Fundamentalism (Religion)
Hair Pulling

Hardiness
Housewives
Industrial Psychology
Marihuana
Personnel Management
Premenstrual Tension
Rational Emotive Therapy
Risk Analysis

Siamese Twins
Social Support Networks
Variance Homogeneity
Venereal Diseases
Volunteer Civilian Personnel
Volunteer Personnel
Workmen's Compensation
    Insurance

The following terms changed from nonpostable to postable status. Consult the Relationship Section for the appropriate "Used For" term.

Acculturation
Algebra
Calculus
Cognitive Behavior Therapy
Disabilities
Distributive Justice
Fibromyalgia
Firearms

Generalized Anxiety Disorder
Geometry
Life Changes
Life Span
Marijuana
Mealtimes
Neuropeptides
Postpartum Psychosis

Premenstrual Syndrome
Resilience (Psychological)
Sexually Transmitted Diseases
Tay-Sachs Disease
Theology
Trichotillomania
Voles

The following nonpostable terms now point to a different postable counterpart. Consult the Relationship Section for the appropriate "Use" term.

Authoritarianism
Concept Validity
Concurrent Validity
Construct Validity

Eating
Eating Patterns
Handicaps
Human Resources

Organizational Psychology
Parasympatholytics
Parental Authoritarianism

Table 4: Changes to Spelling or Text of Terms (19)

The following terms were altered because of changes in spelling, in conceptualization, or to their expansion from their previously truncated forms.

Antisocial Personality Disorder
Formerly
Antisocial Personality

Avoidant Personality Disorder
Formerly
Avoidant Personality

Borderline Personality Disorder
Formerly
Borderline Personality

Dependent Personality Disorder
Formerly
Dependent Personality

Fibromyalgia
Formerly
Fibromyalgia Syndrome

Fundamentalism (Religion)
Formerly
Fundamentalism

Life Changes
Formerly
Life Change

Marijuana Laws
Formerly
Marihuana Laws

Marijuana Legalization
Formerly
Marihuana Legalization

Marijuana Usage
Formerly
Marihuana Usage

Narcissistic Personality Disorder
Formerly
Narcissistic Personality

Paranoid Personality Disorder
Formerly
Paranoid Personality

Passive Aggressive Personality Disorder
Formerly
Passive Aggressive Personality

Psychiatric Classifications (Taxonomies)
Formerly truncated as
Psychiatric Classifications (Taxon)

Obsessive Compulsive Personality Disorder
Formerly
Obsessive Compulsive Personality

Schizoid Personality Disorder
Formerly
Schizoid Personality

Schizotypal Personality Disorder
Formerly
Schizotypal Personality

Therapeutic Techniques (Psychotherapy)
Formerly truncated as
Therapeutic Techniques (Psychother)

Training (Clinical Psychology Graduate)
Formerly truncated as
Training (Clinical Psychology Grad)

Table 5: Term Deletions (30)

Barrett Lennard Relationship Inventory
Barron Welsh Art Scale
California Test of Mental Maturity
California Test of Personality
Cattell Infant Intelligence Scale (*nonpostable term*)
Equimax Rotation
Ethnic Disorders (*nonpostable term*)
Ethnospecific Disorders
Franck Drawing Completion Test
Goldstein Scheerer Object Sort Test
Hidden Figures Test
Hydroxylamine
Idiocy (Amaurotic Familial) (*nonpostable term*)
Incomplete Man Test
Infant Intelligence Scale

Learys Interpersonal Check List
Lorge Thorndike Intelligence Test
Lowenfeld Mosaic Test
Maudsley Personality Inventory
Modern Language Aptitude Test
Omnibus Personality Inventory
Orientals (*nonpostable term*)
Parent Attitude Research Instrument
Purdue Perceptual Motor Survey
Quartimax Rotation
Remote Associates Test
VISTA Volunteers (*nonpostable term*)
Volunteers In Service to America
Welsh Figure Preference Test
Wepman Auditory Discrimination Test

Table 6: Terms Removed and Replaced (24)

Previous Postable Term	Mapped to New Postable Term
Activist Movements	Activism
Amaurotic Familial Idiocy	Tay Sachs Disease
Amygdaloid Body	Amygdala
Cultural Assimilation	Acculturation
Ethnospecific Disorders	Culture Bound Syndromes
Experiment Volunteers	Experimental Subjects
Feeding Practices	Eating Behavior
Fundamentalism (Religion)	Religious Fundamentalism
Hair Pulling	Trichotillomania
Hardiness	Resilience (Psychological)
Housewives	Homemakers
Industrial Psychology	Industrial and Organizational Psychology
Marihuana	Marijuana
Personnel Management	Human Resources Management
Premenstrual Tension	Premenstrual Syndrome
Rational Emotive Therapy	Rational Emotive Behavior Therapy
Risk Analysis	Risk Assessment
Siamese Twins	Conjoined Twins
Social Support Networks	Social Support
Variance Homogeneity	Homogeneity of Variance
Venereal Diseases	Sexually Transmitted Diseases
Volunteer Civilian Personnel	Volunteers
Volunteer Personnel	Volunteers
Workmens Compensation Insurance	Workers' Compensation Insurance

GENERAL INFORMATION

Word Form Conventions

Conventions dealing with singular and plural word forms, direct and indirect entries, abbreviations, acronyms, homographs, and punctuation have been used to ensure standardization of the *Thesaurus* vocabulary. Noun forms are preferred entries, with the plural form used when the term is a noun that can be qualified, for example, **Volunteers, Immunologic Factors,** or **Mental Models** and the singular form when the term refers to processes, properties, or conditions, for example, **Self Regulation, Panic Attack,** or **Community Involvement.** Direct entry or natural word order is preferred when a concept is represented by two or more words, for example, **Mental Health** vs. "Health, Mental" or **Artificial Intelligence** vs. "Intelligence, Artificial."

In cases where ambiguity may occur and to clarify the meaning of homographs, qualifying expressions are included in parentheses, for example, **Debriefing (Psychological), Purging (Eating Disorders),** and **Conservation (Ecological Behavior).**

Also, a selected number of acronyms are used, such as **DOPA, REM Sleep,** and **ROTC Students.**

Term Relationships

The terms in the Relationship Section are displayed to reflect the following relationships:

USE. Directs the user from a term that cannot be used (nonpostable) to a term that can be used (postable) in indexing and searching. The **Use** reference indicates preferred forms of synonyms, abbreviations, spelling, and word sequence:

> Sleep Monitoring
> **Use** Polysomnography

UF (Used For). Reciprocal of the **Use** reference. Terms listed as **UF** (used for) references represent some but not all of the most frequently encountered synonyms, abbreviations, alternate spellings, or word sequences:

> **Polysomnography** 2003
> **UF** Sleep Monitoring

B (Broader Term) and **N (Narrower Term).** Reciprocal designators used to indicate hierarchical relationships:

> **School Based Intervention** 2003
> **B** Intervention 2003

> **Intervention** 2003
> **N** School Based Intervention 2003

R (Related Term). Reciprocal designator used to indicate relationships that are semantic or conceptual, but not hierarchical. Related term references indicate to searchers (or indexers) terms that they may not have considered, but might be related to their topic of interest:

> **Emotional Intelligence** 2003
> **R** Emotional Maturity 1973

RELATIONSHIP SECTION

Each *Thesaurus* term is listed alphabetically and, as appropriate, is cross-referenced and displayed with its broader, narrower, and related terms, also called subterms. Since the beginning of the database in 1967, PsycINFO's indexing vocabulary has been updated periodically with new terms. The date of the term's inclusion in the *Thesaurus* appears as a four-digit superscript. Each postable subterm in a main term's hierarchy also has its date of inclusion shown as well. Fourteen dates can be found: 1967, 1971, 1973, 1978, 1982, 1984, 1985, 1988, 1991, 1994, 1997, 2001, 2003, and 2004. Some of these dates do not correspond with a *Thesaurus* publication year.

The subject code **(SC)** gives the unique five-digit code associated with the term and can be used to retrieve records instead of entering the term text on some online search systems.

Each postable index term in the Relationship Section appears with a posting note **(PN)** reference indicating how many times that term has been used in the indexing of PsycINFO records. Posting notes are based on accumulations of term usage through March 2004. For this edition, PsycINFO records from the past 10 years were retrospectively indexed (re-indexed) with new tenth edition terms. The number of posting notes for these terms reflects the number of records re-indexed. The historical note for each of these terms also indicates this. In past editions, terms that had an indicator PN = 0 were new terms that had yet to accumulate any postings.

Many terms that have ambiguous meanings have scope notes **(SN).** In many cases, a scope note provides a definition and/or information on proper use of the term. The scope note always refers to the one term with which it is associated and does not necessarily have implications for the subterms displayed in the term's hierarchy. The following is an example of a scope note found in the Relationship Section:

Definition and Usage

Qualitative Research [2003]
SN: A type of research methodology that produces descriptive data, with little emphasis given to numerical quantification. Used only when the methodology or research itself is the focus of the discussion.

New to the *Thesaurus* is the historical note **(HN).** The historical note provides information about the historical usage of a term since its introduction to the *Thesaurus*. Specifically, it includes information about changes to a term, the range of years a term was in use, and instructions for searching. In past editions, historical information was captured in the scope note, but with the addition of the historical note (HN), the scope note will be used primarily for definitions of terms.

Change in Usage

Brain Lesions[1967]
HN: Not defined prior to 1982. From 1982 limited to experimentally induced lesions and used primarily for animal populations.

Change in Status

Resilience (Psychological)
HN: In June 2003, this term replaced the discontinued term HARDINESS. HARDINESS was removed from all records containing it and replaced with RESILIENCE (PSYCHO-LOGICAL). Use Psychological Endurance to access references from 1991–1996.

Nonpostable index terms, those not used in the indexing process, are shown in nonbold print with an appropriate **USE** reference. Nonpostable terms are provided as points of entry into the *Thesaurus* vocabulary.

The following example from the Relationship Section illustrates a nonpostable term entry:

Nonpostable Index Term: Work at Home

Postable Index Term: **USE** Telecommuting [2003]

Finally, the Relationship Section uses down arrows ($\downarrow$) in front of any narrower **(N)** or related **(R)** terms that have narrower terms themselves. This feature alerts the user to consider another more specific hierarchical level. The PsycINFO database is indexed to the level of specificity in a given document. In using the Relationship Section and in choosing index terms, consider following any main term's subterms (**N** and **R** terms only) to the lowest level of specificity by turning to the page in the *Thesaurus* where the narrower **(N)** or related **(R)** subterm appears as a main entry to determine if more specific terminology is available. Below is a sample of an index term entry in the Relationship Section.

The following example from the Relationship Section illustrates the various components that may be included in the hierarchy of a postable index term:

Postable Index Term (With year of entry)	**Affective Disorders** 2001
Posting Note and Subject Code (Number of postings)	**PN** 6633 **SC** 09184
Scope Note	**SN** Mental disorders characterized by a disturbance in mood, which is abnormally depressed or elated. Compare EMOTIONAL STABILITY or EMOTIONALLY DISTURBED.
Historical Note	**HN** Use AFFECTIVE DISTURBANCES to access references from 1967–2000.
Used for (Nonpostable terms)	**UF** Affective Disturbances Mood Disorders
Broader Term	**B** Mental Disorders 1967
Narrower Terms (Down arrow indicates more specific terms)	**N** ↓Bipolar Disorder 2001 ↓Major Depression 1988 ↓Mania 1967 Seasonal Affective Disorder 1991
Related Terms (Down arrow indicates more specific terms)	**R** ↓Affective Psychosis 1973 Premenstrual Dysphoric Disorder 2004 Schizoaffective Disorder 1994

ROTATED ALPHABETICAL TERMS SECTION

Many terms represent concepts not expressed in a single word; therefore, postable and nonpostable *Thesaurus* terms in this section are listed in alphabetical order by each word contained within them. The Rotated Alphabetical Terms Section is useful in finding all *Thesaurus* terms that have a particular word in common. This display groups related terms when they may otherwise be separated in the alphabetical Relationship Section. It is important to note that this section should be used in conjunction with the Relationship Section since hierarchies, scope notes, posting notes, and term dates do not appear in the Rotated Alphabetical Terms Section. A term containing three words will appear in three locations in this section as illustrated below:

Animal	Courtship	Behavior
Animal	Courtship	Displays
Animal	Defensive	Behavior

Animal	**Courtship**	Behavior
Animal	**Courtship**	Displays
Human	**Courtship**	

		Displays
Animal	Courtship	Displays
	Auditory	**Displays**

Nonpostable index terms (terms not used for indexing) are represented in nonbold print followed by the appropriate **"Use"** term in italics. All words in the term, just like the postable terms above, appear in different locations depending on how many words are contained in the index term as illustrated below:

	Illumination
	Ilumination Therapy
	USE Phototherapy
Autokinetic	**Illusion**
Hormone	**Therapy**
Illumination	Therapy
	USE Phototherapy
Implosive	**Therapy**

TERM CLUSTERS SECTION

Clusters are collections of index terms that are related to one another conceptually rather than hierarchically, and are displayed together under broad subject categories. This section is useful for viewing all terms in each cluster collectively.

Clusters provide an entry point into the *Thesaurus* vocabulary by allowing a large group of similar terms to be scanned easily and efficiently, thus helping users translate their search vocabulary into *Thesaurus* vocabulary. In a sense, the clusters present an "index" to some of the indexing vocabulary found in the Relationship Section.

It is important to note that the Clusters Section should not be used alone, but in conjunction with the Relationship Section. Useful details regarding particular index terms can be found in the Relationship Section such as scope notes, posting notes, hierarchies, dates for term inclusion, and links to additional search terms.

Not every index term will appear in the Term Clusters Section. Terms appear under nine broad cluster subject areas. The nine subject areas are meant to present index terms for selected subject areas that are frequent in psychological research, but do not cover all subject areas in psychology. There are approximately 2,620 postable index terms in the Clusters Section. Terms may appear in more than one broad cluster area and also in more than one subcluster under any broad subject area, if appropriate. The Term Clusters and Subclusters are listed in Table 7 on page xxi.

Table 7: Term Cluster/Subcluster Subject Areas

Computers Cluster
Applications
Automation
Computers & Communication
Computers & Media
Education & Training
Equipment
Human Machine Systems and Engineering
Information

Disorders Cluster
Antisocial Behavior & Behavior Disorders
Diagnosis
Disorder Characteristics
Learning Disorders & Mental Retardation
Physical & Psychosomatic Disorders
Psychological Disorders
Speech & Language Disorders
Symptomatology

Educational Cluster
Academic Learning & Achievement
Curricula
Educational Personnel & Administration
Educational Testing & Counseling
Schools & Institutions
Special Education
Student Characteristics & Academic
       Environment
Student Populations
Teaching and Teaching Methods

Legal Cluster
Adjudication
Criminal Groups
Criminal Offenses
Criminal Rehabilitation
Laws
Legal Issues
Legal Personnel
Legal Processes

Neuropsychology & Neurology Cluster
Assessment & Diagnosis
Electrophysiology
Neuroanatomy
Neurological Disorders
Neurological Intervention
Neurosciences
Neurotransmitters & Neuroregulators

Occupational & Employment Cluster
Career Areas
Employee, Occupational & Job Characteristics
Occupational Groups
Organizations & Organizational Behavior
Personnel Management & Professional
       Personnel Issues

Statistical Cluster
Design, Analysis & Interpretation
Statistical Reliability & Validity
Statistical Theory & Experimentation

Tests & Testing Cluster
Academic Achievement & Aptitude Measures
Attitude & Interest Measures
Intelligence Measures
Nonprojective Personality Measures
Perceptual Measures
Projective Personality Measures
Testing
Testing Methods

Treatment Cluster
Alternative Therapies
Behavior Modification & Therapy
Counseling
Hospitalization & Institutionalization
Medical & Physical Treatment
Psychotherapy
Rehabilitation
Treatment (General)
Treatment Facilities

Subject Searching in PsycINFO

INTRODUCTION

Using the *Thesaurus of Psychological Index Terms* to search PsycINFO and PsycARTICLES can enhance the precision of your retrieved citations and guide you to closely related topics that you might otherwise miss. The standardized vocabulary in the *Thesaurus* eliminates the need to worry about phraseology used by authors to describe a concept. For effective searches and development of comprehensive search strategies, follow the steps outlined below:

1. Select a search topic

> **Example:** "I'm interested in high school students and bullying."

2. Specifically define the concepts of the topic and develop a list of synonyms that represent the concepts. This can include independent and/or dependent experimental variables and/or a population. A properly defined concept can result in an efficient search with precise retrieval of highly relevant articles, and will also reduce the need to scan and eliminate irrelevant references. The following example shows a more specific and defined topic:

> **Example:** "I'm interested in bullying intervention and educational programs for high school students."

3. Look up your concepts in the *Thesaurus of Psychological Index Terms*. Start in any of the three sections, choosing terms on the basis of your topic and familiarity with the *Thesaurus* vocabulary. See the User Guide on page xvii for a description of each section of the *Thesaurus*.

No matter which section of the *Thesaurus* you look in first, be sure to check the Relationship Section before finalizing your terms. The Relationship Section includes scope notes that define the terms, historical notes that provide information about the historical usage of terms since their introduction, as well as posting notes, subject codes, term dates, and the critical *used for, broader, narrower,* and *related* terms.

The most important things to look for in the Relationship Section are the narrower terms and the dates for main term entry (for material indexed after that date). It is important to note each descriptor's year of entry in the *Thesaurus* (indicated by a four-digit superscript number appended to each term in the Relationship Section) because some new terminology is not "mapped back" to older records to which they are con-

ceptually relevant. For the tenth edition, PsycINFO records from the past 10 years were retrospectively indexed with the new terminology. The posting note number of these terms reflects the number of records that have been re-indexed. The historical note for each of these terms also indicates this.

To retrieve articles relevant to terms before their inclusion in the *Thesaurus*, consider their broader concepts as index terms or use free text strategies to find records added to the database before the starting date.

Also, note each entry's posting note, which is a rough guide to the number of articles you can expect to find under that term.

It is important to remember that all PsycINFO records are indexed to the source document's level of specificity. For example, an article that focuses on "school violence" will be indexed under **"School Violence,"** not the broader and less specific term **"Violence."** Therefore, all applicable narrower terms should be added as synonyms to the list of index terms in your search. Related terms may also closely match a search topic, and should be considered carefully when formulating a strategy.

> **Example 1:**
> a. Bullying
>
> b. School Violence
>
> c. School Based Intervention or Educational Programs (These terms can be used to describe the concept of intervention and educational programs)
>
> d. High School Students or High Schools or Secondary Education (These terms form the context of high school education)

Using these terms, your search statement using Boolean logic would be:

> (Bullying OR School Violence) AND (School Based Intervention OR Educational Programs) AND (High School Students OR High Schools OR Secondary Education)

ELECTRONIC SEARCHING

In search systems, *Thesaurus* terms are located in a descriptor or index term field. Each vendor system that carries PsycINFO operates differently, yet each has the capability to limit a search to the descriptor or index term field. Electronic search systems give you the opportunity to manipulate your search statement to provide precision and recall in retrieval. Formulate your topic and refer to the *Thesaurus* for appropriate terminology, then consult **Appendix E,** a quick reference guide to vendor systems that offer command-line searching, to determine how to focus your search on index terms. Also, refer to **Appendix E** for other specific field names and search examples.

Electronic systems allow the use of Boolean logic in a search. Use the Boolean logical operators **AND, OR,** and **NOT** to combine terms.

Example of Boolean Logic

(Shaded Areas Indicate Retrieval)

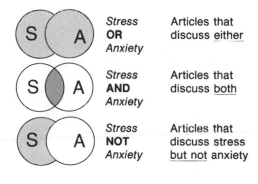

	Stress **OR** *Anxiety*	Articles that discuss either
	Stress **AND** *Anxiety*	Articles that discuss both
	Stress **NOT** *Anxiety*	Articles that discuss stress but not anxiety

Example:
Bullying

OR School Violence

AND (School Based Intervention **OR** Educational Programs)

AND (High School Students **OR** High Schools **OR** Secondary Education)

ELECTRONIC THESAURUS: For added convenience in searching PsycINFO, most vendor systems offer an electronic thesaurus that can automatically display terms along with their broader, narrower, and related concepts. This feature can help reduce typing and enhance the speed of a search, especially when several narrower terms need to be entered, by allowing users to move from term to term and find new appropriate search terms with ease.

EXPLODE FEATURE: The Explode feature is available on some search systems. See the **Master Quick Reference Guide Appendix E** for the systems that make this feature available. When a search system's explode command is used, the system will automatically search the index term and the first level of its narrower terms. Some terms listed as narrower to an index term may have narrower terms of their own—"narrowers of narrowers." In

the *Thesaurus*, narrower terms that have narrower terms of their own are marked with a down-arrow. To achieve comprehensive retrieval, they must be exploded as well.

MAJOR TERMS: Index terms applied to PsycINFO records that represent the primary focus of the reference are designated as "major." Many search systems allow for searching of major terms. See the **Master Quick Reference Guide** in **Appendix E** for each system's label for searching major terms, if applicable.

ADJUSTING YOUR SEARCH RETRIEVAL

If your search retrieves too many records, try making your search more specific by adding another concept. If nearly all of your records appear relevant, but there are still too many, consider restricting your retrieval to recent publication years or a particular language.

If you retrieve too few records, consider dropping a concept, adding synonymous terms, or eliminating restrictions to specific fields.

Content Classification Code Searching

PsycINFO uses a content classification system that divides the field of psychology into 22 major or broad categories and 135 subcategories. Content classification codes can be searched in most systems. Use of the content classification system in searching can shorten online time and screen out undesired references. Content classification codes are particularly useful to retrieve records from a broad subject area in which many different index terms may have been used. Classification codes will limit a search, since only one or two codes are assigned to each record. Keep in mind, however, that a classification code search usually does not retrieve everything in the database that is relevant to a respective topic. A well-constructed search will always include relevant descriptors or index terms.

Search classification codes at their broad level. Using the first two digits of a category retrieves the entire category and enables the search to be executed throughout the entire year range of the database. If more specific information is needed, search one or more four-digit subcategories. Four-digit subcategories were added in 1976; therefore, a search on a four-digit subcategory will limit retrieval to records added in 1976 and later.

A list of the content classification codes appears in **Appendix D** on page xxxi.

Age Group Searching

All search systems use identifying tags for the ages of human populations. A record may have more than one age group tag. Search for age groups in the Age Group field. The following table lists the values that are available in the Age Group field. Values that are indented indicate that they are narrower. When the broader value is searched, the narrower values are automatically searched as well.

Age Group Field Values

```
Childhood (birth–12 yrs)
    Neonatal (birth–1 mo)
    Infancy (1–23 mo)
    Preschool Age (2–5 yrs)
    School Age (6–12 yrs)

Adolescence (13–17 yrs)

Adulthood (18 yrs and older)
    Young Adulthood (18–29 yrs)
    Thirties (30–39 yrs)
    Middle Age (40–64 yrs)
    Aged (65 yrs and older)
        Very Old (85 yrs and older)
```

Population Group Searching

Search for population group characteristics other than age are searched in the Population Group field. The following table lists the values that are available in the Population Group field. A record may have more than one population group value.

Population Group Field Values

```
Human
Animal
Female
Male
Inpatient
Outpatient
```

Form/Content Type Searching

The Form/Content Type field indicates the form of the source document. It is helpful for distinguishing what a source document IS as opposed to what it is ABOUT. For example, if you want to limit your retrieval to literature reviews, you would search LITERATURE REVIEW in the Form/Content Type field. If you want documents that are about how to do a literature review, you would search Literature Review as a *Thesaurus* term.

The following table lists the values available in the Form/Content Type field. A record may have more than one value. Values that are indented indicate that they are narrower. When the broader value is searched, the narrower values are searched as well.

Form/Content Type Field Values

```
Autobiography/Biography
Auxiliary Material Included
Bibliography
Case Study (non-clinical)
Clinical Case Report
Comment
Conference Proceedings/Symposia
Empirical Study
        Clinical Case Report
        Clinical Trial
        Experimental Replication
        Followup Study
        Longitudinal Study
                Prospective Study
                Retrospective Study
        Qualitative Study
        Quantitative Study
                Double Blind Design
                Single Blind Design
        Treatment Outcomes
Erratum/Retraction
```

```
Literature Review
Meta Analysis
Professional Policy/Standard
Program Evaluation
Test/Survey Appended
Reprint
Test/Survey Appended
Journal Abstract
Journal Article
Journal Column/Opinion
Journal Editorial
Journal Information
Journal Letter
Journal Obituary
Journal Review—Book
Journal Review—Software/Video/Other
Book Handbook Manual
Book Reference Work
Book Study Guide/Workbook
Book Textbook
```

Searching for Supplemental Material

The Supplemental Material field lists data that are not part of the original printed source document but are online and supplemental to the document, such as video clips, interactive data sets, and extended charts, tables, and graphs. The Supplemental Material field should not be confused with the Auxiliary Material Included value (located in the Form/Content Type field), which indicates the presence or availability of physical materials accompanying a document, such as audiocassettes, computer software, study guides, data sets, and workbooks. The following table lists the values available in the Supplemental Material field. A record may have more than one value.

Supplemental Material Field Values

3-D Modeling Images
Additional Figures
Appendixes
Audio Clips
Color Figures
Data Sets (Tables)
Data Sets (Interactive)
Expanded Tables
Interactive Web Sites
Video Clips
Other Data Types

Searching for Geographic Locations

In the Ninth Edition of the *Thesaurus*, all geographical location terms were removed. If you are looking for studies done in a particular country, you should now search for it in the Location field.

Searching for Tests and Measures

A Tests and Measures field was added in 2003. Originally, this field contained the names of published tests and measures used in a study (up to 10 names), whether they are the focus of the document or not. It does not replace indexing of tests and measures if they are the focus of the original source document.

HOW TO CONTACT US

To contact us, call our toll-free line at 800-374-2722 in North America, 9:00 a.m. to 5:00 p.m., U.S. Eastern time, Monday through Friday.

For those who do not have toll-free access, we can be contacted at 202-336-5650, FAX 202-336-5633, TTY 202-336-6123, or E-mail at psycinfo@apa.org.

Information on ordering, subscriptions, vendor system documentation, journals covered in PsycINFO, and search aids can also be found on PsycINFO's Web site: http://www.apa.org/psycinfo.

APPENDIX A: Sample Journal Record

FIELD NAME	SAMPLE JOURNAL RECORD
Accession Number:	2004-10204-002
Title:	Bullying and victimization: Cause for concern for both families and schools.
Author:	Ahmed, Eliza; Braithwaite, Valerie
Affiliation:	Australian National University, Research School of Social Sciences, Canberra, ACT, Australia
Correspondence Address:	Ahmed Eliza. Research School of Social Sciences, Australian National University, Canberra, ACT, Australia, 0200, eliza.ahmed@anu.edu.au
Source:	Social Psychology of Education. Vol 7(1) 2004, 35–54. Kluwer Academic Publishers, Netherlands
Publisher URL:	http://www.wkap.nl
Journal URL:	http://www.wkap.nl/journalhome.htm/1381-2890
ISSN:	1381-2890
Publication Year:	2004
Language:	English
Abstract:	This study examines the roles of family variables (authoritarian and authoritative parenting, family disharmony) and school variables (liking school, perceived control of bullying and school hassles) in discriminating non-bully/non-victims, victims and bullies. Participants were parents and their children aged 9–12 years (N=610). Data were analyzed using ANOVA and discriminant function analysis (DFA). Two significant functions emerged, both of which appeared important in discriminating children according to their bullying status. Together they allowed for the correct classification of 76% of the non-bully/non-victims, 57% of victims, and 61% of bullies. The main conclusion is that family and school systems working together may provide the most effective means of intervention for bullying problems. (PsycINFO Database Record © 2004 APA, all rights reserved)
Keywords:	childrearing styles; family disharmony; school variables; liking for school; school hassles; perceived control of bullying; victimization
Index Terms:	*Family Relations; *Parenting Style; * School Environment; *Victimization; *Bullying
Classification Code:	3560-Classroom Dynamics & Student Adjustment & Attitudes
Age Group:	Childhood; Preschool-Age; School-Age; Adulthood
Population:	Human; Male; Female
Location:	Australia
Publication Type:	Empirical Study; Quantitative Study; Journal Article
Format Availability:	Print; Electronic
Format Covered:	Electronic
Update Code:	20040126
Number of References:	64 references present; 64 references displayed

APPENDIX A: Sample Journal Record (Continued)

Cited References:

(1) Ahmed, E. (2001). Shame management: Regulating bullying. In E. Ahmed, N. Harris, J. B. Braithwaite, & V. A. Braithwaite (Eds.), *Shame management through reintegration* (pp. 211–314). Cambridge: Cambridge University Press.

(2) Ahmed, E., & Braithwaite, J. (n.d.). *Shaming, shame, forgiveness and bullying*. Manuscript submitted for publication.

(3) Ahmed, E., Harris, N., Braithwaite, J. B., & Braithwaite, V. A. (Eds.). (2001). *Shame management through reintegration*. Cambridge: Cambridge University Press.

(4) Australian Bureau of Statistics. (1996). *Australian capital territory in focus*. Australian Bureau of Statistics Catalogue. 1307.8, Australia.

(5) Australian Bureau of Statistics. (1997). *Australian social trends. Education—Attainment: Education and employment*. Australia.

(6) Bandura, A. (1986). Social foundations of thought and action: A social cognitive theory. Englewood Cliffs, NJ: Prentice-Hall.

(7) Besag, V. E. (1989). *Bullies and victims in schools*. Milton Keynes: Open University Press.

(8) Block, J. H. (1965). *The child rearing practices report*. Berkeley, CA: Institute of Human Development.

(9) Boulton, M. J., & Smith, P. K. (1994). Bully/victim problems among middle school children: Stability, self-perceived competence, and peer acceptance. *British Journal of Developmental Psychology, 12,* 315–329.

(10) Boulton, M. J., & Underwood, K. (1992). Bully/victim problems among middle school children. *British Journal of Educational Psychology, 62(1),* 73–87.

(references continue)

APPENDIX B: Sample Book Record

FIELD NAME	SAMPLE BOOK RECORD
Accession Number:	2003-88296-000
Title:	Creativity in psychotherapy: Reaching new heights with individuals, couples, and families
Author:	Carson, David K.; Becker, Kent W.
Author Affiliation:	U Wyoming, Dept of Family and Consumer Sciences, Laramie, WY, US (Carson); U Wyoming, Laramie, WY, US (Becker)
Source:	Binghamton, NY, US: Haworth Clinical Practice Press. (2003). xxii, 237pp.
Publisher:	Binghamton, NY, US: Haworth Clinical Practice Press
Publisher URL:	http://www.haworthpress.com
ISBN:	0789015781 (hardcover); 078901579X (paperback)
Publication Year:	2003
Language:	English
Abstract:	(From the cover) Examines the nature, role, and importance of creative thinking in counseling and therapy. The authors combine their backgrounds in marriage and family therapy and counseling to give readers a resource that fills a gap in the therapy literature. The book explores various aspects of creative thinking, personal characteristics of highly creative therapists, creative techniques and interventions, barriers to creative work, and creativity development. This book also features practical techniques and interventions for conducting therapy with children, adults, couples, and families. (PsycINFO Database Record © 2004 APA, all rights reserved)
Keywords:	creativity; psychotherapy; creative thinking; counseling; marriage therapy; family therapy; interventions; individual therapy; couples therapy
Index Terms:	*Counseling; *Couples Therapy; *Creativity; *Family Therapy; *Individual Psychotherapy; Intervention; Marriage Counseling
Classification Code:	3310 Psychotherapy & Psychotherapeutic Counseling
Format Covered:	Print
Population:	Human
Publication Type:	Authored Book
Audience Type:	Psychology: Professional and Research
Table of Contents:	(Abbreviated)
	Preface
	Acknowledgments
	Introduction: Psychotherapy with individuals, couples, and families as a creative enterprise
	Section I: The importance of creativity in individual, couple, and family therapy: Health, dysfunction, and resiliency
	Essential components of creativity in individual, couple, and family treatment
	An overview of the role of creativity in individual mental health, psychopathology, and family dysfunction
	Creativity and resiliency in children, adults, marriages, and families
	[table of contents continues]
Update Code:	20031124
Number of References:	342 references present; 342 references displayed

APPENDIX B: Sample Book Record (Continued)

Cited References:

(1) Ackerman, D. (1999). *Deep play.* New York: Random House.

(2) Adler, A. (1968). *The practice and theory of individual psychology.* New York: Humanities Press.

(3) Ahrons, C. (1995). *The good divorce: Keeping your family together when your marriage comes apart.* New York: HarperCollins.

(4) Albert, R. S. (1996). Some reasons why creativity often fails to make it past puberty and into the real world. *New Directions in Child Development, 72,* 43–56.

(5) Aldwin, C. M. (1994). *Stress, coping, and development: An integrated perspective.* New York: The Guilford Press.

(6) Amabile, T. (1983). *The social psychology of creativity.* New York: Springer-Verlag.

(7) Amabile, T. (1987). The motivation to be creative. In S. G. Isaksen (Ed.), *Frontiers of creativity research* (pp. 223–254). Buffalo, NY: Bearly Limited.

(8) Amabile, T. (1989). *Growing up creative.* New York: Crown.

(9) Amabile, T. M. (1996). *Creativity in context.* Boulder, CO: Westview Press.

(10) Amabile, T. M. (1997). Entrepreneurial creativity through motivational synergy. *Journal of Creative Behavior, 31,* 18–26.

(references continue)

APPENDIX C: Sample Chapter Record

FIELD NAME	SAMPLE CHAPTER RECORD
Accession Number:	2003-88368-011
Chapter Title:	Acute stress disorder among MVA survivors.
Source:	After the crash: Psychological assessment and treatment of survivors of motor vehicle accidents (2nd ed.). (pp.199–212). Washington, DC, US: American Psychological Association. xvii, 475pp.
Author:	Blanchard, Edward B.; Hickling, Edward J.
Affiliation:	State U New York, U at Albany, Ctr for Stress & Anxiety Disorders, Albany NY, US (Blanchard); Private Practice, US (Hickling)
ISBN:	1591470706 (hardcover)
Publisher:	Washington, DC, US: American Psychological Association
Publication Year:	2004
Language:	English
Abstract:	(create) This chapter examined acute stress disorder (ASD) among motor vehicle accident (MVA) survivors. There is a great overlap in the diagnostic criteria for ASD and posttraumatic stress disorder (PTSD), however, there are some important differences. Based on the authors' studies, they did not find that meeting the criteria for ASD within the month following the MVA is at all predictive of short-term (six month) outcome over and above a diagnosis of PTSD two months after the accident. Those individuals who are involved in serious MVAs, and who are likely to have the dissociative symptoms necessary to warrant the diagnosis of ASD, were different in some ways before the accident than MVA victims who develop PTSD but do not develop ASD.
Keywords:	motor vehicle accidents; acute stress disorder; posttraumatic stress disorder; PTSD; dissociative symptoms; diagnostic criteria; survivors
Index Terms:	*Acute Stress Disorder; *Client Characteristics; *Motor Traffic Accidents; *Posttraumatic Stress Disorder; * Survivors; Stress Reactions; Symptoms
Classification Code:	3215 Neuroses & Anxiety Disorders; 4090 Transportation
Age Group:	Adolescence; Adulthood; Young Adulthood; Thirties; Middle Age; Aged
Population:	Human; Male; Female
Location:	US
Publication Type:	Chapter; Empirical Study; Followup Study; Quantitative Study
Format Covered:	Print
Audience Type:	Psychology: Professional & Research
Update Code:	20031222

APPENDIX D: Content Classification System

NOTE: This Classification code system was designed to describe the content of the PsycINFO database, not the field of psychology.

2100 General Psychology
  2140 History & Systems

2200 Psychometrics & Statistics & Methodology
  2220 Tests & Testing
    2221 Sensory & Motor Testing
    2222 Developmental Scales & Schedules
    2223 Personality Scales & Inventories
    2224 Clinical Psychological Testing
    2225 Neuropsychological Assessment
    2226 Health Psychology Testing
    2227 Educational Measurement
    2228 Occupational & Employment Testing
    2229 Consumer Opinion & Attitude Testing
  2240 Statistics & Mathematics
  2260 Research Methods & Experimental Design

2300 Human Experimental Psychology
  2320 Sensory Perception
    2323 Visual Perception
    2326 Auditory & Speech Perception
  2330 Motor Processes
  2340 Cognitive Processes
    2343 Learning & Memory
    2346 Attention
  2360 Motivation & Emotion
  2380 Consciousness States
  2390 Parapsychology

2400 Animal Experimental & Comparative Psychology
  2420 Learning & Motivation
  2440 Social & Instinctive Behavior

2500 Physiological Psychology & Neuroscience
  2510 Genetics
  2520 Neuropsychology & Neurology
  2530 Electrophysiology
  2540 Physiological Processes
  2560 Psychophysiology
  2580 Psychopharmacology

2600 Psychology & the Humanities
  2610 Literature & Fine Arts
  2630 Philosophy

2700 Communication Systems
  2720 Linguistics & Language & Speech
  2750 Mass Media Communications

2800 Developmental Psychology
  2820 Cognitive & Perceptual Development
  2840 Psychosocial & Personality Development
  2860 Gerontology

2900 Social Processes & Social Issues
  2910 Social Structure & Organization
  2920 Religion
  2930 Culture & Ethnology
  2950 Marriage & Family
    2953 Divorce & Remarriage
    2956 Childrearing & Child Care
  2960 Political Processes & Political Issues
  2970 Sex Roles & Womens Issues

2980 Sexual Behavior & Sexual Orientation
2990 Drug & Alcohol Usage (Legal)

3000 Social Psychology
  3020 Group & Interpersonal Processes
  3040 Social Perception & Cognition

3100 Personality Psychology
  3120 Personality Traits & Processes
  3140 Personality Theory
    3143 Psychoanalytic Theory

3200 Psychological & Physical Disorders
  3210 Psychological Disorders
    3211 Affective Disorders
    3213 Schizophrenia & Psychotic States
    3215 Neuroses & Anxiety Disorders
    3217 Personality Disorders
  3230 Behavior Disorders & Antisocial Behavior
    3233 Substance Abuse & Addiction
    3236 Criminal Behavior & Juvenile Delinquency
  3250 Developmental Disorders & Autism
    3253 Learning Disorders
    3256 Mental Retardation
  3260 Eating Disorders
  3270 Speech & Language Disorders
  3280 Environmental Toxins & Health
  3290 Physical & Somatoform & Psychogenic Disorders
    3291 Immunological Disorders
    3293 Cancer
    3295 Cardiovascular Disorders
    3297 Neurological Disorders & Brain Damage
    3299 Vision & Hearing & Sensory Disorders

3300 Health & Mental Health Treatment & Prevention
  3310 Psychotherapy & Psychotherapeutic Counseling
    3311 Cognitive Therapy
    3312 Behavior Therapy & Behavior Modification
    3313 Group & Family Therapy
    3314 Interpersonal & Client Centered & Humanistic Therapy
    3315 Psychoanalytic Therapy
  3340 Clinical Psychopharmacology
  3350 Specialized Interventions
    3351 Clinical Hypnosis
    3353 Self Help Groups
    3355 Lay & Paraprofessional & Pastoral Counseling
    3357 Art & Music & Movement Therapy
  3360 Health Psychology & Medicine
    3361 Behavioral & Psychological Treatment of Physical Illness
    3363 Medical Treatment of Physical Illness
    3365 Promotion & Maintenance of Health & Wellness
  3370 Health & Mental Health Services
    3371 Outpatient Services
    3373 Community & Social Services
    3375 Home Care & Hospice

3377 Nursing Homes & Residential Care
3379 Inpatient & Hospital Services
3380 Rehabilitation
  3383 Drug & Alcohol Rehabilitation
  3384 Occupational & Vocational Rehabilitation
  3385 Speech & Language Therapy
  3386 Criminal Rehabilitation & Penology

3400 Professional Psychological & Health Personnel Issues
  3410 Professional Education & Training
  3430 Professional Personnel Attitudes & Characteristics
  3450 Professional Ethics & Standards & Liability
  3470 Impaired Professionals

3500 Educational Psychology
  3510 Educational Administration & Personnel
  3530 Curriculum & Programs & Teaching Methods
  3550 Academic Learning & Achievement
  3560 Classroom Dynamics & Student Adjustment & Attitudes
  3570 Special & Remedial Education
    3575 Gifted & Talented
  3580 Educational/Vocational Counseling & Student Services

3600 Industrial & Organizational Psychology
  3610 Occupational Interests & Guidance
  3620 Personnel Management & Selection & Training
  3630 Personnel Evaluation & Job Performance
  3640 Management & Management Training
  3650 Personnel Attitudes & Job Satisfaction
  3660 Organizational Behavior
  3670 Working Conditions & Industrial Safety

3700 Sport Psychology & Leisure
  3720 Sports
  3740 Recreation & Leisure

3800 Military Psychology

3900 Consumer Psychology
  3920 Consumer Attitudes & Behavior
  3940 Marketing & Advertising

4000 Engineering & Environmental Psychology
  4010 Human Factors Engineering
  4030 Lifespace & Institutional Design
  4050 Community & Environmental Planning
  4070 Environmental Issues & Attitudes
  4090 Transportation

4100 Intelligent Systems
  4120 Artificial Intelligence & Expert Systems
  4140 Robotics
  4160 Neural Networks

4200 Forensic Psychology & Legal Issues
  4210 Civil Rights & Civil Law
  4230 Criminal Law & Criminal Adjudication
  4250 Mediation & Conflict Resolution
  4270 Crime Prevention
  4290 Police & Legal Personnel

APPENDIX E: PsycINFO Master Quick Reference Guide

The chart on the following pages is a guide to the command syntax for searching PsycINFO record fields on the vendor systems available at the time of this edition's publication. Vendors not listed in this chart do not offer command syntax for searching.

The far left column of the chart contains PsycINFO field names. To find a field's corresponding label and search syntax, read across the field's row to the appropriate vendor column. Blank fields indicate that the field is not searchable in that vendor's interface.

For complete information about searching, users should consult the PsycINFO User Manual (http://www.apa.org/psycinfo/products/userman.html) or contact PsycINFO Customer Relations (psycinfo@apa.org) to obtain vendor-specific documentation or searching information.

PsycINFO MASTER QUICK REFERENCE GUIDE

PsycINFO	Cambridge Scientific Abstracts		Datastar		DIALOG	
FIELD NAME	LABEL	SEARCH EXAMPLES	LABEL	SEARCH EXAMPLES	LABEL	SEARCH EXAMPLES
Accession Number	AN	an=2004-10203-010	AN	2004-10203-010.an.	AA	s aa=2004-10203-010
Publication Type	PT	pt=(peer-reviewed-journal)	PT	pt=peer-reviewed-journal	DT	s dt=peer reviewed journal
Author	AU	au=beck, aaron	AU	beck-a$.au.	AU	s au=beck, aaron?
Author Affiliation	AF	af=(harvard u)	IN	harvard adj u.in.	CS	s cs=(harvard(w)u)
E-mail	EA	ea=barker				
Correspondence Address	CI	ci=(thompson kimberly)			AD	s ad=thompson(w)kimberly
Institutional Author	CA	ca=(national and inst* and child and health)	CA	(national adj inst adj child adj health).ca.		
Title	TI	ti=(multicultural counseling)	TI	multicultural adj counseling.ti.	TI	s multicultural(w)counseling/ti
Source	SO	so=(cognition & instruction and 2003 and dec)	SO	cognition-and-instruction.so.	SO	s so=(cognition and instruction and dec and 2003)
Journal Name	JN	jn=(counseling psychologist)	SO	counseling-psychologist.so.	JN	s jn=counseling psychologist
Special Issue Title	IT	it=(communication research)				[display-only field]
Access URL	IP	ip=academicpress				
DOI	DO	do=10.1016/S0306-4530(03)00030-1				
Book Series Title	SO	so=(behavioral and science)			SE	s se=(behavioral(w)science)
Parent Book Title	SO	so=(understanding and terrorism)			SO	s understanding(w)y terrorism/so
Publisher Publisher URL	PB	pb=(american psychological) pb=www.blackwellpublishing.com	SO	(american adj psychological).so blackwellpublishing.so	PU	s pu=(american(w)psychological)
ISSN	IS	is=0737-0008	SO	0737-0008.so	SN	s sn=0737 0008
Electronic ISSN	EI	ei=1362-3001			SN	s sn=1362-3001
ISBN	IB	ib=0787901253	SO	0-7879-0125-3.so.	BN	s bn=0-7879-0125-3
UMI Dissertation Order Number			UM	aam9835792.um.		[display-only field]
Format Availability	FV	fv=electronic; fv=print				
Format Covered	FC	fc=electronic				
Language	LA	la=english	LG	lg=english	LA	s la=english
Reviewed Item	RW	rw=(handbook and childhood and development			TX	s handbook(w1)childhood(w1)development/tx
Abstract	AB	ab=(solution space analysis)	AB	solution adj space adj analysis.so.	AB	s solution(w)space(w)analysis/ab
Key Concepts (Identifiers)	ID	id=(job retraining)	ID	job with retraining.id.	ID	s job(w)retraining/id
Descriptors All	DE	de=memory	DE	memory.de.	DE	s memory/de
Exact Term	DE	de=(episodic memory)	DE	episodic adj memory.de.	DF	s episodic(w)memory/df
Word/Phrase	DE	de=health care	DE	health care.de.	DE	s health(w)care/de
Explode (with narrower terms)						s antidepressant drugs
Major			MJ	personality-measures.mj.	MAJ	s career change/maj
Subject metalabels (Keywords, Topic, Subject)	KW	kw=(neuroimaging and alzheimer*) searches title, abstract, descriptors & identifiers				

(Continues)

PsycINFO	Cambridge Scientific Abstracts		Datastar		DIALOG	
FIELD NAME	**LABEL**	**SEARCH EXAMPLES**	**LABEL**	**SEARCH EXAMPLES**	**LABEL**	**SEARCH EXAMPLES**
Classification Code	CL	cl=28*; cl=331*; cl=3620	CC	28#.cc.; 331#.cc.; 3620.cc.	SH	s sh=28; s sh=3620
Age Group	PO	po=(school age)	AGE	age=school-age-6-12-yrs	AG	s ag=school age
Population Group	PO	po=human	PO	po=human	PG	s pg=human
Population Location	PO	lo=france	CN	cn=france	GN	s gn=france
Form/Content Type	PT	pt=(empirical study)	AT	at=empirical-study	DT	s dt=literature review?
Intended Audience	TA	ta=professional	TA	psychology.ta.	AI	s ai=psychology?
Conference Information	CF	cf=(forensic and 2004)	CF	(forensic and 2004).cf.	CT	s ct=(forensic and 2004)
Notes	NT	nt=(dubin and lecture)	NT	reprint.nt.		[display-only field]
Table of Contents	TB	tb=(political theor*)	TC	(political theor*).tc.	AB	s political(w)theor?*/tc
Tests & Measures	TM	tm=(wechsler adult); tm=wais	TM	wais.tm.		
Supplemental Data	SD	sd=(interactive web sites)				
Publication Year	PY	py=2004	YR	yr=2004	PY	s py=2004
Number of References	NR	nr=42				
Cited References	RE	re=(costa within 15 1992 within 15 inventory)	CR	(costa near 1992 near neo).cr.	CR	s (costa(3n)neo(12n)1992)/cr
Correction Date	LR	lr=20040126	CD	20040126.cd.		
Release Date	UD	ud=20040301	ED	20040301.ed.	UD	s ud=20040301

PsycINFO MASTER QUICK REFERENCE GUIDE

PsycINFO FIELD NAME	DIMDI LABEL	DIMDI SEARCH EXAMPLES	EBSCO LABEL	EBSCO SEARCH EXAMPLES	NISC LABEL	NISC SEARCH EXAMPLES
Accession Number	ND	find nd=2004-10203-010	AN	AN 2004-10203-010	AA	s aa=2004-10203-010
Publication Type	DTP	find dtp=peer reviewed journal	PT	PT peer reviewed journal	PT	pt=journal article
Author	AU	find au=beck a?	AR, AU	AR beck, aaron*; AUbeck	AU	au=beck
Author Affiliation	CS	find cs=harvard	AA	AA harvard	AD	ad=harvard u
E-mail						
Correspondence Address	RPADDR	find rpaddr=thompson kimberly			AD	ad=thompson kimberly
Institutional Author	CA	find national inst child health/ca	AU	AU national inst of child health		
Title	TI	find multicultural counseling/ti	TI	TI multicultural counseling	TI	ti=multicultural counseling
Source			SO	SO cognition and instruction and dec and 2003	SO	so=cognition & instruction and 2003
Journal Name	JT	find it=counseling psychologist jt=?cognition?	JN	JN cognition & instruction	JN	jn=counseling psychologist
Special Issue Title	JT	find jt–?special issue?		[display-only field]		
Access URL					UR	ur=academicpress
Book Series Title	SE	find behavioral science/se		[display only field]	SE	se=behavioral science
Parent Book Title		[display-only field]		[display only field]	TB	tb=understanding terrorism
Chapter title					CT	ct=crisis management
DOI	DOI	find doi=10.1037//1093-4510.3.1.20	DO	DO 10.1037//1093-4510.3.1.20	UR	ur=10.1037//1093-4510.3.1.20
Publisher	PU	find pu=american psychological	PB	PB american psychological	PB	pu=american psychological
ISSN	ISSN	find issn=0737-0008	IS	IS 07370008	SN	sn= 07370008
Electronic ISSN	ISSN	find issn=1362-3001	IS	1362-3001	SN	sn=1362-3001
ISBN	ISBN	find isbn=0-7879-0125-3	IB	ID 0-7879-0125-3	RN	bn=0787901253
UMI Dissertation Order Number	CN	find cn=aam9835792	DN	DN aam9835792	SO	so=aam9835792
Format Availability						
Format Covered	FSO	find fco=electronic				
Language	LA	find la=english	LA	LA english	LA	la=english
Reviewed Item	REV	find rev=handbook and childhood and development				
Abstract	AB	find solution space analysis/ab	AB	AB solution space analysis	AB	solution near space near analysis
Key Concepts (Identifiers)	KP	find retraining/kp	KP	KP job retraining	KP	kp=job retraining
Descriptors All	CT	find ct=memory	SU	SU memory	KT	kt=memory
Exact Term	CT	find ct=episodic memory	DE	DE episodic memeory	KT	kt=episodic memory
Word/Phrase	CT	find ct=health care	MJ	MJ health care	KT	kt=health care
Explode (with narrower terms)		find ct down antidepressant drugs				kt=exp antidepressant drugs
Major	W1	find ct=problem solving/w1	MC, MM	MJ personality measures	BT	bt=personality-measures
Subject metalabels (Keywords, Topic, Subject)	PQ	find (neuroimaging and alzheimers)/pq searches title, descriptors, key concepts				

(Continues)

PsycINFO	DIMDI		EBSCO		NISC	
FIELD NAME	**LABEL**	**SEARCH EXAMPLES**	**LABEL**	**SEARCH EXAMPLES**	**LABEL**	**SEARCH EXAMPLES**
Classification Code	SC	find sc=28.2.0; find sc down 28	CC	CC 28*; CC 3620	CC	cc=28*; cc=222*; cc=3620
Age Group	AGE	find school age/age	AG	AG school age	AG	ag=adolescence
Population Group	POP	find pop=human	PO	PO human	PO	po=human
Population Location	POPLOC	find poploc=france	PL	PL france	PL	pl=usa
Form/Content Type	DT	find dt=empirical study	CT	CT empirical study	FC	fc=empirical study
Intended Audience	AUD	find aud=psychology?	AI	AI psychology*	TA	ta=psychology*
Conference Information	CF	find cf=(forensic and 2004)	CN	CN (forensic and 2004)	CF	cf=(forensic and 2004)
Notes	NOTE	[display-only field]		[display-only field]	SO	so=dubin
Table of Contents	TC	find tc=political theor?	TC	TC political theor?		political theor*
Tests & Measures	METH	find meth=wechsler adult?; find meth=?wais?			TM	tm=wais; tm=wechsler adult
Supplemental Data	SUP	find sup=interactive web sites				
Publication Year	PY	find py=2004	YR	YR 1997	PY	py=2004
Number of References	RN	find rn=42				
Cited References	RF	find ra=?costa?/ri=psychological assessment/ry=1992			RF	RF=costa near neo near personality near 1992
Reference Author Index	RA		WA	WA costa And WB neo personality And WD 1992		
Reference Title Index			WB			
Reference Year Index	RY		WD			
Reference Source Index	RJ		WC	WC psychological assessment		
Correction Date			CD	CD=20040126		
Release Date	EDAT	find edat=20040301	EM	EM=20040301	RD	rd=20040301

PsycINFO MASTER QUICK REFERENCE GUIDE

FIELD NAME	PsycINFO LABEL	OCLC SEARCH EXAMPLES	Ovid LABEL	Ovid SEARCH EXAMPLES	ProQuest LABEL	ProQuest SEARCH EXAMPLES
Accession Number	NO	no:2004-10203-010	AN	2004-10203-010.an.	NO	no(2004-10203-010)
Publication Type	DT	dt=journal article	PT	journal article.pt.	DT STYPE	dt("journal article"): stype("peer reviewed journal")
Author	AU	au:beck; au=beck,aaron*	AU	beck-aaron$.au.	AU	au("beck aaron")
Author Affiliation	AA	aa:harvard u	IN	harvard u.in.	AA	aa("harvard u")
E-mail			cq	(barker and cuny).cq		
Correspondence Address			cq	(thompson and kimberly).cq		
Institutional Author	CO	co=national inst of child*	CA	(national inst child health).ca	CA	ca(national inst child health)
Title	TI	ti:multicultural counseling	TI	multicultural counseling.ti.	TI	ti(multicultural counseling)
Source Volume Issue	SO vo is	so:cognition & instruction vo:21 is:1	SO vo ip	cognition & instruct$.so. and "21".vo and "1".ip	SO	so(cognition & instruction)
Journal Name	SO	so=counseling psychologist	JN JW	counseling psychologist.jn. brain.jw	JO	jo(counseling psychologist)
Special Issue Title			SI	(communication research) in si		
Access URL	AM	am:academicpress	UR; JU	academicpress.ur; blackwell-publishing.ju	URL	url(http://www.apa.org/journals/law.html*)
Book Series Title	SE	se:behavioral science	ST	behavioral science.st.	SE	se(behavioral science)
Parent Book Title	CB	cb:understanding terrorism	BT	(understanding terrorism).bt.	CB	cb(understanding terrorism)
DOI						
Publisher	PB	pb:american psychological	PU	(american psychological).pu.	PB	pb(american psychological)
ISSN	SN	sn:0737-0008	IS	0737-0008.is.	ISSN SNUM	issn(0737-0008) snum(0737-0008)
Electronic ISSN	SN	sn:1362-3001		1362-3001.is	ISSN SNUM	issn(1362-3001) snum(1362-3001)
ISBN	SN	sn:0787901253	IB	0787901253.ib.	ISBN SNUM	isbn(0787901253): snum(0787901253)
UMI Dissertation Order Number			ON	aai0802081.on.		
Format Availability					FA	fa(electronic)
Format Covered					FC	fc(print)
Language	LN	ln=english	LG	english.lg.	LN	ln(english)
Reviewed Item					RVI	rvi(handbook childhood development)
Abstract	AB	ab:solution space analysis	AB	solution space analysis.ab.	AB	ab("solution space analysis")
Key words (Identifiers)	ID	id:job retraining	ID	job retraining.id.	ID	id(job retraining)
Descriptors/Index Terms All	DE	de: memory	DE	neural plasticity.de.	DE;SU	de(memory)
Exact Term	DE	de=episodic memory	SH	episodic memory.sh.	DE	de("episodic memory")
Word/Phrase	DE	de:health care	HW	health care.hw.	DE	de(health care)
Explode (with narrower terms)	SU	su:anitdepressant drugs		exp antidepressant drugs		

(Continues)

FIELD NAME (PsycINFO)	LABEL (OCLC)	SEARCH EXAMPLES (OCLC)	LABEL (Ovid)	SEARCH EXAMPLES (Ovid)	LABEL (ProQuest)	SEARCH EXAMPLES (ProQuest)
Major	MJ	mj=personality measures		*personality measures	MJ	mj(personality measures)
Subject Metalabels (Keywords, Topic, Subject)	KW	kw:(neuroimaging and alzheimers) searches title, descriptors, abstract, descriptors and TOC	MP	(neuroimaging and alzheimers).mp searches title, keyconcepts, abstract, descriptors and table of contents	SU	su(neuroimaging and alzheimers) searches title, identifiers
	SU	su:neural plasticity searches descriptors, identifiers				
Classification Code	CD	cd=3620*	CC	28.cc. 222.cc. 3620.cc.	CCD	ccd(28*); ccd(3620)
Age Group	AG	ag=180*	AG	school age.ag.	AG	ag(school); ag("adulthood 18 yrs & older")
Population Group	PG	pg=10 human	PO	human.po.	PG	pg(human*)
Population Location	GC	gc=france	LO	france.lo.	LOC; GC	loc(france); gc(france)
Form/Content Type	CT	ct=0800*	FC	empirical study.fc.	AT	at("0800 empirical study")
Intended Audience	IA	ia=juvenile	IA	psychology$.ia.	IA	ia(psychology*)
Conference Information	CN	cn=forensic and 2004	CF	(forensic and 2004).cf.	CN	cn("forensic and 2004")
Notes		[display-only field]	NT	reprint$.nt.		
Table of Contents	TC	tc:job w creation	TC	(political theor$).tc.	TC	tc(political theor*)
Tests & Measures					TM	tm(wechsler adult*); tm(wais)
Supplemental Material						
Publication Year	YR	yr:2004	YR	2004.yr.	PY	py(2004)
Number of References	NR	nr:42			NR	nr(42)
Cited References	CR	cr:(costa w10 neo personality w5 1992)	RF	costa-p$.ca and neo personality.cv and 1992.cb and (psychological assessment).cs	CT	ct(costa w/10 neo personality w/10 1992)
Cited Reference Author			CA			
Cited Reference Title			CV			
Cited Reference Date			CB			
Cited Reference Source			CS			
Last Revision Date	DV	dv:20040126				
Update Code	DA	da:20040301	UP	20040301.up.	UD	ud(20040301)

PsycINFO MASTER QUICK REFERENCE GUIDE

FIELD NAME	PsycNET (APA) LABEL	PsycNET (APA) SEARCH EXAMPLES	Silver-Platter LABEL	Silver-Platter SEARCH EXAMPLES	Thomson ISI LABEL	Thomson ISI SEARCH EXAMPLES
Accession Number	UID	2004-10203-010:uid	AN	(2004-10203-010) in an	IC	ic=(2004-10203-010)
Document Type	doctype	(peer reviewed):doctype	DT	dt=peer-reviewed-journal		
Author	author	'beck aaron':author	AU	beck-aaron* in au	AU	au=(beck aaron)
Author Affiliation	affiliation	'harvard u':affiliation	AF	(harvard u) in af	AD	ad=(harvard u)
E-mail	CRA	(barker and cuny.edu)		barker in cor	AD	ad=(barker and cuny.edu)
Correspondence Address	CRA	'thompson kimberly':cra	COR	(thompson kimberly) in cor	AD	ad=(thompson kimberly)
Institutional Author	author	(national inst* child health):author	CA	(national inst* child health) in ca	IA	ia=(national and inst* and child and health)
Title	title	(multicultural counseling):title	TI	(multicultural counseling) in ti	TI	ti=(multicultural counseling)
Source	source	(cognition and instruction and 2003 and dec):source	SO	(cognition-and-instruction and 2003 dec) in so	SO	so=(cognition & instruction)
Journal Name	source	'rehabilitation psychology':source	JN	rehabilitation-psychology in jn	SO	so=(rehabilitation psychology)
Special Issue Title			SI	(communication research) in si		
Access URL		[display-only field]			IC	ic=(http://www.academic-press.com*)
Book Series Title			ST	(behavioral science) in so		
Parent Book Title			BT	[display-only field]		
DOI		[display-only field]		[display-only field]		
Publisher	PUB	'american psychological':pub	PB	american-psychological in pb		
ISSN	ISSN	(0737-0008):issn	IS	0737-0008 in is	IC	ic=(0737-0008)
Electronic ISSN	ISSN	(1362-3001):issn	ISE	1362-3001 in ise	IC	ic=(1362-3001)
ISBN	ISBN	(0-7879-0125-3):isbn	IB	0787901253 in ib	IC	ic=(0-7879-0125-3)
UMI Dissertation Order Number			UM	um=aai3067687	IC	ic= aam9428690
Format Availability						
Format Covered						
Language	LANG	english:lang	LA	la=english		
Reviewed Item						
Abstract	abstract	(solution near space near analysis):abstract	AB	(solution space analysis) in ab	TS	ts=(solution same space same analysis)
Key words (Identifiers)	ID	(job retraining):keyconcepts	KP	(job retraining) in kp	TS	ts=(job retraining)
Descriptors/Index Terms All	DE	memory:keywords	DE	memory in de	DE	de=memory
Exact Term	DE	'episodic memory':keywords	DE	episodic-memory.de	DE	de=(episodic memory)
Word/Phrase	DE	health:keywords	DE	health- in de	DE	de=health
Explode (with narrower-terms)			DE	exp antidepressant drugs in de		
Major			MJ	personality-measures in mj		

(Continues)

	PsycNET (APA)		Silver-Platter		Thomson ISI	
FIELD NAME	**LABEL**	**SEARCH EXAMPLES**	**LABEL**	**SEARCH EXAMPLES**	**LABEL**	**SEARCH EXAMPLES**
Subject Metalabels **(Keywords, Topic, Subject)**			SU	(neuroimaging and alzheimer*) in su searches descriptors and keyconcepts simultaneously	TS (topic)	ts=(neuroimaging and alzheimer*) searches title, translated title, abstract, keyconcepts, descriptors, TOC
Classification Code	CLS	28*:cls; 3620:cls	CC	cc=28 ; cc=3620	CL	cl=28*; cl=3620
Age Group	AGE	adolescence:age	AG	ag=school-age		
Population Group	POP	human:pop	PO	po=human		
Population Location	LOC	france:loc	LO	lo=france		
Form/Content Type	FORM	'empirical study':form	PT	pt=empirical-study		
Intended Audience			AT	at=psychology*		
Conference Information			CF	(forensic and 2004) in cf	CO	co=(forensic and 2004)
Notes			NT	[display-only field]		
Table of Contents	TOC	(political theor*):toc	TC	political theor* in tc	TS	ts=(politic* theor*)
Tests & Measures	INS	(wechsler adult):ins				
Supplemental Material	SUP	(web sites):sup				
Publication Year	YEAR	2004:year	PY	py=2004		
Number of References						

Cited References
 	
     Reference Author Index
     Reference Title Index
     Reference Year Index
     Reference Source Index
			REF
			
			 RAI
			 RTI
			 RYI
			 RSI
				[display-only field]
				
				 costa-p* in rai
				 (neo personality inventory) in rti
				 ryi=1992
				 psychological-assessment in rsi
					CR	cr=(costa same inventory same 1992)

Correction Date			CD	cd=20040126	IC	ic=20040126
Release Date	RDATE	20040301:rdate	UD	ud=20040301	IC	ic=20040301

RELATIONSHIP SECTION

Abandonment 1997
PN 101   SC 00005
SN Loneliness, anxiety, and emotional and psycho-
logical loss of support resulting from desertion or
neglect. Used for human populations.
UF Desertion
R Attachment Behavior 1985
↓ Child Abuse 1971
Child Neglect 1988
Dependency (Personality) 1967
↓ Emotional States 1973
Loneliness 1973
↓ Relationship Termination 1997
Separation Anxiety 1973
↓ Separation Reactions 1997

Abdomen 1973
PN 224   SC 00010
B Anatomy 1967

Abdominal Wall 1973
PN 9   SC 00020
B Muscles 1967

Abducens Nerve 1973
PN 22   SC 00030
UF Nerve (Abducens)
B Cranial Nerves 1973

Ability 1967
PN 3617   SC 00070
SN Conceptually broad term referring to the skills,
talents, or qualities that enable one to perform a task.
Use a more specific term if possible.
UF Aptitude
Skills
Talent
N Academic Aptitude 1973
↓ Cognitive Ability 1973
↓ Communication Skills 1973
↓ Employee Skills 1970
Learning Ability 1973
↓ Nonverbal Ability 1900
↓ Reading Skills 1973
Self Care Skills 1978
Social Skills 1978
R Ability Grouping 1973
Ability Level 1978
↓ Achievement Potential 1973
↓ Competence 1982
Creativity 1967
Gifted 1967
↓ Intelligence 1967
↓ Performance 1967

Ability Grouping 1973
PN 389   SC 00040
SN Grouping or selection of individuals for instruc-
tional or other purposes based on differences in abil-
ity or achievement.
R ↓ Ability 1967
Ability Level 1978
Academic Aptitude 1973
↓ Education 1967
Educational Placement 1978
Grade Level 1994
Special Education 1967

Ability Level 1978
PN 1811   SC 00050

Ability Level — (cont'd)
SN Demonstrated level of performance. Used in
academic, cognitive, perceptual, or occupational con-
texts, as well as an indicator of a patient's level of
functioning.
UF Functional Status
Level of Functioning
R ↓ Ability 1967
Ability Grouping 1973
Activities of Daily Living 1991
Adaptive Testing 1985

Ability Tests
Use Aptitude Measures

Ablation
Use Lesions

Abnormal Psychology 2003
PN 62   SC 00083
SN Branch of psychology concerned with the study
of mental disorders.
HN This term was introduced in June 2003. Psyc-
INFO records from the past 10 years were re-indexed
with this term. The posting note reflects the number
of records that were re-indexed.
B Psychology 1967
R ↓ Mental Disorders 1967
Psychopathology 1967

Aboriginal Populations
Use Indigenous Populations

Abortion (Induced)
Use Induced Abortion

Abortion (Spontaneous)
Use Spontaneous Abortion

Abortion Laws 1973
PN 101   SC 00110
B Laws 1967
R Induced Abortion 1971

Abreaction
Use Catharsis

Absenteeism (Employee)
Use Employee Absenteeism

Absorption (Physiological) 1973
PN 72   SC 00140
B Physiology 1967
R Bioavailability 1991
↓ Cells (Biology) 1973
Intestines 1973
Skin (Anatomy) 1967

Abstinence (Drugs)
Use Drug Abstinence

Abstinence (Sexual)
Use Sexual Abstinence

Abstraction 1967
PN 1153   SC 00160

Abstraction — (cont'd)
SN Process of selecting or isolating a certain con-
ceptual aspect from a concrete whole.
B Thinking 1967
N ↓ Imagery 1967
R Divergent Thinking 1973

Abuse of Power 1997
PN 61   SC 00165
B Power 1967
R Authority 1967
Coercion 1994
↓ Dominance 1967
↓ Leadership 1967

Abuse Potential (Drugs)
Use Drug Abuse Liability

Abuse Reporting 1997
PN 146   SC 00180
N Child Abuse Reporting 1997
R Battered Females 1988
↓ Child Abuse 1971
Duty to Warn 2001
Elder Abuse 1988
Informants 1988
↓ Laws 1967
Partner Abuse 1001
Physical Abuse 1991
Privileged Communication 1973
Professional Ethics 1973
↓ Sexual Abuse 1988

Academic Achievement 1967
PN 21052   SC 00190
UF Gradepoint Average
Scholastic Achievement
School Achievement
B Achievement 1967
N Academic Overachievement 1967
Academic Underachievement 1967
College Academic Achievement 1067
Mathematics Achievement 1073
Reading Achievement 1973
Science Achievement 1997
R Academic Achievement Motivation 1973
Academic Achievement Prediction 1967
Academic Aptitude 1973
Academic Failure 1978
Academic Self Concept 1997
↓ Education 1967
Educational Attainment Level 1997
School Graduation 1991
School Learning 1967
School Transition 1997

Academic Achievement Motivation 1973
PN 2281   SC 00200
B Achievement Motivation 1967
R ↓ Academic Achievement 1967
Academic Self Concept 1997

Academic Achievement Prediction 1967
PN 2925   SC 00210
SN Prediction of future academic achievement
based on results of tests, inventories, or other mea-
sures.
B Prediction 1967
R ↓ Academic Achievement 1967

Academic Aptitude 1973
PN 1469   SC 00220

Academic Aptitude — (cont'd)
SN Potential ability to perform or achieve in scholastic pursuits.
  UF Aptitude (Academic)
     Scholastic Aptitude
  B Ability 1967
     Achievement Potential 1973
  R Ability Grouping 1973
     ↓ Academic Achievement 1967
     ↓ Education 1967
     ↓ Nonverbal Ability 1988
     Reading Ability 1973
     Student Admission Criteria 1973
     Verbal Ability 1967

Academic Environment 1973
PN 730   **SC** 00230
SN Physical setting or emotional climate where formal instruction takes place.
  B Social Environments 1973
  N Classroom Environment 1973
     Same Sex Education 2003
     ↓ School Environment 1973
  R Learning Environment 2004
     School Violence 2003
     ↓ Single Sex Environments 2001

Academic Failure 1978
PN 1033   **SC** 00233
  B Failure 1967
  R ↓ Academic Achievement 1967
     Academic Underachievement 1967

Academic Grade Level
  Use Grade Level

Academic Overachievement 1967
PN 476   **SC** 00240
SN Academic achievement greater than that anticipated on basis of one's scholastic aptitude score or individual intelligence.
  UF Overachievement (Academic)
  B Academic Achievement 1967

Academic Records
  Use Student Records

Academic Self Concept 1997
PN 539   **SC** 00248
  B Self Concept 1967
  R ↓ Academic Achievement 1967
     Academic Achievement Motivation 1973
     Self Confidence 1994
     Self Efficacy 1985
     Self Perception 1967

Academic Specialization 1973
PN 1976   **SC** 00250
SN Concentration of effort or interest in a special area of knowledge or discipline at an institution of learning.
  UF College Major
     Specialization (Academic)
  R Educational Aspirations 1973
     Professional Specialization 1991

Academic Underachievement 1967
PN 1748   **SC** 00260
SN Academic achievement less than that expected based on one's scholastic aptitude score or individual intelligence.

Academic Underachievement — (cont'd)
  UF Underachievement (Academic)
  B Academic Achievement 1967
  R Academic Failure 1978
     ↓ Failure 1967

Acalculia 1973
PN 142   **SC** 00270
SN Form of aphasia involving impaired ability to perform simple arithmetic calculations.
  UF Dyscalculia
  B Aphasia 1967
  R ↓ Learning Disabilities 1973

Accelerated Speech
  Use Speech Rate

Acceleration Effects 1973
PN 202   **SC** 00290
SN Behavioral, physiological, or psychological effects resulting from acceleration onset/offset or the effects of changes in acceleration rate. Used for both human and animal populations.
  R ↓ Aviation 1967
     Decompression Effects 1973
     Flight Simulation 1973
     ↓ Gravitational Effects 1967
     Physiological Stress 1967
     Spaceflight 1967

Acceptance (Social)
  Use Social Acceptance

Accessory Nerve
  Use Cranial Nerves

Accident Prevention 1973
PN 576   **SC** 00330
  B Prevention 1973
  R ↓ Accidents 1967
     Risk Management 1997
     ↓ Safety 1967
     ↓ Transportation Accidents 1973
     Warning Labels 1997
     ↓ Warnings 1997

Accident Proneness 1973
PN 178   **SC** 00340
  R ↓ Accidents 1967
     ↓ Safety 1967

Accidents 1967
PN 920   **SC** 00350
  N Falls 2004
     Home Accidents 1973
     Industrial Accidents 1973
     Pedestrian Accidents 1973
     ↓ Transportation Accidents 1973
  R Accident Prevention 1973
     Accident Proneness 1973
     ↓ Disasters 1973
     Driving Under the Influence 1988
     ↓ Hazardous Materials 1991
     Hazards 1973
     ↓ Injuries 1973
     ↓ Safety 1967
     Warning Labels 1997
     ↓ Warnings 1997

Acclimatization (Thermal)
  Use Thermal Acclimatization

Accomplishment
  Use Achievement

Accountability 1988
PN 553   **SC** 00385
SN Liability and/or responsibility for specified results or outcomes of an activity over which one has authority.
  B Responsibility 1973
  R Blame 1994
     ↓ Competence 1982
     Consumer Protection 1973
     Criminal Responsibility 1991
     Duty to Warn 2001
     ↓ Management
     Professional Liability 1985
     ↓ Professional Standards 1973
     Quality Control 1988
     Quality of Care 1988

Accountants 1973
PN 344   **SC** 00390
  UF Certified Public Accountants
  B White Collar Workers 1973

Accreditation (Education Personnel) 1973
PN 100   **SC** 00400
SN Professional licensing or certification of teachers, school psychologists, or other educational personnel, usually required for employment.
  UF Teacher Accreditation
  B Professional Certification 1973
     Professional Licensing 1973
  R ↓ Education 1967
     Educational Quality 1997
     Professional Examinations 1994

Accreditation (Educational Programs)
  Use Educational Program Accreditation

Acculturation 2003
PN 3437   **SC** 00410
SN Contact of at least two autonomous cultural groups resulting in change in one or the other, or both groups. Includes the process of a minority group giving up its own cultural traits and absorbing those of a dominant society.
HN In June 2003, this term replaced the discontinued term CULTURAL ASSIMILATION. CULTURAL ASSIMILATION was removed from all records and replaced with ACCULTURATION.
  UF Assimilation (Cultural)
     Cultural Assimilation
  B Culture Change 1967
  R Cross Cultural Communication 1997
     Cross Cultural Psychology 1997
     Cultural Sensitivity 1994
     Multiculturalism 1997

Acetaldehyde 1982
PN 108   **SC** 00415
SN First oxidation product of primary alcohol metabolism. Acetaldehyde has narcotic properties.
  UF Acetic Aldehyde
     Ethanal
     Ethylaldehyde
  R ↓ Alcohols 1967

Acetaldehyde — (cont'd)
↓ Carbohydrate Metabolism 1973
↓ Dopamine Metabolites 1982

Acetazolamide 1973
PN 36   **SC** 00420
B Diuretics 1973
Enzyme Inhibitors 1985
R ↓ Anticonvulsive Drugs 1973

Acetic Aldehyde
Use Acetaldehyde

Acetylcholine 1973
PN 1070   **SC** 00430
B Cholinergic Drugs 1973
Cholinomimetic Drugs 1973
Neurotransmitters 1985
R Acetylcholinesterase 1973
↓ Choline 1973
Cholinergic Nerves 1973
Cholinergic Receptors 2003

Acetylcholine Receptors
Use Cholinergic Receptors

Acetylcholinesterase 1973
PN 399   **SC** 00440
B Esterases 1973
R Acetylcholine 1973
Cholinesterase 1973

Acetylsalicylic Acid
Use Aspirin

Aches
Use Pain

Achievement 1967
PN 3801   **SC** 00470
UF Accomplishment
Attainment (Achievement)
Success
N ↓ Academic Achievement 1967
Occupational Success 1978
R ↓ Achievement Measures 1967
↓ Competence 1982
↓ Failure 1967
↓ Performance 1967

Achievement Measures 1967
PN 2133   **SC** 00490
SN Tests designed to measure knowledge and/or skills acquired from learning, experience, or training.
UF Tests (Achievement)
B Measurement 1967
N Iowa Tests of Basic Skills 1973
Stanford Achievement Test 1973
Wide Range Achievement Test 1973
Woodcock Johnson Psychoeducational
    Battery 2001
R ↓ Achievement 1967
Criterion Referenced Tests 1982

Achievement Motivation 1967
PN 3657   **SC** 00500
SN Need that drives an individual to improve, succeed, or excel.
UF NAch
Need Achievement

Achievement Motivation — (cont'd)
B Motivation 1967
N Academic Achievement Motivation 1973
R ↓ Achievement Potential 1973
Fear of Success 1978
↓ Needs 1967

Achievement Potential 1973
PN 214   **SC** 00510
SN One's general ability to achieve in any area, including academic.
UF Potential (Achievement)
N Academic Aptitude 1973
R ↓ Ability 1967
↓ Achievement Motivation 1967

Achilles Tendon Reflex 1973
PN 16   **SC** 00520
B Reflexes 1971

Achromatic Color 1973
PN 167   **SC** 00530
SN Visual quality which lacks hue and saturation, consequently varying only in brilliance. Includes variations from black through gray to white.
B Color 1967
R ↓ Chromaticity 1997
Color Saturation 1997

Acids 1973
PN 596   **SC** 00550
N ↓ Amino Acids 1973
Ascorbic Acid 1973
Aspirin 1973
Dihydroxyphenylacetic Acid 1991
↓ Fatty Acids 1973
Heparin 1973
Homovanillic Acid 1978
Hydroxyindoleacetic Acid (5-) 1985
Kainic Acid 1988
Lactic Acid 1991
Lysergic Acid Diethylamide 1967
Nicotinic Acid 1973
↓ Nucleic Acids 1973
Taurine 1982
Uric Acid 1973
R ↓ Drugs 1967
↓ Solvents 1982

Acoustic Nerve 1973
PN 137   **SC** 00570
UF Auditory Nerve
Nerve (Acoustic)
B Cranial Nerves 1973

Acoustic Reflex 1973
PN 566   **SC** 00580
SN Bilateral contraction of stapedius muscles when a loud sound is presented.
UF Intra Aural Muscle Reflex
Stapedius Reflex
B Reflexes 1971
R Startle Reflex 1967

Acoustic Stimuli
Use Auditory Stimulation

Acoustics 1997
PN 724   **SC** 00591
SN Structural properties of auditorially perceived stimuli or sounds.
UF Sound Waves

Acoustics — (cont'd)
R ↓ Auditory Perception 1967
↓ Auditory Stimulation 1967
Noise Effects 1973
↓ Speech Characteristics 1973
↓ Stimulus Parameters 1967

Acquaintance Rape 1991
PN 305   **SC** 00593
SN Rape perpetrated by a person or persons known to the victim.
UF Date Rape
B Rape 1973
R ↓ Human Courtship 1973
Social Dating 1973

Acquired Immune Deficiency Syndrome 1988
PN 6790   **SC** 00595
UF AIDS
B Human Immunodeficiency Virus 1991
Sexually Transmitted Diseases 2003
Syndromes 1973
R AIDS (Attitudes Toward) 1997
AIDS Dementia Complex 1997
AIDS Prevention 1994
HIV Testing 1997
Safe Sex 2003
Zidovudine 1994

Acrophobia 1973
PN 61   **SC** 00600
SN Fear of heights.
B Phobias 1967

ACTH (Hormone)
Use Corticotropin

ACTH Releasing Factor
Use Corticotropin Releasing Factor

Acting Out 1967
PN 586   **SC** 00620
SN Behavioral manifestation of those impulses and desires that are unacceptable or irreconcilable with an individual's conscience. When such behavior becomes maladaptive, socially or personally, it is classified as an acting out disorder.
B Symptoms 1967
R ↓ Behavior Disorders 1971
↓ Emotionally Disturbed 1973
Enactments 1997
Rebelliousness 2003

Active Avoidance
Use Avoidance Conditioning

Activism 2003
PN 609   **SC** 00635
SN Doctrines or practices emphasizing direct action (usually political) in support of or opposition to one side of a controversial issue.
HN In June 2003, this term was created to replace the discontinued term ACTIVIST MOVEMENTS. ACTIVIST MOVEMENTS was removed from all records containing it and replaced with ACTIVISM.
UF Activist Movements
B Social Behavior 1967
N Student Activism 1973
R Black Power Movement 1973
Civil Rights Movement 1973

Activism — (cont'd)
              Community Involvement 2003
              Homosexual Liberation Movement 1973
      ↓ Political Attitudes 1973
      ↓ Political Participation 1988
              School Integration 1982
              Social Change 1967
              Social Demonstrations 1973
      ↓ Social Integration 1982
              Womens Liberation Movement 1973

Activism (Student)
  Use Student Activism

Activist Movements
  Use Activism

Activities of Daily Living 1991
PN 1825   **SC** 00655
SN Basic personal care skills such as eating, bathing, dressing, and other personal hygenic skills used to measure functional ability in the elderly and the emotionally and physically disabled. Compare DAILY ACTIVITIES.
  R Ability Level 1978
          Activity Level 1982
          Assisted Living 2003
          Daily Activities 1994
          Geriatric Assessment 1997
          Habilitation 1991
          Hygiene 1994
          Independent Living Programs 1991
          Physical Mobility 1994
      ↓ Rehabilitation 1967
          Self Care Skills 1978

Activity Level 1982
PN 6196   **SC** 00660
SN General energetic state of an organism, frequently used as a measure of drug effects but not restricted to this application.
  B Motor Processes 1967
  R Activities of Daily Living 1991
          Daily Activities 1994
      ↓ Motivation 1967
          Physical Mobility 1994
          Rotational Behavior 1994

Activity Theory 2003
PN 76   **SC** 00664
SN Theory formulated by early 20th century Russian psychologists analyzing behavior based on an individual's activity in or interaction with his or her environment.
HN This term was introduced in June 2003. PsycINFO records from the past 10 years were re-indexed with this term. The posting note reflects the number of records that were re-indexed.
  B Theories 1967
  R ↓ Learning 1967
          ↓ Motivation 1967
          ↓ Participation 1973
              Vygotsky (Lev) 1991

Activity Therapy
  Use Recreation Therapy

Actualization (Self)
  Use Self Actualization

Acupuncture 1973
PN 418   **SC** 00690
  B Alternative Medicine 1997
          Physical Treatment Methods 1973

Acute Alcoholic Intoxication 1973
PN 60   **SC** 00700
SN Temporary mental disturbance marked by muscle incoordination and paresis as the result of excessive alcohol ingestion.
  B Alcohol Intoxication 1973
          Brain Disorders 1967
          Toxic Disorders 1973
  R Toxic Encephalopathies 1973

Acute Paranoid Disorder
  Use Paranoia (Psychosis)

Acute Psychosis 1973
PN 468   **SC** 00710
HN In 1988, this term replaced the discontinued term ACUTE PSYCHOTIC EPISODE. In 2000, ACUTE PSYCHOTIC EPISODE was removed from all records containing it, and replaced with ACUTE PSYCHOSIS.
  UF Acute Psychotic Episode
          Brief Reactive Psychosis
          Psychotic Episode (Acute)
  B Psychosis 1967
  N Acute Schizophrenia 1973

Acute Psychotic Episode
  Use Acute Psychosis

Acute Schizophrenia 1973
PN 646   **SC** 00730
  B Acute Psychosis 1973
          Schizophrenia 1967
  R Postpartum Psychosis 2003

Acute Stress Disorder 2003
PN 95   **SC** 00733
SN Disorder characterized by the development of anxiety and dissociative symptoms as a result of exposure to a traumatic event. Symptoms last at least two days and no longer than four weeks.
HN This term was introduced in June 2003. PsycINFO records from the past 10 years were re-indexed with this term. The posting note reflects the number of records that were re-indexed.
  B Anxiety Disorders 1997
  R Debriefing (Psychological) 2004
          Emotional Trauma 1967
          Posttraumatic Stress Disorder 1985
          Stress Reactions 1973

Adaptability (Personality) 1973
PN 720   **SC** 00740
SN Ability to be flexible and to maximize functioning in the face of environmental changes. See ADJUSTMENT for terms relating to the process of adapting.
  UF Flexibility (Personality)
  B Personality Traits 1967
  R ↓ Adjustment 1967
              Agreeableness 1997
              Coping Behavior 1967
              Openness to Experience 1997
              Resilience (Psychological) 2003

Adaptation 1967
PN 1829   **SC** 00750

Adaptation — (cont'd)
SN Physiological or biological modification of an organism or its morphology in response to the physical environment. For psychological, social, or emotional adaptation, use ADJUSTMENT or one of its narrower or related terms.
  UF Readaptation
  N Environmental Adaptation 1973
      ↓ Sensory Adaptation 1967
          Thermal Acclimatization 1973

Adaptation (Dark)
  Use Dark Adaptation

Adaptation (Environmental)
  Use Environmental Adaptation

Adaptation (Light)
  Use Light Adaptation

Adaptation (Sensory)
  Use Sensory Adaptation

Adaptation (Social)
  Use Social Adjustment

Adaptive Behavior 1991
PN 808   **SC** 00793
SN Behaviors indicating ability to take care of personal needs, function socially, and control problem behavior. Primarily used for disabled or disordered populations.
  B Behavior 1967
  R ↓ Adjustment 1967
          ↓ Mental Disorders 1967
          ↓ Mental Retardation 1967
          ↓ Rehabilitation 1967
              Self Care Skills 1978
              Social Skills 1978
              Special Education 1967

Adaptive Testing 1985
PN 294   **SC** 00795
SN Testing method, usually using a computer, in which test items of varying difficulty levels are selected according to the degree to which the examinee's previous answers were correct.
  UF Tailored Testing
  B Testing Methods 1967
  R Ability Level 1978
          Computer Assisted Testing 1988
          Item Analysis (Statistical) 1973
      ↓ Test Construction 1973

Addiction 1973
PN 1360   **SC** 00800
  B Behavior Disorders 1971
  N ↓ Alcoholism 1967
          ↓ Drug Addiction 1967
              Sexual Addiction 1997
  R Craving 1997
          ↓ Drug Abuse 1973
          ↓ Drug Usage 1971
              Pathological Gambling 1988
              Workaholism 2004

Addisons Disease 1973
PN 19   **SC** 00810
  B Adrenal Gland Disorders 1973
          Syndromes 1973

Addisons Disease — (cont'd)
R ↓ Tuberculosis 1973

Adenosine 1973
PN 534   SC 00820
B Nucleic Acids 1973

ADHD
Use Attention Deficit Disorder with Hyperactivity

Adjectives 1973
PN 494   SC 00830
B Form Classes (Language) 1973

Adjudication 1967
PN 4390   SC 00840
SN Process of judicial decision making.
HN Use ADJUDICATION to access references to JURIES from 1967-1984.
UF Courts
    Juvenile Court
    Sentencing
    Verdict Determination
B Law Enforcement 1978
N Court Referrals 1994
R Criminal Conviction 1973
   ↓ Criminal Justice 1991
   Criminal Responsibility 1991
   Juries 1995
   Jury Selection 1994
   Juvenile Justice 2004
   Legal Decisions 1991
   ↓ Legal Evidence 1991
   Litigation 2003

Adjunctive Behavior 1982
PN 60   SC 00845
SN Noncontingent appropriate or inappropriate behavior that is maintained by an event which acquires its reinforcing characteristics as the result of some other ongoing reinforcement contingency.
B Behavior 1967
N Polydipsia 1982
R ↓ Operant Conditioning 1967
   Pica 1973

Adjustment 1967
PN 9134   SC 00850
SN Conceptually broad term referring to a state of harmony between internal needs and external demands and the processes used in achieving this condition. Use a more specific term if possible. Differentiate from ADAPTATION, which refers to physiological or biological adaptation.
N ↓ Emotional Adjustment 1973
   Occupational Adjustment 1973
   School Adjustment 1967
   Social Adjustment 1973
R Adaptability (Personality) 1973
   Adaptive Behavior 1991
   Adjustment Disorders 1994
   Person Environment Fit 1991
   Well Being 1994
   Work Adjustment Training 1991

Adjustment Disorders 1994
PN 209   SC 00855
SN Maladaptive reaction to psychosocial stressors which impairs social or occupational functioning. Usually a temporary condition that remits after new levels of adaptation are obtained or stressors have been removed.

Adjustment Disorders — (cont'd)
B Mental Disorders 1967
R ↓ Adjustment 1967
   Coping Behavior 1967
   ↓ Emotional Adjustment 1973
   Emotional Trauma 1967
   Occupational Adjustment 1973
   Posttraumatic Stress Disorder 1985
   School Adjustment 1967
   Social Adjustment 1973
   ↓ Stress 1967
   Stress Reactions 1973

Adler (Alfred) 1967
PN 429   SC 00860
SN Identifies biographical or autobiographical studies and discussions of Adler's works.
R Adlerian Psychotherapy 1997
   Individual Psychology 1973
   ↓ Psychologists 1967

Adlerian Psychotherapy 1997
PN 237   SC 00865
UF Individual Psychotherapy (Adlerian)
B Psychoanalysis 1967
   Psychotherapy 1967
R Adler (Alfred) 1967
   Individual Psychology 1973

Administration (Test)
Use Test Administration

Administrators
Use Management Personnel

Administrators (School)
Use School Administrators

Admission (Hospital)
Use Hospital Admission

Admission (Psychiatric Hospital)
Use Psychiatric Hospital Admission

Admission Criteria (Student)
Use Student Admission Criteria

Adolescent Attitudes 1988
PN 4601   SC 00925
SN Attitudes of, not toward, adolescents.
B Attitudes 1967

Adolescent Development 1973
PN 7992   SC 00930
SN Process of physical, cognitive, personality, and psychosocial growth occurring from age 13 through 17. Use a more specific term if possible.
B Human Development 1967
R ↓ Childhood Development 1967
   Developmental Age Groups 1973
   ↓ Developmental Stages 1973
   ↓ Physical Development 1973
   ↓ Psychogenesis 1973
   Sex Linked Developmental Differences 1973
   Sexual Development 1973

Adolescent Fathers 1985
PN 213   SC 00932
SN Fathers aged 13-17 years.

Adolescent Fathers — (cont'd)
UF Teenage Fathers
B Fathers 1967
R Adolescent Pregnancy 1988

Adolescent Mothers 1985
PN 1219   SC 00935
SN Mothers aged 13-17 years. Consider also UNWED MOTHERS.
UF Teenage Mothers
B Mothers 1967
R Adolescent Pregnancy 1988

Adolescent Pregnancy 1988
PN 1213   SC 00936
UF Teenage Pregnancy
B Pregnancy 1967
R Adolescent Fathers 1985
   Adolescent Mothers 1985
   ↓ Social Issues 1991

Adolescent Psychiatry 1985
PN 1222   SC 00937
B Psychiatry 1967
R Adolescent Psychotherapy 1994

Adolescent Psychology 1973
PN 575   SC 00940
SN Branch of developmental psychology devoted to the study and treatment of adolescents. Use a more specific term if possible.
B Developmental Psychology 1973

Adolescent Psychotherapy 1994
PN 712   SC 00945
B Psychotherapy 1967
R Adolescent Psychiatry 1985
   ↓ Child Psychotherapy 1967

Adopted Children 1973
PN 860   SC 00960
B Adoptees 1985
   Family Members 1973
R ↓ Adoption (Child) 1967
   Interracial Adoption 1994

Adoptees 1985
PN 376   SC 00965
SN Anyone who has been formally adopted as a dependent. Limited to human populations.
N Adopted Children 1973
R ↓ Adoption (Child) 1967
   Interracial Adoption 1994

Adoption (Child) 1967
PN 1152   SC 00970
B Legal Processes 1973
N Interracial Adoption 1994
R Adopted Children 1973
   ↓ Adoptees 1985
   Adoptive Parents 1973
   Child Welfare 1988

Adoptive Parents 1973
PN 576   SC 00980
B Parents 1967
R ↓ Adoption (Child) 1967
   Interracial Adoption 1994

Adrenal Cortex Hormones 1973
PN 223   SC 00990

7

Adrenal Cortex Hormones — (cont'd)
B   Hormones 1967
N   Aldosterone 1973
    Corticosterone 1973
    Cortisone 1973
    Deoxycorticosterone 1973
    ↓ Glucocorticoids 1982
    Hydrocortisone 1973
    Prednisolone 1973
R   ↓ Adrenal Glands 1973
    ↓ Adrenal Medulla Hormones 1973
    ↓ Corticosteroids 1973
    ↓ Stress 1967

Adrenal Cortex Steroids
Use   Corticosteroids

Adrenal Gland Disorders 1973
PN 74   **SC** 01010
B   Endocrine Disorders 1973
N   Addisons Disease 1973
    Cushings Syndrome 1973
R   ↓ Endocrine Sexual Disorders 1973
    ↓ Pituitary Disorders 1973

Adrenal Gland Secretion 1973
PN 86   **SC** 01020
B   Endocrine Gland Secretion 1973

Adrenal Glands 1973
PN 515   **SC** 01030
B   Endocrine Glands 1973
N   Hypothalamo Pituitary Adrenal System 1997
R   ↓ Adrenal Cortex Hormones 1973

Adrenal Medulla Hormones 1973
PN 53   **SC** 01040
B   Hormones 1967
N   Norepinephrine 1973
R   ↓ Adrenal Cortex Hormones 1973

Adrenalectomy 1973
PN 394   **SC** 01050
B   Endocrine Gland Surgery 1973

Adrenaline
Use   Epinephrine

Adrenaline Receptors
Use   Adrenergic Receptors

Adrenergic Blocking Drugs 1973
PN 1145   **SC** 01070
UF   Beta Blockers
B   Drugs 1967
N   Alpha Methylparatyrosine 1978
    Dihydroergotamine 1973
    Hydroxydopamine (6-) 1978
    Phenoxybenzamine 1973
    Propranolol 1973
    Yohimbine 1988
R   ↓ Antihypertensive Drugs 1973
    ↓ Ergot Derivatives 1973
    ↓ Sympathetic Nervous System 1973
    ↓ Sympatholytic Drugs 1973
    ↓ Tricyclic Antidepressant Drugs 1997

Adrenergic Drugs 1973
PN 462   **SC** 01080

Adrenergic Drugs — (cont'd)
HN   In 1997, this term replaced the discontinued term ADRENOLYTIC DRUGS. In 2000, ADRE-NOLYTIC DRUGS was removed from all records containing it, and replaced with ADRENERGIC DRUGS.
UF   Adrenolytic Drugs
B   Drugs 1967
N   ↓ Amphetamine 1967
    Dextroamphetamine 1973
    Ephedrine 1973
    Epinephrine 1967
    Methoxamine 1973
    Tyramine 1973
R   ↓ Catecholamines 1973
    Serotonin 1973
    ↓ Sympathetic Nervous System 1973
    ↓ Sympathomimetic Drugs 1973

Adrenergic Nerves 1973
PN 387   **SC** 01090
UF   Nerves (Adrenergic)
B   Autonomic Nervous System 1967

Adrenergic Receptors 2003
PN 76   **SC** 01093
SN   Class of neural receptors that are sensitive to the neurotransmitters epinephrine and norepinephrine.
HN   This term was introduced in June 2003. PsycINFO records from the past 10 years were re-indexed with this term. The posting note reflects the number of records that were re-indexed.
UF   Adrenaline Receptors
    Adrenoceptors
    Receptors (Adrenergic)
B   Neural Receptors 1973
R   ↓ Catecholamines 1973
    Receptor Binding 1985

Adrenoceptors
Use   Adrenergic Receptors

Adrenocorticotropin
Use   Corticotropin

Adrenolytic Drugs
Use   Adrenergic Drugs

Adult Attitudes 1988
PN 7557   **SC** 01122
SN   Attitudes of, not toward, adults.
B   Attitudes 1967

Adult Children
Use   Adult Offspring

Adult Children of Alcoholics
Use   Children of Alcoholics

Adult Day Care 1997
PN 113   **SC** 01125
SN   Home- or center-based care of physically or mentally disabled adults during daytime hours, providing personal, social, and homemaker services.
R   Day Care Centers 1973
    Elder Care 1994
    Home Care 1985
    Home Visiting Programs 1973
    Long Term Care 1994

Adult Development 1978
PN 3707   **SC** 01127
SN   Process of physical, cognitive, personality, and psychosocial growth occurring from age 18. Use a more specific term if possible.
B   Human Development 1967
R   Adult Learning 1997
    Developmental Age Groups 1973
    ↓ Developmental Stages 1973
    Generativity 2001
    Mentor 1985
    Physiological Aging 1967
    ↓ Psychogenesis 1973

Adult Education 1973
PN 1639   **SC** 01130
SN   Formal or informal education for adults, including but not limited to basic education, high school equivalency, vocational education, correspondence courses, continuing education, non-degree coursework, and lifelong learning programs.
UF   High School Equivalency
B   Education 1967
N   ↓ Continuing Education 1985
R   Adult Learning 1997
    Literacy Programs 1997
    Reentry Students 1985

Adult Learning 1997
PN 293   **SC** 01133
B   Learning 1967
R   Adult Development 1978
    ↓ Adult Education 1973
    ↓ Continuing Education 1985
    Reentry Students 1985

Adult Offspring 1985
PN 2699   **SC** 01135
SN   Ages 18 or older.
UF   Adult Children
    Grown Children
B   Family Members 1973
    Offspring 1988
R   Empty Nest 1991

Adultery
Use   Extramarital Intercourse

Advance Directives 1994
PN 293   **SC** 01163
SN   Declaration of personal wishes through legal documents or written instructions pertaining to future medical care if one becomes incapacitated.
UF   Living Wills
R   Assisted Suicide 1997
    ↓ Client Rights 1988
    ↓ Death and Dying 1967
    Euthanasia 1973
    ↓ Legal Processes 1973
    Life Sustaining Treatment 1997
    Palliative Care 1991
    Terminally Ill Patients 1973
    Treatment Refusal 1994
    Treatment Withholding 1988

Advance Organizers 1985
PN 188   **SC** 01165
SN   Structural overview of material to be taught to facilitate incorporation of new material into that previously learned or known.
UF   Structured Overview
B   Instructional Media 1967
    Teaching Methods 1967

Advance Organizers — (cont'd)
R ↓ Learning Strategies   1991
     Study Habits   1973

Adventitious Disorders   2001
PN   52   SC   01168
SN   Disabilities that are accidental or acquired, rather than congenital.
HN   The term ADVENTITIOUSLY HANDICAPPED was used to represent the concept from 1973-1996, and ADVENTITIOUSLY DISABLED was used from 1997-2000. In 2001, ADVENTITIOUS DISORDERS was created to replace the discontinued and deleted term ADVENTITIOUSLY DISABLED. ADVENTITIOUSLY DISABLED and ADVENTITIOUSLY HANDICAPPED were removed from all records containing them and replaced with ADVENTITIOUS DISORDERS.
UF   Adventitiously Handicapped
B   Disorders   1967
R ↓ Congenital Disorders   1973

Adventitiously Handicapped
Use   Adventitious Disorders

Adverbs   1973
PN   78   SC   01180
B   Form Classes (Language)   1973

Advertising   1967
PN   3177   SC   01190
N   Television Advertising   1070
R   Brand Names   1978
     Brand Preferences   1994
  ↓ Consumer Research   1973
     Marketing   1973
  ↓ Mass Media   1907
     Product Design   1997
     Public Relations   1973
  ↓ Quality of Service   1997
     Retailing   1991

Advocacy   1985
PN   1059   SC   01195
SN   The process of defending or pleading the cause of another individual or group.
UF   Child Advocacy
R   Child Welfare   1988
  ↓ Civil Rights   1978
     Empowerment   1991
  ↓ Government Policy Making   1973
     Legislative Processes   1973
     Public Service Announcements   2004
     Right to Treatment   1997

Aerobic Exercise   1908
PN   521   SC   01197
B   Exercise   1973
R ↓ Health Behavior   1982
     Physical Fitness   1073
     Weight Control   1985

Aerospace Personnel   1973
PN   543   SC   01200
UF   Aircraft Crew
     Aviation Personnel
     Flight Attendants
     Navigators (Aircraft)
B   Professional Personnel   1978
N   Aircraft Pilots   1973
     Astronauts   1973
R ↓ Business and Industrial Personnel   1967

Aerospace Personnel — (cont'd)
     Engineers   1967
     Physicists   1973
     Scientists   1967

Aesthetic Preferences   1973
PN   1319   SC   01210
B   Preferences   1967
R   Aesthetics   1967
     Interior Design   1982

Aesthetics   1967
PN   1223   SC   01220
SN   Scientific or philosophical study of beauty or judgments of beauty. Also, the aesthetic qualities themselves.
R   Aesthetic Preferences   1973
  ↓ Arts   1973
     Interior Design   1982

Aetiology
Use   Etiology

Affairs (Sexual)
Use   Extramarital Intercourse

Affection   1973
PN   584   SC   01250
UF   Liking
B   Emotional States   1070
R ↓ Interpersonal Interaction   1967
     Intimacy   1973
     Love   1973
     Physical Contact   1982
  ↓ Psychosexual Behavior   1967
     Romance   1997
     Sexuality   1973

Affective Disorders   2001
PN   6633   SC   01255
SN   Mental disorders characterized by a disturbance in mood which is abnormally depressed or elated. Compare EMOTIONAL STABILITY or EMOTIONALLY DISTURBED.
HN   Use AFFECTIVE DISTURBANCES to access references from 1967-2000.
UF   Affective Disturbances
     Mood Disorders
B   Mental Disorders   1967
N ↓ Bipolar Disorder   2001
  ↓ Major Depression   1988
  ↓ Mania   1967
     Seasonal Affective Disorder   1991
R | Affective Psychosis   1973
     Premenstrual Dysphoric Disorder   2004
     Schizoaffective Disorder   1994

Affective Disturbances
Use   Affective Disorders

Affective Education   1982
PN   488   SC   01265
SN   Curriculum aimed at changing emotional and social behavior of students and enhancing their understanding of such behavior.
UF   Humanistic Education
B   Curriculum   1967
R   Self Actualization   1973
  ↓ Self Concept   1967
     Social Skills   1978

Affective Psychosis   1973
PN   388   SC   01270
B   Psychosis   1967
N   Involutional Depression   1973
R ↓ Affective Disorders   2001
  ↓ Bipolar Disorder   2001

Afferent Pathways   1982
PN   1317   SC   01275
SN   Collections of fibers that carry neural impulses toward neural processing areas from sensory mechanisms or other processing areas.
UF   Sensory Pathways
B   Neural Pathways   1982
N ↓ Lemniscal System   1985
     Spinothalamic Tracts   1973
R   Dorsal Horns   1985
  ↓ Efferent Pathways   1982
  ↓ Receptive Fields   1985
  ↓ Sensory Neurons   1973

Afferent Stimulation   1973
PN   200   SC   01280
SN   Sensory stimulation causing nerve impulses to be carried toward the brain, spinal cord, or sensory relay and processing areas.
UF   Afferentation
B   Stimulation   1967
R ↓ Nervous System   1967
  ↓ Perceptual Stimulation   1973
  ↓ Stereotaxic Techniques   1973
  ↓ Surgery   1971

Afferentation
Use   Afferent Stimulation

Affiliation Motivation   1967
PN   735   SC   01000
SN   Need for association with others and formation of friendships.
UF   Need for Affiliation
B   Motivation   1967
R ↓ Needs   1967

Affirmative Action   1985
PN   410   SC   01305
SN   Programs or policies designed to actively recruit females and minority group members for employment or higher education, in an effort to correct underrepresentative distributions of these groups relative to the general population.
R   Age Discrimination   1994
  ↓ Civil Rights   1978
     Disability Discrimination   1997
     Diversity in the Workplace   2003
     Employment Discrimination   1994
  ↓ Human Resource Management   2003
     Minority Groups   1967
  ↓ Personnel   1967
  ↓ Personnel Recruitment   1973
  ↓ Personnel Selection   1967
     Race and Ethnic Discrimination   1994
     Sex Discrimination   1978
  ↓ Social Discrimination   1982
     Social Equality   1973

African Americans
Use   Blacks

After School Programs   2003
PN   28   SC   01350

After School Programs — (cont'd)

HN This term was introduced in June 2003. Psyc-INFO records from the past 10 years were re-indexed with this term. The posting note reflects the number of records that were re-indexed.
- **R** ↓ Educational Programs 1973
- ↓ Extracurricular Activities 1973

Aftercare 1973
PN 702   **SC** 01320
SN Continuing program of rehabilitation designed to reinforce and maintain the effects of treatment and to help clients adjust to their environment after hospital release.
- **B** Treatment 1967
- **R** Continuum of Care 2004
- Discharge Planning 1994
- Maintenance Therapy 1997
- Outpatient Commitment 1991
- ↓ Outpatient Treatment 1967
- Partial Hospitalization 1985
- Posttreatment Followup 1973
- ↓ Treatment Planning 1997

Aftereffect (Perceptual)
Use Perceptual Aftereffect

Afterimage 1967
PN 277   **SC** 01340
SN Persistence of sensory excitation, usually visual, after cessation of stimulation. This temporary illusory sensation is due to physiological changes in the receptor cells.
- **UF** Successive Contrast
- **B** Perceptual Aftereffect 1967

Age Differences 1967
PN 43955   **SC** 01360
SN Age comparisons of behavioral, developmental, and cognitive variations between individuals or groups. Used for human or animal subjects.
HN In 1982, this term replaced the discontinued term DEVELOPMENTAL DIFFERENCES. In 2000, DEVELOPMENTAL DIFFERENCES was removed from all records containing it, and replaced with AGE DIFFERENCES.
- **UF** Developmental Differences
- **R** Animal Development 1978
- Cohort Analysis 1988
- ↓ Development 1967
- Developmental Age Groups 1973
- Diversity in the Workplace 2003
- Generation Gap 1973
- Grade Level 1994
- ↓ Human Development 1967
- ↓ Physical Development 1973
- ↓ Psychogenesis 1973

Age Discrimination 1994
PN 91   **SC** 01363
HN Use SOCIAL DISCRIMINATION to access references from 1982-1993.
- **B** Social Discrimination 1982
- **R** Affirmative Action 1985
- ↓ Aged (Attitudes Toward) 1978
- Ageism 2003
- Aging (Attitudes Toward) 1985
- ↓ Civil Rights 1978
- Employment Discrimination 1994
- ↓ Prejudice 1967

Age Regression (Hypnotic) 1988
PN 84   **SC** 01365
SN Technique used to recapture early or past life experiences by guiding clients back through their history, usually year by year.
- **B** Hypnosis 1967
- Hypnotherapy 1973
- **R** Early Experience 1967
- Early Memories 1985
- Enactments 1997
- False Memory 1997
- ↓ Life Experiences 1973
- ↓ Psychotherapeutic Techniques 1967
- Repressed Memory 1997

Aged (Attitudes Toward) 1978
PN 1295   **SC** 01372
- **B** Attitudes 1967
- **N** Ageism 2003
- **R** Age Discrimination 1994
- ↓ Aging 1991
- Aging (Attitudes Toward) 1985
- Geriatrics 1967
- Gerontology 1967
- Physiological Aging 1967

Ageism 2003
PN 54   **SC** 01376
HN This term was introduced in June 2003. Psyc-INFO records from the past 10 years were re-indexed with this term. The posting note reflects the number of records that were re-indexed.
- **B** Aged (Attitudes Toward) 1978
- **R** Age Discrimination 1994
- Employment Discrimination 1994
- Stereotyped Attitudes 1967

Agencies (Groups)
Use Organizations

Aggressive Behavior 1967
PN 11646   **SC** 01390
- **UF** Agonistic Behavior
- Fighting
- **B** Social Behavior 1967
- **N** Aggressive Driving Behavior 2004
- ↓ Animal Aggressive Behavior 1973
- Attack Behavior 1973
- Coercion 1994
- ↓ Conflict 1967
- **R** ↓ Behavior Disorders 1071
- Bullying 2003
- Conduct Disorder 1991
- Cruelty 1973
- Retaliation 1991
- ↓ Social Interaction 1967
- Torture 1988

Aggressive Driving Behavior 2004
PN 26   **SC** 01395
HN This term was introduced in June 2004. Psyc-INFO records from the past 10 years were re-indexed with this term. The posting note reflects the number of records that were re-indexed.
- **UF** Road Rage
- **B** Aggressive Behavior 1967
- Driving Behavior 1967
- **R** Highway Safety 1973

Aggressiveness 1973
PN 1833   **SC** 01400
- **B** Personality Traits 1967

Agility (Physical)
Use Physical Agility

Aging 1991
PN 5554   **SC** 01413
- **N** Physiological Aging 1967
- **R** ↓ Aged (Attitudes Toward) 1978
- Aging (Attitudes Toward) 1985
- Developmental Age Groups 1973
- ↓ Developmental Stages 1973
- Generativity 2001
- Geriatric Psychiatry 1997
- Geriatric Psychotherapy 1973
- Geriatrics 1967
- Gerontology 1967
- ↓ Human Development 1967
- Life Changes 2004
- Life Expectancy 1982

Aging (Attitudes Toward) 1985
PN 710   **SC** 01415
SN Attitudes toward the aging process. Includes attitudes toward one's own physical aging and psychological and social maturation.
- **B** Attitudes 1967
- **R** Age Discrimination 1994
- ↓ Aged (Attitudes Toward) 1978
- ↓ Aging 1991
- ↓ Physical Development 1973
- Physiological Aging 1967
- ↓ Psychosocial Development 1973
- Self Perception 1967

Aging (Physiological)
Use Physiological Aging

Agitated Depression
Use Major Depression

Agitation 1991
PN 531   **SC** 01440
SN State usually characterized by restlessness, anxiety, and anguish.
- **R** Akathisia 1991
- ↓ Anxiety 1967
- Distress 1973
- Restlessness 1973

Agnosia 1973
PN 463   **SC** 01450
SN Inability to recognize, understand, or interpret sensory stimuli in the absence of sensory defects. Also, the selective loss of knowledge of specific objects due to emotional disturbance, as seen in schizophrenia, hysteria, or depression.
- **B** Aphasia 1967
- Perceptual Disturbances 1973
- **N** Anosognosia 1994
- Prosopagnosia 1994

Agonistic Behavior
Use Aggressive Behavior

Agoraphobia 1973
PN 2076   **SC** 01480
SN Excessive fear of being alone, or being in public places or situations (e.g., in crowds or elevators) from which there is no easy escape or where help cannot be obtained in the event of an incapacitating reaction or panic.
- **B** Phobias 1967

Agrammatism
Use Aphasia

Agraphia   1973
PN 289   **SC** 01490
SN Inability to write (letters, syllables, words, or phrases) due to an injury to a specific cerebral area or occasionally due to emotional factors.
   B   Aphasia   1967
   R   ↓ Learning Disabilities   1973

Agreeableness   1997
PN 122   **SC** 01495
SN Extent to which an individual is altruistic, sympathetic to others, and eager to help versus being egocentric and skeptical of others' intentions.
   B   Personality Traits   1967
   R   Adaptability (Personality)   1973
         Cooperation   1967
         Cynicism   1973
         Egocentrism   1978
         Empathy   1967
         Five Factor Personality Model   1997
         Likability   1988
         Openmindedness   1978
      ↓ Tolerance   1973

Agricultural Extension Workers   1973
PN 67   **SC** 01500
SN Government employees (usually local, county, or state) who assist with agricultural matters, distribute educational materials, and provide services pertaining to agriculture.
   UF   County Agricultural Agents
         Extension Workers (Agricultural)
   B   Government Personnel   1973
   R   ↓ Agricultural Workers   1973

Agricultural Workers   1973
PN 600   **SC** 01510
   UF   Farmers
         Laborers (Farm)
   B   Nonprofessional Personnel   1982
   N   Migrant Farm Workers   1970
   R   Agricultural Extension Workers   1973
      ↓ Business and Industrial Personnel   1967

AIDS
Use Acquired Immune Deficiency Syndrome

AIDS (Attitudes Toward)   1997
PN 514   **SC** 01516
   B   Physical Illness (Attitudes Toward)   1985
   R   Acquired Immune Deficiency Syndrome   1988
         AIDS Prevention   1994
      ↓ Human Immunodeficiency Virus   1991

AIDS Dementia Complex   1997
PN 61   **SC** 01514
HN Use ACQUIRED IMMUNE DEFICIENCY SYNDROME and DEMENTIA to access references from 1988-1996.
   B   Dementia   1985
   R   Acquired Immune Deficiency Syndrome   1988
      ↓ Human Immunodeficiency Virus   1991

AIDS Prevention   1994
PN 2470   **SC** 01517
SN Health related programs or services directed toward those at risk for HIV/AIDS. Includes prevention of HIV/AIDS and personal risk through health behavior and lifestyle characteristics.

AIDS Prevention — (cont'd)
   B   Prevention   1973
   R   Acquired Immune Deficiency Syndrome   1988
         AIDS (Attitudes Toward)   1997
         Condoms   1991
      ↓ Harm Reduction   2003
      ↓ Health Behavior   1982
      ↓ Health Education   1973
         Health Promotion   1991
         HIV Testing   1997
      ↓ Human Immunodeficiency Virus   1991
         Needle Exchange Programs   2001
         Safe Sex   2003
         Sexual Risk Taking   1997

AIDS Testing
Use HIV Testing

Air Encephalography
Use Pneumoencephalography

Air Force Personnel   1967
PN 1208   **SC** 01530
   B   Military Personnel   1967
   R   National Guardsmen   1973

Air Traffic Accidents   1973
PN 253   **SC** 01540
   B   Transportation Accidents   1973
   R   Air Traffic Control   1973
         Air Transportation   1973
      ↓ Aviation Safety   1973

Air Traffic Control   1973
PN 432   **SC** 01550
   B   Aviation Safety   1973
   R   Air Traffic Accidents   1973
         Air Transportation   1973
      ↓ Transportation Accidents   1973

Air Transportation   1973
PN 258   **SC** 01560
   B   Transportation   1973
   R   Air Traffic Accidents   1973
         Air Traffic Control   1973
      ↓ Aircraft   1973
         Public Transportation   1973
         Spacecraft   1973

Aircraft   1973
PN 302   **SC** 01570
   UF   Airplanes
   N   Helicopters   1973
   R   Air Transportation   1973
         Aircraft Pilots   1973

Aircraft Crew
Use Aerospace Personnel

Aircraft Pilots   1973
PN 1773   **SC** 01580
   UF   Aviators
         Pilots (Aircraft)
   B   Aerospace Personnel   1973
   R   ↓ Aircraft   1973
         Astronauts   1973
      ↓ Aviation Safety   1973

Airplanes
Use Aircraft

Akathisia   1991
PN 252   **SC** 01595
SN The inability to remain in a sitting posture or motor restlessness often resulting from heavy doses of tranquilizing drugs.
   R   Agitation   1991
         Restlessness   1973
      ↓ Side Effects (Drug)   1973
      ↓ Symptoms   1967

Akinesia
Use Apraxia

Alanines   1973
PN 32   **SC** 01610
   B   Amino Acids   1973
   N   ↓ Phenylalanine   1973

Alanon
Use Alcohol Rehabilitation

Alarm Responses   1973
PN 420   **SC** 01620
SN Behavioral, emotional, or physiological reactions to actual or perceived physical threat. Used primarily for animal populations.
   R   ↓ Animal Defensive Behavior   1982
         Animal Distress Calls   1973
         Animal Escape Behavior   1973
      ↓ Animal Ethology   1967
      ↓ Fear   1967
         Startle Reflex   1967
         Tonic Immobility   1978

Alaska Natives   1997
PN 105   **SC** 01635
   UF   Native Alaskans
   B   Indigenous Populations   2001
   R   American Indians   1967
         Inuit   2001
         Minority Groups   1967
      ↓ Pacific Islanders   2001
         Tribes   1973

Alateen
Use Alcohol Rehabilitation

Albinism   1973
PN 73   **SC** 01640
   B   Genetic Disorders   1973
   R   ↓ Eye Disorders   1973
      ↓ Skin Disorders   1973

Albino Rats
Use Rats

Alcohol (Grain)
Use Ethanol

Alcohol Abstinence
Use Sobriety

Alcohol Abuse   1988
PN 6531   **SC** 01660
HN In 1988, this term replaced the discontinued term PROBLEM DRINKING. In 2000, PROBLEM DRINKING was removed from all records containing it, and replaced with ALCOHOL ABUSE.

Alcohol Abuse — (cont'd)
UF Problem Drinking
B   Alcohol Drinking Patterns 1967
     Drug Abuse 1973
N ↓ Alcoholism 1967
R ↓ Alcohol Intoxication 1973
     Alcohol Withdrawal 1994
     Blood Alcohol Concentration 1994
     Codependency 1991
     Drug Abuse Liability 1994
     Polydrug Abuse 1994

Alcohol Addiction
Use Alcoholism

Alcohol Dehydrogenases 1973
PN 95   SC 01670
B   Dehydrogenases 1973
R ↓ Alcohols 1967

Alcohol Drinking Attitudes 1973
PN 1493   SC 01680
SN Attitudes toward the use or abuse of alcohol.
UF Drinking Attitudes
B   Drug Usage Attitudes 1973
R Sobriety 1988

Alcohol Drinking Patterns 1967
PN 9521   SC 01690
UF Drinking (Alcohol)
B   Drinking Behavior 1978
     Drug Usage 1971
N ↓ Alcohol Abuse 1988
   ↓ Alcohol Intoxication 1973
     Social Drinking 1973
R ↓ Alcoholism 1967
     Blood Alcohol Concentration 1994

Alcohol Education
Use Drug Education

Alcohol Intoxication 1973
PN 1486   SC 01700
UF Drunkenness
     Intoxication (Alcohol)
B   Alcohol Drinking Patterns 1967
N   Acute Alcoholic Intoxication 1973
     Chronic Alcoholic Intoxication 1973
R ↓ Alcohol Abuse 1988
   ↓ Alcoholism 1967
     Blood Alcohol Concentration 1994
     Driving Under the Influence 1988
   ↓ Toxic Disorders 1973
     Toxic Psychoses 1973

Alcohol Rehabilitation 1982
PN 4913   SC 01705
SN Treatment for alcoholism or alcohol abuse which may include detoxification, psychotherapy, behavior therapy, Alcoholics Anonymous, and medication.
HN Use DRUG REHABILITATION to access references from 1973-1981.
UF Alanon
     Alateen
B   Drug Rehabilitation 1973
N   Alcoholics Anonymous 1973
     Detoxification 1973
R   Alcohol Withdrawal 1994
     Rehabilitation Counseling 1978
     Sobriety 1988

Alcohol Withdrawal 1994
PN 449   SC 01707
SN Processes and symptomatic effects resulting from abstinence from alcohol. Used for both human and animal populations.
HN Use DRUG WITHDRAWAL to access references from 1973-1993.
B   Drug Withdrawal 1973
R ↓ Alcohol Abuse 1988
   ↓ Alcohol Rehabilitation 1982
   ↓ Alcoholic Psychosis 1973
   ↓ Alcoholism 1967
     Detoxification 1973
     Sobriety 1988

Alcoholic Beverages 1973
PN 787   SC 01710
UF Beverages (Alcoholic)
N   Beer 1973
     Liquor 1973
     Wine 1973
R   Beverages (Nonalcoholic) 1978
   ↓ Drinking Behavior 1978
     Prenatal Exposure 1991

Alcoholic Hallucinosis 1973
PN 48   SC 01720
B   Alcoholic Psychosis 1973
     Hallucinosis 1973
N   Delirium Tremens 1973
     Korsakoffs Psychosis 1973
     Wernickes Syndrome 1973

Alcoholic Offspring
Use Children of Alcoholics

Alcoholic Psychosis 1973
PN 76   SC 01730
B   Alcoholism 1967
     Organic Brain Syndromes 1973
     Psychosis 1967
N ↓ Alcoholic Hallucinosis 1973
R   Alcohol Withdrawal 1994
   ↓ Nutritional Deficiencies 1973
     Toxic Psychoses 1973

Alcoholics Anonymous 1973
PN 628   SC 01740
SN A self-supporting, informal, international fellowship whose primary purpose is to help members achieve sobriety.
B   Alcohol Rehabilitation 1982
     Twelve Step Programs 1997
R ↓ Community Services 1967

Alcoholism 1967
PN 16575   SC 01750
UF Alcohol Addiction
B   Addiction 1973
     Alcohol Abuse 1988
N ↓ Alcoholic Psychosis 1973
R ↓ Alcohol Drinking Patterns 1967
   ↓ Alcohol Intoxication 1973
     Alcohol Withdrawal 1994
     Children of Alcoholics 2003
     Fetal Alcohol Syndrome 1985
   ↓ Nutritional Deficiencies 1973
     Sobriety 1988
   ↓ Toxic Disorders 1973

Alcohols 1967
PN 1728   SC 01760
B   Drugs 1967
N   Ephedrine 1973
     Ethanol 1973
     Isoproterenol 1973
     Methanol 1973
     Methoxamine 1973
     Propranolol 1973
     Tetrahydrocannabinol 1973
     Trihexyphenidyl 1973
R   Acetaldehyde 1982
     Alcohol Dehydrogenases 1973
     Blood Alcohol Concentration 1994
   ↓ Solvents 1982

Aldolases
Use Enzymes

Aldosterone 1973
PN 94   SC 01780
B   Adrenal Cortex Hormones 1973
     Corticosteroids 1973

Alexia 1982
PN 243   SC 01785
SN Inability to read which may be the result of neurological impairment. In a less severe form, often referred to as dyslexia.
UF Word Blindness
B   Dysphasia 1978
N   Dyslexia 1973
R ↓ Reading Disabilities 1967

Alexithymia 1982
PN 959   SC 01788
SN Affective and cognitive disturbances characterized by impaired fantasy life and an inability to verbalize or differentiate emotions. These disturbances overlap diagnostic categories and appear generally in psychosomatic patients.
B   Mental Disorders 1967

Algebra 2003
PN 15   SC 01790
SN Branch of mathematics that generalizes arithmetic by representing numbers with variables.
HN Use MATHEMATICS to access references from 1973 to June 2003.
B   Mathematics 1982

Algorithms 1973
PN 2144   SC 01800
SN Set of well-defined rules established for step-by-step solution of problems in a finite number of steps.
B   Mathematics (Concepts) 1967
R   Computer Programming 2001
     Heuristics 2003

Alienation 1971
PN 1505   SC 01810
SN Withdrawal or estrangement from persons, objects, or positions of former attachment; feelings of detachment from self or avoidance of emotional experiences.
B   Emotional States 1973
R   Anomie 1978
     Depersonalization 1973
   ↓ Separation Reactions 1997

Alkaloids 1973
PN 317   SC 01820

Alkaloids — (cont'd)

HN In 1997, this term replaced the discontinued terms HOMATROPINE, QUINIDINE, and RAUWOLFIA. In 2000, these terms were removed from all records containing them, and replaced with ALKALOIDS.

UF   Homatropine
      Opium Alkaloids
      Quinidine
      Rauwolfia
B   Drugs 1967
N   Apomorphine 1973
      Atropine 1973
      Bromocriptine 1988
      Caffeine 1973
      ↓ Cocaine 1973
      Codeine 1973
      Ephedrine 1973
      ↓ Gamma Aminobutyric Acid Antagonists 1985
      Heroin 1973
      Mescaline 1973
      Morphine 1973
      Nicotine 1973
      Papaverine 1973
      Peyote 1973
      Physostigmine 1973
      Pilocarpine 1973
      Quinine 1973
      Reserpine 1967
      Scopolamine 1973
      Strychnine 1973
      Theophylline 1973
      Tubocurarine 1973
R   ↓ Anti Inflammatory Drugs 1982
      Curare 1973
      ↓ Ergot Derivatives 1973

Allergens
Use Antigens

Allergic Disorders 1973
PN 259   SC 01830
B   Immunologic Disorders 1973
N   Allergic Skin Disorders 1973
     Drug Allergies 1973
     Food Allergies 1973
     Hay Fever 1973
R   Anaphylactic Shock 1973

Allergic Skin Disorders 1973
PN 22   SC 01840
B   Allergic Disorders 1973
     Skin Disorders 1973
R   ↓ Dermatitis 1973
     Eczema 1973
     Neurodermatitis 1973

Alligators
Use Crocodilians

Allocation of Resources
Use Resource Allocation

Allport Vernon Lindzey Study Values
Use Attitude Measures

Alopecia 1973
PN 100   SC 01880
SN Baldness or the loss of hair.
UF Baldness

Alopecia — (cont'd)
     Hair Loss
B   Skin Disorders 1973
R   ↓ Genetic Disorders 1973
     Hair 1973

Alpha Methylparatyrosine 1978
PN 135   SC 01887
UF Alpha Methyltyrosine
B   Adrenergic Blocking Drugs 1973
     Antihypertensive Drugs 1973
     Tyrosine 1973

Alpha Methyltyrosine
Use Alpha Methylparatyrosine

Alpha Rhythm 1973
PN 779   SC 01890
SN Electrically measured impulses or waves of low amplitude and a frequency of 8-13 cycles per second usually observable in the electroencephalogram during wakeful rest.
B   Electrical Activity 1967
     Electroencephalography 1967

Alphabets 1973
PN 177   SC 01900
SN Systems for writing a language.
B   Written Language 1967
N   Initial Teaching Alphabet 1973
     ↓ Letters (Alphabet) 1973
R   Orthography 1973

Alprazolam 1988
PN 572   SC 01903
B   Benzodiazepines 1978
     Minor Tranquilizers 1973
     Sedatives 1973

Alternative Medicine 1997
PN 706   SC 01904
SN Treatments, health care practices, or culturally based healing traditions which are not generally used in conventional medical practice.
UF Complementary Medicine
     Homeopathic Medicine
B   Treatment 1967
N   Acupuncture 1973
     Faith Healing 1973
     Folk Medicine 1973
R   Biofeedback Training 1978
     Dietary Supplements 2001
     Holistic Health 1985
     ↓ Hypnotherapy 1973
     Massage 2001
     Medical Treatment (General) 1973
     ↓ Medicinal Herbs and Plants 2001
     Meditation 1973
     Osteopathic Medicine 2003
     Phototherapy 1991
     ↓ Physical Treatment Methods 1973
     Preventive Medicine 1973
     ↓ Shock Therapy 1973
     Transcultural Psychiatry 1973

Alternative Schools
Use Nontraditional Education

Altitude Effects 1973
PN 220   SC 01910
B   Environmental Effects 1973

Altitude Effects — (cont'd)
R   ↓ Aviation 1967
     ↓ Gravitational Effects 1967

Altruism 1973
PN 1377   SC 01920
SN Consideration for well being of others as opposed to self-love or egoism. Used for human or animal populations.
B   Personality Traits 1967
     Prosocial Behavior 1982
R   ↓ Assistance (Social Behavior) 1973
     Charitable Behavior 1973
     Sharing (Social Behavior) 1978

Aluminum 1994
PN 43   SC 01930
B   Metallic Elements 1973

Alzheimers Disease 1973
PN 12195   SC 01940
UF Dementia of Alzheimers Type
B   Neurodegenerative Diseases 2004
     Organic Brain Syndromes 1973
     Presenile Dementia 1973
R   ↓ Dementia 1985
     Dementia with Lewy Bodies 2001
     Picks Disease 1973
     ↓ Senile Dementia 1973

Amantadine 1978
PN 141   SC 01945
UF Amatadine
B   Antibiotics 1973
     Antitremor Drugs 1973
R   Parkinsons Disease 1973

Amatadine
Use Amantadine

Amaurotic Familial Idiocy
Use Tay Sachs Disease

Ambidexterity
Use Handedness

Ambiguity (Stimulus)
Use Stimulus Ambiguity

Ambiguity (Tolerance)
Use Tolerance for Ambiguity

Ambition
Use Aspirations

Ambivalence 1973
PN 370   SC 01990
B   Emotional States 1973

Amblyopia 1973
PN 227   SC 02000
SN An optically uncorrectable loss of visual acuity without apparent organic change or defect.
B   Eye Disorders 1973
R   ↓ Refraction Errors 1973
     Strabismus 1973

Ambulatory Care
  Use Outpatient Treatment

Amenorrhea 1973
PN 143   **SC** 02010
SN Absence or abnormal cessation of the menses.
  B   Menstrual Disorders 1973

Amentia
  Use Mental Retardation

American Indians 1967
PN 3216   **SC** 02030
  UF   Indians (American)
            Native Americans
  B   Indigenous Populations 2001
  R   Alaska Natives 1997
            Inuit 2001
            Minority Groups 1967
            ↓ Pacific Islanders 2001
            Tribes 1973

Amine Oxidase Inhibitors 1973
PN 14   **SC** 02040
  B   Enzyme Inhibitors 1985
  N   ↓ Dopamine Antagonists 1982
            Iproniazid 1973
            Isocarboxazid 1973
            Lysergic Acid Diethylamide 1967
            Nialamide 1973
  R   ↓ Monoamine Oxidase Inhibitors 1973

Amines 1973
PN 564   **SC** 02060
HN In 1997, this term replaced the discontinued term CHLORISONDAMINE. In 2000, CHLORISON-DAMINE was removed from all records containing it, and replaced with AMINES.
  UF   Chlorisondamine
  B   Drugs 1967
  N   Amitriptyline 1973
            Atropine 1973
            Bufotenine 1973
            Chlordiazepoxide 1973
            Chlorimipramine 1973
            Chlorpromazine 1967
            Chlorprothixene 1973
            ↓ Cocaine 1973
            Diphenhydramine 1973
            Galanthamine 1973
            Guanethidine 1973
            Histamine 1973
            Imipramine 1973
            Mecamylamine 1973
            Meperidine 1973
            Methylphenidate 1973
            Orphenadrine 1973
            Phenethylamines 1985
            Phenoxybenzamine 1973
            Physostigmine 1973
            Puromycin 1973
            Scopolamine 1973
            Serotonin 1973
            ↓ Sympathomimetic Amines 1973
            Thalidomide 1973
            Trihexyphenidyl 1973
            Tryptamine 1973
  R   ↓ Amino Acids 1973

Amino Acids 1973
PN 1175   **SC** 02070
  B   Acids 1973

Amino Acids — (cont'd)
  N   ↓ Alanines 1973
            ↓ Aspartic Acid 1973
            Cysteine 1973
            DOPA 1973
            Gamma Aminobutyric Acid 1978
            Glutamic Acid 1973
            Glutamine 1973
            Glycine 1973
            Histidine 1973
            Leucine 1973
            Methionine 1973
            ↓ Neurokinins 1997
            Proline 1982
            ↓ Tryptophan 1973
            ↓ Tyrosine 1973
  R   ↓ Amines 1973
            Dietary Supplements 2001
            Nerve Growth Factor 1994
            ↓ Neurotransmitters 1985
            ↓ Proteins 1973

Aminotransferases
  Use Transaminases

Amitriptyline 1973
PN 1091   **SC** 02090
  UF   Elavil
  B   Amines 1973
            Tranquilizing Drugs 1967
            Tricyclic Antidepressant Drugs 1997

Amnesia 1967
PN 3004   **SC** 02120
SN Partial or complete loss of memory caused by organic or psychological factors. The loss may be temporary or permanent, and may involve old or recent memories. Compare FORGETTING and MEMORY DECAY.
  B   Memory Disorders 1973
  N   Anterograde Amnesia 2003
            Global Amnesia 1997
            Retrograde Amnesia 2003
  R   Dissociation 2001
            ↓ Dissociative Disorders 2001
            False Memory 1997
            Forgetting
            ↓ Memory 1967
            Repressed Memory 1997

Amniocentesis
  Use Prenatal Diagnosis

Amniotic Fluid 1973
PN 48   **SC** 02130
  B   Body Fluids 1973

Amobarbital 1973
PN 231   **SC** 02140
  UF   Amobarbital Sodium
            Amytal
  B   Barbiturates 1967
            CNS Depressant Drugs 1973
            Hypnotic Drugs 1973
            Sedatives 1973

Amobarbital Sodium
  Use Amobarbital

Amphetamine 1967
PN 3433   **SC** 02160
  UF   Amphetamine (dl-)
            Amphetamine Sulfate
            Benzedrine
  B   Adrenergic Drugs 1973
            Appetite Depressing Drugs 1973
            CNS Stimulating Drugs 1973
            Dopamine Agonists 1985
            Sympathomimetic Amines 1973
            Vasoconstrictor Drugs 1973
  N   Dextroamphetamine 1973
            Methamphetamine 1973
  R   Phenethylamines 1985

Amphetamine (d-)
  Use Dextroamphetamine

Amphetamine (dl-)
  Use Amphetamine

Amphetamine Sulfate
  Use Amphetamine

Amphibia 1973
PN 105   **SC** 02200
  B   Vertebrates 1973
  N   Frogs 1967
            Salamanders 1973
            Toads 1973

Amplifiers (Apparatus) 1973
PN 44   **SC** 02210
  B   Apparatus 1967

Amplitude (Response)
  Use Response Amplitude

Amputation 1973
PN 312   **SC** 02230
HN In 2000, this term replaced the discontinued and deleted term AMPUTEES. AMPUTEES was removed from all records containing it and replaced with AMPUTATION.
  B   Surgery 1971
  N   Mastectomy 1973
  R   Phantom Limbs 1973
            ↓ Prostheses 1973

Amygdala 2003
PN 2626   **SC** 02248
HN In June 2003, this term was created to replace the discontinued term AMYGDALOID BODY. AMYGDALOID BODY was removed from all records containing it and replaced with AMYGDALA.
  UF   Amygdaloid Body
  B   Basal Ganglia 1973
            Limbic System 1973
  R   Medial Forebrain Bundle 1982

Amygdaloid Body
  Use Amygdala

Amytal
  Use Amobarbital

Anabolism 1973
PN 15   **SC** 02280

Anabolism — (cont'd)
SN Constructive part of metabolism concerned especially with macromolecular synthesis.
  B   Metabolism 1967

Anabolites
  Use Metabolites

Anaclitic Depression 1973
PN 42   **SC** 02290
SN Syndrome of withdrawal characterizing infants separated from their mothers for a long period of time.
  B   Major Depression 1988
  R   Attachment Behavior 1985
       Object Relations 1982
     ↓ Parental Absence 1973
     ↓ Separation Reactions 1997

Anagram Problem Solving 1973
PN 306   **SC** 02300
  B   Problem Solving 1967
  R   Anagrams 1973

Anagrams 1973
PN 43   **SC** 02310
SN Words or phrases made by rearranging letters of other words or phrases (e.g., leader from dealer).
  B   Vocabulary 1967
  R   Anagram Problem Solving 1973

Analeptic Drugs 1973
PN 90   **SC** 02320
  UF Antagonists (CNS Depressant Drugs)
       CNS Depressant Drug Antagonists
  D   CNS Stimulating Drugs 1973
  N   Bemegride 1973
       Bicuculline 1994
       Picrotoxin 1973
       Strychnine 1973
  R   Barbiturate Poisoning 1973
       Caffeine 1973
     ↓ Cholinomimetic Drugs 1973
     ↓ Heart Rate Affecting Drugs 1973
       Methylphenidate 1973
       Pentylenetetrazol 1973
       Theophylline 1973

Analgesia 1982
PN 2307   **SC** 02325
SN Pain insensitivity chemically or electrically induced or occurring as a natural phenomenon (e.g., Kiesow's area on the inner cheek).
  B   Pain Perception 1973
  R   ↓ Analgesic Drugs 1973
       Anesthesia (Feeling) 1973
     ↓ Endorphins 1982
       Enkephalins 1982
       Pain Management 1994
       Pain Measurement 1997

Analgesic Drugs 1973
PN 1408   **SC** 02330
  UF Anodynes
       Pain Relieving Drugs
  B   Drugs 1967
  N   Aspirin 1973
       Atropine 1973
       Carbamazepine 1988
       Codeine 1973
       Dihydroergotamine 1973

Analgesic Drugs — (cont'd)
       Heroin 1973
       Meperidine 1973
       Methadone 1973
       Morphine 1973
       Papaverine 1973
       Pentazocine 1991
       Phencyclidine 1982
       Procaine 1982
       Quinine 1973
       Scopolamine 1973
  R   Analgesia 1982
     ↓ Anesthetic Drugs 1973
     ↓ Anti Inflammatory Drugs 1982
     ↓ CNS Depressant Drugs 1973
     ↓ Hypnotic Drugs 1973
     ↓ Narcotic Drugs 1973
     ↓ Pain 1967
       Pain Management 1994
     ↓ Sedatives 1973

Analog Computers 1973
PN 23   **SC** 02340
SN Electronic, mechanical, or electromechanical machines that measure continuous electrical or physical magnitudes (e.g., automobile speedometer) rather than operating on discrete digits.
  B   Computers 1967

Analogy 1991
PN 585   **SC** 02345
  R   Connotations 1973
     ↓ Figurative Language 1985
       Inference 1973
       Logical Thinking 1967
       Metaphor 1982
     ↓ Reasoning 1967

Analysis 1967
PN 2070   **SC** 02370
SN Conceptually broad term referring to the process of examination of a complex problem, its elements, and their relations. Use a more specific term if possible.
  N   ↓ Behavior Analysis 2001
       Causal Analysis 1994
       Cohort Analysis 1988
     ↓ Content Analysis 1978
       Content Analysis (Test) 1967
     ↓ Costs and Cost Analysis 1973
       Error Analysis 1973
       Item Analysis (Test) 1967
       Job Analysis 1967
     ↓ Statistical Analysis 1967
       Systems Analysis 1973
       Task Analysis 1967
  R   Analysis of Covariance 1973
       Analysis of Variance 1967
       Functional Analysis 2001
       Multidimensional Scaling 1982

Analysis of Covariance 1973
PN 533   **SC** 02350
  B   Variability Measurement 1973
  R   ↓ Analysis 1967
       Analysis of Variance 1967
       Multiple Regression 1982
     ↓ Multivariate Analysis 1982

Analysis of Variance 1967
PN 1299   **SC** 02360
  UF ANOVA (Statistics)
  B   Variability Measurement 1973

Analysis of Variance — (cont'd)
  R   ↓ Analysis 1967
       Analysis of Covariance 1973
       Homogeneity of Variance 2003
       Multiple Regression 1982
     ↓ Multivariate Analysis 1982
     ↓ Statistical Regression 1985

Analysts
  Use Psychoanalysts

Analytic Psychology
  Use Jungian Psychology

Analytical Psychotherapy 1973
PN 714   **SC** 02390
SN Form of psychotherapy based on work of C. G. Jung. The unconscious, personal and collective, is disclosed through free association and dream analysis. Therapeutic goals include integration of conscious and unconscious for growth and personality development and a life of fuller awareness.
  UF Jungian Psychotherapy
  B   Psychotherapy 1967
  R   Archetypes 1991
     ↓ Collective Unconscious 1997
       Jung (Carl) 1973
     ↓ Jungian Psychology 1973

Anankastic Personality
  Use Obsessive Compulsive Personality Disorder

Anaphylactic Shock 1973
PN 23   **SC** 02400
SN Immunologic or allergic reaction to antigens such as drugs or foreign proteins to which a hypersensitivity has been established by previous contact.
  UF Protein Sensitization
       Sensitization (Protein)
  B   Immunologic Disorders 1973
  R   ↓ Allergic Disorders 1973
       Shock 1967

Anatomical Systems 1973
PN 48   **SC** 02410
SN Conceptually broad term referring to anatomically related structures (e.g., vascular system). Use a more specific term if possible.
  B   Anatomy 1967
       Systems 1967
  N   ↓ Cardiovascular System 1967
     ↓ Digestive System 1967
     ↓ Endocrine System 1973
     ↓ Musculoskeletal System 1973
     ↓ Nervous System 1967
     ↓ Respiratory System 1973
     ↓ Urogenital System 1973

Anatomically Detailed Dolls 1991
PN 72   **SC** 02415
SN Dolls used in a general play setting or for evaluation and assessment purposes in a therapeutic or legal context.
  B   Toys 1973
  R   ↓ Child Abuse 1971
       Childhood Play Behavior 1978
       Clinical Judgment (Not Diagnosis) 1973
       Doll Play 1973
     ↓ Sexual Abuse 1988

Anatomy 1967
PN 1333   **SC** 02420

Anatomy — (cont'd)

SN Conceptually broad array term referring both to the science of anatomy and the actual structure or morphology of an organism. Use specific anatomical or neuroanatomical terms if possible.

N   Abdomen   1973
    ↓ Anatomical Systems   1973
     Back (Anatomy)   1973
    ↓ Body Fluids   1973
     Breast   1973
    ↓ Cells (Biology)   1973
     Face (Anatomy)   1973
     Feet (Anatomy)   1973
     Hair   1973
     Hand (Anatomy)   1967
     Head (Anatomy)   1973
     Neck (Anatomy)   1973
     Palm (Anatomy)   1973
     Scalp (Anatomy)   1973
    ↓ Sense Organs   1973
     Thigh   1973
    ↓ Tissues (Body)   1973
R   Human Body   2003
     Morphology   1973
     Neuroanatomy   1967
    ↓ Physiology   1967

Ancestors   1973

PN 38   **SC** 02430
UF   Great Grandparents
B   Family Members   1973
N   Grandparents   1973
    ↓ Parents   1967

Androgen Antagonists

Use Antiandrogens

Androgens   1973

PN 702   **SC** 02440
B   Sex Hormones   1973
N   Testosterone   1973
R   Antiandrogens   1982
     Antiestrogens   1982

Androgyny   1982

PN 765   **SC** 02445
SN Combination of masculine and feminine personality characteristics in one individual.

B   Personality Traits   1967
R   Femininity   1967
    ↓ Gender Identity   1985
    ↓ Human Sex Differences   1967
     Masculinity   1967
     Sex Roles   1967

Anemia   1973

PN 191   **SC** 02450
B   Blood and Lymphatic Disorders   1973
R   ↓ Genetic Disorders   1973
     Sickle Cell Disease   1994

Anencephaly   1973

PN 12   **SC** 02460
B   Brain Disorders   1967
     Mental Retardation   1967
     Neonatal Disorders   1973

Anesthesia (Feeling)   1973

PN 234   **SC** 02470
R   Analgesia   1982

Anesthesia (Feeling) — (cont'd)

    ↓ Physical Disorders   1997
    ↓ Sense Organ Disorders   1973
    ↓ Tactual Perception   1967

Anesthesiology   1973

PN 146   **SC** 02480
B   Medical Sciences   1967

Anesthetic Drugs   1973

PN 708   **SC** 02490
B   Drugs   1967
N   ↓ General Anesthetics   1973
     Hexobarbital   1973
     Ketamine   1997
    ↓ Local Anesthetics   1973
     Pentobarbital   1973
     Phencyclidine   1982
     Procaine   1982
R   ↓ Analgesic Drugs   1973
    ↓ Anticonvulsive Drugs   1973
    ↓ Barbiturates   1967
    ↓ CNS Depressant Drugs   1973
    ↓ Hypnotic Drugs   1973
    ↓ Muscle Relaxing Drugs   1973
    ↓ Narcotic Drugs   1973
    ↓ Sedatives   1973

Aneurysms   1973

PN 152   **SC** 02500
B   Cardiovascular Disorders   1967

Anger   1967

PN 3519   **SC** 02510
UF   Rage
B   Emotional States   1973
N   Hostility   1967
R   Anger Control   1997
     Hate   1973
     Jealousy   1973
     Tantrums   1973

Anger Control   1997

PN 279   **SC** 02520
UF   Anger Management
B   Emotional Control   1973
R   Anger   1967
    ↓ Behavior Modification   1973
    ↓ Behavior Therapy   1967
     Explosive Disorder   2001
     Self Control   1973

Anger Management

Use Anger Control

Angina Pectoris   1973

PN 171   **SC** 02530
B   Heart Disorders   1973
R   Myocardial Infarctions   1973

Angiography   1973

PN 48   **SC** 02540
B   Roentgenography   1973

Angiotensin   1973

PN 478   **SC** 02550
B   Neuropeptides   2003
     Peptides   1973
     Vasoconstrictor Drugs   1973
R   Captopril   1991

Anglos   1988

PN 478   **SC** 02553
SN Generally applied to English-speaking White populations of non-Hispanic descent.
HN From 2000, used only to reflect author's terminology.

B   Whites   1982

Angst

Use Anxiety

Anguish

Use Distress

Anhedonia   1985

PN 278   **SC** 02575
SN Loss or absence of ability to experience pleasure.

B   Symptoms   1967
R   Dysthymic Disorder   1988
    ↓ Neurosis   1967
     Pleasure   1973
    ↓ Schizophrenia   1967

Animal Aggressive Behavior   1973

PN 5489   **SC** 02580
B   Aggressive Behavior   1967
     Animal Social Behavior   1967
N   Animal Predatory Behavior   1978
     Attack Behavior   1973
     Muricide   1988
     Threat Postures   1973
R   Animal Dominance   1973
     Territoriality   1967

Animal Assisted Therapy   1994

PN 118   **SC** 02585
SN A type of therapy based on the human-animal companion bond used in an effort to assist in restoring feelings of hope, self worth, responsibility, and communication.

UF   Pet Therapy
B   Psychotherapeutic Techniques   1967
R   ↓ Animals   1967
     Geriatric Psychotherapy   1973
     Interspecies Interaction   1991
     Pets   1982
    ↓ Rehabilitation   1967

Animal Behavior

Use Animal Ethology

Animal Biological Rhythms   1973

PN 514   **SC** 02600
SN Rhythmic and periodic variations in behavioral or physiological functions of animals.
HN Use BIOLOGICAL RHYTHMS to access references from 1967-1972.

UF   Biological Clocks (Animal)
B   Animal Ethology   1967
     Biological Rhythms   1967
N   Animal Circadian Rhythms   1973
R   Animal Sexual Receptivity   1973
     Estrus   1973
     Hibernation   1973

Animal Breeding   1973

PN 3287   **SC** 02610

Animal Breeding — (cont'd)

SN Propagation (or reproduction) of a species in its natural environment or in captive settings. Includes birth rate and breeding success. Compare ANIMAL DOMESTICATION, EUGENICS, and SELECTIVE BREEDING.
- **UF** Breeding (Animal)
- **N** Selective Breeding 1973
- **R** Animal Captivity 1994
  - Animal Domestication 1978
  - ↓ Animal Mating Behavior 1967
  - ↓ Animal Sexual Behavior 1985
  - Animal Strain Differences 1982
  - ↓ Animals 1967
  - Assortative Mating 1991
  - ↓ Genetics 1967
  - Litter Size 1985
  - ↓ Sexual Reproduction 1973

Animal Captivity 1994

PN 620   **SC** 02615
- **UF** Captivity (Animal)
  - Zoo Environment
- **B** Animal Environments 1967
- **R** ↓ Animal Breeding 1973
  - Animal Domestication 1978
  - Animal Rearing 1991
  - Animal Welfare 1985

Animal Circadian Rhythms 1973

PN 2669   **SC** 02620
SN Diurnal cyclical variations or patterns of behavioral or physiological functions of animals.
HN Use BIOLOGICAL RHYTHMS to access references from 1967-1972.
- **UF** Circadian Rhythms (Animal)
  - Daily Biological Rhythms (Animal)
- **B** Animal Biological Rhythms 1973
- **R** Animal Nocturnal Behavior 1973

Animal Coloration 1985

PN 445   **SC** 02625
SN Physical aspect of body color.
- **R** Animal Courtship Displays 1973
  - ↓ Animal Defensive Behavior 1982
  - ↓ Pigments 1973

Animal Communication 1967

PN 1881   **SC** 02630
- **B** Animal Social Behavior 1967
  - Communication 1967
- **N** Animal Distress Calls 1973
- **R** Animal Scent Marking 1985
  - ↓ Animal Vocalizations 1973
  - ↓ Vocalization 1967

Animal Courtship Behavior 1973

PN 1150   **SC** 02640
- **UF** Courtship (Animal)
- **B** Animal Sexual Behavior 1985
  - Animal Social Behavior 1967
- **N** Animal Courtship Displays 1973
- **R** Animal Mate Selection 1982
  - ↓ Animal Mating Behavior 1967

Animal Courtship Displays 1973

PN 351   **SC** 02650
- **UF** Courtship Displays (Animal)
- **B** Animal Courtship Behavior 1973
  - Animal Social Behavior 1967
- **R** Animal Coloration 1985
  - ↓ Animal Mating Behavior 1967
  - Territoriality 1967

Animal Defensive Behavior 1982

PN 2321   **SC** 02652
SN Innate protective responses that occur in presence of predator or other threatening stimulus.
- **UF** Defensive Behavior (Animal)
- **B** Animal Ethology 1967
- **N** Animal Escape Behavior 1973
  - Threat Postures 1973
- **R** Alarm Responses 1973
  - Animal Coloration 1985
  - Animal Distress Calls 1973
  - Attack Behavior 1973
  - Instinctive Behavior 1982
  - Tonic Immobility 1978

Animal Development 1978

PN 3237   **SC** 02655
SN Conceptually broad term. Use a more specific term if possible.
- **B** Development 1967
- **R** Age Differences 1967
  - ↓ Animals 1967
  - ↓ Motor Development 1973
  - Neural Development 1985
  - Perceptual Motor Development 1991
  - ↓ Physical Development 1973
  - ↓ Prenatal Development 1973

Animal Distress Calls 1973

PN 352   **SC** 02660
- **UF** Distress Calls (Animal)
- **B** Animal Communication 1967
  - Animal Vocalizations 1973
- **R** Alarm Responses 1973
  - ↓ Animal Defensive Behavior 1982
  - Instinctive Behavior 1982

Animal Division of Labor 1973

PN 268   **SC** 02670
- **UF** Division of Labor (Animal)
- **B** Animal Social Behavior 1967
  - Division of Labor 1988
- **R** Animal Dominance 1973

Animal Domestication 1978

PN 186   **SC** 02677
SN Adaptation of wild animals to life and breeding in tame conditions according to the interests of human society. Compare ANIMAL BREEDING, EUGENICS, and SELECTIVE BREEDING.
- **UF** Domestication (Animal)
- **R** ↓ Animal Breeding 1973
  - Animal Captivity 1994
  - Pets 1982
  - Selective Breeding 1973

Animal Dominance 1973

PN 2205   **SC** 02680
- **UF** Dominance (Animal)
  - Pecking Order
- **B** Animal Social Behavior 1967
  - Dominance 1967
- **R** ↓ Animal Aggressive Behavior 1973
  - Animal Division of Labor 1973
  - Animal Scent Marking 1985
  - Dominance Hierarchy 1973
  - Territoriality 1967

Animal Drinking Behavior 1973

PN 2052   **SC** 02690
- **UF** Drinking Behavior (Animal)
- **B** Animal Ethology 1967
  - Drinking Behavior 1978

Animal Drinking Behavior — (cont'd)
- **R** ↓ Ingestion 2001
  - Licking 1988
  - Polydipsia 1982
  - Sucking 1978
  - Thirst 1967
  - Water Intake 1967

Animal Emotionality 1978

PN 1109   **SC** 02696
- **UF** Emotionality (Animal)
- **R** Animal Motivation 1967
  - ↓ Emotional Responses 1967

Animal Environments 1967

PN 6858   **SC** 02700
SN Physical and social conditions of an animal's existence or habitat.
- **UF** Habitats (Animal)
- **B** Social Environments 1973
- **N** Animal Captivity 1994
- **R** Animal Rearing 1991
  - ↓ Animals 1967
  - Place Conditioning 1991
  - ↓ Single Sex Environments 2001

Animal Escape Behavior 1973

PN 861   **SC** 02710
- **UF** Escape Behavior (Animal)
- **B** Animal Defensive Behavior 1982
- **R** Alarm Responses 1973

Animal Ethology 1967

PN 5370   **SC** 02720
SN Study of animal behavior especially in relation to ecology, evolution, neuroanatomy, neurophysiology, and genotica. Used for the discipline or the ethological processes themselves. Use a more specific term if possible.
- **UF** Animal Behavior
  - Ethology (Animal)
- **B** Behavior 1967
- **N** ↓ Animal Biological Rhythms 1973
  - ↓ Animal Defensive Behavior 1982
  - Animal Drinking Behavior 1973
  - Animal Exploratory Behavior 1973
  - Animal Feeding Behavior 1973
  - Animal Foraging Behavior 1985
  - Animal Grooming Behavior 1978
  - Animal Hoarding Behavior 1973
  - Animal Homing 1991
  - Animal Nocturnal Behavior 1973
  - Animal Open Field Behavior 1973
  - ↓ Animal Parental Behavior 1982
  - Animal Play 1970
  - Animal Sex Differences 1967
  - ↓ Animal Sexual Behavior 1985
  - ↓ Animal Social Behavior 1967
  - ↓ Animal Vocalizations 1973
  - Hibernation 1973
  - Imprinting 1967
  - Licking 1988
  - Migratory Behavior (Animal) 1973
  - Nest Building 1973
  - Species Recognition 1985
  - Territoriality 1967
- **R** Alarm Responses 1973
  - Animal Motivation 1967
  - ↓ Animals 1967
  - Echolocation 1973
  - Instinctive Behavior 1982
  - Stereotyped Behavior 1973
  - Tool Use 1991

Animal Exploratory Behavior 1973
PN 1956   SC 02730
HN Use EXPLORATORY BEHAVIOR to access references from 1967-1972.
- B   Animal Ethology 1967
-     Exploratory Behavior 1967
- R   Animal Foraging Behavior 1985
-     Instinctive Behavior 1982
-     Neophobia 1985
-     Spontaneous Alternation 1982

Animal Feeding Behavior 1973
PN 5943   SC 02740
- UF   Feeding Behavior (Animal)
- B   Animal Ethology 1967
- R   Animal Foraging Behavior 1985
-     Animal Maternal Behavior 1973
-     Animal Paternal Behavior 1991
-     Cannibalism 2003
-     Food Intake 1967
-     Hunger 1967
-     ↓ Ingestion 2001
-     Sucking 1978

Animal Foraging Behavior 1985
PN 2292   SC 02743
- UF   Foraging (Animal)
- B   Animal Ethology 1967
- R   Animal Exploratory Behavior 1973
-     Animal Feeding Behavior 1973
-     Animal Predatory Behavior 1978

Animal Grooming Behavior 1978
PN 838   SC 02745
- UF   Grooming Behavior (Animal)
- B   Animal Ethology 1967
- R   Licking 1988

Animal Hoarding Behavior 1973
PN 286   SC 02750
- UF   Hoarding Behavior (Animal)
- B   Animal Ethology 1967
-     Hoarding Behavior 2003

Animal Homing 1991
PN 167   SC 02755
SN Returning accurately to one's home or natal area from a distance.
- UF   Homing (Animal)
- B   Animal Ethology 1967
- R   Instinctive Behavior 1982
-     Migratory Behavior (Animal) 1973
-     Territoriality 1967

Animal Human Interaction
   Use   Interspecies Interaction

Animal Innate Behavior
   Use   Instinctive Behavior

Animal Instinctive Behavior
   Use   Instinctive Behavior

Animal Learning 2003
PN 106   SC 02772
SN Used for discussions, hypotheses, or theories of learning in animals; includes theories on cognitive processing. Applicable to all nonhuman species. Compare CONDITIONING.

Animal Learning — (cont'd)
HN This term was introduced in June 2003. PsycINFO records from the past 10 years were re-indexed with this term. The posting note reflects the number of records that were re-indexed.
- B   Learning 1967
- N   Cat Learning 1967
-     Rat Learning 1967
- R   Comparative Psychology 1967
-     ↓ Conditioning 1967
-     Learning Ability 1973

Animal Licking Behavior
   Use   Licking

Animal Locomotion 1982
PN 3409   SC 02775
SN Any form of motor activity resulting in bodily propulsion.
- B   Motor Processes 1967

Animal Mate Selection 1982
PN 1656   SC 02778
SN Ethological processes surrounding the choice of mate for sexual reproduction.
- UF   Mate Selection
- R   ↓ Animal Courtship Behavior 1973
-     ↓ Animal Mating Behavior 1967
-     ↓ Animal Sexual Behavior 1985
-     Assortative Mating 1991
-     ↓ Genetics 1967
-     ↓ Sexual Reproduction 1973

Animal Maternal Behavior 1973
PN 2983   SC 02780
- UF   Maternal Behavior (Animal)
- B   Animal Parental Behavior 1982
- R   Animal Feeding Behavior 1973
-     Animal Maternal Deprivation 1988
-     Animal Paternal Behavior 1991
-     Animal Rearing 1991
-     Licking 1988

Animal Maternal Deprivation 1988
PN 266   SC 02785
HN Consider using ANIMAL MATERNAL BEHAVIOR prior to 1988.
- R   Animal Maternal Behavior 1973
-     Animal Rearing 1991
-     ↓ Social Isolation 1967

Animal Mating Behavior 1967
PN 5768   SC 02790
- UF   Coitus (Animal)
-     Copulation (Animal)
-     Mating Behavior (Animal)
- B   Animal Sexual Behavior 1985
-     Animal Social Behavior 1967
- N   Animal Sexual Receptivity 1973
- R   ↓ Animal Breeding 1973
-     ↓ Animal Courtship Behavior 1973
-     Animal Courtship Displays 1973
-     Animal Mate Selection 1982
-     Assortative Mating 1991
-     Nest Building 1973
-     Pheromones 1973
-     ↓ Sexual Reproduction 1973

Animal Models 1988
PN 5474   SC 02797

Animal Models — (cont'd)
SN Experimentally induced simulations of human conditions in animals designed to investigate the etiology and characteristics of diseases, psychological and psychiatric disorders, or learning processes.
- B   Models 1967
- R   ↓ Animals 1967
-     ↓ Experimental Design 1967
-     ↓ Experimentation 1967

Animal Motivation 1967
PN 1561   SC 02800
- B   Motivation 1967
- R   Animal Emotionality 1978
-     ↓ Animal Ethology 1967
-     ↓ Animals 1967
-     Instinctive Behavior 1982

Animal Navigation
   Use   Migratory Behavior (Animal)

Animal Nocturnal Behavior 1973
PN 166   SC 02820
- UF   Nocturnal Behavior (Animal)
- B   Animal Ethology 1967
- R   Animal Circadian Rhythms 1973

Animal Open Field Behavior 1973
PN 2081   SC 02825
SN Spontaneous animal behavior studied in relatively unrestricted laboratory environments.
HN Prior to 1985 also used for spontaneous animal behavior in natural environments.
- UF   Open Field Behavior (Animal)
- B   Animal Ethology 1967

Animal Parental Behavior 1982
PN 1119   SC 02828
SN Nurturance and care of offspring performed by male and/or female parents.
- UF   Parental Behavior (Animal)
- B   Animal Ethology 1967
-     Animal Social Behavior 1967
- N   Animal Maternal Behavior 1973
-     Animal Paternal Behavior 1991
- R   Animal Rearing 1991
-     Parental Investment 1997

Animal Paternal Behavior 1991
PN 310   SC 02829
- B   Animal Parental Behavior 1982
- R   Animal Feeding Behavior 1973
-     Animal Maternal Behavior 1973
-     Animal Rearing 1991

Animal Play 1973
PN 533   SC 02830
- UF   Play (Animal)
- B   Animal Ethology 1967
- R   ↓ Animal Social Behavior 1967

Animal Predatory Behavior 1978
PN 1928   SC 02834
- UF   Predatory Behavior (Animal)
- B   Animal Aggressive Behavior 1973
- R   Animal Foraging Behavior 1985
-     Attack Behavior 1973
-     Instinctive Behavior 1982
-     Threat Postures 1973

Animal Rearing 1991
PN 832   SC 02836
SN Conditions or environment in which animals are bred, nourished, and raised. Compare ANIMAL PARENTAL BEHAVIOR.
R   Animal Captivity   1994
   ↓ Animal Environments   1967
    Animal Maternal Behavior   1973
    Animal Maternal Deprivation   1988
   ↓ Animal Parental Behavior   1982
    Animal Paternal Behavior   1991

Animal Scent Marking 1985
PN 393   SC 02837
UF   Scent Marking (Animal)
R   ↓ Animal Communication   1967
    Animal Dominance   1973
    Pheromones   1973
    Territoriality   1967

Animal Sex Differences 1967
PN 4215   SC 02840
SN Animal behavioral, developmental, and physiological/anatomical differences between the sexes.
UF   Sex Differences (Animal)
B   Animal Ethology   1967
R   Sex   1967
    Sex Recognition   1997
   ↓ Single Sex Environments   2001

Animal Sexual Behavior 1985
PN 2380   SC 02845
SN Any form of sexual behavior in animals.
B   Animal Ethology   1967
N   ↓ Animal Courtship Behavior   1973
   ↓ Animal Mating Behavior   1967
R   ↓ Animal Breeding   1973
    Animal Mate Selection   1982
    Instinctive Behavior   1982
    Sex   1967

Animal Sexual Receptivity 1973
PN 1368   SC 02850
UF   Lordosis (Animal)
    Sexual Receptivity (Animal)
B   Animal Mating Behavior   1967
R   ↓ Animal Biological Rhythms   1973
    Estrus   1973

Animal Social Behavior 1967
PN 7415   SC 02860
B   Animal Ethology   1967
    Social Behavior   1967
N   ↓ Animal Aggressive Behavior   1973
   ↓ Animal Communication   1967
   ↓ Animal Courtship Behavior   1973
    Animal Courtship Displays   1973
    Animal Division of Labor   1973
    Animal Dominance   1973
   ↓ Animal Mating Behavior   1967
   ↓ Animal Parental Behavior   1982
R   Animal Play   1973
    Interspecies Interaction   1991
    Physical Contact   1982

Animal Strain Differences 1982
PN 3241   SC 02863
SN Anatomical, physiological, and/or behavioral variations between members of different subspecies or strains. Compare SPECIES DIFFERENCES.
HN Use GENETICS and ANIMAL BREEDING together to access references from 1973-1981.

Animal Strain Differences — (cont'd)
UF   Strain Differences (Animal)
R   ↓ Animal Breeding   1973
   ↓ Genetics   1967

Animal Tool Use
Use   Tool Use

Animal Vocalizations 1973
PN 4136   SC 02870
UF   Vocalizations (Animal)
B   Animal Ethology   1967
    Vocalization   1967
N   Animal Distress Calls   1973
R   ↓ Animal Communication   1967
    Echolocation   1973

Animal Welfare 1985
PN 610   SC 02875
R   Animal Captivity   1994
    Experimental Ethics   1978

Animals 1967
PN 3993   SC 02880
SN Conceptually broad term. Use a more specific term if possible (e.g., VERTEBRATES, MAMMALS, DOGS).
N   Female Animals   1973
    Infants (Animal)   1978
   ↓ Invertebrates   1973
    Male Animals   1973
   ↓ Vertebrates   1973
R   Animal Assisted Therapy   1994
   ↓ Animal Breeding   1973
    Animal Development   1978
   ↓ Animal Environments   1967
   ↓ Animal Ethology   1967
    Animal Models   1988
    Animal Motivation   1967
    Biological Symbiosis   1973
    Interspecies Interaction   1991
    Pets   1982
    Species Differences   1982

Animism 1973
PN 90   SC 02890
SN Ascribing life to inanimate objects. Also, the Piagetian stage of development in which children ascribe emotional attributes and intentions to inanimate objects.
B   Philosophies   1967
R   Ethnology   1967
    Myths   1967
    Taboos   1973

Ankle 1973
PN 46   SC 02900
B   Joints (Anatomy)   1973
R   Feet (Anatomy)   1973
    Leg (Anatomy)   1973

Anniversary Events 1994
PN 17   SC 02905
SN Annual occurrence of a specific date that marks a notable event or experience. Includes aspects of both positive or negative reactions to the event or experience.
UF   Anniversary Reactions
B   Experiences (Events)   1973
R   Autobiographical Memory   1994
    Early Experience   1967

Anniversary Events — (cont'd)
    Early Memories   1985
   ↓ Life Experiences   1973
    Life Review   1991
    Reminiscence   1985

Anniversary Reactions
Use   Anniversary Events

Annual Leave
Use   Employee Leave Benefits

Anodynes
Use   Analgesic Drugs

Anomie 1978
PN 211   SC 02940
SN Sense of alienation or despair resulting from the loss or weakening of previously held values. Also, a state of lawlessness or a lack of normative standards within groups or societies.
B   Social Processes   1967
R   Alienation   1971
    Personal Values   1973
    Social Values   1973

Anonymity 1973
PN 258   SC 02945
SN Unknown, unacknowledged, or concealed personal identity.
R   Privileged Communication   1973
    Secrecy   1994
    Self Disclosure   1973
   ↓ Social Perception   1967

Anorexia Nervosa 1973
PN 4973   SC 02950
SN Syndrome in which the primary features include excessive fear of becoming overweight, body image disturbance, significant weight loss, refusal to maintain minimal normal weight, and amenorrhea. This disorder occurs most frequently in adolescent females.
B   Eating Disorders   1997
    Underweight   1973
R   ↓ Body Image Disturbances   1973
    Bulimia   1985
   ↓ Nutritional Deficiencies   1973
   ↓ Somatoform Disorders   2001

Anorexigenic Drugs
Use   Appetite Depressing Drugs

Anosmia 1973
PN 201   SC 02970
SN Loss of the sense of smell.
UF   Olfactory Impairment
B   Sense Organ Disorders   1973
R   ↓ Olfactory Perception   1967
    Taste Disorders   2001

Anosognosia 1994
PN 98   SC 02975
SN Lack of awareness of, or refusal or failure to deal with or recognize that one has a mental or physical disorder.
B   Agnosia   1973
R   Coping Behavior   1967
    Denial   1973
    Illness Behavior   1982

ANOVA (Statistics)
Use Analysis of Variance

Anoxia 1973
PN 640　　　　　　　　　　**SC** 02990
SN Absence or reduction of oxygen in body tissue.
UF Asphyxia
　　Hypoxia
　　Suffocation
B Symptoms 1967
R ↓ Ischemia 1973
　　↓ Respiratory Distress 1973

Antabuse
Use Disulfiram

Antagonism
Use Hostility

Antagonists (CNS Depressant Drugs)
Use Analeptic Drugs

Anterograde Amnesia 2003
PN 30　　　　　　　　　　**SC** 03015
SN Memory loss for events and experiences that occurred after the incident that produced the amnesia.
HN This term was introduced in June 2003. Psyc-INFO records from the past 10 years were re-indexed with this term. The posting note reflects the number of records that were re-indexed.
B Amnesia 1967
R Retrograde Amnesia 2003

Anthropologists 1973
PN 63　　　　　　　　　　**SC** 03030
B Professional Personnel 1978
R Scientists 1967
　　Sociologists 1973

Anthropology 1967
PN 1160　　　　　　　　　　**SC** 03040
SN Science dealing with the study of the interrelations of biological, cultural, geographical, and historical characteristics of the human species. Use a more specific term if possible.
B Social Sciences 1967
R Ethnography 1973
　　Ethnology 1967
　　Folk Psychology 1997

Anti Inflammatory Drugs 1982
PN 359　　　　　　　　　　**SC** 03041
SN Agents which reduce inflammation by acting on body mechanisms, without directly antagonizing the causative agent.
UF Antipyretic Drugs
B Drugs 1967
N Aspirin 1973
　　↓ Glucocorticoids 1982
　　↓ Neurokinins 1997
R ↓ Alkaloids 1973
　　↓ Analgesic Drugs 1973
　　↓ Enzymes 1973
　　↓ Hormones 1967
　　Hydrocortisone 1973
　　Prostaglandins 1982
　　↓ Steroids 1973

Antiadrenergic Drugs
Use Sympatholytic Drugs

Antiandrogens 1982
PN 132　　　　　　　　　　**SC** 03042
SN Substances capable of preventing the normal effects of androgenic hormones on responsive tissues by antagonistic effects on tissue or by inhibiting androgenic effects.
UF Androgen Antagonists
B Drugs 1967
R ↓ Androgens 1973
　　↓ Estrogens 1973
　　↓ Steroids 1973

Antianxiety Drugs
Use Tranquilizing Drugs

Antibiotics 1973
PN 320　　　　　　　　　　**SC** 03050
B Drugs 1967
N Amantadine 1978
　　Cycloheximide 1973
　　Penicillins 1973
　　Puromycin 1973
R Antineoplastic Drugs 1982

Antibodies 1973
PN 629　　　　　　　　　　**SC** 03060
B Globulins 1973
　　Immunologic Factors 2003
R Antigens 1982
　　Blood Serum 1973
　　↓ Drugs 1967
　　Gamma Globulin 1973
　　Immunization 1973
　　↓ Immunoglobulins 1973
　　↓ Neurotoxins 1982

Anticholinergic Drugs
Use Cholinergic Blocking Drugs

Anticholinesterase Drugs
Use Cholinesterase Inhibitors

Anticipation (Serial Learning)
Use Serial Anticipation (Learning)

Anticoagulant Drugs 1973
PN 48　　　　　　　　　　**SC** 03100
B Drugs 1967
N Heparin 1973

Anticonvulsive Drugs 1973
PN 2058　　　　　　　　　　**SC** 03110
HN In 1982, this term replaced the discontinued term ANTIEPILEPTIC DRUGS, and in 1997 it replaced PARALDEHYDE. In 2000, these terms were removed from all records containing them, and replaced with ANTICONVULSIVE DRUGS.
UF Antiepileptic Drugs
　　Paraldehyde
B Drugs 1967
N Carbamazepine 1988
　　Chloral Hydrate 1973
　　Clonazepam 1991
　　Diphenylhydantoin 1973
　　Nitrazepam 1978
　　Oxazepam 1978

Anticonvulsive Drugs — (cont'd)
　　Pentobarbital 1973
　　Phenobarbital 1973
　　Primidone 1973
　　Valproic Acid 1991
R Acetazolamide 1973
　　↓ Anesthetic Drugs 1973
　　↓ Antispasmodic Drugs 1973
　　↓ Barbiturates 1967
　　↓ Benzodiazepines 1978
　　↓ CNS Depressant Drugs 1973
　　↓ Convulsions 1967
　　↓ Epilepsy 1967
　　↓ Hypnotic Drugs 1973
　　↓ Muscle Relaxing Drugs 1973
　　↓ Narcotic Drugs 1973
　　↓ Sedatives 1973
　　↓ Spasms 1973
　　↓ Tranquilizing Drugs 1967

Antidepressant Drugs 1971
PN 8352　　　　　　　　　　**SC** 03120
HN In 1997, this term replaced the discontinued term DEANOL. In 2000, DEANOL was removed from all records and replaced with ANTIDEPRESSANT DRUGS.
UF Deanol
B Drugs 1967
N Bupropion 1994
　　Citalopram 1997
　　Fluoxetine 1991
　　Fluvoxamine 1994
　　Iproniazid 1973
　　Isocarboxazid 1973
　　Lithium Carbonate 1973
　　Methylphenidate 1973
　　Mianserin 1982
　　Moclobemide 1997
　　Molindone 1982
　　Nefazodone 2003
　　Nialamide 1973
　　Nomifensine 1982
　　Paroxetine 1994
　　Phenelzine 1973
　　Pheniprazine 1973
　　Pipradrol 1973
　　Sertraline 1997
　　Sulpiride 1973
　　Tranylcypromine 1973
　　Trazodone 1988
　　↓ Tricyclic Antidepressant Drugs 1997
　　Venlafaxine 2003
　　Zimeldine 1988
R ↓ CNS Stimulating Drugs 1973
　　↓ Lithium 1973
　　↓ Monoamine Oxidase Inhibitors 1973

Antiemetic Drugs 1973
PN 105　　　　　　　　　　**SC** 03140
UF Antinauseant Drugs
B Drugs 1967
N Chlorpromazine 1967
　　Chlorprothixene 1973
　　Fluphenazine 1973
　　Perphenazine 1973
　　Piracetam 1982
　　Prochlorperazine 1973
　　Promethazine 1973
　　Sulpiride 1973
R ↓ Cholinergic Blocking Drugs 1973
　　↓ Hypnotic Drugs 1973
　　Nausea 1973
　　↓ Sedatives 1973
　　↓ Tranquilizing Drugs 1967
　　Vomiting 1973

Antiepileptic Drugs
   Use Anticonvulsive Drugs

Antiestrogens 1982
PN 52   SC 03155
SN Substances capable of preventing the normal effects of estrogenic hormones on responsive tissues by antagonistic effects on tissue or by inhibiting estrogenic effects.
   UF Estrogen Antagonists
   B   Drugs 1967
   R ↓ Androgens 1973
         Antineoplastic Drugs 1982
       ↓ Estrogens 1973
       ↓ Steroids 1973

Antigens 1982
PN 288   SC 03158
SN Substances such as microorganisms or foreign tissues, cells, proteins, toxoids, or exotoxins having the ability to induce antibody formation.
   UF Allergens
         Immunogens
   B   Immunologic Factors 2003
   R   Antibodies 1973
         Blood Groups 1973
       ↓ Immunoglobulins 1973
         Interleukins 1994

Antihistaminic Drugs 1973
PN 306   SC 03160
   B   Drugs 1967
   N   Chlorprothixene 1973
         Cimetidine 1985
         Diphenhydramine 1973
         Mianserin 1982
         Orphenadrine 1973
         Promethazine 1973
   R   Histamine 1973
         Hydroxyzine 1973
       ↓ Hypnotic Drugs 1973
       ↓ Sedatives 1973

Antihypertensive Drugs 1973
PN 291   SC 03170
   B   Drugs 1967
   N   Alpha Methylparatyrosine 1978
         Captopril 1991
         Chlorpromazine 1967
         Clonidine 1973
         Guanethidine 1973
         Hexamethonium 1973
         Hydralazine 1973
         Iproniazid 1973
         Mecamylamine 1973
         Methyldopa 1973
         Pargyline 1973
         Pheniprazine 1973
         Phenoxybenzamine 1973
         Quinpirole 1994
         Reserpine 1967
   R ↓ Adrenergic Blocking Drugs 1973
       ↓ Diuretics 1973
       ↓ Ganglion Blocking Drugs 1973
       ↓ Heart Rate Affecting Drugs 1973
       ↓ Hypertension 1973
       ↓ Hypnotic Drugs 1973
       ↓ Muscle Relaxing Drugs 1973
       ↓ Sedatives 1973
       ↓ Tranquilizing Drugs 1967
       ↓ Vasodilator Drugs 1973

Antinauseant Drugs
   Use Antiemetic Drugs

Antineoplastic Drugs 1982
PN 110   SC 03179
SN Drugs used in the prevention of the development, maturation, or spread of neoplastic cells.
   B   Drugs 1967
   R ↓ Antibiotics 1973
         Antiestrogens 1982
       ↓ Hormones 1967
         Interferons 1994
       ↓ Neoplasms 1967
       ↓ Steroids 1973

Antioxidants 2004
PN 67   SC 58079
SN Substances that inhibit oxidation.
HN This term was introduced in June 2004. PsycINFO records from the past 10 years were re-indexed with this term. The posting note reflects the number of records that were re-indexed.
   N   Ascorbic Acid 1973
   R   Dietary Supplements 2001
         Food Additives 1978
         Oxygen 1973
       ↓ Vitamins 1973

Antiparkinsonian Drugs
   Use Antitremor Drugs

Antipathy
   Use Aversion

Antipsychotic Drugs
   Use Neuroleptic Drugs

Antipyretic Drugs
   Use Anti Inflammatory Drugs

Antischizophrenic Drugs
   Use Neuroleptic Drugs

AntiSemitism 1973
PN 349   SC 03220
   B   Racial and Ethnic Attitudes 1982
         Religious Prejudices 1973
   R   Hate Crimes 2003
         Holocaust 1988
         Jews 1997
         Judaism 1967
       ↓ Prejudice 1967
         Racism 1973

Antisocial Behavior 1971
PN 3903   SC 03230
   UF Deviant Behavior
         Sociopathology
   B   Behavior 1967
   N   Child Neglect 1988
       ↓ Criminal Behavior 2003
         Cruelty 1973
         Elder Abuse 1988
         Emotional Abuse 1991
       ↓ Harassment 2001
       ↓ Juvenile Delinquency 1967
         Partner Abuse 1991
         Patient Abuse 1991
         Persecution 1973
         Physical Abuse 1991
         Recidivism 1973

Antisocial Behavior — (cont'd)
         Runaway Behavior 1973
       ↓ Sexual Abuse 1988
         Terrorism 1982
         Torture 1988
         Verbal Abuse 2003
       ↓ Violence 1973
   R   Antisocial Personality Disorder 1973
       ↓ Behavior Disorders 1971
         Bullying 2003
       ↓ Crime 1967
         Erotomania 1997
         Explosive Disorder 2001
       ↓ Impulse Control Disorders 1997
       ↓ Prosocial Behavior 1982
         Psychopathology 1967
       ↓ Social Behavior 1967

Antisocial Personality Disorder 1973
PN 2182   SC 03240
SN Personality disorder characterized by conflict with others, low frustration tolerance, inadequate conscience development, and rejection of authority and discipline.
HN In 1997, this term replaced the discontinued term PSYCHOPATHY. In 2000, PSYCHOPATHY was removed from all records containing it, and replaced with ANTISOCIAL PERSONALITY.
   UF Psychopath
         Psychopathy
         Sociopath
   B   Personality Disorders 1967
   R ↓ Antisocial Behavior 1971
       ↓ Autism 1967
       ↓ Criminals 1967
       ↓ Juvenile Delinquency 1967
         Narcissistic Personality Disorder 1973

Antispasmodic Drugs 1973
PN 7   SC 03250
SN Drugs that prevent or reduce spasms usually by relaxation of smooth muscle.
   UF Parasympatholytic Drugs
   B   Drugs 1967
   N   Atropine 1973
         Chlorprothixene 1973
         Meperidine 1973
         Orphenadrine 1973
         Papaverine 1973
         Trihexyphenidyl 1973
   R ↓ Anticonvulsive Drugs 1973
       ↓ Cholinergic Blocking Drugs 1973
       ↓ Muscle Relaxing Drugs 1973
       ↓ Spasms 1973

Antitremor Drugs 1973
PN 209   SC 03260
SN Drugs that diminish skeletal muscle tone through action on the central nervous system.
   UF Antiparkinsonian Drugs
   B   Drugs 1967
   N   Amantadine 1978
         Diphenhydramine 1973
         Levodopa 1973
         Nomifensine 1982
         Orphenadrine 1973
         Trihexyphenidyl 1973
   R ↓ Decarboxylase Inhibitors 1982
         Parkinsons Disease 1973
         Tremor 1973

Antitubercular Drugs 1973
PN 15   SC 03270
   B   Drugs 1967

Antitubercular Drugs — (cont'd)
- N   Iproniazid 1973
-     Isoniazid 1973
- R   ↓ Tuberculosis 1973

Antiviral Drugs 1994
PN 247   **SC** 03280
- B   Drugs 1967
- N   Zidovudine 1994

Antonyms 1973
PN 57   **SC** 03290
- B   Semantics 1967
-     Vocabulary 1967
- R   Words (Phonetic Units) 1967

Ants 1973
PN 609   **SC** 03300
- B   Insects 1967
- R   Larvae 1973

Anxiety 1967
PN 23463   **SC** 03310
SN Apprehension or fear of impending actual or imagined danger, vulnerability, or uncertainty.
HN Prior to 1988, also used for anxiety disorders.
- UF   Angst
-     Anxiousness
-     Apprehension
-     Worry
- B   Emotional States 1973
- N   Computer Anxiety 2001
-     Mathematics Anxiety 1985
-     Performance Anxiety 1994
-     Social Anxiety 1985
-     Speech Anxiety 1985
-     Test Anxiety 1967
- R   Agitation 1991
-     ↓ Anxiety Disorders 1997
-     Anxiety Management 1997
-     ↓ Fear 1967
-     Fear of Success 1978
-     Generalized Anxiety Disorder 2004
-     Guilt 1967
-     Jealousy 1973
-     ↓ Neurosis 1967
-     Panic 1973
-     Panic Attack 2003
-     Panic Disorder 1988
-     ↓ Phobias 1967
-     Shame 1994
-     ↓ Stress 1967

Anxiety Disorders 1997
PN 6528   **SC** 03315
SN Disorders characterized by anxiety or dread without apparent object or cause. Symptoms include irritability, anxious expectations, pangs of conscience, anxiety attacks, or phobias.
HN In 1997, this term was created to replace the discontinued term ANXIETY NEUROSIS. In 2000, ANXIETY NEUROSIS was removed from all records containing it, and replaced with ANXIETY DISORDERS.
- UF   Anxiety Neurosis
- B   Mental Disorders 1967
- N   Acute Stress Disorder 2003
-     Castration Anxiety 1973
-     Death Anxiety 1978
-     Generalized Anxiety Disorder 2004
-     Obsessive Compulsive Disorder 1985
-     Panic Disorder 1988
-     ↓ Phobias 1967
-     Posttraumatic Stress Disorder 1985

Anxiety Disorders — (cont'd)
-     Separation Anxiety 1973
- R   ↓ Anxiety 1967
-     Anxiety Management 1997
-     Fear of Success 1978
-     Guilt 1967
-     Hypochondriasis 1973
-     Mathematics Anxiety 1985
-     Panic Attack 2003
-     Performance Anxiety 1994
-     Social Anxiety 1985
-     Speech Anxiety 1985
-     Test Anxiety 1967

Anxiety Management 1997
PN 165   **SC** 03318
- R   ↓ Anxiety 1967
-     ↓ Anxiety Disorders 1997
-     ↓ Behavior Modification 1973
-     ↓ Behavior Therapy 1967
-     ↓ Cognitive Techniques 1985
-     Cognitive Therapy 1982
-     ↓ Relaxation Therapy 1978
-     Stress Management 1985

Anxiety Neurosis
SN Term was discontinued in 1997. In 2000, the term was removed from all records containing it, and replaced with ANXIETY DISORDERS, its postable counterpart.
- **Use** Anxiety Disorders

Anxiety Reducing Drugs
- **Use** Tranquilizing Drugs

Anxiolytic Drugs
- **Use** Tranquilizing Drugs

Anxiousness
- **Use** Anxiety

Aorta 1973
PN 28   **SC** 03360
- B   Arteries (Anatomy) 1973

Apathy 1973
PN 217   **SC** 03380
- UF   Indifference
- B   Emotional States 1973
- R   Hopelessness 1988
-     ↓ Separation Reactions 1997

Apes
- **Use** Primates (Nonhuman)

Aphagia 1973
PN 50   **SC** 03400
SN Not eating, the refusal to eat, or an inability to swallow foods or fluids.
- B   Pain 1967
-     Symptoms 1967
- R   ↓ Eating Disorders 1997

Aphasia 1967
PN 4480   **SC** 03410
SN Partial or complete impairment of language comprehension, formulation, or use due to brain damage.
- UF   Agrammatism
-     Word Deafness

Aphasia — (cont'd)
- B   Brain Disorders 1967
-     Language Disorders 1982
- N   Acalculia 1973
-     ↓ Agnosia 1973
-     Agraphia 1973
-     ↓ Dysphasia 1978
- R   ↓ Learning Disabilities 1973
-     ↓ Perceptual Disturbances 1973

Aphrodisiacs 1973
PN 20   **SC** 03420
- R   ↓ Cannabis 1973

Aplysia
- **Use** Snails

Apnea 1973
PN 187   **SC** 03430
SN Temporary absence of breathing or prolonged respiratory failure.
- B   Respiratory Distress 1973
-     Respiratory Tract Disorders 1973
- N   Sleep Apnea 1991
- R   ↓ Neonatal Disorders 1973
-     Sudden Infant Death 1982

Apolipoproteins 2004
PN 289   **SC** 03435
SN The protein component of lipoproteins
HN This term was introduced in June 2004. Psyc-INFO records from the past 10 years were re-indexed with this term. The posting note reflects the number of records that were re-indexed.
- B   Proteins 1973
- R   Lipoproteins 1973

Apomorphine 1973
PN 1565   **SC** 03440
- UF   Apomorphine Hydrochloride
- B   Alkaloids 1973
-     Dopamine Agonists 1985
-     Emetic Drugs 1973
-     Hypnotic Drugs 1973
-     Narcotic Drugs 1973

Apomorphine Hydrochloride
- **Use** Apomorphine

Apoplexy
- **Use** Cerebrovascular Accidents

Apparatus 1967
PN 3722   **SC** 03480
SN Set of materials, instruments, or equipment designed for specific operation in any setting. Use a more specific term if possible.
HN In 1997, this term replaced the discontinued terms TRANSISTORS (APPARATUS) and VOLT METERS. In 2000, these terms were removed from all records containing them, and replaced with APPARATUS.
- UF   Devices (Experimental)
-     Equipment
-     Experimental Apparatus
-     Transistors (Apparatus)
-     Volt Meters
- N   Amplifiers (Apparatus) 1973
-     Audiometers 1973
-     Cage Apparatus 1973
-     Cameras 1973

Apparatus — (cont'd)
- ↓ Computer Peripheral Devices 1985
- ↓ Computers 1967
- Electrodes 1967
- Generators (Apparatus) 1973
- Incubators (Apparatus) 1973
- Keyboards 1985
- ↓ Mazes 1967
- Metronomes 1973
- Microscopes 1973
- Oscilloscopes 1973
- Polygraphs 1973
- Shuttle Boxes 1973
- Skinner Boxes 1973
- Sonar 1973
- ↓ Stimulators (Apparatus) 1973
- Tachistoscopes 1973
- ↓ Tape Recorders 1973
- Timers (Apparatus) 1973
- Transducers 1973
- Vibrators (Apparatus) 1973
- R ↓ Augmentative Communication 1994
- Polysomnography 2003
- ↓ Television 1967

Apparent Distance 1973
PN 113 **SC** 03490
SN Subjective perception of distance as opposed to actual distance, based on comparison of retinal and familiar sizes.
- B Distance Perception 1973

Apparent Movement 1967
PN 1011 **SC** 03500
SN Subjective perception of movement in the absence of real physical movement.
- UF Stroboscopic Movement
- B Motion Perception 1967
- N Autokinetic Illusion 1967

Apparent Size 1973
PN 265 **SC** 03510
SN Subjective perception of size as opposed to real or actual size.
- UF Size (Apparent)
- B Size Discrimination 1967

Apperception 1973
PN 81 **SC** 03520
SN Process of assimilating new perceptions and relating them to existing body of knowledge.
- R ↓ Attention 1967
- ↓ Perception 1967

Appetite 1973
PN 803 **SC** 03530
SN Indicates an instinctive or acquired motivation, impulse, or desire stemming from internal physiological conditions. Compare HUNGER.
- B Physiology 1967
- N Hunger 1967
- R ↓ Appetite Depressing Drugs 1973
- Craving 1997
- Dietary Restraint 1994
- Eating Attitudes 1994
- ↓ Eating Behavior 2004
- ↓ Eating Disorders 1997
- Satiation 1967

Appetite Depressing Drugs 1973
PN 194 **SC** 03540
- UF Anorexigenic Drugs
- B Drugs 1967

Appetite Depressing Drugs — (cont'd)
- N ↓ Amphetamine 1967
- Dextroamphetamine 1973
- Fenfluramine 1973
- Phenmetrazine 1973
- R ↓ Appetite 1973

Appetite Disorders
Use Eating Disorders

Applied Psychology 1973
PN 755 **SC** 03560
SN Broad discipline in which psychological principles and theories are used to solve practical problems.
- B Psychology 1967
- N ↓ Clinical Psychology 1967
- Community Psychology 1973
- Consumer Psychology 1973
- Counseling Psychology 1973
- ↓ Educational Psychology 1967
- Engineering Psychology 1967
- Environmental Psychology 1982
- Industrial and Organizational Psychology 2003
- Military Psychology 1967
- Political Psychology 1997
- Social Psychology 1967
- Sport Psychology 1982

Apprehension
Use Anxiety

Apprenticeship 1973
PN 177 **SC** 03580
- B Personnel Training 1967
- R ↓ Experiential Learning 1997
- Mentor 1985

Approval (Social)
Use Social Approval

Apraxia 1973
PN 782 **SC** 03600
SN Inability to execute complex coordinated movements resulting from lesions in the motor area of the cortex but involving no sensory impairment or paralysis.
- UF Akinesia
- B Movement Disorders 1985
- Symptoms 1967
- R Parkinsonism 1994
- ↓ Speech Disorders 1967

Aptitude
Use Ability

Aptitude (Academic)
Use Academic Aptitude

Aptitude Measures 1967
PN 2427 **SC** 03630
SN Tests designed to assess capacities or potential abilities in performing tasks, skills, or other acts which have not yet been learned.
HN In 1997, this term replaced the discontinued term SCHOOL AND COLLEGE ABILITY TEST. In 2000, SCHOOL AND COLLEGE ABILITY TEST was removed from all records containing it, and replaced with APTITUDE MEASURES.

Aptitude Measures — (cont'd)
- UF Ability Tests
- School and College Ability Test
- Tests (Aptitude)
- B Measurement 1967
- N Army General Classification Test 1967
- College Entrance Examination Board Scholastic Aptitude Test 2001
- Differential Aptitude Tests 1973
- General Aptitude Test Battery 1973
- Graduate Record Examination 1973

Arabs 1988
PN 615 **SC** 03635
- UF Palestinians
- B Racial and Ethnic Groups 2001
- R Minority Groups 1967

Arachnida 1973
PN 436 **SC** 03640
- UF Spiders
- B Arthropoda 1973

Arachnophobia
Use Phobias

Archetypes 1991
PN 518 **SC** 03650
SN Unconscious representation of inherited collective experience on which the personality is built. Anima, animus, and the shadow are major archetypes.
HN Consider JUNGIAN PSYCHOLOGY to access references from 1973-1990.
- B Collective Unconscious 1997
- R Analytical Psychotherapy 1973
- ↓ Imagery 1967
- Jung (Carl) 1973
- ↓ Jungian Psychology 1973
- Myths 1967
- Unconscious (Personality Factor) 1967

Architects 1973
PN 92 **SC** 03670
- B Business and Industrial Personnel 1967

Architecture 1973
PN 714 **SC** 03680
- B Arts 1973
- N Interior Design 1982
- R Computer Assisted Design 1997
- ↓ Environment 1967
- ↓ Environmental Planning 1982
- Religious Buildings 1973
- Urban Planning 1973

Arecoline 1973
PN 80 **SC** 03690
- UF Arecoline Hydrobromide
- B Cholinomimetic Drugs 1973
- R Bromides 1973

Arecoline Hydrobromide
Use Arecoline

Arguments 1973
PN 663 **SC** 03710
- B Conflict 1967
- Interpersonal Communication 1973
- R Debates 1997

Arithmetic
   Use   Mathematics

Arm (Anatomy) 1973
PN 693   SC 03730
   B   Musculoskeletal System 1973
   R   Elbow (Anatomy) 1973
           Hand (Anatomy) 1967
           Shoulder (Anatomy) 1973
           Wrist 1973

Army General Classification Test 1967
PN 8   SC 03740
   B   Aptitude Measures 1967

Army Personnel 1967
PN 1324   SC 03750
   B   Military Personnel 1967
   R   Draftees 1973
           National Guardsmen 1973

Arousal (Physiological)
   Use   Physiological Arousal

Arousal (Sexual)
   Use   Sexual Arousal

Arrest (Law)
   Use   Legal Arrest

Arrhythmias (Heart) 1973
PN 263   SC 03790
   B   Heart Disorders 1973
   N   Bradycardia 1973
           Fibrillation (Heart) 1973
           Tachycardia 1973

Arson 1985
PN 217   SC 03795
   UF   Firesetting
   B   Crime 1967
   R   ↓ Violent Crime 2003

Art 1967
PN 1661   SC 03800
   SN   Products of aesthetic expression. Not used as a
document type identifier.
   UF   Artwork
   B   Arts 1973
   N   Crafts 1973
           Drawing 1967
           Painting (Art) 1973
           Photographic Art 1973
           Sculpturing 1973

Art Education 1973
PN 645   SC 03810
   B   Curriculum 1967

Art Therapy 1973
PN 1763   SC 03820
   SN   Therapy that uses the creative work of clients for
emotional expression, sublimation, achievement, and
to reveal underlying conflicts.
   B   Creative Arts Therapy 1994
   R   Educational Therapy 1997
           Movement Therapy 1997
           Recreation Therapy 1973

Arterial Pulse 1973
PN 398   SC 03830
   UF   Pulse (Arterial)
   R   Blood Circulation 1973

Arteries (Anatomy) 1973
PN 239   SC 03840
   UF   Coronary Vessels
           Retinal Vessels
   B   Blood Vessels 1973
   N   Aorta 1973
           Carotid Arteries 1973

Arteriosclerosis 1973
PN 46   SC 03850
   B   Cardiovascular Disorders 1967
   N   Atherosclerosis 1973
           Cerebral Arteriosclerosis 1973
   R   ↓ Blood Pressure Disorders 1973

Arthritis 1973
PN 671   SC 03860
   UF   Rheumatism
   B   Joint Disorders 1973
   N   Rheumatoid Arthritis 1973
   R   ↓ Infectious Disorders 1973

Arthropoda 1973
PN 46   SC 03870
   B   Invertebrates 1973
   N   Arachnida 1973
           ↓ Crustacea 1973
           ↓ Insects 1967

Articulation (Speech) 1967
PN 1731   SC 03880
   SN   Production of speech sounds resulting from
vocal tract movements.
   B   Speech Characteristics 1973
           Verbal Communication 1967
   R   Phonetics 1967
           Pronunciation 1973

Articulation Disorders 1973
PN 443   SC 03890
   SN   Speech disorders involving the substitution,
omission, distortion, or addition of phonemes.
   UF   Misarticulation
   B   Speech Disorders 1967
   N   Dysarthria 1973

Artificial Insemination
   Use   Reproductive Technology

Artificial Intelligence 1982
PN 2637   SC 03895
   SN   Study and application of computers to simulate
and perform functions of human information process-
ing.
   B   Computer Applications 1973
   N   ↓ Expert Systems 1991
           Knowledge Engineering 2003
           Machine Learning 2003
           Neural Networks 1991
   R   Automated Speech Recognition 1994
           Automation 1967
           Case Based Reasoning 2003
           ↓ Cognitive Processes 1967
           Cognitive Science 2003
           ↓ Computers 1967
           Cybernetics 1967

Artificial Intelligence — (cont'd)
           Decision Support Systems 1997
           Fuzzy Logic 2003
           Human Machine Systems 1997
           ↓ Intelligence 1967
           Intelligent Tutoring Systems 2003
           Robotics 1985

Artificial Limbs
   Use   Prostheses

Artificial Pacemakers 1973
PN 55   SC 03910
   UF   Pacemakers (Artificial)
   B   Medical Therapeutic Devices 1973

Artificial Respiration 1973
PN 59   SC 03920
   UF   Lifesaving
   B   Physical Treatment Methods 1973
   R   Respiration 1967
           ↓ Respiratory System 1973
           ↓ Respiratory Tract Disorders 1973

Artistic Ability 1973
PN 293   SC 03930
   B   Nonverbal Ability 1988
   N   Musical Ability 1973
   R   Creativity 1967

Artists 1973
PN 1392   SC 03940
   B   Personnel 1967
   N   Musicians 1991
           Writers 1991

Arts 1973
PN 493   SC 03950
   SN   Conceptually broad term referring to all forms of
the arts, including the performing arts. Use a more
specific term if possible.
   UF   Performing Arts
   B   Humanities 2003
   N   ↓ Architecture 1973
           ↓ Art 1967
           Dance 1973
           ↓ Music 1967
           ↓ Theatre 1973
   R   Aesthetics 1967
           Postmodernism 1997

Artwork
   Use   Art

Asbestos
   Use   Hazardous Materials

Asceticism 1973
PN 35   SC 03970
   B   Philosophies 1967
           Religious Practices 1973
   R   Religion 1967
           ↓ Religious Beliefs 1973

Ascorbic Acid 1973
PN 108   SC 03980
   UF   Vitamin C
   B   Acids 1973
           Antioxidants 2004
           Vitamins 1973

Asian Americans
Use Asians

Asians 1982
PN 5032　　　　　SC 04007
HN In 1982, this term was created to replace the discontinued term ASIAN AMERICANS. In 2000, ASIAN AMERICANS was removed from all records and replaced with ASIANS.
UF Asian Americans
B Racial and Ethnic Groups 2001
N Chinese Cultural Groups 1997
　Japanese Cultural Groups 1997
　Korean Cultural Groups 1997
　South Asian Cultural Groups 2004
　↓ Southeast Asian Cultural Groups 2004
　Vietnamese Cultural Groups 1997
R Minority Groups 1967

Aspartic Acid 1973
PN 489　　　　　SC 04010
B Amino Acids 1973
　Neurotransmitters 1985
N N-Methyl-D-Aspartate 1994

Aspergers Syndrome 1991
PN 514　　　　　SC 04015
SN Syndrome or disorder usually first diagnosed in childhood, characterized by severe and sustained impairment in social interactions and restricted, repetitive patterns of behaviors, interests, and activities.
UF Autistic Psychopathy
B Pervasive Developmental Disorders 2001
　Syndromes 1973
R ↓ Autism 1967
　Developmental Disabilities 1982
　Rett Syndrome 1994

Asphyxia
Use Anoxia

Aspiration Level 1973
PN 295　　　　　SC 04030
SN Level of expectations for future achievement.
R ↓ Aspirations 1967

Aspirations 1967
PN 804　　　　　SC 04040
SN Individual desires to achieve goals and ideals. Use a more specific term if possible.
UF Ambition
N Educational Aspirations 1973
　Occupational Aspirations 1973
R Aspiration Level 1973
　Goal Setting 1997
　↓ Goals 1967
　↓ Motivation 1967

Aspirin 1973
PN 145　　　　　SC 04050
UF Acetylsalicylic Acid
B Acids 1973
　Analgesic Drugs 1973
　Anti Inflammatory Drugs 1982

Assassination (Political)
Use Political Assassination

Assertiveness 1973
PN 1934　　　　　SC 04070

Assertiveness — (cont'd)
B Personality Traits 1967
R Assertiveness Training 1978
　Empowerment 1991
　Extraversion 1967
　↓ Resistance 1997

Assertiveness Training 1978
PN 970　　　　　SC 04072
SN Training in the social skills required to be able to refuse requests; to express both positive and negative feelings; to initiate, engage in, and terminate conversation; and to make personal requests without suffering from excessive stress.
B Human Potential Movement 1982
R Assertiveness 1973
　↓ Behavior Modification 1973
　Communication Skills Training 1982
　Human Relations Training 1978
　Social Skills Training 1982

Assessment
Use Measurement

Assessment (Cognitive)
Use Cognitive Assessment

Assessment (Psychological)
Use Psychological Assessment

Assessment Centers 1982
PN 315　　　　　SC 04082
SN Centers specializing in standardized, systematic behavioral evaluation process used to make selection, promotion, development, counseling, and career planning personnel decisions.
R Occupational Guidance 1967
　↓ Personnel Evaluation 1973
　Personnel Placement 1973
　Personnel Promotion 1978
　↓ Personnel Selection 1967

Assessment Criteria
Use Evaluation Criteria

Assimilation (Cultural)
Use Acculturation

Assistance (Social Behavior) 1973
PN 2183　　　　　SC 04100
SN Act of rendering aid or help. Limited to human populations.
UF Helping Behavior
B Interpersonal Interaction 1967
　Prosocial Behavior 1982
N Social Support 2004
R Altruism 1973
　Charitable Behavior 1973
　↓ Help Seeking Behavior 1978
　Volunteers 2003

Assistance Seeking (Professional)
Use Health Care Utilization

Assisted Living 2003
PN 56　　　　　SC 04104
SN Housing and living arrangements for individuals needing a minimal amount of care and supervision.

Assisted Living — (cont'd)
HN This term was introduced in June 2003. PsycINFO records from the past 10 years were re-indexed with this term. The posting note reflects the number of records that were re-indexed.
B Housing 1973
R Activities of Daily Living 1991
　Independent Living Programs 1991
　↓ Living Arrangements 1991
　↓ Residential Care Institutions 1973

Assisted Suicide 1997
PN 398　　　　　SC 04105
SN Provision of support and/or means that gives a patient the power to take his or her own life.
B Suicide 1967
R Advance Directives 1994
　Bioethics 2003
　↓ Death and Dying 1967
　Euthanasia 1973
　Life Sustaining Treatment 1997
　Palliative Care 1991
　Professional Ethics 1973
　Terminally Ill Patients 1973
　Treatment Refusal 1994
　Treatment Withholding 1988

Association (Free)
Use Free Association

Associationism 1973
PN 86　　　　　SC 04120
SN Theory which holds that learning and mental development consist mainly of combinations and recombinations of irreducible mental elements. Also, the basis for theories that explain learning in terms of stimulus and response.
B History of Psychology 1967
　Psychological Theories 2001

Associations (Contextual)
Use Contextual Associations

Associations (Groups)
Use Organizations

Associations (Word)
Use Word Associations

Associative Processes 1967
PN 3361　　　　　SC 04160
SN Development or maintenance of learned or cognitive connections (associations) between events, sensations, ideas, memories, or behavior as the result of functional relationships, similarity-contrast, or spatial-temporal contiguity.
B Cognitive Processes 1967
N Cognitive Contiguity 1973
　Connotations 1973
　Contextual Associations 1967
　Isolation Effect 1973
R Cognitive Generalization 1967
　Connectionism 1994
　Cues 1967
　Word Associations 1967
　Word Recognition 1988

Assortative Mating 1991
PN 109　　　　　SC 04165

Assortative Mating — (cont'd)

SN Nonrandom mating between unrelated individuals with similar characteristics. Used for human or animal populations.
- **UF** Assortive Mating
- **R** ↓ Animal Breeding 1973
   - Animal Mate Selection 1982
   - ↓ Animal Mating Behavior 1967
   - Family Resemblance 1991
   - ↓ Genetics 1967
   - Human Mate Selection 1988
   - Phenotypes 1973
   - Population Genetics 1973
   - ↓ Psychosexual Behavior 1967

Assortive Mating
Use Assortative Mating

Asthenia 1973
PN 55   **SC** 04170
SN Physical weakness, lack of strength and vitality, or a lack of concentration.
- **B** Symptoms 1967
- **N** Myasthenia 1973
- **R** Neurasthenic Neurosis 1973

Asthenic Personality
Use Personality Disorders

Asthma 1967
PN 1688   **SC** 04190
- **B** Dyspnea 1973
- **R** ↓ Immunologic Disorders 1973
   - ↓ Somatoform Disorders 2001

Astrology 1973
PN 115   **SC** 04200
- **R** ↓ Parapsychology 1967
   - Superstitions 1973

Astronauts 1973
PN 133   **SC** 04210
- **B** Aerospace Personnel 1973
- **R** Aircraft Pilots 1973
   - ↓ Military Personnel 1967
   - Spacecraft 1973

Asylums
Use Psychiatric Hospitals

At Risk Populations 1985
PN 15807   **SC** 04225
SN Groups or individuals considered in danger of developing a physical, mental, emotional, behavioral, or other disorder due to adverse internal or external factors.
- **UF** High Risk Populations
   - Risk Populations
- **R** Coronary Prone Behavior 1982
   - ↓ Intervention 2003
   - Predisposition 1973
   - Premorbidity 1978
   - Risk Assessment 2004
   - Risk Factors 2001
   - Susceptibility (Disorders) 1973

Ataractic Drugs
Use Tranquilizing Drugs

Ataraxic Drugs
Use Tranquilizing Drugs

Ataxia 1973
PN 442   **SC** 04250
SN Loss of coordination of voluntary muscular movement.
- **UF** Dysmetria
- **B** Movement Disorders 1985
   - Symptoms 1967
- **R** Hyperkinesis 1973

Atheism 1973
PN 43   **SC** 04260
- **B** Religious Beliefs 1973

Atherosclerosis 1973
PN 152   **SC** 04270
- **B** Arteriosclerosis 1973

Athetosis 1973
PN 27   **SC** 04280
SN Nonprogressive, developmentally-evolving disorder arising from basal ganglia damage in the full term brain characterized by postural reflex impairments, involuntary movements, and dysarthria with preservation of sensation, ocular movement, and frequently, intelligence.
- **B** Brain Disorders 1967
   - Movement Disorders 1985
- **R** Cerebral Palsy 1967

Athletes 1973
PN 3804   **SC** 04287
- **N** College Athletes 1994
- **R** Athletic Participation 1973
   - Athletic Performance 1991
   - Athletic Training 1991
   - ↓ Sports 1967
   - Sports (Attitudes Toward) 2004

Athletic Participation 1973
PN 1377   **SC** 04290
- **B** Participation 1973
   - Recreation 1967
- **R** ↓ Athletes 1973
   - College Athletes 1994
   - ↓ Extracurricular Activities 1973
   - ↓ Sports 1967

Athletic Performance 1991
PN 1386   **SC** 04300
- **UF** Sport Performance
- **B** Performance 1967
- **R** ↓ Athletes 1973
   - Athletic Training 1991
   - College Athletes 1994
   - ↓ Sports 1967
   - ↓ Teams 1988

Athletic Training 1991
PN 426   **SC** 04305
- **UF** Sport Training
   - Training (Athletic)
- **R** ↓ Athletes 1973
   - Athletic Performance 1991
   - Coaches 1988
   - College Athletes 1994
   - ↓ Education 1967
   - ↓ Extracurricular Activities 1973
   - ↓ Sports 1967
   - ↓ Teams 1988

Atmospheric Conditions 1973
PN 489   **SC** 04310
- **UF** Barometric Pressure
   - Climate (Meteorological)
   - Weather
- **B** Environmental Effects 1973
- **R** Pollution 1973
   - ↓ Temperature Effects 1967
   - Thermal Acclimatization 1973

Atomism
Use Reductionism

Atria (Heart)
Use Heart Auricles

Atrial Fibrillation
Use Fibrillation (Heart)

Atrophy (Cerebral)
Use Cerebral Atrophy

Atrophy (Muscular)
Use Muscular Atrophy

Atropine 1973
PN 514   **SC** 04350
- **UF** Hyoscyamine (dl-)
   - Methylatropine
- **B** Alkaloids 1973
   - Amines 1973
   - Analgesic Drugs 1973
   - Antispasmodic Drugs 1973
   - Cholinergic Blocking Drugs 1973
   - Narcotic Drugs 1973
   - Sedatives 1973

Attachment Behavior 1985
PN 6697   **SC** 04355
SN Formation of and investment in significant relationships. Usually refers to the emotional and biological attachment of human or animal infants to caretaking figures.
- **UF** Bonding (Emotional)
- **B** Behavior 1967
- **R** Abandonment 1997
   - Anaclitic Depression 1973
   - Attachment Disorders 2001
   - Dependency (Personality) 1967
   - Emotional Development 1973
   - Erotomania 1997
   - Intimacy 1973
   - Love 1973
   - Object Relations 1982
   - ↓ Parent Child Relations 1967
   - Postpartum Depression 1973
   - Postpartum Psychosis 2003
   - Separation Anxiety 1973
   - Separation Individuation 1982
   - ↓ Separation Reactions 1997
   - Stranger Reactions 1988

Attachment Disorders 2001
PN 77   **SC** 04357
- **UF** Reactive Attachment Disorder
- **R** Attachment Behavior 1985
   - ↓ Child Abuse 1971
   - Child Neglect 1988
   - Failure to Thrive 1988
   - ↓ Parent Child Relations 1967

Attachment Disorders — (cont'd)
- ↓ Relationship Termination   1997
-    Separation Anxiety   1973
- ↓ Separation Reactions   1997

Attack Behavior   1973
- **PN** 790   **SC** 04360
- **SN** Forceful, assaultive behavior. Used for human or animal populations.
- **B**   Aggressive Behavior   1967
-      Animal Aggressive Behavior   1973
- **R**   ↓ Animal Defensive Behavior   1982
-      Animal Predatory Behavior   1978
-      Instinctive Behavior   1982
-      Retaliation   1991

Attainment (Achievement)
- **Use** Achievement

Attainment Level (Education)
- **Use** Educational Attainment Level

Attempted Suicide   1973
- **PN** 4368   **SC** 04380
- **UF**   Parasuicide
-      Suicide (Attempted)
- **B**   Behavior Disorders   1971
-      Self Destructive Behavior   1985
- **R**   Suicidal Ideation   1991
-   ↓ Suicide   1967
-      Suicide Prevention   1973

Attendance (School)
- **Use** School Attendance

Attendants (Institutions)   1973
- **PN** 360   **SC** 04400
- **UF**   Hospital Attendants
-      Residential Care Attendants
- **B**   Paramedical Personnel   1973
- **R**   Prison Personnel   1973
-   ↓ Psychiatric Hospital Staff   1973

Attention   1967
- **PN** 13586   **SC** 04410
- **SN** Condition of perceptual or cognitive awareness of or focusing on some aspect of one's environment. Compare ATTENTION SPAN and VIGILANCE.
- **B**   Awareness   1967
- **N**   Divided Attention   1973
-   ↓ Monitoring   1973
-      Selective Attention   1973
-   ↓ Sustained Attention   1997
-      Vigilance   1967
-      Visual Attention   2004
- **R**   Apperception   1973
-      Attention Span   1970
-      Concentration   1982
-      Distraction   1978
-      Human Channel Capacity   1973
-      Listening (Interpersonal)   1997
-   ↓ Perception   1967
-      Rotary Pursuit   1967
-      Signal Detection (Perception)   1967
-      Time On Task   1988
-   ↓ Tracking   1967

Attention Deficit Disorder   1985
- **PN** 4505   **SC** 04412
- **SN** A disorder characterized by persistent developmentally inappropriate inattention and impulsivity.

Attention Deficit Disorder — (cont'd)
- **N**   Attention Deficit Disorder with Hyperactivity   2001
- **R**   Attention Span   1973
-      Distractibility   1973
-      Impulsiveness   1973
-   ↓ Mental Disorders   1967
-      Minimal Brain Disorders   1973
-      Oppositional Defiant Disorder   1997

Attention Deficit Disorder with Hyperactivity   2001
- **PN** 2042   **SC** 04414
- **SN** A behavior disorder in which the essential features are signs of developmentally inappropriate inattention, impulsivity, and hyperactivity.
- **HN** Use both ATTENTION DEFICIT DISORDER and HYPERKINESIS to access references prior to 2001.
- **UF**   ADHD
- **B**   Attention Deficit Disorder   1985
- **R**   Attention Span   1973
-      Distractibility   1973
-      Hyperkinesis   1973
-      Impulsiveness   1973
-   ↓ Mental Disorders   1967
-      Minimal Brain Disorders   1973
-      Oppositional Defiant Disorder   1997

Attention Span   1973
- **PN** 407   **SC** 04413
- **SN** Temporal duration of concentration or amount of material grasped during exposure to stimuli or information. Compare ATTENTION.
- **B**   Sustained Attention   1997
- **R**   ↓ Attention   1967
-   ↓ Attention Deficit Disorder   1985
-      Attention Deficit Disorder with Hyperactivity   2001
-      Conceptual Tempo   1985
-      Distraction   1978
-      Vigilance   1967

Attitude Change   1967
- **PN** 5346   **SC** 04430
- **SN** Significant alteration in individual or group attitudes or opinions.
- **UF**   Opinion Change
- **R**   ↓ Attitudes   1967
-      Brainwashing   1982

Attitude Formation   1973
- **PN** 810   **SC** 04440
- **SN** Process of developing an opinion or attitude, especially as influenced by psychological, emotional, social, and experiential factors.
- **R**   ↓ Attitudes   1967

Attitude Measurement   1973
- **PN** 947   **SC** 04460
- **SN** Projective, physiological, self-report, or other approaches to the assessment of attitudes.
- **B**   Measurement   1967
- **R**   ↓ Attitude Measures   1967
-   ↓ Attitudes   1967
-      Likert Scales   1994

Attitude Measures   1967
- **PN** 3169   **SC** 04470
- **SN** Instruments or devices used in the assessment of attitudes.

Attitude Measures — (cont'd)
- **HN** In 1997, this term replaced the discontinued terms ALLPORT VERNON LINDZEY STUDY VALUES, MINNESOTA TEACHER ATTITUDE INVENTORY, and OPINION ATTITUDE AND INTEREST SURVEY. In 2000, these terms were removed from all records containing them, and replaced with ATTITUDE MEASURES.
- **UF**   Allport Vernon Lindzey Study Values
-      Minnesota Teacher Attitude Inventory
-      Opinion Attitude and Interest Survey
-      Opinion Questionnaires
-      Opinion Surveys
- **B**   Measurement   1967
- **N**   Wilson Patterson Conservatism Scale   1973
- **R**   Attitude Measurement   1973
-   ↓ Attitudes   1967
-      Likert Scales   1994
-   ↓ Preference Measures   1973
-      Semantic Differential   1967

Attitude Similarity   1973
- **PN** 1043   **SC** 04480
- **R**   ↓ Attitudes   1967

Attitudes   1967
- **PN** 12365   **SC** 04500
- **SN** Conceptually broad term referring to a mental position or feeling toward certain ideas, facts, or persons. Use a more specific term if possible.
- **UF**   Beliefs (Nonreligious)
-      Opinions
- **N**   Adolescent Attitudes   1988
-      Adult Attitudes   1988
-   ↓ Aged (Attitudes Toward)   1978
-      Aging (Attitudes Toward)   1985
-      Child Attitudes   1988
-      Childrearing Attitudes   1973
-   ↓ Client Attitudes   1982
-      Community Attitudes   1973
-      Computer Attitudes   1988
-   ↓ Consumer Attitudes   1973
-      Counselor Attitudes   1973
-      Death Attitudes   1973
-   ↓ Disabled (Attitudes Toward)   1997
-   ↓ Drug Usage Attitudes   1970
-      Eating Attitudes   1994
-   ↓ Employee Attitudes   1967
-      Employer Attitudes   1973
-      Environmental Attitudes   1978
-      Family Planning Attitudes   1973
-      Health Attitudes   1985
-   ↓ Health Personnel Attitudes   1985
-      Homosexuality (Attitudes Toward)   1982
-      Job Applicant Attitudes   1973
-      Marriage Attitudes   1973
-      Obesity (Attitudes Toward)   1997
-      Occupational Attitudes   1973
-   ↓ Parental Attitudes   1973
-   ↓ Physical Illness (Attitudes Toward)   1985
-   ↓ Political Attitudes   1970
-      Psychologist Attitudes   1991
-      Public Opinion   1973
-   ↓ Racial and Ethnic Attitudes   1982
-   ↓ Sex Role Attitudes   1978
-      Sexual Attitudes   1973
-   ↓ Socioeconomic Class Attitudes   1973
-      Sports (Attitudes Toward)   2004
-      Stereotyped Attitudes   1967
-      Student Attitudes   1967
-   ↓ Teacher Attitudes   1967
-      Work (Attitudes Toward)   1973
- **R**   Attitude Change   1967
-      Attitude Formation   1973
-      Attitude Measurement   1973

Attitudes — (cont'd)

- ↓ Attitude Measures 1967
- Attitude Similarity 1973
- Attribution 1973
- ↓ Cognitions 1985
- Hedonism 1973
- Impression Formation 1978
- Irrational Beliefs 1982
- Labeling 1978
- Planned Behavior 1997
- ↓ Prejudice 1967
- ↓ Religious Beliefs 1973
- Stigma 1991
- Superstitions 1973
- World View 1988

Attorneys 1973

PN 885   SC 04510
- **UF** Lawyers
- **B** Legal Personnel 1985
- **R** ↓ Law Enforcement Personnel 1973
- Law Students 1978

Attraction (Interpersonal)

Use Interpersonal Attraction

Attribution 1973

PN 12734   SC 04525
SN Perception of causes of behavior or events or of dispositional properties of an individual or group.
- **B** Social Perception 1967
- **R** ↓ Attitudes 1967
- Blame 1994
- Causal Analysis 1994
- Impression Formation 1978
- Inference 1973
- Internal External Locus of Control 1967
- Learned Helplessness 1978
- Self Fulfilling Prophecies 1997

Attrition (Experimental)

Use Experimental Attrition

Atypical Paranoid Disorder

Use Paranoia (Psychosis)

Atypical Somatoform Disorder

Use Body Dysmorphic Disorder

Audiences 1967

PN 757   SC 04530
SN Groups of spectators or listeners.
- **N** Sports Spectators 1997
- **R** Observers 1973

Audiogenic Seizures 1978

PN 103   SC 04536
- **B** Convulsions 1967
- **R** ↓ Auditory Stimulation 1967

Audiology 1973

PN 203   SC 04540
SN Scientific study of hearing, including: anatomical and functional properties of the ear; hearing disorders and their assessment and treatment; and the rehabilitation of hearing-impaired persons. Consider also AUDIOMETRY and SPEECH AND HEARING MEASURES.
- **B** Paramedical Sciences 1973

Audiometers 1973

PN 19   SC 04550
- **B** Apparatus 1967

Audiometry 1967

PN 1082   SC 04560
SN Specific procedures or audiometric tests used to measure hearing acuity and range in the diagnosis and evaluation of hearing impairments. Consider also AUDIOLOGY and SPEECH AND HEARING MEASURES.
- **UF** Bekesy Audiometry
- **N** Bone Conduction Audiometry 1973
- **R** Auditory Acuity 1988
- ↓ Auditory Stimulation 1967
- ↓ Perceptual Measures 1973

Audiotapes 1973

PN 412   SC 04570
SN Tape recordings of sound used in both educational and noneducational settings.
- **B** Audiovisual Communications Media 1973

Audiovisual Aids (Educational)

Use Educational Audiovisual Aids

Audiovisual Communications Media 1973

PN 316   SC 04590
- **B** Communications Media 1973
- **N** Audiotapes 1973
- ↓ Educational Audiovisual Aids 1973
- Film Strips 1967
- ↓ Motion Pictures 1973
- Photographs 1967
- Radio 1973
- ↓ Television 1967
- Television Advertising 1973
- Videotapes 1973

Audiovisual Instruction 1973

PN 318   SC 04600
- **B** Teaching Methods 1967
- **N** Televised Instruction 1973
- Videotape Instruction 1973
- **R** ↓ Educational Audiovisual Aids 1973

Audition

Use Auditory Perception

Auditory Acuity 1988

PN 191   SC 04615
SN The ability or capacity of a listener to perceive fine detail.
HN Consider AUDITORY THRESHOLDS or AUDITORY DISCRIMINATION to access references prior to 1988.
- **UF** Hearing Acuity
- **B** Auditory Perception 1967
- Perceptual Discrimination 1973
- **R** ↓ Audiometry 1967
- Auditory Discrimination 1967
- Auditory Localization 1973
- Auditory Thresholds 1973

Auditory Cortex 1967

PN 845   SC 04620
- **UF** Cortex (Auditory)
- **B** Temporal Lobe 1973

Auditory Discrimination 1967

PN 3734   SC 04630

Auditory Discrimination — (cont'd)

SN Distinguishing between sounds of different intensity, frequency, pattern, complexity, or other characteristics.
- **B** Auditory Perception 1967
- Perceptual Discrimination 1973
- **R** Auditory Acuity 1988

Auditory Displays 1973

PN 96   SC 04640
SN Presentations of patterned auditory stimulation.
- **B** Auditory Stimulation 1967
- Displays 1967

Auditory Evoked Potentials 1973

PN 3728   SC 04650
- **B** Evoked Potentials 1967
- **R** ↓ Cortical Evoked Potentials 1973

Auditory Feedback 1973

PN 376   SC 04660
SN Return of information on specified behavioral functions or parameters by means of auditory stimulation. Such stimulation may serve to regulate or control subsequent behavior, cognition, perception, or performance. Also, the process of hearing one's own vocalizations, especially as pertains to regulating the parameters of one's speech.
- **B** Auditory Stimulation 1967
- Sensory Feedback 1973
- **N** Delayed Auditory Feedback 1973

Auditory Hallucinations 1973

PN 579   SC 04670
- **B** Hallucinations 1967

Auditory Localization 1973

PN 1014   SC 04680
SN Subjective determination of the specific spatial location of a sound source or relative locations of sound sources.
- **UF** Localization (Sound)
- Sound Localization
- **B** Auditory Perception 1967
- Perceptual Localization 1967
- **R** Auditory Acuity 1988

Auditory Masking 1973

PN 1155   SC 04690
SN Change in perceptual sensitivity to an auditory stimulus due to the presence of a second stimulus in close temporal proximity.
- **B** Masking 1967
- **R** ↓ Auditory Stimulation 1967

Auditory Nerve

Use Acoustic Nerve

Auditory Neurons 1973

PN 312   SC 04710
- **B** Sensory Neurons 1973

Auditory Perception 1967

PN 9019   SC 04720
SN Awareness, detection, or identification of sounds.
- **UF** Audition
- Listening
- **B** Perception 1967
- **N** Auditory Acuity 1988
- Auditory Discrimination 1967

Auditory Perception — (cont'd)

Auditory Localization 1973
↓ Loudness Perception 1973
Music Perception 1997
↓ Pitch Perception 1973
Speech Perception 1967
R   Acoustics 1997
Auditory Thresholds 1973
↓ Ear Disorders 1973
Listening (Interpersonal) 1997
Pattern Discrimination 1967
↓ Rhythm 1991

Auditory Stimulation 1967

PN 9456   SC 04730
UF Acoustic Stimuli
Noise (Sound)
Sound
B   Perceptual Stimulation 1973
N   Auditory Displays 1973
↓ Auditory Feedback 1973
Dichotic Stimulation 1982
Filtered Noise 1973
↓ Loudness 1967
↓ Pitch (Frequency) 1967
White Noise 1973
R   Acoustics 1997
Audiogenic Seizures 1978
↓ Audiometry 1967
Auditory Masking 1973
Bone Conduction Audiometry 1973
Silence 2003
↓ Speech Processing (Mechanical) 1973

Auditory Thresholds 1973

PN 1726   SC 04740
SN The minimal level of auditory stimulation, the minimal difference between any auditory stimuli, or the minimal stimulus change that is perceptually detectable.
B   Thresholds 1967
R   Auditory Acuity 1988
↓ Auditory Perception 1967
↓ Perceptual Measures 1973

Augmentative Communication 1994

PN 595   SC 04750
SN Communication that is supported by keyboards, typewriters, books, gestural systems, or other devices to enable individuals with communication or speech disorders to communicate effectively.
UF Facilitated Communication
B   Communication 1967
N ↓ Manual Communication 1978
R ↓ Apparatus 1967
↓ Communication Disorders 1982
↓ Medical Therapeutic Devices 1973
↓ Speech Disorders 1967
Speech Therapy 1967

Aura 1973

PN 102   SC 04760
SN Sensations experienced immediately prior to the onset of a seizure, migraine headache, or other nervous system disorder symptoms. Also, the patient's recognition of the beginning of an epileptic attack. Use PARAPSYCHOLOGY or PARAPSYCHOLOGICAL PHENOMENA to access references on psychic auras and halos.
B   Symptoms 1967
R ↓ Epilepsy 1967

Aurally Handicapped

Use Hearing Disorders

Auricles (Heart)

Use Heart Auricles

Auricular Fibrillation

Use Fibrillation (Heart)

Authoritarianism 1967

PN 2087   SC 04820
SN Complex of personality characteristics expressed as antidemocratic social attitudes, rigid attachment to traditional values, uncritical acceptance of authority, and intolerance of opposing views.
UF Domination
B   Personality Traits 1967
R   Dogmatism 1978
↓ Dominance 1967
Egalitarianism 1985
Openmindedness 1978

Authoritarianism (Parental)

Use Parenting Style

Authoritarianism Rebellion Scale

Use Nonprojective Personality Measures

Authority 1967

PN 987   SC 04845
SN Ability or vested power to influence thought, attitudes, and behavior.
R   Abuse of Power 1997
Coercion 1994
↓ Dominance 1967
↓ Leadership 1967
Omnipotence 1994
↓ Power 1967
↓ Social Influences 1967
↓ Status 1967

Authors

Use Writers

Autism 1967

PN 5587   SC 04850
B   Mental Disorders 1967
Pervasive Developmental Disorders 2001
N   Early Infantile Autism 1973
R   Antisocial Personality Disorder 1973
Aspergers Syndrome 1991
Autistic Children 1973
Autistic Thinking 1973
Developmental Disabilities 1982
Theory of Mind 2001

Autism Spectrum Disorders

Use Pervasive Developmental Disorders

Autistic Children 1973

PN 3084   SC 04860
B   Emotionally Disturbed 1973
R ↓ Autism 1967
Early Infantile Autism 1973

Autistic Psychopathy

Use Aspergers Syndrome

Autistic Thinking 1973

PN 33   SC 04870
B   Thinking 1967
Thought Disturbances 1973
R ↓ Autism 1967

Autobiographical Memory 1994

PN 788   SC 04875
SN Personal memories of past events that have occurred over the course of one's life. Compare REMINISCENCE and LIFE REVIEW.
B   Memory 1967
R   Anniversary Events 1994
Early Experience 1967
Early Memories 1985
↓ Life Experiences 1973
Life Review 1991
Reminiscence 1985

Autobiography 1973

PN 624   SC 04880
SN Recorded account of one's own life.
B   Biography 1967

Autoeroticism 1997

PN 15   SC 04890
HN Use MASTURBATION to access references from 1973-1996.
R   Eroticism 1973
Masturbation 1973
Narcissism 1967
↓ Psychosexual Behavior 1967

Autogenic Training 1973

PN 480   SC 04900
SN Physiological form of psychotherapy based on studies of sleep and hypnosis and the application of yoga principles.
B   Psychotherapeutic Techniques 1967
Psychotherapy 1967
R   Biofeedback Training 1978
↓ Relaxation Therapy 1978

Autohypnosis 1970

PN 266   SC 04910
SN Practice, process, or hypnotic state resulting from self-induced hypnosis.
UF Self Hypnosis
B   Hypnosis 1967
R   Catalepsy 1973

Autoimmune Disorders

Use Immunologic Disorders

Autokinetic Illusion 1967

PN 251   SC 04930
SN Apparent movement of a fixated light in a dark field.
UF Illusion (Autokinetic)
B   Apparent Movement 1967
Visual Perception 1967

Automated Information Coding 1973

PN 84   SC 04940
B   Automated Information Processing 1973
R ↓ Computers 1967

Automated Information Processing 1973

PN 744   SC 04950
UF Information Processing (Automated)
N   Automated Information Coding 1973

Automated Information Processing —
(cont'd)
  ↓ Automated Information Retrieval 1973
  Automated Information Storage 1973
R ↓ Communication Systems 1973
  ↓ Computers 1967
  ↓ Data Processing 1967
  ↓ Electronic Communication 2001
  ↓ Expert Systems 1991
  Information 1967
  ↓ Information Systems 1991
  Internet 2001

Automated Information Retrieval 1973
PN 370   SC 04960
UF Information Retrieval (Automated)
B   Automated Information Processing 1973
N   Computer Searching 1991
R   Automated Information Storage 1973
  ↓ Computers 1967
  Databases 1991
  Information Services 1988
  ↓ Information Systems 1991

Automated Information Storage 1973
PN 100   SC 04970
B   Automated Information Processing 1973
R ↓ Automated Information Retrieval 1973
  ↓ Computers 1967
  Databases 1991
  ↓ Information Systems 1991

Automated Speech Recognition 1994
PN 248   SC 04975
SN Machine or other apparatus used in the auto-
matic recognition and understanding of human
speech.
UF Automatic Speaker Recognition
B   Speech Processing (Mechanical) 1973
R ↓ Artificial Intelligence 1982
  ↓ Computer Applications 1973
  ↓ Expert Systems 1991
  Speech Perception 1967

Automatic Speaker Recognition
  Use Automated Speech Recognition

Automation 1967
PN 577   SC 04980
SN Use of mechanical and/or electronic devices to
automatically control the operation of an apparatus,
system, or process.
R ↓ Artificial Intelligence 1982
  ↓ Computers 1967

Automatism 1973
PN 238   SC 04990
SN An act or movement performed without con-
scious control.
B   Symptoms 1967

Automobile Accidents
  Use Motor Traffic Accidents

Automobile Safety
  Use Highway Safety

Automobiles 1973
PN 378   SC 05020

Automobiles — (cont'd)
B   Motor Vehicles 1982
R   Drivers 1973

Autonomic Ganglia 1973
PN 25   SC 05050
UF Celiac Plexus
  Hypogastric Plexus
  Myenteric Plexus
  Postganglionic Autonomic Fibers
  Preganglionic Autonomic Fibers
  Stellate Ganglion
  Submucous Plexus
B   Autonomic Nervous System 1967
  Ganglia 1973
R ↓ Peripheral Nervous System 1973

Autonomic Nervous System 1967
PN 1401   SC 05060
B   Peripheral Nervous System 1973
N   Adrenergic Nerves 1973
  Autonomic Ganglia 1973
  Cholinergic Nerves 1973
  ↓ Parasympathetic Nervous System 1973
  ↓ Sympathetic Nervous System 1973
R   Autonomic Nervous System Disorders 1973

Autonomic Nervous System
Disorders 1973
PN 77   SC 05070
B   Nervous System Disorders 1967
R ↓ Autonomic Nervous System 1967

Autonomy (Government) 1973
PN 50   SC 05080
R   Government 1967

Autonomy (Personality)
  Use Independence (Personality)

Autopsy 1973
PN 160   SC 05090
R ↓ Diagnosis 1967
  ↓ Medical Diagnosis 1973
  Psychological Autopsy 1988

Autoregulation
  Use Homeostasis

Autoshaping 1978
PN 399   SC 05106
SN Learned behavior or the experimental paradigm
involving a Pavlovian pairing of a reinforcer and a
stimulus independent of the subject's behavior until
the subject makes a response to the stimulus. At that
point the reinforcer is made contingent on the
acquired response to the stimulus, thereby bringing
the response under operant control.
B   Conditioning 1967
R   Noncontingent Reinforcement 1988
  ↓ Reinforcement 1967

Autosome Disorders 1973
PN 136   SC 05110
B   Chromosome Disorders 1973
N   Crying Cat Syndrome 1973
  Downs Syndrome 1967
  Trisomy 21 1973
R   Autosomes 1973

Autosomes 1973
PN 47   SC 05120
B   Chromosomes 1973
R ↓ Autosome Disorders 1973

Autotomy
  Use Self Mutilation

Aversion 1967
PN 785   SC 05130
UF Antipathy
  Dislike
B   Emotional States 1973
N   Hate 1973
R   Disgust 1994

Aversion Conditioning 1982
PN 2192   SC 05135
SN Conditioning paradigm in which aversive effects
are paired with external stimuli resulting in an aver-
sion to the stimuli. Also, the learned aversion itself.
UF Odor Aversion Conditioning
  Taste Aversion Conditioning
B   Conditioning 1967
N   Covert Sensitization 1988
R   Aversive Stimulation 1973

Aversion Therapy 1973
PN 507   SC 05140
SN Form of behavior therapy designed to eliminate
undesirable behavior patterns through learned asso-
ciations with unpleasant or painful stimuli. Also
known as aversive conditioning therapy.
B   Behavior Therapy 1967
N   Covert Sensitization 1988
R   Counterconditioning 1973
  ↓ Shock Therapy 1973

Aversive Stimulation 1973
PN 1773   SC 05150
SN Presentation of a noxious stimulus. Also, any
noxious stimuli (i.e., stimuli that an organism
attempts to avoid or escape from). Compare PUN-
ISHMENT.
B   Stimulation 1967
R ↓ Aversion Conditioning 1982
  Covert Sensitization 1988

Aviation 1967
PN 750   SC 05160
N   Flight Instrumentation 1973
  Spaceflight 1967
R   Acceleration Effects 1973
  Altitude Effects 1973
  ↓ Aviation Safety 1973
  ↓ Gravitational Effects 1967

Aviation Personnel
  Use Aerospace Personnel

Aviation Safety 1973
PN 227   SC 05170
B   Safety 1967
N   Air Traffic Control 1973
R   Air Traffic Accidents 1973
  Aircraft Pilots 1973
  ↓ Aviation 1967
  ↓ Transportation Accidents 1973

Aviators
  Use Aircraft Pilots

Avoidance 1967
PN 2940   SC 05190
  UF   Escape
  R   Avoidance Conditioning 1967
      Neophobia 1985
      ↓ Resistance 1997

Avoidance Conditioning 1967
PN 6967   SC 05200
SN Learned behavior or the operant conditioning procedure in which the subject learns a behavior that prevents the occurrence of an aversive stimulus. Compare ESCAPE CONDITIONING.
  UF   Active Avoidance
      Conditioning (Avoidance)
      Passive Avoidance
  B   Operant Conditioning 1967
  R   Avoidance 1967

Avoidant Personality Disorder 1994
PN 116   SC 05205
SN Personality disorder characterized by excessive social discomfort, extreme sensitivity to negative perceptions of oneself, pervasive preoccupation with being criticized or rejected in social situations, and low self esteem.
  B   Personality Disorders 1967
  R   Social Anxiety 1985
      Social Phobia 1985

Awareness 1967
PN 3463   SC 05210
SN Conscious realization, perception, or knowledge.
  B   Consciousness States 1971
  N   ↓ Attention 1967
      Body Awareness 1982
      Phonological Awareness 2004
  R   Metacognition 1991
      Sensory Gating 1991

Axons 1973
PN 284   SC 05220
  B   Neurons 1973

Azidothymidine
  Use Zidovudine

AZT
  Use Zidovudine

Babbling
  Use Infant Vocalization

Babinski Reflex 1973
PN 3   SC 05250
  B   Reflexes 1971

Baboons 1973
PN 697   SC 05260
  B   Primates (Nonhuman) 1973

Babysitting
  Use Child Care

Back (Anatomy) 1973
PN 164   SC 05270
  B   Anatomy 1967

Back Pain 1982
PN 1238   SC 05275
  B   Pain 1967
  R   Chronic Pain 1985
      ↓ Physical Disorders 1997

Background (Family)
  Use Family Background

Backward Masking
  Use Masking

Baclofen 1991
PN 167   SC 05293
  B   Muscle Relaxing Drugs 1973

Bacteria
  Use Microorganisms

Bacterial Disorders 1973
PN 102   SC 05300
  B   Infectious Disorders 1973
  N   Bacterial Meningitis 1973
      Gonorrhea 1973
      Pulmonary Tuberculosis 1973
      ↓ Tuberculosis 1973
  R   Pneumonia 1973
      Rheumatic Fever 1973

Bacterial Meningitis 1973
PN 18   SC 05310
  B   Bacterial Disorders 1973
      Meningitis 1973

Balance (Motor Processes)
  Use Equilibrium

Baldness
  Use Alopecia

Ballet
  Use Dance

Bannister Repertory Grid 1970
PN 37   SC 05360
  B   Nonprojective Personality Measures 1973

Baptists
  Use Protestants

Barbital 1973
PN 61   SC 05380
  B   Barbiturates 1967
      CNS Depressant Drugs 1973
      Hypnotic Drugs 1973
      Sedatives 1973

Barbiturate Poisoning 1973
PN 5   SC 05390
  B   Toxic Disorders 1973
  R   ↓ Analeptic Drugs 1973
      ↓ Barbiturates 1967

Barbiturates 1967
PN 264   SC 05400
  B   Drugs 1967
  N   Amobarbital 1973

Barbiturates — (cont'd)
      Barbital 1973
      Hexobarbital 1973
      Methohexital 1973
      Pentobarbital 1973
      Phenobarbital 1973
      Secobarbital 1973
      Thiopental 1973
  R   ↓ Anesthetic Drugs 1973
      ↓ Anticonvulsive Drugs 1973
      Barbiturate Poisoning 1973
      ↓ CNS Depressant Drugs 1973
      ↓ Hypnotic Drugs 1973
      Primidone 1973
      ↓ Sedatives 1973

Bargaining 1973
PN 700   SC 05410
  B   Negotiation 1973

Barium 1973
PN 9   SC 05420
  B   Metallic Elements 1973

Barometric Pressure
  Use Atmospheric Conditions

Baroreceptors 1973
PN 101   SC 05440
  UF   Pressoreceptors
  B   Neural Receptors 1973
      Sensory Neurons 1973
      Sympathetic Nervous System 1973

Basal Ganglia 1973
PN 2844   SC 05470
  UF   Corpus Striatum
      Ventral Striatum
  B   Ganglia 1973
      Telencephalon 1973
  N   Amygdala 2003
      Caudate Nucleus 1973
      Globus Pallidus 1973
      Putamen 1985
      ↓ Striatum 2003
  R   Extrapyramidal Symptoms 1994
      Nucleus Basalis Magnocellularis 1994
      Progressive Supranuclear Palsy 1997
      Substantia Nigra 1994

Basal Metabolism 1973
PN 45   SC 05480
SN The amount of heat produced by the body to maintain life processes at the lowest level of cell activity in the waking state.
  B   Metabolism 1967

Basal Readers
  Use Reading Materials

Basal Skin Resistance 1973
PN 14   SC 05500
SN Baseline or minimum electrical current generated or conducted by the body as measured on the skin surface during a resting state.
  B   Skin Resistance 1973

Baseball 1973
PN 274   SC 05510
  B   Recreation 1967
      Sports 1967

Basic Skills Testing
   Use   Minimum Competency Tests

Basketball   1973
PN 517   SC 05520
   B   Recreation 1967
            Sports 1967

Bass (Fish)   1973
PN 27   SC 05530
   B   Fishes 1967

Bats   1973
PN 377   SC 05550
   UF   Chiroptera
   B   Mammals 1973

Battered Child Syndrome   1973
PN 37   SC 05560
SN   Behavioral pattern, including inability to relate to
others and feelings of rejection, characteristic of
infants and children who have been abused.
   B   Child Abuse 1971
            Syndromes 1973
   R   Physical Abuse 1991

Battered Females   1988
PN 1730   SC 05561
HN   Use FAMILY VIOLENCE to access references
from 1985-1987.
   B   Human Females 1973
   R   ↓ Abuse Reporting 1997
            Family Violence 1982
            Partner Abuse 1991
            Physical Abuse 1991
            Shelters 1991

Bayes Theorem
   Use   Statistical Probability

Bayley Scales of Infant Development   1994
PN 53   SC 05575
   B   Developmental Measures 1994
   R   ↓ Intelligence Measures 1967

Beavers   1973
PN 17   SC 05580
   B   Rodents 1973

Beck Depression Inventory   1988
PN 392   SC 05588
   B   Nonprojective Personality Measures 1973

Bedwetting
   Use   Urinary Incontinence

Beer   1973
PN 146   SC 05590
   B   Alcoholic Beverages 1973

Bees   1973
PN 837   SC 05600
   B   Insects 1967
   R   Larvae 1973

Beetles   1973
PN 246   SC 05610
   B   Insects 1967
   R   Larvae 1973

Behavior   1967
PN 9679   SC 05670
SN   Conceptually broad term referring to any or all
aspects of human or animal behavior. Use a more
specific term if possible.
   N   Adaptive Behavior 1991
          ↓ Adjunctive Behavior 1982
          ↓ Animal Ethology 1967
          ↓ Antisocial Behavior 1971
            Attachment Behavior 1985
            Childhood Play Behavior 1978
            Choice Behavior 1967
            Classroom Behavior 1973
          ↓ Consumer Behavior 1967
            Conservation (Ecological Behavior) 1978
            Coping Behavior 1967
            Coronary Prone Behavior 1982
          ↓ Drinking Behavior 1978
          ↓ Driving Behavior 1967
          ↓ Eating Behavior 2004
          ↓ Exploratory Behavior 1967
          ↓ Health Behavior 1982
          ↓ Hoarding Behavior 2003
            Illness Behavior 1982
            Instinctive Behavior 1982
          ↓ Psychosexual Behavior 1967
            Self Defeating Behavior 1988
          ↓ Self Destructive Behavior 1985
          ↓ Social Behavior 1967
            Stereotyped Behavior 1973
            Voting Behavior 1973
            Wandering Behavior 1991
   R   ↓ Behavior Analysis 2001
            Behavior Change 1973
          ↓ Behavior Disorders 1971
          ↓ Behavior Modification 1973
          ↓ Behavior Problems 1967
          ↓ Behavior Therapy 1967
          ↓ Behavioral Assessment 1982
            Behavioral Contrast 1978
          ↓ Behavioral Sciences 1997
            Behaviorism 1967
            Human Nature 1997
            Planned Behavior 1997

Behavior Analysis   2001
PN 342   SC 05613
SN   Field of psychology emphasizing the experimen-
tal, conceptual, and applied analysis of behavior in
humans and animals.
   B   Analysis 1967
   N   ↓ Behavioral Assessment 1982
   R   ↓ Behavior 1967

Behavior Change   1973
PN 4669   SC 05620
SN   Detectable changes in behavior due to psycho-
therapeutic, behavioral, or other intervention, or
spontaneous occurrence.
   R   ↓ Behavior 1967
          ↓ Behavior Modification 1973
            Lifestyle Changes 1997
            Personality Change 1967

Behavior Contracting   1978
PN 287   SC 05624
SN   Therapeutic technique involving a formal written
contract, usually between two parties, which explicitly
states the relationship between a particular behavior
and its consequences (sanctions). Viewed as a structural means of scheduling reinforcement between the
two parties, it is used as a method of controlling con-
tingencies of reinforcement.
   R   ↓ Behavior Modification 1973

Behavior Contracting   — (cont'd)
          ↓ Behavior Therapy 1967

Behavior Disorders   1971
PN 5258   SC 05630
SN   Disorders characterized by persistent and repet-
itive patterns of behavior that violate societal norms
or rules or that seriously impair a person's function-
ing. Compare BEHAVIOR PROBLEMS.
   B   Disorders 1967
   N   ↓ Addiction 1973
            Attempted Suicide 1973
          ↓ Drug Abuse 1973
          ↓ Homicide 1967
          ↓ Juvenile Delinquency 1967
            Self Mutilation 1973
   R   Acting Out 1967
          ↓ Aggressive Behavior 1967
          ↓ Antisocial Behavior 1971
          ↓ Behavior 1967
          ↓ Behavior Problems 1967
            Body Rocking 1973
            Conduct Disorder 1991
          ↓ Crime 1967
          ↓ Criminal Behavior 2003
            Faking 1973
            Fecal Incontinence 1973
          ↓ Mental Disorders 1967
            Oppositional Defiant Disorder 1997
            Pathological Gambling 1988
          ↓ Self Destructive Behavior 1985
          ↓ Symptoms 1967
            Thumbsucking 1973
            Trichotillomania 2003
            Urinary Incontinence 1973

Behavior Modification   1973
PN 8270   SC 05640
SN   Use of classical conditioning or operant (instru-
mental) learning techniques to modify behavior.
   B   Treatment 1967
   N   ↓ Behavior Therapy 1967
            Biofeedback Training 1978
            Classroom Behavior Modification 1973
          ↓ Contingency Management 1973
            Fading (Conditioning) 1982
            Omission Training 1985
            Overcorrection 1985
          ↓ Self Management 1985
            Time Out 1985
   R   Anger Control 1997
            Anxiety Management 1997
            Assertiveness Training 1978
          ↓ Behavior 1967
            Behavior Change 1973
            Behavior Contracting 1978
          ↓ Behavioral Assessment 1982
            Cognitive Behavior Therapy 2003
            Cognitive Restructuring 1985
            Cognitive Therapy 1982
            Communication Skills Training 1982
            Constant Time Delay 1997
            Counterconditioning 1973
            Functional Analysis 2001
          ↓ Operant Conditioning 1967
          ↓ Prompting 1997
          ↓ Relaxation Therapy 1978
          ↓ Self Help Techniques 1982
            Self Monitoring 1982
            Social Skills Training 1982
            Stress Management 1985

Behavior Problems   1967
PN 12605   SC 05650

Behavior Problems — (cont'd)
SN Disruptive or improper behaviors that generally fall within societal norms and do not seriously impair a person's functioning. Compare BEHAVIOR DISORDERS.
UF Disruptive Behavior
  Misbehavior
  Misconduct
N Tantrums 1973
R ↓ Behavior 1967
  ↓ Behavior Disorders 1971
  Conduct Disorder 1991
  Functional Analysis 2001
  Rebelliousness 2003

Behavior Therapy 1967
PN 9338   **SC** 05660
SN Therapeutic approach that may employ classical conditioning, operant learning techniques, or other behavioral techniques, in an attempt to eliminate or modify problem behavior, addressing itself primarily to the client's overt behavior, as opposed to thoughts, feelings, or other cognitive processes.
B Behavior Modification 1973
  Psychotherapy 1967
N ↓ Aversion Therapy 1973
  ↓ Exposure Therapy 1997
  Implosive Therapy 1973
  Reciprocal Inhibition Therapy 1973
  Response Cost 1997
  Systematic Desensitization Therapy 1973
R Anger Control 1997
  Anxiety Management 1997
  ↓ Behavior 1967
  Behavior Contracting 1978
  Cognitive Behavior Therapy 2003
  Counterconditioning 1973
  Eye Movement Desensitization Therapy 1997
  Paradoxical Techniques 1982

Behavioral Assessment 1982
PN 4423   **SC** 05671
SN Identification and measurement of response units and their controlling environmental and organismic variables for the purposes of understanding and altering human behavior.
B Behavior Analysis 2001
  Psychological Assessment 1967
N Functional Analysis 2001
R ↓ Behavior 1967
  ↓ Behavior Modification 1973
  ↓ Empirical Methods 1973

Behavioral Contrast 1978
PN 286   **SC** 05674
SN Change in response rate or latency following a change in reinforcement of one component of multiple operant discrimination schedules of reinforcement.
R ↓ Behavior 1967
  ↓ Reinforcement 1967
  Response Frequency 1973
  Response Latency 1967
  Stimulus Discrimination 1973

Behavioral Ecology 1997
PN 360   **SC** 57450
SN Study, usually based on naturalistic observations, of the interaction between the environment and the behavior of organisms within that environment.
R ↓ Ecological Factors 1973
  Ecological Psychology 1994

Behavioral Ecology — (cont'd)
  Ecology 1973
  Environmental Psychology 1982
  Research Setting 2001

Behavioral Economics 2003
PN 55   **SC** 58057
SN The application of economic principles to human behavior.
HN This term was introduced in June 2003. PsycINFO records from the past 10 years were re-indexed with this term. The posting note reflects the number of records that were re-indexed.
B Economics 1985
R ↓ Consumer Behavior 1967

Behavioral Genetics 1994
PN 938   **SC** 57405
SN Scientific discipline concerned with the role of genes and gene action in the expression of behavior. Includes analysis of whole populations for specific traits, e.g., intelligence. Used for the scientific discipline or the behavioral genetic processes themselves.
B Genetics 1967
R Biopsychosocial Approach 1991
  ↓ Genetic Disorders 1973
  Genetic Dominance 1973
  Genetic Recessiveness 1973
  Nature Nurture 1994
  Population Genetics 1973
  Psychobiology 1982
  Sociobiology 1982

Behavioral Health
  Use Health Care Psychology

Behavioral Medicine
  Use Health Care Psychology

Behavioral Sciences 1997
PN 245   **SC** 05680
SN Group of scientific disciplines dealing with human and animal action and behavior.
HN Use SOCIAL SCIENCES to access references from 1973-1996.
B Social Sciences 1967
N ↓ Psychology 1967
R ↓ Behavior 1967
  ↓ Sociology 1967

Behaviorism 1967
PN 1898   **SC** 05690
B History of Psychology 1967
  Psychological Theories 2001
R ↓ Behavior 1967
  Positivism (Philosophy) 1967
  Skinner (Burrhus Frederic) 1991
  Watson (John Broadus) 1991

Bekesy Audiometry
  Use Audiometry

Beliefs (Nonreligious)
  Use Attitudes

Beliefs (Religion)
  Use Religious Beliefs

Bem Sex Role Inventory 1988
PN 72   **SC** 05727
B Nonprojective Personality Measures 1973

Bemegride 1973
PN 20   **SC** 05730
B Analeptic Drugs 1973

Benactyzine 1973
PN 26   **SC** 05740
B Cholinergic Blocking Drugs 1973
  Tranquilizing Drugs 1967

Benadryl
  Use Diphenhydramine

Bender Gestalt Test 1967
PN 401   **SC** 05770
B Projective Personality Measures 1973
R ↓ Neuropsychological Assessment 1982

Benign Neoplasms 1973
PN 36   **SC** 05800
B Neoplasms 1967

Benton Revised Visual Retention Test 1973
PN 40   **SC** 05810
B Intelligence Measures 1967
R ↓ Neuropsychological Assessment 1982

Benzedrine
  Use Amphetamine

Benzodiazepine Agonists 1994
PN 175   **SC** 05821
R ↓ Benzodiazepines 1978

Benzodiazepine Antagonists 1985
PN 432   **SC** 05822
R ↓ Benzodiazepines 1978

Benzodiazepines 1978
PN 3057   **SC** 05824
B Drugs 1967
N Alprazolam 1988
  Chlordiazepoxide 1973
  Clonazepam 1991
  Diazepam 1973
  Flunitrazepam 2004
  Flurazepam 1982
  Lorazepam 1988
  Midazolam 1991
  Nitrazepam 1978
  Oxazepam 1978
R ↓ Anticonvulsive Drugs 1973
  Benzodiazepine Agonists 1994
  Benzodiazepine Antagonists 1985
  ↓ Hypnotic Drugs 1973
  ↓ Minor Tranquilizers 1973
  ↓ Muscle Relaxing Drugs 1973
  ↓ Sedatives 1973
  ↓ Tranquilizing Drugs 1967

Bereavement
  Use Grief

Beta Blockers
  Use Adrenergic Blocking Drugs

33

Between Groups Design [1985]
PN 75   SC 05828
SN Experimental design in which the subjects serve in only one treatment condition. Includes designs of matched or correlated groups and randomized groups.
  B   Experimental Design [1967]

Beverages (Alcoholic)
Use Alcoholic Beverages

Beverages (Nonalcoholic) [1978]
PN 226   SC 05833
  UF Coffee
       Tea
  R ↓ Alcoholic Beverages [1973]
     ↓ Drinking Behavior [1978]
      Nutrition [1973]

Bias (Experimenter)
Use Experimenter Bias

Bias (Response)
Use Response Bias

Bias Crimes
Use Hate Crimes

Biased Sampling [1973]
PN 226   SC 05860
SN Inadequate selection of subject samples resulting in an inaccurate representation of the larger population.
  B   Sampling (Experimental) [1973]

Bible [1973]
PN 446   SC 05870
  B   Religious Literature [1973]
  R ↓ Christianity [1973]
      Judaism [1967]
     ↓ Religious Beliefs [1973]

Bibliotherapy [1973]
PN 388   SC 05890
SN Use of reading as adjunct to psychotherapy.
  B   Treatment [1967]
  R   Poetry Therapy [1994]

Bicuculline [1994]
PN 144   SC 05895
HN Use GAMMA AMINOBUTYRIC ACID ANTAGONISTS to access references from 1985-1993.
  B   Analeptic Drugs [1973]
      Gamma Aminobutyric Acid Antagonists [1985]

Big Five Personality Model
Use Five Factor Personality Model

Bile [1973]
PN 19   SC 05900
  B   Body Fluids [1973]
  R   Taurine [1982]

Bilingual Education [1978]
PN 651   SC 05907
SN Education in one's native language as well as the majority language of the country in which one is educated or education in two languages.
  B   Education [1967]

Bilingual Education — (cont'd)
  R   Bilingualism [1973]
      English as Second Language [1997]
      Foreign Language Learning [1967]
      Foreign Languages [1973]
      Multicultural Education [1988]
     ↓ Multilingualism [1973]
     ↓ Teaching [1967]

Bilingualism [1973]
PN 2801   SC 05910
  B   Multilingualism [1973]
  R   Bilingual Education [1978]
      Code Switching [1988]
      Cross Cultural Communication [1997]
      English as Second Language [1997]
     ↓ Language [1967]
      Language Proficiency [1988]
      Native Language [2004]

Binge Eating [1991]
PN 930   SC 05915
SN Eating excessive quantities of food, often after stressful events. Compare BULIMIA.
  B   Eating Behavior [2004]
  R   Bulimia [1985]
     ↓ Eating Disorders [1997]
      Purging (Eating Disorders) [2003]
     ↓ Symptoms [1967]

Binocular Vision [1967]
PN 1597   SC 05920
  B   Visual Perception [1967]

Binomial Distribution [1973]
PN 66   SC 05930
  B   Statistical Probability [1967]
  R ↓ Statistical Sample Parameters [1973]

Bioavailability [1991]
PN 175   SC 05935
SN The degree and rate at which a drug enters the bloodstream and is circulated to specific organs or tissues, as measured by drug concentrations in body fluids or by pharmacologic or therapeutic response.
  UF Bioequivalence
  R   Absorption (Physiological) [1973]
     ↓ Biochemistry [1967]
     ↓ Drug Dosages [1973]
     ↓ Drug Therapy [1967]
     ↓ Drugs [1967]
     ↓ Metabolism [1967]
     ↓ Pharmacology [1973]

Biochemical Markers
Use Biological Markers

Biochemistry [1967]
PN 3972   SC 05940
SN Study of the biological and physiological chemistry of living organisms. Used for the scientific discipline or the biochemical processes themselves.
  B   Chemistry [1967]
  N ↓ Neurochemistry [1973]
  R   Bioavailability [1991]
      Biological Markers [1991]
     ↓ Physiology [1967]

Biodata
Use Biographical Data

Bioequivalence
Use Bioavailability

Bioethics [2003]
PN 65   SC 05944
SN Discipline concerned with the ethical and social implications of biological research and medicine.
HN This term was introduced in June 2003. PsycINFO records from the past 10 years were re-indexed with this term. The posting note reflects the number of records that were re-indexed.
  UF Medical Ethics
  B   Ethics [1967]
  R   Assisted Suicide [1997]
     ↓ Client Rights [1988]
      Euthanasia [1973]
      Experimental Ethics [1978]
     ↓ Genetic Engineering [1994]
     ↓ Health Care Delivery [1978]
     ↓ Medical Sciences [1967]
      Professional Ethics [1973]

Biofeedback [1973]
PN 1466   SC 05945
SN Provision of immediate ongoing information regarding one's own physiological processes.
  B   Feedback [1967]
  N   Biofeedback Training [1978]
  R ↓ Conditioning [1967]
     ↓ Reinforcement [1967]
     ↓ Stimulation [1967]

Biofeedback Training [1978]
PN 2346   SC 05946
SN Self-directed process by which a person uses biofeedback information to gain voluntary control over processes or functions which are primarily under autonomic control. Used in experimental or treatment settings with human subjects.
  B   Behavior Modification [1973]
      Biofeedback [1973]
  R ↓ Alternative Medicine [1997]
      Autogenic Training [1973]

Biographical Data [1978]
PN 961   SC 05948
SN Information identifying an individual's background, life history, or present status.
  UF Biodata
  R   Biographical Inventories [1973]
      Demographic Characteristics [1967]
     ↓ Educational Background [1967]
     ↓ Family Background [1973]
     ↓ Life Experiences [1973]
      Patient History [1973]

Biographical Inventories [1973]
PN 117   SC 05950
SN Sets of items listing information on an individual's background. Not used as a document type identifier.
  B   Inventories [1967]
  R   Biographical Data [1978]

Biography [1967]
PN 747   SC 05960
SN Recorded account of a person's life.
HN From 1967-2000, the term was also used as a document type identifier; however, this usage has been discontinued due to the advent of Form/Content Type field identifiers. References from 1967-2000 can be accessed using either BIOGRAPHY or the Biography Form/Content Type field identifier.

Biography — (cont'd)
B Prose 1973
N Autobiography 1973
R Narratives 1997
 Psychohistory 1978

Biological Clocks (Animal)
Use Animal Biological Rhythms

Biological Family 1988
PN 501 SC 05975
SN The genetic family members of a person in contrast to adoptive or foster families.
UF Birth Parents
 Natural Family
B Family 1967
 Family Members 1973
R Family of Origin 1991

Biological Markers 1991
PN 1805 SC 05977
UF Biochemical Markers
 Clinical Markers
R ↓ Biochemistry 1967
 Interleukins 1994
 ↓ Medical Diagnosis 1973
 Physiological Correlates 1967
 Predisposition 1973
 Prognosis 1973
 ↓ Screening 1982
 Susceptibility (Disorders) 1973

Biological Psychiatry 1994
PN 147 SC 05978
SN A branch of psychiatry focusing on biological, physical, and neurological factors in the etiology and treatment of mental and behavioral disorders.
B Psychiatry 1967
R Neurobiology 1973
 Neuropsychiatry 1973
 Psychobiology 1982

Biological Rhythms 1967
PN 528 SC 05980
SN Rhythmic and periodic variations in physiological and psychological functions. Used for human or animal populations.
N ↓ Animal Biological Rhythms 1973
 Human Biological Rhythms 1973
 Sleep Wake Cycle 1985
R Lunar Synodic Cycle 1973
 Seasonal Variations 1973

Biological Symbiosis 1973
PN 532 SC 06000
SN Intimate relationship between organisms of two or more kinds, particularly one in which the symbiont benefits from the host. Includes parasitic behavior. Limited to animal populations.
UF Parasitism
 Symbiosis (Biological)
R ↓ Animals 1967
 ↓ Biology 1967
 Interspecies Interaction 1991

Biology 1967
PN 2707 SC 06010
SN Branch of science dealing with living organisms. Used for the scientific discipline or the biological processes themselves.
B Sciences 1967
N Botany 1973

Biology — (cont'd)
 Neurobiology 1973
 Sociobiology 1982
 Zoology 1973
R Biological Symbiosis 1973
 Biosynthesis 1973
 Phylogenesis 1973
 Psychobiology 1982

Biopsy 1973
PN 58 SC 06020
B Medical Diagnosis 1973
R ↓ Surgery 1971

Biopsychosocial Approach 1991
PN 1212 SC 06024
SN A systematic integration of biological, psychological, and social approaches to the study, treatment, and understanding of mental health and mental disorders.
UF Biopsychosocial Model
R Behavioral Genetics 1994
 Holistic Health 1985
 Interdisciplinary Treatment Approach 1973
 Psychobiology 1982
 Systems Theory 1988

Biopsychosocial Model
Use Biopsychosocial Approach

Biosynthesis 1973
PN 96 SC 06030
SN Formation of chemical compounds of relatively complex structure from nutrients by enzyme-catalyzed reactions in living cells.
B Metabolism 1967
R ↓ Biology 1967

Bipolar Affective Disorder
Use Bipolar Disorder

Bipolar Disorder 2001
PN 7677 SC 06034
HN The term MANIC DEPRESSIVE PSYCHOSIS was used to represent this concept from 1967-1988, and MANIC DEPRESSION was used from 1988-2000. In 2001, BIPOLAR DISORDER was created to replace these terms. MANIC DEPRESSIVE PSYCHOSIS and MANIC DEPRESSION were removed from all records containing them and replaced with BIPOLAR DISORDER.
UF Bipolar Affective Disorder
 Bipolar Mood Disorder
 Manic Depression
 Manic Depressive Psychosis
B Affective Disorders 2001
N Cyclothymic Personality 1973
R ↓ Affective Psychosis 1973
 ↓ Major Depression 1988
 ↓ Mania 1967

Bipolar Mood Disorder
Use Bipolar Disorder

Biracial Children
Use Interracial Offspring

Birds 1967
PN 6573 SC 06040
UF Fowl

Birds — (cont'd)
B Vertebrates 1973
N Blackbirds 1973
 Budgerigars 1973
 Canaries 1973
 Chickens 1967
 Doves 1973
 Ducks 1973
 Geese 1973
 Owls 1997
 Penguins 1973
 Pigeons 1967
 Quails 1973
 Robins 1973
 Sea Gulls 1973

Birth 1967
PN 2291 SC 06050
UF Childbirth
 Parturition
N Natural Childbirth 1978
 Premature Birth 1973
R Birth Injuries 1973
 Birth Rites 1973
 Birth Trauma 1973
 Birth Weight 1985
 Childbirth Training 1978
 Labor (Childbirth) 1973
 Midwifery 1985
 Obstetrical Complications 1978
 Perinatal Period 1994
 ↓ Pregnancy 1967
 ↓ Sexual Reproduction 1973

Birth Control 1971
PN 1441 SC 06060
UF Contraception
 Population Control
B Family Planning 1973
N ↓ Contraceptive Devices 1973
 Rhythm Method 1973
 Tubal Ligation 1973
 Vasectomy 1973
R Condoms 1991
 Induced Abortion 1071
 Overpopulation 1973
 Premarital Intercourse 1973
 Safe Sex 2003
 Sexual Abstinence 1973
 ↓ Sterilization (Sex) 1973

Birth Control Attitudes
Use Family Planning Attitudes

Birth Injuries 1973
PN 78 SC 06070
SN Physical injuries (such as brain damage) received during birth, mostly in, but not limited to, breech births, instrument deliveries, neonatal anoxia, or premature births. Used for both human and animal populations.
UF Injuries (Birth)
B Injuries 1973
R ↓ Birth 1967
 Birth Trauma 1973
 ↓ Neonatal Disorders 1973
 Obstetrical Complications 1978

Birth Order 1967
PN 1791 SC 06080
B Family Structure 1973

35

Birth Parents
  Use Biological Family

Birth Rate 1982
PN 175   SC 06087
SN Ratio of the number of live births to the number
of individuals in a human population within a speci-
fied time period.
  R   Fertility 1988
        ↓ Population 1973

Birth Rites 1973
PN 92   SC 06090
  B   Rites of Passage 1973
  R ↓ Birth 1967
        Circumcision 2001

Birth Trauma 1973
PN 112   SC 06100
SN Stress, as experienced by infants, of being born
and bombarded with external stimuli that may have
negative influences on subsequent psychological
development. Limited to human populations.
  R ↓ Birth 1967
        Birth Injuries 1973

Birth Weight 1985
PN 975   SC 06105
  UF   Low Birth Weight
  B   Body Weight 1967
  R ↓ Birth 1967
        Premature Birth 1973

Bisexuality 1973
PN 1536   SC 06110
  B   Psychosexual Behavior 1967
        Sexual Orientation 1997
  R   Lesbianism 1973
        Male Homosexuality 1973
        Transsexualism 1973
        Transvestism 1973

Bitterness
  Use Taste Perception

Black Power Movement 1973
PN 43   SC 06130
  B   Social Movements 1967
  R ↓ Activism 2003

Blackbirds 1973
PN 190   SC 06140
  B   Birds 1967

Blacks 1982
PN 23161   SC 06150
HN In 1982, this term was created to replace the
discontinued term NEGROES. In 2000, NEGROES
was removed from all records containing it, and
replaced with BLACKS.
  UF   African Americans
        Negroes
  B   Racial and Ethnic Groups 2001
  R   Minority Groups 1967

Blacky Pictures Test
  Use Projective Personality Measures

Bladder 1973
PN 76   SC 06170

Bladder — (cont'd)
  B   Urogenital System 1973

Blame 1994
PN 472   SC 06175
SN To assign fault or responsibility for an event,
state, or behavior, or the condition of fault or respon-
sibility for something believed to deserve censure.
  R   Accountability 1988
        Attribution 1973
        Guilt 1967
        ↓ Responsibility 1973
        Shame 1994
        ↓ Social Perception 1967

Blind 1967
PN 2920   SC 06180
  B   Vision Disorders 1982
  N   Deaf Blind 1991
  R   Braille 1978

Blink Reflex
  Use Eyeblink Reflex

Block Design Test (Kohs)
  Use Kohs Block Design Test

Blood 1967
PN 1894   SC 06200
  B   Body Fluids 1973
  N ↓ Blood Plasma 1973
  R   Blood Alcohol Concentration 1994
        ↓ Blood and Lymphatic Disorders 1973
        Blood Groups 1973
        Blood Volume 1973
        ↓ Heart 1967

Blood Alcohol Concentration 1994
PN 193   SC 06205
  R ↓ Alcohol Abuse 1988
        ↓ Alcohol Drinking Patterns 1967
        ↓ Alcohol Intoxication 1973
        ↓ Alcohols 1967
        ↓ Blood 1967
        Driving Under the Influence 1988
        Drug Usage Screening 1988

Blood and Lymphatic Disorders 1973
PN 435   SC 06210
  UF   Blood Disorders
        Hematologic Disorders
        Lymphatic Disorders
  B   Physical Disorders 1997
  N   Anemia 1973
        Hemophilia 1973
        Leukemias 1973
        Malaria 1973
        Porphyria 1973
        Rh Incompatibility 1973
        Sickle Cell Disease 1994
  R ↓ Blood 1967

Blood Brain Barrier 1994
PN 65   SC 06215
SN Functional barrier between brain blood vessels
and brain tissues.
  R   Blood Circulation 1973
        ↓ Blood Flow 1973
        ↓ Blood Vessels 1973
        ↓ Brain 1967
        ↓ Cardiovascular System 1967

Blood Brain Barrier — (cont'd)
        Cerebrospinal Fluid 1973
        ↓ Neurochemistry 1973

Blood Cells 1973
PN 183   SC 06220
  B   Cells (Biology) 1973
  N   Erythrocytes 1973
        ↓ Leucocytes 1973

Blood Circulation 1973
PN 172   SC 06230
  UF   Circulation (Blood)
  R   Arterial Pulse 1973
        Blood Brain Barrier 1994
        ↓ Blood Flow 1973
        Blood Volume 1973
        Cerebral Blood Flow 1994

Blood Coagulation 1973
PN 37   SC 06240
  UF   Coagulation (Blood)

Blood Disorders
  Use Blood and Lymphatic Disorders

Blood Donation
  Use Tissue Donation

Blood Flow 1973
PN 792   SC 06270
  N   Cerebral Blood Flow 1994
  R   Blood Brain Barrier 1994
        Blood Circulation 1973
        Blood Volume 1973

Blood Glucose
  Use Blood Sugar

Blood Groups 1973
PN 78   SC 06300
SN Genetically determined classes of human eryth-
rocytes based on specific antigens for which the
groups are named.
  R   Antigens 1982
        ↓ Blood 1967
        Erythrocytes 1973
        ↓ Genetics 1967

Blood Plasma 1973
PN 3814   SC 06310
  UF   Plasma (Blood)
  B   Blood 1967
  N   Blood Serum 1973

Blood Platelets 1973
PN 1153   SC 06320
  UF   Platelets (Blood)

Blood Pressure 1967
PN 3193   SC 06330
  N   Diastolic Pressure 1973
        Systolic Pressure 1973
  R ↓ Blood Pressure Disorders 1973
        Blood Volume 1973
        Cardiovascular Reactivity 1994
        Cerebral Blood Flow 1994
        ↓ Vasoconstrictor Drugs 1973
        ↓ Vasodilator Drugs 1973

Blood Pressure Disorders 1973
PN 32   SC 06340
B   Cardiovascular Disorders 1967
N ↓ Hypertension 1973
     Hypotension 1973
     Syncope 1973
R ↓ Arteriosclerosis 1973
   ↓ Blood Pressure 1967
     Vasoconstriction 1973
     Vasodilation 1973

Blood Proteins 1973
PN 129   SC 06350
B   Proteins 1973
N   Hemoglobin 1973
   ↓ Immunoglobulins 1973
     Serum Albumin 1973

Blood Serum 1973
PN 1714   SC 06360
UF   Serum (Blood)
B   Blood Plasma 1973
R   Antibodies 1973

Blood Sugar 1973
PN 429   SC 06370
UF   Blood Glucose
B   Glucose 1973

Blood Transfusion 1973
PN 51   SC 06380
UF   Transfusion (Blood)
B   Physical Treatment Methods 1973
R   Disease Transmission 2004
     Hemodialysis 1973
     Tissue Donation 1991

Blood Vessels 1973
PN 51   SC 06390
B   Cardiovascular System 1967
N ↓ Arteries (Anatomy) 1973
     Capillaries (Anatomy) 1973
     Veins (Anatomy) 1973
R   Blood Brain Barrier 1991

Blood Volume 1973
PN 141   SC 06400
R ↓ Blood 1967
     Blood Circulation 1973
   ↓ Blood Flow 1973
   ↓ Blood Pressure 1967

Blue Collar Workers 1973
PN 1242   SC 06410
SN Employees whose unskilled, semiskilled, or
skilled occupations involve physical labor.
UF   Laborers (Construction and Industry)
B   Business and Industrial Personnel 1967
N   Industrial Foremen 1973
     Skilled Industrial Workers 1973
     Unskilled Industrial Workers 1973
R   Technical Service Personnel 1973

Boarding Schools 1988
PN 113   SC 06412
SN Elementary or secondary residential educa-
tional institutions for students enrolled in an instruc-
tional program. Primarily used for non-disordered
populations.
B   Schools 1967
R   Institutional Schools 1978

Boards of Education 1978
PN 98   SC 06416
SN Governing bodies responsible for managing
public school systems.
R ↓ Education 1967
     Educational Administration 1967
   ↓ School Administrators 1973

Body Art
   Use Cosmetic Techniques

Body Awareness 1982
PN 767   SC 06425
SN Perception of one's physical self or body at any
particular time.
B   Awareness 1967
R ↓ Body Image 1967
     Human Body 2003
     Self Perception 1967
   ↓ Somesthetic Perception 1967

Body Dysmorphic Disorder 2001
PN 202   SC 06427
SN A preoccupation with a slight or imagined defect
in appearance that causes significant distress or
impairment in social, occupational, or other areas of
functioning. Compare BODY IMAGE DISTUR-
BANCES.
HN In 2001, this term was created to replace the
discontinued term DYSMORPHOPHOBIA. DYS-
MORPHOPHOBIA was removed from all records
containing it and replaced with BODY DYSMORPHIC
DISORDER.
UF   Atypical Somatoform Disorder
     Dysmorphophobia
B   Somatoform Disorders 2001
R ↓ Body Image Disturbances 1973
     Obsessive Compulsive Disorder 1985

Body Fluids 1973
PN 101   SC 06430
B   Anatomy 1967
N   Amniotic Fluid 1973
     Bile 1973
   ↓ Blood 1967
     Cerebrospinal Fluid 1973
     Mucus 1973
     Saliva 1973
     Sweat 1973
     Urine 1973
R ↓ Physiology 1967

Body Height 1973
PN 437   SC 06440
UF   Height (Body)
B   Body Size 1985
R   Physique 1967

Body Image 1967
PN 3653   SC 06450
SN Mental representation of one's body according
to feedback received from one's body, the environ-
ment, and other people.
N ↓ Body Image Disturbances 1973
R   Body Awareness 1982
     Human Body 2003

Body Image Disturbances 1973
PN 782   SC 06460
SN Distortions in the evaluative picture or mental
representation an individual has of his/her body.
Compare BODY DYSMORPHIC DISORDER.

Body Image Disturbances — (cont'd)
B   Body Image 1967
N   Koro 1994
     Phantom Limbs 1973
R   Anorexia Nervosa 1973
     Body Dysmorphic Disorder 2001
     Castration Anxiety 1973

Body Language 1973
PN 385   SC 06470
SN Type of nonverbal communication in which
thoughts, feelings, etc., are expressed through bodily
movement or posture.
UF   Kinesics
B   Interpersonal Communication 1973
     Nonverbal Communication 1971
R   Gestures 1973
     Posture 1973

Body Rocking 1973
PN 63   SC 06480
UF   Rocking (Body)
B   Symptoms 1967
R ↓ Behavior Disorders 1971

Body Rotation
   Use Rotational Behavior

Body Size 1985
PN 1275   SC 06485
SN Used for human or animal populations. For
human populations consider also PHYSIQUE or
SOMATOTYPES.
B   Size 1973
N   Body Height 1973
   ↓ Body Weight 1967
R   Physique 1967

Body Sway Testing 1973
PN 75   SC 06490
B   Measurement 1967
R ↓ Neuropsychological Assessment 1982

Body Temperature 1973
PN 1642   SC 06500
UF   Temperature (Body)
B   Physiology 1967
N   Skin Temperature 1973
     Thermoregulation (Body) 1973
R   Hypothermia 1973

Body Types
   Use Somatotypes

Body Weight 1967
PN 5242   SC 06520
UF   Weight (Body)
B   Body Size 1985
N   Birth Weight 1985
     Obesity 1973
   ↓ Underweight 1973
R   Obesity (Attitudes Toward) 1997
     Physique 1967
     Weight Control 1985

Bombesin 1988
PN 116   SC 06523
B   Neuropeptides 2003
     Peptides 1973

Bonding (Emotional)
  Use   Attachment Behavior

Bone Conduction Audiometry   1973
PN   37   **SC**   06530
  B   Audiometry   1967
  R   ↓ Auditory Stimulation   1967
       ↓ Perceptual Measures   1973

Bone Disorders   1973
PN   123   **SC**   06540
  B   Musculoskeletal Disorders   1973
  N   Osteoporosis   1991

Bone Marrow   1973
PN   238   **SC**   06550
  B   Tissues (Body)   1973
  R   Bones   1973

Bones   1973
PN   170   **SC**   06570
  B   Connective Tissues   1973
       Musculoskeletal System   1973
  R   Bone Marrow   1973
       Jaw   1973
       Spinal Column   1973

Bonobos   1997
PN   72   **SC**   06575
SN   Members of the species Pan panicus. Although not members of the chimpanzee species, Bonobos are often referred to as pygmy chimpanzees.
  UF   Pygmy Chimpanzees
  B   Primates (Nonhuman)   1973
  R   Chimpanzees   1973

Bonuses   1973
PN   37   **SC**   06580
  B   Employee Benefits   1973
  R   Salaries   1973

Books   1973
PN   972   **SC**   06600
SN   Refers to books as a means of communication, as distinct from the document type identifier BOOK.
  B   Printed Communications Media   1973
  N   ↓ Textbooks   1978
  R   Reading Materials   1973

Borderline Mental Retardation   1973
PN   299   **SC**   06610
SN   IQ 71-84.
HN   In 2000, this term replaced the discontinued term SLOW LEARNERS and the discontinued and deleted term BORDERLINE MENTALLY RETARDED. These terms were removed from all records containing them and replaced with BORDERLINE MENTAL RETARDATION.
  UF   Slow Learners
  B   Mental Retardation   1967
  R   Psychosocial Mental Retardation   1973

Borderline Personality Disorder   2001
PN   523   **SC**   06622
SN   Personality disorder with maladaptive patterns of behavior characterized by impulsive and unpredictable actions, mood instability, and unstable interpersonal relationships.
HN   Use BORDERLINE STATES to access references from 1978-2000.
  B   Personality Disorders   1967

Borderline Personality Disorder — (cont'd)
  R   Borderline States   1978
       ↓ Self Destructive Behavior   1985

Borderline States   1978
PN   3757   **SC**   06624
SN   State in which individual has not broken with reality but may become psychotic if exposed to unfavorable circumstances.
  R   Borderline Personality Disorder   2001
       ↓ Mental Disorders   1967
       ↓ Neurosis   1967
       ↓ Psychosis   1967

Boredom   1973
PN   322   **SC**   06630
  B   Emotional States   1973
  R   Monotony   1978

Botany   1973
PN   81   **SC**   06640
  B   Biology   1967
  R   Phylogenesis   1973

Bottle Feeding   1973
PN   123   **SC**   06650
  B   Eating Behavior   2004

Boundaries (Psychological)   1997
PN   281   **SC**   06660
SN   Psychological barriers that separate or divide, and, in some cases, protect the integrity of individuals or groups.
  R   ↓ Group Dynamics   1967
       Intergroup Dynamics   1973
       ↓ Interpersonal Interaction   1967
       Personal Space   1973
       ↓ Personality Processes   1967
       Territoriality   1967

Boundary Violations (Sexual)
  Use   Professional Client Sexual Relations

Bourgeois
  Use   Middle Class

Bowel Disorders
  Use   Colon Disorders

Boys
  Use   Human Males

Brachial Plexus
  Use   Spinal Nerves

Bradycardia   1973
PN   126   **SC**   06730
  B   Arrhythmias (Heart)   1973

Bradykinesia   2001
PN   15   **SC**   06735
SN   Abnormal slowness of movement, which is often a symptom of neurological disorders, particularly Parkinson's disease.
  UF   Hypokinesia
  B   Dyskinesia   1973
  R   Hyperkinesis   1973

Bradykinesia — (cont'd)
       Parkinsonism   1994
       Parkinsons Disease   1973

Braille   1978
PN   164   **SC**   06737
  B   Reading   1967
  R   ↓ Blind   1967
       Braille Instruction   1973
       Reading Education   1973
       Reading Materials   1973
       ↓ Tactual Perception   1967

Braille Instruction   1973
PN   54   **SC**   06740
  B   Curriculum   1967
  R   Braille   1978
       Reading Education   1973

Brain   1967
PN   10188   **SC**   06750
  N   ↓ Brain Stem   1973
       ↓ Forebrain   1985
       ↓ Hindbrain   1997
       ↓ Mesencephalon   1973
  R   Blood Brain Barrier   1994
       ↓ Brain Disorders   1967
       Brain Size   1973
       Brain Weight   1973
       Cerebral Atrophy   1994
       ↓ Cerebral Dominance   1973
       ↓ Lateral Dominance   1967
       Left Brain   1991
       ↓ Neuroimaging   2003
       Ocular Dominance   1973
       Right Brain   1991

Brain Ablation
  Use   Brain Lesions

Brain Concussion   1973
PN   225   **SC**   06770
  UF   Concussion (Brain)
  B   Brain Damage   1967
       Head Injuries   1973

Brain Damage   1967
PN   11857   **SC**   06780
HN   In 2000, this term replaced the discontinued and deleted term BRAIN DAMAGED. BRAIN DAMAGED was removed from all records containing it and replaced with BRAIN DAMAGE.
  B   Brain Disorders   1967
  N   Brain Concussion   1973
       Minimal Brain Disorders   1973
       Traumatic Brain Injury   1997
  R   Cerebral Atrophy   1994
       Cognitive Impairment   2003
       ↓ Congenital Disorders   1973
       ↓ Disorders   1967
       ↓ Epilepsy   1967
       Global Amnesia   1997
       ↓ Head Injuries   1973
       ↓ Mental Retardation   1967
       ↓ Neuropsychological Assessment   1982

Brain Development
  Use   Neural Development

Brain Disorders   1967
PN   2270   **SC**   06800
  B   Central Nervous System Disorders   1973

Brain Disorders — (cont'd)
- **N** Acute Alcoholic Intoxication 1973
  - Anencephaly 1973
  - ↓ Aphasia 1967
  - Athetosis 1973
  - ↓ Brain Damage 1967
  - Brain Neoplasms 1973
  - Cerebral Palsy 1967
  - Cerebrovascular Accidents 1973
  - Chronic Alcoholic Intoxication 1973
  - Encephalitis 1973
  - ↓ Encephalopathies 1982
  - ↓ Epilepsy 1967
  - ↓ Epileptic Seizures 1973
  - Hydrocephaly 1973
  - Microcephaly 1973
  - Minimal Brain Disorders 1973
  - ↓ Organic Brain Syndromes 1973
  - Parkinsons Disease 1973
  - Tay Sachs Disease 2003
- **R** ↓ Brain 1967
  - Cerebral Atrophy 1994
  - ↓ Convulsions 1967
  - ↓ Memory Disorders 1973
  - ↓ Mental Disorders 1967
  - ↓ Neuroimaging 2003
  - Rett Syndrome 1994

Brain Injury (Traumatic)
- **Use** Traumatic Brain Injury

Brain Lesions 1967
PN 9800   **SC** 06830
HN Not defined prior to 1982. From 1982, limited to experimentally induced lesions and used primarily for animal populations.
- **UF** Brain Ablation
  - Cerebral Lesions
  - Subcortical Lesions
- **B** Lesions 1967
- **N** Hypothalamus Lesions 1973
- **R** Decerebration 1973
  - Decortication (Brain) 1973

Brain Mapping
- **Use** Stereotaxic Atlas

Brain Maps
- **Use** Stereotaxic Atlas

Brain Metabolism
- **Use** Neurochemistry

Brain Neoplasms 1973
PN 520   **SC** 06860
- **B** Brain Disorders 1967
  - Nervous System Neoplasms 1973

Brain Self Stimulation 1985
PN 497   **SC** 06864
- **UF** Intracranial Self Stimulation
- **B** Brain Stimulation 1967
  - Self Stimulation 1967

Brain Size 1973
PN 1065   **SC** 06868
- **B** Size 1973
- **R** ↓ Brain 1967
  - Brain Weight 1973
  - Cerebral Atrophy 1994

Brain Stem 1973
PN 1508   **SC** 06870
- **B** Brain 1967
- **N** Locus Ceruleus 1982
  - Medulla Oblongata 1973
  - ↓ Pons 1973
  - Reticular Formation 1967
- **R** ↓ Hindbrain 1997

Brain Stimulation 1967
PN 2277   **SC** 06880
- **B** Stereotaxic Techniques 1973
  - Stimulation 1967
- **N** Brain Self Stimulation 1985
  - Chemical Brain Stimulation 1973
  - Electrical Brain Stimulation 1973
  - Spreading Depression 1967
  - Transcranial Magnetic Stimulation 2003
- **R** Physiological Arousal 1967

Brain Weight 1973
PN 164   **SC** 06882
- **R** ↓ Brain 1967
  - Brain Size 1973
  - Cerebral Atrophy 1994

Brainstorming 1982
PN 143   **SC** 06883
SN Group problem solving technique involving spontaneous contribution of ideas from all group members.
- **B** Group Problem Solving 1973
- **R** Choice Shift 1994
  - ↓ Group Dynamics 1967

Brainwashing 1982
PN 83   **SC** 06884
SN Indoctrination of an individual or group by means of physical or psychological duress in order to alter their political, social, religious, or moral beliefs.
- **UF** Thought Control
- **B** Persuasive Communication 1967
- **R** Attitude Change 1967
  - Coercion 1994
  - Propaganda 1973

Brand Names 1978
PN 926   **SC** 06885
- **B** Names 1985
- **R** ↓ Advertising 1967
  - Brand Preferences 1994
  - ↓ Consumer Behavior 1967
  - ↓ Consumer Research 1973
  - Marketing 1973
  - Retailing 1991

Brand Preferences 1994
PN 500   **SC** 06887
SN Includes loyalty to brand name products or product switching.
- **B** Consumer Attitudes 1973
  - Preferences 1967
- **R** ↓ Advertising 1967
  - Brand Names 1978
  - ↓ Consumer Behavior 1967
  - ↓ Consumer Research 1973
  - Marketing 1973

Bravery
- **Use** Courage

Breakthrough (Psychotherapeutic)
- **Use** Psychotherapeutic Breakthrough

Breakup (Relationship)
- **Use** Relationship Termination

Breast 1973
PN 313   **SC** 06920
- **B** Anatomy 1967

Breast Cancer Screening
- **Use** Cancer Screening

Breast Examination
- **Use** Self Examination (Medical)

Breast Feeding 1973
PN 734   **SC** 06930
- **B** Eating Behavior 2004
- **R** Lactation 1973
  - Weaning 1973

Breast Neoplasms 1973
PN 2123   **SC** 06940
- **UF** Mammary Neoplasms
- **B** Neoplasms 1967
- **R** Mammography 1994
  - Mastectomy 1973

Breathing
- **Use** Respiration

Breeding (Animal)
- **Use** Animal Breeding

Brief Psychotherapy 1967
PN 3352   **SC** 06970
SN Short-term or time-limited methods of psychotherapy.
- **UF** Short Term Psychotherapy
  - Time Limited Psychotherapy
- **B** Psychotherapy 1967
- **R** Solution Focused Therapy 2004

Brief Reactive Psychosis
- **Use** Acute Psychosis

Bright Light Therapy
- **Use** Phototherapy

Brightness Constancy 1985
PN 36   **SC** 06975
SN The tendency to perceive the brightness of stimuli as stable despite objective changes in illumination.
- **B** Brightness Perception 1973
  - Perceptual Constancy 1985

Brightness Contrast 1985
PN 241   **SC** 06977
- **B** Visual Contrast 1985

Brightness Perception 1973
PN 1414   **SC** 06980
- **UF** Luminance Threshold
- **B** Visual Perception 1967

Brightness Perception — (cont'd)
N   Brightness Constancy 1985
R   ↓ Illumination 1967
    Luminance 1982

Broca's Area 2004
PN 15   SC 06985
SN An area located in the left cerebral hemisphere that is highly involved in speech and language processes.
HN This term was introduced in June 2004. PsycINFO records from the past 10 years were re-indexed with this term. The posting note reflects the number of records that were re-indexed.
B   Frontal Lobe 1973

Bromides 1973
PN 45   SC 06990
HN In 1997, this term replaced the discontinued term LITHIUM BROMIDE. In 2000, LITHIUM BROMIDE was removed from all records containing it and replaced with BROMIDES.
UF Lithium Bromide
B   Drugs 1967
R   Arecoline 1973
    Neostigmine 1973
    Scopolamine 1973

Bromocriptine 1988
PN 224   SC 06995
B   Alkaloids 1973
    Enzyme Inhibitors 1985
    Ergot Derivatives 1973

Bronchi 1973
PN 10   SC 07000
B   Respiratory System 1973

Bronchial Disorders 1973
PN 65   SC 07010
B   Respiratory Tract Disorders 1973

Brothers 1973
PN 218   SC 07020
B   Human Males 1973
    Siblings 1967

Bruxism 1985
PN 53   SC 07035
HN Use NOCTURNAL TEETH GRINDING to access references from 1973-1984.
UF Teeth Grinding
N   Nocturnal Teeth Grinding 1973
R   Myofascial Pain 1991

Buddhism 1973
PN 432   SC 07040
B   Religious Affiliation 1973
N   Zen Buddhism 1973
R   Buddhists 1997

Buddhists 1997
PN 29   SC 07045
B   Religious Groups 1997
R   ↓ Buddhism 1973

Budgerigars 1973
PN 85   SC 07050
B   Birds 1967

Budgets 1997
PN 70   SC 07052
HN Use COSTS AND COST ANALYSIS to access references from 1973-1996.
B   Costs and Cost Analysis 1973
R   Cost Containment 1991
    ↓ Economics 1985
    Economy 1973
    Funding 1988
    Income (Economic) 1973
    Money 1967

Bufotenine 1973
PN 18   SC 07060
B   Amines 1973
    Hallucinogenic Drugs 1967
    Vasoconstrictor Drugs 1973

Bulimia 1985
PN 4447   SC 07078
SN Disorder characterized primarily by binge eating and often accompanied by self-induced vomiting and/or misuse of laxatives.
B   Eating Disorders 1997
R   Anorexia Nervosa 1973
    Binge Eating 1991
    Purging (Eating Disorders) 2003
    ↓ Somatoform Disorders 2001

Bulls
Use Cattle

Bullying 2003
PN 377   SC 58064
SN A form of intimidation usually characterized by teasing, threatening, antagonizing, hitting, and victimizing.
HN This term was introduced in June 2003. PsycINFO records from the past 10 years were re-indexed with this term. The posting note reflects the number of records that were re-indexed.
R   ↓ Aggressive Behavior 1967
    ↓ Antisocial Behavior 1971
    ↓ Conflict 1967
    ↓ Dominance 1967
    Emotional Abuse 1991
    ↓ Harassment 2001
    ↓ Perpetrators 1988
    Physical Abuse 1991
    School Violence 2003
    Teasing 2003
    Threat 1967
    Victimization 1973

Bupropion 1994
PN 243   SC 07081
B   Antidepressant Drugs 1971

Burnout
Use Occupational Stress

Burns 1973
PN 396   SC 07090
B   Injuries 1973
R   Electrical Injuries 1973
    ↓ Wounds 1973

Buses
Use Motor Vehicles

Bush Babies
Use Lemurs

Business 1967
PN 1874   SC 07110
UF Commerce
    Industry
    Manufacturing
R   Business Management 1973
    Business Organizations 1973
    Business Students 1973
    Entrepreneurship 1991
    Globalization 2003
    ↓ Management 1967
    Ownership 1985
    Retailing 1991
    Self Employment 1994

Business and Industrial Personnel 1967
PN 5727   SC 07120
UF Businessmen
    Industrial Personnel
B   Personnel 1967
N   Architects 1973
    ↓ Blue Collar Workers 1973
    Industrial Psychologists 1973
    Sales Personnel 1973
    Secretarial Personnel 1973
    ↓ Service Personnel 1991
    Skilled Industrial Workers 1973
    ↓ Technical Personnel 1978
    ↓ White Collar Workers 1973
R   ↓ Aerospace Personnel 1973
    ↓ Agricultural Workers 1973
    Engineers 1967
    ↓ Government Personnel 1973
    ↓ Nonprofessional Personnel 1982
    ↓ Professional Personnel 1978
    Scientists 1967
    Technical Service Personnel 1973

Business Education 1973
PN 489   SC 07123
B   Curriculum 1967
R   Business Management 1973
    ↓ Human Resource Management 2003
    Management Training 1973
    ↓ Personnel Training 1967

Business Management 1973
PN 1021   SC 07130
B   Management 1967
R   Business 1967
    Business Education 1973
    Entrepreneurship 1991
    ↓ Human Resource Management 2003
    ↓ Management Methods 1973

Business Networking
Use Professional Networking

Business Organizations 1973
PN 3142   SC 07140
UF Companies
    Corporations
B   Organizations 1967
    Private Sector 1985
R   Business 1967
    Globalization 2003
    Organizational Learning 2003

Business Students 1973
PN 805   SC 07150
B   Students 1967
R   Business 1967

Businessmen
Use Business and Industrial Personnel

Buspirone 1991
PN 534   SC 07165
B   Minor Tranquilizers 1973
R   Serotonin Agonists 1988

Butterflies 1973
PN 147   SC 07170
B   Insects 1967
R   Larvae 1973

Butyrylperazine
Use Phenothiazine Derivatives

Buying
Use Consumer Behavior

Cadres
Use Social Groups

Caffeine 1973
PN 1359   SC 07210
B   Alkaloids 1973
     CNS Stimulating Drugs 1973
     Diuretics 1973
     Heart Rate Affecting Drugs 1973
     Respiration Stimulating Drugs 1973
R   ↓ Analeptic Drugs 1973

Cage Apparatus 1973
PN 79   SC 07220
B   Apparatus 1967

Calcium 1973
PN 004   SC 07240
B   Chemical Elements 1973
     Metallic Elements 1973
N   Calcium Ions 1973

Calcium Channel Blockers
Use Channel Blockers

Calcium Ions 1973
PN 150   SC 07260
B   Calcium 1973
     Electrolytes 1973

Calculators
Use Digital Computers

Calculus 2003
PN 3   SC 07280
SN   Branch of mathematics concerned with calculation using special symbolic notation.
HN   Use MATHEMATICS to access references from 1973 to June 2003.
B   Mathematics 1982

California F Scale 1973
PN 33   SC 07290

California F Scale — (cont'd)
B   Nonprojective Personality Measures 1973

California Psychological Inventory 1967
PN 302   SC 07300
B   Personality Measures 1967

Calories 1973
PN 372   SC 07330
R   Energy Expenditure 1967

Cameras 1973
PN 53   SC 07350
B   Apparatus 1967

Campaigns (Political)
Use Political Campaigns

Camping 1973
PN 103   SC 07370
B   Recreation 1967
R   Summer Camps (Recreation) 1973
     Vacationing 1973

Camps (Therapeutic)
Use Therapeutic Camps

Campuses 1973
PN 106   SC 07390
B   School Facilities 1973

Canaries 1973
PN 67   SC 07410
B   Birds 1967

Cancer Screening 1997
PN 496   SC 07415
UF   Breast Cancer Screening
     Prostate Cancer Screening
     Skin Cancer Screening
B   Health Screening 1997
R   Health Promotion 2001
     Mammography 1994
     Physical Examination 1988
     Self Examination (Medical) 1988

Cancers
Use Neoplasms

Candidates (Political)
Use Political Candidates

Canids 1997
PN 17   SC 07434
UF   Coyotes
B   Mammals 1973
N   Dogs 1967
     Foxes 1973
     Wolves 1973

Cannabinoids 1982
PN 364   SC 07436
UF   Nabilone
N   Tetrahydrocannabinol 1973
R   ↓ Cannabis 1973

Cannabis 1973
PN 618   SC 07440

Cannabis — (cont'd)
UF   Hemp (Cannabis)
B   Drugs 1967
N   Hashish 1973
     Marijuana 2003
R   Aphrodisiacs 1973
     ↓ Cannabinoids 1982
     ↓ Hallucinogenic Drugs 1967
     ↓ Narcotic Drugs 1973
     Tetrahydrocannabinol 1973

Cannibalism 2003
PN 58   SC 07443
SN   Eating of one's own species. Used for both human and animal populations.
HN   This term was introduced in June 2003. Psyc-INFO records from the past 10 years were re-indexed with this term. The posting note reflects the number of records that were re-indexed.
R   Animal Feeding Behavior 1973
     Death Rites 1973
     Rites (Nonreligious) 1973
     Taboos 1973

Canonical Correlation
Use Multivariate Analysis

Capgras Syndrome 1985
PN 225   SC 07447
SN   Clinical condition in which patient believes an acquaintance, a closely related person, or a close associate has been replaced by a double or an impostor.
B   Psychosis 1967
     Syndromes 1973
R   Delusions 1967
     ↓ Symptoms 1967

Capillaries (Anatomy) 1973
PN 19   SC 07450
B   Blood Vessels 1973

Capital Punishment 1970
PN 490   SC 07460
UF   Death Penalty
     Punishment (Capital)

Capitalism 1973
PN 226   SC 07470
B   Political Economic Systems 1973
R   Entrepreneurship 1991
     Ownership 1985

Capsaicin 1991
PN 189   SC 07475
B   Fatty Acids 1973

Captivity (Animal)
Use Animal Captivity

Captopril 1991
PN 41   SC 07477
B   Antihypertensive Drugs 1973
     Enzyme Inhibitors 1985
R   Angiotensin 1973

Carbachol 1973
PN 233   SC 07480
B   Cholinomimetic Drugs 1973

41

Carbamazepine 1988
PN 855   SC 07483
  B   Analgesic Drugs 1973
       Anticonvulsive Drugs 1973

Carbidopa 1988
PN 37   SC 07485
HN Use DECARBOXYLASES to access references
from 1982-1987.
  B   Decarboxylase Inhibitors 1982
  R   DOPA 1973

Carbohydrate Metabolism 1973
PN 86   SC 07490
  B   Metabolism 1967
  N   Glucose Metabolism 1994
  R   Acetaldehyde 1982
       Guanosine 1985

Carbohydrates 1973
PN 486   SC 07510
  N   Deoxyglucose 1991
     ↓ Sugars 1973

Carbon 1973
PN 14   SC 07520

Carbon Dioxide 1973
PN 352   SC 07530
  R   Respiration 1967

Carbon Monoxide 1973
PN 183   SC 07540
  R ↓ Poisons 1973

Carbon Monoxide Poisoning 1973
PN 78   SC 07550
  UF Carboxyhemoglobinemia
  B   Toxic Disorders 1973

Carbonic Anhydrase
  Use Enzymes

Carboxyhemoglobinemia
  Use Carbon Monoxide Poisoning

Carcinogens 1973
PN 31   SC 07580
  R ↓ Drugs 1967
       Pollution 1973
       Tobacco Smoking 1967

Carcinomas
  Use Neoplasms

Cardiac Arrest
  Use Heart Disorders

Cardiac Disorders
  Use Heart Disorders

Cardiac Rate
  Use Heart Rate

Cardiac Surgery
  Use Heart Surgery

Cardiography 1973
PN 20   SC 07620
  B   Medical Diagnosis 1973
  N   Electrocardiography 1967

Cardiology 1973
PN 63   SC 07630
  B   Medical Sciences 1967
  R ↓ Cardiovascular System 1967

Cardiotonic Drugs
  Use Drugs

Cardiovascular Disorders 1967
PN 3006   SC 07640
  UF Circulatory Disorders
       Coronary Disorders
       Raynauds Disease
       Vascular Disorders
  B   Physical Disorders 1997
  N   Aneurysms 1973
     ↓ Arteriosclerosis 1973
     ↓ Blood Pressure Disorders 1973
     ↓ Cerebrovascular Disorders 1973
       Embolisms 1973
     ↓ Heart Disorders 1973
     ↓ Hemorrhage 1973
     ↓ Hypertension 1973
     ↓ Ischemia 1973
     ↓ Thromboses 1973
  R ↓ Cardiovascular System 1967
       Coronary Prone Behavior 1982
     ↓ Dyspnea 1973
     ↓ Heart Rate Affecting Drugs 1973

Cardiovascular Reactivity 1994
PN 1536   SC 07645
SN Cardiovascular system responses to mental,
physical, or environmental stress or other states due
to intervention or natural occurrence.
  R ↓ Blood Pressure 1967
     ↓ Cardiovascular System 1967
       Heart Rate 1967
       Physiological Arousal 1967
       Physiological Correlates 1967
     ↓ Psychophysiology 1967
       Stress Reactions 1973

Cardiovascular System 1967
PN 1834   SC 07650
  B   Anatomical Systems 1973
  N ↓ Blood Vessels 1973
     ↓ Heart 1967
  R   Blood Brain Barrier 1994
       Cardiology 1973
     ↓ Cardiovascular Disorders 1967
       Cardiovascular Reactivity 1994
       Spleen 1973

Career Aspirations
  Use Occupational Aspirations

Career Change 1978
PN 583   SC 07666
  UF Job Change
  R   Career Development 1985
       Employment History 1978
       Job Satisfaction 1967
       Life Changes 2004
       Occupational Adjustment 1973
       Occupational Aspirations 1973

Career Change — (cont'd)
       Occupational Choice 1967
       Occupational Mobility 1973
    ↓ Occupations 1967
       Professional Development 1982

Career Choice
  Use Occupational Choice

Career Counseling
  Use Occupational Guidance

Career Development 1985
PN 3103   SC 07672
SN Formation of work identity or progression of
career decisions and/or events as influenced by life
or work experience, education, on-the-job training, or
other factors.
  UF Career Transitions
       Management Development
  B   Development 1967
       Human Resource Management 2003
  R   Career Change 1978
       Employment History 1978
    ↓ Management 1967
       Occupational Choice 1967
    ↓ Occupations 1967
       Personnel Placement 1973
       Personnel Promotion 1978
    ↓ Personnel Training 1967
       Professional Development 1982
       Professional Identity 1991
       Professional Networking 2004
       Professional Specialization 1991

Career Education 1978
PN 755   SC 07675
SN Comprehensive educational programs focusing
on individual career development beginning in child-
hood and continuing through the adult years.
  UF Career Exploration
  B   Curriculum 1967
  R   Occupational Guidance 1967

Career Exploration
  Use Career Education

Career Goals
  Use Occupational Aspirations

Career Guidance
  Use Occupational Guidance

Career Maturity
  Use Vocational Maturity

Career Preference
  Use Occupational Preference

Career Transitions
  Use Career Development

Careers
  Use Occupations

Caregiver Burden 1994
PN 1911   SC 07713

Caregiver Burden — (cont'd)

SN Used primarily for family or nonprofessional caregivers and the stress or associated emotional responses experienced when caring for the mentally or physically disabled. Consider OCCUPATIONAL STRESS for professional caregivers, e.g., health care personnel.
R   Caregivers 1988
     Elder Care 1994
     Home Care 1985
     Homebound 1988
     Respite Care 1988
     ↓ Stress 1967

Caregivers 1988

PN 6459   **SC** 07715
SN Family members, professionals, or paraprofessionals who provide care to children or to the mentally or physically disabled.
UF Family Caregivers
R   Caregiver Burden 1994
     ↓ Child Care 1991
     Elder Care 1994
     ↓ Health Care Services 1978
     Home Care 1985
     Home Care Personnel 1997
     Quality of Care 1988
     Respite Care 1988
     ↓ Treatment 1967

Carotid Arteries 1973

PN 152   **SC** 07720
B   Arteries (Anatomy) 1973

Carp 1973

PN 48   **SC** 07740
B   Fishes 1967
N   Goldfish 1973

Cartoons (Humor) 1973

PN 292   **SC** 07780
B   Humor 1967

Case Based Reasoning 2003

PN 35   **SC** 07783
SN Problem solving technique that matches the current problem to previously encountered problems. Used in artificial intelligence discussions.
HN This term was introduced in June 2003. PsycINFO records from the past 10 years were re-indexed with this term. The posting note reflects the number of records that were re-indexed.
B   Reasoning 1967
R   ↓ Artificial Intelligence 1982
     ↓ Expert Systems 1991
     ↓ Inductive Deductive Reasoning 1973
     ↓ Problem Solving 1967

Case History

Use Patient History

Case Management 1991

PN 1349   **SC** 07788
SN Evaluation of health and social service needs of individuals and development and delivery of service or treatment. Includes attention to justification and length of treatment, costs, and health insurance reimbursement.
B   Management 1967
N   Discharge Planning 1994
R   Cost Containment 1991

Case Management — (cont'd)

     ↓ Health Care Administration 1997
     Health Care Costs 1994
     ↓ Health Care Delivery 1978
     ↓ Health Insurance 1973
     Health Service Needs 1997
     Intake Interview 1994
     Long Term Care 1994
     ↓ Managed Care 1994
     Needs Assessment 1985
     Outreach Programs 1997
     Social Casework 1967
     ↓ Treatment 1967
     ↓ Treatment Duration 1988
     ↓ Treatment Planning 1997

Case Report 1967

PN 21978   **SC** 07790
SN Used in records discussing issues involved in the process of conducting exploratory studies of single or multiple clinical cases.
HN From 1967-2000, the term was also used as a mandatory document type identifier; however, this usage has been discontinued due to the advent of Form/Content Type field identifiers. References from 1967-2000 can be accessed using either CASE REPORT or the Case Report Form/Content Type field identifier.

Caseworkers

Use Social Workers

Caste System 1973

PN 226   **SC** 07810
B   Social Structure 1967
     Systems 1967

Castration 1967

PN 308   **SC** 07820
B   Endocrine Gland Surgery 1973
     Sterilization (Sex) 1973
N   Male Castration 1973
     Ovariectomy 1973

Castration Anxiety 1973

PN 164   **SC** 07830
B   Anxiety Disorders 1997
R   ↓ Body Image Disturbances 1973

Cat Learning 1967

PN 121   **SC** 07840
HN Not defined prior to 1982. Use CAT LEARNING or CATS to access references from 1967-1981. From 1982, used for discussions of hypotheses or theories of learning in cats.
B   Animal Learning 2003
     Learning 1967

CAT Scan

Use Tomography

Catabolism 1973

PN 22   **SC** 07850
SN Destructive metabolism involving release of energy (heat) and resulting in breakdown of complex materials within the organism.
B   Metabolism 1967

Catabolites

Use Metabolites

Catalepsy 1973

PN 376   **SC** 07860
SN Condition of muscular semirigidity and trance-like postures. Cataleptic persons make no voluntary motor movements and may display waxy flexibility.
B   Movement Disorders 1985
     Symptoms 1967
R   Autohypnosis 1973
     ↓ Hysteria 1967
     ↓ Schizophrenia 1967
     Suggestibility 1967

Catamnesis

Use Posttreatment Followup

Cataplexy 1973

PN 83   **SC** 07880
SN Temporary loss of muscle tone or weakness following extreme emotion.
B   Movement Disorders 1985
     Muscular Disorders 1973
     Neuromuscular Disorders 1973
R   Narcolepsy 1973

Cataracts 1973

PN 95   **SC** 07890
B   Eye Disorders 1973

Catatonia 1973

PN 494   **SC** 07900
SN Reaction characterized by muscular rigidity or stupor sometimes punctuated by sudden violent outbursts, panic, or hallucinations.
B   Symptoms 1967
R   Catatonic Schizophrenia 1973

Catatonic Schizophrenia 1973

PN 144   **SC** 07910
B   Schizophrenia 1967
R   Catatonia 1973

Catecholamines 1973

PN 2053   **SC** 07920
UF Monoamines (Brain)
B   Neurotransmitters 1985
     Sympathomimetic Amines 1973
N   Dopamine 1973
     Epinephrine 1967
     Norepinephrine 1973
R   ↓ Adrenergic Drugs 1973
     Adrenergic Receptors 2003
     ↓ Decarboxylase Inhibitors 1982
     ↓ Dopamine Antagonists 1982
     Methyldopa 1973

Categorizing

Use Classification (Cognitive Process)

Catharsis 1973

PN 243   **SC** 07940
SN Process of reliving painful experiences and feelings, and the associated emotional responses.
UF Abreaction
B   Personality Processes 1967
R   ↓ Psychoanalysis 1967

Catheterization 1973

PN 103   **SC** 07950
B   Physical Treatment Methods 1973

Cathexis 1973
PN 111   SC 07960
SN Psychoanalytic term designating the attachment of intense emotions to a particular object, person, or oneself.
B   Personality Processes   1967

Cathode Ray Tubes
Use   Video Display Units

Catholicism (Roman)
Use   Roman Catholicism

Catholics 1997
PN 212   SC 07975
B   Christians   1997
R   Roman Catholicism   1973

Cats 1967
PN 6854   SC 07980
B   Felids   1997

Cattell Culture Fair Intelligence Test
Use   Culture Fair Intelligence Test

Cattle 1973
PN 583   SC 08010
UF   Bulls
     Cows
B   Mammals   1973

Caucasians
Use   Whites

Cauda Equina
Use   Spinal Nerves

Caudate Nucleus 1973
PN 1016   SC 08040
B   Basal Ganglia   1973
     Striatum   2003
R   Nucleus Accumbens   1982

Causal Analysis 1994
PN 757   SC 08045
SN Systematic analysis of causal relationships among variables.
B   Analysis   1967
     Methodology   1967
R   Attribution   1973
     ↓ Experimentation   1967
     Path Analysis   1991
     ↓ Statistical Regression   1985
     Structural Equation Modeling   1994

Cecotrophy
Use   Coprophagia

Celebrity
Use   Fame

Celiac Plexus
Use   Autonomic Ganglia

Celibacy
Use   Sexual Abstinence

Cell Nucleus 1973
PN 29   SC 08070
R   ↓ Cells (Biology)   1973

Cells (Biology) 1973
PN 1013   SC 08080
B   Anatomy   1967
N   ↓ Blood Cells   1973
     ↓ Chromosomes   1973
     Cones (Eye)   1973
     Connective Tissue Cells   1973
     Epithelial Cells   1973
     ↓ Neurons   1973
     Sperm   1973
R   Absorption (Physiological)   1973
     Cell Nucleus   1973
     Cytology   1973
     Cytoplasm   1973
     ↓ Physiology   1967

Censorship 1978
PN 87   SC 08086
R   ↓ Civil Rights   1978
     ↓ Communication   1967
     ↓ Communications Media   1973
     Freedom   1978
     Information   1967
     ↓ Laws   1967
     ↓ Social Issues   1991

Centering 1991
PN 11   SC 08088
SN Focusing of attention and concentration on a particular stimulus or on the whole of the present environment and circumstances. Used primarily in, but not limited to, therapeutic settings.
R   ↓ Consciousness States   1971
     Meditation   1973
     ↓ Psychotherapeutic Techniques   1967
     ↓ Self Management   1985

Central Nervous System 1967
PN 2541   SC 08100
B   Nervous System   1967
N   Extrapyramidal Tracts   1973
     Meninges   1973
     Neural Analyzers   1973
     ↓ Neural Pathways   1982
     ↓ Spinal Cord   1973
R   ↓ Central Nervous System Disorders   1973

Central Nervous System Disorders 1973
PN 748   SC 08110
B   Nervous System Disorders   1967
N   ↓ Brain Disorders   1967
     ↓ Chorea   1973
     Dysarthria   1973
     ↓ Meningitis   1973
     ↓ Myelitis   1973
     Neurosyphilis   1973
     Progressive Supranuclear Palsy   1997
R   ↓ Central Nervous System   1967
     Hemiplegia   1978
     Hypothermia   1973
     ↓ Paralysis   1973
     Paraplegia   1978
     Quadriplegia   1985
     ↓ Spinal Cord Injuries   1973

Central Nervous System Drugs
Use   CNS Affecting Drugs

Central Tendency Measures 1973
PN 32   SC 08130
B   Statistical Analysis   1967
     Statistical Measurement   1973
N   Mean   1973
     Median   1973
R   ↓ Population (Statistics)   1973
     T Test   1973
     ↓ Variability Measurement   1973

Central Vision
Use   Foveal Vision

CER (Conditioning)
Use   Conditioned Emotional Responses

Cerebellar Cortex
Use   Cerebellum

Cerebellar Nuclei
Use   Cerebellum

Cerebellopontile Angle
Use   Cerebellum

Cerebellum 1973
PN 1881   SC 08180
UF   Cerebellar Cortex
     Cerebellar Nuclei
     Cerebellopontile Angle
B   Hindbrain   1997
N   Purkinje Cells   1994

Cerebral Aqueduct
Use   Cerebral Ventricles

Cerebral Arteriosclerosis 1973
PN 45   SC 08210
B   Arteriosclerosis   1973
     Cerebrovascular Disorders   1973
R   Cerebrovascular Accidents   1973
     ↓ Senile Dementia   1973

Cerebral Atrophy 1994
PN 508   SC 08215
UF   Atrophy (Cerebral)
     Cortical Atrophy
R   ↓ Brain   1967
     ↓ Brain Damage   1967
     ↓ Brain Disorders   1967
     Brain Size   1973
     Brain Weight   1973
     ↓ Cerebral Cortex   1967
     ↓ Cerebral Dominance   1973

Cerebral Blood Flow 1994
PN 1274   SC 08217
B   Blood Flow   1973
R   Blood Circulation   1973
     ↓ Blood Pressure   1967
     ↓ Cerebral Cortex   1967

Cerebral Cortex 1967
PN 6220   SC 08220
UF   Cortex (Cerebral)
B   Telencephalon   1973
N   Cerebral Ventricles   1973
     Corpus Callosum   1973

Cerebral Cortex — (cont'd)
  ↓ Frontal Lobe   1973
     Left Brain   1991
  ↓ Limbic System   1973
  ↓ Occipital Lobe   1973
  ↓ Parietal Lobe   1973
     Right Brain   1991
  ↓ Temporal Lobe   1973
R   Cerebral Atrophy   1994
     Cerebral Blood Flow   1994
     Interhemispheric Interaction   1985

Cerebral Dominance   1973
PN   4627   **SC**   08230
SN   The control of lower brain centers by the cerebrum or cerebral cortex. Compare LATERAL DOMINANCE.
B   Dominance   1967
N   ↓ Lateral Dominance   1967
R   ↓ Brain   1967
     Cerebral Atrophy   1994
     Interhemispheric Interaction   1985
     Left Brain   1001
     Right Brain   1991

Cerebral Hemorrhage   1973
PN   278   **SC**   08250
B   Cerebrovascular Disorders   1973
     Hemorrhage   1973
R   Cerebrovascular Accidents   1973

Cerebral Ischemia   1973
PN   478   **SC**   08260
B   Cerebrovascular Disorders   1973
     Ischemia   1973
R   Cerebrovascular Accidents   1973

Cerebral Lesions
Use   Brain Lesions

Cerebral Palsy   1967
PN   1235   **SC**   08280
B   Brain Disorders   1967
     Paralysis   1973
R   Athetosis   1973

Cerebral Vascular Disorders
Use   Cerebrovascular Disorders

Cerebral Ventricles   1973
PN   792   **SC**   08310
UF   Cerebral Aqueduct
     Choroid Plexus
     Ependyma
     Ventricles (Cerebral)
B   Cerebral Cortex   1967

Cerebrospinal Fluid   1973
PN   1650   **SC**   08320
UF   Spinal Fluid
B   Body Fluids   1973
R   Blood Brain Barrier   1994

Cerebrovascular Accidents   1973
PN   3592   **SC**   08330
UF   Apoplexy
     Stroke (Cerebrum)
B   Brain Disorders   1967
     Cerebrovascular Disorders   1973
R   Cerebral Arteriosclerosis   1973
     Cerebral Hemorrhage   1973

Cerebrovascular Accidents — (cont'd)
     Cerebral Ischemia   1973
     Coma   1973

Cerebrovascular Disorders   1973
PN   613   **SC**   08340
UF   Cerebral Vascular Disorders
B   Cardiovascular Disorders   1967
N   Cerebral Arteriosclerosis   1973
     Cerebral Hemorrhage   1973
     Cerebral Ischemia   1973
     Cerebrovascular Accidents   1973
R   Coma   1973
   ↓ Hypertension   1973
     Multi Infarct Dementia   1991
   ↓ Nervous System Disorders   1967
   ↓ Vascular Dementia   1997

Certification (Professional)
Use   Professional Certification

Certification Examinations
Use   Professional Examinations

Certified Public Accountants
Use   Accountants

Cervical Plexus
Use   Spinal Nerves

Cervical Sprain Syndrome
Use   Whiplash

Cervix   1973
PN   212   **SC**   08390
B   Uterus   1973

Chance (Fortune)   1973
PN   315   **SC**   08420
SN   The possibility of a favorable or unfavorable outcome in an uncertain situation.
UF   Luck
B   Probability   1967
N   ↓ Statistical Probability   1967
R   Uncertainty   1991

Change (Organizational)
Use   Organizational Change

Change (Social)
Use   Social Change

Channel Blockers   1991
PN   510   **SC**   08450
UF   Calcium Channel Blockers
B   Drugs   1967
R   ↓ Vasodilator Drugs   1973
     Verapamil   1991

Chaos Theory   1997
PN   215   **SC**   09455
B   Theories   1967
R   ↓ Mathematical Modeling   1973
     Predictability (Measurement)   1973
   ↓ Prediction   1967
   ↓ Probability   1967
   ↓ Stochastic Modeling   1973
     Uncertainty   1991

Chaplains   1973
PN   65   **SC**   08460
SN   Clergymen officially attached to branch of military, hospital, institution, court, or university.
B   Clergy   1973
R   Lay Religious Personnel   1973
   ↓ Military Personnel   1967
     Ministers (Religion)   1973
     Priests   1973
     Rabbis   1973

Character
Use   Personality

Character Development
Use   Personality Development

Character Disorders
Use   Personality Disorders

Character Formation
Use   Personality Development

Charisma   1988
PN   233   **SC**   08515
B   Personality Traits   1967
R   Leadership Qualities   1997
     Leadership Style   1973
     Transformational Leadership   2003

Charismatic Leadership
Use   Transformational Leadership

Charitable Behavior   1973
PN   560   **SC**   08520
SN   Generous or spontaneous goodness as manifested in actions for the benefit of others, especially for the needy, poor, or helpless.
B   Interpersonal Interaction   1967
     Prosocial Behavior   1982
R   Altruism   1973
   ↓ Assistance (Social Behavior)   1973
     Sharing (Social Behavior)   1978
     Tissue Donation   1991
     Volunteers   2003

Cheating   1973
PN   385   **SC**   08530
B   Deception   1967
R   Dishonesty   1973
     Fraud   1994
     Test Taking   1985

Chemical Brain Stimulation   1973
PN   996   **SC**   08540
B   Brain Stimulation   1967
     Stereotaxic Techniques   1973

Chemical Elements   1973
PN   222   **SC**   08550
HN   In 1997, this term replaced the discontinued term NONMETALLIC ELEMENTS. In 2000, NONMETALLIC ELEMENTS was removed from all records containing it, and replaced with CHEMICAL ELEMENTS.
UF   Nonmetallic Elements
B   Chemicals   1991
N   ↓ Calcium   1973
R   ↓ Electrolytes   1973

Chemical Elements — (cont'd)
    Food Additives 1978

Chemicals 1991
PN 478   SC 08555
SN May include compounds.
    N ↓ Chemical Elements 1973
    R ↓ Hazardous Materials 1991

Chemistry 1967
PN 447   SC 08560
SN Study of the atomic composition of substances, elements, and their reactions, and the formation, decomposition, and properties of molecules. Used for the scientific discipline or the chemical processes themselves.
    B Sciences 1967
    N ↓ Biochemistry 1967

Chemoreceptors 1973
PN 452   SC 08570
    B Neural Receptors 1973
       Sensory Neurons 1973
    R Olfactory Mucosa 1973
       Taste Buds 1973
       Taste Disorders 2001
       Vomeronasal Sense 1982

Chemotherapy
    Use Drug Therapy

Chess 1973
PN 178   SC 08590
    B Games 1967

Chest
    Use Thorax

Chewing Tobacco
    Use Smokeless Tobacco

Chi Square Test 1973
PN 190   SC 08620
    B Nonparametric Statistical Tests 1967
    R Statistical Significance 1973

Chicanos
    Use Mexican Americans

Chickens 1967
PN 2132   SC 08630
    B Birds 1967

Child Abduction
    Use Kidnapping

Child Abuse 1971
PN 13085   SC 08650
SN Abuse of children or adolescents in a family, institutional, or other setting.
    UF Child Maltreatment
    B Crime 1967
    N Battered Child Syndrome 1973
    R Abandonment 1997
       ↓ Abuse Reporting 1997
       Anatomically Detailed Dolls 1991
       Attachment Disorders 2001

Child Abuse — (cont'd)
       Child Abuse Reporting 1997
       Child Neglect 1988
       Child Welfare 1988
       Emotional Abuse 1991
       Failure to Thrive 1988
       Family Violence 1982
       Munchausen Syndrome by Proxy 1997
       Patient Abuse 1991
       Pedophilia 1973
       Physical Abuse 1991
       ↓ Sexual Abuse 1988
       Verbal Abuse 2003
       ↓ Violent Crime 2003

Child Abuse Reporting 1997
PN 235   SC 08652
SN Reporting of physical abuse, emotional abuse, sexual abuse, verbal abuse, or child neglect by the victim or other individuals.
    B Abuse Reporting 1997
    R ↓ Child Abuse 1971
       Child Neglect 1988
       Child Welfare 1988

Child Advocacy
    Use Advocacy

Child Attitudes 1988
PN 2397   SC 08658
SN Attitudes of, not toward, children.
    B Attitudes 1967

Child Behavior Checklist 1994
PN 166   SC 08659
    B Nonprojective Personality Measures 1973

Child Care 1991
PN 1317   SC 08660
SN Care of children of any age in any setting.
    UF Babysitting
    N Child Day Care 1973
       Child Self Care 1988
    R Caregivers 1988
       ↓ Childrearing Practices 1967
       Foster Care 1978

Child Care Workers 1978
PN 910   SC 08663
SN Mental health, educational, or social services personnel providing day care or residential care for children.
    R Child Day Care 1973
       Day Care Centers 1973
       ↓ Nonprofessional Personnel 1982
       ↓ Service Personnel 1991

Child Custody 1982
PN 1500   SC 08665
SN Legal guardianship of a child.
    B Legal Processes 1973
    R Child Support 1988
       Child Visitation 1988
       Divorce 1973
       Guardianship 1988
       Joint Custody 1988
       ↓ Living Arrangements 1991
       Mediation 1988
       ↓ Parental Absence 1973
       Protective Services 1997

Child Day Care 1973
PN 1698   SC 08670
SN Day care that provides for a child's physical needs and often his/her developmental or educational needs. Kinds of day care include day care centers and school-based programs.
    UF Day Care (Child)
    B Child Care 1991
    R Child Care Workers 1978
       Child Self Care 1988
       Child Welfare 1988
       Day Care Centers 1973
       Quality of Care 1988

Child Discipline 1973
PN 1028   SC 08680
    UF Discipline (Child)
    B Childrearing Practices 1967
       Family Relations 1967
    N Parental Permissiveness 1973
    R ↓ Parent Child Relations 1967
       Parental Role 1973

Child Guidance Clinics 1973
PN 276   SC 08690
SN Facilities which exist for the diagnosis and treatment of behavioral and emotional disorders in childhood.
    UF Child Psychiatric Clinics
    B Clinics 1967
    R ↓ Community Facilities 1973
       Community Mental Health Centers 1973
       ↓ Mental Health Programs 1973
       ↓ Mental Health Services 1978
       Psychiatric Clinics 1973

Child Labor 2003
PN 12   SC 08691
SN The employment of youth.
HN This term was introduced in June 2003. PsycINFO records from the past 10 years were re-indexed with this term. The posting note reflects the number of records that were re-indexed.
    R Child Welfare 1988

Child Maltreatment
    Use Child Abuse

Child Molestation
    Use Pedophilia

Child Neglect 1988
PN 1627   SC 08695
SN Failure of parents or caretakers to provide basic care and emotional support necessary for normal development.
    B Antisocial Behavior 1971
    R Abandonment 1997
       Attachment Disorders 2001
       ↓ Child Abuse 1971
       Child Abuse Reporting 1997
       Child Welfare 1988
       Emotional Abuse 1991
       Failure to Thrive 1988
       Munchausen Syndrome by Proxy 1997

Child Psychiatric Clinics
    Use Child Guidance Clinics

Child Psychiatry 1967
PN 2651   SC 08710

Child Psychiatry — (cont'd)

SN Branch of psychiatry devoted to the study and treatment of behavioral, mental, and emotional disorders of children. Use a more specific term if possible.
B Psychiatry 1967
R Orthopsychiatry 1973

Child Psychology 1967

PN 1132   **SC** 08720
SN Branch of developmental psychology devoted to the study of behavior, adjustment, and development and the treatment of behavioral, mental, and emotional disorders of children. Use a more specific term if possible.
B Developmental Psychology 1973

Child Psychotherapy 1967

PN 2959   **SC** 08730
B Psychotherapy 1967
N Play Therapy 1973
R Adolescent Psychotherapy 1994

Child Self Care 1988

PN 93   **SC** 08733
SN Responsibility for personal care without adult supervision usually before or after the school day. Primarily used for children under age 14.
UF Latchkey Children
B Child Care 1991
R Child Day Care 1973
    Child Welfare 1988
    Self Care Skills 1978

Child Support 1988

PN 126   **SC** 08735
SN Legal obligation of parents or guardians to contribute to the economic maintenance of their children including provision of education, clothing, and food.
R Child Custody 1982
    Divorce 1973
    Joint Custody 1988
    ↓ Marital Separation 1973

Child Visitation 1988

PN 266   **SC** 08737
SN The right of or court-granted permission to parents, grandparents, or guardians to visit children.
UF Visitation Rights
B Legal Processes 1973
R Child Custody 1982

Child Welfare 1988

PN 1639   **SC** 08738
R ↓ Adoption (Child) 1967
    Advocacy 1985
    ↓ Child Abuse 1971
    Child Abuse Reporting 1997
    Child Day Care 1973
    Child Labor 2003
    Child Neglect 1988
    Child Self Care 1988
    Foster Care 1978
    Juvenile Justice 2004
    Protective Services 1997
    Social Casework 1967
    ↓ Social Services 1982

Childbirth

Use Birth

Childbirth (Natural)

Use Natural Childbirth

Childbirth Training 1978

PN 188   **SC** 08746
B Prenatal Care 1991
R ↓ Birth 1967
    Labor (Childbirth) 1973
    Natural Childbirth 1978
    ↓ Obstetrics 1978
    ↓ Pregnancy 1967

Childhood Development 1967

PN 13773   **SC** 08760
SN Process of physical, cognitive, personality, and psychosocial growth occurring from birth through age 12. Use a more specific term if possible.
B Human Development 1967
N ↓ Early Childhood Development 1973
R Adolescent Development 1973
    Developmental Age Groups 1973
    ↓ Developmental Stages 1973
    ↓ Motor Development 1973
    Object Relations 1982
    ↓ Perceptual Development 1973
    ↓ Physical Development 1973
    ↓ Psychogenesis 1973
    ↓ Psychomotor Development 1973
    Separation Individuation 1982
    Transitional Objects 1985

Childhood Memories

Use Early Memories

Childhood Neurosis 1973

PN 203   **SC** 08770
UF Infantile Neurosis
B Neurosis 1967

Childhood Play Behavior 1978

PN 3838   **SC** 08777
UF Play Behavior (Childhood)
B Behavior 1967
R Anatomically Detailed Dolls 1991
    Childhood Play Development 1973
    Childrens Recreational Games 1973
    Doll Play 1973
    ↓ Games 1967
    ↓ Recreation 1967
    Role Playing 1967
    Toy Selection 1973
    ↓ Toys 1973

Childhood Play Development 1973

PN 816   **SC** 08780
UF Play Development (Childhood)
B Psychosocial Development 1973
R Childhood Play Behavior 1978
    Childrens Recreational Games 1973
    Emotional Development 1973

Childhood Psychosis 1967

PN 626   **SC** 08790
UF Infantile Psychosis
B Psychosis 1967
N Childhood Schizophrenia 1967
    Symbiotic Infantile Psychosis 1973
R ↓ Emotionally Disturbed 1973

Childhood Schizophrenia 1967

PN 738   **SC** 08800

Childhood Schizophrenia — (cont'd)

B Childhood Psychosis 1967
    Schizophrenia 1967
R Early Infantile Autism 1973
    Symbiotic Infantile Psychosis 1973

Childlessness 1982

PN 227   **SC** 08805
SN State of having no children.
B Family Structure 1973
    Parenthood Status 1985
R Delayed Parenthood 1985
    Family Planning Attitudes 1973

Childrearing Attitudes 1973

PN 1353   **SC** 08810
B Attitudes 1967
R ↓ Family Relations 1967
    ↓ Parental Attitudes 1973

Childrearing Practices 1967

PN 6044   **SC** 08820
SN Specific methods used by parents to raise children. Compare PARENTING STYLE. Limited to human populations.
B Family Relations 1967
N ↓ Child Discipline 1973
    Toilet Training 1973
    Weaning 1973
R ↓ Child Care 1991
    Father Child Relations 1970
    Mother Child Relations 1967
    ↓ Parent Child Relations 1967
    Parent Training 1978
    ↓ Parental Attitudes 1973
    ↓ Parental Characteristics 1994
    Parental Role 1973
    Parenting Skills 1997
    ↓ Parenting Style 2003
    ↓ Sociocultural Factors 1967

Children of Alcoholics 2003

PN 185   **SC** 08830
HN This term was introduced in June 2003. Psyc-INFO records from the past 10 years were re-indexed with this term. The posting note reflects the number of records that were re-indexed.
UF Adult Children of Alcoholics
    Alcoholic Offspring
    Offspring of Alcoholics
B Offspring 1988
R ↓ Alcoholism 1967
    ↓ Family Background 1973
    ↓ Parent Child Relations 1967
    Transgenerational Patterns 1991

Childrens Apperception Test 1973

PN 38   **SC** 08840
B Projective Personality Measures 1973

Childrens Manifest Anxiety Scale 1973

PN 35   **SC** 08850
B Nonprojective Personality Measures 1973

Childrens Personality Questionnaire 1973

PN 15   **SC** 08860
B Nonprojective Personality Measures 1973

Childrens Recreational Games 1973

PN 85   **SC** 08870
B Games 1967
    Recreation 1967

Childrens Recreational Games — (cont'd)
R   Childhood Play Behavior 1978
     Childhood Play Development 1973
     ↓ Toys 1973

Chimpanzees 1973
PN 1177   SC 08890
B   Mammals 1973
     Primates (Nonhuman) 1973
R   Bonobos 1997

Chinchillas 1973
PN 86   SC 08900
B   Mammals 1973
     Rodents 1973

Chinese Cultural Groups 1997
PN 812   SC 08902
HN   Use ASIANS to access references from 1982-1996.
B   Asians 1982

Chiroptera
Use Bats

Chloral Hydrate 1973
PN 32   SC 08910
B   Anticonvulsive Drugs 1973
     Hypnotic Drugs 1973
     Sedatives 1973

Chloralose
Use Hypnotic Drugs

Chlordiazepoxide 1973
PN 887   SC 08930
UF   Librium
B   Amines 1973
     Benzodiazepines 1978
     Minor Tranquilizers 1973

Chloride Ions 1973
PN 70   SC 08940
B   Electrolytes 1973

Chlorimipramine 1973
PN 941   SC 08950
UF   Clomipramine
B   Amines 1973
     Serotonin Reuptake Inhibitors 1997
     Tricyclic Antidepressant Drugs 1997

Chlorisondamine
Use Amines

Chloroform 1973
PN 9   SC 08970
B   General Anesthetics 1973

Chlorophenylpiperazine
Use Piperazines

Chlorpromazine 1967
PN 1409   SC 08990
UF   Thorazine
B   Amines 1973

Chlorpromazine — (cont'd)
     Antiemetic Drugs 1973
     Antihypertensive Drugs 1973
     CNS Depressant Drugs 1973
     Phenothiazine Derivatives 1973
     Sedatives 1973

Chlorprothixene 1973
PN 22   SC 09000
B   Amines 1973
     Antiemetic Drugs 1973
     Antihistaminic Drugs 1973
     Antispasmodic Drugs 1973
     Minor Tranquilizers 1973
     Phenothiazine Derivatives 1973

Choice Behavior 1967
PN 7206   SC 09010
SN   Motivational or judgmental processes involved in the decision or tendency to select one alternative over another or others. Also used for the choices themselves. Used for human or animal populations.
B   Behavior 1967
     Decision Making 1967
R   Classification (Cognitive Process) 1967
     Freedom 1978
     Human Mate Selection 1988
     Psychological Reactance 1978
     Social Dilemma 2003
     Therapist Selection 1994
     Uncertainty 1991
     Utility Theory 2004
     Volition 1988

Choice Shift 1994
PN 26   SC 09013
SN   In social psychology, the changes or shifts in choices made by groups during decision making processes that may differ from choices made by each group member acting on their own.
UF   Risky Shift
B   Group Decision Making 1978
R   Brainstorming 1982
     Group Discussion 1967
     ↓ Group Dynamics 1967
     ↓ Group Problem Solving 1973
     ↓ Risk Taking 1967

Cholecystokinin 1982
PN 868   SC 09015
SN   Hormone secreted by upper intestinal mucosa on contact with gastric contents, cholecystokini; stimulates contraction of the gallbladder. Also, a neurotransmitter.
UF   Pancreozymin
B   Hormones 1967
     Neuropeptides 2003
     Neurotransmitters 1985
     Peptides 1973

Cholesterol 1973
PN 649   SC 09020
B   Steroids 1973

Choline 1973
PN 471   SC 09030
UF   Choline Chloride
B   Vitamins 1973
N   Lecithin 1991
R   Acetylcholine 1973
     Cholinesterase 1973
     Succinylcholine 1973

Choline Chloride
Use Choline

Cholinergic Blocking Drugs 1973
PN 873   SC 09050
UF   Anticholinergic Drugs
     Cholinolytic Drugs
B   Drugs 1967
N   Atropine 1973
     Benactyzine 1973
     Levodopa 1973
     Nicotine 1973
     Orphenadrine 1973
     Scopolamine 1973
     Trihexyphenidyl 1973
R   ↓ Antiemetic Drugs 1973
     ↓ Antispasmodic Drugs 1973
     Cholinergic Nerves 1973
     Cholinesterase 1973
     ↓ Cholinomimetic Drugs 1973
     ↓ Hallucinogenic Drugs 1967
     ↓ Parasympathetic Nervous System 1973
     ↓ Phenothiazine Derivatives 1973

Cholinergic Drugs 1973
PN 624   SC 09060
UF   Muscarinic Drugs
B   Drugs 1967
N   Acetylcholine 1973
     Physostigmine 1973
     Pilocarpine 1973
R   Cholinergic Receptors 2003
     ↓ Cholinomimetic Drugs 1973

Cholinergic Nerves 1973
PN 838   SC 09070
UF   Nerves (Cholinergic)
B   Autonomic Nervous System 1967
R   Acetylcholine 1973
     ↓ Cholinergic Blocking Drugs 1973
     ↓ Cholinomimetic Drugs 1973

Cholinergic Receptors 2003
PN 115   SC 09075
SN   Class of neural receptors that are sensitive to the neurotransmitter acetylcholine.
HN   This term was introduced in June 2003. Psyc-INFO records from the past 10 years were re-indexed with this term. The posting note reflects the number of records that were re-indexed.
UF   Acetylcholine Receptors
     Cholinoceptors
     Muscarinic Receptors
     Nicotinic Receptors
     Receptors (Cholinergic)
B   Neural Receptors 1973
R   Acetylcholine 1973
     ↓ Cholinergic Drugs 1973
     Receptor Binding 1985

Cholinesterase 1973
PN 117   SC 09080
B   Esterases 1973
R   Acetylcholinesterase 1973
     ↓ Choline 1973
     ↓ Cholinergic Blocking Drugs 1973
     ↓ Cholinesterase Inhibitors 1973

Cholinesterase Inhibitors 1973
PN 710   SC 09090
UF   Anticholinesterase Drugs
B   Enzyme Inhibitors 1985

Cholinesterase Inhibitors — (cont'd)
- N   Galanthamine 1973
-      Neostigmine 1973
-      Physostigmine 1973
- R   Cholinesterase 1973
-     ↓ Cholinomimetic Drugs 1973

Cholinoceptors
- **Use** Cholinergic Receptors

Cholinolytic Drugs
- **Use** Cholinergic Blocking Drugs

Cholinomimetic Drugs 1973
PN 131   SC 09100
- UF Parasympathomimetic Drugs
- B   Drugs 1967
- N   Acetylcholine 1973
-      Arecoline 1973
-      Carbachol 1973
-      Neostigmine 1973
-      Physostigmine 1973
-      Pilocarpine 1973
- R ↓ Analeptic Drugs 1973
-     ↓ Cholinergic Blocking Drugs 1973
-     ↓ Cholinergic Drugs 1973
-     Cholinergic Nerves 1973
-     ↓ Cholinesterase Inhibitors 1973
-     ↓ Parasympathetic Nervous System 1973

Chorda Tympani Nerve
- **Use** Facial Nerve

Chorea 1973
PN 107   SC 09120
- B   Central Nervous System Disorders 1973
-      Movement Disorders 1985
- N   Huntingtons Disease 1973
- R ↓ Infectious Disorders 1973

Choroid
- **Use** Eye (Anatomy)

Choroid Plexus
- **Use** Cerebral Ventricles

Christianity 1973
PN 1935   SC 09150
- B   Religious Affiliation 1973
- N   Protestantism 1973
-      Roman Catholicism 1973
- R   Bible 1973
-     ↓ Christians 1997

Christians 1997
PN 256   SC 09152
- B   Religious Groups 1997
- N   Catholics 1997
-      Protestants 1997
- R ↓ Christianity 1973

Chromaticity 1997
PN 189   SC 09155
- **SN** The collective aspects of a color stimulus determined by its hue (dominant wavelength of light) and its saturation (purity).
- N   Color Saturation 1997
-      Hue 1973
- R   Achromatic Color 1973

Chromaticity — (cont'd)
-     ↓ Color 1967
-     ↓ Color Perception 1967
-     Luminance 1982

Chromosome Disorders 1973
PN 376   SC 09160
- UF Karyotype Disorders
-      Mosaicism
- B   Genetic Disorders 1973
- N ↓ Autosome Disorders 1973
-      Deletion (Chromosome) 1973
-     ↓ Sex Chromosome Disorders 1973
-      Translocation (Chromosome) 1973
-     ↓ Trisomy 1973
-      Williams Syndrome 2003
- R ↓ Chromosomes 1973

Chromosomes 1973
PN 522   SC 09170
- B   Cells (Biology) 1973
- N   Autosomes 1973
-      Sex Chromosomes 1973
- R ↓ Chromosome Disorders 1973
-     ↓ Genes 1973
-      Genetic Linkage 1994
-     ↓ Genetics 1967
-      Genome 2003
-      Mutations 1973

Chronic Alcoholic Intoxication 1973
PN 80   SC 09180
- B   Alcohol Intoxication 1973
-      Brain Disorders 1967
-      Chronic Illness 1991
- R   Toxic Encephalopathies 1973

Chronic Fatigue Syndrome 1997
PN 637   SC 09181
- **SN** Syndrome thought to be caused by a viral organism resulting in chronic fatigue, fever, pain, sore throat, and, in some cases, depression.
- B   Chronic Illness 1991
-      Syndromes 1973
- R ↓ Encephalopathies 1982
-      Epstein Barr Viral Disorder 1994
-      Fatigue 1967
-     ↓ Muscular Disorders 1973
-     ↓ Viral Disorders 1973

Chronic Illness 1991
PN 2463   SC 09183
- **SN** An illness or disorder that persists for a prolonged period of time. Used in conjunction with other specific terms where appropriate.
- N   Chronic Alcoholic Intoxication 1973
-      Chronic Fatigue Syndrome 1997
-     ↓ Chronic Mental Illness 1997
-      Chronic Pain 1985
- R   Chronic Stress 2004
-      Chronicity (Disorders) 1982
-     ↓ Disorders 1967
-     ↓ Mental Disorders 1967
-     ↓ Physical Disorders 1997
-      Severity (Disorders) 1982

Chronic Mental Illness 1997
PN 538   SC 09184
- **SN** A mental illness that persists for a prolonged period of time. Use a more specific term if possible.
- UF Persistent Mental Illness
- B   Chronic Illness 1991

Chronic Mental Illness — (cont'd)
-      Mental Disorders 1967
- N   Chronic Psychosis 1973
- R   Chronicity (Disorders) 1982
-      Prognosis 1973
-      Severity (Disorders) 1982
-     ↓ Treatment Resistant Disorders 1994

Chronic Pain 1985
PN 3547   SC 09185
- B   Chronic Illness 1991
-      Pain 1967
- R   Back Pain 1982
-      Chronic Stress 2004
-      Myofascial Pain 1991
-      Somatoform Pain Disorder 1997

Chronic Psychosis 1973
PN 146   SC 09190
- B   Chronic Mental Illness 1997
-      Psychosis 1967

Chronic Schizophrenia
- **Use** Schizophrenia

Chronic Stress 2004
PN 98   SC 09202
- **SN** Stress that is continual over a long period of time.
- **HN** This term was introduced in June 2004. PsycINFO records from the past 10 years were re-indexed with this term. The posting note reflects the number of records that were re-indexed.
- B   Stress 1967
- R ↓ Chronic Illness 1991
-      Chronic Pain 1985
-      Chronicity (Disorders) 1982
-      Psychological Stress 1973

Chronicity (Disorders) 1982
PN 1975   SC 09203
- **SN** Used only when chronicity itself is a factor, variable, or major focus of the research. Used in conjunction with other specific terms where appropriate.
- R ↓ Chronic Illness 1991
-     ↓ Chronic Mental Illness 1997
-      Chronic Stress 2004
-     ↓ Disorders 1967
-     ↓ Mental Disorders 1967
-     ↓ Physical Disorders 1997
-      Severity (Disorders) 1982

Chunking 2004
PN 22   SC 09204
- **SN** Process of organizing or grouping information into larger units or "chunks."
- **HN** This term was introduced in June 2004. PsycINFO records from the past 10 years were re-indexed with this term. The posting note reflects the number of records that were re-indexed.
- B   Cognitive Processes 1967
- R ↓ Memory 1967
-      Mnemonic Learning 1973
-     ↓ Short Term Memory 1967

Churches
- **Use** Religious Buildings

Cichlids 1973
PN 251   SC 09210
- B   Fishes 1967

Cigarette Smoking
Use Tobacco Smoking

Cimetidine 1985
PN 44 **SC** 09225
B Antihistaminic Drugs 1973

Circadian Rhythms (Animal)
Use Animal Circadian Rhythms

Circadian Rhythms (Human)
Use Human Biological Rhythms

Circulation (Blood)
Use Blood Circulation

Circulatory Disorders
Use Cardiovascular Disorders

Circumcision 2001
PN 69 **SC** 09255
HN From 1973-2000, BIRTH RITES and SURGERY were used together to capture this concept.
UF Female Genital Mutilation
B Surgery 1971
R Birth Rites 1973
↓ Female Genitalia 1973
Gynecology 1978
↓ Male Genitalia 1973
↓ Religious Practices 1973
↓ Rites of Passage 1973

Cirrhosis (Liver) 1973
PN 125 **SC** 09260
B Liver Disorders 1973
R Jaundice 1973

Citalopram 1997
PN 394 **SC** 09265
B Antidepressant Drugs 1971
Serotonin Reuptake Inhibitors 1997

Cities
Use Urban Environments

Citizen Participation
Use Community Involvement

Citizenship 1973
PN 326 **SC** 09280
SN Formal status or social quality of being a member of a community, country, or some other political designation.
R Immigration 1973
↓ Laws 1967
↓ Political Attitudes 1973

Civic Behavior
Use Community Involvement

Civil Law 1994
PN 276 **SC** 09284
B Law (Government) 1973
R ↓ Civil Rights 1978
Disability Laws 1994
↓ Law Enforcement 1978

Civil Law — (cont'd)
↓ Legal Processes 1973
Litigation 2003

Civil Rights 1978
PN 1565 **SC** 09288
SN Rights of personal liberty and equality guaranteed to citizens by constitution and legislation.
B Human Rights 1978
N ↓ Client Rights 1988
Equal Education 1978
R Advocacy 1985
Affirmative Action 1985
Age Discrimination 1994
Censorship 1978
Civil Law 1994
Civil Rights Movement 1973
Democracy 1973
Disability Discrimination 1997
Disability Laws 1994
Empowerment 1991
Freedom 1978
Informed Consent 1985
↓ Justice 1973
↓ Laws 1967
↓ Legal Processes 1973
Race and Ethnic Discrimination 1994
Sex Discrimination 1978
↓ Social Discrimination 1982
Social Equality 1973
↓ Social Integration 1982
↓ Social Issues 1991
↓ Social Movements 1967

Civil Rights Movement 1973
PN 153 **SC** 09290
SN Social and political effort to gain the constitutional rights of citizens, especially by minority groups whose rights have been denied. See SOCIAL MOVEMENTS for more specific terms.
B Social Movements 1967
R ↓ Activism 2003
↓ Civil Rights 1978

Civil Servants
Use Government Personnel

Clairvoyance 1973
PN 126 **SC** 09310
B Extrasensory Perception 1967
N Precognition 1973

Class Attitudes
Use Socioeconomic Class Attitudes

Class Size 2004
PN 34 **SC** 09325
HN This term was introduced in June 2004. Psyc-INFO records from the past 10 years were re-indexed with this term. The posting note reflects the number of records that were re-indexed.
B Group Size 1967
R Classroom Environment 1973
Classrooms 1967

Classical Conditioning 1967
PN 4417 **SC** 09330
SN Learned behavior or the experimental paradigm or procedure used to develop and evoke classically conditioned responses.
UF Conditioning (Classical)

Classical Conditioning — (cont'd)
Pavlovian Conditioning
Respondent Conditioning
B Conditioning 1967
N ↓ Conditioned Emotional Responses 1967
↓ Conditioned Responses 1967
Eyelid Conditioning 1973
Higher Order Conditioning 1997
Unconditioned Responses 1973
R Conditioned Stimulus 1973
Learning Theory 1967
Orienting Responses 1967
Pavlov (Ivan) 1991
Unconditioned Stimulus 1973

Classical Test Theory 2003
PN 16 **SC** 09335
SN A statistical approach in psychological measurement in which observed scores consist of both the true score and error.
HN This term was introduced in June 2003. Psyc-INFO records from the past 10 years were re-indexed with this term. The posting note reflects the number of records that were re-indexed.
B Testing 1967
Theories 1967
R Item Response Theory 1985
Psychometrics 1967
↓ Test Scores 1967

Classification (Cognitive Process) 1967
PN 7914 **SC** 09370
UF Categorizing
Sorting (Cognition)
B Cognitive Processes 1967
R Choice Behavior 1967

Classification Systems
Use Taxonomies

Classmates 1973
PN 70 **SC** 09400
B Students 1967

Classroom Behavior 1973
PN 4253 **SC** 09405
B Behavior 1967
R Classroom Behavior Modification 1973
Classroom Discipline 1973
Classroom Environment 1973
↓ Classroom Management 2004

Classroom Behavior Modification 1973
PN 2144 **SC** 09410
B Behavior Modification 1973
R Classroom Behavior 1973
Classroom Discipline 1973
↓ Classroom Management 2004
↓ Education 1967

Classroom Discipline 1973
PN 1261 **SC** 09420
UF Discipline (Classroom)
B Classroom Management 2004
R Classroom Behavior 1973
Classroom Behavior Modification 1973
↓ Education 1967
School Suspension 1973
Teacher Student Interaction 1973

Classroom Environment 1973
PN 4205 **SC** 09430

Classroom Environment — (cont'd)

SN Physical, social, emotional, psychological, or intellectual characteristics of a classroom, especially as they contribute to the learning process. Includes classroom climate and class size.
B Academic Environment 1973
R Class Size 2004
 Classroom Behavior 1973
 ↓ Classroom Management 2004
 Classrooms 1967
 Learning Environment 2004
 ↓ School Environment 1973
 School Violence 2003

Classroom Instruction

Use Teaching

Classroom Management 2004

PN 42 SC 09445
SN Ways in which teachers organize and manage the classroom environment to ensure order and promote learning.
HN This term was introduced in June 2004. Psyc-INFO records from the past 10 years were re-indexed with this term. The posting note reflects the number of records that were re-indexed.
B Management 1967
N Classroom Discipline 1973
R Classroom Behavior 1973
 Classroom Behavior Modification 1973
 Classroom Environment 1973

Classroom Teachers

Use Teachers

Classrooms 1967

PN 907 SC 09480
B School Facilities 1973
R Class Size 2004
 Classroom Environment 1973

Claustrophobia 1973

PN 84 SC 09470
B Phobias 1967

Cleft Palate 1967

PN 190 SC 09480
B Congenital Disorders 1973
 Neonatal Disorders 1973
R ↓ Speech Disorders 1967

Clergy 1973

PN 614 SC 09490
B Religious Personnel 1973
N Chaplains 1973
 Ministers (Religion) 1973
 Priests 1973
 Rabbis 1973
R Evangelists 1973
 Lay Religious Personnel 1973
 Missionaries 1973
 ↓ Religious Groups 1997

Clerical Personnel 1973

PN 546 SC 09500
UF Keypunch Operators
 Typists
B White Collar Workers 1973
R Secretarial Personnel 1973

Clerical Secretarial Skills 1973

PN 205 SC 09510
UF Secretarial Skills
B Employee Skills 1973
R Proofreading 1988
 Typing 1991
 Word Processing 1991

Client Abuse

Use Patient Abuse

Client Attitudes 1982

PN 6595 SC 09527
SN Attitudes of clients that may affect compliance with a particular treatment modality, or preferences for a particular type of treatment. May include attitudes toward health care professionals.
UF Patient Attitudes
B Attitudes 1967
 Client Characteristics 1973
N Client Satisfaction 1994
R Clients 1973
 Therapist Selection 1994
 Treatment Compliance 1982

Client Centered Therapy 1967

PN 979 SC 09530
UF Nondirective Therapy
 Person Centered Psychotherapy
 Rogerian Therapy
B Humanistic Psychotherapy 2003
 Psychotherapy 1967
R ↓ Humanistic Psychology 1985
 ↓ Psychotherapeutic Techniques 1967
 Rogers (Carl) 1991

Client Characteristics 1973

PN 11584 SC 09540
SN Physical, psychological, emotional, and other traits of individual clients or patients influencing the outcome of the therapeutic process.
UF Patient Characteristics
N ↓ Client Attitudes 1982
 ↓ Health Behavior 1982
 Illness Behavior 1982
 Patient Violence 1994
R Client Participation 1997
 Client Treatment Matching 1997
 Clients 1973
 ↓ Cross Cultural Treatment 1994
 Patient History 1973
 Patient Selection 1997
 ↓ Treatment Planning 1997

Client Compliance

Use Treatment Compliance

Client Counselor Interaction

Use Psychotherapeutic Processes

Client Dropouts

Use Treatment Dropouts

Client Education 1985

PN 1775 SC 09555
SN Informing or instructing patients or clients on the specifics of their disorder and/or its treatment. For client educational level use EDUCATIONAL BACKGROUND.
UF Patient Education
 Pretraining (Therapy)

Client Education — (cont'd)

B Education 1967
R ↓ Health Education 1973
 Health Knowledge 1994
 Health Promotion 1991
 Psychoeducation 1994
 ↓ Therapeutic Processes 1978
 Treatment Compliance 1982

Client Participation 1997

PN 374 SC 09556
UF Patient Participation
B Participation 1973
R ↓ Client Characteristics 1973
 ↓ Client Rights 1988
 Clients 1973
 ↓ Patients 1967
 Treatment Compliance 1982

Client Records 1997

PN 179 SC 57455
UF Patient Records
B Medical Records 1978
R Patient History 1973
 Privileged Communication 1973

Client Rights 1988

PN 939 SC 09557
SN Right of patient or client to be fully informed of benefits or risks of treatment procedures and to make informed decisions to accept or reject treatment.
UF Patient Rights
B Civil Rights 1978
N Right to Treatment 1997
R Advance Directives 1994
 Bioethics 2003
 Client Participation 1997
 Clients 1973
 Empowerment 1991
 Guardianship 1988
 ↓ Human Rights 1978
 Informed Consent 1985
 Involuntary Treatment 1994
 Life Sustaining Treatment 1997
 Quality of Care 1988
 ↓ Treatment 1967
 Treatment Compliance 1982
 Treatment Refusal 1994
 Treatment Withholding 1988

Client Satisfaction 1994

PN 1558 SC 09558
UF Patient Satisfaction
B Client Attitudes 1982
 Satisfaction 1973
R Clients 1973

Client Transfer 1997

PN 48 SC 57465
SN Transfer of client or patient care within or between treatment settings, therapists, or other health care providers.
UF Patient Transfer
R ↓ Facility Discharge 1988
 ↓ Hospital Discharge 1973
 Patient Selection 1997
 Professional Referral 1973
 Psychiatric Hospital Discharge 1978
 ↓ Treatment 1967
 Treatment Refusal 1994
 Treatment Termination 1982

Client Treatment Matching 1997
PN 443   SC 57470
SN Treatment selection based on matching the client's characteristics and needs with appropriate treatment modalities.
UF   Patient Treatment Matching
     Treatment Client Matching
R   ↓ Client Characteristics   1973
     Clinical Judgment (Not Diagnosis)   1973
     Patient Selection   1997
     ↓ Treatment   1967
     Treatment Guidelines   2001
     ↓ Treatment Outcomes   1982
     ↓ Treatment Planning   1997

Client Violence
Use   Patient Violence

Clients 1973
PN 2046   SC 09560
SN Persons receiving psychotherapy, counseling, or other mental health or social service. Consider also PATIENTS or one of its narrower terms.
UF   Counselees
R   ↓ Client Attitudes   1982
     ↓ Client Characteristics   1973
     Client Participation   1997
     ↓ Client Rights   1988
     Client Satisfaction   1994
     Patient Selection   1997

Climacteric Depression
Use   Involutional Depression

Climacteric Paranoia
Use   Involutional Paranoid Psychosis

Climate (Meteorological)
Use   Atmospheric Conditions

Climate (Organizational)
Use   Organizational Climate

Climax (Sexual)
Use   Orgasm

Clinical Judgment (Medical Diagnosis)
Use   Medical Diagnosis

Clinical Judgment (Not Diagnosis) 1973
PN 3613   SC 09620
SN Analysis, evaluation, or prediction of disordered or abnormal behavior, symptoms, or other aspects of psychological functioning. Includes assessing the appropriateness of a particular treatment and the degree or likelihood of clinical improvement.
B   Judgment   1967
R   Anatomically Detailed Dolls   1991
     Client Treatment Matching   1997
     ↓ Diagnosis   1967
     Geriatric Assessment   1997
     Intake Interview   1994
     ↓ Measurement   1967
     Prognosis   1973
     ↓ Psychiatric Evaluation   1997
     ↓ Psychodiagnosis   1967
     ↓ Psychodiagnostic Typologies   1967

Clinical Judgment (Not Diagnosis) — (cont'd)
     ↓ Psychological Assessment   1997
     ↓ Treatment Planning   1997

Clinical Judgment (Psychodiagnosis)
Use   Psychodiagnosis

Clinical Markers
Use   Biological Markers

Clinical Methods Training 1973
PN 2391   SC 09640
SN Instruction and skills training in methods for management and treatment of mental and behavior disorders. Includes training of populations such as parents, teachers, clergy, and administrators as well as mental health or medical personnel.
UF   Training (Clinical Methods)
B   Education   1967
N   ↓ Clinical Psychology Graduate Training   2001
     Clinical Psychology Internship   1973
     ↓ Community Mental Health Training   1973
     Psychiatric Training   1973
     Psychoanalytic Training   1973
     Psychotherapy Training   1973
R   Counselor Education   1973
     Microcounseling   1978
     Personal Therapy   1991
     Practicum Supervision   1978
     Theoretical Orientation   1982

Clinical Psychologists 1973
PN 1250   SC 09650
B   Mental Health Personnel   1967
     Psychologists   1967
R   Clinicians   1973
     Hypnotherapists   1973
     ↓ Psychotherapists   1973

Clinical Psychology 1967
PN 2380   SC 09660
B   Applied Psychology   1973
     Psychology   1967
N   Medical Psychology   1973

Clinical Psychology Graduate Training 2001
PN 1166   SC 09675
HN In 2000, the truncated term CLINICAL PSYCHOLOGY GRAD TRAINING (which was used from 1973-2000) was deleted, removed from all records containing it, and replaced with its expanded form, CLINICAL PSYCHOLOGY GRADUATE TRAINING.
UF   Training (Clinical Psychology Graduate)
B   Clinical Methods Training   1973
     Graduate Psychology Education   1967
     Postgraduate Training   1973
N   Clinical Psychology Internship   1973
R   Practicum Supervision   1978

Clinical Psychology Internship 1973
PN 410   SC 09680
B   Clinical Methods Training   1973
     Clinical Psychology Graduate Training   2001
     Postgraduate Training   1973
R   Practicum Supervision   1978

Clinical Supervision
Use   Professional Supervision

Clinical Trials 2004
PN 259   SC 09687
SN Systematic, planned studies to evaluate the safety and efficacy of drugs, devices, or diagnostic or therapeutic practices. Used only when the methodology is the focus of discussion.
HN This term was introduced in June 2004. PsycINFO records from the past 10 years were re-indexed with this term. The posting note reflects the number of records that were re-indexed.
B   Experimental Design   1967
R   ↓ Drug Therapy   1967
     Evidence Based Practice   2004
     Treatment Effectiveness Evaluation   1973

Clinicians 1973
PN 1195   SC 09690
B   Professional Personnel   1978
R   Clinical Psychologists   1973
     Counseling Psychologists   1988
     ↓ Medical Personnel   1967
     ↓ Mental Health Personnel   1967
     ↓ Physicians   1967
     Psychiatrists   1967
     ↓ Therapists   1967

Clinics 1967
PN 1037   SC 09700
B   Treatment Facilities   1973
N   Child Guidance Clinics   1973
     Psychiatric Clinics   1973
     Walk In Clinics   1973
R   Community Mental Health Centers   1973
     ↓ Crisis Intervention Services   1973
     ↓ Hospitals   1967
     ↓ Treatment   1967

Cliques
Use   Social Groups

Clomipramine
Use   Chlorimipramine

Clonazepam 1991
PN 196   SC 09735
B   Anticonvulsive Drugs   1973
     Benzodiazepines   1978
     Minor Tranquilizers   1973

Clonidine 1973
PN 1052   SC 09740
B   Antihypertensive Drugs   1973
     CNS Stimulating Drugs   1973

Cloning 2003
PN 14   SC 09742
SN Process of asexually reproducing an organism from a single cell of the original organism.
HN This term was introduced in June 2003. PsycINFO records from the past 10 years were re-indexed with this term. The posting note reflects the number of records that were re-indexed.
B   Genetic Engineering   1994
R   Deoxyribonucleic Acid   1973
     Reproductive Technology   1988

Closed Circuit Television 1973
PN 80   SC 09750
B   Television   1967

Closed Head Injuries
  Use   Head Injuries

Closedmindedness
  Use   Openmindedness

Closure (Perceptual)
  Use   Perceptual Closure

Clothing 1967
PN 902   SC 09770
  HN   Use CLOTHING FASHIONS to access references prior to 1991.
  B   Fads and Fashions 1973
  R   ↓ Physical Appearance 1982

Clozapine 1991
PN 2210   SC 09775
  B   Neuroleptic Drugs 1973
       Sedatives 1973

Cloze Testing 1973
PN 262   SC 09780
  SN   Tests or procedures assessing comprehension (e.g., reading or listening) in which the person being tested is required to provide missing components.
  B   Testing Methods 1967
  R   Sentence Completion Tests 1991

Clubs (Social Organizations) 1973
PN 135   SC 09790
  B   Recreation 1967

Cluster Analysis 1973
PN 1198   SC 09800
  UF   Clustering
  R   Statistical Analysis 1967

Clustering
  Use   Cluster Analysis

CNS Affecting Drugs 1973
PN 198   SC 09840
  UF   Central Nervous System Drugs
  B   Drugs 1967
  N   ↓ CNS Depressant Drugs 1973
  .   ↓ CNS Stimulating Drugs 1973
  R   ↓ Heart Rate Affecting Drugs 1973

CNS Depressant Drug Antagonists
  Use   Analeptic Drugs

CNS Depressant Drugs 1973
PN 95   SC 09860
  B   CNS Affecting Drugs 1973
  N   Amobarbital 1973
       Barbital 1973
       Chlorpromazine 1967
       Glutethimide 1973
       Haloperidol 1973
       Scopolamine 1973
  R   ↓ Analgesic Drugs 1973
       ↓ Anesthetic Drugs 1973
       ↓ Anticonvulsive Drugs 1973
       ↓ Barbiturates 1967
       ↓ Dopamine Antagonists 1982
       Flurazepam 1982
       ↓ Hypnotic Drugs 1973
       ↓ Muscle Relaxing Drugs 1973

CNS Depressant Drugs — (cont'd)
       ↓ Narcotic Drugs 1973
       ↓ Sedatives 1973

CNS Stimulating Drugs 1973
PN 1077   SC 09870
  UF   Psychostimulant Drugs
       Stimulants of CNS
  B   CNS Affecting Drugs 1973
  N   ↓ Amphetamine 1967
       ↓ Analeptic Drugs 1973
       Caffeine 1973
       Clonidine 1973
       Dextroamphetamine 1973
       Ephedrine 1973
       Methamphetamine 1973
       Methylphenidate 1973
       Pemoline 1978
       Pentylenetetrazol 1973
       Pipradrol 1973
       Piracetam 1982
  R   ↓ Antidepressant Drugs 1971
       ↓ Emetic Drugs 1973
       ↓ Heart Rate Affecting Drugs 1973
       Smokeless Tobacco 1994

Coaches 1988
PN 547   SC 09880
  HN   Use TEACHERS to access references from 1973-1987.
  R   Athletic Training 1991
       ↓ Sports 1967

Coagulation (Blood)
  Use   Blood Coagulation

Coalition Formation 1973
PN 292   SC 00010
  SN   Temporary alliance of distinct parties, persons, or states for joint action.
  B   Social Processes 1967
  R   ↓ Social Movements 1967

Coast Guard Personnel 1988
PN 21   SC 00915
  B   Military Personnel 1967

Cobalt 1973
PN 21   SC 09920
  B   Metallic Elements 1973

Cocaine 1973
PN 5981   SC 09930
  B   Alkaloids 1973
       Amines 1973
       Local Anesthetics 1973
  N   Crack Cocaine 2003

Cochlea 1973
PN 617   SC 09940
  UF   Organ of Corti
  B   Labyrinth (Anatomy) 1973
  R   Cochlear Implants 1994

Cochlear Implants 1994
PN 336   SC 09945
  B   Hearing Aids 1973
       Prostheses 1973
       Surgery 1971
  R   Cochlea 1973
       ↓ Deaf 1967

Cochlear Implants — (cont'd)
       ↓ Hearing Disorders 1982
       Partially Hearing Impaired 1973

Cochran Q Test 1973
PN 6   SC 09950
  UF   Q Test
  B   Nonparametric Statistical Tests 1967

Cockroaches 1973
PN 177   SC 09960
  B   Insects 1967
  R   Larvae 1973

Code Switching 1988
PN 193   SC 09965
  SN   Alternating use of languages, dialects, or language styles in speech.
  UF   Language Alternation
  B   Oral Communication 1985
  R   Bilingualism 1973
       Sociolinguistics 1985

Codeine 1973
PN 108   SC 09970
  UF   Codeine Sulfate
       Methylmorphine
  B   Alkaloids 1973
       Analgesic Drugs 1973
       Hypnotic Drugs 1973
       Opiates 1973

Codeine Sulfate
  Use   Codeine

Codependency 1991
PN 289   SC 09985
  R   ↓ Alcohol Abuse 1988
       Dependency (Personality) 1967
       Dependent Personality Disorder 1994
       ↓ Drug Abuse 1973
       Dysfunctional Family 1991
       ↓ Emotional Adjustment 1973
       Enabling 1997
       ↓ Family 1967
       ↓ Family Relations 1967
       ↓ Interpersonal Interaction 1967
       ↓ Marital Relations 1967
       ↓ Parent Child Relations 1967
       ↓ Personality Traits 1967

Coeds
  Use   College Students

Coeducation 1973
PN 158   SC 10000
  SN   Education of male and female students at the same institution.
  R   ↓ Education 1967
       Same Sex Education 2003
       ↓ Single Sex Environments 2001

Coercion 1994
PN 468   SC 10020
  B   Aggressive Behavior 1967
       Social Influences 1967
  R   Abuse of Power 1997
       Authority 1967
       Brainwashing 1982
       ↓ Dominance 1967
       Obedience 1973

Coercion — (cont'd)
- ↓ Persuasive Communication 1967
- ↓ Power 1967
- ↓ Punishment 1967
- ↓ Resistance 1997
- Threat 1967
- Torture 1988
- ↓ Violence 1973

Coffee
Use Beverages (Nonalcoholic)

Cognition 1967
PN 6364 **SC** 10040
SN Act or process of knowing which includes awareness and judgment, perceiving, reasoning, and conceiving.
- **R** ↓ Cognitive Development 1973
- Cognitive Impairment 2003
- ↓ Cognitive Processes 1967
- Cognitive Science 2003
- Intuition 1973
- Metacognition 1991
- Need for Cognition 1997

Cognition Enhancing Drugs
Use Nootropic Drugs

Cognitions 1985
PN 3740 **SC** 10045
SN The content of cognitive or thinking processes.
- **UF** Thought Content
- **N** ↓ Expectations 1967
- Irrational Beliefs 1982
- **R** ↓ Attitudes 1967
- Concepts 1967
- Mind 1991
- Rumination (Cognitive Process) 2001
- Schema 1988
- Thought Suppression 2003

Cognitive Ability 1973
PN 20577 **SC** 10050
SN Level of functioning in intellectual tasks.
- **UF** Cognitive Functioning
- Executive Functioning
- Intellectual Functioning
- **B** Ability 1967
- **N** Mathematical Ability 1973
- Reading Ability 1973
- ↓ Spatial Ability 1982
- Verbal Ability 1967
- **R** Cognitive Assessment 1997
- Cognitive Impairment 2003
- Cognitive Processing Speed 1997
- Metacognition 1991

Cognitive Appraisal 2004
PN 73 **SC** 10051
SN Evaluation of an event or situation leading to an emotional response.
HN This term was introduced in June 2004. Psyc-INFO records from the past 10 years were re-indexed with this term. The posting note reflects the number of records that were re-indexed.
- **B** Cognitive Processes 1967
- **R** ↓ Emotional Responses 1967

Cognitive Assessment 1997
PN 1127 **SC** 10053

Cognitive Assessment — (cont'd)
SN Used only for references that focus on the assessment process or the particular assessment itself.
- **UF** Assessment (Cognitive)
- **B** Psychological Assessment 1997
- **R** ↓ Cognitive Ability 1973
- ↓ Cognitive Processes 1967
- ↓ Intelligence 1967
- ↓ Intelligence Measures 1967
- Intelligence Quotient 1967
- ↓ Neuropsychological Assessment 1982
- ↓ Psychiatric Evaluation 1997

Cognitive Behavior Therapy 2003
PN 308 **SC** 10055
SN An integrated approach to psychotherapy that combines the techniques of cognitive and behavior therapy.
HN Use COGNITIVE THERAPY to access references from 1982 to June 2003.
- **B** Psychotherapy 1967
- **R** ↓ Behavior Modification 1973
- ↓ Behavior Therapy 1967
- Cognitive Restructuring 1985
- Cognitive Therapy 1982

Cognitive Complexity 1973
PN 1093 **SC** 10060
SN Conceptual, behavioral, or perceptual dimensions of thinking style that characterize an individual's differentiation or processing of stimuli.
- **UF** Complexity (Cognitive)
- **B** Cognitive Style 1967

Cognitive Contiguity 1973
PN 52 **SC** 10070
SN View of memory organization which holds that events that are experienced together tend to become associated with each other in memory.
- **UF** Contiguity (Cognitive)
- **B** Associative Processes 1967

Cognitive Deficits
Use Cognitive Impairment

Cognitive Development 1973
PN 16613 **SC** 10080
SN Acquisition of conscious thought, reasoning, symbol manipulation, and problem solving abilities beginning in infancy and following an orderly sequence. Compare INTELLECTUAL DEVELOPMENT.
- **B** Psychogenesis 1973
- **N** ↓ Intellectual Development 1973
- ↓ Language Development 1967
- ↓ Perceptual Development 1973
- **R** Cognition 1967
- ↓ Concept Formation 1967
- Conservation (Concept) 1973
- Constructivism 1994
- Egocentrism 1978
- Object Permanence 1985
- Piaget (Jean) 1967
- ↓ Speech Development 1973
- Theory of Mind 2001

Cognitive Discrimination 1973
PN 1153 **SC** 10090
SN Ability to distinguish between examples vs non-examples of a concept, based on the presence or absence of its defining attributes.

Cognitive Discrimination — (cont'd)
- **UF** Discrimination (Cognitive)
- **B** Cognitive Processes 1967
- Concept Formation 1967
- Discrimination 1967
- **R** ↓ Lexical Access 1988
- Lexical Decision 1988
- Stroop Effect 1988
- Visual Search 1982

Cognitive Dissonance 1967
PN 1344 **SC** 10100
SN Psychological conflict resulting from incongruous beliefs or attitudes held simultaneously, or from inconsistency between belief and behavior.
- **UF** Dissonance (Cognitive)
- **R** ↓ Cognitive Processes 1967
- Psychological Reactance 1978

Cognitive Dysfunction
Use Cognitive Impairment

Cognitive Functioning
Use Cognitive Ability

Cognitive Generalization 1967
PN 656 **SC** 10110
SN Ability to evaluate the equivalence of an example of a concept or object across different contexts or modalities.
- **UF** Generalization (Cognitive)
- **B** Cognitive Processes 1967
- Concept Formation 1967
- **R** ↓ Associative Processes 1967
- Semantic Generalization 1973

Cognitive Hypothesis Testing 1982
PN 552 **SC** 10112
SN Problem solving behavior in which the individual derives a set of rules (hypotheses) that are then sampled and tested until the one rule is discovered that consistently results in correct responding to the problem.
HN Use HYPOTHESIS TESTING or other appropriate terms to access references prior to 1982.
- **UF** Hypothesis Testing (Cognitive)
- Rule Learning
- **B** Learning 1967
- Problem Solving 1967
- **R** ↓ Concept Formation 1967
- Heuristics 2003
- ↓ Reasoning 1967

Cognitive Impairment 2003
PN 1288 **SC** 10113
SN Impaired mental or intellectual functioning.
HN This term was introduced in June 2003. Psyc-INFO records from the past 10 years were re-indexed with this term. The posting note reflects the number of records that were re-indexed.
- **UF** Cognitive Deficits
- Cognitive Dysfunction
- **R** ↓ Brain Damage 1967
- Cognition 1967
- ↓ Cognitive Ability 1973
- ↓ Dementia 1985
- ↓ Memory Disorders 1973
- ↓ Mental Retardation 1967
- ↓ Thought Disturbances 1973

Cognitive Load
  Use   Human Channel Capacity

Cognitive Maps   1982
PN   1326   **SC**   10117
SN   Mental representations of spatial environments that allow for the planning and execution of movement within them.
  B   Cognitive Processes   1967
  R   Direction Perception   1997
         Mental Models   2003
         Schema   1988
         Spatial Imagery   1982
         ↓ Spatial Memory   1988
         Spatial Organization   1973
         Spatial Orientation (Perception)   1973

Cognitive Mediation   1967
PN   1232   **SC**   10120
SN   Intervention of cognitive processes between observable stimuli and responses, resulting in a change in subsequent behavior.
  UF   Mediation (Cognitive)
  B   Cognitive Processes   1967
  R   Naming   1988

Cognitive Processes   1967
PN   36190   **SC**   10130
SN   Mental processes involved in the acquisition, processing, and utilization of knowledge or information.
  UF   Human Information Processes
        Information Processes (Human)
  N   ↓ Associative Processes   1967
        Chunking   2004
        Classification (Cognitive Process)   1967
        Cognitive Appraisal   2004
        Cognitive Discrimination   1973
        Cognitive Generalization   1967
        Cognitive Maps   1982
        Cognitive Mediation   1967
        ↓ Comprehension   1967
        Concentration   1982
        ↓ Concept Formation   1967
        ↓ Decision Making   1967
        ↓ Fantasy   1997
        ↓ Ideation   1973
        Imagination   1967
        Intuition   1973
        Mental Rotation   1991
        Metacognition   1991
        Naming   1988
        ↓ Problem Solving   1967
        Rumination (Cognitive Process)   2001
        Schema   1988
        Semantic Generalization   1973
        Social Cognition   1994
        ↓ Thinking   1967
        Thought Suppression   2003
        Transposition (Cognition)   1973
  R   ↓ Artificial Intelligence   1982
        Cognition   1967
        Cognitive Assessment   1997
        Cognitive Dissonance   1967
        Cognitive Processing Speed   1997
        Cognitive Psychology   1985
        ↓ Conflict Resolution   1982
        Connectionism   1994
        Declarative Knowledge   1997
        Generation Effect (Learning)   1991
        Human Information Storage   1973
        ↓ Learning   1967
        ↓ Learning Strategies   1991

Cognitive Processes   —   (cont'd)
        ↓ Memory   1967
        Mind   1991
        Procedural Knowledge   1997
        Questioning   1982
        Reality Testing   1973
        ↓ Spatial Ability   1982
        ↓ Strategies   1967
        Word Associations   1967

Cognitive Processing Speed   1997
PN   672   **SC**   10133
  UF   Information Processing Speed
  R   ↓ Cognitive Ability   1973
        ↓ Cognitive Processes   1967
        ↓ Cognitive Style   1967
        Conceptual Tempo   1985
        Human Channel Capacity   1973
        Reaction Time   1967
        Response Latency   1967

Cognitive Psychology   1985
PN   2442   **SC**   10135
SN   Branch of psychology concerned with aspects of behavior as they relate to mental processes.
  B   Psychology   1967
  R   ↓ Cognitive Processes   1967
        Cognitive Science   2003
        Connectionism   1994

Cognitive Rehabilitation   1985
PN   1043   **SC**   10136
SN   Procedures used to restore or enhance the cognitive functioning level of individuals with mental disability, injury, or disease (e.g., brain damaged stroke patients).
  B   Neuropsychological Rehabilitation   1997
        Rehabilitation   1967
  R   Memory Training   1994

Cognitive Restructuring   1985
PN   440   **SC**   10137
SN   Cognitive technique for altering self-defeating thought patterns by first identifying and analyzing negative self-statements and then developing adaptive self-statements.
  B   Cognitive Techniques   1985
  R   ↓ Behavior Modification   1973
        Cognitive Behavior Therapy   2003
        Cognitive Therapy   1982

Cognitive Science   2003
PN   268   **SC**   10139
SN   Study of cognition from a multidisciplinary approach involving the disciplines of psychology, linguistics, computer science, and artificial intelligence.
HN   This term was introduced in June 2003. Psyc-INFO records from the past 10 years were re-indexed with this term. The posting note reflects the number of records that were re-indexed.
  B   Sciences   1967
  R   ↓ Artificial Intelligence   1982
        Cognition   1967
        Cognitive Psychology   1985
        ↓ Linguistics   1973
        ↓ Neurosciences   1973

Cognitive Style   1967
PN   6714   **SC**   10140
SN   Preferred or habitual style of learning or thinking.
  UF   Learning Style

Cognitive Style   —   (cont'd)
  B   Personality Traits   1967
  N   Cognitive Complexity   1973
        Conceptual Tempo   1985
        Field Dependence   1973
        Impulsiveness   1973
        Reflectiveness   1997
  R   Cognitive Processing Speed   1997
        ↓ Learning Strategies   1991
        Neurolinguistic Programming   2001
        Perceptual Style   1973
        ↓ Personality   1967
        Schema   1988

Cognitive Techniques   1985
PN   1162   **SC**   10142
SN   Methods directed at producing change in thought patterns that may result in changes in affect and behavior.
  B   Treatment   1967
  N   Cognitive Restructuring   1985
        Cognitive Therapy   1982
        Self Instructional Training   1985
  R   Anxiety Management   1997
        Stress Management   1985

Cognitive Therapy   1982
PN   8404   **SC**   10144
SN   Directive therapy based on the belief that the way one perceives and structures the world determines one's feelings and behavior. Treatment aims at altering cognitive schema and hence permitting the patient to change his/her distorted self-view and world view.
  B   Cognitive Techniques   1985
  R   Anxiety Management   1997
        ↓ Behavior Modification   1973
        Cognitive Behavior Therapy   2003
        Cognitive Restructuring   1985
        ↓ Psychotherapy   1967
        Rational Emotive Behavior Therapy   2003
        Self Instructional Training   1985
        ↓ Self Management   1985

Cohabitation   1973
PN   470   **SC**   10150
SN   Primarily, but not exclusively, used for unmarried couples living together.
  B   Living Arrangements   1991
  R   Couples   1982
        ↓ Family   1967
        Living Alone   1994
        Roommates   1973

Cohesion (Group)
  Use   Group Cohesion

Cohort Analysis   1988
PN   542   **SC**   10165
SN   Analysis of the effects attributed to being a member of a group sharing a particular characteristic, experience, or event. Use AGE DIFFERENCES for effects attributable to normal biological, cognitive, or psychosocial maturation.
  B   Analysis   1967
        Experimental Design   1967
        Methodology   1967
  R   Age Differences   1967
        Generation Gap   1973

Coitus
  Use   Sexual Intercourse (Human)

Coitus (Animal)
Use Animal Mating Behavior

Cold Effects 1973
PN 728   **SC** 10200
B Temperature Effects 1967

Colitis 1973
PN 48   **SC** 10220
B Colon Disorders 1973
N Ulcerative Colitis 1973
R Gastrointestinal Ulcers 1967
Irritable Bowel Syndrome 1991

Collaboration
Use Cooperation

Collective Behavior 1967
PN 2918   **SC** 10250
SN Behaviors which characterize groups or individuals acting in groups, usually working toward or achieving a specific goal. Used for human or animal populations.
B Interpersonal Interaction 1967
N Riots 1973
R Contagion 1988
Entrapment Games 1973
↓ Group Dynamics 1967
Group Participation 1973
Mass Hysteria 1973
Social Demonstrations 1973
↓ Sociometry 1991

Collective Unconscious 1997
PN 69   **SC** 10255
SN Genetically determined part of the unconscious shared by all members of a species or race of people.
HN Consider JUNGIAN PSYCHOLOGY to access references prior to 1997.
B Jungian Psychology 1973
N Archetypes 1991
R Analytical Psychotherapy 1973
Jung (Carl) 1973

College Academic Achievement 1967
PN 5195   **SC** 10260
B Academic Achievement 1967

College Athletes 1994
PN 523   **SC** 10270
B Athletes 1973
College Students 1967
R Athletic Participation 1973
Athletic Performance 1991
Athletic Training 1991
↓ Sports 1967
↓ Teams 1988

College Degrees
Use Educational Degrees

College Dropouts 1973
PN 450   **SC** 10290
B School Dropouts 1967

College Education
Use Undergraduate Education

College Entrance Examination Board Scholastic Aptitude Test 2001
PN 354   **SC** 10235
HN In 2001, the truncated term COLL ENT EXAM BD SCHOLASTIC APT TEST (which was used from 1973-2000) was deleted, removed from all records containing it, and replaced with its expanded form, COLLEGE ENTRANCE EXAMINATION BOARD SCHOLASTIC APTITUDE TEST.
UF Preliminary Scholastic Aptitude Test
SAT
Scholastic Aptitude Test
B Aptitude Measures 1967
Entrance Examinations 1973

College Environment 1973
PN 1357   **SC** 10300
SN Social or emotional climate or physical setting of a college or university.
B School Environment 1973
R ↓ Colleges 1967
Community Colleges 1978

College Graduates 1982
PN 383   **SC** 10304
R ↓ College Students 1967
Educational Degrees 1973
School Graduation 1991
School to Work Transition 1994

College Major
Use Academic Specialization

College Students 1967
PN 31320   **SC** 10320
SN Students attending an institution of higher education.
UF Coeds
Undergraduates
B Students 1967
N College Athletes 1994
Community College Students 1973
Education Students 1982
Junior College Students 1973
Nursing Students 1973
ROTC Students 1973
R College Graduates 1982
Graduate Students 1967
Postgraduate Students 1973
Preservice Teachers 1982
Reentry Students 1985

College Teachers 1973
PN 4014   **SC** 10330
UF Professors
B Teachers 1967

Colleges 1967
PN 3023   **SC** 10350
UF Junior Colleges
Universities
B Schools 1967
N Community Colleges 1978
R College Environment 1973
↓ Higher Education 1973
Military Schools 1973

Colon Disorders 1973
PN 350   **SC** 10370
UF Bowel Disorders
B Gastrointestinal Disorders 1973

Colon Disorders — (cont'd)
N ↓ Colitis 1973
Constipation 1973
Diarrhea 1973
Fecal Incontinence 1973
Irritable Bowel Syndrome 1991

Color 1967
PN 2788   **SC** 10380
SN Property of matter or light sources that corresponds to the relative reflectance or absorption of incident light and the wavelength of the incident light or light source. Color is described perceptually by the dimensions of hue, lightness, brightness, and saturation. Compare HUE.
N Achromatic Color 1973
Eye Color 1991
Hue 1973
R ↓ Chromaticity 1997
Color Saturation 1997
↓ Pigments 1973
↓ Visual Stimulation 1973

Color Blindness 1973
PN 295   **SC** 10390
B Eye Disorders 1973
R ↓ Color Perception 1967
↓ Genetic Disorders 1973

Color Constancy 1985
PN 128   **SC** 10395
SN The tendency to perceive hue, brightness, and saturation as stable despite objective changes in context and illumination.
B Color Perception 1967
Perceptual Constancy 1985

Color Contrast 1985
PN 214   **SC** 10397
B Color Perception 1967
Visual Contrast 1985

Color Perception 1967
PN 3970   **SC** 10400
UF Spectral Sensitivity
B Visual Perception 1967
N Color Constancy 1985
Color Contrast 1985
R ↓ Chromaticity 1997
Color Blindness 1973
Color Saturation 1997
Prismatic Stimulation 1973

Color Pyramid Test
Use Projective Personality Measures

Color Saturation 1997
PN 19   **SC** 10420
SN The degree of purity or richness of a color.
UF Saturation (Color)
B Chromaticity 1997
R Achromatic Color 1973
↓ Color 1967
↓ Color Perception 1967
Hue 1973
Luminance 1982

Colostomy 1973
PN 41   **SC** 10430
B Surgery 1971

Columbia Mental Maturity Scale 1973
PN 14   SC 10440
  B   Intelligence Measures 1967

Coma 1973
PN 345   SC 10450
  B   Symptoms 1967
  R ↓ Cerebrovascular Accidents 1973
     ↓ Cerebrovascular Disorders 1973
     ↓ Consciousness Disturbances 1973
     ↓ Epileptic Seizures 1973
     ↓ Injuries 1973
       Insulin Shock Therapy 1973

Combat Experience 1991
PN 849   SC 10452
  SN Direct participation in war.
  R ↓ Experiences (Events) 1973
     ↓ Military Personnel 1967
       Posttraumatic Stress Disorder 1985
     ↓ War 1967

Comfort (Physical)
  Use Physical Comfort

Commerce
  Use Business

Commercials
  Use Television Advertising

Commissioned Officers 1973
PN 271   SC 10470
  SN Military officers who have received a formal cer-
tificate granting rank and authority and who thereby
hold a position of command.
  UF   Military Officers
       Officers (Commissioned)
  B   Military Personnel 1967
  R ↓ Management Personnel 1973
       Volunteer Military Personnel 1973

Commissurotomy 1985
PN 314   SC 10475
  UF   Split Brain
  B   Neurosurgery 1973
  R   Corpus Callosum 1973

Commitment 1985
PN 1624   SC 10478
  SN The process or extent of devoting one's efforts
or resources to an activity, task, or interpersonal rela-
tionship.
  N   Organizational Commitment 1991
  R ↓ Involvement 1973
     ↓ Motivation 1967

Commitment (Outpatient)
  Use Outpatient Commitment

Commitment (Psychiatric) 1973
PN 1225   SC 10480
  B   Hospitalization 1967
       Legal Processes 1973
  N   Outpatient Commitment 1991
  R   Court Referrals 1994
       Guardianship 1988
       Health Care Seeking Behavior 1997
     ↓ Institutional Release 1978

Commitment (Psychiatric) — (cont'd)
       Involuntary Treatment 1994
     ↓ Psychiatric Hospital Admission 1973
       Psychiatric Hospital Discharge 1978
     ↓ Psychiatric Hospitalization 1973
       Right to Treatment 1997
       Self Referral 1991

Communes 1973
PN 105   SC 10510
  B   Communities 1967
  N   Kibbutz 1973

Communicable Diseases
  Use Infectious Disorders

Communication 1967
PN 6168   SC 10570
  SN Conceptually broad term referring to the trans-
mission of verbal or nonverbal information. Use a
more specific term if possible.
  UF   Information Exchange
  N ↓ Animal Communication 1967
     ↓ Augmentative Communication 1994
     ↓ Electronic Communication 2001
     ↓ Interpersonal Communication 1973
     ↓ Nonverbal Communication 1971
     ↓ Persuasive Communication 1967
       Scientific Communication 1973
     ↓ Verbal Communication 1967
  R   Censorship 1978
     ↓ Communication Skills 1973
       Communication Skills Training 1982
     ↓ Communication Systems 1973
       Communication Theory 1973
     ↓ Communications Media 1973
     ↓ Content Analysis 1978
       Emotional Content 1973
       Information 1967
       Messages 1973
       Privileged Communication 1973
       Rhetoric 1991
       Symbolism 1967
     ↓ Vocalization 1967
     ↓ Voice 1973

Communication (Privileged)
  Use Privileged Communication

Communication (Professional)
  Use Scientific Communication

Communication Apprehension
  Use Speech Anxiety

Communication Disorders 1982
PN 871   SC 10533
  SN Impaired ability to communicate usually, due to
speech, language, or hearing disorders.
  B   Disorders 1967
  N ↓ Hearing Disorders 1982
     ↓ Language Disorders 1982
     ↓ Speech Disorders 1967
  R ↓ Augmentative Communication 1994
     ↓ Communication Skills 1973
       Communication Skills Training 1982
       Developmental Disabilities 1982
     ↓ Mental Disorders 1967
     ↓ Physical Disorders 1997
       Speech Anxiety 1985
       Speech Therapy 1967

Communication Skills 1973
PN 3436   SC 10540
  SN Individual ability or competency in any type of
communication. Limited to human populations.
  UF   Communicative Competence
  B   Ability 1967
  N   Language Proficiency 1988
       Rhetoric 1991
       Writing Skills 1985
  R ↓ Communication 1967
     ↓ Communication Disorders 1982
       Communication Skills Training 1982
       Pragmatics 1985
       Social Cognition 1994
     ↓ Verbal Communication 1967

Communication Skills Training 1982
PN 1412   SC 10542
  SN Instruction, usually group oriented, to increase
quality and capability of interpersonal communica-
tion.
  B   Education 1967
  R   Assertiveness Training 1978
     ↓ Behavior Modification 1973
     ↓ Communication 1967
     ↓ Communication Disorders 1982
     ↓ Communication Skills 1973
       Human Relations Training 1978
       Sensitivity Training 1973
     ↓ Skill Learning 1973
       Social Skills Training 1982

Communication Systems 1973
PN 907   SC 10550
  SN Organized schemes for transmitting and receiv-
ing information.
  B   Systems 1967
  N   Internet 2001
       Telephone Systems 1973
  R ↓ Automated Information Processing 1973
     ↓ Communication 1967
     ↓ Electronic Communication 2001
     ↓ Information Systems 1991

Communication Theory 1973
PN 444   SC 10560
  B   Theories 1967
  R ↓ Communication 1967
       Cybernetics 1967
       Information Theory 1967

Communications Media 1973
PN 917   SC 10580
  UF   Media (Communications)
  N ↓ Audiovisual Communications Media 1973
     ↓ Mass Media 1967
     ↓ Telecommunications Media 1973
  R   Censorship 1978
     ↓ Communication 1967
       Computer Mediated Communication 2003
     ↓ Electronic Communication 2001

Communicative Competence
  Use Communication Skills

Communism 1973
PN 636   SC 10590
  UF   Marxism
  B   Political Economic Systems 1973

Communities 1967
PN 4062   SC 10600

Communities — (cont'd)
- B   Social Environments 1973
- N ↓ Communes 1973
  - Neighborhoods 1973
  - Retirement Communities 1997
- R   Community Development 1997
  - Community Involvement 2003

Community Attitudes 1973
PN 1437   SC 10620
SN Attitudes which characterize a group of individuals living in close proximity and organized into a social structure, however tenuous.
- B   Attitudes 1967
- R   Public Opinion 1973

Community College Students 1973
PN 1213   SC 10627
SN Students attending public postsecondary institutions offering 2-year degree programs and transfer components.
- B   College Students 1967
- R   Junior College Students 1973

Community Colleges 1978
PN 431   SC 10630
- B   Colleges 1967
- R   College Environment 1973
-    ↓ Community Facilities 1973

Community Development 1997
PN 228   SC 10635
- UF Rural Development
  - Urban Development
- B   Development 1967
- R ↓ Communities 1967
  - Community Involvement 2003
  - ↓ Community Services 1967
  - Modernization 2003
  - Rural Environments 1967
  - ↓ Urban Environments 1967
  - Urban Planning 1973

Community Facilities 1973
PN 640   SC 10640
- N   Community Mental Health Centers 1973
  - ↓ Housing 1973
  - Public Transportation 1973
  - Shopping Centers 1973
  - Suicide Prevention Centers 1973
- R   Child Guidance Clinics 1973
  - Community Colleges 1978
  - ↓ Community Services 1967
  - Day Care Centers 1973
  - Group Homes 1982
  - Halfway Houses 1973
  - ↓ Libraries 1982
  - ↓ Recreation Areas 1973
  - ↓ Rehabilitation Centers 1973
  - Religious Buildings 1973
  - ↓ Schools 1967
  - Sheltered Workshops 1967
  - Shelters 1991
  - Urban Planning 1973

Community Involvement 2003
PN 87   SC 10644
SN Involvement of an individual in community activities.
HN This term was introduced in June 2003. Psyc-INFO records from the past 10 years were re-indexed with this term. The posting note reflects the number of records that were re-indexed.

Community Involvement — (cont'd)
- UF Citizen Participation
  - Civic Behavior
- B   Involvement 1973
- R ↓ Activism 2003
  - ↓ Communities 1967
  - Community Development 1997
  - ↓ Community Services 1967
  - ↓ Prosocial Behavior 1982
  - Volunteers 2003

Community Mental Health 1973
PN 650   SC 10647
SN General psychological well being or adjustment of persons in a given area.
- B   Mental Health 1967
- R   Community Mental Health Centers 1973
  - Community Mental Health Services 1978
  - ↓ Community Mental Health Training 1973
  - Community Psychiatry 1973
  - Community Psychology 1973
  - Deinstitutionalization 1982
  - ↓ Mental Health Programs 1973

Community Mental Health Centers 1973
PN 1843   SC 10650
- UF Mental Health Centers (Community)
- B   Community Facilities 1973
  - Treatment Facilities 1973
- R   Child Guidance Clinics 1973
  - ↓ Clinics 1967
  - Community Mental Health 1973
  - Community Mental Health Services 1978
  - ↓ Crisis Intervention Services 1973
  - Day Care Centers 1973
  - Hot Line Services 1973
  - ↓ Mental Health Programs 1973
  - ↓ Mental Health Services 1978
  - Psychiatric Clinics 1973
  - Suicide Prevention Centers 1973

Community Mental Health Services 1978
PN 4331   SC 10656
- B   Community Services 1967
  - Mental Health Services 1978
- R   Community Mental Health 1973
  - Community Mental Health Centers 1973
  - Community Psychiatry 1973
  - Community Psychology 1973
  - Deinstitutionalization 1982
  - Group Homes 1982
  - ↓ Mental Health 1967
  - ↓ Mental Health Programs 1973
  - Outreach Programs 1997
  - Supported Employment 1994

Community Mental Health Training 1973
PN 343   SC 10660
- UF Mental Health Training (Community)
  - Training (Community Mental Health)
- B   Clinical Methods Training 1973
- N   Mental Health Inservice Training 1973
- R   Community Mental Health 1973
  - ↓ Mental Health Programs 1973

Community Psychiatry 1973
PN 463   SC 10670
SN Branch of psychiatry concerned with the provision and delivery of community health care needs such as diagnosis; treatment; primary, secondary, and tertiary prevention; rehabilitation; and aftercare. Such services are usually delivered at community mental health centers.

Community Psychiatry — (cont'd)
- B   Psychiatry 1967
- R   Community Mental Health 1973
  - Community Mental Health Services 1978
  - Community Psychology 1973
  - ↓ Mental Health 1967
  - ↓ Mental Health Programs 1973

Community Psychology 1973
PN 966   SC 10680
SN Branch of psychology that emphasizes the analysis of social processes and interactions and design of social interventions within groups and the community.
- B   Applied Psychology 1973
- R   Community Mental Health 1973
  - Community Mental Health Services 1978
  - Community Psychiatry 1973
  - ↓ Mental Health Programs 1973

Community Services 1967
PN 6748   SC 10690
- B   Social Services 1982
- N   Community Mental Health Services 1978
  - Community Welfare Services 1973
  - ↓ Crisis Intervention Services 1973
  - Home Visiting Programs 1973
  - Public Health Services 1973
- R   Alcoholics Anonymous 1973
  - Community Development 1997
  - ↓ Community Facilities 1973
  - Community Involvement 2003
  - ↓ Health Care Services 1978
  - Independent Living Programs 1991
  - Integrated Services 1997
  - ↓ Mental Health Programs 1973
  - ↓ Mental Health Services 1978
  - Outreach Programs 1997
  - ↓ Self Help Techniques 1982
  - Shelters 1991
  - ↓ Support Groups 1991

Community Welfare Services 1973
PN 292   SC 10700
- UF Public Welfare Services
- B   Community Services 1967
- R   Welfare Services (Government) 1973

Commuting (Travel) 1985
PN 108   SC 10705
- R   Geographical Mobility 1978
  - Telecommuting 2003
  - ↓ Transportation 1973
  - Traveling 1973

Comorbidity 1991
PN 6961   SC 10707
SN Coexistence of two or more physical and/or mental disorders.
- R ↓ Diagnosis 1967
  - Differential Diagnosis 1967
  - ↓ Disorders 1967
  - Dual Diagnosis 1991
  - ↓ Mental Disorders 1967
  - Mental Disorders due to General Medical Conditions 2001
  - ↓ Physical Disorders 1997
  - Psychopathology 1967

Companies
Use Business Organizations

Comparative Psychiatry
  Use Transcultural Psychiatry

Comparative Psychology 1967
PN 1274 **SC** 10720
SN Branch of psychology devoted to the study of behavioral differences between organisms of different species. Use SPECIES DIFFERENCES for comparative studies.
  HN Prior to 1982, also used for comparative studies. From 1982, limited to the scientific discipline.
  B Psychology 1967
  R ↓ Animal Learning 2003

Compatibility (Interpersonal)
  Use Interpersonal Compatibility

Compensation (Defense Mechanism) 1973
PN 89 **SC** 10740
SN Defense mechanism of covering up or making up for conscious or unconscious insecurity or feelings of failure.
  B Defense Mechanisms 1967

Compensatory Education 1973
PN 245 **SC** 10745
SN Education designed to enhance intellectual and social skills of disadvantaged students, and to compensate for environmental, experiential, cultural, or economic deficits. Compare REMEDIAL EDUCATION.
  B Curriculum 1967
  R I Educational Programs 1973
  Project Follow Through 1973
  Project Head Start 1973
  ↓ Remedial Education 1985
  Upward Bound 1973

Competence 1982
PN 4478 **SC** 10747
SN Possession of sufficient skills, knowledge, or qualities as required in a given situation.
  N Professional Competence 1997
  R ↓ Ability 1967
  Accountability 1988
  ↓ Achievement 1967
  Competency to Stand Trial 1985
  Minimum Competency Tests 1985
  ↓ Performance 1967
  Social Skills 1978

Competence (Social)
  Use Social Skills

Competency to Stand Trial 1985
PN 488 **SC** 10749
  B Legal Processes 1973
  R ↓ Competence 1982
  Criminal Responsibility 1991
  Forensic Evaluation 1994
  Mentally Ill Offenders 1985

Competition 1967
PN 4084 **SC** 10750
SN Used for human and animal populations.
  B Social Behavior 1967
  R Rivalry 1973

Complementary Medicine
  Use Alternative Medicine

Complexity (Cognitive)
  Use Cognitive Complexity

Complexity (Stimulus)
  Use Stimulus Complexity

Complexity (Task)
  Use Task Complexity

Compliance 1973
PN 2007 **SC** 10810
SN Limited to human populations.
  B Social Behavior 1967
  N Treatment Compliance 1982
  R Obedience 1973
  ↓ Resistance 1997

Comprehension 1967
PN 4692 **SC** 10820
SN Knowledge or understanding of communications, objects, events, or situations as relates to their meaning, significance, relationships, or general principles.
  UF Understanding
  B Cognitive Processes 1967
  N Number Comprehension 1970
  ↓ Verbal Comprehension 1985
  R Intuition 1973
  ↓ Meaning 1967
  Meaningfulness 1967
  Metacognition 1991
  Theory of Mind 2001

Comprehension Tests 1973
PN 65 **SC** 10830
  B Measurement 1967

Compressed Speech 1973
PN 155 **SC** 10840
  B Speech Processing (Mechanical) 1973

Compulsions 1973
PN 813 **SC** 10850
  N Compulsive Repetition 1973
  R ↓ Hoarding Behavior 2003
  Obsessions 1967
  Obsessive Compulsive Disorder 1985
  Obsessive Compulsive Personality Disorder 1973
  Perfectionism 1988

Compulsive Gambling
  Use Pathological Gambling

Compulsive Neurosis
  Use Obsessive Compulsive Disorder

Compulsive Personality Disorder
  Use Obsessive Compulsive Personality Disorder

Compulsive Repetition 1973
PN 186 **SC** 10890
  UF Repetition (Compulsive)
  B Compulsions 1973

Compulsivity (Sexual)
  Use Sexual Addiction

Computer Anxiety 2001
PN 48 **SC** 10897
  B Anxiety 1967
  R Computer Attitudes 1988
  Computer Literacy 1991

Computer Applications 1973
PN 7248 **SC** 10900
SN Application of computers, computer technology, or software to any area.
  N ↓ Artificial Intelligence 1982
  Computer Assisted Design 1997
  Computer Assisted Diagnosis 1973
  ↓ Computer Assisted Instruction 1973
  Computer Assisted Testing 1988
  ↓ Computer Simulation 1973
  Groupware 2003
  Hypermedia 1997
  Hypertext 1997
  R Automated Speech Recognition 1994
  Computer Mediated Communication 2003
  ↓ Computer Peripheral Devices 1985
  Computer Searching 1991
  ↓ Computers 1967
  Databases 1991
  Decision Support Systems 1997
  ↓ Electronic Communication 2001
  ↓ Information Systems 1991
  Internet 2001
  Microcomputers 1985
  Online Therapy 2003
  Virtual Reality 1997
  Word Processing 1991

Computer Assisted Design 1997
PN 82 **SC** 10905
SN Use of a computer system to design a product so that it can be displayed, manipulated, and revised or modified quickly and easily.
  B Computer Applications 1973
  R ↓ Architecture 1973
  ↓ Computer Simulation 1973
  ↓ Computer Software 1967
  ↓ Computers 1967
  ↓ Environmental Planning 1982
  Human Factors Engineering 1973
  Human Machine Systems Design 1997
  Product Design 1997

Computer Assisted Diagnosis 1973
PN 1213 **SC** 10910
  B Computer Applications 1973
  Diagnosis 1967
  R Magnetic Resonance Imaging 1994
  ↓ Medical Diagnosis 1973
  ↓ Neuroimaging 2003
  ↓ Psychodiagnosis 1967
  Telemedicine 2003
  ↓ Tomography 1988

Computer Assisted Instruction 1973
PN 5702 **SC** 10920
SN Use of computers to present instructional materials to students and to assess performance. Compare TEACHING MACHINES.
  UF Computer Based Training
  Instruction (Computer Assisted)
  B Computer Applications 1973
  Teaching Methods 1967
  N Intelligent Tutoring Systems 2003
  R Individualized Instruction 1973
  Programmed Instruction 2001
  Teaching Machines 1973

Computer Assisted Testing [1988]
PN 1209   SC 10921
SN Use of computers in test construction or administration, usually in an educational or employment setting. Not used for diagnosis.
B   Computer Applications 1973
     Testing 1967
R   Adaptive Testing 1985

Computer Attitudes [1988]
PN 1027   SC 10922
B   Attitudes 1967
R   Computer Anxiety 2001
     ↓ Computers 1967

Computer Based Training
Use Computer Assisted Instruction

Computer Conferencing
Use Teleconferencing

Computer Games [1988]
PN 540   SC 10923
UF   Video Games
B   Computers 1967
     Games 1967
R   ↓ Computer Simulation 1973
     ↓ Recreation 1967
     Simulation Games 1973
     ↓ Toys 1973

Computer Literacy [1991]
PN 216   SC 10924
B   Literacy 1973
R   Computer Anxiety 2001
     Computer Searching 1991
     Computer Training 1994
     ↓ Computers 1967

Computer Mediated Communication [2003]
PN 291   SC 58071
SN Use of computer technologies to support human communication. Examples include email, chat, and Internet or local computer network forums.
HN This term was introduced in June 2003. PsycINFO records from the past 10 years were re-indexed with this term. The posting note reflects the number of records that were re-indexed.
UF   Electronic Mail
     Email
B   Electronic Communication 2001
R   ↓ Communications Media 1973
     ↓ Computer Applications 1973
     ↓ Computer Peripheral Devices 1985
     Distance Education 2003
     Groupware 2003
     Human Computer Interaction 1997
     Internet 2001
     Messages 1973
     Online Therapy 2003
     Telemedicine 2003

Computer Peripheral Devices [1985]
PN 189   SC 10925
SN Computer peripheral components and handheld microcomputer devices used for entering data, and collecting, displaying, receiving, and communicating information.
B   Apparatus 1967
N   Video Display Units 1985
R   ↓ Computer Applications 1973

Computer Peripheral Devices — (cont'd)
     Computer Mediated Communication 2003
     ↓ Computers 1967
     Data Collection 1982
     ↓ Electronic Communication 2001
     Human Computer Interaction 1997
     Human Machine Systems 1997
     Keyboards 1985
     ↓ Visual Displays 1973

Computer Programming [2001]
PN 355   SC 10928
HN In 2000, this term was created to update the spelling from the discontinued term COMPUTER PROGRAMING. COMPUTER PROGRAMING was removed from all records containing it and replaced with COMPUTER PROGRAMMING.
UF   Programming (Computer)
R   Algorithms 1973
     Computer Programming Languages 1973
     ↓ Computer Software 1967
     ↓ Computers 1967
     ↓ Data Processing 1967
     Systems Analysis 1973
     ↓ Systems Design 2003

Computer Programming Languages [1973]
PN 764   SC 10930
HN In 2000, this term was created to update the spelling from the discontinued term COMPUTER PROGRAMING LANGUAGES. COMPUTER PROGRAMING LANGUAGES was removed from all records containing it and replaced with COMPUTER PROGRAMMING LANGUAGES.
UF   FORTRAN
     Programming Languages (Computer)
R   Computer Programming 2001
     Computer Training 1994
     ↓ Computers 1967
     ↓ Data Processing 1967

Computer Programs
Use Computer Software

Computer Searching [1991]
PN 406   SC 10945
SN Use of computerized interactive communication system to access and retrieve information.
UF   Online Searching
B   Automated Information Retrieval 1973
R   ↓ Computer Applications 1973
     Computer Literacy 1991
     ↓ Computers 1967
     Databases 1991
     ↓ Electronic Communication 2001
     Human Machine Systems 1997
     Information 1967
     Information Seeking 1973
     Information Services 1988

Computer Simulation [1973]
PN 2536   SC 10950
B   Computer Applications 1973
     Simulation 1967
N   Neural Networks 1991
     Virtual Reality 1997
R   Computer Assisted Design 1997
     Computer Games 1988
     Decision Support Systems 1997
     Simulation Games 1973

Computer Software [1967]
PN 4921   SC 10960

Computer Software — (cont'd)
UF   Computer Programs
N   Decision Support Systems 1997
     Groupware 2003
     Word Processing 1991
R   Computer Assisted Design 1997
     Computer Programming 2001
     ↓ Computers 1967
     ↓ Data Processing 1967
     Databases 1991
     Hypermedia 1997
     Hypertext 1997
     ↓ Systems 1967

Computer Supported Cooperative Work
Use Groupware

Computer Training [1994]
PN 226   SC 10963
B   Curriculum 1967
R   Computer Literacy 1991
     Computer Programming Languages 1973

Computerized Databases
Use Databases

Computers [1967]
PN 3587   SC 10970
B   Apparatus 1967
N   Analog Computers 1973
     Computer Games 1988
     Digital Computers 1973
     Microcomputers 1985
R   ↓ Artificial Intelligence 1982
     Automated Information Coding 1973
     ↓ Automated Information Processing 1973
     ↓ Automated Information Retrieval 1973
     Automated Information Storage 1973
     Automation 1967
     ↓ Computer Applications 1973
     Computer Assisted Design 1997
     Computer Attitudes 1988
     Computer Literacy 1991
     ↓ Computer Peripheral Devices 1985
     Computer Programming 2001
     Computer Programming Languages 1973
     Computer Searching 1991
     ↓ Computer Software 1967
     Cybernetics 1967
     ↓ Data Processing 1967
     Databases 1991
     ↓ Expert Systems 1991
     Human Computer Interaction 1997
     Robotics 1985
     ↓ Systems 1967

Concentration [1982]
PN 420   SC 10977
SN Cognitive effort directed to one object or area of study.
B   Cognitive Processes 1967
     Sustained Attention 1997
R   ↓ Attention 1967
     Distraction 1978
     Rumination (Cognitive Process) 2001
     Selective Attention 1973

Concentration Camps [1973]
PN 377   SC 10980
R   Holocaust 1988
     Prisons 1967

Concept Formation 1967
PN 6176　　　　　　　　SC 11000
SN Developmental or learning process involving identification of common properties of objects, events, or qualities, usually represented by words or symbols, and generalization of those properties to all appropriate objects, events, or qualities.
HN In 1982, this term replaced the discontinued term CONCEPT LEARNING. In 2000, CONCEPT LEARNING was removed from all records containing it and replaced with CONCEPT FORMATION.
UF　Concept Learning
　　Conceptualization
B　Cognitive Processes 1967
N　Cognitive Discrimination 1973
　　Cognitive Generalization 1967
R　↓ Cognitive Development 1973
　　Cognitive Hypothesis Testing 1982
　　Concepts 1967
　　Conservation (Concept) 1973
　　↓ Discrimination Learning 1982
　　↓ Generalization (Learning) 1982
　　↓ Learning 1967

Concept Learning
Use Concept Formation

Concept Validity
Use Test Validity

Concepts 1967
PN 3055　　　　　　　　SC 11030
SN Generic ideas or categories derived from common properties of objects, events, or qualities, usually represented by words or symbols.
R　↓ Cognitions 1985
　　↓ Concept Formation 1967
　　Information 1967
　　↓ Mathematics (Concepts) 1997
　　↓ Terminology 1991

Conceptual Imagery 1973
PN 520　　　　　　　　SC 11040
SN Mental representation of concepts or conceptual relationships.
UF　Imagery (Conceptual)
B　Imagery 1967
R　Imagination 1967
　　Schema 1988

Conceptual Tempo 1985
PN 52　　　　　　　　SC 11045
SN The dimension of cognitive style often measured by response latency or the time required to solve a problem.
B　Cognitive Style 1967
R　Attention Span 1973
　　Cognitive Processing Speed 1997
　　Impulsiveness 1973
　　Perceptual Style 1973
　　Reaction Time 1967
　　Reflectiveness 1997

Conceptualization
Use Concept Formation

Concurrent Reinforcement Schedules 1988
PN 232　　　　　　　　SC 11057
SN Simultaneous use of two or more reinforcement schedules.
B　Reinforcement Schedules 1967

Concurrent Validity
Use Test Validity

Concussion (Brain)
Use Brain Concussion

Conditioned Emotional Responses 1967
PN 682　　　　　　　　SC 11070
UF　CER (Conditioning)
B　Classical Conditioning 1967
　　Conditioned Responses 1967
　　Emotional Responses 1967
　　Operant Conditioning 1967
N　Conditioned Fear 2003

Conditioned Fear 2003
PN 104　　　　　　　　SC 11072
HN This term was introduced in June 2003. Psyc-INFO records from the past 10 years were re-indexed with this term. The posting note reflects the number of records that were re-indexed.
B　Conditioned Emotional Responses 1967
R　↓ Fear 1967

Conditioned Inhibition
Use Conditioned Suppression

Conditioned Place Preference
Use Place Conditioning

Conditioned Reflex
Use Conditioned Responses

Conditioned Responses 1967
PN 3782　　　　　　　　SC 11090
UF　Conditioned Reflex
B　Classical Conditioning 1967
　　Operant Conditioning 1967
　　Responses 1967
N　↓ Conditioned Emotional Responses 1967
　　Conditioned Suppression 1973

Conditioned Stimulus 1973
PN 2371　　　　　　　　SC 11100
SN In classical conditioning, that stimulus (e.g., a light) that acquires the capacity to elicit a conditioned response (e.g., salivation) as a result of that stimulus having been paired consistently with an unconditioned stimulus (e.g., food). In operant conditioning, those stimuli (S+,S-) which differentially signal the presence or absence of reinforcement. Compare CUES.
UF　Discriminative Stimulus
B　Conditioning 1967
R　↓ Classical Conditioning 1967
　　↓ Latent Inhibition 1997
　　↓ Operant Conditioning 1967
　　Preconditioning 1994
　　Secondary Reinforcement 1967
　　↓ Stimulation 1967

Conditioned Suppression 1973
PN 1072　　　　　　　　SC 11110
SN Learned behavior or the conditioning procedure in which the pairing of a neutral stimulus with an aversive stimulus, presented during the performance of a positively-reinforced behavior, results in a decrease of that behavior.
UF　Conditioned Inhibition
　　Suppression (Conditioned)

Conditioned Suppression — (cont'd)
B　Conditioned Responses 1967
R　Prepulse Inhibition 1997

Conditioning 1967
PN 3404　　　　　　　　SC 11120
SN A process or procedure used to modify or change behavior.
B　Learning 1967
N　Autoshaping 1978
　　↓ Aversion Conditioning 1982
　　↓ Classical Conditioning 1967
　　Conditioned Stimulus 1973
　　Counterconditioning 1973
　　↓ Operant Conditioning 1967
　　Place Conditioning 1991
　　Preconditioning 1994
　　Unconditioned Stimulus 1973
R　↓ Animal Learning 2003
　　↓ Biofeedback 1973
　　↓ Latent Inhibition 1997
　　Primary Reinforcement 1973
　　↓ Reinforcement 1967
　　Spontaneous Recovery (Learning) 1973
　　↓ Stimulation 1967

Conditioning (Avoidance)
Use Avoidance Conditioning

Conditioning (Classical)
Use Classical Conditioning

Conditioning (Escape)
Use Escape Conditioning

Conditioning (Eyelid)
Use Eyelid Conditioning

Conditioning (Operant)
Use Operant Conditioning

Conditioning (Verbal)
Use Verbal Learning

Condoms 1991
PN 1292　　　　　　　　SC 11185
B　Contraceptive Devices 1973
R　AIDS Prevention 1994
　　↓ Birth Control 1971
　　↓ Family Planning 1973
　　↓ Prevention 1973
　　Safe Sex 2003
　　↓ Sexually Transmitted Diseases 2003

Conduct Disorder 1991
PN 1643　　　　　　　　SC 11187
SN Repetitive and persistent aggressive or nonaggressive behavior in which basic rights of others or social norms are violated. Self esteem is generally low, and an inability to develop social relationships and lack of concern for others may or may not be present.
HN Consider using BEHAVIOR DISORDERS prior to 1991.
R　↓ Aggressive Behavior 1967
　　↓ Behavior Disorders 1971
　　↓ Behavior Problems 1967
　　Explosive Disorder 2001
　　↓ Impulse Control Disorders 1997

Conduct Disorder — (cont'd)
↓ Mental Disorders 1967
Oppositional Defiant Disorder 1997

Cones (Eye) 1973
PN 579   SC 11190
B   Cells (Biology) 1973
Photoreceptors 1973
Retina 1967
R   Fovea 1982

Confabulation 1973
PN 123   SC 11200
SN Giving untruthful answers to questions about sit-
uations or events that are not recalled due to loss of
memory. Confabulation is not a conscious attempt to
deceive.
B   Thought Disturbances 1973
R   False Memory 1997
Korsakoffs Psychosis 1973

Confession (Legal)
Use Legal Confession

Confession (Religion) 1973
PN 16   SC 11220
B   Religious Practices 1973

Confidence (Self)
Use Self Confidence

Confidence Limits (Statistics) 1973
PN 242   SC 11230
B   Statistical Analysis 1967
R   Effect Size (Statistical) 1985
↓ Hypothesis Testing 1973
Predictability (Measurement) 1973
↓ Statistical Measurement 1973
↓ Statistical Sample Parameters 1973
Statistical Significance 1973
↓ Statistical Tests 1973

Confidentiality of Information
Use Privileged Communication

Confirmatory Factor Analysis
Use Factor Analysis

Conflict 1967
PN 6366   SC 11250
SN Hostile encounter or antagonistic state or action.
B   Aggressive Behavior 1967
Interpersonal Interaction 1967
N   Arguments 1973
↓ Family Conflict 2003
Riots 1973
↓ Violence 1973
↓ War 1967
R   Bullying 2003

Conflict Resolution 1982
PN 3136   SC 11255
SN Process of reducing or removing antagonisms
among individuals, groups, organizations, or political
entities.
N   Mediation 1988
R   ↓ Cognitive Processes 1967
Forgiveness 1988
Litigation 2003
↓ Negotiation 1973
↓ Social Interaction 1967

Conformity (Personality) 1967
PN 1350   SC 11270
B   Personality Traits 1967
Social Behavior 1967
R   Nonconformity (Personality) 1973
Openness to Experience 1997

Confusion (Mental)
Use Mental Confusion

Congenital Disorders 1973
PN 1101   SC 11290
HN The term CONGENITALLY HANDICAPPED
was also used to capture this concept from 1973-
1996, and CONGENITALLY DISABLED was used
from 1997-2000. In 2001, CONGENITAL DISOR-
DERS replaced the discontinued and deleted term
CONGENITALLY DISABLED. CONGENITALLY DIS-
ABLED and CONGENITALLY HANDICAPPED were
removed from all records containing them and
replaced with CONGENITAL DISORDERS.
UF Congenitally Handicapped
B   Disorders 1967
N   Cleft Palate 1967
↓ Drug Induced Congenital Disorders 1973
Hermaphroditism 1973
Microcephaly 1973
Prader Willi Syndrome 1991
Spina Bifida 1978
R   Adventitious Disorders 2001
↓ Brain Damage 1967
Cystic Fibrosis 1985
Deaf Blind 1991
Developmental Disabilities 1982
↓ Genetic Disorders 1973
Hydrocephaly 1973
↓ Mental Disorders 1967
Myotonia 1973
↓ Neonatal Disorders 1973
↓ Physical Disorders 1997
Prenatal Diagnosis 1988
↓ Syphilis 1973
Teratogens 1988

Congenitally Handicapped
Use Congenital Disorders

Conjoined Twins 2003
PN 8   SC 11305
HN In July 2003, this term was created to replace
the discontinued term SIAMESE TWINS. SIAMESE
TWINS was removed from all records containing it
and replaced with CONJOINED TWINS, its postable
counterpart.
UF Siamese Twins
B   Neonatal Disorders 1973
Twins 1967

Conjoint Measurement 1994
PN 42   SC 11307
SN Statistical measurement of a variable that is
composed of two or more components which affect
the variable being measured.
B   Statistical Measurement 1973
R   ↓ Experimental Design 1967
Psychometrics 1967
↓ Statistical Analysis 1967

Conjoint Therapy 1973
PN 422   SC 11310
SN Type of marriage or family therapy in which part-
ners or family members are seen in joint sessions.

Conjoint Therapy — (cont'd)
UF Triadic Therapy
B   Family Therapy 1967
Marriage Counseling 1973
R   Couples Therapy 1994
↓ Group Psychotherapy 1967
↓ Psychotherapeutic Techniques 1967

Connectionism 1994
PN 847   SC 11315
SN Theoretical principles that characterize all learn-
ing and behavior as connected to the stimulus-
response paradigm and the theory that neural link-
ages, whether inherited or acquired, bond these
behaviors.
R   ↓ Associative Processes 1967
↓ Cognitive Processes 1967
Cognitive Psychology 1985
↓ Learning 1967
Learning Theory 1967
Neural Networks 1991

Connective Tissue Cells 1973
PN 18   SC 11320
B   Cells (Biology) 1973
R   ↓ Connective Tissues 1973

Connective Tissues 1973
PN 31   SC 11330
B   Tissues (Body) 1973
N   Bones 1973
R   Connective Tissue Cells 1973

Connotations 1973
PN 226   SC 11340
B   Associative Processes 1967
R   Analogy 1991
↓ Figurative Language 1985
Semantic Generalization 1973
Word Meaning 1973

Consanguineous Marriage 1973
PN 42   SC 11350
B   Endogamous Marriage 1973

Conscience 1967
PN 171   SC 11360
SN Cognitive and affective processes which govern
the individual's standards of behavior, performance,
and morality.
B   Psychoanalytic Personality Factors 1973
Superego 1973

Conscientiousness 1997
PN 216   SC 11365
SN Extent to which an individual is purposeful, well-
organized, strong-willed, and determined.
B   Personality Traits 1967
R   Five Factor Personality Model 1997
Perfectionism 1988
Persistence 1973
↓ Responsibility 1973
Self Monitoring (Personality) 1985

Conscious (Personality Factor) 1973
PN 518   SC 11370
SN That portion of personal mental functioning
which is known to the individual or is observable by
introspection.
HN Use CONSCIOUS (PERSONALITY FACTORS)
prior to 1988.
B   Psychoanalytic Personality Factors 1973

Consciousness Disturbances 1973
PN 201   SC 11380
- N   Delirium 1973
- ↓ Hypnosis 1967
- Place Disorientation 1973
- ↓ Sleep Disorders 1973
- Sleep Talking 1973
- Suggestibility 1967
- Time Disorientation 1973
- R   Coma 1973
- ↓ Consciousness States 1971
- Dissociation 2001
- ↓ Dissociative Disorders 2001
- ↓ Mental Disorders 1967
- ↓ Sleep 1967

Consciousness Raising Groups 1978
PN 132   SC 11387
SN   Disciplined interaction of a small group of people whose exchange of feelings and experiences results in an increased awareness of social issues such as discriminatory social practices and stereotyped thinking.
- B   Human Potential Movement 1982
- R   ↓ Encounter Group Therapy 1973
- ↓ Group Dynamics 1967
- ↓ Group Psychotherapy 1967
- Sensitivity Training 1973

Consciousness States 1971
PN 4245   SC 11390
SN   Conceptually broad term referring to variations in the degree and type of mental awareness. Use a more specific term if possible.
- UF   Deja Vu
- N   ↓ Awareness 1967
- Wakefulness 1973
- R   Centering 1991
- ↓ Consciousness Disturbances 1973
- Dissociation 2001
- Mind 1991
- Physiological Arousal 1967
- ↓ Sleep 1967

Conservation (Concept) 1973
PN 1191   SC 11400
SN   Knowledge of constancy of size, volume, or amount in spite of changed distance or shape; used as measure of cognitive development.
- R   ↓ Cognitive Development 1973
- ↓ Concept Formation 1967
- Object Permanence 1985
- ↓ Perceptual Development 1973
- Piaget (Jean) 1967

Conservation (Ecological Behavior) 1978
PN 767   SC 11403
- UF   Recycling
- B   Behavior 1967
- R   Ecology 1973
- Environmental Attitudes 1978
- Environmental Education 1994

Conservatism 1973
PN 533   SC 11405
- UF   Traditionalism
- B   Personality Traits 1967
- R   Political Conservatism 1973
- Religious Fundamentalism 2003

Conservatism (Political)
- Use   Political Conservatism

Conservatorship
- Use   Guardianship

Consistency (Measurement) 1973
PN 324   SC 11420
- B   Statistical Analysis 1967
- R   Error of Measurement 1985
- ↓ Prediction Errors 1973
- Statistical Reliability 1973
- Statistical Validity 1973

Consonants 1973
PN 1055   SC 11430
- B   Letters (Alphabet) 1973
- Phonemes 1973
- R   Syllables 1973
- Words (Phonetic Units) 1967

Conspecifics 2003
PN 72   SC 11433
SN   An organism that is a member of the same species as another organism.
HN   This term was introduced in June 2003. PsycINFO records from the past 10 years were re-indexed with this term. The posting note reflects the number of records that were re-indexed.
- R   Species Recognition 1985

Constant Time Delay 1997
PN 23   SC 11435
SN   Instruction involving a prompting technique in which dependence on the prompting is faded by a fixed time delay between the presentation of a target stimulus and the delivery of the controlling prompt.
- B   Prompting 1997
- R   ↓ Behavior Modification 1973
- ↓ Learning Strategies 1991
- Task Analysis 1967
- ↓ Teaching Methods 1967

Constipation 1973
PN 83   SC 11440
- B   Colon Disorders 1973

Construct Validity
- Use   Test Validity

Constructionism
- Use   Constructivism

Constructivism 1994
PN 1900   SC 11448
SN   Theoretical perspective that characterizes perceptual experience and reality as constructed by the mind in the observation of the effects of independent actions on objects.
- UF   Constructionism
- B   Theories 1967
- R   ↓ Cognitive Development 1973
- ↓ Learning 1967
- ↓ Perception 1967
- Phenomenology 1967
- Piaget (Jean) 1967

Consultation (Professional)
- Use   Professional Consultation

Consultation Liaison Psychiatry 1991
PN 601   SC 11465

Consultation Liaison Psychiatry — (cont'd)
- B   Professional Consultation 1973
- Psychiatry 1967

Consumer Attitudes 1973
PN 3921   SC 11470
SN   Attitudes of, not toward, consumers.
- B   Attitudes 1967
- N   Brand Preferences 1994
- Consumer Satisfaction 1994
- R   ↓ Consumer Research 1973
- Consumer Surveys 1973
- Public Relations 1973
- ↓ Quality of Services 1997

Consumer Behavior 1967
PN 5945   SC 11480
- UF   Buying
- B   Behavior 1967
- N   Shopping 1997
- R   Behavioral Economics 2003
- Brand Names 1978
- Brand Preferences 1994
- ↓ Consumer Research 1973
- Consumer Satisfaction 1994
- Consumer Surveys 1973
- Retailing 1991
- Shopping Centers 1973
- Supply and Demand 2004

Consumer Fraud
- Use   Fraud

Consumer Product Design
- Use   Product Design

Consumer Protection 1973
PN 143   SC 11490
- R   Accountability 1988
- ↓ Laws 1967
- ↓ Legal Processes 1973
- Product Design 1997
- Warning Labels 1997
- ↓ Warnings 1997

Consumer Psychology 1973
PN 339   SC 11500
SN   Subdiscipline in psychology that has as its emphasis the behavioral and psychological aspects of consumer behavior.
- B   Applied Psychology 1970

Consumer Research 1973
PN 1407   SC 11510
SN   Marketing and advertising research assessing consumer needs, competition, and methods of sale for a product.
- B   Experimentation 1967
- N   Consumer Surveys 1973
- R   ↓ Advertising 1967
- Brand Names 1978
- Brand Preferences 1994
- ↓ Consumer Attitudes 1973
- ↓ Consumer Behavior 1967
- Consumer Satisfaction 1994
- Mail Surveys 1994
- Marketing 1973
- Product Design 1997
- Telephone Surveys 1994

Consumer Satisfaction 1994
PN 642   SC 11515
UF Customer Satisfaction
B   Consumer Attitudes 1973
    Satisfaction 1973
R   ↓ Consumer Behavior 1967
    ↓ Consumer Research 1973
    Consumer Surveys 1973
    Quality Control 1988
    ↓ Quality of Services 1997

Consumer Surveys 1973
PN 250   SC 11520
SN Surveys assessing consumer needs, product usage, and effectiveness of marketing and advertising.
B   Consumer Research 1973
    Surveys 1967
R   ↓ Consumer Attitudes 1973
    ↓ Consumer Behavior 1967
    Consumer Satisfaction 1994
    Mail Surveys 1994
    Product Design 1997
    Telephone Surveys 1994

Contact Lenses 1973
PN 43   SC 11540
B   Optical Aids 1973

Contagion 1988
PN 177   SC 11544
SN Transmission of behavior, attitudes, or emotions to other persons through suggestions, verbal communication, imitation, or gestures. Not used for infectious disorders.
B   Social Behavior 1967
R   ↓ Collective Behavior 1967
    Mass Hysteria 1973

Content Analysis 1978
PN 2417   SC 11548
SN Systematic, objective, quantitative, or qualitative description of the manifest or latent content of communications.
B   Analysis 1967
    Methodology 1967
N   Discourse Analysis 1997
R   ↓ Communication 1967

Content Analysis (Test) 1967
PN 258   SC 11550
SN Systematic examination of a test, primarily to determine whether the test items constitute an adequate sample of the domain or subject matter to be tested.
B   Analysis 1967
    Test Construction 1973
    Testing 1967

Content Validity
Use Test Validity

Contextual Associations 1967
PN 5364   SC 11560
SN In learning and memory, associations made to environmental or internal conditions during learning or memorization. In perception and communication, environmental conditions that affect such aspects as perceptual accuracy, comprehension, or meaning.
UF Associations (Contextual)
B   Associative Processes 1967
R   Place Conditioning 1991

Contextual Associations — (cont'd)
    ↓ Priming 1988
    Semantic Priming 1994
    Word Frequency 1973
    Word Meaning 1973

Contiguity (Cognitive)
Use Cognitive Contiguity

Contingency Management 1973
PN 1062   SC 11580
SN Behavior modification technique in which the stimuli and reinforcers that control a given behavior are manipulated to increase the likelihood of occurrence of the desired behavior.
B   Behavior Modification 1973
N   Token Economy Programs 1973
R   Noncontingent Reinforcement 1988

Contingent Negative Variation 1982
PN 317   SC 11583
SN Cortical evoked potential of slow negativity recorded in the period between stimulus-presentation and responses and which is associated with states of attention or expectancy.
UF Readiness Potential
B   Cortical Evoked Potentials 1973

Continuing Education 1985
PN 556   SC 11590
SN Formal or informal courses, educational programs or services, usually at the postsecondary level, designed to advance or update adult learning for personal, academic, or occupational and professional purposes.
B   Adult Education 1973
N   ↓ Inservice Training 1985
R   Adult Learning 1997
    Distance Education 2003
    ↓ Higher Education 1973
    Individualized Instruction 1973
    Professional Development 1982
    Reentry Students 1985

Continuity of Care
Use Continuum of Care

Continuous Reinforcement
Use Reinforcement Schedules

Continuum of Care 2004
PN 71   SC 11605
SN Provision of continuous, comprehensive, and integrated care that involves health, mental health, and/or social services.
HN This term was introduced in June 2004. Psyc-INFO records from the past 10 years were re-indexed with this term. The posting note reflects the number of records that were re-indexed.
UF Continuity of Care
B   Health Care Services 1978
R   Aftercare 1973
    ↓ Health Care Delivery 1978
    Quality of Care 1988

Contour
Use Form and Shape Perception

Contour Perception
Use Form and Shape Perception

Contraception
Use Birth Control

Contraceptive Devices 1973
PN 272   SC 11630
B   Birth Control 1971
N   Condoms 1991
    Diaphragms (Birth Control) 1973
    Intrauterine Devices 1973
    Oral Contraceptives 1973

Contracts (Psychological)
Use Psychological Contracts

Control (Emotional)
Use Emotional Control

Control (Locus of)
Use Internal External Locus of Control

Control (Self)
Use Self Control

Control (Social)
Use Social Control

Control Groups
Use Experiment Controls

Controls (Instrument)
Use Instrument Controls

Convergent Thinking
Use Inductive Deductive Reasoning

Convergent Validity
Use Test Validity

Conversation 1973
PN 3684   SC 11710
B   Interpersonal Communication 1973
    Verbal Communication 1967
R   Listening (Interpersonal) 1997

Conversion Disorder 2001
PN 533   SC 11717
HN In 2001, this term replaced the discontinued term CONVERSION NEUROSIS. CONVERSION NEUROSIS was removed from all records containing it and replaced with CONVERSION DISORDER.
UF Conversion Hysteria
    Conversion Neurosis
    Hysterical Neurosis (Conversion)
B   Somatoform Disorders 2001
N   Hysterical Paralysis 1973
    Hysterical Vision Disturbances 1973
    Pseudocyesis 1973
R   ↓ Defense Mechanisms 1967
    Histrionic Personality Disorder 1991
    Hypochondriasis 1973
    ↓ Hysteria 1967
    Somatization 1994
    Somatoform Pain Disorder 1997

Conversion Hysteria
Use Conversion Disorder

Conversion Neurosis
  Use Conversion Disorder

Conviction (Criminal)
  Use Criminal Conviction

Convulsions 1967
PN 2988   **SC** 11750
  UF Seizures
  B   Nervous System Disorders 1967
          Symptoms 1967
  N   Audiogenic Seizures 1978
  R   ↓ Anticonvulsive Drugs 1973
          ↓ Brain Disorders 1967
          ↓ Epileptic Seizures 1973
          Experimental Epilepsy 1978
          Hydrocephaly 1973
          ↓ Spasms 1973

Cooperating Teachers 1978
PN 133   **SC** 11756
  SN Experienced elementary or secondary teachers
employed to supervise student teachers or teacher
interns in schools which, although not integral parts
of teacher education institutions, provide experiences
for the student teachers and teacher interns.
  UF Supervising Teachers
  B   Teachers 1967
  R   Practicum Supervision 1978
          Student Teachers 1973
          Student Teaching 1973
          ↓ Teacher Education 1967

Cooperation 1967
PN 5052   **SC** 11700
  SN Used for human or animal populations.
  UF Collaboration
  B   Interpersonal Interaction 1967
          Prosocial Behavior 1982
  R   Agreeableness 1997
          Cooperative Learning 1994
          Groupware 2003
          Volunteers 2002

Cooperative Education 1982
PN 132   **SC** 11765
  SN Combined complementary work and study
experience or program coordinated by a teacher and
designed by the school and the employer to achieve
some occupational goal. Not to be confused with
work study programs which serve as means for financial assistance.
  B   Vocational Education 1973
  R   Curricular Field Experience 1982
          ↓ Educational Programs 1973
          ↓ Experiential Learning 1997

Cooperative Learning 1994
PN 903   **SC** 11766
  SN Learning in small groups where cooperation
among group members determines rewards and per-
formance.
  B   Learning 1967
  R   Cooperation 1967
          Group Instruction 1973
          Individualized Instruction 1973
          Peer Tutoring 1973
          School Learning 1967
          ↓ Teaching 1967
          ↓ Teaching Methods 1967
          ↓ Teams 1988

Cooperative Therapy
  Use Cotherapy

Coordination (Motor)
  Use Motor Coordination

Coordination (Perceptual Motor)
  Use Perceptual Motor Coordination

Coping Behavior 1967
PN 20504   **SC** 11790
  SN Use of conscious or unconscious strategies or
mechanisms in adapting to stress, various disorders,
or environmental demands.
  B   Behavior 1967
  R   Adaptability (Personality) 1973
          Adjustment Disorders 1994
          Anosognosia 1994
          ↓ Emotional Adjustment 1973
          ↓ Emotional Control 1973
          ↓ Helplessness 1997
          Illness Behavior 1982
          Resilience (Psychological) 2003

Copper 1973
PN 97   **SC** 11800
  B   Metallic Elements 1973

Coprophagia 2001
PN   **SC** 11805
  SN Eating of feces. Used for both human and ani-
mal populations.
  UF Cecotrophy
  B   Ingestion 2001
  R   Defecation 1967
          ↓ Eating Disorders 1997
          Fetishism 1973
          Pica 1973

Copulation
  Use Sexual Intercourse (Human)

Copulation (Animal)
  Use Animal Mating Behavior

Cornea 1973
PN 47   **SC** 11830
  B   Eye (Anatomy) 1967

Coronary Disorders
  Use Cardiovascular Disorders

Coronary Heart Disease
  Use Heart Disorders

Coronary Prone Behavior 1982
PN 2334   **SC** 11855
  SN Constellation of behaviors or attitudes constituting a risk factor for coronary heart disease. Traits can
include ambition, competitiveness, sense of time
urgency, devotion to work over relaxation, positive
attitude toward pressure, aggressiveness, impa-
tience, need for recognition, and tendency toward
hostility.
  UF Type A Personality
          Type B Personality
  B   Behavior 1967
  R   At Risk Populations 1985

Coronary Prone Behavior — (cont'd)
          ↓ Cardiovascular Disorders 1967
          Illness Behavior 1982
          ↓ Personality 1967
          ↓ Personality Traits 1967
          Predisposition 1973
          Stress Reactions 1973
          Susceptibility (Disorders) 1973

Coronary Thromboses 1973
PN 7   **SC** 11860
  B   Heart Disorders 1973
          Thromboses 1973
  R   Myocardial Infarctions 1973

Coronary Vessels
  Use Arteries (Anatomy)

Corporal Punishment
  Use Punishment

Corporations
  Use Business Organizations

Corpus Callosum 1973
PN 911   **SC** 11900
  B   Cerebral Cortex 1967
          Neural Pathways 1982
  R   Commissurotomy 1985
          Interhemispheric Interaction 1985
          Left Brain 1991
          Right Brain 1991

Corpus Striatum
  Use Basal Ganglia

Correctional Institutions 1973
PN 1126   **SC** 11910
  UF Institutions (Correctional)
  N   Prisons 1967
          Reformatories 1973
  R   Criminal Rehabilitation 2004
          Halfway Houses 1973
          Incarceration 1973
          Institution Visitation 1973
          Institutional Schools 1978
          Maximum Security Facilities 1985
          Penology 1973

Corrective Lenses
  Use Optical Aids

Correlation (Statistical)
  Use Statistical Correlation

Cortex (Auditory)
  Use Auditory Cortex

Cortex (Cerebral)
  Use Cerebral Cortex

Cortex (Motor)
  Use Motor Cortex

Cortex (Somatosensory)
  Use Somatosensory Cortex

Cortex (Visual)
   Use Visual Cortex

Cortical Atrophy
   Use Cerebral Atrophy

Cortical Evoked Potentials 1973
PN 2147   **SC** 11980
   B   Electrical Activity 1967
       Evoked Potentials 1967
   N   Contingent Negative Variation 1982
   R   Auditory Evoked Potentials 1973
       Olfactory Evoked Potentials 1973
       Somatosensory Evoked Potentials 1973
       Visual Evoked Potentials 1973

Corticoids
   Use Corticosteroids

Corticosteroids 1973
PN 582   **SC** 12000
   UF Adrenal Cortex Steroids
        Corticoids
   B   Steroids 1973
   N   Aldosterone 1973
        Corticosterone 1973
        Cortisone 1973
        Deoxycorticosterone 1973
        Hydrocortisone 1973
        Prednisolone 1973
   R ↓ Adrenal Cortex Hormones 1973

Corticosterone 1973
PN 1329   **SC** 12010
   B   Adrenal Cortex Hormones 1973
        Corticosteroids 1973

Corticotropin 1973
PN 1511   **SC** 12020
   UF ACTH (Hormone)
        Adrenocorticotropin
   B   Neuropeptides 2003
        Pituitary Hormones 1973
   R   Corticotropin Releasing Factor 1994

Corticotropin Releasing Factor 1994
PN 522   **SC** 12025
   UF ACTH Releasing Factor
   B   Hormones 1967
        Neuropeptides 2003
        Peptides 1973
   R   Corticotropin 1973

Cortisol
   Use Hydrocortisone

Cortisone 1973
PN 75   **SC** 12040
   B   Adrenal Cortex Hormones 1973
        Corticosteroids 1973

Cosmetic Techniques 2001
PN 53   **SC** 12035
   UF Body Art
        Piercings
        Tattoos
   R ↓ Fads and Fashions 1973
        Initiation Rites 1973
        ↓ Physical Appearance 1982
        Plastic Surgery 1973

Cosmetic Techniques — (cont'd)
        Rites (Nonreligious) 1973
        Self Mutilation 1973
        Skin (Anatomy) 1967
        Subculture (Anthropological) 1973

Cost Containment 1991
PN 241   **SC** 12041
SN Policies or procedures to restrain or control
expenses in any setting.
   R   Budgets 1997
        ↓ Case Management 1991
        ↓ Costs and Cost Analysis 1973
        Diagnosis Related Groups 1988
        ↓ Economics 1985
        Fee for Service 1994
        Health Care Costs 1994
        ↓ Health Care Services 1978
        Health Maintenance Organizations 1982
        ↓ Managed Care 1994
        Money 1967
        ↓ Professional Fees 1978
        Resource Allocation 1997
        ↓ Treatment 1967

Cost Effectiveness
   Use Costs and Cost Analysis

Costs and Cost Analysis 1973
PN 4835   **SC** 12045
SN Applied to any subject and includes prices,
expenses, or payments; also attachment of dollar
estimates to the costs of an operation and its alterna-
tives.
   UF Cost Effectiveness
        Price
   B   Analysis 1967
   N   Budgets 1997
        Health Care Costs 1994
   R   Cost Containment 1991
        ↓ Economics 1985
        Economy 1973
        Funding 1988
        Money 1967
        ↓ Professional Fees 1978
        Resource Allocation 1997
        Risk Management 1997

Cotherapy 1982
PN 209   **SC** 12047
SN Psychotherapeutic process in which a client or a
group of clients are treated by more than one thera-
pist.
HN Use CONJOINT THERAPY to access refer-
ences from 1973-1981.
   UF Cooperative Therapy
        Multiple Therapy
   B   Psychotherapeutic Techniques 1967
   R   Psychiatric Training 1973
        ↓ Psychotherapy 1967
        Psychotherapy Training 1973

Counselees
   Use Clients

Counseling 1967
PN 9814   **SC** 12080
SN Conceptually broad term referring to a form of
helping process which involves giving advice and
information, in order to assist individuals or groups in
coping with their problems. Use a more specific term
if possible.

Counseling — (cont'd)
   N   Cross Cultural Counseling 2003
        Educational Counseling 1967
        Genetic Counseling 1978
        Group Counseling 1973
        ↓ Marriage Counseling 1973
        Microcounseling 1978
        Occupational Guidance 1967
        Pastoral Counseling 1967
        Peer Counseling 1978
        Premarital Counseling 1973
        ↓ Psychotherapeutic Counseling 1973
        Rehabilitation Counseling 1978
        School Counseling 1982
   R   Counseling Psychology 1973
        ↓ Counselors 1967
        Employee Assistance Programs 1985
        ↓ Family Therapy 1967
        Feminist Therapy 1994
        ↓ Health Care Services 1978
        ↓ Mental Health Services 1978
        Social Casework 1967
        Student Personnel Services 1978
        ↓ Support Groups 1991
        ↓ Treatment 1967

Counseling (Group)
   Use Group Counseling

Counseling Psychologists 1988
PN 292   **SC** 12065
   B   Psychologists 1967
   R   Clinicians 1973
        Counseling Psychology 1973

Counseling Psychology 1973
PN 1183   **SC** 12070
   B   Applied Psychology 1973
   R ↓ Counseling 1967
        Counseling Psychologists 1988

Counselor Attitudes 1973
PN 1250   **SC** 12090
SN Attitudes of, not toward, counselors.
   B   Attitudes 1967
        Counselor Characteristics 1973
   R   Counselor Role 1973
        ↓ Counselors 1967
        ↓ Health Personnel Attitudes 1985
        Psychologist Attitudes 1991

Counselor Characteristics 1973
PN 2740   **SC** 12100
   UF Counselor Effectiveness
        Counselor Personality
   N   Counselor Attitudes 1973
   R ↓ Counselors 1967

Counselor Client Interaction
   Use Psychotherapeutic Processes

Counselor Education 1973
PN 3779   **SC** 12120
   B   Education 1967
   R ↓ Clinical Methods Training 1973
        Counselor Trainees 1973
        Microcounseling 1978
        Practicum Supervision 1978
        ↓ Psychology Education 1978
        Psychotherapy Training 1973
        Rehabilitation Education 1997

Counselor Effectiveness
Use Counselor Characteristics

Counselor Personality
Use Counselor Characteristics

Counselor Role 1973
PN 1056   **SC** 12150
  UF Role (Counselor)
  B Roles 1967
  R Counselor Attitudes 1973
    ↓ Counselors 1967
    Therapist Role 1978

Counselor Trainees 1973
PN 1928   **SC** 12160
  R Counselor Education 1973
    ↓ Counselors 1967
    Therapist Trainees 1973

Counselors 1967
PN 3312   **SC** 12170
  B Professional Personnel 1978
  N Rehabilitation Counselors 1978
    School Counselors 1973
    Vocational Counselors 1973
  R ↓ Counseling 1967
    Counselor Attitudes 1973
    ↓ Counselor Characteristics 1973
    Counselor Role 1973
    Counselor Trainees 1973
    ↓ Health Personnel 1994
    ↓ Mental Health Personnel 1967
    ↓ Psychologists 1967
    ↓ Social Workers 1973
    Sociologists 1973
    ↓ Therapists 1967

Counterconditioning 1973
PN 91   **SC** 12180
SN Technique used to extinguish a response to a certain stimulus by conditioning an alternative, often incompatible response to that stimulus.
  B Conditioning 1967
  R ↓ Aversion Therapy 1973
    ↓ Behavior Modification 1973
    ↓ Behavior Therapy 1967
    Reciprocal Inhibition Therapy 1973

Countertransference 1973
PN 3307   **SC** 12190
SN Conscious or unconscious emotional reaction of the therapist to the patient which may interfere with the treatment.
  B Psychotherapeutic Processes 1967
  R Enactments 1997
    Negative Therapeutic Reaction 1997
    Professional Client Sexual Relations 1994
    Psychotherapeutic Transference 1967

Countries 1967
PN 2219   **SC** 12195
SN Applies to cross-national studies when individual countries are not mentioned or are too numerous to list.
  N Developed Countries 1985
    Developing Countries 1985
  R Geography 1973

County Agricultural Agents
Use Agricultural Extension Workers

Couples 1982
PN 3950   **SC** 12205
SN Two individuals in an intimate relationship.
  R Cohabitation 1973
    Dyads 1973
    ↓ Family 1967
    Romance 1997
    Significant Others 1991
    Social Dating 1973
    ↓ Spouses 1973

Couples Therapy 1994
PN 1034   **SC** 12207
SN Used specifically for unmarried couples. Use MARRIAGE COUNSELING for married couples.
  R Conjoint Therapy 1973
    ↓ Marriage Counseling 1973
    ↓ Psychotherapy 1967
    Sex Therapy 1978

Courage 1973
PN 89   **SC** 12210
  UF Bravery
  B Personality Traits 1967

Course Evaluation 1978
PN 565   **SC** 12215
SN Procedures, materials, or the process involved in the assessment of quality or effectiveness of an academic or vocational course or program by its students or participants. Evaluation may include content, structure, or method of material presentation.
  B Evaluation 1967
  R ↓ Curriculum 1967
    Educational Program Evaluation 1972
    Educational Quality 1997
    Teacher Effectiveness Evaluation 1978
    ↓ Teaching 1967

Course Objectives
Use Educational Objectives

Course of Illness
Use Disease Course

Court Ordered Treatment
Use Court Referrals

Court Referrals 1994
PN 280   **SC** 12219
SN Court ordered assessment, treatment, consultation, or other services for defendants, plaintiffs, or criminals.
  UF Court Ordered Treatment
  B Adjudication 1967
  R ↓ Commitment (Psychiatric) 1973
    ↓ Criminal Justice 1991
    ↓ Criminals 1967
    Defendants 1985
    Forensic Evaluation 1994
    Insanity Defense 1985
    Involuntary Treatment 1994
    Mediation 1988
    Mentally Ill Offenders 1985
    Probation 1973
    Professional Referral 1973
    ↓ Treatment 1967

Courts
Use Adjudication

Courtship (Animal)
Use Animal Courtship Behavior

Courtship (Human)
Use Human Courtship

Courtship Displays (Animal)
Use Animal Courtship Displays

Cousins 1973
PN 19   **SC** 12260
  B Family Members 1973

Covert Sensitization 1988
PN 35   **SC** 12265
SN Form of aversion conditioning in which noxious mental images, thoughts, or feelings are associated with undesirable behavior by verbal cues. Frequently used in therapeutic settings.
  B Aversion Conditioning 1982
    Aversion Therapy 1973
  R Aversive Stimulation 1973

Cows
Use Cattle

Coyotes
Use Canids

Crabs 1973
PN 338   **SC** 12300
  B Crustacea 1973

Crack Cocaine 2003
PN 122   **SC** 12305
SN A highly addictive form of cocaine that is either smoked, injected intravenously, or orally ingested.
HN This term was introduced in June 2003. Psyc-INFO records from the past 10 years were re-indexed with this term. The posting note reflects the number of records that were re-indexed.
  B Cocaine 1973

Crafts 1973
PN 47   **SC** 12310
  UF Handicrafts
  B Art 1967

Cramps (Muscle)
Use Muscular Disorders

Cranial Nerves 1973
PN 152   **SC** 12330
  UF Accessory Nerve
    Glossopharyngeal Nerve
    Hypoglossal Nerve
    Nerve (Accessory)
    Nerves (Cranial)
    Oculomotor Nerve
    Trochlear Nerve
  B Peripheral Nervous System 1973
  N Abducens Nerve 1973
    Acoustic Nerve 1973
    Facial Nerve 1973
    Olfactory Nerve 1973
    Optic Nerve 1973
    Trigeminal Nerve 1973
    Vagus Nerve 1973

Cranial Spinal Cord 1973
PN 5   SC 12340
  B   Spinal Cord 1973

Craving 1997
PN 471   SC 12350
  R ↓ Addiction 1973
     ↓ Appetite 1973
     ↓ Drug Abuse 1973
     ↓ Drug Usage 1971
     ↓ Emotional States 1973
     Food 1978
     ↓ Needs 1967

Crayfish 1973
PN 139   SC 12360
  B   Crustacea 1973

Creative Arts Therapy 1994
PN 172   SC 12365
SN Therapeutic use of the arts in medicine, mental health, or education.
  B   Treatment 1967
  N   Art Therapy 1973
     Dance Therapy 1973
     Music Therapy 1973
     Poetry Therapy 1994
     Recreation Therapy 1973
  R   Improvisation 2004
     Movement Therapy 1997
     ↓ Psychotherapeutic Techniques 1967

Creative Writing 1994
PN 348   SC 12370
HN Use LITERATURE to access references from 1973-1993.
  UF Writing (Creative)
  B   Written Communication 1985
  R ↓ Literature 1967
     Narratives 1997
     Poetry 1973
    ↓ Prose 1973
     Rhetoric 1991
     Storytelling 1988

Creativity 1967
PN 9107   SC 12380
SN Ability to perceive new relationships, and to derive new ideas and solve problems by pursuing nontraditional patterns of thinking. Compare DIVERGENT THINKING.
  UF Innovativeness
     Originality
  B   Personality Traits 1967
  R ↓ Ability 1967
    ↓ Artistic Ability 1973
     Divergent Thinking 1973
     Gifted 1967
     Improvisation 2004
    ↓ Intelligence 1967
     Openness to Experience 1997

Creativity Measurement 1973
PN 412   SC 12390
  B   Measurement 1967

Credibility 1973
PN 1002   SC 12400
  R ↓ Interpersonal Communication 1973
     Reputation 1997
    ↓ Social Perception 1967

Creutzfeldt Jakob Syndrome 1994
PN 148   SC 12410
  B   Encephalopathies 1982
     Presenile Dementia 1973
     Syndromes 1973
     Viral Disorders 1973
  R ↓ Dementia 1985

Cri du Chat Syndrome
  Use Crying Cat Syndrome

Crib Death
  Use Sudden Infant Death

Crime 1967
PN 5912   SC 12430
  UF Felonies
     Misdemeanors
  B   Social Issues 1991
  N   Arson 1985
    ↓ Child Abuse 1971
     Driving Under the Influence 1988
     Drug Distribution 1997
     Hate Crimes 2003
     Kidnapping 1988
    ↓ Sex Offenses 1982
    ↓ Theft 1973
     Vandalism 1978
    ↓ Violent Crime 2003
  R ↓ Antisocial Behavior 1971
    ↓ Behavior Disorders 1971
     Crime Prevention 1985
    ↓ Crime Victims 1982
    ↓ Criminal Behavior 2003
    ↓ Criminal Justice 1991
     Criminal Responsibility 1991
    ↓ Criminals 1967
     Fraud 1994
     Informants 1988
    ↓ Perpetrators 1988
     Self Defense 1985
     Stalking 2001
     Terrorism 1982
     Victimization 1973

Crime Prevention 1985
PN 804   SC 12432
SN Measures aimed at deterring the occurrence of crime or delinquent behavior.
  B   Prevention 1973
  R ↓ Crime 1967
    ↓ Criminal Justice 1991
    ↓ Juvenile Delinquency 1967
    ↓ Law Enforcement 1978

Crime Victims 1982
PN 1589   SC 12434
SN Individuals subjected to and adversely affected by criminal activity.
HN Use VICTIMIZATION to access references from 1973-1981.
  N   Hostages 1988
  R ↓ Crime 1967
     Self Defense 1985
     Victimization 1973

Criminal Behavior 2003
PN 250   SC 12437
HN This term was introduced in June 2003. Psyc-INFO records from the past 10 years were re-indexed with this term. The posting note reflects the number of records that were re-indexed.

Criminal Behavior — (cont'd)
  UF Criminality
  B   Antisocial Behavior 1971
  N ↓ Juvenile Delinquency 1967
  R ↓ Behavior Disorders 1971
    ↓ Crime 1967
     Criminal Rehabilitation 2004
    ↓ Criminals 1967

Criminal Conviction 1973
PN 497   SC 12440
SN Declaration made by a court finding a person guilty and responsible for a criminal offense.
  UF Conviction (Criminal)
  B   Criminal Justice 1991
  R ↓ Adjudication 1967
    ↓ Criminals 1967
     Legal Decisions 1991

Criminal Interrogation
  Use Legal Interrogation

Criminal Justice 1991
PN 1316   SC 12445
SN Used for the system, discipline, or the actual process itself.
  B   Justice 1973
     Legal Processes 1973
  N   Criminal Conviction 1973
     Juvenile Justice 2004
  R ↓ Adjudication 1967
     Court Referrals 1994
    ↓ Crime 1967
     Crime Prevention 1985
     Criminal Law 1973
     Forensic Psychiatry 1973
     Forensic Psychology 1985
    ↓ Law Enforcement 1978
     Legal Decisions 1991
     Litigation 2003
     Penology 1973

Criminal Law 1973
PN 503   SC 12450
  B   Law (Government) 1973
  R ↓ Criminal Justice 1991
     Litigation 2003

Criminal Rehabilitation 2004
PN 69   SC 12452
HN This term was introduced in June 2004. Psyc-INFO records from the past 10 years were re-indexed with this term. The posting note reflects the number of records that were re-indexed.
  B   Rehabilitation 1967
  R ↓ Correctional Institutions 1973
    ↓ Criminal Behavior 2003
    ↓ Criminals 1967
     Parole 1973
    ↓ Prisoners 1967
     Prisons 1967
     Probation 1973

Criminal Responsibility 1991
PN 378   SC 12453
SN State of mind that permits one to be held accountable for criminal acts.
  B   Responsibility 1973
  R   Accountability 1988
    ↓ Adjudication 1967
     Competency to Stand Trial 1985
    ↓ Crime 1967

Criminal Responsibility — (cont'd)
- ↓ Criminals   1967
  - Defendants   1985
  - Insanity Defense   1985
- ↓ Perpetrators   1988

Criminality
- **Use**   Criminal Behavior

Criminally Insane
- **Use**   Mentally Ill Offenders

Criminals   1967
PN   4659   **SC**   12460
- **UF**   Offenders (Adult)
- **B**   Perpetrators   1988
- **N**   Female Criminals   1973
  - Male Criminals   1973
  - Mentally Ill Offenders   1985
- **R**   Antisocial Personality Disorder   1973
  - Court Referrals   1994
  - ↓ Crime   1967
  - ↓ Criminal Behavior   2003
  - Criminal Conviction   1973
  - Criminal Rehabilitation   2004
  - Criminal Responsibility   1991
  - Defendants   1985
  - Forensic Evaluation   1994
  - ↓ Juvenile Delinquency   1967
  - ↓ Prisoners   1967
  - Recidivism   1973

Criminology   1973
PN   480   **SC**   12470
- **R**   Penology   1973

Crises   1971
PN   1120   **SC**   12490
- **N**   Family Crises   1973
  - Identity Crisis   1973
  - Organizational Crises   1973
- **R**   ↓ Crisis Intervention   1973
  - ↓ Crisis Intervention Services   1973
  - ↓ Disasters   1973
  - ↓ Experiences (Events)   1973
  - ↓ Stress   1967

Crisis (Reactions to)
- **Use**   Stress Reactions

Crisis Intervention   1973
PN   1850   **SC**   12510
SN   Brief therapeutic approach which is ameliorative rather than curative of acute psychiatric emergencies. Used in such contexts as emergency rooms of psychiatric or general hospitals, or in the home or place of crisis occurrence, this treatment approach focuses on interpersonal and intrapsychic factors and environmental modification of behavior.
- **B**   Intervention   2003
- **N**   Debriefing (Psychological)   2004
  - Suicide Prevention   1973
- **R**   ↓ Crises   1971
  - ↓ Crisis Intervention Services   1973
  - Family Intervention   2003

Crisis Intervention Services   1973
PN   778   **SC**   12520
SN   Community organizations, programs, or mental health personnel which provide crisis care.
- **B**   Community Services   1967

Crisis Intervention Services — (cont'd)
- Mental Health Programs   1973
- Treatment   1967
- **N**   Hot Line Services   1973
  - Suicide Prevention Centers   1973
- **R**   ↓ Clinics   1967
  - Community Mental Health Centers   1973
  - ↓ Crises   1971
  - ↓ Crisis Intervention   1973
  - Emergency Services   1973
  - ↓ Intervention   2003
  - ↓ Treatment Facilities   1973
  - Walk In Clinics   1973

Criterion Referenced Tests   1982
PN   331   **SC**   12525
SN   Tests in which scores are measured against explicitly stated objectives rather than a group norm.
- **UF**   Mastery Tests
  - Objective Referenced Tests
- **B**   Measurement   1967
- **R**   ↓ Achievement Measures   1967
  - Performance Tests   1973

Criterion Related Validity
- **Use**   Test Validity

Critical Flicker Fusion Threshold   1967
PN   429   **SC**   12530
- **UF**   Flicker Fusion Frequency
- **B**   Visual Thresholds   1973
- **R**   ↓ Perceptual Measures   1973

Critical Incident Debriefing
- **Use**   Debriefing (Psychological)

Critical Period   1988
PN   114   **SC**   12533
- **R**   ↓ Development   1967
  - Imprinting   1967

Critical Scores
- **Use**   Cutting Scores

Criticism   1973
PN   465   **SC**   12540
- **B**   Social Behavior   1967
  - Social Influences   1967
- **N**   Self Criticism   2003
- **R**   Skepticism   2004
  - Social Approval   1967

Crocodilians   1973
PN   24   **SC**   12570
- **UF**   Alligators
- **B**   Reptiles   1967

Cross Cultural Communication   1997
PN   452   **SC**   12580
- **UF**   Intercultural Communication
  - Interethnic Communication
- **B**   Interpersonal Communication   1973
- **R**   Acculturation   2003
  - Bilingualism   1973
  - Cross Cultural Counseling   2003
  - Cross Cultural Differences   1967
  - Cross Cultural Psychology   1997
  - ↓ Cross Cultural Treatment   1994
  - Cultural Sensitivity   1994
  - Multicultural Education   1988
  - Multiculturalism   1997

Cross Cultural Communication — (cont'd)
- Racial and Ethnic Differences   1982
- ↓ Racial and Ethnic Groups   2001
- Racial and Ethnic Relations   1982

Cross Cultural Counseling   2003
PN   59   **SC**   12585
SN   Counseling relationship where the cultural background of the client differs from the counselor or therapist.
HN   This term was introduced in June 2003. PsycINFO records from the past 10 years were re-indexed with this term. The posting note reflects the number of records that were re-indexed.
- **B**   Counseling   1967
  - Cross Cultural Treatment   1994
- **R**   Cross Cultural Communication   1997
  - Cultural Sensitivity   1994
  - ↓ Psychotherapeutic Processes   1967

Cross Cultural Differences   1967
PN   19214   **SC**   12590
SN   Used for comparisons between populations with different psychological, sociological, or cultural mores. Used for comparisons both within and across countries. Compare REGIONAL DIFFERENCES and RACIAL AND ETHNIC DIFFERENCES.
- **UF**   Cultural Differences
- **B**   Sociocultural Factors   1967
- **R**   Cross Cultural Communication   1997
  - Cross Cultural Psychology   1997
  - ↓ Cross Cultural Treatment   1994
  - Cultural Sensitivity   1994
  - Diversity in the Workplace   2000
  - Ethnology   1967
  - Multiculturalism   1997
  - Racial and Ethnic Differences   1982
  - ↓ Racial and Ethnic Groups   2001
  - Regional Differences   2001

Cross Cultural Psychology   1997
PN   622   **SC**   12591
SN   Branch of psychology that studies members of various cultural groups and their specific cultural experiences resulting in similarities and differences in human behavior.
- **B**   Psychology   1967
- **R**   Acculturation   2003
  - Cross Cultural Communication   1997
  - Cross Cultural Differences   1967
  - ↓ Culture (Anthropological)   1967
  - ↓ Culture Bound Syndromes   2004
  - Ethnocentrism   1973
  - Ethnology   1967
  - Racial and Ethnic Differences   1982
  - ↓ Racial and Ethnic Groups   2001
  - ↓ Sociocultural Factors   1967
  - Transcultural Psychiatry   1973

Cross Cultural Treatment   1994
PN   1078   **SC**   12593
SN   Treatment, in any context, where the racial, ethnic, or cultural background of the patient or client is different from that of the health care provider, e.g., therapist, counselor, or physician. Used primarily when the cultural or racial aspects of the treatment paradigm are the major focus.
- **B**   Treatment   1967
- **N**   Cross Cultural Counseling   2003
- **R**   ↓ Client Characteristics   1973
  - Cross Cultural Communication   1997
  - Cross Cultural Differences   1967
  - Cultural Sensitivity   1994

Cross Cultural Treatment — (cont'd)
    Racial and Ethnic Differences 1982
    ↓ Racial and Ethnic Groups 2001
    ↓ Therapist Characteristics 1973
    Transcultural Psychiatry 1973

Cross Disciplinary Research
  Use Interdisciplinary Research

Crossed Eyes
  Use Strabismus

Crowding 1978
PN 538   **SC** 12610
SN Conditions of high population density for a given area. Used for animal or human populations.
  R   Environmental Stress 1973
      Overpopulation 1973
      Personal Space 1973
      Social Density 1978

CRT
  Use Video Display Units

Cruelty 1973
PN 77   **SC** 12620
  B   Antisocial Behavior 1971
      Personality Traits 1967
  R ↓ Aggressive Behavior 1967

Crustacea 1973
PN 370   **SC** 12630
  B   Arthropoda 1973
  N   Crabs 1973
      Crayfish 1973

Crying 1973
PN 638   **SC** 12640
  B   Vocalization 1967
      Voice 1973
  R   Infant Vocalization 1973

Crying Cat Syndrome 1973
PN 34   **SC** 12650
  UF Cri du Chat Syndrome
  B   Autosome Disorders 1973
      Mental Retardation 1967
      Neonatal Disorders 1970
      Syndromes 1973

Cuban Americans
  Use Hispanics

Cued Recall 1994
PN 461   **SC** 12678
  B   Recall (Learning) 1967
  R   Cues 1967
      Forgetting 1973
      Free Recall 1973
    ↓ Memory 1967
    ↓ Prompting 1997

Cues 1967
PN 9694   **SC** 12680
SN Internal or external verbal or nonverbal signals which influence learning, performance, or behavior. Cues are often only obscure secondary stimuli which, though not fully detected, serve to facilitate learning, performance, or behavior. Compare CONDITIONED STIMULUS.

Cues — (cont'd)
  R ↓ Associative Processes 1967
      Cued Recall 1994
      Isolation Effect 1973
    ↓ Memory 1967
      Mnemonic Learning 1973
    ↓ Priming 1988
    ↓ Prompting 1997
      Semantic Priming 1994

Cultism 1973
PN 610   **SC** 12690
  R   Ethn.ology 1967
      Myths 1967
      Occultism 1978
    ↓ Religious Beliefs 1973
      Religious Experiences 1997
      Shamanism 1973
    ↓ Sociocultural Factors 1967

Cultural Assimilation
  Use Acculturation

Cultural Deprivation 1973
PN 215   **SC** 12710
SN Inabllllty of individuals to participate in their society's cultural achievements because of poverty, social discrimination, or other disadvantage. Consider also SOCIAL DEPRIVATION.
  UF Culturally Disadvantaged
  B   Deprivation 1967
      Sociocultural Factors 1967
  R   Disadvantaged 1967
      Multiculturalism 1997
      Poverty Areas 1973
    ↓ Social Deprivation 1973
    ↓ Social Environments 1973

Cultural Differences
  Use Cross Cultural Differences

Cultural Factors
  Use Sociocultural Factors

Cultural Familial Mental Retardation
  Use Psychosocial Mental Retardation

Cultural Pluralism
  Use Multiculturalism

Cultural Psychiatry
  Use Transcultural Psychiatry

Cultural Sensitivity 1994
PN 1867   **SC** 12728
SN Awareness and appreciation of the values, norms, and beliefs unique to a particular cultural, minority, ethnic, or racial group.
  UF Ethnic Sensitivity
  R   Acculturation 2003
      Cross Cultural Communication 1997
      Cross Cultural Counseling 2003
      Cross Cultural Differences 1967
    ↓ Cross Cultural Treatment 1994
    ↓ Culture (Anthropological) 1967
      Ethnic Identity 1973
      Ethnic Values 1973
      Minority Groups 1967
      Multicultural Education 1988

Cultural Sensitivity — (cont'd)
    Multiculturalism 1997
    ↓ Racial and Ethnic Attitudes 1982
    Racial and Ethnic Differences 1982
    ↓ Racial and Ethnic Groups 2001
    Racial and Ethnic Relations 1982
    Sensitivity Training 1973
    ↓ Sociocultural Factors 1967

Cultural Test Bias 1973
PN 835   **SC** 12730
SN Any significant differential performance on tests by different populations (e.g., Hispanics vs. Blacks) as a result of test characteristics that are sensitive to cultural, subcultural, racial, or ethnic factors but which are irrelevant to the variable or construct being measured.
  UF Test Bias (Cultural)
  B   Test Bias 1985
  R   Response Bias 1967
      Test Interpretation 1985

Culturally Disadvantaged
  Use Cultural Deprivation

Culture (Anthropological) 1967
PN 7740   **SC** 12750
  N ↓ Society 1967
      Subculture (Anthropological) 1973
  R   Cross Cultural Psychology 1997
      Cultural Sensitivity 1994
      Ethnology 1967
    ↓ Family Structure 1973
      Multiculturalism 1997
      Popular Culture 2003
    ↓ Racial and Ethnic Groups 2001
    ↓ Sociocultural Factors 1967

Culture Bound Syndromes 2004
PN   **SC** 12755
SN A pathological behavior pattern that is specific to a particular geographic, ethnic, or cultural group.
HN In June 2004, this term was created to replace the deleted term ETHNOSPECIFIC DISORDERS. ETHNOSPECIFIC DISORDERS was removed from all records containing it and replaced with CULTURE BOUND SYNDROMES.
  UF Culture Specific Syndromes
  B   Syndromes 1973
  N   Koro 1904
  R   Cross Cultural Psychology 1997
    ↓ Racial and Ethnic Groups 2001
    ↓ Sociocultural Factors 1967
      Transcultural Psychiatry 1973

Culture Change 1967
PN 621   **SC** 12760
SN Modification in behavior, values, customs, or artifacts over time or as the result of migration to a different cultural environment.
  B   Sociocultural Factors 1967
  N   Acculturation 2003
  R   Culture Shock 1973
      Ethnology 1967
      Modernization 2003
      Multiculturalism 1997

Culture Fair Intelligence Test 1973
PN 35   **SC** 12770
  UF Cattell Culture Fair Intelligence Test
  B   Intelligence Measures 1967

Culture Shock 1973
PN 201   SC 12780
SN Social, psychological, or emotional difficulties in adapting to a new culture or similar difficulties in adapting to one's own culture as the result of rapid social or cultural changes.
R ↓ Culture Change 1967
    Ethnology 1967

Culture Specific Syndromes
Use Culture Bound Syndromes

Curare 1973
PN 27   SC 12790
B Muscle Relaxing Drugs 1973
R ↓ Alkaloids 1973
    Tubocurarine 1973

Curiosity 1967
PN 340   SC 12800
UF Inquisitiveness
B Personality Traits 1967
R ↓ Exploratory Behavior 1967
    Openness to Experience 1997
    Questioning 1982

Curricular Field Experience 1982
PN 407   SC 12805
SN Organizationally or institutionally supervised educational activities, restricted primarily to high school and college, usually undertaken outside the classroom or campus in order to promote practical experience in a specific discipline.
UF Field Instruction
    Field Work (Educational)
B Experiential Learning 1997
R Cooperative Education 1982
  ↓ Curriculum 1967
    Educational Field Trips 1973
  ↓ Educational Programs 1973
  ↓ Practice 1967

Curriculum 1967
PN 7383   SC 12810
SN Set of courses constituting a framework for education in a given subject area.
B Education 1967
N Affective Education 1982
    Art Education 1973
    Braille Instruction 1973
    Business Education 1973
    Career Education 1978
    Compensatory Education 1973
    Computer Training 1994
    Driver Education 1973
    Foreign Language Education 1973
  ↓ Health Education 1973
    Home Economics 1985
  ↓ Language Arts Education 1973
    Mathematics Education 1973
    Music Education 1973
    Physical Education 1967
  ↓ Psychology Education 1978
    Science Education 1973
    Social Studies Education 1978
  ↓ Vocational Education 1973
R Course Evaluation 1978
    Curricular Field Experience 1982
    Curriculum Based Assessment 1994
    Curriculum Development 1973
    Educational Objectives 1978
    Educational Program Accreditation 1994

Curriculum — (cont'd)
    Home Schooling 1994
  ↓ Nontraditional Education 1982

Curriculum Based Assessment 1994
PN 196   SC 12815
B Educational Measurement 1967
R ↓ Curriculum 1967

Curriculum Development 1973
PN 2798   SC 12820
SN Initiating, designing, implementing, and testing of activities designed to create new curricula or to change existing ones.
B Development 1967
R ↓ Curriculum 1967
    Educational Program Planning 1973
  ↓ Program Development 1991

Cursive Writing 1973
PN 65   SC 12830
UF Writing (Cursive)
B Handwriting 1967
R Orthography 1973

Cushings Syndrome 1973
PN 94   SC 12840
B Adrenal Gland Disorders 1973
    Metabolism Disorders 1973
    Syndromes 1973

Customer Satisfaction
Use Consumer Satisfaction

Cutaneous Receptive Fields 1985
PN 73   SC 12845
SN The area of skin being supplied by specific peripheral nerves and localized synaptic distribution in the CNS.
UF Dermatomes
B Receptive Fields 1985

Cutaneous Sense 1967
PN 1413   SC 12850
SN Any of the senses, such as pressure, pain, warmth, cold, and touch, whose receptors lie within or beneath the skin or in the mucous membrane.
UF Haptic Perception
B Somesthetic Perception 1967
N ↓ Tactual Perception 1967

Cutting Scores 1985
PN 147   SC 12855
SN Points at which a continuum of scores may be divided into groups for such purposes as pass/fail decisions or test interpretations.
UF Critical Scores
B Scoring (Testing) 1973
    Test Scores 1967
R Score Equating 1985
    Test Interpretation 1985

Cybercounseling
Use Online Therapy

Cybernetics 1967
PN 525   SC 12860
SN Study of control and communication between humans, machines, animals, and organizations and the parallels between information processing machines and human or animal intellectual or brain function.

Cybernetics — (cont'd)
R ↓ Artificial Intelligence 1982
    Communication Theory 1973
  ↓ Computers 1967
  ↓ Expert Systems 1991
    Human Machine Systems 1997
    Robotics 1985

Cyclic Adenosine Monophosphate 1978
PN 314   SC 12875
B Nucleotides 1978
R Guanosine 1985

Cycloheximide 1973
PN 160   SC 12880
B Antibiotics 1973

Cyclothymic Disorder
Use Cyclothymic Personality

Cyclothymic Personality 1973
PN 122   SC 12890
SN Affective disorder characterized by alternating and recurring periods of depression and elation, similar to manic depressive disorder but of a less severe nature.
UF Cyclothymic Disorder
B Bipolar Disorder 2001
R Hypomania 1973

Cynicism 1973
PN 155   SC 12900
R Personality Traits 1967
R Agreeableness 1997
    Fatalism 1973
    Hopelessness 1988
    Negativism 1973
    Pessimism 1973
    Skepticism 2004

Cysteine 1973
PN 42   SC 12910
B Amino Acids 1973

Cystic Fibrosis 1985
PN 313   SC 12915
B Digestive System Disorders 1973
    Lung Disorders 1973
    Metabolism Disorders 1973
R ↓ Congenital Disorders 1973

Cytochrome Oxidase 1973
PN 131   SC 12920
B Oxidases 1973

Cytokines 2000
PN 92   SC 12925
SN Non-antibody proteins secreted by various cell types that act as intercellular mediators.
HN This term was introduced in June 2003. Psyc-INFO records from the past 10 years were re-indexed with this term. The posting note reflects the number of records that were re-indexed.
B Immunologic Factors 2003
N Interferons 1994
    Interleukins 1994

Cytology 1973
PN 162   SC 12930
R ↓ Cells (Biology) 1973

Cytoplasm 1973
PN 23   SC 12940
R ↓ Cells (Biology) 1973

Daily Activities 1994
PN 855   SC 12955
SN Daily patterns of behavior that are not reflective of functional ability. Compare ACTIVITIES OF DAILY LIVING.
R Activities of Daily Living 1991
    Activity Level 1982
    Hobbies 1988
    ↓ Interests 1967
    Leisure Time 1973
    ↓ Lifestyle 1978
    ↓ Recreation 1967
    Self Care Skills 1978

Daily Biological Rhythms (Animal)
Use Animal Circadian Rhythms

Dance 1973
PN 421   SC 12970
UF Ballet
B Arts 1973
   Recreation 1967
R Dance Therapy 1973
   Improvisation 2004

Dance Therapy 1973
PN 317   SC 12980
B Creative Arts Therapy 1994
R Dance 1973
   Movement Therapy 1997
   Recreation Therapy 1973

Dangerousness 1988
PN 687   SC 12985
R Patient Violence 1994
   ↓ Violence 1973

Dark Adaptation 1973
PN 438   SC 12990
UF Adaptation (Dark)
B Sensory Adaptation 1967
   Visual Perception 1967
R Light Adaptation 1982
   ↓ Perceptual Measures 1973
   ↓ Visual Thresholds 1973

Darwinism 1973
PN 411   SC 13000
SN Biological theory of evolution formulated by C. Darwin, including the fundamental tenet of natural selection as the operating principle of organic change.
B Theories 1967
N Natural Selection 1997
R Evolutionary Psychology 2003
   Theory of Evolution 1967

Data Collection 1982
PN 2012   SC 13005
SN Systematic accumulation, generation, or assembly of information. Compare EXPERIMENTAL METHODS.
B Methodology 1967
R ↓ Computer Peripheral Devices 1985
   ↓ Data Processing 1967
   Information 1967
   ↓ Medical Records 1978

Data Collection — (cont'd)
   Qualitative Research 2003
   Quantitative Methods 2003
   ↓ Sampling (Experimental) 1973
   Statistical Data 1982
   ↓ Statistical Measurement 1973
   ↓ Surveys 1967

Data Pooling
Use Meta Analysis

Data Processing 1967
PN 430   SC 13020
N Word Processing 1991
R ↓ Automated Information Processing 1973
   Computer Programming 2001
   Computer Programming Languages 1973
   ↓ Computer Software 1967
   ↓ Computers 1967
   Data Collection 1982
   ↓ Expert Systems 1991
   Information 1967
   ↓ Information Systems 1991
   ↓ Medical Records 1978

Databases 1991
PN 577   SC 13024
SN Collection of computerized data stored in a computer or on magnetic tape or disks from which information can be accessed and retrieved.
UF Computerized Databases
   Online Databases
R ↓ Automated Information Retrieval 1973
   Automated Information Storage 1973
   ↓ Computer Applications 1973
   Computer Searching 1991
   ↓ Computer Software 1967
   ↓ Computers 1967
   Decision Support Systems 1997
   ↓ Electronic Communication 2001
   ↓ Expert Systems 1991
   Human Machine Systems 1997
   Information 1967
   Information Services 1988
   ↓ Information Systems 1991

Date Rape
Use Acquaintance Rape

Dating (Social)
Use Social Dating

Daughters 1973
PN 1807   SC 13040
B Family Members 1973
   Human Females 1973
   Offspring 1988

Day Camps (Recreation)
Use Summer Camps (Recreation)

Day Care (Child)
Use Child Day Care

Day Care (Treatment)
Use Partial Hospitalization

Day Care Centers 1973
PN 662   SC 13070

Day Care Centers — (cont'd)
SN Facilities for day care of individuals of any age.
R Adult Day Care 1997
   Child Care Workers 1978
   Child Day Care 1973
   ↓ Community Facilities 1973
   Community Mental Health Centers 1973

Day Hospital
Use Partial Hospitalization

Daydreaming 1973
PN 306   SC 13080
R ↓ Fantasy 1997
   Fantasy (Defense Mechanism) 1967

DDT (Insecticide) 1973
PN 7   SC 13090
B Insecticides 1973

Deaf 1967
PN 5543   SC 13100
SN Profoundly or severely hearing impaired. Consider also PARTIALLY HEARING IMPAIRED for severely hearing impaired.
B Hearing Disorders 1982
N Deaf Blind 1991
R Cochlear Implants 1994
   Lipreading 1973
   Partially Hearing Impaired 1973

Deaf Blind 1991
PN 105   SC 13103
B Blind 1967
   Deaf 1967
   Multiple Disabilities 2001
R ↓ Congenital Disorders 1973
   Developmental Disabilities 1982

Deanol
Use Antidepressant Drugs

Death and Dying 1967
PN 8346   SC 13110
UF Dying
   Mortality
N Euthanasia 1973
   Parental Death 2003
R Advance Directives 1994
   Assisted Suicide 1997
   Death Anxiety 1978
   Death Attitudes 1973
   Death Education 1982
   Death Rites 1973
   Grief 1973
   Mortality Rate 1973
   Near Death Experiences 1985
   Palliative Care 1991
   Psychological Autopsy 1988
   Sudden Infant Death 1982
   ↓ Suicide 1967
   Terminal Cancer 1973
   Terminally Ill Patients 1973
   Treatment Withholding 1988

Death Anxiety 1978
PN 991   SC 13115
B Anxiety Disorders 1997
R ↓ Death and Dying 1967
   Death Attitudes 1973

Death Attitudes 1973
PN 2117   SC 13120
B   Attitudes 1967
R   ↓ Death and Dying 1967
     Death Anxiety 1978
     Euthanasia 1973
     ↓ Religious Beliefs 1973

Death Education 1982
PN 345   SC 13124
SN   Education in the process of death and dying. Applies to patients or students of any age including helping professionals.
UF   Thanatology
B   Education 1967
R   ↓ Death and Dying 1967
     ↓ Treatment 1967

Death Instinct 1988
PN 245   SC 13127
UF   Thanatos
B   Psychoanalytic Personality Factors 1973
R   Self Preservation 1997
     Unconscious (Personality Factor) 1967

Death Penalty
Use   Capital Punishment

Death Rate
Use   Mortality Rate

Death Rites 1973
PN 203   SC 10150
UF   Funerals
B   Rites of Passage 1973
R   Cannibalism 2003
     ↓ Death and Dying 1967

Debates 1997
PN 138   SC 13153
UF   Political Debates
     Presidential Debates
R   Arguments 1973
     Group Discussion 1967
     ↓ Persuasive Communication 1967
     Political Campaigns 1973
     Political Candidates 1973
     Political Elections 1973
     ↓ Political Processes 1973
     Public Speaking 1973
     Rhetoric 1991

Debriefing (Experimental) 1991
PN 33   SC 13154
SN   At the conclusion of an experiment, the process that removes any deception and discloses the facts to subjects participating in the research by giving full details of the research purpose and procedures.
UF   Disclosure (Experimental)
R   ↓ Experimental Design 1967
     Experimental Ethics 1978
     Experimental Subjects 1985
     ↓ Experimentation 1967
     Informed Consent 1985

Debriefing (Psychological) 2004
PN 72   SC 13155
SN   Psychological intervention used to reduce distress from psychological trauma.

Debriefing (Psychological) — (cont'd)
HN   This term was introduced in June 2004. Psyc-INFO records from the past 10 years were re-indexed with this term. The posting note reflects the number of records that were re-indexed.
UF   Critical Incident Debriefing
     Psychological Debriefing
B   Crisis Intervention 1973
R   Acute Stress Disorder 2003
     Emotional Trauma 1967
     Posttraumatic Stress Disorder 1985

Decarboxylase Inhibitors 1982
PN 58   SC 13157
B   Enzyme Inhibitors 1985
N   Carbidopa 1988
R   ↓ Antitremor Drugs 1973
     ↓ Catecholamines 1973
     ↓ Dopamine Antagonists 1982
     ↓ Enzymes 1973
     ↓ Serotonin Antagonists 1973

Decarboxylases 1973
PN 93   SC 13160
B   Enzymes 1973

Decentralization 1978
PN 76   SC 13166
SN   Process of distributing or allocating administrative control over organizational functions to authorities that are more local.
R   Educational Administration 1967
     Hospital Administration 1978
     ↓ Organizational Change 1973
     Organizational Development 1973
     Organizational Objectives 1973
     Organizational Structure 1967

Deception 1967
PN 2310   SC 13170
UF   Lying
N   Cheating 1973
     Faking 1973
     Fraud 1994
     Malingering 1973
R   Dishonesty 1973
     Secrecy 1994
     Sincerity 1973

Decerebration 1973
PN 123   SC 13180
SN   Elimination of cerebral functioning by transecting the brain stem or by cutting off the cerebral blood supply.
B   Neurosurgery 1973
R   ↓ Brain Lesions 1967

Decision Making 1967
PN 15822   SC 13190
SN   Cognitive process involving evaluation of the incentives, goals, and outcomes of alternative actions.
B   Cognitive Processes 1967
N   Choice Behavior 1967
     ↓ Group Decision Making 1978
     Management Decision Making 1973
R   Decision Support Systems 1997
     Decision Theory 2003
     ↓ Expert Systems 1991
     Heuristics 2003
     ↓ Judgment 1967

Decision Making — (cont'd)
     ↓ Problem Solving 1967
     Risk Assessment 2004
     Uncertainty 1991
     Utility Theory 2004
     Volition 1988

Decision Support Systems 1997
PN 352   SC 13193
SN   Computer-based planning and decision making systems that provide data on the outcomes or results of alternative decision choices.
B   Computer Software 1967
     Expert Systems 1991
R   ↓ Artificial Intelligence 1982
     ↓ Computer Applications 1973
     ↓ Computer Simulation 1973
     Databases 1991
     ↓ Decision Making 1967
     Decision Theory 2003
     ↓ Information Systems 1991
     Knowledge Engineering 2003

Decision Theory 2003
PN 44   SC 58062
SN   Analytic techniques for modeling decision making in light of possible consequences or outcomes.
HN   This term was introduced in June 2003. Psyc-INFO records from the past 10 years were re-indexed with this term. The posting note reflects the number of records that were re-indexed.
B   Theories 1967
R   ↓ Decision Making 1967
     Decision Support Systems 1997
     ↓ Mathematical Modeling 1070

Declarative Knowledge 1997
PN 340   SC 13194
SN   Knowledge about "how" and "what" things are, which can be modified due to new experiences or internal thought processes. Compare PROCEDURAL KNOWLEDGE.
UF   Factual Knowledge
R   ↓ Cognitive Processes 1967
     Divergent Thinking 1973
     Heuristics 2003
     Information 1967
     ↓ Knowledge Level 1978
     ↓ Memory 1967
     Metacognition 1991
     ↓ Problem Solving 1967
     Procedural Knowledge 1997
     ↓ Reasoning 1967

Decoding
Use   Human Information Storage

Decompression Effects 1973
PN 42   SC 13200
R   Acceleration Effects 1973
     ↓ Gravitational Effects 1967
     Physiological Stress 1967
     Spaceflight 1967
     Underwater Effects 1973

Decortication (Brain) 1973
PN 126   SC 13210
SN   Functional deactivation or physical removal of all or portions of the cortical substance of the brain. Primarily used for experimental contexts.
B   Neurosurgery 1973
R   ↓ Brain Lesions 1967

Deductive Reasoning
Use   Inductive Deductive Reasoning

Deer   1973
PN 241   **SC**   13230
  B   Mammals   1973

Defecation   1967
PN 243   **SC**   13240
  B   Excretion   1967
  R   Coprophagia   2001

Defendants   1985
PN 529   **SC**   13245
SN   Persons who are being sued or prosecuted in a court of law.
  R   Court Referrals   1994
         Criminal Responsibility   1991
         ↓ Criminals   1967
         ↓ Law (Government)   1973

Defense Mechanisms   1967
PN 3393   **SC**   13250
SN   Any intrapsychic strategies that serve to provide relief from emotional conflict or frustration or from unreasonable or undesirable thoughts which lead to anxiety, distress, or depression.
  B   Personality Processes   1967
  N   Compensation (Defense Mechanism)   1973
         Denial   1973
         Displacement (Defense Mechanism)   1973
         Fantasy (Defense Mechanism)   1967
         Grandiosity   1994
         Identification (Defense Mechanism)   1973
         Intellectualization   1973
         Introjection   1973
         Isolation (Defense Mechanism)   1973
         Projection (Defense Mechanism)   1967
         Projective Identification   1994
         Rationalization   1973
         Reaction Formation   1973
         Regression (Defense Mechanism)   1967
         Repression (Defense Mechanism)   1967
         Sublimation   1973
         Suppression (Defense Mechanism)   1973
         Withdrawal (Defense Mechanism)   1973
  R   ↓ Conversion Disorder   2001
         Externalization   1973
         ↓ Internalization   1997
         ↓ Mental Disorders   1967
         ↓ Personality Disorders   1967
         Psychopathology   1967

Defensive Behavior (Animal)
Use   Animal Defensive Behavior

Defensiveness   1967
PN 589   **SC**   13260
  B   Personality Traits   1967

Deformity
Use   Physical Disfigurement

Degrees (Educational)
Use   Educational Degrees

Dehydration   1988
PN 93   **SC**   13285
SN   State of excessively reduced body water or water deficit.

Dehydration — (cont'd)
  R   Homeostasis   1973
         Water Deprivation   1967
         Water Intake   1967

Dehydrogenases   1973
PN 97   **SC**   13290
  B   Enzymes   1973
  N   Alcohol Dehydrogenases   1973
         Lactate Dehydrogenase   1973

Deinstitutionalization   1982
PN 1346   **SC**   13293
SN   Programs emphasizing out-of-hospital treatment and community residence of clients, usually chronic psychiatric or handicapped patients, including those who may never have been hospitalized or who may or may not have experienced normal community life.
  B   Mental Health Programs   1973
  R   Community Mental Health   1973
         Community Mental Health Services   1978
         Discharge Planning   1994
         Habilitation   1991
         ↓ Homeless   1988
         Homeless Mentally Ill   1997
         ↓ Institutional Release   1978
         ↓ Mainstreaming   1991
         Partial Hospitalization   1985
         ↓ Rehabilitation   1967
         Right to Treatment   1997

Deja Vu
Use   Consciousness States

Delay of Gratification   1978
PN 324   **SC**   13297
SN   Voluntary postponement of need satisfaction or fulfillment of desires.
  R   ↓ Impulse Control Disorders   1997
         ↓ Motivation   1967
         ↓ Reinforcement   1967
         Reinforcement Delay   1985
         ↓ Rewards   1967

Delayed Alternation   1994
PN 48   **SC**   13298
SN   Alternation of rewards, usually in maze learning, with a delay between successive trials, forcing experimental subject to also alternate responses in order to receive the reward.
  B   Operant Conditioning   1967
  R   ↓ Learning   1967
         Reinforcement Delay   1985
         Response Variability   1973
         ↓ Rewards   1967
         Spontaneous Alternation   1982

Delayed Auditory Feedback   1973
PN 142   **SC**   13300
  B   Auditory Feedback   1973
         Delayed Feedback   1973

Delayed Development   1973
PN 1838   **SC**   13310
SN   Delays in any or all areas including cognitive, social, language, sensory, and emotional development.
  B   Development   1967
  N   Failure to Thrive   1988
         Language Delay   1988
         Retarded Speech Development   1973
  R   Developmental Age Groups   1973

Delayed Development — (cont'd)
         Developmental Disabilities   1982
         ↓ Human Development   1967
         ↓ Physical Development   1973
         ↓ Psychogenesis   1973

Delayed Feedback   1973
PN 171   **SC**   13320
  B   Feedback   1967
         Perceptual Stimulation   1973
  N   Delayed Auditory Feedback   1973

Delayed Parenthood   1985
PN 50   **SC**   13325
SN   Voluntary decision to postpone parenthood, usually for reasons involving personal development or career interests.
  R   Childlessness   1982
         ↓ Family Planning   1973
         Family Planning Attitudes   1973
         Parental Role   1973

Delayed Reinforcement
Use   Reinforcement Delay

Delayed Speech
Use   Retarded Speech Development

Deletion (Chromosome)   1973
PN 46   **SC**   13340
  B   Chromosome Disorders   1973

Delinquency (Juvenile)
Use   Juvenile Delinquency

Delirium   1973
PN 966   **SC**   13360
  B   Consciousness Disturbances   1973
         Symptoms   1967
  R   Hyperthermia   1973

Delirium Tremens   1973
PN 144   **SC**   13370
SN   Acute alcoholic, psychotic condition characterized by intense tremors, anxiety, hallucinations, and delusions.
  B   Alcoholic Hallucinosis   1973
         Syndromes   1973

Delta Rhythm   1973
PN 124   **SC**   13380
SN   Electrically measured impulses or waves of high amplitude and low frequency (1-3 cycles per second) observable in the electroencephalogram during sleep stages 3 and 4 (moderate to deep sleep).
  B   Electrical Activity   1967
         Electroencephalography   1967

Delusions   1967
PN 2264   **SC**   13390
SN   False personal beliefs held despite contradictory evidence and common sense.
  B   Thought Disturbances   1973
  R   Capgras Syndrome   1985
         Erotomania   1997
         Grandiosity   1994
         ↓ Schizophrenia   1967

Dementia   1985
PN 9332   **SC**   13395

Dementia — (cont'd)

B   Mental Disorders   1967
      Organic Brain Syndromes   1973
N   AIDS Dementia Complex   1997
      Dementia with Lewy Bodies   2001
      ↓ Presenile Dementia   1973
      ↓ Senile Dementia   1973
      ↓ Vascular Dementia   1997
R   Alzheimers Disease   1973
      Cognitive Impairment   2003
      Creutzfeldt Jakob Syndrome   1994
      ↓ Neurodegenerative Diseases   2004
      Parkinsons Disease   1973
      Picks Disease   1973
      Pseudodementia   1985

Dementia (Multi Infarct)
Use   Multi Infarct Dementia

Dementia (Presenile)
Use   Presenile Dementia

Dementia (Senile)
Use   Senile Dementia

Dementia of Alzheimers Type
Use   Alzheimers Disease

Dementia Paralytica
Use   General Paresis

Dementia Praecox
Use   Schizophrenia

Dementia with Lewy Bodies   2001
PN 178   **SC** 13435
SN   Neurodegenerative disease marked by the presence of Lewy body cells in the cerebral cortex and brain stem. Symptoms often include dementia, Parkinsonism, and striking fluctuations in cognitive performance.
UF   Lewy Body Disease
B   Dementia   1985
      Neurodegenerative Diseases   2004
R   Alzheimers Disease   1973
      Parkinsonism   1994
      Parkinsons Disease   1973

Democracy   1973
PN 427   **SC** 13440
B   Political Economic Systems   1973
R   ↓ Civil Rights   1978

Democratic Party
Use   Political Parties

Demographic Characteristics   1967
PN 18774   **SC** 13460
UF   Population Characteristics
R   Biographical Data   1978
      ↓ Population   1973
      Psychosocial Factors   1988

Demonic Possession
Use   Spirit Possession

Demonstrations (Social)
Use   Social Demonstrations

Dendrites   1973
PN 319   **SC** 13490
B   Neurons   1973

Denial   1973
PN 966   **SC** 13500
SN   Exclusion from conscious awareness of unpleasant realities, which would produce anxiety if acknowledged.
B   Defense Mechanisms   1967
R   Anosognosia   1994

Density (Social)
Use   Social Density

Dental Education   1973
PN 75   **SC** 13520
B   Graduate Education   1973

Dental Students   1973
PN 137   **SC** 13530
B   Students   1967
R   Graduate Students   1967

Dental Surgery   1973
PN 93   **SC** 13540
B   Dental Treatment   1973
      Surgery   1971

Dental Treatment   1973
PN 691   **SC** 13550
B   Physical Treatment Methods   1973
N   Dental Surgery   1973

Dentist Patient Interaction
Use   Therapeutic Processes

Dentistry   1973
PN 151   **SC** 13560
B   Medical Sciences   1967

Dentists   1973
PN 203   **SC** 13570
B   Medical Personnel   1967

Deoxycorticosterone   1973
PN 30   **SC** 13580
B   Adrenal Cortex Hormones   1973
      Corticosteroids   1973

Deoxyglucose   1991
PN 99   **SC** 13585
B   Carbohydrates   1973

Deoxyribonucleic Acid   1973
PN 422   **SC** 13590
UF   DNA (Deoxyribonucleic Acid)
B   Nucleic Acids   1973
R   Cloning   2003
      Genome   2003

Dependency (Drug)
Use   Drug Dependency

Dependency (Personality)   1967
PN 2109   **SC** 13620
SN   Lack of self-reliance, reflecting need for security, love, and protection from others.
B   Personality Traits   1967
R   Abandonment   1997
      Attachment Behavior   1985
      Codependency   1991
      Dependent Personality Disorder   1994
      Enabling   1997

Dependent Personality Disorder   1994
PN 73   **SC** 13625
SN   Personality disorder characterized by pervasive patterns of dependent, passive, and submissive behavior.
B   Personality Disorders   1967
R   Codependency   1991
      Dependency (Personality)   1967

Dependent Variables   1973
PN 120   **SC** 13630
SN   Statistical or experimental parameters whose values change as a consequence of changes in one or more other independent variables.
B   Statistical Variables   1973

Depersonalization   1973
PN 389   **SC** 13640
SN   State in which an individual perceives or experiences a sensation of unreality concerning himself or his environment; seen in disorders such as schizophrenia, affective disorders, organic mental disorders, and personality disorders.
B   Dissociative Disorders   2001
      Symptoms   1967
R   Alienation   1971

Depression (Emotion)   1967
PN 17418   **SC** 13650
SN   Mild depression that is not considered clinical depression. For clinical depression, use MAJOR DEPRESSION.
HN   Prior to 1988, also used for major depression in clinical populations.
B   Emotional States   1973
R   ↓ Major Depression   1988
      Sadness   1973
      ↓ Separation Reactions   1997

Depressive Reaction (Neurotic)
Use   Major Depression

Deprivation   1967
PN 1247   **SC** 13680
SN   Removal, denial, or lack of something needed or desired.
N   Cultural Deprivation   1973
      Food Deprivation   1967
      REM Dream Deprivation   1973
      Sleep Deprivation   1967
      ↓ Stimulus Deprivation   1973
      Water Deprivation   1967
R   Environmental Stress   1973
      ↓ Motivation   1967
      Physiological Stress   1967
      Psychological Stress   1973
      ↓ Stress   1967

Depth Perception   1967
PN 2046   **SC** 13690
B   Spatial Perception   1967

Depth Perception — (cont'd)
N Stereoscopic Vision 1973
R Eye Convergence 1982
Linear Perspective 1982
Motion Parallax 1997
Ocular Accommodation 1982

Depth Psychology 1973
PN 263 SC 13700
SN Any of the psychological theories which study the unconscious processes of the personality.
B Psychology 1967

Dermatitis 1973
PN 100 SC 13710
B Skin Disorders 1973
N Eczema 1973
Neurodermatitis 1973
R Allergic Skin Disorders 1973
↓ Infectious Disorders 1973
↓ Toxic Disorders 1973

Dermatomes
Use Cutaneous Receptive Fields

Desegregation
Use Social Integration

Desensitization (Systematic)
Use Systematic Desensitization Therapy

Desertion
Use Abandonment

Design (Experimental)
Use Experimental Design

Design (Man Machine Systems)
Use Human Machine Systems Design

Desipramine 1973
PN 966 SC 13760
B Tricyclic Antidepressant Drugs 1997

Desirability (Social)
Use Social Desirability

Desires
Use Motivation

Detection (Signal)
Use Signal Detection (Perception)

Detention (Legal)
Use Legal Detention

Determinism 1997
PN 101 SC 13815
SN A doctrine that assumes events or objects have antecedent causes that determine their nature.
B Philosophies 1967
R Epistemology 1973
Idealism 1973
Positivism 1973
Volition 1988

Detoxification 1973
PN 882 SC 13820
B Alcohol Rehabilitation 1982
Drug Rehabilitation 1973
R Alcohol Withdrawal 1994
↓ Drug Abstinence 1994
↓ Drug Therapy 1967
↓ Drug Withdrawal 1973
Sobriety 1988

Developed Countries 1985
PN 224 SC 13823
B Countries 1967

Developing Countries 1985
PN 991 SC 13825
UF Third World Countries
Underdeveloped Countries
B Countries 1967
R Modernization 2003

Development 1967
PN 2356 SC 13830
UF Growth
Ontogeny
N Animal Development 1978
Career Development 1985
Community Development 1997
Curriculum Development 1973
↓ Delayed Development 1973
↓ Human Development 1967
Organizational Development 1973
↓ Physical Development 1973
Precocious Development 1973
Professional Development 1982
↓ Program Development 1991
↓ Psychogenesis 1973
R Age Differences 1967
Critical Period 1988
Developmental Age Groups 1973
↓ Developmental Stages 1973
Life Span 2004
Sex Linked Developmental Differences 1973

Developmental Age Groups 1973
PN 639 SC 13840
SN Groups defined by a chronological age span, and characterized by certain physical, behavioral, psychological, and social attributes. Use AGE DIFFERENCES for age comparisons within or between groups.
R Adolescent Development 1973
Adult Development 1978
Age Differences 1967
↓ Aging 1991
↓ Childhood Development 1967
↓ Delayed Development 1973
↓ Development 1967
↓ Developmental Stages 1973
Emotional Development 1973
↓ Human Development 1967
Mental Age 1973
↓ Motor Development 1973
↓ Physical Development 1973
Precocious Development 1973
↓ Psychogenesis 1973

Developmental Differences
Use Age Differences

Developmental Disabilities 1982
PN 5123 SC 13853

Developmental Disabilities — (cont'd)
SN As encompassed in federal legislation for educational assistance to handicapped children, includes disabilities originating before age 18 that constitute substantial barriers to normal functioning. Use a more specific term if possible.
B Disabilities 2003
R Aspergers Syndrome 1991
↓ Autism 1967
↓ Communication Disorders 1982
↓ Congenital Disorders 1973
Deaf Blind 1991
↓ Delayed Development 1973
↓ Genetic Disorders 1973
↓ Human Development 1967
↓ Learning Disorders 1967
↓ Mental Retardation 1967
↓ Nervous System Disorders 1967
↓ Pervasive Developmental Disorders 2001

Developmental Measures 1994
PN 226 SC 13857
N Bayley Scales of Infant Development 1994

Developmental Psychology 1973
PN 2117 SC 13860
B Psychology 1967
N Adolescent Psychology 1973
Child Psychology 1967
Gerontology 1967
R ↓ Human Development 1967

Developmental Stages 1973
PN 2764 SC 13870
SN Phases in an individual's development characterized by certain physical, behavioral, mental, or social attributes, e.g., the latency stage of psychosexual development or the sensorimotor intelligence stage of cognitive development.
N Menopause 1973
↓ Prenatal Developmental Stages 1973
Puberty 1973
R Adolescent Development 1973
Adult Development 1978
↓ Aging 1991
↓ Childhood Development 1967
↓ Development 1967
Developmental Age Groups 1973
Erikson (Erik) 1991
Generativity 2001
↓ Human Development 1967
Life Changes 2004
Object Permanence 1985
↓ Perceptual Development 1973
↓ Physical Development 1973
Piaget (Jean) 1967
↓ Psychogenesis 1973
↓ Rites of Passage 1973

Deviant Behavior
Use Antisocial Behavior

Deviation IQ
Use Standard Scores

Deviations (Sexual)
Use Paraphilias

Devices (Experimental)
Use Apparatus

Dexamethasone 1985
PN 755   SC 13905
SN A synthetic analogue of cortisol.
B   Glucocorticoids 1982
R   Dexamethasone Suppression Test 1988

Dexamethasone Suppression Test 1988
PN 681   SC 13907
SN Laboratory analysis of hypersecretion of cortisol and the body's failure to suppress cortisol after the administration of dexamethasone. Used primarily for diagnosis of major depressive disorders.
B   Medical Diagnosis 1973
R   Dexamethasone 1985

Dexamphetamine
Use Dextroamphetamine

Dexedrine
Use Dextroamphetamine

Dexterity (Physical)
Use Physical Dexterity

Dextroamphetamine 1973
PN 1744   SC 13940
UF Amphetamine (d-)
     Dexamphetamine
     Dexedrine
B   Adrenergic Drugs 1973
     Amphetamine 1967
     Appetite Depressing Drugs 1973
     CNS Stimulating Drugs 1973
     Sympathomimetic Amines 1973

Diabetes 1973
PN 1862   SC 13950
B   Endocrine Disorders 1973
     Metabolism Disorders 1973
N   Diabetes Insipidus 1973
     Diabetes Mellitus 1973

Diabetes Insipidus 1973
PN 101   SC 13960
B   Diabetes 1973
R ↓ Genetic Disorders 1973

Diabetes Mellitus 1973
PN 1307   SC 13970
B   Diabetes 1973

Diacetylmorphine
Use Heroin

Diagnosis 1967
PN 9388   SC 13990
N   Computer Assisted Diagnosis 1973
     Differential Diagnosis 1967
     Educational Diagnosis 1978
     Galvanic Skin Response 1967
  ↓ Medical Diagnosis 1973
  ↓ Psychodiagnosis 1967
R   Autopsy 1973
     Clinical Judgment (Not Diagnosis) 1973
     Comorbidity 1991
     Diagnosis Related Groups 1988
  ↓ Disorders 1967
     Dual Diagnosis 1991

Diagnosis — (cont'd)
     General Health Questionnaire 1991
     Geriatric Assessment 1997
     Intake Interview 1994
     International Classification of Diseases 2001
     Labeling 1978
  ↓ Measurement 1967
  ↓ Mental Disorders 1967
     Misdiagnosis 1997
  ↓ Neuropsychological Assessment 1982
     Pain Measurement 1997
     Patient History 1973
  ↓ Physical Disorders 1997
     Prognosis 1973
     Research Diagnostic Criteria 1994
  ↓ Screening 1982
     Severity (Disorders) 1982
     Symptom Checklists 1991

Diagnosis Related Groups 1988
PN 79   SC 13985
UF DRGs
R   Cost Containment 1991
  ↓ Diagnosis 1967
     Health Care Costs 1994
  ↓ Health Insurance 1973
     Misdiagnosis 1997
  ↓ Professional Fees 1978

Diagnostic and Statistical Manual 1994
PN 1727   SC 13988
SN Used when the current Diagnostic and Statistical Manual or its revisions is the primary focus of the reference. Not used for specific psychodiagnostic categories.
HN Use PSYCHODIAGNOSTIC TYPOLOGIES to access references prior to 1994.
UF DSM
B   Psychodiagnostic Typologies 1967
H   International Classification of Diseases 2001
  ↓ Mental Disorders 1967
  ↓ Psychodiagnosis 1967
     Research Diagnostic Criteria 1994
     Subtypes (Disorders) 2004

Diagnostic Interview Schedule 1991
PN 134   SC 13900
B   Interview Schedules 2001
     Psychodiagnostic Interview 1973
R ↓ Psychodiagnostic Typologies 1967
  ↓ Screening 1982

Dialect 1973
PN 378   SC 14000
SN A variety of language characteristic of a geographical region or ethnic, occupational, socioeconomic, or other group.
B   Language 1967
N   Nonstandard English 1970
R   Ethnolinguistics 1973

Dialectics 1973
PN 482   SC 14010
SN Intellectual investigation through deductive reasoning and juxtaposition of opposing or contradictory ideas.
R ↓ Reasoning 1967

Dialysis 1973
PN 255   SC 14020
B   Physical Treatment Methods 1973
N   Hemodialysis 1973

Diaphragm (Anatomy) 1973
PN 20   SC 14030
B   Muscles 1967
     Respiratory System 1973
R   Thorax 1973

Diaphragms (Birth Control) 1973
PN 12   SC 14040
B   Contraceptive Devices 1973

Diarrhea 1973
PN 92   SC 14050
B   Colon Disorders 1973
R   Fecal Incontinence 1973

Diastolic Pressure 1973
PN 248   SC 14060
B   Blood Pressure 1967

Diazepam 1973
PN 2145   SC 14070
UF Valium
B   Benzodiazepines 1978
     Minor Tranquilizers 1973
     Muscle Relaxing Drugs 1973

Dichoptic Stimulation 1982
PN 140   SC 14075
SN Simultaneous presentation of different stimuli to each eye independently.
B   Visual Stimulation 1973

Dichotic Stimulation 1982
PN 848   SC 14077
SN Simultaneous presentation of different sounds to the two ears.
D   Auditory Stimulation 1967

Dieldrin
Use Insecticides

Diencephalon 1973
PN 302   SC 14110
B   Forebrain 1985
N ↓ Hypothalamus 1967
     Optic Chiasm 1973
  ↓ Thalamus 1967

Dietary Restraint 1994
PN 507   SC 14112
B   Eating Behavior 2004
R ↓ Appetite 1973
     Diets 1978
     Food Intake 1967

Dietary Supplements 2001
PN 130   SC 14113
SN Orally ingested products intended as supplements to the diet, including vitamins, herbs, amino acids, and concentrates, metabolites, and extracts of these substances.
UF Nutritional Supplements
R ↓ Alternative Medicine 1997
  ↓ Amino Acids 1973
  ↓ Antioxidants 2004
     Diets 1978
  ↓ Medicinal Herbs and Plants 2001
     Nutrition 1973
  ↓ Vitamins 1973

Diets   1978
PN 3615   SC 14114
SN Food and drink regularly consumed or pre-scribed for a special reason. Used for human or animal populations.
- R   Dietary Restraint   1994
-     Dietary Supplements   2001
- ↓ Drinking Behavior   1978
- ↓ Eating Behavior   2004
-     Food   1978
-     Food Additives   1978
-     Food Allergies   1973
-     Food Deprivation   1967
-     Food Preferences   1973
- ↓ Health Behavior   1982
-     Nutrition   1973
- ↓ Nutritional Deficiencies   1973
-     Obesity   1973
- ↓ Underweight   1973
-     Weight Control   1985

Differential Aptitude Tests   1973
PN 60   SC 14150
- B   Aptitude Measures   1967

Differential Diagnosis   1967
PN 5340   SC 14160
SN Diagnosis aimed at distinguishing between physical and/or mental disorders of similar character by comparison of symptoms.
- B   Diagnosis   1967
- R   Comorbidity   1991
-     Dual Diagnosis   1991
-     Educational Diagnosis   1978
- ↓ Medical Diagnosis   1973
- ↓ Psychodiagnosis   1967

Differential Limen
Use Thresholds

Differential Personality Inventory
SN Term was discontinued in 1997. In 2000, the term was removed from all records containing it, and replaced with NONPROJECTIVE PERSONALITY MEASURES, its postable counterpart.
Use Nonprojective Personality Measures

Differential Reinforcement   1973
PN 939   SC 14190
SN Selective reinforcement of one response in a defined category (response class) of responses to the exclusion of any other members (responses) of that category. Has application in treatment as well as in experimental contexts.
- B   Reinforcement   1967
- R   ↓ Discrimination Learning   1982
-     Omission Training   1985

Difficulty Level (Test)   1973
PN 331   SC 14200
- UF Test Difficulty
- B   Test Construction   1973
-     Testing   1967
- R   Item Response Theory   1985

Digestion   1973
PN 93   SC 14210
- B   Physiology   1967
- R   ↓ Digestive System   1967
-     ↓ Ingestion   2001
-     Salivation   1973
-     Swallowing   1988

Digestive System   1967
PN 374   SC 14220
- B   Anatomical Systems   1973
- N   Esophagus   1973
-     ↓ Gastrointestinal System   1973
-     Liver   1973
-     Mouth (Anatomy)   1967
-     Pharynx   1973
-     Teeth (Anatomy)   1973
-     ↓ Tongue   1973
- R   Digestion   1973
-     ↓ Digestive System Disorders   1973
-     Salivary Glands   1973

Digestive System Disorders   1973
PN 104   SC 14230
- B   Physical Disorders   1997
- N   Cystic Fibrosis   1985
-     ↓ Gastrointestinal Disorders   1973
-     Jaundice   1973
-     ↓ Liver Disorders   1973
- R   ↓ Digestive System   1967
-     ↓ Infectious Disorders   1973
-     ↓ Neoplasms   1967
-     ↓ Symptoms   1967
-     ↓ Toxic Disorders   1973

Digit Span Testing   1973
PN 266   SC 14240
SN Test of immediate recall involving presentation of a random series of numerals which the subject repeats after the series has been presented.
- B   Measurement   1967

Digital Computers   1973
PN 197   SC 14250
SN Electronic or electromechanical machines that operate directly on binary digits when executing programs and manipulating data (e.g., calculators).
- UF Calculators
- B   Computers   1967

Digits (Mathematics)
Use Numbers (Numerals)

Dihydroergotamine   1973
PN 31   SC 14270
- B   Adrenergic Blocking Drugs   1973
-     Analgesic Drugs   1973
-     Ergot Derivatives   1973
-     Vasoconstrictor Drugs   1973

Dihydroxyphenylacetic Acid   1991
PN 140   SC 14273
- UF DOPAC
- B   Acids   1973
-     Dopamine Metabolites   1982

Dihydroxytryptamine   1991
PN 46   SC 14275
- B   Serotonin Antagonists   1973

Dilantin
Use Diphenylhydantoin

Dilation (Pupil)
Use Pupil Dilation

Diphenhydramine   1973
PN 80   SC 14310

Diphenhydramine — (cont'd)
- UF Benadryl
- B   Amines   1973
-     Antihistaminic Drugs   1973
-     Antitremor Drugs   1973

Diphenylhydantoin   1973
PN 218   SC 14320
- UF Dilantin
-     Diphenylhydantoin Sodium
-     Phenytoin
- B   Anticonvulsive Drugs   1973

Diphenylhydantoin Sodium
Use Diphenylhydantoin

Diptera   1973
PN 362   SC 14350
- UF Flies
- B   Insects   1967
- N   Drosophila   1973
- R   Larvae   1973

Directed Discussion Method   1973
PN 119   SC 14360
- B   Teaching Methods   1967
- R   Lecture Method   1973

Directed Reverie Therapy
Use Guided Imagery

Direction Perception   1997
PN 504   SC 14365
- B   Spatial Perception   1967
- R   Cognitive Maps   1982
-     ↓ Motion Perception   1967
-     ↓ Perceptual Localization   1967
-     ↓ Spatial Memory   1988
-     Spatial Organization   1973

Disabilities   2003
PN 253   SC 14366
HN Use DISORDERS to access references from 2001 to June 2003.
- UF Handicaps
- N   Developmental Disabilities   1982
-     ↓ Learning Disabilities   1973
-     ↓ Multiple Disabilities   2001
-     ↓ Reading Disabilities   1967
- R   Disability Discrimination   1997
-     Disability Laws   1994
-     ↓ Disabled (Attitudes Toward)   1997

Disability Discrimination   1997
PN 120   SC 57480
- B   Social Discrimination   1982
- R   Affirmative Action   1985
-     ↓ Civil Rights   1978
-     ↓ Disabilities   2003
-     Disability Laws   1994
-     ↓ Disabled (Attitudes Toward)   1997
-     ↓ Disorders   1967
-     ↓ Mental Disorders   1967
-     Mental Illness (Attitudes Toward)   1967
-     ↓ Physical Illness (Attitudes Toward)   1985
-     ↓ Prejudice   1967
-     Sensory Disabilities (Attitudes Toward)   2001

Disability Evaluation   1988
PN 196   SC 14367

Disability Evaluation — (cont'd)
SN Evaluation of one's ability to work in order to determine the need for insurance or health benefits.
R ↓ Employee Benefits 1973
   ↓ Insurance 1973
     Social Security 1988

Disability Laws 1994
PN 488   **SC** 57410
SN Rules declared by federal or state governments and enacted by legislative bodies that affect populations with mental or physical disabilities or disorders. Used for the laws themselves, or the interpretation or application of the laws.
B Laws 1967
R Civil Law 1994
   ↓ Civil Rights 1978
   ↓ Disabilities 2003
     Disability Discrimination 1997
     Disabled Personnel 1997

Disability Management 1991
PN 124   **SC** 14368
SN Process of returning an impaired or disabled worker to the workplace. Includes evaluation, assessment, early intervention, and rehabilitation.
B Management 1967
R Disabled Personnel 1997
     Employee Assistance Programs 1985
   ↓ Prevention 1973
   ↓ Rehabilitation 1967
     Vocational Evaluation 1991
   ↓ Vocational Rehabilitation 1967

Disabled (Attitudes Toward) 1997
PN 1794   **SC** 14373
HN In 1997, this term replaced the discontinued term HANDICAPPED (ATTITUDES TOWARD). In 2000, HANDICAPPED (ATTITUDES TOWARD) was removed from all records containing it, and replaced with DISABLED (ATTITUDES TOWARD).
UF Handicapped (Attitudes Toward)
B Attitudes 1967
N Mental Illness (Attitudes Toward) 1967
    Mental Retardation (Attitudes Toward) 2001
    Physical Disabilities (Attitudes Toward) 2001
    Sensory Disabilities (Attitudes Toward) 2001
R ↓ Disabilities 2003
    Disability Discrimination 1997
   ↓ Physical Illness (Attitudes Toward) 1985
    Stereotyped Attitudes 1967

Disabled Personnel 1997
PN 268   **SC** 14369
SN Employees with physical or mental disabilities or injuries resulting from work-related activities.
B Personnel 1967
R Disability Laws 1994
    Disability Management 1991
   ↓ Disorders 1967
    Impaired Professionals 1985
    Supported Employment 1994
    Workers' Compensation Insurance 2003
   ↓ Working Conditions 1973

Disadvantaged 1967
PN 3737   **SC** 14370
SN Individuals deprived of equal access to society's resources, especially as regards education, culture, and employment.
UF Economically Disadvantaged
    Socially Disadvantaged
    Underprivileged

Disadvantaged — (cont'd)
R Cultural Deprivation 1973
   ↓ Homeless 1988
    Poverty 1973
   ↓ Social Class 1967
   ↓ Social Deprivation 1973
   ↓ Socioeconomic Status 1967

Disappointment 1973
PN 78   **SC** 14380
B Emotional States 1973
R Dissatisfaction 1973
   ↓ Separation Reactions 1997

Disasters 1973
PN 938   **SC** 14390
N Natural Disasters 1973
R ↓ Accidents 1967
   ↓ Crises 1971
   ↓ Stress 1967

Discharge Planning 1994
PN 100   **SC** 14395
B Case Management 1991
    Treatment Planning 1997
R Aftercare 1973
    Deinstitutionalization 1982
   ↓ Facility Discharge 1988
   ↓ Hospital Discharge 1973
   ↓ Institutional Release 1978
    Posttreatment Followup 1973
    Psychiatric Hospital Discharge 1978
    Treatment Termination 1982

Discipline (Child)
Use Child Discipline

Discipline (Classroom)
Use Classroom Discipline

Disclosure (Experimental)
Use Debriefing (Experimental)

Disclosure (Self)
Use Self Disclosure

Discourse Analysis 1997
PN 1682   **SC** 14425
SN Analysis of written and spoken language.
B Content Analysis 1978
R ↓ Grammar 1967
   ↓ Language 1967
   ↓ Linguistics 1973
    Morphology (Language) 1973
    Pragmatics 1985
    Rhetoric 1991
   ↓ Semantics 1967
   ↓ Syntax 1971
    Text Structure 1982
   ↓ Verbal Communication 1967

Discovery Teaching Method 1973
PN 138   **SC** 14430
SN Unstructured or guided instruction which encourages independent exploration or discovery.
B Teaching Methods 1967
R ↓ Experiential Learning 1997
    Montessori Method 1973
    Nondirected Discussion Method 1973

Discovery Teaching Method — (cont'd)
    Open Classroom Method 1973
    Self Regulated Learning 2003

Discriminant Validity
Use Test Validity

Discrimination 1967
PN 2737   **SC** 14450
SN Conceptually broad term referring to the general process of differentiation between qualities, entities, or people. Use a more specific term if possible.
N Cognitive Discrimination 1973
    Drug Discrimination 1985
   ↓ Perceptual Discrimination 1973
   ↓ Social Discrimination 1982
    Stimulus Discrimination 1973
R ↓ Discrimination Learning 1982
   ↓ Perception 1967
    Stereotyped Attitudes 1967

Discrimination (Cognitive)
Use Cognitive Discrimination

Discrimination (Social)
Use Social Discrimination

Discrimination Learning 1982
PN 2859   **SC** 14445
SN Learning paradigm in which responses to one stimulus (S+) are reinforced while responses to another stimulus (S-) are either not reinforced or are punished. Also, the learned discriminative responses themselves.
UF Discriminative Learning
B Learning 1967
    Operant Conditioning 1967
N Drug Discrimination 1985
    Matching to Sample 1994
    Nonreversal Shift Learning 1973
    Reversal Shift Learning 1967
R ↓ Concept Formation 1967
    Differential Reinforcement 1973
   ↓ Discrimination 1967
    Extinction (Learning) 1967
    Fading (Conditioning) 1982
   ↓ Generalization (Learning) 1982
    Kinship Recognition 1988
    Stimulus Control 1967
    Stimulus Discrimination 1973

Discriminative Learning
Use Discrimination Learning

Discriminative Stimulus
Use Conditioned Stimulus

Discussion (Group)
Use Group Discussion

Disease Course 1991
PN 4151   **SC** 14470
SN Stages or progression of physical or mental disorders. Compare PROGNOSIS.
UF Course of Illness
    Disorder Course
R ↓ Disorders 1967
   ↓ Mental Disorders 1967
   ↓ Physical Disorders 1997
    Prognosis 1973

Disease Outbreaks
Use Epidemics

Disease Transmission 2004
PN 135 *   SC 14480
SN Transmission of disease from one individual to another.
HN This term was introduced in June 2004. Psyc-INFO records from the past 10 years were re-indexed with this term. The posting note reflects the number of records that were re-indexed.
R Blood Transfusion 1973
     Etiology 1967
  ↓ Infectious Disorders 1973
     Intravenous Drug Usage 1994
  ↓ Sexual Intercourse (Human) 1973
  ↓ Sexually Transmitted Diseases 2003

Diseases (Venereal)
Use Sexually Transmitted Diseases

Disgust 1994
PN 117   SC 14495
B Emotional States 1973
R ↓ Aversion 1967

Dishonesty 1973
PN 149   SC 14500
B Personality Traits 1967
R Cheating 1973
  ↓ Deception 1967
     Fraud 1994
     Sincerity 1973

Dislike
Use Aversion

Disorder Course
Use Disease Course

Disorders 1967
PN 17522   SC 14520
SN Conceptually broad term referring primarily to physical illness. Also used when particular disorders are not specified. Use a more specific term if possible. For general discussions of health impairment consider also the term HEALTH.
HN The term HANDICAPPED was also used to represent this concept from 1967-1996, and DISABLED was used from 1997-2000. In 2000, DISORDERS replaced the discontinued and deleted terms DISABLED and HANDICAPPED. DISABLED and HANDICAPPED were removed from all records containing them and replaced with DISORDERS.
UF Exceptional Children (Handicapped)
N Adventitious Disorders 2001
  ↓ Behavior Disorders 1971
  ↓ Communication Disorders 1982
  ↓ Congenital Disorders 1973
  ↓ Emotionally Disturbed 1973
  ↓ Learning Disorders 1967
  ↓ Mental Disorders 1967
  ↓ Physical Disorders 1997
R ↓ Brain Damage 1967
  ↓ Chronic Illness 1991
     Chronicity (Disorders) 1982
     Comorbidity 1991
  ↓ Diagnosis 1967
     Disability Discrimination 1997
     Disabled Personnel 1997

Disorders — (cont'd)
     Disease Course 1991
     Etiology 1967
     Health Complaints 1997
     Illness Behavior 1982
  ↓ Injuries 1973
     International Classification of Diseases 2001
  ↓ Mental Retardation 1967
     Onset (Disorders) 1973
     Predisposition 1973
     Premorbidity 1978
     Prenatal Exposure 1991
     Prognosis 1973
     Recovery (Disorders) 1973
     Relapse (Disorders) 1973
  ↓ Remission (Disorders) 1973
     Severity (Disorders) 1982
     Special Needs 1994
     Subtypes (Disorders) 2004
     Susceptibility (Disorders) 1973
  ↓ Symptoms 1967
  ↓ Syndromes 1973

Disorientation (Place)
Use Place Disorientation

Disorientation (Time)
Use Time Disorientation

Displacement (Defense Mechanism) 1973
PN 61   SC 14550
B Defense Mechanisms 1967

Displays 1967
PN 382   SC 14560
SN Physical arrangements of stimuli to form a desired pattern; temporal, spatial, or otherwise.
N Auditory Displays 1973
     Graphical Displays 1985
     Tactual Displays 1973
  ↓ Visual Displays 1973
R ↓ Instrument Controls 1985

Disposition
Use Personality

Disruptive Behavior
Use Behavior Problems

Dissatisfaction 1973
PN 324   SC 14590
B Emotional States 1973
R Disappointment 1973
     Frustration 1967
  ↓ Satisfaction 1973

Dissociation 2001
PN 478   SC 14592
SN Used generally to describe the process whereby thoughts, attitudes, emotions, or a coordinated set of activities becomes separated from one's personality or mental processes. Compare DISSOCIATIVE DISORDERS.
HN Consider DISSOCIATIVE PATTERNS from 1973-2000.
R ↓ Amnesia 1967
  ↓ Consciousness Disturbances 1973
  ↓ Consciousness States 1971
  ↓ Dissociative Disorders 2001
  ↓ Neurosis 1967

Dissociative Disorders 2001
PN 1615   SC 14593
SN Mental disorders characterized by disruptions and/or alterations in the normally integrated functions of consciousness, memory, or identity. Compare DISSOCIATION.
HN Consider DISSOCIATIVE PATTERNS to access records from 1973-2000.
UF Dissociative Neurosis
     Dissociative Patterns
     Hysterical Neurosis (Dissociation)
B Mental Disorders 1967
N Depersonalization 1973
     Dissociative Identity Disorder 1997
     Fugue Reaction 1973
R ↓ Amnesia 1967
  ↓ Consciousness Disturbances 1973
     Dissociation 2001
  ↓ Personality Disorders 1967

Dissociative Identity Disorder 1997
PN 1367   SC 14595
HN In 1997, this term was created to replace the discontinued term MULTIPLE PERSONALITY. In 2000, MULTIPLE PERSONALITY was removed from all records and replaced with DISSOCIATIVE IDENTITY DISORDER.
UF Multiple Personality
     Split Personality
B Dissociative Disorders 2001

Dissociative Neurosis
Use Dissociative Disorders

Dissociative Patterns
Use Dissociative Disorders

Dissonance (Cognitive)
Use Cognitive Dissonance

Distance Discrimination
Use Distance Perception

Distance Education 2003
PN 186   SC 14633
SN Type of education where students work at home or at the office and communicate with faculty via various forms of communications media.
HN This term was introduced in June 2003. Psyc-INFO records from the past 10 years were re-indexed with this term. The posting note reflects the number of records that were re-indexed.
UF Distance Learning
B Education 1967
R Computer Mediated Communication 2003
  ↓ Continuing Education 1985
  ↓ Electronic Communication 2001
     Individualized Instruction 1973
  ↓ Nontraditional Education 1982
  ↓ Telecommunications Media 1973

Distance Learning
Use Distance Education

Distance Perception 1973
PN 969   SC 14640
UF Distance Discrimination
B Spatial Perception 1967
N Apparent Distance 1973
     Motion Parallax 1997

Distance Perception — **(cont'd)**
R　Eye Convergence　1982
　　Linear Perspective　1982

Distortion (Perceptual)
Use　Perceptual Distortion

Distractibility　1973
PN　374　　　　　　　　　**SC**　14660
　B　Symptoms　1967
　R　↓ Attention Deficit Disorder　1985
　　　Attention Deficit Disorder with
　　　　　Hyperactivity　2001
　　　Distraction　1978

Distraction　1978
PN　1502　　　　　　　　**SC**　14663
SN　Process or potential cause of interruption of
attention.
　R　↓ Attention　1967
　　　Attention Span　1973
　　　Concentration　1982
　　　Distractibility　1973
　　　Divided Attention　1973
　　　Selective Attention　1973

Distress　1973
PN　6022　　　　　　　　**SC**　14670
SN　Negative emotional state characterized by phys-
ical and/or emotional discomfort, pain, or anguish.
Compare STRESS.
　UF　Anguish
　B　Emotional States　1973
　R　Agitation　1991
　 ┃ Separation Reactions　1997
　 ↓ Stress　1967
　　　Suffering　1973

Distress Calls (Animal)
Use　Animal Distress Calls

Distributed Practice　1973
PN　151　　　　　　　　　**SC**　14690
SN　Practice schedule in which relatively short peri-
ods of practice are spaced with intermittent rest or
periods of activity unrelated to the practiced task.
Compare MASSED PRACTICE.
　B　Learning Schedules　1967
　　　Practice　1967

Distribution (Frequency)
Use　Frequency Distribution

Distributive Justice　2003
PN　8　　　　　　　　　　**SC**　14705
SN　The fairness of resource allocation, responsibil-
ity distribution, and other decision outcomes.
HN　Use JUSTICE to access references from 1988
to June 2003.
　B　Justice　1973
　R　Equity (Payment)　1978
　 ↓ Equity (Social)　1978
　 ↓ Organizational Behavior　1978

Distrust
Use　Suspicion

Disulfiram　1978
PN　187　　　　　　　　　**SC**　14725
　UF　Antabuse
　B　Emetic Drugs　1973

Diuresis　1973
PN　31　　　　　　　　　　**SC**　14730
SN　Increased flow of urine.
　B　Urination　1967
　R　↓ Diuretics　1973

Diuretics　1973
PN　119　　　　　　　　　**SC**　14740
　B　Drugs　1967
　N　Acetazolamide　1973
　　　Caffeine　1973
　　　Theophylline　1973
　R　↓ Antihypertensive Drugs　1973
　　　Diuresis　1973
　　　Probenecid　1982
　　　Purging (Eating Disorders)　2003
　 ↓ Urination　1967

Diurnal Variations
Use　Human Biological Rhythms

Divergent Thinking　1973
PN　677　　　　　　　　　**SC**　14760
SN　Component of intelligence which is manifested
in the ability to generate a wide variety of original
ideas or solutions to a particular problem. Compare
CREATIVITY.
　B　Thinking　1967
　R　↓ Abstraction　1967
　　　Creativity　1967
　　　Declarative Knowledge　1997
　 ↓ Inductive Deductive Reasoning　1973
　 ↓ Intelligence　1967
　　　Procedural Knowledge　1997

Diversity in the Workplace　2003
PN　81　　　　　　　　　　**SC**　14763
SN　All forms of variation among individuals in the
workplace, including but not limited to, ethnicity, gen-
der, age, sexual orientation, religious affiliation, abil-
ity, financial status, and personality.
HN　This term was introduced in June 2003. Psyc-
INFO records from the past 10 years were re-indexed
with this term. The posting note reflects the number
of records that were re-indexed.
　UF　Workforce Diversity
　　　Workplace Diversity
　R　Affirmative Action　1985
　　　Age Differences　1967
　　　Cross Cultural Differences　1967
　 ↓ Employee Characteristics　1988
　 ↓ Human Sex Differences　1967
　　　Individual Differences　1967
　　　Multiculturalism　1997
　 ↓ Organizational Characteristics　1997
　　　Organizational Climate　1973
　　　Racial and Ethnic Differences　1982

Divided Attention　1973
PN　818　　　　　　　　　**SC**　14765
SN　Simultaneous attending to two or more stimuli or
through two or more perceptual modalities. Compare
SELECTIVE ATTENTION.
　B　Attention　1967
　R　Distraction　1978
　　　Selective Attention　1973

Division of Labor　1988
PN　534　　　　　　　　　**SC**　14767
　N　Animal Division of Labor　1973
　R　↓ Economics　1985
　　　Household Management　1985
　 ↓ Occupations　1967

Division of Labor — **(cont'd)**
　　　Sex Roles　1967
　　　Work Load　1982

Division of Labor (Animal)
Use　Animal Division of Labor

Divorce　1973
PN　4688　　　　　　　　**SC**　14780
　B　Marital Separation　1973
　R　Child Custody　1982
　　　Child Support　1988
　　　Divorced Persons　1973
　 ↓ Family　1967
　　　Joint Custody　1988
　　　Life Changes　2004
　　　Mediation　1988
　　　Remarriage　1985

Divorced Persons　1973
PN　789　　　　　　　　　**SC**　14790
　R　Divorce　1973
　 ↓ Family　1967
　 ↓ Marital Separation　1973
　 ↓ Marital Status　1973
　 ↓ Parental Absence　1973

Dizygotic Twins
Use　Heterozygotic Twins

Dizziness
Use　Vertigo

DNA (Deoxyribonucleic Acid)
Use　Deoxyribonucleic Acid

Doctors
Use　Physicians

Dogmatism　1978
PN　544　　　　　　　　　**SC**　14830
　B　Personality Traits　1967
　R　Authoritarianism　1967
　　　Openmindedness　1978
　　　Relativism　1997

Dogs　1967
PN　2203　　　　　　　　**SC**　14840
　B　Canids　1997

Doll Play　1973
PN　110　　　　　　　　　**SC**　14850
　B　Recreation　1967
　R　Anatomically Detailed Dolls　1991
　　　Childhood Play Behavior　1978

Dolphins　1973
PN　257　　　　　　　　　**SC**　14860
　B　Whales　1985
　R　Porpoises　1973

Domestic Service Personnel　1973
PN　46　　　　　　　　　　**SC**　14870
　UF　Maids
　B　Service Personnel　1991
　R　↓ Nonprofessional Personnel　1982

Domestic Violence
Use Family Violence

Domestication (Animal)
Use Animal Domestication

Dominance 1967
PN 1095   **SC** 14900
SN Conceptually broad term referring to relative positions of objects, persons, things, or processes. Use a more specific term if possible.
N Animal Dominance 1973
  ↓ Cerebral Dominance 1973
  Dominance Hierarchy 1973
  Genetic Dominance 1973
R Abuse of Power 1997
  Authoritarianism 1967
  Authority 1967
  Bullying 2003
  Coercion 1994
  Emotional Superiority 1973
  Obedience 1973
  ↓ Power 1967
  ↓ Status 1967

Dominance (Animal)
Use Animal Dominance

Dominance Hierarchy 1973
PN 1130   **SC** 14890
SN Social structure of a group as it relates to the relative social rank or dominance status of its members. Used for human or animal populations.
B Dominance 1967
R Animal Dominance 1973
  ↓ Social Behavior 1967
  ↓ Social Structure 1967

Domination
Use Authoritarianism

DOPA 1973
PN 100   **SC** 14940
B Amino Acids 1973
R Carbidopa 1988
  Dopamine 1973
  Levodopa 1973
  Methyldopa 1973

DOPAC
Use Dihydroxyphenylacetic Acid

Dopamine 1973
PN 7245   **SC** 14950
B Catecholamines 1973
R DOPA 1973
  ↓ Dopamine Metabolites 1982
  ↓ Heart Rate Affecting Drugs 1973
  Homovanillic Acid 1978
  Levodopa 1973
  Methyldopa 1973
  Methylphenyltetrahydropyridine 1994

Dopamine Agonists 1985
PN 1249   **SC** 14951
B Drugs 1967
N ↓ Amphetamine 1967
  Apomorphine 1973
  Morphine 1973
  Quinpirole 1994

Dopamine Antagonists 1982
PN 1349   **SC** 14952
B Amine Oxidase Inhibitors 1973
N Sulpiride 1973
R ↓ Catecholamines 1973
  ↓ CNS Depressant Drugs 1973
  ↓ Decarboxylase Inhibitors 1982
  ↓ Narcotic Drugs 1973
  ↓ Tranquilizing Drugs 1967

Dopamine Metabolites 1982
PN 264   **SC** 14955
SN Molecules generated from the metabolism of dopamine.
B Metabolites 1973
N Dihydroxyphenylacetic Acid 1991
  Homovanillic Acid 1978
R Acetaldehyde 1982
  Dopamine 1973
  ↓ Metabolism 1967

Dormitories 1973
PN 459   **SC** 14960
UF Residence Halls
B Housing 1973
  School Facilities 1973

Dorsal Horns 1985
PN 205   **SC** 14965
SN Longitudinal columns of gray matter (i.e., neuronal cell bodies) in the posterior spinal cord mainly serving sensory mechanisms.
B Spinal Cord 1973
R ↓ Afferent Pathways 1982
  Dorsal Roots 1973

Dorsal Roots 1973
PN 152   **SC** 14970
B Spinal Cord 1973
R Dorsal Horns 1985

Double Bind Interaction 1973
PN 108   **SC** 14990
SN Simultaneous communication of conflicting messages in which the response to either message evokes rejection or disapproval.
B Interpersonal Communication 1973
R Dysfunctional Family 1991
  Schizophrenogenic Family 1967
  Schizophrenogenic Mothers 1973

Doubt 1973
PN 89   **SC** 15000
B Emotional States 1973
R Mental Confusion 1973
  Suspicion 1973
  Uncertainty 1991

Doves 1973
PN 188   **SC** 15010
B Birds 1967

Downs Syndrome 1967
PN 3012   **SC** 15020
UF Mongolism
B Autosome Disorders 1973
  Mental Retardation 1967
  Neonatal Disorders 1973
  Syndromes 1973
R Moderate Mental Retardation 2001
  Trisomy 21 1973

Downsizing 2003
PN 138   **SC** 15017
SN Reduction in workforce within an organization through terminations, retirements, or buyouts.
HN This term was introduced in June 2003. PsycINFO records from the past 10 years were re-indexed with this term. The posting note reflects the number of records that were re-indexed.
B Organizational Change 1973
R Employee Turnover 1973
  Job Security 1978
  Personnel Termination 1973

Doxepin 1994
PN 32   **SC** 15025
HN Use ANTIDEPRESSANT DRUGS or TRANQUILIZING DRUGS to access references from 1973-1993.
B Tranquilizing Drugs 1967
  Tricyclic Antidepressant Drugs 1997

Draftees 1973
PN 59   **SC** 15030
SN Military personnel conscripted for service.
B Enlisted Military Personnel 1973
R Army Personnel 1967
  Navy Personnel 1967

Drama 1973
PN 1017   **SC** 15040
B Theatre 1973
R Improvisation 2004
  ↓ Literature 1967
  Motion Pictures (Entertainment) 1973
  Writers 1991

Drama Therapy
Use Psychodrama

Draw A Man Test
Use Human Figures Drawing

Drawing 1967
PN 2846   **SC** 15050
B Art 1967

Dream Analysis 1973
PN 1701   **SC** 15060
UF Dream Interpretation
B Psychoanalysis 1967
  Psychotherapeutic Techniques 1967
R ↓ Dreaming 1967
  ↓ Parapsychology 1967

Dream Content 1973
PN 1400   **SC** 15070
R ↓ Dreaming 1967
  Nightmares 1973
  ↓ Sleep 1967

Dream Interpretation
Use Dream Analysis

Dream Recall 1973
PN 371   **SC** 15090
R ↓ Dreaming 1967
  Lucid Dreaming 1994

Dreaming 1967
PN 1923   **SC** 15100

Dreaming — (cont'd)
- **N** Lucid Dreaming 1994
- Nightmares 1973
- REM Dreams 1973
- **R** Dream Analysis 1973
- Dream Content 1973
- Dream Recall 1973
- ↓ Sleep 1967

DRGs
- **Use** Diagnosis Related Groups

Drinking (Alcohol)
- **Use** Alcohol Drinking Patterns

Drinking Attitudes
- **Use** Alcohol Drinking Attitudes

Drinking Behavior 1978
PN 327   SC 15127
- **B** Behavior 1967
- **N** ↓ Alcohol Drinking Patterns 1967
- Animal Drinking Behavior 1973
- Water Intake 1967
- **R** ↓ Alcoholic Beverages 1973
- Beverages (Nonalcoholic) 1978
- Diets 1978
- Driving Under the Influence 1988
- ↓ Fluid Intake 1985
- ↓ Ingestion 2001
- Sucking 1978
- Thirst 1967

Drinking Behavior (Animal)
- **Use** Animal Drinking Behavior

Drive
- **Use** Motivation

Driver Education 1973
PN 196   SC 15150
- **B** Curriculum 1967
- **R** Drivers 1973

Driver Safety
- **Use** Highway Safety

Drivers 1973
PN 1583   SC 15170
- **R** Automobiles 1973
- Driver Education 1973
- ↓ Driving Behavior 1967
- Highway Safety 1973
- Motor Traffic Accidents 1973
- ↓ Motor Vehicles 1982

Driving Behavior 1967
PN 3094   SC 15180
SN Manner in which one operates a motor vehicle.
- **B** Behavior 1967
- **N** Aggressive Driving Behavior 2004
- Driving Under the Influence 1988
- **R** Drivers 1973
- Highway Safety 1973
- Motor Traffic Accidents 1973
- Pedestrian Accidents 1973
- Safety Belts 1973

Driving Under the Influence 1988
PN 948   SC 15185
- **UF** Drunk Driving
- **B** Crime 1967
- Driving Behavior 1967
- **R** ↓ Accidents 1967
- ↓ Alcohol Intoxication 1973
- Blood Alcohol Concentration 1994
- ↓ Drinking Behavior 1978
- ↓ Drug Usage 1971
- Highway Safety 1973

Dropouts 1973
PN 288   SC 15190
- **N** Potential Dropouts 1973
- ↓ School Dropouts 1967
- Treatment Dropouts 1978
- **R** ↓ Education 1967
- Experimental Attrition 1994
- ↓ School Enrollment 1973

Drosophila 1973
PN 776   SC 15200
- **UF** Fruit Fly
- **B** Diptera 1973
- **R** Larvae 1973

Drowsiness
- **Use** Sleep Onset

Drug Abstinence 1994
PN 680   SC 15215
SN Voluntary or involuntary abstinence from drugs. For alcohol abstinence, use SOBRIETY.
- **UF** Abstinence (Drugs)
- **N** Sobriety 1988
- **R** Detoxification 1973
- ↓ Drug Abuse 1973
- ↓ Drug Rehabilitation 1973
- ↓ Drug Usage 1971
- ↓ Drug Withdrawal 1973
- Recovery (Disorders) 1973
- Smoking Cessation 1988

Drug Abuse 1973
PN 15982   SC 15220
- **UF** Substance Abuse
- **B** Behavior Disorders 1971
- Drug Usage 1971
- **N** ↓ Alcohol Abuse 1988
- ↓ Drug Dependency 1973
- ↓ Inhalant Abuse 1985
- Polydrug Abuse 1994
- **R** ↓ Addiction 1973
- Codependency 1991
- Craving 1997
- ↓ Drug Abstinence 1994
- Drug Abuse Liability 1994
- Drug Abuse Prevention 1994
- ↓ Drug Addiction 1967
- Drug Distribution 1997
- ↓ Drug Legalization 1997
- Drug Overdoses 1978
- Drug Usage Screening 1988
- ↓ Drugs 1967
- Intravenous Drug Usage 1994
- Needle Exchange Programs 2001
- Needle Sharing 1994
- ↓ Social Issues 1991

Drug Abuse Liability 1994
PN 153   SC 15225

Drug Abuse Liability — (cont'd)
SN Properties of any psychoactive drug or substance which lead to self administration and potentiality for abuse, dependence, and addiction.
- **UF** Abuse Potential (Drugs)
- **R** ↓ Alcohol Abuse 1988
- ↓ Drug Abuse 1973
- ↓ Drug Addiction 1967
- ↓ Drug Dependency 1973
- ↓ Pharmacology 1973
- Psychopharmacology 1967

Drug Abuse Prevention 1994
PN 1428   SC 15227
- **UF** Substance Abuse Prevention
- **B** Prevention 1973
- **R** ↓ Drug Abuse 1973
- Drug Education 1973
- Early Intervention 1982
- ↓ Harm Reduction 2003
- Preventive Medicine 1973
- Primary Mental Health Prevention 1973

Drug Addiction 1967
PN 5297   SC 15230
SN Physical and emotional dependence on a chemical substance. Compare DRUG DEPENDENCY.
- **B** Addiction 1973
- Drug Dependency 1973
- Side Effects (Drug) 1973
- **N** Heroin Addiction 1973
- **R** ↓ Drug Abuse 1973
- Drug Abuse Liability 1994
- Drug Overdoses 1978
- ↓ Drug Withdrawal 1973
- Intravenous Drug Usage 1994
- Methadone Maintenance 1978
- Polydrug Abuse 1994

Drug Administration Methods 1973
PN 2587   SC 15240
SN Techniques, procedures, and routes (e.g., oral, intravenous) of administration of drugs (in experimental or therapeutic contexts) including dosage forms (e.g., liquids, tablets), frequency, and duration of drug administration. Used only when methodological aspects of administering drugs are discussed.
- **N** Drug Self Administration 2004
- ↓ Injections 1973
- **R** ↓ Drug Dosages 1973
- ↓ Drugs 1967

Drug Adverse Reactions
- **Use** Side Effects (Drug)

Drug Allergies 1973
PN 23   SC 15260
- **B** Allergic Disorders 1973
- Side Effects (Drug) 1973
- **R** Drug Sensitivity 1973

Drug Augmentation 2004
PN 187   SC 15263
SN To increase or supplement any drug treatment.
HN This term was introduced in June 2004. PsycINFO records from the past 10 years were re-indexed with this term. The posting note reflects the number of records that were re-indexed.
- **R** ↓ Drug Dosages 1973
- ↓ Drug Therapy 1967

Drug Dependency 1973

PN 5128   SC 15270
SN Psychological craving for or habituation to the use of a chemical substance which may or may not be accompanied by physical dependency. Used for animal or human populations. Compare DRUG ADDICTION.
UF Dependency (Drug)
B   Drug Abuse 1973
    Side Effects (Drug) 1973
N   ↓ Drug Addiction 1967
R   Drug Abuse Liability 1994
    Drug Usage Screening 1988
    Polydrug Abuse 1994

Drug Discrimination 1985

PN 1314   SC 15272
SN A discrimination learning paradigm used to study psychopharmacological and neuropharmacological phenomena. Also, the organism's ability to discriminate the presence, absence, or other qualitative aspects of a chemical substance.
B   Discrimination 1967
    Discrimination Learning 1982
R   ↓ Drugs 1967

Drug Dissociation
Use State Dependent Learning

Drug Distribution 1997

PN 124   SC 15277
B   Crime 1967
R   ↓ Drug Abuse 1973
    ↓ Drug Laws 1973
    ↓ Drug Legalization 1997
    ↓ Drug Usage 1971

Drug Dosages 1973

PN 5614   SC 15280
N   Drug Overdoses 1978
R   Bioavailability 1991
    ↓ Drug Administration Methods 1973
    Drug Augmentation 2004
    Drug Self Administration 2004
    ↓ Drugs 1967

Drug Education 1973

PN 1622   SC 15290
UF Alcohol Education
B   Health Education 1973
R   Drug Abuse Prevention 1994
    ↓ Drugs 1967

Drug Effects
Use Drugs

Drug Induced Congenital Disorders 1973

PN 89   SC 15310
B   Congenital Disorders 1973
    Toxic Disorders 1973
N   Fetal Alcohol Syndrome 1985
R   Thalidomide 1973

Drug Induced Hallucinations 1973

PN 70   SC 15320
B   Hallucinations 1967
R   Psychedelic Experiences 1973

Drug Interactions 1982

PN 4823   SC 15325

Drug Interactions — (cont'd)
SN Chemical and/or pharmacological reactions of drugs in combination, including agonistic and antagonistic interactions.
HN In 1982, this term was created to replace the discontinued terms DRUG POTENTIATION and DRUG SYNERGISM. In 2000, these terms were removed from all records containing them, and replaced with DRUG INTERACTIONS.
UF Drug Potentiation
    Drug Synergism
    Potentiation (Drugs)
R   ↓ Drugs 1967
    ↓ Neurotoxins 1982
    Polydrug Abuse 1994
    Polypharmacy 2004

Drug Laws 1973

PN 452   SC 15330
B   Laws 1967
N   ↓ Marijuana Laws 1973
R   Drug Distribution 1997
    ↓ Drug Legalization 1997
    ↓ Drugs 1967

Drug Legalization 1997

PN 26   SC 15333
N   Marijuana Legalization 1973
R   ↓ Drug Abuse 1973
    Drug Distribution 1997
    ↓ Drug Laws 1973
    ↓ Drug Usage 1971
    ↓ Harm Reduction 2003

Drug Overdoses 1978

PN 527   SC 15335
B   Drug Dosages 1973
R   ↓ Drug Abuse 1973
    ↓ Drug Addiction 1967
    ↓ Drug Therapy 1967
    ↓ Drug Usage 1971

Drug Potentiation
Use Drug Interactions

Drug Rehabilitation 1973

PN 10392   SC 15350
UF Rehabilitation (Drug)
B   Rehabilitation 1967
N   ↓ Alcohol Rehabilitation 1982
    Detoxification 1973
R   ↓ Drug Abstinence 1994
    Drug Usage Screening 1988
    ↓ Drugs 1967
    Employee Assistance Programs 1985
    Methadone Maintenance 1978
    ↓ Psychosocial Rehabilitation 1973
    Rehabilitation Counseling 1978
    Smoking Cessation 1988
    Sobriety 1988
    ↓ Twelve Step Programs 1997

Drug Self Administration 2004

PN 22   SC 15355
SN Administration of drugs or chemicals by one's self. Used clinically or experimentally for humans or animals. Not to be confused with SELF MEDICATION.
HN This term was introduced in June 2004. Psyc-INFO records from the past 10 years were re-indexed with this term. The posting note reflects the number of records that were re-indexed.
UF Self Administration (Drugs)

Drug Self Administration — (cont'd)
B   Drug Administration Methods 1973
R   ↓ Drug Dosages 1973
    ↓ Drug Usage 1971
    ↓ Injections 1973

Drug Sensitivity 1973

PN 1742   SC 15360
SN Behavioral or physical sensitivity, resistance, or reactivity to a particular chemical substance.
UF Sensitivity (Drugs)
B   Side Effects (Drug) 1973
R   Drug Allergies 1973
    Drug Tolerance 1973

Drug Synergism
Use Drug Interactions

Drug Testing
Use Drug Usage Screening

Drug Therapy 1967

PN 53555   SC 15380
SN Mandatory term applied to studies dealing with the use of drugs in the clinical treatment of diseases or psychological disorders. Used for human or animal populations. For the use of drugs in non-clinical contexts, use PHARMACOLOGY or PSYCHOPHARMACOLOGY.
UF Chemotherapy
    Medication
    Pharmacotherapy
    Therapy (Drug)
B   Physical Treatment Methods 1973
N   Hormone Therapy 1994
    ↓ Narcoanalysis 1973
    Polypharmacy 2004
    Vitamin Therapy 1978
R   Bioavailability 1991
    Clinical Trials 2004
    Detoxification 1973
    Drug Augmentation 2004
    Drug Overdoses 1978
    ↓ Drugs 1967
    Maintenance Therapy 1997
    Neuroleptic Malignant Syndrome 1988
    ↓ Outpatient Treatment 1967
    Prescribing (Drugs) 1991
    Prescription Drugs 1991
    Self Medication 1991
    ↓ Side Effects (Drug) 1973
    Sleep Treatment 1973
    Tardive Dyskinesia 1988
    Treatment Resistant Depression 1994

Drug Tolerance 1973

PN 2496   SC 15390
SN Condition in which, after repeated administration, a drug produces a decreased effect and must be administered in larger doses to produce the effect of the original dose.
UF Tolerance (Drug)
R   Drug Sensitivity 1973
    ↓ Drugs 1967
    ↓ Side Effects (Drug) 1973

Drug Usage 1971

PN 8031   SC 15400
SN Act, amount, or mode of using any type of drug. Applies only to humans and should be used when neither abuse nor addiction are the subject matter, regardless of the legality of the particular drug.

Drug Usage — (cont'd)

- **N** ↓ Alcohol Drinking Patterns 1967
- ↓ Drug Abuse 1973
- Intravenous Drug Usage 1994
- Marijuana Usage 1973
- Tobacco Smoking 1967
- **R** ↓ Addiction 1973
- Craving 1997
- Driving Under the Influence 1988
- ↓ Drug Abstinence 1994
- Drug Distribution 1997
- ↓ Drug Legalization 1997
- Drug Overdoses 1978
- Drug Self Administration 2004
- Drug Usage Screening 1988
- ↓ Drugs 1967
- Needle Sharing 1994

Drug Usage Attitudes 1973

PN 1433   **SC** 15410

- **B** Attitudes 1967
- **N** Alcohol Drinking Attitudes 1973
- **R** Health Attitudes 1985
- Marijuana Legalization 1973

Drug Usage Screening 1988

PN 505   **SC** 15415

SN Procedures used to measure or detect prevalence of drug use through analysis of blood, urine, or other body fluids. Not used for measuring the clinical efficacy of therapeutic drugs.

- **UF** Drug Testing
- **B** Screening 1982
- **R** Blood Alcohol Concentration 1994
- ↓ Drug Abuse 1973
- ↓ Drug Dependency 1973
- ↓ Drug Rehabilitation 1973
- ↓ Drug Usage 1971
- ↓ Drugs 1967
- ↓ Health Screening 1997
- ↓ Medical Diagnosis 1973
- Physical Examination 1988
- Urinalysis 1973

Drug Withdrawal 1973

PN 3685   **SC** 15420

SN Processes and symptomatic effects resulting from abstinence from a chemical agent or medication. Used for human or animal populations.

HN In 1982, this term replaced the discontinued term DRUG WITHDRAWAL EFFECTS. DRUG WITHDRAWAL EFFECTS was removed from all records containing it and replaced with DRUG WITHDRAWAL.

- **UF** Drug Withdrawal Effects
- Withdrawal (Drug)
- **N** Alcohol Withdrawal 1994
- Nicotine Withdrawal 1997
- **R** Detoxification 1973
- ↓ Drug Abstinence 1994
- ↓ Drug Addiction 1967

Drug Withdrawal Effects

Use Drug Withdrawal

Drugs 1967

PN 19831   **SC** 15440

SN Conceptually broad term referring to any substance other than food administered for experimental or treatment purposes. Use specific drug classes or names if possible.

Drugs — (cont'd)

HN In 1982, this term replaced the discontinued term DRUG EFFECTS, and in 1997 it replaced CARDIOTONIC DRUGS and NARCOANALYTIC DRUGS. In 2000, these terms were removed from all records containing them, and replaced with DRUGS.

- **UF** Cardiotonic Drugs
- Drug Effects
- Narcoanalytic Drugs
- Psychoactive Drugs
- Psychotropic Drugs
- **N** ↓ Adrenergic Blocking Drugs 1973
- ↓ Adrenergic Drugs 1973
- ↓ Alcohols 1967
- ↓ Alkaloids 1973
- ↓ Amines 1973
- ↓ Analgesic Drugs 1973
- ↓ Anesthetic Drugs 1973
- ↓ Anti Inflammatory Drugs 1982
- Antiandrogens 1982
- ↓ Antibiotics 1973
- ↓ Anticoagulant Drugs 1973
- ↓ Anticonvulsive Drugs 1973
- ↓ Antidepressant Drugs 1971
- ↓ Antiemetic Drugs 1973
- Antiestrogens 1982
- ↓ Antihistaminic Drugs 1973
- ↓ Antihypertensive Drugs 1973
- Antineoplastic Drugs 1982
- ↓ Antispasmodic Drugs 1973
- ↓ Antitremor Drugs 1973
- ↓ Antitubercular Drugs 1973
- ↓ Antiviral Drugs 1994
- ↓ Appetite Depressing Drugs 1973
- ↓ Barbiturates 1967
- ↓ Benzodiazepines 1978
- Bromides 1973
- ↓ Cannabis 1973
- Channel Blockers 1991
- ↓ Cholinergic Blocking Drugs 1973
- ↓ Cholinergic Drugs 1973
- ↓ Cholinomimetic Drugs 1973
- ↓ CNS Affecting Drugs 1973
- ↓ Diuretics 1973
- ↓ Dopamine Agonists 1985
- ↓ Emetic Drugs 1973
- ↓ Enzyme Inhibitors 1985
- ↓ Enzymes 1973
- ↓ Ergot Derivatives 1973
- ↓ Ganglion Blocking Drugs 1973
- ↓ Hallucinogenic Drugs 1967
- ↓ Heart Rate Affecting Drugs 1973
- ↓ Hypnotic Drugs 1973
- ↓ Muscle Relaxing Drugs 1973
- ↓ Narcotic Agonists 1988
- ↓ Narcotic Antagonists 1973
- ↓ Narcotic Drugs 1973
- Nonprescription Drugs 1991
- ↓ Nootropic Drugs 1991
- Prescription Drugs 1991
- ↓ Psychedelic Drugs 1973
- ↓ Psychotomimetic Drugs 1973
- ↓ Respiration Stimulating Drugs 1973
- ↓ Sedatives 1973
- Serotonin Agonists 1988
- ↓ Serotonin Antagonists 1973
- ↓ Steroids 1973
- ↓ Sympatholytic Drugs 1973
- ↓ Sympathomimetic Drugs 1973
- ↓ Tranquilizing Drugs 1967
- ↓ Vasoconstrictor Drugs 1973
- ↓ Vasodilator Drugs 1973
- **R** ↓ Acids 1973
- Antibodies 1973
- Bioavailability 1991

Drugs — (cont'd)

- Carcinogens 1973
- ↓ Drug Abuse 1973
- ↓ Drug Administration Methods 1973
- Drug Discrimination 1985
- ↓ Drug Dosages 1973
- Drug Education 1973
- Drug Interactions 1982
- ↓ Drug Laws 1973
- ↓ Drug Rehabilitation 1973
- ↓ Drug Therapy 1967
- Drug Tolerance 1973
- ↓ Drug Usage 1971
- Drug Usage Screening 1988
- ↓ Hormones 1967
- ↓ Insecticides 1973
- ↓ Peptides 1973
- Placebo 1973
- Prenatal Exposure 1991
- Prescribing (Drugs) 1991
- ↓ Proteins 1973
- Self Medication 1991
- ↓ Side Effects (Drug) 1973
- Teratogens 1988
- ↓ Toxicity 1973
- ↓ Vitamins 1973

Drunk Driving

Use Driving Under the Influence

Drunkenness

Use Alcohol Intoxication

DSM

Use Diagnostic and Statistical Manual

Dual Careers 1982

PN 799   **SC** 15455

SN Situation in which both partners or spouses in a family pursue careers.

- **R** ↓ Family 1967
- ↓ Family Structure 1973
- Family Work Relationship 1997
- Working Women 1978

Dual Diagnosis 1991

PN 904   **SC** 15457

SN Diagnosis based on the coexistence of two or more DSM disorders.

- **R** Comorbidity 1991
- ↓ Diagnosis 1967
- Differential Diagnosis 1967
- ↓ Psychodiagnostic Typologies 1967

Dual Relationships 2003

PN 67   **SC** 15458

SN Occurs when individuals in a helping profession take on more than one role with their client, student, or patient.

HN This term was introduced in June 2003. PsycINFO records from the past 10 years were re-indexed with this term. The posting note reflects the number of records that were re-indexed.

- **R** ↓ Interpersonal Interaction 1967
- Professional Client Sexual Relations 1994
- Professional Ethics 1973
- ↓ Therapeutic Processes 1978

Dualism 1973

PN 1030   **SC** 15460

SN Theory viewing mind and body as two separate and irreducible entities.

Dualism — (cont'd)
UF Mind Body
B Philosophies 1967
R Mind 1991

Duchennes Disease
Use Muscular Disorders

Ducks 1973
PN 335 SC 15480
B Birds 1967

Duodenum
Use Intestines

Duration (Response)
Use Response Duration

Duration (Stimulus)
Use Stimulus Duration

Duty to Warn 2001
PN 32 SC 15525
SN A health care professional's legal and ethical obligation to warn third parties of danger, violence, or the possibility of contracting a serious illness.
R ↓ Abuse Reporting 1997
Accountability 1988
Informants 1988
Informed Consent 1985
Privileged Communication 1973
Professional Ethics 1973
Professional Liability 1985
↓ Professional Standards 1973

Dwarfism (Pituitary)
Use Hypopituitarism

Dyads 1973
PN 2535 SC 15540
B Social Groups 1973
R Couples 1982

Dying
Use Death and Dying

Dying Patients
Use Terminally Ill Patients

Dynamics (Group)
Use Group Dynamics

Dynorphins 1985
PN 144 SC 15575
B Endogenous Opiates 1985
Pituitary Hormones 1973

Dysarthria 1973
PN 330 SC 15580
SN Articulation disorder resulting from central nervous system disease, especially brain damage.
B Articulation Disorders 1973
Central Nervous System Disorders 1973
R Muscular Dystrophy 1973
↓ Paralysis 1973

Dyscalculia
Use Acalculia

Dysfunctional Family 1991
PN 551 SC 15590
SN A family system in which relationships or communication are impaired.
R Codependency 1991
Double Bind Interaction 1973
↓ Family 1967
↓ Family Relations 1967
↓ Family Structure 1973
Marital Conflict 1973
Schizophrenogenic Family 1967

Dyskinesia 1973
PN 784 SC 15600
SN Abnormal involuntary motor processes that occur due to underlying disease processes.
B Movement Disorders 1985
Symptoms 1967
N Bradykinesia 2001
Tardive Dyskinesia 1988
R ↓ Neuromuscular Disorders 1973

Dyslexia 1973
PN 2803 SC 15610
SN Reading disorder involving an inability to understand what is read. Less severe than alexia.
B Alexia 1982
Learning Disabilities 1973
Reading Disabilities 1967
R Educational Diagnosis 1978
↓ Reading 1967

Dysmenorrhea 1973
PN 111 SC 15620
SN Difficult and painful menstruation.
B Menstrual Disorders 1973

Dysmetria
Use Ataxia

Dysmorphophobia
Use Body Dysmorphic Disorder

Dyspareunia 1973
PN 74 SC 15650
B Sexual Function Disturbances 1973
Sexual Intercourse (Human) 1973
R Frigidity 1973
Vaginismus 1973

Dysphagia 2003
PN 38 SC 15654
SN Difficulty swallowing.
HN This term was introduced in June 2003. PsycINFO records from the past 10 years were re-indexed with this term. The posting note reflects the number of records that were re-indexed.
R Esophagus 1973
Pharyngeal Disorders 1973
Swallowing 1988

Dysphasia 1978
PN 247 SC 15655
SN Impairment of language comprehension, formulation, or use due to brain damage. Used only for partial impairments.

Dysphasia — (cont'd)
B Aphasia 1967
N ↓ Alexia 1982

Dysphonia 1973
PN 270 SC 15660
SN Any speech disorder involving problems of voice quality, pitch, or intensity.
UF Voice Disorders
B Speech Disorders 1967

Dysphoria
Use Major Depression

Dyspnea 1973
PN 91 SC 15680
SN Difficulty in breathing which may or may not have an organic cause.
B Respiratory Distress 1973
Respiratory Tract Disorders 1973
Symptoms 1967
N Asthma 1967
R ↓ Cardiovascular Disorders 1967
↓ Lung Disorders 1973
↓ Somatoform Disorders 2001

Dyspraxia
Use Movement Disorders

Dysthymia
Use Dysthymic Disorder

Dysthymic Disorder 1988
PN 1021 SC 15693
SN Chronic affective disorder characterized by either relatively mild depressive symptoms or marked loss of pleasure in usual activities.
HN Consider DEPRESSION (EMOTION) to access references prior to 1988.
UF Dysthymia
B Major Depression 1988
R Anhedonia 1985

Dystonia
Use Muscular Disorders

Dystrophy (Muscular)
Use Muscular Dystrophy

E-Therapy
Use Online Therapy

Eagerness
Use Enthusiasm

Ear (Anatomy) 1967
PN 532 SC 15720
B Sense Organs 1973
N External Ear 1973
↓ Labyrinth (Anatomy) 1973
Middle Ear 1973
↓ Vestibular Apparatus 1967
R ↓ Ear Disorders 1973

Ear Canal
Use External Ear

Ear Disorders   1973
PN   335   SC   15740
SN   Disorders of the external, middle, or inner ear. Use HEARING DISORDERS for pathology involving auditory neural pathways beyond the inner ear.
HN   In 1997, this term replaced the discontinued term OTOSCLEROSIS. In 2000, OTOSCLEROSIS was removed from all records and replaced with EAR DISORDERS.
   UF   Otosclerosis
   B   Sense Organ Disorders   1973
   N   ↓ Labyrinth Disorders   1973
       Tinnitus   1973
   R   ↓ Auditory Perception   1967
       ↓ Ear (Anatomy)   1967
       ↓ Hearing Disorders   1982

Ear Ossicles
   Use   Middle Ear

Early Childhood Development   1973
PN   3271   SC   15770
SN   Process of physical, cognitive, personality, and psychosocial growth occurring from birth through age 5. Use a more specific term if possible.
   B   Childhood Development   1967
   N   ↓ Infant Development   1973
   R   Early Experience   1967
       Early Memories   1985
       ↓ Physical Development   1973
       ↓ Psychogenesis   1973

Early Experience   1967
PN   8856   SC   15780
SN   Any occurrences early in an individual's life. Used for human or animal populations.
   B   Experiences (Events)   1973
   R   Age Regression (Hypnotic)   1988
       Anniversary Events   1994
       Autobiographical Memory   1994
       ↓ Early Childhood Development   1973
       Early Memories   1985
       Enactments   1997
       Life Review   1991

Early Infantile Autism   1973
PN   499   SC   15790
   B   Autism   1967
   R   Autistic Children   1973
       Childhood Schizophrenia   1967
       Symbiotic Infantile Psychosis   1973

Early Intervention   1982
PN   3876   SC   15793
SN   Action taken utilizing medical, family, school, social, or mental health resources and aimed at infants and children at risk for, or in the early stages of mental, physical, learning, or other disorders.
   B   Intervention   2003
   R   Drug Abuse Prevention   1994
       ↓ Prenatal Care   1991
       ↓ Prevention   1973
       Primary Mental Health Prevention   1973
       School Based Intervention   2003
       Special Education   1967
       Special Needs   1994
       ↓ Treatment   1967

Early Memories   1985
PN   985   SC   15796
SN   Memories of events that occurred early in an individual's life.
   UF   Childhood Memories

Early Memories — (cont'd)
   B   Memory   1967
   R   Age Regression (Hypnotic)   1988
       Anniversary Events   1994
       Autobiographical Memory   1994
       ↓ Early Childhood Development   1973
       Early Experience   1967
       False Memory   1997
       Life Review   1991
       Reminiscence   1985
       Repressed Memory   1997

Earthworms   1973
PN   28   SC   15800
   B   Worms   1967

Eating
   Use   Eating Behavior

Eating Attitudes   1994
PN   651   SC   15823
   B   Attitudes   1967
   R   ↓ Appetite   1973
       ↓ Eating Behavior   2004
       Food Preferences   1973
       Obesity (Attitudes Toward)   1997

Eating Behavior   2004
PN   SC   15824
SN   Used for human populations only.
HN   In June 2004, this term was created to replace the discontinued term FEEDING PRACTICES. FEEDING PRACTICES was removed from all records containing it and replaced with EATING BEHAVIOR.
   UF   Eating
       Eating Habits
       Eating Patterns
       Feeding Practices
   B   Behavior   1967
   N   Binge Eating   1991
       Bottle Feeding   1973
       Breast Feeding   1973
       Dietary Restraint   1994
       Weaning   1973
   R   ↓ Appetite   1973
       Diets   1978
       Eating Attitudes   1994
       ↓ Eating Disorders   1997
       Food Intake   1967
       Mealtimes   2004

Eating Disorders   1997
PN   4627   SC   15825
HN   In 1997, this term was created to replace the discontinued term APPETITE DISORDERS. In 2000, APPETITE DISORDERS was removed from all records and replaced with EATING DISORDERS.
   UF   Appetite Disorders
   B   Mental Disorders   1967
   N   Anorexia Nervosa   1973
       Bulimia   1985
       Hyperphagia   1973
       Kleine Levin Syndrome   2001
       Obesity   1973
       Pica   1973
       Purging (Eating Disorders)   2003
   R   Aphagia   1973
       ↓ Appetite   1973
       Binge Eating   1991
       Coprophagia   2001
       ↓ Eating Behavior   2004
       Nausea   1973
       ↓ Nutritional Deficiencies   1973

Eating Disorders — (cont'd)
       ↓ Physical Disorders   1997
       Rumination (Eating)   2001
       ↓ Symptoms   1967
       ↓ Underweight   1973

Eating Habits
   Use   Eating Behavior

Eating Patterns
   Use   Eating Behavior

Echinodermata   1973
PN   39   SC   15840
   UF   Starfish
   B   Invertebrates   1973

Echoencephalography   1973
PN   9   SC   15850
   B   Encephalography   1973
       Medical Diagnosis   1973

Echolalia   1973
PN   113   SC   15870
   B   Language Disorders   1982
   R   Gilles de la Tourette Disorder   1973

Echolocation   1973
PN   220   SC   15880
   R   ↓ Animal Ethology   1967
       ↓ Animal Vocalizations   1973

Eclectic Psychology
   Use   Theoretical Orientation

Eclectic Psychotherapy   1994
PN   124   SC   15887
SN   An approach to psychotherapy that utilizes various therapeutic techniques without concern for theoretical orientation.
   B   Psychotherapy   1967
   R   Integrative Psychotherapy   2003
       Interdisciplinary Treatment Approach   1973
       Multimodal Treatment Approach   1991

Ecological Factors   1973
PN   1145   SC   15890
SN   Elements involved in relations between organisms and their natural environments.
   N   Pollution   1973
       Topography   1973
   R   Behavioral Ecology   1997
       Ecological Psychology   1994
       Ecology   1973
       ↓ Environmental Effects   1973

Ecological Psychology   1994
PN   338   SC   15895
SN   Branch of psychology that studies the frequency or nature of psychological processes or behavior as they occur in natural settings. Compare ENVIRONMENTAL PSYCHOLOGY.
   B   Psychology   1967
   R   Behavioral Ecology   1997
       ↓ Ecological Factors   1973
       Environmental Psychology   1982

Ecology   1973
PN   880   SC   15900
   R   Behavioral Ecology   1997

Ecology — (cont'd)
    Conservation (Ecological Behavior)   1978
  ↓ Ecological Factors   1973
  ↓ Environment   1967
    Environmental Attitudes   1978
    Environmental Education   1994
    Pollution   1973

Economically Disadvantaged
Use   Disadvantaged

Economics   1985
PN 3409   **SC** 15915
SN Social science dealing with the production, distribution, and consumption of goods and services. Used for the discipline or economic factors themselves.
B   Social Sciences   1967
N   Behavioral Economics   2003
R   Budgets   1997
    Cost Containment   1991
  ↓ Costs and Cost Analysis   1973
  ↓ Division of Labor   1988
    Economy   1973
    Globalization   2003
    Health Care Costs   1994
    Human Capital   2003
    Money   1967
  ↓ Political Economic Systems   1973
    Resource Allocation   1997
    Supply and Demand   2004

Economy   1973
PN 1015   **SC** 15920
R   Budgets   1997
  ↓ Costs and Cost Analysis   1973
  ↓ Economics   1985
    Globalization   2003
    Money   1967
  ↓ Political Economic Systems   1973
    Taxation   1985

ECS Therapy
Use   Electroconvulsive Shock Therapy

Ecstasy (Drug)
Use   Methylenedioxymethamphetamine

ECT (Therapy)
Use   Electroconvulsive Shock Therapy

Eczema   1973
PN 47   **SC** 15950
B   Dermatitis   1973
R   Allergic Skin Disorders   1973

Educable Mentally Retarded
Use   Mild Mental Retardation

Education   1967
PN 9076   **SC** 16000
SN Conceptually broad term referring to the process of imparting or obtaining knowledge, skills, and values. Use a more specific term if possible.
UF   Educational Process
    Training
N ↓ Adult Education   1973
    Bilingual Education   1978
    Client Education   1985

Education — (cont'd)
  ↓ Clinical Methods Training   1973
    Communication Skills Training   1982
    Counselor Education   1973
  ↓ Curriculum   1967
    Death Education   1982
    Distance Education   2003
    Elementary Education   1973
  ↓ Family Life Education   1997
    High School Education   2003
  ↓ Higher Education   1973
    Middle School Education   1985
    Multicultural Education   1988
  ↓ Nontraditional Education   1982
    Nursing Education   1973
    Paraprofessional Education   1973
    Parent Training   1978
  ↓ Personnel Training   1967
    Preschool Education   1973
    Private School Education   1973
    Public School Education   1973
    Religious Education   1973
  ↓ Remedial Education   1985
    Secondary Education   1973
    Social Work Education   1973
    Special Education   1967
  ↓ Teacher Education   1967
R   Ability Grouping   1973
  ↓ Academic Achievement   1967
    Academic Aptitude   1973
    Accreditation (Education Personnel)   1973
    Athletic Training   1991
    Boards of Education   1978
    Classroom Behavior Modification   1973
    Classroom Discipline   1973
    Coeducation   1973
  ↓ Dropouts   1973
    Educational Administration   1967
    Educational Aspirations   1973
  ↓ Educational Background   1967
    Educational Counseling   1967
    Educational Degrees   1973
    Educational Diagnosis   1978
    Educational Financial Assistance   1973
    Educational Incentives   1973
  ↓ Educational Laboratories   1973
  ↓ Educational Measurement   1967
    Educational Objectives   1978
  ↓ Educational Personnel   1973
    Educational Placement   1978
    Educational Program Accreditation   1994
  ↓ Educational Programs   1973
  ↓ Educational Psychology   1967
    Educational Quality   1997
    Educational Reform   1997
    Educational Television   1967
    Environmental Education   1994
    Equal Education   1978
  ↓ Extracurricular Activities   1973
    Grade Level   1994
    Home Schooling   1994
    Mainstreaming (Educational)   1978
    Psychoeducation   1994
    Questioning   1982
    School Adjustment   1967
    School Attendance   1973
    School Counseling   1982
  ↓ School Dropouts   1967
  ↓ School Enrollment   1973
  ↓ School Environment   1973
  ↓ School Facilities   1973
    School Graduation   1991
    School Integration   1982
    School Learning   1967
    School Readiness   1973

Education — (cont'd)
    School to Work Transition   1994
    School Transition   1997
    School Truancy   1973
  ↓ Schools   1967
    Student Admission Criteria   1973
    Student Attitudes   1967
  ↓ Student Characteristics   1982
    Student Personnel Services   1978
    Student Records   1978
  ↓ Students   1967
    Study Habits   1973
  ↓ Teacher Characteristics   1973
    Teacher Student Interaction   1973
    Teacher Tenure   1973
  ↓ Teaching   1967
  ↓ Teaching Methods   1967
    Theories of Education   1973

Education Students   1982
PN 533   **SC** 15995
SN Students enrolled in a school or department of education.
B   College Students   1967
R   Preservice Teachers   1982
    Student Teachers   1973
  ↓ Teacher Education   1967

Educational Administration   1967
PN 2486   **SC** 16010
UF   School Administration
    School Organization
B   Management   1967
R   Boards of Education   1978
    Decentralization   1978
  ↓ Education   1967
    Educational Reform   1997

Educational Administrators
Use   School Administrators

Educational Aspirations   1973
PN 1105   **SC** 16020
SN Personal desire for achievement in a certain educational field or to a certain level or degree.
B   Aspirations   1967
R   Academic Specialization   1973
  ↓ Education   1967
    Educational Objectives   1978

Educational Attainment Level   1997
PN 1373   **SC** 16025
SN Completion of a course of study or reaching a specific educational level.
UF   Attainment Level (Education)
B   Educational Background   1967
R ↓ Academic Achievement   1967
    Educational Degrees   1973
    School Graduation   1991
    School to Work Transition   1994

Educational Audiovisual Aids   1973
PN 276   **SC** 16030
UF   Audiovisual Aids (Educational)
B   Audiovisual Communications Media   1973
    Instructional Media   1967
N   Motion Pictures (Educational)   1973
R ↓ Audiovisual Instruction   1973
    Educational Television   1967
    Film Strips   1967
    Televised Instruction   1973
    Videotape Instruction   1973

Educational Background 1967
PN 4224   **SC** 16040
- **N**   Educational Attainment Level 1997
-      Parent Educational Background 1973
- **R**   Biographical Data 1978
-    ↓ Education 1967
-      School Leavers 1988

Educational Background (Parents)
Use   Parent Educational Background

Educational Counseling 1967
PN 2587   **SC** 16060
SN   Assistance offered to school or college students on school program planning, course selection, or academic specialization. Compare SCHOOL COUNSELING.
- **UF**   Educational Guidance
-      Guidance (Educational)
- **B**   Counseling 1967
- **R**   ↓ Education 1967
-      Occupational Guidance 1967
-      Student Personnel Services 1978

Educational Degrees 1973
PN 759   **SC** 16070
- **UF**   College Degrees
-      Degrees (Educational)
-      Graduate Degrees
-      Undergraduate Degrees
- **R**   College Graduates 1982
-    ↓ Education 1967
-      Educational Attainment Level 1997
-      Educational Program Accreditation 1994
-      High School Graduates 1978
-    ↓ Higher Education 1973
-      School Graduation 1991

Educational Diagnosis 1978
PN 2775   **SC** 16075
SN   Identification of cognitive, perceptual, emotional, and other factors which influence academic performance or school adjustment, usually for such purposes as placement of students in curricula or programs suited to their needs, and referral.
- **B**   Diagnosis 1967
- **R**   Differential Diagnosis 1967
-      Dyslexia 1973
-    ↓ Education 1967
-    ↓ Educational Measurement 1967
-      Educational Placement 1978
-    ↓ Learning Disabilities 1973
-    ↓ Learning Disorders 1967
-    ↓ Psychodiagnosis 1967
-      Psychological Report 1988
-    ↓ Reading Disabilities 1967
-      Woodcock Johnson Psychoeducational
-        Battery 2001

Educational Environment
Use   School Environment

Educational Field Trips 1973
PN 80   **SC** 16080
- **UF**   Field Trips (Educational)
- **B**   Teaching Methods 1967
- **R**   Curricular Field Experience 1982
-    ↓ Experiential Learning 1997

Educational Financial Assistance 1973
PN 207   **SC** 16090
- **UF**   Financial Assistance (Educational)

Educational Financial Assistance — (cont'd)
-      Scholarships
-      School Federal Aid
-      School Financial Assistance
-      Stipends
- **R**   ↓ Education 1967
-      Funding 1988
-      Student Personnel Services 1978

Educational Guidance
Use   Educational Counseling

Educational Incentives 1973
PN 134   **SC** 16120
SN   Any type of incentive used or experienced in a school, classroom, or other educational context.
- **B**   Incentives 1967
-      Motivation 1967
- **R**   ↓ Education 1967

Educational Inequality
Use   Equal Education

Educational Intervention
Use   School Based Intervention

Educational Laboratories 1973
PN 181   **SC** 16130
- **UF**   Laboratories (Educational)
- **B**   School Facilities 1973
- **N**   Language Laboratories 1970
- **R**   ↓ Education 1967

Educational Measurement 1967
PN 5837   **SC** 16140
SN   Practices, procedures, methods, and tests used in the assessment of student characteristics or performance, such as academic achievement and school adjustment.
- **B**   Testing 1967
- **N**   Curriculum Based Assessment 1994
-    ↓ Entrance Examinations 1973
-      Grading (Educational) 1973
-      Minimum Competency Tests 1985
- **R**   ↓ Education 1967
-      Educational Diagnosis 1978
-    ↓ Screening 1982

Educational Objectives 1978
PN 1539   **SC** 16145
SN   Specific educational goals toward which one's efforts are directed, or goals proposed or established by educational authorities.
- **UF**   Course Objectives
-      Instructional Objectives
- **B**   Goals 1967
- **R**   ↓ Curriculum 1967
-    ↓ Education 1967
-      Educational Aspirations 1973
-      Educational Quality 1997
-      Educational Reform 1997
-      Mastery Learning 1985

Educational Personnel 1973
PN 3103   **SC** 16150
- **UF**   Faculty
- **B**   Professional Personnel 1978
- **N**   ↓ School Administrators 1973
-      School Counselors 1973
-      School Nurses 1973

Educational Personnel — (cont'd)
-      Teacher Aides 1973
-    ↓ Teachers 1967
- **R**   ↓ Education 1967
-    ↓ Educational Psychologists 1973
-    ↓ Mental Health Personnel 1967
-      Missionaries 1973
-      Professional Supervision 1988
-      Speech Therapists 1973

Educational Placement 1978
PN 1937   **SC** 16155
SN   Assignment of students to classes, programs, or schools according to their abilities and readiness.
- **UF**   Placement (Educational)
- **R**   Ability Grouping 1973
-    ↓ Education 1967
-      Educational Diagnosis 1978
-      Grade Level 1994
-    ↓ Mainstreaming 1991
-      Mainstreaming (Educational) 1978
-      Remedial Reading 1973
-    ↓ Screening 1982
-      Special Education 1967

Educational Process
Use   Education

Educational Program Accreditation 1994
PN 140   **SC** 16165
SN   Recognition and approval of educational programs or institution's maintenance of standards to qualify graduates for professional practice or admission to higher or more specialized educational institutions.
- **UF**   Accreditation (Educational Programs)
-      School Accreditation
- **R**   ↓ Curriculum 1967
-    ↓ Education 1967
-      Educational Degrees 1973
-    ↓ Educational Programs 1973
-      Educational Quality 1997
-    ↓ Graduate Psychology Education 1967
-    ↓ Higher Education 1973
-    ↓ Psychology Education 1978

Educational Program Evaluation 1973
PN 3358   **SC** 16170
SN   Techniques, materials, or process of determining the worth or effectiveness of an educational program in relation to its goals or other criteria.
- **UF**   Program Evaluation (Educational)
- **B**   Program Evaluation 1985
- **R**   Course Evaluation 1978
-    ↓ Educational Programs 1973
-      Educational Quality 1997

Educational Program Planning 1973
PN 1401   **SC** 16180
- **UF**   Program Planning (Educational)
- **B**   Program Development 1991
- **R**   Curriculum Development 1973
-    ↓ Educational Programs 1973

Educational Programs 1973
PN 8022   **SC** 16190
- **UF**   Work Study Programs
- **N**   Foreign Study 1973
-      Literacy Programs 1997
-      Project Follow Through 1973
-      Project Head Start 1973
-      Special Education 1967
-      Upward Bound 1973

Educational Programs — (cont'd)
R   After School Programs 2003
    Compensatory Education 1973
    Cooperative Education 1982
    Curricular Field Experience 1982
    ↓ Education 1967
    Educational Program Accreditation 1994
    Educational Program Evaluation 1973
    Educational Program Planning 1973
    Educational Reform 1997
    Multicultural Education 1988
    ↓ Nontraditional Education 1982
    ↓ Program Development 1991
    School Based Intervention 2003

Educational Psychologists 1973
PN 514   SC 16200
SN Psychologists conducting research and formulating policies in areas of diagnosis and measurement, school adjustment, school learning, and special education.
B   Psychologists 1967
N   School Psychologists 1973
R   ↓ Educational Personnel 1973

Educational Psychology 1967
PN 1847   SC 16210
SN Branch of psychology that emphasizes the application of psychological theories and research findings to educational processes, especially in the areas of learning and motivation.
B   Applied Psychology 1973
N   School Psychology 1973
R   ↓ Education 1967

Educational Quality 1997
PN 237   SC 16205
UF   Quality of Education
R   Accreditation (Education Personnel) 1973
    Course Evaluation 1978
    ↓ Education 1967
    Educational Objectives 1978
    Educational Program Accreditation 1994
    Educational Program Evaluation 1973
    Educational Reform 1997
    Equal Education 1978
    Teacher Effectiveness Evaluation 1978

Educational Reform 1997
PN 714   SC 16217
R   ↓ Education 1967
    Educational Administration 1967
    Educational Objectives 1978
    ↓ Educational Programs 1973
    Educational Quality 1997
    ↓ Policy Making 1988

Educational Supervision
Use Professional Supervision

Educational Television 1967
PN 223   SC 16220
B   Television 1967
R   ↓ Education 1967
    ↓ Educational Audiovisual Aids 1973
    Televised Instruction 1973

Educational Theory
Use Theories of Education

Educational Therapy 1997
PN 25   SC 16225
HN Use SCHOOL COUNSELING to access references from 1982-1996.
R   Art Therapy 1973
    Music Therapy 1973
    Psychoeducation 1994
    ↓ Psychotherapy 1967
    ↓ Remedial Education 1985
    School Counseling 1982
    Special Education 1967
    ↓ Teaching Methods 1967

Educational Toys 1973
PN 39   SC 16230
B   Toys 1973

Edwards Personal Preference Schedule 1967
PN 112   SC 16240
B   Nonprojective Personality Measures 1973

Edwards Personality Inventory 1973
PN 6   SC 16250
B   Nonprojective Personallty Measures 1973

Edwards Social Desirability Scale 1973
PN 14   SC 16260
B   Nonprojective Personality Measures 1973

EEG (Electrophysiology)
Use Electroencephalography

Effect Size (Statistical) 1985
PN 410   SC 16272
SN A statistical estimate that represents the magnitude of a statistically significant result.
UF   Magnitude of Effect (Statistical)
B   Statistical Analysis 1967
R   Confidence Limits (Statistics) 1973
    Statistical Significance 1973

Efferent Pathways 1982
PN 435   SC 16275
SN Collections of fibers that typically carry neural impulses away from central nervous system connections toward muscular and glandular innervations.
UF   Motor Pathways
B   Neural Pathways 1982
    Parasympathetic Nervous System 1973
N   Extrapyramidal Tracts 1973
    Pyramidal Tracts 1973
R   ↓ Afferent Pathways 1982
    Motor Neurons 1973
    ↓ Motor Processes 1967

Efficacy Expectations
Use Self Efficacy

Efficiency (Employee)
Use Employee Efficiency

Effort
Use Energy Expenditure

Egalitarianism 1985
PN 144   SC 16287
B   Personality Traits 1967

Egalitarianism — (cont'd)
R   Authoritarianism 1967
    ↓ Equity (Social) 1978
    Resource Allocation 1997

Ego 1967
PN 4054   SC 16290
B   Psychoanalytic Personality Factors 1973
R   ↓ Ego Development 1991
    Ego Identity 1991

Ego Development 1991
PN 741   SC 16294
SN Gradual development of a part of the id into the ego or an awareness of a child that he or she is a real distinct and separate entity.
B   Personality Development 1967
N   Ego Identity 1991
R   Ego 1967
    ↓ Psychoanalytic Theory 1967

Ego Identity 1991
PN 532   SC 16297
SN The experience of the self as a recognizable entity resulting from one's ego ideal, behavior and social roles, and adjustments to reality.
B   Ego Development 1991
R   Ego 1967
    Erikson (Erik) 1991
    Identity Formation 2004
    ↓ Personality Development 1967
    ↓ Self Concept 1967

Egocentrism 1978
PN 725   SC 16300
SN Self-centered preoccupation or concern regarding one's own needs, wishes, desires, or preferences and usually accompanied by a disregard for the concerns of others. Also, in cognitive development, the inclination to believe that others maintain the same experiential perspective as oneself.
HN Use EGOCENTRISM to access references to role taking or perspective taking from 1978-1981.
R   Agreeableness 1997
    ↓ Cognitive Development 1973
    Narcissism 1967
    ↓ Personality 1967
    ↓ Personality Traits 1967
    Role Taking 1982

Egotism 1973
PN 166   SC 16310
B   Personality Traits 1967
R   Emotional Superiority 1973
    Grandiosity 1994

Eidetic Imagery 1973
PN 138   SC 16320
SN Clear and detailed memory for objects or events perceived, usually visually.
UF   Photographic Memory
B   Memory 1967
R   Episodic Memory 1988
    ↓ Spatial Memory 1988
    ↓ Visual Memory 1994

Ejaculation
Use Male Orgasm

EKG (Electrophysiology)
Use Electrocardiography

Elavil
Use   Amitriptyline

Elbow (Anatomy) 1973
PN 94   SC 16360
B   Joints (Anatomy)   1973
R   Arm (Anatomy)   1973

Elder Abuse 1988
PN 431   SC 16363
SN   Abuse or neglect of elderly persons in a family, institutional, or other setting.
B   Antisocial Behavior   1971
R   ↓ Abuse Reporting   1997
    Emotional Abuse   1991
    Family Violence   1982
    Patient Abuse   1991
    Physical Abuse   1991
    ↓ Sexual Abuse   1988
    Verbal Abuse   2003

Elder Care 1994
PN 920   SC 16364
SN   Informal or formal support systems or programs for the care of the elderly or assistance to the families who have responsibilities for their care.
R   Adult Day Care   1997
    Caregiver Burden   1994
    Caregivers   1988
    Employee Assistance Programs   1985
    ↓ Employee Benefits   1973
    Home Care   1985
    Home Care Personnel   1997
    Home Visiting Programs   1973
    Homebound   1988
    Protective Services   1997

Elected Government Officials
Use   Government Personnel

Elections (Political)
Use   Political Elections

Elective Abortion
Use   Induced Abortion

Elective Mutism 1973
PN 244   SC 16390
UF   Selective Mutism
B   Mental Disorders   1967
    Mutism   1973

Electra Complex 1973
PN 20   SC 16400
B   Psychoanalytic Personality Factors   1973

Electric Fishes 1973
PN 125   SC 16410
B   Fishes   1967

Electrical Activity 1967
PN 9560   SC 16420
SN   Electrically measured responses or response patterns, usually of individual units (i.e., cells) or groups of cells, in any part of the nervous system. Includes neural or neuron impulses; neural depolarization or hyperpolarization; spike, resting, action, generator, graded, presynaptic, or postsynaptic potentials. Compare ELECTROPHYSIOLOGY.

Electrical Activity — (cont'd)
B   Electrophysiology   1973
N   Alpha Rhythm   1973
    ↓ Cortical Evoked Potentials   1973
    Delta Rhythm   1973
    ↓ Evoked Potentials   1967
    Kindling   1985
    Postactivation Potentials   1985
    Theta Rhythm   1973
R   Electrocardiography   1967
    ↓ Electroencephalography   1967
    Polysomnography   2003

Electrical Brain Stimulation 1973
PN 3785   SC 16430
B   Brain Stimulation   1967
    Electrical Stimulation   1973
    Electrophysiology   1973
    Stereotaxic Techniques   1973
R   ↓ Evoked Potentials   1967
    Kindling   1985
    Postactivation Potentials   1985
    ↓ Self Stimulation   1967

Electrical Injuries 1973
PN 30   SC 16440
B   Injuries   1973
R   Burns   1970
    Shock   1967
    ↓ Wounds   1973

Electrical Stimulation 1973
PN 2083   SC 16460
B   Stimulation   1967
N   Electrical Brain Stimulation   1973
    ↓ Electroconvulsive Shock   1967
R   Experimental Epilepsy   1978
    Shock   1967

Electro Oculography 1973
PN 156   SC 16470
UF   EOG (Electrophysiology)
B   Electrophysiology   1973
    Medical Diagnosis   1973
    Ophthalmologic Examination   1973
R   Electroretinography   1967

Electrocardiography 1967
PN 386   SC 16480
UF   EKG (Electrophysiology)
B   Cardiography   1973
    Electrophysiology   1973
R   ↓ Electrical Activity   1967

Electroconvulsive Shock 1967
PN 936   SC 16490
B   Electrical Stimulation   1973
N   Electroconvulsive Shock Therapy   1967
R   Shock   1967

Electroconvulsive Shock Therapy 1967
PN 3070   SC 16500
UF   ECS Therapy
    ECT (Therapy)
    Electroshock Therapy
B   Electroconvulsive Shock   1967
    Shock Therapy   1973

Electrodermal Response
Use   Galvanic Skin Response

Electrodes 1967
PN 314   SC 16520
B   Apparatus   1967
R   ↓ Stimulators (Apparatus)   1973

Electroencephalography 1967
PN 9371   SC 16530
SN   Method of graphically recording the electrical activity (potentials) of the brain by means of intracranial electrodes or electrodes applied to the scalp. Used both for the method as well as the resulting electroencephalogram or the electrophysiological activity itself.
UF   EEG (Electrophysiology)
B   Electrophysiology   1973
    Encephalography   1973
    Medical Diagnosis   1973
N   Alpha Rhythm   1973
    Delta Rhythm   1973
    Theta Rhythm   1973
R   ↓ Electrical Activity   1967
    Magnetoencephalography   1985
    Rheoencephalography   1973

Electrolytes 1973
PN 281   SC 16540
UF   Ions
N   Calcium Ions   1970
    Chloride Ions   1973
    Magnesium Ions   1973
    Potassium Ions   1973
    Sodium Ions   1973
    Zinc   1985
R   ↓ Chemical Elements   1973

Electromyography 1967
PN 2451   SC 16550
UF   EMG (Electrophysiology)
B   Electrophysiology   1973
    Medical Diagnosis   1973

Electronic Communication 2001
PN 562   SC 16555
SN   Conceptually broad term referring to the transmission or telecommunication of verbal or audiovisual information including, but not limited to electronic mail or email, Internet or local computer network Forums, Bulletin Boards, or other electronic messaging systems.
B   Communication   1967
N   Computer Mediated Communication   2003
R   ↓ Automated Information Processing   1973
    ↓ Communication Systems   1973
    ↓ Communications Media   1973
    ↓ Computer Applications   1973
    ↓ Computer Peripheral Devices   1985
    Computer Searching   1991
    Databases   1991
    Distance Education   2003
    Groupware   2003
    Information   1967
    ↓ Information Systems   1991
    Internet   2001
    Messages   1973
    ↓ Technology   1973

Electronic Mail
Use   Computer Mediated Communication

Electronystagmography 1973
PN 9   SC 16560

Electronystagmography — (cont'd)
B   Electrophysiology 1973
      Medical Diagnosis 1973

Electrophysiology 1973
PN 2239   SC 16570
SN Branch of physiology concerned with the study of electrical phenomena within the living organism (i.e., nerve and muscle tissue). Used for the scientific discipline or the electrophysiological processes themselves. Compare ELECTRICAL ACTIVITY.
B   Physiology 1967
N ↓ Electrical Activity 1967
      Electrical Brain Stimulation 1973
      Electro Oculography 1973
      Electrocardiography 1967
      ↓ Electroencephalography 1967
      Electromyography 1967
      Electronystagmography 1973
      Electroplethysmography 1973
      Electroretinography 1967
      Galvanic Skin Response 1967
      ↓ Skin Electrical Properties 1973
      Skin Potential 1973
R ↓ Medical Diagnosis 1973

Electroplethysmography 1973
PN 7   SC 16580
B   Electrophysiology 1973
      Medical Diagnosis 1973
      Plethysmography 1973

Electroretinography 1967
PN 216   SC 16590
B   Electrophysiology 1973
      Medical Diagnosis 1973
      Ophthalmologic Examination 1973
R   Electro Oculography 1973

Electroshock Therapy
    Use Electroconvulsive Shock Therapy

Electrosleep Treatment 1978
PN 15   SC 16605
SN Therapeutic application of a low intensity, intermittent electrical current to the skull, often producing a state of relaxation, but not necessarily sleep.
B   Physical Treatment Methods 1973
R ↓ Shock Therapy 1973
      Sleep Treatment 1973

Elementarism
    Use Reductionism

Elementary Education 1973
PN 1251   SC 16620
B   Education 1967
R   Elementary Schools 1973

Elementary School Students 1967
PN 31265   SC 16630
SN Students in grades 1-6.
B   Students 1967
N   Intermediate School Students 1973
      Primary School Students 1973
R   Grade Level 1994
      Middle School Students 1985

Elementary School Teachers 1973
PN 5567   SC 16640
B   Teachers 1967

Elementary Schools 1973
PN 1073   SC 16650
UF   Grammar Schools
      Primary Schools
B   Schools 1967
R   Elementary Education 1973

Elephants 1973
PN 75   SC 16660
B   Mammals 1973

Elimination (Excretion)
    Use Excretion

Ellis (Albert) 1991
PN 47   SC 16680
SN Identifies biographical or autobiographical studies and discussions of Ellis's works.
R ↓ Psychologists 1967
      Rational Emotive Behavior Therapy 2003
      Self Talk 1988

Email
    Use Computer Mediated Communication

Embarrassment 1973
PN 278   SC 16690
B   Emotional States 1973
R   Shame 1994

Embedded Figures Testing 1967
PN 182   SC 16700
B   Nonprojective Personality Measures 1973

Embolisms 1973
PN 53   SC 16710
B   Cardiovascular Disorders 1967
R ↓ Thromboses 1973

Embryo 1973
PN 257   SC 16720
B   Prenatal Developmental Stages 1973

EMDR
    Use Eye Movement Desensitization Therapy

Emergency Services 1973
PN 1974   SC 16730
R ↓ Crisis Intervention Services 1973
      Natural Disasters 1973

Emetic Drugs 1973
PN 80   SC 16740
UF   Vomit Inducing Drugs
B   Drugs 1967
N   Apomorphine 1973
      Disulfiram 1978
R ↓ CNS Stimulating Drugs 1973
      ↓ Narcotic Drugs 1973
      Vomiting 1973

EMG (Electrophysiology)
    Use Electromyography

Emotional Abuse 1991
PN 894   SC 16755
UF   Psychological Abuse

Emotional Abuse — (cont'd)
B   Antisocial Behavior 1971
R   Bullying 2003
      ↓ Child Abuse 1971
      Child Neglect 1988
      Elder Abuse 1988
      Erotomania 1997
      Family Violence 1982
      Partner Abuse 1991
      Patient Abuse 1991
      Physical Abuse 1991
      Verbal Abuse 2003

Emotional Adjustment 1973
PN 10046   SC 16760
SN Personal acceptance, adaptation, and relation to one's inner self and environment.
UF   Emotional Maladjustment
      Maladjustment (Emotional)
      Personal Adjustment
      Psychological Adjustment
B   Adjustment 1967
N ↓ Emotional Control 1973
      Identity Crisis 1973
R   Adjustment Disorders 1994
      Codependency 1991
      Coping Behavior 1967
      ↓ Emotionally Disturbed 1973
      ↓ Emotions 1967
      ↓ Mental Disorders 1967
      ↓ Mental Health 1967
      ↓ Personality 1967
      Psychopathology 1967
      Resilience (Psychological) 2003

Emotional Content 1973
PN 2012   SC 16765
SN Emotional themes, substance, form, or characteristics of feelings, especially as they are portrayed in various forms of communication (e.g., reading material, motion pictures) or as manifested in specific situations.
R ↓ Communication 1967
      ↓ Emotions 1967

Emotional Control 1973
PN 1164   SC 16770
SN Directing or governing one's own or another's emotions. Not to be confused with EMOTIONAL MATURITY which involves the exhibition of emotional behavior appropriate to one's age.
UF   Control (Emotional)
      Emotional Restraint
B   Emotional Adjustment 1973
N   Anger Control 1997
R   Coping Behavior 1967
      Internal External Locus of Control 1967
      Self Control 1973
      Social Control 1988
      Tantrums 1973

Emotional Development 1973
PN 3061   SC 16780
B   Psychogenesis 1973
R   Attachment Behavior 1985
      Childhood Play Development 1973
      Developmental Age Groups 1973
      Emotional Intelligence 2003
      ↓ Emotions 1967
      Object Relations 1982
      ↓ Personality Development 1967
      ↓ Physical Development 1973
      Psychosexual Development 1982
      ↓ Psychosocial Development 1973

Emotional Expressiveness
Use Emotionality (Personality)

Emotional Immaturity 1973
PN 55   **SC** 16800
SN Tendency to exhibit emotional reactions considered inappropriate for one's age.
UF Immaturity (Emotional)
B Personality Traits 1967
R Emotional Maturity 1973

Emotional Inferiority 1973
PN 63   **SC** 16810
SN Conscious or unconscious feelings of insecurity, insignificance, and inadequacy and of being unable to cope with life's demands.
UF Inferiority (Emotional)
B Personality Traits 1967
R Neuroticism 1973

Emotional Insecurity
Use Emotional Security

Emotional Instability 1973
PN 207   **SC** 16830
SN Tendency to display unpredictable and rapidly changing emotions or moods.
UF Instability (Emotional)
B Personality Traits 1967
R Emotional Stability 1973
   Neuroticism 1973

Emotional Intelligence 2003
PN 260   **SC** 16833
SN Ability to monitor and appraise one's own and others' feelings and emotions, and to use this information to guide thinking and action.
HN This term was introduced in June 2003. Psyc-INFO records from the past 10 years were re-indexed with this term. The posting note reflects the number of records that were re-indexed.
B Intelligence 1967
R Emotional Development 1973
   Emotional Maturity 1973
   ↓ Emotional Responses 1967
   ↓ Emotions 1967

Emotional Maladjustment
Use Emotional Adjustment

Emotional Maturity 1973
PN 580   **SC** 16850
SN Attainment of a level of emotional development and exhibition of emotional patterns commonly associated with persons of a specific age level. Not to be confused with EMOTIONAL CONTROL which involves the suppression or control of direction of one's emotions.
UF Maturity (Emotional)
B Personality Traits 1967
R Emotional Immaturity 1973
   Emotional Intelligence 2003

Emotional Needs
Use Psychological Needs

Emotional Responses 1967
PN 8304   **SC** 16860
SN Use ANIMAL EMOTIONALITY for nonhuman subjects.

Emotional Responses — (cont'd)
HN From 1982, limited to human populations.
B Responses 1967
N ↓ Conditioned Emotional Responses 1967
R Animal Emotionality 1978
   Cognitive Appraisal 2004
   Emotional Intelligence 2003
   ↓ Emotions 1967
   Laughter 1978
   Stranger Reactions 1988

Emotional Restraint
Use Emotional Control

Emotional Security 1973
PN 591   **SC** 16880
SN Possession of inner resources enabling one to cope with unfamiliar or threatening situations, especially as engendered through early nurturance.
UF Emotional Insecurity
   Insecurity (Emotional)
   Security (Emotional)
B Personality Traits 1967
R Emotional Stability 1973

Emotional Stability 1973
PN 468   **SC** 16890
SN Resistance to affective disruption or tendency toward evenness of feelings.
UF Stability (Emotional)
B Personality Traits 1967
R Emotional Instability 1973
   Emotional Security 1973
   Neuroticism 1973
   Resilience (Psychological) 2003

Emotional States 1973
PN 13643   **SC** 16900
UF Moods
B Emotions 1967
N Affection 1973
   Alienation 1971
   Ambivalence 1973
   ↓ Anger 1967
   ↓ Anxiety 1967
   Apathy 1973
   ↓ Aversion 1967
   Boredom 1973
   Depression (Emotion) 1967
   Disappointment 1973
   Disgust 1994
   Dissatisfaction 1973
   Distress 1973
   Doubt 1973
   Embarrassment 1973
   Emotional Trauma 1967
   Enthusiasm 1973
   Euphoria 1973
   ↓ Fear 1967
   Frustration 1967
   Grief 1973
   Guilt 1967
   Happiness 1973
   ↓ Helplessness 1997
   Homesickness 1994
   Hope 1991
   Hopelessness 1988
   Jealousy 1973
   Loneliness 1973
   Love 1973
   ↓ Mania 1967
   Mental Confusion 1973
   Optimism 1973

Emotional States — (cont'd)
   Pessimism 1973
   Pleasure 1973
   Pride 1973
   Restlessness 1973
   Sadness 1973
   Shame 1994
   Suffering 1973
   Suspicion 1973
   Sympathy 1973
R Abandonment 1997
   Craving 1997
   ↓ Emotionally Disturbed 1973
   Irritability 1988
   Learned Helplessness 1978
   Morale 1978
   ↓ Personality 1967

Emotional Superiority 1973
PN 39   **SC** 16910
SN Feeling that one is better than others in ability, virtue, or worth.
UF Superiority (Emotional)
B Personality Traits 1967
R ↓ Dominance 1967
   Egotism 1973
   Grandiosity 1994

Emotional Trauma 1967
PN 6550   **SC** 16920
UF Trauma (Emotional)
B Emotional States 1973
R Acute Stress Disorder 2003
   Adjustment Disorders 1994
   Debriefing (Psychological) 2004
   False Memory 1997
   Posttraumatic Stress Disorder 1985
   Repressed Memory 1997
   ↓ Separation Reactions 1997

Emotionality (Animal)
Use Animal Emotionality

Emotionality (Personality) 1973
PN 1720   **SC** 16930
SN Personality trait characteristic of a person who tends to react strongly or excessively to emotional situations.
UF Emotional Expressiveness
B Personality Traits 1967
R ↓ Emotions 1967
   Neuroticism 1973

Emotionally Disturbed 1973
PN 4775   **SC** 16940
B Disorders 1967
N Autistic Children 1973
R Acting Out 1967
   ↓ Childhood Psychosis 1967
   ↓ Emotional Adjustment 1973
   ↓ Emotional States 1973
   ↓ Emotions 1967

Emotions 1967
PN 11482   **SC** 16960
SN Conceptually broad term referring to the affective aspects of human consciousness. Use a more specific term if possible. Use ANIMAL EMOTIONALITY for nonhuman subjects.
UF Feelings
N ↓ Emotional States 1973
R ↓ Emotional Adjustment 1973
   Emotional Content 1973

Emotions — (cont'd)
    Emotional Development   1973
    Emotional Intelligence   2003
  ↓ Emotional Responses   1967
    Emotionality (Personality)   1973
  ↓ Emotionally Disturbed   1973
    Expressed Emotion   1991
    Human Nature   1997
    Morale   1978
  ↓ Personality   1967

Empathy   1967
PN 4383   **SC** 16970
  B   Personality Traits   1967
  R   Agreeableness   1997

Emphysema (Pulmonary)
  Use Pulmonary Emphysema

Empirical Methods   1973
PN 1449   **SC** 16990
SN Scientific methodology based on experimentation, systematic observation, or measurement, rather than theoretical formulation.
  B   Methodology   1967
  N ↓ Experimental Methods   1967
    Observation Methods   1967
  R ↓ Behavioral Assessment   1982
    Positivism (Philosophy)   1997
    Qualitative Research   2003
    Quantitative Methods   2003

Employability   1973
PN 559   **SC** 17000
SN Potential usefulness of an individual as judged on the basis of job skills, functional literacy, emotional or social maturity, intellectual development, or personal values (e.g., personal responsibility).
  R ↓ Employee Skills   1973
   ↓ Employment Status   1982
   ↓ Personnel   1967
    Supported Employment   1994
    Vocational Evaluation   1991

Employee Absenteeism   1973
PN 962   **SC** 17010
  UF Absenteeism (Employee)
  R ↓ Personnel   1967
    Tardiness   2003

Employee Assistance Programs   1985
PN 1366   **SC** 17015
SN Programs or services provided by the employer to help employees with personal or other matters, including retirement planning or alcohol rehabilitation.
  B   Employee Benefits   1973
  R ↓ Counseling   1967
    Disability Management   1991
   ↓ Drug Rehabilitation   1973
    Elder Care   1994
   ↓ Program Development   1991
   ↓ Support Groups   1991

Employee Attitudes   1967
PN 6541   **SC** 17020
SN Attitudes of, not toward, employees.
  B   Attitudes   1967
    Employee Characteristics   1988
  N   Job Satisfaction   1967
  R   Employee Motivation   1973
    Job Involvement   1978

Employee Attitudes — (cont'd)
  ↓ Job Performance   1967
    Organizational Commitment   1991
    Work (Attitudes Toward)   1973

Employee Benefits   1973
PN 462   **SC** 17030
SN Benefits provided by an employer that may be voluntary or mandated by federal or state law.
  N   Bonuses   1973
    Employee Assistance Programs   1985
   ↓ Employee Health Insurance   1973
    Employee Leave Benefits   1973
    Employee Pension Plans   1973
    Workers' Compensation Insurance   2003
  R   Disability Evaluation   1988
    Elder Care   1994
   ↓ Personnel   1967
    Salaries   1973

Employee Characteristics   1988
PN 1635   **SC** 17035
  N ↓ Employee Attitudes   1967
    Employee Efficiency   1973
    Employee Motivation   1973
    Employee Productivity   1973
   ↓ Employee Skills   1973
    Job Experience Level   1973
    Job Knowledge   1997
  R   Diversity in the Workplace   2003
    Organizational Commitment   1991
   ↓ Personnel   1967
    Professional Competence   1997
    Professional Identity   1991
    Professionalism   2003
    Workaholism   2004

Employee Efficiency   1973
PN 184   **SC** 17040
  UF Efficiency (Employee)
  B   Employee Characteristics   1988
    Job Performance   1967
  R   Employee Productivity   1973

Employee Health Insurance   1973
PN 78   **SC** 17050
  B   Employee Benefits   1973
    Health Insurance   1973
  N   Workers' Compensation Insurance   2003

Employee Interaction   1988
PN 1578   **SC** 17055
SN Dynamics of interpersonal interactions between employees.
  B   Interpersonal Interaction   1967
    Organizational Behavior   1978
  N   Supervisor Employee Interaction   1997
  R   Groupware   2003
   ↓ Personnel   1967

Employee Leave Benefits   1973
PN 160   **SC** 17060
  UF Annual Leave
    Sick Leave
    Vacation Benefits
  B   Employee Benefits   1973

Employee Motivation   1973
PN 1792   **SC** 17080
  B   Employee Characteristics   1988
    Motivation   1967
  R ↓ Employee Attitudes   1967
    Job Involvement   1978

Employee Pension Plans   1973
PN 47   **SC** 17090
  UF Pension Plans (Employee)
  B   Employee Benefits   1973

Employee Productivity   1973
PN 1497   **SC** 17110
  UF Productivity (Employee)
  B   Employee Characteristics   1988
    Job Performance   1967
  R   Employee Efficiency   1973

Employee Selection
  Use Personnel Selection

Employee Skills   1973
PN 651   **SC** 17130
  B   Ability   1967
    Employee Characteristics   1988
  N   Clerical Secretarial Skills   1973
  R   Employability   1973
    Job Knowledge   1997
    Professional Competence   1997
    Supported Employment   1994
    Vocational Evaluation   1991

Employee Supervisor Interaction
  Use Supervisor Employee Interaction

Employee Termination
  Use Personnel Termination

Employee Turnover   1973
PN 1582   **SC** 17140
  UF Personnel Turnover
    Turnover
  R   Downsizing   2003
    Employment History   1978
    Job Security   1978
   ↓ Occupational Tenure   1973
   ↓ Personnel   1967

Employees
  Use Personnel

Employer Attitudes   1973
PN 611   **SC** 17160
SN Attitudes of, not toward, employers.
  B   Attitudes   1967
  R   Organizational Commitment   1991
   ↓ Personnel   1967
    Work (Attitudes Toward)   1973

Employment
  Use Employment Status

Employment Discrimination   1994
PN 323   **SC** 17173
SN Prejudiced and differential treatment of employees or job applicants based on factors other than performance or qualifications.
  UF Job Discrimination
  B   Social Discrimination   1982
  R   Affirmative Action   1985
    Age Discrimination   1994
    Ageism   2003
   ↓ Human Resource Management   2003
    Job Applicant Screening   1973
   ↓ Personnel Evaluation   1973

Employment Discrimination — (cont'd)
- ↓ Personnel Selection 1967
- ↓ Prejudice 1967
- Race and Ethnic Discrimination 1994
- Racism 1973
- Sex Discrimination 1978
- Sexism 1988

Employment History 1978
PN 454　　　　　　　　SC 17174
SN Past record of an individual's working life, including periods of unemployment.
- R Career Change 1978
- Career Development 1985
- Employee Turnover 1973
- ↓ Employment Status 1982
- Job Experience Level 1973
- Occupational Mobility 1973
- Occupational Success 1978
- ↓ Occupational Tenure 1973
- ↓ Occupations 1967
- ↓ Personnel 1967
- Personnel Promotion 1978
- Personnel Termination 1973
- Professional Development 1982
- Retirement 1973
- Unemployment 1967

Employment Interviews
- **Use** Job Applicant Interviews

Employment Processes
- **Use** Personnel Recruitment

Employment Status 1982
PN 4358　　　　　　　SC 17196
SN Condition of employment including full- or part-time, temporary or permanent, and unemployment.
HN Use OCCUPATIONS to access references from 1967-1981.
- UF Employment
- N Self Employment 1994
- Unemployment 1967
- R Employability 1973
- Employment History 1978
- Job Applicants 1985
- ↓ Occupational Tenure 1973
- Reemployment 1991
- Retirement 1973
- Supported Employment 1994
- Working Women 1978

Employment Tests 1973
PN 533　　　　　　　　SC 17200
SN Tests used in personnel selection to measure the suitability of an applicant for a given occupation.
- B Measurement 1967
- R Job Applicant Screening 1973

Empowerment 1991
PN 1745　　　　　　　SC 17203
SN Promotion or attainment of autonomy and freedom of choice for individuals or groups.
- R Advocacy 1985
- Assertiveness 1973
- ↓ Civil Rights 1978
- ↓ Client Rights 1988
- ↓ Helplessness 1997
- Independence (Personality) 1973
- ↓ Involvement 1973
- ↓ Power 1967
- Self Determination 1994

Empty Nest 1991
PN 39　　　　　　　　SC 17205
SN Home environment after children have reached maturity and left home. Also, includes the concept of adult children returning to the home.
- UF Return to Home
- R Adult Offspring 1985
- ↓ Family 1967
- ↓ Family Relations 1967
- Family Size 1973
- ↓ Family Structure 1973
- Home Environment 1973
- Intergenerational Relations 1988
- ↓ Living Arrangements 1991
- ↓ Parent Child Relations 1967

Enabling 1997
PN 32　　　　　　　　SC 17207
- B Social Influences 1967
- R Codependency 1991
- Dependency (Personality) 1967
- ↓ Social Reinforcement 1967

Enactments 1997
PN 132　　　　　　　SC 17209
SN Regressive or defensive interactions between a therapist and client or interaction between two or more people that reenacts past experiences or emotional conflicts of one or more of the persons involved.
- UF Reenactments
- R Acting Out 1967
- Age Regression (Hypnotic) 1988
- Countertransference 1973
- Early Experience 1967
- ↓ Interpersonal Interaction 1967
- Projective Identification 1994
- ↓ Psychotherapeutic Processes 1967
- Psychotherapeutic Transference 1967
- Reminiscence 1985

Encephalitis 1973
PN 358　　　　　　　SC 17210
- B Brain Disorders 1967
- Viral Disorders 1973
- R Encephalomyelitis 1973
- ↓ Infectious Disorders 1973

Encephalography 1973
PN 30　　　　　　　　SC 17220
- B Medical Diagnosis 1973
- Neuroimaging 2003
- N Echoencephalography 1973
- ↓ Electroencephalography 1967
- Pneumoencephalography 1973
- Rheoencephalography 1973
- R ↓ Roentgenography 1973

Encephalography (Air)
- **Use** Pneumoencephalography

Encephalomyelitis 1973
PN 54　　　　　　　　SC 17240
- B Myelitis 1973
- R Encephalitis 1973
- ↓ Infectious Disorders 1973

Encephalopathies 1982
PN 459　　　　　　　SC 17247
SN Degenerative diseases of the brain.
- B Brain Disorders 1967
- N Creutzfeldt Jakob Syndrome 1994

Encephalopathies — (cont'd)
- Toxic Encephalopathies 1973
- Wernickes Syndrome 1973
- R Chronic Fatigue Syndrome 1997
- Thyrotoxicosis 1973

Encoding
- **Use** Human Information Storage

Encopresis
- **Use** Fecal Incontinence

Encounter Group Therapy 1973
PN 257　　　　　　　SC 17270
SN Goal-oriented unstructured groups whose members seek heightened self-awareness and fulfillment of their human potential. The group leader (not necessarily a clinically trained therapist) participates freely in the group activity. Techniques used include role playing, sensory awareness, and physical contact.
- B Group Psychotherapy 1967
- Human Potential Movement 1982
- N Marathon Group Therapy 1973
- R Consciousness Raising Groups 1978
- Human Relations Training 1978
- Sensitivity Training 1973

Encouragement 1973
PN 192　　　　　　　SC 17290
- B Social Interaction 1967
- R ↓ Social Reinforcement 1967

Endocrine Disorders 1973
PN 233　　　　　　　SC 17300
- B Physical Disorders 1997
- N ↓ Adrenal Gland Disorders 1973
- ↓ Diabetes 1973
- Endocrine Neoplasms 1973
- ↓ Endocrine Sexual Disorders 1973
- Parathyroid Disorders 1973
- ↓ Pituitary Disorders 1973
- ↓ Thyroid Disorders 1973
- R ↓ Endocrine System 1973
- Hypothermia 1973
- Migraine Headache 1973
- ↓ Secretion (Gland) 1973
- ↓ Somatoform Disorders 2001

Endocrine Gland Secretion 1973
PN 113　　　　　　　SC 17310
- B Secretion (Gland) 1973
- N Adrenal Gland Secretion 1973
- R ↓ Endocrine Glands 1973

Endocrine Gland Surgery 1973
PN 9　　　　　　　　SC 17320
- B Surgery 1971
- N Adrenalectomy 1973
- ↓ Castration 1967
- Hypophysectomy 1973
- Pinealectomy 1973
- Thyroidectomy 1973

Endocrine Glands 1973
PN 43　　　　　　　　SC 17330
- B Endocrine System 1973
- Glands 1967
- N ↓ Adrenal Glands 1973
- ↓ Gonads 1973
- Parathyroid Glands 1973

Endocrine Glands — (cont'd)

Pineal Body 1973
↓ Pituitary Gland 1973
Thyroid Gland 1973
R ↓ Endocrine Gland Secretion 1973
↓ Hormones 1967
Pancreas 1973

Endocrine Neoplasms 1973

PN 27   SC 17340
B   Endocrine Disorders 1973
Neoplasms 1967

Endocrine Sexual Disorders 1973

PN 77   SC 17350
UF   Ovary Disorders
Testes Disorders
B   Endocrine Disorders 1973
Genital Disorders 1967
N ↓ Hypogonadism 1973
Testicular Feminization Syndrome 1973
R ↓ Adrenal Gland Disorders 1973
↓ Gynecological Disorders 1973
Hermaphroditism 1973
↓ Infertility 1973
↓ Male Genital Disorders 1973
↓ Pituitary Disorders 1973
↓ Thyroid Disorders 1973

Endocrine System 1973

PN 368   SC 17360
B   Anatomical Systems 1973
N ↓ Endocrine Glands 1973
R ↓ Endocrine Disorders 1973
Pancreas 1973

Endocrinology 1973

PN 262   SC 17370
SN Scientific discipline dealing with the study of endocrine glands and internal secretions.
B   Medical Sciences 1967
N   Neuroendocrinology 1985
R   Psychoneuroimmunology 1991

Endogamous Marriage 1973

PN 22   SC 17380
B   Marriage 1967
N   Consanguineous Marriage 1973

Endogenous Depression 1978

PN 1197   SC 17384
B   Major Depression 1988

Endogenous Opiates 1985

PN 510   SC 17385
UF   Opioids (Endogenous)
B   Opiates 1973
Peptides 1973
N   Dynorphins 1985
↓ Endorphins 1982

Endorphins 1982

PN 888   SC 17386
SN Endogenous morphine-like brain polypeptides that can bind to opiate receptors.
B   Endogenous Opiates 1985
Neurotransmitters 1985
Proteins 1973
N   Enkephalins 1982
R   Analgesia 1982
↓ Neuropeptides 2003

Endurance 1973

PN 111   SC 17390
SN Ability to withstand hardship, adversity, or stress. Used for human or animal populations.
N   Physical Endurance 1973
Psychological Endurance 1973
R ↓ Stress 1967

Energy Expenditure 1967

PN 1788   SC 17400
SN Expenditure of mental or physical effort.
UF   Effort
R   Calories 1973
Metabolic Rates 1973

Engineering Psychology 1967

PN 584   SC 17410
SN Branch of applied psychology that emphasizes the study of machine design, the relationship between humans and machines, and the effects of machines on human behavior. Use a more specific term if possible.
B   Applied Psychology 1973
R   Human Factors Engineering 1973

Engineers 1967

PN 765   SC 17420
B   Professional Personnel 1978
R ↓ Aerospace Personnel 1973
↓ Business and Industrial Personnel 1967
Scientists 1967

English as Second Language 1997

PN 803   SC 17450
UF   ESL
R   Bilingual Education 1978
Bilingualism 1973
Foreign Language Education 1973
Foreign Languages 1973
↓ Language 1967
↓ Language Arts Education 1973
Language Proficiency 1988
↓ Multilingualism 1973
Native Language 2004

Enjoyment
Use   Pleasure

Enkephalins 1982

PN 520   SC 17475
SN Endogenous morphine-like brain polypeptides closely related to endorphins.
B   Endorphins 1982
R   Analgesia 1982
↓ Neuropeptides 2003
↓ Peptides 1973

Enlisted Military Personnel 1973

PN 258   SC 17480
SN Military personnel ranking below commissioned officers.
B   Military Personnel 1967
N   Draftees 1973
Noncommissioned Officers 1973
R   Volunteer Military Personnel 1973

Enlistment (Military)
Use   Military Enlistment

Enrollment (School)
Use   School Enrollment

Enteropeptidase
Use   Kinases

Enthusiasm 1973

PN 65   SC 17530
UF   Eagerness
B   Emotional States 1973
R   Morale 1978
↓ Motivation 1967

Entrance Examinations 1973

PN 230   SC 17540
B   Educational Measurement 1967
N   College Entrance Examination Board Scholastic Aptitude Test 2001
R   Student Admission Criteria 1973

Entrapment Games 1973

PN 17   SC 17550
B   Games 1967
R ↓ Collective Behavior 1967
Game Theory 1967
Non Zero Sum Games 1973
Prisoners Dilemma Game 1973

Entrepreneurship 1991

PN 414   SC 17555
SN Initiation, organization, management, and assumption of the attendant risks of a business or enterprise.
R   Business 1967
Business Management 1973
Capitalism 1973
↓ Leadership 1967
↓ Management 1967
Ownership 1985
↓ Private Sector 1985
Self Employment 1994

Enuresis
Use   Urinary Incontinence

Environment 1967

PN 7625   SC 17570
SN Totality of physical, social, psychological, or cultural conditions surrounding an organism.
N ↓ Facility Environment 1988
Learning Environment 2004
↓ Single Sex Environments 2001
↓ Social Environments 1973
↓ Therapeutic Environment 2001
R ↓ Architecture 1973
Ecology 1973
Environmental Adaptation 1973
Environmental Attitudes 1978
Environmental Education 1994
↓ Environmental Planning 1982
Environmental Stress 1973
Geography 1973
↓ Hazardous Materials 1991
Nature Nurture 1994
Person Environment Fit 1991
Physical Comfort 1982
Research Setting 2001
Urban Planning 1973

Environmental Adaptation 1973

PN 529   SC 17590
SN Physiological or biological adaptation to conditions in the physical environment. For psychological, social, or emotional adaptation use ADJUSTMENT or one of its related terms.

Environmental Adaptation — (cont'd)
UF Adaptation (Environmental)
B Adaptation 1967
R ↓ Environment 1967
Mimicry (Biology) 2003
Person Environment Fit 1991

Environmental Attitudes 1978
PN 1803 **SC** 17594
SN Perceptions of or beliefs regarding the physical environment, including factors affecting its quality (e.g., overpopulation, pollution).
B Attitudes 1967
R Conservation (Ecological Behavior) 1978
Ecology 1973
↓ Environment 1967
Environmental Education 1994

Environmental Design
Use Environmental Planning

Environmental Education 1994
PN 193 **SC** 17598
SN Used for educational and noneducational settings.
R Conservation (Ecological Behavior) 1978
Ecology 1973
↓ Education 1967
↓ Environment 1967
Environmental Attitudes 1978
Pollution 1973

Environmental Effects 1973
PN 1660 **SC** 17600
SN Used for the effects of meterological or climatic phenomena, as well as for any effect of a surrounding physical environment on an organism's physical, behavioral, or emotional functioning.
N Altitude Effects 1973
Atmospheric Conditions 1973
↓ Gravitational Effects 1967
Noise Effects 1973
Seasonal Variations 1973
↓ Temperature Effects 1967
Underwater Effects 1973
R ↓ Ecological Factors 1973
Environmental Stress 1973
Home Environment 1973
Lunar Synodic Cycle 1973
Occupational Exposure 1988
Physiological Stress 1967
Prenatal Exposure 1991
↓ Social Environments 1973

Environmental Planning 1982
PN 607 **SC** 17607
SN Planning and design of environment with goals of efficient human-environment interaction and minimal ecological disruption.
UF Environmental Design
N Interior Design 1982
Urban Planning 1973
R ↓ Architecture 1973
Computer Assisted Design 1997
↓ Environment 1967
Person Environment Fit 1991
↓ Recreation Areas 1973

Environmental Psychology 1982
PN 687 **SC** 17609
SN Branch of psychology that studies the relationship between environmental variables and behavior, including manipulation of one by the other.

Environmental Psychology — (cont'd)
B Applied Psychology 1973
R Behavioral Ecology 1997
Ecological Psychology 1994

Environmental Stress 1973
PN 854 **SC** 17610
SN Naturally occurring or experimentally manipulated qualities of the physical environment which result in strain or disequilibrium. Consider also other specific terms (e.g., CROWDING, NOISE EFFECTS).
B Stress 1967
R Crowding 1978
↓ Deprivation 1967
↓ Environment 1967
↓ Environmental Effects 1973
Overpopulation 1973
Physiological Stress 1967
Thermal Acclimatization 1973

Environmental Therapy
Use Milieu Therapy

Envy
Use Jealousy

Enzyme Inhibitors 1985
PN 397 **SC** 17625
SN Any agent that slows or otherwise disrupts the activity of an enzyme, such as antienzymes or enzyme antibodies.
B Drugs 1967
N Acetazolamide 1973
↓ Amine Oxidase Inhibitors 1973
Bromocriptine 1988
Captopril 1991
↓ Cholinesterase Inhibitors 1973
↓ Decarboxylase Inhibitors 1982
Hydroxylase Inhibitors 1985
↓ Monoamine Oxidase Inhibitors 1973
Theophylline 1973
R ↓ Enzymes 1973

Enzymes 1973
PN 1166 **SC** 17630
HN In 1997, this term replaced the discontinued terms ALDOLASES and CARBONIC ANHYDRASE. In 2000, these terms were removed from all records containing them, and replaced with ENZYMES.
UF Aldolases
Carbonic Anhydrase
B Drugs 1967
N Decarboxylases 1973
↓ Dehydrogenases 1973
↓ Esterases 1973
Hydroxylases 1973
Isozymes 1973
Kinases 1982
↓ Oxidases 1973
Phosphatases 1973
Phosphorylases 1973
Proteinases 1973
↓ Transferases 1973
R ↓ Anti Inflammatory Drugs 1982
↓ Decarboxylase Inhibitors 1982
↓ Enzyme Inhibitors 1985
↓ Proteins 1973

EOG (Electrophysiology)
Use Electro Oculography

Ependyma
Use Cerebral Ventricles

Ephedrine 1973
PN 61 **SC** 17660
B Adrenergic Drugs 1973
Alcohols 1967
Alkaloids 1973
CNS Stimulating Drugs 1973
Sympathomimetic Amines 1973
Vasoconstrictor Drugs 1973
R ↓ Local Anesthetics 1973

Epidemics 2001
PN 81 **SC** 17665
SN Sudden increase in the incidence of a disease, injury, or other health-related event.
UF Disease Outbreaks
B Public Health 1988
R Epidemiology 1973
Hygiene 1994
↓ Infectious Disorders 1973
↓ Injuries 1973
↓ Syndromes 1973

Epidemiology 1973
PN 14007 **SC** 17670
SN Study of the occurrence, distribution, and containment of disease or mental disorders. Used for the scientific discipline as a whole or for specific epidemiological factors or findings (e.g., disease incidence or prevalence statistics).
B Medical Sciences 1967
R Epidemics 2001

Epilepsy 1967
PN 6100 **SC** 17680
B Brain Disorders 1967
N ↓ Epileptic Seizures 1973
Experimental Epilepsy 1978
Grand Mal Epilepsy 1973
Petit Mal Epilepsy 1973
R ↓ Anticonvulsive Drugs 1973
Aura 1973
↓ Brain Damage 1967
Fugue Reaction 1973

Epileptic Seizures 1973
PN 1303 **SC** 17690
B Brain Disorders 1967
Epilepsy 1967
N Experimental Epilepsy 1978
R Coma 1973
↓ Convulsions 1967

Epinephrine 1967
PN 913 **SC** 17700
UF Adrenaline
B Adrenergic Drugs 1973
Catecholamines 1973
Heart Rate Affecting Drugs 1973
Hormones 1973
R Vasoconstriction 1973
Vasodilation 1973

Episcopalians
Use Protestants

Episodic Memory 1988
PN 883 **SC** 17705

Episodic Memory — (cont'd)
B   Memory 1967
R   Eidetic Imagery 1973

Epistemology 1973
PN 2003   SC 17710
SN Philosophical study of knowledge, including its origin, nature, and limits.
B   Philosophies 1967
R   Determinism 1997
        Hermeneutics 1991
        Metaphysics 1973
        Positivism (Philosophy) 1997
        Relativism 1997

Epithelial Cells 1973
PN 24   SC 17720
B   Cells (Biology) 1973
R   Skin (Anatomy) 1967

Epithelium
Use Skin (Anatomy)

Epstein Barr Viral Disorder 1994
PN 25   SC 17740
B   Infectious Disorders 1973
        Viral Disorders 1973
R   Chronic Fatigue Syndrome 1997

Equal Education 1978
PN 322   SC 17745
SN Provision of comparable educational opportunities to all individuals irrespective of race, national origin, religion, sex, socioeconomic status, or ability.
UF   Educational Inequality
B   Civil Rights 1978
R   ↓ Education 1967
        Educational Quality 1997
        School Integration 1982
        Social Equality 1973

Equality (Social)
Use Social Equality

Equilibrium 1973
PN 674   SC 17760
SN Maintenance of postural balance. For physiological equilibrium consider HOMEOSTASIS.
UF   Balance (Motor Processes)
R   Falls 2004
      ↓ Perceptual Motor Processes 1967
        Spatial Orientation (Perception) 1973

Equipment
Use Apparatus

Equity (Payment) 1978
PN 684   SC 17784
SN In society, group, or other interpersonal situations, the process of equal allocation of economic resources, rewards, or payoffs.
B   Equity (Social) 1978
R   Distributive Justice 2003
      ↓ Justice 1973
        Money 1967
        Resource Allocation 1997
        Salaries 1973
      ↓ Social Behavior 1967
      ↓ Social Processes 1967

Equity (Social) 1978
PN 960   SC 17786
SN In society, group, or other interpersonal situations, the maintenance of relationships in which the proportions of each member's societal and cultural contributions or benefits are approximately equal.
N   Equity (Payment) 1978
R   Distributive Justice 2003
        Egalitarianism 1985
      ↓ Justice 1973
        Resource Allocation 1997
      ↓ Social Behavior 1967
      ↓ Social Processes 1967

Erection (Penis) 1973
PN 635   SC 17790
B   Psychosexual Behavior 1967
R   Impotence 1973

Ergonomics
Use Human Factors Engineering

Ergot Derivatives 1973
PN 163   SC 17810
B   Drugs 1967
N   Bromocriptine 1988
        Dihydroergotamine 1973
R   ↓ Adrenergic Blocking Drugs 1973
      ↓ Alkaloids 1973
        Lysergic Acid Diethylamide 1967
        Tyramine 1973

Erikson (Erik) 1991
PN 215   SC 17815
SN Identifies biographical or autobiographical studies and discussions of Erikson's works.
R   ↓ Developmental Stages 1973
        Ego Identity 1991
        Generativity 2001
      ↓ Neopsychoanalytic School 1973
      ↓ Psychoanalysis 1967
      ↓ Psychoanalytic Theory 1967
      ↓ Psychologists 1967
      ↓ Psychosocial Development 1973

Eroticism 1973
PN 686   SC 17820
B   Sexual Arousal 1978
R   Autoeroticism 1997
        Inhibited Sexual Desire 1997

Erotomania 1997
PN 39   SC 17823
R   ↓ Antisocial Behavior 1971
        Attachment Behavior 1985
        Delusions 1967
        Emotional Abuse 1991
        Grandiosity 1994
        Hypersexuality 1973
        Love 1973
        Obsessions 1967
        Partner Abuse 1991
      ↓ Psychosexual Behavior 1967
        Sexual Fantasy 1997
        Victimization 1973

Error Analysis 1973
PN 812   SC 17830
SN Collection, classification, and/or analysis of mistakes, especially in task or test performance.
B   Analysis 1967

Error Analysis — (cont'd)
R   ↓ Errors 1967
        Human Machine Systems 1997

Error of Measurement 1985
PN 517   SC 17835
SN Observed differences in obtained scores or measures due to chance variance.
UF   Error Variance
        Measurement Error
        Standard Error of Measurement
B   Errors 1967
        Statistical Analysis 1967
R   Consistency (Measurement) 1973
        Least Squares 1985
      ↓ Scoring (Testing) 1973
        Standard Deviation 1973
      ↓ Statistical Estimation 1985
      ↓ Statistical Measurement 1973
      ↓ Test Bias 1985
        Test Reliability 1973
      ↓ Test Scores 1967

Error Variance
Use Error of Measurement

Errors 1967
PN 3609   SC 17840
SN Inappropriate, inaccurate, or incorrect responses or performance. Also, factual errors or other informational inaccuracies and performance errors on the part of others to which a subject reacts.
UF   Mistakes
N   Error of Measurement 1985
      ↓ Prediction Errors 1973
      ↓ Refraction Errors 1973
R   Error Analysis 1973
        Halo Effect 1982
        Proofreading 1988

Erythroblastosis Fetalis
Use Rh Incompatibility

Erythrocytes 1973
PN 385   SC 17860
UF   Red Blood Cells
B   Blood Cells 1973
R   Blood Groups 1973

Escape
Use Avoidance

Escape Behavior (Animal)
Use Animal Escape Behavior

Escape Conditioning 1973
PN 459   SC 17890
SN Learned behavior or the operant conditioning procedure in which the subject learns a specific behavior that results in the termination of an ongoing aversive stimulus. Consider also NEGATIVE REINFORCEMENT. Compare AVOIDANCE CONDITIONING.
UF   Conditioning (Escape)
B   Operant Conditioning 1967

Eserine
Use Physostigmine

Eskimos
Use Inuit

ESL
Use English as Second Language

Esophagus 1973
PN 125   **SC** 17920
B Digestive System 1967
R Dysphagia 2003

ESP (Parapsychology)
Use Extrasensory Perception

Essay Testing 1973
PN 111   **SC** 17940
B Testing Methods 1967

Essential Hypertension 1973
PN 374   **SC** 17950
B Hypertension 1973

Esterases 1973
PN 47   **SC** 17970
B Enzymes 1973
N Acetylcholinesterase 1973
Cholinesterase 1973
R Hydroxylases 1973
Phosphatases 1973

Estimation 1967
PN 1797   **SC** 17980
SN Subjective judgment or inference about the character, quality, or nature of a person, process, or thing which may or may not involve the inspection or availability of data or pertinent information.
N ↓ Statistical Estimation 1985
Time Estimation 1967
R ↓ Expectations 1967
↓ Prediction 1967

Estradiol 1973
PN 1330   **SC** 18000
B Estrogens 1973

Estrogen Antagonists
Use Antiestrogens

Estrogen Replacement Therapy
Use Hormone Therapy

Estrogens 1973
PN 1268   **SC** 18010
B Sex Hormones 1973
N Estradiol 1973
Estrone 1973
R Antiandrogens 1982
Antiestrogens 1982

Estrone 1973
PN 17   **SC** 18020
B Estrogens 1973

Estrus 1973
PN 740   **SC** 18030
R ↓ Animal Biological Rhythms 1973
Animal Sexual Receptivity 1973

Estrus — (cont'd)
↓ Menstrual Cycle 1973
↓ Menstruation 1973

Ethanal
Use Acetaldehyde

Ethanol 1973
PN 5761   **SC** 18040
UF Alcohol (Grain)
Ethyl Alcohol
B Alcohols 1967
R Fetal Alcohol Syndrome 1985

Ether (Anesthetic) 1973
PN 48   **SC** 18050
UF Ethyl Ether (Anesthetic)
B General Anesthetics 1973

Ethics 1967
PN 2801   **SC** 18060
SN For ethics in social or cultural situations, consider MORALITY.
N Bioethics 2003
Experimental Ethics 1978
Professional Ethics 1973
R Euthanasia 1973
Evil 2003
Integrity 1997
Morality 1967
↓ Religious Beliefs 1973
↓ Social Influences 1967
↓ Values 1967

Ethnic Differences
Use Racial and Ethnic Differences

Ethnic Discrimination
Use Race and Ethnic Discrimination

Ethnic Groups
Use Racial and Ethnic Groups

Ethnic Identity 1973
PN 3633   **SC** 18090
SN Feelings, ties, or associations that an individual experiences as a member of a particular ethnic group.
UF Ethnicity
B Sociocultural Factors 1967
R Cultural Sensitivity 1994
Identity Formation 2004
Ingroup Outgroup 1997
Reference Groups 1994
↓ Self Concept 1967
↓ Social Identity 1988

Ethnic Sensitivity
Use Cultural Sensitivity

Ethnic Values 1973
PN 582   **SC** 18100
B Social Influences 1967
Sociocultural Factors 1967
Values 1967
R Cultural Sensitivity 1994
↓ Racial and Ethnic Groups 2001

Ethnicity
Use Ethnic Identity

Ethnocentrism 1973
PN 385   **SC** 18110
SN Exaggerated tendency to identify with one's own ethnic group, or the inclination to judge others in terms of standards and values of one's own group.
B Racial and Ethnic Attitudes 1982
R Cross Cultural Psychology 1997
↓ Social Identity 1988

Ethnography 1973
PN 1273   **SC** 18120
SN Descriptive study of cultures and societies. Used for the scientific discipline or the descriptive analyses themselves. Consider also ETHNOLOGY.
R Anthropology 1967
Ethnology 1967
Folk Psychology 1997
Kinship Structure 1973
Race (Anthropological) 1973
↓ Rites of Passage 1973
↓ Sociocultural Factors 1967

Ethnolinguistics 1973
PN 261   **SC** 18130
SN A part of anthropological linguistics concerned with the interrelation between a language and the cultural behavior of those who speak it.
B Linguistics 1973
R ↓ Dialect 1973
Ethnology 1967
Metalinguistics 1994
Psycholinguistics 1967
Slang 1973
Sociolinguistics 1985

Ethnology 1967
PN 1684   **SC** 18140
SN Conceptually broad term referring to the study of the origin, distribution, characteristics, and relations of the cultures or ethnic groups of the world. Also, a branch of anthropology dealing with the comparative or analytical study of human culture or societies. Use a more specific term if possible. Consider also ETHNOGRAPHY.
R Animism 1973
Anthropology 1967
Cross Cultural Differences 1967
Cross Cultural Psychology 1997
Cultism 1973
↓ Culture (Anthropological) 1967
↓ Culture Change 1967
Culture Shock 1973
Ethnography 1973
Ethnolinguistics 1973
Folk Medicine 1973
Folk Psychology 1997
Folklore 1991
Kinship 1985
Kinship Structure 1973
Myths 1967
Race (Anthropological) 1973
↓ Racial and Ethnic Attitudes 1982
Racial and Ethnic Differences 1982
↓ Racial and Ethnic Groups 2001
Racial and Ethnic Relations 1982
Shamanism 1973
↓ Sociocultural Factors 1967
Taboos 1973
Transcultural Psychiatry 1973
Witchcraft 1973

Ethology (Animal)
Use Animal Ethology

Ethyl Alcohol
Use Ethanol

Ethyl Ether (Anesthetic)
Use Ether (Anesthetic)

Ethylaldehyde
Use Acetaldehyde

Etiology 1967
PN 12965   **SC** 18190
SN Study of the causes and origins of psychological or physical conditions. Used for the science itself or the specific etiological findings and processes.
    UF Aetiology
        Etiopathogenesis
        Pathogenesis
    R Disease Transmission 2004
      ↓ Disorders 1967
      ↓ Mental Disorders 1967
        Patient History 1973
      ↓ Physical Disorders 1997

Etiopathogenesis
Use Etiology

Etymology 1973
PN 79   **SC** 18200
SN Branch of linguistic science which traces the origin of words and morphemes to their earliest determinable base in a given language group and describes historical changes in words. Used for the discipline or specific etymological aspects of given words.
    UF Word Origins
    B Linguistics 1973
    R Words (Phonetic Units) 1967

Eugenics 1973
PN 97   **SC** 18210
SN Applied science or the biosocial movement which advocates the use of practices aimed at improving the genetic composition of a population. Usually refers to human populations. Compare ANIMAL BREEDING, ANIMAL DOMESTICATION, and SELECTIVE BREEDING.
    B Genetic Engineering 1994
        Genetics 1967
        Sciences 1967
    R ↓ Family Planning 1973
        Genetic Counseling 1978
        Reproductive Technology 1988
        Selective Breeding 1973
      ↓ Sterilization (Sex) 1973

Euphoria 1973
PN 160   **SC** 18230
    B Emotional States 1973
    R Happiness 1973
        Pleasure 1973

Eustachian Tube
Use Middle Ear

Euthanasia 1973
PN 621   **SC** 18255
SN Allowing an incurably ill person to die, usually for reasons of mercy.
    UF Mercy Killing
    B Death and Dying 1967
    R Advance Directives 1994

Euthanasia — (cont'd)
        Assisted Suicide 1997
        Bioethics 2003
        Death Attitudes 1973
      ↓ Ethics 1967
        Professional Ethics 1973
      ↓ Treatment 1967
        Treatment Withholding 1988

Evaluation 1967
PN 6007   **SC** 18260
SN Conceptually broad term referring to the appraisal of the characteristics, significance, importance, or relative value of a person, organization, or thing.
    N Course Evaluation 1978
        Forensic Evaluation 1994
        Geriatric Assessment 1997
        Needs Assessment 1985
        Peer Evaluation 1982
      ↓ Personnel Evaluation 1973
      ↓ Program Evaluation 1985
      ↓ Psychiatric Evaluation 1997
        Risk Assessment 2004
        Self Evaluation 1967
        Treatment Effectiveness Evaluation 1973
        Vocational Evaluation 1991
    R Evaluation Criteria 2001
        Intake Interview 1994
      ↓ Measurement 1967
      ↓ Psychological Assessment 1997
        Psychological Report 1988

Evaluation (Psychiatric)
Use Psychiatric Evaluation

Evaluation (Treatment Effectiveness)
Use Treatment Effectiveness Evaluation

Evaluation Criteria 2001
PN 162   **SC** 18270
SN Specifications that may be used to appraise individuals, organizations, tests, values, or processes.
    UF Assessment Criteria
    R ↓ Evaluation 1967

Evangelists 1973
PN 76   **SC** 18320
    B Religious Personnel 1973
    R ↓ Clergy 1973
        Lay Religious Personnel 1973
        Missionaries 1973

Event Related Potentials
Use Evoked Potentials

Evidence Based Medicine
Use Evidence Based Practice

Evidence Based Practice 2004
PN 102   **SC** 18326
SN Basing clinical practice and decision making on the appraisal of systematic research findings.
HN This term was introduced in June 2004. PsycINFO records from the past 10 years were re-indexed with this term. The posting note reflects the number of records that were re-indexed.
    UF Evidence Based Medicine
    R Clinical Trials 2004
      ↓ Experimentation 1967

Evidence Based Practice — (cont'd)
      ↓ Health Care Delivery 1978

Evil 2003
PN 81   **SC** 18327
HN This term was introduced in June 2003. PsycINFO records from the past 10 years were re-indexed with this term. The posting note reflects the number of records that were re-indexed.
    R ↓ Ethics 1967
        Morality 1967
      ↓ Religious Beliefs 1973
        Sin 1973
        Social Values 1973

Evoked Potentials 1967
PN 4328   **SC** 18330
    UF Event Related Potentials
    B Electrical Activity 1967
    N Auditory Evoked Potentials 1973
      ↓ Cortical Evoked Potentials 1973
        Olfactory Evoked Potentials 1973
        Somatosensory Evoked Potentials 1973
        Visual Evoked Potentials 1973
    R Electrical Brain Stimulation 1973
      ↓ Neuroimaging 2003
        Sensory Gating 1991

Evolution (Theory of)
Use Theory of Evolution

Evolutionary Psychology 2003
PN 221   **SC** 18343
SN A branch of psychology that applies concepts from evolutionary theory to behavior.
HN This term was introduced in June 2003. PsycINFO records from the past 10 years were re-indexed with this term. The posting note reflects the number of records that were re-indexed.
    B Psychology 1967
    R ↓ Darwinism 1973
        Sociobiology 1982
        Theory of Evolution 1967

Exceptional Children (Gifted)
Use Gifted

Exceptional Children (Handicapped)
Use Disorders

Excitation (Physiological)
Use Physiological Arousal

Excretion 1967
PN 619   **SC** 18370
    UF Elimination (Excretion)
    B Physiology 1967
    N Defecation 1967
      ↓ Urination 1967

Executive Functioning
Use Cognitive Ability

Executives
Use Top Level Managers

Exercise 1973
PN 5316   **SC** 18390
    UF Physical Exercise

Exercise — (cont'd)
B Motor Processes 1967
N Aerobic Exercise 1988
   Weightlifting 1994
   Yoga 1973
R ↓ Health Behavior 1982
   Movement Therapy 1997
   Physical Fitness 1973
   Weight Control 1985

Exhaustion
Use Fatigue

Exhibitionism 1973
PN 215   SC 18420
B Paraphilias 1988
R Voyeurism 1973

Existential Therapy 1973
PN 339   SC 18430
SN Form of psychotherapy that deals with the here
and now of the patient's total situation rather than
with his/her past; it emphasizes emotional experi-
ences rather than rational thinking, and stresses a
person's responsibility for his/her own existence.
B Psychotherapy 1967
R ↓ Humanistic Psychotherapy 2003
   Logotherapy 1973

Existentialism 1967
PN 1100   SC 18440
SN Philosophy based on the analysis of the individual's existence in the world which holds that human
existence cannot be completely described in scientific terms. Existentialism also stresses the freedom
and responsibility of the individual as well as the
uniqueness of religious and ethical experiences and
the analysis of subjective phenomena such as anxiety, guilt, and suffering.
B Philosophies 1967
R Relativism 1997
   ↓ Religious Beliefs 1973

Exogamous Marriage 1973
PN 111   SC 18450
UF Interethnic Marriage
    Intermarriage
B Marriage 1967
N Interfaith Marriage 1973
   Interracial Marriage 1973

Expectant Fathers 1985
PN 107   SC 18455
B Expectant Parents 1985
R ↓ Fathers 1967

Expectant Mothers 1985
PN 355   SC 18456
B Expectant Parents 1985
R ↓ Mothers 1967

Expectant Parents 1985
PN 104   SC 18457
N Expectant Fathers 1985
   Expectant Mothers 1985
R ↓ Parents 1967

Expectations 1967
PN 11113   SC 18460
SN Anticipation of future behavior or events. Also
refers to investigations of the effects of that anticipation on behavior.

Expectations — (cont'd)
B Cognitions 1985
N Experimenter Expectations 1973
   Parental Expectations 1997
   Role Expectations 1973
   Teacher Expectations 1978
R ↓ Estimation 1967
   Future 1991
   Halo Effect 1982
   Hope 1991
   Self Efficacy 1985
   Self Fulfilling Prophecies 1997

Experience (Practice)
Use Practice

Experience Level 1988
PN 3468   SC 18495
SN Amount of practical knowledge, skill, or practice
as a result of direct participation in a particular activ-
ity.
UF Expertise
N Job Experience Level 1973
R ↓ Knowledge Level 1978
   ↓ Practice 1967

Experience Level (Job)
Use Job Experience Level

Experiences (Events) 1973
PN 6723   SC 18510
SN Perceptual, emotional, and/or cognitive conse-
quences associated with specific events or contexts.
Compare LIFE EXPERIENCES.
N Anniversary Events 1994
   Early Experience 1967
   ↓ Life Experiences 1973
   Vicarious Experiences 1973
R Combat Experience 1991
   ↓ Crises 1971
   Familiarity 1967
   Homesickness 1994
   Near Death Experiences 1985

Experiences (Life)
Use Life Experiences

Experiential Learning 1997
PN 350   SC 18517
B Learning 1967
   Teaching Methods 1967
N Curricular Field Experience 1982
R Apprenticeship 1970
   Cooperative Education 1982
   Discovery Teaching Method 1973
   Educational Field Trips 1973
   On the Job Training 1973
   School Learning 1967

Experiential Psychotherapy 1973
PN 361   SC 18520
SN Psychotherapeutic approach, having some
roots in existentialism, that emphasizes the concrete,
lived, and felt experience of the client.
B Psychotherapy 1967

Experiment Controls 1973
PN 313   SC 18530
UF Control Groups
R ↓ Experimental Design 1967
   Experimental Subjects 1985

Experiment Controls — (cont'd)
↓ Experimentation 1967
↓ Methodology 1967

Experiment Volunteers
Use Experimental Subjects

Experimental Apparatus
Use Apparatus

Experimental Attrition 1994
PN 125   SC 18555
SN Reduction in the number of experimental sub-
jects over time as a result of resignation or other fac-
tors.
UF Attrition (Experimental)
    Research Dropouts
R ↓ Dropouts 1973
   Experimental Subjects 1985
   ↓ Experimentation 1967

Experimental Design 1967
PN 5271   SC 18560
SN General procedural plan for conducting an
experiment or other research study in view of the
specific data desired. This may include identification
of the independent and dependent variables; selec-
tion of subjects and their assignment to specific
experimental conditions/treatments; the sequence of
experimental conditions/treatments; and a method of
analysis. Consider also EXPERIMENTAL METH-
ODS.
UF Design (Experimental)
    Research Design
N Between Groups Design 1985
   Clinical Trials 2004
   Cohort Analysis 1999
   Followup Studies 1973
   ↓ Hypothesis Testing 1973
   ↓ Longitudinal Studies 1973
   Repeated Measures 1985
R Animal Models 1988
   Conjoint Measurement 1994
   Debriefing (Experimental) 1991
   Experiment Controls 1973
   ↓ Experimental Methods 1967
   ↓ Experimentation 1967
   ↓ Methodology 1967
   ↓ Population (Statistics) 1973
   Psychometrics 1967
   Qualitative Research 2003
   Quantitative Methods 2003
   Quasi Experimental Methods 2003
   Research Setting 2001
   ↓ Sampling (Experimental) 1973
   ↓ Statistical Analysis 1967
   ↓ Statistical Variables 1973
   ↓ Test Construction 1973

Experimental Environment
Use Research Setting

Experimental Epilepsy 1978
PN 202   SC 18564
SN Paroxysmal transient disruption of normal elec-
trical activity in the brain induced by chemical, electri-
cal, or physical stimulation of the brain or by repetitive
sensory stimulation.
B Epilepsy 1967
   Epileptic Seizures 1973
R ↓ Convulsions 1967

Experimental Epilepsy — (cont'd)
↓ Electrical Stimulation 1973
Kindling 1985

Experimental Ethics 1978
PN 1327   SC 18566
B   Ethics 1967
R   Animal Welfare 1985
     Bioethics 2003
     Debriefing (Experimental) 1991
↓ Experimentation 1967
     Fraud 1994
     Informed Consent 1985
     Professional Ethics 1973

Experimental Instructions 1967
PN 2806   SC 18570
SN   Directions given to a subject participating in an experiment.
UF   Instructions (Experimental)
R   ↓ Experimentation 1967
     ↓ Methodology 1967

Experimental Laboratories 1973
PN 444   SC 18580
UF   Laboratories (Experimental)
R   ↓ Experimentation 1967
     ↓ Methodology 1967
     Research Setting 2001

Experimental Methods 1967
PN 5637   SC 18590
SN   System of scientific investigation, usually based on a design and carried out under controlled conditions with the aim of testing a hypothesis, in which one or more variables is manipulated.
UF   Scientific Methods
B   Empirical Methods 1973
N   Quasi Experimental Methods 2003
     ↓ Stimulus Presentation Methods 1973
R   ↓ Experimental Design 1967
     Quantitative Methods 2003

Experimental Neurosis 1973
PN 56   SC 18600
SN   Acute neurotic-like state produced experimentally by requiring discrimination or problem solving responses which are beyond the subject's ability or level of learning. Such states are induced by the repeated delivery of aversive stimulation following failure.
B   Neurosis 1967
R   Experimental Psychosis 1973
     Learned Helplessness 1978

Experimental Psychologists 1973
PN 78   SC 18610
B   Psychologists 1967

Experimental Psychology 1967
PN 879   SC 18620
B   Psychology 1967
R   ↓ Experimentation 1967

Experimental Psychosis 1973
PN 18   SC 18630
SN   Experimentally induced psychotic-like state or condition usually achieved through drug administration. Not to be confused with inadvertent induction of psychotic conditions resulting from toxic side effects in drug therapy. Compare TOXIC PSYCHOSES.
B   Psychosis 1967

Experimental Psychosis — (cont'd)
R   Experimental Neurosis 1973
↓ Hallucinogenic Drugs 1967
↓ Psychotomimetic Drugs 1973

Experimental Replication 1973
PN 3671   SC 18640
SN   Used in records discussing issues involved in the process of conducting a replication of an experiment.
HN   From 1973-2000, the term was also used as a mandatory document type identifier; however, this usage has been discontinued due to the advent of Form/Content Type field identifiers. References from 1973-2000 can be accessed using either EXPERIMENTAL REPLICATION or the Experimental Replication Form/Content Type field identifier.
UF   Replication (Experimental)
R   ↓ Experimentation 1967
     ↓ Methodology 1967

Experimental Setting
Use   Research Setting

Experimental Subjects 1985
PN 1696   SC 18645
SN   Any individual who is, knowingly or unknowingly, a member of an experiment or research population. Used only when methodological or procedural aspects are discussed regarding research subjects. Used primarily for human populations.
HN   In June 2003, this term replaced the discontinued term EXPERIMENT VOLUNTEERS. EXPERIMENT VOLUNTEERS was removed from all records containing it and replaced with EXPERIMENTAL SUBJECTS.
UF   Experiment Volunteers
     Research Subjects
     Volunteers (Experiment)
R   Debriefing (Experimental) 1991
     Experiment Controls 1973
     Experimental Attrition 1994
     ↓ Experimentation 1967

Experimentation 1967
PN 22451   SC 18650
SN   Conceptually broad term referring to any or all aspects of scientific research. Use a more specific term if possible.
UF   Investigation
     Research
N   ↓ Consumer Research 1973
     Interdisciplinary Research 1985
     Qualitative Research 2003
     Quantitative Methods 2003
     Research Setting 2001
R   Animal Models 1988
     Causal Analysis 1994
     Debriefing (Experimental) 1991
     Evidence Based Practice 2004
     Experiment Controls 1973
     Experimental Attrition 1994
     ↓ Experimental Design 1967
     Experimental Ethics 1978
     Experimental Instructions 1967
     Experimental Laboratories 1973
     Experimental Psychology 1967
     Experimental Replication 1973
     Experimental Subjects 1985
     Experimenters 1973
     ↓ Measurement 1967
     ↓ Methodology 1967
     ↓ Population (Statistics) 1973
     Psychometrics 1967

Experimentation — (cont'd)
Psychophysics 1967
↓ Sampling (Experimental) 1973
↓ Statistical Analysis 1967
↓ Statistical Correlation 1967
Statistical Reliability 1973
Statistical Validity 1973
↓ Statistical Variables 1973
↓ Theories 1967

Experimenter Bias 1967
PN 572   SC 18660
SN   Potential and unintentional influence on experimental outcomes caused by the experimenter.
UF   Bias (Experimenter)
R   Experimenter Expectations 1973
     Experimenters 1973
     Halo Effect 1982

Experimenter Expectations 1973
PN 158   SC 18670
SN   Results from experimentation which are anticipated or desired by the researcher in order to confirm a hypothesis and which may serve as a potential factor in experimenter bias.
B   Expectations 1967
R   Experimenter Bias 1967
     Experimenters 1973

Experimenters 1973
PN 595   SC 18680
R   ↓ Experimentation 1967
     Experimenter Bias 1967
     Experimenter Expectations 1973

Expert Systems 1991
PN 1172   SC 18685
UF   Knowledge Based Systems
B   Artificial Intelligence 1982
     Systems 1967
N   Decision Support Systems 1997
R   ↓ Automated Information Processing 1973
     Automated Speech Recognition 1994
     Case Based Reasoning 2003
     ↓ Computers 1967
     Cybernetics 1967
     ↓ Data Processing 1967
     Databases 1991
     ↓ Decision Making 1967
     Heuristics 2003
     Human Machine Systems 1997
     ↓ Information Systems 1991
     Intelligent Tutoring Systems 2003
     Knowledge Engineering 2003
     Machine Learning 2003
     ↓ Problem Solving 1967
     Robotics 1985

Expert Testimony 1973
PN 1405   SC 18690
SN   Legal testimony by persons who by virtue of their training, skills, or expertise are qualified to give evidence concerning some scientific, technical, or professional matter.
UF   Testimony (Expert)
B   Legal Testimony 1982
R   Forensic Evaluation 1994
     Forensic Psychiatry 1973
     Forensic Psychology 1985
     Litigation 2003

Expertise
Use   Experience Level

Explicit Memory　1997
PN　364　　　　　　　SC　18695
SN　Memory of events where one is also aware of learning or experiencing the event.
　B　Memory　1967
　R　Implicit Memory　2003

Exploratory Behavior　1967
PN　764　　　　　　　SC　18700
SN　Locomotor activity or perceptual processes involved in investigating and/or orienting oneself to an environment.
HN　From 1973, limited to human populations. From 1973, use ANIMAL EXPLORATORY BEHAVIOR to access references to nonhumans.
　B　Behavior　1967
　N　Animal Exploratory Behavior　1973
　R　Curiosity　1967
　　　Information Seeking　1973
　　↓ Motivation　1967

Explosive Disorder　2001
PN　58　　　　　　　SC　18705
SN　Disorder characterized by discrete episodes of loss of control of aggressive impulses that may result in serious assault or destruction of property.
HN　In 2000, this term was created to replace the discontinued term EXPLOSIVE PERSONALITY. EXPLOSIVE PERSONALITY was removed from all records containing It and replaced with EXPLOSIVE DISORDER.
　UF　Explosive Personality
　　　Intermittent Explosive Disorder
　B　Impulse Control Disorders　1997
　R　Anger Control　1997
　　↓ Antisocial Behavior　1971
　　　Conduct Disorder　1991
　　↓ Personality Disorders　1967

Explosive Personality
　Use　Explosive Disorder

Exposure Therapy　1997
PN　452　　　　　　　SC　18715
　B　Behavior Therapy　1967
　N　Implosive Therapy　1973
　　　Systematic Desensitization Therapy　1973

Exposure Time (Stimulus)
　Use　Stimulus Duration

Expressed Emotion　1991
PN　598　　　　　　　SC　18725
SN　Frequency and quality of negative emotions, e.g., anger or hostility, expressed by family members or significant others, that often lead to a high relapse rate, especially in schizophrenic patients.
　R　↓ Emotions　1967
　　　Relapse (Disorders)　1973
　　↓ Schizophrenia　1967

Expressions (Facial)
　Use　Facial Expressions

Expressive Psychotherapy　1973
PN　113　　　　　　　SC　18740
SN　Psychotherapeutic method used to promote more effective personality functioning through uninhibited expression of feelings and open discussion of personal problems.
　B　Psychotherapy　1967

Expressive Psychotherapy　— (cont'd)
　R　Improvisation　2004
　　　Supportive Psychotherapy　1997

Expulsion (School)
　Use　School Expulsion

Extended Family　1973
PN　275　　　　　　　SC　18760
　B　Family　1967
　　　Family Structure　1973

Extension Workers (Agricultural)
　Use　Agricultural Extension Workers

External Ear　1973
PN　62　　　　　　　SC　18780
　UF　Ear Canal
　B　Ear (Anatomy)　1967

External Rewards　1973
PN　354　　　　　　　SC　18790
SN　Tangible or overtly identifiable rewards given in return for service or attainment which may act as reinforcement for the activity rewarded. Compare PRIMARY REINFORCEMENT.
　UF　Extrinsic Rewards
　B　Rewards　1967
　R　Extrinsic Motivation　1973
　　　Internal External Locus of Control　1967

Externalization　1973
PN　583　　　　　　　SC　18800
　B　Personality Processes　1967
　R　↓ Defense Mechanisms　1967
　　↓ Internalization　1997
　　↓ Personality Development　1967

Extinction (Learning)　1967
PN　3606　　　　　　　SC　18810
SN　Learned behavior or the experimental paradigm involving withholding reinforcement for a conditioned response and resulting in a gradual reduction and eventual elimination of responding or a return to a rate of responding comparable to levels prior to conditioning. Term may be used in either classical (Pavlovian) or operant (instrumental) conditioning contexts.
　B　Learning　1967
　R　↓ Discrimination Learning　1982
　　↓ Reinforcement　1967

Extracurricular Activities　1973
PN　609　　　　　　　SC　18820
　N　Fraternity Membership　1973
　　　School Club Membership　1973
　　　Sorority Membership　1973
　R　After School Programs　2003
　　　Athletic Participation　1973
　　　Athletic Training　1991
　　↓ Education　1967

Extradimensional Shift Learning
　Use　Nonreversal Shift Learning

Extramarital Intercourse　1973
PN　332　　　　　　　SC　18830
　UF　Adultery
　　　Affairs (Sexual)
　　　Mate Swapping

Extramarital Intercourse　— (cont'd)
　B　Psychosexual Behavior　1967
　　　Sexual Intercourse (Human)　1973
　R　↓ Marital Relations　1967
　　　Monogamy　1997
　　　Promiscuity　1973

Extrapyramidal Symptoms　1994
PN　466　　　　　　　SC　18835
　B　Symptoms　1967
　R　↓ Basal Ganglia　1973
　　　Extrapyramidal Tracts　1973
　　↓ Nervous System Disorders　1967

Extrapyramidal Tracts　1973
PN　123　　　　　　　SC　18840
　B　Central Nervous System　1967
　　　Efferent Pathways　1982
　　　Spinal Cord　1973
　R　Extrapyramidal Symptoms　1994

Extrasensory Perception　1967
PN　731　　　　　　　SC　18850
　UF　ESP (Parapsychology)
　B　Parapsychological Phenomena　1973
　　　Perception　1967
　N　↓ Clairvoyance　1973
　　　Psychokinesis　1973
　R　Telepathy　1973

Extraversion　1967
PN　2861　　　　　　　SC　18854
SN　Personality trait which reflects the extent to which an individual likes people and prefers large gatherings; is assertive, active and talkative; enjoys excitement and stimulation; and tends to have a cheerful disposition.
　B　Personality Traits　1967
　R　Assertiveness　1973
　　　Five Factor Personality Model　1997
　　　Gregariousness　1973
　　　Introversion　1967
　　　Sensation Seeking　1978
　　　Sociability　1973

Extrinsic Motivation　1973
PN　551　　　　　　　SC　18860
SN　Need or desire arising from outside the individual which causes action toward some goal.
　B　Motivation　1967
　R　External Rewards　1973
　　↓ Goals　1967
　　　Internal External Locus of Control　1967
　　↓ Needs　1967

Extrinsic Rewards
　Use　External Rewards

Eye (Anatomy)　1967
PN　1234　　　　　　　SC　18890
　UF　Choroid
　　　Sclera
　B　Sense Organs　1973
　N　Cornea　1973
　　　Eye Color　1991
　　　Fovea　1982
　　　Iris (Eye)　1973
　　　Lens (Eye)　1973
　　　Pupil (Eye)　1973
　　↓ Retina　1967
　R　↓ Eye Disorders　1973
　　↓ Eye Movements　1967

Eye (Anatomy) — (cont'd)
    Ocular Dominance 1973
    Pupil Dilation 1973
    Retinal Image 1973
    ↓ Visual Perception 1967

Eye Accommodation
  Use Ocular Accommodation

Eye Color 1991
PN 24   **SC** 18895
  B   Color 1967
      Eye (Anatomy) 1967
  R   Iris (Eye) 1973
      ↓ Pigments 1973

Eye Contact 1973
PN 633   **SC** 18900
SN Form of nonverbal communication in which two individuals meet each other's glance.
  B   Interpersonal Communication 1973
      Nonverbal Communication 1971
  R   ↓ Social Reinforcement 1967

Eye Convergence 1982
PN 275   **SC** 18902
SN Turning the eyes toward or away from each other when fixating on distal objects.
  UF Vergence Movements
  B   Eye Movements 1967
  R   ↓ Depth Perception 1967
      ↓ Distance Perception 1973
      Strabismus 1973

Eye Disorders 1973
PN 439   **SC** 18910
SN Diseases or defects of the eye. Use VISION DISORDERS for other pathology involving visual neural pathways.
  B   Vision Disorders 1982
  N   Amblyopia 1973
      Cataracts 1973
      Color Blindness 1973
      Glaucoma 1973
      Hemianopia 1973
      Nystagmus 1973
      ↓ Refraction Errors 1973
      Strabismus 1973
      Tunnel Vision 1973
  R   Albinism 1973
      ↓ Eye (Anatomy) 1967
      Hysterical Vision Disturbances 1973
      Ocular Dominance 1973
      ↓ Visual Perception 1967

Eye Dominance
  Use Ocular Dominance

Eye Examination
  Use Ophthalmologic Examination

Eye Fixation 1982
PN 1683   **SC** 18924
SN Orienting one's eye(s) toward and stabilizing one's gaze on a specified visual stimulus.
  UF Gazing
      Ocular Fixation
      Visual Fixation
  B   Visual Perception 1967
  R   Visual Attention 2004
      Visual Field 1967

Eye Movement Desensitization Therapy 1997
PN 284   **SC** 18927
SN Treatment methodology used in the reduction of the emotional impact of trauma-based symptomatology associated with anxiety, nightmares, flashbacks, or intrusive thought processes.
  UF EMDR
  B   Psychotherapy 1967
  R   ↓ Behavior Therapy 1967
      ↓ Eye Movements 1967

Eye Movements 1967
PN 6561   **SC** 18930
  UF Oculomotor Response
      Saccadic Eye Movements
  N   Eye Convergence 1982
      Nystagmus 1973
      Rapid Eye Movement 1971
  R   ↓ Eye (Anatomy) 1967
      Eye Movement Desensitization Therapy 1997
      REM Dreams 1973
      REM Sleep 1973
      Visual Search 1982

Eyeblink Reflex 1973
PN 783   **SC** 18940
  UF Blink Reflex
  B   Reflexes 1971
  R   Startle Reflex 1967

Eyelid Conditioning 1973
PN 724   **SC** 18950
SN Conditioned eye blinking or the classical conditioning paradigm resulting in conditioned eye blinking.
  UF Conditioning (Eyelid)
  B   Classical Conditioning 1967

Eyewitnesses
  Use Witnesses

Eysenck Personality Inventory 1973
PN 496   **SC** 18960
  B   Nonprojective Personality Measures 1973

F Test 1973
PN 95   **SC** 18970
  B   Parametric Statistical Tests 1973
  R   ↓ Variability Measurement 1973

Face (Anatomy) 1973
PN 791   **SC** 18980
  B   Anatomy 1967
  R   Facial Features 1973
      Head (Anatomy) 1973

Face Perception 1985
PN 3094   **SC** 18985
SN Used for human or animal populations.
  UF Face Recognition
  B   Visual Perception 1967
  R   ↓ Facial Expressions 1967
      Facial Features 1973
      Prosopagnosia 1994
      ↓ Social Perception 1967

Face Recognition
  Use Face Perception

Facial Expressions 1967
PN 2892   **SC** 18990
  UF Expressions (Facial)
  B   Nonverbal Communication 1971
  N   Grimaces 1973
      Smiles 1973
  R   Face Perception 1985
      Facial Features 1973

Facial Features 1973
PN 920   **SC** 18993
  R   Face (Anatomy) 1973
      Face Perception 1985
      ↓ Facial Expressions 1967
      ↓ Physical Appearance 1982
      Physical Attractiveness 1973

Facial Muscles 1973
PN 309   **SC** 19000
  B   Muscles 1967

Facial Nerve 1973
PN 166   **SC** 19010
  UF Chorda Tympani Nerve
      Nerve (Facial)
  B   Cranial Nerves 1973

Facilitated Communication
  Use Augmentative Communication

Facilitation (Social)
  Use Social Facilitation

Facility Admission 1988
PN 170   **SC** 19024
  UF Facility Readmission
  N   ↓ Hospital Admission 1973
  R   ↓ Facility Discharge 1988
      ↓ Institutionalization 1967
      ↓ Treatment Facilities 1973

Facility Discharge 1988
PN 94   **SC** 19026
  N   ↓ Hospital Discharge 1973
  R   Client Transfer 1997
      Discharge Planning 1994
      ↓ Facility Admission 1988
      ↓ Institutionalization 1967
      ↓ Treatment Facilities 1973

Facility Environment 1988
PN 487   **SC** 19028
  B   Environment 1967
      Therapeutic Environment 2001
  N   Hospital Environment 1982
  R   ↓ Treatment Facilities 1973

Facility Readmission
  Use Facility Admission

Factitious Disorders 1988
PN 330   **SC** 19035
  UF Ganser Syndrome
  B   Mental Disorders 1967
  N   Munchausen Syndrome 1994
  R   Malingering 1973
      Pseudodementia 1985

Factor Analysis 1967
PN 6203   **SC** 19040

Factor Analysis — (cont'd)
HN Use FACTOR ANALYSIS to access references to the factor structure of psychometric measures from 1967-1984.
UF Confirmatory Factor Analysis
B Multivariate Analysis 1982
N Item Analysis (Statistical) 1973
  ↓ Statistical Rotation 1973
R Factor Structure 1985
  Goodness of Fit 1988
  Path Analysis 1991
  ↓ Statistical Correlation 1967
  Statistical Significance 1973
  Structural Equation Modeling 1994

Factor Structure 1985
PN 5010   **SC** 19045
SN The internal correlational structure of a set of variables said to measure a given construct.
HN Use FACTOR ANALYSIS to access references prior to 1985.
R ↓ Factor Analysis 1967
  ↓ Statistical Rotation 1973
  Structural Equation Modeling 1994

Factorial Validity
Use Statistical Validity

Factory Environments
Use Working Conditions

Factual Knowledge
Use Declarative Knowledge

Faculty
Use Educational Personnel

Fading (Conditioning) 1982
PN 147   **SC** 19087
SN Gradual attenuation of dissimilarity of stimuli dimensions contingent on the subject's mastery of difference between those stimuli. The fading technique is used to facilitate errorless discrimination learning.
B Behavior Modification 1973
  Operant Conditioning 1967
R ↓ Discrimination Learning 1982
  Stimulus Attenuation 1973
  Stimulus Discrimination 1973

Fads and Fashions 1973
PN 124   **SC** 19090
N Clothing 1967
R Cosmetic Techniques 2001
  Popular Culture 2003
  Social Change 1967
  Trends 1991

Failure 1967
PN 1882   **SC** 19100
N Academic Failure 1978
R Academic Underachievement 1967
  ↓ Achievement 1967

Failure to Thrive 1988
PN 235   **SC** 19105
SN Growth disorder of infants and children due to nutritional and/or emotional deprivation and resulting in loss of weight and delayed physical, emotional, and social development.

Failure to Thrive — (cont'd)
B Delayed Development 1973
R Attachment Disorders 2001
  ↓ Child Abuse 1971
  Child Neglect 1988
  ↓ Nutritional Deficiencies 1973

Fainting
Use Syncope

Fairbairnian Theory
Use Object Relations

Fairy Tales
Use Folklore

Faith Healing 1973
PN 392   **SC** 19120
UF Psychic Healing
B Alternative Medicine 1997
  Religious Practices 1973
R Folk Medicine 1973
  Shamanism 1973
  Witchcraft 1973

Faking 1973
PN 501   **SC** 19130
B Deception 1967
R ↓ Behavior Disorders 1971

Falls 2004
PN 105   **SC** 19132
HN This term was introduced in June 2004. Psyc-INFO records from the past 10 years were re-indexed with this term. The posting note reflects the number of records that were re-indexed.
B Accidents 1967
R Equilibrium 1973
  ↓ Injuries 1973

False Memory 1997
PN 695   **SC** 19135
UF Pseudomemory
B Memory 1967
R Age Regression (Hypnotic) 1988
  ↓ Amnesia 1967
  Confabulation 1973
  Early Memories 1985
  Emotional Trauma 1967
  ↓ Hypnosis 1967
  ↓ Hypnotherapy 1970
  Repressed Memory 1997
  Source Monitoring 2004
  Suggestibility 1967

False Pregnancy
Use Pseudocyesis

Fame 1985
PN 101   **SC** 19145
UF Celebrity
R Reputation 1997
  ↓ Social Perception 1967
  ↓ Status 1967

Familial Idiocy (Amaurotic)
Use Tay Sachs Disease

Familiarity 1967
PN 4125   **SC** 19160
SN Knowledge of, or close acquaintance with, an object, stimulus, person, environment, situation, or act.
R ↓ Experiences (Events) 1973
  ↓ Practice 1967
  Stranger Reactions 1988

Family 1967
PN 9069   **SC** 19300
SN Conceptually broad term. Use a more specific term if possible.
N Biological Family 1988
  Extended Family 1973
  Family of Origin 1991
  Interethnic Family 1988
  Interracial Family 1988
  Nuclear Family 1973
  Schizophrenogenic Family 1967
  Stepfamily 1991
R Codependency 1991
  Cohabitation 1973
  Couples 1982
  Divorce 1973
  Divorced Persons 1973
  Dual Careers 1982
  Dysfunctional Family 1991
  Empty Nest 1991
  ↓ Family Background 1973
  Family Crises 1973
  ↓ Family Life Education 1997
  ↓ Family Members 1973
  ↓ Family Planning 1973
  ↓ Family Relations 1967
  Family Resemblance 1991
  ↓ Family Structure 1973
  Kinship 1985
  ↓ Living Arrangements 1991
  ↓ Marital Separation 1973
  ↓ Marital Status 1973
  ↓ Marriage 1967
  Transgenerational Patterns 1991
  Widowers 1973
  Widows 1973
  Working Women 1978

Family Background 1973
PN 4489   **SC** 19170
UF Background (Family)
N Family Socioeconomic Level 1973
  Parent Educational Background 1973
  Parental Occupation 1973
R Biographical Data 1978
  Children of Alcoholics 2003
  ↓ Family 1967
  Family of Origin 1991
  ↓ Marital Status 1973

Family Caregivers
Use Caregivers

Family Conflict 2003
PN 65   **SC** 19178
HN This term was introduced in June 2003. Psyc-INFO records from the past 10 years were re-indexed with this term. The posting note reflects the number of records that were re-indexed.
B Conflict 1967
  Family Relations 1967
N Marital Conflict 1973
R Family Intervention 2003
  Family Violence 1982

Family Conflict — (cont'd)
- Home Environment 1973
- ↓ Parent Child Relations 1967
- Partner Abuse 1991

Family Counseling
- **Use** Family Therapy

Family Crises 1973
PN 567   SC 19190
- **B** Crises 1971
- **R** ↓ Family 1967
- Family Intervention 2003
- ↓ Stress 1967

Family Dynamics
- **Use** Family Relations

Family Environment
- **Use** Home Environment

Family Intervention 2003
PN 152   SC 19195
SN Interventions that involve the family as a whole, or individual family members; includes interventions that are provided by family members on behalf of another family member.
HN This term was introduced in June 2003. Psyc-INFO records from the past 10 years were re-indexed with this term. The posting note reflects the number of records that were re-indexed.
- **B** Intervention 2003
- **R** ↓ Crisis Intervention 1973
- ↓ Family Conflict 2003
- Family Crises 1973
- ↓ Family Relations 1967
- ↓ Family Therapy 1967

Family Life
- **Use** Family Relations

Family Life Education 1997
PN 100   SC 19203
- **UF** Marriage and Family Education
- **B** Education 1967
- **N** Parent Training 1978
- Sex Education 1973
- **R** ↓ Family 1967
- ↓ Family Relations 1967
- ↓ Family Therapy 1967
- Household Management 1985

Family Medicine 1988
PN 389   SC 19205
- **B** Medical Sciences 1967
- **R** Family Physicians 1973
- General Practitioners 1973

Family Members 1973
PN 8855   SC 19210
- **N** Adopted Children 1973
- Adult Offspring 1985
- ↓ Ancestors 1973
- Biological Family 1988
- Cousins 1973
- Daughters 1973
- Foster Children 1973
- Grandchildren 1973
- Grandparents 1973
- Illegitimate Children 1973

Family Members — (cont'd)
- Inlaws 1997
- Orphans 1973
- ↓ Parents 1967
- ↓ Siblings 1967
- Sons 1973
- ↓ Spouses 1973
- Stepchildren 1973
- **R** ↓ Family 1967
- Family of Origin 1991
- Family Resemblance 1991
- ↓ Offspring 1988
- Only Children 1982
- Significant Others 1991

Family of Origin 1991
PN 573   SC 19215
SN Family in which an individual was raised. Compare BIOLOGICAL FAMILY.
- **B** Family 1967
- **R** Biological Family 1988
- ↓ Family Background 1973
- ↓ Family Members 1973
- ↓ Family Structure 1973
- Stepfamily 1991

Family Physicians 1973
PN 852   SC 19220
- **B** Physicians 1967
- **R** Family Medicine 1988
- General Practitioners 1973

Family Planning 1973
PN 673   SC 19230
- **N** ↓ Birth Control 1971
- **R** Condoms 1991
- Delayed Parenthood 1985
- Eugenics 1973
- ↓ Family 1967
- Fertility Enhancement 1973
- Induced Abortion 1971
- ↓ Sterilization (Sex) 1973

Family Planning Attitudes 1973
PN 955   SC 19240
- **UF** Birth Control Attitudes
- **B** Attitudes 1967
- **R** Childlessness 1982
- Delayed Parenthood 1985
- ↓ Family Relations 1967

Family Relations 1967
PN 21859   SC 19250
SN Dynamics of interpersonal interaction and developmental processes taking place between and among members of a biological or socially defined family unit. See FAMILY MEMBERS for references to biological relatives in a family.
- **UF** Family Dynamics
- Family Life
- **B** Interpersonal Relationships 2004
- **N** ↓ Child Discipline 1973
- ↓ Childrearing Practices 1967
- ↓ Family Conflict 2003
- ↓ Marital Relations 1967
- ↓ Parent Child Relations 1967
- Parental Role 1973
- Sibling Relations 1973
- **R** Childrearing Attitudes 1973
- Codependency 1991
- Dysfunctional Family 1991
- Empty Nest 1991
- ↓ Family 1967

Family Relations — (cont'd)
- Family Intervention 2003
- ↓ Family Life Education 1997
- Family Planning Attitudes 1973
- Family Systems Theory 2003
- Family Violence 1982
- Family Work Relationship 1997
- Intergenerational Relations 1988
- Marriage Attitudes 1973
- ↓ Relationship Satisfaction 2001
- Social Support 2004
- Transgenerational Patterns 1991

Family Resemblance 1991
PN 75   SC 19255
- **R** Assortative Mating 1991
- ↓ Family 1967
- ↓ Family Members 1973
- ↓ Genetics 1967
- Transgenerational Patterns 1991
- ↓ Twins 1967

Family Size 1973
PN 894   SC 19260
- **B** Family Structure 1973
- Size 1973
- **R** Empty Nest 1991
- ↓ Parenthood Status 1985

Family Socioeconomic Level 1973
PN 996   SC 19270
- **B** Family Background 1973
- Socioeconomic Status 1967
- **R** Parent Educational Background 1973
- Parental Occupation 1973

Family Structure 1973
PN 3760   SC 19280
- **N** Birth Order 1967
- Childlessness 1982
- Extended Family 1973
- Family Size 1973
- Matriarchy 1973
- Monogamy 1997
- Nuclear Family 1973
- ↓ Parental Absence 1973
- Patriarchy 1973
- Polygamy 1973
- Schizophrenogenic Family 1967
- Stepfamily 1991
- **R** ↓ Culture (Anthropological) 1967
- Dual Careers 1982
- Dysfunctional Family 1991
- Empty Nest 1991
- ↓ Family 1967
- Family of Origin 1991
- Homosexual Parents 1994
- Kinship Structure 1973
- Living Alone 1994
- ↓ Living Arrangements 1991
- Only Children 1982
- ↓ Parenthood Status 1985
- ↓ Single Parents 1978
- ↓ Sociocultural Factors 1967
- Stepchildren 1973
- Stepparents 1973

Family Systems Model
- **Use** Family Systems Theory

Family Systems Theory 2003
PN 91   SC 19284

Family Systems Theory — (cont'd)

SN An approach that utilizes the principles of systems theory to understand and treat families.
HN This term was introduced in June 2003. PsycINFO records from the past 10 years were re-indexed with this term. The posting note reflects the number of records that were re-indexed.
UF   Family Systems Model
R   ↓ Family Relations 1967
    ↓ Family Therapy 1967

Family Therapy 1967

PN 12225   **SC** 19290
UF   Family Counseling
B   Psychotherapeutic Counseling 1973
N   Conjoint Therapy 1973
R   ↓ Counseling 1967
    Family Intervention 2003
    ↓ Family Life Education 1997
    Family Systems Theory 2003
    Social Casework 1967

Family Violence 1982

PN 4024   **SC** 19294
SN Injurious or abusive behavior in family or other domestic interpersonal situations.
UF   Domestic Violence
B   Violence 1973
    Violent Crime 2003
R   Battered Females 1988
    ↓ Child Abuse 1971
    Elder Abuse 1988
    Emotional Abuse 1991
    ↓ Family Conflict 2003
    ↓ Family Relations 1967
    Marital Conflict 1973
    Partner Abuse 1991
    Physical Abuse 1991
    ↓ Sexual Abuse 1988
    Shelters 1991

Family Work Relationship 1997

PN 802   **SC** 19297
UF   Job Family Relationship
    Work Family Relationship
R   Dual Careers 1982
    ↓ Family Relations 1967
    Role Conflicts 1973
    Work (Attitudes Toward) 1973
    ↓ Working Conditions 1973
    Working Women 1978

Fans (Sports)

Use Sports Spectators

Fantasies (Thought Disturbances) 1967

PN 493   **SC** 19310
SN Thinking that severely distorts reality.
B   Thought Disturbances 1973
R   ↓ Fantasy 1997
    Magical Thinking 1973

Fantasy 1997

PN 462   **SC** 19315
HN Use IMAGINATION to access references from 1982-1996.
B   Cognitive Processes 1967
N   Sexual Fantasy 1997
R   Daydreaming 1973
    Fantasies (Thought Disturbances) 1967
    Fantasy (Defense Mechanism) 1967
    ↓ Ideation 1973
    Imagination 1967
    Magical Thinking 1973

Fantasy (Defense Mechanism) 1967

PN 824   **SC** 19320
SN Daydreaming dominated by unconscious material and primary processes for the purpose of wish fulfillment or to alleviate social isolation.
B   Defense Mechanisms 1967
R   Daydreaming 1973
    ↓ Fantasy 1997
    Sexual Fantasy 1997

Farmers

Use Agricultural Workers

Fascism 1973

PN 358   **SC** 19342
UF   Nazism
B   Political Economic Systems 1973
R   Holocaust 1988

Fat Metabolism

Use Lipid Metabolism

Fatalism 1973

PN 96   **SC** 19360
B   Philosophies 1967
R   Cynicism 1973
    Nihilism 1973
    Pessimism 1973

Father Absence 1973

PN 684   **SC** 19370
SN For animals consider ANIMAL PARENTAL BEHAVIOR.
HN From 1982, limited to human populations.
B   Parental Absence 1973
R   Matriarchy 1973

Father Child Communication 1985

PN 114   **SC** 19375
SN Verbal or nonverbal communication between father and child.
B   Parent Child Communication 1973
R   Father Child Relations 1973

Father Child Relations 1973

PN 2676   **SC** 19380
SN For animals consider ANIMAL PARENTAL BEHAVIOR.
HN From 1982, limited to human populations.
B   Parent Child Relations 1967
R   ↓ Childrearing Practices 1967
    Father Child Communication 1985
    ↓ Parental Attitudes 1973
    Parental Permissiveness 1973
    Parental Role 1973

Fathers 1967

PN 4129   **SC** 19390
SN For animals consider ANIMAL PARENTAL BEHAVIOR.
HN From 1982, limited to human populations.
B   Human Males 1973
    Parents 1967
N   Adolescent Fathers 1985
    Single Fathers 1994
R   Expectant Fathers 1985

Fatigue 1967

PN 2116   **SC** 19400
UF   Exhaustion
    Tiredness

Fatigue — (cont'd)

B   Symptoms 1967
R   Chronic Fatigue Syndrome 1997
    Hypersomnia 1994

Fatty Acids 1973

PN 488   **SC** 19410
B   Acids 1973
    Lipids 1973
N   Capsaicin 1991
    ↓ Phosphatides 1973
R   Prostaglandins 1982

Fear 1967

PN 6440   **SC** 19420
B   Emotional States 1973
N   Fear of Success 1978
    Panic 1973
R   Alarm Responses 1973
    ↓ Anxiety 1967
    Conditioned Fear 2003
    Neophobia 1985
    ↓ Neurosis 1967
    Panic Attack 2003
    ↓ Phobias 1967
    Shame 1994
    Social Anxiety 1985
    Stranger Reactions 1988

Fear of Public Speaking

Use Speech Anxiety

Fear of Strangers

Use Stranger Reactions

Fear of Success 1978

PN 406   **SC** 19424
SN Need to inhibit maximum utilization of one's abilities in achievement situations due to expected negative consequences.
B   Fear 1967
    Motivation 1967
R   ↓ Achievement Motivation 1967
    ↓ Anxiety 1967
    ↓ Anxiety Disorders 1997
    Self Handicapping Strategy 1988

Fear Survey Schedule 1973

PN 60   **SC** 19430
B   Nonprojective Personality Measures 1973

Fecal Incontinence 1973

PN 385   **SC** 19440
UF   Encopresis
    Incontinence (Fecal)
B   Colon Disorders 1973
R   ↓ Behavior Disorders 1971
    Diarrhea 1973
    ↓ Symptoms 1967

Fee for Service 1994

PN 85   **SC** 19450
SN Payment for health related services in which the health care provider is reimbursed for services by the client or health insurance carrier.
B   Health Insurance 1973
    Professional Fees 1978
R   Cost Containment 1991
    ↓ Health Care Delivery 1978
    ↓ Health Care Services 1978
    Health Maintenance Organizations 1982
    ↓ Managed Care 1994

Feedback [1967]
PN 6988   SC 19460
SN General concept denoting the return of information that may regulate or control subsequent behavior, cognition, perception, or performance. Use a more specific term if possible.
- N ↓ Biofeedback [1973]
  - ↓ Delayed Feedback [1973]
  - Knowledge of Results [1967]
  - ↓ Sensory Feedback [1973]
- R Intelligent Tutoring Systems [2003]
  - ↓ Learning [1967]
  - ↓ Reinforcement [1967]
  - ↓ Timulation [1967]

Feeding Behavior (Animal)
Use Animal Feeding Behavior

Feeding Practices
Use Eating Behavior

Feelings
Use Emotions

Feet (Anatomy) [1973]
PN 262   SC 19500
- UF Heels (Anatomy)
  - Toes (Anatomy)
- B Anatomy [1967]
  - Musculoskeletal System [1973]
- R Ankle [1973]
  - Leg (Anatomy) [1973]

Felids [1997]
PN 33   SC 19505
- UF Lions
  - Tigers
- B Mammals [1973]
- N Cats [1967]

Felonies
Use Crime

Female Animals [1973]
PN 4039   SC 19520
- B Animals [1967]

Female Criminals [1973]
PN 601   SC 19530
- B Criminals [1967]
  - Human Females [1973]

Female Delinquency [2001]
PN 336   SC 19535
HN In 2000, this term was created to replace the discontinued term FEMALE DELINQUENTS. FEMALE DELINQUENTS was removed from all records containing it and replaced with FEMALE DELINQUENCY.
- B Juvenile Delinquency [1967]
- R ↓ Human Females [1973]
  - Male Delinquency [2001]

Female Genital Mutilation
Use Circumcision

Female Genitalia [1973]
PN 339   SC 19550
SN Used for both human and animal populations.

Female Genitalia — (cont'd)
- UF Genitalia (Female)
- B Urogenital System [1973]
- N Ovaries [1973]
  - ↓ Uterus [1973]
  - Vagina [1973]
- R Circumcision [2001]

Female Homosexuality
Use Lesbianism

Female Only Environments
Use Single Sex Environments

Female Orgasm [1973]
PN 305   SC 19560
SN Used for both human and animal populations.
- B Orgasm [1973]
- R Frigidity [1973]
  - Masturbation [1973]
  - ↓ Sexual Intercourse (Human) [1973]

Females (Human)
Use Human Females

Femininity [1967]
PN 2334   SC 19580
- B Personality Traits [1967]
- R Androgyny [1982]
  - ↓ Gender Identity [1985]
  - Masculinity [1967]
  - Sex Roles [1967]

Feminism [1978]
PN 3957   SC 19585
- R Feminist Therapy [1994]
  - ↓ Sex Role Attitudes [1978]
  - Womens Liberation Movement [1973]

Feminist Therapy [1994]
PN 332   SC 19587
SN An approach to psychotherapy, counseling, or consultation based on the assumptions and tenets of feminism.
- B Psychotherapy [1967]
- R ↓ Counseling [1967]
  - Feminism [1978]

Feminization Syndrome (Testicular)
Use Testicular Feminization Syndrome

Femoral Nerve
Use Spinal Nerves

Fenfluramine [1973]
PN 611   SC 19610
- B Appetite Depressing Drugs [1973]
  - Sympathomimetic Drugs [1973]

Fentanyl [1985]
PN 186   SC 19613
SN Synthetic opiate frequently used illicitly.
- B Opiates [1973]

Fertility [1988]
PN 422   SC 19618
SN The quality or state of being capable of breeding or reproducing. Used for human and animal populations.

Fertility — (cont'd)
- B Sexual Reproduction [1973]
- R Birth Rate [1982]
  - Fertility Enhancement [1973]
  - ↓ Infertility [1973]

Fertility Enhancement [1973]
PN 39   SC 19620
- R ↓ Family Planning [1973]
  - Fertility [1988]
  - ↓ Hormones [1967]
  - Oral Contraceptives [1973]

Fertilization [1973]
PN 126   SC 19630
- R ↓ Pregnancy [1967]
  - Reproductive Technology [1988]
  - ↓ Sexual Reproduction [1973]

Fetal Alcohol Syndrome [1985]
PN 432   SC 19635
- B Drug Induced Congenital Disorders [1973]
  - Syndromes [1973]
- R ↓ Alcoholism [1967]
  - Ethanol [1973]
  - ↓ Mental Retardation [1967]
  - ↓ Prenatal Development [1973]

Fetal Exposure
Use Prenatal Exposure

Fetishism [1973]
PN 245   SC 19640
- UF Sexual Fetishism
- B Paraphilias [1988]
- R Coprophagia [2001]
  - Sexual Masochism [1973]
  - Sexual Sadism [1973]
  - Transvestism [1973]

Fetus [1967]
PN 893   SC 19650
- B Prenatal Developmental Stages [1973]

Fever
Use Hyperthermia

Fibrillation (Heart) [1973]
PN 43   SC 19680
- UF Atrial Fibrillation
  - Auricular Fibrillation
  - Ventricular Fibrillation
- B Arrhythmias (Heart) [1973]

Fibromyalgia [2004]
PN   SC 19685
SN A common nonarticular rheumatic condition that is characterized by muscle pain, tenderness, and stiffness.
HN Use MUSCULAR DISORDERS to access references from 1994 to June 2004.
- B Muscular Disorders [1973]
- R ↓ Pain [1967]

Fiction
Use Literature

Field Dependence [1973]
PN 2095   SC 19710

Field Dependence — (cont'd)

SN Aspect of cognitive style as seen in relative lack of autonomy from external referents, the inability to overcome embedding contexts, or the reliance on visual rather than gravitational cues in perception of the upright. Used also for reciprocal concept of field independence.
B　Cognitive Style　1967

Field Experiment

Use　Observation Methods

Field Instruction

Use　Curricular Field Experience

Field Trips (Educational)

Use　Educational Field Trips

Field Work (Educational)

Use　Curricular Field Experience

Fighting

Use　Aggressive Behavior

Figurative Language　1985

PN　445　　　　　　**SC**　19736
SN Verbal expressions that signify one concept by using words that would normally be used to signify some other concept as a result of a conceptual analogy or qualitative similarity between the concepts.
UF　Figures of Speech
　　　Simile
B　Language　1967
N　Metaphor　1982
R　Analogy　1991
　　　Connotations　1973
　　　Symbolism　1967
　　　↓ Verbal Meaning　1973

Figure Ground Discrimination　1973

PN　745　　　　　　**SC**　19740
SN Discrimination of a portion of a visual configuration as a coherent figure distinct from the background.
B　Perceptual Discrimination　1973
R　Form and Shape Perception　1967
　　　Pattern Discrimination　1967
　　　↓ Spatial Perception　1967

Figures of Speech

Use　Figurative Language

Film Strips　1967

PN　542　　　　　　**SC**　19750
SN Strips of film for still projection.
B　Audiovisual Communications Media　1973
R　↓ Educational Audiovisual Aids　1973

Filtered Noise　1973

PN　79　　　　　　**SC**　19760
B　Auditory Stimulation　1967

Filtered Speech　1973

PN　50　　　　　　**SC**　19770
B　Speech Processing (Mechanical)　1973

Financial Assistance (Educational)

Use　Educational Financial Assistance

Fine Motor Skill Learning　1973

PN　179　　　　　　**SC**　19790
B　Perceptual Motor Learning　1967
　　　Skill Learning　1973

Finger Tapping　1973

PN　436　　　　　　**SC**　19800
B　Motor Performance　1973

Fingers (Anatomy)　1973

PN　640　　　　　　**SC**　19820
B　Musculoskeletal System　1973
N　Thumb　1973
R　Hand (Anatomy)　1967

Fingerspelling　1973

PN　85　　　　　　**SC**　19830
B　Manual Communication　1978
R　Sign Language　1973

Fire Fighters　1991

PN　202　　　　　　**SC**　19845
R　Fire Prevention　1973
　　　↓ Government Personnel　1973
　　　↓ Paramedical Personnel　1973

Fire Prevention　1973

PN　52　　　　　　**SC**　19850
B　Prevention　1973
R　Fire Fighters　1991
　　　↓ Safety　1967

Firearms　2003

PN　14　　　　　　**SC**　19855
HN Use WEAPONS to access references from 1973 to June 2003.
UF　Guns
B　Weapons　1978
R　Gun Control Laws　1973

Firesetting

Use　Arson

FIRO-B

Use　Fundamental Interpersonal Relation Orientation Behavior Ques

First Experiences　2004

PN　60　　　　　　**SC**　19867
SN Initial experience of an event in an individual's life.
HN This term was introduced in June 2004. PsycINFO records from the past 10 years were re-indexed with this term. The posting note reflects the number of records that were re-indexed.
R　↓ Life Experiences　1973

First Language

Use　Native Language

Fishes　1967

PN　2509　　　　　　**SC**　19870
B　Vertebrates　1973
N　Bass (Fish)　1973
　　　↓ Carp　1973
　　　Cichlids　1973
　　　Electric Fishes　1973
　　　Salmon　1973
　　　Sticklebacks　1973
R　Larvae　1973

Five Factor Personality Model　1997

PN　853　　　　　　**SC**　19875
SN A model of personality dimensions that encompass five broad factors: neuroticism, extraversion, openness to experience, agreeableness, and conscientiousness.
UF　Big Five Personality Model
B　Personality Theory　1967
R　Agreeableness　1997
　　　Conscientiousness　1997
　　　Extraversion　1967
　　　NEO Personality Inventory　1997
　　　Neuroticism　1973
　　　Openness to Experience　1997
　　　↓ Personality　1967
　　　↓ Personality Development　1967
　　　↓ Personality Traits　1967

Fixed Interval Reinforcement　1973

PN　796　　　　　　**SC**　19880
UF　Interval Reinforcement
B　Reinforcement Schedules　1967

Fixed Ratio Reinforcement　1973

PN　825　　　　　　**SC**　19890
UF　Ratio Reinforcement
B　Reinforcement Schedules　1967

Flashbacks

Use　Hallucinations

Flexibility (Personality)

Use　Adaptability (Personality)

Flexion Reflex　1973

PN　152　　　　　　**SC**　19910
B　Reflexes　1071

Flextime

Use　Work Scheduling

Flicker Fusion Frequency

Use　Critical Flicker Fusion Threshold

Flies

Use　Diptera

Flight Attendants

Use　Aerospace Personnel

Flight Instrumentation　1973

PN　193　　　　　　**SC**　19930
UF　Instrumentation (Flight)
B　Aviation　1967
　　　Instrument Controls　1985

Flight Simulation　1973

PN　664　　　　　　**SC**　19940
B　Simulation　1967
R　Acceleration Effects　1973
　　　↓ Gravitational Effects　1967

Flooding Therapy

Use　Implosive Therapy

Fluency

Use　Verbal Fluency

Fluid Intake 1985
PN 1024   SC 19965
SN Ingestion of liquids or solutions. Frequently used as an objective measure of physiological or motivational state or learning. Used for human or animal populations.
B   Ingestion 2001
N   Water Intake 1967
R   ↓ Drinking Behavior 1978
     Thirst 1967

Flunitrazepam 2004
PN 35   SC 19966
SN A benzodiazepine with sedative and hypnotic properties.
HN This term was introduced in June 2004. PsycINFO records from the past 10 years were re-indexed with this term. The posting note reflects the number of records that were re-indexed.
UF   Rohypnol
B   Benzodiazepines 1978

Fluoxetine 1991
PN 2085   SC 19967
UF   Prozac
B   Antidepressant Drugs 1971
     Serotonin Reuptake Inhibitors 1997

Fluphenazine 1973
PN 489   SC 19970
UF   Prolixin
B   Antiemetic Drugs 1973
     Phenothiazine Derivatives 1973

Flurazepam 1982
PN 97   SC 19974
SN Organic heterocyclic compound, used as a benzodiazepine tranquilizer and a nonbarbiturate sedative.
B   Benzodiazepines 1978
     Hypnotic Drugs 1973
     Sedatives 1973
R   ↓ CNS Depressant Drugs 1973

Fluvoxamine 1994
PN 516   SC 19975
B   Antidepressant Drugs 1971
     Serotonin Reuptake Inhibitors 1997

Focusing (Visual)
     Use   Ocular Accommodation

Folic Acid 1973
PN 139   SC 19980
B   Vitamins 1973

Folie A Deux 1973
PN 108   SC 19990
UF   Shared Paranoid Disorder
B   Paranoia (Psychosis) 1967
R   Involutional Paranoid Psychosis 1973
     Paranoid Schizophrenia 1967

Folk Medicine 1973
PN 617   SC 20000
B   Alternative Medicine 1997
R   Ethnology 1967
     Faith Healing 1973
     ↓ Medical Sciences 1967
     Shamanism 1967
     Transcultural Psychiatry 1973

Folk Psychology 1997
PN 84   SC 20005
SN Branch of psychology that deals with legends, beliefs, folklore, and customs of a race or people, especially primitive societies.
B   Psychology 1967
R   Anthropology 1967
     Ethnography 1973
     Ethnology 1967
     Folklore 1991
     Social Psychology 1967
     Transcultural Psychiatry 1973

Folklore 1991
PN 323   SC 20010
HN Use MYTHS to access references from 1973-1990.
UF   Fairy Tales
     Folktales
R   Ethnology 1967
     Folk Psychology 1997
     ↓ Literature 1967
     Myths 1967
     Storytelling 1988

Folktales
     Use   Folklore

Follicle Stimulating Hormone 1991
PN 35   SC 20025
B   Gonadotropic Hormones 1973

Followup (Posttreatment)
     Use   Posttreatment Followup

Followup Studies 1973
PN 12298   SC 20040
SN Used in records discussing issues involved in the process of conducting studies with individuals or groups who are followed and reexamined to assess and compare present findings with the original observations or measurements.
HN From 1973-2000, the term was also used as a mandatory document type identifier; however, this usage has been discontinued due to the advent of Form/Content Type field identifiers. References from 1973-2000 can be accessed using either FOLLOWUP STUDIES or the Followup Studies Form/Content Type field identifier.
UF   Studies (Followup)
B   Experimental Design 1967
R   ↓ Longitudinal Studies 1973

Food 1978
PN 2014   SC 20045
R   Craving 1997
     Diets 1978
     Food Additives 1978
     Food Allergies 1973
     Food Intake 1967
     Food Preferences 1973
     Nutrition 1973

Food Additives 1978
PN 121   SC 20047
R   ↓ Antioxidants 2004
     ↓ Chemical Elements 1973
     Diets 1978
     Food 1978
     Nutrition 1973

Food Allergies 1973
PN 80   SC 20050
B   Allergic Disorders 1973
R   Diets 1978
     Food 1978

Food Deprivation 1967
PN 2168   SC 20060
SN Absence of ad libitum food access. In experimental settings, food deprivation is used to achieve a definable level of motivation within the organism.
B   Deprivation 1967
     Stimulus Deprivation 1973
R   Diets 1978
     Hunger 1967
     ↓ Nutritional Deficiencies 1973
     Starvation 1973

Food Intake 1967
PN 7181   SC 20070
SN Ingestion of food. Frequently used as an objective measure of physiological or motivational state or learning. Used for human or animal populations.
B   Ingestion 2001
R   Animal Feeding Behavior 1973
     Dietary Restraint 1994
     ↓ Eating Behavior 2004
     Food 1978
     Rumination (Eating) 2001
     Sucking 1978
     Weight Control 1985

Food Preferences 1973
PN 1959   SC 20080
B   Preferences 1967
R   Diets 1978
     Eating Attitudes 1994
     Food 1978

Football 1973
PN 263   SC 20090
B   Recreation 1967
     Sports 1967

Foraging (Animal)
     Use   Animal Foraging Behavior

Forced Choice (Testing Method) 1967
PN 291   SC 20100
SN Assessment method requiring a choice between equally unlikely or undesirable alternatives, designed to reduce the effects of social desirability on the selection of test answers.
UF   True False Tests
B   Testing Methods 1967

Forebrain 1985
PN 834   SC 20105
UF   Prosencephalon
B   Brain 1967
N   ↓ Diencephalon 1973
     Nucleus Basalis Magnocellularis 1994
     ↓ Telencephalon 1973

Foreign Language Education 1973
PN 1089   SC 20110
SN Curriculum, teaching methods, and educational programs used in the instruction of a language that is not native to the learner.
UF   Immersion Programs
     Second Language Education
B   Curriculum 1967

Foreign Language Education — (cont'd)
R   English as Second Language 1997

Foreign Language Learning 1967
PN 2884   SC 20120
B   Learning 1967
R   Bilingual Education 1978
       Foreign Languages 1973
       ↓ Language Development 1967
       Language Laboratories 1973
       Language Proficiency 1988

Foreign Language Translation 1973
PN 3595   SC 20130
SN Rendering from one language to another. Use
with foreign language test translations.
R   Foreign Languages 1973

Foreign Languages 1973
PN 1417   SC 20140
SN Second or nonnative languages.
B   Language 1967
R   Bilingual Education 1978
       English as Second Language 1997
       Foreign Language Learning 1967
       Foreign Language Translation 1973

Foreign Nationals 1985
PN 126   SC 20145
SN Persons living in a country other than their own,
generally with intent to return to their home country.
N   Foreign Students 1973
       Foreign Workers 1985
R   Immigration 1070

Foreign Organizations 1973
PN 43   SC 20150
SN Organizations located in or originating from a
foreign country.
B   Organizations 1967
R   International Organizations 1973

Foreign Policy Making 1973
PN 277   SC 20160
UF   Policy Making (Foreign)
B   Government Policy Making 1973
R   Government 1967
       International Relations 1967
       Peace 1988
       ↓ War 1967

Foreign Students 1973
PN 987   SC 20168
SN Persons attending school or a training program
in a country other than their own, generally with intent
to return to their home country.
B   Foreign Nationals 1985
       Students 1967
R   Foreign Study 1973

Foreign Study 1973
PN 125   SC 20170
SN Pursuit of an educational program in a country
other than one's own, generally with intent to return
to the home country.
B   Educational Programs 1973
R   Foreign Students 1973

Foreign Workers 1985
PN 223   SC 20175

Foreign Workers — (cont'd)
SN Persons employed in a country other than their
own, generally with intent to return to their home
country.
UF   Guest Workers
B   Foreign Nationals 1985
R   Migrant Farm Workers 1973

Foremen (Industrial)
Use Industrial Foremen

Forensic Evaluation 1994
PN 882   SC 20185
B   Evaluation 1967
       Legal Processes 1973
       Psychiatric Evaluation 1997
R   Competency to Stand Trial 1985
       Court Referrals 1994
       ↓ Criminals 1967
       Expert Testimony 1973
       Forensic Psychiatry 1973
       Forensic Psychology 1985
       Insanity Defense 1985
       Mentally Ill Offenders 1985
       ↓ Psychodiagnosis 1967
       ↓ Psychological Assessment 1997
       Psychological Report 1988

Forensic Psychiatry 1973
PN 1531   SC 20190
SN Branch of psychiatry devoted to legal issues
relating to disordered behavior and mental disorders,
including legal responsibility, competency to stand
trial, and commitment issues.
B   Psychiatry 1967
R   ↓ Criminal Justice 1991
       Expert Testimony 1973
       Forensic Evaluation 1994
       Forensic Psychology 1985
       Insanity Defense 1985

Forensic Psychology 1985
PN 1114   SC 20195
UF   Legal Psychology
B   Psychology 1967
R   ↓ Criminal Justice 1991
       Expert Testimony 1973
       Forensic Evaluation 1994
       Forensic Psychiatry 1973
       Psychological Autopsy 1988

Forgetting 1973
PN 1079   SC 20200
SN Inability to recall, recollect, or reproduce previ-
ously learned material, behavior, or experience.
Compare AMNESIA and MEMORY DECAY.
R   ↓ Amnesia 1967
       Cued Recall 1994
       Free Recall 1973
       Fugue Reaction 1973
       ↓ Interference (Learning) 1967
       ↓ Latent Inhibition 1997
       ↓ Learning 1967
       ↓ Memory 1967
       Memory Decay 1973
       Memory Training 1994
       Reminiscence 1985
       ↓ Retention 1967
       Serial Recall 1994
       Suppression (Defense Mechanism) 1973

Forgiveness 1988
PN 446   SC 20205

Forgiveness — (cont'd)
R   ↓ Conflict Resolution 1982
       ↓ Religious Beliefs 1973
       ↓ Social Interaction 1967

Form and Shape Perception 1967
PN 4884   SC 20210
SN Perception of the physical form or shape of
objects through any of the senses, usually haptic or
visual.
UF   Contour
       Contour Perception
       Form Perception
       Shape Perception
B   Perception 1967
R   Figure Ground Discrimination 1973
       Motion Parallax 1997
       Object Recognition 1997
       Pattern Discrimination 1967

Form Classes (Language) 1973
PN 508   SC 20220
UF   Words (Form Classes)
B   Language 1967
       Syntax 1971
N   Adjectives 1973
       Adverbs 1973
       Nouns 1973
       Pronouns 1973
       Verbs 1973

Form Perception
Use Form and Shape Perception

Fornix 1982
PN 266   SC 20234
SN Arched white fiber tract extending from the hip-
pocampal formation to the septum, anterior nucleus
of the thalamus, and mammillary body.
UF   Hippocampal Commissure
       Trigonum Cerebrale
B   Limbic System 1973
       Neural Pathways 1982
R   Medial Forebrain Bundle 1982
       Septal Nuclei 1982

FORTRAN
Use Computer Programming Languages

Forward Masking
Use Masking

Foster Care 1978
PN 1551   SC 20245
SN Family care provided by persons other than the
natural or adoptive parents.
UF   Foster Homes
R   ↓ Child Care 1991
       Child Welfare 1988
       Foster Children 1973
       Foster Parents 1973
       Protective Services 1997

Foster Children 1973
PN 603   SC 20250
B   Family Members 1973
R   Foster Care 1978

Foster Homes
Use Foster Care

Foster Parents 1973
PN 423   SC 20260
B   Parents 1967
R   Foster Care 1978
    Surrogate Parents (Humans) 1973

Fovea 1982
PN 187   SC 20265
SN Centrally located and depressed portion of the retina containing only cone photoreceptors.
B   Eye (Anatomy) 1967
R   Cones (Eye) 1973
    Foveal Vision 1988
    Visual Field 1967

Foveal Vision 1988
PN 311   SC 20267
UF Central Vision
B   Visual Perception 1967
R   Fovea 1982

Fowl
Use Birds

Foxes 1973
PN 89   SC 20290
B   Canids 1997

Fragile X Syndrome 1994
PN 274   SC 20295
B   Sex Linked Hereditary Disorders 1973
    Syndromes 1973
R   ↓ Mental Retardation 1967
    ↓ Sex Chromosome Disorders 1973

Fragmentation (Schizophrenia) 1973
PN 12   SC 20300
UF Loosening of Associations
B   Thought Disturbances 1973
R   ↓ Schizophrenia 1967

Frail
Use Health Impairments

Frankness
Use Honesty

Fraternal Twins
Use Heterozygotic Twins

Fraternity Membership 1973
PN 201   SC 20340
SN Belonging to a club traditionally restricted to males. Used also for fraternity organizations.
B   Extracurricular Activities 1973

Fraud 1994
PN 88   SC 20345
UF Consumer Fraud
B   Deception 1967
R   Cheating 1973
    ↓ Crime 1967
    Dishonesty 1973
    Experimental Ethics 1978

Free Association 1994
PN 137   SC 20347

Free Association — (cont'd)
SN Spontaneous association of ideas or mental images restricted by consciousness. Primarily used in, but not restricted to, psychoanalysis or Jungian analysis as a method to gain access to the organization and content of a patient's mind.
UF Association (Free)
R   ↓ Jungian Psychology 1973
    ↓ Psychoanalysis 1967
    ↓ Psychoanalytic Theory 1967
    ↓ Psychotherapeutic Techniques 1967
    Unconscious (Personality Factor) 1967

Free Recall 1973
PN 2059   SC 20350
SN Method of measuring the retention of learned material in which a subject is asked to recall as much of the material as possible, in any order, without the aid of external cues. Compare SERIAL ANTICIPATION (LEARNING) and RECONSTRUCTION (LEARNING).
B   Recall (Learning) 1967
R   Cued Recall 1994
    Forgetting 1973
    ↓ Memory 1967
    Serial Recall 1994

Free Will
Use Volition

Freedom 1978
PN 514   SC 20354
R   Censorship 1978
    Choice Behavior 1967
    ↓ Civil Rights 1978
    ↓ Justice 1973
    ↓ Political Processes 1973
    Psychological Reactance 1978
    Volition 1988

Frequency (Pitch)
Use Pitch (Frequency)

Frequency (Response)
Use Response Frequency

Frequency (Stimulus)
Use Stimulus Frequency

Frequency Distribution 1973
PN 418   SC 20380
UF Distribution (Frequency)
B   Statistical Analysis 1967
    Statistical Measurement 1973
N   Normal Distribution 1973
    Skewed Distribution 1973
R   Standard Deviation 1973

Freud (Sigmund) 1967
PN 4477   SC 20390
SN Identifies biographical or autobiographical studies and discussions of Freud's works.
R   Freudian Psychoanalytic School 1973
    ↓ Neopsychoanalytic School 1973
    ↓ Psychoanalysis 1967
    ↓ Psychoanalytic Theory 1967
    ↓ Psychologists 1967

Freudian Psychoanalytic School 1973
PN 775   SC 20400

**Freudian Psychoanalytic School —
    (cont'd)**
UF Psychoanalytic School (Freudian)
B   History of Psychology 1967
    Psychoanalytic Theory 1967
    Psychological Theories 2001
R   Freud (Sigmund) 1967
    Metapsychology 1994
    ↓ Neopsychoanalytic School 1973
    Psychoanalytic Interpretation 1967

Friendship 1967
PN 3754   SC 20410
B   Interpersonal Relationships 2004
R   Interpersonal Compatibility 1973
    Peer Pressure 1994
    ↓ Peer Relations 1967
    Relationship Quality 2004
    ↓ Relationship Satisfaction 2001
    ↓ Relationship Termination 1997
    Significant Others 1991
    Social Dating 1973
    Social Support 2004

Frigidity 1973
PN 55   SC 20420
B   Sexual Function Disturbances 1973
R   Dyspareunia 1973
    Female Orgasm 1973
    Impotence 1973
    ↓ Orgasm 1973
    ↓ Symptoms 1967
    Vaginismus 1973

Frogs 1967
PN 934   SC 20430
B   Amphibia 1973
R   Larvae 1973

Frontal Lobe 1973
PN 4410   SC 20440
B   Cerebral Cortex 1967
N   Broca's Area 2004
    Gyrus Cinguli 1973
    Motor Cortex 1973
    Prefrontal Cortex 1994

**Frostig Developmental Test of Visual
    Perception** 2001
PN 34
HN In 2001, the truncated term FROSTIG DEVELOPMENT TEST VIS PERCEPT (which was used from 1973-2000) was deleted, removed from all records containing it, and replaced with its expanded form FROSTIG DEVELOPMENTAL TEST OF VISUAL PERCEPTION.
B   Intelligence Measures 1967

Fruit Fly
Use Drosophila

Frustration 1967
PN 1341   SC 20470
B   Emotional States 1973
R   Dissatisfaction 1973
    Mental Confusion 1973

Fugue Reaction 1973
PN 44   SC 20480

Fugue Reaction — (cont'd)

SN Dissociative reaction characterized by extensive amnesia and a sudden change in one's lifestyle. Upon recovery, prefugue events are remembered but those that occurred during the fugue are forgotten.

B Dissociative Disorders 2001
R ↓ Epilepsy 1967
Forgetting 1973

Fulfillment
Use Satisfaction

Functional Analysis 2001
PN 211 **SC** 20496
SN A part of behavioral assessment concerned with the experimental manipulation of environmental events that are maintaining or suppressing a target behavior.

B Behavioral Assessment 1982
R ↓ Analysis 1967
↓ Behavior Modification 1973
↓ Behavior Problems 1967
↓ Methodology 1967

Functional Knowledge
Use Procedural Knowledge

Functional Status
Use Ability Level

Functionalism 1973
PN 260 **SC** 20500
SN Doctrine or system of psychology which holds (contrary to structural psychology) that mental processes are the proper subject matter of psychology and that an essential feature of all psychological processes is the part they play in the adaptive functions of an organism.

B History of Psychology 1967
Psychological Theories 2001
R James (William) 1991

Fundamental Interpersonal Relation Orientation Behavior Ques 2001
PN 57 **SC** 20515
HN In 2001, the truncated term FUND INTERPER RELA ORIENTAT BEH QUES (which was used from 1973-2000) was deleted, removed from all records containing it, and mapped to its expanded form FUNDAMENTAL INTERPERSONAL RELATION ORIENTATION BEHAVIOR QUES.

UF FIRO-B
B Nonprojective Personality Measures 1973

Fundamentalism (Religious)
Use Religious Fundamentalism

Funding 1988
PN 834 **SC** 20524
R Budgets 1997
↓ Costs and Cost Analysis 1973
Educational Financial Assistance 1973
↓ Government Policy Making 1973
↓ Government Programs 1973
Money 1967
Resource Allocation 1997

Funerals
Use Death Rites

Furniture 1985
PN 40 **SC** 20527
R Human Factors Engineering 1973
Interior Design 1982
Physical Comfort 1982

Future 1991
PN 980 **SC** 20528
R ↓ Expectations 1967
↓ History 1973
↓ Prediction 1967
Social Change 1967
↓ Time 1967
Trends 1991

Fuzzy Logic 2003
PN 34 **SC** 58067
SN A mathematical technique used to deal with imprecise data and problems.
HN This term was introduced in June 2003. PsycINFO records from the past 10 years were re-indexed with this term. The posting note reflects the number of records that were re-indexed.

R ↓ Artificial Intelligence 1982
Fuzzy Set Theory 1991
↓ Mathematical Modeling 1973

Fuzzy Set Theory 1991
PN 236 **SC** 20529
SN Mathematical theory of sets in which membership is a matter of degree and boundaries are indistinct.

B Statistical Analysis 1967
Theories 1967
R Fuzzy Logic 2003
↓ Mathematical Modeling 1973
↓ Psychophysical Measurement 1967
↓ Statistical Probability 1967

GABA Agonists
Use Gamma Aminobutyric Acid Agonists

GABA Antagonists
Use Gamma Aminobutyric Acid Antagonists

Galanin
Use Peptides

Galantamine
Use Galanthamine

Galanthamine 1973
PN 58 **SC** 20530
UF Galantamine
B Amines 1973
Cholinesterase Inhibitors 1973

Galvanic Skin Response 1967
PN 1925 **SC** 20550
SN Means of assessing sympathetic nervous system activity (i.e., arousal) by measuring onset of palmar sweat gland response.

UF Electrodermal Response
GSR (Electrophysiology)
Psychogalvanic Reflex
B Diagnosis 1967
Electrophysiology 1973
Medical Diagnosis 1973
R Skin Potential 1973
↓ Skin Resistance 1973

Gamblers Anonymous
Use Twelve Step Programs

Gambling 1973
PN 863 **SC** 20560
B Recreation 1967
Risk Taking 1967
Social Behavior 1967
N Pathological Gambling 1988
R ↓ Games 1967

Game Theory 1967
PN 631 **SC** 20570
SN Mathematical theory which attempts to analyze and model the decision making process involved in gain-loss situations.

B Theories 1967
R Entrapment Games 1973
↓ Games 1967
Non Zero Sum Games 1973
Prisoners Dilemma Game 1973
↓ Simulation 1967

Games 1967
PN 2077 **SC** 20580
N Chess 1973
Childrens Recreational Games 1973
Computer Games 1988
Entrapment Games 1973
Non Zero Sum Games 1973
Prisoners Dilemma Game 1973
Simulation Games 1973
R Childhood Play Behavior 1978
↓ Gambling 1973
Game Theory 1967
↓ Recreation 1967
↓ Toys 1973

Gamma Aminobutyric Acid 1978
PN 1689 **SC** 20585
B Amino Acids 1973
Neurotransmitters 1985
R ↓ Gamma Aminobutyric Acid Agonists 1985
↓ Gamma Aminobutyric Acid Antagonists 1985

Gamma Aminobutyric Acid Agonists 1985
PN 402 **SC** 20587
UF GABA Agonists
N Muscimol 1994
R Gamma Aminobutyric Acid 1978

Gamma Aminobutyric Acid Antagonists 1985
PN 321 **SC** 20589
UF GABA Antagonists
B Alkaloids 1973
N Bicuculline 1994
Picrotoxin 1973
R Gamma Aminobutyric Acid 1978

Gamma Globulin 1973
PN 12 **SC** 20590
B Immunoglobulins 1973
R Antibodies 1973

Ganglia 1973
PN 259 **SC** 20600
B Nervous System 1967
N Autonomic Ganglia 1973
↓ Basal Ganglia 1973
Spinal Ganglia 1973

Ganglion Blocking Drugs 1973
PN 15   SC 20610
B   Drugs 1967
N   Hexamethonium 1973
    Mecamylamine 1973
    Nicotine 1973
R   ↓ Antihypertensive Drugs 1973

Ganglion Cells (Retina) 1985
PN 189   SC 20615
UF   Retinal Ganglion Cells
B   Neurons 1973
    Retina 1967

Gangs (Juvenile)
Use   Juvenile Gangs

Ganser Syndrome
Use   Factitious Disorders

Gastrointestinal Disorders 1973
PN 652   SC 20630
B   Digestive System Disorders 1973
N   ↓ Colon Disorders 1973
    Gastrointestinal Ulcers 1967
    Vomiting 1973
R   Influenza 1973
    ↓ Neoplasms 1967
    ↓ Somatoform Disorders 2001
    ↓ Toxic Disorders 1973

Gastrointestinal System 1973
PN 354   SC 20640
B   Digestive System 1967
N   Intestines 1973
    Stomach 1973
R   Pancreas 1973

Gastrointestinal Ulcers 1967
PN 589   SC 20650
UF   Peptic Ulcers
    Ulcers (Gastrointestinal)
B   Gastrointestinal Disorders 1973
R   ↓ Colitis 1973

Gastropods
Use   Mollusca

Gates MacGinitie Reading Tests 1973
PN 18   SC 20670
UF   Gates Reading Readiness Tests
    Gates Reading Test
B   Reading Measures 1973

Gates Reading Readiness Tests
Use   Gates MacGinitie Reading Tests

Gates Reading Test
Use   Gates MacGinitie Reading Tests

Gating (Sensory)
Use   Sensory Gating

Gaussian Distribution
Use   Normal Distribution

Gay Liberation Movement
Use   Homosexual Liberation Movement

Gay Males
Use   Male Homosexuality

Gay Parents
Use   Homosexual Parents

Gazing
Use   Eye Fixation

Geese 1973
PN 115   SC 20710
B   Birds 1967

Gender Differences
Use   Human Sex Differences

Gender Identity 1985
PN 2198   SC 20717
SN   Inner conviction that one is male or female or inner sense of being masculine or feminine.
UF   Sexual Identity (Gender)
N   Transsexualism 1973
R   Androgyny 1982
    Femininity 1967
    ↓ Gender Identity Disorder 1997
    Masculinity 1967
    ↓ Personality 1967
    Psychosexual Development 1982
    ↓ Self Concept 1967
    Sex Roles 1967
    ↓ Sexual Orientation 1997

Gender Identity Disorder 1997
PN 171   SC 20719
HN   Consider GENDER IDENTITY to access references from 1985-1996.
B   Mental Disorders 1967
N   Transsexualism 1973
R   ↓ Gender Identity 1985
    Hermaphroditism 1973
    ↓ Sexual Orientation 1997
    Transvestism 1973

Gender Role Attitudes
Use   Sex Role Attitudes

Gender Roles
Use   Sex Roles

Gene Expression 2004
PN 139   SC 20726
SN   Process by which messenger RNA is transcribed and then translated into proteins.
HN   This term was introduced in June 2004. PsycINFO records from the past 10 years were re-indexed with this term. The posting note reflects the number of records that were re-indexed.
R   ↓ Genes 1973
    ↓ Genetics 1967
    Quantitative Trait Loci 2004
    Ribonucleic Acid 1973

General Anesthetics 1973
PN 173   SC 20720

General Anesthetics — (cont'd)
B   Anesthetic Drugs 1973
N   Chloroform 1973
    Ether (Anesthetic) 1973
    Methohexital 1973
    Thiopental 1973

General Aptitude Test Battery 1973
PN 61   SC 20730
B   Aptitude Measures 1967

General Health Questionnaire 1991
PN 155   SC 20740
B   Personality Measures 1967
    Questionnaires 1967
R   ↓ Diagnosis 1967
    ↓ Health 1973
    ↓ Screening Tests 1982

General Paresis 1973
PN 51   SC 20750
UF   Dementia Paralytica
    Paresis (General)
B   Paralysis 1973
R   Neurosyphilis 1973
    ↓ Syphilis 1973

General Practitioners 1973
PN 1610   SC 20760
B   Physicians 1967
R   Family Medicine 1988
    Family Physicians 1973

Generalization (Cognitive)
Use   Cognitive Generalization

Generalization (Learning) 1982
PN 1583   SC 20775
SN   Responding in a similar manner to different stimuli that have some common property as the result of a conditioned or learned similarity. Also known as secondary generalization. Also includes generalization of any learned behavior to a new context or setting. Compare TRANSFER (LEARNING) or STIMULUS GENERALIZATION.
B   Learning 1967
N   Response Generalization 1973
    Stimulus Generalization 1967
R   ↓ Concept Formation 1967
    ↓ Discrimination Learning 1982
    ↓ Transfer (Learning) 1967

Generalization (Response)
Use   Response Generalization

Generalization (Semantic)
Use   Semantic Generalization

Generalization (Stimulus)
Use   Stimulus Generalization

Generalized Anxiety Disorder 2004
PN   SC 20801
SN   An anxiety disorder characterized by free-floating, persistent, and excessive worry for at least six months.
HN   Use ANXIETY DISORDERS to access references from 1994 to June 2004.
B   Anxiety Disorders 1997
R   ↓ Anxiety 1967

Generation Effect (Learning) 1991

PN 113   **SC** 20802
SN In learning or memory contexts, the effect of generating a stimuli oneself rather than having it presented by external sources.
B Learning 1967
R ↓ Cognitive Processes 1967
   ↓ Memory 1967

Generation Gap 1973

PN 236   **SC** 20805
SN Differences in values, morals, attitudes, and behavior of young adults and older adults in contemporary society.
R Age Differences 1967
   Cohort Analysis 1988
   Intergenerational Relations 1988
   ↓ Parent Child Relations 1967
   Transgenerational Patterns 1991

Generativity 2001

PN 54   **SC** 20807
SN The concern with passing on to the next generation knowledge and guidance which will outlive oneself. The conflict between generativity vs self-absorption is the seventh of E. Erikson's eight stages of man, and often occurs during middle adulthood.
R Adult Development 1978
   ↓ Aging 1991
   ↓ Developmental Stages 1973
   Erikson (Erik) 1991
   Intergenerational Relations 1988
   ↓ Prosocial Behavior 1982
   ↓ Psychosocial Development 1973

Generators (Apparatus) 1973

PN 32   **SC** 20810
B Apparatus 1967

Genes 1973

PN 2929   **SC** 20820
N Quantitative Trait Loci 2004
R ↓ Chromosomes 1973
   Gene Expression 2004
   Genetic Linkage 1994
   ↓ Genetics 1967
   Genome 2003

Genetic Counseling 1978

PN 566   **SC** 20826
SN Presentation and discussion, usually with prospective parents, of factors involved in potential inheritance of disorders.
B Counseling 1967
R Eugenics 1973
   ↓ Genetic Disorders 1973
   ↓ Genetic Engineering 1994
   Genetic Testing 2003
   ↓ Genetics 1967

Genetic Disorders 1973

PN 1166   **SC** 20830
UF Hereditary Disorders
B Physical Disorders 1997
N Albinism 1973
   ↓ Chromosome Disorders 1973
   Huntingtons Disease 1973
   Phenylketonuria 1973
   Porphyria 1973
   Rh Incompatibility 1973
   ↓ Sex Linked Hereditary Disorders 1973
   Sickle Cell Disease 1994

Genetic Disorders — (cont'd)

   Tay Sachs Disease 2003
   Williams Syndrome 2003
R Alopecia 1973
   Anemia 1973
   Behavioral Genetics 1994
   Color Blindness 1973
   ↓ Congenital Disorders 1973
   Developmental Disabilities 1982
   Diabetes Insipidus 1973
   Genetic Counseling 1978
   ↓ Genetic Engineering 1994
   Genetic Testing 2003
   ↓ Genetics 1967
   Hypopituitarism 1973
   Mutations 1973
   Picks Disease 1973
   Prenatal Diagnosis 1988
   ↓ Refraction Errors 1973

Genetic Dominance 1973

PN 68   **SC** 20840
B Dominance 1967
R Behavioral Genetics 1994
   Genetic Recessiveness 1973
   ↓ Genetics 1967

Genetic Engineering 1994

PN 92   **SC** 20845
N Cloning 2003
   Eugenics 1973
R Bioethics 2003
   Genetic Counseling 1978
   ↓ Genetic Disorders 1973
   Genetic Linkage 1994
   ↓ Genetics 1967
   Population Genetics 1973
   Reproductive Technology 1988
   Selective Breeding 1973

Genetic Linkage 1994

PN 722   **SC** 20847
SN Linkage of genes at different loci on the same chromosome and analysis of how genes are inherited together.
UF Linkage Analysis
R ↓ Chromosomes 1973
   ↓ Genes 1973
   ↓ Genetic Engineering 1994
   ↓ Genetics 1967
   Genotypes 1973
   Quantitative Trait Loci 2004

Genetic Recessiveness 1973

PN 41   **SC** 20850
UF Recessiveness (Genetic)
R Behavioral Genetics 1994
   Genetic Dominance 1973
   ↓ Genetics 1967

Genetic Screening

Use Genetic Testing

Genetic Testing 2003

PN 116   **SC** 20855
SN Screening for presence or predisposition to a particular trait or disease that may be passed on to one's offspring.
HN This term was introduced in June 2003. PsycINFO records from the past 10 years were re-indexed with this term. The posting note reflects the number of records that were re-indexed.

Genetic Testing — (cont'd)

UF Genetic Screening
B Health Screening 1997
R Genetic Counseling 1978
   ↓ Genetic Disorders 1973
   ↓ Medical Diagnosis 1973
   Preventive Medicine 1973

Genetics 1967

PN 13433   **SC** 20860
SN Conceptually broad term referring both to the science of heredity and the biological process of transmission of characteristics from progenitor to offspring.
UF Heredity
N Behavioral Genetics 1994
   Eugenics 1973
   Genome 2003
   Population Genetics 1973
R ↓ Animal Breeding 1973
   Animal Mate Selection 1982
   Animal Strain Differences 1982
   Assortative Mating 1991
   Blood Groups 1973
   ↓ Chromosomes 1973
   Family Resemblance 1991
   Gene Expression 2004
   ↓ Genes 1973
   Genetic Counseling 1978
   ↓ Genetic Disorders 1973
   Genetic Dominance 1973
   ↓ Genetic Engineering 1994
   Genetic Linkage 1994
   Genetic Recessiveness 1973
   Genotypes 1973
   Hybrids (Biology) 1973
   Instinctive Behavior 1982
   Mutations 1973
   Natural Selection 1997
   Nature Nurture 1994
   ↓ Nucleic Acids 1973
   Phenotypes 1973
   Polymorphism 2003
   Predisposition 1973
   Quantitative Trait Loci 2004
   Reproductive Technology 1988
   Selective Breeding 1973
   ↓ Sexual Reproduction 1973
   Species Differences 1982
   Translocation (Chromosome) 1973
   ↓ Twins 1967

Geniculate Bodies (Thalamus) 1973

PN 512   **SC** 20870
B Thalamus 1967
R Visual Receptive Fields 1982

Genital Disorders 1967

PN 208   **SC** 20880
UF Sex Differentiation Disorders
   Sexual Disorders (Physiological)
B Urogenital Disorders 1973
N ↓ Endocrine Sexual Disorders 1973
   ↓ Gynecological Disorders 1973
   Hermaphroditism 1973
   ↓ Infertility 1973
   ↓ Male Genital Disorders 1973
R Sex 1967

Genital Herpes

Use Herpes Genitalis

Genitalia (Female)
Use Female Genitalia

Genitalia (Male)
Use Male Genitalia

Geniuses
Use Gifted

Genocide 1988
PN 178   SC 20915
SN Deliberate and systematic destruction of a racial, political, or cultural group.
B   Homicide 1967
N   Holocaust 1988

Genome 2003
PN 58   SC 20917
SN An organism's complete gene complement contained in a set of chromosomes.
HN This term was introduced in June 2003. PsycINFO records from the past 10 years were re-indexed with this term. The posting note reflects the number of records that were re-indexed.
UF   Human Genome
B   Genetics 1967
R   ↓ Chromosomes 1973
    Deoxyribonucleic Acid 1973
    ↓ Genes 1973
    Quantitative Trait Loci 2004

Genotypes 1973
PN 1216   SC 20920
R   Genetic Linkage 1994
    ↓ Genetics 1967
    Phenotypes 1973
    Polymorphism 2003

Genuineness
Use Sincerity

Geographic Regions
Use Geography

Geographical Differences
Use Regional Differences

Geographical Mobility 1978
PN 460   SC 20924
SN Capacity or facility of individuals to move from one geographic region to another. Includes job- or study-related commuting.
UF   Mobility (Geographical)
R   Commuting (Travel) 1985
    ↓ Human Migration 1973

Geography 1973
PN 1125   SC 20925
SN Science dealing with the description of the topographical features of the earth and the distribution of life on earth. Also, geographic areas or their features.
UF   Geographic Regions
    Physical Divisions (Geographic)
    Physical Geography
    Political Divisions (Geographic)
B   Sciences 1967
R   ↓ Countries 1967
    ↓ Environment 1967
    Regional Differences 2001

Geomagnetism
Use Magnetism

Geometry 2003
PN 15   SC 20930
SN Branch of mathematics concerned with the relationships of points, lines, angles, curves, space, and surfaces.
HN Use MATHEMATICS to access references from 1973 to June 2003.
B   Mathematics 1982

Gerbils 1973
PN 714   SC 20940
B   Rodents 1973

Geriatric Assessment 1997
PN 404   SC 20945
B   Evaluation 1967
R   Activities of Daily Living 1991
    Clinical Judgment (Not Diagnosis) 1973
    ↓ Diagnosis 1967
    Geriatric Patients 1973
    Geriatric Psychiatry 1997
    Geriatrics 1967
    Gerontology 1967
    ↓ Measurement 1967
    Needs Assessment 1985
    ↓ Psychiatric Evaluation 1997
    ↓ Psychological Assessment 1997
    ↓ Screening 1982

Geriatric Patients 1973
PN 5237   SC 20950
SN Older persons suffering from mental or physical diseases and disabilities and under some form of treatment.
B   Patients 1967
R   Geriatric Assessment 1997

Geriatric Psychiatry 1997
PN 442   SC 20955
B   Psychiatry 1967
R   ↓ Aging 1991
    Geriatric Assessment 1997
    Geriatric Psychotherapy 1973
    Geriatrics 1967
    Gerontology 1967

Geriatric Psychotherapy 1973
PN 332   SC 20960
B   Psychotherapy 1967
R   ↓ Aging 1991
    Animal Assisted Therapy 1994
    Geriatric Psychiatry 1997
    Geriatrics 1967
    Gerontology 1967
    Physiological Aging 1967

Geriatrics 1967
PN 1839   SC 20970
SN Medical subdiscipline which deals with the problems of old age and aging.
HN Use GERIATRICS or GERONTOLOGY to access references on the aged (elderly) from 1967-1972.
B   Medical Sciences 1967
R   ↓ Aged (Attitudes Toward) 1978
    ↓ Aging 1991
    Geriatric Assessment 1997
    Geriatric Psychiatry 1997
    Geriatric Psychotherapy 1973

Geriatrics — (cont'd)
    Gerontology 1967
    Physiological Aging 1967

German Measles
Use Rubella

Gerontology 1967
PN 2271   SC 21000
SN Scientific study of old age and the phenomena associated with old age.
HN Use GERONTOLOGY or GERIATRICS to access references to the aged (elderly) from 1967-1972.
B   Developmental Psychology 1973
R   ↓ Aged (Attitudes Toward) 1978
    ↓ Aging 1991
    Geriatric Assessment 1997
    Geriatric Psychiatry 1997
    Geriatric Psychotherapy 1973
    Geriatrics 1967
    Life Review 1991

Gestalt Psychology 1967
PN 878   SC 21010
SN School of psychology concerned with the study of the individual's perception of and response to configurational wholes.
B   History of Psychology 1967
    Psychological Theories 2001

Gestalt Therapy 1973
PN 895   SC 21020
SN Type of psychotherapy which emphasizes treatment of the individual as a whole and focuses on sensory awareness of present experience.
B   Human Potential Movement 1982
    Psychotherapy 1967
R   ↓ Humanistic Psychotherapy 2003

Gestation
Use Pregnancy

Gestures 1973
PN 1130   SC 21040
B   Nonverbal Communication 1971
R   Body Language 1973

Ghettoes 1973
PN 105   SC 21050
UF   Urban Ghettoes
B   Urban Environments 1967
R   Poverty Areas 1973

Gifted 1967
PN 5620   SC 21060
UF   Exceptional Children (Gifted)
    Geniuses
    Intellectually Gifted
    Talented
R   ↓ Ability 1967
    Creativity 1967
    ↓ Intelligence 1967
    Savants 2001

Gilles de la Tourette Disorder 1973
PN 1390   SC 21070
UF   Tourette Syndrome
B   Neuromuscular Disorders 1973
R   Echolalia 1973

Gipsies
  Use Gypsies

Girls
  Use Human Females

Glands 1967
PN 671   **SC** 21080
  N ↓ Endocrine Glands 1973
        Mammary Glands 1973
        Pancreas 1973
        Salivary Glands 1973
  R Pheromones 1973

Glaucoma 1973
PN 72   **SC** 21090
  B Eye Disorders 1973

Global Amnesia 1997
PN 55   **SC** 21095
  HN Use AMNESIA to access references from 1967-1996.
  B Amnesia 1967
  R ↓ Brain Damage 1967

Globalization 2003
PN 142   **SC** 21098
  SN Refers to the emergence of a global cultural system brought about by advances in communications technology; the internationalization of consumerism; the world-wide influence of popular culture; and the increasing development, activism, connectivity, and interdependence of the world's markets and businesses.
  HN This term was introduced in June 2003. Psyc-INFO records from the past 10 years were re-indexed with this term. The posting note reflects the number of records that were re-indexed.
  R Business 1967
        Business Organizations 1973
        ↓ Economics 1905
        Economy 1973
        Modernization 2003
        Popular Culture 2003

Globulins 1973
PN 137   **SC** 21100
  UF Glycoproteins
  B Proteins 1973
  N Antibodies 1973
        ↓ Immunoglobulins 1973

Globus Pallidus 1972
PN 431   **SC** 21110
  B Basal Ganglia 1973
  R ↓ Striatum 2003

Glossolalia 1973
PN 47   **SC** 21130
  SN Unintelligible speech occurring in hypnotic or mediumistic trances, religious experiences, or some mental disorders.
  R ↓ Mental Disorders 1967
        ↓ Religious Practices 1973

Glossopharyngeal Nerve
  Use Cranial Nerves

Glucagon 1973
PN 72   **SC** 21150

Glucagon — (cont'd)
  B Hormones 1967
        Neuropeptides 2003

Glucocorticoids 1982
PN 542   **SC** 21155
  SN Any steroid-like compound capable of significantly influencing intermediary metabolism. Glucocorticoids are also clinically useful anti-inflammatory agents.
  B Adrenal Cortex Hormones 1973
        Anti Inflammatory Drugs 1982
  N Dexamethasone 1985

Glucose 1973
PN 1297   **SC** 21160
  B Sugars 1973
  N Blood Sugar 1973
  R Glucose Metabolism 1994
        Glycogen 1973

Glucose Metabolism 1994
PN 469   **SC** 21165
  B Carbohydrate Metabolism 1973
  R ↓ Glucose 1973
        ↓ Neurochemistry 1973

Glue Sniffing 1973
PN 61   **SC** 21170
  B Inhalant Abuse 1985

Glutamate
  Use Glutamic Acid

Glutamic Acid 1973
PN 971   **SC** 21180
  UF Glutamate
  B Amino Acids 1973
        Neurotransmitters 1985
  R Kainic Acid 1988

Glutamine 1973
PN 219   **SC** 21190
  B Amino Acids 1973

Glutethimide 1973
PN 16   **SC** 21210
  B CNS Depressant Drugs 1973
        Hypnotic Drugs 1973
        Sedatives 1973

Glycine 1973
PN 234   **SC** 21220
  B Amino Acids 1973
        Neurotransmitters 1985

Glycogen 1973
PN 67   **SC** 21230
  R ↓ Glucose 1973

Glycoproteins
  Use Globulins

Goal Setting 1997
PN 625   **SC** 21237
  R ↓ Aspirations 1967
        ↓ Goals 1967
        ↓ Motivation 1967

Goals 1967
PN 5332   **SC** 21240
  SN Aims toward which an individual or a group aspire or toward which effort is directed. Use a more specific term if possible.
  UF Objectives
  N Educational Objectives 1978
        Organizational Objectives 1973
  R ↓ Aspirations 1967
        Extrinsic Motivation 1973
        Goal Setting 1997
        ↓ Incentives 1967
        Intention 1988
        Intrinsic Motivation 1973
        ↓ Motivation 1967
        ↓ Needs 1967

Goats 1973
PN 162   **SC** 21250
  B Mammals 1973

God Concepts 1973
PN 554   **SC** 21260
  B Religious Beliefs 1973
  R Theology 2003

Goiters 1973
PN 18   **SC** 21270
  B Thyroid Disorders 1973
  R Hyperthyroidism 1973
        Hypothyroidism 1973

Goldfish 1973
PN 514   **SC** 21280
  B Carp 1973

Gonadotropic Hormones 1973
PN 414   **SC** 21300
  UF Gonadotropin
  B Hormones 1967
  N Follicle Stimulating Hormone 1991
        Luteinizing Hormone 1978
        Prolactin 1973
  R ↓ Pituitary Hormones 1973
        ↓ Sex Hormones 1973

Gonadotropin
  Use Gonadotropic Hormones

Gonads 1973
PN 149   **SC** 21320
  B Endocrine Glands 1973
        Urogenital System 1973
  N Ovaries 1973
        Testes 1973

Gonorrhea 1973
PN 52   **SC** 21330
  B Bacterial Disorders 1973
        Sexually Transmitted Diseases 2003

Goodenough Harris Draw A Person Test 1967
PN 128   **SC** 21340
  B Intelligence Measures 1967
  R Human Figures Drawing 1973

Goodness of Fit 1988
PN 372   **SC** 21350
  B Statistical Analysis 1967
  R ↓ Factor Analysis 1967

Goodness of Fit — (cont'd)
↓ Mathematical Modeling   1973
    Maximum Likelihood   1985
    Statistical Significance   1973

Gorillas   1973
PN   269   SC   21370
  B   Primates (Nonhuman)   1973

Gossip   1982
PN   121   SC   21375
SN   Idle personal talk or communication of unsubstantiated information.
  UF   Rumors
  B   Interpersonal Communication   1973
  R   Messages   1973

Gough Adjective Check List   1973
PN   25   SC   21380
  B   Nonprojective Personality Measures   1973

Government   1967
PN   973   SC   21390
  UF   Government Bureaucracy
  B   Public Sector   1985
  R   Autonomy (Government)   1973
       Foreign Policy Making   1973
       Government Agencies   1973
       ↓ Government Personnel   1973
       ↓ Government Policy Making   1973
       ↓ Government Programs   1973
       Gun Control Laws   1973
       Job Corps   1973
       ↓ Law (Government)   1973
       ↓ Law Enforcement   1978
       ↓ Laws   1967
       ↓ Legal Processes   1973
       Legislative Processes   1973
       ↓ Marijuana Laws   1973
       Marijuana Legalization   1973
       Peace Corps   1973
       ↓ Political Economic Systems   1973
       ↓ Politics   1967
       Project Follow Through   1973
       Project Head Start   1973
       Taxation   1985
       Upward Bound   1973
       Welfare Services (Government)   1973

Government Agencies   1973
PN   814   SC   21400
  B   Organizations   1967
       Public Sector   1985
  R   Government   1967

Government Bureaucracy
  Use   Government

Government Personnel   1973
PN   1528   SC   21420
  UF   Civil Servants
       Elected Government Officials
  B   Personnel   1967
  N   Agricultural Extension Workers   1973
       ↓ Law Enforcement Personnel   1973
       ↓ Military Personnel   1967
       Police Personnel   1973
       Public Health Service Nurses   1973
  R   ↓ Business and Industrial Personnel   1967
       Fire Fighters   1991
       Government   1967

Government Policy Making   1973
PN   5495   SC   21430
  UF   Policy Making (Government)
       Public Policy
  B   Policy Making   1988
  N   Foreign Policy Making   1973
       ↓ Laws   1967
       Legislative Processes   1973
  R   Advocacy   1985
       Funding   1988
       Government   1967
       Health Care Policy   1994
       ↓ Legal Processes   1973
       ↓ War   1967

Government Programs   1973
PN   1282   SC   21440
  UF   Programs (Government)
  N   Job Corps   1973
       Medicaid   1994
       Medicare   1988
       Peace Corps   1973
       Project Follow Through   1973
       Project Head Start   1973
       Social Security   1988
       Upward Bound   1973
       Welfare Services (Government)   1973
  R   Funding   1988
       Government   1967
       ↓ Program Development   1991
       Shelters   1991
       ↓ Social Services   1982

Grade Level   1994
PN   470   SC   21445
  UF   Academic Grade Level
  R   Ability Grouping   1973
       Age Differences   1967
       ↓ Education   1967
       Educational Placement   1978
       ↓ Elementary School Students   1967
       High School Students   1967
       Junior High School Students   1971
       Kindergarten Students   1973
       School Transition   1997
       Special Education Students   1973
       Transfer Students   1973

Gradepoint Average
  Use   Academic Achievement

Grading (Educational)   1973
PN   679   SC   21460
SN   Rating of achievement level by means of established scales or standards. Consider also SCORING (TESTING) or TEST SCORES.
  B   Educational Measurement   1967
  R   ↓ Scoring (Testing)   1973

Graduate Degrees
  Use   Educational Degrees

Graduate Education   1973
PN   793   SC   21480
  B   Higher Education   1973
  N   Dental Education   1973
       ↓ Graduate Psychology Education   1967
       ↓ Medical Education   1973
       Rehabilitation Education   1997

Graduate Psychology Education   1967
PN   2999   SC   21490

Graduate Psychology Education — (cont'd)
  UF   Training (Graduate Psychology)
  B   Graduate Education   1973
       Psychology Education   1978
  N   ↓ Clinical Psychology Graduate Training   2001
  R   Educational Program Accreditation   1994

Graduate Record Examination   1973
PN   158   SC   21500
  B   Aptitude Measures   1967

Graduate Schools   1973
PN   102   SC   21510
  B   Schools   1967
  R   ↓ Higher Education   1973

Graduate Students   1967
PN   3722   SC   21520
SN   Students pursuing academic studies past the college level.
  B   Students   1967
  R   ↓ College Students   1967
       Dental Students   1973
       Law Students   1978
       Medical Students   1967
       Postgraduate Students   1973

Graduation (School)
  Use   School Graduation

Grammar   1967
PN   3082   SC   21530
SN   Science of the structure of language including universal grammar, descriptive and prescriptive grammar, and the rules and principles of syntax, phonology, and semantics applied in verbal communication. Compare SYNTAX.
  B   Linguistics   1973
  N   Morphology (Language)   1973
       ↓ Phonology   1973
       ↓ Semantics   1967
       ↓ Syntax   1971
       Transformational Generative Grammar   1973
  R   Discourse Analysis   1997
       ↓ Language   1967
       ↓ Verbal Communication   1967
       Words (Phonetic Units)   1967

Grammar Schools
  Use   Elementary Schools

Grand Mal Epilepsy   1973
PN   34   SC   21550
  B   Epilepsy   1967

Grandchildren   1973
PN   399   SC   21560
  B   Family Members   1973

Grandiosity   1994
PN   39   SC   21565
  B   Defense Mechanisms   1967
  R   Delusions   1967
       Egotism   1973
       Emotional Superiority   1973
       Erotomania   1997
       Narcissism   1967
       Omnipotence   1994

Grandparents 1973
PN 994   SC 21570
  B   Ancestors 1973
      Family Members 1973

Graphical Displays 1985
PN 984   SC 21575
SN Pictorial rendering of data (e.g., bar graphs, continuous line graphs, and data plots).
HN Consider VISUAL DISPLAYS to access references from 1973-1984.
  B   Displays 1967
  R   Statistical Data 1982
     ↓ Statistical Measurement 1973

Graphology
  Use Handwriting

Grasping 1997
PN 299   SC 21585
  B   Motor Processes 1967

Grasshoppers 1973
PN 100   SC 21590
  B   Insects 1967
  R   Larvae 1973

Gravitational Effects 1967
PN 295   SC 21600
  B   Environmental Effects 1973
  N   Weightlessness 1967
  R   Acceleration Effects 1973
     Altitude Effects 1973
     ↓ Aviation 1967
     Decompression Effects 1973
     Flight Simulation 1973
     Spaceflight 1967
     Underwater Effects 1973

Great Grandparents
  Use Ancestors

Gregariousness 1973
PN 26   SC 21660
  B   Personality Traits 1967
  R   Extraversion 1967
     Sociability 1973

Grief 1973
PN 5580   SC 21680
  UF Bereavement
     Mourning
  B   Emotional States 1973
  R   ↓ Death and Dying 1967
     ↓ Separation Reactions 1997
     Suffering 1973

Grimaces 1973
PN 14   SC 21690
  B   Facial Expressions 1967

Grooming Behavior (Animal)
  Use Animal Grooming Behavior

Gross Motor Skill Learning 1973
PN 190   SC 21700
  B   Perceptual Motor Learning 1967
     Skill Learning 1973

Ground Transportation 1973
PN 148   SC 21710
  B   Transportation 1973
  N   ↓ Motor Vehicles 1982
     Railroad Trains 1973
  R   Highway Safety 1973

Grounded Theory 2004
PN 116   SC 21715
SN Methodological approach to constructing theories based on systematically analyzing qualitative data.
HN This term was introduced in June 2004. PsycINFO records from the past 10 years were re-indexed with this term. The posting note reflects the number of records that were re-indexed.
  B   Methodology 1967
  R   Qualitative Research 2003
     Theory Formulation 1973

Group Cohesion 1973
PN 1285   SC 21730
SN Mutual bonds formed among the members of a group as a consequence of their combined efforts toward a common goal or purpose.
  UF Cohesion (Group)
  B   Group Dynamics 1967
  R   Group Development 1997

Group Counseling 1973
PN 3585   SC 21740
  UF Counseling (Group)
  B   Counseling 1967
  R   ↓ Self Help Techniques 1982
     ↓ Support Groups 1991
     ↓ Twelve Step Programs 1997

Group Decision Making 1978
PN 1783   SC 21745
SN Process of arriving at a decision or judgment by a group.
  B   Decision Making 1967
  N   Choice Shift 1994
  R   Management Decision Making 1973

Group Development 1997
PN 244   SC 21747
SN Used in treatment and nontreatment settings.
  B   Group Dynamics 1967
  R   Group Cohesion 1973
     Group Participation 1973
     ↓ Group Psychotherapy 1967
     ↓ Group Size 1967
     Group Structure 1967

Group Discussion 1967
PN 2275   SC 21750
  UF Discussion (Group)
  B   Group Dynamics 1967
     Interpersonal Communication 1973
  R   Choice Shift 1994
     Debates 1997

Group Dynamics 1967
PN 8476   SC 21760
  UF Dynamics (Group)
  N   Group Cohesion 1973
     Group Development 1997
     Group Discussion 1967
     Group Participation 1973
     Group Performance 1967
     ↓ Group Size 1967
     Group Structure 1967

Group Dynamics — (cont'd)
     Intergroup Dynamics 1973
  R   Boundaries (Psychological) 1997
     Brainstorming 1982
     Choice Shift 1994
     ↓ Collective Behavior 1967
     Consciousness Raising Groups 1978
     Group Instruction 1973
     ↓ Group Problem Solving 1973
     ↓ Group Psychotherapy 1967
     Human Relations Training 1978
     Ingroup Outgroup 1997
     ↓ Organizational Behavior 1978
     Peer Pressure 1994
     Reference Groups 1994
     Sensitivity Training 1973
     ↓ Sociometry 1991
     ↓ Teams 1988

Group Health Plans
  Use Health Maintenance Organizations

Group Homes 1982
PN 749   SC 21767
SN Housing for groups of patients, children, or others who need or desire emotional and physical support.
  B   Housing 1973
  R   ↓ Community Facilities 1973
     Community Mental Health Services 1978
     ↓ Residential Care Institutions 1973
     Retirement Communities 1997
     Shelters 1991

Group Instruction 1973
PN 950   SC 21770
  B   Teaching Methods 1967
  R   Cooperative Learning 1994
     ↓ Group Dynamics 1967

Group Participation 1973
PN 1738   SC 21780
SN Involvement in a group's purpose or activities.
  B   Group Dynamics 1967
     Interpersonal Interaction 1967
     Participation 1973
  R   ↓ Collective Behavior 1967
     Group Development 1997
     Social Loafing 2003

Group Performance 1967
PN 2042   SC 21790
SN Process and effectiveness of a group in accomplishing an intended goal.
  B   Group Dynamics 1967
     Interpersonal Interaction 1967
     Performance 1967

Group Problem Solving 1973
PN 1321   SC 21800
SN Dynamics of group interaction during the process of analyzing, defining, and attaining the solution to a problem.
  B   Problem Solving 1967
  N   Brainstorming 1982
  R   Choice Shift 1994
     ↓ Group Dynamics 1967

Group Psychotherapy 1967
PN 10866   SC 21810
  UF Group Therapy
  B   Psychotherapy 1967

Group Psychotherapy — (cont'd)
N ↓ Encounter Group Therapy 1973
    Therapeutic Community 1967
R Conjoint Therapy 1973
    Consciousness Raising Groups 1978
    Group Development 1997
    ↓ Group Dynamics 1967
    ↓ Human Potential Movement 1982
    Psychodrama 1967
    Sensitivity Training 1973
    ↓ Support Groups 1991
    Transactional Analysis 1973
    ↓ Twelve Step Programs 1997

Group Size 1967
PN 1602   SC 21820
UF Size (Group)
B Group Dynamics 1967
    Size 1973
N Class Size 2004
R Group Development 1997

Group Structure 1967
PN 1172   SC 21830
SN Patterns of organization, behavior, and communication of a group that determine the interpersonal relations of its members.
B Group Dynamics 1967
R Group Development 1997

Group Testing 1973
PN 222   SC 21840
B Measurement 1967
R Test Administration 1973

Group Therapy
Use Group Psychotherapy

Groups (Organizations)
Use Organizations

Groups (Social)
Use Social Groups

Groupware 2003
PN 38   SC 21892
SN Computer software and other technology designed to enable communication and foster productivity both within and among groups of people working together on a task.
HN This term was introduced in June 2003. PsycINFO records from the past 10 years were re-indexed with this term. The posting note reflects the number of records that were re-indexed.
UF Computer Supported Cooperative Work
B Computer Applications 1973
    Computer Software 1967
R Computer Mediated Communication 2003
    Cooperation 1967
    ↓ Electronic Communication 2001
    ↓ Employee Interaction 1988
    Supervisor Employee Interaction 1997
    ↓ Technology 1973
    Teleconferencing 1997
    ↓ Work Teams 2001
    ↓ Working Conditions 1973

Grown Children
Use Adult Offspring

Growth
Use Development

Growth Centers
Use Human Potential Movement

Growth Hormone
Use Somatotropin

Growth Hormone Inhibitor
Use Somatostatin

GSR (Electrophysiology)
Use Galvanic Skin Response

Guanethidine 1973
PN 37   SC 21930
B Amines 1973
    Antihypertensive Drugs 1973
R Norepinephrine 1973

Guanosine 1985
PN 77   SC 21929
R ↓ Carbohydrate Metabolism 1973
    Cyclic Adenosine Monophosphate 1978
    ↓ Nucleic Acids 1973

Guardianship 1988
PN 177   SC 21932
SN Court appointment of an individual to act as a guardian or conservator and to legally act and speak in the interest of a minor or a physically or mentally disabled adult.
UF Conservatorship
B Legal Processes 1973
R Child Custody 1982
    ↓ Client Rights 1988
    ↓ Commitment (Psychiatric) 1973
    Informed Consent 1985
    Protective Services 1997

Guessing 1973
PN 257   SC 21933
SN Responding to questions or test items on the basis of little or no knowledge of the correct answer.
R Intuition 1973
    Questioning 1982
    ↓ Strategies 1967
    Test Taking 1985

Guest Workers
Use Foreign Workers

Guidance (Educational)
Use Educational Counseling

Guidance (Occupational)
Use Occupational Guidance

Guidance Counseling
Use School Counseling

Guided Fantasy
Use Guided Imagery

Guided Imagery 2001
PN 362   SC 21957
SN Mind-body technique involving the deliberate prompting of mental images, used in the treatment of mental disorders, for performance enhancement, and in helping patients cope with diseases and their symptoms.
UF Directed Reverie Therapy
    Guided Fantasy
B Psychotherapeutic Techniques 1967
    Psychotherapy 1967
R ↓ Hypnotherapy 1973
    ↓ Imagery 1967
    Relaxation 1973
    ↓ Relaxation Therapy 1978

Guilford Zimmerman Temperament Survey 2001
PN 19   SC 21965
HN In 2001, the truncated term GUILFORD ZIMMERMAN TEMPERAMENT SURV (which was used from 1973-2000) was deleted, removed from all records containing it, and replaced with its expanded form GUILFORD ZIMMERMAN TEMPERAMENT SURVEY.
B Nonprojective Personality Measures 1973

Guilt 1967
PN 2088   SC 21970
B Emotional States 1973
R ↓ Anxiety 1967
    ↓ Anxiety Disorders 1997
    Blame 1994
    Shame 1994

Guinea Pigs 1967
PN 964   SC 21980
B Rodents 1973

Gulls
Use Sea Gulls

Gun Control Laws 1973
PN 88   SC 22000
B Laws 1967
R Firearms 2003
    Government 1967

Guns
Use Firearms

Gustatory Perception
Use Taste Perception

Gymnastic Therapy
Use Recreation Therapy

Gynecological Disorders 1973
PN 238   SC 22040
B Genital Disorders 1967
    Urogenital Disorders 1973
N ↓ Menstrual Disorders 1973
R ↓ Endocrine Sexual Disorders 1973
    Hermaphroditism 1973
    ↓ Hypogonadism 1973
    ↓ Infertility 1973
    Pseudocyesis 1973
    Sterility 1973

Gynecologists 1973
PN 82　　　　　　　　　　SC 22050
　B　Physicians 1967
　R　Obstetricians 1978
　　　Surgeons 1973

Gynecology 1978
PN 214　　　　　　　　　SC 22053
SN Medical specialty dealing with the female endocrine system, reproductive physiology, and diseases of the genital tract. Used for the medical specialty or the specific gynecological issues or findings.
　B　Medical Sciences 1967
　R　Circumcision 2001
　　↓ Obstetrics 1978

Gypsies 1973
PN 79　　　　　　　　　　SC 22055
　UF　Gipsies
　B　Racial and Ethnic Groups 2001
　R　↓ Human Migration 1973
　　　Minority Groups 1967

Gyrus Cinguli 1973
PN 503　　　　　　　　　SC 22060
　B　Frontal Lobe 1973
　　　Limbic System 1973

Habilitation 1991
PN 77　　　　　　　　　　SC 22065
SN Establishment, not restoration, of fundamental capabilities, knowledge, experiences, and attitudes before or along with the usual rehabilitation procedures as a means of increasing patient awareness and developing their potential. Used primarily for physically or mentally disabled populations. Compare REHABILITATION
　R　Activities of Daily Living 1991
　　　Deinstitutionalization 1982
　　　Independent Living Programs 1991
　　↓ Mainstreaming 1991
　　↓ Rehabilitation 1967
　　↓ Skill Learning 1973

Habitat Selection
　Use Territoriality

Habitats (Animal)
　Use Animal Environments

Habits 1967
PN 554　　　　　　　　　SC 22080
　UF　Mannerisms
　N　Nail Biting 1973
　　　Thumbsucking 1973
　　　Tobacco Smoking 1967
　　　Trichotillomania 2003
　R　↓ Learning 1967

Habituation 1967
PN 2508　　　　　　　　SC 22090
SN Progressive attenuation of a response elicited by repetitive stimulation.
　R　↓ Sensory Adaptation 1967

Hair 1973
PN 236　　　　　　　　　SC 22100
　B　Anatomy 1967
　R　Alopecia 1973
　　　Scalp (Anatomy) 1973
　　　Skin (Anatomy) 1967

Hair Loss
　Use Alopecia

Hair Pulling
　Use Trichotillomania

Halcion
　Use Triazolam

Halfway Houses 1973
PN 242　　　　　　　　　SC 22140
SN Facilities for psychiatric, drug, or alcohol rehabilitation patients or mentally retarded individuals who no longer need hospitalization or institutionalization, but who are not yet fully prepared to return to their communities.
　B　Residential Care Institutions 1973
　　　Treatment Facilities 1973
　R　↓ Community Facilities 1973
　　↓ Correctional Institutions 1973
　　↓ Psychiatric Hospital Programs 1967
　　　Psychiatric Hospitals 1967

Hallucinations 1967
PN 1249　　　　　　　　SC 22150
SN Perceptions through any sense modality in the absence of an appropriate stimulus. (Usually indicative of abnormality but may be experienced occasionally by normal persons).
　UF　Flashbacks
　B　Perceptual Disturbances 1973
　N　Auditory Hallucinations 1973
　　　Drug Induced Hallucinations 1973
　　　Hypnagogic Hallucinations 1973
　　　Visual Hallucinations 1973
　R　↓ Hallucinogenic Drugs 1967
　　↓ Hallucinosis 1973
　　　Near Death Experiences 1985

Hallucinogenic Drugs 1967
PN 484　　　　　　　　　SC 22160
　B　Drugs 1967
　N　Bufotenine 1973
　　　Lysergic Acid Diethylamide 1967
　　　Mescaline 1973
　　　Peyote 1973
　　　Phencyclidine 1982
　　　Psilocybin 1973
　R　↓ Cannabis 1973
　　↓ Cholinergic Blocking Drugs 1973
　　　Experimental Psychosis 1973
　　↓ Hallucinations 1967
　　↓ Psychedelic Drugs 1973
　　↓ Psychotomimetic Drugs 1973
　　　Tetrahydrocannabinol 1973

Hallucinosis 1973
PN 63　　　　　　　　　　SC 22170
SN Mental disorder characterized by hallucinations occurring in a normal state of consciousness and attributable to specific organic factors.
　B　Psychosis 1967
　N　↓ Alcoholic Hallucinosis 1973
　R　↓ Hallucinations 1967

Halo Effect 1982
PN 146　　　　　　　　　SC 22177
SN Tendency to rate individuals too high or too low on the basis of one outstanding trait or an erroneous overall impression. Often the source of error in rating scales.

Halo Effect — (cont'd)
　R　↓ Errors 1967
　　↓ Expectations 1967
　　　Experimenter Bias 1967
　　　Rating 1967
　　↓ Social Perception 1967

Haloperidol 1973
PN 3521　　　　　　　　SC 22180
　B　CNS Depressant Drugs 1973
　　　Sedatives 1973
　　　Tranquilizing Drugs 1967

Halstead Reitan Neuropsychological Battery 2001
PN 117　　　　　　　　　SC 22185
HN In 2000, the truncated term HALSTEAD REITAN NEUROPSYCH BATTERY (which was used from 1991-2000) was deleted, removed from all records containing it, and replaced with its expanded form HALSTEAD REITAN NEUROPSYCHOLOGICAL BATTERY. Use NEUROPSYCHOLOGICAL ASSESSMENT to access references from 1982-1990.
　B　Neuropsychological Assessment 1982

Hamsters 1973
PN 1518　　　　　　　　SC 22190
　B　Rodents 1973

Hand (Anatomy) 1967
PN 1367　　　　　　　　SC 22200
　B　Anatomy 1967
　　　Musculoskeletal System 1973
　R　Arm (Anatomy) 1973
　　↓ Fingers (Anatomy) 1973
　　　Palm (Anatomy) 1973
　　　Wrist 1973

Handedness 1978
PN 2891　　　　　　　　SC 22210
SN Learned or spontaneous differential dexterity with and tendency to use one hand rather than the other.
　UF　Ambidexterity
　B　Lateral Dominance 1967

Handicapped (Attitudes Toward)
　Use Disabled (Attitudes Toward)

Handicaps
　Use Disabilities

Handicrafts
　Use Crafts

Handwriting 1967
PN 1014　　　　　　　　SC 22250
　UF　Graphology
　　　Writing (Handwriting)
　B　Verbal Communication 1967
　　　Written Language 1967
　N　Cursive Writing 1973
　　　Handwriting Legibility 1973
　　　Printing (Handwriting) 1973

Handwriting Legibility 1973
PN 71　　　　　　　　　　SC 22260
　UF　Legibility (Handwriting)

Handwriting Legibility — (cont'd)
B   Handwriting 1967
      Legibility 1978

Happiness 1973
PN 1360   SC 22270
UF   Joy
B   Emotional States 1973
R   Euphoria 1973
      Pleasure 1973

Haptic Perception
Use   Cutaneous Sense

Harassment 2001
PN 98   SC 22282
B   Antisocial Behavior 1971
N   Sexual Harassment 1985
      Stalking 2001
R   Bullying 2003
      Hate Crimes 2003
      ↓ Perpetrators 1988
      Threat 1967
      Victimization 1973

Harassment (Sexual)
Use   Sexual Harassment

Hardiness
Use   Resilience (Psychological)

Harm Reduction 2003
PN 140   SC 22287
SN   Pragmatic approach concerned with reducing potential harm to individuals participating in high risk behaviors.
HN   This term was introduced in June 2003. PsycINFO records from the past 10 years were re-indexed with this term. The posting note reflects the number of records that were re-indexed.
N   Needle Exchange Programs 2001
R   AIDS Prevention 1994
      Drug Abuse Prevention 1994
      ↓ Drug Legalization 1997
      Risk Management 1997

Hashish 1973
PN 74   SC 22290
B   Cannabis 1973
R   Marijuana 2003
      Tetrahydrocannabinol 1973

Hate 1973
PN 356   SC 22300
B   Aversion 1967
R   ↓ Anger 1967
      Hate Crimes 2003
      Hostility 1967

Hate Crimes 2003
PN 59   SC 22301
SN   A crime committed against an individual, a small group, or a large population in which the perpetrator is motivated by a bias against the victim because of his or her race, ethnicity, religion, sex, national origin, or sexual orientation.
HN   This term was introduced in June 2003. PsycINFO records from the past 10 years were re-indexed with this term. The posting note reflects the number of records that were re-indexed.
UF   Bias Crimes

Hate Crimes — (cont'd)
B   Crime 1967
R   AntiSemitism 1973
      ↓ Harassment 2001
      Hate 1973
      ↓ Prejudice 1967
      ↓ Racial and Ethnic Attitudes 1982
      Racism 1973
      ↓ Religious Prejudices 1973
      ↓ Sexual Orientation 1997
      Victimization 1973
      ↓ Violence 1973

Hawaii Natives 2001
PN 15   SC 22315
UF   Native Hawaiians
B   Pacific Islanders 2001
R   Minority Groups 1967

Hay Fever 1973
PN 14   SC 22320
B   Allergic Disorders 1973
      Respiratory Tract Disorders 1973
R   ↓ Somatoform Disorders 2001

Hazardous Materials 1991
PN 257   SC 22325
UF   Asbestos
      Toxic Waste
N   ↓ Insecticides 1973
      ↓ Poisons 1973
      Teratogens 1988
R   ↓ Accidents 1967
      ↓ Chemicals 1991
      ↓ Environment 1967
      Occupational Exposure 1988
      Pollution 1973
      ↓ Safety 1967
      ↓ Toxicity 1973

Hazards 1973
PN 369   SC 22330
R   ↓ Accidents 1967
      Risk Perception 1997
      ↓ Safety 1967
      ↓ Safety Devices 1973
      Warning Labels 1997
      ↓ Warnings 1997

Head (Anatomy) 1973
PN 740   SC 22340
B   Anatomy 1967
R   Face (Anatomy) 1973
      Scalp (Anatomy) 1973
      Skin (Anatomy) 1967

Head Banging 1973
PN 56   SC 22350
B   Self Destructive Behavior 1985

Head Injuries 1973
PN 2996   SC 22360
UF   Closed Head Injuries
B   Injuries 1973
N   Brain Concussion 1973
R   ↓ Brain Damage 1967
      Traumatic Brain Injury 1997
      Whiplash 1997
      ↓ Wounds 1973

Head Start
Use   Project Head Start

Headache 1973
PN 1358   SC 22380
B   Pain 1967
      Symptoms 1967
N   Migraine Headache 1973
      Muscle Contraction Headache 1973
R   ↓ Somatoform Disorders 2001

Health 1973
PN 12512   SC 22390
UF   Wellness
N   Holistic Health 1985
      ↓ Mental Health 1967
      ↓ Public Health 1988
R   General Health Questionnaire 1991
      Health Attitudes 1985
      ↓ Health Behavior 1982
      Health Complaints 1997
      Health Knowledge 1994
      Hygiene 1994
      Preventive Medicine 1973
      Public Health Services 1973
      Well Being 1994

Health Attitudes 1985
PN 4434   SC 22391
UF   Health Locus of Control
B   Attitudes 1967
R   ↓ Drug Usage Attitudes 1973
      ↓ Health 1973
      ↓ Health Behavior 1982
      Health Knowledge 1994
      Health Promotion 1991
      Lifestyle Changes 1997
      Obesity (Attitudes Toward) 1997
      ↓ Physical Illness (Attitudes Toward) 1985

Health Behavior 1982
PN 6336   SC 22392
SN   Individual lifestyle and behavior which may or may not enhance or maintain good health.
B   Behavior 1967
      Client Characteristics 1973
N   Safe Sex 2003
R   Aerobic Exercise 1988
      AIDS Prevention 1994
      Diets 1978
      ↓ Exercise 1973
      ↓ Health 1973
      Health Attitudes 1985
      Health Knowledge 1994
      Health Promotion 1991
      Holistic Health 1985
      Hygiene 1994
      ↓ Lifestyle 1978
      Lifestyle Changes 1997
      ↓ Prenatal Care 1991
      Preventive Medicine 1973
      Self Examination (Medical) 1988
      Self Referral 1991
      Weight Control 1985

Health Care Administration 1997
PN 274   SC 57485
B   Management 1967
N   Hospital Administration 1978
R   ↓ Case Management 1991
      ↓ Health Care Delivery 1978
      Health Care Policy 1994
      ↓ Health Care Services 1978
      ↓ Mental Health Programs 1973
      ↓ Mental Health Services 1978
      ↓ Treatment Facilities 1973

Health Care Costs 1994

PN 1638   **SC** 22393
- **UF** Medical Care Costs
        Mental Health Care Costs
- **B**   Costs and Cost Analysis 1973
- **R** ↓ Case Management 1991
        Cost Containment 1991
        Diagnosis Related Groups 1988
        ↓ Economics 1985
        ↓ Health Care Delivery 1978
        ↓ Health Care Services 1978
        Health Care Utilization 1985
        ↓ Health Insurance 1973
        Health Maintenance Organizations 1982
        ↓ Managed Care 1994
        ↓ Mental Health Services 1978
        ↓ Professional Fees 1978
        ↓ Treatment 1967

Health Care Delivery 1978

PN 7335   **SC** 22394
SN Practices, policies, or referral processes that contribute to making mental and/or medical health care personnel, services, or facilities available to persons in need of such care.
- **N**   Home Care 1985
        Hospice 1982
        ↓ Managed Care 1994
        Telemedicine 2003
- **R**   Bioethics 2003
        ↓ Case Management 1991
        Continuum of Care 2004
        Evidence Based Practice 2004
        Fee for Service 1994
        ↓ Health Care Administration 1997
        Health Care Costs 1994
        Health Care Policy 1994
        ↓ Health Care Services 1978
        Health Care Utilization 1985
        Health Maintenance Organizations 1982
        Health Service Needs 1997
        ↓ Mental Health Programs 1973
        ↓ Mental Health Services 1978
        Needs Assessment 1985
        Outreach Programs 1997
        Palliative Care 1991
        ↓ Prevention 1973
        Primary Health Care 1988
        Private Practice 1978
        Quality of Care 1988
        ↓ Quality of Services 1997
        ↓ Treatment 1967
        ↓ Treatment Planning 1997

Health Care Policy 1994

PN 1557   **SC** 57415
- **UF** Mental Health Care Policy
- **B**   Policy Making 1988
- **R** ↓ Government Policy Making 1973
        ↓ Health Care Administration 1997
        ↓ Health Care Delivery 1978
        ↓ Health Care Services 1978
        ↓ Health Insurance 1973
        Medicaid 1994
        Medicare 1988
        ↓ Mental Health Services 1978

Health Care Professionals
Use Health Personnel

Health Care Psychology 1985

PN 1694   **SC** 22398
- **UF** Behavioral Health

Health Care Psychology — (cont'd)
        Behavioral Medicine
        Health Psychology
- **N**   Medical Psychology 1973
- **R**   Interdisciplinary Treatment Approach 1973
        Psychosomatic Medicine 1978

Health Care Seeking Behavior 1997

PN 868   **SC** 22399
HN Consider HELP SEEKING BEHAVIOR or HEALTH CARE UTILIZATION to access references from 1978-1984 and 1985-1996, respectively.
- **UF** Treatment Seeking Behavior
- **B**   Help Seeking Behavior 1978
- **R** ↓ Commitment (Psychiatric) 1973
        ↓ Health Care Services 1978
        Health Care Utilization 1985
        Health Service Needs 1997
        ↓ Hospital Admission 1973
        ↓ Mental Health Services 1978
        Online Therapy 2003
        Self Referral 1991
        ↓ Treatment 1967

Health Care Services 1978

PN 5760   **SC** 22396
- **B**   Treatment 1967
- **N**   Continuum of Care 2004
        Long Term Care 1994
        ↓ Mental Health Services 1978
        Palliative Care 1991
        Primary Health Care 1988
- **R**   Caregivers 1988
        ↓ Community Services 1967
        Cost Containment 1991
        ↓ Counseling 1967
        Fee for Service 1994
        ↓ Health Care Administration 1997
        Health Care Costs 1994
        ↓ Health Care Delivery 1978
        Health Care Policy 1994
        Health Care Seeking Behavior 1997
        Health Care Utilization 1985
        Health Maintenance Organizations 1982
        Health Service Needs 1997
        Integrated Services 1997
        ↓ Managed Care 1994
        ↓ Mental Health Programs 1973
        Outreach Programs 1997
        ↓ Prenatal Care 1991
        ↓ Prevention 1973
        Quality of Care 1988
        ↓ Quality of Services 1997
        ↓ Rehabilitation 1967
        Self Referral 1991
        Social Casework 1967
        ↓ Social Services 1982
        Telemedicine 2003

Health Care Utilization 1985

PN 5614   **SC** 22397
SN Processes involved in or factors affecting usage of professional or nonprofessional health services or programs. Use HEALTH CARE SEEKING BEHAVIOR for factors involved in seeking treatment.
HN Use HELP SEEKING BEHAVIOR to access references from 1978-1984.
- **UF** Assistance Seeking (Professional)
        Health Service Utilization
        Utilization (Health Care)
- **R**   Health Care Costs 1994
        ↓ Health Care Delivery 1978
        Health Care Seeking Behavior 1997

Health Care Utilization — (cont'd)
        ↓ Health Care Services 1978
        ↓ Help Seeking Behavior 1978
        Self Referral 1991

Health Complaints 1997

PN 245   **SC** 22402
- **R** ↓ Disorders 1967
        ↓ Health 1973
        Symptom Checklists 1991
        ↓ Symptoms 1967

Health Education 1973

PN 4342   **SC** 22400
SN Instruction or programs in school, institutional, or community settings which present material about factors affecting health behavior and attitudes.
- **B**   Curriculum 1967
- **N**   Drug Education 1973
        Sex Education 1973
- **R**   AIDS Prevention 1994
        Client Education 1985
        Health Knowledge 1994
        Health Promotion 1991
        ↓ Prenatal Care 1991
        ↓ Prevention 1973
        Psychoeducation 1994

Health Impairments 2001

PN 624   **SC** 22415
HN In 2001, this term was created to replace the discontinued and deleted term HEALTH IMPAIRED. HEALTH IMPAIRED was removed from all records containing it and replaced with HEALTH IMPAIRMENTS.
- **UF** Frail
- **B**   Physical Disorders 1997
- **R**   Homebound 1988

Health Insurance 1973

PN 1010   **SC** 22420
- **B**   Insurance 1973
- **N** ↓ Employee Health Insurance 1973
        Fee for Service 1994
        Health Maintenance Organizations 1982
        Medicaid 1994
        Medicare 1988
- **R** ↓ Case Management 1991
        Diagnosis Related Groups 1988
        Health Care Costs 1994
        Health Care Policy 1994
        ↓ Hospitalization 1967
        ↓ Managed Care 1994

Health Knowledge 1994

PN 1824   **SC** 22421
SN Knowledge or understanding of illness, health, or mental health and health related issues.
- **B**   Knowledge Level 1978
- **R**   Client Education 1985
        ↓ Health 1973
        Health Attitudes 1985
        ↓ Health Behavior 1982
        ↓ Health Education 1973
        Health Promotion 1991
        Mental Illness (Attitudes Toward) 1967
        ↓ Physical Illness (Attitudes Toward) 1985
        Telemedicine 2003

Health Locus of Control
Use Health Attitudes

Health Maintenance Organizations 1982
PN 531   SC 22425
SN Organizations providing comprehensive, coordi-
nated medical services to voluntarily enrolled mem-
bers on a prepaid basis.
UF   Group Health Plans
      HMO
B   Health Insurance 1973
      Managed Care 1994
      Organizations 1967
R   Cost Containment 1991
      Fee for Service 1994
      Health Care Costs 1994
      ↓ Health Care Delivery 1978
      ↓ Health Care Services 1978
      Health Promotion 1991
      Preventive Medicine 1973

Health Personnel 1994
PN 2316   SC 57420
SN Personnel working in a medical or mental health
profession. Used for unspecified health care profes-
sionals or when both medical and mental health pro-
fessionals are discussed. Use a more specific term if
possible.
HN Consider MEDICAL PERSONNEL or MENTAL
HEALTH PERSONNEL to access references prior to
1994.
UF   Health Care Professionals
B   Professional Personnel 1978
N   ↓ Medical Personnel 1967
      ↓ Mental Health Personnel 1967
R   ↓ Counselors 1967
      Home Care Personnel 1997
      ↓ Social Workers 1973
      ↓ Therapists 1967

Health Personnel Attitudes 1985
PN 5173   SC 22426
SN Attitudes of persons working in health or medi-
cal professions.
B   Attitudes 1967
N   ↓ Therapist Attitudes 1978
R   Counselor Attitudes 1973
      Psychologist Attitudes 1991

Health Promotion 1991
PN 3128   SC 22423
SN Education or other types of interventions used
to improve and encourage both physical and mental
health.
HN Consider using HEALTH EDUCATION to
access references from 1973-1990.
R   AIDS Prevention 1994
      Cancer Screening 1997
      Client Education 1985
      Health Attitudes 1985
      ↓ Health Behavior 1982
      ↓ Health Education 1973
      Health Knowledge 1994
      Health Maintenance Organizations 1982
      ↓ Health Screening 1997
      Lifestyle Changes 1997
      ↓ Prevention 1973
      Preventive Medicine 1973
      ↓ Public Health 1988
      Public Service Announcements 2004
      ↓ Screening 1982

Health Psychology
Use   Health Care Psychology

Health Screening 1997
PN 365   SC 22431
HN Consider PHYSICAL EXAMINATION to access
references from 1988-1996.
B   Screening 1982
N   Cancer Screening 1997
      Genetic Testing 2003
      HIV Testing 1997
      Physical Examination 1988
R   Drug Usage Screening 1988
      Health Promotion 1991
      Mammography 1994
      ↓ Medical Diagnosis 1973
      Preventive Medicine 1973
      ↓ Public Health 1988

Health Service Needs 1997
PN 1061   SC 22432
UF   Mental Health Service Needs
B   Needs 1967
R   ↓ Case Management 1991
      ↓ Health Care Delivery 1978
      Health Care Seeking Behavior 1997
      ↓ Health Care Services 1978
      Intake Interview 1994
      ↓ Mental Health Services 1978
      Needs Assessment 1985

Health Service Utilization
Use   Health Care Utilization

Hearing Acuity
Use   Auditory Acuity

Hearing Aids 1973
PN 565   SC 22430
B   Medical Therapeutic Devices 1973
N   Cochlear Implants 1994

Hearing Disorders 1982
PN 2849   SC 22435
SN Disorders involving the hearing mechanisms,
specifically the sensorineural pathways.
HN The term AURALLY HANDICAPPED was also
used to represent this concept from 1973-1996, and
AURALLY DISABLED was used from 1997-2000. In
2000, HEARING DISORDERS replaced the discon-
tinued and deleted term AURALLY DISABLED.
AURALLY DISABLED and AURALLY HANDI-
CAPPED were removed from all records containing
them and replaced with HEARING DISORDERS.
UF   Aurally Handicapped
      Sensorineural Hearing Loss
B   Communication Disorders 1982
N   ↓ Deaf 1967
R   Cochlear Implants 1994
      ↓ Ear Disorders 1973

Hearing Impaired (Partially)
Use   Partially Hearing Impaired

Hearing Measures
Use   Speech and Hearing Measures

Heart 1967
PN 525   SC 22460
B   Cardiovascular System 1967
N   Heart Auricles 1973
      Heart Valves 1973

Heart — (cont'd)
      Heart Ventricles 1973
      Myocardium 1973
R   ↓ Blood 1967
      Vagus Nerve 1973

Heart Attacks
Use   Heart Disorders

Heart Auricles 1973
PN 12   SC 22470
UF   Atria (Heart)
      Auricles (Heart)
B   Heart 1967

Heart Beat
Use   Heart Rate

Heart Disorders 1973
PN 2386   SC 22480
UF   Cardiac Arrest
      Cardiac Disorders
      Coronary Heart Disease
      Heart Attacks
B   Cardiovascular Disorders 1967
N   Angina Pectoris 1973
      ↓ Arrhythmias (Heart) 1973
      Coronary Thromboses 1973
      Myocardial Infarctions 1973
R   Rheumatic Fever 1973
      Williams Syndrome 2003

Heart Rate 1967
PN 6625   SC 22490
UF   Cardiac Rate
      Heart Beat
      Heartbeat
R   Cardiovascular Reactivity 1994

Heart Rate Affecting Drugs 1973
PN 73   SC 22500
B   Drugs 1967
N   Caffeine 1973
      Epinephrine 1967
      Theophylline 1973
      Verapamil 1991
R   ↓ Analeptic Drugs 1973
      ↓ Antihypertensive Drugs 1973
      ↓ Cardiovascular Disorders 1967
      ↓ CNS Affecting Drugs 1973
      ↓ CNS Stimulating Drugs 1973
      Dopamine 1973
      ↓ Muscle Relaxing Drugs 1973
      ↓ Vasoconstrictor Drugs 1973
      ↓ Vasodilator Drugs 1973

Heart Surgery 1973
PN 648   SC 22510
UF   Cardiac Surgery
B   Surgery 1971
R   Organ Transplantation 1973

Heart Transplants
Use   Organ Transplantation

Heart Valves 1973
PN 50   SC 22530
UF   Valves (Heart)
B   Heart 1967

Heart Ventricles 1973
PN 59   **SC** 22540
  UF   Ventricles (Heart)
  B   Heart 1967

Heartbeat
  Use   Heart Rate

Heat Effects 1973
PN 673   **SC** 22560
  B   Temperature Effects 1967

Hebephrenic Schizophrenia
  Use   Schizophrenia (Disorganized Type)

Hedonism 1973
PN 139   **SC** 22580
  R   ↓ Attitudes 1967
      ↓ Philosophies 1967

Heels (Anatomy)
  Use   Feet (Anatomy)

Height (Body)
  Use   Body Height

Helicopters 1973
PN 75   **SC** 22610
  B   Aircraft 1973

Helium 1973
PN 29   **SC** 22620

Help Seeking Behavior 1978
PN 1887   **SC** 22624
SN   Searching for or requesting help from others
through formal or informal mechanisms.
HN   From 1978-1004 used primarily for the seeking
or utilization of professional care or services. From
1997, use HEALTH CARE SEEKING BEHAVIOR to
access references on help seeking in a treatment
context.
  B   Social Behavior 1967
  N   Health Care Seeking Behavior 1997
  R   ↓ Assistance (Social Behavior) 1973
      Health Care Utilization 1985
      Self Referral 1991

Helping Behavior
  Use   Assistance (Social Behavior)

Helplessness 1997
PN 143   **SC** 22627
  B   Emotional States 1973
  N   Learned Helplessness 1978
  R   Coping Behavior 1967
      Empowerment 1991
      Hopelessness 1988
      Internal External Locus of Control 1967
      ↓ Power 1967
      Self Control 1973
      Self Determination 1994
      Self Efficacy 1985

Helplessness (Learned)
  Use   Learned Helplessness

Hematologic Disorders
  Use   Blood and Lymphatic Disorders

Hematoma 1973
PN 71   **SC** 22640
  B   Hemorrhage 1973
      Symptoms 1967
  R   ↓ Injuries 1973

Hemianopia 1973
PN 160   **SC** 22650
  UF   Hemiopia
  B   Eye Disorders 1973
  R   ↓ Nervous System Disorders 1967

Hemiopia
  Use   Hemianopia

Hemiplegia 1978
PN 310   **SC** 22675
SN   Paralysis of one side of the body resulting from
disease or injury to the brain or spinal cord.
  B   Paralysis 1973
  R   ↓ Central Nervous System Disorders 1973
      ↓ Injuries 1973
      ↓ Musculoskeletal Disorders 1973
      Paraplegia 1978
      Quadriplegia 1985
      ↓ Spinal Cord Injuries 1973

Hemispherectomy 1973
PN 131   **SC** 22680
  B   Neurosurgery 1973

Hemispheric Specialization
  Use   Lateral Dominance

Hemodialysis 1973
PN 550   **SC** 22690
  B   Dialysis 1973
  R   Blood Transfusion 1973

Hemoglobin 1973
PN 113   **SC** 22700
  B   Blood Proteins 1973
      Pigments 1973

Hemophilia 1973
PN 245   **SC** 22710
  B   Blood and Lymphatic Disorders 1973
      Sex Linked Hereditary Disorders 1973

Hemorrhage 1973
PN 80   **SC** 22720
  B   Cardiovascular Disorders 1967
      Symptoms 1967
  N   Cerebral Hemorrhage 1973
      Hematoma 1973

Hemp (Cannabis)
  Use   Cannabis

Henmon Nelson Tests of Mental Ability
  Use   Intelligence Measures

Heparin 1973
PN 22   **SC** 22750

Heparin — (cont'd)
  B   Acids 1973
      Anticoagulant Drugs 1973

Hepatic Disorders
  Use   Liver Disorders

Hepatitis 1973
PN 356   **SC** 22770
  B   Liver Disorders 1973
  N   Toxic Hepatitis 1973
  R   ↓ Infectious Disorders 1973
      Jaundice 1973

Hereditary Disorders
  Use   Genetic Disorders

Heredity
  Use   Genetics

Hermaphroditism 1973
PN 120   **SC** 22800
  UF   Intersexuality
      Pseudohermaphroditism
  B   Congenital Disorders 1973
      Genital Disorders 1967
  R   ↓ Endocrine Sexual Disorders 1973
      ↓ Gender Identity Disorder 1997
      ↓ Gynecological Disorders 1973
      ↓ Male Genital Disorders 1973
      Sterility 1973
      Testicular Feminization Syndrome 1973

Hermeneutics 1991
PN 471   **SC** 22805
SN   Theory and method of interpreting meaning.
Originally, the term referred to interpretation of the
scriptures.
  B   Philosophies 1967
  R   Epistemology 1973
      Metaphysics 1973
      Phenomenology 1967
      Positivism (Philosophy) 1997
      Rhetoric 1991
      ↓ Semiotics 1985

Heroin 1973
PN 900   **SC** 22810
  UF   Diacetylmorphine
  B   Alkaloids 1973
      Analgesic Drugs 1973
      Opiates 1973
      Sedatives 1973
  R   Heroin Addiction 1973

Heroin Addiction 1973
PN 1521   **SC** 22820
  B   Drug Addiction 1967
  R   Heroin 1973
      Methadone Maintenance 1978

Herpes Genitalis 1988
PN 80   **SC** 22825
  UF   Genital Herpes
  B   Sexually Transmitted Diseases 2003
      Viral Disorders 1973

Herpes Simplex 1973
PN 271   **SC** 22830

Herpes Simplex — (cont'd)
- **B** Skin Disorders 1973
  Viral Disorders 1973

Heterogeneity of Variance
- **Use** Homogeneity of Variance

Heterosexism
- **Use** Homosexuality (Attitudes Toward)

Heterosexual Interaction
- **Use** Male Female Relations

Heterosexuality 1973
PN 1578   SC 22840
- **B** Psychosexual Behavior 1967
  Sexual Orientation 1997
- **R** Lesbianism 1973
  Male Female Relations 1988
  Male Homosexuality 1973
  Sex Linked Developmental Differences 1973
  Sexual Development 1973

Heterozygotic Twins 1973
PN 824   SC 22850
- **UF** Dizygotic Twins
  Fraternal Twins
- **B** Twins 1967

Heuristic Modeling 1973
PN 491   SC 22860
- **B** Simulation 1967
- **R** Heuristics 2003
  ↓ Mathematical Modeling 1973

Heuristics 2003
PN 137   SC 22862
- **SN** Informal techniques for problem solving based on simple rules or prior experience.
- **HN** This term was introduced in June 2003. PsycINFO records from the past 10 years were re-indexed with this term. The posting note reflects the number of records that were re-indexed.
- **B** Problem Solving 1967
- **R** Algorithms 1973
  Cognitive Hypothesis Testing 1982
  ↓ Decision Making 1967
  Declarative Knowledge 1997
  ↓ Expert Systems 1991
  Heuristic Modeling 1973
  ↓ Inductive Deductive Reasoning 1973
  ↓ Reasoning 1967
  ↓ Strategies 1967

Hexamethonium 1973
PN 32   SC 22870
- **B** Antihypertensive Drugs 1973
  Ganglion Blocking Drugs 1973

Hexobarbital 1973
PN 30   SC 22880
- **B** Anesthetic Drugs 1973
  Barbiturates 1967
  Hypnotic Drugs 1973
  Sedatives 1973

Hibernation 1973
PN 85   SC 22890
- **B** Animal Ethology 1967
- **R** ↓ Animal Biological Rhythms 1973

High Risk Populations
- **Use** At Risk Populations

High School Education 2003
PN 90   SC 22921
- **SN** Education for grades 9 through 12.
- **HN** This term was introduced in June 2003. PsycINFO records from the past 10 years were re-indexed with this term. The posting note reflects the number of records that were re-indexed.
- **B** Education 1967
- **R** High Schools 1973
  Secondary Education 1973

High School Equivalency
- **Use** Adult Education

High School Graduates 1978
PN 319   SC 22924
- **R** Educational Degrees 1973
  High School Students 1967
  School Graduation 1991
  School to Work Transition 1994

High School Personality Questionnaire 2001
PN 32   SC 22927
- **HN** In 2000, the truncated term HIGH SCH PERSONALITY QUESTIONNAIRE (which was used from 1973-2000) was deleted, removed from all records containing it, and replaced with its expanded form HIGH SCHOOL PERSONALITY QUESTIONNAIRE.
- **B** Nonprojective Personality Measures 1973

High School Students 1967
PN 19245   SC 22930
- **SN** Students in grades 9-12.
- **B** Students 1967
- **R** Grade Level 1994
  High School Graduates 1978
  Reentry Students 1985

High School Teachers 1973
PN 2668   SC 22940
- **B** Teachers 1967

High Schools 1973
PN 1005   SC 22950
- **B** Schools 1967
- **R** High School Education 2003
  Military Schools 1973
  Secondary Education 1973

Higher Education 1973
PN 1827   SC 22960
- **SN** College or university education beyond the successful completion of high school or grammar school, or the attainment of an approved equivalent.
- **B** Education 1967
- **N** ↓ Graduate Education 1973
  ↓ Postgraduate Training 1973
  Undergraduate Education 1978
- **R** ↓ Colleges 1967
  ↓ Continuing Education 1985
  Educational Degrees 1973
  Educational Program Accreditation 1994
  Graduate Schools 1973
  Professional Specialization 1991
  School Graduation 1991

Higher Order Conditioning 1997
PN 24   SC 22970
- **SN** A classical conditioning method in which the original conditioned stimulus is used as the unconditioned stimulus in a new experimental setting.
- **UF** Second Order Conditioning
- **B** Classical Conditioning 1967

Highway Safety 1973
PN 981   SC 22980
- **UF** Automobile Safety
  Driver Safety
- **B** Safety 1967
- **R** Aggressive Driving Behavior 2004
  Drivers 1973
  ↓ Driving Behavior 1967
  Driving Under the Influence 1988
  ↓ Ground Transportation 1973
  Motor Traffic Accidents 1973
  ↓ Transportation Accidents 1973

Hindbrain 1997
PN 22   SC 22985
- **UF** Rhombencephalon
- **B** Brain 1967
- **N** ↓ Cerebellum 1973
  Medulla Oblongata 1973
  ↓ Pons 1973
- **R** ↓ Brain Stem 1973
  Raphe Nuclei 1982

Hinduism 1973
PN 327   SC 22990
- **B** Religious Affiliation 1973
- **R** Hindus 1997

Hindus 1997
PN 51   SC 22995
- **B** Religious Groups 1997
- **R** Hinduism 1973

Hippies
- **Use** Subculture (Anthropological)

Hippocampal Commissure
- **Use** Fornix

Hippocampus 1967
PN 7510   SC 23010
- **B** Limbic System 1973
- **R** Medial Forebrain Bundle 1982
  Septal Nuclei 1982

Hips 1973
PN 179   SC 23020
- **B** Musculoskeletal System 1973

Hiring
- **Use** Personnel Selection

Hispanics 1982
PN 7023   SC 23035
- **UF** Cuban Americans
  Latinos/Latinas
  Puerto Rican Americans
  Spanish Americans
- **B** Racial and Ethnic Groups 2001
- **N** Mexican Americans 1973
- **R** Minority Groups 1967

Histamine 1973

PN 292   SC 23050
- **B**   Amines 1973
-     Neurotransmitters 1985
- **R** ↓ Antihistaminic Drugs 1973
-     Histidine 1973

Histidine 1973

PN 38   SC 23060
- **B**   Amino Acids 1973
- **R**   Histamine 1973

Histology 1973

PN 172   SC 23070
SN Branch of anatomy dealing with the structure of cells, tissues, and organs in relation to their functions. Used for the scientific discipline or the organic structure itself.
- **R**   Morphology 1973
-    ↓ Physiology 1967
-    ↓ Tissues (Body) 1973

History 1973

PN 10230   SC 23075
SN Recording and/or explanation of previous events, experiences, trends, and treatments.
- **N** ↓ History of Psychology 1967
- **R**   Future 1991
-     Psychohistory 1978
-     Trends 1991

History of Psychology 1967

PN 8269   SC 23080
- **B**   History 1973
- **N**   Associationism 1973
-     Behaviorism 1967
-     Freudian Psychoanalytic School 1973
-     Functionalism 1973
-     Gestalt Psychology 1967
-    ↓ Neopsychoanalytic School 1973
-     Structuralism 1973
- **R**   Phenomenology 1967
-    ↓ Psychological Theories 2001
-    ↓ Psychology 1967
-    ↓ Theories 1967

Histrionic Personality Disorder 1991

PN 294   SC 23082
SN Personality disorder characterized by emotional instability, excitability, overreaction, self-dramatization, self-centeredness, and over-dependence on others.
HN In 2000, this term replaced the discontinued term HYSTERICAL PERSONALITY. HYSTERICAL PERSONALITY was removed from all records containing it, and replaced with HISTRIONIC PERSONALITY DISORDER.
- **UF** Hysterical Personality
- **B**   Personality Disorders 1967
- **R** ↓ Conversion Disorder 2001
-    ↓ Hysteria 1967

HIV

Use Human Immunodeficiency Virus

HIV Testing 1997

PN 279   SC 23084
- **UF** AIDS Testing
- **B**   Health Screening 1997
-     Medical Diagnosis 1973
- **R**   Acquired Immune Deficiency Syndrome 1988
-     AIDS Prevention 1994
-    ↓ Human Immunodeficiency Virus 1991

HMO

Use Health Maintenance Organizations

Hoarding Behavior 2003

PN 39   SC 23089
SN Accumulating and storing things for a possible future need. Often considered a compulsive behavior.
HN This term was introduced in June 2003. PsycINFO records from the past 10 years were re-indexed with this term. The posting note reflects the number of records that were re-indexed.
- **B**   Behavior 1967
- **N**   Animal Hoarding Behavior 1973
- **R** ↓ Compulsions 1973
-     Obsessive Compulsive Disorder 1985

Hoarding Behavior (Animal)

Use Animal Hoarding Behavior

Hobbies 1988

PN 54   SC 23100
HN Use RECREATION to access references from 1973-1988.
- **R**   Daily Activities 1994
-    ↓ Interests 1967
-     Leisure Time 1973
-    ↓ Recreation 1967

Hoffmanns Reflex 1973

PN 49   SC 23110
SN Flexing of the thumb and some other finger resulting from a sudden tapping of the nail of the index, middle, or ring finger. Also known as digital reflex, finger flexion reflex, snapping reflex, H reflex, or Hoffmann's (H) response.
- **B**   Reflexes 1971

Holidays 1988

PN 84   SC 23113
SN Days marked by general suspension of work in commemoration or celebration of an event.
- **R**   Leisure Time 1973
-    ↓ Recreation 1967
-     Tourism 2003
-     Vacationing 1973

Holistic Health 1985

PN 668   SC 23115
SN Personal practices or medical or psychological diagnosis and treatment based on the concept that humans are composed of body, mind, and spirit. An observed disorder or dysfunction in one component implies the need for treatment of the whole organism to restore health.
- **UF** Wholistic Health
- **B**   Health 1973
- **R** ↓ Alternative Medicine 1997
-     Biopsychosocial Approach 1991
-    ↓ Health Behavior 1982
-    ↓ Lifestyle 1978
-     Meditation 1973
-    ↓ Physical Treatment Methods 1973
-     Preventive Medicine 1973
-    ↓ Psychotherapy 1967

Holocaust 1988

PN 463   SC 23117
SN Nazi persecution and genocide of Jews and others in Europe between 1933 and 1945.
- **B**   Genocide 1988
- **R**   AntiSemitism 1973

Holocaust — (cont'd)

-     Concentration Camps 1973
-     Fascism 1973
-     Holocaust Survivors 1988
-     Jews 1997
-     Judaism 1967

Holocaust Survivors 1988

PN 559   SC 23118
- **B**   Survivors 1994
- **R**   Holocaust 1988
-     Jews 1997

Holtzman Inkblot Technique 1967

PN 145   SC 23120
- **B**   Projective Personality Measures 1973
-     Projective Techniques 1967

Homatropine

Use Alkaloids

Home Accidents 1973

PN 61   SC 23140
- **B**   Accidents 1967

Home Birth

Use Midwifery

Home Care 1985

PN 1762   SC 23145
SN Health and personal care provided in the home environment, usually by family members.
- **B**   Health Care Delivery 1978
- **R**   Adult Day Care 1997
-     Caregiver Burden 1994
-     Caregivers 1988
-     Elder Care 1994
-     Home Care Personnel 1997
-     Home Visiting Programs 1973
-     Homebound 1988
-     Hospice 1982
-     Long Term Care 1994
-    ↓ Outpatient Treatment 1967
-     Quality of Care 1988
-     Respite Care 1988

Home Care Personnel 1997

PN 83   SC 23146
SN Personnel providing personal care, nursing services, medical treatment, or followup care to patients in their homes.
- **UF** Home Health Aides
- **B**   Paraprofessional Personnel 1973
- **R**   Caregivers 1988
-     Elder Care 1994
-    ↓ Health Personnel 1994
-     Home Care 1985
-     Home Visiting Programs 1973
-    ↓ Paramedical Personnel 1973

Home Economics 1985

PN 66   SC 23147
- **B**   Curriculum 1967
- **R**   Household Management 1985

Home Environment 1973

PN 4867   SC 23150
- **UF** Family Environment
- **B**   Social Environments 1973
- **R**   Empty Nest 1991
-    ↓ Environmental Effects 1973

Home Environment — (cont'd)
↓ Family Conflict 2003
   Learning Environment 2004
   Living Alone 1994
↓ Living Arrangements 1991
↓ Single Sex Environments 2001

Home Health Aides
Use Home Care Personnel

Home Reared Mentally Retarded 1973
PN 50   **SC** 23160
B Mental Retardation 1967
R Institutionalized Mentally Retarded 1973

Home Schooling 1994
PN 55   **SC** 23165
SN Provision of compulsory education in the home.
B Nontraditional Education 1982
R ↓ Curriculum 1967
   ↓ Education 1967
   ↓ Teaching Methods 1967

Home Visiting Programs 1973
PN 709   **SC** 23170
SN Planned educational, health, or counseling procedures or activities that take place in the home.
B Community Services 1967
   Mental Health Programs 1973
R Adult Day Care 1997
   Elder Care 1994
   Home Care 1985
   Home Care Personnel 1997
   Homebound 1988
   ↓ Program Development 1991

Homebound 1988
PN 50   **SC** 23173
SN Individuals restricted to place of residence for health or disability reasons.
R Caregiver Burden 1994
   Elder Care 1994
   Health Impairments 2001
   Home Care 1985
   Home Visiting Programs 1973

Homeless 1988
PN 2276   **SC** 23174
B Social Issues 1991
N Homeless Mentally Ill 1997
R Deinstitutionalization 1982
   Disadvantaged 1967
   Poverty 1973
   Shelters 1991
   ↓ Social Deprivation 1973

Homeless Mentally Ill 1997
PN 292   **SC** 23171
UF Mentally Ill Homeless
B Homeless 1988
R Deinstitutionalization 1982
   ↓ Mental Disorders 1967
   Psychopathology 1967

Homemakers 2003
PN 429   **SC** 23176
HN In June 2003, this term was created to replace the discontinued term HOUSEWIVES. HOUSEWIVES was removed from all records containing it and replaced with HOMEMAKERS.
UF Housewives
R Household Management 1985

Homemaking
Use Household Management

Homeopathic Medicine
Use Alternative Medicine

Homeostasis 1973
PN 404   **SC** 23180
SN Tendency of an organism to maintain a state of physiological equilibrium and the processes by which such a stable internal environment is maintained.
UF Autoregulation
B Physiology 1967
R Dehydration 1988
   Instinctive Behavior 1982

Homesickness 1994
PN 47   **SC** 23183
B Emotional States 1973
R ↓ Experiences (Events) 1973
   ↓ Life Experiences 1973
   Loneliness 1973
   Reminiscence 1985
   Sadness 1973
   ↓ Separation Reactions 1997

Homework 1988
PN 339   **SC** 23185
SN Assignment given to students or clients to be completed outside regular classroom period or therapeutic setting.
R Note Taking 1991
   ↓ Psychotherapeutic Techniques 1967
   Study Habits 1973

Homicide 1967
PN 2519   **SC** 23190
UF Murder
B Behavior Disorders 1971
   Violent Crime 2003
N ↓ Genocide 1988
   Infanticide 1978
   Serial Homicide 2003

Homing (Animal)
Use Animal Homing

Homogeneity of Variance 2003
PN 130   **SC** 23198
SN Extent to which the variance in two or more statistical samples is similar or different.
HN In June 2003, this term was created to replace the discontinued term VARIANCE HOMOGENEITY. VARIANCE HOMOGENEITY was removed from all records containing it and replaced with HOMOGENEITY of VARIANCE.
UF Heterogeneity of Variance
   Variance Homogeneity
B Statistical Measurement 1973
R Analysis of Variance 1967
   Standard Deviation 1973

Homographs 1973
PN 100   **SC** 23200
SN Words identical in spelling but different in derivation, pronunciation, and meaning.
B Vocabulary 1967
R Homonyms 1973
   Orthography 1973
   Words (Phonetic Units) 1967

Homonyms 1973
PN 96   **SC** 23210
B Semantics 1967
   Vocabulary 1967
R Homographs 1973
   Words (Phonetic Units) 1967

Homophobia
Use Homosexuality (Attitudes Toward)

Homosexual Liberation Movement 1973
PN 63   **SC** 23220
UF Gay Liberation Movement
B Social Movements 1967
R ↓ Activism 2003

Homosexual Parents 1994
PN 184   **SC** 23225
UF Gay Parents
   Lesbian Parents
B Parents 1967
R ↓ Family Structure 1973
   Lesbianism 1973
   Male Homosexuality 1973
   Significant Others 1991

Homosexuality 1967
PN 2864   **SC** 23230
B Psychosexual Behavior 1967
   Sexual Orientation 1997
N Lesbianism 1973
   Male Homosexuality 1973
R Homosexuality (Attitudes Toward) 1982
   Transsexualism 1973
   Transvestism 1973

Homosexuality (Attitudes Toward) 1982
PN 1717   **SC** 23233
SN Attitudes regarding sexual contact between persons of the same sex.
UF Heterosexism
   Homophobia
B Attitudes 1967
R ↓ Homosexuality 1967
   ↓ Sexual Orientation 1997
   Stereotyped Attitudes 1967

Homovanillic Acid 1978
PN 646   **SC** 23235
SN Excretion product of dopamine metabolism.
B Acids 1973
   Dopamine Metabolites 1982
R Dopamine 1973

Honesty 1973
PN 433   **SC** 23240
UF Frankness
B Personality Traits 1967
R Integrity 1997

Hope 1991
PN 550   **SC** 23247
B Emotional States 1973
R ↓ Expectations 1967
   Hopelessness 1988
   Optimism 1973
   Positivism 1973
   Trust (Social Behavior) 1967

Hopelessness 1988
PN 764   **SC** 23250

Hopelessness — (cont'd)
SN Feeling that one's physical, emotional, or social
state is beyond improvement.
B   Emotional States 1973
R   Apathy 1973
     Cynicism 1973
     ↓ Helplessness 1997
     Hope 1991
     Pessimism 1973

Hormone Therapy 1994
PN 589   SC 23255
UF   Estrogen Replacement Therapy
B   Drug Therapy 1967
R   ↓ Hormones 1967

Hormones 1967
PN 3250   SC 23260
N   ↓ Adrenal Cortex Hormones 1973
     ↓ Adrenal Medulla Hormones 1973
     Cholecystokinin 1982
     Corticotropin Releasing Factor 1994
     Epinephrine 1967
     Glucagon 1973
     ↓ Gonadotropic Hormones 1973
     Insulin 1973
     Leptin 2004
     Melatonin 1973
     Parathyroid Hormone 1973
     ↓ Pituitary Hormones 1973
     ↓ Progestational Hormones 1985
     ↓ Sex Hormones 1973
     ↓ Thyroid Hormones 1973
R   ↓ Anti Inflammatory Drugs 1982
     Antineoplastic Drugs 1982
     ↓ Drugs 1967
     ↓ Endocrine Glands 1973
     Fertility Enhancement 1979
     Hormone Therapy 1994
     Pheromones 1973
     Prostaglandins 1982
     ↓ Steroids 1973

Horses 1973
PN 308   SC 23270
B   Mammals 1973

Hospice 1982
PN 805   SC 23275
SN Supportive palliative care of terminally ill
patients, usually in their own home, by a treatment
team and family members; sometimes involves resi-
dential care.
B   Health Care Delivery 1978
R   Home Care 1985
     Palliative Care 1991
     Terminally Ill Patients 1973

Hospital Accreditation 1973
PN 19   SC 23280
SN Recognition of a hospital as maintaining stan-
dards set by a government agency.
R   ↓ Hospitals 1967

Hospital Addiction Syndrome
Use Munchausen Syndrome

Hospital Administration 1978
PN 346   SC 23286
B   Health Care Administration 1997
R   Decentralization 1978

Hospital Administration — (cont'd)
     ↓ Hospitals 1967
     ↓ Medical Records 1978

Hospital Admission 1973
PN 583   SC 23290
UF   Admission (Hospital)
     Readmission (Hospital)
B   Facility Admission 1988
     Hospitalization 1967
N   ↓ Psychiatric Hospital Admission 1973
R   Health Care Seeking Behavior 1997
     ↓ Hospital Discharge 1973
     ↓ Institutional Release 1978
     ↓ Psychiatric Hospitalization 1973

Hospital Attendants
Use Attendants (Institutions)

Hospital Discharge 1973
PN 605   SC 23303
B   Facility Discharge 1988
     Hospitalization 1967
     Institutional Release 1978
N   Psychiatric Hospital Discharge 1978
R   Client Transfer 1997
     Discharge Planning 1994
     ↓ Hospital Admission 1973
     ↓ Psychiatric Hospital Admission 1973
     Psychiatric Hospital Readmission 1973
     ↓ Psychiatric Hospitalization 1973
     Treatment Termination 1982

Hospital Environment 1982
PN 990   SC 23304
SN Physical, organizational, or psychological char-
acteristics of a hospital, and their potential impact on
hospital staff and patients.
B   Facility Environment 1988
R   ↓ Hospitals 1967
     Intensive Care 1988

Hospital Programs 1978
PN 1588   SC 23306
SN Organized plans for care, including psychiatric
treatment, or training in general medical hospital set-
tings.
N   ↓ Psychiatric Hospital Programs 1967
R   Intensive Care 1988
     Partial Hospitalization 1985
     ↓ Program Development 1991
     Psychiatric Units 1991

Hospital Psychiatric Units
Use Psychiatric Units

Hospital Staff
Use Medical Personnel

Hospitalization 1967
PN 2031   SC 23320
B   Institutionalization 1967
N   ↓ Commitment (Psychiatric) 1973
     ↓ Hospital Admission 1973
     ↓ Hospital Discharge 1973
     ↓ Psychiatric Hospitalization 1973
R   ↓ Health Insurance 1973
     Long Term Care 1994
     Patient Seclusion 1994
     Psychiatric Units 1991

Hospitalized Patients 1973
PN 6357   SC 23330
B   Patients 1967

Hospitals 1967
PN 2326   SC 23340
UF   Infirmaries
B   Residential Care Institutions 1973
     Treatment Facilities 1973
N   Psychiatric Hospitals 1967
     Sanatoriums 1973
R   ↓ Clinics 1967
     Hospital Accreditation 1973
     Hospital Administration 1978
     Hospital Environment 1982
     Intensive Care 1988
     Maximum Security Facilities 1985
     Nursing Homes 1973
     Psychiatric Clinics 1973
     Psychiatric Units 1991

Hostages 1988
PN 96   SC 23347
HN Use CRIME VICTIMS to access references
from 1982-1987.
B   Crime Victims 1982
R   Kidnapping 1988
     Prisoners of War 1973
     Terrorism 1982

Hostility 1967
PN 2721   SC 23350
UF   Antagonism
     Resentment
B   Anger 1967
R   Hate 1973
     Retaliation 1991

Hot Line Services 1973
PN 499   SC 23360
SN Telephone information, counseling, and crisis
intervention services.
UF   Telephone Hot Lines
B   Crisis Intervention Services 1973
     Mental Health Programs 1973
R   Community Mental Health Centers 1973
     Information Services 1988
     Suicide Prevention Centers 1973

Household Management 1985
PN 758   SC 23365
SN Activities carried out for the regular mainte-
nance of home and personal belongings.
UF   Homemaking
     Housework
B   Management 1967
R   ↓ Division of Labor 1988
     ↓ Family Life Education 1997
     Home Economics 1985
     Homemakers 2003

Household Structure
Use Living Arrangements

Housewives
Use Homemakers

Housework
Use Household Management

Housing 1973
PN 1528   **SC** 23380
B   Community Facilities 1973
N   Assisted Living 2003
         Dormitories 1973
         Group Homes 1982
         Retirement Communities 1997
         Shelters 1991
R ↓ Living Arrangements 1991
       ↓ Social Programs 1973

Hue 1973
PN 320   **SC** 23390
SN One of the perceived dimensions of color corresponding to the wavelength of the light. Compare COLOR.
B   Chromaticity 1997
         Color 1967
R   Color Saturation 1997

Human Animal Interaction
Use Interspecies Interaction

Human Biological Rhythms 1973
PN 2644   **SC** 23400
SN Periodic variations in human physiological and psychological functions.
HN Use BIOLOGICAL RHYTHMS to access references from 1967-1972.
UF   Circadian Rhythms (Human)
         Diurnal Variations
B   Biological Rhythms 1967

Human Body 2003
PN 77   **SC** 23402
SN The body as an artistic, cultural, sociological, or physical concept.
HN This term was introduced in June 2003. PsycINFO records from the past 10 years were re-indexed with this term. The posting note reflects the number of records that were re-indexed.
R ↓ Anatomy 1967
         Body Awareness 1982
       ↓ Body Image 1967
         Physique 1967
         Soul 2004

Human Capital 2003
PN 45   **SC** 23405
SN Investment of resources including, time, money, education, and training to increase productivity and profits.
HN This term was introduced in June 2003. PsycINFO records from the past 10 years were re-indexed with this term. The posting note reflects the number of records that were re-indexed.
R ↓ Economics 1985
       ↓ Personnel Supply 1973
         Resource Allocation 1997
         Social Capital 2004

Human Channel Capacity 1973
PN 1579   **SC** 23410
SN Number of signals or information volume which can be processed simultaneously.
UF   Cognitive Load
         Mental Load
R ↓ Attention 1967
         Cognitive Processing Speed 1997
         Human Information Storage 1973
         Work Load 1982

Human Computer Interaction 1997
PN 1625   **SC** 23415
UF   Human Computer Interface
R   Computer Mediated Communication 2003
       ↓ Computer Peripheral Devices 1985
       ↓ Computers 1967
         Human Factors Engineering 1973
         Human Machine Systems 1997
         Human Machine Systems Design 1997
         Keyboards 1985

Human Computer Interface
Use Human Computer Interaction

Human Courtship 1973
PN 310   **SC** 23420
UF   Courtship (Human)
B   Psychosexual Behavior 1967
N   Social Dating 1973
R   Acquaintance Rape 1991
         Human Mate Selection 1988
         Male Female Relations 1988
         Monogamy 1997
       ↓ Relationship Termination 1997
         Romance 1997

Human Development 1967
PN 3959   **SC** 23430
SN Conceptually broad term. Use a more specific term if possible.
UF   Maturation
B   Development 1967
N   Adolescent Development 1973
         Adult Development 1978
       ↓ Childhood Development 1967
R   Age Differences 1967
       ↓ Aging 1991
       ↓ Delayed Development 1973
         Developmental Age Groups 1973
         Developmental Disabilities 1982
       ↓ Developmental Psychology 1973
       ↓ Developmental Stages 1973
         Life Expectancy 1982
         Nature Nurture 1994
       ↓ Physical Development 1973
       ↓ Psychogenesis 1973

Human Factors Engineering 1973
PN 2737   **SC** 23440
UF   Ergonomics
         Usability (Systems)
R   Computer Assisted Design 1997
         Engineering Psychology 1967
         Furniture 1985
         Human Computer Interaction 1997
         Human Machine Systems 1997
       ↓ Instrument Controls 1985
         Quality Control 1988
       ↓ Working Conditions 1973

Human Females 1973
PN 35877   **SC** 23450
SN Used for all-female populations when sex is pertinent to the focus of the study. For comparison of sexes use HUMAN SEX DIFFERENCES.
UF   Females (Human)
         Girls
         Women
N   Battered Females 1988
         Daughters 1973
         Female Criminals 1973
       ↓ Mothers 1967
         Sisters 1973

Human Females — (cont'd)
         Widows 1973
         Wives 1973
         Working Women 1978
R   Female Delinquency 2001
       ↓ Human Sex Differences 1967
         Sex Linked Developmental Differences 1973

Human Figures Drawing 1973
PN 687   **SC** 23460
SN Projective measures or techniques designed to yield information from drawings of human figures and responses to questions about the drawings.
UF   Draw A Man Test
B   Projective Personality Measures 1973
R   Goodenough Harris Draw A Person Test 1967
         Mirror Image 1991

Human Genome
Use Genome

Human Immunodeficiency Virus 1991
PN 9115   **SC** 23465
UF   HIV
B   Immunologic Disorders 1973
         Sexually Transmitted Diseases 2003
         Viral Disorders 1973
N   Acquired Immune Deficiency Syndrome 1988
R   AIDS (Attitudes Toward) 1997
         AIDS Dementia Complex 1997
         AIDS Prevention 1994
         HIV Testing 1997
         Safe Sex 2003
         Zidovudine 1994

Human Information Processes
Use Cognitive Processes

Human Information Storage 1973
PN 8453   **SC** 23480
SN Process of information perception, encoding, or storage, and retrieval of material from memory.
UF   Decoding
         Encoding
         Information Storage (Human)
R ↓ Cognitive Processes 1967
         Human Channel Capacity 1973
         Information 1967
       ↓ Lexical Access 1988
         Lexical Decision 1988
       ↓ Memory 1967
         Word Recognition 1988

Human Machine Systems 1997
PN 1954   **SC** 23485
SN Systems based on the human engineering concept that views human operators and the machines they operate as functionally integrated parts of a larger goal-oriented system.
HN In 1997, this term was created to replace the discontinued term MAN MACHINE SYSTEMS. In 2000, MAN MACHINE SYSTEMS was removed from all records containing it, and replaced with HUMAN MACHINE SYSTEMS.
UF   Man Machine Systems
B   Systems 1967
R ↓ Artificial Intelligence 1982
       ↓ Computer Peripheral Devices 1985
         Computer Searching 1991
         Cybernetics 1967
         Databases 1991
         Error Analysis 1973

Human Machine Systems — (cont'd)

  ↓ Expert Systems   1991
  Human Computer Interaction   1997
  Human Factors Engineering   1973
  Human Machine Systems Design   1997
  Systems Analysis   1973
  Virtual Reality   1997

Human Machine Systems Design   1997

PN   2266   **SC**   23487
HN   In 1997, this term was created to replace the discontinued term MAN MACHINE SYSTEMS DESIGN. In 2000, MAN MACHINE SYSTEMS DESIGN was removed from all records containing it, and replaced with HUMAN MACHINE SYSTEMS DESIGN.

UF   Design (Man Machine Systems)
      Man Machine Systems Design
B   Systems Design   2003
R   Computer Assisted Design   1997
      Human Computer Interaction   1997
      Human Machine Systems   1997
      ↓ Instrument Controls   1985
      ↓ Systems   1967
      Systems Analysis   1973

Human Males   1973

PN   12193   **SC**   23490
SN   Used for all-male populations when sex is pertinent to the focus of the study. For comparison of sexes use HUMAN SEX DIFFERENCES.

UF   Boys
      Males (Human)
      Men
N   Brothers   1973
      ↓ Fathers   1967
      Husbands   1973
      Male Criminals   1973
      Sons   1970
      Widowers   1973
R   ↓ Human Sex Differences   1967
      Male Delinquency   2001
      Sex Linked Developmental Differences   1973

Human Mate Selection   1988

PN   540   **SC**   23495
UF   Mate Selection
R   Assortative Mating   1991
      Choice Behavior   1967
      ↓ Human Courtship   1973
      ↓ Interpersonal Attraction   1967
      Interpersonal Compatibility   1973
      ↓ Psychosexual Behavior   1967
      Romance   1997

Human Migration   1973

PN   1409   **SC**   23500
SN   Movement of residence from one place to another. Includes nomadism; labor or seasonal migration; patterns of rural, urban, or suburban migration; or voluntary or forced relocation.

UF   Migration (Human)
      Population Shifts
B   Social Processes   1967
N   Refugees   1988
R   Geographical Mobility   1978
      Gypsies   1973
      Immigration   1973
      Migrant Farm Workers   1973

Human Nature   1997

PN   265   **SC**   23502
R   ↓ Behavior   1967

Human Nature — (cont'd)

  ↓ Emotions   1967
  Instinctive Behavior   1982
  Mind   1991
  ↓ Personality   1967

Human Potential Movement   1982

PN   235   **SC**   23504
SN   Movement aimed at the enhancement of personal psychological growth. Formats used include Gestalt therapy, sensory awakening, sensory awareness, meditation, encounter groups, transactional analysis, assertiveness training, and humanistic psychology.

UF   Growth Centers
      Personal Growth Techniques
N   Assertiveness Training   1978
      Consciousness Raising Groups   1978
      ↓ Encounter Group Therapy   1973
      Gestalt Therapy   1973
      Human Relations Training   1978
      Sensitivity Training   1973
      Transactional Analysis   1973
R   ↓ Group Psychotherapy   1967
      Humanism   1973
      ↓ Humanistic Psychology   1985
      Maslow (Abraham Harold)   1991
      Meditation   1973
      Self Actualization   1973

Human Relations Training   1978

PN   499   **SC**   23506
SN   Techniques aimed at promoting awareness of feelings and needs of others in order to facilitate positive interpersonal interactions.

UF   T Groups
B   Human Potential Movement   1982
R   Assertiveness Training   1978
      Communication Skills Training   1982
      ↓ Encounter Group Therapy   1973
      ↓ Group Dynamics   1967
      Marathon Group Therapy   1973
      Parent Training   1978
      ↓ Personnel Training   1967
      Sensitivity Training   1973
      Social Skills Training   1982

Human Resource Management   2003

PN   2138   **SC**   58070
HN   In June 2003, this term was created to replace the discontinued term PERSONNEL MANAGEMENT. PERSONNEL MANAGEMENT was removed from all records containing it and replaced with HUMAN RESOURCE MANAGEMENT.

UF   Human Resources
      Personnel Management
N   Career Development   1985
      Job Analysis   1967
      Labor Management Relations   1967
      ↓ Personnel Evaluation   1973
      ↓ Personnel Recruitment   1973
      ↓ Personnel Selection   1967
      Personnel Termination   1973
R   Affirmative Action   1985
      Business Education   1973
      Business Management   1973
      Employment Discrimination   1994
      ↓ Personnel   1967
      Supervisor Employee Interaction   1997
      Supported Employment   1994

Human Resources

Use   Human Resource Management

Human Rights   1978

PN   757   **SC**   23508
SN   Fundamental rights of every human being to life, freedom, and equality. Often used for freedom from arbitrary governmental interference.

B   Social Issues   1991
N   ↓ Civil Rights   1978
R   ↓ Client Rights   1988
      Social Equality   1973
      ↓ Social Movements   1967
      ↓ Social Processes   1967
      Treatment Withholding   1988

Human Sex Differences   1967

PN   54740   **SC**   23510
UF   Gender Differences
      Sex Differences (Human)
N   Sex Linked Developmental Differences   1973
R   Androgyny   1982
      Diversity in the Workplace   2003
      ↓ Human Females   1973
      ↓ Human Males   1973
      Sex   1967
      Sex Recognition   1997
      ↓ Single Sex Environments   2001

Humanism   1973

PN   771   **SC**   23520
SN   Philosophy that asserts commitment to the use of reason and observation to serve human need and interest.

B   Philosophies   1967
R   ↓ Human Potential Movement   1982
      ↓ Humanistic Psychology   1985
      ↓ Humanistic Psychotherapy   2003

Humanistic Education

Use   Affective Education

Humanistic Psychology   1985

PN   717   **SC**   23527
SN   School of psychology emphasizing a holistic approach including self-actualization, creativity, and free choice.

B   Psychology   1967
N   Transpersonal Psychology   1988
R   Client Centered Therapy   1967
      ↓ Human Potential Movement   1982
      Humanism   1973
      ↓ Humanistic Psychotherapy   2003
      Maslow (Abraham Harold)   1991
      Neurolinguistic Programming   2001
      Rogers (Carl)   1991
      Self Psychology   1988

Humanistic Psychotherapy   2003

PN   24   **SC**   23528
SN   Approach to psychotherapy based on humanistic philosophy that focuses on the client as a whole and recognizes the individual's capacity for self-healing.

HN   This term was introduced in June 2003. PsycINFO records from the past 10 years were re-indexed with this term. The posting note reflects the number of records that were re-indexed.

B   Psychotherapy   1967
N   Client Centered Therapy   1967
R   Existential Therapy   1973
      Gestalt Therapy   1973
      Humanism   1973
      ↓ Humanistic Psychology   1985
      Rogers (Carl)   1991

Humanities 2003
PN 24   SC 23535
SN Branches of learning such as literature, art, and philosophy that are concerned with human thought and culture.
HN This term was introduced in June 2003. Psyc-INFO records from the past 10 years were re-indexed with this term. The posting note reflects the number of records that were re-indexed.
  N ↓ Arts 1973
    ↓ Literature 1967
    ↓ Philosophies 1967
     Theology 2003

Humor 1967
PN 1940   SC 23540
  N Cartoons (Humor) 1973
    Jokes 1973
  R Laughter 1978

Hunger 1967
PN 586   SC 23560
SN Need or desire for food. May also be defined operationally in experimental settings as the duration of food deprivation or the organism's percentage of normal body weight following food deprivation. Compare APPETITE.
  B Appetite 1973
    Motivation 1967
  R Animal Feeding Behavior 1973
    Food Deprivation 1967
    Starvation 1973

Huntingtons Chorea
  Use Huntingtons Disease

Huntingtons Disease 1973
PN 954   SC 23570
HN In 1997, this term replaced the discontinued term HUNTINGTONS CHOREA. In 2000, HUNTINGTONS CHOREA was removed from all records containing it, and replaced with HUNTINGTONS DISEASE.
  UF Huntingtons Chorea
  B Chorea 1973
    Genetic Disorders 1973

Husbands 1973
PN 1466   SC 23590
  B Human Males 1973
    Spouses 1973

Hybrids (Biology) 1973
PN 109   SC 23600
  R ↓ Genetics 1967

Hydralazine 1973
PN 10   SC 23620
  B Antihypertensive Drugs 1973
    Sympatholytic Drugs 1973

Hydrocephaly 1973
PN 318   SC 23630
  B Brain Disorders 1967
  R ↓ Congenital Disorders 1973
    ↓ Convulsions 1967
    ↓ Infectious Disorders 1973
    ↓ Mental Retardation 1967
    ↓ Neonatal Disorders 1973

Hydrocortisone 1973
PN 2775   SC 23640
  UF Cortisol
  B Adrenal Cortex Hormones 1973
    Corticosteroids 1973
  R ↓ Anti Inflammatory Drugs 1982

Hydrogen 1973
PN 16   SC 23650

Hydroxydopamine (6-) 1978
PN 662   SC 23656
  UF Oxidopamine
  B Adrenergic Blocking Drugs 1973

Hydroxyindoleacetic Acid (5-) 1985
PN 469   SC 23658
SN Major metabolic product of serotonin.
  B Acids 1973
    Serotonin Metabolites 1978

Hydroxylase Inhibitors 1985
PN 30   SC 23665
  B Enzyme Inhibitors 1985
  R Hydroxylases 1973

Hydroxylases 1973
PN 333   SC 23670
  B Enzymes 1973
  R ↓ Esterases 1973
    Hydroxylase Inhibitors 1985
    Phosphatases 1973

Hydroxytryptamine (5-)
  Use Serotonin

Hydroxytryptophan (5-) 1991
PN 107   SC 23685
  B Tryptophan 1973

Hydroxyzine 1973
PN 29   SC 23690
  B Minor Tranquilizers 1973
  R ↓ Antihistaminic Drugs 1973

Hygiene 1994
PN 105   SC 23700
HN Use HEALTH to access references from 1973-1993.
  R Activities of Daily Living 1991
    Epidemics 2001
    ↓ Health 1973
    ↓ Health Behavior 1982
    Self Care Skills 1978

Hyoscine
  Use Scopolamine

Hyoscyamine (dl-)
  Use Atropine

Hyperactivity
  Use Hyperkinesis

Hyperalgesia
  Use Somatosensory Disorders

Hypercholesterolemia
  Use Metabolism Disorders

Hyperesthesia
  Use Somatosensory Disorders

Hyperglycemia 1985
PN 101   SC 23745
  B Metabolism Disorders 1973
    Symptoms 1967

Hypericum Perforatum 2003
PN 113   SC 23747
HN This term was introduced in June 2003. Psyc-INFO records from the past 10 years were re-indexed with this term. The posting note reflects the number of records that were re-indexed.
  UF Saint John's Wort
    St. John's Wort
  B Medicinal Herbs and Plants 2001

Hyperkinesis 1973
PN 5817   SC 23760
SN Excessive and usually inappropriate motor activity accompanied by poor attention span and restlessness. Consider also ATTENTION DEFICIT DISORDER.
  UF Hyperactivity
  B Nervous System Disorders 1967
    Symptoms 1967
  R Ataxia 1973
    Attention Deficit Disorder with Hyperactivity 2001
    Bradykinesia 2001
    Minimal Brain Disorders 1973
    ↓ Neuromuscular Disorders 1973
    Oppositional Defiant Disorder 1997
    Restlessness 1973

Hypermedia 1997
PN 245   SC 23780
SN Computerized multimedia that contain images, video clips, and sounds in addition to or instead of text, and include highlighted elements that, when selected by the user, instruct the computer program to retrieve one or more of the computerized media.
  B Computer Applications 1973
  R ↓ Computer Software 1967
    Hypertext 1997

Hyperparathyroidism
  Use Parathyroid Disorders

Hyperphagia 1973
PN 328   SC 23800
  UF Polyphagia
  B Eating Disorders 1997
    Symptoms 1967
  R Kleine Levin Syndrome 2001
    Obesity 1973
    ↓ Somatoform Disorders 2001

Hypersensitivity (Immunologic)
  Use Immunologic Disorders

Hypersexuality 1973
PN 99   SC 23820
  UF Nymphomania
  B Psychosexual Behavior 1967
  R Erotomania 1997

Hypersexuality — (cont'd)
Promiscuity 1973
Sex Drive 1973
Sexual Addiction 1997

Hypersomnia 1994
PN 58   SC 23825
SN Excessive sleepiness.
B   Sleep Disorders 1973
R   Fatigue 1967
Kleine Levin Syndrome 2001
Narcolepsy 1973
↓ Symptoms 1967

Hypertension 1973
PN 2316   SC 23830
B   Blood Pressure Disorders 1973
Cardiovascular Disorders 1967
N   Essential Hypertension 1973
R   ↓ Antihypertensive Drugs 1973
↓ Cerebrovascular Disorders 1973

Hypertext 1997
PN 144   SC 23835
SN Computer-readable text that contains high-lighted words or phrases that, when selected by the user, instruct the computer program to retrieve one or more similar documents.
B   Computer Applications 1973
R   ↓ Computer Software 1967
Hypermedia 1997

Hyperthermia 1973
PN 333   SC 23840
UF Fever
B   Symptoms 1967
R   Delirium 1973
Thermoregulation (Body) 1973

Hyperthyroidism 1973
PN 150   SC 23850
B   Thyroid Disorders 1973
R   Goiters 1973
Tachycardia 1973
Thyrotoxicosis 1973
↓ Underweight 1973

Hyperventilation 1973
PN 320   SC 23860
B   Respiratory Distress 1973
Respiratory Tract Disorders 1973
Symptoms 1967
R   ↓ Somatoform Disorders 2001

Hypesthesia
Use Somatosensory Disorders

Hypnagogic Hallucinations 1973
PN 42   SC 23870
SN False sensory perceptions without actual appropriate stimuli, occurring while falling asleep.
B   Hallucinations 1967
R   ↓ Sleep Disorders 1973

Hypnoanalysis
Use Hypnotherapy

Hypnosis 1967
PN 3973   SC 23890

Hypnosis — (cont'd)
SN Trance-like state induced by effective suggestion and characterized by increased suggestibility to the hypnotist. For hypnosis used in treatment, use HYPNOTHERAPY.
B   Consciousness Disturbances 1973
N   Age Regression (Hypnotic) 1988
Autohypnosis 1973
R   False Memory 1997
↓ Hypnotherapy 1973
Posthypnotic Suggestions 1994

Hypnotherapists 1973
PN 49   SC 23900
SN Persons conducting treatment by means of hypnosis.
B   Hypnotists 1973
Psychotherapists 1973
R   Clinical Psychologists 1973
Psychiatrists 1967
Psychoanalysts 1973

Hypnotherapy 1973
PN 2936   SC 23910
SN Use of hypnosis in treatment.
UF Hypnoanalysis
B   Psychotherapy 1967
N   Age Regression (Hypnotic) 1988
R   ↓ Alternative Medicine 1997
False Memory 1997
Guided Imagery 2001
↓ Hypnosis 1967
Posthypnotic Suggestions 1994
Progressive Relaxation Therapy 1978
↓ Psychoanalysis 1967
↓ Relaxation Therapy 1978

Hypnotic Drugs 1973
PN 835   SC 23920
HN In 1973, this term replaced the discontinued term CHLORALOSE. In 2000, CHLORALOSE was removed from all records containing it, and replaced with HYPNOTIC DRUGS.
UF Chloralose
Sleep Inducing Drugs
B   Drugs 1967
N   Amobarbital 1973
Apomorphine 1973
Barbital 1973
Chloral Hydrate 1973
Codeine 1973
Flurazepam 1982
Glutethimide 1973
Hexobarbital 1973
Meprobamate 1973
Methaqualone 1973
Nitrazepam 1978
Pentobarbital 1973
Phenobarbital 1973
Secobarbital 1973
Thalidomide 1973
Thiopental 1973
Triazolam 1988
R   ↓ Analgesic Drugs 1973
↓ Anesthetic Drugs 1973
↓ Anticonvulsive Drugs 1973
↓ Antiemetic Drugs 1973
↓ Antihistaminic Drugs 1973
↓ Antihypertensive Drugs 1973
↓ Barbiturates 1967
↓ Benzodiazepines 1978
↓ CNS Depressant Drugs 1973
↓ Narcotic Drugs 1973
↓ Sedatives 1973

Hypnotic Susceptibility 1973
PN 1604   SC 23930
SN Personal characteristic or state of being receptive to hypnosis.
UF Susceptibility (Hypnotic)
B   Personality Traits 1967
R   Openness to Experience 1997
Posthypnotic Suggestions 1994

Hypnotists 1973
PN 32   SC 23940
SN Persons conducting scientific experiments by means of hypnosis.
B   Personnel 1967
N   Hypnotherapists 1973

Hypoactive Sexual Desire Disorder
Use Inhibited Sexual Desire

Hypochondriasis 1973
PN 691   SC 23950
B   Somatoform Disorders 2001
R   ↓ Anxiety Disorders 1997
↓ Conversion Disorder 2001
Somatization 1994
Somatoform Pain Disorder 1997

Hypogastric Plexus
Use Autonomic Ganglia

Hypoglossal Nerve
Use Cranial Nerves

Hypoglycemia 1973
PN 204   SC 23980
B   Metabolism Disorders 1973
Symptoms 1967

Hypogonadism 1973
PN 62   SC 24000
B   Endocrine Sexual Disorders 1973
N   Klinefelters Syndrome 1973
Turners Syndrome 1973
R   ↓ Gynecological Disorders 1973
Hypopituitarism 1973
↓ Male Genital Disorders 1973
Sterility 1973

Hypokinesia
Use Bradykinesia

Hypomania 1973
PN 283   SC 24010
SN Mild form of mania.
B   Mania 1967
R   Cyclothymic Personality 1973

Hyponatremia 1997
PN 74   SC 24015
SN Abnormally low blood sodium level.
B   Metabolism Disorders 1973
R   Polydipsia 1982
↓ Sodium 1973
↓ Toxic Disorders 1973

Hypoparathyroidism
Use Parathyroid Disorders

Hypophysectomy 1973
PN 121   SC 24030
UF   Pituitary Gland Surgery
B   Endocrine Gland Surgery   1973

Hypophysis Disorders
  Use   Pituitary Disorders

Hypopituitarism 1973
PN 73   SC 24050
UF   Dwarfism (Pituitary)
      Pituitary Dwarfism
B   Pituitary Disorders   1973
R   ↓ Genetic Disorders   1973
    ↓ Hypogonadism   1973

Hypotension 1973
PN 142   SC 24060
B   Blood Pressure Disorders   1973

Hypothalamo Hypophyseal System 1973
PN 419   SC 24070
B   Hypothalamus   1967
      Pituitary Gland   1973
R   Hypothalamo Pituitary Adrenal System   1997
   ↓ Pituitary Hormones   1973

**Hypothalamo Pituitary Adrenal
    System** 1997
PN 667   SC 24075
B   Adrenal Glands   1973
      Hypothalamus   1967
      Pituitary Gland   1973
R   Hypothalamo Hypophyseal System   1973

Hypothalamus 1967
PN 4718   SC 24080
UF   Mammillary Bodies (Hypothalamic)
B   Diencephalon   1973
N   Hypothalamo Hypophyseal System   1973
      Hypothalamo Pituitary Adrenal System   1997
      Preoptic Area   1994
R   Medial Forebrain Bundle   1982

Hypothalamus Lesions 1973
PN 908   SC 24090
HN   Not defined prior to 1982. From 1982, limited to experimentally induced lesions and used primarily for animal populations.
B   Brain Lesions   1967

Hypothermia 1973
PN 500   SC 24100
B   Symptoms   1967
R   ↓ Body Temperature   1973
   ↓ Central Nervous System Disorders   1973
   ↓ Endocrine Disorders   1973
      Thermoregulation (Body)   1973

Hypothesis Testing 1973
PN 1092   SC 24110
SN   Application of statistical tests to determine whether a research hypothesis should be accepted or rejected.
HN   From 1982, limited to discussions of statistical procedures. Use HYPOTHESIS TESTING or other appropriate terms to access references to COGNITIVE HYPOTHESIS TESTING prior to 1982.
B   Experimental Design   1967
N   Null Hypothesis Testing   1973
R   Confidence Limits (Statistics)   1973

Hypothesis Testing — (cont'd)
      Predictability (Measurement)   1973
   ↓ Prediction Errors   1973
   ↓ Probability   1967
   ↓ Statistical Analysis   1967
      Statistical Power   1991
      Statistical Significance   1973
   ↓ Theories   1967
      Theory Formulation   1973
      Theory Verification   1973

Hypothesis Testing (Cognitive)
  Use   Cognitive Hypothesis Testing

Hypothyroidism 1973
PN 279   SC 24120
UF   Myxedema
B   Thyroid Disorders   1973
R   Goiters   1973
   ↓ Infertility   1973
   ↓ Metabolism Disorders   1973
      Thyrotropin   1973
      Thyroxine   1973

Hypoxia
  Use   Anoxia

Hysterectomy 1973
PN 248   SC 24150
B   Sterilization (Sex)   1973
      Surgery   1971
R   Ovariectomy   1973

Hysteria 1967
PN 1024   SC 24160
B   Mental Disorders   1967
N   Mass Hysteria   1973
R   Catalepsy   1973
   ↓ Conversion Disorder   2001
      Histrionic Personality Disorder   1991
      Suggestibility   1967

Hysterical Blindness
  Use   Hysterical Vision Disturbances

Hysterical Neurosis (Conversion)
  Use   Conversion Disorder

Hysterical Neurosis (Dissociation)
  Use   Dissociative Disorders

Hysterical Paralysis 1973
PN 27   SC 24220
UF   Paralysis (Hysterical)
B   Conversion Disorder   2001

Hysterical Personality
  Use   Histrionic Personality Disorder

Hysterical Vision Disturbances 1973
PN 25   SC 24240
UF   Hysterical Blindness
      Vision Disturbances (Hysterical)
B   Conversion Disorder   2001
R   ↓ Eye Disorders   1973

Iatrogenic Effects
  Use   Side Effects (Treatment)

Ibotenic Acid 1991
PN 83   SC 24245
B   Insecticides   1973
      Neurotoxins   1982
N   Muscimol   1994

ICD
  Use   International Classification of Diseases

Iconic Memory 1985
PN 96   SC 24248
SN   Brief sensory memory, usually lasting only fractions of a second.
B   Short Term Memory   1967

Id 1973
PN 85   SC 24250
B   Psychoanalytic Personality Factors   1973
R   Unconscious (Personality Factor)   1967

Ideal Self
  Use   Self Concept

Idealism 1973
PN 176   SC 24260
B   Philosophies   1967
R   Determinism   1997

Ideation 1973
PN 376   SC 24270
SN   Process of idea or image formation.
B   Cognitive Processes   1967
N   Imagination   1967
      Suicidal Ideation   1991
R   ↓ Fantasy   1997

Identical Twins
  Use   Monozygotic Twins

Identification (Defense Mechanism) 1973
PN 868   SC 24290
B   Defense Mechanisms   1967
R   Introjection   1973
      Projective Identification   1994

Identity (Personal)
  Use   Self Concept

Identity (Professional)
  Use   Professional Identity

Identity Crisis 1973
PN 335   SC 24320
B   Crises   1971
      Emotional Adjustment   1973
R   ↓ Personality Development   1967
   ↓ Self Concept   1967
   ↓ Stress   1967

Identity Formation 2004
PN 128   SC 24322
SN   The process of developing one's identity based on early influences and experiences.
HN   This term was introduced in June 2004. PsycINFO records from the past 10 years were re-indexed with this term. The posting note reflects the number of records that were re-indexed.
R   Ego Identity   1991

Identity Formation — (cont'd)
    Ethnic Identity   1973
    ↓ Personality Development   1967
    ↓ Self Concept   1967
    ↓ Social Identity   1988

Idiot Savants
    Use   Savants

Ileum
    Use   Intestines

Illegitimate Children   1973
PN   52   **SC**   24380
    B   Family Members   1973

Illinois Test of Psycholinguistic Abilities   2001
PN   171   **SC**   24391
HN   In 2000, the truncated term ILLINOIS TEST PSYCHOLINGUIST ABIL (which was used from 1973-2000) was deleted, removed from all records containing it, and replaced with its expanded form ILLINOIS TEST OF PSYCHOLINGUISTIC ABILITIES.
    B   Intelligence Measures   1967

Illiteracy
    Use   Literacy

Illness (Physical)
    Use   Physical Disorders

Illness Behavior   1982
PN   1737   **SC**   24415
SN   Adaptive or nonadaptive behaviors exhibited by an individual during the course of an illness or dysfunction.
    B   Behavior   1967
           Client Characteristics   1973
    R   Anosognosia   1994
           Coping Behavior   1967
           Coronary Prone Behavior   1982
           ↓ Disorders   1967
           ↓ Physical Disorders   1997
           ↓ Physical Illness (Attitudes Toward)   1985
           Recovery (Disorders)   1973
           Somatization   1994
           ↓ Somatoform Disorders   2001
           Treatment Compliance   1982

Illumination   1967
PN   4852   **SC**   24420
SN   Visible portion of the electromagnetic radiation spectrum but may include ultraviolet and infrared light. May also refer more generally to ambient light. Compare LUMINANCE.
    UF   Light
           Photic Threshold
    B   Visual Stimulation   1973
    N   Photopic Stimulation   1973
           Scotopic Stimulation   1973
    R   ↓ Brightness Perception   1973
           Light Adaptation   1982
           ↓ Light Refraction   1982
           Luminance   1982

Illumination Therapy
    Use   Phototherapy

Illusion (Autokinetic)
    Use   Autokinetic Illusion

Illusions (Perception)   1967
PN   3112   **SC**   24440
SN   Misperception or alteration of reality in subjective perception.
    UF   Optical Illusions
    B   Perception   1967
    N   Mueller Lyer Illusion   1988
           ↓ Perceptual Aftereffect   1967
           Spatial Distortion   1973
    R   ↓ Perceptual Distortion   1982
           ↓ Perceptual Disturbances   1973

Image (Retinal)
    Use   Retinal Image

Imagery   1967
PN   7147   **SC**   24470
    UF   Visualization
    B   Abstraction   1967
    N   Conceptual Imagery   1973
           Spatial Imagery   1982
    R   Archetypes   1991
           Guided Imagery   2001
           Imagination   1967

Imagery (Conceptual)
    Use   Conceptual Imagery

Imagination   1967
PN   2426   **SC**   24490
SN   Process of forming mental images of objects, qualities, situations, or relationships, which are not immediately apparent to the senses.
    B   Cognitive Processes   1967
           Ideation   1973
    R   Conceptual Imagery   1973
           ↓ Fantasy   1997
           ↓ Imagery   1967
           Magical Thinking   1973
           Vicarious Experiences   1973

Imaginativeness
    Use   Openness to Experience

Imipramine   1973
PN   2009   **SC**   24520
    UF   Tofranil
    B   Amines   1973
           Tricyclic Antidepressant Drugs   1997

Imitation (Learning)   1967
PN   3932   **SC**   24530
SN   Imitation by human or animal subjects to learn a model's behavior or responses.
    UF   Modeling Behavior
    B   Social Learning   1973
    R   Observational Learning   1973
           Role Models   1982

Immaturity (Emotional)
    Use   Emotional Immaturity

Immersion Programs
    Use   Foreign Language Education

Immigrants
    Use   Immigration

Immigration   1973
PN   3840   **SC**   24560
SN   Permanent resettlement in a country other than the country of one's origin.
    UF   Immigrants
    B   Social Processes   1967
    R   Citizenship   1973
           ↓ Foreign Nationals   1985
           ↓ Human Migration   1973
           Refugees   1988

Immunization   1973
PN   412   **SC**   24570
    UF   Vaccination
    B   Physical Treatment Methods   1973
    R   Antibodies   1973

Immunogens
    Use   Antigens

Immunoglobulins   1973
PN   300   **SC**   24580
    B   Blood Proteins   1973
           Globulins   1973
           Immunologic Factors   2003
    N   Gamma Globulin   1973
    R   Antibodies   1973
           Antigens   1982
           ↓ Immunologic Disorders   1973
           Immunoreactivity   1994
           Interferons   1994

Immunologic Disorders   1973
PN   571   **SC**   24590
    UF   Autoimmune Disorders
           Hypersensitivity (Immunologic)
    B   Physical Disorders   1997
    N   ↓ Allergic Disorders   1973
           Anaphylactic Shock   1973
           ↓ Human Immunodeficiency Virus   1991
           Rh Incompatibility   1973
    R   Asthma   1967
           ↓ Immunoglobulins   1973

Immunologic Factors   2003
PN   33   **SC**   24594
SN   Substances that affect the functioning of the immune system.
HN   This term was introduced in June 2003. PsycINFO records from the past 10 years were re-indexed with this term. The posting note reflects the number of records that were re-indexed.
    N   Antibodies   1973
           Antigens   1982
           ↓ Cytokines   2003
           ↓ Immunoglobulins   1973
    R   ↓ Immunology   1973
           Immunoreactivity   1994

Immunology   1973
PN   2273   **SC**   24600
SN   Medical science dealing with the study of immunity. Used for the scientific discipline or the immunological processes themselves.
    UF   Immunopathology
    B   Medical Sciences   1967
    N   Psychoneuroimmunology   1991
    R   ↓ Immunologic Factors   2003
           Immunoreactivity   1994

Immunopathology
Use Immunology

Immunoreactivity 1994
PN 1230 **SC** 24613
HN Use IMMUNOLOGY to access references from 1973-1993.
R ↓ Immunoglobulins 1973
↓ Immunologic Factors 2003
↓ Immunology 1973
Interleukins 1994

Impaired Professionals 1985
PN 304 **SC** 24615
SN Professional personnel who are physically or psychologically disordered to the extent that such disorders interfere with the performance of professional duties or conflict with professional standards. Does not include handicaps that do not interfere with professional performance.
R Disabled Personnel 1997
↓ Medical Personnel 1967
↓ Mental Health Personnel 1967
Personal Therapy 1991
Professional Ethics 1973
Professional Liability 1985
↓ Professional Personnel 1978
↓ Professional Standards 1973

Implicit Learning 2004
PN 129 **SC** 24617
SN Learning that occurs without awareness of how the knowledge or skills were acquired. Not to be confused with INCIDENTAL LEARNING.
HN This term was introduced in June 2004. PsycINFO records from the past 10 years were re-indexed with this term. The posting note reflects the number of records that were re-indexed.
B Learning 1967
R Implicit Memory 2003

Implicit Memory 2003
PN 275 **SC** 24618
SN Memory of events without specific awareness of learning or experiencing the event.
HN This term was introduced in June 2003. PsycINFO records from the past 10 years were re-indexed with this term. The posting note reflects the number of records that were re-indexed.
B Memory 1967
R Explicit Memory 1997
Implicit Learning 2004

Implosive Therapy 1973
PN 384 **SC** 24620
SN Behavioral therapy involving flooding the client with anxiety through intense or prolonged real-life or imagined exposure to feared objects or situations, thereby demonstrating that they cause no harm. The aim is gradual extinction of anxiety or phobic responses.
UF Flooding Therapy
B Behavior Therapy 1967
Exposure Therapy 1997

Impotence 1973
PN 545 **SC** 24630
B Sexual Function Disturbances 1973
R Erection (Penis) 1973
Frigidity 1973
↓ Male Orgasm 1973
↓ Orgasm 1973
Premature Ejaculation 1973

Impression Formation 1978
PN 1585 **SC** 24634
SN Process by which an individual transforms various perceptions and observations about another person or group into an overall impression or set of attitudes toward or about that person or group.
B Social Perception 1967
R ↓ Attitudes 1967
Attribution 1973
Impression Management 1978

Impression Management 1978
PN 920 **SC** 24636
SN Techniques of image cultivation or impression formation designed to obtain good evaluations of one's self and to win approval from others. Used for both individuals and groups.
UF Ingratiation
R Impression Formation 1978
Self Monitoring (Personality) 1985
↓ Social Behavior 1967
↓ Social Perception 1967
Uncertainty 1991

Imprinting 1967
PN 481 **SC** 24640
SN Rapid learning process that takes place during early critical periods of development. Establishes the basis for patterns of social behavior. Used for both human and animal populations.
B Animal Ethology 1967
Social Learning 1973
R Critical Period 1988
Species Recognition 1985

Improvisation 2004
PN 92 **SC** 24642
SN Creating dialogue, movement, or music in a spontaneous, unscripted fashion. Used in clinical and nonclinical settings.
HN This term was introduced in June 2004. PsycINFO records from the past 10 years were re-indexed with this term. The posting note reflects the number of records that were re-indexed.
R ↓ Creative Arts Therapy 1994
Creativity 1967
Dance 1973
Drama 1973
Expressive Psychotherapy 1973
Psychodrama 1967
↓ Psychotherapeutic Techniques 1967

Impulse Control Disorders 1997
PN 122 **SC** 24645
SN Mental disorders characterized by an intense need to gratify one's immediate desires and failure to resist the impulse or temptation.
B Mental Disorders 1967
N Explosive Disorder 2001
R ↓ Antisocial Behavior 1971
Conduct Disorder 1991
Delay of Gratification 1978
Impulsiveness 1973
Kleptomania 1973
↓ Paraphilias 1988
Pathological Gambling 1988
Pyromania 1973
Self Control 1973

Impulsiveness 1973
PN 2526 **SC** 24650
B Cognitive Style 1967
R ↓ Attention Deficit Disorder 1985

Impulsiveness — (cont'd)
Attention Deficit Disorder with Hyperactivity 2001
Conceptual Tempo 1985
↓ Impulse Control Disorders 1997
Kleptomania 1973
Pathological Gambling 1988
Pyromania 1973
Reflectiveness 1997

In Vitro Fertilization
Use Reproductive Technology

Inadequate Personality 1973
PN 5 **SC** 24660
SN Inadequate responses to physical, social, and emotional demands; general ineptness and instability, despite absence of actual physical or mental deficit.
B Personality 1967

Incarceration 1973
PN 1157 **SC** 24670
B Institutionalization 1967
Law Enforcement 1978
R ↓ Correctional Institutions 1973
Institution Visitation 1973
↓ Institutional Release 1978

Incentives 1967
PN 1297 **SC** 24680
SN Events or objects which increase or induce drives or determination. Popularly described as one's expectation of reward. May be used for human or animal populations. Compare REWARDS and REINFORCEMENT.
B Motivation 1967
N Educational Incentives 1973
Monetary Incentives 1973
R ↓ Goals 1967
↓ Needs 1967
↓ Rewards 1967
Temptation 1973

Incest 1973
PN 2022 **SC** 24690
B Paraphilias 1988
Sexual Abuse 1988
Sexual Intercourse (Human) 1973
R Pedophilia 1973
↓ Perpetrators 1988
↓ Sex Offenses 1982

Incidental Learning 1967
PN 907 **SC** 24700
SN Learning that occurs unintentionally, usually as a result of some other unrelated activity. Not to be confused with IMPLICIT LEARNING. Use LATENT LEARNING for animal populations.
HN From 1982, limited to human populations.
B Learning 1967
N Latent Learning 1973

Inclusion (Educational)
Use Mainstreaming (Educational)

Income (Economic) 1973
PN 756 **SC** 24710
SN Monetary gain (such as wages, interest, dividends, profits) received by individuals or nations within a given period for labor or services rendered or from capital resources.

Income (Economic) — (cont'd)

R   Budgets 1997
↓ Income Level 1973
Poverty 1973
Salaries 1973
↓ Socioeconomic Status 1967
Taxation 1985

Income Level 1973

PN 1405   **SC** 24720
SN Total amount of monetary gain received within a given period that is associated with socioeconomic status.
B   Socioeconomic Status 1967
N   Lower Income Level 1973
Middle Income Level 1973
Upper Income Level 1973
R   Income (Economic) 1973
Salaries 1973
↓ Social Class 1967

Incompatibility (Rh)

Use Rh Incompatibility

Incontinence (Fecal)

Use Fecal Incontinence

Incontinence (Urinary)

Use Urinary Incontinence

Incorporation (Psychological)

Use Internalization

Incubators (Apparatus) 1973

PN 9   **SC** 24780
B   Apparatus 1967

Independence (Personality) 1973

PN 2369   **SC** 24790
UF Autonomy (Personality)
B   Personality Traits 1967
R   Empowerment 1991
Internal External Locus of Control 1967
↓ Resistance 1997
Self Determination 1994

Independent Living

Use Self Care Skills

Independent Living Programs 1991

PN 218   **SC** 24798
SN Community-based programs or services to assist disabled individuals performing all or most of their daily functions, thus increasing self sufficiency and self determination and eliminating a need to depend on others.
R   Activities of Daily Living 1991
Assisted Living 2003
↓ Community Services 1967
Habilitation 1991
↓ Mainstreaming 1991
↓ Program Development 1991
↓ Rehabilitation 1967
Self Care Skills 1978
Supported Employment 1994

Independent Party (Political)

Use Political Parties

Independent Study

Use Individualized Instruction

Independent Variables 1973

PN 129   **SC** 24810
SN Statistical or experimental parameters that are manipulated in an attempt to analyze their relative effect on specified dependent variables.
B   Statistical Variables 1973

Indians (American)

Use American Indians

Indifference

Use Apathy

Indigenous Populations 2001

PN 273   **SC** 24845
UF Aboriginal Populations
Maori
Natives
B   Racial and Ethnic Groups 2001
N   Alaska Natives 1997
American Indians 1967
Inuit 2001
↓ Pacific Islanders 2001
R   Minority Groups 1967

Individual Counseling

Use Individual Psychotherapy

Individual Differences 1967

PN 9465   **SC** 24860
SN Any specific characteristic or quantitative difference in a quality or trait that can serve to distinguish one individual from another. Used for both human and animal populations.
R   Diversity in the Workplace 2003
↓ Personality 1967
Personality Correlates 1967
↓ Personality Theory 1967

Individual Problem Solving

Use Problem Solving

Individual Psychology 1973

PN 1009   **SC** 24880
SN Theory and practice of Adlerian psychology, stressing the unique wholeness of the individual and viewing the striving to overcome and master obstacles as the primary motivating force.
B   Neopsychoanalytic School 1973
R   Adler (Alfred) 1967
Adlerian Psychotherapy 1997

Individual Psychotherapy 1973

PN 1801   **SC** 24890
SN Psychotherapy occurring on a one-on-one basis as compared to a group setting or environment. Use ADLERIAN PSYCHOTHERAPY to access references on Adlerian individual psychotherapy.
UF Individual Counseling
Individual Therapy
Psychotherapy (Individual)
B   Psychotherapy 1967

Individual Psychotherapy (Adlerian)

Use Adlerian Psychotherapy

Individual Testing 1973

PN 104   **SC** 24900
B   Measurement 1967
R   Test Administration 1973

Individual Therapy

Use Individual Psychotherapy

Individualism

Use Individuality

Individuality 1973

PN 1552   **SC** 24930
UF Individualism
B   Personality Traits 1967
R   Nonconformity (Personality) 1973
Self Determination 1994

Individualized Instruction 1973

PN 2141   **SC** 24940
SN Instruction adapted to individual needs or instruction in which a student works alone or only with a teacher. Also, self-initiated study with or without formal academic guidance or involvement.
UF Independent Study
Instruction (Individualized)
Self Directed Learning
Self Instruction
B   Teaching Methods 1967
R   ↓ Computer Assisted Instruction 1973
↓ Continuing Education 1985
Cooperative Learning 1994
Distance Education 2003
↓ Learning 1967
Open Classroom Method 1970
Programmed Instruction 2001
Self Regulated Learning 2003
↓ Tutoring 1973

Induced Abortion 1971

PN 1302   **SC** 24950
UF Abortion (Induced)
Elective Abortion
Therapeutic Abortion
B   Surgery 1971
R   Abortion Laws 1973
↓ Birth Control 1971
↓ Family Planning 1973
Spontaneous Abortion 1971

Inductive Deductive Reasoning 1973

PN 1528   **SC** 24960
UF Convergent Thinking
Deductive Reasoning
Syllogistic Reasoning
B   Reasoning 1967
N   Inference 1973
R   Case Based Reasoning 2003
Divergent Thinking 1973
Heuristics 2003
Logical Thinking 1967
↓ Problem Solving 1967

Industrial Accidents 1973

PN 597   **SC** 24970
B   Accidents 1967
R   Occupational Exposure 1988
Occupational Safety 1973
Work Related Illnesses 1994

Industrial and Organizational Psychology 2003

PN 1840   SC 25012

HN In June 2003, this term was created to replace the discontinued term INDUSTRIAL PSYCHOLOGY. INDUSTRIAL PSYCHOLOGY was removed from all records and replaced with INDUSTRIAL and ORGANIZATIONAL PSYCHOLOGY.

UF   Industrial Psychology
     Organizational Psychology
B   Applied Psychology 1973

Industrial Arts Education

Use Vocational Education

Industrial Foremen 1973

PN 60   SC 24980

UF   Foremen (Industrial)
B   Blue Collar Workers 1973
R   ↓ Management Personnel 1973

Industrial Personnel

Use Business and Industrial Personnel

Industrial Psychologists 1973

PN 125   SC 25000

B   Business and Industrial Personnel 1967
     Psychologists 1967
R   Social Psychologists 1973

Industrial Psychology

Use Industrial and Organizational Psychology

Industrial Safety

Use Occupational Safety

Industrialization 1973

PN 454   SC 25030

B   Social Processes 1967
R   Modernization 2003
     ↓ Technology 1973
     Urbanization 1973

Industry

Use Business

Infant Development 1973

PN 5225   SC 25060

B   Early Childhood Development 1973
N   Neonatal Development 1973
R   ↓ Physical Development 1973
     ↓ Psychogenesis 1973

Infant Vocalization 1973

PN 676   SC 25080

UF   Babbling
     Vocalization (Infant)
B   Voice 1973
R   Crying 1973

Infanticide 1978

PN 402   SC 25085

UF   Neonaticide
B   Homicide 1967

Infantile Neurosis

Use Childhood Neurosis

Infantile Paralysis

Use Poliomyelitis

Infantile Psychosis

Use Childhood Psychosis

Infantilism 1973

PN 24   SC 25120

R   ↓ Mental Disorders 1967

Infants (Animal) 1978

PN 5659   SC 25134

UF   Neonates (Animal)
B   Animals 1967

Infarctions (Myocardial)

Use Myocardial Infarctions

Infections

Use Infectious Disorders

Infectious Disorders 1973

PN 622   SC 25160

UF   Communicable Diseases
     Infections
     Neuroinfections
B   Physical Disorders 1997
N   ↓ Bacterial Disorders 1973
     Epstein Barr Viral Disorder 1994
     ↓ Parasitic Disorders 1973
     ↓ Sexually Transmitted Diseases 2003
     ↓ Viral Disorders 1973
R   ↓ Arthritis 1973
     ↓ Chorea 1973
     ↓ Dermatitis 1973
     ↓ Digestive System Disorders 1973
     Disease Transmission 2004
     Encephalitis 1973
     Encephalomyelitis 1973
     Epidemics 2001
     ↓ Hepatitis 1973
     Hydrocephaly 1973
     Jaundice 1973
     ↓ Liver Disorders 1973
     ↓ Myelitis 1973

Inference 1973

PN 2872   SC 25180

B   Inductive Deductive Reasoning 1973
R   Analogy 1991
     Attribution 1973

Inferior Colliculus 1973

PN 277   SC 25190

B   Mesencephalon 1973

Inferiority (Emotional)

Use Emotional Inferiority

Infertility 1973

PN 825   SC 25210

B   Genital Disorders 1967
N   Sterility 1973
R   ↓ Endocrine Sexual Disorders 1973
     Fertility 1988
     ↓ Gynecological Disorders 1973
     Hypothyroidism 1973
     Klinefelters Syndrome 1973
     ↓ Male Genital Disorders 1973

Infirmaries

Use Hospitals

Inflammation 2004

PN 74   SC 25225

SN Local response to injury or irritation characterized by swelling, redness, pain, heat, and/or loss of function.

HN This term was introduced in June 2004. PsycINFO records from the past 10 years were re-indexed with this term. The posting note reflects the number of records that were re-indexed.

R   ↓ Injuries 1973
     ↓ Pathology 1973
     ↓ Symptoms 1967

Inflection 1973

PN 511   SC 25230

SN A grammatically functional change in the pitch or loudness of the voice. Also, the syntactic change in words to designate such factors as case, gender, or tense.

B   Prosody 1991
R   ↓ Phonology 1973
     ↓ Speech Characteristics 1973
     ↓ Syntax 1971

Influence (Interpersonal)

Use Interpersonal Influences

Influences (Social)

Use Social Influences

Influenza 1973

PN 163   SC 25260

B   Viral Disorders 1973
R   ↓ Gastrointestinal Disorders 1973
     ↓ Nervous System Disorders 1967
     ↓ Respiratory Tract Disorders 1973

Informants 1988

PN 110   SC 25270

SN Persons who provide information against another person who is suspected of committing a violation.

UF   Whistleblowing
R   ↓ Abuse Reporting 1997
     ↓ Crime 1967
     Duty to Warn 2001
     Labor Management Relations 1967
     ↓ Organizational Behavior 1978
     ↓ Social Behavior 1967

Information 1967

PN 5292   SC 25360

SN Conceptually broad term referring to a body of knowledge. Use a more specific term if possible. Differentiate from KNOWLEDGE LEVEL which is the amount of information acquired or received by an individual or group.

R   ↓ Automated Information Processing 1973
     Censorship 1978
     ↓ Communication 1967
     Computer Searching 1991
     Concepts 1967
     Data Collection 1982
     ↓ Data Processing 1967
     Databases 1991
     Declarative Knowledge 1997
     ↓ Electronic Communication 2001
     Human Information Storage 1973

Information — (cont'd)
- Information Seeking 1973
- Information Services 1988
- ↓ Information Specialists 1988
- ↓ Information Systems 1991
- Information Theory 1967
- ↓ Knowledge Level 1978
- ↓ Libraries 1982
- Messages 1973
- Privileged Communication 1973
- Procedural Knowledge 1997

Information (Messages)
Use Messages

Information Exchange
SN Consider HUMAN COMPUTER INTERACTION for exchanges between humans and computers.
Use Communication

Information Processes (Human)
Use Cognitive Processes

Information Processing (Automated)
Use Automated Information Processing

Information Processing Speed
Use Cognitive Processing Speed

Information Retrieval (Automated)
Use Automated Information Retrieval

Information Seeking 1973
PN 1528   **SC** 25330
R Computer Searching 1991
↓ Exploratory Behavior 1967
Information 1967
Questioning 1982

Information Services 1988
PN 223   **SC** 25335
R ↓ Automated Information Retrieval 1973
Computer Searching 1991
Databases 1991
Hot Line Services 1973
Information 1967
↓ Information Systems 1991
↓ Libraries 1982

Information Specialists 1988
PN 26   **SC** 25338
B Professional Personnel 1978
N Librarians 1988
R Information 1967

Information Storage (Human)
Use Human Information Storage

Information Systems 1991
PN 1144   **SC** 25345
SN Collection, organization, and storage of data or the operational functions used to process information.
UF Management Information Systems
B Systems 1967
N Internet 2001
R ↓ Automated Information Processing 1973
↓ Automated Information Retrieval 1973

Information Systems — (cont'd)
- Automated Information Storage 1973
- ↓ Communication Systems 1973
- ↓ Computer Applications 1973
- ↓ Data Processing 1967
- Databases 1991
- Decision Support Systems 1997
- ↓ Electronic Communication 2001
- ↓ Expert Systems 1991
- Information 1967
- Information Services 1988
- Knowledge Engineering 2003
- Word Processing 1991

Information Theory 1967
PN 567   **SC** 25350
SN Branch of science which deals statistically with the transmission of information and its measurable characteristics. Used for the scientific discipline or for application of information theory to specific areas of investigation.
B Theories 1967
R Communication Theory 1973
Information 1967
↓ Stochastic Modeling 1973

Informed Consent 1985
PN 1334   **SC** 25363
SN Process of making rational decisions regarding one's treatment or participation in experimental procedures.
R ↓ Civil Rights 1978
↓ Client Rights 1988
Debriefing (Experimental) 1991
Duty to Warn 2001
Experimental Ethics 1978
Guardianship 1988
Involuntary Treatment 1994
↓ Legal Processes 1973
Professional Ethics 1973
Treatment Compliance 1982
Treatment Refusal 1994
Treatment Withholding 1988

Ingestion 2001
PN 2477   **SC** 25364
SN Oral intake of food, liquids, medicine, etc. Used for both human and animal populations.
HN In 2001, this term was created to replace the discontinued term EATING. EATING was removed from all records containing it and replaced with INGESTION. In June 2004, EATING became nonpostable to EATING BEHAVIOR.
B Physiology 1967
N Coprophagia 2001
↓ Fluid Intake 1985
Food Intake 1967
R Animal Drinking Behavior 1973
Animal Feeding Behavior 1973
Digestion 1967
↓ Drinking Behavior 1978
Pica 1973
Swallowing 1988

Ingratiation
Use Impression Management

Ingroup Outgroup 1997
PN 1038   **SC** 25366
UF Outgroup Ingroup
B Social Groups 1973
R Ethnic Identity 1973
↓ Group Dynamics 1967

Ingroup Outgroup — (cont'd)
- Intergroup Dynamics 1973
- Self Perception 1967
- ↓ Social Identity 1988
- Social Networks 1994
- ↓ Social Perception 1967

Inhalant Abuse 1985
PN 265   **SC** 25367
SN Inhalation of vapors from volatile chemical substances (such as aerosol sprays, solvents, and anesthetics) in order to produce mind-altering effects.
UF Solvent Abuse
B Drug Abuse 1973
N Glue Sniffing 1973
R ↓ Solvents 1982

Inhibited Sexual Desire 1997
PN 66   **SC** 25370
SN Lack of sexual interest or feelings.
UF Hypoactive Sexual Desire Disorder
B Sexual Function Disturbances 1973
R Eroticism 1973
Libido 1973
Sex Drive 1973
↓ Sexual Arousal 1978

Inhibition (Personality) 1973
PN 937   **SC** 25380
B Personality Processes 1967

Inhibition (Proactive)
Use Proactive Inhibition

Inhibition (Retroactive)
Use Retroactive Inhibition

Initial Teaching Alphabet 1973
PN 17   **SC** 25410
SN A system developed in England in 1959 that uses a phoneme-grapheme correspondence to stress consistency between symbol and sound for beginning reading instruction.
B Alphabets 1973
R ↓ Language Arts Education 1973
Phonics 1973
↓ Reading 1967
Reading Education 1973
↓ Teaching Methods 1967

Initiation Rites 1973
PN 79   **SC** 25420
B Rites of Passage 1973
R Cosmetic Techniques 2001

Initiative 1973
PN 158   **SC** 25430
B Personality Traits 1967

Injections 1973
PN 372   **SC** 25440
B Drug Administration Methods 1973
N Intramuscular Injections 1973
Intraperitoneal Injections 1973
Intravenous Injections 1973
Subcutaneous Injections 1973
R Drug Self Administration 2004

Injuries 1973
PN 2663   **SC** 25450
UF Physical Trauma

Injuries — (cont'd)

Trauma (Physical)
- **N** Birth Injuries 1973
  - Burns 1973
  - Electrical Injuries 1973
  - ↓ Head Injuries 1973
  - ↓ Spinal Cord Injuries 1973
  - ↓ Wounds 1973
- **R** ↓ Accidents 1967
  - Coma 1973
  - ↓ Disorders 1967
  - Epidemics 2001
  - Falls 2004
  - Hematoma 1973
  - Hemiplegia 1978
  - Inflammation 2004
  - Paraplegia 1978
  - Physical Disfigurement 1978
  - ↓ Physical Disorders 1997
  - Quadriplegia 1985
  - ↓ Safety 1967
  - Shock 1967

Injuries (Birth)
Use Birth Injuries

Inlaws 1997
PN 34 **SC** 25465
- **B** Family Members 1973
- **R** ↓ Parents 1967
  - ↓ Spouses 1973

Inmates (Prison)
Use Prisoners

Innate Behavior (Animal)
Use Instinctive Behavior

Inner City
Use Urban Environments

Inner Ear
Use Labyrinth (Anatomy)

Inner Speech
Use Self Talk

Innovativeness
Use Creativity

Inquisitiveness
Use Curiosity

Insanity
Use Mental Disorders

Insanity Defense 1985
PN 663 **SC** 25525
SN Legal defense designed to invoke an exemption from criminal responsibility on the basis of a mental disorder at the time of the alleged criminal offense.
- **B** Legal Processes 1973
- **R** Court Referrals 1994
  - Criminal Responsibility 1991
  - Forensic Evaluation 1994
  - Forensic Psychiatry 1973
  - ↓ Mental Disorders 1967

Insanity Defense — (cont'd)
Mentally Ill Offenders 1985

Insecticides 1973
PN 215 **SC** 25530
HN In 1997, this term replaced the discontinued term DIELDRIN. In 2000, DIELDRIN was removed from all records containing it, and replaced with INSECTICIDES.
- **UF** Dieldrin
  - Pesticides
- **B** Hazardous Materials 1991
- **N** DDT (Insecticide) 1973
  - ↓ Ibotenic Acid 1991
  - Parathion 1973
- **R** ↓ Drugs 1967
  - ↓ Insects 1967
  - ↓ Neurotoxins 1982
  - Nicotine 1973
  - ↓ Poisons 1973

Insects 1967
PN 1596 **SC** 25540
- **B** Arthropoda 1973
- **N** Ants 1973
  - Bees 1973
  - Beetles 1973
  - Butterflies 1973
  - Cockroaches 1973
  - ↓ Diptera 1973
  - Grasshoppers 1973
  - Larvae 1973
  - Mantis 1973
  - Moths 1973
  - Wasps 1982
- **R** ↓ Insecticides 1973

Insecurity (Emotional)
Use Emotional Security

Insensitivity (Personality)
Use Sensitivity (Personality)

Inservice Teacher Education 1973
PN 1497 **SC** 25570
SN Course or program designed to provide teachers with growth in job-related competencies or skills. Usually school sponsored.
- **B** Inservice Training 1985
  - Teacher Education 1967
- **R** On the Job Training 1973
  - Professional Development 1982

Inservice Training 1985
PN 432 **SC** 25575
- **B** Continuing Education 1985
  - Personnel Training 1967
- **N** Inservice Teacher Education 1973
  - Mental Health Inservice Training 1973
- **R** On the Job Training 1973
  - Professional Development 1982

Inservice Training (Mental Health)
Use Mental Health Inservice Training

Insight 1973
PN 657 **SC** 25590
- **B** Personality Processes 1967
- **R** Intuition 1973
  - Perceptiveness (Personality) 1973

Insight (Psychotherapeutic Process) 1973
PN 256 **SC** 25600
- **B** Psychotherapeutic Processes 1967

Insight Therapy 1973
PN 164 **SC** 25610
SN Psychotherapeutic method which seeks to uncover the causes of the client's conflicts through conscious awareness (i.e., insight) into unconscious dynamics of feelings, responses, and behavior.
- **B** Psychotherapy 1967

Insomnia 1973
PN 1577 **SC** 25620
- **UF** Sleeplessness
- **B** Sleep Disorders 1973
  - Symptoms 1967

Instability (Emotional)
Use Emotional Instability

Instinctive Behavior 1982
PN 1279 **SC** 25638
SN Stereotyped, unlearned, largely stimulus-bound, adaptive behavior limited in its expression by the inherent properties of the nervous system and genetic factors. Used for human or animal populations.
HN In 1982, this term was created to replace the discontinued terms ANIMAL INNATE BEHAVIOR and ANIMAL INSTINCTIVE BEHAVIOR. In 2000, these terms were removed from all records containing it, and replaced with INSTINCTIVE BEHAVIOR.
- **UF** Animal Innate Behavior
  - Animal Instinctive Behavior
  - Innate Behavior (Animal)
- **B** Behavior 1967
- **R** ↓ Animal Defensive Behavior 1982
  - Animal Distress Calls 1973
  - ↓ Animal Ethology 1967
  - Animal Exploratory Behavior 1973
  - Animal Homing 1991
  - Animal Motivation 1967
  - Animal Predatory Behavior 1978
  - ↓ Animal Sexual Behavior 1985
  - Attack Behavior 1973
  - ↓ Genetics 1967
  - Homeostasis 1973
  - Human Nature 1997
  - ↓ Motivation 1967
  - Neophobia 1985
  - ↓ Nervous System 1967
  - ↓ Physiology 1967
  - ↓ Reflexes 1971
  - Self Preservation 1997
  - Species Recognition 1985
  - Spontaneous Alternation 1982

Institution Visitation 1973
PN 128 **SC** 25650
SN Visiting a patient or convict in an institution (e.g., hospital, prison, or nursing home) by someone from outside the institution (e.g., friends or family).
- **UF** Visitation (Institution)
- **R** ↓ Correctional Institutions 1973
  - Incarceration 1973
  - ↓ Residential Care Institutions 1973

Institutional Release 1978
PN 204 **SC** 25664
SN Discharge or release of an individual from any type of correctional or therapeutic residential facility.
- **B** Institutionalization 1967

Institutional Release — (cont'd)

- **N** ↓ Hospital Discharge 1973
- **R** ↓ Commitment (Psychiatric) 1973
  - Deinstitutionalization 1982
  - Discharge Planning 1994
  - ↓ Hospital Admission 1973
  - Incarceration 1973
  - ↓ Psychiatric Hospital Admission 1973
  - ↓ Psychiatric Hospitalization 1973

Institutional Schools 1978

PN 231   **SC** 25666
SN Schools that are part of larger residential institutions such as hospitals or prisons.

- **B** Schools 1967
- **R** Boarding Schools 1988
  - ↓ Correctional Institutions 1973
  - ↓ Residential Care Institutions 1973
  - ↓ Treatment Facilities 1973

Institutionalization 1967

PN 2008   **SC** 25670

- **N** ↓ Hospitalization 1967
  - Incarceration 1973
  - ↓ Institutional Release 1978
- **R** ↓ Facility Admission 1988
  - ↓ Facility Discharge 1988
  - Orphanages 1973

Institutionalized Mentally Retarded 1973

PN 1378   **SC** 25680

- **B** Mental Retardation 1967
- **R** Home Reared Mentally Retarded 1973
  - ↓ Residential Care Institutions 1973

Institutions (Correctional)

Use Correctional Institutions

Institutions (Residential Care)

Use Residential Care Institutions

Instruction

Use Teaching

Instruction (Computer Assisted)

Use Computer Assisted Instruction

Instruction (Individualized)

Use Individualized Instruction

Instruction (Programmed)

Use Programmed Instruction

Instructional Media 1967

PN 1350   **SC** 25740
SN Formats or technologies for conveyance of didactic content, including print, film, computers, phonographic records, and magnetic tape.

- **B** Teaching 1967
- **N** Advance Organizers 1985
  - ↓ Educational Audiovisual Aids 1973
  - Reading Materials 1973
  - Teaching Machines 1973
  - ↓ Textbooks 1978

Instructional Objectives

Use Educational Objectives

Instructions (Experimental)

Use Experimental Instructions

Instructors

Use Teachers

Instrument Controls 1985

PN 125   **SC** 25765
SN May include knobs, handles, levers, latches, dials, switches, buttons, and any other mechanism used to control the operation of machines and instruments.
HN Consider VISUAL DISPLAYS to access references from 1973-1984.

- **UF** Controls (Instrument)
- **N** Flight Instrumentation 1973
- **R** ↓ Displays 1967
  - Human Factors Engineering 1973
  - Human Machine Systems Design 1997
  - Keyboards 1985

Instrumental Conditioning

Use Operant Conditioning

Instrumental Learning

Use Operant Conditioning

Instrumentality 1991

PN 136   **SC** 25785

- **R** ↓ Motivation 1967
  - ↓ Personality Traits 1967
  - Self Efficacy 1985

Instrumentation (Flight)

Use Flight Instrumentation

Insulin 1973

PN 873   **SC** 25800

- **B** Hormones 1967
- **R** Insulin Shock Therapy 1973

Insulin Shock Therapy 1973

PN 36   **SC** 25820

- **B** Shock Therapy 1973
- **R** Coma 1973
  - Insulin 1973

Insurance 1973

PN 202   **SC** 25830

- **N** ↓ Health Insurance 1973
  - Life Insurance 1973
  - Social Security 1988
- **R** Disability Evaluation 1988
  - Risk Management 1997

Insurance Agents

Use Sales Personnel

Intake Interview 1994

PN 151   **SC** 25845
SN Initial evaluation, assessment, or screening of clients or patients to determine needs and appropriate health, mental health, rehabilitation, or other services.

- **B** Interviews 1967
- **R** ↓ Case Management 1991
  - Clinical Judgment (Not Diagnosis) 1973

Intake Interview — (cont'd)

- ↓ Diagnosis 1967
- ↓ Evaluation 1967
- Health Service Needs 1997
- ↓ Interview Schedules 2001
- Needs Assessment 1985
- ↓ Psychiatric Evaluation 1997
- ↓ Psychodiagnostic Interview 1973
- ↓ Screening 1982

Integrated Services 1997

PN 813   **SC** 25847
SN Collaboration and cooperation among social service, education, health, or community service providers.

- **UF** Interagency Services
- **R** ↓ Community Services 1967
  - ↓ Health Care Services 1978
  - Interdisciplinary Treatment Approach 1973
  - ↓ Mental Health Programs 1973
  - ↓ Mental Health Services 1978
  - Multimodal Treatment Approach 1991
  - Public Health Services 1973
  - ↓ Social Programs 1973
  - ↓ Social Services 1982

Integration (Racial)

Use Social Integration

Integrative Psychotherapy 2003

PN 64   **SC** 25853
SN Integration of two or more theoretical approaches and clinical methods of psychotherapy.
HN This term was introduced in June 2003. PsycINFO records from the past 10 years were re-indexed with this term. The posting note reflects the number of records that were re-indexed.

- **B** Psychotherapy 1967
- **R** Eclectic Psychotherapy 1994
  - Interdisciplinary Treatment Approach 1973
  - Multimodal Treatment Approach 1991

Integrity 1997

PN 150   **SC** 25855

- **B** Personality Traits 1967
- **R** ↓ Ethics 1967
  - Honesty 1973
  - Morality 1967
  - ↓ Values 1967

Intellectual Development 1973

PN 1660   **SC** 25860
SN Acquisition of factual knowledge. Consider COGNITIVE DEVELOPMENT for acquisition of reasoning, thought, and problem solving abilities.

- **B** Cognitive Development 1973
- **N** Language Development 1967
- **R** ↓ Intelligence 1967

Intellectual Functioning

Use Cognitive Ability

Intellectualism 1973

PN 40   **SC** 25870
SN Doctrine which attempts to explain emotion and volition in terms of cognitive processes.

- **B** Philosophies 1967

Intellectualization 1973

PN 15   **SC** 25880

Intellectualization — (cont'd)
SN Defense mechanism in which distressful emotional content of a painful situation is avoided by focusing on intellectual (cognitive) aspects of the situation or by engaging in abstract thinking.
B   Defense Mechanisms   1967
R   Isolation (Defense Mechanism)   1973

Intellectually Gifted
Use   Gifted

Intelligence   1967
PN 9268   **SC** 25900
SN General ability to think, reason, learn, apply knowledge, or deal effectively with the environment. Consider also INTELLIGENCE QUOTIENT.
N   Emotional Intelligence   2003
R   ↓ Ability   1967
     ↓ Artificial Intelligence   1982
     Cognitive Assessment   1997
     Creativity   1967
     Divergent Thinking   1973
     Gifted   1967
     ↓ Intellectual Development   1973
     Intelligence Quotient   1967
     Mental Age   1973
     ↓ Reasoning   1967
     ↓ Thinking   1967
     Wisdom   1994

Intelligence Age
Use   Mental Age

Intelligence Measures   1967
PN 4477   **SC** 25910
HN In 1997, this term replaced the discontinued terms HENMON NELSON TESTS OF MENTAL ABILITY, LEITER ADULT INTELLIGENCE SCALE, TEMPORAL SPATIAL CONCEPT SCALE, and VANE KINDERGARTEN TEST. In 2000, these terms were removed from all records containing them, and replaced with INTELLIGENCE MEASURES.
UF   Henmon Nelson Tests of Mental Ability
     Leiter Adult Intelligence Scale
     Temporal Spatial Concept Scale
     Tests (Intelligence)
     Vane Kindergarten Test
B   Measurement   1967
N   Benton Revised Visual Retention Test   1973
     Columbia Mental Maturity Scale   1973
     Culture Fair Intelligence Test   1973
     Frostig Developmental Test of Visual Perception   2001
     Goodenough Harris Draw A Person Test   1967
     Illinois Test of Psycholinguistic Abilities   2001
     Kaufman Assessment Battery for Children   2001
     Kohs Block Design Test   1973
     Miller Analogies Test   1973
     Peabody Picture Vocabulary Test   1973
     Porteus Maze Test   1973
     Raven Coloured Progressive Matrices   1973
     Raven Progressive Matrices   1978
     Slosson Intelligence Test   2001
     Stanford Binet Intelligence Scale   1967
     Wechsler Adult Intelligence Scale   1967
     Wechsler Bellevue Intelligence Scale   1967
     Wechsler Intelligence Scale for Children   2001
     Wechsler Preschool Primary Scale   1988
R   Bayley Scales of Infant Development   1994
     Cognitive Assessment   1997

Intelligence Quotient   1967
PN 4150   **SC** 25920
SN Relative intelligence of an individual expressed as a score on a standardized test of intelligence. Consider also INTELLIGENCE.
B   Test Scores   1967
R   Cognitive Assessment   1997
     ↓ Intelligence   1967
     Mental Age   1973

Intelligent Tutoring Systems   2003
PN 23   **SC** 25930
SN Systems which provide individualized instruction and performance assessment in response to a learner's actions. Used in artificial intelligence discussions.
HN This term was introduced in June 2003. PsycINFO records from the past 10 years were re-indexed with this term. The posting note reflects the number of records that were re-indexed.
B   Computer Assisted Instruction   1973
R   ↓ Artificial Intelligence   1982
     ↓ Expert Systems   1991
     ↓ Feedback   1967
     ↓ Learning   1967

Intensity (Stimulus)
Use   Stimulus Intensity

Intensive Care   1988
PN 539   **SC** 25942
R   Hospital Environment   1982
     ↓ Hospital Programs   1978
     ↓ Hospitals   1967

Intention   1988
PN 3264   **SC** 25945
SN Determination to act in a certain manner.
R   ↓ Goals   1967
     ↓ Motivation   1967
     Planned Behavior   1997

Intentional Learning   1973
PN 349   **SC** 25950
SN Purposive or motivated learning.
B   Learning   1967

Interaction (Interpersonal)
Use   Interpersonal Interaction

Interaction (Social)
Use   Social Interaction

Interaction Analysis (Statistics)   1973
PN 144   **SC** 25990
B   Statistical Analysis   1967
R   Interaction Variance   1973

Interaction Variance   1973
PN 36   **SC** 26000
B   Variability Measurement   1973
R   Interaction Analysis (Statistics)   1973

Interagency Services
Use   Integrated Services

Intercourse (Sexual)
Use   Sexual Intercourse (Human)

Intercultural Communication
Use   Cross Cultural Communication

Interdisciplinary Research   1985
PN 719   **SC** 26025
SN Any research effort coordinated or executed by members of two or more specialties, disciplines, or theoretical orientations.
UF   Cross Disciplinary Research
     Multidisciplinary Research
B   Experimentation   1967
R   Interdisciplinary Treatment Approach   1973

Interdisciplinary Treatment Approach   1973
PN 3655   **SC** 26030
SN Combination of two or more disciplines in the prevention, diagnosis, treatment, or rehabilitation of mental or physical disorders.
UF   Multidisciplinary Treatment Approach
B   Treatment   1967
R   Biopsychosocial Approach   1991
     Eclectic Psychotherapy   1994
     ↓ Health Care Psychology   1985
     Integrated Services   1997
     Integrative Psychotherapy   2003
     Interdisciplinary Research   1985
     Multimodal Treatment Approach   1991
     Partial Hospitalization   1985
     ↓ Teams   1988

Interest Inventories   1973
PN 501   **SC** 26040
B   Inventories   1967

Interest Patterns
Use   Interests

Interests   1967
PN 1605   **SC** 26080
HN In 1982, this term replaced the discontinued term INTEREST PATTERNS. In 2000, INTEREST PATTERNS was removed from all records containing it, and replaced with INTERESTS.
UF   Interest Patterns
N   Occupational Interests   1967
R   Daily Activities   1994
     Hobbies   1988

Interethnic Communication
Use   Cross Cultural Communication

Interethnic Family   1988
PN 27   **SC** 26070
B   Family   1967
R   Interracial Adoption   1994
     Interracial Family   1988
     Racial and Ethnic Differences   1982

Interethnic Marriage
Use   Exogamous Marriage

Interfaith Marriage   1973
PN 59   **SC** 26090
B   Exogamous Marriage   1973

Interference (Learning)   1967
PN 3626   **SC** 26100

Interference (Learning) — (cont'd)

SN Inhibition of learning due to negative transfer effects of competing memories, thoughts, or learned behavior. Effects include slower learning and poorer memory.
B   Learning   1967
N   ↓ Latent Inhibition   1997
     Proactive Inhibition   1973
     Retroactive Inhibition   1973
R   Forgetting   1973
   ↓ Memory   1967
   ↓ Retention   1967
     Stroop Effect   1988

Interferons   1994

PN   187   SC   26103
B   Cytokines   2003
     Proteins   1973
R   Antineoplastic Drugs   1982
   ↓ Immunoglobulins   1973

Intergenerational Relations   1988

PN   1556   SC   26105
SN Contact between related or nonrelated persons of different generational age groups.
R   Empty Nest   1991
   ↓ Family Relations   1967
     Generation Gap   1973
     Generativity   2001
     Transgenerational Patterns   1991

Intergenerational Transmission

Use   Transgenerational Patterns

Intergroup Dynamics   1973

PN   1513   SC   26110
B   Group Dynamics   1967
R   Boundaries (Psychological)   1997
     Ingroup Outgroup   1997

Interhemispheric Interaction   1985

PN   919   SC   26112
SN Any neurophysiological, electrophysiological, or neurochemical exchange occurring between the cerebral hemispheres.
UF   Interhemispheric Transfer
R   ↓ Cerebral Cortex   1967
   ↓ Cerebral Dominance   1973
     Corpus Callosum   1973
     Left Brain   1991
     Right Brain   1991

Interhemispheric Transfer

Use   Interhemispheric Interaction

Interior Design   1982

PN   262   SC   26115
SN Practice or resultant product of planning and implementing the design of architectural interiors and furnishings.
B   Architecture   1973
     Environmental Planning   1982
R   Aesthetic Preferences   1973
     Aesthetics   1967
     Furniture   1985

Interleukins   1994

PN   529   SC   26117
SN Compounds produced by lymphocytes that regulate immune system functioning and individual cell mediated immunity.

Interleukins — (cont'd)

B   Cytokines   2003
R   Antigens   1982
     Biological Markers   1991
     Immunoreactivity   1994
     Lymphocytes   1973

Intermarriage

Use   Exogamous Marriage

Intermediate School Students   1973

PN   74   SC   26130
SN Includes the middle and/or upper elementary school grades, usually grades 4, 5, and 6. Use ELEMENTARY SCHOOL STUDENTS unless specific reference is made to population as intermediate school students.
B   Elementary School Students   1967

Intermittent Explosive Disorder

Use   Explosive Disorder

Intermittent Reinforcement

Use   Reinforcement Schedules

Internal Consistency

Use   Test Reliability

Internal External Locus of Control   1967

PN   10800   SC   26150
UF   Control (Locus of)
     Locus of Control
B   Personality Traits   1967
R   Attribution   1973
   ↓ Emotional Control   1973
     External Rewards   1973
     Extrinsic Motivation   1973
   ↓ Helplessness   1997
     Independence (Personality)   1973
     Internal Rewards   1973
     Intrinsic Motivation   1973
     Self Control   1973
     Self Determination   1994

Internal Rewards   1973

PN   141   SC   26160
SN Satisfaction of a personal value or intrinsic criteria of behavior through action or attainment. Compare SECONDARY REINFORCEMENT.
UF   Intrinsic Rewards
B   Rewards   1967
R   Internal External Locus of Control   1967
     Intrinsic Motivation   1973

Internalization   1997

PN   603   SC   26165
UF   Incorporation (Psychological)
B   Personality Processes   1967
N   Introjection   1973
R   ↓ Defense Mechanisms   1967
     Externalization   1973
     Object Permanence   1985
     Object Relations   1982
   ↓ Personality Development   1967
   ↓ Psychotherapeutic Processes   1967

International Classification of Diseases   2001

PN   260   SC   26168

International Classification of Diseases — (cont'd)

SN Used when the International Classification of Diseases or its revisions is the primary focus of the reference. Not used for specific psychodiagnostic categories.
HN Consider PSYCHODIAGNOSTIC TYPOLOGIES to access references prior to 1997. In 2000, the truncated term INTERNATIONAL CLASS OF DISEASES was deleted and removed from all records containing it, and replaced with INTERNATIONAL CLASSIFICATION OF DISEASES, its expanded form.
UF   ICD
B   Psychodiagnostic Typologies   1967
R   ↓ Diagnosis   1967
     Diagnostic and Statistical Manual   1994
   ↓ Disorders   1967
   ↓ Mental Disorders   1967
   ↓ Psychodiagnosis   1967
     Research Diagnostic Criteria   1994

International Organizations   1973

PN   632   SC   26170
B   Organizations   1967
R   Foreign Organizations   1973

International Relations   1967

PN   1274   SC   26180
R   Foreign Policy Making   1973
     Peace   1988

Internet   2001

PN   2105   SC   26185
SN A global system of linked computer networks that facilitates information retrieval and international communication.
UF   World Wide Web (WWW)
B   Communication Systems   1973
     Information Systems   1991
R   ↓ Automated Information Processing   1973
   ↓ Computer Applications   1973
     Computer Mediated Communication   2003
   ↓ Electronic Communication   2001
     Online Therapy   2003
   ↓ Telecommunications Media   1973
     Telemedicine   2003

Internet Counseling

Use   Online Therapy

Internists   1973

PN   148   SC   26190
B   Physicians   1967

Internship (Medical)

Use   Medical Internship

Interobserver Reliability

Use   Interrater Reliability

Interocular Transfer   1985

PN   121   SC   26207
SN Any neurophysiological, electrophysiological, or perceptual interaction between the two eyes.
B   Visual Perception   1967
R   Ocular Dominance   1973
   ↓ Perceptual Aftereffect   1967
   ↓ Sensory Adaptation   1967

Interpersonal Attraction 1967
PN 2773   SC 26210
UF   Attraction (Interpersonal)
B   Interpersonal Interaction 1967
N   Sexual Attraction 2003
R   Human Mate Selection 1988
↓ Interpersonal Relationships 2004
Likability 1988
Physical Attractiveness 1973

Interpersonal Communication 1973
PN 8984   SC 26220
B   Communication 1967
Interpersonal Interaction 1967
N   Arguments 1973
Body Language 1973
Conversation 1973
Cross Cultural Communication 1997
Double Bind Interaction 1973
Eye Contact 1973
Gossip 1982
Group Discussion 1967
Interviewing 1973
↓ Interviews 1967
Job Applicant Interviews 1973
Listening (Interpersonal) 1997
↓ Negotiation 1973
↓ Parent Child Communication 1973
R   Credibility 1973
Neurolinguistic Programming 2001
Pragmatics 1985
Scientific Communication 1973
Self Disclosure 1973
Self Reference 1994
Speech Anxiety 1985

Interpersonal Compatibility 1973
PN 419   SC 26230
UF   Compatibility (Interpersonal)
B   Interpersonal Interaction 1967
R   Friendship 1967
Human Mate Selection 1988
↓ Interpersonal Relationships 2004

Interpersonal Competence
Use   Social Skills

Interpersonal Distance
Use   Personal Space

Interpersonal Influences 1967
PN 3997   SC 26240
SN   Effect one individual has on another with or without apparent intention or direct exercise of command.
UF   Influence (Interpersonal)
B   Interpersonal Interaction 1967
Social Influences 1967
N   Peer Pressure 1994
R   ↓ Persuasive Communication 1967
Reference Groups 1994
Suggestibility 1967

Interpersonal Interaction 1967
PN 20910   SC 26250
UF   Interaction (Interpersonal)
Rapport
B   Social Interaction 1967
N   ↓ Assistance (Social Behavior) 1973
Charitable Behavior 1973
↓ Collective Behavior 1967
↓ Conflict 1967

Interpersonal Interaction — (cont'd)
Cooperation 1967
↓ Employee Interaction 1988
Group Participation 1973
Group Performance 1967
↓ Interpersonal Attraction 1967
↓ Interpersonal Communication 1973
Interpersonal Compatibility 1973
↓ Interpersonal Influences 1967
Male Female Relations 1988
↓ Participation 1973
↓ Peer Relations 1967
Persecution 1973
Rivalry 1973
Social Dating 1973
Stranger Reactions 1988
R   Affection 1973
Boundaries (Psychological) 1997
Codependency 1991
Dual Relationships 2003
Enactments 1997
↓ Interpersonal Relationships 2004
Intimacy 1973
Mentor 1985
Mirroring 1997
Popularity 1988
↓ Relationship Satisfaction 2001
Retaliation 1991
Social Cognition 1994
Social Networks 1994

Interpersonal Perception
Use   Social Perception

Interpersonal Psychotherapy 1997
PN 298   SC 26263
SN   Technique formulated by H. S. Sullivan based on the study of the patient's interpersonal relationships both within and outside of the psychotherapeutic situation.
B   Psychotherapy 1967
R   ↓ Psychotherapeutic Techniques 1967

Interpersonal Relationship Satisfaction
Use   Relationship Satisfaction

Interpersonal Relationships 2004
PN 188   SC 58084
HN   This term was introduced in June 2004. Psyc-INFO records from the past 10 years were re-indexed with this term. The posting note reflects the number of records that were re-indexed.
UF   Personal Relationships
N   ↓ Family Relations 1967
Friendship 1967
Kinship 1985
↓ Marital Relations 1967
R   ↓ Interpersonal Attraction 1967
Interpersonal Compatibility 1973
↓ Interpersonal Interaction 1967
Relationship Quality 2004
↓ Relationship Satisfaction 2001

Interracial Adoption 1994
PN 97   SC 26265
UF   Transracial Adoption
B   Adoption (Child) 1967
R   Adopted Children 1973
↓ Adoptees 1985
Adoptive Parents 1973
Interethnic Family 1988
Interracial Family 1988

Interracial Family 1988
PN 47   SC 26270
B   Family 1967
R   Interethnic Family 1988
Interracial Adoption 1994
Interracial Marriage 1973
Interracial Offspring 1988
Racial and Ethnic Differences 1982
Racial and Ethnic Relations 1982

Interracial Marriage 1973
PN 187   SC 26280
UF   Miscegenous Marriage
B   Exogamous Marriage 1973
R   Interracial Family 1988
Interracial Offspring 1988
Racial and Ethnic Relations 1982

Interracial Offspring 1988
PN 191   SC 26282
UF   Biracial Children
B   Offspring 1988
R   Interracial Family 1988
Interracial Marriage 1973
Racial and Ethnic Differences 1982
Racial and Ethnic Relations 1982

Interrater Reliability 1982
PN 1924   SC 26284
SN   Statistically measured correspondence between judgments by observers of a common event.
UF   Interobserver Reliability
R   Observation Methods 1967
Rating 1967
Statistical Reliability 1973
Test Reliability 1973

Interresponse Time 1973
PN 294   SC 26290
SN   Interval between successive responses.
B   Response Parameters 1973
Time 1967
R   Response Frequency 1973

Intersensory Integration
Use   Sensory Integration

Intersensory Processes 1978
PN 1250   SC 26295
B   Perception 1967
N   Sensory Integration 1991
Synesthesia 2003
R   Perceptual Motor Development 1991
↓ Perceptual Motor Processes 1967

Intersexuality
Use   Hermaphroditism

Interspecies Interaction 1991
PN 1047   SC 26297
SN   Social behavior involving members of two or more animal species including humans and animals.
UF   Animal Human Interaction
Human Animal Interaction
B   Social Behavior 1967
R   Animal Assisted Therapy 1994
↓ Animal Social Behavior 1967
↓ Animals 1967
Biological Symbiosis 1973
Pets 1982
Species Differences 1982

Interstimulus Interval 1967
PN 2281 **SC** 26300
SN In conditioning contexts, the temporal interval separating the conditioned stimulus and unconditioned stimulus or the temporal interval between the elements of a multiple component (i.e., compound) stimulus.
B Stimulus Intervals 1973
R Reinforcement Delay 1985

Intertrial Interval 1973
PN 1007 **SC** 26310
SN Temporal interval between successive discrete trials in conditioning or learning contexts.
B Stimulus Intervals 1973

Interval Reinforcement
Use Fixed Interval Reinforcement AND Variable Interval Reinforcement

Intervention 2003
PN 1041 **SC** 26323
SN Intervening on the behalf of one or more individuals. Use a more specific term if possible.
HN This term was introduced in June 2003. PsycINFO records from the past 10 years were re-indexed with this term. The posting note reflects the number of records that were re-indexed.
N ↓ Crisis Intervention 1973
Early Intervention 1982
Family Intervention 2003
School Based Intervention 2003
R At Risk Populations 1985
↓ Crisis Intervention Services 1973
| Prevention 1070
↓ Rehabilitation 1967
↓ Treatment 1967

Interview Schedules 2001
PN 22 **SC** 26325
SN Precoded questionnaires for gathering data, which are completed during interviews.
B Interviews 1967
N Diagnostic Interview Schedule 1991
Structured Clinical Interview 2001
R Intake Interview 1994
↓ Psychiatric Evaluation 1997
↓ Psychological Assessment 1997

Interviewers 1988
PN 260 **SC** 26330
R Interviewing 1973
↓ Interviews 1967

Interviewing 1973
PN 1741 **SC** 26340
SN Used for the methods, techniques, principles, and practice of interviewing.
B Interpersonal Communication 1973
R Interviewers 1988
↓ Interviews 1967
Legal Interrogation 1994
Microcounseling 1978
Questioning 1982

Interviews 1967
PN 3013 **SC** 26350
B Interpersonal Communication 1973
N Intake Interview 1994
↓ Interview Schedules 2001
Job Applicant Interviews 1973
↓ Psychodiagnostic Interview 1973

Interviews — (cont'd)
R Interviewers 1988
Interviewing 1973
↓ Measurement 1967
Qual3itative Research 2003
Questioning 1982

Intestines 1973
PN 169 **SC** 26360
UF Duodenum
Ileum
B Gastrointestinal System 1973
R Absorption (Physiological) 1973

Intimacy 1973
PN 3183 **SC** 26370
R Affection 1973
Attachment Behavior 1985
↓ Interpersonal Interaction 1967
Love 1973
Physical Contact 1982
Romance 1997

Intoxication
Use Toxic Disorders

Intoxication (Alcohol)
Use Alcohol Intoxication

Intra Aural Muscle Reflex
Use Acoustic Reflex

Intracranial Self Stimulation
Use Brain Self Stimulation

Intramuscular Injections 1973
PN 55 **SC** 26400
B Injections 1973

Intraperitoneal Injections 1973
PN 73 **SC** 26410
B Injections 1973

Intrauterine Devices 1973
PN 28 **SC** 26420
B Contraceptive Devices 1973

Intravenous Drug Usage 1994
PN 1207 **SC** 26425
UF IV Drug Usage
B Drug Usage 1971
R Disease Transmission 2004
↓ Drug Abuse 1973
↓ Drug Addiction 1967
Intravenous Injections 1973
Needle Exchange Programs 2001
Needle Sharing 1994

Intravenous Injections 1973
PN 605 **SC** 26430
B Injections 1973
R Intravenous Drug Usage 1994
Needle Sharing 1994

Intrinsic Motivation 1973
PN 1575 **SC** 26440
SN Need or desire which arises from within the individual and causes action toward some goal.

Intrinsic Motivation — (cont'd)
B Motivation 1967
R ↓ Goals 1967
Internal External Locus of Control 1967
Internal Rewards 1973
Need for Cognition 1997
↓ Needs 1967

Intrinsic Rewards
Use Internal Rewards

Introjection 1973
PN 142 **SC** 26460
B Defense Mechanisms 1967
Internalization 1997
R Identification (Defense Mechanism) 1973

Introspection 1973
PN 316 **SC** 26470
B Personality Processes 1967
R Reflectiveness 1997
Self Monitoring (Personality) 1985
Self Perception 1967

Introversion 1967
PN 1237 **SC** 26480
B Personality Traits 1967
R Extraversion 1967

Intuition 1973
PN 739 **SC** 26485
B Cognitive Processes 1967
R Cognition 1967
↓ Comprehension 1967
Guessing 1973
Insight 1973

Inuit 2001
PN 269 **SC** 26487
HN In 2001, this term was created to replace the discontinued term ESKIMOS. ESKIMOS was removed from all records containing it and replaced with INUIT.
UF Eskimos
B Indigenous Populations 2001
R Alaska Natives 1997
American Indians 1967
Minority Groups 1967
↓ Pacific Islanders 2001

Inventories 1967
PN 4730 **SC** 26490
B Measurement 1967
N Biographical Inventories 1973
Interest Inventories 1973

Invertebrates 1070
PN 244 **SC** 26540
B Animals 1967
N ↓ Arthropoda 1973
Echinodermata 1973
↓ Mollusca 1973
↓ Worms 1967
R ↓ Vertebrates 1973

Investigation
Use Experimentation

Involuntary Treatment 1994
PN 392 **SC** 26555
B Treatment 1967

145

Involuntary Treatment — (cont'd)
R ↓ Client Rights 1988
  ↓ Commitment (Psychiatric) 1973
  Court Referrals 1994
  Informed Consent 1985
  Right to Treatment 1997
  Treatment Compliance 1982
  Treatment Dropouts 1978
  Treatment Refusal 1994

Involutional Depression 1973
PN 64   SC 26560
UF Climacteric Depression
B Affective Psychosis 1973
  Major Depression 1988

Involutional Paranoid Psychosis 1973
PN 7   SC 26570
UF Climacteric Paranoia
B Paranoia (Psychosis) 1967
R Folie A Deux 1973
  Paranoid Schizophrenia 1967

Involvement 1973
PN 2584   SC 26575
B Social Behavior 1967
N Community Involvement 2003
  Job Involvement 1978
R ↓ Commitment 1985
  Empowerment 1991
  ↓ Participation 1973

Ions
Use Electrolytes

Iowa Tests of Basic Skills 1973
PN 51   SC 26590
B Achievement Measures 1967

Iproniazid 1973
PN 16   SC 26600
B Amine Oxidase Inhibitors 1973
  Antidepressant Drugs 1971
  Antihypertensive Drugs 1973
  Antitubercular Drugs 1973
  Monoamine Oxidase Inhibitors 1973

Iris (Eye) 1973
PN 53   SC 26630
B Eye (Anatomy) 1967
R Eye Color 1991

Iron 1973
PN 162   SC 26640
B Metallic Elements 1973

Irradiation
Use Radiation

Irrational Beliefs 1982
PN 746   SC 26654
SN Erroneous or distorted convictions or ideas firmly held despite objective and obvious contradictory proof or evidence.
B Cognitions 1985
R ↓ Attitudes 1967
  Superstitions 1973

Irritability 1988
PN 255   SC 26658

Irritability — (cont'd)
SN Used for human or animal populations.
B Personality Traits 1967
R ↓ Emotional States 1973

Irritable Bowel Syndrome 1991
PN 273   SC 26659
SN Functional disorder of the colon that is generally psychosomatic.
B Colon Disorders 1973
  Syndromes 1973
R ↓ Colitis 1973
  ↓ Somatoform Disorders 2001

Ischemia 1973
PN 391   SC 26660
B Cardiovascular Disorders 1967
N Cerebral Ischemia 1973
R Anoxia 1973

Islam 1973
PN 476   SC 26670
B Religious Affiliation 1973
R Muslims 1997

Isocarboxazid 1973
PN 32   SC 26680
B Amine Oxidase Inhibitors 1973
  Antidepressant Drugs 1971
  Monoamine Oxidase Inhibitors 1973

Isoenzymes
Use Isozymes

Isolation (Defense Mechanism) 1973
PN 149   SC 26700
SN Unconscious separation of an unacceptable impulse, idea, or act from its original memory source, removing the emotional charge associated with the original memory.
B Defense Mechanisms 1967
R Intellectualization 1973

Isolation (Social)
Use Social Isolation

Isolation Effect 1973
PN 221   SC 26720
SN Facilitating effect of isolation of distinctive features of an item (e.g., type face, color) in learning.
B Associative Processes 1967
R Cues 1967
  Stimulus Salience 1973
  ↓ Verbal Learning 1967

Isoniazid 1973
PN 29   SC 26730
B Antitubercular Drugs 1973

Isoproterenol 1973
PN 151   SC 26740
B Alcohols 1967
  Sympathomimetic Drugs 1973

Isozymes 1973
PN 55   SC 26750
UF Isoenzymes
B Enzymes 1973

Itching
Use Pruritus

Item Analysis (Statistical) 1973
PN 975   SC 26800
SN Quantitative analysis of a test item, especially regarding its difficulty level and validity.
B Factor Analysis 1967
R Adaptive Testing 1985
  Item Response Theory 1985
  Statistical Weighting 1985
  Test Items 1973

Item Analysis (Test) 1967
PN 1524   SC 26810
SN Qualitative analysis of a test item, especially regarding its content and form.
B Analysis 1967
  Test Construction 1973
  Testing 1967
R Item Content (Test) 1973
  Test Items 1973

Item Bias
Use Test Bias

Item Content (Test) 1973
PN 488   SC 26820
SN Topics or subject matter covered in test questions, units, or tasks.
B Test Construction 1973
  Testing 1967
R Item Analysis (Test) 1967
  Test Forms 1988
  Test Items 1973

Item Response Theory 1985
PN 1608   SC 26825
SN A statistical approach in psychological measurement. Also known as item characteristic curve theory.
UF Latent Trait Theory
  Logistic Models
  Rasch Model
B Testing 1967
  Theories 1967
R Classical Test Theory 2003
  Difficulty Level (Test) 1973
  Item Analysis (Statistical) 1973
  Psychometrics 1967
  ↓ Test Scores 1967

IV Drug Usage
Use Intravenous Drug Usage

Jails
Use Prisons

James (William) 1991
PN 200   SC 26855
SN Identifies biographical or autobiographical studies and discussions of James's works.
R Functionalism 1973
  ↓ Psychologists 1967

Japanese Americans 1973
PN 40   SC 26863

Japanese Cultural Groups 1997
PN 282   SC 26865

Japanese Cultural Groups — (cont'd)
HN Use ASIANS to access references from 1982-1996.
B Asians 1982

Jaundice 1973
PN 34   SC 26870
B Digestive System Disorders 1973
Liver Disorders 1973
R Cirrhosis (Liver) 1973
↓ Hepatitis 1973
↓ Infectious Disorders 1973

Jaw 1973
PN 283   SC 26880
UF Mandibula
Maxilla
B Musculoskeletal System 1973
R Bones 1973

Jealousy 1973
PN 692   SC 26890
UF Envy
B Emotional States 1973
R ↓ Anger 1967
↓ Anxiety 1967

Jews 1997
PN 498   SC 26900
HN Use JUDAISM to access references prior to 1997.
B Religious Groups 1997
R AntiSemitism 1973
Holocaust 1988
Holocaust Survivors 1988
Judaism 1967
Minority Groups 1967

Job Analysis 1967
PN 1635   SC 26910
SN Analysis specifying job duties, responsibilities, and technical components.
B Analysis 1967
Human Resource Management 2003
R ↓ Job Characteristics 1985
Task Analysis 1967
Work Load 1982

Job Applicant Attitudes 1973
PN 262   SC 26920
SN Attitudes of, not toward, job applicants.
B Attitudes 1967
R Job Applicants 1985
Job Search 1985
Occupational Attitudes 1973
↓ Personnel 1967

Job Applicant Interviews 1973
PN 791   SC 26930
UF Employment Interviews
B Interpersonal Communication 1973
Interviews 1967
Personnel Selection 1967
R Job Search 1985
↓ Personnel Evaluation 1973
↓ Personnel Recruitment 1973

Job Applicant Screening 1973
PN 730   SC 26940
UF Testing (Job Applicants)
B Personnel Selection 1967
Screening 1982

Job Applicant Screening — (cont'd)
R Employment Discrimination 1994
Employment Tests 1973
Job Search 1985
↓ Personnel Evaluation 1973
↓ Personnel Recruitment 1973

Job Applicants 1985
PN 628   SC 26953
SN Persons seeking employment.
R ↓ Employment Status 1982
Job Applicant Attitudes 1973
Job Search 1985
↓ Personnel 1967

Job Change
Use Career Change

Job Characteristics 1985
PN 2659   SC 26957
SN Responsibilities or tasks that characterize a specific job.
N Work Load 1982
R Job Analysis 1967
↓ Occupations 1967
Quality of Work Life 1988

Job Corps 1973
PN 35   SC 26960
SN U.S. Government program of vocational and psychosocial training and counseling for disadvantaged adolescents and adults.
B Government Programs 1973
R Government 1967

Job Discrimination
Use Employment Discrimination

Job Enrichment 1973
PN 128   SC 26980
SN Formal or informal programs or techniques used to enhance the quality of a job or to further challenge the employee.
B Working Conditions 1973
R Job Experience Level 1973
Job Satisfaction 1967
Occupational Guidance 1967
Occupational Mobility 1973
↓ Personnel Training 1967

Job Experience Level 1973
PN 2215   SC 26990
UF Experience Level (Job)
B Employee Characteristics 1988
Experience Level 1988
R Employment History 1978
Job Enrichment 1973
Job Knowledge 1997
Occupational Status 1978

Job Family Relationship
Use Family Work Relationship

Job Involvement 1978
PN 1290   SC 26994
B Involvement 1973
R ↓ Employee Attitudes 1967
Employee Motivation 1973
↓ Job Performance 1967
Job Satisfaction 1967

Job Involvement — (cont'd)
Organizational Commitment 1991
Participative Management 1988
Work (Attitudes Toward) 1973

Job Knowledge 1997
PN 270   SC 26996
B Employee Characteristics 1988
Knowledge Level 1978
R ↓ Employee Skills 1973
Job Experience Level 1973
↓ Job Performance 1967

Job Mobility
Use Occupational Mobility

Job Performance 1967
PN 8885   SC 27010
B Performance 1967
N Employee Efficiency 1973
Employee Productivity 1973
R ↓ Employee Attitudes 1967
Job Involvement 1978
Job Knowledge 1997
Organizational Commitment 1991
↓ Personnel 1967
↓ Personnel Evaluation 1973
Personnel Promotion 1978
Work Load 1982

Job Promotion
Use Personnel Promotion

Job Reentry
Use Reemployment

Job Satisfaction 1967
PN 9529   SC 27040
SN Positive attitudes toward one's work when tangible and/or intangible rewards fulfill expectations.
UF Work Satisfaction
B Employee Attitudes 1967
Satisfaction 1973
R Career Change 1978
Job Enrichment 1973
Job Involvement 1978
Organizational Commitment 1991
Quality of Work Life 1988
Role Satisfaction 1994

Job Search 1985
PN 489   SC 27043
SN Process of seeking employment. For consideration of career alternatives use CAREER EDUCATION.
R Job Applicant Attitudes 1970
Job Applicant Interviews 1973
Job Applicant Screening 1973
Job Applicants 1985
Reemployment 1991
Unemployment 1967

Job Security 1978
PN 279   SC 27045
SN Probable assurance of continued employment.
R Downsizing 2003
Employee Turnover 1973
↓ Occupational Tenure 1973
Personnel Termination 1973
Retirement 1973
Unemployment 1967

Job Selection
  Use Occupational Choice

Job Status
  Use Occupational Status

Job Stress
  Use Occupational Stress

Job Training
  Use Personnel Training

Jobs
  Use Occupations

Joint Custody 1988
PN 104   **SC** 27065
  R Child Custody 1982
    Child Support 1988
    Divorce 1973

Joint Disorders 1973
PN 103   **SC** 27070
  B Musculoskeletal Disorders 1973
  N ↓ Arthritis 1973
  R ↓ Joints (Anatomy) 1973

Joints (Anatomy) 1973
PN 189   **SC** 27080
  B Musculoskeletal System 1973
  N Ankle 1973
    Elbow (Anatomy) 1973
    Knee 1973
    Shoulder (Anatomy) 1973
    Wrist 1973
  R ↓ Joint Disorders 1973

Jokes 1973
PN 267   **SC** 27090
  B Humor 1967
  R Teasing 2003

Journalists 1973
PN 182   **SC** 27100
  B Professional Personnel 1978
  R ↓ News Media 1997

Joy
  Use Happiness

Judaism 1967
PN 1580   **SC** 27130
  B Religious Affiliation 1973
  R AntiSemitism 1973
    Bible 1973
    Holocaust 1988
    Jews 1997
    Rabbis 1973

Judges 1985
PN 370   **SC** 27135
  B Legal Personnel 1985

Judgment 1967
PN 7010   **SC** 27140
  SN Mental act of comparing or evaluating choices within a given set of values frequently with the purpose of choosing a course of action.

Judgment — (cont'd)
  N Clinical Judgment (Not Diagnosis) 1973
    Probability Judgment 1978
  R ↓ Decision Making 1967
    Judgment Disturbances 1973
    Uncertainty 1991
    Wisdom 1994

Judgment Disturbances 1973
PN 15   **SC** 27150
  SN Maladaptive judgment resulting from wish-fulfilling, impulsive decisions based on need for immediate infantile gratification.
  B Thought Disturbances 1973
  R ↓ Judgment 1967

Judo 1973
PN 48   **SC** 27160
  B Recreation 1967
    Sports 1967
  R Martial Arts 1985

Jumping 1973
PN 130   **SC** 27170
  B Motor Performance 1973
    Motor Processes 1967

Jung (Carl) 1973
PN 879   **SC** 27180
  SN Identifies biographical or autobiographical studies and discussions of Jung's works.
  R Analytical Psychotherapy 1973
    Archetypes 1991
    ↓ Collective Unconscious 1997
    ↓ Jungian Psychology 1973
    ↓ Psychologists 1967

Jungian Psychology 1973
PN 2264   **SC** 27190
  SN Analytical psychology characterized by theories of the collective unconscious, the archetype, the complex, and psychological types.
  UF Analytic Psychology
  B Neopsychoanalytic School 1973
  N ↓ Collective Unconscious 1997
  R Analytical Psychotherapy 1973
    Archetypes 1991
    Free Association 1994
    Jung (Carl) 1973

Jungian Psychotherapy
  Use Analytical Psychotherapy

Junior College Students 1973
PN 206   **SC** 27200
  SN Students in two-year colleges.
  B College Students 1967
  R Community College Students 1973

Junior Colleges
  Use Colleges

Junior High School Students 1971
PN 10652   **SC** 27220
  SN Students in 7th and 8th grade. Sometimes includes students in 9th grade.
  B Students 1967
  R Grade Level 1994
    Middle School Students 1985

Junior High School Teachers 1973
PN 1542   **SC** 27230
  B Teachers 1967
  R Middle School Teachers 2003

Junior High Schools 1973
PN 319   **SC** 27240
  B Schools 1967
  R Middle Schools 2003
    Secondary Education 1973

Juries 1985
PN 1097   **SC** 27245
  SN Bodies of persons sworn to give a verdict in a court of law. Also used for mock and simulated juries.
  HN Use ADJUDICATION to access references from 1973-1984.
  R ↓ Adjudication 1967
    Jury Selection 1994
    ↓ Legal Personnel 1985

Jury Selection 1994
PN 45   **SC** 27252
  HN Use JURIES to access references from 1985-1993.
  R ↓ Adjudication 1967
    Juries 1985

Justice 1973
PN 2218   **SC** 27260
  SN Used for the impartial and fair settlement of conflict and differences, or the designation of rewards or punishment.
  N ↓ Criminal Justice 1991
    Distributive Justice 2003
    Procedural Justice 2003
  R ↓ Civil Rights 1978
    Equity (Payment) 1978
    ↓ Equity (Social) 1978
    Freedom 1978
    ↓ Law (Government) 1973
    ↓ Law Enforcement 1978
    Morality 1967
    Reward Allocation 1988
    Social Equality 1973
    ↓ Social Issues 1991

Juvenile Court
  Use Adjudication

Juvenile Delinquency 1967
PN 7950   **SC** 27280
  SN Behavior of children or adolescents that is antisocial, dangerous, or criminal, and usually subject to legal action. The age at which juveniles become adults varies across countries and cultures, but usually ranges from 15-18 years.
  HN In 2000, this term became the postable counterpart for the discontinued term JUVENILE DELINQUENTS. JUVENILE DELINQUENTS was removed from all records containing it and replaced with JUVENILE DELINQUENCY.
  UF Delinquency (Juvenile)
    Offenders (Juvenile)
  B Antisocial Behavior 1971
    Behavior Disorders 1971
    Criminal Behavior 2003
  N Female Delinquency 2001
    Male Delinquency 2001
  R Antisocial Personality Disorder 1973
    Crime Prevention 1985
    ↓ Criminals 1967

Juvenile Delinquency — (cont'd)
　　Juvenile Gangs 1973
　　Juvenile Justice 2004
　　Predelinquent Youth 1978

Juvenile Gangs 1973
PN 549　　　　　　　SC 27300
　UF　Gangs (Juvenile)
　R　↓ Juvenile Delinquency 1967
　　　Juvenile Justice 2004

Juvenile Justice 2004
PN 83　　　　　　　SC 27303
　SN　Conceptually broad term referring to the laws, legal services and programs, and judicial institutions that deal with delinquent and/or exploited children and adolescents.
　HN　This term was introduced in June 2004. Psyc INFO records from the past 10 years were re-indexed with this term. The posting note reflects the number of records that were re-indexed.
　B　Criminal Justice 1991
　R　↓ Adjudication 1967
　　　Child Welfare 1988
　　↓ Juvenile Delinquency 1967
　　　Juvenile Gangs 1973
　　　Predelinquent Youth 1978

Kainic Acid 1988
PN 197　　　　　　　SC 27305
　B　Acids 1973
　R　Glutamic Acid 1973
　　↓ Neurotoxins 1982

Kangaroos 1973
PN 20　　　　　　　SC 27310
　B　Marsupials 1973

Karate
　Use　Martial Arts

Karyotype Disorders
　Use　Chromosome Disorders

Kaufman Assessment Battery for Children 2001
PN 177　　　　　　　SC 27323
　HN　In 2000, the truncated term KAUFMAN ASSESSMENT BATTERY CHILDREN (which was used from 1988-2000) was deleted, removed from all records containing it, and replaced with its expanded form KAUFMAN ASSESSMENT BATTERY FOR CHILDREN.
　B　Intelligence Measures 1967

Ketamine 1997
PN 221　　　　　　　SC 27327
　B　Anesthetic Drugs 1973

Keyboards 1985
PN 93　　　　　　　SC 27328
　B　Apparatus 1967
　R　↓ Computer Peripheral Devices 1985
　　　Human Computer Interaction 1997
　　↓ Instrument Controls 1985
　　　Typing 1991

Keypunch Operators
　Use　Clerical Personnel

Kibbutz 1973
PN 370　　　　　　　SC 27340
　B　Communes 1973

Kidnapping 1988
PN 112　　　　　　　SC 27345
　UF　Child Abduction
　B　Crime 1967
　R　Hostages 1988
　　↓ Violent Crime 2003

Kidney Diseases 1988
PN 524　　　　　　　SC 27347
　UF　Renal Diseases
　B　Urogenital Disorders 1973

Kidney Transplants
　Use　Organ Transplantation

Kidneys 1973
PN 305　　　　　　　SC 27360
　B　Urogenital System 1973

Kinases 1982
PN 571　　　　　　　SC 27366
　SN　Enzymes that catalyze the conversion of proenzymes to active enzymes or the transfer of phosphate groups to form triphosphates (ATP).
　UF　Enteropeptidase
　B　Enzymes 1973

Kindergarten Students 1973
PN 3573　　　　　　　SC 27370
　SN　Students in kindergarten.
　B　Students 1967
　R　Grade Level 1994
　　↓ Preschool Students 1982

Kindergartens 1973
PN 315　　　　　　　SC 27380
　B　Schools 1967

Kindling 1985
PN 361　　　　　　　SC 27385
　SN　Afterdischarges and generalized convulsions produced by repeated brain stimulation, usually electrical. Often used as an experimental model of epilepsy.
　B　Electrical Activity 1967
　R　Electrical Brain Stimulation 1973
　　　Experimental Epilepsy 1978

Kinesics
　Use　Body Language

Kinesthetic Perception 1967
PN 1182　　　　　　　SC 27390
　SN　Sensory modality involving awareness of body movement, position, and posture, and movement of body parts, such as muscles, tendons, and joints. Used for human or animal populations.
　B　Somesthetic Perception 1967
　R　Spatial Orientation (Perception) 1973

Kinship 1985
PN 614　　　　　　　SC 27395
　SN　The state of being related such as by birth, common ancestry, or marriage. Used for human or animal populations.

Kinship — (cont'd)
　B　Interpersonal Relationships 2004
　R　Ethnology 1967
　　↓ Family 1967
　　　Kinship Recognition 1988
　　　Kinship Structure 1973

Kinship Recognition 1988
PN 386　　　　　　　SC 27399
　R　↓ Discrimination Learning 1982
　　　Kinship 1985
　　　Species Recognition 1985

Kinship Structure 1973
PN 209　　　　　　　SC 27400
　R　Ethnography 1973
　　　Ethnology 1967
　　↓ Family Structure 1973
　　　Kinship 1985
　　↓ Sociocultural Factors 1967

Kirton Adaption Innovation Inventory 2001
PN 9　　　　　　　SC 27411
　HN　In 2000, the truncated term KIRTON ADAPTION INNOVATION INVEN (which was used from 1997-2000) was deleted, removed from all records containing it, and replaced with its expanded form KIRTON ADAPTION INNOVATION INVENTORY.
　B　Personality Measures 1967

Kleine Levin Syndrome 2001
PN 6　　　　　　　SC 27415
　SN　A condition characterized by recurrent hypersomnia and hyperphagia and marked by such symptoms as mental confusion, excessive sleep requirements, restlessness, and hallucinations.
　B　Eating Disorders 1997
　　　Sleep Disorders 1973
　　　Syndromes 1973
　R　Hyperphagia 1973
　　　Hypersomnia 1994

Kleptomania 1973
PN 78　　　　　　　SC 27420
　R　↓ Impulse Control Disorders 1997
　　　Impulsiveness 1973
　　↓ Personality Disorders 1967

Klinefelters Syndrome 1973
PN 88　　　　　　　SC 27430
　B　Hypogonadism 1973
　　　Male Genital Disorders 1973
　　　Neonatal Disorders 1973
　　　Sex Chromosome Disorders 1973
　　　Syndromes 1973
　R　↓ Infertility 1973
　　↓ Mental Retardation 1967

Knee 1973
PN 151　　　　　　　SC 27440
　B　Joints (Anatomy) 1973
　R　Leg (Anatomy) 1973

Knowledge Based Systems
　Use　Expert Systems

Knowledge Engineering 2003
PN 22　　　　　　　SC 27444
　SN　The process of creating intelligent systems. Used in artificial intelligence discussions.

Knowledge Engineering — (cont'd)
HN This term was introduced in June 2003. Psyc-INFO records from the past 10 years were re-indexed with this term. The posting note reflects the number of records that were re-indexed.
B Artificial Intelligence 1982
R Decision Support Systems 1997
↓ Expert Systems 1991
↓ Information Systems 1991

Knowledge Level 1978
PN 11104   SC 27446
SN Range of received or acquired information, understanding, or awareness. Limited to human populations.
N Health Knowledge 1994
Job Knowledge 1997
R Declarative Knowledge 1997
↓ Experience Level 1988
Information 1967
Procedural Knowledge 1997
Wisdom 1994

Knowledge of Results 1967
PN 607   SC 27450
B Feedback 1967

Kohlberg (Lawrence) 1991
PN 99   SC 27455
SN Identifies biographical or autobiographical studies and discussions of Kohlberg's works.
R Moral Development 1973
↓ Psychologists 1967

Kohs Block Design Test 1973
PN 31   SC 27460
UF Block Design Test (Kohs)
B Intelligence Measures 1967

Kolmogorov Smirnov Test 1973
PN 4   SC 27470
B Nonparametric Statistical Tests 1967

Korean Cultural Groups 1997
PN 283   SC 27483
HN Use ASIANS to access references from 1982-1996.
B Asians 1982

Koro 1994
PN 39   SC 27485
SN A mental disorder characterized by fear or delusions of the shrinkage of the penis, labia, or breasts into the abdomen or chest. Observed primarily in Southern Chinese and some African cultures.
B Body Image Disturbances 1973
Culture Bound Syndromes 2004
Mental Disorders 1967

Korsakoffs Psychosis 1973
PN 498   SC 27490
B Alcoholic Hallucinosis 1973
R Confabulation 1973

Kuder Occupational Interest Survey 1973
PN 48   SC 27510
B Occupational Interest Measures 1973

Kuder Preference Record 1973
PN 20   SC 27520
B Preference Measures 1973

Kupfer Detre Self Rating Scale
Use Nonprojective Personality Measures

Kwashiorkor 1973
PN 8   SC 27550
B Protein Deficiency Disorders 1973

L Dopa
Use Levodopa

Labeling 1978
PN 1372   SC 27565
SN In social or therapeutic settings, designating the condition of an individual or group by a simplistic word or phrase which may serve to indicate status, stigma, or other characteristics.
R ↓ Attitudes 1967
↓ Diagnosis 1967
↓ Names 1985
↓ Psychodiagnostic Typologies 1967
↓ Social Perception 1967
Stereotyped Attitudes 1967
Stigma 1991

Labor (Childbirth) 1973
PN 424   SC 27570
R ↓ Birth 1967
Childbirth Training 1978
Midwifery 1985
Obstetrical Complications 1978

Labor Management Relations 1967
PN 784   SC 27580
UF Labor Relations
B Human Resource Management 2003
R Informants 1988
Labor Unions 1973
↓ Management 1967
Mediation 1988
↓ Organizational Behavior 1978
Psychological Contracts 2003
Strikes 1973
Supervisor Employee Interaction 1997

Labor Relations
Use Labor Management Relations

Labor Union Members 1973
PN 268   SC 27600
R ↓ Personnel 1967

Labor Unions 1973
PN 501   SC 27610
B Organizations 1967
R Labor Management Relations 1967

Laboratories (Educational)
Use Educational Laboratories

Laboratories (Experimental)
Use Experimental Laboratories

Laborers (Construction and Industry)
Use Blue Collar Workers

Laborers (Farm)
Use Agricultural Workers

Labyrinth (Anatomy) 1973
PN 145   SC 27660
SN The bony structure of the inner ear that houses the membranous labyrinth (i.e., the cochlea, vestibule, semicircular canals, utricle, and saccule). May also refer to these latter membranous structures.
UF Inner Ear
B Ear (Anatomy) 1967
N Cochlea 1973
R ↓ Vestibular Apparatus 1967

Labyrinth (Apparatus)
Use Mazes

Labyrinth Disorders 1973
PN 69   SC 27680
B Ear Disorders 1973
N Menieres Disease 1973
Motion Sickness 1973
R ↓ Somesthetic Perception 1967
Vertigo 1973

Lactate Dehydrogenase 1973
PN 24   SC 27690
B Dehydrogenases 1973

Lactation 1973
PN 675   SC 27700
B Secretion (Gland) 1973
R Breast Feeding 1973
Postnatal Period 1973

Lactic Acid 1991
PN 94   SC 27720
UF Sodium Lactate
B Acids 1973

Language 1967
PN 10155   SC 27740
N ↓ Dialect 1973
↓ Figurative Language 1985
Foreign Languages 1973
↓ Form Classes (Language) 1973
Native Language 2004
Phrases 1973
Profanity 1991
Rhetoric 1991
Sentences 1967
Sign Language 1973
Spelling 1973
↓ Vocabulary 1967
↓ Written Language 1967
R Bilingualism 1973
Discourse Analysis 1997
English as Second Language 1997
↓ Grammar 1967
↓ Language Development 1967
↓ Linguistics 1973
↓ Literacy 1973
Metalinguistics 1994
Monolingualism 1973
↓ Multilingualism 1973
Neurolinguistics 1991
Symbolism 1967
↓ Verbal Communication 1967

Language Alternation
Use Code Switching

Language Arts Education 1973
PN 2121   SC 27750

Language Arts Education — (cont'd)

SN Education in subjects aimed at development of comprehension and use of written and oral language.
- **B** Curriculum 1967
- **N** Phonics 1973
  - Reading Education 1973
  - Spelling 1973
- **R** English as Second Language 1997
  - Initial Teaching Alphabet 1973
  - ↓ Literacy 1973
  - Literacy Programs 1997

Language Delay 1988

PN 424   **SC** 27755
- **B** Delayed Development 1973
  - Language Development 1967
- **R** ↓ Language Disorders 1982
  - Retarded Speech Development 1973

Language Development 1967

PN 12494   **SC** 27760
SN Acquisition of the rules governing the structure of language (e.g., syntax) and meaning. Use SPEECH DEVELOPMENT for acquisition of speech sound production. Compare VERBAL LEARNING.
- **B** Cognitive Development 1973
  - Intellectual Development 1973
- **N** Language Delay 1988
- **R** Foreign Language Learning 1967
  - ↓ Language 1967
  - ↓ Language Disorders 1982
  - Metalinguistics 1994
  - Reading Development 1997
  - ↓ Speech Development 1973
  - ↓ Verbal Communication 1967
  - Vygotsky (Lev) 1991

Language Disorders 1982

PN 3310   **SC** 27763
SN Disorders, usually due to cognitive or neurological dysfunction, resulting in problems in symbolization or in delays in language and speech development.
- **B** Communication Disorders 1982
- **N** ↓ Aphasia 1967
  - Echolalia 1973
  - ↓ Mutism 1973
- **R** Language Delay 1988
  - ↓ Language Development 1967
  - Neurolinguistics 1991
  - ↓ Speech Disorders 1967

Language Laboratories 1973

PN 7   **SC** 27770
- **B** Educational Laboratories 1973
- **R** Foreign Language Learning 1967
  - Learning Centers (Educational) 1973

Language Proficiency 1988

PN 1253   **SC** 27773
SN Accuracy and fluency of verbal communication in a second language learning or bilingual context. Includes concept of Limited English Proficiency, which is knowledge of English without sufficient proficiency to communicate or participate in an English-speaking society. Consider VERBAL FLUENCY for other contexts.
- **UF** Limited English Proficiency
- **B** Communication Skills 1973
  - Verbal Communication 1967
- **R** Bilingualism 1973
  - English as Second Language 1997
  - Foreign Language Learning 1967

Language Proficiency — (cont'd)
- Verbal Ability 1967
- Verbal Fluency 1973

Larvae 1973

PN 327   **SC** 27780
- **B** Insects 1967
- **R** Ants 1973
  - Bees 1973
  - Beetles 1973
  - Butterflies 1973
  - Cockroaches 1973
  - ↓ Diptera 1973
  - Drosophila 1973
  - ↓ Fishes 1967
  - Frogs 1967
  - Grasshoppers 1973
  - Mantis 1973
  - Moths 1973
  - Salamanders 1973
  - Toads 1973
  - Wasps 1982

Laryngeal Disorders 1973

PN 107   **SC** 27790
- **B** Respiratory Tract Disorders 1973

Larynx 1973

PN 182   **SC** 27800
- **B** Respiratory System 1973
- **N** Vocal Cords 1973

Laser Irradiation 1973

PN 35   **SC** 27810
- **B** Radiation 1967

Latchkey Children
Use Child Self Care

Latency (Response)
Use Response Latency

Lateness
Use Tardiness

Latent Inhibition 1997

PN 333   **SC** 27825
- **B** Interference (Learning) 1967
- **N** Proactive Inhibition 1973
  - Retroactive Inhibition 1973
- **R** Conditioned Stimulus 1973
  - ↓ Conditioning 1967
  - Forgetting 1973
  - ↓ Memory 1967
  - Prepulse Inhibition 1997

Latent Learning 1973

PN 120   **SC** 27830
SN Learning that is not immediately manifested in performance but which remains dormant until activated by some contingency. Use INCIDENTAL LEARNING for human populations.
HN From 1982, limited to animal populations.
- **B** Incidental Learning 1967

Latent Trait Theory
Use Item Response Theory

Lateral Dominance 1967

PN 7656   **SC** 27840
SN The tendency for the right or left hemisphere to be dominant over the other for most functions, leading to a differential primacy, functional asymmetry, or preference for one side of the body. Compare CEREBRAL DOMINANCE.
- **UF** Hemispheric Specialization
- **B** Cerebral Dominance 1973
- **N** Handedness 1978
  - Ocular Dominance 1973
- **R** ↓ Brain 1967
  - Left Brain 1991
  - Right Brain 1991

Latinos/Latinas
Use Hispanics

Laughter 1978

PN 327   **SC** 27855
- **B** Vocalization 1967
- **R** ↓ Emotional Responses 1967
  - ↓ Humor 1967
  - ↓ Nonverbal Communication 1971
  - Smiles 1973

Law (Government) 1973

PN 318   **SC** 27860
SN Science and philosophy of law as sanctioned by governmental authority. For specific laws or statutes, use LAWS.
- **N** Civil Law 1994
  - Criminal Law 1973
- **R** Defendants 1985
  - Government 1967
  - ↓ Justice 1973
  - ↓ Law Enforcement 1978
  - ↓ Laws 1967
  - Political Psychology 1997

Law Enforcement 1978

PN 838   **SC** 27865
- **B** Legal Processes 1973
- **N** ↓ Adjudication 1967
  - Incarceration 1973
  - Legal Arrest 1973
  - Legal Detention 1973
- **R** Civil Law 1994
  - Crime Prevention 1985
  - ↓ Criminal Justice 1991
  - Government 1967
  - ↓ Justice 1973
  - ↓ Law (Government) 1973
  - ↓ Laws 1967
  - ↓ Legal Evidence 1991
  - Legal Interrogation 1994
  - Parole 1973
  - Probation 1973

Law Enforcement Personnel 1973

PN 459   **SC** 27870
- **B** Government Personnel 1973
  - Legal Personnel 1985
- **N** Parole Officers 1973
  - Police Personnel 1973
  - Prison Personnel 1973
  - Probation Officers 1973
- **R** Attorneys 1973
  - ↓ Social Workers 1973

Law Students 1978

PN 203   **SC** 27875
- **B** Students 1967

Law Students — (cont'd)
R   Attorneys 1973
    Graduate Students 1967

Laws 1967
PN 4927   SC 27880
SN Rules of conduct made obligatory by some legal or controlling authority; includes statutes enacted by a legislative body.
B   Government Policy Making 1973
N   Abortion Laws 1973
    Disability Laws 1994
    ↓ Drug Laws 1973
    Gun Control Laws 1973
R   ↓ Abuse Reporting 1997
    Censorship 1978
    Citizenship 1973
    ↓ Civil Rights 1978
    Consumer Protection 1973
    Government 1967
    ↓ Law (Government) 1973
    ↓ Law Enforcement 1978
    Legal Decisions 1991
    ↓ Legal Processes 1973
    Legislative Processes 1973
    Litigation 2003

Lawsuits
Use Litigation

Lawyers
Use Attorneys

Lay Religious Personnel 1973
PN 82   SC 27900
SN Participants or members of a religious group or organization who perform various functional and ceremonial tasks not requiring a member of the clergy.
B   Religious Personnel 1973
R   Chaplains 1973
    ↓ Clergy 1973
    Evangelists 1973
    Missionaries 1973

Lead (Metal) 1973
PN 260   SC 27910
B   Metallic Elements 1973

Lead Poisoning 1973
PN 357   SC 27920
B   Toxic Disorders 1973
R   Pica 1973

Leadership 1967
PN 6081   SC 27930
B   Social Behavior 1967
N   Leadership Qualities 1997
    Leadership Style 1973
    Transformational Leadership 2003
R   Abuse of Power 1997
    Authority 1967
    Entrepreneurship 1991
    ↓ Management 1967

Leadership Qualities 1997
PN 412   SC 27935
B   Leadership 1967
R   Charisma 1988
    Leadership Style 1973
    ↓ Management 1967
    ↓ Personality Traits 1967

Leadership Style 1973
PN 2877   SC 27940
B   Leadership 1967
    Social Behavior 1967
R   Charisma 1988
    Leadership Qualities 1997
    Transformational Leadership 2003

Learned Helplessness 1978
PN 1631   SC 27945
SN Learned expectation that one's responses are independent of reward and, hence, do not predict or control the occurrence of rewards. Learned helplessness derives from a history, experimentally induced or naturally occurring, of having received punishment/aversive stimulation regardless of responses made. Such circumstances result in an impaired ability to learn. Used for human or animal populations.
UF Helplessness (Learned)
B   Helplessness 1997
R   Attribution 1973
    ↓ Emotional States 1973
    Experimental Neurosis 1973

Learning 1967
PN 18220   SC 28030
SN Conceptually broad term referring to the process of acquiring knowledge, skills, or behaviors by instruction, study, or experience. Use a more specific term if possible.
N   Adult Learning 1997
    ↓ Animal Learning 2003
    Cat Learning 1967
    Cognitive Hypothesis Testing 1982
    ↓ Conditioning 1967
    Cooperative Learning 1994
    ↓ Discrimination Learning 1982
    ↓ Experiential Learning 1997
    Extinction (Learning) 1967
    Foreign Language Learning 1967
    ↓ Generalization (Learning) 1982
    Generation Effect (Learning) 1991
    Implicit Learning 2004
    ↓ Incidental Learning 1967
    Intentional Learning 1973
    ↓ Interference (Learning) 1967
    Mastery Learning 1985
    Maze Learning 1967
    Mnemonic Learning 1973
    Nonverbal Learning 1973
    Observational Learning 1973
    Organizational Learning 2003
    Overlearning 1967
    ↓ Perceptual Motor Learning 1967
    Probability Learning 1967
    Rat Learning 1967
    Relearning 1973
    School Learning 1967
    Self Regulated Learning 2003
    Sequential Learning 1973
    ↓ Serial Learning 1967
    ↓ Skill Learning 1973
    ↓ Social Learning 1973
    Spatial Learning 1994
    Spontaneous Recovery (Learning) 1973
    State Dependent Learning 1982
    ↓ Transfer (Learning) 1967
    Trial and Error Learning 1973
    ↓ Verbal Learning 1967
R   Activity Theory 2003
    ↓ Cognitive Processes 1967
    ↓ Concept Formation 1967
    Connectionism 1994
    Constructivism 1994
    Delayed Alternation 1994

Learning — (cont'd)
    ↓ Feedback 1967
    Forgetting 1973
    ↓ Habits 1967
    Individualized Instruction 1973
    Intelligent Tutoring Systems 2003
    Learning Ability 1973
    ↓ Learning Disorders 1967
    Learning Environment 2004
    Learning Rate 1973
    ↓ Learning Schedules 1967
    ↓ Learning Strategies 1991
    Learning Theory 1967
    Machine Learning 2003
    ↓ Memory 1967
    Metacognition 1991
    Primacy Effect 1973
    ↓ Prompting 1967
    Recency Effect 1973
    ↓ Reinforcement 1967
    ↓ Retention 1967
    ↓ Serial Position Effect 1982
    Spontaneous Alternation 1982
    ↓ Strategies 1967
    Time On Task 1988

Learning Ability 1973
PN 1335   SC 27960
SN Capacity to acquire a behavior, skill, or knowledge from experience, formal instruction, or conditioning. Used for animal or human populations.
B   Ability 1967
R   ↓ Animal Learning 2003
    ↓ Learning 1967

Learning Centers (Educational) 1973
PN 88   SC 27970
B   School Facilities 1973
R   Language Laboratories 1973

Learning Disabilities 1973
PN 13757   SC 27980
SN According to U.S. federal legislation, disabilities involved in understanding or using language, manifested in impaired listening, thinking, talking, reading, writing, or arithmetic skills. Includes perceptual handicaps, brain injury, minimal brain dysfunction, and developmental aphasia. Compare LEARNING DISORDERS.
B   Disabilities 2003
    Learning Disorders 1967
N   Dyslexia 1973
R   Acalculia 1973
    Agraphia 1973
    ↓ Aphasia 1967
    Educational Diagnosis 1978
    Minimal Brain Disorders 1973
    ↓ Perceptual Disturbances 1973

Learning Disorders 1967
PN 1512   SC 27990
SN According to U.S. federal legislation, learning problems that are due to visual, hearing, or motor handicaps, mental retardation, emotional disturbance or environmental, cultural, or economic disadvantage. Compare LEARNING DISABILITIES.
B   Disorders 1967
N   ↓ Learning Disabilities 1973
    ↓ Reading Disabilities 1967
R   Developmental Disabilities 1982
    Educational Diagnosis 1978
    ↓ Learning 1967
    ↓ Mental Disorders 1967
    ↓ Physical Disorders 1997

Learning Environment 2004
PN 131   SC 27991
SN Used for any environment where learning can occur. Not limited to educational settings.
HN This term was introduced in June 2004. Psyc-INFO records from the past 10 years were re-indexed with this term. The posting note reflects the number of records that were re-indexed.
B   Environment 1967
R ↓ Academic Environment 1973
    Classroom Environment 1973
    Home Environment 1973
   ↓ Learning 1967
   ↓ Learning Strategies 1991
   ↓ School Environment 1973

Learning Organizations
   Use Organizational Learning

Learning Rate 1973
PN 596   SC 28000
R ↓ Learning 1967
   ↓ Serial Position Effect 1982

Learning Schedules 1967
PN 113   SC 28010
UF Schedules (Learning)
N   Distributed Practice 1973
    Massed Practice 1973
R ↓ Learning 1967

Learning Strategies 1991
PN 2661   SC 28013
SN Techniques, methods, or tactics used for learning.
UF Strategies (Learning)
B   Strategies 1967
N   Mnemonic Learning 1973
    Observational Learning 1973
   ↓ Social Learning 1973
    Trial and Error Learning 1973
R   Advance Organizers 1985
   ↓ Cognitive Processes 1967
   ↓ Cognitive Style 1967
    Constant Time Delay 1997
   ↓ Learning 1967
    Learning Environment 2004
    Memory Training 1994
    Metacognition 1991
    Note Taking 1991
   ↓ Prompting 1997
    Self Regulated Learning 2003
    Study Habits 1973
    Time Management 1994

Learning Style
   Use Cognitive Style

Learning Theory 1967
PN 2136   SC 28020
B   Theories 1967
R ↓ Classical Conditioning 1967
    Connectionism 1994
   ↓ Learning 1967
   ↓ Operant Conditioning 1967

Least Preferred Coworker Scale 1973
PN 62   SC 28050
B   Preference Measures 1973

Least Squares 1985
PN 207   SC 28055

Least Squares — (cont'd)
SN Method of estimating the curve-of-best-fit or regression line of a set of points representing statistical data.
B   Statistical Estimation 1985
R   Error of Measurement 1985
   ↓ Statistical Regression 1985

Lecithin 1991
PN 8   SC 28058
B   Choline 1973
    Phosphatides 1973

Lecture Method 1973
PN 671   SC 28060
B   Teaching Methods 1967
R   Directed Discussion Method 1973

Left Brain 1991
PN 669   SC 28070
SN Used only when the left hemisphere of the brain is the focus of the document.
B   Cerebral Cortex 1967
R ↓ Brain 1967
   ↓ Cerebral Dominance 1973
    Corpus Callosum 1973
    Interhemispheric Interaction 1985
   ↓ Lateral Dominance 1967
    Ocular Dominance 1973
    Right Brain 1991

Leg (Anatomy) 1973
PN 377   SC 28080
B   Musculoskeletal System 1973
R   Ankle 1973
    Feet (Anatomy) 1973
    Knee 1973
    Thigh 1973

Legal Arrest 1973
PN 551   SC 28090
SN Taking custody, under legal authority, of a person for the purpose of holding or detaining him/her to answer criminal charges or civil demands.
UF Arrest (Law)
B   Law Enforcement 1978

Legal Confession 2003
PN 14   SC 28093
SN Disclosure of information that could be considered damaging to the person confessing.
HN This term was introduced in June 2003. Psyc-INFO records from the past 10 years were re-indexed with this term. The posting note reflects the number of records that were re-indexed.
UF Confession (Legal)
B   Legal Processes 1973
R ↓ Legal Evidence 1991
    Legal Interrogation 1994
   ↓ Legal Testimony 1982
    Self Disclosure 1973

Legal Decisions 1991
PN 767   SC 28095
SN Used for discussions of the implications or the effects of specific judicial decisions. Not used for the actual process of judicial decision making.
R ↓ Adjudication 1967
    Criminal Conviction 1973
   ↓ Criminal Justice 1991
   ↓ Laws 1967
   ↓ Legal Processes 1973

Legal Decisions — (cont'd)
    Legislative Processes 1973
    Litigation 2003

Legal Detention 1973
PN 138   SC 28100
SN Being detained (e.g., in jail) by law enforcers for having committed or for being suspected of having committed a crime, especially immediately prior to a legal court disposition.
UF Detention (Legal)
B   Law Enforcement 1978
R   Legal Interrogation 1994

Legal Evidence 1991
PN 404   SC 28103
SN Testimony, records, documents, objects, and diagrams submitted to a court during a hearing or trial.
B   Legal Processes 1973
N ↓ Legal Testimony 1982
R ↓ Adjudication 1967
   ↓ Law Enforcement 1978
    Legal Confession 2003
    Legal Interrogation 1994
    Litigation 2003
    Witnesses 1985

Legal Interrogation 1994
PN 167   SC 28104
UF Criminal Interrogation
    Police Interrogation
B   Legal Processes 1973
R   Interviewing 1973
   ↓ Law Enforcement 1978
    Legal Confession 2003
    Legal Detention 1973
   ↓ Legal Evidence 1991
   ↓ Legal Testimony 1982
    Polygraphs 1973
    Questioning 1982
    Witnesses 1985

Legal Liability (Professional)
   Use Professional Liability

Legal Personnel 1985
PN 226   SC 28107
UF Paralegal Personnel
B   Professional Personnel 1978
N   Attorneys 1973
    Judges 1985
   ↓ Law Enforcement Personnel 1973
R   Juries 1985

Legal Processes 1973
PN 7007   SC 28110
SN Broad concept encompassing psychological and behavioral aspects of the law--its formation, enforcement, impact, and implications. Also includes reference to the legal justice system and legislative processes as they relate to psychology.
N ↓ Adoption (Child) 1967
    Child Custody 1982
    Child Visitation 1988
   ↓ Commitment (Psychiatric) 1973
    Competency to Stand Trial 1985
   ↓ Criminal Justice 1991
    Forensic Evaluation 1994
    Guardianship 1988
    Insanity Defense 1985
   ↓ Law Enforcement 1978
    Legal Confession 2003

Legal Processes — (cont'd)
  ↓ Legal Evidence 1991
    Legal Interrogation 1994
  ↓ Legal Testimony 1982
    Legislative Processes 1973
    Litigation 2003
    Parole 1973
    Probation 1973
R Advance Directives 1994
    Civil Law 1994
  ↓ Civil Rights 1978
    Consumer Protection 1973
    Government 1967
  ↓ Government Policy Making 1973
    Informed Consent 1985
  ↓ Laws 1967
    Legal Decisions 1991
    Professional Liability 1985
    Protective Services 1997
    Risk Management 1997
  ↓ Social Issues 1991

Legal Psychology
Use Forensic Psychology

Legal Testimony 1982
PN 924   **SC** 28115
SN Evidence presented by a witness under oath or affirmation (as distinguished from evidence derived from other sources) either orally or written as a deposition or an affidavit.
B Legal Evidence 1991
    Legal Processes 1973
N Expert Testimony 1973
R Legal Confession 2003
    Legal Interrogation 1994
    Litigation 2003
    Witnesses 1985

Legalization (Marihuana)
Use Marijuana Legalization

Legibility 1978
PN 53   **SC** 28127
N Handwriting Legibility 1973
R Readability 1978
  ↓ Written Language 1967

Legibility (Handwriting)
Use Handwriting Legibility

Legislative Processes 1973
PN 691   **SC** 28140
B Government Policy Making 1973
    Legal Processes 1973
R Advocacy 1985
    Government 1967
  ↓ Laws 1967
    Legal Decisions 1991

Leisure Time 1973
PN 2096   **SC** 28150
R Daily Activities 1994
    Hobbies 1988
    Holidays 1988
  ↓ Recreation 1967
    Relaxation 1973

Leiter Adult Intelligence Scale
Use Intelligence Measures

Lemniscal System 1985
PN 18   **SC** 28165
SN Long ascending sensory neural pathways projecting to the diencephalon. This system includes the medial lemniscus, lateral lemniscus, spinothalamic tracts, and secondary trigeminal projections.
B Afferent Pathways 1982
N Spinothalamic Tracts 1973
R Reticular Formation 1967

Lemurs 1973
PN 350   **SC** 28170
UF Bush Babies
B Mammals 1973

Length of Stay
Use Treatment Duration

Lens (Eye) 1973
PN 64   **SC** 28180
B Eye (Anatomy) 1967
R ↓ Light Refraction 1982
    Ocular Accommodation 1982

Leptin 2004
PN 119   **SC** 28182
SN A peptide hormone that regulates food intake and energy balance.
HN This term was introduced in June 2004. PsycINFO records from the past 10 years were re-indexed with this term. The posting note reflects the number of records that were re-indexed.
B Hormones 1967
    Peptides 1973

Lesbian Parents
Use Homosexual Parents

Lesbianism 1973
PN 3221   **SC** 28190
UF Female Homosexuality
B Homosexuality 1967
R Bisexuality 1973
    Heterosexuality 1973
    Homosexual Parents 1994
    Male Homosexuality 1973

Lesions 1967
PN 2230   **SC** 28200
HN Not defined prior to 1982. From 1982, limited to experimentally induced lesions and used primarily for animal populations.
UF Ablation
    Sectioning (Lesion)
N ↓ Brain Lesions 1967
    Neural Lesions 1973
R ↓ Surgery 1971

Lesson Plans 1973
PN 177   **SC** 28220
B Teaching Methods 1967

Letters (Alphabet) 1973
PN 1978   **SC** 28230
B Alphabets 1973
N Consonants 1973
    Vowels 1973

Leucine 1973
PN 52   **SC** 28240
B Amino Acids 1973

Leucocytes 1973
PN 391   **SC** 28250
UF Leukocytes
    White Blood Cells
B Blood Cells 1973
N Lymphocytes 1973
    Natural Killer Cells 2003

Leukemias 1973
PN 417   **SC** 28260
B Blood and Lymphatic Disorders 1973
    Neoplasms 1967

Leukocytes
Use Leucocytes

Leukotomy
Use Psychosurgery

Level of Functioning
Use Ability Level

Levodopa 1973
PN 885   **SC** 28290
UF L Dopa
B Antitremor Drugs 1973
    Cholinergic Blocking Drugs 1973
R DOPA 1973
    Dopamine 1973

Lewy Body Disease
Use Dementia with Lewy Bodies

Lexical Access 1988
PN 1972   **SC** 29293
N Lexical Decision 1988
R Cognitive Discrimination 1973
    Human Information Storage 1973
    Semantic Memory 1988
  ↓ Verbal Memory 1994
    Word Meaning 1973
    Words (Phonetic Units) 1967

Lexical Decision 1988
PN 1806   **SC** 29296
B Lexical Access 1988
R Cognitive Discrimination 1973
    Human Information Storage 1973
    Semantic Memory 1988
  ↓ Verbal Memory 1994
    Word Meaning 1973
    Words (Phonetic Units) 1967

Liberalism 1973
PN 206   **SC** 28298
B Personality Traits 1967
R Political Liberalism 1973

Liberalism (Political)
Use Political Liberalism

Libido 1973
PN 262   **SC** 28310
B Psychoanalytic Personality Factors 1973
R Inhibited Sexual Desire 1997
    Sex Drive 1973

Librarians 1988
PN 61   **SC** 28314

Librarians — (cont'd)
B   Information Specialists 1988
R   ↓ Professional Personnel 1978

Libraries 1982
PN 134   SC 28317
N   School Libraries 1973
R   ↓ Community Facilities 1973
     Information 1967
     Information Services 1988

Libraries (School)
Use   School Libraries

Librium
Use   Chlordiazepoxide

Licensing (Professional)
Use   Professional Licensing

Licensure Examinations
Use   Professional Examinations

Licking 1988
PN 205   SC 28345
SN   Used for human or animal populations.
UF   Animal Licking Behavior
B   Animal Ethology 1967
     Motor Processes 1967
R   Animal Drinking Behavior 1973
     Animal Grooming Behavior 1978
     Animal Maternal Behavior 1973

Lidocaine 1973
PN 208   SC 28350
UF   Xylocaine
B   Local Anesthetics 1973

Life Changes 2004
PN   SC 28351
SN   Changes in one's life that may be considered
significant and may have an effect on lifestyle, health,
or well-being.
HN   Use LIFE EXPERIENCES to access references
from 1985 to June 2004.
UF   Life Transitions
B   Life Experiences 1973
R   ↓ Aging 1991
     Career Change 1978
    ↓ Developmental Stages 1973
     Divorce 1973
     Life Span 2004
     Lifestyle Changes 1997
    ↓ Marriage 1967
     Menopause 1973
     Parental Death 2003
    ↓ Parenthood Status 1985
    ↓ Pregnancy 1967
    ↓ Quality of Life 1985
     Well Being 1994

Life Course
Use   Life Span

Life Expectancy 1982
PN 670   SC 28352
SN   Anticipated number of years of life for an individual, based on statistical probability. Used for both
human and animal populations.
HN   Use AGED and PHYSIOLOGICAL AGING
together to access references from 1973-1981.

Life Expectancy — (cont'd)
UF   Longevity
R   ↓ Aging 1991
    ↓ Human Development 1967
     Life Span 2004
     Physiological Aging 1967

Life Experiences 1973
PN 7695   SC 28355
SN   Specific events which are commonly considered
noteworthy or memorable (e.g., college graduation,
wedding) or are considered unusual or otherwise sig-
nificant (e.g., life change due to illness). Compare
EXPERIENCES (EVENTS).
UF   Experiences (Life)
B   Experiences (Events) 1973
N   Life Changes 2004
R   Age Regression (Hypnotic) 1988
     Anniversary Events 1994
     Autobiographical Memory 1994
     Biographical Data 1978
     First Experiences 2004
     Homesickness 1994
     Life Review 1991
     Life Satisfaction 1985
     Life Span 2004

Life Insurance 1973
PN 23   SC 28360
B   Insurance 1973

Life Review 1991
PN 314   SC 28361
SN   Reflection on and return to past life experiences
in order to think about and reintegrate them into
present life circumstances. Usually performed in a
treatment or intervention setting. Not limited to elderly populations
HN   Consider using REMINISCENCE to access references from 1985-1990.
R   Anniversary Events 1994
     Autobiographical Memory 1994
     Early Experience 1967
     Early Memories 1985
     Gerontology 1967
    ↓ Life Experiences 1970
     Narratives 1997
     Reminiscence 1985
    ↓ Treatment 1967

Life Satisfaction 1985
PN 2877   SC 28362
B   Satisfaction 1973
R   ↓ Life Experiences 1973
     Lifestyle Changes 1997
    ↓ Quality of Life 1985
     Role Satisfaction 1994
     Well Being 1994

Life Span 2004
PN   SC 28365
HN   Use LIFE EXPECTANCY to access references
from 1002 to June 2004.
UF   Life Course
R   ↓ Development 1967
     Life Changes 2004
     Life Expectancy 1982
    ↓ Life Experiences 1973

Life Sustaining Treatment 1997
PN 166   SC 28368
B   Treatment 1967
R   Advance Directives 1994

Life Sustaining Treatment — (cont'd)
     Assisted Suicide 1997
    ↓ Client Rights 1988
     Medical Treatment (General) 1973
     Palliative Care 1991
     Terminally Ill Patients 1973
     Treatment Refusal 1994
     Treatment Withholding 1988

Life Transitions
Use   Life Changes

Lifesaving
Use   Artificial Respiration

Lifestyle 1978
PN 2763   SC 28375
SN   Typical way of life or manner of living character-
istic of an individual or groups.
N   Lifestyle Changes 1997
R   Daily Activities 1994
    ↓ Health Behavior 1982
     Holistic Health 1985
    ↓ Personality 1967
    ↓ Personality Processes 1967
    ↓ Quality of Life 1985

Lifestyle Changes 1997
PN 274   SC 28380
B   Lifestyle 1978
R   Behavior Change 1973
     Health Attitudes 1985
    ↓ Health Behavior 1982
     Health Promotion 1991
     Life Changes 2004
     Life Satisfaction 1985
    ↓ Quality of Life 1985
     Well Being 1994

Light
Use   Illumination

Light Adaptation 1982
PN 311   SC 28393
SN   Change in the general level of sensitivity of the
photoreceptors as a result of exposure to light.
UF   Adaptation (Light)
B   Sensory Adaptation 1967
R   Dark Adaptation 1973
    ↓ Illumination 1967
    ↓ Visual Thresholds 1973

Light Refraction 1982
PN 47   SC 28395
SN   Deflection of light from a straight path when
passing obliquely through the interface of two media
that have different densities.
N   ↓ Refraction Errors 1973
R   ↓ Illumination 1967
     Lens (Eye) 1973

Light Therapy
Use   Phototherapy

Likability 1988
PN 154   SC 28387
B   Personality Traits 1967
R   Agreeableness 1997
    ↓ Interpersonal Attraction 1967
     Peer Pressure 1994

Likability — (cont'd)
Social Approval 1967
↓ Social Perception 1967

Likert Scales 1994
PN 109   SC 28388
B   Rating Scales 1967
R   Attitude Measurement 1973
↓ Attitude Measures 1967
Self Report 1982
Semantic Differential 1967
↓ Surveys 1967

Liking
Use Affection

Limbic System 1973
PN 1492   SC 28410
B   Cerebral Cortex 1967
Neural Pathways 1982
N   Amygdala 2003
Fornix 1982
Gyrus Cinguli 1973
Hippocampus 1967
Medial Forebrain Bundle 1982
Olfactory Bulb 1973
Septal Nuclei 1982
R   Nucleus Accumbens 1982
Raphe Nuclei 1982

Limen
Use Thresholds

Limited English Proficiency
Use Language Proficiency

Linear Perspective 1982
PN 217   SC 28427
SN Apparent convergence of parallel contours that are projected into the plane of sight of the observer.
UF Visual Perspective
B   Vision 1967
R ↓ Depth Perception 1967
↓ Distance Perception 1973
↓ Size Discrimination 1967
↓ Visual Stimulation 1973

Linear Regression 1973
PN 358   SC 28430
B   Statistical Correlation 1967
Statistical Regression 1985
R   Multiple Regression 1982

Linguistics 1973
PN 3538   SC 28450
N   Ethnolinguistics 1973
Etymology 1973
↓ Grammar 1967
Metalinguistics 1994
Neurolinguistics 1991
Orthography 1973
Psycholinguistics 1967
Sociolinguistics 1985
R   Cognitive Science 2003
Discourse Analysis 1997
↓ Language 1967
Pragmatics 1985
↓ Prosody 1991
↓ Semiotics 1985
↓ Verbal Communication 1967

Linkage Analysis
Use Genetic Linkage

Lions
Use Felids

Lipid Metabolism 1973
PN 176   SC 28460
UF Fat Metabolism
B   Metabolism 1967
R ↓ Lipids 1973

Lipid Metabolism Disorders 1973
PN 56   SC 28470
B   Metabolism Disorders 1973
N   Tay Sachs Disease 2003

Lipids 1973
PN 830   SC 28480
N ↓ Fatty Acids 1973
R   Lipid Metabolism 1973
↓ Steroids 1973

Lipoproteins 1973
PN 355   SC 28490
R   Apolipoproteins 2004
↓ Proteins 1973

Lipreading 1973
PN 345   SC 28500
UF Speechreading
R ↓ Deaf 1967
Speech Perception 1967
↓ Visual Perception 1967

Lips (Face) 1973
PN 149   SC 28510
R   Mouth (Anatomy) 1967

Liquor 1973
PN 51   SC 28520
B   Alcoholic Beverages 1973

Listening
Use Auditory Perception

Listening (Interpersonal) 1997
PN 240   SC 28535
B   Interpersonal Communication 1973
R ↓ Attention 1967
↓ Auditory Perception 1967
Conversation 1973
Listening Comprehension 1973
Social Skills 1978

Listening Comprehension 1973
PN 1513   SC 28540
B   Verbal Comprehension 1985
R   Listening (Interpersonal) 1997

Literacy 1973
PN 2676   SC 28550
UF Illiteracy
N   Computer Literacy 1991
R ↓ Language 1967
↓ Language Arts Education 1973
Literacy Programs 1997
Phonological Awareness 2004
Reading Development 1997

Literacy — (cont'd)
Reading Education 1973
↓ Reading Skills 1973
Writing Skills 1985

Literacy Programs 1997
PN 258   SC 28555
B   Educational Programs 1973
R ↓ Adult Education 1973
↓ Language Arts Education 1973
↓ Literacy 1973
Reading Education 1973
↓ Reading Skills 1973
↓ Social Services 1982
Writing Skills 1985

Literature 1967
PN 5855   SC 28560
UF Fiction
B   Humanities 2003
N   Poetry 1973
↓ Prose 1973
R   Creative Writing 1994
Drama 1973
Folklore 1991
Metaphor 1982
Myths 1967
Narratives 1997
Postmodernism 1997
↓ Religious Literature 1973
Writers 1991

Literature Review 1967
PN 21986   SC 28580
SN Used in records discussing issues involved in the process of conducting surveys of previously published material.
HN From 1967-2000, the term was also used as a mandatory document type identifier; however, this usage has been discontinued due to the advent of Form/Content Type field identifiers. References from 1967-2000 can be accessed using either LITERATURE REVIEW or the Literature Review Form/Content Type field identifier. In 1973, this term replaced the discontinued term REVIEW (OF LITERATURE). In 2000, REVIEW (OF LITERATURE) was removed from all records containing it, and replaced with LITERATURE REVIEW.
UF Review (of Literature)
R   Meta Analysis 1985

Lithium 1973
PN 3477   SC 28590
SN Used for documents that do not specify the type of lithium used, e.g., carbonate, chloride, or bromide. Use a more specific term if possible.
B   Metallic Elements 1973
N   Lithium Carbonate 1973
R ↓ Antidepressant Drugs 1971
↓ Tricyclic Antidepressant Drugs 1997

Lithium Bromide
Use Bromides

Lithium Carbonate 1973
PN 741   SC 28610
B   Antidepressant Drugs 1971
Lithium 1973

Litigation 2003
PN 163   SC 28612
SN A lawsuit or formal court action intended to resolve disputes between two parties.

Litigation — (cont'd)

HN This term was introduced in June 2003. Psyc-INFO records from the past 10 years were re-indexed with this term. The posting note reflects the number of records that were re-indexed.
  UF Lawsuits
  B Legal Processes 1973
  R ↓ Adjudication 1967
    Civil Law 1994
    ↓ Conflict Resolution 1982
    ↓ Criminal Justice 1991
    Criminal Law 1973
    Expert Testimony 1973
    ↓ Laws 1967
    Legal Decisions 1991
    ↓ Legal Evidence 1991
    ↓ Legal Testimony 1982

Litter Size 1985
PN 133   SC 28615
SN Used for animal populations only.
  B Size 1973
  R ↓ Animal Breeding 1973

Liver 1973
PN 403   SC 28620
  B Digestive System 1967

Liver Disorders 1973
PN 278   SC 28630
  UF Hepatic Disorders
  B Digestive System Disorders 1973
  N Cirrhosis (Liver) 1973
    ↓ Hepatitis 1973
    Jaundice 1973
  R ↓ Infectious Disorders 1973
    ↓ Neoplasms 1967
    ↓ Toxic Disorders 1973

Living Alone 1994
PN 59   SC 28633
HN Use LIVING ARRANGEMENTS to access references from 1991-1993.
  B Living Arrangements 1991
  R Cohabitation 1973
    ↓ Family Structure 1973
    Home Environment 1973
    ↓ Marital Status 1973
    Single Persons 1973

Living Arrangements 1991
PN 1060   SC 28635
  UF Household Structure
  N Cohabitation 1973
    Living Alone 1994
  R Assisted Living 2003
    Child Custody 1982
    Empty Nest 1991
    ↓ Family 1967
    ↓ Family Structure 1973
    Home Environment 1973
    ↓ Housing 1973
    ↓ Marital Status 1973
    Retirement Communities 1997
    Roommates 1973
    Shelters 1991
    ↓ Single Sex Environments 2001

Living Wills
  Use Advance Directives

Lizards 1973
PN 531   SC 28640
  B Reptiles 1967

Lobectomy
  Use Psychosurgery

Lobotomy
  Use Psychosurgery

Local Anesthetics 1973
PN 107   SC 28660
  B Anesthetic Drugs 1973
  N ↓ Cocaine 1973
    Lidocaine 1973
    Quinine 1973
  R Ephedrine 1973
    Methoxamine 1973

Localization (Perceptual)
  Use Perceptual Localization

Localization (Sound)
  Use Auditory Localization

Locus Ceruleus 1982
PN 454   SC 28687
SN Pigmented nucleus in the brain stem that synthesizes norepinephrine.
  B Brain Stem 1973
  R Reticular Formation 1967

Locus of Control
  Use Internal External Locus of Control

Logic (Philosophy) 1973
PN 372   SC 28700
  R Philosophies 1967

Logical Thinking 1967
PN 1862   SC 28710
  UF Ratiocination
  B Thinking 1967
  R Analogy 1991
    ↓ Inductive Deductive Reasoning 1973

Logistic Models
  Use Item Response Theory

Logistic Regression 2003
PN 62   SC 28718
SN A type of regression analysis used to predict whether or not something will happen. Most often used when the dependent variable is dichotomous or categorical.
HN This term was introduced in June 2003. Psyc-INFO records from the past 10 years were re-indexed with this term. The posting note reflects the number of records that were re-indexed.
  B Statistical Correlation 1967
    Statistical Regression 1985
  R Multiple Regression 1982

Logotherapy 1973
PN 349   SC 28720
SN Existential analysis based on spiritual values and emphasizing search for the meaning of human existence.

Logotherapy — (cont'd)
  B Psychotherapy 1967
  R Existential Therapy 1973

Loneliness 1973
PN 1586   SC 28730
  B Emotional States 1973
  R Abandonment 1997
    Homesickness 1994

Long Term Care 1994
PN 954   SC 28735
SN Delivery of health or mental health services over a prolonged or extended period. Care can be in an institutional setting or in the community, e.g., at home, and delivered by health care professionals, family, or friends.
  B Health Care Services 1978
    Treatment Duration 1988
  R Adult Day Care 1997
    ↓ Case Management 1991
    Home Care 1985
    ↓ Hospitalization 1967
    ↓ Mental Health Services 1978
    Nursing Homes 1973
    Palliative Care 1991

Long Term Memory 1973
PN 2113   SC 28740
SN Retention of events or learned material for relatively long periods, presumed to be based on permanent encoding and storage of information transferred from short term memory. Consider also RETENTION.
  B Memory 1967

Long Term Potentiation
  Use Postactivation Potentials

Longevity
  Use Life Expectancy

Longitudinal Studies 1973
PN 14055   SC 28760
SN Used in records discussing issues involved in the process of conducting observations or measurements of the same individual or group over an extended period.
HN From 1973-2000, the term was also used as a mandatory document type identifier; however, this usage has been discontinued due to the advent of Form/Content Type field identifiers. References from 1973-2000 can be accessed using either LONGITUDINAL STUDIES or the Longitudinal Studies Form/Content Type field identifier.
  UF Studies (Longitudinal)
  B Experimental Design 1967
  N Prospective Studies 1997
  R Followup Studies 1973
    Retrospective Studies 1997

Loosening of Associations
  Use Fragmentation (Schizophrenia)

Lorazepam 1988
PN 401   SC 28765
  B Benzodiazepines 1978
    Minor Tranquilizers 1973

Lordosis (Animal)
  Use Animal Sexual Receptivity

Loudness 1967
PN 523   SC 28780
  UF   Sound Pressure Level
  B   Auditory Stimulation 1967
  N   Noise Levels (Work Areas) 1973

Loudness Discrimination 1973
PN 185   SC 28790
  B   Loudness Perception 1973

Loudness Perception 1973
PN 331   SC 28800
  B   Auditory Perception 1967
  N   Loudness Discrimination 1973

Love 1973
PN 2013   SC 28830
  B   Emotional States 1973
  R   Affection 1973
        Attachment Behavior 1985
        Erotomania 1997
        Intimacy 1973
        Romance 1997

Low Birth Weight
  Use   Birth Weight

Lower Class 1973
PN 943   SC 28850
  B   Social Class 1967
        Socioeconomic Status 1967

Lower Class Attitudes 1973
PN 70   SC 28860
SN Attitudes of, not toward, the lower class.
  B   Socioeconomic Class Attitudes 1973

Lower Income Level 1973
PN 2261   SC 28870
  B   Income Level 1973
  R   Poverty 1973

Loxapine 1982
PN 52   SC 28875
SN Organic heterocyclic compound used as a tranquilizing agent.
  UF   Oxilapine
  B   Minor Tranquilizers 1973

Loyalty 1973
PN 304   SC 28880
  B   Personality Traits 1967

LSD (Drug)
  Use   Lysergic Acid Diethylamide

Lucid Dreaming 1994
PN 41   SC 28893
  B   Dreaming 1967
  R   Dream Recall 1973
        REM Dreams 1973
        REM Sleep 1973
        ↓ Sleep 1967

Luck
  Use   Chance (Fortune)

Lumbar Spinal Cord 1973
PN 150   SC 28900

Lumbar Spinal Cord — (cont'd)
  B   Spinal Cord 1973

Lumbrosacral Plexus
  Use   Spinal Nerves

Luminance 1982
PN 1425   SC 28930
SN Product of multiplying the physical intensity of a light wave by the spectral sensitivity of the typical observer's visual system for that specific wavelength. Compare ILLUMINATION.
  R   ↓ Brightness Perception 1973
        ↓ Chromaticity 1997
        Color Saturation 1997
        ↓ Illumination 1967
        Stimulus Intensity 1967
        ↓ Visual Thresholds 1973

Luminance Threshold
  Use   Brightness Perception AND Visual Thresholds

Lunar Synodic Cycle 1973
PN 114   SC 28950
SN Successive phases of the moon reflecting its motion around the earth.
  R   ↓ Biological Rhythms 1967
        ↓ Environmental Effects 1973

Lung 1973
PN 159   SC 28960
  B   Respiratory System 1973

Lung Disorders 1973
PN 469   SC 28970
  UF   Pulmonary Disorders
  B   Respiratory Tract Disorders 1973
  N   Cystic Fibrosis 1985
        Pneumonia 1973
        Pulmonary Emphysema 1973
        Pulmonary Tuberculosis 1973
  R   ↓ Dyspnea 1973

Lupus 1973
PN 300   SC 28980
  B   Skin Disorders 1973
  R   ↓ Tuberculosis 1973

Luria Nebraska Neuropsychological Battery 2001
PN 84   SC 28983
HN In 2000, the truncated term LURIA NEBRASKA NEUROPSYCH BATTERY (which was used from 1991-2000) was deleted, removed from all records containing It, and replaced with its expanded form LURIA NEBRASKA NEUROPSYCHOLOGICAL BATTERY. Use NEUROPSYCHOLOGICAL ASSESSMENT to access references from 1982-1990.
  B   Neuropsychological Assessment 1982

Luteinizing Hormone 1978
PN 472   SC 28985
  B   Gonadotropic Hormones 1973
  R   ↓ Pituitary Hormones 1973
        ↓ Sex Hormones 1973

Lutherans
  Use   Protestants

Lying
  Use   Deception

Lymphatic Disorders
  Use   Blood and Lymphatic Disorders

Lymphocytes 1973
PN 720   SC 29060
  B   Leucocytes 1973
  R   Interleukins 1994

Lysergic Acid Diethylamide 1967
PN 848   SC 29070
  UF   LSD (Drug)
  B   Acids 1973
        Amine Oxidase Inhibitors 1973
        Hallucinogenic Drugs 1967
        Psychedelic Drugs 1973
        Psychotomimetic Drugs 1973
        Serotonin Antagonists 1973
  R   ↓ Ergot Derivatives 1973

Machiavellianism 1973
PN 399   SC 29087
SN Extent to which an individual feels that any means, however unscrupulous, can justifiably be used to achieve power.
  B   Personality Traits 1967

Machine Learning 2003
PN 79   SC 29088
SN Changes in systems that perform tasks associated with artificial intelligence.
HN This term was introduced in June 2003. PsycINFO records from the past 10 years were re-indexed with this term. The posting note reflects the number of records that were re-indexed.
  B   Artificial Intelligence 1982
  R   ↓ Expert Systems 1991
        ↓ Learning 1967
        Neural Networks 1991

Magazines 1973
PN 498   SC 29090
  B   Printed Communications Media 1973

Magical Thinking 1973
PN 165   SC 29100
SN Belief that one's utterances, thoughts, or behavior can have a controlling influence on specific events or prevent their occurrence by means that operate beyond the normal laws of cause and effect.
  B   Thinking 1967
        Thought Disturbances 1973
  R   Fantasies (Thought Disturbances) 1967
        ↓ Fantasy 1997
        Imagination 1967
        Omnipotence 1994

Magnesium 1973
PN 189   SC 29110
  B   Metallic Elements 1973
  N   Magnesium Ions 1973

Magnesium Ions 1973
PN 17   SC 29120
  B   Electrolytes 1973
        Magnesium 1973

Magnet Schools
  Use Nontraditional Education

Magnetic Resonance Imaging 1994
PN 1892   **SC** 29133
  UF MRI
  B Neuroimaging 2003
       Tomography 1988
  R Computer Assisted Diagnosis 1973
       Magnetoencephalography 1985

Magnetism 1985
PN 678   **SC** 29135
  UF Geomagnetism
  R Magnetoencephalography 1985
       Physics 1973
       Transcranial Magnetic Stimulation 2003

Magnetoencephalography 1985
PN 341   **SC** 29136
  R ↓ Electroencephalography 1967
       Magnetic Resonance Imaging 1994
       Magnetism 1985

Magnitude Estimation 1991
PN 177   **SC** 29138
  SN Unidimensional scaling method used in statistics and psychophysics for quantitative judgment and ratio estimation.
  B Psychophysical Measurement 1967
       Statistical Estimation 1985
  R Scaling (Testing) 1967

Magnitude of Effect (Statistical)
  Use Effect Size (Statistical)

Maids
  Use Domestic Service Personnel

Mail Surveys 1994
PN 139   **SC** 29141
  B Surveys 1967
  R ↓ Consumer Research 1973
       Consumer Surveys 1973
       ↓ Methodology 1967
       ↓ Questionnaires 1967
       Telephone Surveys 1994

Mainstreaming 1991
PN 319   **SC** 29144
  SN Integration or transition into society of individuals who have been considered for institutionalization or other type of isolation, but are now considered able to learn from education or community involvement.
  N Mainstreaming (Educational) 1978
  R Deinstitutionalization 1982
       Educational Placement 1978
       Habilitation 1991
       Independent Living Programs 1991
       ↓ Rehabilitation 1967
       School to Work Transition 1994
       ↓ Social Integration 1982
       Special Education 1967
       Special Needs 1994

Mainstreaming (Educational) 1978
PN 3283   **SC** 29145
  SN Integration of students with special education needs into classes or schools with regular students.

Mainstreaming (Educational) — (cont'd)
  UF Inclusion (Educational)
  B Mainstreaming 1991
  R ↓ Education 1967
       Educational Placement 1978
       School Integration 1982
       Special Education 1967

Maintenance Therapy 1997
PN 306   **SC** 29142
  SN Treatment or therapy that is designed to maintain patients in a stable condition and to promote either gradual healing or to prevent the relapse of a disorder or condition. Used primarily, but not exclusively, in drug therapy settings.
  R Aftercare 1973
       ↓ Drug Therapy 1967
       Methadone Maintenance 1978
       ↓ Outpatient Treatment 1967
       Relapse Prevention 1994
       ↓ Treatment Duration 1988

Major Depression 1988
PN 37459   **SC** 29143
  SN Affective disorder marked by dysphoric mood, inactivity, lack of interest, insomnia, feelings of worthlessness, diminished ability to think, and thoughts of suicide. Use DEPRESSION (EMOTION) for nonclinical depression.
  HN Consider DEPRESSION (EMOTION) to access references prior to 1988. In 1988, this term replaced the discontinued term PSYCHOTIC DEPRESSIVE REACTION, and in 2000 it replaced the term NEUROTIC DEPRESSIVE REACTION. In 2000, those terms were removed from all records containing it, and replaced with MAJOR DEPRESSION.
  UF Agitated Depression
       Depressive Reaction (Neurotic)
       Dysphoria
       Melancholia
       Neurotic Depressive Reaction
       Psychotic Depressive Reaction
       Unipolar Depression
  B Affective Disorders 2001
  N Anaclitic Depression 1973
       Dysthymic Disorder 1988
       Endogenous Depression 1978
       Involutional Depression 1973
       Postpartum Depression 1973
       Reactive Depression 1970
       Recurrent Depression 1994
       Treatment Resistant Depression 1994
  R ↓ Bipolar Disorder 2001
       Depression (Emotion) 1967
       ↓ Neurosis 1967
       Pseudodementia 1985
       Seasonal Affective Disorder 1991

Major Tranquilizers
  Use Neuroleptic Drugs

Maladjustment (Emotional)
  Use Emotional Adjustment

Maladjustment (Social)
  Use Social Adjustment

Malaria 1973
PN 76   **SC** 29180
  B Blood and Lymphatic Disorders 1973
       Parasitic Disorders 1973
  R ↓ Nervous System Disorders 1967

Male Animals 1973
PN 4247   **SC** 29190
  B Animals 1967

Male Castration 1973
PN 694   **SC** 29200
  SN Used for both human and animal populations.
  B Castration 1967

Male Criminals 1973
PN 1304   **SC** 29210
  B Criminals 1967
       Human Males 1973

Male Delinquency 2001
PN 1140   **SC** 29215
  HN In 2001, this term was created to replace the discontinued term MALE DELINQUENTS. MALE DELINQUENTS was removed from all records containing it and replaced with MALE DELINQUENCY.
  B Juvenile Delinquency 1967
  R Female Delinquency 2001
       ↓ Human Males 1973

Male Female Relations 1988
PN 2307   **SC** 29225
  SN Relationships or interactions between the sexes. Limited to human populations.
  UF Heterosexual Interaction
  B Interpersonal Interaction 1967
  R Heterosexuality 1973
       ↓ Human Courtship 1973
       ↓ Marital Relations 1967
       ↓ Relationship Satisfaction 2001
       ↓ Relationship Termination 1997
       Social Dating 1973
       Social Skills 1970

Male Genital Disorders 1973
PN 49   **SC** 29230
  B Genital Disorders 1967
  N Klinefelters Syndrome 1973
       Testicular Feminization Syndrome 1973
  R ↓ Endocrine Sexual Disorders 1973
       Hermaphroditism 1973
       ↓ Hypogonadism 1973
       ↓ Infertility 1973
       Sterility 1973

Male Genitalia 1973
PN 184   **SC** 29240
  SN Used for both human and animal populations.
  UF Genitalia (Male)
  R Urogenital System 1973
  N Penis 1973
       Prostate 1973
       Testes 1973
  R Circumcision 2001

Male Homosexuality 1973
PN 4759   **SC** 29250
  UF Gay Males
  B Homosexuality 1967
  R Bisexuality 1973
       Heterosexuality 1973
       Homosexual Parents 1994
       Lesbianism 1973

Male Only Environments
  Use Single Sex Environments

Male Orgasm 1973
PN 316   SC 29260
SN Used for both human and animal populations.
UF Ejaculation
B Orgasm 1973
N Nocturnal Emission 1973
    Premature Ejaculation 1973
R Impotence 1973
    Masturbation 1973
    ↓ Sexual Intercourse (Human) 1973

Males (Human)
Use Human Males

Malignant Neoplasms
Use Neoplasms

Malingering 1973
PN 878   SC 29290
SN Feigning or exaggerating illness or symptoms, usually in order to escape work, evoke sympathy, or gain compensation.
B Deception 1967
R ↓ Factitious Disorders 1988
    ↓ Mental Disorders 1967
    Munchausen Syndrome 1994
    ↓ Physical Disorders 1997
    ↓ Somatoform Disorders 2001

Malnutrition
Use Nutritional Deficiencies

Malpractice
Use Professional Liability

Mammals 1973
PN 1648   SC 29310
B Vertebrates 1973
N Bats 1973
    ↓ Canids 1997
    Cattle 1973
    Chimpanzees 1973
    Chinchillas 1973
    Deer 1973
    Elephants 1973
    ↓ Felids 1997
    Goats 1973
    Horses 1973
    Lemurs 1973
    ↓ Marsupials 1973
    ↓ Primates (Nonhuman) 1973
    Rabbits 1967
    ↓ Rodents 1973
    Seals (Animal) 1973
    Sheep 1973
    ↓ Whales 1985

Mammary Glands 1973
PN 19   SC 29320
B Glands 1967

Mammary Neoplasms
Use Breast Neoplasms

Mammillary Bodies (Hypothalamic)
Use Hypothalamus

Mammography 1994
PN 315   SC 29345

Mammography — (cont'd)
B Roentgenography 1973
R Breast Neoplasms 1973
    Cancer Screening 1997
    ↓ Health Screening 1997
    ↓ Medical Diagnosis 1973
    Physical Examination 1988
    Preventive Medicine 1973

Man Machine Systems
Use Human Machine Systems

Man Machine Systems Design
Use Human Machine Systems Design

Managed Care 1994
PN 1735   SC 29365
SN Competitive prepaid plan of health care delivery to contain costs and provide access to quality health care.
HN Use CASE MANAGEMENT to access references from 1991-1993.
B Health Care Delivery 1978
N Health Maintenance Organizations 1982
R ↓ Case Management 1991
    Cost Containment 1991
    Fee for Service 1994
    Health Care Costs 1994
    ↓ Health Care Services 1978
    ↓ Health Insurance 1973
    Quality of Care 1988
    ↓ Treatment Planning 1997

Management 1967
PN 2576   SC 29420
SN Conceptually broad term referring to the process of manipulation of human or material resources to accomplish given goals. Use a more specific term if possible.
N Business Management 1973
    ↓ Case Management 1991
    ↓ Classroom Management 2004
    Disability Management 1991
    Educational Administration 1967
    ↓ Health Care Administration 1997
    Household Management 1985
    Risk Management 1997
    ↓ Self Management 1985
    Stress Management 1985
    Time Management 1994
R Accountability 1988
    Business 1967
    Career Development 1985
    Entrepreneurship 1991
    Labor Management Relations 1967
    ↓ Leadership 1967
    Leadership Qualities 1997
    Management Decision Making 1973
    ↓ Management Methods 1973
    ↓ Management Personnel 1973
    Management Planning 1973
    Management Training 1973
    Transformational Leadership 2003
    ↓ Work Teams 2001

Management Decision Making 1973
PN 1665   SC 29370
B Decision Making 1967
R ↓ Group Decision Making 1978
    ↓ Management 1967
    ↓ Management Methods 1973
    Management Planning 1973
    Participative Management 1988

Management Development
Use Career Development

Management Information Systems
Use Information Systems

Management Methods 1973
PN 3462   SC 29380
N Participative Management 1988
    Self Managing Work Teams 2001
R Business Management 1973
    ↓ Management 1967
    Management Decision Making 1973
    Management Planning 1973
    Supervisor Employee Interaction 1997
    ↓ Teams 1988
    Work Scheduling 1973
    ↓ Work Teams 2001

Management Personnel 1973
PN 9148   SC 29390
UF Administrators
    Supervisors
B White Collar Workers 1973
N Middle Level Managers 1973
    Top Level Managers 1973
R Commissioned Officers 1973
    Industrial Foremen 1973
    ↓ Management 1967
    ↓ School Administrators 1973
    Supervisor Employee Interaction 1997

Management Planning 1973
PN 439   SC 29400
UF Planning (Management)
R ↓ Management 1967
    Management Decision Making 1973
    ↓ Management Methods 1973
    Marketing 1973

Management Training 1973
PN 1464   SC 29410
B Personnel Training 1967
R Business Education 1973
    ↓ Management 1967
    Wilderness Experience 1991

Manager Employee Interaction
Use Supervisor Employee Interaction

Mandibula
Use Jaw

Mania 1967
PN 2452   SC 29450
B Affective Disorders 2001
    Emotional States 1973
N Hypomania 1973
R ↓ Bipolar Disorder 2001

Manic Depression
Use Bipolar Disorder

Manic Depressive Psychosis
Use Bipolar Disorder

Mann Whitney U Test 1973
PN 18   SC 29470
B Nonparametric Statistical Tests 1967

Mannerisms
Use Habits

Manpower
Use Personnel Supply

Mantis 1973
PN 29   **SC** 29500
UF Praying Mantis
B Insects 1967
R Larvae 1973

Manual Communication 1978
PN 161   **SC** 29505
SN Form of communication used by the deaf in which sign language and finger spelling are substituted for speech. Also, an unsystematic or informal method of communication with gestures.
B Augmentative Communication 1994
Nonverbal Communication 1971
Verbal Communication 1967
N Fingerspelling 1973
Sign Language 1973

Manufacturing
Use Business

Maori
Use Indigenous Populations

Maprotiline 1982
PN 211   **SC** 29527
B Tricyclic Antidepressant Drugs 1997

Marathon Group Therapy 1973
PN 138   **SC** 29540
SN Encounter group that meets for extended sessions and that aims to develop the ability to express oneself emotionally and to initiate intimate interpersonal interactions.
B Encounter Group Therapy 1973
R Human Relations Training 1978
Sensitivity Training 1973

Marihuana
Use Marijuana

Marijuana 2003
PN 922   **SC** 29590
HN In June 2003, this term replaced the discontinued term MARIHUANA. MARIHUANA was removed from all records and replaced with MARIJUANA.
UF Marihuana
B Cannabis 1973
R Hashish 1970
↓ Marijuana Laws 1973
Marijuana Usage 1973
Tetrahydrocannabinol 1973

Marijuana Laws 1973
PN 29   **SC** 29560
B Drug Laws 1973
N Marijuana Legalization 1973
R Government 1967
Marijuana 2003
Marijuana Usage 1973

Marijuana Legalization 1973
PN 39   **SC** 29570

Marijuana Legalization — (cont'd)
UF Legalization (Marihuana)
B Drug Legalization 1997
Marijuana Laws 1973
R ↓ Drug Usage Attitudes 1973
Government 1967

Marijuana Usage 1973
PN 1291   **SC** 29580
B Drug Usage 1971
R Marijuana 2003
↓ Marijuana Laws 1973

Marine Personnel 1973
PN 224   **SC** 29600
B Military Personnel 1967

Marital Adjustment
Use Marital Relations

Marital Conflict 1973
PN 1843   **SC** 29620
B Family Conflict 2003
Marital Relations 1967
R Dysfunctional Family 1991
Family Violence 1982
↓ Relationship Termination 1997

Marital Fidelity
Use Monogamy

Marital Relations 1967
PN 7868   **SC** 29640
UF Marital Adjustment
B Family Relations 1967
Interpersonal Relationships 2004
N Marital Conflict 1973
Marital Satisfaction 1988
R Codependency 1991
Extramarital Intercourse 1973
Male Female Relations 1988
↓ Relationship Termination 1997
Romance 1997

Marital Satisfaction 1988
PN 1825   **SC** 29645
B Marital Relations 1967
Relationship Satisfaction 2001
Satisfaction 1973
R Relationship Quality 2004
↓ Relationship Termination 1997
Role Satisfaction 1994

Marital Separation 1973
PN 908   **SC** 29650
UF Separation (Marital)
B Relationship Termination 1997
N Divorce 1973
R Child Support 1988
Divorced Persons 1973
↓ Family 1967
↓ Marital Status 1973
↓ Parental Absence 1973

Marital Status 1973
PN 2301   **SC** 29660
N Never Married 1994
R Divorced Persons 1973
↓ Family 1967
↓ Family Background 1973

Marital Status — (cont'd)
Living Alone 1994
↓ Living Arrangements 1991
↓ Marital Separation 1973
↓ Marriage 1967
Remarriage 1985
↓ Single Parents 1978
Single Persons 1973
Widowers 1973
Widows 1973

Marital Therapy
Use Marriage Counseling

Marketing 1973
PN 3441   **SC** 29670
R ↓ Advertising 1967
Brand Names 1978
Brand Preferences 1994
↓ Consumer Research 1973
Management Planning 1973
Product Design 1997
↓ Quality of Services 1997
Retailing 1991

Markov Chains 1973
PN 277   **SC** 29680
SN Statistical model representing conditional and sequential probabilities to determine the future values of a random variable.
B Simulation 1967
Stochastic Modeling 1973

Marlowe Crowne Social Desirability Scale 2001
PN 55   **SC** 29691
HN In 2001, the truncated term MARLOWE CROWNE SOC DESIRABIL SCALE (which was used from 1973-2000) was deleted, removed from all records containing it, and replaced with its expanded form MARLOWE CROWNE SOCIAL DESIRABILITY SCALE.
B Nonprojective Personality Measures 1973

Marriage 1967
PN 2281   **SC** 29700
N ↓ Endogamous Marriage 1973
↓ Exogamous Marriage 1973
Monogamy 1997
Polygamy 1973
Remarriage 1985
R ↓ Family 1967
Life Changes 2004
↓ Marital Status 1973
Marriage Rites 1973
Romance 1997

Marriage and Family Education
Use Family Life Education

Marriage Attitudes 1973
PN 853   **SC** 29710
SN General attitudes toward marriage and divorce, or attitudes toward a specific marital relationship.
B Attitudes 1967
R ↓ Family Relations 1967

Marriage Counseling 1973
PN 3264   **SC** 29720
UF Marital Therapy
Marriage Therapy
B Counseling 1967

Marriage Counseling — (cont'd)
N   Conjoint Therapy 1973
R   Couples Therapy 1994
   ↓ Psychotherapeutic Counseling 1973
   ↓ Psychotherapy 1967
    Sex Therapy 1978

Marriage Rites 1973
PN 56   SC 29730
B   Rites of Passage 1973
R   ↓ Marriage 1967

Marriage Therapy
Use   Marriage Counseling

Married Couples
Use   Spouses

Marsupials 1973
PN 65   SC 29760
B   Mammals 1973
N   Kangaroos 1973
    Opossums 1973

Martial Arts 1985
PN 158   SC 29765
UF   Karate
B   Recreation 1967
    Sports 1967
R   Judo 1973
    Meditation 1973
    Self Defense 1985

Marxism
Use   Communism

Masculinity 1967
PN 2746   SC 29780
B   Personality Traits 1967
R   Androgyny 1982
    Femininity 1967
   ↓ Gender Identity 1985
    Sex Roles 1967

Masking 1967
PN 725   SC 29790
SN   Changes in perceptual sensitivity to a stimulus due to the presence of a second stimulus in close temporal proximity.
UF   Backward Masking
    Forward Masking
N   Auditory Masking 1973
    Visual Masking 1973
R   ↓ Perceptual Stimulation 1973

Maslow (Abraham Harold) 1991
PN 71   SC 29795
SN   Identifies biographical or autobiographical studies and discussions of Maslow's works.
R   ↓ Human Potential Movement 1982
   ↓ Humanistic Psychology 1985
   ↓ Psychologists 1967
    Self Actualization 1973

Masochism 1973
PN 356   SC 29800
SN   Pleasure derived from being physically or psychologically abused.
B   Sadomasochism 1973
N   Sexual Masochism 1973

Masochism — (cont'd)
R   Masochistic Personality 1973
   ↓ Sadism 1973
   ↓ Self Destructive Behavior 1985

Masochistic Personality 1973
PN 67   SC 29810
SN   Personality marked by self-destructiveness or self-defeating behavior, a conscious or unconscious need to suffer, and seeking out opportunities for suffering or self-injury.
B   Sadomasochistic Personality 1973
R   ↓ Masochism 1973
   ↓ Self Destructive Behavior 1985
    Sexual Masochism 1973

Mass Culture
Use   Popular Culture

Mass Hysteria 1973
PN 79   SC 29820
B   Hysteria 1967
R   ↓ Collective Behavior 1967
    Contagion 1988

Mass Media 1967
PN 2574   SC 29830
B   Communications Media 1973
N   ↓ Motion Pictures 1973
   ↓ News Media 1997
   ↓ Printed Communications Media 1973
    Radio 1973
   ↓ Television 1967
R   ↓ Advertising 1967
    Popular Culture 2003
    Public Service Announcements 2004

Massage 2001
PN 43   SC 29835
SN   Systematic manipulation of body tissues. Used in both therapeutic and non-therapeutic situations.
B   Tactual Stimulation 1973
R   ↓ Alternative Medicine 1997
    Physical Contact 1982
    Physical Therapy 1973
   ↓ Physical Treatment Methods 1973

Massed Practice 1973
PN 158   SC 29840
SN   Practice schedule with trials that are closely spaced and continuous over a long period. Compare DISTRIBUTED PRACTICE.
B   Learning Schedules 1967
    Practice 1967

Mastectomy 1973
PN 268   SC 29850
B   Amputation 1973
R   Breast Neoplasms 1973

Mastery Learning 1985
PN 269   SC 29855
SN   Educational approach involving specification of educational objectives and success criteria and individual pacing in attaining them.
B   Learning 1967
R   Educational Objectives 1978
    School Learning 1967
    Sequential Learning 1973
   ↓ Teaching Methods 1967

Mastery Tests
Use   Criterion Referenced Tests

Masticatory Muscles 1973
PN 51   SC 29860
B   Muscles 1967

Masturbation 1973
PN 380   SC 29870
B   Psychosexual Behavior 1967
R   Autoeroticism 1997
    Female Orgasm 1973
   ↓ Male Orgasm 1973

Matching Test
Use   Matching to Sample

Matching to Sample 1994
PN 596   SC 29873
UF   Matching Test
B   Discrimination Learning 1982
R   ↓ Memory 1967
   ↓ Recognition (Learning) 1967

Mate Selection
Use   Animal Mate Selection AND Human Mate Selection

Mate Swapping
Use   Extramarital Intercourse

Materialism 1973
PN 333   SC 29890
B   Philosophies 1967

Maternal Behavior (Animal)
Use   Animal Maternal Behavior

Maternal Behavior (Human)
Use   Mother Child Relations

Maternal Investment
Use   Parental Investment

Mates (Humans)
Use   Spouses

Mathematical Ability 1973
PN 2319   SC 29930
UF   Numerical Ability
B   Cognitive Ability 1973
    Nonverbal Ability 1988
R   ↓ Mathematics (Concepts) 1967
    Mathematics Anxiety 1985

Mathematical Modeling 1973
PN 5393   SC 29940
SN   Use of mathematical formulas or equations to analyze or systematize data for description in quantitative terms.
B   Simulation 1967
N   Structural Equation Modeling 1994
R   Chaos Theory 1997
    Decision Theory 2003
    Fuzzy Logic 2003
    Fuzzy Set Theory 1991
    Goodness of Fit 1988

Mathematical Modeling — (cont'd)
Heuristic Modeling 1973
↓ Stochastic Modeling 1973

Mathematical Psychology 1973
PN 200　　　　SC 29950
SN Discipline that attempts to systematize the data of psychology by means of mathematical and statistical models and applications.
B　Psychology 1967

Mathematicians 1973
PN 52　　　　SC 29960
B　Professional Personnel 1978
R　Physicists 1973
Scientists 1967

Mathematics 1982
PN 1769　　　　SC 29965
SN Science of numbers and the operations performed on them. Compare MATHEMATICS (CONCEPTS).
UF　Arithmetic
B　Sciences 1967
N　Algebra 2003
Calculus 2003
Geometry 2003
Statistics 1982
R　Mathematics Anxiety 1985

Mathematics (Concepts) 1967
PN 2756　　　　SC 29970
SN Specific principles that are cognitively internalized or are to be learned concerning numbers, their relations, and mathematical operations performed on them. Compare MATHEMATICS.
N　Algorithms 1973
Number Systems 1973
Numbers (Numerals) 1967
R　Concepts 1967
Mathematical Ability 1973
Mathematics Achievement 1973
Mathematics Education 1973
↓ Statistical Analysis 1967

Mathematics Achievement 1973
PN 4147　　　　SC 29980
B　Academic Achievement 1967
R　↓ Mathematics (Concepts) 1967
Mathematics Anxiety 1985
Mathematics Education 1973
Science Achievement 1997

Mathematics Anxiety 1985
PN 316　　　　SC 29985
SN Fear or tension associated with the study or performance of arithmetic and mathematical tasks.
B　Anxiety 1967
R　↓ Anxiety Disorders 1997
Mathematical Ability 1973
↓ Mathematics 1982
Mathematics Achievement 1973

Mathematics Education 1973
PN 4146　　　　SC 29990
B　Curriculum 1967
R　↓ Mathematics (Concepts) 1967
Mathematics Achievement 1973
Science Achievement 1997

Mating Behavior (Animal)
Use　Animal Mating Behavior

Matriarchy 1973
PN 35　　　　SC 30010
B　Family Structure 1973
R　Father Absence 1973
Patriarchy 1973
↓ Sex Role Attitudes 1978
Sex Roles 1967

Matriculation
Use　School Enrollment

Maturation
Use　Human Development

Maturity (Emotional)
Use　Emotional Maturity

Maturity (Physical)
Use　Physical Maturity

Maturity (Vocational)
Use　Vocational Maturity

Maxilla
Use　Jaw

Maximum Likelihood 1985
PN 357　　　　SC 30075
SN Method of estimating population parameters from sample data by selecting parameter values that maximize the likelihood of the occurrence of the observed sample results.
B　Statistical Estimation 1985
R　Goodness of Fit 1988

Maximum Security Facilities 1985
PN 156　　　　SC 30077
R　↓ Correctional Institutions 1973
↓ Hospitals 1967

Maze Learning 1967
PN 2570　　　　SC 30080
SN Learning the correct route through a maze to obtain reinforcement. Used for human or animal populations.
B　Learning 1967
R　Spatial Learning 1994

Maze Pathways 1973
PN 139　　　　SC 30090
SN Use when specifically referring to pathway choice, discrimination, or spatial organization of pathway. Used for human or animal populations. When comparing types of mazes, use MAZES.
UF　Runways (Maze)
B　Mazes 1967

Mazes 1967
PN 453　　　　SC 30110
SN System of pathways consisting of a number of blind alleys and one or more correct paths leading to a goal/reinforcement. Used to study learning and motivation in humans and animals.
UF　Labyrinth (Apparatus)
B　Apparatus 1967
N　Maze Pathways 1973
T Mazes 1973

MCPP
Use　Piperazines

MDMA
Use　Methylenedioxymethamphetamine

Mealtimes 2004
PN　　　　SC 30150
SN Use for human populations only.
HN Use FEEDING PRACTICES to access references from 1973 to June 2004.
R　↓ Eating Behavior 2004

Mean 1973
PN 290　　　　SC 30160
B　Central Tendency Measures 1973
R　Standard Scores 1985

Meaning 1967
PN 3737　　　　SC 30170
SN Generally refers to the significance, sense, connotation, or denotation conveyed by any form of information.
N　Nonverbal Meaning 1973
↓ Verbal Meaning 1973
R　↓ Comprehension 1967
Meaningfulness 1967

Meaningfulness 1967
PN 1314　　　　SC 30180
R　↓ Comprehension 1967
↓ Meaning 1967

Measles 1973
PN 24　　　　SC 30190
B　Viral Disorders 1973
R　Rubella 1973

Measurement 1967
PN 22388　　　　SC 30200
SN Conceptually broad term referring to the process and tools used in psychological assessment of human subjects. Use specific test names or procedures if possible. For other types of measurement that do not involve psychological tests, consider METHODOLOGY, EVALUATION, or other appropriate terms.
UF　Assessment
Tests
N　↓ Achievement Measures 1967
↓ Aptitude Measures 1967
Attitude Measurement 1973
↓ Attitude Measures 1967
Body Sway Testing 1973
Comprehension Tests 1973
Creativity Measurement 1973
Criterion Referenced Tests 1982
Digit Span Testing 1973
Employment Tests 1973
Group Testing 1973
Individual Testing 1973
↓ Intelligence Measures 1967
↓ Inventories 1967
Multidimensional Scaling 1982
Needs Assessment 1985
↓ Occupational Interest Measures 1973
Pain Measurement 1997
↓ Perceptual Measures 1973
Performance Tests 1973
↓ Personality Measures 1967
Posttesting 1973
↓ Preference Measures 1973

Measurement — (cont'd)

Pretesting 1973
Professional Examinations 1994
Profiles (Measurement) 1973
Projective Testing Technique 1973
↓ Psychiatric Evaluation 1997
↓ Psychological Assessment 1997
Psychometrics 1967
↓ Questionnaires 1967
↓ Rating Scales 1967
↓ Reading Measures 1973
↓ Retention Measures 1973
↓ Screening 1982
↓ Screening Tests 1982
↓ Selection Tests 1973
Sensorimotor Measures 1973
Sociometric Tests 1967
Speech and Hearing Measures 1973
Standardized Tests 1985
↓ Statistical Measurement 1973
Subtests 1973
↓ Surveys 1967
Symptom Checklists 1991
↓ Testing 1967
Verbal Tests 1973

R   Clinical Judgment (Not Diagnosis) 1973
↓ Diagnosis 1967
↓ Evaluation 1967
↓ Experimentation 1967
Geriatric Assessment 1997
↓ Interviews 1967
↓ Methodology 1967
Piagetian Tasks 1973
↓ Prediction Errors 1973
Response Bias 1967
Semantic Differential 1967
Sociograms 1973
↓ Statistical Analysis 1967
↓ Test Construction 1973
Test Norms 1973
↓ Test Scores 1967
↓ Testing Methods 1967
Testwiseness 1978

Measurement Error

Use   Error of Measurement

Mecamylamine 1973

PN 174   **SC** 30220
B   Amines 1973
Antihypertensive Drugs 1973
Ganglion Blocking Drugs 1973

Mechanical Aptitude 1973

PN 72   **SC** 30230
B   Nonverbal Ability 1988

Mechanoreceptors 1973

PN 223   **SC** 30250
B   Neural Receptors 1973
Sensory Neurons 1973

Media (Communications)

Use   Communications Media

Medial Forebrain Bundle 1982

PN 192   **SC** 30286

Medial Forebrain Bundle — (cont'd)

SN Complex group of nerve fibers arising from basal olfactory regions, the periamygdaloid region, and the septal nuclei passing to, and through, the lateral preoptic and hypothalamic regions. This bundle provides the chief pathway for reciprocal connections between the hypothalamus and the biogenic amine systems of the brain stem.
B   Limbic System 1973
R   Amygdala 2003
Fornix 1982
Hippocampus 1967
↓ Hypothalamus 1967
Septal Nuclei 1982

Median 1973

PN 20   **SC** 30290
B   Central Tendency Measures 1973

Median Nerve

Use   Spinal Nerves

Mediated Responses 1967

PN 113   **SC** 30310
SN Intervening or anticipatory responses aroused by stimuli and subsequently responsible for the initiation of behavior.
B   Responses 1967

Mediation 1988

PN 1214   **SC** 30315
SN Intervention by independent and impartial third party or parties to promote reconciliation, settlement, or compromise between conflicting parties.
B   Conflict Resolution 1982
R   Child Custody 1982
Court Referrals 1994
Divorce 1973
Labor Management Relations 1967
↓ Negotiation 1973

Mediation (Cognitive)

Use   Cognitive Mediation

Medicaid 1994

PN 305   **SC** 30323
SN Government health care program for impoverished citizens administered by most local public assistance offices. Compare MEDICARE.
B   Government Programs 1973
Health Insurance 1973
R   Health Care Policy 1994
Medicare 1988
Social Security 1988
Welfare Services (Government) 1973

Medical Care Costs

Use   Health Care Costs

Medical Diagnosis 1973

PN 3598   **SC** 30330
SN Diagnosis of mental or physical disorders through use of medical methods or tests. Compare PSYCHODIAGNOSIS.
UF   Clinical Judgment (Medical Diagnosis)
B   Diagnosis 1967
N   Biopsy 1973
↓ Cardiography 1973
Dexamethasone Suppression Test 1988
Echoencephalography 1973
Electro Oculography 1973

Medical Diagnosis — (cont'd)

↓ Electroencephalography 1967
Electromyography 1967
Electronystagmography 1973
Electroplethysmography 1973
Electroretinography 1967
↓ Encephalography 1973
Galvanic Skin Response 1967
HIV Testing 1997
↓ Ophthalmologic Examination 1973
↓ Plethysmography 1973
Pneumoencephalography 1973
Prenatal Diagnosis 1988
Rheoencephalography 1973
↓ Roentgenography 1973
↓ Tomography 1988
Urinalysis 1973
R   Autopsy 1973
Biological Markers 1991
Computer Assisted Diagnosis 1973
Differential Diagnosis 1967
Drug Usage Screening 1988
↓ Electrophysiology 1973
Genetic Testing 2003
↓ Health Screening 1997
Mammography 1994
Patient History 1973
Physical Examination 1988
Prognosis 1973
Psychological Report 1988

Medical Education 1973

PN 3558   **SC** 30340
B   Graduate Education 1973
N   Medical Internship 1973
Medical Residency 1973
Psychiatric Training 1973
R   Nursing Education 1973

Medical Ethics

Use   Bioethics

Medical History

Use   Patient History

Medical Internship 1973

PN 161   **SC** 30350
UF   Internship (Medical)
B   Medical Education 1973
Postgraduate Training 1973

Medical Model 1978

PN 722   **SC** 30355
SN Conceptual approach to disorders originally applied to the study and treatment of physical illness. Also known as the disease or faulty mechanism model.
B   Models 1967

Medical Patients 1973

PN 4453   **SC** 30360
B   Patients 1967

Medical Personnel 1967

PN 2995   **SC** 30370
UF   Hospital Staff
B   Health Personnel 1994
N   Dentists 1973
Military Medical Personnel 1973
↓ Nurses 1967
Optometrists 1973
↓ Paramedical Personnel 1973

Medical Personnel — (cont'd)
    Pharmacists 1991
    Physical Therapists 1973
  ↓ Physicians 1967
  ↓ Psychiatric Hospital Staff 1973
R Clinicians 1973
    Impaired Professionals 1985
  ↓ Medical Sciences 1967
  ↓ Mental Health Personnel 1967
    Scientists 1967

Medical Personnel Supply 1973
PN 25   **SC** 30380
SN Manpower needs and availability of medical personnel.
B Personnel Supply 1973

Medical Psychology 1973
PN 306   **SC** 30390
SN Subspecialty of clinical psychology concerned with physical health and illness.
B Clinical Psychology 1967
    Health Care Psychology 1985
R ↓ Medical Sciences 1967

Medical Records 1978
PN 531   **SC** 30395
HN Use MEDICAL RECORDS KEEPING to access references from 1978-1996.
N Client Records 1997
R Data Collection 1982
  ↓ Data Processing 1967
    Hospital Administration 1078
    Patient History 1973
  ↓ Treatment 1967

Medical Regimen Compliance
Use Treatment Compliance

Medical Residency 1973
PN 1650   **SC** 30400
SN Required hospital training in a medical specialty for a medical graduate and licensed physician.
UF Psychiatric Residency
    Residency (Medical)
B Medical Education 1973
    Postgraduate Training 1973

Medical Sciences 1967
PN 2057   **SC** 30410
UF Medicine (Science of)
B Sciences 1967
N Anesthesiology 1973
    Cardiology 1973
    Dentistry 1973
  ↓ Endocrinology 1973
    Epidemiology 1973
    Family Medicine 1988
    Geriatrics 1967
    Gynecology 1978
  ↓ Immunology 1973
    Neurology 1967
  ↓ Obstetrics 1978
    Ophthalmology 1973
    Osteopathic Medicine 2003
  ↓ Pathology 1973
    Pediatrics 1973
  ↓ Psychiatry 1967
    Psychosomatic Medicine 1978
    Radiology 1973
  ↓ Surgery 1971
    Veterinary Medicine 1973
R Bioethics 2003

Medical Sciences — (cont'd)
    Folk Medicine 1973
  ↓ Medical Personnel 1967
    Medical Psychology 1973
  ↓ Neurosciences 1973
  ↓ Paramedical Sciences 1973

Medical Students 1967
PN 3888   **SC** 30420
B Students 1967
R Graduate Students 1967

Medical Therapeutic Devices 1973
PN 530   **SC** 30430
SN Equipment designed for rehabilitation or treatment of abnormal or undesirable conditions.
UF Therapeutic Devices (Medical)
N Artificial Pacemakers 1973
  ↓ Hearing Aids 1973
  ↓ Optical Aids 1973
  ↓ Prostheses 1973
R ↓ Augmentative Communication 1994
    Mobility Aids 1978

Medical Treatment (General) 1973
PN 2538   **SC** 30440
SN Use for medical treatment as a broad topic.
B Treatment 1967
R ↓ Alternative Medicine 1997
    Life Sustaining Treatment 1997
  ↓ Physical Treatment Methods 1973

Medicare 1988
PN 240   **SC** 30445
SN Government health care program for the aged administered through the Social Security Administration or the US Health Care Financing Administration. Compare MEDICAID.
B Government Programs 1973
    Health Insurance 1973
R Health Care Policy 1994
    Medicaid 1994
    Social Security 1988

Medication
Use Drug Therapy

Medicinal Herbs and Plants 2001
PN 325   **SC** 30455
SN Herbs and plants whose roots, leaves, seeds, bark, or other constituents possess therapeutic qualities when administered in a treatment capacity.
N Hypericum Perforatum 2003
R ↓ Alternative Medicine 1997
    Dietary Supplements 2001

Medicine (Science of)
Use Medical Sciences

Medics
Use Paramedical Personnel

Meditation 1973
PN 1365   **SC** 30480
SN Family of contemplative techniques all of which involve a conscious attempt to focus one's attention in a nonanalytical way and to refrain from ruminating, discursive thought. Sometimes considered a spiritual or religious practice.
B Religious Practices 1973
R ↓ Alternative Medicine 1997

Meditation — (cont'd)
    Centering 1991
    Holistic Health 1985
  ↓ Human Potential Movement 1982
    Martial Arts 1985
    Prayer 1973
  ↓ Relaxation Therapy 1978

Medulla Oblongata 1973
PN 493   **SC** 30490
B Brain Stem 1973
    Hindbrain 1997

Melancholia
Use Major Depression

Melancholy
Use Sadness

Melanin 1973
PN 41   **SC** 30530
B Pigments 1973
R Melanocyte Stimulating Hormone 1985
    Melatonin 1973
  ↓ Tyrosine 1973

Melanocyte Stimulating Hormone 1985
PN 103   **SC** 30535
UF Melanotropin
B Peptides 1973
    Pituitary Hormones 1973
R Melanin 1973
    Melatonin 1973

Melanotropin
Use Melanocyte Stimulating Hormone

Melatonin 1973
PN 781   **SC** 30540
B Hormones 1967
R Melanin 1973
    Melanocyte Stimulating Hormone 1985
    Pineal Body 1973

Mellaril
Use Thioridazine

Membranes 1973
PN 251   **SC** 30560
B Tissues (Body) 1973
N Meninges 1973
  ↓ Nasal Mucosa 1973
    Nictitating Membrane 1973

Memory 1967
PN 27892   **SC** 30570
N Autobiographical Memory 1994
    Early Memories 1985
    Eidetic Imagery 1973
    Episodic Memory 1988
    Explicit Memory 1997
    False Memory 1997
    Implicit Memory 2003
    Long Term Memory 1973
    Memory Decay 1973
    Memory Trace 1973
    Reminiscence 1985
    Repressed Memory 1997
  ↓ Short Term Memory 1967
  ↓ Spatial Memory 1988

Memory — (cont'd)
    Spontaneous Recovery (Learning) 1973
    ↓ Verbal Memory 1994
    ↓ Visual Memory 1994
  R ↓ Amnesia 1967
    Chunking 2004
    ↓ Cognitive Processes 1967
    Cued Recall 1994
    Cues 1967
    Declarative Knowledge 1997
    Forgetting 1973
    Free Recall 1973
    Generation Effect (Learning) 1991
    Human Information Storage 1973
    ↓ Interference (Learning) 1967
    ↓ Latent Inhibition 1997
    ↓ Learning 1967
    Matching to Sample 1994
    ↓ Memory Disorders 1973
    Memory Training 1994
    Metacognition 1991
    Note Taking 1991
    Procedural Knowledge 1997
    ↓ Prompting 1997
  R ↓ Recall (Learning) 1967
    Relearning 1973
    ↓ Retention 1967
    Rote Learning 1973
    Serial Recall 1994
    Source Monitoring 2004

Memory Decay 1973
PN 384   **SC** 30580
SN Fading of memory traces over time. Compare FORGETTING and AMNESIA.
  B   Memory 1967
  R   Forgetting 1973
      Memory Training 1994

Memory Disorders 1973
PN 1633   **SC** 30590
  B   Thought Disturbances 1973
  N   ↓ Amnesia 1967
  R   ↓ Brain Disorders 1967
      Cognitive Impairment 2003
      ↓ Memory 1967
      Memory Training 1994
      ↓ Mental Disorders 1967
      ↓ Physical Disorders 1997

Memory Enhancing Drugs
  Use Nootropic Drugs

Memory for Designs Test 1973
PN 32   **SC** 30610
  B   Nonprojective Personality Measures 1973
  R   ↓ Neuropsychological Assessment 1982

Memory Trace 1973
PN 437   **SC** 30620
SN Hypothetical change in nerve cells or brain activity that accompanies the storage of information.
  B   Memory 1967

Memory Training 1994
PN 305   **SC** 30623
  R   Cognitive Rehabilitation 1985
      Forgetting 1973
      ↓ Learning Strategies 1991
      ↓ Memory 1967
      Memory Decay 1973
      ↓ Memory Disorders 1973
      Mnemonic Learning 1973

Memory Training — (cont'd)
    ↓ Neuropsychological Rehabilitation 1997
    ↓ Practice 1967
    ↓ Recall (Learning) 1967
    ↓ Recognition (Learning) 1967
    ↓ Retention 1967

Men
  Use Human Males

Menarche 1973
PN 206   **SC** 30630
  B   Menstruation 1973
  R   Puberty 1973

Menieres Disease 1973
PN 63   **SC** 30640
  B   Labyrinth Disorders 1973
      Syndromes 1973
  R   Vertigo 1973

Meninges 1973
PN 30   **SC** 30650
  B   Central Nervous System 1967
      Membranes 1973

Meningitis 1973
PN 65   **SC** 30660
  B   Central Nervous System Disorders 1973
  N   Bacterial Meningitis 1973

Meningomyelocele
  Use Spina Bifida

Menopause 1973
PN 1137   **SC** 30670
  B   Developmental Stages 1973
  R   Life Changes 2004
      ↓ Menstrual Cycle 1973

Menstrual Cycle 1973
PN 1243   **SC** 30680
  N   ↓ Menstruation 1973
      Ovulation 1973
  R   Estrus 1973
      Menopause 1973
      Premenstrual Dysphoric Disorder 2004
      Premenstrual Syndrome 2003

Menstrual Disorders 1973
PN 206   **SC** 30690
  B   Gynecological Disorders 1973
  N   Amenorrhea 1973
      Dysmenorrhea 1973
      Premenstrual Dysphoric Disorder 2004
  R   Premenstrual Syndrome 2003

Menstruation 1973
PN 371   **SC** 30700
  B   Menstrual Cycle 1973
  N   Menarche 1973
  R   Estrus 1973

Mental Age 1973
PN 289   **SC** 30710
SN Intelligence level expressed in units of chronological age and determined by comparison with other individuals of the same age using intelligence test scores.
  UF Intelligence Age

Mental Age — (cont'd)
  R   Developmental Age Groups 1973
      ↓ Intelligence 1967
      Intelligence Quotient 1967

Mental Confusion 1973
PN 455   **SC** 30720
  UF Confusion (Mental)
  B   Emotional States 1973
  R   Doubt 1973
      Frustration 1967
      ↓ Thought Disturbances 1973
      Wandering Behavior 1991

Mental Deficiency
  Use Mental Retardation

Mental Disorders 1967
PN 30077   **SC** 30740
SN Conceptually broad term referring to all forms of psychopathology. Use a more specific term if possible.
  UF Insanity
      Mental Illness
      Nervous Breakdown
      Psychiatric Disorders
  B   Disorders 1967
  N   Adjustment Disorders 1994
      ↓ Affective Disorders 2001
      Alexithymia 1982
      ↓ Anxiety Disorders 1997
      ↓ Autism 1967
      ↓ Chronic Mental Illness 1997
      ↓ Dementia 1985
      ↓ Dissociative Disorders 2001
      ↓ Eating Disorders 1997
      Elective Mutism 1973
      ↓ Factitious Disorders 1988
      ↓ Gender Identity Disorder 1997
      ↓ Hysteria 1967
      ↓ Impulse Control Disorders 1997
      Koro 1994
      Mental Disorders due to General Medical Conditions 2001
      ↓ Neurosis 1967
      ↓ Paraphilias 1988
      ↓ Personality Disorders 1967
      ↓ Pervasive Developmental Disorders 2001
      Pseudodementia 1985
      ↓ Psychosis 1967
      Schizoaffective Disorder 1994
  R   Abnormal Psychology 2003
      Adaptive Behavior 1991
      ↓ Attention Deficit Disorder 1985
      Attention Deficit Disorder with Hyperactivity 2001
      ↓ Behavior Disorders 1971
      Borderline States 1978
      ↓ Brain Disorders 1967
      ↓ Chronic Illness 1991
      Chronicity (Disorders) 1982
      ↓ Communication Disorders 1982
      Comorbidity 1991
      Conduct Disorder 1991
      ↓ Congenital Disorders 1973
      ↓ Consciousness Disturbances 1973
      ↓ Defense Mechanisms 1967
      ↓ Diagnosis 1967
      Diagnostic and Statistical Manual 1994
      Disability Discrimination 1997
      Disease Course 1991
      ↓ Emotional Adjustment 1973
      Etiology 1967
      Glossolalia 1973

Mental Disorders — (cont'd)

    Homeless Mentally Ill 1997
    Infantilism 1973
    Insanity Defense 1985
    International Classification of Diseases 2001
    ↓ Learning Disorders 1967
    Malingering 1973
    ↓ Memory Disorders 1973
    Mental Illness (Attitudes Toward) 1967
    ↓ Mental Retardation 1967
    Mentally Ill Offenders 1985
    Microcephaly 1973
    Narcissism 1967
    Onset (Disorders) 1973
    ↓ Organic Brain Syndromes 1973
    ↓ Perceptual Disturbances 1973
    ↓ Personality Processes 1967
    ↓ Physical Disorders 1997
    Porphyria 1973
    Predisposition 1973
    Premorbidity 1978
    Prognosis 1973
    Psychiatric Patients 1967
    Psychiatric Symptoms 1997
    ↓ Psychodiagnosis 1967
    ↓ Psychological Assessment 1997
    Psychopathology 1967
    Recovery (Disorders) 1973
    Relapse (Disorders) 1973
    ↓ Remission (Disorders) 1973
    Research Diagnostic Criteria 1994
    Rett Syndrome 1994
    ↓ Sadomasochism 1973
    Savants 2001
    Schizophrenogenic Family 1967
    Severity (Disorders) 1982
    ↓ Sexual Function Disturbances 1973
    ↓ Sleep Disorders 1973
    Special Needs 1994
    Structured Clinical Interview 2001
    ↓ Suicide 1967
    Susceptibility (Disorders) 1973
    ↓ Symptoms 1967
    ↓ Syndromes 1973
    ↓ Thought Disturbances 1973
    ↓ Toxic Disorders 1973
    ↓ Treatment Resistant Disorders 1994
    Work Related Illnesses 1994

Mental Disorders due to General Medical Conditions 2001

PN 12   **SC** 30745
SN Used for disorders characterized by the presence of mental symptoms judged to be the direct physiological consequence of a general medical condition. Use only for disorders described by this or more specific phraseology. This could include "Catatonic Disorder due to a General Medical Condition," "Dementia due to a General Medical Condition," etc. For a more specific disorder, also use a term for the symptom (e.g., CATATONIA, DEMENTIA). Compare COMORBIDITY.
  B   Mental Disorders 1967
  R   Comorbidity 1991

Mental Health 1967

PN 11436   **SC** 30750
  B   Health 1973
  N   Community Mental Health 1973
  R   Community Mental Health Services 1978
      Community Psychiatry 1973
      ↓ Emotional Adjustment 1973
      ↓ Mental Health Personnel 1967
      ↓ Mental Health Programs 1973

Mental Health — (cont'd)

    ↓ Mental Health Services 1978
    Primary Mental Health Prevention 1973
    Well Being 1994

Mental Health Care Costs
  Use Health Care Costs

Mental Health Care Policy
  Use Health Care Policy

Mental Health Centers (Community)
  Use Community Mental Health Centers

Mental Health Consultation
  Use Professional Consultation

Mental Health Inservice Training 1973

PN 486   **SC** 30780
  UF   Inservice Training (Mental Health)
      Training (Mental Health Inservice)
  B   Community Mental Health Training 1973
      Inservice Training 1985
  R   ↓ Mental Health Programs 1973
      Professional Development 1982

Mental Health Personnel 1967

PN 6097   **SC** 30790
  B   Health Personnel 1994
  N   Clinical Psychologists 1973
      ↓ Psychiatric Hospital Staff 1973
      Psychiatric Nurses 1973
      Psychiatric Social Workers 1973
      Psychiatrists 1967
      ↓ Psychotherapists 1973
      School Psychologists 1973
  R   Clinicians 1973
      ↓ Counselors 1967
      ↓ Educational Personnel 1973
      Impaired Professionals 1985
      ↓ Medical Personnel 1967
      ↓ Mental Health 1967
      Mental Health Personnel Supply 1973
      Occupational Therapists 1973
      ↓ Paraprofessional Personnel 1973
      Personal Therapy 1991
      Professional Supervision 1988
      ↓ Psychologists 1967
      ↓ Social Workers 1973
      ↓ Therapists 1967

Mental Health Personnel Supply 1973

PN 118   **SC** 30800
  B   Personnel Supply 1973
  R   ↓ Mental Health Personnel 1967

Mental Health Program Evaluation 1973

PN 1471   **SC** 30810
SN Methodology or procedures for assessment of any mental health program in relation to previously established goals or other criteria. Also used for the formal evaluations themselves. For effectiveness of particular treatment modes, use the specific type of treatment (e.g., DRUG THERAPY). For efficacy of treatment for a particular disorder, use the specific disorder (e.g., MANIA).
  UF   Program Evaluation (Mental Health)
  B   Program Evaluation 1985
  R   ↓ Mental Health Programs 1973
      Psychotherapeutic Outcomes 1973

Mental Health Program Evaluation — (cont'd)

    ↓ Treatment 1967
    Treatment Effectiveness Evaluation 1973
    ↓ Treatment Outcomes 1982

Mental Health Programs 1973

PN 2568   **SC** 30820
SN Programs for the maintenance of mental health.
  UF   Programs (Mental Health)
  N   ↓ Crisis Intervention Services 1973
      Deinstitutionalization 1982
      Home Visiting Programs 1973
      Hot Line Services 1973
      Suicide Prevention Centers 1973
  R   Child Guidance Clinics 1973
      Community Mental Health 1973
      Community Mental Health Centers 1973
      Community Mental Health Services 1978
      ↓ Community Mental Health Training 1973
      Community Psychiatry 1973
      Community Psychology 1973
      ↓ Community Services 1967
      ↓ Health Care Administration 1997
      ↓ Health Care Delivery 1978
      ↓ Health Care Services 1978
      Integrated Services 1997
      ↓ Mental Health 1967
      Mental Health Inservice Training 1973
      Mental Health Program Evaluation 1973
      ↓ Mental Health Services 1978
      Outreach Programs 1997
      Partial Hospitalization 1985
      Primary Mental Health Prevention 1973
      ↓ Program Development 1991
      Psychiatric Clinics 1973
      Public Health Services 1973

Mental Health Service Needs
  Use Health Service Needs

Mental Health Services 1978

PN 10781   **SC** 30825
SN Services available for maintenance of mental health and treatment of mental disorders.
  B   Health Care Services 1978
  N   Community Mental Health Services 1978
  R   Child Guidance Clinics 1973
      Community Mental Health Centers 1973
      ↓ Community Services 1967
      ↓ Counseling 1967
      ↓ Health Care Administration 1997
      Health Care Costs 1994
      ↓ Health Care Delivery 1978
      Health Care Policy 1994
      Health Care Seeking Behavior 1997
      Health Service Needs 1997
      Integrated Services 1997
      Long Term Care 1994
      ↓ Mental Health 1967
      ↓ Mental Health Programs 1973
      Outreach Programs 1997
      ↓ Prevention 1973
      ↓ Psychiatric Hospital Programs 1967
      Quality of Care 1988
      ↓ Quality of Services 1997
      School Counseling 1982
      Social Casework 1967
      ↓ Social Services 1982
      Student Personnel Services 1978
      ↓ Support Groups 1991
      ↓ Twelve Step Programs 1997

Mental Health Training (Community)
Use Community Mental Health Training

Mental Hospitals
Use Psychiatric Hospitals

Mental Illness
Use Mental Disorders

Mental Illness (Attitudes Toward) 1967
PN 1877   **SC** 30860
B Disabled (Attitudes Toward) 1997
R Disability Discrimination 1997
Health Knowledge 1994
↓ Mental Disorders 1967

Mental Load
Use Human Channel Capacity

Mental Models 2003
PN 283   **SC** 30867
SN Mental representations of real, imaginary, or hypothetical situations. The structure of the model corresponds to the structure it represents.
HN This term was introduced in June 2003. Psyc-INFO records from the past 10 years were re-indexed with this term. The posting note reflects the number of records that were re-indexed.
B Models 1967
R Cognitive Maps 1982
Schema 1988

Mental Retardation 1967
PN 16931   **SC** 30870
SN Impaired intellectual (IQ below 70) and adaptive functioning manifested during the developmental period. Use a more specific term if possible. Use for both the concept of the disorder itself and for populations of mentally retarded persons.
HN In 2000, this term replaced the discontinued and deleted term MENTALLY RETARDED. MENTALLY RETARDED was removed from all records containing it and replaced with MENTAL RETARDATION.
UF Amentia
Mental Deficiency
Oligophrenia
Retardation (Mental)
N Anencephaly 1973
Borderline Mental Retardation 1973
Crying Cat Syndrome 1973
Downs Syndrome 1967
Home Reared Mentally Retarded 1973
Institutionalized Mentally Retarded 1973
Mild Mental Retardation 2001
Moderate Mental Retardation 2001
Profound Mental Retardation 2001
Psychosocial Mental Retardation 1973
Severe Mental Retardation 2001
Tay Sachs Disease 2003
R Adaptive Behavior 1991
↓ Brain Damage 1967
Cognitive Impairment 2003
Developmental Disabilities 1982
↓ Disorders 1967
Fetal Alcohol Syndrome 1985
Fragile X Syndrome 1994
Hydrocephaly 1973
Klinefelters Syndrome 1973
↓ Mental Disorders 1967
Mental Retardation (Attitudes Toward) 2001

Mental Retardation — (cont'd)
Microcephaly 1973
Phenylketonuria 1973
Prader Willi Syndrome 1991
Rett Syndrome 1994
Savants 2001
Williams Syndrome 2003

Mental Retardation (Attitudes Toward) 2001
PN 643   **SC** 30881
HN In 2000, the truncated term MENTAL RETAR-DATION (ATTIT TOWARD) (which was used from 1973-2000) was deleted, removed from all records containing it, and replaced with its expanded form MENTAL RETARDATION (ATTITUDES TOWARD).
B Disabled (Attitudes Toward) 1997
R ↓ Mental Retardation 1967

Mental Rotation 1991
PN 455   **SC** 30883
B Cognitive Processes 1967
R Mirror Image 1991
↓ Spatial Ability 1982
Spatial Imagery 1982
Spatial Organization 1973
↓ Spatial Perception 1967

Mentally Ill Homeless
Use Homeless Mentally Ill

Mentally Ill Offenders 1985
PN 1811   **SC** 30885
UF Criminally Insane
B Criminals 1967
R Competency to Stand Trial 1985
Court Referrals 1994
Forensic Evaluation 1994
Insanity Defense 1985
↓ Mental Disorders 1967

Mentor 1985
PN 1113   **SC** 30895
SN An individual who befriends and facilitates the development of a less experienced individual, especially within a profession, business, trade, or academic environment.
R Adult Development 1978
Apprenticeship 1973
↓ Interpersonal Interaction 1967
Occupational Aspirations 1973
Occupational Guidance 1967
Peer Counseling 1978
Professional Development 1982
Significant Others 1991
↓ Social Influences 1967
Supervisor Employee Interaction 1997
Vocational Counselors 1973

Meperidine 1973
PN 72   **SC** 30900
B Amines 1973
Analgesic Drugs 1973
Antispasmodic Drugs 1973
Narcotic Drugs 1973
Sedatives 1973

Mephenesin
Use Muscle Relaxing Drugs

Meprobamate 1973
PN 62   **SC** 30920

Meprobamate — (cont'd)
B Hypnotic Drugs 1973
Muscle Relaxing Drugs 1973
Sedatives 1973
Tranquilizing Drugs 1967

Mercury (Metal) 1973
PN 87   **SC** 30930
B Metallic Elements 1973

Mercury Poisoning 1973
PN 96   **SC** 30940
B Toxic Disorders 1973

Mercy Killing
Use Euthanasia

Mescaline 1973
PN 113   **SC** 30950
B Alkaloids 1973
Hallucinogenic Drugs 1967
Psychotomimetic Drugs 1973
R Peyote 1973

Mesencephalon 1973
PN 1695   **SC** 30960
UF Midbrain
Red Nucleus
B Brain 1967
N Inferior Colliculus 1973
Optic Lobe 1973
Substantia Nigra 1994
Superior Colliculus 1973
↓ Tegmentum 1991

Mesoridazine 1973
PN 35   **SC** 30970
B Phenothiazine Derivatives 1973

Messages 1973
PN 1586   **SC** 30980
SN Informational content of communications transmitted between persons or systems.
UF Information (Messages)
R ↓ Communication 1967
Computer Mediated Communication 2003
↓ Electronic Communication 2001
Gossip 1982
Information 1967

Meta Analysis 1985
PN 2493   **SC** 30985
SN Used in records discussing issues involved in the process of conducting a statistical analysis of a large collection of integrated findings.
HN From 1985-2000, the term was also used as a document type identifier; however, this usage has been discontinued due to the advent of Form/Content Type field identifiers. References from 1985-2000 can be accessed using either META ANALYSIS or the Meta Analysis Form/Content Type field identifier.
UF Data Pooling
B Methodology 1967
Statistical Analysis 1967
R Literature Review 1967

Metabolic Rates 1973
PN 254   **SC** 30990
R Energy Expenditure 1967
↓ Metabolism 1967
↓ Physiology 1967

Metabolism 1967
PN 2784   SC 31000
SN Biochemical changes in the cells, digestive system, and body tissues by which energy is provided, new material is incorporated, and substances, such as drugs, are disposed.
B   Physiology 1967
N   Anabolism 1973
     Basal Metabolism 1973
     Biosynthesis 1973
   ↓ Carbohydrate Metabolism 1973
     Catabolism 1973
     Lipid Metabolism 1973
   ↓ Metabolites 1973
     Protein Metabolism 1973
R   Bioavailability 1991
   ↓ Dopamine Metabolites 1982
     Metabolic Rates 1973
   ↓ Metabolism Disorders 1973
   ↓ Norepinephrine Metabolites 1982
     Thermoregulation (Body) 1973

Metabolism Disorders 1973
PN 488   SC 31020
UF Hypercholesterolemia
B   Physical Disorders 1997
N   Cushings Syndrome 1973
     Cystic Fibrosis 1985
   ↓ Diabetes 1973
     Hyperglycemia 1985
     Hypoglycemia 1973
     Hyponatremia 1997
   ↓ Lipid Metabolism Disorders 1973
     Phenylketonuria 1973
     Porphyria 1973
R   Hypothyroidism 1973
   ↓ Metabolism 1967
   ↓ Nutritional Deficiencies 1973

Metabolites 1973
PN 1074   SC 31030
SN Biochemical products of metabolism.
UF Anabolites
     Catabolites
B   Metabolism 1967
N ↓ Dopamine Metabolites 1982
   ↓ Norepinephrine Metabolites 1982
   ↓ Serotonin Metabolites 1978

Metacognition 1991
PN 1782   SC 31040
SN Awareness, monitoring, and knowledge of one's own cognitive processes and activities including memory and comprehension.
UF Metamemory
B   Cognitive Processes 1967
R ↓ Awareness 1967
     Cognition 1967
   ↓ Cognitive Ability 1973
   ↓ Comprehension 1967
     Declarative Knowledge 1997
   ↓ Learning 1967
   ↓ Learning Strategies 1991
   ↓ Memory 1967
     Metalinguistics 1994
     Procedural Knowledge 1997
     School Learning 1967

Metalinguistics 1994
PN 160   SC 31045
SN Branch of linguistics concerned with how language is used, the role of language in culture, and the use of particular linguistic forms.
B   Linguistics 1973

Metalinguistics — (cont'd)
R   Ethnolinguistics 1973
   ↓ Language 1967
   ↓ Language Development 1967
     Metacognition 1991
     Pragmatics 1985
     Psycholinguistics 1967
     Sociolinguistics 1985
     Verbal Ability 1967
   ↓ Verbal Communication 1967

Metallic Elements 1973
PN 320   SC 31050
B   Metals 1991
N   Aluminum 1994
     Barium 1973
   ↓ Calcium 1973
     Cobalt 1973
     Copper 1973
     Iron 1973
     Lead (Metal) 1973
   ↓ Lithium 1973
   ↓ Magnesium 1973
     Mercury (Metal) 1973
   ↓ Potassium 1973
   ↓ Sodium 1973
     Zinc 1985

Metals 1991
PN 52   SC 31052
SN May include alloys.
N ↓ Metallic Elements 1973

Metamemory
  Use Metacognition

Metaphor 1982
PN 2062   SC 31057
SN Figures of speech used to suggest an analogy between one kind of object or idea and another.
B   Figurative Language 1985
R   Analogy 1991
   ↓ Literature 1967
     Myths 1967
   ↓ Semantics 1967
     Symbolism 1967

Metaphysics 1973
PN 369   SC 31060
SN Branch of philosophy concerned with the fundamental nature of things and existence.
B   Philosophies 1967
R   Epistemology 1973
     Hermeneutics 1991
     Reality 1973
     Relativism 1997

Metapsychology 1994
PN 191   SC 31070
B   Psychology 1967
R   Freudian Psychoanalytic School 1973
     Object Relations 1982
   ↓ Psychoanalytic Theory 1967

Methadone 1973
PN 746   SC 31080
B   Analgesic Drugs 1973
     Narcotic Drugs 1973
R   Methadone Maintenance 1978

Methadone Maintenance 1978
PN 1803   SC 31083

Methadone Maintenance — (cont'd)
SN Rehabilitation of heroin addicts by substituting methadone for heroin, enabling the addict to lead a relatively normal life. Methadone maintenance does not actually treat the addiction.
R ↓ Drug Addiction 1967
   ↓ Drug Rehabilitation 1973
     Heroin Addiction 1973
     Maintenance Therapy 1997
     Methadone 1973

Methamphetamine 1973
PN 727   SC 31090
UF Methedrine
B   Amphetamine 1967
     CNS Stimulating Drugs 1973
     Vasoconstrictor Drugs 1973
R   Methylenedioxymethamphetamine 1991

Methanol 1973
PN 36   SC 31100
UF Methyl Alcohol
B   Alcohols 1967

Methaqualone 1973
PN 44   SC 31110
UF Quaalude
B   Hypnotic Drugs 1973
     Sedatives 1973

Methedrine
  Use Methamphetamine

Methionine 1973
PN 125   SC 31130
B   Amino Acids 1973

Methodists
  Use Protestants

Methodology 1967
PN 17926   SC 31140
SN Conceptually broad term that refers generally to strategies, techniques, or procedures used in applied, descriptive, or empirical studies. Compare EXPERIMENTAL METHODS.
UF Research Methods
N   Causal Analysis 1994
     Cohort Analysis 1988
   ↓ Content Analysis 1978
     Data Collection 1982
   ↓ Empirical Methods 1973
     Grounded Theory 2004
     Meta Analysis 1985
     Qualitative Research 2003
     Quantitative Methods 2003
     Self Report 1982
R   Experiment Controls 1973
   ↓ Experimental Design 1967
     Experimental Instructions 1967
     Experimental Laboratories 1973
     Experimental Replication 1973
   ↓ Experimentation 1967
     Functional Analysis 2001
     Mail Surveys 1994
   ↓ Measurement 1967
   ↓ Surveys 1967
     Telephone Surveys 1994
     Theory Formulation 1973
     Theory Verification 1973

Methohexital 1973
PN 44   SC 31150
  B   Barbiturates 1967
      General Anesthetics 1973

Methoxamine 1973
PN 22   SC 31160
  B   Adrenergic Drugs 1973
      Alcohols 1967
      Sympathomimetic Amines 1973
      Vasoconstrictor Drugs 1973
  R ↓ Local Anesthetics 1973

Methoxyhydroxyphenylglycol (3,4) 1991
PN 171   SC 31165
  UF MHPG
  B   Norepinephrine Metabolites 1982

Methyl Alcohol
  Use Methanol

Methylatropine
  Use Atropine

Methyldiphenylhydramine
  Use Orphenadrine

Methyldopa 1973
PN 55   SC 31190
  B   Antihypertensive Drugs 1973
  R ↓ Catecholamines 1973
      DOPA 1973
      Dopamine 1973

Methylenedioxymethamphetamine 1991
PN 465   SC 31195
  UF Ecstasy (Drug)
      MDMA
  R   Methamphetamine 1973

Methylmorphine
  Use Codeine

Methylphenidate 1973
PN 1502   SC 31210
  UF Ritalin
  B   Amines 1973
      Antidepressant Drugs 1971
      CNS Stimulating Drugs 1973
  R ↓ Analeptic Drugs 1973

Methylphenyltetrahydropyridine 1994
PN 60   SC 31213
  UF MPTP
  B   Neurotoxins 1982
  R   Dopamine 1973

Methysergide
  Use Serotonin Antagonists

Metrazole
  Use Pentylenetetrazol

Metronomes 1973
PN 27   SC 31230
  B   Apparatus 1967

Metropolitan Readiness Tests 1978
PN 40   SC 31240
HN Use METROPOLITAN READING READINESS
TEST to access references from 1973-1977.
  B   Reading Measures 1973

Mexican Americans 1973
PN 3318   SC 31250
SN Populations of Mexican descent residing perma-
nently in the U.S.
  UF Chicanos
  B   Hispanics 1982

MHPG
  Use Methoxyhydroxyphenylglycol (3,4)

Mianserin 1982
PN 319   SC 31266
SN Organic heterocyclic compound having antiser-
otonin properties and used as an antihistamine.
  B   Antidepressant Drugs 1971
      Antihistaminic Drugs 1973
      Serotonin Antagonists 1973

Mice 1973
PN 13673   SC 31270
  B   Rodents 1973

Microcephaly 1973
PN 69   SC 31280
SN Smallness of the head produced by incomplete
development of the brain, often associated with
below normal mental and cognitive development.
  B   Brain Disorders 1967
      Congenital Disorders 1973
  R ↓ Mental Disorders 1967
     ↓ Mental Retardation 1967
     ↓ Neonatal Disorders 1973

Microcomputers 1985
PN 976   SC 31282
  UF Personal Computers
  B   Computers 1967
  R ↓ Computer Applications 1973

Microcounseling 1978
PN 96   SC 31284
SN Short-term technique for teaching basic inter-
viewing skills using role playing, videotape analysis,
and feedback in prepracticum training.
  B   Counseling 1967
  R ↓ Clinical Methods Training 1973
      Counselor Education 1973
      Interviewing 1973
      Paraprofessional Education 1973

Microorganisms 1985
PN 99   SC 31287
SN Single-celled microscopic or ultramicroscopic
organisms.
  UF Bacteria
      Single Cell Organisms
  N   Protozoa 1973

Microscopes 1973
PN 14   SC 31290
  B   Apparatus 1967

Micturition
  Use Urination

Midazolam 1991
PN 260   SC 31303
  B   Benzodiazepines 1978
      Minor Tranquilizers 1973

Midbrain
  Use Mesencephalon

Middle Class 1973
PN 837   SC 31320
  UF Bourgeois
  B   Social Class 1967

Middle Class Attitudes 1973
PN 62   SC 31330
SN Attitudes of, not toward, the middle class.
  B   Socioeconomic Class Attitudes 1973

Middle Ear 1973
PN 156   SC 31340
  UF Ear Ossicles
      Eustachian Tube
      Tympanic Membrane
  B   Ear (Anatomy) 1967

Middle Income Level 1973
PN 110   SC 31350
  B   Income Level 1973

Middle Level Managers 1973
PN 715   SC 31360
SN Second-line managers or supervisors primarily
responsible for daily work flow and production in a
business or industrial organization.
  B   Management Personnel 1973
  R   Top Level Managers 1973

Middle School Education 1985
PN 282   SC 31364
SN Education for grades six through eight (some-
times five through eight) using methods and materi-
als specifically focusing on the needs and
characteristics of early adolescents.
  B   Education 1967
  R   Middle Schools 2003

Middle School Students 1985
PN 2347   SC 31367
SN Students in 6th, 7th, and 8th grades. Sometimes
may include students in 5th grade. Use ELEMEN-
TARY SCHOOL STUDENTS or JUNIOR HIGH
SCHOOL STUDENTS, as appropriate, unless spe-
cific reference is made to the population as middle
school students.
  R ↓ Elementary School Students 1967
      Junior High School Students 1971

Middle School Teachers 2003
PN 45   SC 31366
HN This term was introduced in June 2003. Psyc-
INFO records from the past 10 years were re-indexed
with this term. The posting note reflects the number
of records that were re-indexed.
  B   Teachers 1967
  R   Junior High School Teachers 1973

Middle Schools 2003
PN 39   SC 31365

Middle Schools — (cont'd)
HN This term was introduced in June 2003. Psyc-INFO records from the past 10 years were re-indexed with this term. The posting note reflects the number of records that were re-indexed.
- **B** Schools 1967
- **R** Junior High Schools 1973
  Middle School Education 1985

Midwifery 1985
PN 123   **SC** 31368
- **UF** Home Birth
- **B** Obstetrics 1978
- **R** ↓ Birth 1967
  Labor (Childbirth) 1973

Migraine Headache 1973
PN 1601   **SC** 31370
- **B** Headache 1973
- **R** ↓ Endocrine Disorders 1973
  Nausea 1973
  ↓ Somatoform Disorders 2001

Migrant Farm Workers 1973
PN 134   **SC** 31380
- **B** Agricultural Workers 1973
- **R** Foreign Workers 1985
  ↓ Human Migration 1973

Migration (Human)
Use Human Migration

Migratory Behavior (Animal) 1973
PN 773   **SC** 31400
- **UF** Animal Navigation
- **B** Animal Ethology 1967
- **R** Animal Homing 1991

Mild Mental Retardation 2001
PN 0510   **SC** 31405
SN IQ 50-70.
HN In 2000, this term was created to replace the discontinued term EDUCABLE MENTALLY RETARDED and the discontinued and deleted term MILDLY MENTALLY RETARDED. These terms were removed from all records containing them and replaced with MILD MENTAL RETARDATION.
- **UF** Educable Mentally Retarded
- **B** Mental Retardation 1967

Milieu Therapy 1988
PN 257   **SC** 31420
SN Modification or manipulation of patient's personal life circumstances or environment through controlled and stimulatory environments. Treatment setting can be a hospital, therapeutic community, or home.
HN Use THERAPEUTIC COMMUNITY to access references from 1973-1987.
- **UF** Environmental Therapy
  Socioenvironmental Therapy
- **B** Treatment 1967
- **R** Sociotherapy 1973
  Therapeutic Community 1967
  ↓ Therapeutic Environment 2001

Militancy 1973
PN 76   **SC** 31430
- **B** Social Behavior 1967

Military Enlistment 1973
PN 279   **SC** 31440
- **UF** Enlistment (Military)
- **R** Military Recruitment 1973

Military Medical Personnel 1973
PN 204   **SC** 31450
- **B** Medical Personnel 1967
  Military Personnel 1967

Military Officers
Use Commissioned Officers

Military Personnel 1967
PN 3395   **SC** 31470
- **UF** Servicemen
- **B** Government Personnel 1973
- **N** Air Force Personnel 1967
  Army Personnel 1967
  Coast Guard Personnel 1988
  Commissioned Officers 1973
  ↓ Enlisted Military Personnel 1973
  Marine Personnel 1973
  Military Medical Personnel 1973
  Military Psychologists 1997
  National Guardsmen 1973
  Navy Personnel 1967
  ROTC Students 1973
  Volunteer Military Personnel 1973
- **R** Astronauts 1973
  Chaplains 1973
  Combat Experience 1991
  Military Veterans 1973

Military Psychologists 1997
PN 20   **SC** 31475
- **R** Military Personnel 1967
  Psychologists 1967
- **R** Military Psychology 1967

Military Psychology 1967
PN 592   **SC** 31480
- **B** Applied Psychology 1973
- **R** Military Psychologists 1997

Military Recruitment 1973
PN 248   **SC** 31490
- **UF** Recruitment (Military)
- **B** Personnel Recruitment 1973
- **R** Military Enlistment 1973

Military Schools 1973
PN 170   **SC** 31500
- **B** Schools 1967
- **R** ↓ Colleges 1967
  High Schools 1973

Military Training 1973
PN 1371   **SC** 31510
- **B** Personnel Training 1967

Military Veterans 1973
PN 3462   **SC** 31520
- **UF** Veterans (Military)
- **R** ↓ Military Personnel 1967
  ↓ Personnel 1967

Miller Analogies Test 1973
PN 15   **SC** 31530
- **B** Intelligence Measures 1967

Millon Clinical Multiaxial Inventory 1988
PN 417   **SC** 31540
- **B** Nonprojective Personality Measures 1973

Mimicry (Biology) 2003
PN 29   **SC** 31543
SN Evolutionary process by which one species mimics the appearance or characteristics of another species. Use only for animal populations. Consider also IMITATION (LEARNING).
HN This term was introduced in June 2003. Psyc-INFO records from the past 10 years were re-indexed with this term. The posting note reflects the number of records that were re-indexed.
- **R** Environmental Adaptation 1973
  ↓ Physical Appearance 1982
  Theory of Evolution 1967

Mind 1991
PN 2047   **SC** 31550
SN Conceptually broad term referring to the organized totality of conscious and unconscious mental processes or psychic activities of an individual.
- **UF** Psyche
- **R** ↓ Cognitions 1985
  ↓ Cognitive Processes 1967
  ↓ Consciousness States 1971
  Dualism 1973
  Human Nature 1997
  ↓ Perception 1967
  Soul 2004
  Theory of Mind 2001
  Unconscious (Personality Factor) 1967

Mind Blindness
Use Theory of Mind

Mind Body
Use Dualism

Mini Mental State Examination 1994
PN 275   **SC** 31548
- **B** Neuropsychological Assessment 1982

Minimal Brain Disorders 1973
PN 500   **SC** 31560
HN In 2000, this term replaced the discontinued and deleted term MINIMALLY BRAIN DAMAGED. MINIMALLY BRAIN DAMAGED was removed from all records containing it and replaced with MINIMAL BRAIN DISORDERS.
- **B** Brain Damage 1967
  Brain Disorders 1967
- **R** ↓ Attention Deficit Disorder 1985
  Attention Deficit Disorder with
  Hyperactivity 2001
  Hyperkinesis 1970
  ↓ Learning Disabilities 1973

Minimum Competency Tests 1985
PN 129   **SC** 31585
- **UF** Basic Skills Testing
- **B** Educational Measurement 1967
- **R** ↓ Competence 1982

Ministers (Religion) 1973
PN 556   **SC** 31590
- **UF** Pastors
- **B** Clergy 1973
- **R** Chaplains 1973
  Missionaries 1973

Minks 1973
PN 44   SC 31600
B   Rodents 1973

Minnesota Multiphasic Personality Inventory 2001
PN 4542   SC 31611
HN In 2000, the truncated term MINN MULTIPHA-SIC PERSONALITY INVEN (which was used from 1967-2000) was deleted, removed from all records containing it, and replaced with its expanded form MINNESOTA MULTIPHASIC PERSONALITY INVENTORY.
UF   MMPI
B   Nonprojective Personality Measures 1973

Minnesota Teacher Attitude Inventory
Use   Attitude Measures

Minor Tranquilizers 1973
PN 179   SC 31630
B   Tranquilizing Drugs 1967
N   Alprazolam 1988
     Buspirone 1991
     Chlordiazepoxide 1973
     Chlorprothixene 1973
     Clonazepam 1991
     Diazepam 1973
     Hydroxyzine 1973
     Lorazepam 1988
     Loxapine 1982
     Midazolam 1991
     Oxazepam 1978
R ↓ Benzodiazepines 1978

Minority Group Discrimination
Use   Race and Ethnic Discrimination

Minority Groups 1967
PN 4090   SC 31640
SN Includes ethnic and linguistic minority groups and in/out social groups.
B   Social Groups 1973
R   Affirmative Action 1985
     Alaska Natives 1997
     American Indians 1967
     Arabs 1988
  ↓ Asians 1982
     Blacks 1082
     Cultural Sensitivity 1994
     Gypsies 1973
     Hawaii Natives 2001
  ↓ Hispanics 1982
  ↓ Indigenous Populations 2001
     Inuit 2001
     Jews 1997
     Multiculturalism 1997
  ↓ Pacific Islanders 2001
     Race and Ethnic Discrimination 1994
  ↓ Racial and Ethnic Groups 2001
  ↓ Social Identity 1988

Mirror Image 1991
PN 277   SC 31645
R   Human Figures Drawing 1973
     Mental Rotation 1991
  ↓ Perceptual Discrimination 1973
     Self Perception 1967
  ↓ Visual Perception 1967

Mirroring 1997
PN 41   SC 31647

Mirroring — (cont'd)
SN Reflecting or emulating another person's behavior or other qualities in interactional or psychotherapeutic contexts. Also a technique in psychodrama.
B   Psychotherapeutic Techniques 1967
R ↓ Interpersonal Interaction 1967
     Psychodrama 1967
  ↓ Psychotherapeutic Processes 1967
     Self Psychology 1988

Misanthropy 1973
PN 55   SC 31650
UF   Misogyny
B   Personality Traits 1967

Misarticulation
Use   Articulation Disorders

Misbehavior
Use   Behavior Problems

Miscarriage
Use   Spontaneous Abortion

Miscegenous Marriage
Use   Interracial Marriage

Misconduct
Use   Behavior Problems

Misdemeanors
Use   Crime

Misdiagnosis 1997
PN 116   SC 31705
R ↓ Diagnosis 1967
     Diagnosis Related Groups 1988
     Patient History 1973
     Professional Liability 1985
  ↓ Psychodiagnostic Typologies 1967
  ↓ Screening 1982

Misogyny
Use   Misanthropy

Missionaries 1973
PN 155   SC 31720
B   Religious Personnel 1973
R ↓ Clergy 1973
  ↓ Educational Personnel 1973
     Evangelists 1973
     Lay Religious Personnel 1973
     Ministers (Religion) 1973
     Nuns 1973
     Priests 1973

Mistakes
Use   Errors

MMPI
Use   Minnesota Multiphasic Personality Inventory

Mnemonic Learning 1973
PN 939   SC 31750
SN Use of artificial ways (e.g., imagery) to facilitate learning, memory, recognition, and recall of material learned.
B   Learning 1967

Mnemonic Learning — (cont'd)
     Learning Strategies 1991
R   Chunking 2004
     Cues 1967
     Memory Training 1994
     Note Taking 1991

Mobility (Geographical)
Use   Geographical Mobility

Mobility (Occupational)
Use   Occupational Mobility

Mobility (Social)
Use   Social Mobility

Mobility Aids 1978
PN 296   SC 31774
UF   Seeing Eye Dogs
     Tactual Maps
     Wheelchairs
R ↓ Medical Therapeutic Devices 1973
     Physical Mobility 1994

Moclobemide 1997
PN 133   SC 31780
B   Antidepressant Drugs 1971
     Monoamine Oxidase Inhibitors 1973

Modeling
Use   Simulation

Modeling Behavior
Use   Imitation (Learning)

Models 1967
PN 34784   SC 31805
SN Quantitative or descriptive representations of how systems function, or criteria used for comparison purposes. Not to be used for role models.
N   Animal Models 1988
     Medical Model 1978
     Mental Models 2003

Moderate Mental Retardation 2001
PN 1757   SC 31807
SN IQ 35-49.
HN In 2000, this term was created to replace the discontinued term TRAINABLE MENTALLY RETARDED and the discontinued and deleted term MODERATELY MENTALLY RETARDED. These terms were removed from all records containing them and replaced with MODERATE MENTAL RETARDATION.
UF   Trainable Mentally Retarded
B   Mental Retardation 1967
R   Downs Syndrome 1967

Modernization 2003
PN 44   SC 31822
SN Process of change in which the most current ways or ideas are adopted.
HN This term was introduced in June 2003. Psyc-INFO records from the past 10 years were re-indexed with this term. The posting note reflects the number of records that were re-indexed.
B   Social Processes 1967
R   Community Development 1997
  ↓ Culture Change 1967
     Developing Countries 1985

Modernization — (cont'd)
Globalization 2003
Industrialization 1973
Social Change 1967
Urbanization 1973

Molindone 1982
PN 36   SC 31833
SN Organic heterocyclic indole having antiserotonin
properties and used as an antidepressant, sedative,
and tranquilizer.
B   Antidepressant Drugs 1971
      Neuroleptic Drugs 1973
      Sedatives 1973
      Serotonin Antagonists 1973

Mollusca 1973
PN 424   SC 31840
UF   Gastropods
B   Invertebrates 1973
N   Octopus 1973
      Snails 1973

Monetary Incentives 1973
PN 668   SC 31850
SN Money expected or promised in return for ser-
vice or attainment which may encourage the contin-
ued occurrence of the activity being rewarded.
B   Incentives 1967
      Motivation 1967
R   Monetary Rewards 1973
      ↓ Needs 1967

Monetary Rewards 1973
PN 509   SC 31860
SN Money given in return for service or attainment
which may act as reinforcement for the activity being
rewarded.
B   Rewards 1967
R   Monetary Incentives 1973

Money 1967
PN 1594   SC 31870
R   Budgets 1997
      Cost Containment 1991
      ↓ Costs and Cost Analysis 1973
      ↓ Economics 1985
      Economy 1973
      Equity (Payment) 1978
      Funding 1988
      ↓ Professional Fees 1978
      Resource Allocation 1997

Mongolism
Use Downs Syndrome

Monitoring 1973
PN 1351   SC 31800
SN Systematic observation or recording of events,
processes, or individuals.
B   Attention 1967
N   Polysomnography 2003
      Self Monitoring 1982
      Source Monitoring 2004
      Vigilance 1967
R   Selective Attention 1973
      ↓ Tracking 1967

Monkeys 1967
PN 12077   SC 31900
B   Primates (Nonhuman) 1973

Monoamine Oxidase Inhibitors 1973
PN 1062   SC 31920
B   Enzyme Inhibitors 1985
N   Iproniazid 1973
      Isocarboxazid 1973
      Moclobemide 1997
      Nialamide 1973
      Pargyline 1973
      Phenelzine 1973
      Pheniprazine 1973
      Tranylcypromine 1973
R   ↓ Amine Oxidase Inhibitors 1973
      ↓ Antidepressant Drugs 1971
      Monoamine Oxidases 1973
      ↓ Tricyclic Antidepressant Drugs 1997

Monoamine Oxidases 1973
PN 684   SC 31930
B   Oxidases 1973
R   ↓ Monoamine Oxidase Inhibitors 1973

Monoamines (Brain)
Use Catecholamines

Monocular Vision 1973
PN 778   SC 31940
B   Visual Perception 1967
R   Motion Parallax 1007

Monogamy 1997
PN 115   SC 31945
SN Used for human or animal populations.
UF   Marital Fidelity
B   Family Structure 1973
      Marriage 1967
      Psychosexual Behavior 1967
R   Extramarital Intercourse 1973
      ↓ Human Courtship 1973
      Polygamy 1973

Monolingualism 1973
PN 209   SC 31950
R   ↓ Language 1967

Monotony 1978
PN 73   SC 31955
SN Quality of task or stimulation characterized by
tedious or wearisome sameness and uniformity.
R   Boredom 1973

Monozygotic Twins 1973
PN 1224   SC 31960
UF   Identical Twins
B   Twins 1967

Montessori Method 1973
PN 87   SC 31970
SN Method of early childhood education developed
by M. Montessori, stressing individual instruction and
guidance and emphasizing practical life activities.
B   Teaching Methods 1967
R   Discovery Teaching Method 1973
      Open Classroom Method 1973

Mood Disorders
Use Affective Disorders

Moodiness 1973
PN 55   SC 31980
B   Personality Traits 1967

Moods
Use Emotional States

Mooney Problem Check List 1973
PN 11   SC 32000
B   Nonprojective Personality Measures 1973

Moral Development 1973
PN 3653   SC 32006
SN Process of acquiring ethical judgment.
B   Psychogenesis 1973
R   Kohlberg (Lawrence) 1991
      Morality 1967
      ↓ Personality Development 1967
      ↓ Psychosocial Development 1973

Morale 1978
PN 666   SC 32008
SN Prevailing spirit or attitude of an individual or
group characterized by self confidence and motiva-
tion and sense of purpose.
R   ↓ Emotional States 1973
      ↓ Emotions 1967
      Enthusiasm 1973

Morality 1967
PN 4559   SC 32010
SN Subjective or objective standards of right or
wrong, based on societal norms or ethical principles.
HN In 1982, this term replaced the discontinued
term MORALS. In 2000, MORALS was removed from
all records and replaced with MORALITY.
UF   Morals
R   ↓ Ethics 1967
      Evil 2003
      Integrity 1997
      ↓ Justice 1973
      Moral Development 1973
      Personal Values 1973
      ↓ Religious Beliefs 1973
      Reputation 1997
      Shame 1994
      Social Values 1973
      ↓ Values 1967

Morals
Use Morality

Mores
Use Values

Morita Therapy 1994
PN 34   SC 32035
B   Psychotherapeutic Techniques 1967

Morphemes 1973
PN 355   SC 32050
SN Minimum meaningful linguistic units that contain
no smaller meaningful units.
R   Morphology (Language) 1973
      Phonetics 1967

Morphine 1973
PN 4064   SC 32060
B   Alkaloids 1973
      Analgesic Drugs 1973
      Dopamine Agonists 1985
      Opiates 1973

Morphology 1973
PN 1315   SC 32070
SN Branch of biology that deals with the structure and form of plants and animals. Used for the scientific discipline or the morphological structure itself.
R ↓ Anatomy 1967
    Histology 1973
↓ Physiology 1967
    Polymorphism 2003

Morphology (Language) 1973
PN 932   SC 32080
SN Study of morphemes, including both their phonology and semantics. Used for the linguistic discipline or the specific morphological principles or characteristics of words. Compare MORPHEMES.
B Grammar 1967
R Discourse Analysis 1997
    Morphemes 1973
↓ Phonology 1973
↓ Prosody 1991
↓ Semantics 1967
↓ Syntax 1971
    Words (Phonetic Units) 1967

Mortality
Use Death and Dying

Mortality Rate 1973
PN 2311   SC 32100
UF Death Rate
R ↓ Death and Dying 1967
↓ Population 1973

Mosaicism
Use Chromosome Disorders

Moslems
Use Muslims

Mother Absence 1973
PN 285   SC 32120
SN For animals use ANIMAL MATERNAL DEPRIVATION.
HN From 1982, limited to human populations.
B Parental Absence 1973
R Patriarchy 1973

Mother Child Communication 1985
PN 1353   SC 32125
SN Verbal or nonverbal communication between mother and child.
B Parent Child Communication 1973
R Mother Child Relations 1967

Mother Child Relations 1967
PN 11371   SC 32130
SN For animals consider ANIMAL MATERNAL BEHAVIOR.
HN From 1982, limited to human populations.
UF Maternal Behavior (Human)
B Parent Child Relations 1967
R ↓ Childrearing Practices 1967
    Mother Child Communication 1985
↓ Parental Attitudes 1973
    Parental Permissiveness 1973
    Parental Role 1973
    Postpartum Depression 1973
    Postpartum Psychosis 2003
    Schizophrenogenic Mothers 1973
    Separation Individuation 1982

Mother Child Relations — (cont'd)
    Symbiotic Infantile Psychosis 1973

Mothers 1967
PN 15912   SC 32140
SN For animals consider ANIMAL MATERNAL BEHAVIOR.
HN From 1982, limited to human populations.
B Human Females 1973
    Parents 1967
N Adolescent Mothers 1985
    Schizophrenogenic Mothers 1973
    Single Mothers 1994
    Unwed Mothers 1973
R Expectant Mothers 1985
    Primipara 2001

Moths 1973
PN 171   SC 32150
B Insects 1967
R Larvae 1973

Motion Parallax 1997
PN 67   SC 32155
SN Monocular distance cues for motion perception based on observer movements and the resultant movements of objects in the visual field.
B Distance Perception 1973
    Motion Perception 1967
R ↓ Depth Perception 1967
    Form and Shape Perception 1967
    Monocular Vision 1973

Motion Perception 1967
PN 5576   SC 32160
UF Movement Perception
B Spatial Perception 1967
N ↓ Apparent Movement 1967
    Motion Parallax 1997
R Direction Perception 1997

Motion Pictures 1973
PN 509   SC 32170
SN Use a more specific term if possible.
B Audiovisual Communications Media 1973
    Mass Media 1967
N Motion Pictures (Educational) 1973
    Motion Pictures (Entertainment) 1973

Motion Pictures (Educational) 1973
PN 166   SC 32180
SN Films produced for educational purposes.
B Educational Audiovisual Aids 1973
    Motion Pictures 1973

Motion Pictures (Entertainment) 1973
PN 1073   SC 32190
UF Movies
B Motion Pictures 1973
R Drama 1973
    Photographic Art 1973

Motion Sickness 1973
PN 382   SC 32200
B Labyrinth Disorders 1973

Motivation 1967
PN 15585   SC 32210
UF Desires
    Drive
N ↓ Achievement Motivation 1967
    Affiliation Motivation 1967

Motivation — (cont'd)
    Animal Motivation 1967
    Educational Incentives 1973
    Employee Motivation 1973
    Extrinsic Motivation 1973
    Fear of Success 1978
    Hunger 1967
↓ Incentives 1967
    Intrinsic Motivation 1973
    Monetary Incentives 1973
    Procrastination 1985
    Sex Drive 1973
    Temptation 1973
    Thirst 1967
R Activity Level 1982
    Activity Theory 2003
↓ Aspirations 1967
↓ Commitment 1985
    Delay of Gratification 1978
↓ Deprivation 1967
    Enthusiasm 1973
↓ Exploratory Behavior 1967
    Goal Setting 1997
↓ Goals 1967
    Instinctive Behavior 1982
    Instrumentality 1991
    Intention 1988
    Motivation Training 1973
↓ Needs 1967
    Persistence 1973
    Planned Behavior 1997
↓ Reinforcement 1967
    Satiation 1967

Motivation Training 1973
PN 153   SC 32220
UF Training (Motivation)
R ↓ Motivation 1967

Motor Coordination 1973
PN 1590   SC 32230
UF Coordination (Motor)
B Motor Processes 1967
R ↓ Motor Performance 1973
    Motor Skills 1973
↓ Perceptual Motor Coordination 1973
↓ Physical Agility 1973

Motor Cortex 1973
PN 1156   SC 32240
UF Cortex (Motor)
B Frontal Lobe 1973

Motor Development 1973
PN 2009   SC 32250
B Physical Development 1973
N Perceptual Motor Development 1991
↓ Psychomotor Development 1973
R Animal Development 1978
↓ Childhood Development 1967
    Developmental Age Groups 1973
↓ Motor Processes 1967
    Physical Mobility 1994

Motor Disorders
Use Nervous System Disorders

Motor Evoked Potentials
Use Somatosensory Evoked Potentials

Motor Neurons 1973
PN 719   SC 32290

Motor Neurons — (cont'd)
B   Neurons 1973
R   ↓ Efferent Pathways 1982

Motor Pathways
  Use Efferent Pathways

Motor Performance 1973
PN 5689   SC 32300
B   Motor Processes 1967
      Performance 1967
N   Finger Tapping 1973
      Jumping 1973
      Running 1973
      Walking 1973
R   Motor Coordination 1973

Motor Processes 1967
PN 11569   SC 32310
UF   Physical Activity
N   Activity Level 1982
      Animal Locomotion 1982
      ↓ Exercise 1973
      Grasping 1997
      Jumping 1973
      Licking 1988
      Motor Coordination 1973
      ↓ Motor Performance 1973
      Motor Skills 1973
      ↓ Physical Agility 1973
      Physical Mobility 1994
      Rotational Behavior 1994
      Sucking 1978
      Swallowing 1988
      Swimming 1973
      Tonic Immobility 1978
      Tool Use 1991
      Wandering Behavior 1991
R   ↓ Efferent Pathways 1982
      ↓ Motor Development 1973
      Muscle Tone 1985
      ↓ Perceptual Motor Processes 1967
      Physical Restraint 1982
      Posture 1970

Motor Skill Learning
  Use Perceptual Motor Learning

Motor Skills 1973
PN 1589   SC 32330
B   Motor Processes 1967
      Nonverbal Ability 1988
R   Motor Coordination 1973
      ↓ Tracking 1967

Motor Traffic Accidents 1973
PN 1756   SC 32340
UF   Automobile Accidents
      Traffic Accidents (Motor)
B   Transportation Accidents 1973
R   Drivers 1973
      ↓ Driving Behavior 1967
      Highway Safety 1973
      Pedestrian Accidents 1973

Motor Vehicles 1982
PN 368   SC 32350
SN Automotive vehicles not operated on rails.
UF   Buses
      Motorcycles
      Trucks

Motor Vehicles — (cont'd)
B   Ground Transportation 1973
N   Automobiles 1973
R   Drivers 1973

Motorcycles
  Use Motor Vehicles

Mourning
  Use Grief

Mouse Killing
  Use Muricide

Mouth (Anatomy) 1967
PN 452   SC 32370
B   Digestive System 1967
R   Lips (Face) 1973
      Salivary Glands 1973
      Teeth (Anatomy) 1973
      ↓ Tongue 1973

Movement Disorders 1985
PN 830   SC 32375
SN Physically- or psychologically-based abnormalities in motor processes relating primarily to posture, coordination, or locomotion.
UF   Dyspraxia
B   Nervous System Disorders 1967
N   Apraxia 1973
      Ataxia 1973
      Athetosis 1973
      Catalepsy 1973
      Cataplexy 1973
      ↓ Chorea 1973
      ↓ Dyskinesia 1973
      Myasthenia Gravis 1973
      Myoclonia 1973
      ↓ Paralysis 1973
      ↓ Spasms 1973
      Tics 1973
      Torticollis 1973
      Tremor 1973
R   ↓ Muscular Disorders 1973
      ↓ Musculoskeletal Disorders 1973
      ↓ Neuromuscular Disorders 1973
      ↓ Symptoms 1967

Movement Perception
  Use Motion Perception

Movement Therapy 1997
PN 148   SC 32385
SN Therapeutic technique utilizing bodily movements and rhythmic exercises used to improve psychological and/or physical functioning of patients or clients.
B   Treatment 1967
R   Art Therapy 1973
      ↓ Creative Arts Therapy 1994
      Dance Therapy 1973
      ↓ Exercise 1973
      Music Therapy 1973
      Recreation Therapy 1973

Movies
  Use Motion Pictures (Entertainment)

MPTP
  Use Methylphenyltetrahydropyridine

MRI
  Use Magnetic Resonance Imaging

Mucus 1973
PN 26   SC 32440
B   Body Fluids 1973

Mueller Lyer Illusion 1988
PN 96   SC 32439
B   Illusions (Perception) 1967

Multi Infarct Dementia 1991
PN 301   SC 32442
UF   Dementia (Multi Infarct)
B   Vascular Dementia 1997
R   ↓ Cerebrovascular Disorders 1973

Multicultural Education 1988
PN 677   SC 32441
SN Educational program involving two or more ethnic or cultural groups designed to help participants define their own ethnic or cultural identity and to appreciate that of others. The primary purposes are to reduce prejudice and stereotyping, and to promote cultural pluralism.
B   Education 1967
R   Bilingual Education 1978
      Cross Cultural Communication 1997
      Cultural Sensitivity 1994
      ↓ Educational Programs 1973
      Multiculturalism 1997

Multiculturalism 1997
PN 1221   SC 57500
UF   Cultural Pluralism
R   Acculturation 2003
      Cross Cultural Communication 1997
      Cross Cultural Differences 1967
      Cultural Deprivation 1973
      Cultural Sensitivity 1994
      ↓ Culture (Anthropological) 1967
      ↓ Culture Change 1967
      Diversity in the Workplace 2003
      Minority Groups 1967
      Multicultural Education 1988
      ↓ Racial and Ethnic Attitudes 1982
      Racial and Ethnic Differences 1982
      ↓ Racial and Ethnic Groups 2001
      Racial and Ethnic Relations 1982
      ↓ Sociocultural Factors 1967

Multidimensional Scaling 1982
PN 736   SC 32443
SN Set of psychological data analysis techniques that represent perceived stimuli in multidimensional spatial or pictorial configurations.
B   Measurement 1967
R   ↓ Analysis 1967
      ↓ Rating Scales 1967
      Scaling (Testing) 1967

Multidisciplinary Research
  Use Interdisciplinary Research

Multidisciplinary Treatment Approach
  Use Interdisciplinary Treatment Approach

Multidrug Abuse
  Use Polydrug Abuse

Multilingualism 1973
PN 178   SC 32450
 N   Bilingualism 1973
 R   Bilingual Education 1978
     English as Second Language 1997
     ↓ Language 1967

Multimodal Treatment Approach 1991
PN 994   SC 32455
SN Use of different therapeutic techniques based
on the theoretical principles from one medical or psy-
chological specialty or discipline. Compare INTER-
DISCIPLINARY TREATMENT APPROACH.
 B   Treatment 1967
 R   Eclectic Psychotherapy 1994
     Integrated Services 1997
     Integrative Psychotherapy 2003
     Interdisciplinary Treatment Approach 1973

Multiple Births 1973
PN 43   SC 32460
SN Birth of more than one child at the same time to
the same parents. Also used to refer to the children
themselves. Use a more specific term if possible.
Limited to human populations.
 B   Siblings 1967
 N   Triplets 1973
     ↓ Twins 1967

Multiple Choice (Testing Method) 1973
PN 755   SC 32470
 B   Testing Methods 1967

Multiple Disabilities 2001
PN 991   SC 32473
HN The term MULTIPLY HANDICAPPED was used
to represent this concept from 1973-1996, and MUL-
TIPLY DISABLED was used from 1997-2000. In
2000, MULTIPLE DISABILITIES was created to
replace the discontinued and deleted term MULTIPLY
DISABLED. MULTIPLY DISABLED and MULTIPLY
HANDICAPPED were removed from all records con-
taining them and replaced with MULTIPLE DISABILI-
TIES.
 UF Multiply Handicapped
 B   Disabilities 2003
 N   Deaf Blind 1991

Multiple Personality
 Use Dissociative Identity Disorder

Multiple Regression 1982
PN 358   SC 32485
SN Method of analyzing the collective and separate
influences of two or more independent variables on
the variation of a criterion variable.
 B   Multivariate Analysis 1982
     Statistical Regression 1985
 R   Analysis of Covariance 1973
     Analysis of Variance 1967
     Linear Regression 1973
     Logistic Regression 2003
     Nonlinear Regression 1973
     Path Analysis 1991
     ↓ Statistical Correlation 1967

Multiple Sclerosis 1973
PN 1555   SC 32490
 B   Sclerosis (Nervous System) 1973
 R   ↓ Myelitis 1973

Multiple Therapy
 Use Cotherapy

Multiply Handicapped
 Use Multiple Disabilities

Multivariate Analysis 1982
PN 1095   SC 32513
SN Any statistical technique designed to measure
the influence of many independent variables acting
simultaneously on more than one dependent vari-
able.
 UF Canonical Correlation
 B   Statistical Analysis 1967
 N   ↓ Factor Analysis 1967
     Multiple Regression 1982
     Path Analysis 1991
 R   Analysis of Covariance 1973
     Analysis of Variance 1967
     ↓ Statistical Correlation 1967
     ↓ Statistical Regression 1985

Munchausen Syndrome 1994
PN 58   SC 32517
SN A disorder characterized by plausible presenta-
tions of physical symptoms or an acute illness that
are under the individual's control, and often resulting
in multiple, unnecessary hospitalizations.
HN Use FACTITIOUS DISORDERS to access refer-
ences from 1988-1993.
 UF Hospital Addiction Syndrome
 B   Factitious Disorders 1988
 R   Malingering 1973
     Munchausen Syndrome by Proxy 1997
     ↓ Somatoform Disorders 2001

Munchausen Syndrome by Proxy 1997
PN 114   SC 32519
SN A phenomenon in which symptoms of an acute
illness are fabricated by an individual other than the
patient (e.g., a caregiver or parent) resulting in habitual seeking of medical care.
 R   ↓ Child Abuse 1971
     Child Neglect 1988
     Munchausen Syndrome 1994

Murder
 Use Homicide

Muricide 1988
PN 42   SC 32523
 UF Mouse Killing
 B   Animal Aggressive Behavior 1973

Muscarinic Drugs
 Use Cholinergic Drugs

Muscarinic Receptors
 Use Cholinergic Receptors

Muscimol 1994
PN 161   SC 32525
HN Use GAMMA AMINOBUTYRIC ACID AGO-
NISTS to access references from 1985-1993.
 UF Pantherine
 B   Gamma Aminobutyric Acid Agonists 1985
     Ibotenic Acid 1991

Muscle Contraction Headache 1973
PN 572   SC 32530
 UF Tension Headache
 B   Headache 1973

Muscle Contractions 1973
PN 676   SC 32540
 UF Rigidity (Muscles)
 R   Muscle Relaxation 1973
     Muscle Tone 1985
     ↓ Muscles 1967
     Parkinsonism 1994
     ↓ Reflexes 1971

Muscle Cramps
 Use Muscular Disorders

Muscle Relaxation 1973
PN 486   SC 32557
 R   Muscle Contractions 1973
     ↓ Muscles 1967
     Progressive Relaxation Therapy 1978
     Relaxation 1973
     ↓ Relaxation Therapy 1978

Muscle Relaxation Therapy
 Use Relaxation Therapy

Muscle Relaxing Drugs 1973
PN 178   SC 32560
HN In 1997, this term replaced the discontinued
term MEPHENESIN. In 2000, MEPHENESIN was
removed from all records and replaced with MUSCLE
RELAXING DRUGS.
 UF Mephenesin
     Neuromuscular Blocking Drugs
 B   Drugs 1967
 N   Baclofen 1991
     Curare 1973
     Diazepam 1973
     Meprobamate 1973
     Orphenadrine 1973
     Papaverine 1973
     Succinylcholine 1973
     Theophylline 1973
     Tubocurarine 1973
 R   ↓ Anesthetic Drugs 1973
     ↓ Anticonvulsive Drugs 1973
     ↓ Antihypertensive Drugs 1973
     ↓ Antispasmodic Drugs 1973
     ↓ Benzodiazepines 1978
     ↓ CNS Depressant Drugs 1973
     ↓ Heart Rate Affecting Drugs 1973
     ↓ Tranquilizing Drugs 1967
     Vasodilation 1973

Muscle Spasms 1973
PN 85   SC 32570
 B   Spasms 1973
 R   ↓ Muscles 1967

Muscle Tone 1985
PN 99   SC 32575
 R   ↓ Motor Processes 1967
     Muscle Contractions 1973
     ↓ Reflexes 1971

Muscles 1967
PN 1860   SC 32580
 B   Musculoskeletal System 1973
 N   Abdominal Wall 1973

Muscles — (cont'd)
Diaphragm (Anatomy) 1973
Facial Muscles 1973
Masticatory Muscles 1973
Oculomotor Muscles 1973
R   Muscle Contractions 1973
Muscle Relaxation 1973
Muscle Spasms 1973
↓ Tissues (Body) 1973

Muscular Atrophy 1973
PN 46   SC 32590
UF   Atrophy (Muscular)
B   Muscular Disorders 1973

Muscular Disorders 1973
PN 1014   SC 32600
UF   Cramps (Muscle)
Duchennes Disease
Dystonia
Muscle Cramps
B   Musculoskeletal Disorders 1973
N   Cataplexy 1973
Fibromyalgia 2004
Muscular Atrophy 1973
Muscular Dystrophy 1973
Myasthenia Gravis 1973
Myoclonia 1973
Myofascial Pain 1991
Myotonia 1973
Torticollis 1973
R   Chronic Fatigue Syndrome 1997
↓ Movement Disorders 1985
↓ Neuromuscular Disorders 1973

Muscular Dystrophy 1973
PN 188   SC 32610
UF   Dystrophy (Muscular)
B   Muscular Disorders 1973
Neuromuscular Disorders 1973
R   Dysarthria 1973
↓ Peripheral Nerve Disorders 1973

Musculocutaneous Nerve
Use   Spinal Nerves

Musculoskeletal Disorders 1973
PN 613   SC 32630
UF   Skeletomuscular Disorders
Temporomandibular Joint Syndrome
B   Physical Disorders 1997
N   ↓ Bone Disorders 1973
↓ Joint Disorders 1973
↓ Muscular Disorders 1973
R   Hemiplegia 1978
↓ Movement Disorders 1985
↓ Musculoskeletal System 1973
↓ Neuromuscular Disorders 1973
↓ Paralysis 1973
Paraplegia 1978
Poliomyelitis 1973
Quadriplegia 1985
↓ Tuberculosis 1973

Musculoskeletal System 1973
PN 145   SC 32640
B   Anatomical Systems 1973
N   Arm (Anatomy) 1973
Bones 1973
Feet (Anatomy) 1973
↓ Fingers (Anatomy) 1973
Hand (Anatomy) 1967

Musculoskeletal System — (cont'd)
Hips 1973
Jaw 1973
↓ Joints (Anatomy) 1973
Leg (Anatomy) 1973
↓ Muscles 1967
Skull 1973
Spinal Column 1973
Tendons 1973
Thorax 1973
R   ↓ Musculoskeletal Disorders 1973
↓ Nose 1973
Osteopathic Medicine 2003

Music 1967
PN 4774   SC 32650
UF   Songs
B   Arts 1973
N   Musical Instruments 1973
Rock Music 1991
R   Music Perception 1997
Musicians 1991
↓ Rhythm 1991
Singing 1997
Tempo 1997

Music Education 1973
PN 1196   SC 32660
B   Curriculum 1967

Music Perception 1997
PN 653   SC 32665
B   Auditory Perception 1967
R   ↓ Music 1967
Musical Ability 1973
↓ Pitch Perception 1973
↓ Rhythm 1991
Singing 1997
Tempo 1997

Music Therapy 1973
PN 1308   SC 32670
B   Creative Arts Therapy 1994
R   Educational Therapy 1997
Movement Therapy 1997
Recreation Therapy 1973

Musical Ability 1973
PN 959   SC 32680
B   Artistic Ability 1973
R   Music Perception 1997

Musical Instruments 1973
PN 295   SC 32690
UF   Piano
B   Music 1967

Musicians 1991
PN 703   SC 32695
B   Artists 1973
R   ↓ Music 1967

Muslims 1997
PN 210   SC 32700
HN   Use ISLAM to access references prior to 1997.
UF   Moslems
B   Religious Groups 1997
R   Islam 1973

Mutations 1973
PN 1021   SC 32710

Mutations — (cont'd)
SN   Individual, strain, or species genetic variation resulting from an abrupt or unusual change in gene structure. Also, an externally induced or naturally occurring change in gene characteristics that is propagated in subsequent divisions of the cell.
R   ↓ Chromosomes 1973
↓ Genetic Disorders 1973
↓ Genetics 1967
Translocation (Chromosome) 1973

Mutilation (Self)
Use   Self Mutilation

Mutism 1973
PN 245   SC 32730
B   Language Disorders 1982
N   Elective Mutism 1973

Mutual Storytelling Technique 1973
PN 54   SC 32740
UF   Storytelling Technique
B   Psychotherapeutic Techniques 1967

Myasthenia 1973
PN 9   SC 32750
SN   Anomaly of the muscles, resulting in muscular debility, weakness, lack of tone, fatigue, or exhaustion.
B   Asthenia 1973

Myasthenia Gravis 1973
PN 63   SC 32760
B   Movement Disorders 1985
Muscular Disorders 1973
Neuromuscular Disorders 1973
Peripheral Nerve Disorders 1973

Myelin Sheath 1973
PN 125   SC 32780
B   Nerve Tissues 1973

Myelitis 1973
PN 9   SC 32790
B   Central Nervous System Disorders 1973
N   Encephalomyelitis 1973
Poliomyelitis 1973
R   ↓ Infectious Disorders 1973
Multiple Sclerosis 1973

Myelomeningocele
Use   Spina Bifida

Myenteric Plexus
Use   Autonomic Ganglia

Myers Briggs Type Indicator 1973
PN 522   SC 32810
B   Nonprojective Personality Measures 1973

Myocardial Infarctions 1973
PN 1118   SC 32820
UF   Infarctions (Myocardial)
B   Heart Disorders 1973
R   Angina Pectoris 1973
Coronary Thromboses 1973

Myocardium 1973
PN 27   SC 32830

Myocardium — (cont'd)
B   Heart   1967

Myoclonia   1973
PN   210   SC   32840
B   Movement Disorders   1985
    Muscular Disorders   1973

Myofascial Pain   1991
PN   119   SC   32845
B   Muscular Disorders   1973
    Pain   1967
R   ↓ Bruxism   1985
    Chronic Pain   1985
    ↓ Somatoform Disorders   2001
    ↓ Syndromes   1973

Myopia   1973
PN   135   SC   32850
UF   Nearsightedness
B   Refraction Errors   1973

Myotonia   1973
PN   48   SC   32860
B   Muscular Disorders   1973
R   ↓ Congenital Disorders   1973

Mysticism   1967
PN   516   SC   32870
UF   Visions (Mysticism)
B   Philosophies   1967
R   Occultism   1978
    ↓ Parapsychology   1967
    ↓ Religious Beliefs   1973
    Religious Experiences   1997
    ↓ Religious Practices   1973
    Witchcraft   1973

Myths   1967
PN   1676   SC   32890
R   Animism   1973
    Archetypes   1991
    Cultism   1973
    Ethnology   1967
    Folklore   1991
    ↓ Literature   1967
    Metaphor   1982
    Storytelling   1988
    Transcultural Psychiatry   1973

Myxedema
Use   Hypothyroidism

N-Methyl-D-Aspartate   1994
PN   1753   SC   32905
UF   NMDA
B   Aspartic Acid   1973

Nabilone
Use   Cannabinoids

NAch
Use   Achievement Motivation

Nail Biting   1973
PN   87   SC   32920
B   Habits   1967

Nalorphine   1973
PN   47   SC   32940

Nalorphine — (cont'd)
B   Narcotic Antagonists   1973

Naloxone   1978
PN   1948   SC   32944
B   Narcotic Antagonists   1973

Naltrexone   1988
PN   826   SC   32945
B   Narcotic Antagonists   1973

Names   1985
PN   573   SC   32947
N   Brand Names   1978
R   Labeling   1978
    Nouns   1973

Naming   1988
PN   2053   SC   32948
SN   Process of identifying an object or concept with a word or phrase.
B   Cognitive Processes   1967
R   Cognitive Mediation   1967
    Object Recognition   1997

Napping   1994
PN   91   SC   32949
B   Sleep   1967
R   Sleep Onset   1973
    Sleep Wake Cycle   1985

Narcissism   1967
PN   2038   SC   32950
SN   Self-love in which all sources of pleasure are unrealistically believed to emanate from within oneself, resulting in a false sense of omnipotence, and in which the libido is no longer attached to external love objects, but is redirected to one's self.
B   Personality Traits   1967
R   Autoeroticism   1997
    Egocentrism   1978
    Grandiosity   1994
    ↓ Mental Disorders   1967
    Narcissistic Personality Disorder   1973
    Selfishness   1973

Narcissistic Personality Disorder   1973
PN   1028   SC   32960
SN   Personality disorder characterized by excessive self-love, egocentrism, grandiosity, exhibitionism, excessive needs for attention, and sensitivity to criticism.
B   Personality Disorders   1967
R   Antisocial Personality Disorder   1973
    Narcissism   1967

Narcoanalysis   1973
PN   20   SC   32970
SN   Sleep-like state induced by medication or hypnosis and used in the treatment of mental disorders.
B   Drug Therapy   1967
    Physical Treatment Methods   1973
N   Sleep Treatment   1973

Narcoanalytic Drugs
Use   Drugs

Narcolepsy   1973
PN   403   SC   32990
UF   Paroxysmal Sleep
B   Sleep Disorders   1973

Narcolepsy — (cont'd)
R   Cataplexy   1973
    Hypersomnia   1994

Narcosis   1973
PN   75   SC   33000
B   Toxic Disorders   1973
R   ↓ Narcotic Drugs   1973

Narcotic Agonists   1988
PN   860   SC   32995
UF   Opiate Agonists
B   Drugs   1967
N   Pentazocine   1991
R   ↓ Narcotic Drugs   1973

Narcotic Antagonists   1973
PN   1008   SC   33010
UF   Opiate Antagonists
    Opioid Antagonists
B   Drugs   1967
N   Nalorphine   1973
    Naloxone   1978
    Naltrexone   1988
R   ↓ Narcotic Drugs   1973

Narcotic Drugs   1973
PN   493   SC   33020
B   Drugs   1967
N   Apomorphine   1973
    Atropine   1973
    Meperidine   1973
    Methadone   1973
    ↓ Opiates   1973
R   ↓ Analgesic Drugs   1973
    ↓ Anesthetic Drugs   1973
    ↓ Anticonvulsive Drugs   1973
    ↓ Cannabis   1973
    ↓ CNS Depressant Drugs   1973
    ↓ Dopamine Antagonists   1982
    ↓ Emetic Drugs   1973
    ↓ Hypnotic Drugs   1973
    Narcosis   1973
    ↓ Narcotic Agonists   1988
    ↓ Narcotic Antagonists   1973
    ↓ Tranquilizing Drugs   1967

Narcotics Anonymous
Use   Twelve Step Programs

Narratives   1997
PN   2854   SC   33025
SN   Construction or reconstruction of an event or story.
B   Verbal Communication   1967
R   ↓ Biography   1967
    Creative Writing   1994
    Life Review   1991
    ↓ Literature   1967
    Storytelling   1988

Nasal Mucosa   1973
PN   51   SC   33030
B   Membranes   1973
    Nose   1973
N   Olfactory Mucosa   1973

National Guardsmen   1973
PN   64   SC   33040
B   Military Personnel   1967
R   Air Force Personnel   1967
    Army Personnel   1967

National Guardsmen — (cont'd)
Volunteer Military Personnel 1973

Nationalism 1967
PN 459   SC 33050
B   Political Attitudes 1973

Native Alaskans
Use Alaska Natives

Native Americans
Use American Indians

Native Hawaiians
Use Hawaii Natives

Native Language 2004
PN 45   SC 58074
HN   This term was introduced in June 2004. Psyc-
INFO records from the past 10 years were re-indexed
with this term. The posting note reflects the number
of records that were re-indexed.
UF   First Language
B   Language 1967
R   Bilingualism 1973
     English as Second Language 1997

Natives
Use Indigenous Populations

Natural Childbirth 1978
PN 52   SC 33056
UF   Childbirth (Natural)
B   Birth 1967
R   Childbirth Training 1978

Natural Disasters 1973
PN 836   SC 33060
SN   Calamity caused by natural forces resulting in
substantial damage, loss, and distress.
B   Disasters 1973
R   Emergency Services 1973
     ↓ Stress 1967

Natural Family
Use Biological Family

Natural Killer Cells 2003
PN 7   SC 33072
SN   White blood cells that kill tumor- and virus-
infected cells as part of the body's immune system.
HN   This term was introduced in June 2003. Psyc-
INFO records from the past 10 years were re-indexed
with this term. The posting note reflects the number
of records that were re-indexed.
B   Leucocytes 1973

Natural Selection 1997
PN 207   SC 33073
SN   Natural evolutionary process that results in the
survival of organisms best suited to changing living
conditions through the perpetuation of desirable
genetic qualities and the elimination of undesirable
ones.
HN   Consider DARWINISM to access references
from 1973-1996.
B   Darwinism 1973
R   ↓ Genetics 1967
     Theory of Evolution 1967

Naturalistic Observation
Use Observation Methods

Nature Nurture 1994
PN 614   SC 33075
SN   Debatable issue concerning the controversial
role of genetics or heredity versus environment or
experience in normal or abnormal developmental
processes.
R   Behavioral Genetics 1994
     ↓ Environment 1967
     ↓ Genetics 1967
     ↓ Human Development 1967
     Predisposition 1973
     ↓ Psychogenesis 1973

Nausea 1973
PN 320   SC 33080
B   Symptoms 1967
R   ↓ Antiemetic Drugs 1973
     ↓ Eating Disorders 1997
     Migraine Headache 1973
     Vomiting 1973

Navigators (Aircraft)
Use Aerospace Personnel

Navy Personnel 1967
PN 1219   SC 33100
B   Military Personnel 1967
R   Draftees 1973

Nazism
Use Fascism

Near Death Experiences 1985
PN 352   SC 00105
SN   Psychological and sensory phenomena
reported by persons who were near clinical death.
B   Parapsychological Phenomena 1973
R   ↓ Death and Dying 1967
     ↓ Experiences (Events) 1973
     ↓ Hallucinations 1967
     Out of Body Experiences 1988

Nearsightedness
Use Myopia

Neck (Anatomy) 1973
PN 265   SC 33120
B   Anatomy 1967

Need Achievement
Use Achievement Motivation

Need for Affiliation
Use Affiliation Motivation

Need for Approval 1997
PN 40   SC 33160
B   Personality Traits 1967
R   ↓ Needs 1967
     Social Acceptance 1967
     Social Approval 1967
     Social Desirability 1967

Need for Cognition 1997
PN 91   SC 33167
B   Personality Traits 1967

Need for Cognition — (cont'd)
R   Cognition 1967
     Intrinsic Motivation 1973
     ↓ Needs 1967

Need Satisfaction 1973
PN 629   SC 33170
B   Satisfaction 1973
R   ↓ Needs 1967
     Psychological Needs 1997

Needle Exchange Programs 2001
PN 58   SC 33173
B   Harm Reduction 2003
     Social Programs 1973
R   AIDS Prevention 1994
     ↓ Drug Abuse 1973
     Intravenous Drug Usage 1994
     Needle Sharing 1994
     Outreach Programs 1997

Needle Sharing 1994
PN 237   SC 33175
R   ↓ Drug Abuse 1973
     ↓ Drug Usage 1971
     Intravenous Drug Usage 1994
     Intravenous Injections 1973
     Needle Exchange Programs 2001
     Sharing (Social Behavior) 1978

Needs 1967
PN 4211   SC 33180
N   Health Service Needs 1997
     Psychological Needs 1997
R   ↓ Achievement Motivation 1967
     Affiliation Motivation 1967
     Craving 1997
     Extrinsic Motivation 1973
     ↓ Goals 1967
     ↓ Incentives 1967
     Intrinsic Motivation 1973
     Monetary Incentives 1973
     ↓ Motivation 1967
     Need for Approval 1997
     Need for Cognition 1997
     Need Satisfaction 1973
     Needs Assessment 1985
     Nurturance 1985
     Special Needs 1994

Needs Assessment 1985
PN 1805   SC 33185
SN   Systematic identification of needs of an individ-
ual or a group.
B   Evaluation 1967
     Measurement 1967
R   ↓ Case Management 1991
     Geriatric Assessment 1997
     ↓ Health Care Delivery 1978
     Health Service Needs 1997
     Intake Interview 1994
     ↓ Needs 1967
     ↓ Psychological Assessment 1997
     Psychological Needs 1997
     Special Needs 1994
     ↓ Surveys 1967
     ↓ Treatment Planning 1997

Nefazodone 2003
PN 210   SC 33188

Nefazodone — (cont'd)
HN This term was introduced in June 2003. Psyc-INFO records from the past 10 years were re-indexed with this term. The posting note reflects the number of records that were re-indexed.
  B   Antidepressant Drugs 1971

Negative and Positive Symptoms
  Use   Positive and Negative Symptoms

Negative Reinforcement 1973
PN 417   **SC** 33200
SN A stimulus or stimulus situation that, when withdrawn or discontinued following a response, increases the probability of occurrence of that response. Consider also ESCAPE CONDITIONING.
  B   Reinforcement 1967

Negative Therapeutic Reaction 1997
PN 26   **SC** 33205
SN In psychoanalysis, after a period of successful and constructive treatment, the worsening of a patient's symptoms and neurotic behavior.
  B   Psychotherapeutic Processes 1967
  R   Countertransference 1973
     ↓ Psychoanalysis 1967
       Psychotherapeutic Resistance 1973
       Psychotherapeutic Transference 1967

Negative Transfer 1973
PN 197   **SC** 33210
SN Previous learning or practice that hinders the acquisition of new material or skills as the result of dissimilar characteristics of the prior and current learning situation.
  B   Transfer (Learning) 1967

Negativism 1973
PN 450   **SC** 33220
SN State of mind or behavior characterized by extreme skepticism and persistent opposition or resistance to outside suggestions or advice.
  B   Personality Traits 1967
  R   Cynicism 1973
       Pessimism 1973
       Skepticism 2004

Negotiation 1973
PN 1786   **SC** 33230
  B   Interpersonal Communication 1973
  N   Bargaining 1973
  R   ↓ Conflict Resolution 1982
       Mediation 1988

Negroes
  Use   Blacks

Neighborhoods 1973
PN 1141   **SC** 33260
  B   Communities 1967

Nembutal
  Use   Pentobarbital

NEO Personality Inventory 1997
PN 189   **SC** 33275
  B   Personality Measures 1967
  R   Five Factor Personality Model 1997

NeoFreudian School
  Use   Neopsychoanalytic School

Neologisms 1973
PN 45   **SC** 33290
  B   Vocabulary 1967
  R   Words (Phonetic Units) 1967

Neonatal Development 1973
PN 834   **SC** 33320
SN Process of physical, cognitive, personality, and psychosocial growth occurring during the first month of life. Use a more specific term if possible.
  B   Infant Development 1973
  R   Neonatal Period 2001
     ↓ Physical Development 1973
     ↓ Psychogenesis 1973

Neonatal Disorders 1973
PN 162   **SC** 33330
  B   Physical Disorders 1997
  N   Anencephaly 1973
       Cleft Palate 1967
       Conjoined Twins 2003
       Crying Cat Syndrome 1973
       Downs Syndrome 1967
       Klinefelters Syndrome 1973
       Phenylketonuria 1973
       Tay Sachs Disease 2003
       Turners Syndrome 1973
  R   ↓ Apnea 1973
       Birth Injuries 1973
     ↓ Congenital Disorders 1973
       Hydrocephaly 1973
       Microcephaly 1973
       Rh Incompatibility 1973
       Sleep Apnea 1991

Neonatal Period 2001
PN 140   **SC** 33340
SN Usually the period from age 0 through 1 month. Compare PERINATAL PERIOD. Used for both human and animal populations.
  R   Neonatal Development 1973

Neonates (Animal)
  Use   Infants (Animal)

Neonaticide
  Use   Infanticide

Neophobia 1985
PN 170   **SC** 33368
SN Fearful or cautious exploration or reaction to novel objects, situations, or stimuli. Usually examined in subhuman species.
  R   Animal Exploratory Behavior 1973
       Avoidance 1967
     ↓ Fear 1967
       Instinctive Behavior 1982
       Stimulus Novelty 1973

Neoplasms 1967
PN 7175   **SC** 33370
  UF   Cancers
       Carcinomas
       Malignant Neoplasms
       Sarcomas
       Tumors
  B   Physical Disorders 1997
  N   Benign Neoplasms 1973

Neoplasms — (cont'd)
       Breast Neoplasms 1973
       Endocrine Neoplasms 1973
       Leukemias 1973
     ↓ Nervous System Neoplasms 1973
       Terminal Cancer 1973
  R   Antineoplastic Drugs 1982
     ↓ Digestive System Disorders 1973
     ↓ Gastrointestinal Disorders 1973
     ↓ Liver Disorders 1973

Neopsychoanalytic School 1973
PN 62   **SC** 33380
SN School of psychoanalysis originating with Jung and Adler which differs from Freudian psychoanalysis in emphasizing the importance of social and cultural factors in development of an individual's personality.
  UF   NeoFreudian School
  B   History of Psychology 1967
       Psychological Theories 2001
  N   Individual Psychology 1973
     ↓ Jungian Psychology 1973
  R   Erikson (Erik) 1991
       Freud (Sigmund) 1967
       Freudian Psychoanalytic School 1973
     ↓ Psychoanalytic Theory 1967

Neostigmine 1973
PN 47   **SC** 33390
  UF   Proserine
  B   Cholinesterase Inhibitors 1973
       Cholinomimetic Drugs 1973
  R   Bromides 1973

Neostriatum
  Use   Striatum

Nerve (Abducens)
  Use   Abducens Nerve

Nerve (Accessory)
  Use   Cranial Nerves

Nerve (Acoustic)
  Use   Acoustic Nerve

Nerve (Facial)
  Use   Facial Nerve

Nerve Cells
  Use   Neurons

Nerve Endings 1973
PN 39   **SC** 33450
  B   Nervous System 1967
  N   ↓ Neural Receptors 1973
       Proprioceptors 1973
       Synapses 1973
       Thermoreceptors 1973

Nerve Growth Factor 1994
PN 350   **SC** 33455
SN Polypeptide proteins that stimulate growth and development of peripheral, sympathetic, and sensory neurons.
  B   Peptides 1973
  R   ↓ Amino Acids 1973
     ↓ Nervous System 1967
       Neural Development 1985

Nerve Growth Factor — (cont'd)
  ↓ Neurons 1973

Nerve Tissues 1973
PN 133　　　　　　　　　　SC 33460
  B　　Nervous System 1967
　　　　Tissues (Body) 1973
  N　　Myelin Sheath 1973
  R　↓ Neurons 1973

Nerves (Adrenergic)
  Use　Adrenergic Nerves

Nerves (Cholinergic)
  Use　Cholinergic Nerves

Nerves (Cranial)
  Use　Cranial Nerves

Nerves (Peripheral)
  Use　Peripheral Nervous System

Nerves (Spinal)
  Use　Spinal Nerves

Nervous Breakdown
  Use　Mental Disorders

Nervous System 1967
PN 842　　　　　　　　　　SC 33530
  B　　Anatomical Systems 1970
  N　↓ Central Nervous System 1967
　　↓ Ganglia 1973
　　↓ Nerve Endings 1973
　　↓ Nerve Tissues 1973
　　↓ Neurons 1973
　　↓ Peripheral Nervous System 1973
　　↓ Receptive Fields 1985
  R　　Afferent Stimulation 1973
　　　　Instinctive Behavior 1982
　　　　Nerve Growth Factor 1994
　　↓ Nervous System Disorders 1967
　　　　Neural Development 1985
　　　　Neural Networks 1991
　　　　Neural Plasticity 1994
　　↓ Stereotaxic Techniques 1973

Nervous System Disorders 1967
PN 5536　　　　　　　　　　SC 33540
  UF　Motor Disorders
　　　　Neuroinfections
　　　　Neurological Disorders
　　　　Neuropathy
  B　　Physical Disorders 1997
  N　　Autonomic Nervous System Disorders 1973
　　↓ Central Nervous System Disorders 1973
　　↓ Convulsions 1967
　　　　Hyperkinesis 1973
　　↓ Movement Disorders 1985
　　↓ Nervous System Neoplasms 1973
　　↓ Neurodegenerative Diseases 2004
　　↓ Neuromuscular Disorders 1973
　　↓ Peripheral Nerve Disorders 1973
　　↓ Sclerosis (Nervous System) 1973
  R　↓ Cerebrovascular Disorders 1973
　　　　Developmental Disabilities 1982
　　　　Extrapyramidal Symptoms 1994
　　　　Hemianopia 1973
　　　　Influenza 1973

Nervous System Disorders — (cont'd)
　　　　Malaria 1973
　　↓ Nervous System 1967
　　　　Nystagmus 1973
　　　　Parkinsonism 1994
　　　　Somatosensory Disorders 2001
　　↓ Symptoms 1967
　　↓ Tuberculosis 1973

Nervous System Neoplasms 1973
PN 28　　　　　　　　　　SC 33550
  B　　Neoplasms 1967
　　　　Nervous System Disorders 1967
  N　　Brain Neoplasms 1973

Nervous System Plasticity
  Use　Neural Plasticity

Nervousness 1973
PN 69　　　　　　　　　　SC 33560
  B　　Personality Traits 1967

Nest Building 1973
PN 704　　　　　　　　　　SC 33570
  B　　Animal Ethology 1967
  R　↓ Animal Mating Behavior 1967

Networks (Social)
  Use　Social Networks

Neural Analyzers 1973
PN 24　　　　　　　　　　SC 33600
  SN　The peripheral sensory receptors or nerve endings (e.g., visual analyzer, acoustic analyzer) that select and transform stimuli and their associated projections and terminations in the central nervous system where synthesis of the transformations occurs.
  B　　Central Nervous System 1967

Neural Development 1985
PN 2805　　　　　　　　　　SC 33605
  SN　Functional and morphological development of central and peripheral nervous systems and supportive tissue.
  UF　Brain Development
　　　　Neural Regeneration
　　　　Reinnervation
  B　　Physical Development 1973
  R　　Animal Development 1978
　　　　Nerve Growth Factor 1994
　　↓ Nervous System 1967
　　　　Neural Plasticity 1994
　　　　Neural Transplantation 1985

Neural Lesions 1973
PN 1021　　　　　　　　　　SC 33610
  HN　Not defined prior to 1982. From 1982, limited to experimentally induced neural lesions and used primarily for animal populations.
  B　　Lesions 1967

Neural Networks 1991
PN 3807　　　　　　　　　　SC 33612
  SN　Computer simulation that duplicates the neural structure and cognitive processes of the human or animal brain.
  B　　Artificial Intelligence 1982
　　　　Computer Simulation 1973
  R　　Connectionism 1994
　　　　Machine Learning 2003

Neural Networks — (cont'd)
  ↓ Nervous System 1967
　　Neuroanatomy 1967

Neural Pathways 1982
PN 1996　　　　　　　　　　SC 33615
  SN　Collections of central or peripheral neural fibers having a common neurological function and serving to connect neuroanatomical systems such as sensory or motor mechanisms or central nervous system nuclei.
  B　　Central Nervous System 1967
　　　　Peripheral Nervous System 1973
  N　↓ Afferent Pathways 1982
　　　　Corpus Callosum 1973
　　↓ Efferent Pathways 1982
　　　　Fornix 1982
　　↓ Limbic System 1973
　　　　Optic Chiasm 1973
　　　　Optic Tract 1982
　　　　Reticular Formation 1967

Neural Plasticity 1994
PN 1470　　　　　　　　　　SC 33617
  SN　Change in reactivity of the nervous system and its components as a result of constant successive activations.
  UF　Nervous System Plasticity
  R　↓ Nervous System 1967
　　　　Neural Development 1985
　　　　Postactivation Potentials 1985
　　↓ Receptive Fields 1985

Neural Receptors 1973
PN 7730　　　　　　　　　　SC 33620
  UF　Receptors (Neural)
  B　　Nerve Endings 1973
  N　　Adrenergic Receptors 2003
　　　　Baroreceptors 1973
　　　　Chemoreceptors 1973
　　　　Cholinergic Receptors 2003
　　　　Mechanoreceptors 1973
　　　　Nociceptors 1985
　　↓ Photoreceptors 1973
　　　　Proprioceptors 1973
　　　　Thermoreceptors 1973
  R　　Receptor Binding 1985

Neural Regeneration
  Use　Neural Development

Neural Transmission
  Use　Neurotransmission

Neural Transplantation 1985
PN 379　　　　　　　　　　SC 33628
  R　　Neural Development 1985
　　　　Organ Transplantation 1973
　　　　Tissue Donation 1991

Neuralgia 1973
PN 114　　　　　　　　　　SC 33630
  B　　Pain 1967
　　　　Peripheral Nerve Disorders 1973
  N　　Trigeminal Neuralgia 1973

Neurasthenic Neurosis 1973
PN 146　　　　　　　　　　SC 33640
  B　　Neurosis 1967
  R　↓ Asthenia 1973

Neuroanatomy 1967
PN 3745　　　　　　　　　　SC 33660
SN Branch of neurology concerned with the anatomy of the nervous system. Used for the scientific discipline or the anatomical structures themselves.
B　Neurosciences 1973
R　↓ Anatomy 1967
　　Neural Networks 1991

Neurobiology 1973
PN 2419　　　　　　　　　　SC 33670
SN Biology of the nervous system. Used for the scientific discipline or the neurobiological processes themselves.
B　Biology 1967
　　Neurosciences 1973
R　Biological Psychiatry 1994

Neurochemistry 1973
PN 9774　　　　　　　　　　SC 33680
SN Chemical makeup and metabolism of nervous tissue. Used for the scientific discipline or the neurochemical processes themselves.
UF　Brain Metabolism
B　Biochemistry 1967
　　Neurosciences 1973
N　Neuroendocrinology 1985
　　Receptor Binding 1985
R　Blood Brain Barrier 1994
　　Glucose Metabolism 1994

Neurodegenerative Diseases 2004
PN 35　　　　　　　　　　SC 33692
SN Neurologic disorders characterized by progressive nervous system dysfunction and loss of neural tissue.
HN This term was introduced in June 2004. PsycINFO records from the past 10 years were re-indexed with this term. The posting note reflects the number of records that were re-indexed.
B　Nervous System Disorders 1967
N　Alzheimers Disease 1973
　　Dementia with Lewy Bodies 2001
　　Parkinsons Disease 1973
R　↓ Dementia 1985
　　Neuropathology 1973

Neurodermatitis 1973
PN 31　　　　　　　　　　SC 33690
B　Dermatitis 1973
　　Somatoform Disorders 2001
R　Allergic Skin Disorders 1973

Neuroendocrinology 1985
PN 1397　　　　　　　　　　SC 33695
SN Study of the biological, chemical, and physical relations between the nervous system and endocrine glands. Used for the scientific discipline or neuroendocrinological processes themselves.
B　Endocrinology 1973
　　Neurochemistry 1973
　　Neurophysiology 1973

Neuroimaging 2003
PN 397　　　　　　　　　　SC 33698
SN Conceptually broad term referring to techniques that provide in-depth portraits of regional brain structure, activity, and function. The techniques involve extensive computer analysis and are often used for the assessment and diagnosis of brain impairment.

Neuroimaging — (cont'd)
HN This term was introduced in June 2003. PsycINFO records from the past 10 years were re-indexed with this term. The posting note reflects the number of records that were re-indexed.
N　↓ Encephalography 1973
　　Magnetic Resonance Imaging 1994
　　↓ Roentgenography 1973
　　↓ Tomography 1988
R　↓ Brain 1967
　　↓ Brain Disorders 1967
　　Computer Assisted Diagnosis 1973
　　↓ Evoked Potentials 1967

Neuroinfections
Use Infectious Disorders AND Nervous System Disorders

Neurokinins 1997
PN 87　　　　　　　　　　SC 33705
B　Amino Acids 1973
　　Anti Inflammatory Drugs 1982
　　Neurotransmitters 1985
　　Peptides 1973
N　Substance P 1985

Neuroleptic Drugs 1973
PN 8948　　　　　　　　　　SC 33710
HN In 1982, this term replaced the discontinued terms ANTIPSYCHOTIC DRUGS and ANTISCHIZOPHRENIC DRUGS. In 2000, these terms were removed from all records containing them, and replaced with NEUROLEPTIC DRUGS.
UF　Antipsychotic Drugs
　　Antischizophrenic Drugs
　　Major Tranquilizers
B　Tranquilizing Drugs 1967
N　Clozapine 1991
　　Molindone 1982
　　Nialamide 1973
　　Olanzapine 2003
　　Quetiapine 2004
　　Reserpine 1967
　　Risperidone 1997
　　Spiroperidol 1991
　　Sulpiride 1973
　　Tetrabenazine 1973
R　Neuroleptic Malignant Syndrome 1988
　　Prostaglandins 1982
　　Tardive Dyskinesia 1988

Neuroleptic Malignant Syndrome 1988
PN 509　　　　　　　　　　SC 33715
B　Syndromes 1973
　　Toxic Disorders 1973
R　↓ Drug Therapy 1967
　　↓ Neuroleptic Drugs 1973
　　↓ Side Effects (Drug) 1973

Neurolinguistic Programming 2001
PN 115　　　　　　　　　　SC 33718
SN R. Bandler's model of techniques and strategies for interpersonal communication based on elements of transformational grammar and preferred sensory representations for learning and self expression. Also, self intervention method in humanistic psychology aimed at personal growth and human potential.
HN In 2000, this term was created to update the spelling from the discontinued term NEUROLINGUISTIC PROGRAMING. NEUROLINGUISTIC PROGRAMING was removed from all records containing them and replaced with NEUROLINGUISTIC PROGRAMMING.

Neurolinguistic Programming — (cont'd)
R　↓ Cognitive Style 1967
　　↓ Humanistic Psychology 1985
　　↓ Interpersonal Communication 1973
　　Neurolinguistics 1991
　　Perceptual Style 1973

Neurolinguistics 1991
PN 301　　　　　　　　　　SC 33719
SN Study of the neurological mechanisms involved in the development, acquisition, and use of language. Used for the scientific discipline or the neurolinguistic processes themselves.
B　Linguistics 1973
R　↓ Language 1967
　　↓ Language Disorders 1982
　　Neurolinguistic Programming 2001
　　Psycholinguistics 1967
　　↓ Verbal Communication 1967

Neurological Disorders
Use Nervous System Disorders

Neurologists 1973
PN 160　　　　　　　　　　SC 33730
UF　Neuropathologists
B　Physicians 1967
R　Surgeons 1973

Neurology 1967
PN 6244　　　　　　　　　　SC 33740
SN Scientific discipline dealing with the anatomy, physiology, and organic diseases of the nervous system. Used for the scientific discipline or the neurological findings themselves.
B　Medical Sciences 1967
　　Neurosciences 1973
R　Neuropathology 1973
　　↓ Neurosurgery 1973

Neuromuscular Blocking Drugs
Use Muscle Relaxing Drugs

Neuromuscular Disorders 1973
PN 275　　　　　　　　　　SC 33760
B　Nervous System Disorders 1967
N　Cataplexy 1973
　　Gilles de la Tourette Disorder 1973
　　Muscular Dystrophy 1973
　　Myasthenia Gravis 1973
　　↓ Paralysis 1973
R　↓ Dyskinesia 1973
　　Hyperkinesis 1973
　　↓ Movement Disorders 1985
　　↓ Muscular Disorders 1973
　　↓ Musculoskeletal Disorders 1973
　　↓ Sclerosis (Nervous System) 1973
　　↓ Spinal Cord Injuries 1973

Neurons 1973
PN 5854　　　　　　　　　　SC 33770
UF　Nerve Cells
B　Cells (Biology) 1973
　　Nervous System 1967
N　Axons 1973
　　Dendrites 1973
　　Ganglion Cells (Retina) 1985
　　Motor Neurons 1973
　　Purkinje Cells 1994
　　↓ Sensory Neurons 1973
R　Nerve Growth Factor 1994

Neurons — (cont'd)
↓ Nerve Tissues 1973
   Visual Receptive Fields 1982

Neuropathologists
Use Neurologists

Neuropathology 1973
PN 3739   **SC** 33790
SN Branch of medicine dealing with morphological and other aspects of nervous system disorders. Used for the scientific discipline or the neuropathological findings themselves.
B   Neurosciences 1973
     Pathology 1973
R ↓ Neurodegenerative Diseases 2004
     Neurology 1967

Neuropathy
Use Nervous System Disorders

Neuropeptide Y 2004
PN 197   **SC** 33804
SN A 36-amino acid peptide located in the nervous system that is associated with feeding behavior.
HN This term was introduced in June 2004. PsycINFO records from the past 10 years were re-indexed with this term. The posting note reflects the number of records that were re-indexed.
B   Neuropeptides 2003

Neuropeptides 2003
PN 67   **SC** 33805
SN Peptides located in neural tissue.
HN Use PEPTIDES to access references from 1994 to June 2003.
B   Peptides 1973
N   Angiotensin 1973
     Bombesin 1988
     Cholecystokinin 1982
     Corticotropin 1973
     Corticotropin Releasing Factor 1994
     Glucagon 1973
     Neuropeptide Y 2004
     Neurotensin 1985
     Prolactin 1973
     Somatostatin 1991
     Somatotropin 1973
     Thyrotropin 1973
     Vasopressin 1973
R ↓ Endorphins 1982
     Enkephalins 1982
  ↓ Neurotransmitters 1985
  ↓ Proteins 1973

Neurophysiology 1973
PN 5707   **SC** 33810
SN Physiology of the nervous system. Used for the scientific discipline, the neurophysiological processes, or neurophysiological structures themselves.
B   Neurosciences 1973
     Physiology 1967
N   Neuroendocrinology 1985
     Neurotransmission 2003
     Receptor Binding 1985

Neuropsychiatrists
Use Psychiatrists

Neuropsychiatry 1973
PN 1132   **SC** 33830

Neuropsychiatry — (cont'd)
SN Medical specialty that combines psychiatry and neurology. Used for the scientific discipline or the neuropsychiatric findings themselves.
B   Neurosciences 1973
     Psychiatry 1967
R   Biological Psychiatry 1994

Neuropsychological Assessment 1982
PN 6907   **SC** 33835
SN Use of tests, including intelligence, motor, and lateralization measures, to diagnose brain damage or other neurological dysfunction.
B   Psychological Assessment 1997
N   Halstead Reitan Neuropsychological
      Battery 2001
     Luria Nebraska Neuropsychological
      Battery 2001
     Mini Mental State Examination 1994
     Wechsler Memory Scale 1988
     Wisconsin Card Sorting Test 1994
R   Bender Gestalt Test 1967
     Benton Revised Visual Retention Test 1973
     Body Sway Testing 1973
  ↓ Brain Damage 1967
     Cognitive Assessment 1997
  ↓ Diagnosis 1967
     Memory for Designs Test 1973
  ↓ Neuropsychological Rehabilitation 1997
  ↓ Testing 1967
     Traumatic Brain Injury 1997

Neuropsychological Rehabilitation 1997
PN 461   **SC** 33837
B   Rehabilitation 1967
N   Cognitive Rehabilitation 1988
R   Memory Training 1994
  ↓ Neuropsychological Assessment 1982

Neuropsychology 1973
PN 8356   **SC** 33840
SN Branch of clinical psychology emphasizing the relationship between brain and behavior, including the diagnosis of brain pathology using cognitive or psychological tests. Used for the discipline or the neuropsychological functions themselves.
B   Neurosciences 1973
     Physiological Psychology 1967
R   Psychoneuroimmunology 1991

Neurosciences 1973
PN 1154   **SC** 33850
SN Scientific disciplines concerned with the development, structure, function, chemistry, and pathology of the nervous system.
B   Sciences 1967
N   Neuroanatomy 1967
     Neurobiology 1973
  ↓ Neurochemistry 1973
     Neurology 1967
     Neuropathology 1973
  ↓ Neurophysiology 1973
     Neuropsychiatry 1973
     Neuropsychology 1973
R   Cognitive Science 2003
  ↓ Medical Sciences 1967

Neurosis 1967
PN 4943   **SC** 33860

Neurosis — (cont'd)
SN Psychoanalytic term referring to mental conditions characterized primarily by anxiety, fears, obsessive thoughts, compulsions, dissociation, and depression. Neuroses have no organic origins and are believed to be a product of unconscious processes resulting from internal conflicts. Compare PSYCHOSIS.
UF Psychoneurosis
B   Mental Disorders 1967
N   Childhood Neurosis 1973
     Experimental Neurosis 1973
     Neurasthenic Neurosis 1973
     Occupational Neurosis 1973
     Traumatic Neurosis 1973
R   Anhedonia 1985
  ↓ Anxiety 1967
     Borderline States 1978
     Dissociation 2001
  ↓ Fear 1967
  ↓ Major Depression 1988
     Obsessive Compulsive Disorder 1985

Neurosurgeons
Use Surgeons

Neurosurgery 1973
PN 1001   **SC** 33890
B   Surgery 1971
N   Commissurotomy 1985
     Decerebration 1973
     Decortication (Brain) 1973
     Hemispherectomy 1973
  ↓ Psychosurgery 1973
     Pyramidotomy 1970
     Sympathectomy 1973
     Tractotomy 1973
     Vagotomy 1970
R   Neurology 1967

Neurosyphilis 1973
PN 43   **SC** 33900
B   Central Nervous System Disorders 1973
     Syphilis 1973
R   General Paresis 1973

Neurotensin 1985
PN 189   **SC** 33905
B   Neuropeptides 2003
     Neurotransmitters 1985
     Peptides 1973

Neurotic Depressive Reaction
Use Major Depression

Neuroticism 1973
PN 2219   **SC** 33915
SN Personality trait that contrasts adjustment or emotional stability with maladjustment. Experience of anxiety, anger, disgust, sadness, embarrassment, and a variety of other negative emotions.
B   Personality Traits 1967
R   Emotional Inferiority 1973
     Emotional Instability 1973
     Emotional Stability 1973
     Emotionality (Personality) 1973
     Five Factor Personality Model 1997

Neurotoxicity 2003
PN 138   **SC** 33918
SN Toxicity to nerves and/or nervous tissues.

Neurotoxicity — (cont'd)
HN This term was introduced in June 2003. Psyc-INFO records from the past 10 years were re-indexed with this term. The posting note reflects the number of records that were re-indexed.
B Toxicity 1973
R ↓ Neurotoxins 1982

Neurotoxins 1982
PN 1399 **SC** 33920
SN Bacterial, chemical, or pharmacological substances that are destructive to nerve tissue.
B Poisons 1973
N ↓ Ibotenic Acid 1991
Methylphenyltetrahydropyridine 1994
R Antibodies 1973
Drug Interactions 1982
↓ Insecticides 1973
Kainic Acid 1988
Neurotoxicity 2003
↓ Toxic Disorders 1973
↓ Toxicity 1973

Neurotransmission 2003
PN 253 **SC** 33923
SN The transmission of nerve impulses across a synapse via chemical substances or electrical signals.
HN This term was introduced in June 2003. Psyc-INFO records from the past 10 years were re-indexed with this term. The posting note reflects the number of records that were re-indexed.
UF Neural Transmission
Synaptic Transmission
B Neurophysiology 1973
R ↓ Neurotransmitters 1985
Synapses 1973

Neurotransmitters 1985
PN 1589 **SC** 33924
SN Chemical substances, synthesized and released by nerve cells, or glandular hormones that excite or inhibit other nerve, muscle, or gland cells by producing a brief alteration in the postsynaptic membrane of the receiving cell. Use a more specific term if possible.
N Acetylcholine 1973
↓ Aspartic Acid 1973
↓ Catecholamines 1973
Cholecystokinin 1982
↓ Endorphins 1982
Gamma Aminobutyric Acid 1978
Glutamic Acid 1973
Glycine 1973
Histamine 1973
↓ Neurokinins 1997
Neurotensin 1985
Serotonin 1973
Substance P 1985
R ↓ Amino Acids 1973
↓ Neuropeptides 2003
Neurotransmission 2003
Nitric Oxide 2003
↓ Peptides 1973

Neutrality (Psychotherapeutic)
Use Psychotherapeutic Neutrality

Never Married 1994
PN 69 **SC** 33926
B Marital Status 1973
R ↓ Single Parents 1978
Single Persons 1973
Unwed Mothers 1973

News Media 1997
PN 415 **SC** 33945
B Mass Media 1967
N Newspapers 1973
R Journalists 1973
Radio 1973
↓ Television 1967

Newsletters (Professional)
Use Scientific Communication

Newspapers 1973
PN 663 **SC** 33960
B News Media 1997
Printed Communications Media 1973

Niacin
Use Nicotinic Acid

Niacinamide
Use Nicotinamide

Nialamide 1973
PN 40 **SC** 33990
B Amine Oxidase Inhibitors 1973
Antidepressant Drugs 1971
Monoamine Oxidase Inhibitors 1973
Neuroleptic Drugs 1973

Nicotinamide 1973
PN 39 **SC** 34000
UF Niacinamide
Nicotinic Acid Amide
B Vitamins 1973
R Nicotinic Acid 1973
Pellagra 1973

Nicotine 1973
PN 2972 **SC** 34010
UF Tobacco (Drug)
B Alkaloids 1973
Cholinergic Blocking Drugs 1973
Ganglion Blocking Drugs 1973
R ↓ Insecticides 1973
Nicotine Withdrawal 1997
Smokeless Tobacco 1994
Tobacco Smoking 1967

Nicotine Withdrawal 1997
PN 149 **SC** 34015
B Drug Withdrawal 1973
R Nicotine 1973
Smokeless Tobacco 1994
Smoking Cessation 1988
Tobacco Smoking 1967

Nicotinic Acid 1973
PN 87 **SC** 34020
UF Niacin
B Acids 1973
Vasodilator Drugs 1973
Vitamins 1973
R Nicotinamide 1973

Nicotinic Acid Amide
Use Nicotinamide

Nicotinic Receptors
Use Cholinergic Receptors

Nictitating Membrane 1973
PN 324 **SC** 34040
SN Fold of transparent or semitransparent mucous membrane present in many vertebrates that can be drawn over the eye like a third eyelid. This membrane cleans and moistens the cornea without occluding light.
B Membranes 1973

Night Terrors
Use Sleep Disorders

Nightmares 1973
PN 411 **SC** 34050
B Dreaming 1967
R Dream Content 1973

Nihilism 1973
PN 21 **SC** 34060
B Philosophies 1967
R Fatalism 1973
Pessimism 1973

Nitrazepam 1978
PN 58 **SC** 34066
B Anticonvulsive Drugs 1973
Benzodiazepines 1978
Hypnotic Drugs 1973
Sedatives 1973

Nitric Oxide 2003
PN 400 **SC** 34068
SN Free radical gas produced by catalyzed nitric oxide synthase that acts like a neurotransmitter. Not to be confused with Nitrous Oxide which acts as an anesthetic.
HN This term was introduced in June 2003. Psyc-INFO records from the past 10 years were re-indexed with this term. The posting note reflects the number of records that were re-indexed.
R ↓ Neurotransmitters 1985
Nitrogen 1973
Oxygen 1973

Nitrogen 1973
PN 337 **SC** 34070
R Nitric Oxide 2003

NMDA
Use N-Methyl-D-Aspartate

Nociception
Use Pain Perception

Nociceptors 1985
PN 457 **SC** 34080
UF Pain Receptors
B Neural Receptors 1973
Sensory Neurons 1973

Nocturnal Behavior (Animal)
Use Animal Nocturnal Behavior

Nocturnal Emission 1973
PN 8 **SC** 34100
B Male Orgasm 1973

Nocturnal Teeth Grinding 1973
PN 47 **SC** 34110

Nocturnal Teeth Grinding — (cont'd)
HN   Use NOCTURNAL TEETH GRINDING to access references to BRUXISM from 1973-1984.
B   Bruxism   1985
R   ↓ Sleep   1967

Noise (Sound)
   Use   Auditory Stimulation

Noise Effects   1973
PN   1691   SC   34150
SN   Behavioral, physiological, or psychological effects of environmental or experimentally manipulated noise on an organism.
B   Environmental Effects   1973
R   Acoustics   1997
     Pollution   1973

Noise Levels (Work Areas)   1973
PN   272   SC   34160
B   Loudness   1967
     Working Conditions   1973

Nomenclature (Psychological)
   Use   Psychological Terminology

Nomifensine   1982
PN   138   SC   34175
SN   Organic heterocyclic compound used as an anti-parkinson agent and antidepressive agent.
B   Antidepressant Drugs   1971
     Antitremor Drugs   1973

Non Zero Sum Games   1973
PN   34   SC   34180
SN   Quantitative games in which all players may win points as opposed to zero sum games in which points won by one player must be lost by another or others.
B   Games   1967
R   Entrapment Games   1973
     Game Theory   1967
     Prisoners Dilemma Game   1973

Noncommissioned Officers   1973
PN   43   SC   34200
SN   Subordinate military officers (e.g., sergeants) appointed from enlisted personnel.
UF   Officers (Noncommissioned)
B   Enlisted Military Personnel   1973

Nonconformity (Personality)   1973
PN   98   SC   34210
B   Personality Traits   1967
R   Conformity (Personality)   1967
     Individuality   1973
     Rebelliousness   2003

Noncontingent Reinforcement   1988
PN   127   SC   34215
SN   Presentation of reinforcement (punishment or positive rewards) independently of behavior.
B   Reinforcement   1967
R   Autoshaping   1978
     ↓ Contingency Management   1973

Nondirected Discussion Method   1973
PN   22   SC   34220

**Nondirected Discussion Method —
(cont'd)**
SN   Teaching method which encourages students' spontaneity and restricts the leader's role to that of a moderator.
B   Teaching Methods   1967
R   Discovery Teaching Method   1973

Nondirective Therapy
   Use   Client Centered Therapy

Nongraded Schools   1973
PN   11   SC   34250
SN   Schools that group students according to such characteristics as academic achievement, mental and physical ability, or emotional development, rather than by age or grade level.
B   Schools   1967

Nonlinear Regression   1973
PN   78   SC   34260
B   Statistical Correlation   1967
     Statistical Regression   1985
R   Multiple Regression   1982

Nonmetallic Elements
   Use   Chemical Elements

Nonparametric Statistical Tests   1967
PN   370   SC   34280
B   Statistical Tests   1973
N   Chi Square Test   1973
     Cochran Q Test   1973
     Kolmogorov Smirnov Test   1973
     Mann Whitney U Test   1973
     Sign Test   1973
     Wilcoxon Sign Rank Test   1973

Nonprescription Drugs   1991
PN   153   SC   34285
SN   Drugs or medication sold legally without prescription.
UF   Over the Counter Drugs
B   Drugs   1967
R   Prescription Drugs   1991
     Self Medication   1991

Nonprofessional Personnel   1982
PN   132   SC   34290
SN   Conceptually broad term. Use a more specific term if possible.
HN   Use PARAPROFESSIONAL PERSONNEL to access references from 1973-1981.
B   Personnel   1967
N   ↓ Agricultural Workers   1973
R   ↓ Business and Industrial Personnel   1967
     Child Care Workers   1978
     Domestic Service Personnel   1973
     ↓ Paraprofessional Personnel   1973
     ↓ Professional Personnel   1978
     ↓ Service Personnel   1991
     Technical Service Personnel   1973

Nonprofit Organizations   1973
PN   315   SC   34300
B   Organizations   1967

Nonprojective Personality Measures   1973
PN   1266   SC   34304

**Nonprojective Personality Measures —
(cont'd)**
SN   Direct assessment of personality traits through scoring of a subject's responses to questions on structured, standardized tests. Use a more specific term if possible.
HN   In 1997, this term replaced the discontinued terms AUTHORITARIANISM REBELLION SCALE, DIFFERENTIAL PERSONALITY INVENTORY, KUPFER DETRE SELF RATING SCALE, and WHITE BETZ A B SCALE. In 2000, these terms were removed from all records containing them, and replaced with NONPROJECTIVE PERSONALITY MEASURES.
UF   Authoritarianism Rebellion Scale
     Differential Personality Inventory
     Kupfer Detre Self Rating Scale
     White Betz A B Scale
B   Personality Measures   1967
N   Bannister Repertory Grid   1973
     Beck Depression Inventory   1988
     Bern Sex Role Inventory   1988
     California F Scale   1973
     Child Behavior Checklist   1994
     Childrens Manifest Anxiety Scale   1973
     Childrens Personality Questionnaire   1973
     Edwards Personal Preference Schedule   1967
     Edwards Personality Inventory   1973
     Edwards Social Desirability Scale   1973
     Embedded Figures Testing   1967
     Eysenck Personality Inventory   1973
     Fear Survey Schedule   1973
     Fundamental Interpersonal Relation
       Orientation Behavior Ques   2001
     Gough Adjective Check List   1973
     Guilford Zimmerman Temperament
       Survey   2001
     High School Personality Questionnaire   2001
     Marlowe Crowne Social Desirability
       Scale   2001
     Memory for Designs Test   1973
     Millon Clinical Multiaxial Inventory   1988
     Minnesota Multiphasic Personality
       Inventory   2001
     Mooney Problem Check List   1973
     Myers Briggs Type Indicator   1973
     Personal Orientation Inventory   1973
     Psychological Screening Inventory   1973
     Repression Sensitization Scale   1973
     Rod and Frame Test   1973
     Rokeach Dogmatism Scale   1973
     Rotter Internal External Locus of Control
       Scale   2001
     Sixteen Personality Factors
       Questionnaire   2001
     State Trait Anxiety Inventory   1973
     Taylor Manifest Anxiety Scale   1973
     Tennessee Self Concept Scale   1973
     Vineland Social Maturity Scale   1973
     Zungs Self Rating Depression Scale   1973

Nonrapid Eye Movement Sleep
   Use   NREM Sleep

NonREM Sleep
   Use   NREM Sleep

Nonreversal Shift Learning   1973
PN   48   SC   34330

Nonreversal Shift Learning — (cont'd)
SN Experimental technique used for the demonstration of mediating processes in concept formation that assesses the ability to shift dimensions in stimulus discrimination tasks, as, for example, from size to color.
UF Extradimensional Shift Learning
B Discrimination Learning 1982

Nonsense Syllable Learning 1967
PN 172   SC 34340
SN Verbal learning paradigm in which collections or lists of letters, which have no obvious meaning (e.g., XAB, GZL), are used as stimulus items. Also, the actual acquisition, retention, and retrieval of such stimulus items.
B Verbal Learning 1967

Nonstandard English 1973
PN 286   SC 34350
B Dialect 1973
R Slang 1973

Nontraditional Careers 1985
PN 346   SC 34352
SN Occupations in which certain groups (usually males or females) have traditionally been underrepresented.
B Occupations 1967
R Occupational Choice 1967
    Sex Roles 1967

Nontraditional Education 1982
PN 643   SC 34355
SN Alternative educational programs within or without the formal educational system that provide flexible and innovative teaching, curriculum, grading, or degree requirements.
UF Alternative Schools
    Magnet Schools
    Open Universities
B Education 1967
N Home Schooling 1994
R ↓ Curriculum 1967
    Distance Education 2003
    ↓ Educational Programs 1973
    ↓ Teaching Methods 1967

Nonverbal Ability 1088
PN 382   SC 34357
SN Ability in nonlanguage areas such as spatial relations, mathematics, or music.
B Ability 1967
N ↓ Artistic Ability 1973
    Mathematical Ability 1973
    Mechanical Aptitude 1973
    Motor Skills 1973
    ↓ Spatial Ability 1982
R Academic Aptitude 1973
    ↓ Nonverbal Communication 1971

Nonverbal Communication 1971
PN 3837   SC 34360
B Communication 1967
N Body Language 1973
    Eye Contact 1973
    ↓ Facial Expressions 1967
    Gestures 1973
    ↓ Manual Communication 1978
R Laughter 1978
    ↓ Nonverbal Ability 1988
    Silence 2003

Nonverbal Learning 1973
PN 253   SC 34370
SN Acquisition, retention, and retrieval of knowledge or skills that do not involve verbally presented information or language, such as perceptual responses or motor activities.
B Learning 1967

Nonverbal Meaning 1973
PN 73   SC 34380
B Meaning 1967

Nonverbal Reinforcement 1973
PN 32   SC 34390
B Social Reinforcement 1967

Nonviolence 1991
PN 68   SC 34393
B Social Interaction 1967
R Pacifism 1973
    ↓ Political Attitudes 1973
    ↓ Violence 1973

Nootropic Drugs 1991
PN 366   SC 34395
UF Cognition Enhancing Drugs
    Memory Enhancing Drugs
B Drugs 1967
N Piracetam 1982

Noradrenaline
Use Norepinephrine

Norepinephrine 1973
PN 3463   SC 34410
UF Noradrenaline
B Adrenal Medulla Hormones 1973
    Catecholamines 1973
    Vasoconstrictor Drugs 1973
R Guanethidine 1973
    ↓ Norepinephrine Metabolites 1982

Norepinephrine Metabolites 1982
PN 300   SC 34413
SN Molecules generated from the metabolism of norepinephrine.
B Metabolites 1973
N Methoxyhydroxyphenylglycol (3,4) 1991
R ↓ Metabolism 1967
    Norepinephrine 1973

Normal Distribution 1973
PN 163   SC 34420
UF Gaussian Distribution
B Frequency Distribution 1973
R ↓ Statistical Sample Parameters 1973

Normalization (Test)
Use Test Standardization

Norms (Social)
Use Social Norms

Norms (Statistical)
Use Statistical Norms

Norms (Test)
Use Test Norms

Nortriptyline 1994
PN 198   SC 34485
HN Use ANTIDEPRESSANT DRUGS to access references from 1978-1993.
B Tricyclic Antidepressant Drugs 1997

Norway Rats 1973
PN 138   SC 34500
B Rats 1967

Nose 1973
PN 105   SC 34510
B Respiratory System 1973
N ↓ Nasal Mucosa 1973
R ↓ Musculoskeletal System 1973

Note Taking 1991
PN 126   SC 34515
R Homework 1988
    ↓ Learning Strategies 1991
    ↓ Memory 1967
    Mnemonic Learning 1973
    ↓ Strategies 1967
    Study Habits 1973
    ↓ Written Communication 1985

Nouns 1973
PN 1037   SC 34520
B Form Classes (Language) 1973
R ↓ Names 1985

Novel Stimuli
Use Stimulus Novelty

Novelty Seeking
Use Sensation Seeking

Novocaine
Use Procaine

NREM Sleep 1973
PN 782   SC 34550
UF Nonrapid Eye Movement Sleep
    NonREM Sleep
    Slow Wave Sleep
B Sleep 1967

Nuclear Family 1973
PN 238   SC 34560
B Family 1967
    Family Structure 1973

Nuclear Technology 1985
PN 474   SC 34565
B Technology 1973

Nuclear War 1985
PN 548   SC 34567
B War 1967

Nucleic Acids 1973
PN 67   SC 34570
B Acids 1973
N Adenosine 1973
    Deoxyribonucleic Acid 1973
    ↓ Nucleotides 1978
    Ribonucleic Acid 1973
R ↓ Genetics 1967
    Guanosine 1985

Nucleotides 1978
PN 247   **SC** 34573
  B Nucleic Acids 1973
  N Cyclic Adenosine Monophosphate 1978

Nucleus Accumbens 1982
PN 1635   **SC** 34574
SN One of the largest nuclei in the septal region lying anteriorly and medially to the junction of the caudate nucleus and putamen and laterally to the septal nuclei.
  R Caudate Nucleus 1973
    ↓ Limbic System 1973
    Septal Nuclei 1982

Nucleus Basalis Magnocellularis 1994
PN 142   **SC** 57425
  B Forebrain 1985
  R ↓ Basal Ganglia 1973

Nudity 1973
PN 61   **SC** 34575
  R Obscenity 1978
    ↓ Physical Appearance 1982
    Pornography 1973

Null Hypothesis Testing 1970
PN 246   **SC** 34580
SN Application of statistical tests to determine whether a null hypothesis should be accepted or rejected. Limited to discussions of statistical procedures.
  B Hypothesis Testing 1973

Number Comprehension 1973
PN 549   **SC** 34590
SN Knowledge or understanding of the meaning significance, and relationships symbolized by numerals.
  B Comprehension 1967

Number Systems 1070
PN 70   **SC** 34600
  B Mathematics (Concepts) 1967
    Systems 1967
  R Numbers (Numerals) 1967

Numbers (Numerals) 1967
PN 1234   **SC** 34610
SN Symbol of a member of an abstract mathematical system which is subject to rules of succession, addition, and multiplication.
  UF Digits (Mathematics)
  B Mathematics (Concepts) 1967
    Written Language 1967
  R Number Systems 1973
    Numerosity Perception 1967

Numerical Ability
  Use Mathematical Ability

Numerosity Perception 1967
PN 535   **SC** 34630
SN Perception of quantities in stimulus sets in visual, auditory, or other perceptual modes.
  B Perception 1967
  R Numbers (Numerals) 1967

Nuns 1973
PN 154   **SC** 34640
  B Religious Personnel 1973

Nuns — (cont'd)
  R Missionaries 1973

Nurse Patient Interaction
  Use Therapeutic Processes

Nursery School Students 1973
PN 416   **SC** 34650
SN Students attending a nursery school, usually ages 2, 3, and 4.
  B Preschool Students 1982

Nursery Schools 1973
PN 167   **SC** 34660
  B Schools 1967

Nurses 1967
PN 6332   **SC** 34670
  B Medical Personnel 1967
  N Psychiatric Nurses 1973
    Public Health Service Nurses 1973
    School Nurses 1973

Nursing 1973
PN 3151   **SC** 34680
  B Paramedical Sciences 1973

Nursing Education 1973
PN 1298   **SC** 34690
  B Education 1967
  R ↓ Medical Education 1973

Nursing Homes 1973
PN 3493   **SC** 34700
SN Establishments where maintenance and personal or nursing care are provided for persons (as the aged or chronically ill) who are unable to care for themselves.
  B Residential Care Institutions 1973
    Treatment Facilities 1973
  R ↓ Hospitals 1967
    Long Term Care 1994
    Psychiatric Units 1991
    Retirement Communities 1997
    Sanatoriums 1973

Nursing Students 1973
PN 1616   **SC** 34710
  B College Students 1967

Nurturance 1085
PN 324   **SC** 34714
SN Need, tendency, or process of providing care and support to others. For animal populations, use ANIMAL MATERNAL BEHAVIOR or ANIMAL PARENTAL BEHAVIOR.
  B Personality Traits 1967
    Social Behavior 1967
  R ↓ Needs 1967
    ↓ Parent Child Relations 1967

Nutrition 1973
PN 2232   **SC** 34720
  R Beverages (Nonalcoholic) 1978
    Dietary Supplements 2001
    Diets 1978
    Food 1978
    Food Additives 1978
    ↓ Nutritional Deficiencies 1973
    ↓ Physiology 1967

Nutritional Deficiencies 1973
PN 1156   **SC** 34730
  UF Malnutrition
  B Physical Disorders 1997
  N ↓ Protein Deficiency Disorders 1973
    Starvation 1973
    ↓ Vitamin Deficiency Disorders 1973
  R ↓ Alcoholic Psychosis 1973
    ↓ Alcoholism 1967
    Anorexia Nervosa 1973
    Diets 1978
    ↓ Eating Disorders 1997
    Failure to Thrive 1988
    Food Deprivation 1967
    ↓ Metabolism Disorders 1973
    Nutrition 1973
    ↓ Underweight 1973

Nutritional Supplements
  Use Dietary Supplements

Nymphomania
  Use Hypersexuality

Nystagmus 1973
PN 659   **SC** 34760
SN Eye movement reflex stabilizing the retinal image of a visual stimulus to compensate for head or stimulus movement. Also, eye movement defects resulting from neurological, muscular, or genetic disorders.
  UF Optokinetic Nystagmus
    Vestibular Nystagmus
  B Eye Disorders 1973
    Eye Movements 1967
    Reflexes 1971
  R ↓ Nervous System Disorders 1967

Obedience 1973
PN 360   **SC** 34770
SN Limited to human populations.
  UF Submissiveness
  B Personality Traits 1967
  R Coercion 1994
    ↓ Compliance 1973
    ↓ Dominance 1967
    ↓ Resistance 1997

Obesity 1973
PN 4416   **SC** 34780
  UF Overweight
  B Body Weight 1967
    Eating Disorders 1997
    Symptoms 1967
  R Diets 1978
    Hyperphagia 1973
    Obesity (Attitudes Toward) 1997
    ↓ Somatoform Disorders 2001

Obesity (Attitudes Toward) 1997
PN 78   **SC** 34783
  B Attitudes 1967
  R ↓ Body Weight 1967
    Eating Attitudes 1994
    Health Attitudes 1985
    Obesity 1973
    Weight Control 1985

Object Permanence 1985
PN 255   **SC** 34788
SN Knowledge of the continued existence of an object even when it is not directly perceived.

Object Permanence — (cont'd)
R ↓ Cognitive Development 1973
    Conservation (Concept) 1973
   ↓ Developmental Stages 1973
   ↓ Internalization 1997
   ↓ Perceptual Constancy 1985

Object Recognition 1997
PN 1502   SC 34789
B Perception 1967
    Recognition (Learning) 1967
R Form and Shape Perception 1967
    Naming 1988
   ↓ Perceptual Discrimination 1973

Object Relations 1982
PN 4081   SC 34786
SN Psychoanalytic description of emotional attachments formed with other persons, as opposed to interest and love for oneself; individual's mode of relation to others and self.
UF Fairbairnian Theory
    Winnicottian Theory
R Anaclitic Depression 1973
    Attachment Behavior 1985
   ↓ Childhood Development 1967
    Emotional Development 1973
   ↓ Internalization 1997
    Metapsychology 1994
   ↓ Psychoanalytic Theory 1967
   ↓ Psychosocial Development 1973
    Self Psychology 1988
    Separation Individuation 1982
    Transitional Objects 1985

Objective Referenced Tests
Use Criterion Referenced Tests

Objectives
Use Goals

Objectives (Organizational)
Use Organizational Objectives

Objectivity 1973
PN 604   SC 34810
B Personality Traits 1967
R Subjectivity 1994

Oblique Rotation 1973
PN 69   SC 34820
B Statistical Rotation 1973

Obscenity 1978
PN 89   SC 34826
R Nudity 1973
    Pornography 1973
    Profanity 1991

Observation Methods 1967
PN 2825   SC 34830
SN In research, any techniques used in the intentional examination of persons or processes in natural or manipulated settings for the purpose of obtaining facts or reporting conclusions.
UF Field Experiment
    Naturalistic Observation
B Empirical Methods 1973
R Interrater Reliability 1982
    Qualitative Research 2003
    Self Monitoring 1982

Observational Learning 1973
PN 854   SC 34840
SN Learning by observation of others by human or animal subjects or learning by visualization of behavior without actually performing an act and experiencing its consequences. Compare SOCIAL LEARNING.
B Learning 1967
    Learning Strategies 1991
R Imitation (Learning) 1967
   ↓ Social Learning 1973

Observers 1973
PN 693   SC 34850
SN Individuals who examine, record, or rate specified events, behaviors, or processes in experimental, social, or therapeutic situations.
R ↓ Audiences 1967

Obsessions 1967
PN 867   SC 34860
B Thought Disturbances 1973
R ↓ Compulsions 1973
    Erotomania 1997
    Obsessive Compulsive Disorder 1985
    Obsessive Compulsive Personality
      Disorder 1973

Obsessive Compulsive Disorder 1985
PN 4602   SC 34865
SN Disorder characterized by recurrent obsessions or compulsions that may interfere with the individual's daily functioning or serve as a source of distress.
HN In 2000, this term replaced the discontinued term OBSESSIVE COMPULSIVE NEUROSIS. OBSESSIVE COMPULSIVE NEUROSIS was removed from all records containing it and replaced with OBSESSIVE COMPULSIVE DISORDER.
UF Compulsive Neurosis
    Obsessive Compulsive Neurosis
    Obsessive Neurosis
B Anxiety Disorders 1997
R Body Dysmorphic Disorder 2001
   ↓ Compulsions 1973
   ↓ Hoarding Behavior 2003
   ↓ Neurosis 1967
    Obsessions 1967
    Obsessive Compulsive Personality
      Disorder 1973

Obsessive Compulsive Neurosis
Use Obsessive Compulsive Disorder

**Obsessive Compulsive Personality
Disorder** 1973
PN 331   SC 34880
SN Personality disorder characterized by perfectionism, indecisiveness, excessive devotion to work, inability to express warm emotions, and insistence that things be done in accord with one's own preferences.
UF Anankastic Personality
    Compulsive Personality Disorder
B Personality Disorders 1967
R ↓ Compulsions 1973
    Obsessions 1967
    Obsessive Compulsive Disorder 1985

Obsessive Neurosis
Use Obsessive Compulsive Disorder

Obstetrical Complications 1978
PN 711   SC 34895

Obstetrical Complications — (cont'd)
R ↓ Birth 1967
    Birth Injuries 1973
    Labor (Childbirth) 1973
   ↓ Obstetrics 1978
    Postsurgical Complications 1973
   ↓ Pregnancy 1967
    Premature Birth 1973

Obstetricians 1978
PN 80   SC 34900
B Physicians 1967
R Gynecologists 1973
    Surgeons 1973

Obstetrics 1978
PN 249   SC 34910
HN Use OBSTETRICS GYNECOLOGY to access references from 1973-1977.
B Medical Sciences 1967
N Midwifery 1985
R Childbirth Training 1978
    Gynecology 1978
    Obstetrical Complications 1978
   ↓ Prenatal Care 1991

Obturator Nerve
Use Spinal Nerves

Occipital Lobe 1973
PN 666   SC 34930
B Cerebral Cortex 1967
N Visual Cortex 1967

Occultism 1978
PN 156   SC 34935
R Cultism 1973
    Mysticism 1967
   ↓ Parapsychological Phenomena 1973
   ↓ Parapsychology 1967
   ↓ Religious Beliefs 1973
    Spirit Possession 1997
    Witchcraft 1973

Occupation (Parental)
Use Parental Occupation

Occupational Adjustment 1973
PN 1274   SC 34950
SN Personal adaptation to one's vocation.
UF Vocational Adjustment
B Adjustment 1967
R Adjustment Disorders 1994
    Career Change 1978
    Occupational Neurosis 1973
   ↓ Occupations 1967
    School to Work Transition 1994
    Work Adjustment Training 1991

Occupational Aspirations 1973
PN 2290   SC 34960
UF Career Aspirations
    Career Goals
    Vocational Aspirations
B Aspirations 1967
R Career Change 1978
    Mentor 1985
   ↓ Occupations 1967
    Professional Development 1982

Occupational Attitudes 1973
PN 2035   **SC** 34970
SN Attitudes toward specific occupations or careers.
  B   Attitudes 1967
  R   Job Applicant Attitudes 1973
    ↓ Occupations 1967
      Vocational Maturity 1978
      Work (Attitudes Toward) 1973

Occupational Choice 1967
PN 4268   **SC** 34980
  UF Career Choice
      Job Selection
      Vocational Choice
  R   Career Change 1978
      Career Development 1985
      Nontraditional Careers 1985
      Occupational Preference 1973
    ↓ Occupations 1967
      Professional Specialization 1991
      Reemployment 1991
      Vocational Maturity 1978

Occupational Exposure 1988
PN 485   **SC** 34985
SN Exposure to conditions, substances, or apparatus in the workplace that may be harmful to health.
  R ↓ Environmental Effects 1973
    ↓ Hazardous Materials 1991
      Industrial Accidents 1973
      Occupational Safety 1973
    ↓ Occupations 1967
      Work Related Illnesses 1994
    ↓ Working Conditions 1973

Occupational Guidance 1967
PN 4882   **SC** 34990
SN Assistance in career selection or development; assessment of interests, abilities, or aptitude; compilation of occupational and economic information; and referral to placement services.
  UF Career Counseling
      Career Guidance
      Guidance (Occupational)
      Vocational Counseling
      Vocational Guidance
  B   Counseling 1967
  R   Assessment Centers 1982
      Career Education 1978
      Educational Counseling 1967
      Job Enrichment 1973
      Mentor 1985
      Occupational Success Prediction 1973
    ↓ Occupations 1967
      Student Personnel Services 1978
      Vocational Counselors 1973

Occupational Interest Measures 1973
PN 754   **SC** 35000
  B   Measurement 1967
  N   Kuder Occupational Interest Survey 1973
      Strong Vocational Interest Blank 1967

Occupational Interests 1967
PN 1858   **SC** 35010
  UF Vocational Interests
  B   Interests 1967
  R ↓ Occupations 1967
      Vocational Maturity 1978

Occupational Mobility 1973
PN 610   **SC** 35020

Occupational Mobility — (cont'd)
SN The capacity or actual tendency toward upward progression in occupational status or occupational attainment.
  UF Job Mobility
      Mobility (Occupational)
      Vocational Mobility
  R   Career Change 1978
      Employment History 1978
      Job Enrichment 1973
    ↓ Occupational Tenure 1973
    ↓ Occupations 1967

Occupational Neurosis 1973
PN 26   **SC** 35030
SN Neurotic disorder developed as a consequence of occupational stress, inappropriate occupational choice, overwork, job dissatisfaction, or other job-related stress.
  B   Neurosis 1967
  R   Occupational Adjustment 1973
      Occupational Stress 1973

Occupational Preference 1973
PN 997   **SC** 35040
  UF Career Preference
      Vocational Preference
  B   Preferences 1967
  R   Occupational Choice 1967
    ↓ Occupations 1967
      Professional Specialization 1991
      Vocational Maturity 1978

Occupational Safety 1973
PN 919   **SC** 35050
  UF Industrial Safety
  B   Safety 1967
      Working Conditions 1973
  R   Industrial Accidents 1973
      Occupational Exposure 1988
    ↓ Occupations 1967
      Work Related Illnesses 1994

Occupational Status 1978
PN 1969   **SC** 35056
SN Occupational rank or position achieved by employee, usually based on abilities or competence. Also, social prestige attributed to specific occupations.
  UF Job Status
      Prestige (Occupational)
  B   Status 1967
  R   Job Experience Level 1973
    ↓ Occupational Tenure 1973
    ↓ Occupations 1967
      Personnel Promotion 1978

Occupational Stress 1973
PN 8152   **SC** 35060
  UF Burnout
      Job Stress
      Work Stress
  B   Stress 1967
  R   Occupational Neurosis 1973
    ↓ Occupations 1967
      Quality of Work Life 1988
      Work Related Illnesses 1994
      Workaholism 2004

Occupational Success 1978
PN 1421   **SC** 35067
  B   Achievement 1967
  R   Employment History 1978

Occupational Success — (cont'd)
      Occupational Success Prediction 1973
    ↓ Occupations 1967
      Personnel Promotion 1978

Occupational Success Prediction 1973
PN 764   **SC** 35070
  B   Personnel Evaluation 1973
      Prediction 1967
  R   Occupational Guidance 1967
      Occupational Success 1978

Occupational Tenure 1973
PN 552   **SC** 35080
  UF Tenure (Occupational)
  N   Teacher Tenure 1973
  R   Employee Turnover 1973
      Employment History 1978
    ↓ Employment Status 1982
      Job Security 1978
      Occupational Mobility 1973
      Occupational Status 1978
    ↓ Occupations 1967
      Personnel Termination 1973

Occupational Therapists 1973
PN 717   **SC** 35090
  B   Therapists 1967
  R ↓ Mental Health Personnel 1967
    ↓ Paraprofessional Personnel 1973
    ↓ Psychiatric Hospital Staff 1973

Occupational Therapy 1967
PN 2230   **SC** 35100
SN Method of treatment for physical or mental disorders that involves engagement of patients in useful or creative activities or work as a means of improving functional skills in the areas of work, daily living, or vocational activities.
  B   Rehabilitation 1967
  R   Physical Therapy 1973

Occupations 1967
PN 4128   **SC** 35110
SN Conceptually broad term referring to work specialties as defined by duties and required skills. Use a more specific term if possible.
HN Use OCCUPATIONS to access references on employment status from 1967-1981.
  UF Careers
      Jobs
      Vocations
  N   Nontraditional Careers 1985
  R   Career Change 1978
      Career Development 1985
    ↓ Division of Labor 1988
      Employment History 1978
    ↓ Job Characteristics 1985
      Occupational Adjustment 1973
      Occupational Aspirations 1973
      Occupational Attitudes 1973
      Occupational Choice 1967
      Occupational Exposure 1988
      Occupational Guidance 1967
      Occupational Interests 1967
      Occupational Mobility 1973
      Occupational Preference 1973
      Occupational Safety 1973
      Occupational Status 1978
      Occupational Stress 1973
      Occupational Success 1978
    ↓ Occupational Tenure 1973
    ↓ Personnel 1967

Occupations — (cont'd)
  ↓ Professional Personnel   1978
  ↓ Vocational Education   1973
     Vocational Maturity   1978
     Working Women   1978

Octopus   1973
PN   56   SC   35120
  B   Mollusca   1973

Ocular Accommodation   1982
PN   323   SC   35127
SN   Process of focusing an image on the retina by means of a flattening or bulging of the lens.
  UF   Eye Accommodation
       Focusing (Visual)
  B   Reflexes   1971
  R   ↓ Depth Perception   1967
       Lens (Eye)   1973
     ↓ Refraction Errors   1973

Ocular Dominance   1973
PN   343   SC   35130
  UF   Eye Dominance
  B   Lateral Dominance   1967
  R   ↓ Brain   1967
     ↓ Eye (Anatomy)   1967
     ↓ Eye Disorders   1973
       Interocular Transfer   1985
       Left Brain   1991
       Right Brain   1991

Ocular Fixation
  Use   Eye Fixation

Oculomotor Muscles   1973
PN   146   SC   35140
  B   Muscles   1967

Oculomotor Nerve
  Use   Cranial Nerves

Oculomotor Response
  Use   Eye Movements

Odor Aversion Conditioning
  Use   Aversion Conditioning

Odor Discrimination   1973
PN   1252   SC   35170
  B   Olfactory Perception   1967
       Perceptual Discrimination   1973
  R   Olfactory Thresholds   1973

Oedipal Complex   1973
PN   1234   SC   35180
  B   Psychoanalytic Personality Factors   1973

Offenders (Adult)
  Use   Criminals

Offenders (Juvenile)
  Use   Juvenile Delinquency

Office Environment
  Use   Working Conditions

Officers (Commissioned)
  Use   Commissioned Officers

Officers (Noncommissioned)
  Use   Noncommissioned Officers

Offspring   1988
PN   2146   SC   35230
SN   Used specifically for children, regardless of age, whose parents had significant experiences or conditions, e.g., alcoholism, fame, or political persecution. Limited to human populations.
  N   Adult Offspring   1985
       Children of Alcoholics   2003
       Daughters   1973
       Interracial Offspring   1988
       Sons   1973
  R   ↓ Family Members   1973

Offspring of Alcoholics
  Use   Children of Alcoholics

Olanzapine   2003
PN   840   SC   35236
HN   This term was introduced in June 2003. Psyc-INFO records from the past 10 years were re-indexed with this term. The posting note reflects the number of records that were re-indexed.
  B   Neuroleptic Drugs   1973

Olfactory Bulb   1973
PN   773   SC   35247
  B   Limbic System   1973

Olfactory Evoked Potentials   1973
PN   123   SC   35250
  B   Evoked Potentials   1967
  R   ↓ Cortical Evoked Potentials   1973

Olfactory Impairment
  Use   Anosmia

Olfactory Mucosa   1973
PN   69   SC   35260
  B   Nasal Mucosa   1973
  R   Chemoreceptors   1973

Olfactory Nerve   1973
PN   131   SC   35270
  B   Cranial Nerves   1973

Olfactory Perception   1967
PN   2652   SC   35280
  UF   Smell Perception
  B   Perception   1967
  N   Odor Discrimination   1973
       Olfactory Thresholds   1973
  R   Anosmia   1973
       Taste Perception   1967
       Vomeronasal Sense   1982

Olfactory Stimulation   1978
PN   1235   SC   35285
  B   Perceptual Stimulation   1973

Olfactory Thresholds   1973
PN   230   SC   35290
  B   Olfactory Perception   1967

Olfactory Thresholds — (cont'd)
       Thresholds   1967
  R   Odor Discrimination   1973
     ↓ Perceptual Measures   1973

Oligophrenia
  Use   Mental Retardation

Oligophrenia (Phenylpyruvic)
  Use   Phenylketonuria

Omission Training   1985
PN   17   SC   35315
SN   Removal of positive reinforcement upon occurrence of undesirable behavior. Has applications in both therapeutic and experimental contexts.
  B   Behavior Modification   1973
       Operant Conditioning   1967
  R   Differential Reinforcement   1973
       Time Out   1985

Omnipotence   1994
PN   35   SC   35325
  B   Personality Traits   1967
  R   Authority   1967
       Grandiosity   1994
       Magical Thinking   1973
     ↓ Power   1967

On the Job Training   1973
PN   225   SC   35330
  B   Personnel Training   1967
  R   ↓ Experiential Learning   1997
       Inservice Teacher Education   1973
     ↓ Inservice Training   1985

Online Databases
  Use   Databases

Online Searching
  Use   Computer Searching

Online Therapy   2003
PN   64   SC   35334
SN   Therapy in which clinician and client are geographically separated and communicate via computer or other telecommunications media.
HN   This term was introduced in June 2003. Psyc-INFO records from the past 10 years were re-indexed with this term. The posting note reflects the number of records that were re-indexed.
  UF   Cybercounseling
       E-Therapy
       Internet Counseling
       Teletherapy
       Web Based Mental Health Services
  B   Treatment   1967
  R   ↓ Computer Applications   1973
       Computer Mediated Communication   2003
       Health Care Seeking Behavior   1997
       Internet   2001
     ↓ Psychotherapy   1967
     ↓ Telecommunications Media   1973

Only Children   1982
PN   118   SC   35335
SN   Children having no siblings.
  R   ↓ Family Members   1973
     ↓ Family Structure   1973

Onomatopoeia and Images Test
Use Projective Personality Measures

Onset (Disorders) 1973
PN 4038   **SC** 35350
SN Beginning or first appearance of a mental or physical disorder.
R ↓ Disorders 1967
    ↓ Mental Disorders 1967
    ↓ Physical Disorders 1997
    Premorbidity 1978
    Prodrome 2004

Ontogeny
Use Development

Open Classroom Method 1973
PN 376   **SC** 35370
SN Approach to teaching and learning emphasizing the student's right to make decisions and viewing the teacher as a facilitator of learning rather than a transmitter of knowledge. May include grouping of students across grades, independent study, individualized rates of progression, open-plan schools without interior walls, or unstructured time and curricula.
B Teaching Methods 1967
R Discovery Teaching Method 1973
    Individualized Instruction 1973
    Montessori Method 1973
    Team Teaching Method 1973

Open Field Behavior (Animal)
Use Animal Open Field Behavior

Open Universities
Use Nontraditional Education

Openmindedness 1978
PN 188   **SC** 35376
SN Willingness to consider new and unconventional ideas, and readiness to reexamine social, political, and religious values.
UF Closedmindedness
B Personality Traits 1967
R Agreeableness 1997
    Authoritarianism 1967
    Dogmatism 1978

Openness to Experience 1997
PN 163   **SC** 35378
SN A broad experiential trait manifested in active imagination, aesthetic sensitivity, attentiveness to inner feelings, preference for variety, intellectual curiosity, and independence of judgment.
UF Imaginativeness
B Personality Traits 1967
R Adaptability (Personality) 1973
    Conformity (Personality) 1967
    Creativity 1967
    Curiosity 1967
    Five Factor Personality Model 1997
    Hypnotic Susceptibility 1973
    Rigidity (Personality) 1967
    ↓ Tolerance 1973

Operant Conditioning 1967
PN 7147   **SC** 35380

Operant Conditioning — (cont'd)
SN Learned behavior or the experimental paradigm in which reinforcers (positive or negative) or punishers immediately and contingently follow the performance of some behavior, the frequency of which changes as a direct consequence of such contingent reinforcement.
UF Conditioning (Operant)
    Instrumental Conditioning
    Instrumental Learning
B Conditioning 1967
N Avoidance Conditioning 1967
    ↓ Conditioned Emotional Responses 1967
    ↓ Conditioned Responses 1967
    Delayed Alternation 1994
    ↓ Discrimination Learning 1982
    Escape Conditioning 1973
    Fading (Conditioning) 1982
    Omission Training 1985
    Time Out 1985
R ↓ Adjunctive Behavior 1982
    ↓ Behavior Modification 1973
    Conditioned Stimulus 1973
    Learning Theory 1967
    Polydipsia 1982
    ↓ Reinforcement 1967
    ↓ Self Stimulation 1967
    Skinner (Burrhus Frederic) 1991
    Unconditioned Stimulus 1973

Operation (Surgery)
Use Surgery

Ophidiophobia 1973
PN 262   **SC** 35400
SN Fear of snakes.
UF Snake Phobia
B Phobias 1967

Ophthalmologic Examination 1973
PN 84   **SC** 35410
UF Eye Examination
B Medical Diagnosis 1973
N Electro Oculography 1973
    Electroretinography 1967

Ophthalmology 1973
PN 49   **SC** 35420
B Medical Sciences 1967
R Optometry 1973

Opiate Agonists
Use Narcotic Agonists

Opiate Antagonists
Use Narcotic Antagonists

Opiates 1973
PN 3475   **SC** 35430
UF Opioids
    Opium Alkaloids
    Opium Derivatives
B Narcotic Drugs 1973
N Codeine 1973
    ↓ Endogenous Opiates 1985
    Fentanyl 1985
    Heroin 1973
    Morphine 1973
    Papaverine 1973

Opinion (Public)
Use Public Opinion

Opinion Attitude and Interest Survey
Use Attitude Measures

Opinion Change
Use Attitude Change

Opinion Questionnaires
Use Attitude Measures

Opinion Surveys
Use Attitude Measures

Opinions
Use Attitudes

Opioid Antagonists
Use Narcotic Antagonists

Opioids
Use Opiates

Opioids (Endogenous)
Use Endogenous Opiates

Opium Alkaloids
Use Alkaloids AND Opiates

Opium Derivatives
Use Opiates

Opossums 1973
PN 94   **SC** 35530
B Marsupials 1973

Oppositional Defiant Disorder 1997
PN 391   **SC** 35535
SN A psychopathological disorder, usually beginning in childhood, consisting of negativism, disobedience, and hostile behavior toward authority figures.
R ↓ Attention Deficit Disorder 1985
    Attention Deficit Disorder with
       Hyperactivity 2001
    ↓ Behavior Disorders 1971
    Conduct Disorder 1991
    Hyperkinesis 1973

Optic Chiasm 1973
PN 79   **SC** 35540
B Diencephalon 1973
    Neural Pathways 1982
R Optic Nerve 1973

Optic Lobe 1973
PN 133   **SC** 35550
B Mesencephalon 1973

Optic Nerve 1973
PN 238   **SC** 35560
B Cranial Nerves 1973
R Optic Chiasm 1973

Optic Tract 1982
PN 82   SC 35563
SN Portion of the optic pathway that extends poste-
riorly from the optic chiasm in two nerve fiber bundles
to synapse near the superior colliculi and in the lateral geniculate body of the thalamus.
  B   Neural Pathways   1982

Optical Aids 1973
PN 192   SC 35565
  UF   Corrective Lenses
  B   Medical Therapeutic Devices   1973
  N   Contact Lenses   1973

Optical Illusions
  Use Illusions (Perception)

Optimism 1973
PN 1183   SC 35580
SN Attitude characterized by a positive and cheerful
disposition and inclination to anticipate the most
favorable outcome of events or actions.
  B   Emotional States   1973
       Personality Traits   1967
  R   Hope   1991
       Pessimism   1973
       Positive Psychology   2003
       Positivism   1973

Optokinetic Nystagmus
  Use Nystagmus

Optometrists 1973
PN 44   SC 35590
  B   Medical Personnel   1967

Optometry 1973
PN 167   SC 35600
  B   Paramedical Sciences   1973
  R   Ophthalmology   1973

Oral Communication 1985
PN 5376   SC 35610
SN Expression of information in oral form.
HN Use VERBAL COMMUNICATION to access ref-
erences from 1967-1984.
  UF   Speech
       Verbalization
  B   Verbal Communication   1967
  N   Code Switching   1988
       Oral Reading   1973
       Public Speaking   1973
       Self Talk   1988
       Singing   1997
       ↓ Speech Characteristics   1973
  R   Rhetoric   1991
       Verbal Ability   1967
       Verbal Fluency   1973
       ↓ Vocalization   1967
       ↓ Voice   1973

Oral Contraceptives 1973
PN 343   SC 35620
  B   Contraceptive Devices   1973
  R   Fertility Enhancement   1973

Oral Reading 1973
PN 1215   SC 35630
SN Reading aloud by individuals or groups or the
condition of being read to by others.
  UF   Reading Aloud
  B   Oral Communication   1985

Oral Reading — (cont'd)
       Reading   1967

Organ Donation
  Use Tissue Donation

Organ of Corti
  Use Cochlea

Organ Transplantation 1973
PN 1028   SC 35660
  UF   Heart Transplants
       Kidney Transplants
       Renal Transplantation
       Transplants (Organ)
  B   Surgery   1971
  R   Heart Surgery   1973
       Neural Transplantation   1985
       Tissue Donation   1991

Organic Brain Syndromes 1973
PN 792   SC 35670
  B   Brain Disorders   1967
       Syndromes   1973
  N   ↓ Alcoholic Psychosis   1973
       Alzheimers Disease   1973
       ↓ Dementia   1985
       Toxic Psychoses   1973
  R   ↓ Mental Disorders   1967
       Postpartum Depression   1973
       Postpartum Psychosis   2003

Organic Therapies
  Use Physical Treatment Methods

Organizational Behavior 1978
PN 8511   SC 35695
SN Behavior of organizations and of individuals
within organizational settings.
  B   Social Behavior   1967
  N   ↓ Employee Interaction   1988
       Organizational Effectiveness   1985
  R   Distributive Justice   2003
       ↓ Group Dynamics   1967
       Informants   1988
       Labor Management Relations   1967
       ↓ Organizational Characteristics   1997
       Organizational Commitment   1991
       Organizational Learning   2003
       Organizational Structure   1967
       ↓ Organizations   1967
       Procedural Justice   2003
       Professional Networking   2004
       Psychological Contracts   2003
       ↓ Sociometry   1991

Organizational Change 1973
PN 3584   SC 35700
  UF   Change (Organizational)
  N   Downsizing   2003
       Organizational Merger   1973
  R   Decentralization   1978
       Organizational Climate   1973
       Organizational Crises   1973
       Organizational Development   1973
       Organizational Learning   2003

Organizational Characteristics 1997
PN 1155   SC 35705
  N   Organizational Climate   1973
       Organizational Structure   1967

Organizational Characteristics — (cont'd)
  R   Diversity in the Workplace   2003
       ↓ Organizational Behavior   1978
       Organizational Commitment   1991
       Organizational Learning   2003
       Organizational Objectives   1973
       Quality of Work Life   1988

Organizational Climate 1973
PN 4121   SC 35710
SN Social or environmental characteristics of an
organization which affect the behavior or perfor-
mance of its members.
  UF   Climate (Organizational)
       Organizational Culture
  B   Organizational Characteristics   1997
  R   Diversity in the Workplace   2003
       ↓ Organizational Change   1973
       Organizational Crises   1973
       Organizational Structure   1967
       Quality of Work Life   1988
       ↓ Working Conditions   1973

Organizational Commitment 1991
PN 1721   SC 35715
SN Commitment of organizations and of individuals
within organizational settings.
  B   Commitment   1985
  R   ↓ Employee Attitudes   1967
       ↓ Employee Characteristics   1988
       Employer Attitudes   1973
       Job Involvement   1978
       ↓ Job Performance   1967
       Job Satisfaction   1967
       ↓ Organizational Behavior   1978
       ↓ Organizational Characteristics   1997
       Organizational Effectiveness   1985
       Organizational Objectives   1973
       Psychological Contracts   2003

Organizational Crises 1973
PN 201   SC 35720
  B   Crises   1971
  R   ↓ Organizational Change   1973
       Organizational Climate   1973
       ↓ Stress   1967

Organizational Culture
  Use Organizational Climate

Organizational Development 1973
PN 2137   SC 35730
SN Application of behavioral, management, or other
techniques to organizations in order to integrate indi-
viduals' or members' needs with organizational goals
and objectives.
  B   Development   1967
  R   Decentralization   1978
       ↓ Organizational Change   1973
       Organizational Learning   2003
       Organizational Objectives   1973
       Organizational Structure   1967

Organizational Effectiveness 1985
PN 1889   SC 35735
SN Measure of the ability of an organization to meet
the needs of its environment, including personnel
needs.
  UF   Organizational Performance
  B   Organizational Behavior   1978
  R   Organizational Commitment   1991
       Organizational Learning   2003
       Organizational Objectives   1973

Organizational Effectiveness — (cont'd)
     Quality Control   1988

Organizational Goals
   Use   Organizational Objectives

Organizational Learning   2003
PN 197   **SC** 35748
SN Conceptually broad term referring to the ability of an organization to adapt, learn, and change with its environment, and to the process of obtaining, sharing, and utilizing knowledge in an organizational setting.
HN This term was introduced in June 2003. Psyc-INFO records from the past 10 years were re-indexed with this term. The posting note reflects the number of records that were re-indexed.
   UF   Learning Organizations
   B   Learning   1967
   R   Business Organizations   1973
     ↓ Organizational Behavior   1978
     ↓ Organizational Change   1973
     ↓ Organizational Characteristics   1997
     Organizational Development   1973
     Organizational Effectiveness   1985

Organizational Merger   1973
PN 104   **SC** 35750
   B   Organizational Change   1973
   R   Organizational Structure   1967

Organizational Objectives   1973
PN 747   **SC** 35760
   UF   Objectives (Organizational)
     Organizational Goals
   B   Goals   1967
   R   Decentralization   1978
     ↓ Organizational Characteristics   1997
     Organizational Commitment   1991
     Organizational Development   1973
     Organizational Effectiveness   1985
     Quality Control   1988

Organizational Performance
   Use   Organizational Effectiveness

Organizational Policy Making
   Use   Policy Making

Organizational Psychology
   Use   Industrial and Organizational Psychology

Organizational Structure   1967
PN 3582   **SC** 35770
   B   Organizational Characteristics   1997
   R   Decentralization   1978
     ↓ Organizational Behavior   1978
     Organizational Climate   1973
     Organizational Development   1973
     Organizational Merger   1973
     ↓ Organizations   1967
     Self Managing Work Teams   2001
     ↓ Work Teams   2001

Organizations   1967
PN 3188   **SC** 35780
   UF   Agencies (Groups)
     Associations (Groups)
     Groups (Organizations)

Organizations — (cont'd)
   N   Business Organizations   1973
     Foreign Organizations   1973
     Government Agencies   1973
     Health Maintenance Organizations   1982
     International Organizations   1973
     Labor Unions   1973
     Nonprofit Organizations   1973
     Professional Organizations   1973
     Religious Organizations   1991
   R   ↓ Organizational Behavior   1978
     Organizational Structure   1967

Orgasm   1973
PN 123   **SC** 35790
   UF   Climax (Sexual)
   B   Psychosexual Behavior   1967
   N   Female Orgasm   1973
     ↓ Male Orgasm   1973
   R   Frigidity   1973
     Impotence   1973
     Sexual Satisfaction   1994

Orientation (Perceptual)
   Use   Perceptual Orientation

Orientation (Spatial)
   Use   Spatial Orientation (Perception)

Orienting Reflex   1967
PN 916   **SC** 35820
SN Innate physiological responses, such as pupil dilation, galvanic skin response, and EEG activity, to novel stimuli.
   B   Reflexes   1971
     Sensory Adaptation   1007

Orienting Responses   1967
PN 1136   **SC** 35830
SN Behavioral reactions in an organism, such as arrest of movement or head turning, to novel stimuli; behavioral correlate of orienting reflex.
   B   Responses   1967
     Sensory Adaptation   1967
   R   ↓ Classical Conditioning   1967

Originality
   Use   Creativity

Orphanages   1973
PN 93   **SC** 35850
   B   Residential Care Institutions   1973
   R   ↓ Institutionalization   1967
     Orphans   1973

Orphans   1973
PN 162   **SC** 35860
   B   Family Members   1973
   R   Orphanages   1973

Orphenadrine   1973
PN 14   **SC** 35870
   UF   Methyldiphenylhydramine
   B   Amines   1973
     Antihistaminic Drugs   1973
     Antispasmodic Drugs   1973
     Antitremor Drugs   1973
     Cholinergic Blocking Drugs   1973
     Muscle Relaxing Drugs   1973

Orthogonal Rotation   1973
PN 105   **SC** 35880
   B   Statistical Rotation   1973
   N   Varimax Rotation   1973

Orthography   1973
PN 1430   **SC** 35890
SN Art and formal rules of writing and spelling according to accepted usage. Also used to refer to the representation of the sounds of a language by written symbols.
   B   Linguistics   1973
   R   ↓ Alphabets   1973
     Cursive Writing   1973
     Homographs   1973
     Proofreading   1988
     Spelling   1973
     ↓ Written Language   1967

Orthopedically Handicapped
   Use   Physical Disorders

Orthopsychiatry   1973
PN 23   **SC** 35910
SN Interdisciplinary approach combining psychiatry, psychology, pediatrics, and other related fields for prevention and early treatment of mental disorders, particularly in children and adolescents.
   B   Psychiatry   1967
   R   Child Psychiatry   1967

Oscilloscopes   1973
PN 26   **SC** 35920
   B   Apparatus   1967

Osteopathic Medicine   2003
PN 5   **SC** 35928
SN A system of therapy and medicine based on the theory that diseases are chiefly due to a loss of structural integrity, which can be restored by manipulation of the skeleton and muscles.
HN This term was introduced in June 2003. Psyc-INFO records from the past 10 years were re-indexed with this term. The posting note reflects the number of records that were re-indexed.
   UF   Osteopathy
   B   Medical Sciences   1967
   R   ↓ Alternative Medicine   1997
     ↓ Musculoskeletal System   1973
     ↓ Physical Treatment Methods   1973

Osteopathy
   Use   Osteopathic Medicine

Osteoporosis   1001
PN 167   **SC** 35930
   B   Bone Disorders   1973

Otosclerosis
   Use   Ear Disorders

Out of Body Experiences   1988
PN 92   **SC** 35945
   B   Parapsychological Phenomena   1973
   R   Near Death Experiences   1985

Outcomes (Psychotherapeutic)
   Use   Psychotherapeutic Outcomes

Outcomes (Treatment)
  Use Treatment Outcomes

Outgroup Ingroup
  Use Ingroup Outgroup

Outpatient Commitment 1991
PN 96   **SC** 35957
SN Legally mandated psychiatric or psychological treatment on an outpatient basis.
  UF Commitment (Outpatient)
  B   Commitment (Psychiatric) 1973
      Outpatient Treatment 1967
  R   Aftercare 1973
      Partial Hospitalization 1985

Outpatient Psychiatric Clinics
  Use Psychiatric Clinics

Outpatient Treatment 1967
PN 3419   **SC** 35970
SN Treatment in private practice, clinic, or hospital for ambulatory, non-hospitalized patients. Compare PARTIAL HOSPITALIZATION.
  UF Ambulatory Care
  B   Treatment 1967
  N   Outpatient Commitment 1991
  R   Aftercare 1973
      ↓ Drug Therapy 1967
      Home Care 1985
      Maintenance Therapy 1997
      Outpatients 1973
      Psychiatric Clinics 1973

Outpatients 1973
PN 2217   **SC** 35980
  B   Patients 1967
  R   ↓ Outpatient Treatment 1967

Outreach Programs 1997
PN 314   **SC** 35983
  B   Social Programs 1973
      Social Services 1982
  R   ↓ Case Management 1991
      Community Mental Health Services 1978
      ↓ Community Services 1967
      ↓ Health Care Delivery 1978
      ↓ Health Care Services 1978
      ↓ Mental Health Programs 1973
      ↓ Mental Health Services 1978
      Needle Exchange Programs 2001
      Social Casework 1967
      ↓ Support Groups 1991

Outward Bound
  Use Wilderness Experience

Ovariectomy 1973
PN 946   **SC** 35990
  B   Castration 1967
  R   Hysterectomy 1973

Ovaries 1973
PN 204   **SC** 36000
  B   Female Genitalia 1973
      Gonads 1973

Ovary Disorders
  Use Endocrine Sexual Disorders

Over the Counter Drugs
  Use Nonprescription Drugs

Overachievement (Academic)
  Use Academic Overachievement

Overcorrection 1985
PN 45   **SC** 36025
SN Therapeutic technique involving restitution and/or intensive practice of appropriate behavior following the occurrence of disruptive or inappropriate behavior.
  B   Behavior Modification 1973
  R   Overlearning 1967
      ↓ Practice 1967

Overlearning 1967
PN 236   **SC** 36030
SN Learning in which practice continues beyond the point of mastery of the material or task.
  B   Learning 1967
  R   Overcorrection 1985

Overpopulation 1973
PN 194   **SC** 36040
  B   Population 1973
  R   ↓ Birth Control 1971
      Crowding 1978
      Environmental Stress 1973
      Social Density 1978

Overweight
  Use Obesity

Ovulation 1973
PN 157   **SC** 36060
  B   Menstrual Cycle 1973

Owls 1997
PN 68   **SC** 36063
  B   Birds 1967

Ownership 1985
PN 441   **SC** 36065
  UF Possession
      Property
  R   Business 1967
      Capitalism 1973
      Entrepreneurship 1991
      ↓ Private Sector 1985
      Self Employment 1994

Oxazepam 1978
PN 121   **SC** 36075
  B   Anticonvulsive Drugs 1973
      Benzodiazepines 1978
      Minor Tranquilizers 1973

Oxidases 1973
PN 106   **SC** 36080
  B   Enzymes 1973
  N   Cytochrome Oxidase 1973
      Monoamine Oxidases 1973

Oxidopamine
  Use Hydroxydopamine (6-)

Oxilapine
  Use Loxapine

Oxygen 1973
PN 390   **SC** 36090
  R   ↓ Antioxidants 2004
      Nitric Oxide 2003

Oxygenation 1973
PN 114   **SC** 36100
  B   Physiology 1967

Oxytocin 1973
PN 445   **SC** 36120
  B   Pituitary Hormones 1973

Pacemakers (Artificial)
  Use Artificial Pacemakers

Pacific Islanders 2001
PN 45   **SC** 36133
  B   Indigenous Populations 2001
  N   Hawaii Natives 2001
  R   Alaska Natives 1997
      American Indians 1967
      Inuit 2001
      Minority Groups 1967

Pacifism 1973
PN 37   **SC** 36140
  B   Philosophies 1967
  R   Nonviolence 1991

Pain 1967
PN 6052   **SC** 36150
  UF Aches
  B   Symptoms 1967
  N   Aphagia 1973
      Back Pain 1982
      Chronic Pain 1985
      ↓ Headache 1973
      Myofascial Pain 1991
      ↓ Neuralgia 1973
      Somatoform Pain Disorder 1997
  R   ↓ Analgesic Drugs 1973
      Fibromyalgia 2004
      Pain Management 1994
      Pain Measurement 1997
      ↓ Pain Perception 1973
      Pain Thresholds 1973
      ↓ Physical Disorders 1997
      ↓ Spasms 1973
      Suffering 1973

Pain (Psychogenic)
  Use Somatoform Pain Disorder

Pain Disorder
  Use Somatoform Pain Disorder

Pain Management 1994
PN 2218   **SC** 36165
  B   Treatment 1967
  R   Analgesia 1982
      ↓ Analgesic Drugs 1973
      ↓ Pain 1967
      Pain Measurement 1997
      ↓ Pain Perception 1973
      Pain Thresholds 1973
      Palliative Care 1991
      ↓ Physical Treatment Methods 1973
      Somatoform Pain Disorder 1997

Pain Measurement 1997
PN 348   SC 36167
SN Tests, scales, or other techniques used to assess or evaluate pain in human or animal populations. Used only when the methodology is the focus of the reference.
B   Measurement 1967
R   Analgesia 1982
   ↓ Diagnosis 1967
   ↓ Pain 1967
   Pain Management 1994
   ↓ Pain Perception 1973
   Pain Thresholds 1973
   ↓ Perceptual Measures 1973

Pain Perception 1973
PN 4737   SC 36170
UF Nociception
B   Somesthetic Perception 1967
N   Analgesia 1982
   Pain Thresholds 1973
R ↓ Pain 1967
   Pain Management 1994
   Pain Measurement 1997
   Somatosensory Disorders 2001

Pain Receptors
Use Nociceptors

Pain Relieving Drugs
Use Analgesic Drugs

Pain Thresholds 1973
PN 1127   SC 36190
B   Pain Perception 1973
   Thresholds 1967
R ↓ Pain 1967
   Pain Management 1994
   Pain Measurement 1997
   ↓ Perceptual Measures 1973

Painting (Art) 1973
PN 669   SC 36200
B   Art 1967

Paired Associate Learning 1967
PN 2816   SC 36210
B   Verbal Learning 1967
R   Word Associations 1967

Palestinians
Use Arabs

Palliative Care 1991
PN 1069   SC 36219
B   Health Care Services 1978
R   Advance Directives 1994
   Assisted Suicide 1997
   ↓ Death and Dying 1967
   ↓ Health Care Delivery 1978
   Hospice 1982
   Life Sustaining Treatment 1997
   Long Term Care 1994
   Pain Management 1994
   Terminally Ill Patients 1973

Palm (Anatomy) 1973
PN 44   SC 36220
B   Anatomy 1967
R   Hand (Anatomy) 1967

Palsy
Use Paralysis

Pancreas 1973
PN 133   SC 36240
B   Glands 1967
R ↓ Endocrine Glands 1973
   ↓ Endocrine System 1973
   ↓ Gastrointestinal System 1973

Pancreozymin
Use Cholecystokinin

Panic 1973
PN 1192   SC 36260
HN Prior to 1988, also used for PANIC DISORDER.
B   Fear 1967
R ↓ Anxiety 1967
   Panic Attack 2003
   Panic Disorder 1988

Panic Attack 2003
PN 230   SC 36261
SN An episode of intense fear and anxiety that may be accompanied by one or more of the following symptoms: heart palpitations, sweating, shortness of breath, chest pain, nausea, dizziness, and trembling. Generally, attacks are unexpected and last no longer than 15 minutes.
HN This term was introduced in June 2003. PsycINFO records from the past 10 years were re-indexed with this term. The posting note reflects the number of records that were re indexed.
R ↓ Anxiety 1967
   ↓ Anxiety Disorders 1997
   ↓ Fear 1967
   Panic 1973
   Panic Disorder 1988

Panic Disorder 1988
PN 4587   SC 36265
HN Consider PANIC to access references from 1973-1987.
B   Anxiety Disorders 1997
R ↓ Anxiety 1967
   Panic 1973
   Panic Attack 2003

Pantherine
Use Muscimol

Papaverine 1973
PN 34   SC 36270
B   Alkaloids 1973
   Analgesic Drugs 1973
   Antispasmodic Drugs 1973
   Muscle Relaxing Drugs 1973
   Opiates 1973

Parachlorophenylalanine 1978
PN 186   SC 36275
B   Phenylalanine 1973
   Serotonin Antagonists 1973

Paradigmatic Techniques
Use Paradoxical Techniques

Paradoxical Sleep
Use REM Sleep

Paradoxical Techniques 1982
PN 453   SC 36282
SN Techniques designed to disrupt dysfunctional behavior patterns through systematically encouraging them, thus allaying anticipatory anxiety, creating resistance to the symptomatic behavior, or enabling clients to achieve voluntary control over this behavior.
UF Paradigmatic Techniques
   Reframing
   Symptom Prescription
B   Psychotherapeutic Techniques 1967
R ↓ Behavior Therapy 1967
   ↓ Psychotherapy 1967

Paragraphs 1973
PN 71   SC 36300
B   Written Language 1967

Paraldehyde
Use Anticonvulsive Drugs

Paralegal Personnel
Use Legal Personnel

Paralysis 1973
PN 365   SC 36320
UF Palsy
B   Movement Disorders 1985
   Neuromuscular Disorders 1973
N   Cerebral Palsy 1967
   General Paresis 1973
   Hemiplegia 1978
   Paraplegia 1978
   Quadriplegia 1985
R ↓ Central Nervous System Disorders 1973
   Dysarthria 1973
   ↓ Musculoskeletal Disorders 1973
   Parkinsons Disease 1973
   ↓ Peripheral Nerve Disorders 1973
   Poliomyelitis 1973
   ↓ Sclerosis (Nervous System) 1973
   ↓ Spinal Cord Injuries 1973

Paralysis (Hysterical)
Use Hysterical Paralysis

Paralysis (Infantile)
Use Poliomyelitis

Paralysis Agitans
Use Parkinsons Disease

Paramedical Personnel 1973
PN 296   SC 36360
HN In 1997, this term replaced the discontinued term MEDICS. In 2000, MEDICS was removed from all records containing it and replaced with PARAMEDICAL PERSONNEL.
UF Medics
B   Medical Personnel 1967
   Paraprofessional Personnel 1973
N   Attendants (Institutions) 1973
   Psychiatric Aides 1973
R   Fire Fighters 1991
   Home Care Personnel 1997
   ↓ Paramedical Sciences 1973
   ↓ Psychiatric Hospital Staff 1973

Paramedical Sciences 1973
PN 13   SC 36370

Paramedical Sciences — (cont'd)
- **N** Audiology 1973
  - Nursing 1973
  - Optometry 1973
  - ↓ Pharmacology 1973
  - Physical Therapy 1973
- **R** ↓ Medical Sciences 1967
  - ↓ Paramedical Personnel 1973

Parameter Estimation
Use Statistical Estimation

Parameters (Response)
Use Response Parameters

Parameters (Stimulus)
Use Stimulus Parameters

Parametric Statistical Tests 1973
PN 135   **SC** 36400
- **B** Statistical Tests 1973
- **N** F Test 1973
  - T Test 1973

Paranoia 1988
PN 263   **SC** 36410
SN Mild paranoia in nonpsychotic persons.
- **B** Personality Traits 1967
- **R** Paranoid Personality Disorder 1973

Paranoia (Psychosis) 1967
PN 920   **SC** 36420
SN Gradual development of an elaborate and complex delusional system, usually involving persecutory or grandiose delusions with few other signs of personality or thought disturbance.
- **UF** Acute Paranoid Disorder
  - Atypical Paranoid Disorder
  - Paranoid Disorder
- **B** Psychosis 1967
- **N** Folie A Deux 1973
  - Involutional Paranoid Psychosis 1973
- **R** Paranoid Personality Disorder 1973
  - Paranoid Schizophrenia 1967

Paranoid Disorder
Use Paranoia (Psychosis)

Paranoid Personality Disorder 1973
PN 188   **SC** 36430
SN Nonpsychotic personality disorder marked by hypersensitivity, jealousy, and unwarranted suspicion with tendency to blame others for one's shortcomings.
- **B** Personality Disorders 1967
- **R** Paranoia 1988
  - ↓ Paranoia (Psychosis) 1967
  - Paranoid Schizophrenia 1967

Paranoid Schizophrenia 1967
PN 1449   **SC** 36440
SN Type of schizophrenia characterized by grandiosity, suspiciousness, and delusions of persecution, often with hallucinations.
- **B** Schizophrenia 1967
- **R** Folie A Deux 1973
  - Involutional Paranoid Psychosis 1973
  - ↓ Paranoia (Psychosis) 1967
  - Paranoid Personality Disorder 1973
  - ↓ Psychosis 1967

Paraphilias 1988
PN 1491   **SC** 36443
SN Sexual urges, fantasies, or behaviors generally involving themes of suffering, humiliation, sexual activity with non-consenting partners, or an orientation toward non-human objects for sexual arousal.
HN In 2000, the term's status changed from non-postable to postable. SEXUAL DEVIATIONS was removed from all records containing it and replaced with PARAPHILIAS.
- **UF** Deviations (Sexual)
  - Perversions (Sexual)
  - Sexual Deviations
- **B** Mental Disorders 1967
  - Psychosexual Behavior 1967
- **N** Exhibitionism 1973
  - Fetishism 1973
  - Incest 1973
  - Pedophilia 1973
  - Sexual Masochism 1973
  - Sexual Sadism 1973
  - Transvestism 1973
  - Voyeurism 1973
- **R** ↓ Impulse Control Disorders 1997
  - Pornography 1973
  - ↓ Sex Offenses 1982
  - ↓ Sexual Abuse 1988
  - Sexual Addiction 1997

Paraplegia 1978
PN 175   **SC** 36446
SN Paralysis of the lower limbs and trunk.
- **B** Paralysis 1973
- **R** ↓ Central Nervous System Disorders 1973
  - Hemiplegia 1978
  - ↓ Injuries 1973
  - ↓ Musculoskeletal Disorders 1973
  - Quadriplegia 1985
  - ↓ Spinal Cord Injuries 1973

Paraprofessional Education 1973
PN 604   **SC** 36450
SN Training or education of aides, such as paramedical and paralegal personnel, who assist professional persons.
- **B** Education 1967
- **R** Microcounseling 1978

Paraprofessional Personnel 1973
PN 1154   **SC** 36460
SN Persons with minimal or special training in a profession working as aides or assistants to professionals.
HN Use PARAPROFESSIONAL PERSONNEL to access references to nonprofessional personnel from 1973-1981.
- **B** Personnel 1967
- **N** Home Care Personnel 1997
  - ↓ Paramedical Personnel 1973
  - Teacher Aides 1973
- **R** ↓ Mental Health Personnel 1967
  - ↓ Nonprofessional Personnel 1982
  - Occupational Therapists 1973
  - ↓ Professional Personnel 1978

Parapsychological Phenomena 1973
PN 1462   **SC** 36470
- **B** Parapsychology 1967
- **N** ↓ Extrasensory Perception 1967
  - Near Death Experiences 1985
  - Out of Body Experiences 1988
  - Telepathy 1973
- **R** Occultism 1978

Parapsychological Phenomena — (cont'd)
- Religious Experiences 1997
- Spirit Possession 1997
- Superstitions 1973

Parapsychology 1967
PN 1079   **SC** 36480
- **N** ↓ Parapsychological Phenomena 1973
- **R** Astrology 1973
  - Dream Analysis 1973
  - Mysticism 1967
  - Occultism 1978
  - Witchcraft 1973

Parasitic Disorders 1973
PN 151   **SC** 36490
- **B** Infectious Disorders 1973
- **N** Malaria 1973

Parasitism
Use Biological Symbiosis

Parasuicide
Use Attempted Suicide

Parasympathetic Nervous System 1973
PN 96   **SC** 36500
- **B** Autonomic Nervous System 1967
- **N** ↓ Efferent Pathways 1982
  - Vagus Nerve 1973
- **R** ↓ Cholinergic Blocking Drugs 1973
  - ↓ Cholinomimetic Drugs 1973

Parasympatholytic Drugs
Use Antispasmodic Drugs

Parasympathomimetic Drugs
Use Cholinomimetic Drugs

Parathion 1973
PN 9   **SC** 36530
- **B** Insecticides 1973

Parathyroid Disorders 1973
PN 60   **SC** 36540
- **UF** Hyperparathyroidism
  - Hypoparathyroidism
- **B** Endocrine Disorders 1973

Parathyroid Glands 1973
PN 9   **SC** 36550
- **B** Endocrine Glands 1973
- **R** Parathyroid Hormone 1973

Parathyroid Hormone 1973
PN 16   **SC** 36560
- **B** Hormones 1967
- **R** Parathyroid Glands 1973

Parent Child Communication 1973
PN 2096   **SC** 36580
SN For animals consider ANIMAL PARENTAL BEHAVIOR or ANIMAL MATERNAL BEHAVIOR.
HN From 1982, limited to human populations.
- **B** Interpersonal Communication 1973
- **N** Father Child Communication 1985
  - Mother Child Communication 1985
- **R** ↓ Parent Child Relations 1967

Parent Child Communication — (cont'd)
↓ Parental Characteristics 1994

Parent Child Relations 1967
PN 14096   SC 36590
SN For animals consider ANIMAL PARENTAL BEHAVIOR or ANIMAL MATERNAL BEHAVIOR.
HN From 1982, limited to human populations.
- UF   Parental Influence
- B   Family Relations 1967
- N   Father Child Relations 1973
      Mother Child Relations 1967
     ↓ Parental Attitudes 1973
      Parental Permissiveness 1973
- R   Attachment Behavior 1985
      Attachment Disorders 2001
     ↓ Child Discipline 1973
     ↓ Childrearing Practices 1967
      Children of Alcoholics 2003
      Codependency 1991
      Empty Nest 1991
     ↓ Family Conflict 2003
      Generation Gap 1973
      Nurturance 1985
     ↓ Parent Child Communication 1973
      Parent School Relationship 1982
      Parent Training 1978
     ↓ Parental Characteristics 1994
      Parental Expectations 1997
      Parental Investment 1997
      Parental Role 1973
      Parenting Skills 1997
     ↓ Parenting Style 2003
      Transgenerational Patterns 1991

Parent Educational Background 1973
PN 888   SC 36600
- UF   Educational Background (Parents)
- B   Educational Background 1967
      Family Background 1973
      Parental Characteristics 1994
- R   Family Socioeconomic Level 1973
      Parental Occupation 1973

Parent Effectiveness Training
  Use Parent Training

Parent School Relationship 1982
PN 1504   SC 36605
SN Interaction between parents and school and/or educational personnel, such as parent-teacher conferences.
- UF   PTA
- R   ↓ Parent Child Relations 1967
      Parent Training 1978
     ↓ Teacher Attitudes 1967

Parent Training 1978
PN 3578   SC 36606
SN Educational materials, information, or instruction for parents.
- UF   Parent Effectiveness Training
- B   Education 1967
      Family Life Education 1997
- R   ↓ Childrearing Practices 1967
      Human Relations Training 1978
     ↓ Parent Child Relations 1967
      Parent School Relationship 1982
      Parental Role 1973
      Parenting Skills 1997

Parental Absence 1973
PN 602   SC 36610

Parental Absence — (cont'd)
SN For animals consider ANIMAL PARENTAL BEHAVIOR or ANIMAL MATERNAL BEHAVIOR.
HN From 1982, limited to human populations.
- B   Family Structure 1973
- N   Father Absence 1973
      Mother Absence 1973
- R   Anaclitic Depression 1973
      Child Custody 1982
      Divorced Persons 1973
     ↓ Marital Separation 1973
     ↓ Parental Characteristics 1994
      Parental Death 2003
     ↓ Single Parents 1978
      Widowers 1973
      Widows 1973

Parental Attitudes 1973
PN 8854   SC 36620
SN Attitudes of, not toward, parents.
- B   Attitudes 1967
      Parent Child Relations 1967
      Parental Characteristics 1994
- N   Parental Expectations 1997
- R   Childrearing Attitudes 1973
     ↓ Childrearing Practices 1967
      Father Child Relations 1973
      Mother Child Relations 1967
      Parental Permissiveness 1973
      Parental Role 1973

Parental Authoritarianism
  Use Parenting Style

Parental Behavior (Animal)
  Use Animal Parental Behavior

Parental Characteristics 1994
PN 3033   SC 36637
- N   Parent Educational Background 1973
     ↓ Parental Attitudes 1973
      Parental Occupation 1973
      Parental Permissiveness 1973
      Parental Role 1973
      Parenting Skills 1997
     ↓ Parenting Style 2003
- R   ↓ Childrearing Practices 1967
     ↓ Parent Child Communication 1973
     ↓ Parent Child Relations 1967
     ↓ Parental Absence 1973
      Parental Investment 1997
     ↓ Parents 1967

Parental Death 2003
PN 39   SC 36638
SN Death of parents.
HN This term was introduced in June 2003. Psyc-INFO records from the past 10 years were re-indexed with this term. The posting note reflects the number of records that were re-indexed.
- B   Death and Dying 1967
- R   Life Changes 2004
     ↓ Parental Absence 1973
     ↓ Parents 1967

Parental Expectations 1997
PN 232   SC 36639
SN Expectations or aspirations for a level of behavior, achievement, or performance (e.g., in school, life, or career) that parents have for their children.
- B   Expectations 1967
      Parental Attitudes 1973

Parental Expectations — (cont'd)
- R   ↓ Parent Child Relations 1967
      Parental Investment 1997
      Parental Role 1973
     ↓ Parents 1967

Parental Influence
  Use Parent Child Relations

Parental Investment 1997
PN 466   SC 36645
SN Parental provision of resources and/or care to offspring. Used for both human and animal populations.
- UF   Maternal Investment
      Paternal Investment
- R   ↓ Animal Parental Behavior 1982
     ↓ Parent Child Relations 1967
     ↓ Parental Characteristics 1994
      Parental Expectations 1997

Parental Occupation 1973
PN 410   SC 36650
- UF   Occupation (Parental)
- B   Family Background 1973
      Parental Characteristics 1994
- R   Family Socioeconomic Level 1973
      Parent Educational Background 1973

Parental Permissiveness 1973
PN 490   SC 36660
- UF   Permissiveness (Parental)
- B   Child Discipline 1973
      Parent Child Relations 1967
      Parental Characteristics 1994
      Parenting Style 2003
- R   Father Child Relations 1973
      Mother Child Relations 1967
     ↓ Parental Attitudes 1973
      Parental Role 1973

Parental Role 1973
PN 3065   SC 36670
SN Descriptions, perceptions, and attitudes about the social, psychological, behavioral, or emotional role of parents.
- B   Family Relations 1967
      Parental Characteristics 1994
      Roles 1967
- R   ↓ Child Discipline 1973
     ↓ Childrearing Practices 1967
      Delayed Parenthood 1985
      Father Child Relations 1973
      Mother Child Relations 1967
     ↓ Parent Child Relations 1967
      Parent Training 1978
     ↓ Parental Attitudes 1973
      Parental Expectations 1997
      Parental Permissiveness 1973

Parenthood Status 1985
PN 975   SC 36675
SN State of having or not having children, or the number of children one has.
- N   Childlessness 1982
- R   Family Size 1973
     ↓ Family Structure 1973
      Life Changes 2004

Parenting Skills 1997
PN 944   SC 36677
- B   Parental Characteristics 1994

Parenting Skills — (cont'd)
R ↓ Childrearing Practices 1967
    ↓ Parent Child Relations 1967
    Parent Training 1978

Parenting Style 2003
PN 200   SC 36678
SN Characteristic manner in which parents raise their children. Compare CHILDREARING PRACTICES.
HN This term was introduced in June 2003. PsycINFO records from the past 10 years were re-indexed with this term. The posting note reflects the number of records that were re-indexed.
UF Authoritarianism (Parental)
    Parental Authoritarianism
B Parental Characteristics 1994
N Parental Permissiveness 1973
R ↓ Childrearing Practices 1967
    ↓ Parent Child Relations 1967

Parents 1967
PN 14211   SC 36680
SN For animals consider ANIMAL PARENTAL BEHAVIOR or ANIMAL MATERNAL BEHAVIOR.
HN From 1982, limited to human populations.
B Ancestors 1973
    Family Members 1973
N Adoptive Parents 1973
    ↓ Fathers 1967
    Foster Parents 1973
    Homosexual Parents 1994
    ↓ Mothers 1967
    ↓ Single Parents 1978
    Stepparents 1973
    Surrogate Parents (Humans) 1973
R ↓ Expectant Parents 1985
    Inlaws 1997
    ↓ Parental Characteristics 1994
    Parental Death 2003
    Parental Expectations 1997
    ↓ Spouses 1973

Paresis (General)
Use General Paresis

Paresthesia
Use Somatosensory Disorders

Pargyline 1973
PN 81   SC 36700
B Antihypertensive Drugs 1973
    Monoamine Oxidase Inhibitors 1973

Parietal Lobe 1973
PN 1519   SC 36710
B Cerebral Cortex 1967
N Somatosensory Cortex 1973

Parkinsonism 1994
PN 476   SC 36715
SN Clinical state, usually drug induced, characterized by tremors, muscle rigidity, postural reflex dysfunction, and akinesia. Compare PARKINSONS DISEASE.
R Apraxia 1973
    Bradykinesia 2001
    Dementia with Lewy Bodies 2001
    Muscle Contractions 1973
    ↓ Nervous System Disorders 1967
    Parkinsons Disease 1973
    ↓ Reflexes 1971

Parkinsonism — (cont'd)
    ↓ Symptoms 1967
    Tremor 1973

Parkinsons Disease 1973
PN 3977   SC 36720
SN A disease characterized as a progressive motor disability manifested by tremors, shaking, muscular rigidity, and lack of postural reflexes.
UF Paralysis Agitans
B Brain Disorders 1967
    Neurodegenerative Diseases 2004
R Amantadine 1978
    ↓ Antitremor Drugs 1973
    Bradykinesia 2001
    ↓ Dementia 1985
    Dementia with Lewy Bodies 2001
    ↓ Paralysis 1973
    Parkinsonism 1994
    Tremor 1973

Parks (Recreational)
Use Recreation Areas

Parochial School Education
Use Private School Education

Parole 1973
PN 344   SC 36750
SN Conditional release of a prisoner serving an indeterminate or unexpired sentence.
UF Parolees
B Legal Processes 1973
R Criminal Rehabilitation 2004
    ↓ Law Enforcement 1978
    Probation 1973

Parole Officers 1973
PN 57   SC 36760
B Law Enforcement Personnel 1973
R Probation Officers 1973

Parolees
Use Parole

Paroxetine 1994
PN 869   SC 36770
B Antidepressant Drugs 1971
    Serotonin Reuptake Inhibitors 1007

Paroxysmal Sleep
Use Narcolepsy

Partial Hospitalization 1985
PN 1282   SC 36775
SN Ambulatory treatment program of intensive, multidisciplinary care. Involves stabilization, rehabilitation, and/or maintenance of patients through more comprehensive treatment than is possible in an outpatient setting. Compare OUTPATIENT TREATMENT.
UF Day Care (Treatment)
    Day Hospital
B Treatment 1967
R Aftercare 1973
    Deinstitutionalization 1982
    ↓ Hospital Programs 1978
    Interdisciplinary Treatment Approach 1973
    ↓ Mental Health Programs 1973
    Outpatient Commitment 1991

Partial Hospitalization — (cont'd)
    ↓ Rehabilitation 1967

Partial Reinforcement
Use Reinforcement Schedules

Partially Hearing Impaired 1973
PN 2680   SC 36790
UF Hearing Impaired (Partially)
R Cochlear Implants 1994
    ↓ Deaf 1967

Partially Sighted 1973
PN 136   SC 36800

Participation 1973
PN 2976   SC 36810
SN Taking part in an activity. Use a more specific term if possible.
B Interpersonal Interaction 1967
N Athletic Participation 1973
    Client Participation 1997
    Group Participation 1973
    Participative Management 1988
R Activity Theory 2003
    ↓ Involvement 1973

Participative Management 1988
PN 517   SC 36820
SN Management technique permitting nonmanagement personnel to be involved in the governance, management, or policy-making processes of an institution or organization.
UF Quality Circles
B Management Methods 1973
    Participation 1973
R Job Involvement 1978
    Management Decision Making 1973
    Quality Control 1988
    Self Managing Work Teams 2001

Partner Abuse 1991
PN 2166   SC 36825
SN Includes married and unmarried persons.
UF Spouse Abuse
B Antisocial Behavior 1971
R ↓ Abuse Reporting 1997
    Battered Females 1988
    Emotional Abuse 1991
    Erotomania 1997
    ↓ Family Conflict 2003
    Family Violence 1982
    Physical Abuse 1991
    ↓ Sexual Abuse 1988
    Verbal Abuse 2003
    ↓ Violence 1973

Parturition
Use Birth

Passive Aggressive Personality Disorder 1973
PN 55   SC 36850
B Personality Disorders 1967

Passive Avoidance
Use Avoidance Conditioning

Passiveness 1973
PN 257   SC 36870

Passiveness — (cont'd)
B　　Personality Traits　1967

Pastoral Counseling　1967
PN　1415　　　　　　　　SC　36880
SN　Provision of counseling by religious personnel.
B　　Counseling　1967
R　↓ Psychotherapy　1967

Pastors
Use　Ministers (Religion)

Paternal Investment
Use　Parental Investment

Path Analysis　1991
PN　146　　　　　　　　SC　36895
SN　Quantification of the causal relationships that exist among variables.
B　　Multivariate Analysis　1982
R　　Causal Analysis　1994
　　↓ Factor Analysis　1967
　　Multiple Regression　1982

Pathogenesis
Use　Etiology

Pathological Gambling　1988
PN　818　　　　　　　　SC　36905
UF　Compulsive Gambling
B　　Gambling　1973
R　↓ Addiction　1973
　↓ Behavior Disorders　1971
　↓ Impulse Control Disorders　1997
　　Impulsiveness　1973

Pathologists　1970
PN　26　　　　　　　　SC　36920
B　　Physicians　1967
R　　Surgeons　1973

Pathology　1973
PN　945　　　　　　　　SC　36930
B　　Medical Sciences　1967
N　　Neuropathology　1973
　　Psychopathology　1967
R　　Inflammation　2004

Patient Abuse　1991
PN　100　　　　　　　　SC　36935
UF　Client Abuse
B　　Antisocial Behavior　1971
R　↓ Child Abuse　1971
　　Elder Abuse　1988
　　Emotional Abuse　1991
　　Patient Violence　1994
　↓ Patients　1967
　　Physical Abuse　1991
　　Professional Client Sexual Relations　1994
　　Professional Liability　1985
　↓ Professional Standards　1973
　↓ Sexual Abuse　1988
　↓ Therapeutic Processes　1978
　↓ Treatment　1967
　　Verbal Abuse　2003

Patient Attitudes
Use　Client Attitudes

Patient Care Planning
Use　Treatment Planning

Patient Characteristics
Use　Client Characteristics

Patient Dropouts
Use　Treatment Dropouts

Patient Education
Use　Client Education

Patient History　1973
PN　3032　　　　　　　　SC　36955
UF　Case History
　　Medical History
　　Psychiatric History
R　　Biographical Data　1978
　↓ Client Characteristics　1973
　　Client Records　1997
　↓ Diagnosis　1967
　　Etiology　1967
　↓ Medical Diagnosis　1973
　↓ Medical Records　1978
　　Misdiagnosis　1997
　　Premorbidity　1978
　　Prognosis　1973
　↓ Psychodiagnosis　1967
　↓ Treatment　1967

Patient Participation
Use　Client Participation

Patient Records
Use　Client Records

Patient Rights
Use　Client Rights

Patient Satisfaction
Use　Client Satisfaction

Patient Seclusion　1994
PN　125　　　　　　　　SC　36959
UF　Seclusion (Patient)
B　　Social Isolation　1967
R　↓ Hospitalization　1967
　　Patient Violence　1994
　↓ Patients　1967
　↓ Psychiatric Hospitalization　1973
　　Psychiatric Hospitals　1967
　　Psychiatric Units　1991

Patient Selection　1997
PN　41　　　　　　　　SC　57505
SN　Selection of patients or clients for participation in research studies or for specific treatment modalities.
R　↓ Client Characteristics　1973
　　Client Transfer　1997
　　Client Treatment Matching　1997
　　Clients　1973
　↓ Patients　1967
　　Therapist Selection　1994

Patient Therapist Interaction
Use　Psychotherapeutic Processes

Patient Therapist Sexual Relations
Use　Professional Client Sexual Relations

Patient Transfer
Use　Client Transfer

Patient Treatment Matching
Use　Client Treatment Matching

Patient Violence　1994
PN　488　　　　　　　　SC　36965
SN　Violence or behavioral disruptions by psychiatric or medical patients directed toward other patients, institutional staff, or themselves.
UF　Client Violence
B　　Client Characteristics　1973
　　Violence　1973
R　　Dangerousness　1988
　　Patient Abuse　1991
　　Patient Seclusion　1994
　↓ Patients　1967
　　Physical Restraint　1982
　↓ Therapeutic Processes　1978

Patients　1967
PN　3263　　　　　　　　SC　36970
SN　Persons under medical care. Use a more specific term if possible. Consider also CLIENTS.
N　　Geriatric Patients　1973
　　Hospitalized Patients　1973
　　Medical Patients　1973
　　Outpatients　1970
　　Psychiatric Patients　1967
　　Surgical Patients　1973
　　Terminally Ill Patients　1970
R　　Client Participation　1007
　　Patient Abuse　1991
　　Patient Seclusion　1994
　　Patient Selection　1997
　　Patient Violence　1994

Patriarchy　1973
PN　216　　　　　　　　SC　36980
B　　Family Structure　1973
R　　Matriarchy　1973
　　Mother Absence　1973
　↓ Sex Role Attitudes　1978
　　Sex Roles　1967

Pattern Discrimination　1967
PN　3448　　　　　　　　SC　37000
SN　Distinguishing temporal, spatial, or pictorial/symbolic regularities (patterns) of visual, auditory, or other types of stimuli. Includes the concept of pattern perception.
B　　Perceptual Discrimination　1973
R　↓ Auditory Perception　1967
　　Figure Ground Discrimination　1973
　　Form and Shape Perception　1967
　　Perceptual Closure　1973
　↓ Rhythm　1991
　　Texture Perception　1982
　　Visual Acuity　1982
　　Visual Search　1982

Pavlov (Ivan)　1991
PN　92　　　　　　　　SC　37005
SN　Identifies biographical or autobiographical studies and discussions of Pavlov's works.
R　↓ Classical Conditioning　1967
　↓ Psychologists　1967

Pavlovian Conditioning
Use Classical Conditioning

Pay
Use Salaries

PCP
Use Phencyclidine

Peabody Picture Vocabulary Test 1973
PN 297   **SC** 37030
B Intelligence Measures 1967

Peace 1988
PN 560   **SC** 37038
B Social Interaction 1967
   Social Issues 1991
R Foreign Policy Making 1973
   International Relations 1967
   ↓ Social Movements 1967
   ↓ War 1967

Peace Corps 1973
PN 26   **SC** 37040
B Government Programs 1973
R Government 1967

Pearson Product Moment Correlation
   Coefficient
Use Statistical Correlation

Pecking Order
Use Animal Dominance

Pedagogy
Use Teaching

Pederasty
Use Pedophilia

Pedestrian Accidents 1973
PN 106   **SC** 37090
B Accidents 1967
R ↓ Driving Behavior 1967
   Motor Traffic Accidents 1973
   Pedestrians 1973

Pedestrians 1973
PN 206   **SC** 37100
R Pedestrian Accidents 1973

Pediatricians 1973
PN 501   **SC** 37110
B Physicians 1967

Pediatrics 1973
PN 1957   **SC** 37120
B Medical Sciences 1967

Pedophilia 1973
PN 717   **SC** 37130
UF Child Molestation
   Pederasty
B Paraphilias 1988
R ↓ Child Abuse 1971
   Incest 1973
   ↓ Sex Offenses 1982
   ↓ Sexual Abuse 1988

Peer Counseling 1978
PN 728   **SC** 37135
SN Supervised performance of limited counselor functions by a person of approximately the same age or status as the counselee.
B Counseling 1967
R Mentor 1985
   ↓ Peer Relations 1967
   Peer Tutoring 1973
   Peers 1978

Peer Evaluation 1982
PN 1090   **SC** 37137
SN Appraisal by one's peers.
UF Peer Review
B Evaluation 1967
R ↓ Peer Relations 1967
   ↓ Personnel Evaluation 1973
   Professional Competence 1997
   ↓ Professional Fees 1978
   ↓ Professional Standards 1973

Peer Pressure 1994
PN 253   **SC** 37138
B Interpersonal Influences 1967
   Peer Relations 1967
R Friendship 1967
   ↓ Group Dynamics 1967
   Likability 1988
   Peers 1978
   ↓ Persuasive Communication 1967
   Social Acceptance 1967
   Social Approval 1967
   Temptation 1973

Peer Relations 1967
PN 8831   **SC** 37140
B Interpersonal Interaction 1967
N Peer Pressure 1994
R Friendship 1967
   Peer Counseling 1978
   Peer Evaluation 1982
   Peers 1978
   Reference Groups 1994
   ↓ Relationship Termination 1997
   ↓ Sociometry 1991
   Teasing 2003

Peer Review
Use Peer Evaluation

Peer Tutoring 1973
PN 859   **SC** 37150
SN Teaching method in which students provide individual instruction for other students, not necessarily of the same age or grade level.
B Tutoring 1973
R Cooperative Learning 1994
   Peer Counseling 1978
   Peers 1978

Peers 1978
PN 1872   **SC** 37154
R Peer Counseling 1978
   Peer Pressure 1994
   ↓ Peer Relations 1967
   Peer Tutoring 1973
   Significant Others 1991

Pellagra 1973
PN 10   **SC** 37160
B Vitamin Deficiency Disorders 1973

Pellagra — (cont'd)
R Nicotinamide 1973

Pemoline 1978
PN 97   **SC** 37175
B CNS Stimulating Drugs 1973

Penguins 1973
PN 69   **SC** 37180
B Birds 1967

Penicillins 1973
PN 72   **SC** 37190
B Antibiotics 1973

Penis 1973
PN 275   **SC** 37200
B Male Genitalia 1973

Penis Envy 1973
PN 75   **SC** 37210
R ↓ Psychoanalytic Personality Factors 1973

Penitentiaries
Use Prisons

Penology 1973
PN 243   **SC** 37230
R ↓ Correctional Institutions 1973
   ↓ Criminal Justice 1991
   Criminology 1973

Pension Plans (Employee)
Use Employee Pension Plans

Pentazocine 1991
PN 31   **SC** 37245
B Analgesic Drugs 1973
   Narcotic Agonists 1988

Pentobarbital 1973
PN 741   **SC** 37250
UF Nembutal
   Sodium Pentobarbital
B Anesthetic Drugs 1973
   Anticonvulsive Drugs 1973
   Barbiturates 1967
   Hypnotic Drugs 1973
   Sedatives 1973

Pentothal
Use Thiopental

Pentylenetetrazol 1973
PN 297   **SC** 37270
UF Metrazole
   Pentylenetetrazole
B CNS Stimulating Drugs 1973
R ↓ Analeptic Drugs 1973

Pentylenetetrazole
Use Pentylenetetrazol

Peptic Ulcers
Use Gastrointestinal Ulcers

Peptides 1973
PN 3073   SC 37330
UF   Galanin
N   Angiotensin 1973
     Bombesin 1988
     Cholecystokinin 1982
     Corticotropin Releasing Factor 1994
     ↓ Endogenous Opiates 1985
     Leptin 2004
     Melanocyte Stimulating Hormone 1985
     Nerve Growth Factor 1994
     ↓ Neurokinins 1997
     ↓ Neuropeptides 2003
     Neurotensin 1985
     Somatostatin 1991
     Substance P 1985
R   ↓ Drugs 1967
     Enkephalins 1982
     ↓ Neurotransmitters 1985
     ↓ Proteins 1973

Perception 1967
PN 6488   SC 37350
SN   Conceptually broad term referring to the pro-
cess of obtaining cognitive or sensory information
about the environment. Use a more specific term if
possible.
UF   Sensation
N   ↓ Auditory Perception 1967
     ↓ Extrasensory Perception 1967
     Form and Shape Perception 1967
     ↓ Illusions (Perception) 1967
     ↓ Intersensory Processes 1978
     Numerosity Perception 1967
     Object Recognition 1997
     ↓ Olfactory Perception 1967
     Perceptual Closure 1973
     ↓ Perceptual Constancy 1985
     ↓ Perceptual Discrimination 1973
     ↓ Perceptual Distortion 1982
     ↓ Perceptual Localization 1967
     ↓ Perceptual Motor Learning 1967
     ↓ Perceptual Motor Processes 1967
     ↓ Perceptual Orientation 1973
     Perceptual Style 1973
     Risk Perception 1997
     Role Perception 1973
     Self Perception 1967
     Sensory Gating 1991
     ↓ Social Perception 1967
     ↓ Somesthetic Perception 1967
     ↓ Spatial Perception 1967
     Subliminal Perception 1973
     Taste Perception 1967
     ↓ Time Perception 1967
     ↓ Visual Perception 1967
R   Apperception 1973
     ↓ Attention 1967
     Constructivism 1994
     ↓ Discrimination 1967
     Mind 1991
     ↓ Perceptual Development 1973
     ↓ Perceptual Disturbances 1973
     ↓ Perceptual Measures 1973
     ↓ Perceptual Stimulation 1973
     ↓ Priming 1988
     ↓ Rhythm 1991
     Sensory Neglect 1994
     Signal Detection (Perception) 1967

Perceptiveness (Personality) 1973
PN 42   SC 37360
SN   Demonstrating insight or sympathetic under-
standing or keen powers of observation.

Perceptiveness (Personality) — (cont'd)
B   Personality Traits 1967
R   Insight 1973
     Sensitivity (Personality) 1967
     ↓ Social Perception 1967

Perceptual Aftereffect 1967
PN 1180   SC 37370
SN   Subjective perceptual alterations resulting from
prolonged exposure to preceding sensory stimula-
tion.
UF   Aftereffect (Perceptual)
B   Illusions (Perception) 1967
N   Afterimage 1967
R   Interocular Transfer 1985

Perceptual Closure 1973
PN 182   SC 37380
SN   Perception of units which together form a closed
unit or whole, being organized together and per-
ceived as a whole.
UF   Closure (Perceptual)
     Perceptual Fill
B   Perception 1967
R   Pattern Discrimination 1967

Perceptual Constancy 1985
PN 149   SC 37385
SN   Stable perception of a stimulus in any sensory
modality despite changes in its objective properties.
B   Perception 1967
N   Brightness Constancy 1985
     Color Constancy 1985
     Size Constancy 1985
R   Object Permanence 1988

Perceptual Development 1973
PN 3281   SC 37390
SN   The acquisition of sensory skills or abilities in
the natural course of physical and psychological mat-
uration.
B   Cognitive Development 1973
N   Perceptual Motor Development 1991
R   ↓ Childhood Development 1967
     Conservation (Concept) 1973
     ↓ Developmental Stages 1973
     ↓ Perception 1967
     ↓ Physical Development 1973
     ↓ Psychomotor Development 1973

Perceptual Discrimination 1973
PN 1216   SC 37400
B   Discrimination 1967
     Perception 1967
N   Auditory Acuity 1988
     Auditory Discrimination 1967
     Figure Ground Discrimination 1973
     Odor Discrimination 1973
     Pattern Discrimination 1967
     Visual Discrimination 1967
R   Mirror Image 1991
     Object Recognition 1997
     Stroop Effect 1988

Perceptual Distortion 1982
PN 235   SC 37410
SN   Lack of correspondence between the common
perception of a stimulus and the perception by an
individual. Perceptual distortion does not involve hal-
lucinatory or illusory components, but rather is a
function of individual differences.
UF   Distortion (Perceptual)
B   Perception 1967

Perceptual Distortion — (cont'd)
N   Spatial Distortion 1973
R   ↓ Illusions (Perception) 1967
     ↓ Perceptual Disturbances 1973
     Sensory Neglect 1994

Perceptual Disturbances 1973
PN 584   SC 37420
N   ↓ Agnosia 1973
     ↓ Hallucinations 1967
R   ↓ Aphasia 1967
     ↓ Illusions (Perception) 1967
     ↓ Learning Disabilities 1973
     ↓ Mental Disorders 1967
     ↓ Perception 1967
     ↓ Perceptual Distortion 1982
     Sensory Neglect 1994

Perceptual Fill
Use Perceptual Closure

Perceptual Localization 1967
PN 993   SC 37440
SN   Discrimination of the physical displacement or
spatial location of a stimulus in any sensory modality.
UF   Localization (Perceptual)
B   Perception 1967
N   Auditory Localization 1973
R   Direction Perception 1997
     ↓ Tracking 1967

Perceptual Measures 1973
PN 761   SC 37450
D   Measurement 1967
N   Rod and Frame Test 1973
     Stroop Color Word Test 1973
R   ↓ Audiometry 1967
     Auditory Thresholds 1973
     Bone Conduction Audiometry 1973
     Critical Flicker Fusion Threshold 1967
     Dark Adaptation 1973
     Olfactory Thresholds 1973
     Pain Measurement 1997
     Pain Thresholds 1973
     ↓ Perception 1967
     ↓ Psychophysical Measurement 1967
     Sensorimotor Measures 1973
     Speech and Hearing Measures 1973
     ↓ Thresholds 1967
     Vibrotactile Thresholds 1973
     ↓ Visual Thresholds 1973

Perceptual Motor Coordination 1973
PN 1491   SC 37460
UF   Coordination (Perceptual Motor)
B   Perceptual Motor Processes 1967
N   Physical Dexterity 1973
H   Motor Coordination 1973
     Perceptual Motor Development 1991

Perceptual Motor Development 1991
PN 434   SC 37470
HN   Use MOTOR DEVELOPMENT and PERCEP-
TUAL DEVELOPMENT to access references from
1973-1990.
UF   Sensorimotor Development
B   Motor Development 1973
     Perceptual Development 1973
R   Animal Development 1978
     ↓ Intersensory Processes 1978
     ↓ Perceptual Motor Coordination 1973
     ↓ Perceptual Motor Learning 1967

Perceptual Motor Development —
(cont'd)
   ↓ Perceptual Motor Processes 1967
   ↓ Psychomotor Development 1973

Perceptual Motor Learning 1967
PN 2057   SC 37480
  UF Motor Skill Learning
  B   Learning 1967
      Perception 1967
  N   Fine Motor Skill Learning 1973
      Gross Motor Skill Learning 1973
  R   Perceptual Motor Development 1991
    ↓ Skill Learning 1973
    ↓ Tracking 1967

Perceptual Motor Measures
  Use Sensorimotor Measures

Perceptual Motor Processes 1967
PN 7185   SC 37490
  UF Psychomotor Processes
      Sensorimotor Processes
  B   Perception 1967
  N ↓ Perceptual Motor Coordination 1973
      Sensory Integration 1991
    ↓ Tracking 1967
  R   Equilibrium 1973
    ↓ Intersensory Processes 1978
    ↓ Motor Processes 1967
      Perceptual Motor Development 1991

Perceptual Neglect
  Use Sensory Neglect

Perceptual Orientation 1973
PN 996   SC 37500
SN Awareness of one's position in time and space.
  UF Orientation (Perceptual)
  B   Perception 1967
  N   Spatial Orientation (Perception) 1973
  R   Time Perspective 1978

Perceptual Stimulation 1973
PN 565   SC 37510
  B   Stimulation 1967
  N ↓ Auditory Stimulation 1967
    ↓ Delayed Feedback 1973
      Olfactory Stimulation 1978
    ↓ Sensory Feedback 1973
    ↓ Somesthetic Stimulation 1973
      Taste Stimulation 1967
    ↓ Visual Stimulation 1973
  R   Afferent Stimulation 1973
    ↓ Masking 1967
    ↓ Perception 1967
      Sensory Gating 1991

Perceptual Style 1973
PN 549   SC 37520
SN Manner in which sensory information or stimuli are organized meaningfully by an individual.
  B   Perception 1967
  R ↓ Cognitive Style 1967
      Conceptual Tempo 1985
      Neurolinguistic Programming 2001
      Schema 1988

Perfectionism 1988
PN 471   SC 37523
  B   Personality Traits 1967

Perfectionism — (cont'd)
  R ↓ Compulsions 1973
      Conscientiousness 1997
      Self Criticism 2003

Performance 1967
PN 7730   SC 37525
SN Conceptually broad term, having application across broad disciplines and subject matter contexts in which execution or accomplishment of a specified task or objective is of concern. Use terms describing specific activity or performance when possible.
  N   Athletic Performance 1991
      Group Performance 1967
    ↓ Job Performance 1967
    ↓ Motor Performance 1973
  R ↓ Ability 1967
    ↓ Achievement 1967
    ↓ Competence 1982
      Performance Anxiety 1994

Performance Anxiety 1994
PN 180   SC 37527
  B   Anxiety 1967
  R ↓ Anxiety Disorders 1997
    ↓ Performance 1967

Performance Tests 1973
PN 888   SC 37530
SN Tests requiring nonverbal responses, for example, the manipulation of objects or the performance of motor skills.
  B   Measurement 1967
  R   Criterion Referenced Tests 1982

Performing Arts
  Use Arts

Periaqueductal Gray 1985
PN 381   SC 37550
SN Mesencephalic cells in the gray area surrounding the cerebral aqueduct important for visceral and limbic mechanisms.
  B   Tegmentum 1991

Perinatal Period 1994
PN 482   SC 37555
SN Usually the period just preceding or just following birth. Compare NEONATAL PERIOD. Used for both human and animal populations.
  R ↓ Birth 1967
      Postnatal Period 1973
    ↓ Pregnancy 1967
    ↓ Prenatal Development 1973

Peripheral Nerve Disorders 1973
PN 145   SC 37560
  B   Nervous System Disorders 1967
  N   Myasthenia Gravis 1973
    ↓ Neuralgia 1973
  R   Muscular Dystrophy 1973
    ↓ Paralysis 1973
    ↓ Peripheral Nervous System 1973

Peripheral Nervous System 1973
PN 432   SC 37570
SN Anatomical systems of structures outside the brain and spinal cord composed of neural tissue.
HN Use PERIPHERAL NERVES to access references from 1973-1993.
  UF Nerves (Peripheral)

Peripheral Nervous System — (cont'd)
  B   Nervous System 1967
  N ↓ Autonomic Nervous System 1967
    ↓ Cranial Nerves 1973
    ↓ Neural Pathways 1982
      Spinal Nerves 1973
  R   Autonomic Ganglia 1973
    ↓ Peripheral Nerve Disorders 1973

Peripheral Vision 1988
PN 419   SC 37580
  B   Visual Perception 1967
  R   Visual Field 1967

Permissiveness (Parental)
  Use Parental Permissiveness

Perpetrators 1988
PN 2767   SC 37595
  N ↓ Criminals 1967
  R   Bullying 2003
    ↓ Crime 1967
      Criminal Responsibility 1991
    ↓ Harassment 2001
      Incest 1973
      Stalking 2001
      Victimization 1973

Perphenazine 1973
PN 140   SC 37600
  B   Antiemetic Drugs 1973
      Phenothiazine Derivatives 1973

Persecution 1973
PN 158   SC 37610
  B   Antisocial Behavior 1971
      Interpersonal Interaction 1967
  R   Torture 1988
      Victimization 1973

Perseverance
  Use Persistence

Perseveration 1967
PN 299   SC 37630
SN Persistent repetition of a response to different and perhaps inappropriate stimuli which may be due to a refusal or an inability to interrupt one's behavior or to change from one task to another. Also, pathological repetition of thoughts, acts, or verbalizations.
  B   Thought Disturbances 1973

Persistence 1973
PN 1157   SC 37640
SN Maintenance of particular behavior despite effort, opposition, or cessation of initiating stimulus. Used for human or animal populations.
  UF Perseverance
  B   Personality Traits 1967
  R   Conscientiousness 1997
    ↓ Motivation 1967

Persistent Mental Illness
  Use Chronic Mental Illness

Person Centered Psychotherapy
  Use Client Centered Therapy

Person Environment Fit 1991
PN 685   SC 37645

Person Environment Fit — (cont'd)
SN Compatibility between individuals and their sur-
roundings.
　R　↓ Adjustment 1967
　　　↓ Environment 1967
　　　Environmental Adaptation 1973
　　　↓ Environmental Planning 1982
　　　↓ Personality 1967
　　　↓ Systems 1967
　　　↓ Working Conditions 1973

Personal Adjustment
　Use Emotional Adjustment

Personal Computers
　Use Microcomputers

Personal Construct Theory
　Use Personality Theory

Personal Defense
　Use Self Defense

Personal Growth Techniques
　Use Human Potential Movement

Personal Orientation Inventory 1973
PN 119　　　　　　　　　　SC 37670
　B　Nonprojective Personality Measures 1973

Personal Relationships
　Use Interpersonal Relationships

Personal Space 1973
PN 1170　　　　　　　　　SC 37680
SN Minimal spatial distance preferred by an individ-
ual in his/her relations with others.
　UF　Interpersonal Distance
　R　Boundaries (Psychological) 1997
　　　Crowding 1978
　　　Physical Contact 1982
　　　↓ Social Behavior 1967
　　　Social Density 1978

Personal Therapy 1991
PN 90　　　　　　　　　　SC 37685
SN Therapy for professionals working in the mental
health field, for example, psychologists, psychiatrists,
or social workers.
　B　Treatment 1967
　R　↓ Clinical Methods Training 1973
　　　Impaired Professionals 1985
　　　↓ Mental Health Personnel 1967
　　　↓ Professional Consultation 1973
　　　Professional Supervision 1988
　　　Psychoanalytic Training 1973
　　　Self Analysis 1994

Personal Values 1973
PN 2565　　　　　　　　　SC 37690
SN Set of ideals that an individual deems worth-
while and that influence his/her behavior.
　B　Values 1967
　R　Anomie 1978
　　　Morality 1967

Personality 1967
PN 11502　　　　　　　　SC 37870
SN Conceptually broad term referring to the totality
of an individual's behavioral or emotional characteristics. Use a more specific term if possible.

Personality — (cont'd)
　UF　Character
　　　Disposition
　　　Temperament
　N　Inadequate Personality 1973
　　　↓ Personality Traits 1967
　　　↓ Psychoanalytic Personality Factors 1973
　R　↓ Cognitive Style 1967
　　　Coronary Prone Behavior 1982
　　　Egocentrism 1978
　　　↓ Emotional Adjustment 1973
　　　↓ Emotional States 1973
　　　↓ Emotions 1967
　　　Five Factor Personality Model 1997
　　　↓ Gender Identity 1985
　　　Human Nature 1997
　　　Individual Differences 1967
　　　↓ Lifestyle 1978
　　　Person Environment Fit 1991
　　　Personality Change 1967
　　　Personality Correlates 1967
　　　↓ Personality Development 1967
　　　↓ Personality Disorders 1967
　　　↓ Personality Processes 1967
　　　↓ Personality Theory 1967
　　　Predisposition 1973
　　　Psychodynamics 1973
　　　Self Actualization 1973
　　　↓ Self Concept 1967
　　　Self Disclosure 1973
　　　Self Evaluation 1967
　　　Self Monitoring (Personality) 1985
　　　Self Perception 1967
　　　Somatotypes 1973
　　　Teacher Personality 1973

Personality Assessment
　Use Personality Measures

Personality Change 1967
PN 1433　　　　　　　　　SC 37720
SN Process or fact of change associated either with
development and maturity, or as the result of stress,
illness, treatment, or other factors.
　B　Personality Processes 1967
　R　Behavior Change 1973
　　　↓ Personality 1967
　　　↓ Personality Development 1967

Personality Correlates 1967
PN 4970　　　　　　　　　SC 37740
SN Description of numerous or unspecified person-
ality traits which bear a mutual or reciprocal relation-
ship to a particular phenomenon or behavior.
　R　Individual Differences 1967
　　　↓ Personality 1967

Personality Development 1967
PN 6042　　　　　　　　　SC 37750
　UF　Character Development
　　　Character Formation
　B　Psychosocial Development 1973
　N　↓ Ego Development 1991
　　　Separation Individuation 1982
　R　Ego Identity 1991
　　　Emotional Development 1973
　　　Externalization 1973
　　　Five Factor Personality Model 1997
　　　Identity Crisis 1973
　　　Identity Formation 2004
　　　↓ Internalization 1997
　　　Moral Development 1973
　　　↓ Personality 1967

Personality Development — (cont'd)
　　　Personality Change 1967
　　　↓ Personality Theory 1967

Personality Disorders 1967
PN 5168　　　　　　　　　SC 37760
HN In 1997, this term replaced the discontinued
term ASTHENIC PERSONALITY. In 2000,
ASTHENIC PERSONALITY was removed from all
records containing it, and replaced with PERSONAL-
ITY DISORDERS.
　UF　Asthenic Personality
　　　Character Disorders
　B　Mental Disorders 1967
　N　Antisocial Personality Disorder 1973
　　　Avoidant Personality Disorder 1994
　　　Borderline Personality Disorder 2001
　　　Dependent Personality Disorder 1994
　　　Histrionic Personality Disorder 1991
　　　Narcissistic Personality Disorder 1973
　　　Obsessive Compulsive Personality
　　　　Disorder 1973
　　　Paranoid Personality Disorder 1973
　　　Passive Aggressive Personality
　　　　Disorder 1973
　　　↓ Sadomasochistic Personality 1973
　　　Schizoid Personality Disorder 1973
　　　Schizotypal Personality Disorder 1991
　R　↓ Defense Mechanisms 1967
　　　↓ Dissociative Disorders 2001
　　　Explosive Disorder 2001
　　　Kleptomania 1973
　　　↓ Personality 1967
　　　↓ Personality Processes 1967
　　　↓ Personality Theory 1967
　　　Pyromania 1973

Personality Factors
　Use Personality Traits

Personality Factors (Psychoanalytic)
　Use Psychoanalytic Personality Factors

Personality Measures 1967
PN 9494　　　　　　　　　SC 37790
　UF　Personality Assessment
　　　Personality Tests
　　　Tests (Personality)
　B　Measurement 1967
　N　California Psychological Inventory 1967
　　　General Health Questionnaire 1991
　　　Kirton Adaption Innovation Inventory 2001
　　　NEO Personality Inventory 1997
　　　↓ Nonprojective Personality Measures 1973
　　　↓ Projective Personality Measures 1973
　　　Rokeach Dogmatism Scale 1973
　　　Sensation Seeking Scale 1973
　　　Sentence Completion Tests 1991

Personality Processes 1967
PN 1487　　　　　　　　　SC 37800
SN Conceptually broad term referring to the interac-
tion among personality structures (e.g., ego, id) or
pattern of characteristic tendencies, often but not
exclusively from a psychoanalytic perspective. Use a
more specific term if possible.
　N　Catharsis 1973
　　　Cathexis 1973
　　　↓ Defense Mechanisms 1967
　　　Externalization 1973
　　　Inhibition (Personality) 1973
　　　Insight 1973
　　　↓ Internalization 1997

Personality Processes — (cont'd)

Introspection 1973
Personality Change 1967
R   Boundaries (Psychological) 1997
↓ Lifestyle 1978
↓ Mental Disorders 1967
↓ Personality 1967
↓ Personality Disorders 1967
↓ Psychoanalytic Personality Factors 1973
↓ Psychoanalytic Theory 1967
Reality Testing 1973

Personality Tests

Use   Personality Measures

Personality Theory 1967

PN 3414   **SC** 37850
UF   Personal Construct Theory
N   Five Factor Personality Model 1997
R   Individual Differences 1967
↓ Personality 1967
↓ Personality Development 1967
↓ Personality Disorders 1967
Self Perception 1967
Self Psychology 1988

Personality Traits 1967

PN 24145   **SC** 37860
UF   Personality Factors
B   Personality 1967
N   Adaptability (Personality) 1973
Aggressiveness 1973
Agreeableness 1997
Altruism 1973
Androgyny 1982
Assertiveness 1973
Authoritarianism 1967
Charisma 1988
↓ Cognitive Style 1967
Conformity (Personality) 1967
Conscientiousness 1997
Conservatism 1973
Courage 1973
Creativity 1967
Cruelty 1973
Curiosity 1967
Cynicism 1973
Defensiveness 1967
Dependency (Personality) 1967
Dishonesty 1973
Dogmatism 1978
Egalitarianism 1985
Egotism 1973
Emotional Immaturity 1973
Emotional Inferiority 1973
Emotional Instability 1973
Emotional Maturity 1973
Emotional Security 1973
Emotional Stability 1973
Emotional Superiority 1973
Emotionality (Personality) 1973
Empathy 1967
Extraversion 1967
Femininity 1967
Gregariousness 1973
Honesty 1973
Hypnotic Susceptibility 1973
Independence (Personality) 1973
Individuality 1973
Initiative 1973
Integrity 1997
Internal External Locus of Control 1967
Introversion 1967
Irritability 1988

Personality Traits — (cont'd)

Liberalism 1973
Likability 1988
Loyalty 1973
Machiavellianism 1973
Masculinity 1967
Misanthropy 1973
Moodiness 1973
Narcissism 1967
Need for Approval 1997
Need for Cognition 1997
Negativism 1973
Nervousness 1973
Neuroticism 1973
Nonconformity (Personality) 1973
Nurturance 1985
Obedience 1973
Objectivity 1973
Omnipotence 1994
Openmindedness 1978
Openness to Experience 1997
Optimism 1973
Paranoia 1988
Passiveness 1973
Perceptiveness (Personality) 1973
Perfectionism 1988
Persistence 1973
Pessimism 1973
Positivism 1973
Psychoticism 1978
Rebelliousness 2003
Repression Sensitization 1973
Resilience (Psychological) 2003
Rigidity (Personality) 1967
↓ Risk Taking 1967
Self Control 1973
Selfishness 1973
Sensation Seeking 1978
Sensitivity (Personality) 1967
Seriousness 1973
Sexuality 1973
Sincerity 1973
Sociability 1973
Subjectivity 1994
Suggestibility 1967
Timidity 1973
↓ Tolerance 1973
R   Codependency 1991
Coronary Prone Behavior 1982
Egocentrism 1978
Five Factor Personality Model 1997
Instrumentality 1991
Leadership Qualities 1997

Personnel 1967

PN 4954   **SC** 37980
SN Conceptually broad term referring to the body of persons employed by a given organization or associated with a particular occupation. Use a more specific term if possible.
UF   Employees
      Workers
N ↓ Artists 1973
↓ Business and Industrial Personnel 1967
Disabled Personnel 1997
↓ Government Personnel 1973
↓ Hypnotists 1973
↓ Nonprofessional Personnel 1982
↓ Paraprofessional Personnel 1973
↓ Professional Personnel 1978
↓ Religious Personnel 1973
↓ Social Workers 1973
R   Affirmative Action 1985
Employability 1973
Employee Absenteeism 1973

Personnel — (cont'd)

↓ Employee Benefits 1973
↓ Employee Characteristics 1988
↓ Employee Interaction 1988
Employee Turnover 1973
Employer Attitudes 1973
Employment History 1978
↓ Human Resource Management 2003
Job Applicant Attitudes 1973
Job Applicants 1985
↓ Job Performance 1967
Labor Union Members 1973
Military Veterans 1973
↓ Occupations 1967
↓ Personnel Supply 1973
↓ Personnel Training 1967
Reemployment 1991
Retirement 1973
↓ Teams 1988
Unemployment 1967
Work (Attitudes Toward) 1973
↓ Working Conditions 1973
Working Women 1978

Personnel Development

Use   Personnel Training

Personnel Evaluation 1973

PN 2992   **SC** 37900
B   Evaluation 1967
Human Resource Management 2003
N   Occupational Success Prediction 1973
Teacher Effectiveness Evaluation 1978
R   Assessment Centers 1982
Employment Discrimination 1994
Job Applicant Interviews 1973
Job Applicant Screening 1973
↓ Job Performance 1967
Peer Evaluation 1982
Personnel Promotion 1978
↓ Personnel Selection 1967
Professional Competence 1997

Personnel Management

Use   Human Resource Management

Personnel Placement 1973

PN 358   **SC** 37920
UF   Placement (Personnel)
R   Assessment Centers 1982
Career Development 1985

Personnel Promotion 1978

PN 502   **SC** 37925
UF   Job Promotion
R   Assessment Centers 1982
Career Development 1985
Employment History 1978
↓ Job Performance 1967
Occupational Status 1978
Occupational Success 1978
↓ Personnel Evaluation 1973

Personnel Recruitment 1973

PN 607   **SC** 37930
UF   Employment Processes
      Recruitment (Personnel)
B   Human Resource Management 2003
N   Military Recruitment 1973
Teacher Recruitment 1973
R   Affirmative Action 1985
Job Applicant Interviews 1973

Personnel Recruitment — (cont'd)
   Job Applicant Screening 1973

Personnel Selection 1967
PN 3552   SC 37940
   UF   Employee Selection
        Hiring
        Selection (Personnel)
   B   Human Resource Management 2003
   N   Job Applicant Interviews 1973
        Job Applicant Screening 1973
   R   Affirmative Action 1985
        Assessment Centers 1982
        Employment Discrimination 1994
        ↓ Personnel Evaluation 1973
        ↓ Screening 1982

Personnel Supply 1973
PN 123   SC 37950
SN Availability of manpower or human resources
required for an occupation or service in order to meet
demands.
   UF   Manpower
   N   Medical Personnel Supply 1973
        Mental Health Personnel Supply 1973
   R   Human Capital 2003
        ↓ Personnel 1967

Personnel Termination 1973
PN 545   SC 37960
   UF   Employee Termination
   B   Human Resource Management 2003
   R   Downsizing 2003
        Employment History 1978
        Job Security 1978
        ↓ Occupational Tenure 1973
        Retirement 1973
        Unemployment 1967

Personnel Training 1967
PN 4347   SC 37970
   UF   Job Training
        Personnel Development
        Training (Personnel)
   B   Education 1967
   N   Apprenticeship 1973
        ↓ Inservice Training 1985
        Management Training 1973
        Military Training 1973
        On the Job Training 1973
   R   Business Education 1973
        Career Development 1985
        Human Relations Training 1978
        Job Enrichment 1973
        ↓ Personnel 1967
        Sensitivity Training 1973

Personnel Turnover
   Use Employee Turnover

Perspective Taking
   Use Role Taking

Perspiration
   Use Sweat

Persuasion Therapy 1973
PN 13   SC 38000
SN Limited directive therapy in which the client is
encouraged to follow the therapist's advice to deal
with current crises.

Persuasion Therapy — (cont'd)
   B   Psychotherapy 1967

Persuasive Communication 1967
PN 2937   SC 38010
SN Communication, in written or oral form, aimed at
influencing others to accept a position, belief, or
course of action.
   B   Communication 1967
   N   Brainwashing 1982
   R   Coercion 1994
        Debates 1997
        ↓ Interpersonal Influences 1967
        Peer Pressure 1994
        Propaganda 1973
        Public Service Announcements 2004
        Rhetoric 1991

Pervasive Developmental Disorders 2001
PN 183   SC 38016
SN Broad term for disorders, usually first diagnosed
in children prior to age 4, characterized by severe
and profound impairment in social interaction, com-
munication, and the presence of stereotyped behav-
iors, interests, and activities. Compare
DEVELOPMENTAL DISABILITIES.
   UF   Autism Spectrum Disorders
   B   Mental Disorders 1967
   N   Aspergers Syndrome 1991
        ↓ Autism 1967
        Rett Syndrome 1994
   R   Developmental Disabilities 1982
        Stereotyped Behavior 1973

Perversions (Sexual)
   Use Paraphilias

Pessimism 1973
PN 507   SC 38020
SN Attitude characterized by a gloomy and desper-
ate temperament and inclination to emphasize and
expect the worst possible outcome of events and
actions.
   B   Emotional States 1973
        Personality Traits 1967
   R   Cynicism 1973
        Fatalism 1973
        Hopelessness 1988
        Negativism 1973
        Nihilism 1973
        Optimism 1973
        Skepticism 2004

Pesticides
   Use Insecticides

Pet Therapy
   Use Animal Assisted Therapy

Petit Mal Epilepsy 1973
PN 44   SC 38030
   B   Epilepsy 1967

Pets 1982
PN 594   SC 38035
SN Domesticated animals kept primarily for plea-
sure rather than utility.
   R   Animal Assisted Therapy 1994
        Animal Domestication 1978
        ↓ Animals 1967
        Interspecies Interaction 1991

Peyote 1973
PN 7   SC 38050
   B   Alkaloids 1973
        Hallucinogenic Drugs 1967
        Psychotomimetic Drugs 1973
   R   Mescaline 1973

Phantom Limbs 1973
PN 191   SC 38060
   B   Body Image Disturbances 1973
   R   ↓ Amputation 1973

Pharmacists 1991
PN 171   SC 38065
   B   Medical Personnel 1967

Pharmacology 1973
PN 1868   SC 38070
SN The study of the chemistry, actions, and effects
of drugs on living organisms or tissues. Used for
intended effects of drugs; for adverse or undesired
effects of drugs, use SIDE EFFECTS (DRUG). For
the use of drugs in a treatment capacity, use DRUG
THERAPY.
   B   Paramedical Sciences 1973
   N   Psychopharmacology 1967
   R   Bioavailability 1991
        Drug Abuse Liability 1994

Pharmacotherapy
   Use Drug Therapy

Pharyngeal Disorders 1973
PN 32   SC 38090
   B   Respiratory Tract Disorders 1973
   R   Dysphagia 2003

Pharynx 1973
PN 47   SC 38100
   B   Digestive System 1967
        Respiratory System 1973

Phenaglycodol
   Use Sedatives

Phencyclidine 1982
PN 790   SC 38125
SN Piperadine having hallucinogenic, anesthetic,
and analgesic properties.
   UF   PCP
   B   Analgesic Drugs 1973
        Anesthetic Drugs 1973
        Hallucinogenic Drugs 1967

Phenelzine 1973
PN 308   SC 38130
   B   Antidepressant Drugs 1971
        Monoamine Oxidase Inhibitors 1973

Phenethylamines 1985
PN 126   SC 38135
   UF   Phenylethylamines
   B   Amines 1973
   R   ↓ Amphetamine 1967

Pheniprazine 1973
PN 6   SC 38140
   B   Antidepressant Drugs 1971
        Antihypertensive Drugs 1973
        Monoamine Oxidase Inhibitors 1973

Phenmetrazine 1973
PN 14   SC 38150
  B   Appetite Depressing Drugs 1973
       Sympathomimetic Amines 1973

Phenobarbital 1973
PN 346   SC 38160
  B   Anticonvulsive Drugs 1973
       Barbiturates 1967
       Hypnotic Drugs 1973
       Sedatives 1973

Phenomenology 1967
PN 2687   SC 38180
  B   Philosophies 1967
  R   Constructivism 1994
       Hermeneutics 1991
       ↓ History of Psychology 1967

Phenothiazine Derivatives 1973
PN 224   SC 38190
  HN   In 1997, this term replaced the discontinued
  terms BUTYRYLPERAZINE and TRIFLUPRO-
  MAZINE. In 2000, these terms were removed from all
  records containing them, and replaced with PHE-
  NOTHIAZINE DERIVATIVES.
  UF   Butyrylperazine
       Triflupromazine
  B   Tranquilizing Drugs 1967
  N   Chlorpromazine 1967
       Chlorprothixene 1973
       Fluphenazine 1973
       Mesoridazine 1973
       Perphenazine 1973
       Prochlorperazine 1973
       Promazine 1973
       Thioridazine 1973
       Trifluoperazine 1973
  R   ↓ Cholinergic Blocking Drugs 1973

Phenotypes 1973
PN 1033   SC 38200
  R   Assortative Mating 1991
       ↓ Genetics 1967
       Genotypes 1973
       Polymorphism 2003

Phenoxybenzamine 1973
PN 73   SC 38210
  B   Adrenergic Blocking Drugs 1973
       Amines 1973
       Antihypertensive Drugs 1973

Phenylalanine 1973
PN 195   SC 38220
  B   Alanines 1973
  N   Parachlorophenylalanine 1978

Phenylethylamines
  Use Phenethylamines

Phenylketonuria 1973
PN 227   SC 38230
  UF   Oligophrenia (Phenylpyruvic)
       PKU (Hereditary Disorder)
  B   Genetic Disorders 1973
       Metabolism Disorders 1973
       Neonatal Disorders 1973
  R   ↓ Mental Retardation 1967

Phenytoin
  Use Diphenylhydantoin

Pheromones 1973
PN 913   SC 38240
  SN   Chemical substances released by an organism
  that may influence the behavior of other organisms of
  the same species in characteristic ways.
  R   ↓ Animal Mating Behavior 1967
       Animal Scent Marking 1985
       ↓ Glands 1967
       ↓ Hormones 1967

Phi Coefficient 1973
PN 25   SC 38250
  B   Statistical Correlation 1967

Philosophies 1967
PN 6153   SC 38270
  B   Humanities 2003
  N   Animism 1973
       Asceticism 1973
       Determinism 1997
       Dualism 1973
       Epistemology 1973
       Existentialism 1967
       Fatalism 1973
       Hermeneutics 1991
       Humanism 1973
       Idealism 1973
       Intellectualism 1973
       Logic (Philosophy) 1973
       Materialism 1973
       Metaphysics 1973
       Mysticism 1967
       Nihilism 1973
       Pacifism 1973
       Phenomenology 1967
       Positivism (Philosophy) 1997
       Postmodernism 1997
       Pragmatism 1973
       Realism (Philosophy) 1973
       Reductionism 1973
       Relativism 1997
  R   Hedonism 1973

Philosophy of Life
  Use World View

Phobias 1967
PN 2995   SC 38280
  SN   Disorders characterized by persistent, unrealis-
  tic, intense fear of an object, activity, or situation.
  HN   In 1988, this term replaced the discontinued
  term PHOBIC NEUROSIS. In 2000, PHOBIC NEU-
  ROSIS was removed from all records containing it,
  and replaced with PHOBIAS.
  UF   Arachnophobia
       Phobic Neurosis
       Spider Phobia
  B   Anxiety Disorders 1997
  N   Acrophobia 1973
       Agoraphobia 1973
       Claustrophobia 1973
       Ophidiophobia 1973
       School Phobia 1973
       Social Phobia 1985
  R   ↓ Anxiety 1967
       ↓ Fear 1967

Phobic Neurosis
  Use Phobias

Phonemes 1973
PN 1514   SC 38300
  SN   Members of the set of the smallest units of
  speech that serve to distinguish one utterance from
  another, such as the p of pat and the f of fat. Used
  both for the concept of phonemes as well as the dis-
  cipline of phonemics. Compare PHONOLOGY.
  B   Phonology 1973
  N   Consonants 1973
  R   Phonetics 1967
       Phonological Awareness 2004
       ↓ Prosody 1991
       Vowels 1973

Phonemic Awareness
  Use Phonological Awareness

Phonetics 1967
PN 1405   SC 38310
  SN   Science, study, analysis, and classification of
  sounds including their production in speech, transmission and perception. Used for the linguistic discipline or the specific phonetic characteristics of
  utterances themselves.
  B   Phonology 1973
  R   Articulation (Speech) 1967
       Morphemes 1973
       ↓ Phonemes 1973
       Syllables 1973

Phonics 1973
PN 251   SC 38320
  SN   Science of sound. Also, a method of teaching
  beginners to read and pronounce words by hearing
  the phonetic value of letters, letter groups, and espe-
  cially syllables.
  B   Language Arts Education 1973
  R   Initial Teaching Alphabet 1973
       Reading Education 1973

Phonological Awareness 2004
PN 255   SC 38327
  SN   Ability to recognize various speech sounds
  including, syllables, rhymes, and phonemes.
  HN   This term was introduced in June 2004. Psyc-
  INFO records from the past 10 years were re-indexed
  with this term. The posting note reflects the number
  of records that were re-indexed.
  UF   Phonemic Awareness
  B   Awareness 1967
  R   ↓ Literacy 1973
       ↓ Phonemes 1973
       ↓ Phonology 1973
       Reading Development 1997
       Reading Readiness 1973
       Rhyme 2004
       Word Recognition 1988

Phonology 1973
PN 3939   SC 38330
  SN   Study of the ways in which speech sounds (phonemes) and phonetic features form systems and patterns at a given point in time or from a historical
  perspective. Used for the linguistic discipline or the
  specific phonological processes or factors themselves. Compare PHONEMES.
  B   Grammar 1967
  N   ↓ Phonemes 1973
       Phonetics 1973
       ↓ Prosody 1991
       Syllables 1973
       Vowels 1973
  R   Inflection 1973

Phonology — (cont'd)

    Morphology (Language) 1973
    Phonological Awareness 2004
    Rhyme 2004
  ↓ Semantics 1967
  ↓ Syntax 1971

Phosphatases 1973

PN 161   **SC** 38340
  B   Enzymes 1973
  R ↓ Esterases 1973
       Hydroxylases 1973

Phosphatides 1973

PN 303   **SC** 38350
  UF   Phospholipids
  B   Fatty Acids 1973
  N   Lecithin 1991

Phospholipids

  Use Phosphatides

Phosphorus 1973

PN 89   **SC** 38370

Phosphorylases 1973

PN 55   **SC** 38380
  B   Enzymes 1973

Photic Threshold

  Use Illumination AND Visual Thresholds

Photographic Art 1973

PN 63   **SC** 38400
  B   Art 1967
  R   Motion Pictures (Entertainment) 1973

Photographic Memory

  Use Eidetic Imagery

Photographs 1967

PN 951   **SC** 38410
SN Use for photographs as stimuli.
  B   Audiovisual Communications Media 1973
  R   Pictorial Stimuli 1978

Photopic Stimulation 1973

PN 274   **SC** 38420
SN Presentation of light at intensity levels characteristic of daylight illumination, activating cone photoreceptors in the retina.
  B   Illumination 1967
  R   Scotopic Stimulation 1973

Photoreceptors 1973

PN 440   **SC** 38430
  B   Neural Receptors 1973
       Sensory Neurons 1973
  N   Cones (Eye) 1973
       Rods (Eye) 1973
  R   Visual Receptive Fields 1982

Phototherapy 1991

PN 416   **SC** 38435
  UF   Bright Light Therapy
       Illumination Therapy
       Light Therapy
  B   Physical Treatment Methods 1973

Phototherapy — (cont'd)

  R ↓ Alternative Medicine 1997
    ↓ Psychotherapy 1967
      Seasonal Affective Disorder 1991

Phrases 1973

PN 335   **SC** 38440
SN Groups of words that function as an element in grammatical structure.
  B   Language 1967
  R ↓ Syntax 1971

Phrenic Nerve

  Use Spinal Nerves

Phylogenesis 1973

PN 282   **SC** 38460
  R ↓ Biology 1967
      Botany 1973

Physical Abuse 1991

PN 2558   **SC** 38465
  B   Antisocial Behavior 1971
       Violent Crime 2003
  R ↓ Abuse Reporting 1997
      Battered Child Syndrome 1973
      Battered Females 1988
      Bullying 2003
    ↓ Child Abuse 1971
      Elder Abuse 1988
      Emotional Abuse 1991
      Family Violence 1982
      Partner Abuse 1991
      Patient Abuse 1991
    ↓ Sexual Abuse 1988
      Verbal Abuse 2003
    ↓ Violence 1973

Physical Activity

  Use Motor Processes

Physical Agility 1970

PN 117   **SC** 38470
  UF   Agility (Physical)
  B   Motor Processes 1967
  N   Physical Dexterity 1973
  R   Motor Coordination 1973
       Physical Mobility 1994

Physical Appearance 1982

PN 895   **SC** 38473
SN Externally visible characteristics or features of a person.
  N   Physique 1967
  R   Clothing 1967
       Cosmetic Techniques 2001
       Facial Features 1973
       Mimicry (Biology) 2003
       Nudity 1973
       Physical Attractiveness 1973
       Somatotypes 1973

Physical Attractiveness 1973

PN 1865   **SC** 38475
  R   Facial Features 1973
    ↓ Interpersonal Attraction 1967
    ↓ Physical Appearance 1982
      Sexual Attraction 2003

Physical Comfort 1982

PN 249   **SC** 38477

Physical Comfort — (cont'd)

SN Perceived degree of physical well-being in response to internal or environmental conditions.
  UF   Comfort (Physical)
  R ↓ Environment 1967
      Furniture 1985
    ↓ Satisfaction 1973

Physical Contact 1982

PN 1016   **SC** 38478
SN Bodily contact. Used for human or animal populations.
  UF   Touching
  B   Social Interaction 1967
  R   Affection 1973
    ↓ Animal Social Behavior 1967
      Intimacy 1973
      Massage 2001
      Personal Space 1973
    ↓ Tactual Perception 1967

Physical Development 1973

PN 2014   **SC** 38480
  UF   Physical Growth
  B   Development 1967
  N ↓ Motor Development 1973
      Neural Development 1985
    ↓ Prenatal Development 1973
      Sexual Development 1973
  R   Adolescent Development 1973
      Age Differences 1967
      Aging (Attitudes Toward) 1985
      Animal Development 1978
    ↓ Childhood Development 1967
    ↓ Delayed Development 1973
      Developmental Age Groups 1973
    ↓ Developmental Stages 1973
    ↓ Early Childhood Development 1970
      Emotional Development 1973
    ↓ Human Development 1967
    ↓ Infant Development 1973
      Neonatal Development 1973
    ↓ Perceptual Development 1973
      Physical Maturity 1973
      Precocious Development 1973
    ↓ Psychogenesis 1973
      Sex Linked Developmental Differences 1973

Physical Dexterity 1973

PN 202   **SC** 38490
  UF   Dexterity (Physical)
  B   Perceptual Motor Coordination 1973
       Physical Agility 1973
  R   Physical Mobility 1994

Physical Disabilities (Attitudes Toward) 2001

PN 686   **SC** 38485
HN In 2000, the truncated terms PHYSICAL DISABILITIES (ATTIT TOWARD) (which was used from 1997-2000) and PHYSICAL HANDICAPS (ATTIT TOWARD) (which was used from 1973-1996) were deleted, removed from all records containing them, and replaced with the expanded form PHYSICAL DISABILITIES (ATTITUDES TOWARD).
  UF   Physical Handicaps (Attitudes Toward)
  B   Disabled (Attitudes Toward) 1997

Physical Disfigurement 1978

PN 250   **SC** 38492
  UF   Deformity
  R ↓ Injuries 1973
    ↓ Physical Disorders 1997

Physical Disorders [1997]
PN 4785   SC 38493
HN Consider DISORDERS to access references prior to 1997. The term PHYSICALLY HANDICAPPED was also used to represent this concept from 1967-1996, and PHYSICALLY DISABLED was used from 1997-2000. In 2000, PHYSICAL DISORDERS replaced the discontinued and deleted term PHYSICALLY DISABLED. PHYSICALLY DISABLED and PHYSICALLY HANDICAPPED were removed from all records containing them and replaced with PHYSICAL DISORDERS.
　UF　Illness (Physical)
　　　Orthopedically Handicapped
　　　Physical Illness
　　　Physically Handicapped
　B　Disorders [1967]
　N　↓ Blood and Lymphatic Disorders [1973]
　　　↓ Cardiovascular Disorders [1967]
　　　↓ Digestive System Disorders [1973]
　　　↓ Endocrine Disorders [1973]
　　　↓ Genetic Disorders [1973]
　　　Health Impairments [2001]
　　　↓ Immunologic Disorders [1973]
　　　↓ Infectious Disorders [1973]
　　　↓ Metabolism Disorders [1973]
　　　↓ Musculoskeletal Disorders [1973]
　　　↓ Neonatal Disorders [1973]
　　　↓ Neoplasms [1967]
　　　↓ Nervous System Disorders [1967]
　　　↓ Nutritional Deficiencies [1973]
　　　↓ Respiratory Tract Disorders [1973]
　　　↓ Sense Organ Disorders [1973]
　　　↓ Sensory System Disorders [2001]
　　　↓ Skin Disorders [1973]
　　　↓ Toxic Disorders [1973]
　　　↓ Urogenital Disorders [1973]
　　　↓ Vision Disorders [1982]
　R　Anesthesia (Feeling) [1973]
　　　Back Pain [1982]
　　　↓ Chronic Illness [1991]
　　　Chronicity (Disorders) [1982]
　　　↓ Communication Disorders [1982]
　　　Comorbidity [1991]
　　　↓ Congenital Disorders [1973]
　　　↓ Diagnosis [1967]
　　　Disease Course [1991]
　　　↓ Eating Disorders [1997]
　　　Etiology [1967]
　　　Illness Behavior [1982]
　　　↓ Injuries [1973]
　　　↓ Learning Disorders [1967]
　　　Malingering [1973]
　　　↓ Memory Disorders [1973]
　　　↓ Mental Disorders [1967]
　　　Onset (Disorders) [1973]
　　　↓ Pain [1967]
　　　Physical Disfigurement [1978]
　　　Predisposition [1973]
　　　Premorbidity [1978]
　　　Prenatal Exposure [1991]
　　　Prognosis [1973]
　　　Recovery (Disorders) [1973]
　　　Relapse (Disorders) [1973]
　　　↓ Remission (Disorders) [1973]
　　　Rett Syndrome [1994]
　　　Severity (Disorders) [1982]
　　　↓ Sexual Function Disturbances [1973]
　　　↓ Sleep Disorders [1973]
　　　Special Needs [1994]
　　　Susceptibility (Disorders) [1973]
　　　↓ Symptoms [1967]
　　　↓ Syndromes [1973]
　　　↓ Treatment Resistant Disorders [1994]
　　　Work Related Illnesses [1994]

Physical Divisions (Geographic)
　Use　Geography

Physical Education [1967]
PN 1675   SC 38500
　B　Curriculum [1967]

Physical Endurance [1973]
PN 289   SC 38510
　B　Endurance [1973]
　R　Physical Fitness [1973]
　　　Physical Strength [1973]
　　　Physiological Stress [1967]

Physical Examination [1988]
PN 485   SC 38515
SN Examination or screening of an individual's overall physical health.
　B　Health Screening [1997]
　R　Cancer Screening [1997]
　　　Drug Usage Screening [1988]
　　　Mammography [1994]
　　　↓ Medical Diagnosis [1973]
　　　Preventive Medicine [1973]
　　　Self Examination (Medical) [1988]

Physical Exercise
　Use　Exercise

Physical Fitness [1973]
PN 1523   SC 38530
　R　Aerobic Exercise [1988]
　　　↓ Exercise [1973]
　　　Physical Endurance [1973]
　　　Physical Strength [1973]

Physical Geography
　Use　Geography

Physical Growth
　Use　Physical Development

Physical Handicaps (Attitudes Toward)
　Use　Physical Disabilities (Attitudes Toward)

Physical Illness
　Use　Physical Disorders

Physical Illness (Attitudes Toward) [1985]
PN 1719   SC 38557
SN Attitudes toward one's own or other's physical illness.
　B　Attitudes [1967]
　N　AIDS (Attitudes Toward) [1997]
　R　Disability Discrimination [1997]
　　　↓ Disabled (Attitudes Toward) [1997]
　　　Health Attitudes [1985]
　　　Health Knowledge [1994]
　　　Illness Behavior [1982]

Physical Maturity [1973]
PN 108   SC 38560
SN Attainment of a stage of physical development commonly associated with persons of a given age level.
　UF　Maturity (Physical)
　R　↓ Physical Development [1973]

Physical Mobility [1994]
PN 384   SC 38563
SN Ability to move within one's environment. May be used for mobility problems associated with aging or handicapping conditions. Used for human populations only.
　B　Motor Processes [1967]
　R　Activities of Daily Living [1991]
　　　Activity Level [1982]
　　　Mobility Aids [1978]
　　　↓ Motor Development [1973]
　　　↓ Physical Agility [1973]
　　　Physical Dexterity [1973]

Physical Restraint [1982]
PN 1113   SC 38566
SN Use of any physical means to restrict the movement of a client or subject, human or animal.
　UF　Restraint (Physical)
　R　↓ Motor Processes [1967]
　　　Patient Violence [1994]
　　　↓ Physical Treatment Methods [1973]
　　　↓ Treatment [1967]

Physical Strength [1973]
PN 510   SC 38570
　UF　Strength (Physical)
　R　Physical Endurance [1973]
　　　Physical Fitness [1973]

Physical Therapists [1973]
PN 136   SC 38580
　B　Medical Personnel [1967]
　　　Therapists [1967]

Physical Therapy [1973]
PN 617   SC 38590
SN Treatment of disorder or injury by physical means, such as light, heat, cold, water, electricity, or by mechanical apparatus or kinesitherapy.
　UF　Physiotherapy
　B　Paramedical Sciences [1973]
　　　Rehabilitation [1967]
　R　Massage [2001]
　　　Occupational Therapy [1967]

Physical Trauma
　Use　Injuries

Physical Treatment Methods [1973]
PN 919   SC 38610
HN In 2000, this term became the postable counterpart for the discontinued term ORGANIC THERAPIES. ORGANIC THERAPIES was removed from all records containing it and replaced with PHYSICAL TREATMENT METHODS.
　UF　Organic Therapies
　　　Treatment Methods (Physical)
　B　Treatment [1967]
　N　Acupuncture [1973]
　　　Artificial Respiration [1973]
　　　Blood Transfusion [1973]
　　　Catheterization [1973]
　　　↓ Dental Treatment [1973]
　　　↓ Dialysis [1973]
　　　↓ Drug Therapy [1967]
　　　Electrosleep Treatment [1978]
　　　Immunization [1973]
　　　↓ Narcoanalysis [1973]
　　　Phototherapy [1991]
　　　↓ Psychosurgery [1973]
　　　Radiation Therapy [1973]
　　　↓ Shock Therapy [1973]

Physical Treatment Methods — (cont'd)
  ↓ Surgery   1971
    Transcranial Magnetic Stimulation   2003
  R ↓ Alternative Medicine   1997
    Holistic Health   1985
    Massage   2001
    Medical Treatment (General)   1973
    Osteopathic Medicine   2003
    Pain Management   1994
    Physical Restraint   1982

Physically Handicapped
  Use   Physical Disorders

Physician Patient Interaction
  Use   Therapeutic Processes

Physicians   1967
PN 6454   **SC** 38640
  UF   Doctors
  B   Medical Personnel   1967
  N   Family Physicians   1973
    General Practitioners   1973
    Gynecologists   1973
    Internists   1973
    Neurologists   1973
    Obstetricians   1978
    Pathologists   1973
    Pediatricians   1973
    Psychiatrists   1967
    Surgeons   1973
  R   Clinicians   1973

Physicists   1973
PN 34   **SC** 38650
  B   Professional Personnel   1978
  R ↓ Aerospace Personnel   1973
    Mathematicians   1973
    Scientists   1967

Physics   1973
PN 938   **SC** 38660
  B   Sciences   1967
  R   Magnetism   1985
    Relativism   1997

Physiological Aging   1967
PN 3858   **SC** 38670
  SN   Biological changes which occur in an organism with the passage of time.
  UF   Aging (Physiological)
  B   Aging   1991
  R   Adult Development   1978
    ↓ Aged (Attitudes Toward)   1978
    Aging (Attitudes Toward)   1985
    Geriatric Psychotherapy   1973
    Geriatrics   1967
    Life Expectancy   1982
    ↓ Physiology   1967
    ↓ Senile Dementia   1973

Physiological Arousal   1967
PN 4286   **SC** 38680
  SN   Condition of alertness and readiness to respond as evidenced by physiological signs such as heart rate or blood pressure.
  UF   Arousal (Physiological)
    Excitation (Physiological)
  R ↓ Brain Stimulation   1967
    Cardiovascular Reactivity   1994
    ↓ Consciousness States   1971
    Physiological Stress   1967

Physiological Arousal — (cont'd)
  ↓ Physiology   1967
  ↓ Sexual Arousal   1978

Physiological Correlates   1967
PN 8242   **SC** 38690
  SN   Numerous or unspecified physiological processes which accompany a particular psychological or physical action, state, or characteristic.
  R   Biological Markers   1991
    Cardiovascular Reactivity   1994
    Physiological Stress   1967
    ↓ Physiology   1967
    ↓ Symptoms   1967

Physiological Psychology   1967
PN 519   **SC** 38700
  SN   Branch of psychology concerned with the physiological correlates of cognitive, emotional, and behavioral processes. Use PHYSIOLOGY, PSYCHOPHYSIOLOGY, or a more specific term for the specific physiological processes themselves.
  B   Psychology   1967
  N   Neuropsychology   1973
  R ↓ Psychophysiology   1967

Physiological Stress   1967
PN 2202   **SC** 38710
  B   Stress   1967
  R   Acceleration Effects   1973
    Decompression Effects   1973
    ↓ Deprivation   1967
    ↓ Environmental Effects   1973
    Environmental Stress   1973
    Physical Endurance   1973
    Physiological Arousal   1967
    Physiological Correlates   1967
    ↓ Physiology   1967
    Pollution   1973
    Thermal Acclimatization   1973

Physiology   1967
PN 2353   **SC** 38720
  SN   Conceptually broad term referring both to a branch of biological science and the functions and processes of living organisms. Use a more specific term if possible.
  N   Absorption (Physiological)   1973
    ↓ Appetite   1973
    ↓ Body Temperature   1973
    Digestion   1973
    ↓ Electrophysiology   1973
    ↓ Excretion   1967
    Homeostasis   1973
    ↓ Ingestion   2001
    ↓ Metabolism   1967
    ↓ Neurophysiology   1973
    Oxygenation   1973
    ↓ Psychophysiology   1967
    ↓ Reflexes   1971
    ↓ Secretion (Gland)   1973
    ↓ Sexual Reproduction   1973
    Thermal Acclimatization   1973
  R ↓ Anatomy   1967
    ↓ Biochemistry   1967
    ↓ Body Fluids   1973
    ↓ Cells (Biology)   1973
    Histology   1973
    Instinctive Behavior   1982
    Metabolic Rates   1973
    Morphology   1973
    Nutrition   1973
    Physiological Aging   1967

Physiology — (cont'd)
  Physiological Arousal   1967
  Physiological Correlates   1967
  Physiological Stress   1967

Physiotherapy
  Use   Physical Therapy

Physique   1967
PN 659   **SC** 38740
  SN   Overall body structure and appearance, including size, musculature, and posture. Limited primarily to human populations. Consider also BODY SIZE or SOMATOTYPES.
  B   Physical Appearance   1982
  R   Body Height   1973
    ↓ Body Size   1985
    ↓ Body Weight   1967
    Human Body   2003
    Posture   1973
    Somatotypes   1973

Physostigmine   1973
PN 568   **SC** 38750
  UF   Eserine
  B   Alkaloids   1973
    Amines   1973
    Cholinergic Drugs   1973
    Cholinesterase Inhibitors   1973
    Cholinomimetic Drugs   1973

Piaget (Jean)   1967
PN 1354   **SC** 38755
  SN   Identifies biographical or autobiographical studies and discussions of Piaget's works.
  R ↓ Cognitive Development   1070
    Conservation (Concept)   1973
    Constructivism   1994
    ↓ Developmental Stages   1973
    Piagetian Tasks   1973
    ↓ Psychologists   1967

Piagetian Tasks   1973
PN 831   **SC** 38757
  SN   In measurement context, tasks used to assess children's cognitive abilities, based on Piaget's theory of cognitive development.
  R ↓ Measurement   1967
    Piaget (Jean)   1967

Piano
  Use   Musical Instruments

Pica   1973
PN 139   **SC** 38770
  B   Eating Disorders   1997
  R ↓ Adjunctive Behavior   1982
    Coprophagia   2001
    ↓ Ingestion   2001
    Lead Poisoning   1973
    Toxicomania   1973

Picketing
  Use   Social Demonstrations

Picks Disease   1973
PN 153   **SC** 38790
  B   Presenile Dementia   1973
  R   Alzheimers Disease   1973
    ↓ Dementia   1985
    ↓ Genetic Disorders   1973

Picrotoxin 1973
PN 237 SC 38800
B Analeptic Drugs 1973
Gamma Aminobutyric Acid Antagonists 1985

Pictorial Stimuli 1978
PN 4093 SC 38805
SN Drawings, pictures, or other visual stimuli not composed of letters or digits.
R Photographs 1967
↓ Stimulus Presentation Methods 1973
↓ Visual Displays 1973
↓ Visual Stimulation 1973

Piercings
Use Cosmetic Techniques

Pigeons 1967
PN 5203 SC 38810
B Birds 1967

Pigments 1973
PN 275 SC 38820
N Hemoglobin 1973
Melanin 1973
Rhodopsin 1985
R Animal Coloration 1985
↓ Color 1967
Eye Color 1991

Pigs 1973
PN 764 SC 38830
B Vertebrates 1973

Pilocarpine 1973
PN 165 SC 38840
B Alkaloids 1973
Cholinergic Drugs 1973
Cholinomimetic Drugs 1973

Pilots (Aircraft)
Use Aircraft Pilots

Pimozide 1973
PN 459 SC 38860
B Tranquilizing Drugs 1967

Pineal Body 1973
PN 254 SC 38870
B Endocrine Glands 1973
R Melatonin 1973

Pinealectomy 1973
PN 82 SC 38880
B Endocrine Gland Surgery 1973

Piperazines 1994
PN 148 SC 38885
UF Chlorophenylpiperazine
MCPP
N Trazodone 1988

Pipradrol 1973
PN 14 SC 38890
B Antidepressant Drugs 1971
CNS Stimulating Drugs 1973

Piracetam 1982
PN 169 SC 38900

Piracetam — (cont'd)
B Antiemetic Drugs 1973
CNS Stimulating Drugs 1973
Nootropic Drugs 1991

Pitch (Frequency) 1967
PN 2634 SC 38910
SN Perceived changes in auditory stimuli that are a function of the sound's frequency usually measured in hertz. Also, in linguistics, a phonetic element marking the fundamental frequency of a component of speech.
UF Frequency (Pitch)
Tone (Frequency)
B Auditory Stimulation 1967
N Speech Pitch 1973
Ultrasound 1973

Pitch Discrimination 1973
PN 645 SC 38920
B Pitch Perception 1973

Pitch Perception 1973
PN 556 SC 38930
B Auditory Perception 1967
N Pitch Discrimination 1973
R Music Perception 1997

Pituitary Disorders 1973
PN 55 SC 38940
UF Hypophysis Disorders
B Endocrine Disorders 1973
N Hypopituitarism 1973
R ↓ Adrenal Gland Disorders 1973
↓ Endocrine Sexual Disorders 1973
↓ Thyroid Disorders 1973

Pituitary Dwarfism
Use Hypopituitarism

Pituitary Gland 1973
PN 393 SC 38960
B Endocrine Glands 1973
N Hypothalamo Hypophyseal System 1973
Hypothalamo Pituitary Adrenal System 1997

Pituitary Gland Surgery
Use Hypophysectomy

Pituitary Hormones 1973
PN 284 SC 38980
B Hormones 1967
N Corticotropin 1973
Dynorphins 1985
Melanocyte Stimulating Hormone 1985
Oxytocin 1973
Somatotropin 1973
Thyrotropin 1973
Vasopressin 1973
R ↓ Gonadotropic Hormones 1973
Hypothalamo Hypophyseal System 1973
Luteinizing Hormone 1978

PKU (Hereditary Disorder)
Use Phenylketonuria

Place Conditioning 1991
PN 723 SC 39005
SN Learned behavior or the conditioning procedure in which a stimulus is paired with an environment, location, or physical position.

Place Conditioning — (cont'd)
UF Conditioned Place Preference
B Conditioning 1967
R ↓ Animal Environments 1967
Contextual Associations 1967

Place Disorientation 1973
PN 71 SC 39010
SN Impaired awareness of place, often characteristic of organic mental disorders.
UF Disorientation (Place)
B Consciousness Disturbances 1973
R Wandering Behavior 1991

Placebo 1973
PN 1231 SC 39020
SN Any effect of therapeutic intervention that cannot be attributed to the specific action of a drug or the treatment. Also, the specific substance used as a control in experiments testing the effect of a particular drug. Term is used selectively for studies of the placebo effect or other methodological issues.
R ↓ Drugs 1967

Placement (Educational)
Use Educational Placement

Placement (Personnel)
Use Personnel Placement

Placenta 1973
PN 77 SC 39040
R ↓ Pregnancy 1967
↓ Uterus 1973

Planarians 1973
PN 33 SC 39060
B Worms 1967

Planned Behavior 1997
PN 559 SC 39065
SN Based on I. Ajzen's theory that behavioral intentions are determined by one's perceived control over the behavior, attitude toward the behavior, and subjective norms.
R ↓ Attitudes 1967
↓ Behavior 1967
Intention 1988
↓ Motivation 1967

Planning (Management)
Use Management Planning

Plasma (Blood)
Use Blood Plasma

Plastic Surgery 1973
PN 173 SC 39090
B Surgery 1971
R Cosmetic Techniques 2001

Platelets (Blood)
Use Blood Platelets

Play
Use Recreation

Play (Animal)
  Use Animal Play

Play Behavior (Childhood)
  Use Childhood Play Behavior

Play Development (Childhood)
  Use Childhood Play Development

Play Therapy 1973
PN 1330   SC 39150
  B   Child Psychotherapy 1967

Playgrounds 1973
PN 154   SC 39160
  B   Recreation Areas 1973
  R ↓ School Facilities 1973

Pleasure 1973
PN 939   SC 39170
  UF   Enjoyment
  B   Emotional States 1973
  R   Anhedonia 1985
       Euphoria 1973
       Happiness 1973

Plethysmography 1973
PN 76   SC 39180
  B   Medical Diagnosis 1973
  N   Electroplethysmography 1973

PMS
  Use Premenstrual Syndrome

Pneumoencephalography 1973
PN 29   SC 39190
  UF   Air Encephalography
       Encephalography (Air)
  B   Encephalography 1973
       Medical Diagnosis 1973
       Roentgenography 1973

Pneumonia 1973
PN 79   SC 39200
  B   Lung Disorders 1973
  R ↓ Bacterial Disorders 1973
     ↓ Viral Disorders 1973

Poetry 1973
PN 1064   SC 39210
  B   Literature 1967
  R   Creative Writing 1994
       Rhyme 2004

Poetry Therapy 1994
PN 48   SC 39215
  B   Creative Arts Therapy 1994
  R   Bibliotherapy 1973
     ↓ Psychotherapeutic Techniques 1967

Point Biserial Correlation 1973
PN 21   SC 39220
  B   Statistical Correlation 1967

Poisoning
  Use Toxic Disorders

Poisons 1973
PN 526   SC 39240
  UF   Toxins
  B   Hazardous Materials 1991
  N ↓ Neurotoxins 1982
  R   Carbon Monoxide 1973
     ↓ Insecticides 1973
       Prenatal Exposure 1991
       Teratogens 1988

Poisson Distribution
  Use Skewed Distribution

Police Interrogation
  Use Legal Interrogation

Police Personnel 1973
PN 2779   SC 39270
  B   Government Personnel 1973
       Law Enforcement Personnel 1973

Policy Making 1988
PN 2628   SC 39278
  UF   Organizational Policy Making
  N ↓ Government Policy Making 1973
       Health Care Policy 1994
  R   Educational Reform 1997

Policy Making (Foreign)
  Use Foreign Policy Making

Policy Making (Government)
  Use Government Policy Making

Poliomyelitis 1973
PN 68   SC 39300
  UF   Infantile Paralysis
       Paralysis (Infantile)
  B   Myelitis 1973
       Viral Disorders 1973
  R ↓ Musculoskeletal Disorders 1973
     ↓ Paralysis 1973
     ↓ Respiratory Tract Disorders 1973

Political Assassination 1973
PN 75   SC 39320
  UF   Assassination (Political)
  B   Violent Crime 2003

Political Attitudes 1973
PN 3095   SC 39330
  B   Attitudes 1967
       Politics 1967
  N   Nationalism 1967
       Political Conservatism 1973
       Political Liberalism 1973
       Political Radicalism 1973
  R ↓ Activism 2003
       Citizenship 1973
       Nonviolence 1991
       Political Socialization 1988
       Voting Behavior 1973

Political Campaigns 1973
PN 349   SC 39340
  UF   Campaigns (Political)
  B   Political Processes 1973
  R   Debates 1997
       Political Candidates 1973
       Political Elections 1973

Political Campaigns — (cont'd)
       Political Issues 1973
       Political Parties 1973
       Politicians 1978

Political Candidates 1973
PN 477   SC 39350
  UF   Candidates (Political)
  B   Politics 1967
  R   Debates 1997
       Political Campaigns 1973
       Political Elections 1973
       Politicians 1978

Political Conservatism 1973
PN 308   SC 39360
  UF   Conservatism (Political)
  B   Political Attitudes 1973
  R   Conservatism 1973

Political Debates
  Use Debates

Political Divisions (Geographic)
  Use Geography

Political Economic Systems 1973
PN 429   SC 39370
  B   Systems 1967
  N   Capitalism 1973
       Communism 1973
       Democracy 1973
       Fascism 1973
       Socialism 1973
       Totalitarianism 1973
  R ↓ Economics 1985
       Economy 1973
       Government 1967
       Political Psychology 1997

Political Elections 1973
PN 510   SC 39380
  UF   Elections (Political)
  B   Political Processes 1973
  R   Debates 1997
       Political Campaigns 1973
       Political Candidates 1973
       Political Parties 1973
       Politicians 1978
       Voting Behavior 1973

Political Involvement
  Use Political Participation

Political Issues 1973
PN 844   SC 39390
  B   Politics 1967
  R   Political Campaigns 1973
     ↓ Social Issues 1991
       Voting Behavior 1973

Political Liberalism 1973
PN 237   SC 39400
  UF   Liberalism (Political)
  B   Political Attitudes 1973
  R   Liberalism 1973

Political Participation 1988
PN 473   SC 39405
  UF   Political Involvement

Political Participation — (cont'd)
B   Politics   1967
N   Voting Behavior   1973
R   ↓ Activism   2003
     Political Psychology   1997
     Social Demonstrations   1973
     ↓ Social Movements   1967

Political Parties   1973
PN   393   SC   39410
UF   Democratic Party
     Independent Party (Political)
     Republican Party
B   Politics   1967
R   Political Campaigns   1973
     Political Elections   1973

Political Processes   1973
PN   1314   SC   39420
B   Politics   1967
N   Political Campaigns   1973
     Political Elections   1973
     Voting Behavior   1973
R   Debates   1997
     Freedom   1978
     Political Psychology   1997
     Political Revolution   1973
     ↓ Social Processes   1967

Political Psychology   1997
PN   184   SC   39425
B   Applied Psychology   1973
R   ↓ Law (Government)   1973
     ↓ Political Economic Systems   1973
     ↓ Political Participation   1988
     ↓ Political Processes   1973
     ↓ Politics   1967
     Public Opinion   1973
     Voting Behavior   1973

Political Radicalism   1973
PN   152   SC   39430
UF   Radicalism (Political)
B   Political Attitudes   1973

Political Refugees
Use   Refugees

Political Revolution   1973
PN   165   SC   39440
UF   Revolutions (Political)
B   Radical Movements   1973
R   ↓ Political Processes   1973
     Terrorism   1982

Political Socialization   1988
PN   172   SC   39443
SN   Transmission of political norms through social agents, e.g., school, parents, peers, or mass media.
B   Socialization   1967
R   ↓ Political Attitudes   1973

Politicians   1978
PN   902   SC   39445
R   Political Campaigns   1973
     Political Candidates   1973
     Political Elections   1973
     ↓ Politics   1967

Politics   1967
PN   2756   SC   39450

Politics — (cont'd)
N   ↓ Political Attitudes   1973
     Political Candidates   1973
     Political Issues   1973
     ↓ Political Participation   1988
     Political Parties   1973
     ↓ Political Processes   1973
R   Government   1967
     Political Psychology   1997
     Politicians   1978

Pollution   1973
PN   403   SC   39460
B   Ecological Factors   1973
R   Atmospheric Conditions   1973
     Carcinogens   1973
     Ecology   1973
     Environmental Education   1994
     ↓ Hazardous Materials   1991
     Noise Effects   1973
     Physiological Stress   1967
     ↓ Temperature Effects   1967

Polydipsia   1982
PN   430   SC   39465
SN   Noncontingent excessive drinking behavior usually produced and maintained by operant schedules of reinforcement involving food as a reinforcer. Also used for disordered human populations.
B   Adjunctive Behavior   1982
R   Animal Drinking Behavior   1973
     Hyponatremia   1997
     ↓ Operant Conditioning   1967

Polydrug Abuse   1994
PN   276   SC   39467
UF   Multidrug Abuse
B   Drug Abuse   1973
R   ↓ Alcohol Abuse   1988
     ↓ Drug Addiction   1967
     ↓ Drug Dependency   1973
     Drug Interactions   1982

Polygamy   1973
PN   139   SC   39470
SN   Used for human or animal populations.
B   Family Structure   1973
     Marriage   1967
R   Monogamy   1997

Polygraphs   1973
PN   306   SC   39480
B   Apparatus   1967
R   Legal Interrogation   1994

Polymorphism   2003
PN   478   SC   39485
SN   Expression of more than one morphologic type.
HN   This term was introduced in June 2003. PsycINFO records from the past 10 years were re-indexed with this term. The posting note reflects the number of records that were re-indexed.
R   ↓ Genetics   1967
     Genotypes   1973
     Morphology   1973
     Phenotypes   1973

Polyphagia
Use   Hyperphagia

Polypharmacy   2004
PN   36   SC   39492

Polypharmacy — (cont'd)
SN   Simultaneous administration of multiple medications to treat the same illness.
HN   This term was introduced in June 2004. PsycINFO records from the past 10 years were re-indexed with this term. The posting note reflects the number of records that were re-indexed.
B   Drug Therapy   1967
R   Drug Interactions   1982
     Prescribing (Drugs)   1991

Polysomnography   2003
PN   22   SC   39495
SN   Simultaneous recording of electrophysiologic activity during sleep.
UF   Sleep Monitoring
B   Monitoring   1973
R   ↓ Apparatus   1967
     ↓ Electrical Activity   1967
     ↓ Sleep   1967
     ↓ Sleep Disorders   1973

Pons   1973
PN   611   SC   39510
B   Brain Stem   1973
     Hindbrain   1997
N   Raphe Nuclei   1982

Popular Culture   2003
PN   52   SC   39515
SN   Expressions or characteristics from art, literature, film, television, sports, or fashion that are widely disseminated and commercialized through the media and society.
HN   This term was introduced in June 2003. PsycINFO records from the past 10 years were re-indexed with this term. The posting note reflects the number of records that were re-indexed.
UF   Mass Culture
R   ↓ Culture (Anthropological)   1967
     ↓ Fads and Fashions   1973
     Globalization   2003
     ↓ Mass Media   1967
     ↓ Society   1967
     Subculture (Anthropological)   1973
     Trends   1991

Popularity   1988
PN   329   SC   39520
HN   Use SOCIAL APPROVAL to access references from 1973-1987.
R   ↓ Interpersonal Interaction   1967
     Reputation   1997
     Social Acceptance   1967
     Social Approval   1967
     ↓ Social Influences   1967
     ↓ Social Perception   1967

Population   1973
PN   483   SC   39530
SN   Total number of organisms (human or animal) inhabiting a given locality.
N   Overpopulation   1973
     ↓ Population (Statistics)   1973
R   Birth Rate   1982
     Demographic Characteristics   1967
     Mortality Rate   1973
     Social Density   1978

Population (Statistics)   1973
PN   760   SC   39540
SN   All the objects or people of a given class.
B   Population   1973

Population (Statistics) — (cont'd)

N ↓ Statistical Samples 1973
R ↓ Central Tendency Measures 1973
↓ Experimental Design 1967
↓ Experimentation 1967
↓ Sampling (Experimental) 1973
↓ Statistical Analysis 1967
Statistical Reliability 1973
↓ Statistical Variables 1973

Population Characteristics

Use Demographic Characteristics

Population Control

Use Birth Control

Population Density

Use Social Density

Population Genetics 1973

PN 163　　　　　　　　**SC** 39570
SN Study of the genetic composition of human or animal populations; gene interactions and alterations that promote population changes and evolution.
B Genetics 1967
R Assortative Mating 1991
Behavioral Genetics 1994
↓ Genetic Engineering 1994

Population Shifts

Use Human Migration

Pornography 1973

PN 562　　　　　　　　**SC** 39580
UF X Rated Materials
R Nudity 1973
Obscenity 1978
↓ Paraphilias 1988
↓ Psychosexual Behavior 1967
Sex 1967
↓ Sex Offenses 1982

Porphyria 1973

PN 46　　　　　　　　**SC** 39590
B Blood and Lymphatic Disorders 1973
Genetic Disorders 1973
Metabolism Disorders 1973
R ↓ Mental Disorders 1967

Porpoises 1973

PN 10　　　　　　　　**SC** 39600
B Whales 1985
R Dolphins 1973

Porteus Maze Test 1973

PN 23　　　　　　　　**SC** 39610
B Intelligence Measures 1967

Positive and Negative Symptoms 1997

PN 1015　　　　　　　**SC** 39618
UF Negative and Positive Symptoms
B Symptoms 1967
R ↓ Schizophrenia 1967

Positive Psychology 2003

PN 178　　　　　　　　**SC** 39619
SN Approach to psychology that emphasizes optimism and positive human functioning instead of focusing on psychopathology and dysfunction.

Positive Psychology — (cont'd)

HN This term was introduced in June 2003. PsycINFO records from the past 10 years were re-indexed with this term. The posting note reflects the number of records that were re-indexed.
B Psychology 1967
R Optimism 1973
Positivism 1973
Well Being 1994

Positive Reinforcement 1973

PN 984　　　　　　　　**SC** 39620
SN Presentation of a positive reinforcer contingent on the performance of some behavior. Also, the positively reinforcing object or event itself which, when made to follow the performance of some behavior, results in an increase in the frequency of occurrence of that behavior. Compare REWARDS.
B Reinforcement 1967
N Praise 1973

Positive Transfer 1973

PN 171　　　　　　　　**SC** 39630
SN Previous learning or practice which aids the acquisition of new material or skills as the result of common characteristics shared by the prior and current learning situation.
B Transfer (Learning) 1967

Positivism 1973

PN 400　　　　　　　　**SC** 39640
SN Personal quality or state of being positive or confident. Compare OPTIMISM.
B Personality Traits 1967
R Determinism 1997
Hope 1991
Optimism 1973
Positive Psychology 2003

Positivism (Philosophy) 1997

PN 47　　　　　　　　**SC** 39642
SN Philosophical view that scientific knowledge comes only from direct observation and application of empirical methods.
B Philosophies 1967
R Behaviorism 1967
↓ Empirical Methods 1973
Epistemology 1973
Hermeneutics 1991
Reductionism 1973

Positron Emission Tomography

Use Tomography

Possession

Use Ownership

Postactivation Potentials 1985

PN 804　　　　　　　　**SC** 39650
SN Enhancement of synaptic and cellular responses induced by brief high frequency electrical stimulation.
UF Long Term Potentiation
Short Term Potentiation
B Electrical Activity 1967
R Electrical Brain Stimulation 1973
Neural Plasticity 1994

Postganglionic Autonomic Fibers

Use Autonomic Ganglia

Postgraduate Students 1973

PN 182　　　　　　　　**SC** 39684
SN Students involved in study or research after having completed a master's or doctoral degree. Such students are not necessarily pursuing a degree.
B Students 1967
R ↓ College Students 1967
Graduate Students 1967

Postgraduate Training 1973

PN 397　　　　　　　　**SC** 39685
SN Studies or research beyond master's or doctoral degree.
B Higher Education 1973
N ↓ Clinical Psychology Graduate Training 2001
Clinical Psychology Internship 1973
Medical Internship 1973
Medical Residency 1973
R Professional Specialization 1991

Posthypnotic Suggestions 1994

PN 85　　　　　　　　**SC** 39687
R ↓ Hypnosis 1967
↓ Hypnotherapy 1973
Hypnotic Susceptibility 1973
↓ Relaxation Therapy 1978
Suggestibility 1967

Postmodernism 1997

PN 732　　　　　　　　**SC** 39689
B Philosophies 1967
R ↓ Arts 1973
↓ Literature 1967

Postnatal Depression

Use Postpartum Depression

Postnatal Dysphoria

Use Postpartum Depression

Postnatal Period 1973

PN 1909　　　　　　　**SC** 39690
R Lactation 1973
Perinatal Period 1994
Postpartum Depression 1973
Postpartum Psychosis 2003
↓ Pregnancy 1967

Postpartum Depression 1973

PN 1098　　　　　　　**SC** 39700
UF Postnatal Depression
Postnatal Dysphoria
Puerperal Depression
B Major Depression 1988
R Attachment Behavior 1985
Mother Child Relations 1967
↓ Organic Brain Syndromes 1973
Postnatal Period 1973
Postpartum Psychosis 2003

Postpartum Psychosis 2003

PN 6　　　　　　　　**SC** 39705
SN Psychotic reaction occurring after childbirth.
HN Use POSTPARTUM DEPRESSION to access references from 1988 to June 2003.
UF Puerperal Psychosis
B Psychosis 1967
R Acute Schizophrenia 1973
Attachment Behavior 1985
Mother Child Relations 1967
↓ Organic Brain Syndromes 1973

Postpartum Psychosis — (cont'd)
Postnatal Period 1973
Postpartum Depression 1973

Postsurgical Complications 1973
PN 288   SC 39710
- UF Surgical Complications
- R Obstetrical Complications 1978
  Recovery (Disorders) 1973
  Relapse (Disorders) 1973
  ↓ Surgery 1971
  ↓ Treatment Outcomes 1982

Posttesting 1973
PN 113   SC 39720
SN Measurement performed after experimental manipulation, treatment, or program intervention. Comparison of pretest and posttest scores gives a measure of effectiveness of independent variables such as treatments or programs.
- B Measurement 1967
- R Repeated Measures 1985
  ↓ Testing Methods 1967

Posttraumatic Stress Disorder 1985
PN 7783   SC 39727
SN Acute, chronic, or delayed reactions to traumatic events such as military combat, assault, or natural disaster.
HN Use TRAUMATIC NEUROSIS or STRESS REACTIONS to access references from 1973-1984.
- B Anxiety Disorders 1997
- R Acute Stress Disorder 2003
  Adjustment Disorders 1994
  Combat Experience 1991
  Debriefing (Psychological) 2004
  Emotional Trauma 1967
  Stress Reactions 1973
  Traumatic Neurosis 1973

Posttreatment Followup 1973
PN 848   SC 39730
SN Periodic check-ups of patients. Usually part of a comprehensive aftercare treatment.
- UF Catamnesis
  Followup (Posttreatment)
- R Aftercare 1973
  Discharge Planning 1994
  ↓ Treatment 1967
  ↓ Treatment Planning 1997

Posture 1973
PN 1600   SC 39740
- R Body Language 1973
  ↓ Motor Processes 1967
  Physique 1967

Potassium 1973
PN 265   SC 39750
- B Metallic Elements 1973
- N Potassium Ions 1973

Potassium Ions 1973
PN 86   SC 39770
- B Electrolytes 1973
  Potassium 1973

Potential (Achievement)
Use Achievement Potential

Potential Dropouts 1973
PN 151   SC 39790

Potential Dropouts — (cont'd)
- B Dropouts 1973

Potentiation (Drugs)
Use Drug Interactions

Poverty 1973
PN 1681   SC 39820
- B Social Issues 1991
- R Disadvantaged 1967
  ↓ Homeless 1988
  Income (Economic) 1973
  Lower Income Level 1973
  ↓ Socioeconomic Status 1967

Poverty Areas 1973
PN 134   SC 39830
- UF Slums
- B Social Environments 1973
- R Cultural Deprivation 1973
  Ghettoes 1973

Power 1967
PN 4803   SC 39840
SN Social control an individual has over others.
- B Social Influences 1967
- N Abuse of Power 1007
- R Authority 1967
  Coercion 1994
  ↓ Dominance 1967
  Empowerment 1991
  ↓ Helplessness 1997
  Omnipotence 1994

Practical Knowledge
Use Procedural Knowledge

Practice 1967
PN 4946   SC 39850
HN In 1982, this term replaced the discontinued term PRACTICE EFFECTS. In 2000, PRACTICE EFFECTS was removed from all records and replaced with PRACTICE.
- UF Experience (Practice)
  Practice Effects
  Rehearsal
- N Distributed Practice 1973
  Massed Practice 1973
- R Curricular Field Experience 1982
  ↓ Experience Level 1988
  Familiarity 1967
  Memory Training 1994
  Overcorrection 1985
  Test Coaching 1997

Practice Effects
Use Practice

Practicum Supervision 1978
PN 883   SC 39865
SN Supervision of students involved in practical application of learned material.
- R ↓ Clinical Methods Training 1973
  ↓ Clinical Psychology Graduate Training 2001
  Clinical Psychology Internship 1973
  Cooperating Teachers 1978
  Counselor Education 1973
  ↓ Teacher Education 1967

Prader Willi Syndrome 1991
PN 155   SC 39867

Prader Willi Syndrome — (cont'd)
- B Congenital Disorders 1973
  Syndromes 1973
- R ↓ Mental Retardation 1967

Pragmatics 1985
PN 1183   SC 39868
SN Study of the rules governing the use of language in context. Also used for the actual social interaction aspects of communication.
- B Semiotics 1985
  Verbal Communication 1967
- R ↓ Communication Skills 1973
  Discourse Analysis 1997
  ↓ Interpersonal Communication 1973
  ↓ Linguistics 1973
  Metalinguistics 1994

Pragmatism 1973
PN 194   SC 39870
- B Philosophies 1967

Praise 1973
PN 550   SC 39880
- B Positive Reinforcement 1973
  Verbal Reinforcement 1973

Prayer 1973
PN 226   SC 39890
- B Religious Practices 1973
- R Meditation 1973

Praying Mantis
Use Mantis

Precocious Development 1973
PN 105   SC 39910
- B Development 1967
- R Developmental Age Groups 1973
  ↓ Physical Development 1973
  ↓ Psychogenesis 1973

Precognition 1973
PN 136   SC 39920
- B Clairvoyance 1973

Preconditioning 1994
PN 42   SC 39923
SN Presentation of two stimuli in a consecutive manner without reinforcement to determine if a subject will respond to both stimuli in a conditioning paradigm.
- UF Sensory Preconditioning
- B Conditioning 1967
- R Conditioned Stimulus 1973

Predatory Behavior (Animal)
Use Animal Predatory Behavior

Predelinquent Youth 1978
PN 119   SC 39927
SN Children considered at risk for developing delinquent behavior because their sociocultural and family backgrounds and early behavior patterns parallel those of juvenile delinquents.
- R ↓ Juvenile Delinquency 1967
  Juvenile Justice 2004

Predictability (Measurement) 1973
PN 351   SC 39930

Predictability (Measurement) — (cont'd)

SN Statistical procedures used to forecast the value of the criterion variables (such as behavior, performance, or outcomes) on the basis of selected predictor variables.

B   Statistical Analysis   1967
     Statistical Measurement   1973
R   Chaos Theory   1997
     Confidence Limits (Statistics)   1973
     ↓ Hypothesis Testing   1973
     ↓ Prediction   1967
     ↓ Prediction Errors   1973
     ↓ Probability   1967
     ↓ Statistical Estimation   1985

Prediction   1967

PN 11072   **SC** 39940
N   Academic Achievement Prediction   1967
     Occupational Success Prediction   1973
R   Chaos Theory   1997
     ↓ Estimation   1967
     Future   1991
     Predictability (Measurement)   1973
     ↓ Prediction Errors   1973
     Prognosis   1973
     Self Fulfilling Prophecies   1997

Prediction Errors   1973

PN 96   **SC** 39950
B   Errors   1067
N   Type I Errors   1973
     Type II Errors   1973
R   Consistency (Measurement)   1973
     ↓ Hypothesis Testing   1973
     ↓ Measurement   1967
     Predictability (Measurement)   1973
     ↓ Prediction   1967
     ↓ Statistical Analysis   1967
     Statistical Power   1991
     Statistical Reliability   1973
     Statistical Validity   1973
     ↓ Statistical Variables   1973

Predictive Validity

   Use   Statistical Validity

Predisposition   1973

PN 2685   **SC** 39970
SN Proneness toward disorders or propensity toward certain behaviors due to physical, psychological, social, or situational factors. Consider also SUSCEPTIBILITY (DISORDERS).

R   At Risk Populations   1985
     Biological Markers   1991
     Coronary Prone Behavior   1982
     ↓ Disorders   1967
     ↓ Genetics   1967
     ↓ Mental Disorders   1967
     Nature Nurture   1994
     ↓ Personality   1967
     ↓ Physical Disorders   1997
     Premorbidity   1978
     Response Bias   1967
     Risk Factors   2001
     Susceptibility (Disorders)   1973

Prednisolone   1973

PN 52   **SC** 39980
B   Adrenal Cortex Hormones   1973
     Corticosteroids   1973

Preference Measures   1973

PN 710   **SC** 39990
B   Measurement   1967
N   Kuder Preference Record   1973
     Least Preferred Coworker Scale   1973
R   ↓ Attitude Measures   1967
     ↓ Preferences   1967

Preferences   1967

PN 8111   **SC** 39995
N   Aesthetic Preferences   1973
     Brand Preferences   1994
     Food Preferences   1973
     Occupational Preference   1973
R   ↓ Preference Measures   1973
     Preferred Rewards   1973

Preferred Rewards   1973

PN 166   **SC** 40030
B   Rewards   1967
R   ↓ Preferences   1967

Prefrontal Cortex   1994

PN 2119   **SC** 40035
B   Frontal Lobe   1973

Preganglionic Autonomic Fibers

   Use   Autonomic Ganglia

Pregnancy   1967

PN 6058   **SC** 40050
UF   Gestation
N   Adolescent Pregnancy   1988
R   ↓ Birth   1967
     Childbirth Training   1978
     Fertilization   1973
     Life Changes   2004
     Obstetrical Complications   1978
     Perinatal Period   1994
     Placenta   1973
     Postnatal Period   1973
     ↓ Prenatal Care   1991
     Primipara   2001
     Reproductive Technology   1988
     Safe Sex   2003
     ↓ Sexual Reproduction   1973
     Sexual Risk Taking   1997

Pregnancy (False)

   Use   Pseudocyesis

Prejudice   1967

PN 2148   **SC** 40070
B   Social Influences   1967
N   ↓ Religious Prejudices   1973
R   Age Discrimination   1994
     AntiSemitism   1973
     ↓ Attitudes   1967
     Disability Discrimination   1997
     Employment Discrimination   1994
     Hate Crimes   2003
     Race and Ethnic Discrimination   1994
     ↓ Racial and Ethnic Attitudes   1982
     Racial and Ethnic Relations   1982
     Racism   1973
     Sex Discrimination   1978
     Sexism   1988
     Stereotyped Attitudes   1967
     Stigma   1991

Preliminary Scholastic Aptitude Test

   Use   College Entrance Examination Board Scholastic Aptitude Test

Premarital Counseling   1973

PN 180   **SC** 40090
B   Counseling   1967
R   ↓ Psychotherapeutic Counseling   1973

Premarital Intercourse   1973

PN 350   **SC** 40100
B   Sexual Intercourse (Human)   1973
R   ↓ Birth Control   1971
     Promiscuity   1973
     Social Dating   1973
     Unwed Mothers   1973
     Virginity   1973

Premature Birth   1973

PN 1833   **SC** 40110
B   Birth   1967
R   Birth Weight   1985
     Obstetrical Complications   1978

Premature Ejaculation   1973

PN 174   **SC** 40120
B   Male Orgasm   1973
     Sexual Function Disturbances   1973
R   Impotence   1973

Premenstrual Dysphoric Disorder   2004

PN 89   **SC** 40113
SN A more severe and disabling form of premenstrual syndrome in which mood symptoms are the primary characteristic.
HN This term was introduced in June 2004. PsycINFO records from the past 10 years were re-indexed with this term. The posting note reflects the number of records that were re-indexed.
B   Menstrual Disorders   1973
R   ↓ Affective Disorders   2001
     ↓ Menstrual Cycle   1973
     Premenstrual Syndrome   2003

Premenstrual Syndrome   2003

PN 1094   **SC** 40115
SN Physiological, emotional, and mental stress related to the period of time immediately preceding menstruation.
HN In June 2003, this term replaced the discontinued term PREMENSTRUAL TENSION. PREMENSTRUAL TENSION was removed from all records containing it and replaced with PREMENSTRUAL SYNDROME.
UF   PMS
     Premenstrual Tension
B   Syndromes   1973
R   ↓ Menstrual Cycle   1973
     ↓ Menstrual Disorders   1973
     Premenstrual Dysphoric Disorder   2004

Premenstrual Tension

   Use   Premenstrual Syndrome

Premorbidity   1978

PN 885   **SC** 40135
SN Condition of an individual before onset of illness or disorder.
R   At Risk Populations   1985
     ↓ Disorders   1967

Premorbidity — (cont'd)
 ↓ Mental Disorders 1967
　Onset (Disorders) 1973
　Patient History 1973
 ↓ Physical Disorders 1997
　Predisposition 1973
　Susceptibility (Disorders) 1973

Prenatal Care 1991
PN 474　　　　　　SC 40137
SN Medical, health, and educational services pro-
vided or obtained during pregnancy. Includes mater-
nal health behavior affecting prenatal development.
 N　Childbirth Training 1978
 R　Early Intervention 1982
 ↓ Health Behavior 1982
 ↓ Health Care Services 1978
 ↓ Health Education 1973
 ↓ Obstetrics 1978
 ↓ Pregnancy 1967
 ↓ Prenatal Development 1973
　Prenatal Diagnosis 1988
 ↓ Prevention 1973
　Preventive Medicine 1973

Prenatal Development 1973
PN 2425　　　　　　SC 40140
SN Development of an organism prior to birth. Used
for human or animal populations.
 B　Physical Development 1973
 N ↓ Prenatal Developmental Stages 1973
 R　Animal Development 1978
　Fetal Alcohol Syndrome 1985
　Perinatal Period 1994
 ↓ Prenatal Care 1991
　Prenatal Diagnosis 1988
　Prenatal Exposure 1991
 ↓ Psychogenesis 1973
　Teratogens 1988

Prenatal Developmental Stages 1973
PN 43　　　　　　SC 40150
 B　Developmental Stages 1973
　Prenatal Development 1973
 N　Embryo 1973
　Fetus 1967

Prenatal Diagnosis 1988
PN 241　　　　　　SC 40152
SN Techniques or procedures used to detect or
identify specific abnormalities or characteristics of
the fetus.
 UF　Amniocentesis
 B　Medical Diagnosis 1973
 R ↓ Congenital Disorders 1973
 ↓ Genetic Disorders 1973
 ↓ Prenatal Care 1991
 ↓ Prenatal Development 1973
　Reproductive Technology 1988

Prenatal Exposure 1991
PN 2361　　　　　　SC 40156
SN Exposure to chemicals or other environmental
factors prior to birth. Used for human and animal
populations.
 UF　Fetal Exposure
 R ↓ Alcoholic Beverages 1973
 ↓ Disorders 1967
 ↓ Drugs 1967
 ↓ Environmental Effects 1973
 ↓ Physical Disorders 1997
 ↓ Poisons 1973
 ↓ Prenatal Development 1973
　Teratogens 1988

Prenatal Exposure — (cont'd)
　Thalidomide 1973
　Tobacco Smoking 1967

Preoptic Area 1994
PN 233　　　　　　SC 40158
HN Consider HYPOTHALAMUS to access refer-
ences prior to 1994.
 B　Hypothalamus 1967

Prepulse Inhibition 1997
PN 382　　　　　　SC 40159
SN Markedly reduced startle response resulting
from a weaker stimulus preceding a stronger startle-
inducing stimulus.
 R　Conditioned Suppression 1973
 ↓ Latent Inhibition 1997
　Sensory Gating 1991
　Startle Reflex 1967

Presbyterians
 Use　Protestants

Preschool Education 1973
PN 1809　　　　　　SC 40170
 B　Education 1967
 R　Project Head Start 1973

Preschool Students 1982
PN 3159　　　　　　SC 40173
SN Students from infancy to entrance in kindergar-
ten or 1st grade.
 B　Students 1967
 N　Nursery School Students 1973
 R　Kindergarten Students 1973

Preschool Teachers 1985
PN 601　　　　　　SC 40176
 B　Teachers 1967

Prescribing (Drugs) 1991
PN 1080　　　　　　SC 40177
 R ↓ Drug Therapy 1967
 ↓ Drugs 1967
　Polypharmacy 2004
 ↓ Treatment 1967

Prescription Drugs 1991
PN 342　　　　　　SC 40178
 B　Drugs 1967
 R ↓ Drug Therapy 1967
　Nonprescription Drugs 1991
　Self Medication 1991

Presenile Dementia 1973
PN 220　　　　　　SC 40180
 UF　Dementia (Presenile)
 B　Dementia 1985
 N　Alzheimers Disease 1973
　Creutzfeldt Jakob Syndrome 1994
　Picks Disease 1973
 R ↓ Senile Dementia 1973

Preservice Teachers 1982
PN 1085　　　　　　SC 40205
SN Education students or graduates prior to
employment as teachers.
 B　Teachers 1967
 R ↓ College Students 1967
　Education Students 1982
　Student Teachers 1973

Preservice Teachers — (cont'd)
 ↓ Teacher Education 1967

Presidential Debates
 Use　Debates

Pressoreceptors
 Use　Baroreceptors

Pressors (Drugs)
 Use　Vasoconstrictor Drugs

Pressure Sensation 1973
PN 103　　　　　　SC 40270
 R　Somatosensory Disorders 2001
 ↓ Somesthetic Perception 1967

Prestige (Occupational)
 Use　Occupational Status

Pretesting 1973
PN 171　　　　　　SC 40280
SN Running preliminary trials to establish a base-
line. Comparison of pretest and posttest scores gives
a measure of effectiveness of independent variables
such as treatments or programs.
 B　Measurement 1967
 R　Repeated Measures 1985
 ↓ Testing Methods 1967

Pretraining (Therapy)
 Use　Client Education

Prevention 1973
PN 9418　　　　　　SC 40290
SN Conceptually broad term referring to any pro-
cess that acts to deter undesirable occurrences. Use
a more specific term if possible.
 N　Accident Prevention 1973
　AIDS Prevention 1994
　Crime Prevention 1985
　Drug Abuse Prevention 1994
　Fire Prevention 1973
　Preventive Medicine 1973
　Primary Mental Health Prevention 1973
　Relapse Prevention 1994
　Suicide Prevention 1973
 R　Condoms 1991
　Disability Management 1991
　Early Intervention 1982
 ↓ Health Care Delivery 1978
 ↓ Health Care Services 1978
 ↓ Health Education 1973
　Health Promotion 1991
 ↓ Intervention 2003
 ↓ Mental Health Services 1978
 ↓ Prenatal Care 1991
　Public Service Announcements 2004
　Risk Management 1997
　Risk Perception 1997
 ↓ Safety 1967
　Suicide Prevention Centers 1973
 ↓ Treatment 1967

Preventive Medicine 1973
PN 841　　　　　　SC 40300
 B　Prevention 1973
　Treatment 1967
 R ↓ Alternative Medicine 1997
　Drug Abuse Prevention 1994

Preventive Medicine — (cont'd)
Genetic Testing   2003
↓ Health   1973
↓ Health Behavior   1982
Health Maintenance Organizations   1982
Health Promotion   1991
↓ Health Screening   1997
Holistic Health   1985
Mammography   1994
Physical Examination   1988
↓ Prenatal Care   1991
Relapse Prevention   1994

Price
Use   Costs and Cost Analysis

Pride   1973
PN   166   **SC**   40310
B   Emotional States   1973

Priests   1973
PN   243   **SC**   40320
B   Clergy   1973
R   Chaplains   1973
     Missionaries   1973

Primacy Effect   1973
PN   254   **SC**   40328
SN   Component of the serial position effect which is manifested by a greater ease in learning items that occur at the beginning of a series rather than those toward the middle. Compare RECENCY EFFECT.
B   Serial Position Effect   1982
R   ↓ Learning   1967
     Recency Effect   1973

Primal Therapy   1978
PN   52   **SC**   40329
SN   Combination of intensive individual therapy and group psychotherapy with emphasis on experiencing and expression of blocked traumatic events or feelings (primals) and their integration into total life functioning.
B   Psychotherapy   1967
R   ↓ Psychotherapeutic Techniques   1967

Primary Health Care   1988
PN   3212   **SC**   40331
SN   Health care provided by a medical professional with whom a patient has initial contact when entering the health care system and by whom a patient may be referred to a specialist.
B   Health Care Services   1978
R   ↓ Health Care Delivery   1978

Primary Mental Health Prevention   1973
PN   1716   **SC**   40330
SN   Mental health programs designed to prevent onset or occurrence of mental illness in high risk or target populations.
B   Prevention   1973
R   Drug Abuse Prevention   1994
     Early Intervention   1982
     ↓ Mental Health   1967
     ↓ Mental Health Programs   1973
     Relapse Prevention   1994

Primary Reinforcement   1973
PN   59   **SC**   40340

Primary Reinforcement — (cont'd)
SN   Presentation of a primary reinforcer. Also, objects or events which do not require prior pairing with other reinforcers in order to maintain reinforcing properties. Also known as unconditioned reinforcers or unconditioned stimuli. Compare EXTERNAL REWARDS.
B   Reinforcement   1967
R   ↓ Conditioning   1967
     Unconditioned Stimulus   1973

Primary School Students   1973
PN   723   **SC**   40350
SN   Students in kindergarten through 3rd grade. Use ELEMENTARY SCHOOL STUDENTS or KINDERGARTEN STUDENTS unless specific reference is made to population as primary school students.
B   Elementary School Students   1967

Primary Schools
Use   Elementary Schools

Primates (Nonhuman)   1973
PN   2095   **SC**   40370
UF   Apes
B   Mammals   1973
N   Baboons   1973
     Bonobos   1997
     Chimpanzees   1973
     Gorillas   1973
     Monkeys   1967

Primidone   1973
PN   19   **SC**   40380
B   Anticonvulsive Drugs   1973
R   ↓ Barbiturates   1967

Priming   1988
PN   2781   **SC**   40385
N   Semantic Priming   1994
R   Contextual Associations   1967
     Cues   1967
     ↓ Perception   1967
     ↓ Prompting   1997
     ↓ Semantics   1967

Primipara   2001
PN   18   **SC**   40325
SN   Pregnant with, or having borne, only one child or offspring.
R   ↓ Mothers   1967
     ↓ Pregnancy   1967

Printed Communications Media   1973
PN   618   **SC**   40390
B   Mass Media   1967
N   ↓ Books   1973
     Magazines   1973
     Newspapers   1973

Printing (Handwriting)   1973
PN   49   **SC**   40400
B   Handwriting   1967

Prismatic Stimulation   1973
PN   217   **SC**   40410
SN   Visual stimulation technique in which special lenses are used to spatially distort or invert visual images or the visual field. Also includes prisms that differentially refract light of different wavelengths to produce an array or spectrum of colors.

Prismatic Stimulation — (cont'd)
B   Visual Stimulation   1973
R   ↓ Color Perception   1967
     Spatial Distortion   1973

Prison Personnel   1973
PN   569   **SC**   40420
B   Law Enforcement Personnel   1973
R   Attendants (Institutions)   1973

Prisoners   1967
PN   4572   **SC**   40430
UF   Inmates (Prison)
N   Prisoners of War   1973
R   Criminal Rehabilitation   2004
     ↓ Criminals   1967

Prisoners Dilemma Game   1973
PN   437   **SC**   40440
SN   Nonzero-sum game in which individual outcomes are determined by joint actions of two players. Incentives for both cooperation and competition exist, and no communication is permitted between the two players.
B   Games   1967
R   Entrapment Games   1973
     Game Theory   1967
     Non Zero Sum Games   1973
     Social Dilemma   2003

Prisoners of War   1973
PN   221   **SC**   40450
B   Prisoners   1967
R   Hostages   1988

Prisons   1967
PN   1520   **SC**   40460
UF   Jails
     Penitentiaries
B   Correctional Institutions   1973
R   Concentration Camps   1973
     Criminal Rehabilitation   2004
     Reformatories   1973

Privacy   1973
PN   650   **SC**   40467
R   Privileged Communication   1973
     Secrecy   1994
     ↓ Social Behavior   1967

Private Practice   1978
PN   578   **SC**   40469
SN   Employment of professional personnel in independent for-profit practices (as opposed to public offices or nonprofit settings) in which there is direct contact with clients and payment for services rendered. Private practitioners may function in individual practices, partnerships, or incorporated business settings.
R   ↓ Health Care Delivery   1978

Private School Education   1973
PN   575   **SC**   40470
SN   Schools or formal education in schools supported and administered by organizations not affiliated with the government.
UF   Parochial School Education
B   Education   1967
R   Religious Education   1973

Private Sector   1985
PN   505   **SC**   40475

Private Sector — (cont'd)
SN Any type of non-government organization, service, or sphere of involvement.
N Business Organizations 1973
R Entrepreneurship 1991
Ownership 1985

Privileged Communication 1973
PN 1211 · SC 40480
SN Confidential communication between doctors, lawyers, or therapists and their clients which, by legal sanction, may not be revealed to others. Also, any documents or recorded statements of such communication which can be legally withheld from public inspection.
UF Communication (Privileged)
Confidentiality of Information
R ↓ Abuse Reporting 1997
Anonymity 1973
Client Records 1997
↓ Communication 1967
Duty to Warn 2001
Information 1967
Privacy 1973
Professional Ethics 1973
↓ Psychotherapeutic Processes 1967

Proactive Inhibition 1973
PN 755 · SC 40490
SN The theory that previous learning of material can interfere with the retention of newly-learned material. Also, the actual proactive interference itself.
UF Inhibition (Proactive)
B Interference (Learning) 1967
Latent Inhibition 1997

Probability 1967
PN 1912 · SC 40500
SN The likelihood of the chance occurrence of specific events. May include the mathematical study of probability theory.
N ↓ Chance (Fortune) 1973
Response Probability 1973
↓ Statistical Probability 1967
R Chaos Theory 1997
↓ Hypothesis Testing 1973
Predictability (Measurement) 1973
Probability Judgment 1978
Probability Learning 1967

Probability Judgment 1978
PN 1147 · SC 40505
SN Process of ascertaining or estimating the degree of likelihood that certain specified conditions or events have, can, or will occur.
B Judgment 1967
R ↓ Probability 1967
Probability Learning 1967

Probability Learning 1967
PN 605 · SC 40510
SN Experimental paradigm in which subjects are asked to guess or estimate whether an experimentally controlled event will occur or choose which of various alternative events will occur. As learning occurs, the proportion of correct responses tends to approach the actual probability proportion of event occurrences. Used for the experimental paradigm or task as well as the learned behavior itself.
B Learning 1967
R ↓ Probability 1967
Probability Judgment 1978

Probation 1973
PN 557 · SC 40520
SN Period of suspended sentence of a convicted offender following good behavior and during which the offender is not incarcerated but is under the supervision of a probation officer.
B Legal Processes 1973
R Court Referrals 1994
Criminal Rehabilitation 2004
↓ Law Enforcement 1978
Parole 1973

Probation Officers 1973
PN 234 · SC 40530
B Law Enforcement Personnel 1973
R Parole Officers 1973

Probenecid 1982
PN 15 · SC 40535
SN Agent that promotes the urinary excretion of uric acid.
R ↓ Diuretics 1973

Problem Drinking
Use Alcohol Abuse

Problem Solving 1967
PN 13412 · SC 40550
SN Process of determining a correct sequence of alternatives leading to a desired goal or to successful completion or performance of a task.
UF Individual Problem Solving
B Cognitive Processes 1967
N Anagram Problem Solving 1973
Cognitive Hypothesis Testing 1982
↓ Group Problem Solving 1973
Heuristics 2003
R Case Based Reasoning 2003
↓ Decision Making 1967
Declarative Knowledge 1997
↓ Expert Systems 1991
↓ Inductive Deductive Reasoning 1973
↓ Reasoning 1967
Solution Focused Therapy 2004

Procaine 1982
PN 92 · SC 40560
HN In 1982, this term replaced the discontinued term NOVOCAINE. In 2000, NOVOCAINE was removed from all records and replaced with PROCAINE.
UF Novocaine
B Analgesic Drugs 1973
Anesthetic Drugs 1973

Procedural Justice 2003
PN 141 · SC 40563
SN The perceived fairness of the process by which decisions are made and outcomes are determined.
HN This term was introduced in June 2003. PsycINFO records from the past 10 years were re-indexed with this term. The posting note reflects the number of records that were re-indexed.
B Justice 1973
R ↓ Organizational Behavior 1978

Procedural Knowledge 1997
PN 389 · SC 40565
SN Knowledge regarding how to do things. Compare DECLARATIVE KNOWLEDGE.
UF Functional Knowledge
Practical Knowledge

Procedural Knowledge — (cont'd)
R ↓ Cognitive Processes 1967
Declarative Knowledge 1997
Divergent Thinking 1973
Information 1967
↓ Knowledge Level 1978
↓ Memory 1967
Metacognition 1991
↓ Reasoning 1967

Process Psychosis 1973
PN 65 · SC 40570
UF Process Schizophrenia
B Psychosis 1967

Process Schizophrenia
Use Process Psychosis AND Schizophrenia

Prochlorperazine 1973
PN 17 · SC 40640
B Antiemetic Drugs 1973
Phenothiazine Derivatives 1973

Procrastination 1985
PN 238 · SC 40645
SN Habitual, often counterproductive postponing.
HN Use STUDY HABITS to access references in educational contexts from 1973-1984.
B Motivation 1967

Prodrome 2004
PN 11 · SC 40646
SN A premonitory symptom or early warning sign of a mental or physical disorder.
HN This term was introduced in June 2004. PsycINFO records from the past 10 years were re-indexed with this term. The posting note reflects the number of records that were re-indexed.
B Symptoms 1967
R Onset (Disorders) 1973

Product Design 1997
PN 438 · SC 40647
SN Process of conceptualizing, planning, researching, developing, and field testing products or goods.
UF Consumer Product Design
R ↓ Advertising 1967
Computer Assisted Design 1997
Consumer Protection 1973
↓ Consumer Research 1973
Consumer Surveys 1973
Marketing 1973

Productivity (Employee)
Use Employee Productivity

Profanity 1991
PN 15 · SC 40655
B Language 1967
R Obscenity 1978

Professional Certification 1973
PN 789 · SC 40660
SN In general, certification constitutes permission to use a particular professional title contingent on fulfilling requisite educational and training programs.
UF Certification (Professional)
N Accreditation (Education Personnel) 1973
R Professional Development 1982
Professional Examinations 1994
↓ Professional Licensing 1973

Professional Certification — (cont'd)
  ↓ Professional Personnel 1978

Professional Client Sexual Relations 1994
PN 337   SC 40665
SN Sexual relations, intimacy, or affectionate behavior between a professional (e.g., therapist, lawyer, religious personnel, or educator) and his or her clients or patients.
  UF Boundary Violations (Sexual)
      Patient Therapist Sexual Relations
      Sexual Boundary Violations
      Therapist Patient Sexual Relations
  R   Countertransference 1973
      Dual Relationships 2003
      Patient Abuse 1991
      Professional Ethics 1973
      ↓ Professional Standards 1973
      ↓ Psychosexual Behavior 1967
      ↓ Psychotherapeutic Processes 1967
      Psychotherapeutic Transference 1967
      ↓ Sexual Abuse 1988
      Sexual Harassment 1985
      ↓ Therapeutic Processes 1978

Professional Communication
  Use Scientific Communication

Professional Competence 1997
PN 811   SC 40675
SN Possessing the knowledge and qualifications of a particular profession.
  B   Competence 1982
  R   ↓ Employee Characteristics 1988
      ↓ Employee Skills 1973
      Peer Evaluation 1982
      ↓ Personnel Evaluation 1973
      Professional Development 1982
      Professional Liability 1985
      ↓ Professional Standards 1973
      Professionalism 2003

Professional Consultation 1973
PN 4384   SC 40680
SN Advisory services offered by specialists in a particular field which may be client or colleague oriented or focus on policy setting, planning, and programs of an organization.
  HN In 1982, this term replaced the discontinued term MENTAL HEALTH CONSULTATION. In 2000, MENTAL HEALTH CONSULTATION was removed from all records containing it and replaced with PROFESSIONAL CONSULTATION.
  UF Consultation (Professional)
      Mental Health Consultation
  N   Consultation Liaison Psychiatry 1991
  R   Personal Therapy 1991
      ↓ Professional Personnel 1978
      Professional Supervision 1988

Professional Development 1982
PN 3093   SC 40715
SN Participation in activities which promote professional career development.
  B   Development 1967
  R   Career Change 1978
      Career Development 1985
      ↓ Continuing Education 1985
      Employment History 1978
      Inservice Teacher Education 1973
      ↓ Inservice Training 1985
      Mental Health Inservice Training 1973
      Mentor 1985

Professional Development — (cont'd)
      Occupational Aspirations 1973
      ↓ Professional Certification 1973
      Professional Competence 1997
      Professional Identity 1991
      ↓ Professional Personnel 1978
      Professional Specialization 1991
      ↓ Professional Standards 1973

Professional Ethics 1973
PN 7136   SC 40720
SN Moral principles of conducting professional research or practices.
  B   Ethics 1967
  R   ↓ Abuse Reporting 1997
      Assisted Suicide 1997
      Bioethics 2003
      Dual Relationships 2003
      Duty to Warn 2001
      Euthanasia 1973
      Experimental Ethics 1978
      Impaired Professionals 1985
      Informed Consent 1985
      Privileged Communication 1973
      Professional Client Sexual Relations 1994
      Professional Liability 1985
      ↓ Professional Personnel 1978
      ↓ Professional Standards 1973

Professional Examinations 1994
PN 170   SC 40723
SN Required examinations for licensure or certification in order to practice a profession.
  UF Certification Examinations
      Licensure Examinations
      State Board Examinations
  B   Measurement 1967
  R   Accreditation (Education Personnel) 1973
      ↓ Professional Certification 1973
      ↓ Professional Licensing 1973

Professional Fees 1978
PN 369   SC 40724
  N   Fee for Service 1994
  R   Cost Containment 1991
      ↓ Costs and Cost Analysis 1973
      Diagnosis Related Groups 1988
      Health Care Costs 1994
      Money 1967
      Peer Evaluation 1982
      ↓ Professional Personnel 1978
      Salaries 1973

Professional Identity 1991
PN 877   SC 40725
SN Concept of self and role within a professional domain.
  UF Identity (Professional)
  B   Social Identity 1988
  R   Career Development 1985
      ↓ Employee Characteristics 1988
      Professional Development 1982
      ↓ Professional Personnel 1978
      Professionalism 2003
      Role Perception 1973
      ↓ Self Concept 1967

Professional Liability 1985
PN 1064   SC 40727
SN Legal liabilities relating to the conduct of one's profession.
  UF Legal Liability (Professional)
      Malpractice
  B   Professional Standards 1973

Professional Liability — (cont'd)
  R   Accountability 1988
      Duty to Warn 2001
      Impaired Professionals 1985
      ↓ Legal Processes 1973
      Misdiagnosis 1997
      Patient Abuse 1991
      Professional Competence 1997
      Professional Ethics 1973
      ↓ Responsibility 1973
      Risk Management 1997

Professional Licensing 1973
PN 606   SC 40730
SN Permission from an authority (e.g., government review board) to use a particular professional title as well as to practice the profession. Professional licensing laws also specify what activities constitute the legal or legitimate practice of the profession. One does not necessarily need to be certified (professionally) in order to be licensed.
  UF Licensing (Professional)
  N   Accreditation (Education Personnel) 1973
  R   ↓ Professional Certification 1973
      Professional Examinations 1994
      ↓ Professional Personnel 1978

Professional Networking 2004
PN 14   SC 40740
SN A linkage, association, or partnership of individuals or groups who collaborate to achieve professional goals or objectives.
  HN This term was introduced in June 2004. PsycINFO records from the past 10 years were re-indexed with this term. The posting note reflects the number of records that were re-indexed.
  UF Business Networking
  R   Career Development 1985
      ↓ Organizational Behavior 1978
      Social Networks 1994

Professional Newsletters
  Use Scientific Communication

Professional Organizations 1973
PN 2908   SC 40760
  B   Organizations 1967
  R   ↓ Professional Personnel 1978

Professional Orientation
  Use Theoretical Orientation

Professional Personnel 1978
PN 2242   SC 40765
SN Conceptually broad term referring to members of professions requiring prolonged and specialized training. Use a more specific term if possible.
  B   Personnel 1967
  N   ↓ Aerospace Personnel 1973
      Anthropologists 1973
      Clinicians 1973
      ↓ Counselors 1967
      ↓ Educational Personnel 1973
      Engineers 1967
      ↓ Health Personnel 1994
      ↓ Information Specialists 1988
      Journalists 1973
      ↓ Legal Personnel 1985
      Mathematicians 1973
      Physicists 1973
      ↓ Psychologists 1967
      Scientists 1967

Professional Personnel — (cont'd)

Sociologists 1973
↓ Therapists 1967
R ↓ Business and Industrial Personnel 1967
Impaired Professionals 1985
Librarians 1988
↓ Nonprofessional Personnel 1982
↓ Occupations 1967
↓ Paraprofessional Personnel 1973
↓ Professional Certification 1973
↓ Professional Consultation 1973
Professional Development 1982
Professional Ethics 1973
↓ Professional Fees 1978
Professional Identity 1991
↓ Professional Licensing 1973
Professional Organizations 1973
Professional Referral 1973
Professional Specialization 1991
↓ Professional Standards 1973
Professional Supervision 1988
↓ Religious Personnel 1973

Professional Referral 1973

PN 2070 SC 40770
SN Act of directing a client to a professional or agency for assessment, treatment, or consultation.
UF Referral (Professional)
R Client Transfer 1997
Court Referrals 1994
↓ Professional Personnel 1978
Self Referral 1991

Professional Specialization 1991

PN 540 SC 40775
SN Training in or choice of a speciality within a profession.
UF Specialization (Professional)
R Academic Specialization 1973
Career Development 1985
↓ Higher Education 1973
Occupational Choice 1967
Occupational Preference 1973
↓ Postgraduate Training 1973
Professional Development 1982
↓ Professional Personnel 1978

Professional Standards 1973

PN 3248 SC 40780
SN Minimally acceptable levels of quality professional care or services maintained in order to promote the welfare of those who make use of such services.
UF Standards (Professional)
N Professional Liability 1985
R Accountability 1988
Duty to Warn 2001
Impaired Professionals 1985
Patient Abuse 1991
Peer Evaluation 1982
Professional Client Sexual Relations 1994
Professional Competence 1997
Professional Development 1982
Professional Ethics 1973
↓ Professional Personnel 1978
Professionalism 2003
↓ Quality of Services 1997
Treatment Guidelines 2001

Professional Supervision 1988

PN 2393 SC 40785
SN Processes or techniques of supervision of fully trained educational or mental health personnel.

Professional Supervision — (cont'd)

UF Clinical Supervision
Educational Supervision
Supervision (Professional)
R ↓ Educational Personnel 1973
↓ Mental Health Personnel 1967
Personal Therapy 1991
↓ Professional Consultation 1973
↓ Professional Personnel 1978

Professionalism 2003

PN 85 SC 40788
SN Conduct, attitudes, and methods attributed to professionals.
HN This term was introduced in June 2003. PsycINFO records from the past 10 years were re-indexed with this term. The posting note reflects the number of records that were re-indexed.
R ↓ Employee Characteristics 1988
Professional Competence 1997
Professional Identity 1991
↓ Professional Standards 1973
Work (Attitudes Toward) 1973

Professors

Use College Teachers

Profiles (Measurement) 1973

PN 1671 SC 40800
SN Usually a composite of scores obtained through psychological testing utilizing instruments which yield separate measures and which comprises a picture or profile of the individual's characteristics across several areas.
B Measurement 1967

Profound Mental Retardation 2001

PN 1436 SC 40805
SN IQ below 20.
HN In 2000, this term replaced the discontinued and deleted term PROFOUNDLY MENTALLY RETARDED. PROFOUNDLY MENTALLY RETARDED was removed from all records containing it and replaced with PROFOUND MENTAL RETARDATION.
B Mental Retardation 1967

Progestational Hormones 1985

PN 108 SC 40815
UF Progestins
B Hormones 1967
N Progesterone 1973

Progesterone 1973

PN 1080 SC 40820
B Progestational Hormones 1985
Sex Hormones 1973
Steroids 1973

Progestins

Use Progestational Hormones

Prognosis 1973

PN 2944 SC 40830
SN Prediction of the course, duration, and outcome of a disorder. Compare DISEASE COURSE.
R Biological Markers 1991
↓ Chronic Mental Illness 1997
Clinical Judgment (Not Diagnosis) 1973
↓ Diagnosis 1967
Disease Course 1991

Prognosis — (cont'd)

↓ Disorders 1967
↓ Medical Diagnosis 1973
↓ Mental Disorders 1967
Patient History 1973
↓ Physical Disorders 1997
↓ Prediction 1967
↓ Psychodiagnosis 1967
Severity (Disorders) 1982
↓ Treatment 1967

Program Development 1991

PN 2210 SC 40832
SN Formulation and/or implementation of programs in any setting.
UF Program Planning
B Development 1967
N Educational Program Planning 1973
R Curriculum Development 1973
↓ Educational Programs 1973
Employee Assistance Programs 1985
↓ Government Programs 1973
Home Visiting Programs 1973
↓ Hospital Programs 1978
Independent Living Programs 1991
↓ Mental Health Programs 1973
↓ Program Evaluation 1985
↓ Psychiatric Hospital Programs 1967
↓ Social Programs 1973

Program Evaluation 1985

PN 3508 SC 40835
SN Assessment of programs in any setting.
B Evaluation 1967
N Educational Program Evaluation 1973
Mental Health Program Evaluation 1973
R ↓ Program Development 1991

Program Evaluation (Educational)

Use Educational Program Evaluation

Program Evaluation (Mental Health)

Use Mental Health Program Evaluation

Program Planning

Use Program Development

Program Planning (Educational)

Use Educational Program Planning

Programmed Instruction 2001

PN 951 SC 40870
HN In 2000, this term was created to update the spelling from the discontinued term PROGRAMED INSTRUCTION. PROGRAMED INSTRUCTION was removed from all records containing it and replaced with PROGRAMMED INSTRUCTION.
UF Instruction (Programmed)
B Teaching Methods 1967
R ↓ Computer Assisted Instruction 1973
Individualized Instruction 1973
Programmed Textbooks 2001
↓ Prompting 1997
Teaching Machines 1973

Programmed Textbooks 2001

PN 41 SC 40900
SN Textbooks prepared for use with programmed instruction. Not used as a document type identifier.

Programmed Textbooks — (cont'd)

HN In 2000, this term was created to update the spelling from the discontinued term PROGRAMED TEXTBOOKS. PROGRAMED TEXTBOOKS was removed from all records containing it and replaced with PROGRAMMED TEXTBOOKS.
B   Textbooks   1978
R   Programmed Instruction   2001

Programming (Computer)
Use   Computer Programming

Programming Languages (Computer)
Use   Computer Programming Languages

Programs (Government)
Use   Government Programs

Programs (Mental Health)
Use   Mental Health Programs

Progressive Relaxation Therapy   1978
PN 597   **SC** 40945
SN Therapeutic procedures which teach clients to tense and relax muscle groups, focusing on the sensations involved in relaxation. This method provides clients with practice in recognizing the sensation of tension which will serve as a cue to produce a state of muscle relaxation.
B   Relaxation Therapy   1978
R   ↓ Hypnotherapy   1973
     Muscle Relaxation   1973
     Systematic Desensitization Therapy   1973

Progressive Supranuclear Palsy   1997
PN 59   **SC** 40947
SN A progressive neurological disorder characterized by ophthalmoplegia, dystonia, memory impairment, personality disorders, and dementia. Etiology is unknown.
B   Central Nervous System Disorders   1973
R   ↓ Basal Ganglia   1973
     ↓ Senile Dementia   1973

Project Follow Through   1973
PN 41   **SC** 40950
SN U.S. Government educational program for disadvantaged elementary school students to supplement Project Head Start and encourage academic and psychosocial growth.
B   Educational Programs   1973
     Government Programs   1973
R   Compensatory Education   1973
     Government   1967

Project Head Start   1973
PN 651   **SC** 40960
SN U.S. Government program for disadvantaged 3-5 yr olds aimed at improving children's educational potential by encouraging their psychosocial development and by providing economic assistance to their families.
UF   Head Start
B   Educational Programs   1973
     Government Programs   1973
R   Compensatory Education   1973
     Government   1967
     Preschool Education   1973
     School Readiness   1973

Projection (Defense Mechanism)   1967
PN 530   **SC** 40970
B   Defense Mechanisms   1967
R   Projective Identification   1994

Projective Identification   1994
PN 305   **SC** 40975
B   Defense Mechanisms   1967
R   Enactments   1997
     Identification (Defense Mechanism)   1973
     Projection (Defense Mechanism)   1967

Projective Personality Measures   1973
PN 955   **SC** 40980
SN Tests which derive an indirect and global assessment of personality through the analysis of meaning or structure freely imposed by the subject upon unstructured or ambiguous materials. Use a more specific term if possible. Compare NON-PROJECTIVE PERSONALITY MEASURES.
HN In 1997, this term replaced the discontinued terms BLACKY PICTURES TEST, COLOR PYRAMID TEST, and ONOMATOPOEIA AND IMAGES TEST. In 2000, these terms were removed from all records containing them, and replaced with PROJECTIVE PERSONALITY MEASURES.
UF   Blacky Pictures Test
     Color Pyramid Test
     Onomatopoeia and Images Test
B   Personality Measures   1967
     Projective Techniques   1967
N   Bender Gestalt Test   1967
     Childrens Apperception Test   1973
     Holtzman Inkblot Technique   1967
     Human Figures Drawing   1973
     Rorschach Test   1967
     Rosenzweig Picture Frustration Study   1967
     Rotter Incomplete Sentences Blank   1973
     Sentence Completion Tests   1991
     Szondi Test   1973
     Thematic Apperception Test   1967
     Zulliger Z Test   1973
R   Psychoanalytic Interpretation   1967

Projective Techniques   1967
PN 1673   **SC** 40990
SN Utilization of ambiguous or unstructured stimuli designed to elicit responses which are believed to reveal an individual's attitudes, defense modes or motivations, and personality structure. Also, the specific tests or techniques themselves. Use a more specific term if possible.
UF   Projective Tests
N   Holtzman Inkblot Technique   1967
     ↓ Projective Personality Measures   1973
R   Psychoanalytic Interpretation   1967

Projective Testing Technique   1973
PN 378   **SC** 41000
SN Administration, construction, scoring, and interpretation of projective tests.
B   Measurement   1967

Projective Tests
Use   Projective Techniques

Prolactin   1973
PN 1658   **SC** 41020
B   Gonadotropic Hormones   1973
     Neuropeptides   2003

Proline   1982
PN 21   **SC** 41027
B   Amino Acids   1973

Prolixin
Use   Fluphenazine

Promazine   1973
PN 25   **SC** 41040
B   Phenothiazine Derivatives   1973

Promethazine   1973
PN 40   **SC** 41050
B   Antiemetic Drugs   1973
     Antihistaminic Drugs   1973
     Sedatives   1973

Promiscuity   1973
PN 127   **SC** 41060
UF   Sexual Delinquency
B   Psychosexual Behavior   1967
R   Extramarital Intercourse   1973
     Hypersexuality   1973
     Premarital Intercourse   1973
     Prostitution   1973
     Sexual Addiction   1997

Prompting   1997
PN 127   **SC** 41065
N   Constant Time Delay   1997
R   ↓ Behavior Modification   1973
     Cued Recall   1994
     Cues   1967
     ↓ Learning   1967
     ↓ Learning Strategies   1991
     ↓ Memory   1967
     ↓ Priming   1988
     Programmed Instruction   2001
     ↓ Teaching Methods   1967

Pronouns   1973
PN 469   **SC** 41070
B   Form Classes (Language)   1973

Pronunciation   1973
PN 547   **SC** 41080
B   Speech Characteristics   1973
R   Articulation (Speech)   1967

Proofreading   1988
PN 57   **SC** 41085
R   Clerical Secretarial Skills   1973
     ↓ Errors   1967
     Orthography   1973
     ↓ Reading   1967
     Verbal Ability   1967
     ↓ Written Communication   1985

Propaganda   1973
PN 85   **SC** 41090
B   Social Influences   1967
R   Brainwashing   1982
     ↓ Persuasive Communication   1967

Property
Use   Ownership

Propranolol   1973
PN 611   **SC** 41100
B   Adrenergic Blocking Drugs   1973

Propranolol — (cont'd)
Alcohols 1967

Proprioceptors 1973
PN 196   **SC** 41110
- **B**   Nerve Endings 1973
     Neural Receptors 1973
     Sensory Neurons 1973

Prose 1973
PN 916   **SC** 41120
- **B**   Literature 1967
- **N** ↓ Biography 1967
- **R**   Creative Writing 1994
     Text Structure 1982

Prosencephalon
Use Forebrain

Proserine
Use Neostigmine

Prosocial Behavior 1982
PN 1630   **SC** 41133
SN Positive social behavior generally concerned with promotion of the welfare of others. Limited to human populations.
- **B**   Social Behavior 1967
- **N**   Altruism 1973
-    ↓ Assistance (Social Behavior) 1973
     Charitable Behavior 1973
     Cooperation 1967
     Sharing (Social Behavior) 1978
     Trust (Social Behavior) 1967
- **R** ↓ Antisocial Behavior 1971
     Community Involvement 2003
     Generativity 2001
     Volunteers 2003

Prosody 1991
PN 585   **SC** 41134
SN Physical characteristics of speech that indicate linguistic features such as stress, intonation, intensity, and duration of speech sounds.
HN Use INFLECTION to access references from 1988-1990.
- **B**   Phonology 1973
- **N**   Inflection 1973
- **R** ↓ Linguistics 1973
     Morphology (Language) 1973
-    ↓ Phonemes 1973
     Sentence Structure 1973
-    ↓ Speech Characteristics 1973

Prosopagnosia 1994
PN 132   **SC** 41135
SN A visual agnosia usually due to brain damage and characterized by an inability to recognize familiar faces, and in some cases, one's own face.
- **B**   Agnosia 1973
- **R**   Face Perception 1985

Prospective Studies 1997
PN 266   **SC** 41137
SN Used in records discussing issues involved in the process of conducting studies of observations of the same individual or group over an extended period of time, usually to generate prognostic data or incidence rates related to a particular disorder, event, or behavior.

Prospective Studies — (cont'd)
HN From 1997-2000, the term was also used as a mandatory document type identifier; however, this usage has been discontinued due to the advent of Form/Content Type field identifiers. References from 1997-2000 can be accessed using either PROSPECTIVE STUDIES or the Prospective Studies Form/Content Type field identifier.
- **B**   Longitudinal Studies 1973
- **R**   Retrospective Studies 1997

Prostaglandins 1982
PN 237   **SC** 41136
SN Physiologically potent compounds of ubiquitous occurrence formed from essential fatty acids and affecting the nervous system, female reproductive organs, and metabolism.
- **R** ↓ Anti Inflammatory Drugs 1982
-    ↓ Fatty Acids 1973
-    ↓ Hormones 1967
-    ↓ Neuroleptic Drugs 1973
-    ↓ Sympathomimetic Drugs 1973

Prostate 1973
PN 194   **SC** 41140
- **B**   Male Genitalia 1973

Prostate Cancer Screening
Use Cancer Screening

Prostheses 1973
PN 274   **SC** 41150
- **UF** Artificial Limbs
- **B**   Medical Therapeutic Devices 1973
- **N**   Cochlear Implants 1994
- **R** ↓ Amputation 1973

Prostitution 1973
PN 771   **SC** 41160
- **B**   Psychosexual Behavior 1967
- **R**   Promiscuity 1973

Protective Services 1997
PN 470   **SC** 41170
- **B**   Social Services 1982
- **R**   Child Custody 1982
     Child Welfare 1988
     Elder Care 1994
     Foster Care 1978
     Guardianship 1988
-    ↓ Legal Processes 1973
     Shelters 1991
     Social Casework 1967

Protein Deficiency Disorders 1973
PN 43   **SC** 41180
- **B**   Nutritional Deficiencies 1973
- **N**   Kwashiorkor 1973

Protein Metabolism 1973
PN 198   **SC** 41190
- **B**   Metabolism 1967

Protein Sensitization
Use Anaphylactic Shock

Proteinases 1973
PN 56   **SC** 41210
- **B**   Enzymes 1973

Proteins 1973
PN 3006   **SC** 41220
- **N**   Apolipoproteins 2004
-    ↓ Blood Proteins 1973
-    ↓ Endorphins 1982
-    ↓ Globulins 1973
     Interferons 1994
- **R** ↓ Amino Acids 1973
-    ↓ Drugs 1967
-    ↓ Enzymes 1973
     Lipoproteins 1973
-    ↓ Neuropeptides 2003
-    ↓ Peptides 1973

Protest (Student)
Use Student Activism

Protestantism 1973
PN 505   **SC** 41250
- **B**   Christianity 1973
- **R**   Protestants 1997

Protestants 1997
PN 213   **SC** 41253
- **UF** Baptists
     Episcopalians
     Lutherans
     Methodists
     Presbyterians
- **B**   Christians 1997
- **R**   Protestantism 1973

Protozoa 1973
PN 22   **SC** 41255
- **B**   Microorganisms 1985

Prozac
Use Fluoxetine

Pruritus 1973
PN 55   **SC** 41260
- **UF** Itching
- **B**   Skin Disorders 1973
     Symptoms 1967
- **R**   Scratching 1973

Pseudocyesis 1973
PN 84   **SC** 41270
- **UF** False Pregnancy
     Pregnancy (False)
     Pseudopregnancy
- **B**   Conversion Disorder 2001
- **R** ↓ Gynecological Disorders 1973

Pseudodementia 1985
PN 109   **SC** 41280
SN Dementia-like disorder in the absence of organic brain disease.
- **B**   Mental Disorders 1967
- **R** ↓ Dementia 1985
-    ↓ Factitious Disorders 1988
-    ↓ Major Depression 1988

Pseudohermaphroditism
Use Hermaphroditism

Pseudomemory
Use False Memory

Pseudopregnancy
  Use Pseudocyesis

Pseudopsychopathic Schizophrenia
  Use Schizophrenia

Psilocybin 1973
PN 48   SC 41310
  B Hallucinogenic Drugs 1967

Psyche
  Use Mind

Psychedelic Drugs 1973
PN 114   SC 41320
  B Drugs 1967
  N Lysergic Acid Diethylamide 1967
  R ↓ Hallucinogenic Drugs 1967
  ↓ Psychotomimetic Drugs 1973

Psychedelic Experiences 1973
PN 52   SC 41330
  R Drug Induced Hallucinations 1973

Psychiatric Aides 1973
PN 87   SC 41340
  B Paramedical Personnel 1973
  Psychiatric Hospital Staff 1973

Psychiatric Classifications (Taxonomies)
  Use Psychodiagnostic Typologies

Psychiatric Clinics 1973
PN 658   SC 41370
  UF Outpatient Psychiatric Clinics
  B Clinics 1967
  R Child Guidance Clinics 1973
  Community Mental Health Centers 1973
  ↓ Hospitals 1967
  ↓ Mental Health Programs 1973
  ↓ Outpatient Treatment 1967
  Walk In Clinics 1973

Psychiatric Disorders
  Use Mental Disorders

Psychiatric Evaluation 1997
PN 505   SC 41385
  UF Evaluation (Psychiatric)
  B Evaluation 1967
  Measurement 1967
  N Forensic Evaluation 1994
  R Clinical Judgment (Not Diagnosis) 1973
  Cognitive Assessment 1997
  Geriatric Assessment 1997
  Intake Interview 1994
  ↓ Interview Schedules 2001
  ↓ Psychodiagnosis 1967
  ↓ Psychodiagnostic Interview 1973
  ↓ Psychological Assessment 1997
  Psychological Report 1988
  ↓ Screening 1982
  ↓ Screening Tests 1982

Psychiatric History
  Use Patient History

Psychiatric Hospital Admission 1973
PN 1165   SC 41390
  UF Admission (Psychiatric Hospital)
  B Hospital Admission 1973
  Psychiatric Hospitalization 1973
  N Psychiatric Hospital Readmission 1973
  R ↓ Commitment (Psychiatric) 1973
  ↓ Hospital Discharge 1973
  ↓ Institutional Release 1978
  Psychiatric Hospital Discharge 1978

Psychiatric Hospital Discharge 1978
PN 811   SC 41395
  B Hospital Discharge 1973
  Psychiatric Hospitalization 1973
  R Client Transfer 1997
  ↓ Commitment (Psychiatric) 1973
  Discharge Planning 1994
  ↓ Psychiatric Hospital Admission 1973
  Psychiatric Hospital Readmission 1973
  Treatment Termination 1982

Psychiatric Hospital Programs 1967
PN 1764   SC 41400
  SN Organized plans for care or training in psychiatric hospitals.
  B Hospital Programs 1978
  N Therapeutic Community 1967
  R Halfway Houses 1973
  ↓ Mental Health Services 1978
  ↓ Program Development 1991
  Token Economy Programs 1973

Psychiatric Hospital Readmission 1973
PN 701   SC 41410
  UF Readmission (Psychiatric Hospital)
  B Psychiatric Hospital Admission 1973
  Psychiatric Hospitalization 1973
  R ↓ Hospital Discharge 1973
  Psychiatric Hospital Discharge 1978

Psychiatric Hospital Staff 1973
PN 838   SC 41420
  B Medical Personnel 1967
  Mental Health Personnel 1967
  N Psychiatric Aides 1973
  R Attendants (Institutions) 1973
  Occupational Therapists 1973
  ↓ Paramedical Personnel 1973
  Psychiatric Nurses 1973
  Psychiatrists 1967

Psychiatric Hospitalization 1973
PN 4603   SC 41430
  B Hospitalization 1967
  N ↓ Psychiatric Hospital Admission 1973
  Psychiatric Hospital Discharge 1978
  Psychiatric Hospital Readmission 1973
  R ↓ Commitment (Psychiatric) 1973
  ↓ Hospital Admission 1973
  ↓ Hospital Discharge 1973
  ↓ Institutional Release 1978
  Patient Seclusion 1994

Psychiatric Hospitals 1967
PN 4022   SC 41440
  UF Asylums
  Mental Hospitals
  State Hospitals
  B Hospitals 1967
  R Halfway Houses 1973
  Patient Seclusion 1994

Psychiatric Hospitals — (cont'd)
  Psychiatric Units 1991
  Sanatoriums 1973

Psychiatric Nurses 1973
PN 1224   SC 41450
  B Mental Health Personnel 1967
  Nurses 1967
  R ↓ Psychiatric Hospital Staff 1973

Psychiatric Patients 1967
PN 21529   SC 41460
  B Patients 1967
  R ↓ Mental Disorders 1967
  Psychiatric Symptoms 1997
  Psychopathology 1967

Psychiatric Report
  Use Psychological Report

Psychiatric Residency
  Use Medical Residency AND Psychiatric Training

Psychiatric Social Workers 1973
PN 72   SC 41470
  B Mental Health Personnel 1967
  Social Workers 1973

Psychiatric Symptoms 1997
PN 3646   SC 41475
  UF Psychotic Symptoms
  B Symptoms 1967
  R ↓ Mental Disorders 1967
  Psychiatric Patients 1967
  Psychopathology 1967
  Symptom Checklists 1991
  Symptom Remission 1973

Psychiatric Training 1973
PN 2150   SC 41480
  UF Psychiatric Residency
  Training (Psychiatric)
  B Clinical Methods Training 1973
  Medical Education 1973
  R Cotherapy 1982
  Psychoanalytic Training 1973
  Psychotherapy Training 1973

Psychiatric Units 1991
PN 697   SC 41485
  SN Units in a general hospital or inpatient care facility specializing in psychiatric care of acutely disturbed patients.
  UF Hospital Psychiatric Units
  R ↓ Hospital Programs 1978
  ↓ Hospitalization 1967
  ↓ Hospitals 1967
  Nursing Homes 1973
  Patient Seclusion 1994
  Psychiatric Hospitals 1967
  ↓ Residential Care Institutions 1973

Psychiatrists 1967
PN 4914   SC 41490
  UF Neuropsychiatrists
  B Mental Health Personnel 1967
  Physicians 1967
  R Clinicians 1973
  Hypnotherapists 1973
  ↓ Psychiatric Hospital Staff 1973
  Psychoanalysts 1973

Psychiatrists — (cont'd)
↓ Psychologists 1967
↓ Psychotherapists 1973

Psychiatry 1967
PN 8291   SC 41500
B   Medical Sciences 1967
N   Adolescent Psychiatry 1985
     Biological Psychiatry 1994
     Child Psychiatry 1967
     Community Psychiatry 1973
     Consultation Liaison Psychiatry 1991
     Forensic Psychiatry 1973
     Geriatric Psychiatry 1997
     Neuropsychiatry 1973
     Orthopsychiatry 1973
     Social Psychiatry 1967
     Transcultural Psychiatry 1973
R   ↓ Psychology 1967
     ↓ Treatment 1967

Psychic Healing
Use Faith Healing

Psychoactive Drugs
Use Drugs

Psychoanalysis 1967
PN 22512   SC 41520
UF   Psychoanalytic Therapy
B   Psychotherapy 1967
N   Adlerian Psychotherapy 1997
     Dream Analysis 1973
     Self Analysis 1994
R   Catharsis 1973
     Erikson (Erik) 1991
     Free Association 1994
     Freud (Sigmund) 1967
     ↓ Hypnotherapy 1973
     Negative Therapeutic Reaction 1997
     ↓ Psychoanalytic Theory 1967
     Psychodynamic Psychotherapy 2003
     Psychotherapeutic Neutrality 1997
     ↓ Psychotherapeutic Processes 1967
     Transactional Analysis 1973

Psychoanalysts 1973
PN 3084   SC 41530
UF   Analysts
B   Psychotherapists 1973
R   Hypnotherapists 1973
     Psychiatrists 1967

Psychoanalytic Interpretation 1967
PN 7393   SC 41540
SN Description or formulation of the meaning or significance of any particular event, condition, or process (e.g., patient's productions, art, literature, or historical biographies) from a psychoanalytic perspective.
B   Theoretical Interpretation 1988
R   Freudian Psychoanalytic School 1973
     ↓ Projective Personality Measures 1973
     ↓ Projective Techniques 1967
     ↓ Psychoanalytic Theory 1967
     Psychohistory 1978

Psychoanalytic Personality Factors 1973
PN 605   SC 41550
UF   Personality Factors (Psychoanalytic)
B   Personality 1967

Psychoanalytic Personality Factors — (cont'd)
N   Conscience 1967
     Conscious (Personality Factor) 1973
     Death Instinct 1988
     Ego 1967
     Electra Complex 1973
     Id 1973
     Libido 1973
     Oedipal Complex 1973
     Subconscious 1973
     ↓ Superego 1973
     Unconscious (Personality Factor) 1967
R   Penis Envy 1973
     ↓ Personality Processes 1967

Psychoanalytic School (Freudian)
Use Freudian Psychoanalytic School

Psychoanalytic Theory 1967
PN 15440   SC 41570
N   Freudian Psychoanalytic School 1973
R   ↓ Ego Development 1991
     Erikson (Erik) 1991
     Free Association 1994
     Freud (Sigmund) 1967
     Metapsychology 1994
     ↓ Neopsychoanalytic School 1973
     Object Relations 1982
     ↓ Personality Processes 1967
     ↓ Psychoanalysis 1967
     Psychoanalytic Interpretation 1967
     Self Psychology 1988

Psychoanalytic Therapy
Use Psychoanalysis

Psychoanalytic Training 1973
PN 906   SC 41590
UF   Training (Psychoanalytic)
B   Clinical Methods Training 1973
R   Personal Therapy 1991
     Psychiatric Training 1973
     Psychotherapy Training 1973
     Self Analysis 1994

Psychoanalytically Oriented Psychotherapy
Use Psychodynamic Psychotherapy

Psychobiology 1982
PN 1058   SC 41595
SN Scientific discipline emphasizing the holistic functioning of the individual in the environment in relation to normal or abnormal behavior.
B   Sciences 1967
R   Behavioral Genetics 1994
     Biological Psychiatry 1994
     ↓ Biology 1967
     Biopsychosocial Approach 1991
     ↓ Psychology 1967

Psychodiagnosis 1967
PN 16324   SC 41600
SN Diagnosis of mental disorders through the use of psychological methods or tests. Compare MEDICAL DIAGNOSIS.
UF   Clinical Judgment (Psychodiagnosis)
B   Diagnosis 1967
N   ↓ Psychodiagnostic Interview 1973
R   Clinical Judgment (Not Diagnosis) 1973

Psychodiagnosis — (cont'd)
     Computer Assisted Diagnosis 1973
     Diagnostic and Statistical Manual 1994
     Differential Diagnosis 1967
     Educational Diagnosis 1978
     Forensic Evaluation 1994
     International Classification of Diseases 2001
     ↓ Mental Disorders 1967
     Patient History 1973
     Prognosis 1973
     ↓ Psychiatric Evaluation 1997
     ↓ Psychodiagnostic Typologies 1967
     ↓ Psychological Assessment 1997
     Psychological Report 1988
     Research Diagnostic Criteria 1994
     Structured Clinical Interview 2001

Psychodiagnostic Interview 1973
PN 1824   SC 41630
B   Interviews 1967
     Psychodiagnosis 1967
N   Diagnostic Interview Schedule 1991
     Structured Clinical Interview 2001
R   Intake Interview 1994
     ↓ Psychiatric Evaluation 1997
     ↓ Psychological Assessment 1997

Psychodiagnostic Typologies 1967
PN 6130   SC 41640
SN Systematic classification of mental, cognitive, emotional, or behavioral disorders.
UF   Psychiatric Classifications (Taxonomies)
     Typologies (Psychodiagnostic)
N   Diagnostic and Statistical Manual 1994
     International Classification of Diseases 2001
     Research Diagnostic Criteria 2001
R   Clinical Judgment (Not Diagnosis) 1973
     Diagnostic Interview Schedule 1991
     Dual Diagnosis 1991
     Labeling 1978
     Misdiagnosis 1997
     ↓ Psychodiagnosis 1967
     Structured Clinical Interview 2001
     Subtypes (Disorders) 2004
     Taxonomies 1973

Psychodrama 1967
PN 976   SC 41650
SN Projective technique and method of group psychotherapy in which personality make-up, interpersonal relations, conflicts, and emotional problems are explored through dramatization of meaningful situations.
UF   Drama Therapy
B   Psychotherapeutic Techniques 1967
     Psychotherapy 1967
R   ↓ Group Psychotherapy 1967
     Improvisation 2004
     Mirroring 1997
     Role Playing 1967

Psychodynamic Psychotherapy 2003
PN 182   SC 41657
SN An approach to psychotherapy that emphasizes inner conflict and ongoing intense psychological processes within the individual. Therapy is generally not as lengthy or intensive as psychoanalysis.
HN This term was introduced in June 2003. PsycINFO records from the past 10 years were re-indexed with this term. The posting note reflects the number of records that were re-indexed.
UF   Psychoanalytically Oriented Psychotherapy
B   Psychotherapy 1967
R   ↓ Psychoanalysis 1967

Psychodynamics 1973
PN 7201   SC 41660
SN Human behavior and emotions in terms of conscious and unconscious motivations.
- UF Psychological Correlates
- R ↓ Personality 1967
  Psychosocial Factors 1988
 ↓ Social Behavior 1967
 ↓ Social Interaction 1967

Psychoeducation 1994
PN 1088   SC 41665
- R Client Education 1985
- ↓ Education 1967
 Educational Therapy 1997
- ↓ Health Education 1973
- ↓ Treatment 1967

Psychogalvanic Reflex
Use Galvanic Skin Response

Psychogenesis 1973
PN 1108   SC 41670
SN Development of mental functions, traits, or states.
- UF Psychological Development
- B Development 1967
- N ↓ Cognitive Development 1973
 Emotional Development 1973
 Moral Development 1973
 ↓ Psychosocial Development 1973
- R Adolescent Development 1973
 Adult Development 1978
 Age Differences 1967
 ↓ Childhood Development 1967
 ↓ Delayed Development 1973
 Developmental Age Groups 1973
 ↓ Developmental Stages 1973
 ↓ Early Childhood Development 1978
 ↓ Human Development 1967
 ↓ Infant Development 1973
 Nature Nurture 1994
 Neonatal Development 1973
 ↓ Physical Development 1973
 Precocious Development 1973
 ↓ Prenatal Development 1973
 Sex Linked Developmental Differences 1973
 Sexual Development 1973

Psychogenic Pain
Use Somatoform Pain Disorder

Psychohistory 1978
PN 1232   SC 41685
SN Psychological, often psychoanalytical, interpretation of historical events and personalities. Includes psychobiographies, historical group fantasies and processes, studies of childhood from an historical perspective, and historical psychodynamics.
- R ↓ Biography 1967
- ↓ History 1973
 Psychoanalytic Interpretation 1967

Psychoimmunology
Use Psychoneuroimmunology

Psychokinesis 1973
PN 230   SC 41690
- UF Telekinesis
- B Extrasensory Perception 1967

Psycholinguistics 1967
PN 2478   SC 41700
SN Discipline that combines the techniques of linguistics and psychology in the study of the relationship of language and behavior and cognitive processes. Used for the discipline as well as specific psycholinguistic processes themselves.
- B Linguistics 1973
- R Ethnolinguistics 1973
 Metalinguistics 1994
 Neurolinguistics 1991
 Vygotsky (Lev) 1991

Psychological Abuse
Use Emotional Abuse

Psychological Adjustment
Use Emotional Adjustment

Psychological Assessment 1997
PN 3009   SC 41706
SN Assessment of a patient/client by interviews, observations, or psychological tests to evaluate personality, adjustment, abilities, interests, cognitive functioning, or functioning in other areas of life. Used for references that focus on the assessment process or the assessment itself.
- UF Assessment (Psychological)
- B Measurement 1967
- N ↓ Behavioral Assessment 1982
 Cognitive Assessment 1997
 ↓ Neuropsychological Assessment 1982
- R Clinical Judgment (Not Diagnosis) 1973
 ↓ Evaluation 1967
 Forensic Evaluation 1994
 Geriatric Assessment 1997
 ↓ Interview Schedules 2001
 ↓ Mental Disorders 1967
 Needs Assessment 1985
 ↓ Psychiatric Evaluation 1997
 ↓ Psychodiagnosis 1967
 ↓ Psychodiagnostic Interview 1973
 Psychological Report 1988
 Psychopathology 1967
 Structured Clinical Interview 2001

Psychological Autopsy 1988
PN 118   SC 41705
SN Psychological profile developed after an individual's death by examination of personal letters or by interviewing acquaintances and relatives. Such autopsies are usually done following suicidal deaths and suspicious cases of death.
- R Autopsy 1973
- ↓ Death and Dying 1967
 Forensic Psychology 1965
- ↓ Suicide 1967

Psychological Contracts 2003
PN 91   SC 58068
SN An implicit agreement between two individuals, an individual and an organization, or members of a group that represents the expectations that both parties have in the relationship.
HN This term was introduced in June 2003. PsycINFO records from the past 10 years were re-indexed with this term. The posting note reflects the number of records that were re-indexed.
- UF Contracts (Psychological)
- R Labor Management Relations 1967
- ↓ Organizational Behavior 1978
 Organizational Commitment 1991
 Supervisor Employee Interaction 1997

Psychological Correlates
Use Psychodynamics

Psychological Debriefing
Use Debriefing (Psychological)

Psychological Development
Use Psychogenesis

Psychological Endurance 1973
PN 515   SC 41710
- B Endurance 1973
- R Psychological Stress 1973
 Resilience (Psychological) 2003
 Stress Reactions 1973

Psychological Interpretation
Use Theoretical Interpretation

Psychological Needs 1997
PN 340   SC 41715
- UF Emotional Needs
- B Needs 1967
- R Need Satisfaction 1973
 Needs Assessment 1985

Psychological Reactance 1978
PN 309   SC 41716
SN Decrease in the attractiveness of an activity, behavior, or attitude as a result of having been forced or induced by external sources to engage in the activity or behavior, or to maintain the attitude. Such reactions may appear as emotional dissatisfaction, involvement and performance decrements, or negative attitude.
- UF Reactance
- R Choice Behavior 1997
 Cognitive Dissonance 1967
 Freedom 1978

Psychological Report 1988
PN 152   SC 41718
- UF Psychiatric Report
- R Educational Diagnosis 1978
- ↓ Evaluation 1967
 Forensic Evaluation 1994
- ↓ Medical Diagnosis 1973
- ↓ Psychiatric Evaluation 1997
- ↓ Psychodiagnosis 1967
- ↓ Psychological Assessment 1997

Psychological Screening Inventory 1973
PN 48   SC 41720
- B Nonprojective Personality Measures 1973
 Screening Tests 1982
 Selection Tests 1973

Psychological Stress 1973
PN 4827   SC 41730
- B Stress 1967
- R Chronic Stress 2004
- ↓ Deprivation 1967
 Psychological Endurance 1973
 Resilience (Psychological) 2003

Psychological Terminology 1973
PN 1380   SC 41740
SN Definitions, analysis, evaluation, or review of individual terms or nomenclature in the field of psychology. Compare GLOSSARY.

Psychological Terminology — (cont'd)
- **UF** Nomenclature (Psychological)
  Terminology (Psychological)
- **B** Terminology 1991
- **R** Scientific Communication 1973

Psychological Testing
- **Use** Psychometrics

Psychological Theories 2001
PN 581　　　　　　　　　SC 41746
- **B** Theories 1967
- **N** Associationism 1973
  Behaviorism 1967
  Freudian Psychoanalytic School 1973
  Functionalism 1973
  Gestalt Psychology 1967
  ↓ Neopsychoanalytic School 1973
  Structuralism 1973
- **R** ↓ History of Psychology 1967
  ↓ Psychology 1967

Psychologist Attitudes 1991
PN 621　　　　　　　　　SC 41747
- **SN** Attitudes of, not toward, psychologists.
- **B** Attitudes 1967
- **R** Counselor Attitudes 1973
  ↓ Health Personnel Attitudes 1985
  ↓ Psychologists 1967
  ↓ Therapist Attitudes 1978

Psychologists 1967
PN 7509　　　　　　　　　SC 41750
- **B** Professional Personnel 1978
- **N** Clinical Psychologists 1973
  Counseling Psychologists 1988
  ↓ Educational Psychologists 1973
  Experimental Psychologists 1973
  Industrial Psychologists 1973
  Military Psychologists 1997
  Social Psychologists 1973
- **R** Adler (Alfred) 1967
  ↓ Counselors 1967
  Ellis (Albert) 1991
  Erikson (Erik) 1991
  Freud (Sigmund) 1967
  James (William) 1991
  Jung (Carl) 1973
  Kohlberg (Lawrence) 1991
  Maslow (Abraham Harold) 1991
  ↓ Mental Health Personnel 1967
  Pavlov (Ivan) 1991
  Piaget (Jean) 1967
  Psychiatrists 1967
  Psychologist Attitudes 1991
  ↓ Psychotherapists 1973
  Rogers (Carl) 1991
  Scientists 1967
  Skinner (Burrhus Frederic) 1991
  ↓ Social Workers 1973
  Vygotsky (Lev) 1991
  Watson (John Broadus) 1991

Psychology 1967
PN 10020　　　　　　　　SC 41760
- **B** Behavioral Sciences 1997
- **N** Abnormal Psychology 2003
  ↓ Applied Psychology 1973
  ↓ Clinical Psychology 1967
  Cognitive Psychology 1985
  Comparative Psychology 1967
  Cross Cultural Psychology 1997
  Depth Psychology 1973

Psychology — (cont'd)
- ↓ Developmental Psychology 1973
  Ecological Psychology 1994
  Evolutionary Psychology 2003
  Experimental Psychology 1967
  Folk Psychology 1997
  Forensic Psychology 1985
  ↓ Humanistic Psychology 1985
  Mathematical Psychology 1973
  Metapsychology 1994
  ↓ Physiological Psychology 1967
  Positive Psychology 2003
  Self Psychology 1988
- **R** ↓ History of Psychology 1967
  ↓ Psychiatry 1967
  Psychobiology 1982
  ↓ Psychological Theories 2001
  ↓ Psychophysiology 1967

Psychology Education 1978
PN 3256　　　　　　　　　SC 41765
- **B** Curriculum 1967
- **N** ↓ Graduate Psychology Education 1967
- **R** Counselor Education 1973
  Educational Program Accreditation 1994
  Theoretical Orientation 1982

Psychometrics 1967
PN 5981　　　　　　　　　SC 41770
- **SN** Subdiscipline within psychology dealing with the development and application of statistical techniques to the analysis of psychological data. Also, psychological measurement in which numerical estimates are obtained of a specific aspect of performance.
- **UF** Psychological Testing
- **B** Measurement 1967
- **R** Classical Test Theory 2003
  Conjoint Measurement 1994
  ↓ Experimental Design 1967
  ↓ Experimentation 1967
  Item Response Theory 1985
  Psychophysics 1967
  ↓ Statistical Analysis 1967
  Test Interpretation 1985
  ↓ Testing 1967

Psychomotor Development 1973
PN 398　　　　　　　　　SC 41780
- **B** Motor Development 1973
- **N** ↓ Speech Development 1973
- **R** ↓ Childhood Development 1967
  ↓ Perceptual Development 1973
  Perceptual Motor Development 1991

Psychomotor Processes
- **Use** Perceptual Motor Processes

Psychoneuroimmunology 1991
PN 663　　　　　　　　　SC 41795
- **SN** Study of the interrelationship among immune responses, psychological processes, and the nervous system. Used for the scientific discipline or the psychoneuroimmunologic processes themselves.
- **UF** Psychoimmunology
- **B** Immunology 1973
  Psychophysiology 1967
- **R** ↓ Endocrinology 1973
  Neuropsychology 1973

Psychoneurosis
- **Use** Neurosis

Psychopath
- **Use** Antisocial Personality Disorder

Psychopathology 1967
PN 12284　　　　　　　　SC 41820
- **SN** Study of mental disorders, emotional problems, or maladaptive behaviors. Used for the scientific discipline or for unspecified dysfunctions.
- **B** Pathology 1973
- **R** Abnormal Psychology 2003
  ↓ Antisocial Behavior 1971
  Comorbidity 1991
  ↓ Defense Mechanisms 1967
  ↓ Emotional Adjustment 1973
  Homeless Mentally Ill 1997
  ↓ Mental Disorders 1967
  Psychiatric Patients 1967
  Psychiatric Symptoms 1997
  ↓ Psychological Assessment 1997

Psychopathy
- **Use** Antisocial Personality Disorder

Psychopharmacology 1967
PN 3482　　　　　　　　　SC 41840
- **SN** The study of the effect of drugs on behavior or other psychological processes. For the use of drugs in a treatment capacity, use DRUG THERAPY.
- **B** Pharmacology 1973
- **R** Drug Abuse Liability 1994

Psychophysical Measurement 1967
PN 1837　　　　　　　　　SC 41850
- **SN** Techniques or methodology used to assess perceptual sensitivities and functions of any sensory modality as related to the parameters of stimulation.
- **N** Magnitude Estimation 1991
- **R** Fuzzy Set Theory 1991
  ↓ Perceptual Measures 1973
  Signal Detection (Perception) 1967
  Threshold Determination 1973

Psychophysics 1967
PN 1147　　　　　　　　　SC 41860
- **R** ↓ Experimentation 1967
  Psychometrics 1967

Psychophysiologic Disorders
- **Use** Somatoform Disorders

Psychophysiology 1967
PN 3698　　　　　　　　　SC 41880
- **SN** Study of the physiological correlates of mental, somatic, and behavioral processes.
- **B** Physiology 1967
- **N** Psychoneuroimmunology 1991
- **R** Cardiovascular Reactivity 1994
  ↓ Physiological Psychology 1967
  ↓ Psychology 1967

Psychosexual Behavior 1967
PN 10899　　　　　　　　SC 41890
- **SN** Human sexual behavior which includes both mental and somatic aspects of sexuality.
- **UF** Sexual Behavior
- **B** Behavior 1967
- **N** Bisexuality 1973
  Erection (Penis) 1973
  Extramarital Intercourse 1973
  Heterosexuality 1973
  ↓ Homosexuality 1967

Psychosexual Behavior — (cont'd)

- ↓ Human Courtship 1973
- Hypersexuality 1973
- Masturbation 1973
- Monogamy 1997
- ↓ Orgasm 1973
- ↓ Paraphilias 1988
- Promiscuity 1973
- Prostitution 1973
- Safe Sex 2003
- Seduction 1994
- Sex Roles 1967
- Sexual Abstinence 1973
- ↓ Sexual Arousal 1978
- ↓ Sexual Function Disturbances 1973
- ↓ Sexual Intercourse (Human) 1973
- Sexual Risk Taking 1997
- Transsexualism 1973
- Transvestism 1973
- Virginity 1973
- **R** Affection 1973
- Assortative Mating 1991
- Autoeroticism 1997
- Erotomania 1997
- Human Mate Selection 1988
- Pornography 1973
- Professional Client Sexual Relations 1994
- Psychosexual Development 1982
- Romance 1997
- Sex 1967
- Sex Linked Developmental Differences 1973
- Sexual Addiction 1997
- Sexual Attitudes 1973
- Sexual Attraction 2003
- Sexual Development 1973
- Sexual Fantasy 1997
- ↓ Sexual Orientation 1997
- Sexual Partners 2000
- Sexual Satisfaction 1994

Psychosexual Development 1982

PN 1889   **SC** 41895
SN Psychological maturation and development of sexual identity, desires, beliefs, and attitudes throughout the life cycle.
- **B** Psychosocial Development 1973
- **R** Emotional Development 1973
- ↓ Gender Identity 1985
- ↓ Psychosexual Behavior 1967
- Sex 1967
- Sexual Attitudes 1973
- Sexual Development 1973
- Sexuality 1973

Psychosis 1967

PN 9540   **SC** 41910
- **B** Mental Disorders 1967
- **N** ↓ Acute Psychosis 1973
- ↓ Affective Psychosis 1973
- ↓ Alcoholic Psychosis 1973
- Capgras Syndrome 1985
- ↓ Childhood Psychosis 1967
- Chronic Psychosis 1973
- Experimental Psychosis 1973
- ↓ Hallucinosis 1973
- ↓ Paranoia (Psychosis) 1967
- Postpartum Psychosis 2003
- Process Psychosis 1973
- Reactive Psychosis 1973
- ↓ Schizophrenia 1967
- Senile Psychosis 1973
- Toxic Psychoses 1973
- **R** Borderline States 1978
- Paranoid Schizophrenia 1967

Psychosocial Development 1973

PN 8984   **SC** 41920
SN Process of psychological and social maturation occurring at any time during the life cycle.
- **UF** Social Development
- **B** Psychogenesis 1973
- **N** Childhood Play Development 1973
- ↓ Personality Development 1967
- Psychosexual Development 1982
- **R** Aging (Attitudes Toward) 1985
- Emotional Development 1973
- Erikson (Erik) 1991
- Generativity 2001
- Moral Development 1973
- Object Relations 1982

Psychosocial Factors 1988

PN 13996   **SC** 41925
- **R** Demographic Characteristics 1967
- Psychodynamics 1973
- Risk Factors 2001
- ↓ Social Influences 1967
- ↓ Sociocultural Factors 1967

Psychosocial Mental Retardation 1973

PN 50   **SC** 41930
SN Reversible mental retardation due to environmental and/or social factors with no organic etiological component.
- **UF** Cultural Familial Mental Retardation
- **B** Mental Retardation 1967
- **R** Borderline Mental Retardation 1973

Psychosocial Readjustment 1973

PN 1204   **SC** 41940
SN Attainment of attitudes and skills which will facilitate an individual's reintegration or functioning in society, usually following traumatic or unusual personal experiences.
HN In 1982, this term replaced the discontinued term PSYCHOSOCIAL RESOCIALIZATION. In 2000, PSYCHOSOCIAL RESOCIALIZATION was removed from all records and replaced with PSYCHOSOCIAL READJUSTMENT.
- **UF** Psychosocial Resocialization
- Readjustment (Psychosocial)
- Resocialization (Psychosocial)
- **R** ↓ Psychosocial Rehabilitation 1973
- ↓ Treatment 1967

Psychosocial Rehabilitation 1973

PN 2086   **SC** 41950
SN Programs, techniques, or processes of treatment by which individuals, institutionalized or otherwise removed from normal community life (e.g., prisoners), acquire psychological and social skills and attitudes which facilitate community reentry.
- **UF** Rehabilitation (Psychosocial)
- **B** Rehabilitation 1967
- **N** Therapeutic Social Clubs 1973
- ↓ Vocational Rehabilitation 1967
- **R** ↓ Drug Rehabilitation 1973
- Psychosocial Readjustment 1973
- Rehabilitation Counseling 1978

Psychosocial Resocialization

  Use Psychosocial Readjustment

Psychosomatic Disorders

  Use Somatoform Disorders

Psychosomatic Medicine 1978

PN 627   **SC** 41975
SN Medical specialty dealing with the diagnosis and treatment of psychosomatic disorders.
- **B** Medical Sciences 1967
- **R** ↓ Health Care Psychology 1985
- Somatization Disorder 2001
- ↓ Somatoform Disorders 2001

Psychostimulant Drugs

  Use CNS Stimulating Drugs

Psychosurgery 1973

PN 343   **SC** 41980
- **UF** Leukotomy
- Lobectomy
- Lobotomy
- **B** Neurosurgery 1973
- Physical Treatment Methods 1973
- **N** Thalamotomy 1973
- **R** Sympathectomy 1973
- Tractotomy 1973

Psychotherapeutic Breakthrough 1973

PN 78   **SC** 41990
- **UF** Breakthrough (Psychotherapeutic)
- **B** Psychotherapeutic Processes 1967

Psychotherapeutic Counseling 1973

PN 1003   **SC** 42000
- **B** Counseling 1967
- Psychotherapy 1967
- **N** ↓ Family Therapy 1967
- **R** ↓ Marriage Counseling 1973
- Premarital Counseling 1973

Psychotherapeutic Methods

  Use Psychotherapeutic Techniques

Psychotherapeutic Neutrality 1997

PN 47   **SC** 42025
- **UF** Neutrality (Psychotherapeutic)
- **R** ↓ Psychoanalysis 1967
- ↓ Psychotherapeutic Processes 1967
- ↓ Psychotherapeutic Techniques 1967

Psychotherapeutic Outcomes 1973

PN 3362   **SC** 42030
SN Limited to treatment results that are a direct function of specific characteristics of clients or therapists or a function of unique or specifically-described circumstances of the treatment itself.
- **UF** Outcomes (Psychotherapeutic)
- **D** Treatment Outcomes 1982
- **R** Mental Health Program Evaluation 1973
- Treatment Dropouts 1978
- Treatment Effectiveness Evaluation 1973

Psychotherapeutic Processes 1967

PN 20218   **SC** 42040
SN Experiential, attitudinal, emotional, or behavioral phenomena occurring during the course of psychotherapy. Applies to the client or psychotherapist individually or to their interaction.
- **UF** Client Counselor Interaction
- Counselor Client Interaction
- Patient Therapist Interaction
- Therapist Patient Interaction
- **B** Therapeutic Processes 1978
- **N** Countertransference 1973
- Insight (Psychotherapeutic Process) 1973

Psychotherapeutic Processes — (cont'd)

Negative Therapeutic Reaction 1997
Psychotherapeutic Breakthrough 1973
Psychotherapeutic Resistance 1973
Psychotherapeutic Transference 1967
Therapeutic Alliance 1994
R Cross Cultural Counseling 2003
Enactments 1997
↓ Internalization 1997
Mirroring 1997
Privileged Communication 1973
Professional Client Sexual Relations 1994
↓ Psychoanalysis 1967
Psychotherapeutic Neutrality 1997
↓ Psychotherapy 1967
↓ Treatment Outcomes 1982

Psychotherapeutic Resistance 1973

PN 949   **SC** 42050
SN Conscious or unconscious defensive attempts by the client to prevent repressed material from coming to consciousness.
UF Resistance (Psychotherapeutic)
B Psychotherapeutic Processes 1967
Resistance 1997
R Negative Therapeutic Reaction 1997
Treatment Refusal 1994

Psychotherapeutic Techniques 1967

PN 12351   **SC** 42060
UF Psychotherapeutic Methods
Therapeutic Techniques (Psychotherapy)
B Treatment 1967
N Animal Assisted Therapy 1994
Autogenic Training 1973
Cotherapy 1982
Dream Analysis 1973
Guided Imagery 2001
Mirroring 1997
Morita Therapy 1994
Mutual Storytelling Technique 1973
Paradoxical Techniques 1982
Psychodrama 1967
R Age Regression (Hypnotic) 1988
Centering 1991
Client Centered Therapy 1967
Conjoint Therapy 1973
↓ Creative Arts Therapy 1994
Free Association 1994
Homework 1988
Improvisation 2004
Interpersonal Psychotherapy 1997
Poetry Therapy 1994
Primal Therapy 1978
Psychotherapeutic Neutrality 1997
↓ Psychotherapy 1967
Rational Emotive Behavior Therapy 2003
Reality Therapy 1973
↓ Relaxation Therapy 1978
Role Playing 1967
↓ Self Help Techniques 1982
Self Talk 1988
↓ Twelve Step Programs 1997
Wilderness Experience 1991

Psychotherapeutic Transference 1967

PN 3694   **SC** 42070
SN Unconscious projection of feelings, thoughts, and wishes to the therapist that were originally associated with important figures from the client's past.
UF Transference (Psychotherapeutic)
B Psychotherapeutic Processes 1967
R Countertransference 1973
Enactments 1997

Psychotherapeutic Transference — (cont'd)

Negative Therapeutic Reaction 1997
Professional Client Sexual Relations 1994
Therapeutic Alliance 1994

Psychotherapist Attitudes 1973

PN 913   **SC** 42080
SN Attitudes of, not toward, psychotherapists.
B Therapist Attitudes 1978
R ↓ Psychotherapists 1973
Therapist Role 1978

Psychotherapist Trainees

Use Therapist Trainees

Psychotherapists 1973

PN 3896   **SC** 42100
B Mental Health Personnel 1967
Therapists 1967
N Hypnotherapists 1973
Psychoanalysts 1973
R Clinical Psychologists 1973
Psychiatrists 1967
↓ Psychologists 1967
Psychotherapist Attitudes 1973

Psychotherapy 1967

PN 21523   **SC** 42110
UF Reconstructive Psychotherapy
B Treatment 1967
N Adlerian Psychotherapy 1997
Adolescent Psychotherapy 1994
Analytical Psychotherapy 1973
Autogenic Training 1973
↓ Behavior Therapy 1967
Brief Psychotherapy 1967
↓ Child Psychotherapy 1967
Client Centered Therapy 1967
Cognitive Behavior Therapy 2003
Eclectic Psychotherapy 1994
Existential Therapy 1973
Experiential Psychotherapy 1973
Expressive Psychotherapy 1973
Eye Movement Desensitization Therapy 1997
Feminist Therapy 1994
Geriatric Psychotherapy 1973
Gestalt Therapy 1973
↓ Group Psychotherapy 1967
Guided Imagery 2001
↓ Humanistic Psychotherapy 2003
↓ Hypnotherapy 1973
Individual Psychotherapy 1973
Insight Therapy 1973
Integrative Psychotherapy 2003
Interpersonal Psychotherapy 1997
Logotherapy 1973
Persuasion Therapy 1973
Primal Therapy 1978
↓ Psychoanalysis 1967
Psychodrama 1967
Psychodynamic Psychotherapy 2003
↓ Psychotherapeutic Counseling 1973
Rational Emotive Behavior Therapy 2003
Reality Therapy 1973
Relationship Therapy 1973
Solution Focused Therapy 2004
Supportive Psychotherapy 1997
Transactional Analysis 1973
R Cognitive Therapy 1982
Cotherapy 1982
Couples Therapy 1994
Educational Therapy 1997

Psychotherapy — (cont'd)

Holistic Health 1985
↓ Marriage Counseling 1973
Online Therapy 2003
Paradoxical Techniques 1982
Pastoral Counseling 1967
Phototherapy 1991
↓ Psychotherapeutic Processes 1967
↓ Psychotherapeutic Techniques 1967
Recreation Therapy 1973
Spontaneous Remission 1973
Theoretical Orientation 1982

Psychotherapy (Individual)

Use Individual Psychotherapy

Psychotherapy Training 1973

PN 1704   **SC** 42120
UF Training (Psychotherapy)
B Clinical Methods Training 1973
R Cotherapy 1982
Counselor Education 1973
Psychiatric Training 1973
Psychoanalytic Training 1973

Psychotic Depressive Reaction

Use Major Depression

Psychotic Episode (Acute)

Use Acute Psychosis

Psychotic Symptoms

Use Psychiatric Symptoms

Psychoticism 1978

PN 572   **SC** 42145
B Personality Traits 1967

Psychotomimetic Drugs 1973

PN 54   **SC** 42150
B Drugs 1967
N Lysergic Acid Diethylamide 1967
Mescaline 1973
Peyote 1973
R Experimental Psychosis 1973
↓ Hallucinogenic Drugs 1967
↓ Psychedelic Drugs 1973

Psychotropic Drugs

Use Drugs

PTA

Use Parent School Relationship

Puberty 1973

PN 765   **SC** 42160
B Developmental Stages 1973
R Menarche 1973

Pubescence

Use Sexual Development

Public Attitudes

Use Public Opinion

Public Health 1988

PN 1158   **SC** 42185

Public Health — (cont'd)
- **B** Health 1973
- **N** Epidemics 2001
- **R** Health Promotion 1991
  - ↓ Health Screening 1997
  - Public Health Services 1973
  - Public Service Announcements 2004

Public Health Service Nurses 1973
PN 176   **SC** 42190
- **B** Government Personnel 1973
  - Nurses 1967
- **R** Public Health Services 1973

Public Health Services 1973
PN 975   **SC** 42200
- **B** Community Services 1967
- **R** ↓ Health 1973
  - Integrated Services 1997
  - ↓ Mental Health Programs 1973
  - ↓ Public Health 1988
  - Public Health Service Nurses 1973

Public Opinion 1973
PN 2405   **SC** 42210
- **UF** Opinion (Public)
  - Public Attitudes
- **B** Attitudes 1967
- **R** Community Attitudes 1973
  - Political Psychology 1997
  - Public Relations 1973

Public Policy
- **Use** Government Policy Making

Public Relations 1973
PN 315   **SC** 42220
- **SN** The business of attempting to influence or persuade individuals or the public to have an understanding or concern for, or positive disposition toward, a particular person, organization, idea, policy, practice, or activity.
- **R** ↓ Advertising 1967
  - ↓ Consumer Attitudes 1973
  - Public Opinion 1973

Public School Education 1973
PN 1298   **SC** 42230
- **SN** Education in free tax-supported schools controlled by a local governmental authority.
- **B** Education 1967

Public Sector 1985
PN 773   **SC** 42235
- **SN** Any type of government-related or public organization, service, or sphere of involvement.
- **N** Government 1967
  - Government Agencies 1973

Public Service Announcements 2004
PN 27   **SC** 42232
- **HN** This term was introduced in June 2004. Psyc-INFO records from the past 10 years were re-indexed with this term. The posting note reflects the number of records that were re-indexed.
- **R** Advocacy 1985
  - Health Promotion 1991
  - ↓ Mass Media 1967
  - ↓ Persuasive Communication 1967
  - ↓ Prevention 1973

Public Service Announcements — (cont'd)
- ↓ Public Health 1988
- Television Advertising 1973

Public Speaking 1973
PN 590   **SC** 42240
- **SN** Formal or informal speech in a group or public setting.
- **B** Oral Communication 1985
- **R** Debates 1997
  - Speech Anxiety 1985

Public Transportation 1973
PN 143   **SC** 42250
- **B** Community Facilities 1973
  - Transportation 1973
- **R** Air Transportation 1973
  - Railroad Trains 1973

Public Welfare Services
- **Use** Community Welfare Services

Puerperal Depression
- **Use** Postpartum Depression

Puerperal Psychosis
- **Use** Postpartum Psychosis

Puerto Rican Americans
- **Use** Hispanics

Pulmonary Disorders
- **Use** Lung Disorders

Pulmonary Emphysema 1973
PN 43   **SC** 42290
- **UF** Emphysema (Pulmonary)
- **B** Lung Disorders 1973

Pulmonary Tuberculosis 1973
PN 16   **SC** 42300
- **B** Bacterial Disorders 1973
  - Lung Disorders 1973
  - Tuberculosis 1973

Pulse (Arterial)
- **Use** Arterial Pulse

Punishment 1967
PN 3037   **SC** 42320
- **SN** Presentation of a punisher contingent on the performance of some behavior. Also, the punishing event or object itself which, when following the performance of some behavior, results in a reduction in the occurrence or frequency of that behavior. Compare AVERSIVE STIMULATION. Used for both human and animal populations.
- **UF** Corporal Punishment
- **B** Reinforcement 1967
- **N** Response Cost 1997
- **R** Coercion 1994
  - Threat 1967

Punishment (Capital)
- **Use** Capital Punishment

Pupil (Eye) 1973
PN 154   **SC** 42340
- **B** Eye (Anatomy) 1967

Pupil Dilation 1973
PN 333   **SC** 42360
- **UF** Dilation (Pupil)
- **R** ↓ Eye (Anatomy) 1967

Purging (Eating Disorders) 2003
PN 39   **SC** 42383
- **SN** Compensatory behaviors including self-induced vomiting, misuse of laxatives, diuretics, or enemas for the purpose of preventing weight gain.
- **HN** This term was introduced in June 2003. Psyc-INFO records from the past 10 years were re-indexed with this term. The posting note reflects the number of records that were re-indexed.
- **B** Eating Disorders 1997
- **R** Binge Eating 1991
  - Bulimia 1985
  - ↓ Diuretics 1973
  - Vomiting 1973

Purkinje Cells 1994
PN 164   **SC** 42385
- **B** Cerebellum 1973
  - Neurons 1973

Puromycin 1973
PN 37   **SC** 42390
- **B** Amines 1973
  - Antibiotics 1973

Putamen 1985
PN 316   **SC** 42405
- **SN** The largest and most lateral part of the basal ganglia which, together with the caudate nucleus and globus pallidus, forms the corpus striatum.
- **B** Basal Ganglia 1973
  - Striatum 2003

Pygmalion Effect
- **Use** Self Fulfilling Prophecies

Pygmy Chimpanzees
- **Use** Bonobos

Pyramidal Tracts 1973
PN 144   **SC** 42410
- **B** Efferent Pathways 1982
  - Spinal Cord 1973

Pyramidotomy 1973
PN 10   **SC** 42420
- **B** Neurosurgery 1973
- **R** Tractotomy 1973

Pyromania 1973
PN 46   **SC** 42430
- **R** ↓ Impulse Control Disorders 1997
  - Impulsiveness 1973
  - ↓ Personality Disorders 1967

Q Sort Testing Technique 1967
PN 187   **SC** 42440
- **B** Testing Methods 1967

Q Test
 Use   Cochran Q Test

Quaalude
 Use   Methaqualone

Quadriplegia 1985
 PN 109   SC 42470
 SN Paralysis of both arms and both legs.
 B   Paralysis 1973
 R ↓ Central Nervous System Disorders 1973
     Hemiplegia 1978
   ↓ Injuries 1973
   ↓ Musculoskeletal Disorders 1973
     Paraplegia 1978
   ↓ Spinal Cord Injuries 1973

Quails 1973
 PN 423   SC 42480
 B   Birds 1967

Qualitative Methods
 Use   Qualitative Research

Qualitative Research 2003
 PN 290   SC 42481
 SN A type of research methodology that produces
 descriptive data, with little emphasis given to numeri-
 cal quantification. Used only when the methodology
 or research itself is the focus of discussion.
 HN This term was introduced in June 2003. Psyc-
 INFO records from the past 10 years were re-indexed
 with this term. The posting note reflects the number
 of records that were re-indexed.
 UF   Qualitative Methods
 B   Experimentation 1967
      Methodology 1967
 R   Data Collection 1982
    ↓ Empirical Methods 1973
    ↓ Experimental Design 1967
      Grounded Theory 2004
    ↓ Interviews 1967
      Observation Methods 1967

Quality Circles
 Use   Participative Management

Quality Control 1900
 PN 466   SC 42483
 SN Efforts or techniques directed at the detection of
 imperfections or shortcomings in products or ser-
 vices.
 R   Accountability 1988
      Consumer Satisfaction 1994
      Human Factors Engineering 1973
      Organizational Effectiveness 1985
      Organizational Objectives 1973
      Participative Management 1988
    ↓ Quality of Services 1997

Quality of Care 1988
 PN 2319   SC 42484
 SN Quality of medical or mental health care.
 B   Quality of Services 1997
 R   Accountability 1988
      Caregivers 1988
      Child Day Care 1973
    ↓ Client Rights 1988
      Continuum of Care 2004

Quality of Care — (cont'd)
   ↓ Health Care Delivery 1978
   ↓ Health Care Services 1978
     Home Care 1985
   ↓ Managed Care 1994
   ↓ Mental Health Services 1978
   ↓ Treatment 1967

Quality of Education
 Use   Educational Quality

Quality of Life 1985
 PN 6837   SC 42485
 N   Quality of Work Life 1988
 R   Life Changes 2004
      Life Satisfaction 1985
    ↓ Lifestyle 1978
      Lifestyle Changes 1997
      Well Being 1994

Quality of Services 1997
 PN 828   SC 57510
 SN Used for health care and non-health care ser-
 vices. Consider QUALITY of CARE for health care
 services.
 UF   Service Quality
 N   Quality of Care 1988
 R ↓ Advertising 1967
   ↓ Consumer Attitudes 1973
     Consumer Satisfaction 1994
   ↓ Health Care Delivery 1978
   ↓ Health Care Services 1978
     Marketing 1973
   ↓ Mental Health Services 1978
   ↓ Professional Standards 1973
     Quality Control 1988
     Retailing 1991
     Treatment Guidelines 2001

Quality of Work Life 1988
 PN 477   SC 42487
 SN Includes aspects such as salary, benefits,
 safety, and efficiency, as well as variety and chal-
 lenge, responsibility, contribution, and recognition.
 B   Quality of Life 1985
 R ↓ Job Characteristics 1985
     Job Satisfaction 1967
     Occupational Stress 1973
   ↓ Organizational Characteristics 1997
     Organizational Climate 1973
   ↓ Working Conditions 1973

Quantitative Methods 2003
 PN 62   SC 42488
 SN Form of research methodology in which experi-
 mental variables and relationships are assigned
 numerical value. Used only when the methodology or
 research itself is the focus of discussion.
 HN This term was introduced in June 2003. Psyc-
 INFO records from the past 10 years were re-indexed
 with this term. The posting note reflects the number
 of records that were re-indexed.
 UF   Quantitative Research
 B   Experimentation 1967
      Methodology 1967
 R   Data Collection 1982
    ↓ Empirical Methods 1973
    ↓ Experimental Design 1967
    ↓ Experimental Methods 1967
    ↓ Statistical Analysis 1967
      Statistical Data 1982
    ↓ Statistical Measurement 1973

Quantitative Research
 Use   Quantitative Methods

Quantitative Trait Loci 2004
 PN 38   SC 58075
 SN Locations of genes that control variation in
 quantitative traits.
 HN This term was introduced in June 2004. Psyc-
 INFO records from the past 10 years were re-indexed
 with this term. The posting note reflects the number
 of records that were re-indexed.
 B   Genes 1973
 R   Gene Expression 2004
      Genetic Linkage 1994
    ↓ Genetics 1967
      Genome 2003

Quasi Experimental Methods 2003
 PN 18   SC 42492
 SN Research conducted in settings or environments
 where normal or traditional controls are not, or can-
 not be applied.
 HN This term was introduced in June 2003. Psyc-
 INFO records from the past 10 years were re-indexed
 with this term. The posting note reflects the number
 of records that were re-indexed.
 B   Experimental Methods 1967
 R ↓ Experimental Design 1967

Questioning 1982
 PN 1576   SC 42495
 R ↓ Cognitive Processes 1967
     Curiosity 1967
   ↓ Education 1967
     Guessing 1973
     Information Seeking 1973
     Interviewing 1973
   ↓ Interviews 1967
     Legal Interrogation 1994
   ↓ Teaching Methods 1967

Questionnaires 1967
 PN 7290   SC 42500
 B   Measurement 1967
 N   General Health Questionnaire 1991
 R   Mail Surveys 1994
    ↓ Surveys 1967
      Telephone Surveys 1994

Quetiapine 2004
 PN 208   SC 42510
 HN This term was introduced in June 2004. Psyc-
 INFO records from the past 10 years were re-indexed
 with this term. The posting note reflects the number
 of records that were re-indexed.
 B   Neuroleptic Drugs 1973

Quinidine
 Use   Alkaloids

Quinine 1973
 PN 188   SC 42560
 B   Alkaloids 1973
      Analgesic Drugs 1973
      Local Anesthetics 1973

Quinpirole 1994
 PN 145   SC 42570
 B   Antihypertensive Drugs 1973
      Dopamine Agonists 1985

Rabbis   1973
PN 51   SC 42580
B   Clergy   1973
R   Chaplains   1973
     Judaism   1967

Rabbits   1967
PN 2909   SC 42590
B   Mammals   1973

Race (Anthropological)   1973
PN 685   SC 42600
R   Ethnography   1973
     Ethnology   1967
  ↓ Racial and Ethnic Attitudes   1982
     Racial and Ethnic Differences   1982
  ↓ Racial and Ethnic Groups   2001
  ↓ Sociocultural Factors   1967
  ↓ Whites   1982

Race and Ethnic Discrimination   1994
PN 855   SC 42605
HN   Use SOCIAL DISCRIMINATION to access references from 1982-1993. In 1994, this term replaced the discontinued terms MINORITY GROUP DISCRIMINATION and RACIAL DISCRIMINATION. In 2000, these terms were removed from all records containing them, and replaced with RACE AND ETHNIC DISCRIMINATION.
UF   Ethnic Discrimination
     Minority Group Discrimination
     Racial Discrimination
B   Social Discrimination   1982
R   Affirmative Action   1985
  ↓ Civil Rights   1978
     Employment Discrimination   1994
     Minority Groups   1967
  ↓ Prejudice   1967
  ↓ Racial and Ethnic Attitudes   1982
     Racial and Ethnic Differences   1982
     Racism   1973

Race Attitudes
Use   Racial and Ethnic Attitudes

Race Relations
Use   Racial and Ethnic Relations

Racial and Ethnic Attitudes   1982
PN 3834   SC 42617
SN   Attitudes about race or ethnicity or toward members of a given racial or ethnic group. Not to be used for the general attitudes of individuals of a specific racial or ethnic group.
HN   In 1982, this term was created to replace the discontinued term RACE ATTITUDES. In 2000, RACE ATTITUDES was removed from all records containing it and replaced with RACIAL AND ETHNIC ATTITUDES.
UF   Race Attitudes
B   Attitudes   1967
N   AntiSemitism   1973
     Ethnocentrism   1973
     Racism   1973
R   Cultural Sensitivity   1994
     Ethnology   1967
     Hate Crimes   2003
     Multiculturalism   1997
  ↓ Prejudice   1967
     Race (Anthropological)   1973
     Race and Ethnic Discrimination   1994
  ↓ Racial and Ethnic Groups   2001

Racial and Ethnic Attitudes   — (cont'd)
     Racial and Ethnic Relations   1982
     Stereotyped Attitudes   1967

Racial and Ethnic Differences   1982
PN 15491   SC 42618
SN   Differences between two or more racial or ethnic groups. Use CROSS CULTURAL DIFFERENCES for cultural comparisons, and use REGIONAL DIFFERENCES for geographical comparisons.
HN   In 1982, this term replaced the discontinued term RACIAL DIFFERENCES. In 2000, RACIAL DIFFERENCES was removed from all records containing it, and replaced with RACIAL AND ETHNIC DIFFERENCES.
UF   Ethnic Differences
     Racial Differences
R   Cross Cultural Communication   1997
     Cross Cultural Differences   1967
     Cross Cultural Psychology   1997
  ↓ Cross Cultural Treatment   1994
     Cultural Sensitivity   1994
     Diversity in the Workplace   2003
     Ethnology   1967
     Interethnic Family   1988
     Interracial Family   1988
     Interracial Offspring   1988
     Multiculturalism   1997
     Race (Anthropological)   1973
     Race and Ethnic Discrimination   1994
  ↓ Racial and Ethnic Groups   2001
     Racism   1973

Racial and Ethnic Groups   2001
PN 5261   SC 42616
HN   In 2000, this term was created to replace the discontinued term ETHNIC GROUPS. ETHNIC GROUPS was removed from all records and replaced with RACIAL AND ETHNIC GROUPS.
UF   Ethnic Groups
N   Arabs   1988
  ↓ Asians   1982
     Blacks   1982
     Gypsies   1973
  ↓ Hispanics   1982
  ↓ Indigenous Populations   2001
  ↓ Whites   1982
R   Cross Cultural Communication   1997
     Cross Cultural Differences   1967
     Cross Cultural Psychology   1997
  ↓ Cross Cultural Treatment   1994
     Cultural Sensitivity   1994
  ↓ Culture (Anthropological)   1967
  ↓ Culture Bound Syndromes   2004
     Ethnic Values   1973
     Ethnology   1967
     Minority Groups   1967
     Multiculturalism   1997
     Race (Anthropological)   1973
  ↓ Racial and Ethnic Attitudes   1982
     Racial and Ethnic Differences   1982
  ↓ Religious Groups   1997
  ↓ Sociocultural Factors   1967
     Tribes   1973

Racial and Ethnic Relations   1982
PN 1512   SC 42619
SN   Contact and interaction between and among different racial and ethnic groups.
HN   In 1982, this term was created to replace the discontinued term RACE RELATIONS. In 2000, RACE RELATIONS was removed from all records containing it, and replaced with RACIAL AND ETHNIC RELATIONS.
UF   Race Relations

Racial and Ethnic Relations   — (cont'd)
B   Social Behavior   1967
R   Cross Cultural Communication   1997
     Cultural Sensitivity   1994
     Ethnology   1967
     Interracial Family   1988
     Interracial Marriage   1973
     Interracial Offspring   1988
     Multiculturalism   1997
  ↓ Prejudice   1967
  ↓ Racial and Ethnic Attitudes   1982
     School Integration   1982
  ↓ Social Discrimination   1982
     Social Equality   1973
  ↓ Social Integration   1982

Racial Differences
Use   Racial and Ethnic Differences

Racial Discrimination
Use   Race and Ethnic Discrimination

Racial Integration
Use   Social Integration

Racial Segregation (Schools)
Use   School Integration

Racism   1973
PN 1578   SC 42660
SN   Belief that racial differences produce inherent superiority of a particular race.
B   Racial and Ethnic Attitudes   1982
R   AntiSemitism   1973
     Employment Discrimination   1994
     Hate Crimes   2003
  ↓ Prejudice   1967
     Race and Ethnic Discrimination   1994
     Racial and Ethnic Differences   1982
  ↓ Social Discrimination   1982
  ↓ Social Issues   1991

Radial Nerve
Use   Spinal Nerves

Radiation   1967
PN 592   SC 42680
UF   Irradiation
N   Laser Irradiation   1973
R   Radiation Therapy   1973
  ↓ Roentgenography   1973

Radiation Therapy   1973
PN 270   SC 42690
UF   X Ray Therapy
B   Physical Treatment Methods   1973
R   ↓ Radiation   1967

Radical Movements   1973
PN 87   SC 42700
N   Political Revolution   1973
R   ↓ Social Movements   1967
     Terrorism   1982

Radicalism (Political)
Use   Political Radicalism

Radio   1973
PN 348   SC 42730

Radio — (cont'd)
- **B** Audiovisual Communications Media 1973
  - Mass Media 1967
  - Telecommunications Media 1973
- **R** ↓ News Media 1997

Radiography
- **Use** Roentgenography

Radiology 1973
- **PN** 75   **SC** 42740
- **B** Medical Sciences 1967

Rage
- **Use** Anger

Railroad Trains 1973
- **PN** 164   **SC** 42760
- **UF** Trains (Railroad)
- **B** Ground Transportation 1973
- **R** Public Transportation 1973

Random Sampling 1973
- **PN** 232   **SC** 42780
- **B** Sampling (Experimental) 1973

Rank Difference Correlation 1973
- **PN** 31   **SC** 42790
- **UF** Spearman Rho
- **B** Statistical Correlation 1967

Rank Order Correlation 1973
- **PN** 116   **SC** 42800
- **B** Statistical Correlation 1967

Rape 1973
- **PN** 2699   **SC** 42810
- **B** Sexual Abuse 1988
  - Sexual Intercourse (Human) 1973
  - Violent Crime 2003
- **N** Acquaintance Rape 1991

Raphe Nuclei 1982
- **PN** 531   **SC** 42815
- **SN** Serotonin synthesizing neurons in and near the median plane of the brain stem lying dorsally in the pons. These nuclei are sometimes grouped with the reticular formation and are thought to function as part of the limbic system.
- **B** Pons 1973
- **R** ↓ Hindbrain 1997
  - ↓ Limbic System 1973
  - Reticular Formation 1967

Rapid Eye Movement 1971
- **PN** 366   **SC** 42820
- **UF** REM
- **B** Eye Movements 1967
- **R** REM Dream Deprivation 1973
  - REM Dreams 1973
  - REM Sleep 1973

Rapid Eye Movement Dreams
- **Use** REM Dreams

Rapid Eye Movement Sleep
- **Use** REM Sleep

Rapid Heart Rate
- **Use** Tachycardia

Rapport
- **Use** Interpersonal Interaction

Rasch Model
- **Use** Item Response Theory

Rat Learning 1967
- **PN** 2261   **SC** 42860
- **HN** Not defined prior to 1982. Use RAT LEARNING or RATS to access references from 1967-1981. From 1982 used for discussions of hypotheses or theories of learning in rats.
- **B** Animal Learning 2003
  - Learning 1967

Rating 1967
- **PN** 2236   **SC** 42880
- **SN** Measurement technique involving relative evaluation or estimate of characteristics or qualities of a person, process, or thing. Used when rating as a technique is the object of interest.
- **B** Testing 1967
- **R** Halo Effect 1982
  - Interrater Reliability 1982

Rating Scales 1967
- **PN** 12152   **SC** 42890
- **B** Measurement 1967
- **N** Likert Scales 1994
- **R** Multidimensional Scaling 1982

Ratio Reinforcement
- **Use** Fixed Ratio Reinforcement AND Variable Ratio Reinforcement

Ratiocination
- **Use** Logical Thinking

Rational Emotive Behavior Therapy 2003
- **PN** 1177   **SC** 42914
- **SN** A directive, interpretative, and philosophical therapy developed by Albert Ellis that stresses the reciprocal interactions among cognition, emotion, and behavior and views the goal of treatment as the client's development of rational as opposed to irrational beliefs about his or her problem.
- **HN** In June 2003, this term was created to replace the discontinued term RATIONAL EMOTIVE THERAPY. RATIONAL EMOTIVE THERAPY was removed from all records containing it and replaced with RATIONAL EMOTIVE BEHAVIOR THERAPY.
- **UF** Rational Emotive Therapy
- **B** Psychotherapy 1967
- **R** Cognitive Therapy 1982
  - Ellis (Albert) 1991
  - ↓ Psychotherapeutic Techniques 1967

Rational Emotive Therapy
- **Use** Rational Emotive Behavior Therapy

Rationalization 1973
- **PN** 215   **SC** 42920
- **B** Defense Mechanisms 1967

Rats 1967
- **PN** 66113   **SC** 42930

Rats — (cont'd)
- **UF** Albino Rats
  - White Rats
- **B** Rodents 1973
- **N** Norway Rats 1973

Rauwolfia
- **Use** Alkaloids

Raven Coloured Progressive Matrices 1973
- **PN** 122   **SC** 42950
- **B** Intelligence Measures 1967

Raven Progressive Matrices 1978
- **PN** 249   **SC** 42960
- **HN** Use RAVENS PROGRESSIVE MATRICES to access references from 1973-1977.
- **B** Intelligence Measures 1967

Raynauds Disease
- **Use** Cardiovascular Disorders

RDC
- **Use** Research Diagnostic Criteria

Reactance
- **Use** Psychological Reactance

Reaction Formation 1973
- **PN** 31   **SC** 42990
- **SN** Defense mechanism that leads to the formation of behaviors and attitudes opposite to the repressed anxiety-inducing behavior or feelings.
- **B** Defense Mechanisms 1967

Reaction Time 1967
- **PN** 9851   **SC** 43000
- **SN** Minimal time interval between the onset of a stimulus and the beginning of a subject's response to that stimulus. Compare RESPONSE LATENCY.
- **UF** Response Lag
  - Response Speed
  - Response Time
  - RT (Response)
  - Speed (Response)
- **B** Response Parameters 1973
- **R** Cognitive Processing Speed 1997
  - Conceptual Tempo 1985

Reactive Attachment Disorder
- **Use** Attachment Disorders

Reactive Depression 1973
- **PN** 268   **SC** 43020
- **B** Major Depression 1988

Reactive Psychosis 1973
- **PN** 203   **SC** 43030
- **UF** Reactive Schizophrenia
  - Traumatic Psychosis
- **B** Psychosis 1967

Reactive Schizophrenia
- **Use** Reactive Psychosis AND Schizophrenia

Readability 1978
- **PN** 462   **SC** 43045

Readability — (cont'd)
SN Textual difficulty or other qualitative aspects of reading material that facilitate comprehension. May include clarity of graphic displays.
　B　Written Language　1967
　R　↓ Legibility　1978
　　　↓ Reading　1967
　　　Reading Comprehension　1973
　　　Reading Materials　1973

Readaptation
　Use　Adaptation

Readiness Potential
　Use　Contingent Negative Variation

Reading　1967
PN　4986　　　　　　　　　**SC**　43080
　N　Braille　1978
　　　Oral Reading　1973
　　　Remedial Reading　1973
　　　Silent Reading　1973
　R　Dyslexia　1973
　　　Initial Teaching Alphabet　1973
　　　Proofreading　1988
　　　Readability　1978
　　　Reading Ability　1973
　　　Reading Achievement　1973
　　　Reading Comprehension　1973
　　　Reading Development　1997
　　　↓ Reading Disabilities　1967
　　　Reading Education　1973
　　　Reading Materials　1973
　　　Reading Readiness　1973
　　　↓ Reading Skills　1973
　　　Reading Speed　1973
　　　Sight Vocabulary　1973

Reading Ability　1973
PN　4098　　　　　　　　　**SC**　43090
SN　Perceptual and intellectual capacity or efficiency in reading.
　B　Cognitive Ability　1973
　R　Academic Aptitude　1973
　　　↓ Reading　1967
　　　Reading Development　1997
　　　↓ Reading Skills　1973

Reading Achievement　1973
PN　3723　　　　　　　　　**SC**　43100
　B　Academic Achievement　1967
　R　↓ Reading　1967

Reading Aloud
　Use　Oral Reading

Reading Comprehension　1973
PN　5863　　　　　　　　　**SC**　43110
　B　Reading Skills　1973
　　　Verbal Comprehension　1985
　R　Readability　1978
　　　↓ Reading　1967

Reading Development　1997
PN　778　　　　　　　　　**SC**　43115
　R　↓ Language Development　1967
　　　↓ Literacy　1973
　　　Phonological Awareness　2004
　　　↓ Reading　1967
　　　Reading Ability　1973
　　　Reading Readiness　1973

Reading Development — (cont'd)
　　　↓ Reading Skills　1973

Reading Disabilities　1967
PN　3333　　　　　　　　　**SC**　43120
　B　Disabilities　2003
　　　Learning Disorders　1967
　N　Dyslexia　1973
　R　↓ Alexia　1982
　　　Educational Diagnosis　1978
　　　↓ Reading　1967

Reading Education　1973
PN　4085　　　　　　　　　**SC**　43130
　B　Language Arts Education　1973
　R　Braille　1978
　　　Braille Instruction　1973
　　　Initial Teaching Alphabet　1973
　　　↓ Literacy　1973
　　　Literacy Programs　1997
　　　Phonics　1973
　　　↓ Reading　1967
　　　Remedial Reading　1973

Reading Materials　1973
PN　1283　　　　　　　　　**SC**　43140
　UF　Basal Readers
　B　Instructional Media　1967
　R　↓ Books　1973
　　　Braille　1978
　　　Readability　1978
　　　↓ Reading　1967
　　　Text Structure　1982
　　　↓ Textbooks　1978

Reading Measures　1973
PN　744　　　　　　　　　**SC**　43150
　B　Measurement　1967
　N　Gates MacGinitie Reading Tests　1973
　　　Metropolitan Readiness Tests　1978

Reading Readiness　1973
PN　410　　　　　　　　　**SC**　43160
SN　Developmental level at which language skills; cognitive, perceptual and motor abilities; experience; and interest combine to enable a child to profit from specific reading activities. Compare SCHOOL READINESS.
　R　Phonological Awareness　2004
　　　↓ Reading　1967
　　　Reading Development　1997

Reading Skills　1973
PN　2349　　　　　　　　　**SC**　43170
SN　Proficiency in reading developed through practice and influenced by ability. Includes word recognition, pronunciation, and comprehension.
　B　Ability　1967
　N　Reading Comprehension　1973
　　　Reading Speed　1973
　R　↓ Literacy　1973
　　　Literacy Programs　1997
　　　↓ Reading　1967
　　　Reading Ability　1973
　　　Reading Development　1997
　　　Sight Vocabulary　1973
　　　Word Recognition　1988

Reading Speed　1973
PN　780　　　　　　　　　**SC**　43180
　B　Reading Skills　1973
　R　↓ Reading　1967

Readjustment (Psychosocial)
　Use　Psychosocial Readjustment

Readmission (Hospital)
　Use　Hospital Admission

Readmission (Psychiatric Hospital)
　Use　Psychiatric Hospital Readmission

Realism (Philosophy)　1973
PN　249　　　　　　　　　**SC**　43220
　B　Philosophies　1967

Reality　1973
PN　1473　　　　　　　　　**SC**　43230
　R　Metaphysics　1973
　　　Reality Testing　1973
　　　Reality Therapy　1973

Reality Testing　1973
PN　281　　　　　　　　　**SC**　43240
SN　Cognitive process of evaluation and judgment for differentiation between objective perceptions originating outside of the self and subjective stimuli or fantasies.
　R　↓ Cognitive Processes　1967
　　　↓ Personality Processes　1967
　　　Reality　1973

Reality Therapy　1973
PN　446　　　　　　　　　**SC**　43250
SN　Method of psychotherapeutic treatment based on assumption of client's personal responsibility for his/her behavior. Therapist actively guides client to accurate self-perception for fulfillment of needs of self-worth and respect for others.
　B　Psychotherapy　1967
　R　↓ Psychotherapeutic Techniques　1967
　　　Reality　1973

Reasoning　1967
PN　5508　　　　　　　　　**SC**　43260
　B　Thinking　1967
　N　Case Based Reasoning　2003
　　　↓ Inductive Deductive Reasoning　1973
　R　Analogy　1991
　　　Cognitive Hypothesis Testing　1982
　　　Declarative Knowledge　1997
　　　Dialectics　1973
　　　Heuristics　2003
　　　↓ Intelligence　1967
　　　↓ Problem Solving　1967
　　　Procedural Knowledge　1997

Rebelliousness　2003
PN　11　　　　　　　　　**SC**　43265
HN　This term was introduced in June 2003. PsycINFO records from the past 10 years were re-indexed with this term. The posting note reflects the number of records that were re-indexed.
　B　Personality Traits　1967
　R　Acting Out　1967
　　　↓ Behavior Problems　1967
　　　Nonconformity (Personality)　1973

Recall (Learning)　1967
PN　11265　　　　　　　　　**SC**　43290
　B　Retention　1967
　N　Cued Recall　1994
　　　Free Recall　1973
　　　Serial Recall　1994

Recall (Learning) — (cont'd)
R ↓ Memory 1967
    Memory Training 1994
    Reminiscence 1985

Recency Effect 1973
PN 373   **SC** 43298
SN Component of the serial position effect which is manifested by a greater ease in learning items which occur at the end of a series rather than those toward the middle.
B   Serial Position Effect 1982
R ↓ Learning 1967
    Primacy Effect 1973

Receptive Fields 1985
PN 195   **SC** 43299
SN Spatially discrete patterns of peripheral and central neuronal innervation of sensory mechanisms.
B   Nervous System 1967
N   Cutaneous Receptive Fields 1985
    Visual Receptive Fields 1982
R ↓ Afferent Pathways 1982
    Neural Plasticity 1994
    Sensory Neglect 1994
    ↓ Sensory Neurons 1973

Receptor Binding 1985
PN 3240   **SC** 43297
SN Affinity processes occurring between chemical substances and specific cellular sites in the body (e.g., blood platelet or neural receptor binding of an adrenergic drug.) Consider also NEURAL RECEPTORS.
B   Neurochemistry 1973
    Neurophysiology 1973
R   Adrenergic Receptors 2003
    Cholinergic Receptors 2003
    ↓ Neural Receptors 1973

Receptors (Adrenergic)
Use Adrenergic Receptors

Receptors (Cholinergic)
Use Cholinergic Receptors

Receptors (Neural)
Use Neural Receptors

Recessiveness (Genetic)
Use Genetic Recessiveness

Recidivism 1973
PN 1853   **SC** 43320
SN Repetition or recurrence of previous condition or behavior pattern (e.g., behavior disorder or criminal or delinquent behavior), especially when recurrence leads to recommitment or a second conviction.
B   Antisocial Behavior 1971
R ↓ Criminals 1967

Reciprocal Inhibition Therapy 1973
PN 70   **SC** 43330
SN Form of behavior therapy which seeks to evoke one response in order to bring about a suppression or decrease in the strength of a simultaneous response. Used to weaken unadaptive habits, particularly anxiety responses.
B   Behavior Therapy 1967

Reciprocal Inhibition Therapy — (cont'd)
R   Counterconditioning 1973
    Systematic Desensitization Therapy 1973

Reciprocity 1973
PN 1007   **SC** 43340
B   Social Behavior 1967
R   Retaliation 1991

Recognition (Learning) 1967
PN 7920   **SC** 43350
B   Retention 1967
N   Object Recognition 1997
R   Matching to Sample 1994
    Memory Training 1994
    Word Recognition 1988

Reconstruction (Learning) 1973
PN 148   **SC** 43360
SN Recalling memorized items in the order in which they were originally presented. Compare FREE RECALL.
B   Retention 1967

Reconstructive Psychotherapy
Use Psychotherapy

Recorders (Tape)
Use Tape Recorders

Recovery (Disorders) 1973
PN 3810   **SC** 43390
R ↓ Disorders 1967
    ↓ Drug Abstinence 1994
    Illness Behavior 1982
    ↓ Mental Disorders 1967
    ↓ Physical Disorders 1997
    Postsurgical Complications 1973
    Relapse Prevention 1994
    ↓ Remission (Disorders) 1973
    Sobriety 1988
    ↓ Treatment Outcomes 1982

Recreation 1967
PN 2290   **SC** 43400
UF   Play
N   Athletic Participation 1973
    Baseball 1973
    Basketball 1973
    Camping 1973
    Childrens Recreational Games 1973
    Clubs (Social Organizations) 1973
    Dance 1973
    Doll Play 1973
    Football 1973
    ↓ Gambling 1973
    Judo 1973
    Martial Arts 1985
    Soccer 1994
    Summer Camps (Recreation) 1973
    Swimming 1973
    Television Viewing 1973
    Tennis 1973
    Traveling 1973
    Vacationing 1973
    Weightlifting 1994
R   Childhood Play Behavior 1978
    Computer Games 1988
    Daily Activities 1994
    ↓ Games 1967
    Hobbies 1988
    Holidays 1988

Recreation — (cont'd)
    Leisure Time 1973
    Relaxation 1973
    ↓ Sports 1967
    Tourism 2003
    ↓ Toys 1973
    Wilderness Experience 1991

Recreation Areas 1973
PN 365   **SC** 43410
UF   Parks (Recreational)
N   Playgrounds 1973
R ↓ Community Facilities 1973
    ↓ Environmental Planning 1982
    Urban Planning 1973

Recreation Therapy 1973
PN 534   **SC** 43420
UF   Activity Therapy
    Gymnastic Therapy
B   Creative Arts Therapy 1994
R   Art Therapy 1973
    Dance Therapy 1973
    Movement Therapy 1997
    Music Therapy 1973
    ↓ Psychotherapy 1967
    Therapeutic Camps 1978

Recreational Day Camps
Use Summer Camps (Recreation)

Recruitment (Military)
Use Military Recruitment

Recruitment (Personnel)
Use Personnel Recruitment

Recruitment (Teachers)
Use Teacher Recruitment

Recurrence (Disorders)
Use Relapse (Disorders)

Recurrent Depression 1994
PN 257   **SC** 43465
B   Major Depression 1988
R   Relapse (Disorders) 1973
    Seasonal Affective Disorder 1991

Recycling
Use Conservation (Ecological Behavior)

Red Blood Cells
Use Erythrocytes

Red Nucleus
Use Mesencephalon

Reductionism 1973
PN 239   **SC** 43480
UF   Atomism
    Elementarism
B   Philosophies 1967
R   Positivism (Philosophy) 1997

Reemployment 1991
PN 262   **SC** 43485

Reemployment — (cont'd)

SN Returning to work following a period of absence, e.g., unemployment or retirement.
- UF Job Reentry
  - Return to Work
- R ↓ Employment Status 1982
  - Job Search 1985
  - Occupational Choice 1967
  - ↓ Personnel 1967
  - Retirement 1973
  - Unemployment 1967

Reenactments

Use Enactments

Reentry Students 1985

PN 352   SC 43495
SN Persons reentering school or an educational program after an extended absence; for example, middle-aged adults enrolled in undergraduate programs.
- B Students 1967
- R ↓ Adult Education 1973
  - Adult Learning 1997
  - ↓ College Students 1967
  - ↓ Continuing Education 1985
  - High School Students 1967
  - ↓ School Dropouts 1967

Reference Groups 1994

PN 139   SC 43497
SN Social groups used as sources for personal and behavioral identification, motivation, and evaluation of one's own status.
- B Social Groups 1973
- R Ethnic Identity 1973
  - ↓ Group Dynamics 1967
  - ↓ Interpersonal Influences 1967
  - ↓ Peer Relations 1967
  - ↓ Self Concept 1967
  - ↓ Social Identity 1988
  - ↓ Social Influences 1967
  - Social Support 2004
  - ↓ Socialization 1967

Referral (Professional)

Use Professional Referral

Referral (Self)

Use Self Referral

Reflectiveness 1997

PN 270   SC 43505
HN Use IMPULSIVENESS to access references from 1985-1996.
- B Cognitive Style 1967
- R Conceptual Tempo 1985
  - Impulsiveness 1973
  - Introspection 1973
  - Reminiscence 1985
  - Self Monitoring (Personality) 1985
  - Self Perception 1967

Reflexes 1971

PN 1707   SC 43530
SN Simple automatic involuntary neuromuscular responses to stimuli.
- UF Unconditioned Reflex
- B Physiology 1967
- N Achilles Tendon Reflex 1973
  - Acoustic Reflex 1973

Reflexes — (cont'd)

- Babinski Reflex 1973
- Eyeblink Reflex 1973
- Flexion Reflex 1973
- Hoffmanns Reflex 1973
- Nystagmus 1973
- Ocular Accommodation 1982
- Orienting Reflex 1967
- Startle Reflex 1967
- Yawning 1988
- R Instinctive Behavior 1982
  - Muscle Contractions 1973
  - Muscle Tone 1985
  - Parkinsonism 1994

Reformatories 1973

PN 53   SC 43540
SN Specific type of correctional institution to which young or first offenders are committed for training and reformation.
- B Correctional Institutions 1973
- R Prisons 1967

Refraction Errors 1973

PN 107   SC 43550
- B Errors 1967
  - Eye Disorders 1973
  - Light Refraction 1982
- N Myopia 1973
- R Amblyopia 1973
  - ↓ Genetic Disorders 1973
  - Ocular Accommodation 1982

Reframing

Use Paradoxical Techniques

Refugees 1988

PN 1276   SC 43555
SN Uprooted, homeless, voluntary or involuntary migrants who flee their native country, usually to escape danger or persecution because of their race, religion, or political views, and who no longer possess protection of their former government.
HN Use HUMAN MIGRATION to access references from 1982-1987.
- UF Political Refugees
- B Human Migration 1973
- R Immigration 1973
  - ↓ Social Processes 1967

Refusal (Treatment)

Use Treatment Refusal

Regional Differences 2001

PN 318   SC 43558
SN Used for comparisons between similar populations whose attributes differ primarily due to their geographical region of residence. Used for comparisons both within and across countries. Compare CROSS CULTURAL DIFFERENCES.
- UF Geographical Differences
- R Cross Cultural Differences 1967
  - Geography 1973
  - ↓ Sociocultural Factors 1967

Regression (Defense Mechanism) 1967

PN 590   SC 43560
- B Defense Mechanisms 1967

Regression Analysis

Use Statistical Regression

Regression Artifact

Use Statistical Regression

Regurgitation

Use Vomiting

Rehabilitation 1967

PN 6486   SC 43580
SN Treatment designed to restore or bring a client to a condition of health or useful and constructive activity. Used for populations including sensory handicapped, retarded, delinquent, criminal, or disordered. Use a more specific term if possible.
- B Treatment 1967
- N Cognitive Rehabilitation 1985
  - Criminal Rehabilitation 2004
  - ↓ Drug Rehabilitation 1973
  - ↓ Neuropsychological Rehabilitation 1997
  - Occupational Therapy 1967
  - Physical Therapy 1973
  - ↓ Psychosocial Rehabilitation 1973
- R Activities of Daily Living 1991
  - Adaptive Behavior 1991
  - Animal Assisted Therapy 1994
  - Deinstitutionalization 1982
  - Disability Management 1991
  - Habilitation 1991
  - ↓ Health Care Services 1978
  - Independent Living Programs 1991
  - ↓ Intervention 2003
  - ↓ Mainstreaming 1991
  - Partial Hospitalization 1985
  - ↓ Rehabilitation Centers 1973
  - Rehabilitation Counseling 1978
  - Self Care Skills 1978
  - ↓ Support Groups 1991
  - ↓ Twelve Step Programs 1997
  - Wilderness Experience 1991

Rehabilitation (Drug)

Use Drug Rehabilitation

Rehabilitation (Psychosocial)

Use Psychosocial Rehabilitation

Rehabilitation (Vocational)

Use Vocational Rehabilitation

Rehabilitation Centers 1973

PN 315   SC 43620
- N Sheltered Workshops 1967
- R ↓ Community Facilities 1973
  - ↓ Rehabilitation 1967

Rehabilitation Counseling 1978

PN 782   SC 43624
- B Counseling 1967
- R ↓ Alcohol Rehabilitation 1982
  - ↓ Drug Rehabilitation 1973
  - ↓ Psychosocial Rehabilitation 1973
  - ↓ Rehabilitation 1967
  - Rehabilitation Education 1997
  - ↓ Vocational Rehabilitation 1967
  - Work Adjustment Training 1991

Rehabilitation Counselors 1978

PN 779   SC 43626
- B Counselors 1967
- R Rehabilitation Education 1997
  - ↓ Social Workers 1973

Rehabilitation Education 1997

PN 132   **SC** 43627

SN Graduate education to train students in rehabilitation processes or counseling in such areas as drug rehabilitation, vocational rehabilitation, or occupational rehabilitation.

B Graduate Education 1973
R Counselor Education 1973
      Rehabilitation Counseling 1978
      Rehabilitation Counselors 1978

Rehearsal
Use Practice

Reinforcement 1967

PN 7202   **SC** 43630

SN Presentation of a reinforcer contingent on the performance of some behavior. Also, the reinforcing event or object itself (i.e., the reinforcer) which, when made to follow the performance of some behavior, results in a change in the frequency of occurrence of that behavior. Compare REWARDS and INCENTIVES.

N Differential Reinforcement 1973
      Negative Reinforcement 1973
      Noncontingent Reinforcement 1988
      ↓ Positive Reinforcement 1973
      Primary Reinforcement 1973
      ↓ Punishment 1967
      Reinforcement Amounts 1973
      ↓ Reinforcement Schedules 1967
      ↓ Rewards 1967
      Secondary Reinforcement 1967
      Self Reinforcement 1973
      ↓ Social Reinforcement 1967
R Autoshaping 1978
      Behavioral Contrast 1978
      ↓ Biofeedback 1973
      ↓ Conditioning 1967
      Delay of Gratification 1978
      Extinction (Learning) 1967
      ↓ Feedback 1967
      ↓ Learning 1967
      ↓ Motivation 1967
      ↓ Operant Conditioning 1967
      ↓ Self Stimulation 1967
      Vicarious Experiences 1973

Reinforcement (Vicarious)
Use Vicarious Experiences

Reinforcement Amounts 1973

PN 1025   **SC** 43640

B Reinforcement 1967
R Reinforcement Delay 1985

Reinforcement Delay 1985

PN 423   **SC** 43645

SN Time delay between the occurrence of a conditioned response and the administration of reinforcement in an operant conditioning paradigm. Consider INTERSTIMULUS INTERVAL for classical conditioning studies.

UF Delayed Reinforcement
B Reinforcement Schedules 1967
R Delay of Gratification 1978
      Delayed Alternation 1994
      Interstimulus Interval 1967
      Reinforcement Amounts 1973
      ↓ Stimulus Intervals 1973

Reinforcement Schedules 1967

PN 5157   **SC** 43650

UF Continuous Reinforcement
      Intermittent Reinforcement
      Partial Reinforcement
      Schedules (Reinforcement)
B Reinforcement 1967
N Concurrent Reinforcement Schedules 1988
      Fixed Interval Reinforcement 1973
      Fixed Ratio Reinforcement 1973
      Reinforcement Delay 1985
      Variable Interval Reinforcement 1973
      Variable Ratio Reinforcement 1973

Reinnervation
Use Neural Development

Rejection (Social)
Use Social Acceptance

Relapse (Disorders) 1973

PN 2843   **SC** 43660

SN Recurrence of symptoms after apparent cure or period of improvement.

UF Recurrence (Disorders)
R ↓ Disorders 1967
      Expressed Emotion 1991
      ↓ Mental Disorders 1967
      ↓ Physical Disorders 1997
      Postsurgical Complications 1973
      Recurrent Depression 1994
      Relapse Prevention 1994
      ↓ Treatment Outcomes 1982

Relapse Prevention 1994

PN 668   **SC** 43670

B Prevention 1973
R Maintenance Therapy 1997
      Preventive Medicine 1973
      Primary Mental Health Prevention 1973
      Recovery (Disorders) 1973
      Relapse (Disorders) 1973
      ↓ Remission (Disorders) 1973
      ↓ Treatment 1967
      ↓ Treatment Outcomes 1982

Relationship Quality 2004

PN 95   **SC** 43674

SN Used for spouses, couples, friends, or family members.

HN This term was introduced in June 2004. PsycINFO records from the past 10 years were re-indexed with this term. The posting note reflects the number of records that were re-indexed.

R Friendship 1967
      ↓ Interpersonal Relationships 2004
      Marital Satisfaction 1988
      ↓ Relationship Satisfaction 2001

Relationship Satisfaction 2001

PN 471   **SC** 43675

SN Used for satisfaction in relationships, including those between married and unmarried individuals, same-sex couples, relatives, and friends.

UF Interpersonal Relationship Satisfaction
B Satisfaction 1973
N Marital Satisfaction 1988
R ↓ Family Relations 1967
      Friendship 1967
      ↓ Interpersonal Interaction 1967
      ↓ Interpersonal Relationships 2004

Relationship Satisfaction — (cont'd)
      Male Female Relations 1988
      Relationship Quality 2004
      ↓ Relationship Termination 1997
      Role Satisfaction 1994

Relationship Termination 1997

PN 228   **SC** 43680

SN Voluntary or involuntary ending of a relationship.

UF Breakup (Relationship)
N ↓ Marital Separation 1973
R Abandonment 1997
      Attachment Disorders 2001
      Friendship 1967
      ↓ Human Courtship 1973
      Male Female Relations 1988
      Marital Conflict 1973
      ↓ Marital Relations 1967
      Marital Satisfaction 1988
      ↓ Peer Relations 1967
      ↓ Relationship Satisfaction 2001
      Romance 1997
      ↓ Separation Anxiety 1973
      ↓ Separation Reactions 1997
      Social Dating 1973

Relationship Therapy 1973

PN 67   **SC** 43690

SN Psychotherapeutic approach in which the relationship between the therapist and client serves as the basis for the therapy. The therapist provides a supportive setting in which the client can grow and develop and gradually reach differentiation from the therapist and come to perceive his/her own self as separate and distinct.

B Psychotherapy 1967

Relativism 1997

PN 66   **SC** 43694

B Philosophies 1967
R Dogmatism 1978
      Epistemology 1973
      Existentialism 1967
      Metaphysics 1973
      Physics 1973

Relaxation 1973

PN 1180   **SC** 43697

SN Tranquil and restful state, activity, or pasttime of lessened muscle tension, stress, or attention.

R Guided Imagery 2001
      Leisure Time 1973
      Muscle Relaxation 1973
      ↓ Recreation 1967
      Yoga 1973

Relaxation Therapy 1978

PN 2416   **SC** 43700

SN Therapy emphasizing relaxation and teaching a person or patient how to relax in order to reduce psychological tensions.

UF Muscle Relaxation Therapy
B Treatment 1967
N Progressive Relaxation Therapy 1978
R Anxiety Management 1997
      Autogenic Training 1973
      ↓ Behavior Modification 1973
      Guided Imagery 2001
      ↓ Hypnotherapy 1973
      Meditation 1973
      Muscle Relaxation 1973
      Posthypnotic Suggestions 1994
      ↓ Psychotherapeutic Techniques 1967
      Systematic Desensitization Therapy 1973

Relearning 1973
PN 145   SC 43710
  B   Learning 1967
  R ↓ Memory 1967

Reliability (Statistical)
  SN   Term was discontinued in 1973. In 2000, the term was stripped from all records containing it, and replaced with STATISTICAL RELIABILITY, its postable counterpart.
  Use   Statistical Reliability

Reliability (Test)
  Use   Test Reliability

Religion 1967
PN 4118   SC 43740
  SN   Conceptually broad term. Use a more specific term if possible.
  R   Asceticism 1973
     ↓ Religious Beliefs 1973
      Religious Buildings 1973
      Religious Education 1973
      Religious Experiences 1997
     ↓ Religious Literature 1973
      Religious Organizations 1991
     ↓ Religious Personnel 1973
     ↓ Religious Practices 1973
     ↓ Religious Prejudices 1973
      Spirituality 1988
      Theology 2003

Religiosity 1973
PN 2500   SC 43750
  SN   Degree of one's religious involvement, devotion to religious beliefs, or adherence to religious observances.
  B   Religious Beliefs 1973
  R   Religious Fundamentalism 2003
      Spirituality 1988

Religious Affiliation 1973
PN 1426   SC 43760
  B   Religious Beliefs 1973
  N ↓ Buddhism 1973
     ↓ Christianity 1973
      Hinduism 1973
      Islam 1973
      Judaism 1967
      Shamanism 1973
      Sikhism 2004
  R   Religious Fundamentalism 2003
     ↓ Religious Groups 1997
     ↓ Religious Practices 1973
      Theology 2003

Religious Beliefs 1973
PN 4477   SC 43770
  UF   Beliefs (Religion)
  N   Atheism 1973
      God Concepts 1973
      Religiosity 1973
     ↓ Religious Affiliation 1973
      Religious Fundamentalism 2003
      Sin 1973
  R   Asceticism 1973
     ↓ Attitudes 1967
      Bible 1973
      Cultism 1973
      Death Attitudes 1973
     ↓ Ethics 1967
      Evil 2003

Religious Beliefs — (cont'd)
      Existentialism 1967
      Forgiveness 1988
      Morality 1967
      Mysticism 1967
      Occultism 1978
      Religion 1967
      Religious Education 1973
      Religious Experiences 1997
     ↓ Religious Literature 1973
     ↓ Religious Practices 1973
     ↓ Religious Prejudices 1973
      Soul 2004
      Spirit Possession 1997
      Spirituality 1988
      Superstitions 1973
      Theology 2003
      Witchcraft 1973

Religious Buildings 1973
PN 70   SC 43780
  UF   Churches
  R ↓ Architecture 1973
     ↓ Community Facilities 1973
      Religion 1967

Religious Education 1973
PN 584   SC 43790
  B   Education 1967
  R   Private School Education 1973
      Religion 1967
     ↓ Religious Beliefs 1973
     ↓ Religious Personnel 1973
      Seminaries 1973

Religious Experiences 1997
PN 266   SC 43795
  R   Cultism 1973
      Mysticism 1967
     ↓ Parapsychological Phenomena 1973
      Religion 1967
     ↓ Religious Beliefs 1973
      Spirituality 1988

Religious Fundamentalism 2003
PN 205   SC 43796
  SN   Conservative religious beliefs and practices that emphasize literal interpretation of scriptures and strict adherence to traditional principles and practices.
  HN   In June 2003, this term was created to replace the discontinued term FUNDAMENTALISM (RELIGIOUS). FUNDAMENTALISM (RELIGIOUS) was removed from all records containing it and replaced with RELIGIOUS FUNDAMENTALISM.
  UF   Fundamentalism (Religious)
  B   Religious Beliefs 1973
  R   Conservatism 1973
      Religiosity 1973
     ↓ Religious Affiliation 1973

Religious Groups 1997
PN 240   SC 43797
  SN   Groups and their members sharing common religious beliefs and belonging to the same religious affiliation.
  N   Buddhists 1997
     ↓ Christians 1997
      Hindus 1997
      Jews 1997
      Muslims 1997
      Sikhs 2004
  R ↓ Clergy 1973

Religious Groups — (cont'd)
     ↓ Racial and Ethnic Groups 2001
     ↓ Religious Affiliation 1973
      Religious Organizations 1991
     ↓ Religious Practices 1973

Religious Literature 1973
PN 148   SC 43800
  N   Bible 1973
  R ↓ Literature 1967
      Religion 1967
     ↓ Religious Beliefs 1973
      Theology 2003

Religious Occupations
  Use   Religious Personnel

Religious Organizations 1991
PN 294   SC 43815
  SN   Any type of agency, organization, or institution operated by religious groups or persons. Includes, but not limited to, church, social service, educational, fraternal, recreational, missionary, or rehabilitation organizations.
  B   Organizations 1967
  R   Religion 1967
     ↓ Religious Groups 1997

Religious Personnel 1973
PN 342   SC 43820
  UF   Religious Occupations
  B   Personnel 1967
  N ↓ Clergy 1973
      Evangelists 1973
      Lay Religious Personnel 1973
      Missionaries 1973
      Nuns 1973
      Seminarians 1973
  R ↓ Professional Personnel 1978
      Religion 1967
      Religious Education 1973

Religious Practices 1973
PN 1529   SC 43830
  UF   Rites (Religion)
      Rituals (Religion)
      Worship
  N   Asceticism 1973
      Confession (Religion) 1973
      Faith Healing 1973
      Meditation 1973
      Prayer 1973
      Yoga 1973
  R   Circumcision 2001
      Glossolalia 1973
      Mysticism 1967
      Religion 1967
     ↓ Religious Affiliation 1973
     ↓ Religious Beliefs 1973
     ↓ Religious Groups 1997

Religious Prejudices 1973
PN 49   SC 43840
  B   Prejudice 1967
  N   AntiSemitism 1973
  R   Hate Crimes 2003
      Religion 1967
     ↓ Religious Beliefs 1973

REM
  Use   Rapid Eye Movement

REM Dream Deprivation 1973
PN 26   SC 43860
- B   Deprivation 1967
- R   Rapid Eye Movement 1971

REM Dreams 1973
PN 109   SC 43870
- UF   Rapid Eye Movement Dreams
- B   Dreaming 1967
- R   ↓ Eye Movements 1967
  - Lucid Dreaming 1994
  - Rapid Eye Movement 1971
  - REM Sleep 1973

REM Sleep 1973
PN 2168   SC 43880
- UF   Paradoxical Sleep
  - Rapid Eye Movement Sleep
- B   Sleep 1967
- R   ↓ Eye Movements 1967
  - Lucid Dreaming 1994
  - Rapid Eye Movement 1971
  - REM Dreams 1973

Remarriage 1985
PN 526   SC 43885
- B   Marriage 1967
- R   Divorce 1973
  - ↓ Marital Status 1973
  - Stepfamily 1991

Remedial Education 1985
PN 627   SC 43887
- SN   Specialized instruction designed to raise academic competence of students with below-normal achievement or learning difficulties. Compare COMPENSATORY EDUCATION.
- B   Education 1967
- N   Remedial Reading 1973
- R   Compensatory Education 1973
  - Educational Therapy 1997
  - Special Education 1967

Remedial Reading 1973
PN 847   SC 43890
- SN   Specialized instruction designed to correct faulty reading habits or to improve imperfectly learned reading skills.
- B   Reading 1967
  - Remedial Education 1985
- R   Educational Placement 1978
  - Reading Education 1973

Remembering
- Use   Retention

Reminiscence 1985
PN 766   SC 43905
- SN   Process of recalling past experiences.
- B   Memory 1967
- R   Anniversary Events 1994
  - Autobiographical Memory 1994
  - Early Memories 1985
  - Enactments 1997
  - Forgetting 1973
  - Homesickness 1994
  - Life Review 1991
  - ↓ Recall (Learning) 1967
  - Reflectiveness 1997
  - ↓ Retention 1967

Remission (Disorders) 1973
PN 823   SC 43910
- SN   Diminution or disappearance of symptoms.
- N   Spontaneous Remission 1973
  - Symptom Remission 1973
- R   ↓ Disorders 1967
  - ↓ Mental Disorders 1967
  - ↓ Physical Disorders 1997
  - Recovery (Disorders) 1973
  - Relapse Prevention 1994
  - ↓ Treatment Outcomes 1982

Renal Diseases
- Use   Kidney Diseases

Renal Transplantation
- Use   Organ Transplantation

Repairmen
- Use   Technical Service Personnel

Repeated Measures 1985
PN 286   SC 43935
- SN   Experimental design in which the subjects serve in all experimental, treatment, or control conditions.
- UF   Within Subjects Design
- B   Experimental Design 1967
  - Testing 1967
- R   Posttesting 1973
  - Pretesting 1973

Repetition (Compulsive)
- Use   Compulsive Repetition

Repetitive Transcranial Magnetic Stimulation
- Use   Transcranial Magnetic Stimulation

Replication (Experimental)
- Use   Experimental Replication

Repressed Memory 1997
PN 459   SC 43955
- B   Memory 1967
- R   Age Regression (Hypnotic) 1988
  - ↓ Amnesia 1967
  - Early Memories 1985
  - Emotional Trauma 1967
  - False Memory 1997
  - Repression (Defense Mechanism) 1967

Repression (Defense Mechanism) 1967
PN 927   SC 43960
- B   Defense Mechanisms 1967
- R   Repressed Memory 1997
  - Suppression (Defense Mechanism) 1973

Repression Sensitization 1973
PN 278   SC 43968
- SN   Personality continuum which characterizes individual's defensive response to threat, with avoidance (repression or denial) at one extreme and approach (worry or intellectualization) at the other.
- UF   Sensitization Repression
- B   Personality Traits 1967

Repression Sensitization Scale 1973
PN 28   SC 43970
- B   Nonprojective Personality Measures 1973

Reproductive Technology 1988
PN 458   SC 43975
- UF   Artificial Insemination
  - In Vitro Fertilization
  - Test Tube Babies
- R   Cloning 2003
  - Eugenics 1973
  - Fertilization 1973
  - ↓ Genetic Engineering 1994
  - ↓ Genetics 1967
  - ↓ Pregnancy 1967
  - Prenatal Diagnosis 1988
  - Selective Breeding 1973
  - ↓ Sexual Reproduction 1973

Reptiles 1967
PN 84   SC 43980
- B   Vertebrates 1973
- N   Crocodilians 1973
  - Lizards 1973
  - Snakes 1973
  - Turtles 1973

Republican Party
- Use   Political Parties

Reputation 1997
PN 136   SC 43995
- R   Credibility 1973
  - Fame 1985
  - Morality 1967
  - Popularity 1988
  - Social Approval 1967
  - Social Cognition 1994
  - ↓ Social Perception 1967
  - ↓ Status 1967

Research
- Use   Experimentation

Research Design
- Use   Experimental Design

Research Diagnostic Criteria 1994
PN 45   SC 44013
- SN   Used when the Research Diagnostic Criteria or its revisions are the focus of the reference. Not used for specific psychodiagnostic categories.
- HN   Use PSYCHODIAGNOSTIC TYPOLOGIES to access references prior to 1994.
- UF   RDC
- B   Psychodiagnostic Typologies 1967
- R   ↓ Diagnosis 1967
  - Diagnostic and Statistical Manual 1994
  - International Classification of Diseases 2001
  - ↓ Mental Disorders 1967
  - ↓ Psychodiagnosis 1967

Research Dropouts
- Use   Experimental Attrition

Research Methods
- Use   Methodology

Research Setting 2001
PN 63   SC 44024
- UF   Experimental Environment
  - Experimental Setting
- B   Experimentation 1967
- R   Behavioral Ecology 1997

Research Setting — (cont'd)
↓ Environment 1967
↓ Experimental Design 1967
   Experimental Laboratories 1973

Research Subjects
Use Experimental Subjects

Resentment
Use Hostility

Reserpine 1967
PN 328   SC 44040
  UF Serpasil
  B   Alkaloids 1973
      Antihypertensive Drugs 1973
      Neuroleptic Drugs 1973
      Sedatives 1973
      Sympatholytic Drugs 1973

Residence Halls
Use Dormitories

Residency (Medical)
Use Medical Residency

Residential Care Attendants
Use Attendants (Institutions)

Residential Care Institutions 1973
PN 5315   SC 44080
SN Facilities where individuals or patients live and receive appropriate treatment or care.
  UF Institutions (Residential Care)
  N   Halfway Houses 1970
    ↓ Hospitals 1967
      Nursing Homes 1973
      Orphanages 1973
  R   Assisted Living 2003
      Group Homes 1982
      Institution Visitation 1973
      Institutional Schools 1978
      Institutionalized Mentally Retarded 1970
      Psychiatric Units 1991
      Retirement Communities 1997
    ↓ Treatment Facilities 1973

Resilience (Psychological) 2003
PN 1156   SC 44085
HN In June 2003, this term replaced the discontinued term HARDINESS. HARDINESS was removed from all records containing it and replaced with RESILIENCE (PSYCHOLOGICAL). Use PSYCHOLOGICAL ENDURANCE to access references from 1991-1996.
  UF Hardiness
  B   Personality Traits 1967
  R   Adaptability (Personality) 1973
      Coping Behavior 1967
    ↓ Emotional Adjustment 1973
      Emotional Stability 1973
      Psychological Endurance 1973
      Psychological Stress 1973

Resistance 1997
PN 427   SC 44087
  N   Psychotherapeutic Resistance 1973
  R   Assertiveness 1973
      Avoidance 1967
      Coercion 1994

Resistance — (cont'd)
↓ Compliance 1973
  Independence (Personality) 1973
  Obedience 1973
  School Refusal 1994
  Temptation 1973
  Treatment Refusal 1994

Resistance (Psychotherapeutic)
Use Psychotherapeutic Resistance

Resocialization (Psychosocial)
Use Psychosocial Readjustment

Resonance
Use Vibration

Resource Allocation 1997
PN 550   SC 44125
  UF Allocation of Resources
  R   Cost Containment 1991
    ↓ Costs and Cost Analysis 1973
    ↓ Economics 1985
      Egalitarianism 1985
      Equity (Payment) 1978
    ↓ Equity (Social) 1978
      Funding 1988
      Human Capital 2003
      Money 1967
      Reward Allocation 1988

Resource Teachers 1973
PN 111   SC 44130
SN Teachers with special competencies who supplement regular curricula or programs or who assist other teachers in specified areas.
  B   Teachers 1967
  R   Special Education Teachers 1973

Respiration 1967
PN 2750   SC 44140
  UF Breathing
  R   Artificial Respiration 1973
      Carbon Dioxide 1973
    ↓ Respiration Stimulating Drugs 1973
    ↓ Respiratory Distress 1973
    ↓ Respiratory System 1973
    ↓ Respiratory Tract Disorders 1973
      Yawning 1988

Respiration Stimulating Drugs 1973
PN 13   SC 44160
  B   Drugs 1967
  N   Caffeine 1973
  R   Respiration 1967

Respiratory Distress 1973
PN 163   SC 44170
  B   Symptoms 1967
  N   ↓ Apnea 1973
    ↓ Dyspnea 1973
      Hyperventilation 1973
  R   Anoxia 1973
      Respiration 1967

Respiratory System 1973
PN 117   SC 44180
  B   Anatomical Systems 1973
  N   Bronchi 1973
      Diaphragm (Anatomy) 1973

Respiratory System — (cont'd)
↓ Larynx 1973
  Lung 1973
↓ Nose 1973
  Pharynx 1973
  Thorax 1973
  Trachea 1973
  R   Artificial Respiration 1973
      Respiration 1967

Respiratory Tract Disorders 1973
PN 490   SC 44190
  B   Physical Disorders 1997
  N   ↓ Apnea 1973
      Bronchial Disorders 1973
    ↓ Dyspnea 1973
      Hay Fever 1973
      Hyperventilation 1973
      Laryngeal Disorders 1973
    ↓ Lung Disorders 1973
      Pharyngeal Disorders 1973
  R   Artificial Respiration 1973
      Influenza 1973
      Poliomyelitis 1973
      Respiration 1967

Respite Care 1988
PN 260   SC 44195
SN Provision of care, relief, or support to caregivers of physically or mentally disabled persons.
  R   Caregiver Burden 1994
      Caregivers 1988
      Home Care 1985

Respondent Conditioning
Use Classical Conditioning

Response Amplitude 1973
PN 868   SC 44210
  UF Amplitude (Response)
  B   Response Parameters 1973

Response Bias 1967
PN 2242   SC 44220
SN Tendency to respond with different styles or criteria as a result of motivational or physical influences. Response bias frequently serves as a source of measurement error in psychophysical, personality, and other types of measurement.
  UF Bias (Response)
  R   Cultural Test Bias 1973
    ↓ Measurement 1967
      Predisposition 1973
    ↓ Test Bias 1985
      Test Taking 1985

Response Consistency
Use Response Variability

Response Cost 1997
PN 24   SC 44228
SN Punishment procedure in which positive reinforcer is lost when a specified behavior is performed.
  B   Behavior Therapy 1967
      Punishment 1967
  R   Token Economy Programs 1973

Response Duration 1973
PN 464   SC 44230
  UF Duration (Response)
  B   Response Parameters 1973

Response Frequency 1973
PN 1897   SC 44240
SN Number of responses measured during a fixed time period.
UF Frequency (Response)
    Response Rate
B Response Parameters 1973
R Behavioral Contrast 1978
    Interresponse Time 1973

Response Generalization 1973
PN 465   SC 44250
SN Learning phenomenon in which an emitted response is functionally identical to the originally-conditioned response but which, unlike the conditioned response, was never specifically conditioned. Compare GENERALIZATION (LEARNING) and STIMULUS GENERALIZATION.
UF Generalization (Response)
B Generalization (Learning) 1982
    Response Parameters 1973

Response Inhibition 2004
PN 53   SC 44255
SN The inhibition of response to certain stimuli.
HN This term was introduced in June 2004. Psyc-INFO records from the past 10 years were re-indexed with this term. The posting note reflects the number of records that were re-indexed.
B Response Parameters 1973

Response Lag
Use Reaction Time

Response Latency 1967
PN 2465   SC 44270
SN Duration of the interval between a stimulus and the onset of the elicited response. Compare REACTION TIME.
UF Latency (Response)
B Response Parameters 1973
R Behavioral Contrast 1978
    Cognitive Processing Speed 1997

Response Parameters 1973
PN 1448   SC 44280
UF Parameters (Response)
N Interresponse Time 1973
    Reaction Time 1967
    Response Amplitude 1973
    Response Duration 1973
    Response Frequency 1973
    Response Generalization 1973
    Response Inhibition 2004
    Response Latency 1967
    Response Probability 1973
    Response Set 1967
    Response Variability 1973
R ↓ Responses 1967

Response Probability 1973
PN 223   SC 44290
B Probability 1967
    Response Parameters 1973

Response Rate
Use Response Frequency

Response Set 1967
PN 651   SC 44300

Response Set — (cont'd)
SN Cognitive state of concentration or behavioral readiness to respond. Also, deliberate or inadvertent style or tendency to respond to test items in characteristic ways (e.g., with socially desirable answers) that detract from the validity of the obtained measures.
UF Set (Response)
B Response Parameters 1973

Response Speed
Use Reaction Time

Response Time
Use Reaction Time

Response Variability 1973
PN 740   SC 44330
UF Response Consistency
    Variability (Response)
B Response Parameters 1973
R Delayed Alternation 1994
    Spontaneous Alternation 1982

Responses 1967
PN 3511   SC 44340
N ↓ Conditioned Responses 1967
  ↓ Emotional Responses 1967
    Mediated Responses 1067
    Orienting Responses 1967
    Unconditioned Responses 1973
R ↓ Response Parameters 1973

Responsibility 1973
PN 3000   SC 44345
B Social Behavior 1967
N Accountability 1988
    Criminal Responsibility 1991
R Blame 1994
    Conscientiousness 1997
    Professional Liability 1985

Restlessness 1973
PN 186   SC 44350
B Emotional States 1973
    Symptoms 1967
R Agitation 1991
    Akathisia 1991
    Hyperkinesis 1973

Restraint (Physical)
Use Physical Restraint

Restricted Environmental Stimulation
Use Stimulus Deprivation

Retail Stores
Use Retailing

Retailing 1991
PN 612   SC 44362
UF Retail Stores
R ↓ Advertising 1967
    Brand Names 1978
    Business 1967
  ↓ Consumer Behavior 1967
    Marketing 1973
  ↓ Quality of Services 1997
    Sales Personnel 1973

Retailing — (cont'd)
    Self Employment 1994
    Shopping 1997
    Shopping Centers 1973

Retaliation 1991
PN 160   SC 44364
HN Use RECIPROCITY to access references from 1973-1990.
UF Revenge
B Social Behavior 1967
R ↓ Aggressive Behavior 1967
    Attack Behavior 1973
    Hostility 1967
  ↓ Interpersonal Interaction 1967
    Reciprocity 1973

Retardation (Mental)
Use Mental Retardation

Retarded Speech Development 1973
PN 157   SC 44390
SN Speech development that is below normal for a specific age level.
UF Delayed Speech
B Delayed Development 1973
    Speech Development 1973
R Language Delay 1988
  ↓ Speech Disorders 1967

Retention 1967
PN 5369   SC 44400
SN Persistence of a learned act, information, or experience as measured by reproduction, recall, recognition, or relearning. Consider also LONG TERM MEMORY or SHORT TERM MEMORY. Used for both human and animal populations.
UF Remembering
N ↓ Recall (Learning) 1967
  ↓ Recognition (Learning) 1967
    Reconstruction (Learning) 1973
R Forgetting 1973
  ↓ Interference (Learning) 1967
  ↓ Learning 1967
  ↓ Memory 1967
    Memory Training 1994
    Reminiscence 1985
  ↓ Retention Measures 1973

Retention (School)
Use School Retention

Retention Measures 1973
PN 161   SC 44410
B Measurement 1967
N Wechsler Memory Scale 1988
R ↓ Retention 1967

Reticular Formation 1967
PN 551   SC 44420
B Brain Stem 1973
    Neural Pathways 1982
R ↓ Lemniscal System 1985
    Locus Ceruleus 1982
    Raphe Nuclei 1982

Retina 1967
PN 1610   SC 44430
B Eye (Anatomy) 1967
N Cones (Eye) 1973
    Ganglion Cells (Retina) 1985

Retina — (cont'd)
Rods (Eye) 1973
R ↓ Retinal Eccentricity 1991

Retinal Eccentricity 1991
PN 170   SC 44435
R ↓ Retina 1967
Retinal Image 1973
Spatial Organization 1973
↓ Visual Perception 1967
Visual Receptive Fields 1982
↓ Visual Thresholds 1973

Retinal Ganglion Cells
Use Ganglion Cells (Retina)

Retinal Image 1973
PN 637   SC 44450
UF Image (Retinal)
R ↓ Eye (Anatomy) 1967
Retinal Eccentricity 1991

Retinal Vessels
Use Arteries (Anatomy)

Retirement 1973
PN 1557   SC 44470
R Employment History 1978
↓ Employment Status 1982
Job Security 1978
↓ Personnel 1967
Personnel Termination 1973
Reemployment 1991
Retirement Communities 1997
Unemployment 1967

Retirement Communities 1997
PN 94   SC 44473
B Communities 1967
Housing 1973
R Group Homes 1982
↓ Living Arrangements 1991
Nursing Homes 1070
↓ Residential Care Institutions 1973
Retirement 1973

Retroactive Inhibition 1973
PN 559   SC 44480
SN The theory that learning new material can interfere with the retention of previously learned material. Also, the actual retroactive interference itself.
UF Inhibition (Retroactive)
B Interference (Learning) 1967
Latent Inhibition 1997

Retrograde Amnesia 2003
PN 115   SC 58073
SN Memory loss for events and experiences that occurred before the incident that produced the amnesia.
HN This term was introduced in June 2003. PsycINFO records from the past 10 years were re-indexed with this term. The posting note reflects the number of records that were re-indexed.
B Amnesia 1967
R Anterograde Amnesia 2003

Retrospective Studies 1997
PN 259   SC 44481

Retrospective Studies — (cont'd)
SN Used in records discussing issues involved in the process of conducting studies which utilize data about experiences or events that occurred in the past, usually to study etiologic hypotheses or causative factors related to a disorder, behavior, or phenomenon.
HN From 1997-2000, the term was also used as a document type identifier; however, this usage has been discontinued due to the advent of Form/Content Type field identifiers. References from 1997-2000 can be accessed using either RETROSPECTIVE STUDIES or the Retrospective Studies Form/Content Type field identifier.
R ↓ Longitudinal Studies 1973
Prospective Studies 1997

Rett Syndrome 1994
PN 186   SC 44482
B Pervasive Developmental Disorders 2001
Syndromes 1973
R Aspergers Syndrome 1991
↓ Brain Disorders 1967
↓ Mental Disorders 1967
↓ Mental Retardation 1967
↓ Physical Disorders 1997

Return to Home
Use Empty Nest

Return to Work
Use Reemployment

Revenge
Use Retaliation

Reversal Shift Learning 1967
PN 714   SC 44490
SN Experimental technique for demonstration of mediating processes in concept formation which assesses ability to learn to reverse responses in stimulus discrimination task, so that the subject is required to respond to a formerly negative stimulus and not to respond to the formerly positive discriminative stimulus.
B Discrimination Learning 1982

Review (of Literature)
Use Literature Review

Revolutions (Political)
Use Political Revolution

Reward Allocation 1988
PN 217   SC 44515
R ↓ Justice 1973
Resource Allocation 1997
↓ Rewards 1967
↓ Social Perception 1967

Rewards 1967
PN 3566   SC 44520
SN Events or objects subjectively deemed to be pleasant to a recipient. Compare INCENTIVES, REINFORCEMENT, and POSITIVE REINFORCEMENT.
B Reinforcement 1967
N External Rewards 1973
Internal Rewards 1973

Rewards — (cont'd)
Monetary Rewards 1973
Preferred Rewards 1973
R Delay of Gratification 1978
Delayed Alternation 1994
↓ Incentives 1967
Reward Allocation 1988

Rh Incompatibility 1973
PN 7   SC 44530
UF Erythroblastosis Fetalis
Incompatibility (Rh)
B Blood and Lymphatic Disorders 1973
Genetic Disorders 1973
Immunologic Disorders 1973
R ↓ Neonatal Disorders 1973

Rheoencephalography 1973
PN 19   SC 44540
B Encephalography 1973
Medical Diagnosis 1973
R ↓ Electroencephalography 1967

Rhetoric 1991
PN 532   SC 44545
B Communication Skills 1973
Language 1967
R ↓ Communication 1967
Creative Writing 1994
Debates 1997
Discourse Analysis 1997
Hermeneutics 1991
↓ Oral Communication 1985
↓ Persuasive Communication 1967
↓ Written Communication 1985

Rheumatic Fever 1973
PN 29   SC 44550
R ↓ Bacterial Disorders 1973
↓ Heart Disorders 1973
Rheumatoid Arthritis 1973

Rheumatism
Use Arthritis

Rheumatoid Arthritis 1973
PN 914   SC 44570
B Arthritis 1973
R Rheumatic Fever 1973

Rhodopsin 1985
PN 11   SC 44575
SN A red pigment localized in the outer segments of rod cells in the retina.
B Pigments 1973
R Rods (Eye) 1973

Rhombencephalon
Use Hindbrain

Rhyme 2004
PN 65   SC 58081
HN This term was introduced in June 2004. PsycINFO records from the past 10 years were re-indexed with this term. The posting note reflects the number of records that were re-indexed.
R Phonological Awareness 2004
↓ Phonology 1973
Poetry 1973
Words (Phonetic Units) 1967

Rhythm 1991
PN 421   **SC** 44577
  N   Speech Rhythm 1973
  R   ↓ Auditory Perception 1967
       ↓ Music 1967
       Music Perception 1997
       Pattern Discrimination 1967
       ↓ Perception 1967
       Speech Perception 1967
       Tempo 1997

Rhythm Method 1973
PN 5   **SC** 44580
  B   Birth Control 1971

Ribonucleic Acid 1973
PN 699   **SC** 44600
  UF RNA (Ribonucleic Acid)
  B   Nucleic Acids 1973
  R   Gene Expression 2004

Right Brain 1991
PN 927   **SC** 44610
SN Used only when the right hemisphere of the brain is the focus of the document.
  B   Cerebral Cortex 1967
  R ↓ Brain 1967
      ↓ Cerebral Dominance 1973
      Corpus Callosum 1973
      Interhemispheric Interaction 1985
      ↓ Lateral Dominance 1967
      Left Brain 1991
      Ocular Dominance 1973

Right to Treatment 1997
PN 19   **SC** 44615
  B   Client Rights 1988
  R   Advocacy 1985
      ↓ Commitment (Psychiatric) 1973
      Deinstitutionalization 1982
      Involuntary Treatment 1994
      Self Referral 1991

Rigidity (Muscles)
  Use Muscle Contractions

Rigidity (Personality) 1967
PN 258   **SC** 44620
  B   Personality Traits 1967
  R   Openness to Experience 1997

Riots 1973
PN 135   **SC** 44640
  B   Collective Behavior 1967
      Conflict 1967
  R ↓ Violence 1973

Risk Analysis
  Use Risk Assessment

Risk Assessment 2004
PN   **SC** 58083
HN In June 2004, this term was created to replace the discontinued term RISK ANALYSIS. RISK ANALYSIS was removed from all records containing it and replaced with RISK ASSESSMENT.
  UF Risk Analysis
  B   Evaluation 1967
  R   At Risk Populations 1985
      ↓ Decision Making 1967

Risk Assessment — (cont'd)
      Risk Factors 2001
      Risk Management 1997

Risk Factors 2001
PN 4262   **SC** 44642
SN Personal behaviors or lifestyles, environmental effects, or inborn characteristics which epidemiological evidence has shown to be associated with the increased rate of a behavior or health-related condition.
  R   At Risk Populations 1985
      Predisposition 1973
      Psychosocial Factors 1988
      Risk Assessment 2004
      ↓ Sociocultural Factors 1967
      Susceptibility (Disorders) 1973
      ↓ Symptoms 1967

Risk Management 1997
PN 674   **SC** 44644
SN Reducing and preventing loss, damage, harm, or danger to a business, group, or individual through safety and protective measures. Used for clinical and nonclinical environments.
  B   Management 1967
  R   Accident Prevention 1973
      ↓ Costs and Cost Analysis 1973
      ↓ Harm Reduction 2003
      ↓ Insurance 1973
      ↓ Legal Processes 1973
      ↓ Prevention 1973
      Professional Liability 1985
      Risk Assessment 2004
      ↓ Risk Taking 1967
      ↓ Safety 1967

Risk Perception 1997
PN 1379   **SC** 44646
SN Awareness of, or attitudes toward, potential risk. Primarily used for risk associated with disease or behavior.
  B   Perception 1967
  R   Hazards 1973
      ↓ Prevention 1973
      ↓ Risk Taking 1967
      ↓ Safety 1967
      Sexual Risk Taking 1997

Risk Populations
  Use At Risk Populations

Risk Taking 1967
PN 4901   **SC** 44650
  B   Personality Traits 1967
      Social Behavior 1967
  N ↓ Gambling 1973
      Sexual Risk Taking 1997
  R   Choice Shift 1994
      Risk Management 1997
      Risk Perception 1997

Risky Shift
  Use Choice Shift

Risperidone 1997
PN 1201   **SC** 44657
  B   Neuroleptic Drugs 1973

Ritalin
  Use Methylphenidate

Ritanserin 1997
PN 61   **SC** 44665
  B   Serotonin Antagonists 1973

Rites (Nonreligious) 1973
PN 697   **SC** 44670
  UF Rituals (Nonreligious)
  R   Cannibalism 2003
      Cosmetic Techniques 2001
      ↓ Rites of Passage 1973

Rites (Religion)
  Use Religious Practices

Rites of Passage 1973
PN 184   **SC** 44690
  B   Sociocultural Factors 1967
  N   Birth Rites 1973
      Death Rites 1973
      Initiation Rites 1973
      Marriage Rites 1973
  R   Circumcision 2001
      ↓ Developmental Stages 1973
      Ethnography 1973
      Rites (Nonreligious) 1973
      Taboos 1973

Rituals (Nonreligious)
  Use Rites (Nonreligious)

Rituals (Religion)
  Use Religious Practices

Rivalry 1973
PN 74   **SC** 44720
  B   Interpersonal Interaction 1967
  R   Competition 1967

RNA (Ribonucleic Acid)
  Use Ribonucleic Acid

Road Rage
  Use Aggressive Driving Behavior

Robbery
  Use Theft

Robins 1973
PN 52   **SC** 44750
  B   Birds 1967

Robotics 1985
PN 613   **SC** 44755
  R ↓ Artificial Intelligence 1982
      ↓ Computers 1967
      Cybernetics 1967
      ↓ Expert Systems 1991

Rock Music 1991
PN 138   **SC** 44757
  B   Music 1967

Rocking (Body)
  Use Body Rocking

Rod and Frame Test 1973
PN 134   **SC** 44770

Rod and Frame Test — (cont'd)
B   Nonprojective Personality Measures 1973
    Perceptual Measures 1973

Rodents 1973
PN 1236   SC 44780
B   Mammals 1973
N   Beavers 1973
    Chinchillas 1973
    Gerbils 1973
    Guinea Pigs 1967
    Hamsters 1973
    Mice 1973
    Minks 1973
    ↓ Rats 1967
    Squirrels 1973
    Voles 2004

Rods (Eye) 1973
PN 277   SC 44790
B   Photoreceptors 1973
    Retina 1967
R   Rhodopsin 1985

Roentgenography 1973
PN 173   SC 44800
UF Radiography
    X Ray Diagnosis
B   Medical Diagnosis 1973
    Neuroimaging 2003
N   Angiography 1973
    Mammography 1994
    Pneumoencephalography 1973
R   ↓ Encephalography 1973
    ↓ Radiation 1967
    ↓ Tomography 1988

Rogerian Therapy
Use Client Centered Therapy

Rogers (Carl) 1991
PN 136   SC 44805
SN Identifies biographical or autobiographical stud-
ies and discussions of Rogers's works.
R   Client Centered Therapy 1967
    ↓ Humanistic Psychology 1985
    ↓ Humanistic Psychotherapy 2003
    ↓ Psychologists 1967

Rohypnol
Use Flunitrazepam

Rokeach Dogmatism Scale 1973
PN 31   SC 44810
B   Nonprojective Personality Measures 1973
    Personality Measures 1967

Role (Counselor)
Use Counselor Role

Role Conflicts 1973
PN 2465   SC 44830
UF Role Strain
R   Family Work Relationship 1997
    Role Satisfaction 1994
    ↓ Roles 1967

Role Expectations 1973
PN 1119   SC 44840

Role Expectations — (cont'd)
SN Functional patterns or types of behavior
expected from an individual in a specific social or pro-
fessional position or situation.
B   Expectations 1967
R   Role Satisfaction 1994
    ↓ Roles 1967

Role Models 1982
PN 549   SC 44845
SN Real or theoretical persons consciously or
unconsciously perceived as being a standard for
emulation in one or more of their roles.
R   Imitation (Learning) 1967
    Role Perception 1973
    ↓ Roles 1967
    Significant Others 1991
    ↓ Social Influences 1967

Role Perception 1973
PN 2418   SC 44850
SN Views or understanding of one's own or others'
function or behavior in particular situations.
B   Perception 1967
R   Professional Identity 1991
    Role Models 1982
    Role Satisfaction 1994
    Role Taking 1982
    ↓ Roles 1967

Role Playing 1967
PN 1574   SC 44860
SN Psychological or behavioral enactment of social
roles other than one's own, typically seen in child's
play, or used as an experimental, instructional, or
psychotherapeutic technique. Compare ROLE TAK-
ING.
R   Childhood Play Behavior 1978
    Psychodrama 1967
    ↓ Psychotherapeutic Techniques 1967
    Role Taking 1982
    ↓ Roles 1967

Role Satisfaction 1994
PN 102   SC 44863
B   Satisfaction 1973
R   Job Satisfaction 1967
    Life Satisfaction 1985
    Marital Satisfaction 1988
    ↓ Relationship Satisfaction 2001
    Role Conflicts 1973
    Role Expectations 1973
    Role Perception 1973
    ↓ Roles 1967
    ↓ Self Concept 1967

Role Strain
Use Role Conflicts

Role Taking 1982
PN 786   SC 44865
SN Perceiving, understanding, or experiencing the
social, emotional or physical aspects of a situation
from a standpoint of another person or persons.
Compare ROLE PLAYING.
HN Use EGOCENTRISM to access references from
1978-1981.
UF Perspective Taking
R   Egocentrism 1978
    Role Perception 1973
    Role Playing 1967
    ↓ Roles 1967

Role Taking — (cont'd)
    Symbolic Interactionism 1988

Roles 1967
PN 5453   SC 44870
N   Counselor Role 1973
    Parental Role 1973
    Sex Roles 1967
    Therapist Role 1978
R   Role Conflicts 1973
    Role Expectations 1973
    Role Models 1982
    Role Perception 1973
    Role Playing 1967
    Role Satisfaction 1994
    Role Taking 1982

Roman Catholicism 1973
PN 798   SC 44880
UF Catholicism (Roman)
B   Christianity 1973
R   Catholics 1997

Romance 1997
PN 735   SC 44883
R   Affection 1973
    Couples 1982
    ↓ Human Courtship 1973
    Human Mate Selection 1988
    Intimacy 1973
    Love 1973
    ↓ Marital Relations 1967
    ↓ Marriage 1967
    ↓ Psychosexual Behavior 1967
    ↓ Relationship Termination 1997
    Significant Others 1991
    Social Dating 1973

Roommates 1973
PN 151   SC 44890
SN Individuals residing in common abodes.
R   Cohabitation 1973
    ↓ Living Arrangements 1991

Rorschach Test 1967
PN 2936   SC 44900
B   Projective Personality Measures 1973

Rosenzweig Picture Frustration Study 1967
PN 51   SC 44910
B   Projective Personality Measures 1973

Rotary Pursuit 1967
PN 203   SC 44920
B   Tracking 1967
R   ↓ Attention 1967

Rotation Methods (Statistical)
Use Statistical Rotation

Rotational Behavior 1994
PN 186   SC 44935
SN Used primarily for animal populations.
UF Body Rotation
B   Motor Processes 1967
R   Activity Level 1982

ROTC Students 1973
PN 72   SC 44940
B   College Students 1967

ROTC Students — (cont'd)
Military Personnel 1967
R   Volunteer Military Personnel 1973

Rote Learning 1973
PN 134   SC 44950
SN   Verbatim memorization of information which requires no understanding.
R   ↓ Memory 1967

Rotter Incomplete Sentences Blank 1973
PN 19   SC 44960
B   Projective Personality Measures 1973

Rotter Internal External Locus of Control Scale 2001
PN 155
HN   In 2000, the truncated term ROTTER INTERN EXTERN LOCUS CONT SCAL (which was used from 1973-2000) was deleted, removed from all records containing it, and replaced with its expanded form ROTTER INTERNAL EXTERNAL LOCUS OF CONTROL SCALE.
B   Nonprojective Personality Measures 1973

RT (Response)
Use   Reaction Time

Rubella 1973
PN 47   SC 45000
UF   German Measles
B   Viral Disorders 1973
R   Measles 1973

Rule Learning
Use   Cognitive Hypothesis Testing

Rumination (Cognitive Process) 2001
PN 97   SC 45007
SN   Constant preoccupation with particular thoughts which may provoke anxiety and distress. Can be associated with obsessive compulsive disorder and depression.
B   Cognitive Processes 1967
R   ↓ Cognitions 1985
Concentration 1982
↓ Thought Disturbances 1973
Thought Suppression 2003

Rumination (Eating) 2001
PN 5   SC 45008
SN   Characterized by regurgitating partially digested food and chewing it again. Often used to describe an eating disorder of infancy or early childhood.
R   ↓ Eating Disorders 1997
Food Intake 1967
Vomiting 1973

Rumors
Use   Gossip

Runaway Behavior 1973
PN 428   SC 45015
B   Antisocial Behavior 1971
R   Shelters 1991

Running 1973
PN 776   SC 45020
B   Motor Performance 1973

Runways (Maze)
Use   Maze Pathways

Rural Development
Use   Community Development

Rural Environments 1967
PN 5511   SC 45040
B   Social Environments 1973
R   Community Development 1997

Saccadic Eye Movements
Use   Eye Movements

Saccharin 1973
PN 511   SC 45050
R   ↓ Sugars 1973

SAD
Use   Seasonal Affective Disorder

Sadism 1973
PN 108   SC 45070
B   Sadomasochism 1973
N   Sexual Sadism 1973
R   ↓ Masochism 1973

Sadness 1973
PN 593   SC 45090
UF   Melancholy
B   Emotional States 1973
R   Depression (Emotion) 1967
Homesickness 1994
↓ Separation Reactions 1997

Sadomasochism 1973
PN 171   SC 45100
SN   Derivation of pleasure from infliction of physical or mental pain on others and oneself, with presence of high degree of destructiveness.
N   ↓ Masochism 1973
↓ Sadism 1973
R   ↓ Mental Disorders 1967
↓ Sadomasochistic Personality 1973

Sadomasochistic Personality 1973
PN 15   SC 45110
B   Personality Disorders 1967
N   Masochistic Personality 1973
R   ↓ Sadomasochism 1973

Safe Sex 2003
PN 171   SC 45115
SN   Sexual behavior or practices which reduce one's risk of pregnancy or transmission of HIV and other sexually transmitted diseases.
HN   This term was introduced in June 2003. PsycINFO records from the past 10 years were re-indexed with this term. The posting note reflects the number of records that were re-indexed.
B   Health Behavior 1982
Psychosexual Behavior 1967
R   Acquired Immune Deficiency Syndrome 1988
AIDS Prevention 1994
↓ Birth Control 1971
Condoms 1991
↓ Human Immunodeficiency Virus 1991
↓ Pregnancy 1967
Sex Education 1973

Safe Sex — (cont'd)
↓ Sexual Intercourse (Human) 1973
Sexual Risk Taking 1997

Safety 1967
PN 1667   SC 45120
N   ↓ Aviation Safety 1973
Highway Safety 1973
Occupational Safety 1973
Water Safety 1973
R   Accident Prevention 1973
Accident Proneness 1973
↓ Accidents 1967
Fire Prevention 1973
↓ Hazardous Materials 1991
Hazards 1973
↓ Injuries 1973
↓ Prevention 1973
Risk Management 1997
Risk Perception 1997
↓ Safety Devices 1973
Warning Labels 1997
↓ Warnings 1997

Safety Belts 1973
PN 308   SC 45130
UF   Seat Belts
B   Safety Devices 1973
R   ↓ Driving Behavior 1967
↓ Transportation Accidents 1973

Safety Devices 1973
PN 264   SC 45140
N   Safety Belts 1973
R   Hazards 1973
↓ Safety 1967
Warning Labels 1997
↓ Warnings 1997

Safety Warnings
Use   Warnings

Saint John's Wort
Use   Hypericum Perforatum

Salamanders 1973
PN 244   SC 45150
B   Amphibia 1973
R   Larvae 1973

Salaries 1973
PN 1551   SC 45160
UF   Pay
Wages
R   Bonuses 1973
↓ Employee Benefits 1973
Equity (Payment) 1978
Income (Economic) 1973
↓ Income Level 1973
↓ Professional Fees 1978

Sales Personnel 1973
PN 1236   SC 45170
UF   Insurance Agents
B   Business and Industrial Personnel 1967
White Collar Workers 1973
R   Retailing 1991
↓ Service Personnel 1991

Salience (Stimulus)
Use   Stimulus Salience

Saliva 1973
PN 453   SC 45200
- B   Body Fluids   1973
- R   Salivation   1973

Salivary Glands 1973
PN 50   SC 45210
- B   Glands   1967
- R   ↓ Digestive System   1967
-     Mouth (Anatomy)   1967

Salivation 1973
PN 240   SC 45220
- B   Secretion (Gland)   1973
- R   Digestion   1973
-     Saliva   1973

Salmon 1973
PN 90   SC 45230
- B   Fishes   1967

Saltiness
- Use   Taste Perception

Same Sex Education 2003
PN 27   SC 45242
HN This term was introduced in June 2003. Psyc-INFO records from the past 10 years were re-indexed with this term. The posting note reflects the number of records that were re-indexed.
- UF   Single Sex Education
- B   Academic Environment   1973
-     Single Sex Environments   2001
- R   Coeducation   1973

Same Sex Environments
- Use   Single Sex Environments

Sample Size 1997
PN 180   SC 45245
- B   Statistical Sample Parameters   1973
- R   ↓ Sampling (Experimental)   1973

Sampling (Experimental) 1973
PN 892   SC 45250
SN Systematic selection of part of a larger population of individual responses, individuals, or groups for use in empirical study or research. Results about the entire population are then generalized from this smaller sample.
- N   Biased Sampling   1973
-     Random Sampling   1973
- R   Data Collection   1982
-     ↓ Experimental Design   1967
-     ↓ Experimentation   1967
-     ↓ Population (Statistics)   1973
-     Sample Size   1997
-     ↓ Statistical Analysis   1967
-     Statistical Power   1991
-     Statistical Reliability   1973
-     ↓ Statistical Samples   1973
-     ↓ Statistical Variables   1973

Sanatoriums 1973
PN 14   SC 45260
- B   Hospitals   1967
- R   Nursing Homes   1973
-     Psychiatric Hospitals   1967

Sarcomas
- Use   Neoplasms

SAT
- Use   College Entrance Examination Board Scholastic Aptitude Test

Satiation 1967
PN 961   SC 45280
SN Primarily limited to gratification or satisfaction of a physiologically-based motivation (e.g., need for food and water) but may also refer to gratification of a psychic goal or motivation. Consider also SATISFACTION or NEED SATISFACTION for the latter concept.
- R   ↓ Appetite   1973
-     ↓ Motivation   1967

Satisfaction 1973
PN 5099   SC 45290
- UF   Fulfillment
- N   Client Satisfaction   1994
-     Consumer Satisfaction   1994
-     Job Satisfaction   1967
-     Life Satisfaction   1985
-     Marital Satisfaction   1988
-     Need Satisfaction   1973
-     ↓ Relationship Satisfaction   2001
-     Role Satisfaction   1994
-     Sexual Satisfaction   1994
- R   Dissatisfaction   1973
-     Physical Comfort   1982

Saturation (Color)
- Use   Color Saturation

Savants 2001
PN 125   SC 45297
HN In 2000, this term was created to replace the discontinued term IDIOT SAVANTS. IDIOT SAVANTS was removed from all records and replaced with SAVANTS.
- UF   Idiot Savants
- R   Gifted   1967
-     ↓ Mental Disorders   1967
-     ↓ Mental Retardation   1967

Scaling (Testing) 1967
PN 1621   SC 45360
- B   Testing   1967
-     Testing Methods   1967
- R   Magnitude Estimation   1991
-     Multidimensional Scaling   1982

Scalp (Anatomy) 1973
PN 70   SC 45370
- B   Anatomy   1967
- R   Hair   1973
-     Head (Anatomy)   1973
-     Skin (Anatomy)   1967

Scalp Disorders
- Use   Skin Disorders

Scent Marking (Animal)
- Use   Animal Scent Marking

Schedules (Learning)
- Use   Learning Schedules

Schedules (Reinforcement)
- Use   Reinforcement Schedules

Scheduling (Work)
- Use   Work Scheduling

Schema 1988
PN 2680   SC 45425
SN Cognitive structure used for comprehension, perception, and interpretation of stimuli.
- UF   Scripts
- B   Cognitive Processes   1967
- R   ↓ Cognitions   1985
-     Cognitive Maps   1982
-     ↓ Cognitive Style   1967
-     Conceptual Imagery   1973
-     Mental Models   2003
-     Perceptual Style   1973
-     Social Cognition   1994

Schizoaffective Disorder 1994
PN 1323   SC 45427
SN Mental disorder characterized by the presence of both affective disorder and schizophrenia-like symptoms.
- B   Mental Disorders   1967
- R   ↓ Affective Disorders   2001
-     ↓ Schizophrenia   1967

Schizoid Personality Disorder 1973
PN 466   SC 45430
SN Personality disorder characterized by alienation, shyness, oversensitivity, seclusiveness, egocentricity, avoidance of intimate relationships, autistic thinking, and withdrawal from and lack of response to the environment.
- B   Personality Disorders   1967
- R   ↓ Schizophrenia   1967
-     Schizotypal Personality Disorder   1991

Schizophrenia 1967
PN 37757   SC 45440
HN In 1988, this term replaced the terms CHRONIC SCHIZOPHRENIA, PSEUDOPSYCHOPATHIC SCHIZOPHRENIA, and SIMPLE SCHIZOPHRENIA. In 2000, these terms were removed from all records containing them, and replaced with SCHIZOPHRENIA.
- UF   Chronic Schizophrenia
-     Dementia Praecox
-     Process Schizophrenia
-     Pseudopsychopathic Schizophrenia
-     Reactive Schizophrenia
-     Schizophrenia (Residual Type)
-     Simple Schizophrenia
- B   Psychosis   1967
- N   Acute Schizophrenia   1973
-     Catatonic Schizophrenia   1973
-     Childhood Schizophrenia   1967
-     Paranoid Schizophrenia   1967
-     Schizophrenia (Disorganized Type)   1973
-     Schizophreniform Disorder   1994
-     Undifferentiated Schizophrenia   1973
- R   Anhedonia   1985
-     Catalepsy   1973
-     Delusions   1967
-     Expressed Emotion   1991
-     Fragmentation (Schizophrenia)   1973
-     Positive and Negative Symptoms   1997
-     Schizoaffective Disorder   1994
-     Schizoid Personality Disorder   1973
-     Schizotypal Personality Disorder   1991

Schizophrenia (Disorganized Type) 1973
PN 147   SC 45445
HN In 2000, the term's status changed from non-postable to postable. HEBEPHRENIC SCHIZO-PHRENIA was removed from all records containing it, and replaced with SCHIZOPHRENIA (DISORGA-NIZED TYPE).
UF   Hebephrenic Schizophrenia
B   Schizophrenia 1967

Schizophrenia (Residual Type)
Use   Schizophrenia

Schizophreniform Disorder 1994
PN 210   SC 45447
HN Use ACUTE SCHIZOPHRENIA to access references from 1988-1993.
B   Schizophrenia 1967

Schizophrenogenic Family 1967
PN 309   SC 45450
B   Family 1967
    Family Structure 1973
R   Double Bind Interaction 1973
    Dysfunctional Family 1991
    ↓ Mental Disorders 1967
    Schizophrenogenic Mothers 1973

Schizophrenogenic Mothers 1973
PN 38   SC 45460
B   Mothers 1967
R   Double Bind Interaction 1973
    Mother Child Relations 1967
    Schizophrenogenic Family 1967

Schizotypal Personality Disorder 1991
PN 605   SC 45465
SN Personality disorder characterized by eccentric thoughts and appearance, inappropriate affect and behavior, extreme social anxiety, and limited interpersonal interaction.
HN Consider using SCHIZOID PERSONALITY to access references from 1973-1990.
B   Personality Disorders 1967
R   Schizoid Personality Disorder 1973
    ↓ Schizophrenia 1967

Scholarships
Use   Educational Financial Assistance

Scholastic Achievement
Use   Academic Achievement

Scholastic Aptitude
Use   Academic Aptitude

Scholastic Aptitude Test
Use   College Entrance Examination Board
    Scholastic Aptitude Test

School Accreditation
Use   Educational Program Accreditation

School Achievement
Use   Academic Achievement

School Adjustment 1967
PN 4024   SC 45510

School Adjustment — (cont'd)
SN Process of adjusting to school environment and to the role of a student.
UF   Student Adjustment
B   Adjustment 1967
R   Adjustment Disorders 1994
    ↓ Education 1967
    School Transition 1997

School Administration
Use   Educational Administration

School Administrators 1973
PN 2559   SC 45530
UF   Administrators (School)
    Educational Administrators
B   Educational Personnel 1973
N   School Principals 1973
    School Superintendents 1973
R   Boards of Education 1978
    ↓ Management Personnel 1973

School and College Ability Test
Use   Aptitude Measures

School Attendance 1973
PN 1277   SC 45560
SN Regular presence of students in school or classes or absenteeism due to factors other than truancy. Compare SCHOOL ENROLLMENT.
UF   Attendance (School)
R   ↓ Education 1967
    ↓ School Enrollment 1973
    School Refusal 1994
    School Retention 1994
    Student Attrition 1991
    Tardiness 2003

School Based Intervention 2003
PN 420   SC 45563
SN Intervening with an individual or group of individuals in a school setting for the purpose of influencing or reorienting one's behavior or approach to learning.
HN This term was introduced in June 2003. PsycINFO records from the past 10 years were re-indexed with this term. The posting note reflects the number of records that were re-indexed.
UF   Educational Intervention
B   Intervention 2003
R   Early Intervention 1982
    ↓ Educational Programs 1973
    School Counseling 1982
    Student Personnel Services 1978

School Club Membership 1973
PN 39   SC 45570
B   Extracurricular Activities 1973

School Counseling 1982
PN 3361   SC 45579
SN Counseling services provided by counselors or teacher counselors in order to help school, college, or university students cope with adjustment problems. Compare EDUCATIONAL COUNSELING.
UF   Guidance Counseling
    School Guidance
B   Counseling 1967
R   ↓ Education 1967
    Educational Therapy 1997
    ↓ Mental Health Services 1978

School Counseling — (cont'd)
    School Based Intervention 2003
    School Counselors 1973
    Student Personnel Services 1978

School Counselors 1973
PN 1935   SC 45580
B   Counselors 1967
    Educational Personnel 1973
R   School Counseling 1982
    School Psychologists 1973
    Vocational Counselors 1973

School Dropouts 1967
PN 1413   SC 45590
B   Dropouts 1973
N   College Dropouts 1973
R   ↓ Education 1967
    Reentry Students 1985
    School Refusal 1994
    School Retention 1994
    Student Attrition 1991

School Enrollment 1973
PN 537   SC 45600
SN Number of students registered to attend school, college or university. Also, the act of enrolling in school. Compare SCHOOL ATTENDANCE.
UF   Enrollment (School)
    Matriculation
N   School Expulsion 1973
    School Suspension 1973
    Student Attrition 1991
R   ↓ Dropouts 1973
    ↓ Education 1967
    School Attendance 1973
    School Retention 1994
    School Truancy 1973

School Environment 1973
PN 5088   SC 45610
SN School characteristics, including overall social and physical atmosphere or school climate.
UF   Educational Environment
B   Academic Environment 1973
N   College Environment 1973
R   Classroom Environment 1973
    ↓ Education 1967
    Learning Environment 2004
    ↓ School Facilities 1973
    School Violence 2003
    ↓ Schools 1967

School Expulsion 1973
PN 74   SC 45620
UF   Expulsion (School)
B   School Enrollment 1973
R   School Suspension 1973
    Student Attrition 1991

School Facilities 1973
PN 145   SC 45630
N   Campuses 1973
    Classrooms 1967
    Dormitories 1973
    ↓ Educational Laboratories 1973
    Learning Centers (Educational) 1973
    School Libraries 1973
R   ↓ Education 1967
    Playgrounds 1973
    ↓ School Environment 1973
    ↓ Schools 1967

School Federal Aid
　Use Educational Financial Assistance

School Financial Assistance
　Use Educational Financial Assistance

School Graduation 1991
PN 196　　　　　　　　　SC 45653
SN Completion of a course of study resulting in the award or acceptance of a diploma or degree.
　UF Graduation (School)
　R ↓ Academic Achievement 1967
　　　College Graduates 1982
　　↓ Education 1967
　　　Educational Attainment Level 1997
　　　Educational Degrees 1973
　　　High School Graduates 1978
　　↓ Higher Education 1973
　　　School to Work Transition 1994
　　　School Transition 1997

School Guidance
　Use School Counseling

School Integration 1982
PN 658　　　　　　　　　SC 45658
SN Incorporation of students of different racial, ethnic, or other types of groups into the same school.
HN In 1982, this term was created to replace the discontinued term SCHOOL INTEGRATION (RACIAL). In 2000, SCHOOL INTEGRATION (RACIAL) was removed from all records containing it, and replaced with SCHOOL INTEGRATION.
　UF Racial Segregation (Schools)
　　　School Integration (Racial)
　B Social Integration 1982
　R ↓ Activism 2003
　　↓ Education 1967
　　　Equal Education 1978
　　　Mainstreaming (Educational) 1978
　　　Racial and Ethnic Relations 1982

School Integration (Racial)
　Use School Integration

School Learning 1967
PN 5318　　　　　　　　　SC 45670
SN Learning in an academic environment. For educational performance use ACADEMIC ACHIEVEMENT or one of its narrower terms.
　B Learning 1967
　R ↓ Academic Achievement 1967
　　　Cooperative Learning 1994
　　↓ Education 1967
　　↓ Experiential Learning 1997
　　　Mastery Learning 1985
　　　Metacognition 1991

School Leavers 1988
PN 85　　　　　　　　　SC 45675
SN British term referring to persons who have recently left school, generally after the completion of a basic education program and satisfaction of government requirements.
　R ↓ Educational Background 1967
　　　School Retention 1994
　　　Student Attrition 1991

School Libraries 1973
PN 97　　　　　　　　　SC 45680

School Libraries — (cont'd)
　UF Libraries (School)
　B Libraries 1982
　　　School Facilities 1973

School Nurses 1973
PN 83　　　　　　　　　SC 45690
　B Educational Personnel 1973
　　　Nurses 1967

School Organization
　Use Educational Administration

School Phobia 1973
PN 282　　　　　　　　　SC 45710
　B Phobias 1967
　R School Refusal 1994
　　　Separation Anxiety 1973
　　　Student Attitudes 1967

School Principals 1973
PN 2544　　　　　　　　　SC 45720
　B School Administrators 1973

School Psychologists 1973
PN 1956　　　　　　　　　SC 45730
SN Psychologists usually associated with elementary or secondary schools who provide counseling, testing, or diagnostic services to students, teachers, or parents.
　B Educational Psychologists 1973
　　　Mental Health Personnel 1967
　R School Counselors 1973

School Psychology 1973
PN 1478　　　　　　　　　SC 45740
SN Branch of psychology that emphasizes training and certification of school psychologists.
　B Educational Psychology 1967

School Readiness 1973
PN 600　　　　　　　　　SC 45750
SN Developmental level at which a child is prepared to adjust to school and the student role. Compare READING READINESS.
　R ↓ Education 1967
　　　Project Head Start 1973

School Refusal 1994
PN 156　　　　　　　　　SC 45755
SN Unwillingness of students to attend school or classes.
　R ↓ Resistance 1997
　　　School Attendance 1973
　　↓ School Dropouts 1967
　　　School Phobia 1973
　　　School Truancy 1973
　　　Separation Anxiety 1973
　　　Student Attitudes 1967

School Retention 1994
PN 310　　　　　　　　　SC 45757
SN Retention of students in school or educational programs.
　UF Retention (School)
　R School Attendance 1973
　　↓ School Dropouts 1967
　　↓ School Enrollment 1973
　　　School Leavers 1988
　　　School Truancy 1973

School Retention — (cont'd)
　　　Student Attrition 1991
　　↓ Students 1967

School Superintendents 1973
PN 471　　　　　　　　　SC 45760
SN Administrators who coordinate and direct the operations and activities of a school system at the district, city, or state level.
　UF Superintendents (School)
　B School Administrators 1973

School Suspension 1973
PN 186　　　　　　　　　SC 45770
SN Temporary, forced withdrawal of a student from school, usually for disciplinary reasons.
　UF Suspension (School)
　B School Enrollment 1973
　R Classroom Discipline 1973
　　　School Expulsion 1973

School to Work Transition 1994
PN 383　　　　　　　　　SC 45775
SN Transition following school graduation or termination and entry into the work force. Used for normal and disordered populations.
　R College Graduates 1982
　　↓ Education 1967
　　　Educational Attainment Level 1997
　　　High School Graduates 1978
　　↓ Mainstreaming 1991
　　　Occupational Adjustment 1973
　　　School Graduation 1991
　　↓ Vocational Rehabilitation 1967

School Transition 1997
PN 279　　　　　　　　　SC 45777
SN Movement or advancement from one grade, school, or program to the next.
　R ↓ Academic Achievement 1967
　　↓ Education 1967
　　　Grade Level 1994
　　　School Adjustment 1967
　　　School Graduation 1991

School Truancy 1973
PN 248　　　　　　　　　SC 45780
SN Student's deliberate, often chronic absence from school without an accepted medical or other justifiable reason.
　B Truancy 1973
　R ↓ Education 1967
　　↓ School Enrollment 1973
　　　School Refusal 1994
　　　School Retention 1994

School Violence 2003
PN 142　　　　　　　　　SC 45783
HN This term was introduced in June 2003. PsycINFO records from the past 10 years were re-indexed with this term. The posting note reflects the number of records that were re-indexed.
　B Violence 1973
　R ↓ Academic Environment 1973
　　　Bullying 2003
　　　Classroom Environment 1973
　　↓ School Environment 1973

Schools 1967
PN 3046　　　　　　　　　SC 45790
　N Boarding Schools 1988
　　↓ Colleges 1967
　　　Elementary Schools 1973

Schools — (cont'd)

Graduate Schools 1973
High Schools 1973
Institutional Schools 1978
Junior High Schools 1973
Kindergartens 1973
Middle Schools 2003
Military Schools 1973
Nongraded Schools 1973
Nursery Schools 1973
Seminaries 1973
Technical Schools 1973
R ↓ Community Facilities 1973
↓ Education 1967
↓ School Environment 1973
↓ School Facilities 1973

Sciatic Nerve
Use Spinal Nerves

SCID
Use Structured Clinical Interview

Science Achievement 1997
PN 259 SC 45815
B Academic Achievement 1967
R Mathematics Achievement 1973
Mathematics Education 1973
Science Education 1973

Science Education 1973
PN 4176 SC 45820
B Curriculum 1967
R Science Achievement 1997

Sciences 1967
PN 2652 SC 45825
N ↓ Biology 1967
↓ Chemistry 1967
Cognitive Science 2003
Eugenics 1973
Geography 1973
↓ Mathematics 1982
↓ Medical Sciences 1967
↓ Neurosciences 1973
Physics 1973
Psychobiology 1982
↓ Social Sciences 1967
R ↓ Technology 1973

Scientific Communication 1973
PN 10541 SC 45830
SN Formal or informal communication among professionals.
UF Communication (Professional)
Newsletters (Professional)
Professional Communication
Professional Newsletters
B Communication 1967
R ↓ Interpersonal Communication 1973
Psychological Terminology 1973
↓ Terminology 1991

Scientific Methods
Use Experimental Methods

Scientists 1967
PN 1308 SC 45850
SN Conceptually broad term. Use a more specific term if possible.

Scientists — (cont'd)
B Professional Personnel 1978
R ↓ Aerospace Personnel 1973
Anthropologists 1973
↓ Business and Industrial Personnel 1967
Engineers 1967
Mathematicians 1973
↓ Medical Personnel 1967
Physicists 1973
↓ Psychologists 1967
Sociologists 1973

Sclera
Use Eye (Anatomy)

Sclerosis (Nervous System) 1973
PN 324 SC 45870
B Nervous System Disorders 1967
N Multiple Sclerosis 1973
R ↓ Neuromuscular Disorders 1973
↓ Paralysis 1973

Scopolamine 1973
PN 1275 SC 45880
UF Hyoscine
Scopolamine Hydrobromide
B Alkaloids 1973
Amines 1973
Analgesic Drugs 1973
Cholinergic Blocking Drugs 1973
CNS Depressant Drugs 1973
Sedatives 1973
R Bromides 1973

Scopolamine Hydrobromide
Use Scopolamine

Score Equating 1985
PN 281 SC 45895
SN Techniques, procedures, or methods used to allow comparison of scores obtained from various editions of the same test or from different tests measuring the same trait.
UF Test Equating
R Cutting Scores 1985
↓ Scoring (Testing) 1973
Standard Scores 1985

Scores (Test)
Use Test Scores

Scoring (Testing) 1973
PN 2189 SC 45910
SN Assignment of numerical values or other types of codes, or the application of comments to test results in order to evaluate a test performance in reference to some established standard or other criterion. Compare GRADING (EDUCATIONAL) or TEST SCORES.
B Testing 1967
N Cutting Scores 1985
R Error of Measurement 1985
Grading (Educational) 1973
Score Equating 1985
Standard Scores 1985
Statistical Weighting 1985
Test Interpretation 1985
↓ Test Scores 1967

Scotopic Stimulation 1973
PN 136 SC 45940

Scotopic Stimulation — (cont'd)
SN Presentation of light at intensity levels characteristic of nighttime illumination, activating rod photoreceptors in the retina.
B Illumination 1967
R Photopic Stimulation 1973

Scratching 1973
PN 81 SC 45950
B Symptoms 1967
R Pruritus 1973

Screening 1982
PN 2169 SC 45960
SN Preliminary use of testing procedures or instruments to identify individuals at risk for a particular problem, or in need of a more thorough evaluation, or to determine an individual's suitability for a specific treatment, education, or occupation.
B Measurement 1967
N Drug Usage Screening 1988
↓ Health Screening 1997
Job Applicant Screening 1973
R Biological Markers 1991
↓ Diagnosis 1967
Diagnostic Interview Schedule 1991
↓ Educational Measurement 1967
Educational Placement 1978
Geriatric Assessment 1997
Health Promotion 1991
Intake Interview 1994
Misdiagnosis 1997
↓ Personnel Selection 1967
↓ Psychiatric Evaluation 1997
↓ Screening Tests 1982
Symptom Checklists 1991

Screening Tests 1982
PN 2567 SC 45980
B Measurement 1967
N Psychological Screening Inventory 1973
R General Health Questionnaire 1991
↓ Psychiatric Evaluation 1997
↓ Screening 1982

Scripts
Use Schema

Sculpturing 1973
PN 72 SC 45990
B Art 1967

Sea Gulls 1973
PN 194 SC 46010
UF Gulls
B Birds 1967

Seals (Animal) 1973
PN 167 SC 46020
B Mammals 1973

Seasonal Affective Disorder 1991
PN 611 SC 46025
UF SAD
Winter Depression
B Affective Disorders 2001
R ↓ Major Depression 1988
Phototherapy 1991
Recurrent Depression 1994

Seasonal Variations 1973
PN 1731   SC 46030
SN Periodic changes in behavioral, psychological, or physiological responses in relation to seasonal changes. Used for human or animal populations.
B   Environmental Effects 1973
R   ↓ Biological Rhythms 1967
     ↓ Temperature Effects 1967

Seat Belts
  Use Safety Belts

Seclusion (Patient)
  Use Patient Seclusion

Secobarbital 1973
PN 53   SC 46040
UF Seconal
B   Barbiturates 1967
    Hypnotic Drugs 1973
    Sedatives 1973

Seconal
  Use Secobarbital

Second Language Education
  Use Foreign Language Education

Second Order Conditioning
  Use Higher Order Conditioning

Secondary Education 1973
PN 1440   SC 46060
SN Education provided by comprehensive schools, grammar schools, junior high or high schools, typically for grades 7-12.
B   Education 1967
R   High School Education 2003
    High Schools 1973
    Junior High Schools 1973

Secondary Reinforcement 1967
PN 376   SC 46070
SN Presentation of a secondary reinforcer. Also, objects or events which acquire reinforcing properties only through having been consistently paired or associated with other reinforcers. Also known as conditioned reinforcers. Compare INTERNAL REWARDS.
UF Token Reinforcement
B   Reinforcement 1967
R   Conditioned Stimulus 1973

Secrecy 1994
PN 163   SC 46075
R   Anonymity 1973
    ↓ Deception 1967
    Privacy 1973
    Self Disclosure 1973

Secretarial Personnel 1973
PN 163   SC 46080
B   Business and Industrial Personnel 1967
    White Collar Workers 1973
R   Clerical Personnel 1973

Secretarial Skills
  Use Clerical Secretarial Skills

Secretion (Gland) 1973
PN 173   SC 46100
B   Physiology 1967
N   ↓ Endocrine Gland Secretion 1973
    Lactation 1973
    Salivation 1973
    Sweating 1973
R   ↓ Endocrine Disorders 1973

Sectioning (Lesion)
  Use Lesions

Security (Emotional)
  Use Emotional Security

Sedatives 1973
PN 581   SC 46130
HN In 1997, this term replaced the discontinued term PHENAGLYCODOL. In 2000, PHENAGLYCODOL was removed from all records and replaced with SEDATIVES.
UF Phenaglycodol
B   Drugs 1967
N   Alprazolam 1988
    Amobarbital 1973
    Atropine 1973
    Barbital 1973
    Chloral Hydrate 1973
    Chlorpromazine 1967
    Clozapine 1991
    Flurazepam 1982
    Glutethimide 1973
    Haloperidol 1973
    Heroin 1973
    Hexobarbital 1973
    Meperidine 1973
    Meprobamate 1973
    Methaqualone 1973
    Molindone 1982
    Nitrazepam 1978
    Pentobarbital 1973
    Phenobarbital 1973
    Promethazine 1973
    Reserpine 1967
    Scopolamine 1973
    Secobarbital 1973
    Thalidomide 1973
    Thiopental 1973
    Triazolam 1988
R   ↓ Analgesic Drugs 1973
    ↓ Anesthetic Drugs 1973
    ↓ Anticonvulsive Drugs 1973
    ↓ Antiemetic Drugs 1973
    ↓ Antihistaminic Drugs 1973
    ↓ Antihypertensive Drugs 1973
    ↓ Barbiturates 1967
    ↓ Benzodiazepines 1978
    ↓ CNS Depressant Drugs 1973
    ↓ Hypnotic Drugs 1973
    ↓ Tranquilizing Drugs 1967

Seduction 1994
PN 99   SC 46133
B   Psychosexual Behavior 1967

Seeing Eye Dogs
  Use Mobility Aids

Segregation (Racial)
  Use Social Integration

Seizures
  Use Convulsions

Selection (Personnel)
  Use Personnel Selection

Selection (Therapist)
  Use Therapist Selection

Selection Tests 1973
PN 514   SC 46170
SN Tests developed to assess specific traits or skills with the purpose of screening or selecting individuals for occupational or educational placement.
B   Measurement 1967
N   Psychological Screening Inventory 1973

Selective Attention 1973
PN 3052   SC 46175
SN Focusing of awareness on a limited range of stimuli. Compare DIVIDED ATTENTION.
B   Attention 1967
R   Concentration 1982
    Distraction 1978
    Divided Attention 1973
    ↓ Monitoring 1973
    Sensory Gating 1991
    Vigilance 1967

Selective Breeding 1973
PN 371   SC 46180
SN Systematic approach to the development of genotype-dependent differences in a physical or behavioral trait. Compare ANIMAL BREEDING, ANIMAL DOMESTICATION, and EUGENICS.
B   Animal Breeding 1973
R   Animal Domestication 1978
    Eugenics 1973
    ↓ Genetic Engineering 1994
    ↓ Genetics 1967
    Reproductive Technology 1988

Selective Mutism
  Use Elective Mutism

Self Acceptance
  Use Self Perception

Self Actualization 1973
PN 2293   SC 46190
SN According to A. Maslow's theory, the process of striving to fulfull one's talents, capacities, and potentialities for maximum self realization, ideally with integration of physical, social, intellectual, and emotional needs.
UF Actualization (Self)
    Self Realization
R   Affective Education 1982
    ↓ Human Potential Movement 1982
    Maslow (Abraham Harold) 1991
    ↓ Personality 1967
    Self Determination 1994
    ↓ Self Help Techniques 1982

Self Administration (Drugs)
  Use Drug Self Administration

Self Analysis 1994
PN 113   SC 46195

Self Analysis — (cont'd)

SN A psychotherapist's application of psychoanalytic principles to his or her personal feelings, drives, and behaviors.

B Psychoanalysis 1967
R Personal Therapy 1991
     Psychoanalytic Training 1973

Self Assessment

Use Self Evaluation

Self Care Skills 1978

PN 1994   **SC** 46215
SN Skills such as personal hygiene, feeding, independent housekeeping, public transportation use, which are often taught in rehabilitation programs for persons with mental, physical, or emotional handicaps.

UF Independent Living
B Ability 1967
R Activities of Daily Living 1991
     Adaptive Behavior 1991
     Child Self Care 1988
     Daily Activities 1994
     Hygiene 1994
     Independent Living Programs 1991
     ↓ Rehabilitation 1967
     ↓ Skill Learning 1973
     Special Education 1967

Self Concept 1967

PN 22264   **SC** 46220
UF Ideal Self
     Identity (Personal)
     Self Image
N Academic Self Concept 1997
     Self Confidence 1994
     Self Esteem 1973
R Affective Education 1982
     Ego Identity 1991
     Ethnic Identity 1973
     ↓ Gender Identity 1985
     Identity Crisis 1973
     Identity Formation 2004
     ↓ Personality 1967
     Professional Identity 1991
     Reference Groups 1994
     Role Satisfaction 1994
     Self Congruence 1978
     Self Criticism 2003
     Self Perception 1967
     ↓ Social Identity 1990
     Symbolic Interactionism 1988

Self Confidence 1994

PN 792   **SC** 46230
HN Use SELF ESTEEM to access references from 1973-1993.
UF Confidence (Self)
B Self Concept 1967
R Academic Self Concept 1997
     Self Efficacy 1985
     Self Esteem 1973
     Self Perception 1967

Self Congruence 1978

PN 300   **SC** 46235
SN State of harmony between actual and ideal selves, or congruence between experience, personality, and self-concept.
R ↓ Self Concept 1967

Self Consciousness

Use Self Perception

Self Control 1973

PN 3966   **SC** 46240
SN The ability to repress or the practice of repressing one's behavior, impulsive reactions, emotions, or desires.
UF Control (Self)
     Willpower
B Personality Traits 1967
R Anger Control 1997
     ↓ Emotional Control 1973
     ↓ Helplessness 1997
     ↓ Impulse Control Disorders 1997
     Internal External Locus of Control 1967
     Self Regulation 2003
     Temptation 1973

Self Criticism 2003

PN 67   **SC** 46242
HN This term was introduced in June 2003. PsycINFO records from the past 10 years were re-indexed with this term. The posting note reflects the number of records that were re-indexed.
B Criticism 1973
R Perfectionism 1988
     ↓ Self Concept 1967
     Self Esteem 1973
     Self Evaluation 1967
     Self Monitoring 1982

Self Defeating Behavior 1988

PN 188   **SC** 46243
SN Behavior that blocks one's own goals and wishes, e.g., the tendency to compete so aggressively that one cannot hold a job.
B Behavior 1967
R ↓ Self Destructive Behavior 1985
     Self Handicapping Strategy 1988

Self Defense 1985

PN 143   **SC** 46245
SN Protecting one's self or property against crime.
UF Personal Defense
R ↓ Crime 1967
     ↓ Crime Victims 1982
     Martial Arts 1985
     Self Preservation 1997
     ↓ Violence 1973

Self Destructive Behavior 1985

PN 1595   **SC** 46244
UF Self Injurious Behavior
B Behavior 1967
N Attempted Suicide 1973
     Head Banging 1973
     Self Inflicted Wounds 1973
     Self Mutilation 1973
     ↓ Suicide 1967
R ↓ Behavior Disorders 1971
     Borderline Personality Disorder 2001
     ↓ Masochism 1973
     Masochistic Personality 1973
     Self Defeating Behavior 1988
     Trichotillomania 2003

Self Determination 1994

PN 575   **SC** 46246
SN The power of individuals to determine their own destiny or actions.

Self Determination — (cont'd)

R Empowerment 1991
     ↓ Helplessness 1997
     Independence (Personality) 1973
     Individuality 1973
     Internal External Locus of Control 1967
     Self Actualization 1973
     ↓ Self Management 1985
     Volition 1988
     World View 1988

Self Directed Learning

Use Individualized Instruction

Self Disclosure 1973

PN 3657   **SC** 46250
UF Disclosure (Self)
R Anonymity 1973
     ↓ Interpersonal Communication 1973
     Legal Confession 2003
     ↓ Personality 1967
     Secrecy 1994

Self Efficacy 1985

PN 5834   **SC** 46255
SN Cognitive mechanism based on expectations or beliefs about one's ability to perform actions necessary to produce a given effect. Also, a theoretical component of behavior change in various therapeutic treatments.
UF Efficacy Expectations
R Academic Self Concept 1997
     ↓ Expectations 1967
     ↓ Helplessness 1997
     Instrumentality 1991
     Self Confidence 1994
     Self Evaluation 1967
     Self Fulfilling Prophecies 1997
     Self Perception 1967

Self Employment 1994

PN 51   **SC** 46257
B Employment Status 1982
R Business 1967
     Entrepreneurship 1991
     Ownership 1985
     Retailing 1991

Self Esteem 1973

PN 13349   **SC** 46260
UF Self Respect
B Self Concept 1967
R Self Confidence 1994
     Self Criticism 2003
     Self Perception 1967

Self Evaluation 1967

PN 5206   **SC** 46270
UF Self Assessment
B Evaluation 1967
R ↓ Personality 1967
     Self Criticism 2003
     Self Efficacy 1985
     ↓ Self Management 1985
     Self Monitoring 1982
     Self Report 1982
     Social Comparison 1985

Self Examination (Medical) 1988

PN 282   **SC** 46273

Self Examination (Medical) — (cont'd)

SN Self examination for detection of medical conditions or disorders, e.g., breast or testicular cancer. Also used for self administration of medical diagnostic procedures.
- **UF** Breast Examination
- **R** Cancer Screening 1997
  - ↓ Health Behavior 1982
  - Physical Examination 1988

Self Fulfilling Prophecies 1997

PN 66　　　　　**SC** 46271
SN Expectations or predictions that turn out just as one prophesized. The fulfillment of expectations is usually due to behavior that optimizes the outcome.
- **UF** Pygmalion Effect
- **R** Attribution 1973
  - ↓ Expectations 1967
  - ↓ Prediction 1967
  - Self Efficacy 1985
  - Social Cognition 1994
  - ↓ Social Perception 1967

Self Handicapping Strategy 1988

PN 168　　　　　**SC** 46274
SN Conscious or unconscious efforts to lessen one's chances of performing well at a task in which one is ego-involved and fears failure so that poor performance or lack of ability may be attributed to circumstance.
- **R** Fear of Success 1978
  - Self Defeating Behavior 1900

Self Help Techniques 1982

PN 1922　　　　　**SC** 46275
SN Techniques, materials, or processes designed to assist individuals in solving their own problems. Consider also SUPPORT GROUPS.
- **N** ↓ Self Management 1985
- **R** ↓ Behavior Modification 1973
  - ↓ Community Services 1967
  - Group Counseling 1973
  - ↓ Psychotherapeutic Techniques 1967
  - Self Actualization 1973
  - Self Monitoring 1982
  - Self Referral 1991
  - ↓ Support Groups 1991
  - ↓ Treatment 1967
  - ↓ Twelve Step Programs 1997

Self Hypnosis

Use Autohypnosis

Self Image

Use Self Concept

Self Inflicted Wounds 1973

PN 566　　　　　**SC** 46290
SN Any injury to body tissue (including bones) resulting from self directed physical violence. Compare SELF MUTILATION.
- **B** Self Destructive Behavior 1985
  - Wounds 1973
- **R** Self Mutilation 1973

Self Injurious Behavior

Use Self Destructive Behavior

Self Instruction

Use Individualized Instruction

Self Instructional Training 1985

PN 220　　　　　**SC** 46294
SN Cognitive technique for overcoming cognitive deficits in areas such as problem solving, verbal mediation, and information seeking. Overt verbalizations of thought processes are modeled for and imitated by the client. Covert self-verbalizations follow which result in the client gaining verbal control over behavior.
- **B** Cognitive Techniques 1985
  - Self Management 1985
- **R** Cognitive Therapy 1982

Self Management 1985

PN 2103　　　　　**SC** 46295
SN Self-regulated modification and/or maintenance of behavior by self-governing of behavioral consequences. Used with disordered or normal populations of all ages.
- **B** Behavior Modification 1973
  - Management 1967
  - Self Help Techniques 1982
- **N** Self Instructional Training 1985
- **R** Centering 1991
  - Cognitive Therapy 1982
  - Self Determination 1994
  - Self Evaluation 1967
  - Self Monitoring 1982
  - Self Regulation 2003
  - Self Reinforcement 1973
  - Time Management 1994

Self Managing Work Teams 2001

PN 36　　　　　**SC** 46299
SN Autonomous groups of employees who share the responsibility for and have been given the authority to oversee and control all work processes.
- **B** Management Methods 1973
  - Work Teams 2001
- **R** Organizational Structure 1967
  - Participative Management 1988

Self Medication 1991

PN 229　　　　　**SC** 46298
SN Medicating one's self without the advice or consent of a physician. Not to be confused with DRUG SELF ADMINISTRATION.
- **R** ↓ Drug Therapy 1967
  - ↓ Drugs 1967
  - Nonprescription Drugs 1991
  - Prescription Drugs 1991

Self Monitoring 1982

PN 1495　　　　　**SC** 46296
SN Systematic observation and recording of one's own behavior usually for the purpose of changing the behavior by means of behavior modification techniques.
- **UF** Self Observation
- **B** Monitoring 1973
- **R** ↓ Behavior Modification 1973
  - Observation Methods 1967
  - Self Criticism 2003
  - Self Evaluation 1967
  - ↓ Self Help Techniques 1982
  - ↓ Self Management 1985
  - Self Regulation 2003
  - Self Report 1982

Self Monitoring (Personality) 1985

PN 564　　　　　**SC** 46297

Self Monitoring (Personality) — (cont'd)

SN The process of subjectively observing and comparing one's own behaviors and expressions with those of others in social interactions for the purpose of regulating and controlling one's own verbal and nonverbal behaviors.
- **R** Conscientiousness 1997
  - Impression Management 1978
  - Introspection 1973
  - ↓ Personality 1967
  - Reflectiveness 1997
  - Self Perception 1967
  - Self Regulation 2003
  - Social Comparison 1985
  - ↓ Social Interaction 1967

Self Mutilation 1973

PN 751　　　　　**SC** 46300
SN Act of inflicting permanent physical damage to oneself, such as cutting off or destroying a limb or other part of the body. Compare SELF INFLICTED WOUNDS.
- **UF** Autotomy
  - Mutilation (Self)
- **B** Behavior Disorders 1971
  - Self Destructive Behavior 1985
- **R** Cosmetic Techniques 2001
  - Self Inflicted Wounds 1973

Self Observation

Use Self Monitoring

Self Perception 1967

PN 12999　　　　　**SC** 46310
SN Physical and social awareness and perceptions of oneself.
- **UF** Self Acceptance
  - Self Consciousness
- **D** Perception 1967
- **R** Academic Self Concept 1967
  - Aging (Attitudes Toward) 1985
  - Body Awareness 1982
  - Ingroup Outgroup 1967
  - Introspection 1973
  - Mirror Image 1991
  - ↓ Personality 1967
  - ↓ Personality Theory 1967
  - Reflectiveness 1967
  - ↓ Self Concept 1967
  - Self Confidence 1994
  - Self Efficacy 1985
  - Self Esteem 1973
  - Self Monitoring (Personality) 1985
  - Self Reference 1994
  - Self Report 1982

Self Preservation 1997

PN 112　　　　　**SC** 46312
- **UF** Survival Instinct
- **R** Death Instinct 1988
  - Instinctive Behavior 1982
  - Self Defense 1985
  - Theory of Evolution 1967

Self Psychology 1988

PN 1494　　　　　**SC** 46315
SN Psychological theory and approach to psychotherapy focusing on interpretation of behavior in reference to self. Includes the psychoanalytic concept of an individual's need to organize the psyche into a cohesive whole, the self.
- **B** Psychology 1967
- **R** ↓ Humanistic Psychology 1985

Self Psychology — (cont'd)
    Mirroring 1997
    Object Relations 1982
    ↓ Personality Theory 1967
    ↓ Psychoanalytic Theory 1967

Self Realization
  Use Self Actualization

Self Reference 1994
PN 194   **SC** 46323

  R ↓ Interpersonal Communication 1973
    Self Perception 1967
    ↓ Social Perception 1967

Self Referral 1991
PN 105   **SC** 46325
SN Act of directing oneself to an agency, service, or professional for assessment, diagnosis, treatment, or consultation.
  UF Referral (Self)
  R ↓ Commitment (Psychiatric) 1973
    ↓ Health Behavior 1982
    Health Care Seeking Behavior 1997
    ↓ Health Care Services 1978
    Health Care Utilization 1985
    ↓ Help Seeking Behavior 1978
    Professional Referral 1973
    Right to Treatment 1997
    ↓ Self Help Techniques 1982

Self Regulated Learning 2003
PN 132   **SC** 46328
SN Approach to learning that involves self adjustment, self monitoring, strategy use, and goal setting.
HN This term was introduced in June 2003. PsycINFO records from the past 10 years were re-indexed with this term. The posting note reflects the number of records that were re-indexed.
  B Learning 1967
  R Discovery Teaching Method 1973
    Individualized Instruction 1973
    ↓ Learning Strategies 1991
    Self Regulation 2003

Self Regulation 2003
PN 495   **SC** 46327
SN Process of adjusting one's behavior to achieve or avoid a particular outcome.
HN This term was introduced in June 2003. PsycINFO records from the past 10 years were re-indexed with this term. The posting note reflects the number of records that were re-indexed.
  R Self Control 1973
    ↓ Self Management 1985
    Self Monitoring 1982
    Self Monitoring (Personality) 1985
    Self Regulated Learning 2003

Self Reinforcement 1973
PN 1437   **SC** 46330
SN Used for human and animal populations.
  B Reinforcement 1967
  R ↓ Self Management 1985
    ↓ Self Stimulation 1967

Self Report 1982
PN 5523   **SC** 46335

Self Report — (cont'd)
SN Method for obtaining information through the elicitation of overt verbal responses, oral or written, from the subject/client by the use of questions or directives. Used only when self-report is discussed in reference to methodological considerations.
  B Methodology 1967
  R Likert Scales 1994
    Self Evaluation 1967
    Self Monitoring 1982
    Self Perception 1967

Self Respect
  Use Self Esteem

Self Stimulation 1967
PN 2135   **SC** 46350
  B Stimulation 1967
  N Brain Self Stimulation 1985
  R Electrical Brain Stimulation 1973
    ↓ Operant Conditioning 1967
    ↓ Reinforcement 1967
    Self Reinforcement 1973
    Stereotyped Behavior 1973

Self Talk 1988
PN 425   **SC** 46355
SN Vocalized or unvocalized speech that is directed to oneself or an imaginary recipient.
  UF Inner Speech
  B Oral Communication 1985
  R Ellis (Albert) 1991
    ↓ Psychotherapeutic Techniques 1967
    Subvocalization 1973

Selfishness 1973
PN 107   **SC** 46360
  B Personality Traits 1967
  R Narcissism 1967

Semantic Differential 1967
PN 872   **SC** 46370
SN Technique or test which uses subjective ratings of an idea, concept, or object by means of scaling opposite adjectives in order to study connotative meaning. Also used to assess interactions between people and situations and for attitude assessment.
  R ↓ Attitude Measures 1967
    Likert Scales 1994
    ↓ Measurement 1967

Semantic Generalization 1973
PN 179   **SC** 46380
SN Conditioning of a reaction to a nonverbal stimulus and subsequent generalization of the response to verbal signs representative of the original stimulus. The types include generalization from object to sign, from sign to sign, and from sign to object.
  UF Generalization (Semantic)
  B Cognitive Processes 1967
  R Cognitive Generalization 1967
    Connotations 1973

Semantic Memory 1988
PN 1295   **SC** 46385
SN Organized knowledge about words, their meanings, and their relations.
  B Verbal Memory 1994
  R ↓ Lexical Access 1988
    Lexical Decision 1988
    Semantic Priming 1994
    ↓ Semantics 1967

Semantic Priming 1994
PN 718   **SC** 46387
  B Priming 1988
  R Contextual Associations 1967
    Cues 1967
    Semantic Memory 1988
    ↓ Semantics 1967

Semantics 1967
PN 6123   **SC** 46390
SN Linguistic science dealing with the relations between language symbols (words, expressions, phrases) and the objects or concepts to which they refer. Also includes the study of changes in the meanings of words. Used for the discipline or the specific semantic characteristics of linguistic symbols.
  B Grammar 1967
  N Antonyms 1973
    Homonyms 1973
    Synonyms 1973
  R Discourse Analysis 1997
    Metaphor 1982
    Morphology (Language) 1973
    ↓ Phonology 1973
    ↓ Priming 1988
    Semantic Memory 1988
    Semantic Priming 1994
    ↓ Syntax 1971
    ↓ Verbal Meaning 1973
    ↓ Vocabulary 1967
    Words (Phonetic Units) 1967

Semicircular Canals 1973
PN 66   **SC** 46400
  B Vestibular Apparatus 1967

Seminarians 1973
PN 211   **SC** 46410
  B Religious Personnel 1973
    Students 1967

Seminaries 1973
PN 34   **SC** 46420
SN Institutions for training for ministry, priesthood, or rabbinate.
  B Schools 1967
  R Religious Education 1973

Semiotics 1985
PN 434   **SC** 46425
SN Analysis of signs and symbols, especially their syntactic, semantic, and pragmatic functions in language.
  N Pragmatics 1985
  R Hermeneutics 1991
    ↓ Linguistics 1973
    Symbolism 1967

Senile Dementia 1973
PN 926   **SC** 46440
  UF Dementia (Senile)
  B Dementia 1985
    Syndromes 1973
  N Senile Psychosis 1973
  R Alzheimers Disease 1973
    Cerebral Arteriosclerosis 1973
    Physiological Aging 1967
    ↓ Presenile Dementia 1973
    Progressive Supranuclear Palsy 1997

Senile Psychosis 1973
PN 16   **SC** 46450

Senile Psychosis — (cont'd)
- **B**   Psychosis   1967
  - Senile Dementia   1973

Sensation
- **Use**   Perception

Sensation Seeking   1978
PN   1077   SC   46477
SN   Need for novel experience or stimulation in order to reach optimal levels of arousal. Limited to human populations.
- **UF**   Novelty Seeking
  - Stimulation Seeking (Personality)
- **B**   Personality Traits   1967
- **R**   Extraversion   1967

Sensation Seeking Scale   1973
PN   88   SC   46480
- **B**   Personality Measures   1967

Sense Organ Disorders   1973
PN   46   SC   46490
- **B**   Physical Disorders   1997
  - Sensory System Disorders   2001
- **N**   Anosmia   1973
  - ↓ Ear Disorders   1973
  - Taste Disorders   2001
  - ↓ Vision Disorders   1982
- **R**   Anesthesia (Feeling)   1973
  - ↓ Sense Organs   1973

Sense Organs   1973
PN   112   SC   46500
- **B**   Anatomy   1967
- **N**   ↓ Ear (Anatomy)   1967
  - ↓ Eye (Anatomy)   1967
  - Taste Buds   1973
- **R**   ↓ Sense Organ Disorders   1973
  - ↓ Sensory System Disorders   2001
  - Taste Disorders   2001

Sensitivity (Drugs)
- **Use**   Drug Sensitivity

Sensitivity (Personality)   1967
PN   1404   SC   46520
- **UF**   Insensitivity (Personality)
- **B**   Personality Traits   1967
- **R**   Perceptiveness (Personality)   1973

Sensitivity Training   1973
PN   1101   SC   46530
SN   Group training that focuses on interpersonal relations within the group and enhancement of self-confidence, self-perception, behavioral skills, and role flexibility.
- **B**   Human Potential Movement   1982
- **R**   Communication Skills Training   1982
  - Consciousness Raising Groups   1978
  - Cultural Sensitivity   1994
  - ↓ Encounter Group Therapy   1973
  - ↓ Group Dynamics   1967
  - ↓ Group Psychotherapy   1967
  - Human Relations Training   1978
  - Marathon Group Therapy   1973
  - ↓ Personnel Training   1967
  - Social Skills Training   1982

Sensitization (Protein)
- **Use**   Anaphylactic Shock

Sensitization Repression
- **Use**   Repression Sensitization

Sensorially Handicapped
- **Use**   Sensory System Disorders

Sensorimotor Development
- **Use**   Perceptual Motor Development

Sensorimotor Measures   1973
PN   355   SC   46550
- **UF**   Perceptual Motor Measures
- **B**   Measurement   1967
- **R**   ↓ Perceptual Measures   1973

Sensorimotor Processes
- **Use**   Perceptual Motor Processes

Sensorineural Hearing Loss
- **Use**   Hearing Disorders

Sensory Adaptation   1967
PN   2179   SC   46560
SN   Change in sensitivity of sensory systems or components as a result of ongoing or prolonged stimulation.
- **UF**   Adaptation (Sensory)
- **B**   Adaptation   1967
  - Thresholds   1967
- **N**   Dark Adaptation   1973
  - Light Adaptation   1982
  - Orienting Reflex   1967
  - Orienting Responses   1967
- **R**   Habituation   1967
  - Interocular Transfer   1985
  - Sensory Integration   1991

Sensory Deprivation   1967
PN   1206   SC   46570
SN   Restriction of sensory or environmental stimulation through surgical or other techniques. Used primarily for animal populations. Consider STIMULUS DEPRIVATION for human populations.
- **B**   Stimulus Deprivation   1973

Sensory Disabilities (Attitudes Toward)   2001
PN   131   SC   46576
HN   In 2000, the truncated terms SENSORY DISABILITIES (ATTIT TOWARD) (which was used from 1997-2000) and SENSORY HANDICAPS (ATTIT TOWARD) (which was used from 1973-1996) were deleted, removed from all records containing them, and replaced with the expanded form SENSORY DISABILITIES (ATTITUDES TOWARD).
- **UF**   Sensory Handicaps (Attitudes Toward)
- **B**   Disabled (Attitudes Toward)   1997
- **R**   Disability Discrimination   1997

Sensory Feedback   1973
PN   454   SC   46580
SN   Return of afferent neural signals or information from sensory receptors. Sensory feedback may function in the regulation of behavior in general but is especially important in the control of bodily movement. Use a more specific term if possible.
- **B**   Feedback   1967
  - Perceptual Stimulation   1973
- **N**   ↓ Auditory Feedback   1973
  - Visual Feedback   1973

Sensory Gating   1991
PN   386   SC   46585
SN   The internal process of blocking one or more sensory stimuli while attention is focused on another sensory stimuli or sensory channel.
- **UF**   Gating (Sensory)
- **B**   Perception   1967
- **R**   ↓ Awareness   1967
  - ↓ Evoked Potentials   1967
  - ↓ Perceptual Stimulation   1973
  - Prepulse Inhibition   1997
  - Selective Attention   1973

Sensory Handicaps (Attitudes Toward)
- **Use**   Sensory Disabilities (Attitudes Toward)

Sensory Integration   1991
PN   672   SC   46595
SN   Neural processes of organizing sensory inputs from the environment and producing an adaptive response. In treatment, the environment's sensory input is manipulated to facilitate environmental interaction.
- **UF**   Intersensory Integration
- **B**   Intersensory Processes   1978
  - Perceptual Motor Processes   1967
- **R**   ↓ Sensory Adaptation   1967
  - ↓ Treatment   1967

Sensory Neglect   1994
PN   862   SC   46597
- **UF**   Perceptual Neglect
  - Spatial Neglect
  - Visual Neglect
- **R**   ↓ Perception   1967
  - ↓ Perceptual Distortion   1982
  - ↓ Perceptual Disturbances   1973
  - ↓ Receptive Fields   1985

Sensory Neurons   1973
PN   1139   SC   46610
- **B**   Neurons   1973
- **N**   Auditory Neurons   1973
  - Baroreceptors   1973
  - Chemoreceptors   1973
  - Mechanoreceptors   1973
  - Nociceptors   1985
  - ↓ Photoreceptors   1973
  - Proprioceptors   1973
  - Taste Buds   1973
  - Thermoreceptors   1973
- **R**   ↓ Afferent Pathways   1982
  - ↓ Receptive Fields   1985
  - Taste Disorders   2001

Sensory Pathways
- **Use**   Afferent Pathways

Sensory Preconditioning
- **Use**   Preconditioning

Sensory System Disorders   2001
PN   156   SC   46599
SN   Disorders of the sense organs or of the somatosensory system.

Sensory System Disorders — (cont'd)

HN The term SENSORIALLY HANDICAPPED was used to represent this concept from 1994-1996, and SENSORIALLY DISABLED was used from 1997-2000. In 2000, SENSORY SYSTEM DISORDERS was created to replace the discontinued and deleted term SENSORIALLY DISABLED. SENSORIALLY DISABLED and SENSORIALLY HANDICAPPED were removed from all records containing them and replaced with SENSORY SYSTEM DISORDERS.

UF   Sensorially Handicapped
B   Physical Disorders   1997
N   ↓ Sense Organ Disorders   1973
     Somatosensory Disorders   2001
R   ↓ Sense Organs   1973
     Somatosensory Cortex   1973
     Synesthesia   2003

Sentence Completion Tests   1991
PN 57   **SC** 46617
B   Personality Measures   1967
     Projective Personality Measures   1973
R   Cloze Testing   1973

Sentence Comprehension   1973
PN 2243   **SC** 46620
B   Verbal Comprehension   1985

Sentence Structure   1973
PN 2050   **SC** 46630
SN Specific characteristics of a sentence's construction, including such aspects as its syntax, length, and complexity. Compare SYNTAX.
R   ↓ Prosody   1991
   ↓ Syntax   1971
     Text Structure   1982

Sentences   1967
PN 2006   **SC** 46640
SN Grammatically and syntactically arranged words that constitute a grammatically complete and meaningful unit.
B   Language   1967

Sentencing
Use   Adjudication

Separation (Marital)
Use   Marital Separation

Separation Anxiety   1973
PN 926   **SC** 46660
B   Anxiety Disorders   1997
     Separation Reactions   1997
R   Abandonment   1997
     Attachment Behavior   1985
     Attachment Disorders   2001
   ↓ Relationship Termination   1997
     School Phobia   1973
     School Refusal   1994
     Stranger Reactions   1988

Separation Individuation   1982
PN 1544   **SC** 46665
SN Normal process begun in infancy of disengagement from one's mother and development of a separate, individual identity. Limited to human populations.
B   Personality Development   1967
R   Attachment Behavior   1985

Separation Individuation — (cont'd)
   ↓ Childhood Development   1967
     Mother Child Relations   1967
     Object Relations   1982
     Transitional Objects   1985

Separation Reactions   1997
PN 222   **SC** 46670
N   Separation Anxiety   1973
R   Abandonment   1997
     Alienation   1971
     Anaclitic Depression   1973
     Apathy   1973
     Attachment Behavior   1985
     Attachment Disorders   2001
     Depression (Emotion)   1967
     Disappointment   1973
     Distress   1973
     Emotional Trauma   1967
     Grief   1973
     Homesickness   1994
   ↓ Relationship Termination   1997
     Sadness   1973
     Withdrawal (Defense Mechanism)   1973

Septal Nuclei   1982
PN 636   **SC** 46676
SN Subcallosal nuclei that form an integral part of the limbic system. These nuclei contribute to the medial forebrain bundle and have processes synapsing in the hippocampus.
UF   Septum
B   Limbic System   1973
R   Fornix   1982
     Hippocampus   1967
     Medial Forebrain Bundle   1982
     Nucleus Accumbens   1982

Septum
Use   Septal Nuclei

Sequential Learning   1973
PN 536   **SC** 46690
SN Type of learning in which a particular task is completed before the next task is given. The learning of each subsequent task is dependent on the previous task completed.
B   Learning   1967
R   Mastery Learning   1985

Serial Anticipation (Learning)   1973
PN 140   **SC** 46700
SN Learning paradigm which involves the initial presentation of a list of items or a series of events with a short interval between the items or elements in the series. Upon subsequent presentation of the list/series, the subject attempts to guess or anticipate the next item/element in the sequence. Thus, each item/element serves as a cue for the recall of the next. Compare FREE RECALL.
UF   Anticipation (Serial Learning)
B   Serial Learning   1967
R   ↓ Verbal Learning   1967

Serial Homicide   2003
PN 28   **SC** 46715
HN This term was introduced in June 2003. PsycINFO records from the past 10 years were re-indexed with this term. The posting note reflects the number of records that were re-indexed.
UF   Serial Murder
B   Homicide   1967

Serial Learning   1967
PN 1463   **SC** 46720
SN Learning, usually memorization, of items in a list according to a prescribed order.
B   Learning   1967
N   Serial Anticipation (Learning)   1973
R   ↓ Serial Position Effect   1982
     Serial Recall   1994
   ↓ Verbal Learning   1967

Serial Murder
Use   Serial Homicide

Serial Position Effect   1982
PN 341   **SC** 46724
SN Effect of the relative position of an item in a series on the rate of learning that item.
N   Primacy Effect   1973
     Recency Effect   1973
R   ↓ Learning   1967
     Learning Rate   1973
   ↓ Serial Learning   1967
     Serial Recall   1994

Serial Recall   1994
PN 299   **SC** 46727
B   Recall (Learning)   1967
R   Forgetting   1973
     Free Recall   1973
   ↓ Memory   1967
   ↓ Serial Learning   1967
   ↓ Serial Position Effect   1982

Seriousness   1973
PN 27   **SC** 46730
B   Personality Traits   1967

Serotonin   1973
PN 6665   **SC** 46740
UF   Hydroxytryptamine (5-)
B   Amines   1973
     Neurotransmitters   1985
     Vasoconstrictor Drugs   1973
R   ↓ Adrenergic Drugs   1973
     Serotonin Agonists   1988
   ↓ Serotonin Antagonists   1973
   ↓ Serotonin Metabolites   1978
   ↓ Serotonin Precursors   1978

Serotonin Agonists   1988
PN 1523   **SC** 46745
B   Drugs   1967
R   Buspirone   1991
     Serotonin   1973
   ↓ Serotonin Antagonists   1973

Serotonin Antagonists   1973
PN 2133   **SC** 46750
UF   Methysergide
B   Drugs   1967
N   Dihydroxytryptamine   1991
     Lysergic Acid Diethylamide   1967
     Mianserin   1982
     Molindone   1982
     Parachlorophenylalanine   1978
     Ritanserin   1997
     Tetrabenazine   1973
R   ↓ Decarboxylase Inhibitors   1982
     Serotonin   1973
     Serotonin Agonists   1988
   ↓ Serotonin Precursors   1978
   ↓ Serotonin Reuptake Inhibitors   1997

Serotonin Metabolites   1978
PN 176   **SC** 46754
B Metabolites   1973
N Hydroxyindoleacetic Acid (5-)   1985
R Serotonin   1973
↓ Serotonin Precursors   1978

Serotonin Precursors   1978
PN 99   **SC** 46756
N ↓ Tryptophan   1973
R Serotonin   1973
↓ Serotonin Antagonists   1973
↓ Serotonin Metabolites   1978

Serotonin Reuptake Inhibitors   1997
PN 1317   **SC** 46758
HN Consider using SEROTONIN ANTAGONISTS to access references from 1973-1996.
N Chlorimipramine   1973
Citalopram   1997
Fluoxetine   1991
Fluvoxamine   1994
Paroxetine   1994
Zimeldine   1988
R ↓ Serotonin Antagonists   1973

Serpasil
Use Reserpine

Sertraline   1997
PN 563   **SC** 46765
B Antidepressant Drugs   1971

Serum (Blood)
Use Blood Serum

Serum Albumin   1973
PN 41   **SC** 46780
B Blood Proteins   1973

Service Personnel   1991
PN 491   **SC** 46785
SN Employees who have direct contact with the public; generally nonprofessional and nonsales personnel. Includes hotel, airline, and restaurant personnel, but does not include health care personnel.
B Business and Industrial Personnel   1967
N Domestic Service Personnel   1973
Technical Service Personnel   1973
R Child Care Workers   1978
↓ Nonprofessional Personnel   1982
Sales Personnel   1973
↓ Technical Personnel   1978

Service Quality
Use Quality of Services

Servicemen
Use Military Personnel

Set (Response)
Use Response Set

Severe Mental Retardation   2001
PN 2232   **SC** 46800
SN IQ 20-34.

Severe Mental Retardation   — (cont'd)
HN In 2000, this term replaced the discontinued and deleted term SEVERELY MENTALLY RETARDED. SEVERELY MENTALLY RETARDED was removed from all records containing it and replaced with SEVERE MENTAL RETARDATION.
B Mental Retardation   1967

Severity (Disorders)   1982
PN 5508   **SC** 46824
SN Degree of severity of mental or physical disorder.
R ↓ Chronic Illness   1991
↓ Chronic Mental Illness   1997
Chronicity (Disorders)   1982
↓ Diagnosis   1967
↓ Disorders   1967
↓ Mental Disorders   1967
↓ Physical Disorders   1997
Prognosis   1973

Sex   1967
PN 1022   **SC** 46950
SN Conceptually broad term referring to the structural, functional, or behavioral characteristics of males and females of a given species. Use a more specific term if possible. For comparisons of the sexes use HUMAN SEX DIFFERENCES or ANIMAL SEX DIFFERENCES.
R Animal Sex Differences   1967
↓ Animal Sexual Behavior   1985
↓ Genital Disorders   1967
↓ Human Sex Differences   1967
Pornography   1973
↓ Psychosexual Behavior   1967
Psychosexual Development   1982
Sex Change   1988
Sex Chromosomes   1973
Sex Discrimination   1978
Sex Drive   1973
Sex Education   1973
↓ Sex Hormones   1973
↓ Sex Offenses   1982
Sex Recognition   1997
↓ Sex Role Attitudes   1978
Sex Therapy   1978
Sexual Attitudes   1973
Sexual Development   1973
Sexual Harassment   1985
↓ Sexual Reproduction   1973
Sexuality   1973

Sex Change   1988
PN 168   **SC** 46828
UF Sexual Reassignment
B Surgery   1971
R Sex   1967
Transsexualism   1973

Sex Chromosome Disorders   1973
PN 177   **SC** 46830
B Chromosome Disorders   1973
N Klinefelters Syndrome   1973
R Fragile X Syndrome   1994
↓ Sex Linked Hereditary Disorders   1973

Sex Chromosomes   1973
PN 109   **SC** 46840
B Chromosomes   1973
R Sex   1967

Sex Differences (Animal)
Use Animal Sex Differences

Sex Differences (Human)
Use Human Sex Differences

Sex Differentiation Disorders
Use Genital Disorders

Sex Discrimination   1978
PN 1191   **SC** 46875
SN Prejudiced and differential treatment on the basis of sex rather than on the basis of merit.
B Social Discrimination   1982
R Affirmative Action   1985
↓ Civil Rights   1978
Employment Discrimination   1994
↓ Prejudice   1967
Sex   1967
Sexism   1988

Sex Drive   1973
PN 378   **SC** 46880
B Motivation   1967
R Hypersexuality   1973
Inhibited Sexual Desire   1997
Libido   1973
Sex   1967
↓ Sexual Arousal   1978

Sex Education   1973
PN 1456   **SC** 46890
B Family Life Education   1997
Health Education   1973
R Safe Sex   2003
Sex   1967

Sex Hormones   1973
PN 777   **SC** 46900
B Hormones   1967
N ↓ Androgens   1973
↓ Estrogens   1973
Progesterone   1973
R ↓ Gonadotropic Hormones   1973
Luteinizing Hormone   1978
Sex   1967

Sex Linked Developmental Differences   1973
PN 1387   **SC** 46920
SN Differential variation between males and females in specified areas of development. Limited to human populations.
B Human Sex Differences   1967
R Adolescent Development   1973
↓ Development   1967
Heterosexuality   1973
↓ Human Females   1973
↓ Human Males   1973
↓ Physical Development   1973
↓ Psychogenesis   1973
↓ Psychosexual Behavior   1967
Sexual Development   1973

Sex Linked Hereditary Disorders   1973
PN 145   **SC** 46930
SN Disorders occurring in either sex and which are transmitted by genes in the sex chromosomes.
B Genetic Disorders   1973
N Fragile X Syndrome   1994
Hemophilia   1973
Testicular Feminization Syndrome   1973
Turners Syndrome   1973
R ↓ Sex Chromosome Disorders   1973

Sex Offenses　1982
PN　2752　　　　　　　　　　SC　46933
- B　Crime　1967
- N　↓ Sexual Abuse　1988
- R　Incest　1973
　↓ Paraphilias　1988
　Pedophilia　1973
　Pornography　1973
　Sex　1967
　Sexual Harassment　1985

Sex Recognition　1997
PN　52　　　　　　　　　　SC　46934
- R　Animal Sex Differences　1967
　↓ Human Sex Differences　1967
　Sex　1967

Sex Role Attitudes　1978
PN　6779　　　　　　　　　　SC　46935
SN　Attitudes toward culturally- or socially-pre-scribed patterns of behavior for males and females.
- UF　Gender Role Attitudes
　Sex Role Stereotyping
- B　Attitudes　1967
- N　Sexism　1988
- R　Feminism　1978
　Matriarchy　1973
　Patriarchy　1973
　Sex　1967
　Sex Roles　1967
　Stereotyped Attitudes　1967

Sex Role Stereotyping
- Use　Sex Role Attitudes

Sex Roles　1967
PN　10509　　　　　　　　　SC　46940
SN　Behavioral patterns in a given society which are deemed appropriate to one sex or the other.
- UF　Gender Roles
- B　Psychosexual Behavior　1967
　Roles　1967
- R　Androgyny　1982
　↓ Division of Labor　1988
　Femininity　1967
　↓ Gender Identity　1985
　Masculinity　1967
　Matriarchy　1973
　Nontraditional Careers　1985
　Patriarchy　1973
　↓ Sex Role Attitudes　1978
　Social Norms　1985

Sex Therapy　1978
PN　1137　　　　　　　　　　SC　46945
SN　Treatment of specific sexual function distur-bances or therapy aimed at improving sexual rela-tionships.
- B　Treatment　1967
- R　Couples Therapy　1994
　↓ Marriage Counseling　1973
　Sex　1967

Sexism　1988
PN　613　　　　　　　　　　SC　46955
- B　Sex Role Attitudes　1978
- R　Employment Discrimination　1994
　↓ Prejudice　1967
　Sex Discrimination　1978
　Stereotyped Attitudes　1967

Sexual Abstinence　1973
PN　166　　　　　　　　　　SC　46960
- UF　Abstinence (Sexual)
　Celibacy
- B　Psychosexual Behavior　1967
- R　↓ Birth Control　1971
　Virginity　1973

Sexual Abuse　1988
PN　8994　　　　　　　　　　SC　46965
- B　Antisocial Behavior　1971
　Sex Offenses　1982
- N　Incest　1973
　↓ Rape　1973
- R　↓ Abuse Reporting　1997
　Anatomically Detailed Dolls　1991
　↓ Child Abuse　1971
　Elder Abuse　1988
　Family Violence　1982
　↓ Paraphilias　1988
　Partner Abuse　1991
　Patient Abuse　1991
　Pedophilia　1973
　Physical Abuse　1991
　Professional Client Sexual Relations　1994
　Sexual Harassment　1985
　↓ Violent Crime　2003

Sexual Addiction　1997
PN　205　　　　　　　　　　SC　46967
- UF　Compulsivity (Sexual)
　Sexual Compulsivity
- B　Addiction　1973
- R　Hypersexuality　1973
　↓ Paraphilias　1988
　Promiscuity　1973
　↓ Psychosexual Behavior　1967

Sexual Arousal　1978
PN　1223　　　　　　　　　　SC　46970
SN　Physiological and/or emotional state of sexual excitation.
- UF　Arousal (Sexual)
- B　Psychosexual Behavior　1967
- N　Eroticism　1973
- R　Inhibited Sexual Desire　1997
　Physiological Arousal　1967
　Sex Drive　1973
　Sexual Attraction　2003
　Sexual Fantasy　1997
　Sexual Satisfaction　1994

Sexual Attitudes　1973
PN　3511　　　　　　　　　　SC　46980
SN　Opinions or beliefs about sexual development and behavior.
- B　Attitudes　1967
- R　↓ Psychosexual Behavior　1967
　Psychosexual Development　1982
　Sex　1967
　Sexual Attraction　2003
　↓ Sexual Orientation　1997
　Sexual Risk Taking　1997
　Sexual Satisfaction　1994

Sexual Attraction　2003
PN　42　　　　　　　　　　SC　46984
HN　This term was introduced in June 2003. Psyc-INFO records from the past 10 years were re-indexed with this term. The posting note reflects the number of records that were re-indexed.
- B　Interpersonal Attraction　1967

Sexual Attraction　— (cont'd)
- R　Physical Attractiveness　1973
　↓ Psychosexual Behavior　1967
　↓ Sexual Arousal　1978
　Sexual Attitudes　1973
　↓ Sexual Orientation　1997

Sexual Behavior
- Use　Psychosexual Behavior

Sexual Boundary Violations
- Use　Professional Client Sexual Relations

Sexual Compulsivity
- Use　Sexual Addiction

Sexual Delinquency
- Use　Promiscuity

Sexual Development　1973
PN　902　　　　　　　　　　SC　47010
HN　Prior to 1982 used for maturation of cognitive, emotional, and physical aspects of sexuality in humans or animals. From 1982 consider PSYCHO-SEXUAL DEVELOPMENT for references on cogni-tive and emotional aspects.
- UF　Pubescence
- B　Physical Development　1973
- R　Adolescent Development　1973
　Heterosexuality　1973
　↓ Psychogenesis　1973
　↓ Psychosexual Behavior　1967
　Psychosexual Development　1982
　Sex　1967
　Sex Linked Developmental Differences　1973

Sexual Deviations
- Use　Paraphilias

Sexual Disorders (Physiological)
- Use　Genital Disorders

Sexual Fantasy　1997
PN　125　　　　　　　　　　SC　47035
- B　Fantasy　1997
- R　Erotomania　1997
　Fantasy (Defense Mechanism)　1967
　↓ Psychosexual Behavior　1967
　↓ Sexual Arousal　1978
　Sexuality　1973

Sexual Fetishism
- Use　Fetishism

Sexual Function Disturbances　1973
PN　2570　　　　　　　　　　SC　47050
- B　Psychosexual Behavior　1967
- N　Dyspareunia　1973
　Frigidity　1973
　Impotence　1973
　Inhibited Sexual Desire　1997
　Premature Ejaculation　1973
　Vaginismus　1973
- R　↓ Mental Disorders　1967
　↓ Physical Disorders　1997
　↓ Somatoform Disorders　2001
　↓ Urogenital Disorders　1973

Sexual Harassment 1985
PN 1131   SC 47055
SN Physical or psychological sexual threats or attempts to willfully subject a person to involuntary sexual activity usually for the purpose of social control.
UF Harassment (Sexual)
B   Harassment 2001
R   Professional Client Sexual Relations 1994
    Sex 1967
    ↓ Sex Offenses 1982
    ↓ Sexual Abuse 1988
    Victimization 1973

Sexual Identity (Gender)
Use Gender Identity

Sexual Intercourse (Human) 1973
PN 1080   SC 47060
UF Coitus
    Copulation
    Intercourse (Sexual)
B   Psychosexual Behavior 1967
N   Dyspareunia 1973
    Extramarital Intercourse 1973
    Incest 1973
    Premarital Intercourse 1973
    ↓ Rape 1973
R   Disease Transmission 2004
    Female Orgasm 1973
    ↓ Male Orgasm 1973
    Safe Sex 2003
    Sexual Partners 2003
    ↓ Sexual Reproduction 1973
    Sexual Satisfaction 1994

Sexual Masochism 1973
PN 57   SC 47070
B   Masochism 1973
    Paraphilias 1988
R   Fetishism 1973
    Masochistic Personality 1973
    Sexual Sadism 1973

Sexual Orientation 1997
PN 917   SC 47072
N   Bisexuality 1973
    Heterosexuality 1973
    ↓ Homosexuality 1967
R   ↓ Gender Identity 1985
    ↓ Gender Identity Disorder 1997
    Hate Crimes 2003
    Homosexuality (Attitudes Toward) 1982
    ↓ Psychosexual Behavior 1967
    Sexual Attitudes 1973
    Sexual Attraction 2003

Sexual Partners 2003
PN 65   SC 58061
HN This term was introduced in June 2003. PsycINFO records from the past 10 years were re-indexed with this term. The posting note reflects the number of records that were re-indexed.
R   ↓ Psychosexual Behavior 1967
    ↓ Sexual Intercourse (Human) 1973
    Sexual Risk Taking 1997

Sexual Reassignment
Use Sex Change

Sexual Receptivity (Animal)
Use Animal Sexual Receptivity

Sexual Reproduction 1973
PN 1523   SC 47090
B   Physiology 1967
N   Fertility 1988
R   ↓ Animal Breeding 1973
    Animal Mate Selection 1982
    ↓ Animal Mating Behavior 1967
    ↓ Birth 1967
    Fertilization 1973
    ↓ Genetics 1967
    ↓ Pregnancy 1967
    Reproductive Technology 1988
    Sex 1967
    ↓ Sexual Intercourse (Human) 1973
    Sperm 1973

Sexual Risk Taking 1997
PN 2094   SC 47095
B   Psychosexual Behavior 1967
    Risk Taking 1967
R   AIDS Prevention 1994
    ↓ Pregnancy 1967
    Risk Perception 1997
    Safe Sex 2003
    Sexual Attitudes 1973
    Sexual Partners 2003
    ↓ Sexually Transmitted Diseases 2003

Sexual Sadism 1973
PN 67   SC 47100
B   Paraphilias 1988
    Sadism 1973
R   Fetishism 1973
    Sexual Masochism 1973

Sexual Satisfaction 1994
PN 273   SC 47110
B   Satisfaction 1973
R   ↓ Orgasm 1973
    ↓ Psychosexual Behavior 1967
    ↓ Sexual Arousal 1978
    Sexual Attitudes 1973
    ↓ Sexual Intercourse (Human) 1973
    Sexuality 1973

Sexuality 1973
PN 3613   SC 47120
B   Personality Traits 1967
R   Affection 1973
    Psychosexual Development 1982
    Sex 1967
    Sexual Fantasy 1997
    Sexual Satisfaction 1994

Sexually Transmitted Diseases 2003
PN 1091   SC 47125
HN In June 2003, this term replaced the discontinued term VENEREAL DISEASES. VENEREAL DISEASES was removed from all records containing it and replaced with SEXUALLY TRANSMITTED DISEASES.
UF Diseases (Venereal)
    Venereal Diseases
B   Infectious Disorders 1973
N   Acquired Immune Deficiency Syndrome 1988
    Gonorrhea 1973
    Herpes Genitalis 1988
    ↓ Human Immunodeficiency Virus 1991
    ↓ Syphilis 1973
R   Condoms 1991
    Disease Transmission 2004
    Sexual Risk Taking 1997
    ↓ Urogenital Disorders 1973

Shamanism 1973
PN 276   SC 47130
B   Religious Affiliation 1973
R   Cultism 1973
    Ethnology 1967
    Faith Healing 1973
    Folk Medicine 1973
    Transcultural Psychiatry 1973
    ↓ Treatment 1967
    Witchcraft 1973

Shame 1994
PN 889   SC 47140
HN Use GUILT to access references from 1973-1993.
B   Emotional States 1973
R   ↓ Anxiety 1967
    Blame 1994
    Embarrassment 1973
    ↓ Fear 1967
    Guilt 1967
    Morality 1967

Shape Perception
Use Form and Shape Perception

Shared Paranoid Disorder
Use Folie A Deux

Sharing (Social Behavior) 1978
PN 466   SC 47155
B   Prosocial Behavior 1982
R   Altruism 1973
    Charitable Behavior 1973
    Needle Sharing 1994

Sheep 1973
PN 700   SC 47170
B   Mammals 1973

Sheltered Workshops 1967
PN 342   SC 47180
SN Places which provide handicapped individuals with job training and work experience.
B   Rehabilitation Centers 1973
R   ↓ Community Facilities 1973
    Supported Employment 1994

Shelters 1991
PN 369   SC 47185
B   Housing 1973
R   Battered Females 1988
    ↓ Community Facilities 1973
    ↓ Community Services 1997
    Family Violence 1982
    ↓ Government Programs 1973
    Group Homes 1982
    ↓ Homeless 1988
    ↓ Living Arrangements 1991
    Protective Services 1997
    Runaway Behavior 1973
    ↓ Social Services 1982

Shifts (Workday)
Use Workday Shifts

Shock 1967
PN 3083   SC 47200
B   Symptoms 1967
R   Anaphylactic Shock 1973
    Electrical Injuries 1973

Shock — (cont'd)
↓ Electrical Stimulation 1973
↓ Electroconvulsive Shock 1967
↓ Injuries 1973
↓ Shock Therapy 1973
  Shock Units 1973
  Syncope 1973

Shock Therapy 1973
PN 44   **SC** 47210
B   Physical Treatment Methods 1973
N   Electroconvulsive Shock Therapy 1967
    Insulin Shock Therapy 1973
R ↓ Alternative Medicine 1997
   ↓ Aversion Therapy 1973
    Electrosleep Treatment 1978
    Shock 1967

Shock Units 1973
PN 28   **SC** 47220
B   Stimulators (Apparatus) 1973
R   Shock 1967

Shoplifting 1973
PN 134   **SC** 47230
B   Theft 1973

Shopping 1997
PN 273   **SC** 47240
HN Use CONSUMER BEHAVIOR to access references prior to 1997.
B   Consumer Behavior 1967
R   Retailing 1991
    Shopping Centers 1973

Shopping Centers 1973
PN 155   **SC** 47250
B   Community Facilities 1973
R ↓ Consumer Behavior 1967
    Retailing 1991
    Shopping 1997

Short Term Memory 1967
PN 7829   **SC** 47260
SN Retention of information for very brief periods, usually seconds; also referred to as working memory. Consider also RETENTION.
UF Working Memory
B   Memory 1967
N   Iconic Memory 1985
R   Chunking 2004

Short Term Potentiation
Use Postactivation Potentials

Short Term Psychotherapy
Use Brief Psychotherapy

Shoulder (Anatomy) 1973
PN 125   **SC** 47290
B   Joints (Anatomy) 1973
R   Arm (Anatomy) 1973

Shuttle Box Grids
Use Shuttle Boxes

Shuttle Box Hurdles
Use Shuttle Boxes

Shuttle Boxes 1973
PN 92   **SC** 47320
HN In 1997, this term replaced the discontinued terms SHUTTLE BOX GRIDS and SHUTTLE BOX HURDLES. In 2000, these terms were removed from all records and replaced with SHUTTLE BOXES.
UF Shuttle Box Grids
    Shuttle Box Hurdles
B   Apparatus 1967

Shyness
Use Timidity

Siamese Twins
Use Conjoined Twins

Sibling Relations 1973
PN 1451   **SC** 47350
B   Family Relations 1967

Siblings 1967
PN 2627   **SC** 47360
B   Family Members 1973
N   Brothers 1973
   ↓ Multiple Births 1973
    Sisters 1973

Sick Leave
Use Employee Leave Benefits

Sickle Cell Disease 1994
PN 257   **SC** 47380
B   Blood and Lymphatic Disorders 1973
    Genetic Disorders 1973
R   Anemia 1973

Side Effects (Drug) 1973
PN 11493   **SC** 47390
SN Acute or chronic and often undesirable effects of drugs occurring in addition to the intended or therapeutic objective.
HN In 1982, this term replaced the discontinued term DRUG ADVERSE REACTIONS. In 2000, DRUG ADVERSE REACTIONS was removed from all records containing it, and replaced with SIDE EFFECTS (DRUG).
UF Drug Adverse Reactions
B   Side Effects (Treatment) 1988
N ↓ Drug Addiction 1967
    Drug Allergies 1973
   ↓ Drug Dependency 1973
    Drug Sensitivity 1973
R   Akathisia 1991
   ↓ Drug Therapy 1967
    Drug Tolerance 1973
   ↓ Drugs 1967
    Neuroleptic Malignant Syndrome 1988
    Tardive Dyskinesia 1988

Side Effects (Treatment) 1988
PN 974   **SC** 47392
SN Acute or chronic and often undesirable effects of treatment other than drug therapy occurring in addition to the intended or therapeutic objective. For side effects of drug therapy use SIDE EFFECTS (DRUG).
UF Iatrogenic Effects
N ↓ Side Effects (Drug) 1973
R ↓ Treatment 1967
   ↓ Treatment Outcomes 1982

Sight Vocabulary 1973
PN 151   **SC** 47400
SN Words that one recognizes immediately while reading.
B   Vocabulary 1967
R ↓ Reading 1967
   ↓ Reading Skills 1973
    Word Recognition 1988

Sign Language 1973
PN 1461   **SC** 47410
SN System of hand gestures for communication in which the gestures function as words.
B   Language 1967
    Manual Communication 1978
R   Fingerspelling 1973

Sign Rank Test
Use Wilcoxon Sign Rank Test

Sign Test 1973
PN 5   **SC** 47430
B   Nonparametric Statistical Tests 1967
R   Statistical Significance 1973

Signal Detection (Perception) 1967
PN 2980   **SC** 47440
SN Psychophysical technique that permits the estimation of the bias of the observer as well as the detectability of the signal (i.e., stimulus) in any sensory modality. Compare THRESHOLDS.
UF Detection (Signal)
R ↓ Attention 1967
   ↓ Perception 1967
   ↓ Psychophysical Measurement 1967
    Threshold Determination 1973
    Visual Search 1982

Signal Intensity
Use Stimulus Intensity

Significance (Statistical)
Use Statistical Significance

Significant Others 1991
PN 674   **SC** 47465
SN Includes teachers, peers, family members, friends, and unmarried persons or couples.
R   Couples 1982
   ↓ Family Members 1973
    Friendship 1967
    Homosexual Parents 1994
    Mentor 1985
    Peers 1978
    Role Models 1982
    Romance 1997
    Social Support 2004
   ↓ Spouses 1973

Sikhism 2004
PN 5   **SC** 47466
SN A monotheistic religion founded in 16th century India, that combines elements of Hinduism and Islam.
HN This term was introduced in June 2004. PsycINFO records from the past 10 years were re-indexed with this term. The posting note reflects the number of records that were re-indexed.
B   Religious Affiliation 1973
R   Sikhs 2004

Sikhs 2004
PN 5   SC 47467
HN This term was introduced in June 2004. Psyc-INFO records from the past 10 years were re-indexed with this term. The posting note reflects the number of records that were re-indexed.
B   Religious Groups 1997
R   Sikhism 2004

Silence 2003
PN 88   SC 47468
HN This term was introduced in June 2003. Psyc-INFO records from the past 10 years were re-indexed with this term. The posting note reflects the number of records that were re-indexed.
R   ↓ Auditory Stimulation 1967
    ↓ Nonverbal Communication 1971

Silent Reading 1973
PN 278   SC 47470
B   Reading 1967

Similarity (Stimulus)
  Use   Stimulus Similarity

Simile
  Use   Figurative Language

Simple Schizophrenia
  Use   Schizophrenia

Simulation 1967
PN 2967   3C 47510
UF   Modeling
    Simulators
N   ↓ Computer Simulation 1973
    Flight Simulation 1973
    Heuristic Modeling 1973
    Markov Chains 1973
    ↓ Mathematical Modeling 1973
    Simulation Games 1973
    ↓ Stochastic Modeling 1970
R   Game Theory 1967

Simulation Games 1973
PN 488   SC 47520
B   Games 1967
    Simulation 1967
R   Computer Games 1988
    ↓ Computer Simulation 1973

Simulators
  Use   Simulation

Sin 1973
PN 77   SC 47540
B   Religious Beliefs 1973
R   Evil 2003

Sincerity 1973
PN 67   SC 47550
UF   Genuineness
B   Personality Traits 1967
R   ↓ Deception 1967
    Dishonesty 1973

Singing 1997
PN 167   SC 47552

Singing — (cont'd)
SN Use ANIMAL VOCALIZATIONS for singing in animal populations.
B   Oral Communication 1985
R   ↓ Music 1967
    Music Perception 1997
    ↓ Vocalization 1967
    ↓ Voice 1973

Single Cell Organisms
  Use   Microorganisms

Single Fathers 1994
PN 44   SC 47554
HN Use SINGLE PARENTS to access references from 1978-1993.
B   Fathers 1967
    Single Parents 1978
R   Single Persons 1973

Single Mothers 1994
PN 423   SC 47555
HN Use SINGLE PARENTS to access references from 1978-1993.
B   Mothers 1967
    Single Parents 1978
R   Single Persons 1973
    Unwed Mothers 1973
    Working Women 1978

Single Parents 1978
PN 1041   SC 47556
SN Parents rearing children alone.
B   Parents 1967
N   Single Fathers 1994
    Single Mothers 1994
R   ↓ Family Structure 1973
    ↓ Marital Status 1973
    Never Married 1994
    ↓ Parental Absence 1973
    Single Persons 1973
    Unwed Mothers 1973

Single Persons 1973
PN 462   SC 47560
SN Persons who are not married.
R   Living Alone 1994
    ↓ Marital Status 1973
    Never Married 1994
    Single Fathers 1994
    Single Mothers 1994
    ↓ Single Parents 1978

Single Sex Education
  Use   Same Sex Education

Single Sex Environments 2001
PN 49   SC 47565
SN Used for both human and animal populations. Use only when gender is pertinent to the focus of the study.
UF   Female Only Environments
    Male Only Environments
    Same Sex Environments
B   Environment 1967
N   Same Sex Education 2003
R   ↓ Academic Environment 1973
    ↓ Animal Environments 1967
    Animal Sex Differences 1967
    Coeducation 1973
    Home Environment 1973

Single Sex Environments — (cont'd)
    ↓ Human Sex Differences 1967
    ↓ Living Arrangements 1991

Sisters 1973
PN 198   SC 47570
B   Human Females 1973
    Siblings 1967

Sixteen Personality Factors Questionnaire 2001
PN 433   SC 47591
HN In 2000, the truncated term SIXTEEN PERSONALITY FACTORS QUESTION (which was used from 1973-2000) was deleted, removed from all records containing it, and replaced with its expanded form SIXTEEN PERSONALITY FACTORS QUESTIONNAIRE.
B   Nonprojective Personality Measures 1973

Size 1973
PN 984   SC 47610
SN Relative physical dimensions of objects or stimuli.
B   Stimulus Parameters 1967
N   ↓ Body Size 1985
    Brain Size 1973
    Family Size 1973
    ↓ Group Size 1967
    Litter Size 1985
    Size Constancy 1985
    ↓ Size Discrimination 1967

Size (Apparent)
  Use   Apparent Size

Size (Group)
  Use   Group Size

Size Constancy 1985
PN 42   SC 47635
SN The tendency for the perceived size of stimuli to remain constant despite objective changes in context and stimulus parameters.
B   Perceptual Constancy 1985
    Size 1973
R   ↓ Size Discrimination 1967

Size Discrimination 1967
PN 951   SC 47640
B   Size 1973
    Spatial Perception 1967
N   Apparent Size 1973
R   Linear Perspective 1982
    Size Constancy 1985

Skeletomuscular Disorders
  Use   Musculoskeletal Disorders

Skepticism 2004
PN 22   SC 47670
HN This term was introduced in June 2004. Psyc-INFO records from the past 10 years were re-indexed with this term. The posting note reflects the number of records that were re-indexed.
R   ↓ Criticism 1973
    Cynicism 1973
    Negativism 1973
    Pessimism 1973
    Uncertainty 1991

Skewed Distribution   1973
PN 101   **SC** 47680
UF Poisson Distribution
B Frequency Distribution   1973

Skill Learning   1973
PN 2518   **SC** 47690
B Learning   1967
N Fine Motor Skill Learning   1973
     Gross Motor Skill Learning   1973
R Communication Skills Training   1982
     Habilitation   1991
     ↓ Perceptual Motor Learning   1967
     Self Care Skills   1978
     Social Skills Training   1982

Skilled Industrial Workers   1973
PN 281   **SC** 47700
SN Blue collar workers who perform skilled labor in an industrial setting.
B Blue Collar Workers   1973
     Business and Industrial Personnel   1967

Skills
Use Ability

Skin (Anatomy)   1967
PN 951   **SC** 47720
UF Epithelium
B Tissues (Body)   1973
R Absorption (Physiological)   1973
     Cosmetic Techniques   2001
     Epithelial Cells   1973
     Hair   1973
     Head (Anatomy)   1973
     Scalp (Anatomy)   1973

Skin Cancer Screening
Use Cancer Screening

Skin Conduction
Use Skin Resistance

Skin Disorders   1973
PN 579   **SC** 47740
UF Scalp Disorders
B Physical Disorders   1997
N Allergic Skin Disorders   1973
     Alopecia   1973
     ↓ Dermatitis   1973
     Herpes Simplex   1973
     Lupus   1973
     Pruritus   1973
R Albinism   1973
     ↓ Somatoform Disorders   2001
     Sweating   1973
     ↓ Tuberculosis   1973

Skin Electrical Properties   1973
PN 106   **SC** 47750
SN General electrodermal characteristics and responses as measured on the skin surface. Use a more specific term if possible.
B Electrophysiology   1973
N Skin Potential   1973
     ↓ Skin Resistance   1973

Skin Potential   1973
PN 102   **SC** 47760

Skin Potential — (cont'd)
SN Degree of electrical charge of the skin.
B Electrophysiology   1973
     Skin Electrical Properties   1973
R Galvanic Skin Response   1967
     ↓ Skin Resistance   1973

Skin Resistance   1973
PN 1446   **SC** 47770
SN Resistance of the skin to the flow of electric current; reciprocal of skin conductance.
UF Skin Conduction
B Skin Electrical Properties   1973
N Basal Skin Resistance   1973
R Galvanic Skin Response   1967
     Skin Potential   1973

Skin Temperature   1973
PN 645   **SC** 47780
B Body Temperature   1973

Skinner (Burrhus Frederic)   1991
PN 255   **SC** 47785
SN Identifies biographical or autobiographical studies and discussions of Skinner's works.
R Behaviorism   1967
     ↓ Operant Conditioning   1967
     ↓ Psychologists   1967
     Skinner Boxes   1973

Skinner Boxes   1973
PN 23   **SC** 47790
B Apparatus   1967
R Skinner (Burrhus Frederic)   1991

Skull   1973
PN 34   **SC** 47800
B Musculoskeletal System   1973

Slang   1973
PN 59   **SC** 47810
B Vocabulary   1967
R Ethnolinguistics   1973
     Nonstandard English   1973

Sleep   1967
PN 6588   **SC** 47820
N Napping   1994
     NREM Sleep   1973
     REM Sleep   1973
R ↓ Consciousness Disturbances   1973
     ↓ Consciousness States   1971
     Dream Content   1973
     ↓ Dreaming   1967
     Lucid Dreaming   1994
     Nocturnal Teeth Grinding   1973
     Polysomnography   2003
     Sleep Apnea   1991
     Sleep Deprivation   1967
     ↓ Sleep Disorders   1973
     Sleep Onset   1973
     Sleep Talking   1973
     Sleep Treatment   1973
     Sleep Wake Cycle   1985

Sleep Apnea   1991
PN 325   **SC** 47825
SN Temporary absence of breathing or prolonged respiratory failure occurring during sleep.
B Apnea   1973
R ↓ Neonatal Disorders   1973

Sleep Apnea — (cont'd)
     ↓ Sleep   1967
     ↓ Sleep Disorders   1973
     Sudden Infant Death   1982

Sleep Deprivation   1967
PN 1492   **SC** 47830
B Deprivation   1967
R ↓ Sleep   1967
     ↓ Sleep Disorders   1973

Sleep Disorders   1973
PN 2149   **SC** 47840
UF Night Terrors
B Consciousness Disturbances   1973
N Hypersomnia   1994
     Insomnia   1973
     Kleine Levin Syndrome   2001
     Narcolepsy   1973
     Sleepwalking   1973
R Hypnagogic Hallucinations   1973
     ↓ Mental Disorders   1967
     ↓ Physical Disorders   1997
     Polysomnography   2003
     ↓ Sleep   1967
     Sleep Apnea   1991
     Sleep Deprivation   1967

Sleep Inducing Drugs
Use Hypnotic Drugs

Sleep Monitoring
Use Polysomnography

Sleep Onset   1973
PN 784   **SC** 47860
UF Drowsiness
R Napping   1994
     ↓ Sleep   1967

Sleep Talking   1973
PN 17   **SC** 47870
B Consciousness Disturbances   1973
R ↓ Sleep   1967

Sleep Treatment   1973
PN 65   **SC** 47880
SN Prolonged sleep or rest used in the treatment of mental disorders. Such sleep may be induced by drugs, hypnosis, or other means. For sleep withdrawal therapy, which is the deprivation of sleep for therapeutic purposes, use SLEEP DEPRIVATION.
B Narcoanalysis   1973
R ↓ Drug Therapy   1967
     Electrosleep Treatment   1978
     ↓ Sleep   1967

Sleep Wake Cycle   1985
PN 1486   **SC** 47885
B Biological Rhythms   1967
R Napping   1994
     ↓ Sleep   1967
     Wakefulness   1973

Sleeplessness
Use Insomnia

Sleepwalking   1973
PN 147   **SC** 47890

Sleepwalking — (cont'd)

HN In 1982, this term replaced the discontinued term SOMNAMBULISM. In 2000, SOMNAMBULISM was removed from all records containing it, and replaced with SLEEPWALKING.
UF Somnambulism
B Sleep Disorders 1973

Slosson Intelligence Test 2001

PN 68   **SC** 47901
HN In 2000, the truncated term SLOSSON INTELLIGENCE TEST FOR CHILD (which was used from 1991-2000) was deleted, removed from all records containing it, and replaced with its new form SLOSSON INTELLIGENCE TEST.
B Intelligence Measures 1967

Slow Learners

Use Borderline Mental Retardation

Slow Wave Sleep

Use NREM Sleep

Slums

Use Poverty Areas

Smell Perception

Use Olfactory Perception

Smiles 1973

PN 360   **SC** 47950
B Facial Expressions 1967
R Laughter 1978

Smokeless Tobacco 1994

PN 147   **SC** 47060
UF Chewing Tobacco
     Snuff
     Tobacco (Smokeless)
R ↓ CNS Stimulating Drugs 1973
     Nicotine 1973
     Nicotine Withdrawal 1007
     Tobacco Smoking 1967

Smoking (Tobacco)

Use Tobacco Smoking

Smoking Cessation 1988

PN 2763   **SC** 47980
SN Used for cigarette smoking rehabilitation programs or stopping the habit of smoking.
HN Use DRUG REHABILITATION and TOBACCO SMOKING to access references prior to 1988.
R ↓ Drug Abstinence 1994
     ↓ Drug Rehabilitation 1973
     Nicotine Withdrawal 1997
     Tobacco Smoking 1967

Snails 1973

PN 492   **SC** 47990
UF Aplysia
B Mollusca 1973

Snake Phobia

Use Ophidiophobia

Snakes 1973

PN 353   **SC** 48010

Snakes — (cont'd)

B Reptiles 1967

Snuff

Use Smokeless Tobacco

Sobriety 1988

PN 661   **SC** 48020
UF Alcohol Abstinence
B Drug Abstinence 1994
R Alcohol Drinking Attitudes 1973
     ↓ Alcohol Rehabilitation 1982
     Alcohol Withdrawal 1994
     ↓ Alcoholism 1967
     Detoxification 1973
     ↓ Drug Rehabilitation 1973
     Recovery (Disorders) 1973

Soccer 1994

PN 184   **SC** 48025
B Recreation 1967
     Sports 1967

Sociability 1973

PN 446   **SC** 48030
B Personality Traits 1967
R Extraversion 1967
     Gregariousness 1973

Social Acceptance 1967

PN 2378   **SC** 48040
SN Degree to which an individual is incorporated by others in their activities or is welcomed to interact with others informally. Limited to human populations.
UF Acceptance (Social)
     Rejection (Social)
     Social Rejection
B Social Behavior 1967
R Need for Approval 1997
     Peer Pressure 1994
     Popularity 1988
     Social Approval 1967
     Stigma 1991
     ↓ Tolerance 1973

Social Adaptation

Use Social Adjustment

Social Adjustment 1973

PN 6439   **SC** 48060
UF Adaptation (Social)
     Maladjustment (Social)
     Social Adaptation
     Social Maladjustment
B Adjustment 1967
     Social Behavior 1967
R Adjustment Disorders 1994

Social Anxiety 1985

PN 1081   **SC** 48065
SN Apprehension or fear of social interaction or social situations in general. Compare SOCIAL PHOBIA.
B Anxiety 1967
R ↓ Anxiety Disorders 1997
     Avoidant Personality Disorder 1994
     ↓ Fear 1967
     ↓ Social Interaction 1967
     ↓ Social Isolation 1967
     Speech Anxiety 1985

Social Anxiety Disorder

Use Social Phobia

Social Approval 1967

PN 1799   **SC** 48070
SN Favorable direct or indirect judgment by member or members of a given social group of another member or members, based on conduct, physical makeup, or other characteristics.
UF Approval (Social)
B Social Behavior 1967
     Social Influences 1967
R ↓ Criticism 1973
     Likability 1988
     Need for Approval 1997
     Peer Pressure 1994
     Popularity 1988
     Reputation 1997
     Social Acceptance 1967
     ↓ Social Reinforcement 1967
     Stigma 1991

Social Behavior 1967

PN 6939   **SC** 48080
B Behavior 1967
N ↓ Activism 2003
     ↓ Aggressive Behavior 1967
     ↓ Animal Social Behavior 1967
     Competition 1967
     ↓ Compliance 1973
     Conformity (Personality) 1967
     Contagion 1988
     ↓ Criticism 1973
     ↓ Gambling 1973
     ↓ Help Seeking Behavior 1978
     Interspecies Interaction 1991
     ↓ Involvement 1973
     ↓ Leadership 1967
     Leadership Style 1973
     Militancy 1973
     Nurturance 1985
     ↓ Organizational Behavior 1978
     ↓ Prosocial Behavior 1982
     Racial and Ethnic Relations 1982
     Reciprocity 1973
     ↓ Responsibility 1973
     Retaliation 1991
     ↓ Risk Taking 1967
     Social Acceptance 1967
     Social Adjustment 1973
     Social Approval 1967
     Social Cognition 1994
     Social Demonstrations 1973
     Social Drinking 1973
     Social Facilitation 1973
     ↓ Social Interaction 1967
     Social Loafing 2003
     ↓ Social Perception 1967
     ↓ Social Reinforcement 1967
     Social Skills 1978
R ↓ Antisocial Behavior 1971
     Dominance Hierarchy 1973
     Equity (Payment) 1978
     ↓ Equity (Social) 1978
     Impression Management 1978
     Informants 1988
     Personal Space 1973
     Privacy 1973
     Psychodynamics 1973
     Social Change 1967
     ↓ Social Influences 1967

Social Capital 2004

PN 112   **SC** 48085

Social Capital — (cont'd)

SN Investing in social relationships by establishing trust, norms, and networks to create social cohesion and facilitate cooperative communities.

HN This term was introduced in June 2004. Psyc-INFO records from the past 10 years were re-indexed with this term. The posting note reflects the number of records that were re-indexed.

- **B** Social Processes 1967
- **R** Human Capital 2003
   Social Networks 1994

Social Casework 1967

PN 5167   **SC** 48090

- **UF** Social Work
- **B** Treatment 1967
- **R** ↓ Case Management 1991
   Child Welfare 1988
   ↓ Counseling 1967
   ↓ Family Therapy 1967
   ↓ Health Care Services 1978
   ↓ Mental Health Services 1978
   Outreach Programs 1997
   Protective Services 1997
   ↓ Social Services 1982

Social Caseworkers

Use Social Workers

Social Change 1967

PN 4444   **SC** 48110

- **UF** Change (Social)
- **R** ↓ Activism 2003
   ↓ Fads and Fashions 1973
   Future 1991
   Modernization 2003
   ↓ Social Behavior 1967
   ↓ Social Influences 1967
   ↓ Social Movements 1967
   ↓ Social Processes 1967
   ↓ Social Programs 1973
   Trends 1991

Social Class 1967

PN 2831   **SC** 48120

- **B** Social Structure 1967
   Socioeconomic Status 1967
- **N** Lower Class 1973
   Middle Class 1973
   Upper Class 1973
- **R** Disadvantaged 1967
   ↓ Income Level 1973
   ↓ Socioeconomic Class Attitudes 1973

Social Class Attitudes

Use Socioeconomic Class Attitudes

Social Clubs (Therapeutic)

Use Therapeutic Social Clubs

Social Cognition 1994

PN 2800   **SC** 48143

SN Cognitive processes and activity that accompany and mediate social interaction.

- **B** Cognitive Processes 1967
   Social Behavior 1967
- **R** ↓ Communication Skills 1973
   ↓ Interpersonal Interaction 1967
   Reputation 1997
   Schema 1988
   Self Fulfilling Prophecies 1997

Social Cognition — (cont'd)

- ↓ Social Interaction 1967
- ↓ Social Perception 1967
   Social Skills Training 1982

Social Comparison 1985

PN 1335   **SC** 48145

SN Subjective evaluation of personal characteristics (e.g., ability level, personality traits, accomplishments) of oneself or another person in relation to the perceived characteristics of others.

- **B** Social Perception 1967
- **R** Self Evaluation 1967
   Self Monitoring (Personality) 1985
   ↓ Social Influences 1967

Social Competence

Use Social Skills

Social Control 1988

PN 773   **SC** 48148

SN Power of institutions, organizations, or laws of society to influence or regulate behavior or attitudes of groups or individuals. Consider POWER to access references that describe the control an individual has over other persons.

- **UF** Control (Social)
- **B** Social Processes 1967
- **R** ↓ Emotional Control 1973
   ↓ Social Influences 1967

Social Dating 1973

PN 1612   **SC** 48150

- **UF** Dating (Social)
- **B** Human Courtship 1973
   Interpersonal Interaction 1967
- **R** Acquaintance Rape 1991
   Couples 1982
   Friendship 1967
   Male Female Relations 1988
   Premarital Intercourse 1973
   ↓ Relationship Termination 1997
   Romance 1997

Social Demonstrations 1973

PN 98   **SC** 48160

- **UF** Demonstrations (Social)
   Picketing
- **B** Social Behavior 1967
- **R** ↓ Activism 2003
   ↓ Collective Behavior 1967
   ↓ Political Participation 1988
   ↓ Social Movements 1967
   Student Activism 1973

Social Density 1978

PN 554   **SC** 48165

SN Number of animals or humans per given space unit. For specifically high density conditions use CROWDING.

- **UF** Density (Social)
   Population Density
- **R** Crowding 1978
   Overpopulation 1973
   Personal Space 1973
   ↓ Population 1973
   ↓ Social Environments 1973

Social Deprivation 1973

PN 366   **SC** 48170

Social Deprivation — (cont'd)

SN Limited access to society's resources due to poverty, neglect, social discrimination, or other disadvantage. For a lack of social contact use SOCIAL ISOLATION. Consider also CULTURAL DEPRIVATION.

- **B** Social Processes 1967
   Stimulus Deprivation 1973
- **N** ↓ Social Isolation 1967
- **R** Cultural Deprivation 1973
   Disadvantaged 1967
   ↓ Homeless 1988

Social Desirability 1967

PN 1575   **SC** 48180

- **UF** Desirability (Social)
- **B** Social Influences 1967
- **R** Need for Approval 1997

Social Development

Use Psychosocial Development

Social Dilemma 2003

PN 32   **SC** 48184

SN Situation where an individual's self-interest creates a potentially negative outcome for the rest of the group members.

HN This term was introduced in June 2003. Psyc-INFO records from the past 10 years were re-indexed with this term. The posting note reflects the number of records that were re-indexed.

- **B** Social Processes 1967
- **R** Choice Behavior 1967
   Prisoners Dilemma Game 1973
   ↓ Social Issues 1991

Social Discrimination 1982

PN 1316   **SC** 48185

SN Prejudiced and differential treatment based on religion, sex, race, ethnicity, disability, or other personal characteristics rather than on the basis of merit. Use a more specific term if possible.

- **UF** Discrimination (Social)
- **B** Discrimination 1967
   Social Issues 1991
- **N** Age Discrimination 1994
   Disability Discrimination 1997
   Employment Discrimination 1994
   Race and Ethnic Discrimination 1994
   Sex Discrimination 1978
- **R** Affirmative Action 1985
   ↓ Civil Rights 1978
   Racial and Ethnic Relations 1982
   Racism 1973
   ↓ Social Integration 1982
   Stereotyped Attitudes 1967
   Stigma 1991

Social Drinking 1973

PN 557   **SC** 48190

SN Consumption of alcoholic beverages in social settings.

- **B** Alcohol Drinking Patterns 1967
   Social Behavior 1967

Social Environments 1973

PN 3074   **SC** 48200

- **B** Environment 1967
- **N** ↓ Academic Environment 1973
   ↓ Animal Environments 1967
   ↓ Communities 1967
   Home Environment 1973

Social Environments — (cont'd)
Poverty Areas 1973
Rural Environments 1967
Suburban Environments 1967
Towns 1973
↓ Urban Environments 1967
↓ Working Conditions 1973
R   Cultural Deprivation 1973
↓ Environmental Effects 1973
Social Density 1978

Social Equality 1973
PN 1145   SC 48210
UF   Equality (Social)
B   Social Issues 1991
R   Affirmative Action 1985
↓ Civil Rights 1978
Equal Education 1978
↓ Human Rights 1978
↓ Justice 1973
Racial and Ethnic Relations 1982
↓ Social Integration 1982

Social Facilitation 1973
PN 497   SC 48220
SN   Process whereby activity is increased in the
presence of conspecifics.
UF   Facilitation (Social)
B   Social Behavior 1967
R   ↓ Social Influences 1967
Social Loafing 2003

Social Groups 1973
PN 1483   SC 48230
UF   Cadres
Cliques
Groups (Social)
N   Dyads 1973
Ingroup Outgroup 1997
Minority Groups 1967
Reference Groups 1994
R   Social Networks 1994

Social Identity 1988
PN 3174   SC 48235
SN   An aspect of self image based on in-group pref-
erence or ethnocentrism and a perception of belong-
ing to a social or cultural group.
N   Professional Identity 1991
R   Ethnic Identity 1973
Ethnocentrism 1973
Identity Formation 2004
Ingroup Outgroup 1997
Minority Groups 1967
Reference Groups 1994
↓ Self Concept 1967

Social Immobility
Use Social Mobility

Social Influences 1967
PN 6711   SC 48250
UF   Influences (Social)
N   Coercion 1994
↓ Criticism 1973
Enabling 1997
Ethnic Values 1973
↓ Interpersonal Influences 1967
↓ Power 1967
↓ Prejudice 1967
Propaganda 1973
Social Approval 1967
Social Desirability 1967

Social Influences — (cont'd)
Social Norms 1985
Social Values 1973
Superstitions 1973
Taboos 1973
R   Authority 1967
↓ Ethics 1967
Mentor 1985
Popularity 1988
Psychosocial Factors 1988
Reference Groups 1994
Role Models 1982
↓ Social Behavior 1967
Social Change 1967
Social Comparison 1985
Social Control 1988
Social Facilitation 1973
Social Loafing 2003
↓ Social Movements 1967
↓ Social Reinforcement 1967

Social Integration 1982
PN 1368   SC 48258
SN   Process of uniting diverse groups (e.g., racial,
ethnic, religious, or disabled) of a society or organiza-
tion.
HN   In 1982, this term was created to replace the
discontinued term RACIAL INTEGRATION. In 2000,
RACIAL INTEGRATION was removed from all
records containing it, and replaced with SOCIAL
INTEGRATION.
UF   Desegregation
Integration (Racial)
Racial Integration
Segregation (Racial)
B   Social Issues 1991
Social Processes 1967
N   School Integration 1982
R   ↓ Activism 2003
↓ Civil Rights 1978
↓ Mainstreaming 1991
Racial and Ethnic Relations 1982
↓ Social Discrimination 1982
Social Equality 1973

Social Interaction 1967
PN 9189   SC 48260
UF   Interaction (Social)
B   Social Behavior 1967
N   Encouragement 1973
↓ Interpersonal Interaction 1967
Nonviolence 1991
Peace 1988
Physical Contact 1982
Teasing 2003
Victimization 1973
R   ↓ Aggressive Behavior 1967
↓ Conflict Resolution 1982
Forgiveness 1988
Psychodynamics 1973
Self Monitoring (Personality) 1985
Social Anxiety 1985
Social Cognition 1994
Social Networks 1994
Social Support 2004
Symbolic Interactionism 1988

Social Isolation 1967
PN 3353   SC 48270
SN   Voluntary or involuntary absence of contact with
others. Used for human or animal populations.
UF   Isolation (Social)
B   Social Deprivation 1973
Stimulus Deprivation 1973

Social Isolation — (cont'd)
N   Patient Seclusion 1994
R   Animal Maternal Deprivation 1988
Social Anxiety 1985

Social Issues 1991
PN 1641   SC 48275
SN   Social concerns, including but not limited to
problems or conditions perceived to have social
causes, definitions, consequences, or possible solu-
tions.
UF   Social Problems
N   ↓ Crime 1967
↓ Homeless 1988
↓ Human Rights 1978
Peace 1988
Poverty 1973
↓ Social Discrimination 1982
Social Equality 1973
↓ Social Integration 1982
Unemployment 1967
↓ War 1967
R   Adolescent Pregnancy 1988
Censorship 1978
↓ Civil Rights 1978
↓ Drug Abuse 1973
↓ Justice 1973
↓ Legal Processes 1973
Political Issues 1973
Racism 1973
Social Dilemma 2003
↓ Social Movements 1967
↓ Social Processes 1967
↓ Social Programs 1973

Social Learning 1973
PN 1790   SC 48280
B   Learning 1967
Learning Strategies 1991
N   Imitation (Learning) 1967
Imprinting 1967
R   Observational Learning 1973
↓ Social Reinforcement 1967

Social Loafing 2003
PN 39   SC 48284
SN   Tendency of individuals to exert less effort on a
task when working together in a group than working
alone.
HN   This term was introduced in June 2003. Psyc-
INFO records from the past 10 years were re-indexed
with this term. The posting note reflects the number
of records that were re-indexed.
B   Social Behavior 1967
R   Group Participation 1973
Social Facilitation 1973
↓ Social Influences 1967

Social Maladjustment
Use Social Adjustment

Social Mobility 1967
PN 395   SC 48300
SN   Change in social status by an individual or a
group.
UF   Mobility (Social)
Social Immobility
Upward Mobility
B   Social Processes 1967

Social Movements 1967
PN 1167   SC 48310
N   Black Power Movement 1973

Social Movements — (cont'd)

Civil Rights Movement 1973
Homosexual Liberation Movement 1973
Womens Liberation Movement 1973
R ↓ Civil Rights 1978
    Coalition Formation 1973
  ↓ Human Rights 1978
    Peace 1988
  ↓ Political Participation 1988
  ↓ Radical Movements 1973
    Social Change 1967
    Social Demonstrations 1973
  ↓ Social Influences 1967
  ↓ Social Issues 1991
  ↓ Social Programs 1973

Social Networks 1994

PN 1212   **SC** 48313
SN A formal or informal linkage, association, or network of individuals or groups that share common interests, contacts, knowledge, or resources. Compare SOCIAL SUPPORT NETWORKS and SUPPORT GROUPS.
UF Networks (Social)
R Ingroup Outgroup 1997
  ↓ Interpersonal Interaction 1967
    Professional Networking 2004
    Social Capital 2004
  ↓ Social Groups 1973
  ↓ Social Interaction 1967
    Social Support 2004
    Sociograms 1973
  ↓ Sociometry 1991
  ↓ Support Groups 1991

Social Norms 1985

PN 2132   **SC** 48315
SN Rules for social conduct, or standards which comprise a cultural definition of desirable or acceptable behavior. Also, patterns or traits seen as typical in the behavior of a social group.
UF Norms (Social)
B Social Influences 1967
R Sex Roles 1967
    Social Values 1973

Social Perception 1967

PN 17902   **SC** 48320
SN Awareness of social phenomena, including attitudes or behaviors of persons or groups, especially as they relate to one's self.
UF Interpersonal Perception
B Perception 1967
    Social Behavior 1967
N Attribution 1973
    Impression Formation 1978
    Social Comparison 1985
R Anonymity 1973
    Blame 1994
    Credibility 1973
    Face Perception 1985
    Fame 1985
    Halo Effect 1982
    Impression Management 1978
    Ingroup Outgroup 1997
    Labeling 1978
    Likability 1988
    Perceptiveness (Personality) 1973
    Popularity 1988
    Reputation 1997
    Reward Allocation 1988
    Self Fulfilling Prophecies 1997
    Self Reference 1994
    Social Cognition 1994

Social Perception — (cont'd)

Stereotyped Attitudes 1967
Stigma 1991
Stranger Reactions 1988
Theory of Mind 2001

Social Phobia 1985

PN 1422   **SC** 48325
SN Extreme apprehension or fear of social interaction or social situations in general. Compare SOCIAL ANXIETY.
UF Social Anxiety Disorder
B Phobias 1967
R Avoidant Personality Disorder 1994

Social Problems

Use Social Issues

Social Processes 1967

PN 3398   **SC** 48330
N Anomie 1978
    Coalition Formation 1973
  ↓ Human Migration 1973
    Immigration 1973
    Industrialization 1973
    Modernization 2003
    Social Capital 2004
    Social Control 1988
  ↓ Social Deprivation 1973
    Social Dilemma 2003
  ↓ Social Integration 1982
    Social Mobility 1967
  ↓ Socialization 1967
  ↓ Status 1967
    Urbanization 1973
R Equity (Payment) 1978
  ↓ Equity (Social) 1978
  ↓ Human Rights 1978
  ↓ Political Processes 1973
    Refugees 1988
    Social Change 1967
  ↓ Social Issues 1991
  ↓ Sociocultural Factors 1967
    Trends 1991

Social Programs 1973

PN 751   **SC** 48340
N Needle Exchange Programs 2001
    Outreach Programs 1997
R ↓ Housing 1973
    Integrated Services 1997
  ↓ Program Development 1991
    Social Change 1967
  ↓ Social Issues 1991
  ↓ Social Movements 1967
  ↓ Social Services 1982

Social Psychiatry 1967

PN 245   **SC** 48350
SN Branch of psychiatry concerned with the role of ecological, social, cultural, and economic factors in the etiology, incidence, and manifestations of mental disorders. Differentiate from COMMUNITY PSYCHIATRY, which emphasizes the practical and clinical applications of social psychiatry.
B Psychiatry 1967
R Social Psychology 1967

Social Psychologists 1973

PN 138   **SC** 48360
B Psychologists 1967
R Industrial Psychologists 1973
    Sociologists 1973

Social Psychology 1967

PN 4063   **SC** 48370
SN Branch of psychology concerned with the study of individuals in groups and the interpersonal interactions within and between groups.
B Applied Psychology 1973
R Folk Psychology 1997
    Social Psychiatry 1967

Social Reinforcement 1967

PN 1362   **SC** 48380
B Reinforcement 1967
    Social Behavior 1967
N Nonverbal Reinforcement 1973
  ↓ Verbal Reinforcement 1973
R Enabling 1997
    Encouragement 1973
    Eye Contact 1973
    Social Approval 1967
  ↓ Social Influences 1967
  ↓ Social Learning 1973

Social Rejection

Use Social Acceptance

Social Sciences 1967

PN 2476   **SC** 48390
SN Group of scientific disciplines which study social institutions, their functioning, and the interpersonal relationships and behavior of individuals of those institutions.
B Sciences 1967
N Anthropology 1967
  ↓ Behavioral Sciences 1997
  ↓ Economics 1985
  ↓ Sociology 1967
R Theoretical Orientation 1982

Social Security 1988

PN 166   **SC** 48392
SN Government program providing for economic security and social welfare of individuals or families upon retirement, death, or disability. Used for US and non-US programs.
B Government Programs 1973
    Insurance 1973
R Disability Evaluation 1988
    Medicaid 1994
    Medicare 1988

Social Services 1982

PN 3308   **SC** 48393
SN Activities designed to promote social welfare, usually associated with government or a helping organization (e.g., a church).
N ↓ Community Services 1967
    Outreach Programs 1997
    Protective Services 1997
R Child Welfare 1988
  ↓ Government Programs 1973
  ↓ Health Care Services 1978
    Integrated Services 1997
    Literacy Programs 1997
  ↓ Mental Health Services 1978
    Shelters 1991
    Social Casework 1967
  ↓ Social Programs 1973
  ↓ Support Groups 1991

Social Skills 1978

PN 6108   **SC** 48395
UF Competence (Social)
    Interpersonal Competence

Social Skills — (cont'd)

      Social Competence
B   Ability 1967
      Social Behavior 1967
R   Adaptive Behavior 1991
      Affective Education 1982
    ↓ Competence 1982
      Listening (Interpersonal) 1997
      Male Female Relations 1988
      Social Skills Training 1982

Social Skills Training 1982

PN 2716   **SC** 48397
SN Instruction, usually group oriented, to increase quality and capability of interpersonal interaction.
R   Assertiveness Training 1978
    ↓ Behavior Modification 1973
      Communication Skills Training 1982
      Human Relations Training 1978
      Sensitivity Training 1973
    ↓ Skill Learning 1973
      Social Cognition 1994
      Social Skills 1978

Social Stigma

Use Stigma

Social Stress 1973

PN 1039   **SC** 48400
B   Stress 1967

Social Structure 1967

PN 2307   **SC** 48410
B   Society 1967
N   Caste System 1973
    ↓ Social Class 1967
R   Dominance Hierarchy 1973
    ↓ Status 1967

Social Studies Education 1978

PN 645   **SC** 48415
SN Social sciences education in elementary, junior high, and high schools. Includes history, current events, and political science.
B   Curriculum 1967

Social Support 2004

PN   **SC** 48416
SN Family members or friends who provide social, emotional, or psychological support or comfort to an individual. Consider also SUPPORT GROUPS.
HN In June 2004, this term was created to replace the discontinued term SOCIAL SUPPORT NETWORKS. SOCIAL SUPPORT NETWORKS was removed from all records containing it and replaced with SOCIAL SUPPORT.
UF Social Support Networks
B   Assistance (Social Behavior) 1973
R ↓ Family Relations 1967
      Friendship 1967
      Reference Groups 1994
      Significant Others 1991
    ↓ Social Interaction 1967
      Social Networks 1994
    ↓ Support Groups 1991

Social Support Networks

Use Social Support

Social Values 1973

PN 2248   **SC** 48420

Social Values — (cont'd)

B   Social Influences 1967
      Values 1967
R   Anomie 1978
      Evil 2003
      Morality 1967
      Social Norms 1985
    ↓ Society 1967

Social Work

Use Social Casework

Social Work Education 1973

PN 1233   **SC** 48440
B   Education 1967

Social Workers 1973

PN 3826   **SC** 48450
UF Caseworkers
      Social Caseworkers
B   Personnel 1967
N   Psychiatric Social Workers 1973
R ↓ Counselors 1967
    ↓ Health Personnel 1994
    ↓ Law Enforcement Personnel 1973
    ↓ Mental Health Personnel 1967
    ↓ Psychologists 1967
      Rehabilitation Counselors 1978
      Sociologists 1973
    ↓ Therapists 1967
      Vocational Counselors 1973

Socialism 1973

PN 287   **SC** 48460
B   Political Economic Systems 1973

Socialization 1967

PN 4500   **SC** 48470
SN Process by which individuals acquire social skills and other characteristics necessary to function effectively in society or in a particular group.
B   Social Processes 1967
N   Political Socialization 1988
R   Reference Groups 1994

Socially Disadvantaged

Use Disadvantaged

Society 1967

PN 1919   **SC** 48490
B   Culture (Anthropological) 1967
N ↓ Social Structure 1967
    ↓ Socioeconomic Status 1967
R   Popular Culture 2003
      Social Values 1973

Sociobiology 1982

PN 563   **SC** 48495
SN Systematic study of the biological basis of all aspects of social behavior. Used for both human and animal populations.
B   Biology 1967
      Sociology 1967
R   Behavioral Genetics 1994
      Evolutionary Psychology 2003

Sociocultural Factors 1967

PN 15195   **SC** 48500
UF Cultural Factors
N   Cross Cultural Differences 1967
      Cultural Deprivation 1973

Sociocultural Factors — (cont'd)

    ↓ Culture Change 1967
      Ethnic Identity 1973
      Ethnic Values 1973
    ↓ Rites of Passage 1973
R ↓ Childrearing Practices 1967
      Cross Cultural Psychology 1997
      Cultism 1973
      Cultural Sensitivity 1994
    ↓ Culture (Anthropological) 1967
    ↓ Culture Bound Syndromes 2004
      Ethnography 1973
      Ethnology 1967
    ↓ Family Structure 1973
      Kinship Structure 1973
      Multiculturalism 1997
      Psychosocial Factors 1988
      Race (Anthropological) 1973
    ↓ Racial and Ethnic Groups 2001
      Regional Differences 2001
      Risk Factors 2001
    ↓ Social Processes 1967

Socioeconomic Class Attitudes 1973

PN 324   **SC** 48510
SN Attitudes of, not toward, members of a particular socioeconomic class.
UF Class Attitudes
      Social Class Attitudes
B   Attitudes 1967
N   Lower Class Attitudes 1973
      Middle Class Attitudes 1973
      Upper Class Attitudes 1973
R ↓ Social Class 1967
    ↓ Socioeconomic Status 1967

Socioeconomic Status 1967

PN 9715   **SC** 48520
SN The combination of one's social class and income level. Includes socioeconomic differences between individuals or groups.
B   Society 1967
      Status 1967
N   Family Socioeconomic Level 1973
    ↓ Income Level 1973
      Lower Class 1973
    ↓ Social Class 1967
R   Disadvantaged 1967
      Income (Economic) 1973
      Poverty 1973
    ↓ Socioeconomic Class Attitudes 1973

Socioenvironmental Therapy

Use Milieu Therapy

Sociograms 1973

PN 52   **SC** 48530
SN Diagrams in which interactions between group members are analyzed on the basis of mutual attractions or antipathies.
B   Sociometry 1991
R ↓ Measurement 1967
      Social Networks 1994

Sociolinguistics 1985

PN 527   **SC** 48535
SN The study of the sociological aspects of language, concerned with the part language plays in maintaining the social roles in a community.
B   Linguistics 1973
R   Code Switching 1988
      Ethnolinguistics 1973
      Metalinguistics 1994

Sociolinguistics — (cont'd)
↓ Sociology   1967
Symbolic Interactionism   1988

Sociologists   1973
PN   131   SC   48540
B   Professional Personnel   1978
R   Anthropologists   1973
    ↓ Counselors   1967
    Scientists   1967
    Social Psychologists   1973
    ↓ Social Workers   1973

Sociology   1967
PN   2068   SC   48550
B   Social Sciences   1967
N   Sociobiology   1982
R   ↓ Behavioral Sciences   1997
    Sociolinguistics   1985
    Symbolic Interactionism   1988

Sociometric Tests   1967
PN   430   SC   48560
SN   Tests or techniques used to identify preferences, likes, or dislikes of group members with respect to each other, as well as to identify various patterns of group structure or interaction.
B   Measurement   1967
    Sociometry   1991

Sociometry   1991
PN   242   SC   48565
SN   Used for the scientific discipline or the sociometric processes and properties themselves.
N   Sociograms   1973
    Sociometric Tests   1967
R   ↓ Collective Behavior   1967
    ↓ Group Dynamics   1967
    ↓ Organizational Behavior   1978
    ↓ Peer Relations   1967
    Social Networks   1994

Sociopath
Use   Antisocial Personality Disorder

Sociopathology
Use   Antisocial Behavior

Sociotherapy   1973
PN   103   SC   48580
SN   Any therapy in which the main emphasis is on socioenvironmental and interpersonal factors. Sometimes used to refer to a therapeutic community.
B   Treatment   1967
R   Milieu Therapy   1988
    Therapeutic Community   1967

Sodium   1973
PN   1024   SC   48590
B   Metallic Elements   1973
N   Sodium Ions   1973
R   Hyponatremia   1997

Sodium Ions   1973
PN   98   SC   48610
B   Electrolytes   1973
    Sodium   1973

Sodium Lactate
Use   Lactic Acid

Sodium Pentobarbital
Use   Pentobarbital

Solution Focused Therapy   2004
PN   41   SC   48621
SN   Approach to psychotherapy that focuses on solutions instead of problems.
HN   This term was introduced in June 2004. PsycINFO records from the past 10 years were re-indexed with this term. The posting note reflects the number of records that were re-indexed.
B   Psychotherapy   1967
R   Brief Psychotherapy   1967
    ↓ Problem Solving   1967

Solvent Abuse
Use   Inhalant Abuse

Solvents   1982
PN   337   SC   48625
SN   Substances that react chemically with a solid to bring it into solution. Also, liquids that dissolve another substance (solute) without any change in chemical composition.
N   Toluene   1991
R   ↓ Acids   1973
    ↓ Alcohols   1967
    ↓ Inhalant Abuse   1985

Somatization   1994
PN   985   SC   57430
SN   Process of organically manifesting and expressing cognitive and emotional disturbances through bodily symptoms. Primarily used in nonclinical contexts.
R   ↓ Conversion Disorder   2001
    Hypochondriasis   1973
    Illness Behavior   1982
    Somatization Disorder   2001
    ↓ Somatoform Disorders   2001
    Somatoform Pain Disorder   1997
    ↓ Symptoms   1967

Somatization Disorder   2001
PN   57   SC   48627
SN   Pattern of recurring polysymptomatic somatic complaints resulting in medical treatment or impaired daily function. Usually begins before age 30 and extends over a period of years.
HN   Consider PSYCHOSOMATIC DISORDERS to access records from 1967-2000.
B   Somatoform Disorders   2001
R   Psychosomatic Medicine   1978
    Somatization   1994

Somatoform Disorders   2001
PN   5088   SC   48628
SN   Disorders characterized by bodily symptoms caused by psychological factors.
HN   Consider PSYCHOSOMATIC DISORDERS to access references from 1967-2000.
UF   Psychophysiologic Disorders
    Psychosomatic Disorders
N   Body Dysmorphic Disorder   2001
    ↓ Conversion Disorder   2001
    Hypochondriasis   1973
    Neurodermatitis   1973
    Somatization Disorder   2001
    Somatoform Pain Disorder   1997
R   Anorexia Nervosa   1973
    Asthma   1967
    Bulimia   1985

Somatoform Disorders — (cont'd)
↓ Dyspnea   1973
↓ Endocrine Disorders   1973
↓ Gastrointestinal Disorders   1973
Hay Fever   1973
↓ Headache   1973
Hyperphagia   1973
Hyperventilation   1973
Illness Behavior   1982
Irritable Bowel Syndrome   1991
Malingering   1973
Migraine Headache   1973
Munchausen Syndrome   1994
Myofascial Pain   1991
Obesity   1973
Psychosomatic Medicine   1978
↓ Sexual Function Disturbances   1973
↓ Skin Disorders   1973
Somatization   1994
↓ Symptoms   1967
↓ Urinary Function Disorders   1973
↓ Urogenital Disorders   1973

Somatoform Pain Disorder   1997
PN   316   SC   48629
HN   In 1997, this term was created to replace the discontinued term PSYCHOGENIC PAIN. In 2000, PSYCHOGENIC PAIN was removed from all records containing it, and replaced with SOMATOFORM PAIN DISORDER.
UF   Pain (Psychogenic)
    Pain Disorder
    Psychogenic Pain
B   Pain   1967
    Somatoform Disorders   2001
R   Chronic Pain   1985
    ↓ Conversion Disorder   2001
    Hypochondriasis   1973
    Pain Management   1994
    Somatization   1994

Somatosensory Cortex   1973
PN   893   SC   48630
UF   Cortex (Somatosensory)
B   Parietal Lobe   1973
R   ↓ Sensory System Disorders   2001

Somatosensory Disorders   2001
PN   92   SC   48635
SN   Disorders of sensory information received from the skin and deep tissue of the body that are associated with impaired or abnormal somatic sensation. Such disorders may affect proprioception, tactile, thermal, and pressure sensation, and pain perception.
UF   Hyperalgesia
    Hyperesthesia
    Hypesthesia
    Paresthesia
B   Sensory System Disorders   2001
R   ↓ Nervous System Disorders   1967
    ↓ Pain Perception   1973
    Pressure Sensation   1973
    ↓ Somesthetic Perception   1967
    Temperature Perception   1973

Somatosensory Evoked Potentials   1973
PN   1022   SC   48640
UF   Motor Evoked Potentials
B   Evoked Potentials   1967
R   ↓ Cortical Evoked Potentials   1973

Somatostatin   1991
PN   194   SC   48645

Somatostatin — (cont'd)
UF Growth Hormone Inhibitor
B Neuropeptides 2003
  Peptides 1973
R Somatotropin 1973

Somatotropin 1973
PN 820   **SC** 48650
UF Growth Hormone
B Neuropeptides 2003
  Pituitary Hormones 1973
R Somatostatin 1991

Somatotypes 1973
PN 203   **SC** 48660
SN Body types as derived from any of various classifications of body build and which usually imply a correlation with personality characteristics.
UF Body Types
R ↓ Personality 1967
  ↓ Physical Appearance 1982
  Physique 1967

Somesthetic Perception 1967
PN 997   **SC** 48670
SN Awareness of bodily condition or stimuli, including kinesthetic and cutaneous perception.
B Perception 1967
N ↓ Cutaneous Sense 1967
  Kinesthetic Perception 1967
  ↓ Pain Perception 1973
  Temperature Perception 1973
  Weight Perception 1967
R Body Awareness 1982
  ↓ Labyrinth Disorders 1973
  Pressure Sensation 1973
  Somatosensory Disorders 2001

Somesthetic Stimulation 1970
PN 763   **SC** 48680
UF Vestibular Stimulation
B Perceptual Stimulation 1973
N ↓ Tactual Stimulation 1973
R Weightlessness 1967

Somnambulism
  Use Sleepwalking

Sonar 1973
PN 47   **SC** 48700
B Apparatus 1967

Songs
  Use Music

Sons 1973
PN 1105   **SC** 48710
B Family Members 1973
  Human Males 1973
  Offspring 1988

Sorority Membership 1973
PN 146   **SC** 48720
SN Belonging to a club traditionally restricted to females. Used also for sorority organizations.
B Extracurricular Activities 1973

Sorting (Cognition)
  Use Classification (Cognitive Process)

Soul 2004
PN 100   **SC** 48735
HN This term was introduced in June 2004. Psyc-INFO records from the past 10 years were re-indexed with this term. The posting note reflects the number of records that were re-indexed.
R Human Body 2003
  Mind 1991
  ↓ Religious Beliefs 1973
  Spirituality 1988

Sound
  Use Auditory Stimulation

Sound Localization
  Use Auditory Localization

Sound Pressure Level
  Use Loudness

Sound Waves
  Use Acoustics

Source Monitoring 2004
PN 94   **SC** 48768
SN The cognitive capacity to differentiate between experienced memories and to be able to attribute them to the particular source.
HN This term was introduced in June 2004. Psyc-INFO records from the past 10 years were re-indexed with this term. The posting note reflects the number of records that were re-indexed.
B Monitoring 1973
R False Memory 1997
  ↓ Memory 1967

Sourness
  Use Taste Perception

South Asian Cultural Groups 2004
PN 204   **SC** 48780
SN Cultural groups from the subcontinent of India, including Bangladesh, Nepal, Pakistan, Sri Lanka, Maldives, and Bhutan.
HN This term was introduced in June 2004. Psyc-INFO records from the past 10 years were re-indexed with this term. The posting note reflects the number of records that were re-indexed.
B Asians 1982

South East Asian Cultural Groups
  Use Southeast Asian Cultural Groups

Southeast Asian Cultural Groups 2004
PN 58   **SC** 48785
SN Cultural groups from countries south of China and east of India, including Brunei, Cambodia, Laos, Vietnam, Thailand, Singapore, Malaysia, Indonesia, Philippines, Myanmar, and East Timor.
HN This term was introduced in June 2004. Psyc-INFO records from the past 10 years were re-indexed with this term. The posting note reflects the number of records that were re-indexed.
UF South East Asian Cultural Groups
B Asians 1982
N Vietnamese Cultural Groups 1997

Spacecraft 1973
PN 54   **SC** 48820

Spacecraft — (cont'd)
R Air Transportation 1973
  Astronauts 1973

Spaceflight 1967
PN 333   **SC** 48830
B Aviation 1967
R Acceleration Effects 1973
  Decompression Effects 1973
  ↓ Gravitational Effects 1967
  Weightlessness 1967

Spanish Americans
  Use Hispanics

Spasms 1973
PN 120   **SC** 48850
B Movement Disorders 1985
  Symptoms 1967
N Muscle Spasms 1973
R ↓ Anticonvulsive Drugs 1973
  ↓ Antispasmodic Drugs 1973
  ↓ Convulsions 1967
  ↓ Pain 1967

Spatial Ability 1982
PN 2240   **SC** 48855
SN Potential or actual performance on tasks involving mental manipulation of objects or judgments of spatial relationships with respect to actual or imagined bodily orientation.
B Cognitive Ability 1973
  Nonverbal Ability 1988
N ↓ Visuospatial Ability 1997
R ↓ Cognitive Processes 1967
  Mental Rotation 1991
  Spatial Imagery 1982
  Spatial Learning 1994
  Spatial Orientation (Perception) 1973

Spatial Discrimination
  Use Spatial Perception

Spatial Distortion 1973
PN 198   **SC** 48870
SN Alterations of an organism's normal spatial perception in any sensory modality. Distortions may be induced by such means as optical lenses, prisms, mirror displays or images, and left-right inversion of sound stimuli.
B Illusions (Perception) 1967
  Perceptual Distortion 1982
  Spatial Perception 1967
R Prismatic Stimulation 1973

Spatial Frequency 1982
PN 1664   **SC** 48872
SN Number of alternating cycles (e.g., patterns of vertical stripes of light and dark light) occurring in a specified visual angle as, for example, in sine wave or square wave displays.
B Stimulus Parameters 1967
R Temporal Frequency 1985
  ↓ Visual Displays 1973
  ↓ Visual Stimulation 1973

Spatial Imagery 1982
PN 509   **SC** 48875
SN Mental representation of spatial relationships.
B Imagery 1967
R Cognitive Maps 1982

Spatial Imagery — (cont'd)
Mental Rotation 1991
↓ Spatial Ability 1982
↓ Spatial Memory 1988
Spatial Organization 1973
Spatial Orientation (Perception) 1973

Spatial Learning 1994
PN 1153   SC 48876
B   Learning 1967
R   Maze Learning 1967
↓ Spatial Ability 1982
↓ Spatial Memory 1988
↓ Spatial Perception 1967

Spatial Memory 1988
PN 2165   SC 48877
B   Memory 1967
N   Visuospatial Memory 1997
R   Cognitive Maps 1982
Direction Perception 1997
Eidetic Imagery 1973
Spatial Imagery 1982
Spatial Learning 1994
↓ Visual Memory 1994

Spatial Neglect
Use Sensory Neglect

Spatial Organization 1973
PN 3446   SC 48880
SN Perception of spatial relationships. Also, the actual pattern or physical arrangement of objects or stimuli, including the dimensions of proximity, continuation, and relative position.
B   Spatial Perception 1967
R   Cognitive Maps 1982
Direction Perception 1997
Mental Rotation 1991
Retinal Eccentricity 1991
Spatial Imagery 1982

Spatial Orientation (Perception) 1973
PN 4579   SC 48890
SN Ability to perceive or orient oneself or external stimuli in space with respect to environmentally or egocentrically defined reference points.
UF   Orientation (Spatial)
B   Perceptual Orientation 1973
Spatial Perception 1967
R   Cognitive Maps 1982
Equilibrium 1973
Kinesthetic Perception 1967
↓ Spatial Ability 1982
Spatial Imagery 1982

Spatial Perception 1967
PN 5386   SC 48900
UF   Spatial Discrimination
B   Perception 1967
N   ↓ Depth Perception 1967
Direction Perception 1997
↓ Distance Perception 1973
↓ Motion Perception 1967
↓ Size Discrimination 1967
Spatial Distortion 1973
Spatial Organization 1973
Spatial Orientation (Perception) 1973
R   Figure Ground Discrimination 1973
Mental Rotation 1991
Spatial Learning 1994
Visual Acuity 1982

Spearman Brown Test 1973
PN 15   SC 48910
B   Statistical Tests 1973
R   Statistical Reliability 1973

Spearman Rho
Use Rank Difference Correlation

Special Education 1967
PN 13860   SC 48930
SN Educational programs and services for students with disabilities or gifted students whose characteristics and educational needs differ from those who can be taught through standard methods and materials.
B   Education 1967
Educational Programs 1973
R   Ability Grouping 1973
Adaptive Behavior 1991
Early Intervention 1982
Educational Placement 1978
Educational Therapy 1997
↓ Mainstreaming 1991
Mainstreaming (Educational) 1978
↓ Remedial Education 1985
Self Care Skills 1978
Special Needs 1994

Special Education Students 1973
PN 4286   SC 49010
B   Students 1967
R   Grade Level 1994

Special Education Teachers 1973
PN 2174   SC 49020
B   Teachers 1967
R   Resource Teachers 1973

Special Needs 1994
PN 893   SC 49025
SN Unspecified disorder, disability, or other problem that requires special services or intervention practices. Use a more specific term if possible.
R   ↓ Disorders 1967
Early Intervention 1982
↓ Mainstreaming 1991
↓ Mental Disorders 1967
↓ Needs 1967
Needs Assessment 1985
↓ Physical Disorders 1997
Special Education 1967

Specialization (Academic)
Use Academic Specialization

Specialization (Professional)
Use Professional Specialization

Species Differences 1982
PN 2140   SC 49035
SN Anatomical, physiological, and/or behavioral variations between members of different species. May be used for comparisons between human and animal populations. Compare ANIMAL STRAIN DIFFERENCES.
HN Consider COMPARATIVE PSYCHOLOGY to access references from 1967-1981.
R   ↓ Animals 1967
↓ Genetics 1967
Interspecies Interaction 1991

Species Recognition 1985
PN 420   SC 49037
SN Ability of members of a given species to identify and recognize other members of the same species.
B   Animal Ethology 1967
R   Conspecifics 2003
Imprinting 1967
Instinctive Behavior 1982
Kinship Recognition 1988

Spectral Sensitivity
Use Color Perception

Speech
Use Oral Communication

Speech and Hearing Measures 1973
PN 670   SC 49060
SN Consider also AUDIOLOGY and AUDIOMETRY.
UF   Hearing Measures
Speech Measures
B   Measurement 1967
R   ↓ Perceptual Measures 1973

Speech Anxiety 1985
PN 402   SC 49065
SN Anxiety or fear associated with actual or anticipated oral communication with others.
UF   Communication Apprehension
Fear of Public Speaking
B   Anxiety 1967
R   ↓ Anxiety Disorders 1997
↓ Communication Disorders 1982
↓ Interpersonal Communication 1973
Public Speaking 1973
Social Anxiety 1985

Speech Characteristics 1973
PN 4457   SC 49070
B   Oral Communication 1985
N   Articulation (Speech) 1967
Pronunciation 1967
Speech Pauses 1973
Speech Pitch 1973
Speech Rate 1973
Speech Rhythm 1973
R   Acoustics 1997
Inflection 1973
↓ Prosody 1991

Speech Development 1973
PN 1819   SC 49080
B   Psychomotor Development 1973
N   Retarded Speech Development 1973
R   ↓ Cognitive Development 1973
↓ Language Development 1967

Speech Disorders 1967
PN 2481   SC 49090
HN The term SPEECH HANDICAPPED was also used to represent this concept from 1973-1996, and SPEECH DISABLED was used from 1997-2000. In 2000, SPEECH DISORDERS replaced the discontinued and deleted term SPEECH DISABLED. SPEECH DISABLED and SPEECH HANDICAPPED were removed from all records containing them and replaced with SPEECH DISORDERS.
UF   Speech Handicapped
B   Communication Disorders 1982
N   ↓ Articulation Disorders 1973
Dysphonia 1973
Stuttering 1967

Speech Disorders — (cont'd)
- **R**   Apraxia   1973
- ↓ Augmentative Communication   1994
- Cleft Palate   1967
- ↓ Language Disorders   1982
- Retarded Speech Development   1973

Speech Handicapped
- **Use**   Speech Disorders

Speech Measures
- **Use**   Speech and Hearing Measures

Speech Pauses   1973
PN 299   **SC** 49120
- **B**   Speech Characteristics   1973

Speech Perception   1967
PN 5724   **SC** 49130
- **B**   Auditory Perception   1967
- **R**   Automated Speech Recognition   1994
- Lipreading   1973
- ↓ Rhythm   1991
- Word Recognition   1988

Speech Pitch   1973
PN 351   **SC** 49140
- **B**   Pitch (Frequency)   1967
- Speech Characteristics   1973

Speech Processing (Mechanical)   1973
PN 270   **SC** 49150
- **N**   Automated Speech Recognition   1994
- Compressed Speech   1973
- Filtered Speech   1973
- Synthetic Speech   1973
- **R**   ↓ Auditory Stimulation   1967
- ↓ Verbal Communication   1967

Speech Rate   1973
PN 722   **SC** 49160
- **UF**   Accelerated Speech
- **B**   Speech Characteristics   1973
- **R**   Tempo   1997
- Verbal Fluency   1973

Speech Rhythm   1973
PN 202   **SC** 49170
- **B**   Rhythm   1991
- Speech Characteristics   1973
- **R**   Tempo   1997

Speech Therapists   1973
PN 478   **SC** 49180
- **B**   Therapists   1967
- **R**   ↓ Educational Personnel   1973

Speech Therapy   1967
PN 2373   **SC** 49190
- **B**   Treatment   1967
- **R**   ↓ Augmentative Communication   1994
- ↓ Communication Disorders   1982

Speechreading
- **Use**   Lipreading

Speed
- **Use**   Velocity

Speed (Response)
- **Use**   Reaction Time

Spelling   1973
PN 1973   **SC** 49220
SN Instruction, ability, or performance in the formation of words from letters according to accepted orthographic standards.
- **B**   Language   1967
- Language Arts Education   1973
- **R**   Orthography   1973

Sperm   1973
PN 222   **SC** 49230
- **B**   Cells (Biology)   1973
- **R**   ↓ Sexual Reproduction   1973

Sperm Donation
- **Use**   Tissue Donation

Spider Phobia
- **Use**   Phobias

Spiders
- **Use**   Arachnida

Spina Bifida   1978
PN 363   **SC** 49245
SN Birth defect involving inadequate closure of the bony casement of the spinal cord, through which the spinal membranes, with or without spinal cord tissue, may protrude.
- **UF**   Meningomyelocele
- Myelomeningocele
- **B**   Congenital Disorders   1973

Spinal Column   1973
PN 105   **SC** 49250
- **B**   Musculoskeletal System   1973
- **R**   Bones   1973
- ↓ Spinal Cord   1973

Spinal Cord   1973
PN 1225   **SC** 49260
- **B**   Central Nervous System   1967
- **N**   Cranial Spinal Cord   1973
- Dorsal Horns   1985
- Dorsal Roots   1973
- Extrapyramidal Tracts   1973
- Lumbar Spinal Cord   1973
- Pyramidal Tracts   1973
- Spinothalamic Tracts   1973
- Ventral Roots   1973
- **R**   Spinal Column   1973

Spinal Cord Injuries   1973
PN 967   **SC** 49270
- **B**   Injuries   1973
- **N**   Whiplash   1997
- **R**   ↓ Central Nervous System Disorders   1973
- Hemiplegia   1978
- ↓ Neuromuscular Disorders   1973
- ↓ Paralysis   1973
- Paraplegia   1978
- Quadriplegia   1985

Spinal Fluid
- **Use**   Cerebrospinal Fluid

Spinal Ganglia   1973
PN 48   **SC** 49290
- **B**   Ganglia   1973

Spinal Nerves   1973
PN 478   **SC** 49300
- **UF**   Brachial Plexus
- Cauda Equina
- Cervical Plexus
- Femoral Nerve
- Lumbrosacral Plexus
- Median Nerve
- Musculocutaneous Nerve
- Nerves (Spinal)
- Obturator Nerve
- Phrenic Nerve
- Radial Nerve
- Sciatic Nerve
- Thoracic Nerves
- Ulnar Nerve
- **B**   Peripheral Nervous System   1973

Spinothalamic Tracts   1973
PN 62   **SC** 49310
- **B**   Afferent Pathways   1982
- Lemniscal System   1985
- Spinal Cord   1973

Spiperone
- **Use**   Spiroperidol

Spirit Possession   1997
PN 71   **SC** 49314
- **UF**   Demonic Possession
- **R**   Occultism   1978
- ↓ Parapsychological Phenomena   1973
- ↓ Religious Beliefs   1973

Spirituality   1988
PN 3178   **SC** 49315
SN Degree of involvement or state of awareness or devotion to a higher being or life philosophy. Not always related to conventional religious beliefs.
- **R**   Religion   1967
- Religiosity   1973
- ↓ Religious Beliefs   1973
- Religious Experiences   1997
- Soul   2004

Spiroperidol   1991
PN 45   **SC** 49317
- **UF**   Spiperone
- **B**   Neuroleptic Drugs   1973

Spleen   1973
PN 76   **SC** 49320
- **R**   ↓ Cardiovascular System   1967

Split Brain
- **Use**   Commissurotomy

Split Personality
- **Use**   Dissociative Identity Disorder

Spontaneous Abortion   1971
PN 332   **SC** 49350
- **UF**   Abortion (Spontaneous)
- Miscarriage
- **R**   Induced Abortion   1971

Spontaneous Alternation 1982
PN 205   SC 49352
SN Instinctive successive alternation of responses between alternatives in a situation involving discrete choices or exploration.
R   Animal Exploratory Behavior 1973
       Delayed Alternation 1994
       Instinctive Behavior 1982
       ↓ Learning 1967
       Response Variability 1973

Spontaneous Recovery (Learning) 1973
PN 111   SC 49357
SN Recurrence of a conditioned response following experimental extinction. The response is weaker than when originally conditioned and will extinguish rapidly if not reinforced.
B   Learning 1967
       Memory 1967
R   ↓ Conditioning 1967

Spontaneous Remission 1973
PN 77   SC 49360
B   Remission (Disorders) 1973
R   ↓ Psychotherapy 1967
       ↓ Treatment 1967

Sport Performance
   Use Athletic Performance

Sport Psychology 1982
PN 982   SC 49365
SN Branch of psychology that investigates and applies psychological and physiological principles relating to athletic activity. Also used for psychological processes and their manifestations in such activity.
B   Applied Psychology 1973

Sport Training
   Use Athletic Training

Sports 1967
PN 3245   SC 49370
N   Baseball 1973
       Basketball 1973
       Football 1973
       Judo 1973
       Martial Arts 1985
       Soccer 1994
       Swimming 1973
       Tennis 1973
       Weightlifting 1994
R   ↓ Athletes 1973
       Athletic Participation 1973
       Athletic Performance 1991
       Athletic Training 1991
       Coaches 1988
       College Athletes 1994
       ↓ Recreation 1967
       Sports (Attitudes Toward) 2004
       Sports Spectators 1997
       ↓ Teams 1988
       Wilderness Experience 1991

Sports (Attitudes Toward) 2004
PN 26   SC 49371
SN Used for the attitudes of participants and spectators of sports.

Sports (Attitudes Toward) — (cont'd)
HN This term was introduced in June 2004. PsycINFO records from the past 10 years were re-indexed with this term. The posting note reflects the number of records that were re-indexed.
UF   Sportsmanship
       Sportspersonship
B   Attitudes 1967
R   ↓ Athletes 1973
       ↓ Sports 1967
       Sports Spectators 1997

Sports Spectators 1997
PN 140   SC 49373
UF   Fans (Sports)
B   Audiences 1967
R   ↓ Sports 1967
       Sports (Attitudes Toward) 2004

Sportsmanship
   Use Sports (Attitudes Toward)

Sportspersonship
   Use Sports (Attitudes Toward)

Spouse Abuse
   Use Partner Abuse

Spouses 1973
PN 7525   SC 49380
SN Married persons
UF   Married Couples
       Mates (Humans)
B   Family Members 1973
N   Husbands 1973
       Wives 1973
R   Couples 1982
       Inlaws 1997
       ↓ Parents 1967
       Significant Others 1991

Spreading Depression 1967
PN 160   SC 49390
SN Cerebral cortex cellular depolarization and a depressed electrical activity in depolarized cortical areas resulting from application of intense localized electrical stimulation or local application of a chemical or localized trauma to the cerebral cortex.
B   Brain Stimulation 1967

Squirrels 1973
PN 362   SC 49400
B   Rodents 1973

St. John's Wort
   Use Hypericum Perforatum

Stability (Emotional)
   Use Emotional Stability

Stage Plays
   Use Theatre

Stalking 2001
PN 150   SC 49435
SN Willful, malicious, and repeated nonconsensual contact with and harassing of another individual.
B   Harassment 2001
R   ↓ Crime 1967

Stalking — (cont'd)
       ↓ Perpetrators 1988
       Victimization 1973

Stammering
   Use Stuttering

Standard Deviation 1973
PN 136   SC 49450
B   Variability Measurement 1973
R   Error of Measurement 1985
       ↓ Frequency Distribution 1973
       Homogeneity of Variance 2003
       Standard Scores 1985

Standard Error of Measurement
   Use Error of Measurement

Standard Scores 1985
PN 93   SC 49455
SN Test scores measuring the distance of individual scores from the mean of the normative group, expressed in terms of the standard deviation.
UF   Deviation IQ
       Stanines
       Z Scores
B   Test Scores 1967
R   Mean 1973
       Score Equating 1086
       ↓ Scoring (Testing) 1973
       Standard Deviation 1973

Standardization (Test)
   Use Test Standardization

Standardized Tests 1985
PN 576   SC 49465
SN Tests with established norms, administration and scoring procedures, and validity and reliability data.
B   Measurement 1967
R   Test Norms 1973
       Test Standardization 1973

Standards (Professional)
   Use Professional Standards

Stanford Achievement Test 1973
PN 62   SC 49480
B   Achievement Measures 1967

Stanford Binet Intelligence Scale 1967
PN 366   SC 49490
B   Intelligence Measures 1967

Stanines
   Use Standard Scores

Stapedius Reflex
   Use Acoustic Reflex

Starfish
   Use Echinodermata

Startle Reflex 1967
PN 1406   SC 49510
B   Reflexes 1971

Startle Reflex — (cont'd)
R   Acoustic Reflex   1973
     Alarm Responses   1973
     Eyeblink Reflex   1973
     Prepulse Inhibition   1997

Starvation   1973
PN   129   **SC**   49520
B   Nutritional Deficiencies   1973
R   Food Deprivation   1967
     Hunger   1967

State Board Examinations
Use   Professional Examinations

State Dependent Learning   1982
PN   132   **SC**   49525
SN   Learning phenomenon wherein the transfer of a response that was learned in the context of specific internal or external cues is dependent on the constancy of the stimulus complex in the new situation to which the behavior is to transfer.
UF   Drug Dissociation
B   Learning   1967

State Hospitals
Use   Psychiatric Hospitals

State Trait Anxiety Inventory   1973
PN   228   **SC**   49540
B   Nonprojective Personality Measures   1973

Statistical Analysis   1967
PN   8203   **SC**   49550
SN   Application of statistical procedures to the interpretation of numerical data.
B   Analysis   1967
N   ↓ Central Tendency Measures   1973
     Cluster Analysis   1973
     Confidence Limits (Statistics)   1973
     Consistency (Measurement)   1973
     Effect Size (Statistical)   1985
     Error of Measurement   1985
     ↓ Frequency Distribution   1973
     Fuzzy Set Theory   1991
     Goodness of Fit   1988
     Interaction Analysis (Statistics)   1970
     Meta Analysis   1985
     ↓ Multivariate Analysis   1982
     Predictability (Measurement)   1973
     ↓ Statistical Correlation   1967
     Statistical Data   1982
     ↓ Statistical Estimation   1985
     Statistical Norms   1971
     ↓ Statistical Probability   1967
     ↓ Statistical Regression   1985
     Statistical Reliability   1973
     Statistical Significance   1973
     ↓ Statistical Tests   1973
     Statistical Validity   1973
     Statistical Weighting   1985
     Time Series   1985
     ↓ Variability Measurement   1973
R   Conjoint Measurement   1994
     ↓ Experimental Design   1967
     ↓ Experimentation   1967
     ↓ Hypothesis Testing   1973
     ↓ Mathematics (Concepts)   1967
     ↓ Measurement   1967
     ↓ Population (Statistics)   1973
     ↓ Prediction Errors   1973
     Psychometrics   1967

Statistical Analysis — (cont'd)
     Quantitative Methods   2003
     ↓ Sampling (Experimental)   1973
     ↓ Statistical Measurement   1973
     ↓ Statistical Variables   1973
     Uncertainty   1991

Statistical Correlation   1967
PN   3519   **SC**   49560
UF   Correlation (Statistical)
     Pearson Product Moment Correlation Coefficient
B   Statistical Analysis   1967
N   Linear Regression   1973
     Logistic Regression   2003
     Nonlinear Regression   1973
     Phi Coefficient   1973
     Point Biserial Correlation   1973
     Rank Difference Correlation   1973
     Rank Order Correlation   1973
     Tetrachoric Correlation   1973
R   ↓ Experimentation   1967
     ↓ Factor Analysis   1967
     Multiple Regression   1982
     ↓ Multivariate Analysis   1982
     Statistical Data   1982
     ↓ Statistical Regression   1985
     Statistical Significance   1973
     Statistical Validity   1973
     ↓ Statistical Variables   1973
     ↓ Variability Measurement   1973

Statistical Data   1982
PN   898   **SC**   49564
SN   Sets of quantitative values that summarize, through mathematical operation, or express the parameters that represent a population or some other sample (e.g., response frequency).
B   Statistical Analysis   1967
R   Data Collection   1982
     Graphical Displays   1985
     Quantitative Methods   2003
     ↓ Statistical Correlation   1967
     ↓ Statistical Measurement   1973
     Statistical Tables   1982
     ↓ Statistical Variables   1973
     Time Series   1985

Statistical Estimation   1985
PN   1359   **SC**   49567
SN   Any inferential mathematical derivation of an estimate of a parameter from one or more samples. Includes interval estimation.
UF   Parameter Estimation
B   Estimation   1967
     Statistical Analysis   1967
N   Least Squares   1985
     Magnitude Estimation   1991
     Maximum Likelihood   1985
R   Error of Measurement   1985
     Predictability (Measurement)   1973

Statistical Measurement   1973
PN   768   **SC**   49570
SN   Process of or products derived from the collection or manipulation of statistical data in order to derive basic summarizing quantitative values which describe a set of measurements.
B   Measurement   1967
N   ↓ Central Tendency Measures   1973
     Conjoint Measurement   1994
     ↓ Frequency Distribution   1973
     Homogeneity of Variance   2003
     Predictability (Measurement)   1973

Statistical Measurement — (cont'd)
     Statistical Norms   1971
     ↓ Statistical Probability   1967
     ↓ Variability Measurement   1973
R   Confidence Limits (Statistics)   1973
     Data Collection   1982
     Error of Measurement   1985
     Graphical Displays   1985
     Quantitative Methods   2003
     ↓ Statistical Analysis   1967
     Statistical Data   1982
     Statistical Significance   1973
     ↓ Statistical Tests   1973

Statistical Norms   1971
PN   314   **SC**   49580
UF   Norms (Statistical)
B   Statistical Analysis   1967
     Statistical Measurement   1973
R   ↓ Statistical Sample Parameters   1973

Statistical Power   1991
PN   317   **SC**   49585
SN   The ability of a statistic to reject a false hypothesis.
B   Statistical Probability   1967
R   ↓ Hypothesis Testing   1973
     ↓ Prediction Errors   1973
     ↓ Sampling (Experimental)   1973
     Statistical Significance   1973
     ↓ Statistical Tests   1973
     Type I Errors   1973
     Type II Errors   1973

Statistical Probability   1967
PN   1252   **SC**   49590
UF   Bayes Theorem
B   Chance (Fortune)   1973
     Probability   1967
     Statistical Analysis   1967
     Statistical Measurement   1973
N   Binomial Distribution   1973
     Statistical Power   1991
R   Fuzzy Set Theory   1991

Statistical Regression   1985
PN   649   **SC**   49595
SN   Statistical comparison of the frequency distributions of one variable while the other(s) are held constant for the purpose of discovering predictive and functional relationships between variables.
HN   Use ANALYSIS OF VARIANCE or more specific terms prior to 1985.
UF   Regression Analysis
     Regression Artifact
B   Statistical Analysis   1967
N   Linear Regression   1973
     Logistic Regression   2003
     Multiple Regression   1982
     Nonlinear Regression   1973
R   Analysis of Variance   1967
     Causal Analysis   1994
     Least Squares   1985
     ↓ Multivariate Analysis   1982
     ↓ Statistical Correlation   1967

Statistical Reliability   1973
PN   2691   **SC**   49600
HN   In 1973, this term was created to replace the discontinued term RELIABILITY (STATISTICAL). In 2000, RELIABILITY (STATISTICAL) was removed from all records containing it, and replaced with STATISTICAL RELIABILITY.
UF   Reliability (Statistical)

Statistical Reliability — (cont'd)

B Statistical Analysis 1967
R Consistency (Measurement) 1973
  ↓ Experimentation 1967
  Interrater Reliability 1982
  ↓ Population (Statistics) 1973
  ↓ Prediction Errors 1973
  ↓ Sampling (Experimental) 1973
  Spearman Brown Test 1973
  Statistical Validity 1973

Statistical Rotation 1973

PN 79   SC 49610
UF Rotation Methods (Statistical)
B Factor Analysis 1967
N Oblique Rotation 1973
  ↓ Orthogonal Rotation 1973
R Factor Structure 1985

Statistical Sample Parameters 1973

PN 444   SC 49620
SN Quantities and qualities describing a statistical population.
B Statistical Samples 1973
N Sample Size 1997
R Binomial Distribution 1973
  Confidence Limits (Statistics) 1973
  Normal Distribution 1973
  Statistical Norms 1971

Statistical Samples 1973

PN 313   SC 49630
SN Portion of a population taken as representative of the whole population.
B Population (Statistics) 1973
N ↓ Statistical Sample Parameters 1973
R ↓ Sampling (Experimental) 1973

Statistical Significance 1973

PN 764   SC 49640
UF Significance (Statistical)
B Statistical Analysis 1967
R Chi Square Test 1973
  Confidence Limits (Statistics) 1973
  Effect Size (Statistical) 1985
  ↓ Factor Analysis 1967
  Goodness of Fit 1988
  ↓ Hypothesis Testing 1973
  Sign Test 1973
  ↓ Statistical Correlation 1967
  ↓ Statistical Measurement 1973
  Statistical Power 1991
  ↓ Statistical Tests 1973
  T Test 1973

Statistical Tables 1982

PN 137   SC 49647
SN Systematically organized displays of statistical values or distributions or summary data derived from statistical calculation. The table of critical values of the F distribution is an example of the first category, and a contingency table showing test score means as related to the variables of sex and age is an example of the second category.
R Statistical Data 1982
  ↓ Statistical Variables 1973

Statistical Tests 1973

PN 682   SC 49650
SN Specific mathematical techniques used to analyze data in order to assess the probability that a set of results could have occurred by chance and hence to test for the probable correctness of empirical hypotheses.

Statistical Tests — (cont'd)

UF Tests (Statistical)
B Statistical Analysis 1967
N ↓ Nonparametric Statistical Tests 1967
  ↓ Parametric Statistical Tests 1973
  Spearman Brown Test 1973
R Confidence Limits (Statistics) 1973
  ↓ Statistical Measurement 1973
  Statistical Power 1991
  Statistical Significance 1973

Statistical Validity 1973

PN 13777   SC 49660
HN In 2000, this term became the postable counterpart for the terms FACTORIAL VALIDITY and PREDICTIVE VALIDITY. These terms were removed from all records containing them and replaced with STATISTICAL VALIDITY.
UF Factorial Validity
  Predictive Validity
  Validity (Statistical)
B Statistical Analysis 1967
R Consistency (Measurement) 1973
  ↓ Experimentation 1967
  ↓ Prediction Errors 1973
  ↓ Statistical Correlation 1967
  Statistical Reliability 1973
  ↓ Statistical Variables 1973

Statistical Variables 1973

PN 894   SC 49670
N Dependent Variables 1973
  Independent Variables 1973
R ↓ Experimental Design 1967
  ↓ Experimentation 1967
  ↓ Population (Statistics) 1973
  ↓ Prediction Errors 1973
  ↓ Sampling (Experimental) 1973
  ↓ Statistical Analysis 1967
  ↓ Statistical Correlation 1967
  Statistical Data 1982
  Statistical Tables 1982
  Statistical Validity 1973

Statistical Weighting 1985

PN 203   SC 49671
SN A coefficient or mathematical constant that determines the relative contribution of a statistic to a total numeric value. Also, the process of assigning such statistical weights.
UF Weight (Statistics)
B Statistical Analysis 1967
R Item Analysis (Statistical) 1973
  ↓ Scoring (Testing) 1973
  Test Interpretation 1985
  ↓ Test Scores 1967

Statistics 1982

PN 1016   SC 49672
SN Subdiscipline of mathematics that deals with the gathering and evaluation of numerical data for making inferences from the data.
B Mathematics 1982

Status 1967

PN 2244   SC 49675
SN General term used to indicate relative social position or rank.
B Social Processes 1967
N Occupational Status 1978
  ↓ Socioeconomic Status 1967
R Authority 1967
  ↓ Dominance 1967

Status — (cont'd)

Fame 1985
Reputation 1997
↓ Social Structure 1967

Stealing

Use Theft

Stelazine

Use Trifluoperazine

Stellate Ganglion

Use Autonomic Ganglia

Stepchildren 1973

PN 299   SC 49720
B Family Members 1973
R ↓ Family Structure 1973
  Stepfamily 1991

Stepfamily 1991

PN 399   SC 49725
B Family 1967
  Family Structure 1973
R Family of Origin 1991
  Remarriage 1985
  Stepchildren 1973
  Stepparents 1973

Stepparents 1973

PN 528   SC 49730
B Parents 1967
R ↓ Family Structure 1973
  Stepfamily 1991

Stereopsis

Use Stereoscopic Vision

Stereoscopic Presentation 1973

PN 206   SC 49750
SN Simultaneous presentation of separate two-dimensional pictures (taken from slightly different angles) to each eye of one subject, resulting in a perception of depth.
B Stimulus Presentation Methods 1973
  Visual Stimulation 1973

Stereoscopic Vision 1973

PN 898   SC 49760
UF Stereopsis
B Depth Perception 1967
  Visual Perception 1967

Stereotaxic Atlas 1973

PN 1030   SC 49770
UF Brain Mapping
  Brain Maps
R ↓ Stereotaxic Techniques 1973

Stereotaxic Techniques 1973

PN 162   SC 49780
SN Methods, procedures, or apparatus which permit precise spatial positioning of electrodes or other probes into the brain for experimental or surgical purposes.
B Surgery 1971
N ↓ Brain Stimulation 1967
  Chemical Brain Stimulation 1973
  Electrical Brain Stimulation 1973

Stereotaxic Techniques — (cont'd)
- R   Afferent Stimulation 1973
- ↓ Nervous System 1967
-   Stereotaxic Atlas 1973

Stereotyped Attitudes 1967
PN 6127   SC 49790
SN Oversimplified, rigid, often negative preconceptions of individuals, groups, or social classes who identify with a particular ethnicity, gender, religion, sexual orientation, or other group. Compare STIGMA.
- UF Stereotyping
- B   Attitudes 1967
- R   Ageism 2003
- ↓ Disabled (Attitudes Toward) 1997
- ↓ Discrimination 1967
-   Homosexuality (Attitudes Toward) 1982
-   Labeling 1978
- ↓ Prejudice 1967
- ↓ Racial and Ethnic Attitudes 1982
- ↓ Sex Role Attitudes 1978
-   Sexism 1988
- ↓ Social Discrimination 1982
- ↓ Social Perception 1967
-   Stigma 1991

Stereotyped Behavior 1973
PN 2430   SC 49795
SN Highly repetitive, often non-functional, rhythmic behaviors that occur at a high frequency. Used for animal or disordered human populations.
- B   Behavior 1967
- R   ↓ Animal Ethology 1967
- ↓ Pervasive Developmental Disorders 2001
- ↓ Self Stimulation 1967
- ↓ Symptoms 1967

Stereotyping
Use Stereotyped Attitudes

Sterility 1973
PN 50   SC 49810
- B   Infertility 1973
- R   ↓ Gynecological Disorders 1973
-   Hermaphroditism 1973
- ↓ Hypogonadism 1973
- ↓ Male Genital Disorders 1973
-   Testicular Feminization Syndrome 1973
-   Turners Syndrome 1973

Sterilization (Sex) 1973
PN 137   SC 49820
- N   ↓ Castration 1967
-   Hysterectomy 1973
-   Tubal Ligation 1973
-   Vasectomy 1973
- R   ↓ Birth Control 1971
-   Eugenics 1973
- ↓ Family Planning 1973

Steroids 1973
PN 1001   SC 49830
- B   Drugs 1967
- N   Cholesterol 1973
- ↓ Corticosteroids 1973
-   Progesterone 1973
- R   ↓ Anti Inflammatory Drugs 1982
-   Antiandrogens 1982
-   Antiestrogens 1982
-   Antineoplastic Drugs 1982
- ↓ Hormones 1967
- ↓ Lipids 1973

Sticklebacks 1973
PN 208   SC 49840
- B   Fishes 1967

Stigma 1991
PN 1124   SC 49843
SN Perception of a distinguishing personal characteristic or condition, e.g., a physical or psychological disorder, race, or religion, which carries or is believed to carry a physical, psychological, or social disadvantage.
- UF Social Stigma
- R   ↓ Attitudes 1967
-   Labeling 1978
- ↓ Prejudice 1967
-   Social Acceptance 1967
-   Social Approval 1967
- ↓ Social Discrimination 1982
- ↓ Social Perception 1967
-   Stereotyped Attitudes 1967

Stimulants of CNS
Use CNS Stimulating Drugs

Stimulation 1967
PN 1481   SC 49850
- N   Afferent Stimulation 1973
-   Aversive Stimulation 1973
- ↓ Brain Stimulation 1967
- ↓ Electrical Stimulation 1973
- ↓ Perceptual Stimulation 1973
- ↓ Self Stimulation 1967
-   Subliminal Stimulation 1985
-   Verbal Stimuli 1982
- R   ↓ Biofeedback 1973
-   Conditioned Stimulus 1973
- ↓ Conditioning 1967
- ↓ Feedback 1967
-   Stimulus Ambiguity 1967
-   Stimulus Change 1973
-   Stimulus Control 1967
- ↓ Stimulus Deprivation 1973
-   Stimulus Discrimination 1973
-   Stimulus Generalization 1967
- ↓ Stimulus Parameters 1967
- ↓ Stimulus Presentation Methods 1973
-   Unconditioned Stimulus 1973

Stimulation Seeking (Personality)
Use Sensation Seeking

Stimulators (Apparatus) 1973
PN 57   SC 49860
- B   Apparatus 1967
- N   Shock Units 1973
- R   Electrodes 1967
-   Vibrators (Apparatus) 1973

Stimulus (Unconditioned)
Use Unconditioned Stimulus

Stimulus Ambiguity 1967
PN 1008   SC 49890
- UF Ambiguity (Stimulus)
- R   ↓ Stimulation 1967
-   Stimulus Generalization 1967
-   Stroop Effect 1988

Stimulus Attenuation 1973
PN 143   SC 49900

Stimulus Attenuation — (cont'd)
SN Controlled, progressive, or otherwise manipulated reduction in the intensity, clarity, salience, or other such distinguishing qualities of a stimulus.
- B   Stimulus Parameters 1967
- R   Fading (Conditioning) 1982

Stimulus Change 1973
PN 584   SC 49910
- R   ↓ Stimulation 1967

Stimulus Complexity 1971
PN 1878   SC 49920
- UF Complexity (Stimulus)
- B   Stimulus Parameters 1967

Stimulus Control 1967
PN 1459   SC 49930
SN Change in the probability of occurrence of a conditioned response as a direct function of the onset, offset, or changes in a conditioned stimulus.
- R   ↓ Discrimination Learning 1982
- ↓ Stimulation 1967
-   Stimulus Generalization 1967

Stimulus Deprivation 1973
PN 173   SC 49940
- UF Restricted Environmental Stimulation
- B   Deprivation 1967
- N   Food Deprivation 1967
-   Sensory Deprivation 1967
- ↓ Social Deprivation 1973
- ↓ Social Isolation 1967
-   Water Deprivation 1967
- R   ↓ Stimulation 1967

Stimulus Discrimination 1973
PN 2341   SC 49950
- B   Discrimination 1967
- R   Behavioral Contrast 1978
- ↓ Discrimination Learning 1982
-   Fading (Conditioning) 1982
- ↓ Stimulation 1967
-   Stimulus Generalization 1967

Stimulus Duration 1973
PN 2840   SC 49960
- UF Duration (Stimulus)
-   Exposure Time (Stimulus)
- B   Stimulus Parameters 1967

Stimulus Frequency 1973
PN 1497   SC 49980
SN Number of stimulus presentations within a given trial or per unit time.
- UF Frequency (Stimulus)
- B   Stimulus Parameters 1967
- R   Temporal Frequency 1985

Stimulus Generalization 1967
PN 900   SC 49990
SN Responding in a similar manner to different stimuli which have some common physical property. Also known as primary generalization. Compare GENERALIZATION (LEARNING) and RESPONSE GENERALIZATION.
- UF Generalization (Stimulus)
- B   Generalization (Learning) 1982
- R   ↓ Stimulation 1967
-   Stimulus Ambiguity 1967
-   Stimulus Control 1967
-   Stimulus Discrimination 1973

Stimulus Intensity 1967
PN 3405   SC 50000
  UF   Intensity (Stimulus)
      Signal Intensity
  B   Stimulus Parameters 1967
  R   Luminance 1982

Stimulus Intervals 1973
PN 1359   SC 50010
SN Temporal intervals between stimuli presented in any sensory modality. Use INTERSTIMULUS INTERVAL in conditioning contexts.
  B   Stimulus Parameters 1967
  N   Interstimulus Interval 1967
      Intertrial Interval 1973
  R   Reinforcement Delay 1985

Stimulus Novelty 1973
PN 2334   SC 50020
SN New, unexpected, or unfamiliar quality of a stimulus.
  UF   Novel Stimuli
  B   Stimulus Parameters 1967
  R   Neophobia 1985

Stimulus Offset 1985
PN 90   SC 50023
  B   Stimulus Parameters 1967

Stimulus Onset 1982
PN 638   SC 50025
  B   Stimulus Parameters 1967

Stimulus Parameters 1967
PN 6878   SC 50030
SN Applied when quantifiable or descriptive characteristics of stimuli in a study are emphasized. Use a more specific term if possible.
  UF   Parameters (Stimulus)
  N   ↓ Size 1973
      Spatial Frequency 1982
      Stimulus Attenuation 1973
      Stimulus Complexity 1971
      Stimulus Duration 1973
      Stimulus Frequency 1973
      Stimulus Intensity 1967
      ↓ Stimulus Intervals 1973
      Stimulus Novelty 1973
      Stimulus Offset 1985
      Stimulus Onset 1982
      Stimulus Salience 1973
      Stimulus Similarity 1967
      Stimulus Variability 1973
      Temporal Frequency 1985
  R   Acoustics 1997
      ↓ Stimulation 1967

Stimulus Pattern
  Use Stimulus Variability

Stimulus Presentation Methods 1973
PN 2816   SC 50050
SN Methodological, procedural, or technical aspects of stimulus presentation. Use a more specific term if possible, e.g., VISUAL STIMULATION for visual stimulus presentation.
  B   Experimental Methods 1967
  N   Stereoscopic Presentation 1973
      Tachistoscopic Presentation 1973
  R   Pictorial Stimuli 1978
      ↓ Stimulation 1967
      Verbal Stimuli 1982

Stimulus Salience 1973
PN 1051   SC 50060
SN Relative prominence or distinctiveness of a stimulus.
  UF   Salience (Stimulus)
  B   Stimulus Parameters 1967
  R   Isolation Effect 1973

Stimulus Similarity 1967
PN 2395   SC 50070
SN Conceptual or physical resemblance of two or more stimuli.
  UF   Similarity (Stimulus)
  B   Stimulus Parameters 1967

Stimulus Variability 1973
PN 1635   SC 50080
  UF   Stimulus Pattern
      Variability (Stimulus)
  B   Stimulus Parameters 1967

Stipends
  Use Educational Financial Assistance

Stochastic Modeling 1973
PN 632   SC 50100
SN Statistical modeling for sequences of events whose probabilities are constantly changing.
  B   Simulation 1967
  N   Markov Chains 1973
  R   Chaos Theory 1997
      Information Theory 1967
      ↓ Mathematical Modeling 1973
      Time Series 1985

Stomach 1973
PN 151   SC 50120
  B   Gastrointestinal System 1973

Storytelling 1988
PN 1560   SC 50125
  B   Verbal Communication 1967
  R   Creative Writing 1994
      Folklore 1991
      Myths 1967
      Narratives 1997

Storytelling Technique
  Use Mutual Storytelling Technique

Strabismus 1973
PN 205   SC 50140
  UF   Crossed Eyes
  B   Eye Disorders 1973
  R   Amblyopia 1973
      Eye Convergence 1982

Strain Differences (Animal)
  Use Animal Strain Differences

Stranger Reactions 1988
PN 292   SC 50148
SN Emotional or behavioral responses to unfamiliar persons. Used for all age groups.
  UF   Fear of Strangers
      Xenophobia
  B   Interpersonal Interaction 1967
  R   Attachment Behavior 1985
      ↓ Emotional Responses 1967
      Familiarity 1967

Stranger Reactions — (cont'd)
      ↓ Fear 1967
      Separation Anxiety 1973
      ↓ Social Perception 1967

Strategies 1967
PN 8102   SC 50150
SN Methods, techniques, or tactics used in accomplishing a given goal or task.
  N   ↓ Learning Strategies 1991
  R   ↓ Cognitive Processes 1967
      Guessing 1973
      Heuristics 2003
      ↓ Learning 1967
      Note Taking 1991

Strategies (Learning)
  Use Learning Strategies

Strength (Physical)
  Use Physical Strength

Stress 1967
PN 21534   SC 50170
SN Refers to the emotional, psychological, or physical effects as well as the sources of agitation, strain, tension, or pressure. Compare DISTRESS. Used for both human and animal populations.
  N   Chronic Stress 2004
      Environmental Stress 1973
      Occupational Stress 1973
      Physiological Stress 1967
      Psychological Stress 1973
      Social Stress 1973
      Stress Reactions 1973
  R   Adjustment Disorders 1994
      ↓ Adrenal Cortex Hormones 1973
      ↓ Anxiety 1967
      Caregiver Burden 1994
      ↓ Crises 1971
      ↓ Deprivation 1967
      ↓ Disasters 1973
      Distress 1973
      ↓ Endurance 1973
      Family Crises 1973
      Identity Crisis 1973
      Natural Disasters 1973
      Organizational Crises 1973
      Stress Management 1985

Stress Management 1985
PN 2276   SC 50175
SN Techniques or services designed to alleviate the effects and/or causes of stress.
  B   Management 1967
  R   Anxiety Management 1997
      ↓ Behavior Modification 1973
      ↓ Cognitive Techniques 1985
      ↓ Stress 1967
      ↓ Treatment 1967

Stress Reactions 1973
PN 6755   SC 50180
SN Reactions to stressful events in everyday life or in experimental settings. Differentiate from POST-TRAUMATIC STRESS DISORDER which refers to reactions that seriously impair a person's functioning.
  UF   Crisis (Reactions to)
  B   Stress 1967
  R   Acute Stress Disorder 2003
      Adjustment Disorders 1994
      Cardiovascular Reactivity 1994

Stress Reactions — (cont'd)
    Coronary Prone Behavior 1982
    Posttraumatic Stress Disorder 1985
    Psychological Endurance 1973

Striate Cortex
Use Visual Cortex

Striatum 2003
PN 374   **SC** 50187
SN Part of the corpus striatum that includes the caudate nucleus and putamen. For STRIATE COR- TEX use VISUAL CORTEX.
HN This term was introduced in June 2003. Psyc- INFO records from the past 10 years were re-indexed with this term. The posting note reflects the number of records that were re-indexed.
UF Neostriatum
B   Basal Ganglia 1973
N   Caudate Nucleus 1973
     Putamen 1985
R   Globus Pallidus 1973

Strikes 1973
PN 139   **SC** 50190
R   Labor Management Relations 1967

Stroboscopic Movement
Use Apparent Movement

Stroke (Cerebrum)
Use Cerebrovascular Accidents

Strong Vocational Interest Blank 1967
PN 224   **SC** 50220
B   Occupational Interest Measures 1973

Stroop Color Word Test 1973
PN 452   **SC** 50250
B   Perceptual Measures 1973
R   Stroop Effect 1988

Stroop Effect 1988
PN 548   **SC** 50255
SN Interference in information or perceptual pro- cessing due to presentation of stimuli that are contra- dictory in different dimensions as a measure of cognitive control, e.g., stimulus word "red" printed in the color green.
R   Cognitive Discrimination 1973
    ↓ Interference (Learning) 1967
    ↓ Perceptual Discrimination 1973
     Stimulus Ambiguity 1967
     Stroop Color Word Test 1973

Structural Equation Modeling 1994
PN 849   **SC** 50257
B   Mathematical Modeling 1973
R   Causal Analysis 1994
    ↓ Factor Analysis 1967
     Factor Structure 1985

Structuralism 1973
PN 261   **SC** 50260
B   History of Psychology 1967
     Psychological Theories 2001

Structured Clinical Interview 2001
PN 59   **SC** 50263

Structured Clinical Interview — (cont'd)
UF SCID
B   Interview Schedules 2001
     Psychodiagnostic Interview 1973
R   ↓ Mental Disorders 1967
    ↓ Psychodiagnosis 1967
    ↓ Psychodiagnostic Typologies 1967
    ↓ Psychological Assessment 1997

Structured Overview
Use Advance Organizers

Strychnine 1973
PN 134   **SC** 50270
B   Alkaloids 1973
     Analeptic Drugs 1973

Student Activism 1973
PN 245   **SC** 50280
UF Activism (Student)
     Protest (Student)
     Student Protest
B   Activism 2003
R   Social Demonstrations 1973

Student Adjustment
Use School Adjustment

Student Admission Criteria 1973
PN 781   **SC** 50290
UF Admission Criteria (Student)
R   Academic Aptitude 1973
    ↓ Education 1967
    ↓ Entrance Examinations 1973

Student Attitudes 1967
PN 17027   **SC** 50300
CN Attitudes of, not toward, students.
B   Attitudes 1967
     Student Characteristics 1982
R   ↓ Education 1967
     School Phobia 1973
     School Refusal 1994

Student Attrition 1991
PN 170   **SC** 50301
SN Reduction in students enrolled in school as a result of transfers or dropouts.
B   School Enrollment 1973
R   School Attendance 1973
    ↓ School Dropouts 1967
     School Expulsion 1973
     School Leavers 1988
     School Retention 1994
    ↓ Students 1967

Student Characteristics 1982
PN 3802   **SC** 50303
SN Distinguishing traits or qualities of a student.
N   Student Attitudes 1967
R   ↓ Education 1967
    ↓ Students 1967

Student Personnel Services 1978
PN 1661   **SC** 50305
SN Services offered by schools, colleges, or univer- sities related to health, housing, employment, or other student concerns.
R   ↓ Counseling 1967
    ↓ Education 1967
     Educational Counseling 1967

Student Personnel Services — (cont'd)
    Educational Financial Assistance 1973
    ↓ Mental Health Services 1978
     Occupational Guidance 1967
     School Based Intervention 2003
     School Counseling 1982

Student Protest
Use Student Activism

Student Records 1978
PN 73   **SC** 50315
UF Academic Records
R   ↓ Education 1967

Student Teachers 1973
PN 1460   **SC** 50320
SN Students engaged in practice teaching under the supervision of a cooperating master teacher as partial fulfillment of an education degree.
B   Teachers 1967
R   Cooperating Teachers 1978
     Education Students 1982
     Preservice Teachers 1982

Student Teaching 1973
PN 305   **SC** 50330
SN College students teaching under the supervision of a regular teacher in a real school situation. Part of the graduation requirement for education majors.
UF Teaching Internship
B   Teacher Education 1967
R   Cooperating Teachers 1978

Students 1967
PN 7547   **SC** 50340
SN Persons attending school. Use a more specific term if possible.
N   Business Students 1973
     Classmates 1973
    ↓ College Students 1967
     Dental Students 1973
    ↓ Elementary School Students 1967
     Foreign Students 1973
     Graduate Students 1967
     High School Students 1967
     Junior High School Students 1971
     Kindergarten Students 1973
     Law Students 1978
     Medical Students 1967
     Postgraduate Students 1973
    ↓ Preschool Students 1982
     Reentry Students 1985
     Seminarians 1973
     Special Education Students 1973
     Transfer Students 1973
     Vocational School Students 1973
R   ↓ Education 1967
     School Retention 1994
     Student Attrition 1991
    ↓ Student Characteristics 1982

Students T Test
Use T Test

Studies (Followup)
Use Followup Studies

Studies (Longitudinal)
Use Longitudinal Studies

Study Habits 1973
PN 1824   SC 50380
  UF Study Skills
  R Advance Organizers 1985
    ↓ Education 1967
    Homework 1988
    ↓ Learning Strategies 1991
    Note Taking 1991
    Test Taking 1985
    Time Management 1994

Study Skills
  Use Study Habits

Stuttering 1967
PN 2422   SC 50390
HN In 1982, this term replaced the discontinued term STAMMERING. In 2000, STAMMERING was removed from all records containing it, and replaced with STUTTERING.
  UF Stammering
  B Speech Disorders 1967

Subconscious 1973
PN 99   SC 50410
  B Psychoanalytic Personality Factors 1973

Subcortical Lesions
  Use Brain Lesions

Subculture (Anthropological) 1973
PN 589   SC 50430
  UF Hippies
  B Culture (Anthropological) 1967
  R Cosmetic Techniques 2001
    Popular Culture 2003

Subcutaneous Injections 1973
PN 53   SC 50440
  B Injections 1973

Subjectivity 1994
PN 917   SC 50450
HN Use OBJECTIVITY to access references from 1973-1993.
  B Personality Traits 1967
  R Objectivity 1973

Sublimation 1973
PN 114   SC 50460
  B Defense Mechanisms 1967

Subliminal Perception 1973
PN 367   SC 50470
SN Perceptual response to a stimulus that is below the threshold for conscious detection.
  B Perception 1967
  R Subliminal Stimulation 1985

Subliminal Stimulation 1985
PN 324   SC 50475
SN Below-threshold stimulation.
  B Stimulation 1967
  R Subliminal Perception 1973

Submarines 1973
PN 44   SC 50480
  B Water Transportation 1973

Submissiveness
  Use Obedience

Submucous Plexus
  Use Autonomic Ganglia

Substance Abuse
  Use Drug Abuse

Substance Abuse Prevention
  Use Drug Abuse Prevention

Substance P 1985
PN 344   SC 50527
  B Neurokinins 1997
    Neurotransmitters 1985
    Peptides 1973

Substantia Nigra 1994
PN 219   SC 50530
HN Use MESENCEPHALON to access references from 1973-1993.
  B Mesencephalon 1973
  R ↓ Basal Ganglia 1973

Subtests 1973
PN 1352   SC 50540
  B Measurement 1967
  R ↓ Testing Methods 1967

Subtypes (Disorders) 2004
PN 336   SC 50545
SN Subtypes of a particular disorder, e.g., Bulimia Nervosa Purging Type or Non-purging Type.
HN This term was introduced in June 2004. Psyc-INFO records from the past 10 years were re-indexed with this term. The posting note reflects the number of records that were re-indexed.
  R Diagnostic and Statistical Manual 1994
    ↓ Disorders 1967
    ↓ Psychodiagnostic Typologies 1967

Suburban Environments 1967
PN 637   SC 50550
  B Social Environments 1973

Subvocalization 1973
PN 97   SC 50555
SN Covert speech behavior which involves movement of the tongue, mouth, and larynx without producing audible sounds.
  B Vocalization 1967
  R Self Talk 1988

Success
  Use Achievement

Successive Contrast
  Use Afterimage

Succinylcholine 1973
PN 13   SC 50580
  B Muscle Relaxing Drugs 1973
  R ↓ Choline 1973

Sucking 1978
PN 433   SC 50585
  B Motor Processes 1967

Sucking — (cont'd)
  R Animal Drinking Behavior 1973
    Animal Feeding Behavior 1973
    ↓ Drinking Behavior 1978
    Food Intake 1967
    Weaning 1973

Sudden Infant Death 1982
PN 212   SC 50587
SN Unexpected death of an apparently healthy infant during sleep.
  UF Crib Death
  R ↓ Apnea 1973
    ↓ Death and Dying 1967
    Sleep Apnea 1991
    ↓ Syndromes 1973

Suffering 1973
PN 530   SC 50590
  B Emotional States 1973
  R Distress 1973
    Grief 1973
    ↓ Pain 1967
    Torture 1988

Suffocation
  Use Anoxia

Sugars 1973
PN 1023   SC 50600
  B Carbohydrates 1973
  N ↓ Glucose 1973
  R Saccharin 1973

Suggestibility 1967
PN 979   SC 50610
  B Consciousness Disturbances 1973
    Personality Traits 1967
  R Catalepsy 1973
    False Memory 1997
    ↓ Hysteria 1967
    ↓ Interpersonal Influences 1967
    Posthypnotic Suggestions 1994

Suicidal Ideation 1991
PN 1865   SC 50605
SN Thoughts of or an unusual preoccupation with suicide.
  B Ideation 1973
  R Attempted Suicide 1973
    ↓ Suicide 1967

Suicide 1967
PN 9657   SC 50620
  B Self Destructive Behavior 1985
  N Assisted Suicide 1997
  R Attempted Suicide 1973
    ↓ Death and Dying 1967
    ↓ Mental Disorders 1967
    Psychological Autopsy 1988
    Suicidal Ideation 1991
    Suicide Prevention 1973

Suicide (Attempted)
  Use Attempted Suicide

Suicide Prevention 1973
PN 1499   SC 50640
  B Crisis Intervention 1973
    Prevention 1973
  R Attempted Suicide 1973

Suicide Prevention — (cont'd)
↓ Suicide 1967
Suicide Prevention Centers 1973

Suicide Prevention Centers 1973
PN 102   SC 50650
B   Community Facilities 1973
     Crisis Intervention Services 1973
     Mental Health Programs 1973
R   Community Mental Health Centers 1973
     Hot Line Services 1973
     ↓ Prevention 1973
     Suicide Prevention 1973

Sulpiride 1973
PN 444   SC 50660
B   Antidepressant Drugs 1971
     Antiemetic Drugs 1973
     Dopamine Antagonists 1982
     Neuroleptic Drugs 1973

Summer Camps (Recreation) 1973
PN 154   SC 50670
UF Day Camps (Recreation)
     Recreational Day Camps
B   Recreation 1967
R   Camping 1973
     Vacationing 1973

Superego 1973
PN 448   SC 50690
B   Psychoanalytic Personality Factors 1973
N   Conscience 1967

Superintendents (School)
Use School Superintendents

Superior Colliculus 1973
PN 624   SC 50700
B   Mesencephalon 1973

Superiority (Emotional)
Use Emotional Superiority

Superstitions 1973
PN 176   SC 50720
B   Social Influences 1967
R   Astrology 1973
     ↓ Attitudes 1967
     Irrational Beliefs 1982
     ↓ Parapsychological Phenomena 1973
     ↓ Religious Beliefs 1973
     Taboos 1973

Supervising Teachers
Use Cooperating Teachers

Supervision (Professional)
Use Professional Supervision

Supervisor Employee Interaction 1997
PN 754   SC 50729
UF Employee Supervisor Interaction
     Manager Employee Interaction
B   Employee Interaction 1988
R   Groupware 2003
     ↓ Human Resource Management 2003
     Labor Management Relations 1967

Supervisor Employee Interaction — (cont'd)
↓ Management Methods 1973
↓ Management Personnel 1973
Mentor 1985
Psychological Contracts 2003

Supervisors
Use Management Personnel

Supply and Demand 2004
PN 13   SC 50735
HN This term was introduced in June 2004. Psyc-INFO records from the past 10 years were re-indexed with this term. The posting note reflects the number of records that were re-indexed.
R   ↓ Consumer Behavior 1967
     ↓ Economics 1985

Support Groups 1991
PN 1771   SC 50740
SN Groups, organizations, or institutions providing social and emotional support to an individual. Compare SOCIAL NETWORKS and SELF HELP TECHNIQUES.
HN Consider SOCIAL SUPPORT NETWORKS to access references from 1982-1990.
N   ↓ Twelve Step Programs 1997
R   ↓ Community Services 1967
     ↓ Counseling 1967
     Employee Assistance Programs 1985
     Group Counseling 1973
     ↓ Group Psychotherapy 1967
     ↓ Mental Health Services 1978
     Outreach Programs 1997
     ↓ Rehabilitation 1967
     ↓ Self Help Techniques 1982
     Social Networks 1994
     ↓ Social Services 1982
     Social Support 2004

Supported Employment 1994
PN 361   SC 50745
SN Competitive employment in an integrated setting for persons with disabilities who require ongoing support to perform their jobs.
B   Vocational Rehabilitation 1967
R   Community Mental Health Services 1978
     Disabled Personnel 1997
     Employability 1973
     ↓ Employee Skills 1973
     ↓ Employment Status 1982
     ↓ Human Resource Management 2003
     Independent Living Programs 1991
     Sheltered Workshops 1967
     Work Adjustment Training 1991

Supportive Psychotherapy 1997
PN 156   SC 50750
SN Psychotherapy aimed at supporting or reinforcing strengths and coping mechanisms, rather than interpreting or uncovering deeper psychological conflicts. May entail guidance, reassurance, advice, encouragement, and assistance.
HN Use PSYCHOTHERAPY to access references from 1973-1996.
B   Psychotherapy 1967
R   Expressive Psychotherapy 1973

Suppression (Conditioned)
Use Conditioned Suppression

Suppression (Defense Mechanism) 1973
PN 198   SC 50770
B   Defense Mechanisms 1967
R   Forgetting 1973
     Repression (Defense Mechanism) 1967

Surgeons 1973
PN 162   SC 50780
UF Neurosurgeons
B   Physicians 1967
R   Gynecologists 1973
     Neurologists 1973
     Obstetricians 1978
     Pathologists 1973

Surgery 1971
PN 2495   SC 50790
UF Operation (Surgery)
B   Medical Sciences 1967
     Physical Treatment Methods 1973
N   ↓ Amputation 1973
     Circumcision 2001
     Cochlear Implants 1994
     Colostomy 1973
     Dental Surgery 1973
     ↓ Endocrine Gland Surgery 1973
     Heart Surgery 1973
     Hysterectomy 1973
     Induced Abortion 1971
     ↓ Neurosurgery 1973
     Organ Transplantation 1973
     Plastic Surgery 1973
     Sex Change 1988
     ↓ Stereotaxic Techniques 1973
     Vasectomy 1973
R   Afferent Stimulation 1973
     Biopsy 1973
     ↓ Lesions 1967
     Postsurgical Complications 1973

Surgical Complications
Use Postsurgical Complications

Surgical Patients 1973
PN 1853   SC 50810
B   Patients 1967

Surrogate Parents (Humans) 1973
PN 141   SC 50820
B   Parents 1967
R   Foster Parents 1973

Surveys 1967
PN 3070   SC 50830
B   Measurement 1967
N   Consumer Surveys 1973
     Mail Surveys 1994
     Telephone Surveys 1994
R   Data Collection 1982
     Likert Scales 1994
     ↓ Methodology 1967
     Needs Assessment 1985
     ↓ Questionnaires 1967

Survival Instinct
Use Self Preservation

Survivors 1994
PN 1812   SC 50850

Survivors — (cont'd)

SN Family members, significant others, or individuals surviving traumatic life events.
N   Holocaust Survivors 1988

Susceptibility (Disorders) 1973

PN 1948   **SC** 50880
SN Vulnerability to mental or physical disorders due to genetic, immunologic, or other characteristics. Consider also PREDISPOSITION.
UF   Vulnerability (Disorders)
R   At Risk Populations 1985
      Biological Markers 1991
      Coronary Prone Behavior 1982
      ↓ Disorders 1967
      ↓ Mental Disorders 1967
      ↓ Physical Disorders 1997
      Predisposition 1973
      Premorbidity 1978
      Risk Factors 2001

Susceptibility (Hypnotic)

Use   Hypnotic Susceptibility

Suspension (School)

Use   School Suspension

Suspicion 1973

PN 159   **SC** 50910
UF   Distrust
B   Emotional States 1973
R   Doubt 1973
      Uncertainty 1991

Sustained Attention 1997

PN 297   **SC** 50915
SN Focusing or attending to one or more stimuli over an extended period.
B   Attention 1967
N   Attention Span 1973
      Concentration 1982
      Vigilance 1967

Swallowing 1988

PN 131   **SC** 50920
B   Motor Processes 1967
R   Digestion 1973
      Dysphagia 2003
      ↓ Ingestion 2001

Sweat 1973

PN 40   **SC** 50930
UF   Perspiration
B   Body Fluids 1973
R   Sweating 1973

Sweating 1973

PN 86   **SC** 50940
B   Secretion (Gland) 1973
R   ↓ Skin Disorders 1973
      Sweat 1973

Sweetness

Use   Taste Perception

Swimming 1973

PN 767   **SC** 50970
B   Motor Processes 1967
      Recreation 1967
      Sports 1967

Syllables 1973

PN 1087   **SC** 50990
B   Phonology 1973
R   Consonants 1973
      Phonetics 1967
      Vowels 1973

Syllogistic Reasoning

Use   Inductive Deductive Reasoning

Symbiosis (Biological)

Use   Biological Symbiosis

Symbiotic Infantile Psychosis 1973

PN 23   **SC** 51020
B   Childhood Psychosis 1967
R   Childhood Schizophrenia 1967
      Early Infantile Autism 1973
      Mother Child Relations 1967

Symbolic Interactionism 1988

PN 343   **SC** 51025
SN Sociological theory that assumes that self concept is created through interpretation of symbolic gestures, words, actions, and appearances expressed by others during social interaction.
R   Role Taking 1982
      ↓ Self Concept 1967
      ↓ Social Interaction 1967
      Sociolinguistics 1985
      ↓ Sociology 1967

Symbolism 1967

PN 2875   **SC** 51030
R   ↓ Communication 1967
      ↓ Figurative Language 1985
      ↓ Language 1967
      Metaphor 1982
      ↓ Semiotics 1985

Sympathectomy 1973

PN 57   **SC** 51050
B   Neurosurgery 1973
R   ↓ Psychosurgery 1973

Sympathetic Nervous System 1973

PN 476   **SC** 51060
B   Autonomic Nervous System 1967
N   Baroreceptors 1973
R   ↓ Adrenergic Blocking Drugs 1973
      ↓ Adrenergic Drugs 1973
      ↓ Sympatholytic Drugs 1973
      ↓ Sympathomimetic Drugs 1973

Sympatholytic Drugs 1973

PN 26   **SC** 51080
UF   Antiadrenergic Drugs
B   Drugs 1967
N   Hydralazine 1973
      Reserpine 1967
R   ↓ Adrenergic Blocking Drugs 1973
      ↓ Sympathetic Nervous System 1973
      ↓ Sympathomimetic Drugs 1973

Sympathomimetic Amines 1973

PN 13   **SC** 51090
B   Amines 1973
      Sympathomimetic Drugs 1973
N   ↓ Amphetamine 1967
      ↓ Catecholamines 1973
      Dextroamphetamine 1973

Sympathomimetic Amines — (cont'd)

      Ephedrine 1973
      Methoxamine 1973
      Phenmetrazine 1973
      Tyramine 1973

Sympathomimetic Drugs 1973

PN 94   **SC** 51100
B   Drugs 1967
N   Fenfluramine 1973
      Isoproterenol 1973
      ↓ Sympathomimetic Amines 1973
R   ↓ Adrenergic Drugs 1973
      Prostaglandins 1982
      ↓ Sympathetic Nervous System 1973
      ↓ Sympatholytic Drugs 1973

Sympathy 1973

PN 183   **SC** 51110
B   Emotional States 1973

Symptom Checklists 1991

PN 327   **SC** 51124
B   Measurement 1967
R   ↓ Diagnosis 1967
      Health Complaints 1997
      Psychiatric Symptoms 1997
      ↓ Screening 1982
      ↓ Symptoms 1967

Symptom Prescription

Use   Paradoxical Techniques

Symptom Remission 1973

PN 159   **SC** 51130
B   Remission (Disorders) 1973
R   Psychiatric Symptoms 1997
      ↓ Symptoms 1967

Symptoms 1967

PN 18579   **SC** 51140
N   Acting Out 1967
      Anhedonia 1985
      Anoxia 1973
      Aphagia 1973
      Apraxia 1973
      ↓ Asthenia 1973
      Ataxia 1973
      Aura 1973
      Automatism 1973
      Body Rocking 1973
      Catalepsy 1973
      Catatonia 1973
      Coma 1973
      ↓ Convulsions 1967
      Delirium 1973
      Depersonalization 1973
      Distractibility 1973
      ↓ Dyskinesia 1973
      ↓ Dyspnea 1973
      Extrapyramidal Symptoms 1994
      Fatigue 1967
      ↓ Headache 1973
      Hematoma 1973
      ↓ Hemorrhage 1973
      Hyperglycemia 1985
      Hyperkinesis 1973
      Hyperphagia 1973
      Hyperthermia 1973
      Hyperventilation 1973
      Hypoglycemia 1973
      Hypothermia 1973
      Insomnia 1973

Symptoms — (cont'd)

Nausea 1973
Obesity 1973
↓ Pain 1967
Positive and Negative Symptoms 1997
Prodrome 2004
Pruritus 1973
Psychiatric Symptoms 1997
↓ Respiratory Distress 1973
Restlessness 1973
Scratching 1973
Shock 1967
↓ Spasms 1973
Syncope 1973
Tics 1973
Tremor 1973
↓ Underweight 1973
Vertigo 1973
Vomiting 1973
R   Akathisia 1991
↓ Behavior Disorders 1971
Binge Eating 1991
Capgras Syndrome 1985
↓ Digestive System Disorders 1973
↓ Disorders 1967
↓ Eating Disorders 1997
Fecal Incontinence 1973
Frigidity 1973
Health Complaints 1997
Hypersomnia 1994
Inflammation 2004
↓ Mental Disorders 1967
↓ Movement Disorders 1985
↓ Nervous System Disorders 1967
Parkinsonism 1994
↓ Physical Disorders 1997
Physiological Correlates 1967
Risk Factors 2001
Somatization 1994
↓ Somatoform Disorders 2001
Stereotyped Behavior 1973
Symptom Checklists 1991
Symptom Remission 1973
Urinary Incontinence 1973
Wandering Behavior 1991

Synapses 1973

PN 1830   **SC** 51150
B   Nerve Endings 1973
R   Neurotransmission 2003

Synaptic Transmission

Use Neurotransmission

Syncope 1973

PN 103   **SC** 51160
UF   Fainting
B   Blood Pressure Disorders 1973
Symptoms 1967
R   Shock 1967
Vertigo 1973

Syndromes 1973

PN 3922   **SC** 51170
N   Acquired Immune Deficiency Syndrome 1988
Addisons Disease 1973
Aspergers Syndrome 1991
Battered Child Syndrome 1973
Capgras Syndrome 1985
Chronic Fatigue Syndrome 1997
Creutzfeldt Jakob Syndrome 1994
Crying Cat Syndrome 1973
↓ Culture Bound Syndromes 2004

Syndromes — (cont'd)

Cushings Syndrome 1973
Delirium Tremens 1973
Downs Syndrome 1967
Fetal Alcohol Syndrome 1985
Fragile X Syndrome 1994
Irritable Bowel Syndrome 1991
Kleine Levin Syndrome 2001
Klinefelters Syndrome 1973
Menieres Disease 1973
Neuroleptic Malignant Syndrome 1988
↓ Organic Brain Syndromes 1973
Prader Willi Syndrome 1991
Premenstrual Syndrome 2003
Rett Syndrome 1994
↓ Senile Dementia 1973
Testicular Feminization Syndrome 1973
Turners Syndrome 1973
Wernickes Syndrome 1973
Williams Syndrome 2003
R   ↓ Disorders 1967
Epidemics 2001
↓ Mental Disorders 1967
Myofascial Pain 1991
↓ Physical Disorders 1997
Sudden Infant Death 1982

Synesthesia 2003

PN 27   **SC** 51172
SN Condition in which experiences that normally arouse sensation in one particular sensory modality also arouse sensation in another (e.g., colors may be experienced as odor).
HN This term was introduced in June 2003. Psyc-INFO records from the past 10 years were re-indexed with this term. The posting note reflects the number of records that were re-indexed.
B   Intersensory Processes 1978
R   ↓ Sensory System Disorders 2001

Synonyms 1973

PN 119   **SC** 51190
B   Semantics 1967
Vocabulary 1967
R   Words (Phonetic Units) 1967

Syntax 1971

PN 3596   **SC** 51220
SN Study and rules of the relation of morphemes to one another as expressions of ideas and as structural components of sentences; the study and science of sentence construction; and, the actual grouping and specific combination and relationship of words in a sentence. Compare GRAMMAR and SENTENCE STRUCTURE.
B   Grammar 1967
N   ↓ Form Classes (Language) 1973
R   Discourse Analysis 1997
Inflection 1973
Morphology (Language) 1973
↓ Phonology 1973
Phrases 1973
↓ Semantics 1967
Sentence Structure 1973
Transformational Generative Grammar 1973

Synthetic Speech 1973

PN 366   **SC** 51230
SN Sounds having similar characteristics and functional properties of natural speech but which are made by means other than natural vocalization mechanisms (e.g., computer-generated speech sounds).
B   Speech Processing (Mechanical) 1973

Syphilis 1973

PN 83   **SC** 51240
B   Sexually Transmitted Diseases 2003
N   Neurosyphilis 1973
R   ↓ Congenital Disorders 1973
General Paresis 1973

Systematic Desensitization Therapy 1973

PN 1592   **SC** 51250
UF   Desensitization (Systematic)
B   Behavior Therapy 1967
Exposure Therapy 1997
R   Progressive Relaxation Therapy 1978
Reciprocal Inhibition Therapy 1973
↓ Relaxation Therapy 1978

Systems 1967

PN 1017   **SC** 51270
SN Conceptually broad term referring to interrelated elements acting as or constituting a unified whole. Use a more specific term if possible.
N   ↓ Anatomical Systems 1973
Caste System 1973
↓ Communication Systems 1973
↓ Expert Systems 1991
Human Machine Systems 1997
↓ Information Systems 1991
Number Systems 1973
↓ Political Economic Systems 1973
R   ↓ Computer Software 1967
↓ Computers 1967
Human Machine Systems Design 1997
Person Environment Fit 1991
Systems Analysis 1973
↓ Systems Design 2003
Systems Theory 1988

Systems Analysis 1973

PN 651   **SC** 51260
B   Analysis 1967
R   Computer Programming 2001
Human Machine Systems 1997
Human Machine Systems Design 1997
↓ Systems 1967
↓ Systems Design 2003
Systems Theory 1988
Task Analysis 1967

Systems Design 2003

PN 26   **SC** 51262
SN A process of defining the hardware and software architecture, components, modules, interfaces, and data for a system to satisfy specified requirements.
HN This term was introduced in June 2003. Psyc-INFO records from the past 10 years were re-indexed with this term. The posting note reflects the number of records that were re-indexed.
N   Human Machine Systems Design 1997
R   Computer Programming 2001
↓ Systems 1967
Systems Analysis 1973

Systems Theory 1988

PN 3121   **SC** 51265
SN Examination of organizations, structures, or procedures from a macroscopic perspective that integrates constituent parts into a whole.
B   Theories 1967
R   Biopsychosocial Approach 1991
↓ Systems 1967
Systems Analysis 1973

Systolic Pressure 1973
PN 337   SC 51280
B   Blood Pressure 1967

Szondi Test 1973
PN 36   SC 51290
B   Projective Personality Measures 1973

T Groups
Use Human Relations Training

T Mazes 1973
PN 88   SC 51310
B   Mazes 1967

T Test 1973
PN 130   SC 51320
UF   Students T Test
B   Parametric Statistical Tests 1973
R   ↓ Central Tendency Measures 1973
     Statistical Significance 1973

Taboos 1973
PN 161   SC 51330
B   Social Influences 1967
R   Animism 1973
     Cannibalism 2003
     Ethnology 1967
     ↓ Rites of Passage 1973
     Superstitions 1973
     Transcultural Psychiatry 1973

Tachistoscopes 1973
PN 41   SC 51340
SN   Apparatus used in experimental studies for pre-
sentation of visual stimuli for controlled stimulus inter-
vals, intensities, and durations.
B   Apparatus 1967

Tachistoscopic Presentation 1973
PN 469   SC 51350
B   Stimulus Presentation Methods 1973
     Visual Stimulation 1973

Tachycardia 1973
PN 97   SC 51360
UF   Rapid Heart Rate
B   Arrhythmias (Heart) 1973
R   Hyperthyroidism 1973

Tactual Discrimination
Use Tactual Perception

Tactual Displays 1973
PN 103   SC 51380
SN   Materials or apparatus designed to present
information or patterns by means of touch or manipulation. Also, any information or patterns conveyed by
such means.
B   Displays 1967
     Tactual Stimulation 1973

Tactual Maps
Use Mobility Aids

Tactual Perception 1967
PN 2249   SC 51390
SN   Awareness of the qualities or characteristics of
objects, substances, or surfaces by means of touch.

Tactual Perception — (cont'd)
UF   Tactual Discrimination
     Touch
B   Cutaneous Sense 1967
N   Texture Perception 1982
     Vibrotactile Thresholds 1973
R   Anesthesia (Feeling) 1973
     Braille 1978
     Physical Contact 1982

Tactual Stimulation 1973
PN 1477   SC 51400
SN   Perceptual arousal or excitation of an organism
by means of touch.
B   Somesthetic Stimulation 1973
N   Massage 2001
     Tactual Displays 1973

Tailored Testing
Use Adaptive Testing

Talent
Use Ability

Talented
Use Gifted

Tantrums 1973
PN 82   SC 51440
B   Behavior Problems 1967
R   ↓ Anger 1967
     ↓ Emotional Control 1973

Tape Recorders 1973
PN 90   SC 51450
UF   Recorders (Tape)
B   Apparatus 1967
N   Videotape Recorders 1973

Tardiness 2003
PN 16   SC 51455
HN   This term was introduced in June 2003. Psyc-
INFO records from the past 10 years were re-indexed
with this term. The posting note reflects the number
of records that were re-indexed.
UF   Lateness
R   Employee Absenteeism 1973
     School Attendance 1973

Tardive Dyskinesia 1988
PN 1063   SC 51460
B   Dyskinesia 1973
R   ↓ Drug Therapy 1967
     ↓ Neuroleptic Drugs 1973
     ↓ Side Effects (Drug) 1973

Task Analysis 1967
PN 1738   SC 51470
B   Analysis 1967
R   Constant Time Delay 1997
     Job Analysis 1967
     Systems Analysis 1973
     Task Complexity 1973

Task Complexity 1973
PN 4595   SC 51480
UF   Complexity (Task)
     Task Difficulty
R   Task Analysis 1967

Task Difficulty
Use Task Complexity

Taste Aversion Conditioning
Use Aversion Conditioning

Taste Buds 1973
PN 214   SC 51500
B   Sense Organs 1973
     Sensory Neurons 1973
     Tongue 1973
R   Chemoreceptors 1973
     Taste Disorders 2001

Taste Discrimination
Use Taste Perception

Taste Disorders 2001
PN 3   SC 51515
SN   Disorders involving abnormal gustatory function
or perception.
B   Sense Organ Disorders 1973
R   Anosmia 1973
     Chemoreceptors 1973
     ↓ Sense Organs 1973
     ↓ Sensory Neurons 1973
     Taste Buds 1973
     ↓ Tongue 1973

Taste Perception 1967
PN 3688   SC 51520
UF   Bitterness
     Gustatory Perception
     Saltiness
     Sourness
     Sweetness
     Taste Discrimination
B   Perception 1967
R   ↓ Olfactory Perception 1967

Taste Stimulation 1967
PN 946   SC 51530
B   Perceptual Stimulation 1973

Tattoos
Use Cosmetic Techniques

Taurine 1982
PN 53   SC 51545
SN   Suspected neurotransmitter or membrane stabi-
lizer located in the posterior pituitary gland as well as
other mammalian tissue.
B   Acids 1973
R   Bile 1973

Taxation 1985
PN 198   SC 51547
R   Economy 1973
     Government 1967
     Income (Economic) 1973

Taxonomies 1973
PN 4136   SC 51550
UF   Classification Systems
     Typologies (General)
R   ↓ Psychodiagnostic Typologies 1967

Tay Sachs Disease 2003
PN 24   SC 51560

Tay Sachs Disease — (cont'd)

HN In June 2003, this term replaced the discontinued term AMAUROTIC FAMILIAL IDIOCY. AMAUROTIC FAMILIAL IDIOCY was removed from all records containing it and replaced with TAY SACHS DISEASE.

UF   Amaurotic Familial Idiocy
      Familial Idiocy (Amaurotic)
B   Brain Disorders   1967
      Genetic Disorders   1973
      Lipid Metabolism Disorders   1973
      Mental Retardation   1967
      Neonatal Disorders   1973

Taylor Manifest Anxiety Scale   1973

PN   34   **SC**   51570
B   Nonprojective Personality Measures   1973

Tea

Use   Beverages (Nonalcoholic)

Teacher Accreditation

Use   Accreditation (Education Personnel)

Teacher Aides   1973

PN   156   **SC**   51600
SN Paraprofessional school personnel who assist teachers in the instructional process or other classroom duties.

B   Educational Personnel   1973
      Paraprofessional Personnel   1973

Teacher Attitudes   1967

PN   10402   **SC**   51610
SN Attitudes of, not toward, teachers.

B   Attitudes   1967
      Teacher Characteristics   1973
N   ↓ Teacher Expectations   1978
R   Parent School Relationship   1982
      Teacher Personality   1973
      Teacher Student Interaction   1973

Teacher Characteristics   1973

PN   5003   **SC**   51615
UF   Teacher Effectiveness
N   ↓ Teacher Attitudes   1967
      Teacher Personality   1973
R   ↓ Education   1967
      Teacher Effectiveness Evaluation   1978
      Teacher Expectations   1978
      Teacher Student Interaction   1973
      ↓ Teachers   1967
      ↓ Teaching   1967

Teacher Education   1967

PN   4509   **SC**   51620
UF   Teacher Training
B   Education   1967
N   Inservice Teacher Education   1973
      Student Teaching   1973
R   Cooperating Teachers   1978
      Education Students   1982
      Practicum Supervision   1978
      Preservice Teachers   1982

Teacher Effectiveness

Use   Teacher Characteristics

Teacher Effectiveness Evaluation   1978

PN   1474   **SC**   51625

Teacher Effectiveness Evaluation — (cont'd)

SN Techniques, materials, or the procedural aspects of judging teachers' performance by peers, students, or others based on stated criteria.

HN Use PERSONNEL EVALUATION and TEACHERS (or a more specific term, e.g., COLLEGE TEACHERS) to access references from 1973-1977.

B   Personnel Evaluation   1973
R   Course Evaluation   1978
      Educational Quality   1997
      ↓ Teacher Characteristics   1973

Teacher Expectations   1978

PN   774   **SC**   51627
B   Expectations   1967
      Teacher Attitudes   1967
R   ↓ Teacher Characteristics   1973
      Teacher Student Interaction   1973

Teacher Personality   1973

PN   503   **SC**   51630
B   Teacher Characteristics   1973
R   ↓ Personality   1967
      ↓ Teacher Attitudes   1967
      Teacher Student Interaction   1973

Teacher Recruitment   1973

PN   55   **SC**   51640
SN Process of attracting candidates to the teaching profession or finding teachers to fill vacancies.

UF   Recruitment (Teachers)
B   Personnel Recruitment   1973

Teacher Student Interaction   1973

PN   5577   **SC**   51650
R   Classroom Discipline   1973
      ↓ Education   1967
      ↓ Teacher Attitudes   1967
      ↓ Teacher Characteristics   1973
      Teacher Expectations   1978
      Teacher Personality   1973

Teacher Tenure   1973

PN   143   **SC**   51670
UF   Tenure (Teacher)
B   Occupational Tenure   1973
R   ↓ Education   1967

Teacher Training

Use   Teacher Education

Teachers   1967

PN   9473   **SC**   51690
UF   Classroom Teachers
      Instructors
      Tutors
B   Educational Personnel   1973
N   College Teachers   1973
      Cooperating Teachers   1978
      Elementary School Teachers   1973
      High School Teachers   1973
      Junior High School Teachers   1973
      Middle School Teachers   2003
      Preschool Teachers   1985
      Preservice Teachers   1982
      Resource Teachers   1973
      Special Education Teachers   1973
      Student Teachers   1973
      Vocational Education Teachers   1988
R   ↓ Teacher Characteristics   1973

Teaching   1967

PN   5269   **SC**   51700
UF   Classroom Instruction
      Instruction
      Pedagogy
N   ↓ Instructional Media   1967
      ↓ Teaching Methods   1967
R   Bilingual Education   1967
      Cooperative Learning   1994
      Course Evaluation   1978
      ↓ Education   1967
      ↓ Teacher Characteristics   1973

Teaching Internship

Use   Student Teaching

Teaching Machines   1973

PN   67   **SC**   51730
SN Mechanical, electronic, or electrically controlled apparatus for the presentation of programed instructional material or texts for independent, self-paced education. Compare COMPUTER ASSISTED INSTRUCTION.

B   Instructional Media   1967
R   ↓ Computer Assisted Instruction   1973
      Programmed Instruction   2001

Teaching Methods   1967

PN   20401   **SC**   51740
B   Teaching   1967
N   Advance Organizers   1985
      ↓ Audiovisual Instruction   1973
      ↓ Computer Assisted Instruction   1973
      Directed Discussion Method   1973
      Discovery Teaching Method   1973
      Educational Field Trips   1973
      ↓ Experiential Learning   1997
      Group Instruction   1973
      Individualized Instruction   1973
      Lecture Method   1973
      Lesson Plans   1973
      Montessori Method   1973
      Nondirected Discussion Method   1973
      Open Classroom Method   1973
      Programmed Instruction   2001
      Team Teaching Method   1973
      ↓ Tutoring   1973
R   Constant Time Delay   1997
      Cooperative Learning   1994
      ↓ Education   1967
      Educational Therapy   1997
      Home Schooling   1994
      Initial Teaching Alphabet   1973
      Mastery Learning   1985
      ↓ Nontraditional Education   1982
      ↓ Prompting   1997
      Questioning   1982

Team Teaching Method   1973

PN   177   **SC**   51750
B   Teaching Methods   1967
R   Open Classroom Method   1973
      ↓ Teams   1988

Teams   1988

PN   2465   **SC**   51751
N   ↓ Work Teams   2001
R   Athletic Performance   1991
      Athletic Training   1991
      College Athletes   1994
      Cooperative Learning   1994
      ↓ Group Dynamics   1967
      Interdisciplinary Treatment Approach   1973

Teams — (cont'd)
  ↓ Management Methods   1973
  ↓ Personnel   1967
  ↓ Sports   1967
  Team Teaching Method   1973

Teasing   2003
PN   50   SC   51752
SN   To annoy, taunt, or joke with in a manner that is considered either petty, harassing, or playful.
HN   This term was introduced in June 2003. Psyc-INFO records from the past 10 years were re-indexed with this term. The posting note reflects the number of records that were re-indexed.
  B   Social Interaction   1967
  R   Bullying   2003
       Jokes   1973
       ↓ Peer Relations   1967
       Victimization   1973

Technical Education Teachers
  Use   Vocational Education Teachers

Technical Personnel   1978
PN   448   SC   51755
  B   Business and Industrial Personnel   1967
  N   Technical Service Personnel   1973
  R   ↓ Service Personnel   1991

Technical Schools   1973
PN   179   SC   51760
SN   Schools that teach specific job skills, usually at the postsecondary level, often emphasizing underlying sciences and supporting mathematics as well as skills, methods, materials, and processes of a specialized field of technology.
  UF   Vocational Schools
  B   Schools   1967

Technical Service Personnel   1973
PN   140   SC   51770
  UF   Repairmen
  B   Service Personnel   1991
       Technical Personnel   1978
  R   ↓ Blue Collar Workers   1973
       ↓ Business and Industrial Personnel   1967
       ↓ Nonprofessional Personnel   1982

Technology   1973
PN   4275   SC   51805
  N   Nuclear Technology   1985
  R   ↓ Electronic Communication   2001
       Groupware   2003
       Industrialization   1973
       ↓ Sciences   1967

Teenage Fathers
  Use   Adolescent Fathers

Teenage Mothers
  Use   Adolescent Mothers

Teenage Pregnancy
  Use   Adolescent Pregnancy

Teeth (Anatomy)   1973
PN   261   SC   51820
  B   Digestive System   1967
  R   Mouth (Anatomy)   1967

Teeth Grinding
  Use   Bruxism

Tegmentum   1991
PN   504   SC   51835
  UF   Ventral Tegmental Area
  B   Mesencephalon   1973
  N   Periaqueductal Gray   1985

Telecommunications Media   1973
PN   607   SC   51840
  B   Communications Media   1973
  N   Radio   1973
       Telephone Systems   1973
       ↓ Television   1967
       Television Advertising   1973
  R   Distance Education   2003
       Internet   2001
       Online Therapy   2003
       Telecommuting   2003
       Teleconferencing   1997
       Telemedicine   2003
       Telemetry   1973

Telecommuting   2003
PN   38   SC   51842
SN   Working at home via computer and telecommunications media.
HN   This term was introduced in June 2003. Psyc-INFO records from the past 10 years were re-indexed with this term. The posting note reflects the number of records that were re-indexed.
  UF   Work at Home
  R   Commuting (Travel)   1985
       ↓ Telecommunications Media   1973
       Teleconferencing   1997
       ↓ Working Conditions   1973

Teleconferencing   1997
PN   259   SC   51845
SN   Communication between persons remote from one another by means of a telecommunication system with audio and/or visual links.
  UF   Computer Conferencing
  R   Groupware   2003
       ↓ Telecommunications Media   1973
       Telecommuting   2003
       Telephone Systems   1973
       ↓ Television   1967

Telehealth
  Use   Telemedicine

Telekinesis
  Use   Psychokinesis

Telemedicine   2003
PN   145   SC   51858
SN   Provision of health care via various forms of telecommunications media.
HN   This term was introduced in June 2003. Psyc-INFO records from the past 10 years were re-indexed with this term. The posting note reflects the number of records that were re-indexed.
  UF   Telehealth
  B   Health Care Delivery   1978
  R   Computer Assisted Diagnosis   1973
       Computer Mediated Communication   2003
       ↓ Health Care Services   1978
       Health Knowledge   1994
       Internet   2001

Telemedicine — (cont'd)
  ↓ Telecommunications Media   1973
  ↓ Therapeutic Processes   1978

Telemetry   1973
PN   58   SC   51860
SN   Process of measuring and transmitting quantitative information and recording at a remote location.
  R   ↓ Telecommunications Media   1973

Telencephalon   1973
PN   421   SC   51870
  B   Forebrain   1985
  N   ↓ Basal Ganglia   1973
       ↓ Cerebral Cortex   1967

Telepathy   1973
PN   147   SC   51880
  B   Parapsychological Phenomena   1973
  R   ↓ Extrasensory Perception   1967

Telephone Hot Lines
  Use   Hot Line Services

Telephone Surveys   1994
PN   163   SC   51895
  B   Surveys   1967
  R   ↓ Consumer Research   1973
       Consumer Surveys   1973
       Mail Surveys   1994
       ↓ Methodology   1967
       ↓ Questionnaires   1967
       Telephone Systems   1973

Telephone Systems   1973
PN   879   SC   51900
  B   Communication Systems   1973
       Telecommunications Media   1973
  R   Teleconferencing   1997
       Telephone Surveys   1994

Teletherapy
  Use   Online Therapy

Televised Instruction   1973
PN   199   SC   51910
  B   Audiovisual Instruction   1973
  R   ↓ Educational Audiovisual Aids   1973
       Educational Television   1967

Television   1967
PN   2218   SC   51920
  B   Audiovisual Communications Media   1973
       Mass Media   1967
       Telecommunications Media   1973
  N   Closed Circuit Television   1973
       Educational Television   1967
       Television Advertising   1973
  R   ↓ Apparatus   1967
       ↓ News Media   1997
       Teleconferencing   1997
       Video Display Units   1985

Television Advertising   1973
PN   925   SC   51930
  UF   Commercials
  B   Advertising   1967
       Audiovisual Communications Media   1973
       Telecommunications Media   1973
       Television   1967
  R   Public Service Announcements   2004

Television Viewing 1973
PN 2332   SC 51940
B   Recreation 1967

Temperament
Use   Personality

Temperature (Body)
Use   Body Temperature

Temperature Effects 1967
PN 1417   SC 51990
UF   Thermal Factors
B   Environmental Effects 1973
N   Cold Effects 1973
    Heat Effects 1973
R   Atmospheric Conditions 1973
    Pollution 1973
    Seasonal Variations 1973
    Thermal Acclimatization 1973

Temperature Perception 1973
PN 373   SC 52000
B   Somesthetic Perception 1967
R   Somatosensory Disorders 2001

Tempo 1997
PN 135   SC 52005
R   ↓ Music 1967
    Music Perception 1997
    ↓ Rhythm 1991
    Speech Rate 1973
    Speech Rhythm 1973
    ↓ Time Perception 1967

Temporal Frequency 1985
PN 798   SC 52015
SN   Number of alternating cycles (e.g., patterns of vertical stripes of light and dark light) occurring during a specified time interval. Usually expressed in terms of cycles per second (Hz) as, for example, in sine or square wave visual displays.
B   Stimulus Parameters 1967
R   Spatial Frequency 1982
    Stimulus Frequency 1973
    ↓ Visual Displays 1973
    ↓ Visual Stimulation 1973

Temporal Lobe 1973
PN 3506   SC 52010
B   Cerebral Cortex 1967
N   Auditory Cortex 1967

Temporal Spatial Concept Scale
Use   Intelligence Measures

Temporomandibular Joint Syndrome
Use   Musculoskeletal Disorders

Temptation 1973
PN 143   SC 52030
B   Motivation 1967
R   ↓ Incentives 1967
    Peer Pressure 1994
    ↓ Resistance 1997
    Self Control 1973

Tendons 1973
PN 19   SC 52050

Tendons — (cont'd)
B   Musculoskeletal System 1973

Tennessee Self Concept Scale 1973
PN 50   SC 52060
B   Nonprojective Personality Measures 1973

Tennis 1973
PN 247   SC 52070
B   Recreation 1967
    Sports 1967

Tension Headache
Use   Muscle Contraction Headache

Tenure (Occupational)
Use   Occupational Tenure

Tenure (Teacher)
Use   Teacher Tenure

Teratogens 1988
PN 284   SC 52105
SN   Drugs or other agents that cause developmental malformations.
B   Hazardous Materials 1991
R   ↓ Congenital Disorders 1973
    ↓ Drugs 1967
    ↓ Poisons 1973
    ↓ Prenatal Development 1973
    Prenatal Exposure 1991
    Thalidomide 1973
    ↓ Toxicity 1973

Terminal Cancer 1973
PN 596   SC 52110
B   Neoplasms 1967
R   ↓ Death and Dying 1967
    Terminally Ill Patients 1973

Terminally Ill Patients 1973
PN 2152   SC 52120
UF   Dying Patients
B   Patients 1967
R   Advance Directives 1994
    Assisted Suicide 1997
    ↓ Death and Dying 1967
    Hospice 1982
    Life Sustaining Treatment 1997
    Palliative Care 1991
    Terminal Cancer 1973

Terminology 1991
PN 667   SC 52125
SN   Definitions, analysis, evaluation, or review of individual terms or nomenclature in any field.
N   Psychological Terminology 1973
R   Concepts 1967
    Scientific Communication 1973

Terminology (Psychological)
Use   Psychological Terminology

Territoriality 1967
PN 2032   SC 52140
SN   Behavioral patterns characteristic of defense or occupation of a territory. Used for both human and animal populations.
UF   Habitat Selection
B   Animal Ethology 1967
R   ↓ Animal Aggressive Behavior 1973

Territoriality — (cont'd)
    Animal Courtship Displays 1973
    Animal Dominance 1973
    Animal Homing 1991
    Animal Scent Marking 1985
    Boundaries (Psychological) 1997

Terrorism 1982
PN 980   SC 52150
SN   Violence or threats of violence in order to achieve political, economic, or social goals.
B   Antisocial Behavior 1971
    Violent Crime 2003
R   ↓ Crime 1967
    Hostages 1988
    Political Revolution 1973
    ↓ Radical Movements 1973
    ↓ Violence 1973

Test Administration 1973
PN 2093   SC 52180
SN   Instructions, timing, preparation of test materials, testing conditions, mode of presentation, and other factors involved in the administration of tests.
UF   Administration (Test)
B   Testing 1967
R   Group Testing 1973
    Individual Testing 1973
    ↓ Testing Methods 1967

Test Anxiety 1967
PN 2101   SC 52190
SN   Fear or tension in anticipation of formal examination frequently resulting in performance decrement and contributing to measurement error.
B   Anxiety 1967
R   ↓ Anxiety Disorders 1997
    Test Taking 1985

Test Bias 1985
PN 572   SC 52196
SN   Any significant differential performance on tests by different populations (e.g., males versus females) as a result of test characteristics which are irrelevant to the variable or construct being measured.
UF   Item Bias
B   Test Construction 1973
    Testing 1967
N   Cultural Test Bias 1973
R   Error of Measurement 1985
    Response Bias 1967

Test Bias (Cultural)
Use   Cultural Test Bias

Test Coaching 1997
PN 34   SC 52205
R   ↓ Practice 1967
    Test Taking 1985
    ↓ Testing 1967
    Testwiseness 1978
    ↓ Tutoring 1973

Test Construction 1973
PN 13111   SC 52210
SN   Planning, selection, writing, editing, and statistical analysis of test items, and design of instructions for test administration and scoring.
N   Content Analysis (Test) 1967
    Difficulty Level (Test) 1973
    Item Analysis (Test) 1967
    Item Content (Test) 1973

Test Construction — (cont'd)

   ↓ Test Bias   1985
      Test Forms   1988
      Test Items   1973
      Test Reliability   1973
      Test Standardization   1973
      Test Validity   1973
R   Adaptive Testing   1985
   ↓ Experimental Design   1967
   ↓ Measurement   1967

Test Difficulty
Use   Difficulty Level (Test)

Test Equating
Use   Score Equating

Test Forms   1988
PN   2251   **SC**   52214
SN   Includes different versions or schedules of a test.
B   Test Construction   1973
      Testing   1967
R   Item Content (Test)   1973

Test Interpretation   1985
PN   1166   **SC**   52215
SN   Judgment and explanation of the significance, meaning, application, or limitation of an assessment instrument and an obtained score or scores.
B   Testing   1967
R   Cultural Test Bias   1973
      Cutting Scores   1985
      Psychometrics   1967
   ↓ Scoring (Testing)   1973
      Statistical Weighting   1985
   ↓ Test Scores   1967
      Test Validity   1973

Test Items   1973
PN   1476   **SC**   52220
B   Test Construction   1973
      Testing   1967
R   Item Analysis (Statistical)   1973
      Item Analysis (Test)   1967
      Item Content (Test)   1973

Test Normalization
Use   Test Standardization

Test Norms   1973
PN   1587   **SC**   52240
UF   Norms (Test)
R   ↓ Measurement   1967
      Standardized Tests   1985

Test Reliability   1973
PN   15939   **SC**   52250
SN   Consistency, dependability, and reproducibility of test scores, expressed as a reliability coefficient.
UF   Internal Consistency
      Reliability (Test)
B   Test Construction   1973
      Testing   1967
R   Error of Measurement   1985
      Interrater Reliability   1982
      Test Standardization   1973

Test Scores   1967
PN   4572   **SC**   52260

Test Scores — (cont'd)
SN   Quantitative values or evaluations assigned to describe test performance of individuals. Compare SCORING (TESTING) and GRADING (EDUCATIONAL).
UF   Scores (Test)
N   Cutting Scores   1985

      Intelligence Quotient   1967
      Standard Scores   1985
R   Classical Test Theory   2003
      Error of Measurement   1985
      Item Response Theory   1985
   ↓ Measurement   1967
   ↓ Scoring (Testing)   1973
      Statistical Weighting   1985
      Test Interpretation   1985

Test Standardization   1973
PN   974   **SC**   52270
UF   Normalization (Test)
      Standardization (Test)
      Test Normalization
B   Test Construction   1973
      Testing   1967
R   Standardized Tests   1985
      Test Reliability   1973
      Test Validity   1973

Test Taking   1985
PN   807   **SC**   52275
SN   Strategies, attitudes, behaviors, or other factors associated with taking any type of test.
R   Cheating   1973
      Guessing   1973
      Response Bias   1967
      Study Habits   1973
      Test Anxiety   1967
      Test Coaching   1997
   ↓ Testing   1967
      Testwiseness   1978

Test Tube Babies
Use   Reproductive Technology

Test Validity   1973
PN   24094   **SC**   52280
SN   Extent to which a test measures what it was designed to measure.
UF   Concept Validity
      Concurrent Validity
      Construct Validity
      Content Validity
      Convergent Validity
      Criterion Related Validity
      Discriminant Validity
      Validity (Test)
B   Test Construction   1973
      Testing   1967
R   Test Interpretation   1985
      Test Standardization   1973

Testes   1973
PN   206   **SC**   52290
B   Gonads   1973
      Male Genitalia   1973

Testes Disorders
Use   Endocrine Sexual Disorders

Testicular Feminization Syndrome   1973
PN   9   **SC**   52310

Testicular Feminization Syndrome — (cont'd)
UF   Feminization Syndrome (Testicular)
B   Endocrine Sexual Disorders   1973
      Male Genital Disorders   1973
      Sex Linked Hereditary Disorders   1973
      Syndromes   1973
R   Hermaphroditism   1973
      Sterility   1973

Testimony (Expert)
Use   Expert Testimony

Testing   1967
PN   3617   **SC**   52330
SN   Administration of tests, and analysis and interpretation of test scores in order to measure differences between individuals or between test performances of the same individual on different occasions.
B   Measurement   1967
N   Classical Test Theory   2003
      Computer Assisted Testing   1988
      Content Analysis (Test)   1967
      Difficulty Level (Test)   1973
   ↓ Educational Measurement   1967
      Item Analysis (Test)   1967
      Item Content (Test)   1973
      Item Response Theory   1985
      Rating   1967
      Repeated Measures   1985
      Scaling (Testing)   1967
   ↓ Scoring (Testing)   1973
      Test Administration   1973
   ↓ Test Bias   1985
      Test Forms   1988
      Test Interpretation   1985
      Test Items   1973
      Test Reliability   1973
      Test Standardization   1973
      Test Validity   1973
R   ↓ Neuropsychological Assessment   1982
      Psychometrics   1967
      Test Coaching   1997
      Test Taking   1985
      Testwiseness   1978

Testing (Job Applicants)
Use   Job Applicant Screening

Testing Methods   1967
PN   1300   **SC**   52370
N   Adaptive Testing   1985
      Cloze Testing   1973
      Essay Testing   1973
      Forced Choice (Testing Method)   1967
      Multiple Choice (Testing Method)   1973
      Q Sort Testing Technique   1967
      Scaling (Testing)   1967
R   ↓ Measurement   1967
      Posttesting   1973
      Pretesting   1973
      Subtests   1973
      Test Administration   1973

Testosterone   1973
PN   2391   **SC**   52380
B   Androgens   1973

Tests
Use   Measurement

Tests (Achievement)
Use Achievement Measures

Tests (Aptitude)
Use Aptitude Measures

Tests (Intelligence)
Use Intelligence Measures

Tests (Personality)
Use Personality Measures

Tests (Statistical)
Use Statistical Tests

Testwiseness   1978
PN 116   **SC** 52415
SN High degree of sophistication in test-taking skills resulting in advantage over others with same knowledge or ability.
R ↓ Measurement 1967
    Test Coaching 1997
    Test Taking 1985
    ↓ Testing 1967

Tetrabenazine   1973
PN 45   **SC** 52430
B Neuroleptic Drugs 1973
    Serotonin Antagonists 1973

Tetrachoric Correlation   1973
PN 14   **SC** 52450
B Statistical Correlation 1967

Tetrahydrocannabinol   1973
PN 725   **SC** 52470
B Alcohols 1967
    Cannabinoids 1982
R ↓ Cannabis 1973
    ↓ Hallucinogenic Drugs 1967
    Hashish 1973
    Marijuana 2003

Text Structure   1982
PN 2018   **SC** 52473
SN Arrangement of sentence or paragraph segments, concepts, or physical format of reading material.
R Discourse Analysis 1997
    ↓ Prose 1973
    Reading Materials 1973
    Sentence Structure 1973
    ↓ Verbal Communication 1967

Textbooks   1978
PN 1037   **SC** 52475
SN Books focusing on principles of a specific subject and used as basis of instruction. Use BOOK to access references that are in themselves textbooks. Use TEXTBOOKS when textbooks are the object of discussion or study (e.g., analyses of best format for textbook chapters).
B Books 1973
    Instructional Media 1967
N Programmed Textbooks 2001
R Reading Materials 1973

Texture Perception   1982
PN 681   **SC** 52485

Texture Perception — (cont'd)
SN Perception of the surface characteristics (frequently patterned) or appearance of objects or substances, usually through the visual or haptic senses.
B Tactual Perception 1967
    Visual Perception 1967
R Pattern Discrimination 1967

Thalamic Nuclei   1973
PN 569   **SC** 52500
B Thalamus 1967

Thalamotomy   1973
PN 33   **SC** 52510
B Psychosurgery 1973

Thalamus   1967
PN 1394   **SC** 52520
B Diencephalon 1973
N Geniculate Bodies (Thalamus) 1973
    Thalamic Nuclei 1973

Thalidomide   1973
PN 19   **SC** 52530
B Amines 1973
    Hypnotic Drugs 1973
    Sedatives 1973
R ↓ Drug Induced Congenital Disorders 1973
    Prenatal Exposure 1991
    Teratogens 1988

Thanatology
Use Death Education

Thanatos
Use Death Instinct

Theatre   1973
PN 359   **SC** 52540
UF Stage Plays
B Arts 1973
N Drama 1973

Theft   1973
PN 553   **SC** 52550
UF Robbery
    Stealing
B Crime 1967
N Shoplifting 1973

Thematic Apperception Test   1967
PN 604   **SC** 52560
B Projective Personality Measures 1973

Theology   2003
PN 24   **SC** 52570
SN Study of religious beliefs, practices, and experience, as well as the relationship between God and the world.
HN Use RELIGION to access references from 1973 to June 2003.
B Humanities 2003
R God Concepts 1973
    Religion 1967
    ↓ Religious Affiliation 1973
    ↓ Religious Beliefs 1973
    ↓ Religious Literature 1973

Theophylline   1973
PN 93   **SC** 52580

Theophylline — (cont'd)
B Alkaloids 1973
    Diuretics 1973
    Enzyme Inhibitors 1985
    Heart Rate Affecting Drugs 1973
    Muscle Relaxing Drugs 1973
R ↓ Analeptic Drugs 1973
    Vasodilation 1973

Theoretical Interpretation   1988
PN 985   **SC** 52582
SN Description or analysis of any particular event, condition, or process from a specific psychological perspective. Usually used in conjunction with other index terms, e.g., humanistic psychology.
UF Psychological Interpretation
N Psychoanalytic Interpretation 1967
R ↓ Theories 1967

Theoretical Orientation   1982
PN 4054   **SC** 52584
SN Adherence to a particular school of thought, theoretical movement, or practice in a scientific or other area of knowledge.
UF Eclectic Psychology
    Professional Orientation
R ↓ Clinical Methods Training 1973
    ↓ Psychology Education 1978
    ↓ Psychotherapy 1967
    ↓ Social Sciences 1967
    ↓ Theories 1967
    ↓ Therapist Characteristics 1973

Theories   1967
PN 28581   **SC** 52590
SN Conceptually broad term referring to the systematic deductive derivation of secondary principles explaining observed phenomena. Use a more specific term if possible.
N Activity Theory 2003
    Chaos Theory 1997
    Classical Test Theory 2003
    Communication Theory 1973
    Constructivism 1994
    ↓ Darwinism 1973
    Decision Theory 2003
    Fuzzy Set Theory 1991
    Game Theory 1967
    Information Theory 1967
    Item Response Theory 1985
    Learning Theory 1967
    ↓ Psychological Theories 2001
    Systems Theory 1988
    Theories of Education 1973
    Theory of Evolution 1967
    Utility Theory 2004
R ↓ Experimentation 1967
    ↓ History of Psychology 1967
    ↓ Hypothesis Testing 1973
    ↓ Theoretical Interpretation 1988
    Theoretical Orientation 1982
    Theory Formulation 1973
    Theory Verification 1973

Theories of Education   1973
PN 808   **SC** 52587
SN Principles and supporting data concerning the educational process, with application for educational practice.
UF Educational Theory
B Theories 1967
R ↓ Education 1967

Theory Formulation 1973
PN 1630   SC 52600
SN Advancement of propositions and formulation of
hypotheses concerning description, explanation, or
interpretation of facts. Applies both to principles of
theory formulation and presentation of new theories.
R   Grounded Theory 2004
     ↓ Hypothesis Testing 1973
     ↓ Methodology 1967
     ↓ Theories 1967
     Theory Verification 1973

Theory of Evolution 1967
PN 3708   SC 52610
SN Theories explaining the origins of living organ-
isms and the process by which they evolved into their
present forms. For C. Darwin's theory of evolution,
use DARWINISM.
UF   Evolution (Theory of)
B   Theories 1967
R   ↓ Darwinism 1973
     Evolutionary Psychology 2003
     Mimicry (Biology) 2003
     Natural Selection 1997
     Self Preservation 1997

Theory of Mind 2001
PN 522   SC 52615
SN Ability to attribute mental states, cognitions, atti-
tudes, beliefs, and emotions to oneself and other
individuals. Used for both human and animal popula-
tions.
UF   Mind Blindness
R   ↓ Autism 1967
     ↓ Cognitive Development 1973
     ↓ Comprehension 1967
     Mind 1991
     ↓ Social Perception 1967

Theory Verification 1973
PN 1726   SC 52620
SN Process of proving or disproving theoretical
assumptions using empirical data. Applies both to
principles of theory testing and their applications.
UF   Verification (of Theories)
R   ↓ Hypothesis Testing 1973
     ↓ Methodology 1967
     ↓ Theories 1967
     Theory Formulation 1973

Therapeutic Abortion
Use Induced Abortion

Therapeutic Alliance 1994
PN 873   SC 52633
UF   Working Alliance
B   Psychotherapeutic Processes 1967
R   Psychotherapeutic Transference 1967
     ↓ Treatment 1967

Therapeutic Camps 1978
PN 151   SC 52635
SN Camps, usually for children, staffed by mental
health personnel and offering treatment programs as
well as outdoor activities fostering personal growth
and accomplishment.
UF   Camps (Therapeutic)
B   Treatment Facilities 1973
R   Recreation Therapy 1973
     Wilderness Experience 1991

Therapeutic Community 1967
PN 1613   SC 52640
SN Institutional or residential treatment setting
emphasizing social and environmental factors in ther-
apy and management and rehabilitation, usually of
psychiatric or drug rehabilitation patients.
B   Group Psychotherapy 1967
     Psychiatric Hospital Programs 1967
R   Milieu Therapy 1988
     Sociotherapy 1973

Therapeutic Devices (Medical)
Use Medical Therapeutic Devices

Therapeutic Environment 2001
PN 115   SC 52621
UF   Treatment Environment
B   Environment 1967
N   ↓ Facility Environment 1988
R   Milieu Therapy 1988
     ↓ Therapeutic Processes 1978
     ↓ Treatment Facilities 1973

Therapeutic Outcomes
Use Treatment Outcomes

Therapeutic Processes 1978
PN 7189   SC 52655
SN Experiential, attitudinal, emotional, or behavioral
phenomena occurring during the course of treatment.
Applies to the patient or therapist (i.e., nurse, doctor,
etc.) individually or to their interaction.
UF   Dentist Patient Interaction
     Nurse Patient Interaction
     Physician Patient Interaction
N   ↓ Psychotherapeutic Processes 1967
R   Client Education 1985
     Dual Relationships 2003
     Patient Abuse 1991
     Patient Violence 1994
     Professional Client Sexual Relations 1994
     Telemedicine 2003
     ↓ Therapeutic Environment 2001
     Therapist Selection 1994
     ↓ Treatment 1967
     ↓ Treatment Outcomes 1982
     Treatment Termination 1982

Therapeutic Social Clubs 1973
PN 81   SC 52660
SN Associations of persons, usually patients or
former patients, who engage in regular social activi-
ties stressing self-help and psychosocial rehabilita-
tion.
UF   Social Clubs (Therapeutic)
B   Psychosocial Rehabilitation 1973
R   ↓ Treatment 1967

Therapeutic Techniques (Psychotherapy)
Use Psychotherapeutic Techniques

Therapist Attitudes 1978
PN 1463   SC 52680
SN Attitudes of, not toward, therapists.
B   Health Personnel Attitudes 1985
     Therapist Characteristics 1973
N   Psychotherapist Attitudes 1973
R   Psychologist Attitudes 1991
     Therapist Role 1978

Therapist Characteristics 1973
PN 3803   SC 52690
SN Traits or qualities of therapists, including but not
limited to effectiveness, experience level, and per-
sonality.
UF   Therapist Effectiveness
     Therapist Experience
     Therapist Personality
N   ↓ Therapist Attitudes 1978
R   ↓ Cross Cultural Treatment 1994
     Theoretical Orientation 1982
     Therapist Selection 1994
     ↓ Therapists 1967

Therapist Effectiveness
Use Therapist Characteristics

Therapist Experience
Use Therapist Characteristics

Therapist Patient Interaction
Use Psychotherapeutic Processes

Therapist Patient Sexual Relations
Use Professional Client Sexual Relations

Therapist Personality
Use Therapist Characteristics

Therapist Role 1978
PN 1204   SC 52735
B   Roles 1967
R   Counselor Role 1973
     Psychotherapist Attitudes 1973
     ↓ Therapist Attitudes 1978

Therapist Selection 1994
PN 32   SC 52737
SN Motivational and judgmental processes involved
in the decision to choose a particular therapist or
counselor.
UF   Selection (Therapist)
R   Choice Behavior 1967
     ↓ Client Attitudes 1982
     Patient Selection 1997
     ↓ Therapeutic Processes 1978
     ↓ Therapist Characteristics 1973
     ↓ Therapists 1967
     ↓ Treatment 1967

Therapist Trainees 1973
PN 1009   SC 52740
UF   Psychotherapist Trainees
R   Counselor Trainees 1973
     ↓ Therapists 1967

Therapists 1967
PN 2331   SC 52750
SN Conceptually broad term referring to persons
trained in the treatment of problems including mental
disorders and behavior disorders. Use a more spe-
cific term if possible.
B   Professional Personnel 1978
N   Occupational Therapists 1973
     Physical Therapists 1973
     ↓ Psychotherapists 1973
     Speech Therapists 1973
R   Clinicians 1973
     ↓ Counselors 1967
     ↓ Health Personnel 1994

Therapists — (cont'd)
- ↓ Mental Health Personnel 1967
- ↓ Social Workers 1973
- ↓ Therapist Characteristics 1973
- Therapist Selection 1994
- Therapist Trainees 1973

Therapy
Use Treatment

Therapy (Drug)
Use Drug Therapy

Thermal Acclimatization 1973
PN 71 **SC** 52830
SN Adjustment to ambient temperature ranges that may be different from the organism's typical experience or that may be typical but cyclical in nature (e.g., seasonal changes in temperature). Compare THERMOREGULATION (BODY).
- **UF** Acclimatization (Thermal)
- **B** Adaptation 1967
- Physiology 1967
- **R** Atmospheric Conditions 1973
- Environmental Stress 1973
- Physiological Stress 1967
- ↓ Temperature Effects 1967
- Thermoregulation (Body) 1973

Thermal Factors
Use Temperature Effects

Thermoreceptors 1973
PN 51 **SC** 52840
- **B** Nerve Endings 1973
- Neural Receptors 1973
- Sensory Neurons 1973

Thermoregulation (Body) 1973
PN 652 **SC** 52850
SN Homeostatic behavioral or physiological responses that maintain body temperature within a viable range. Compare THERMAL ACCLIMATIZATION.
- **B** Body Temperature 1973
- **R** Hyperthermia 1973
- Hypothermia 1973
- ↓ Metabolism 1967
- Thermal Acclimatization 1973

Theta Rhythm 1973
PN 406 **SC** 52860
SN Electrically measured impulses or waves of low amplitude and a frequency of 4-7 cycles per second observable in the electroencephalogram during stage 1 sleep.
- **B** Electrical Activity 1967
- Electroencephalography 1967

Thigh 1973
PN 12 **SC** 52870
- **B** Anatomy 1967
- **R** Leg (Anatomy) 1973

Thinking 1967
PN 4742 **SC** 52880
SN Cognitive process involved in the manipulation of concepts and ideas.
- **B** Cognitive Processes 1967
- **N** ↓ Abstraction 1967

Thinking — (cont'd)
- Autistic Thinking 1973
- Divergent Thinking 1973
- Logical Thinking 1967
- Magical Thinking 1973
- ↓ Reasoning 1967
- **R** ↓ Intelligence 1967

Thiopental 1973
PN 33 **SC** 52890
- **UF** Pentothal
- **B** Barbiturates 1967
- General Anesthetics 1973
- Hypnotic Drugs 1973
- Sedatives 1973

Thioridazine 1973
PN 340 **SC** 52900
- **UF** Mellaril
- **B** Phenothiazine Derivatives 1973

Thiothixene 1973
PN 104 **SC** 52910
- **B** Tranquilizing Drugs 1967

Third World Countries
Use Developing Countries

Thirst 1967
PN 310 **SC** 52920
- **B** Motivation 1967
- **R** Animal Drinking Behavior 1973
- ↓ Drinking Behavior 1978
- ↓ Fluid Intake 1985
- Water Deprivation 1067

Thoracic Nerves
Use Spinal Nerves

Thorax 1973
PN 135 **SC** 52960
- **UF** Chest
- **B** Musculoskeletal System 1973
- Respiratory System 1073
- **R** Diaphragm (Anatomy) 1973

Thorazine
Use Chlorpromazine

Thought Content
Use Cognitions

Thought Control
Use Brainwashing

Thought Disturbances 1973
PN 1209 **SC** 52980
SN Disturbances of thinking that affect thought content, language, and/or communication marked by delusions, incoherence, and profound loosening of associations.
- **N** Autistic Thinking 1973
- Confabulation 1973
- Delusions 1967
- Fantasies (Thought Disturbances) 1967
- Fragmentation (Schizophrenia) 1973
- Judgment Disturbances 1973
- Magical Thinking 1973
- ↓ Memory Disorders 1973

Thought Disturbances — (cont'd)
- Obsessions 1967
- Perseveration 1967
- **R** Cognitive Impairment 2003
- Mental Confusion 1973
- ↓ Mental Disorders 1967
- Rumination (Cognitive Process) 2001

Thought Suppression 2003
PN 75 **SC** 52984
SN Active process of attempting not to think about a particular thought or event.
HN This term was introduced in June 2003. Psyc-INFO records from the past 10 years were re-indexed with this term. The posting note reflects the number of records that were re-indexed.
- **B** Cognitive Processes 1967
- **R** ↓ Cognitions 1985
- Rumination (Cognitive Process) 2001

Threat 1967
PN 2266 **SC** 52990
- **R** Bullying 2003
- Coercion 1994
- ↓ Harassment 2001
- ↓ Punishment 1967
- Threat Postures 1973

Threat Postures 1973
PN 114 **SC** 53000
- **B** Animal Aggressive Behavior 1973
- Animal Defensive Behavior 1982
- **R** Animal Predatory Behavior 1970
- Threat 1967

Threshold Determination 1973
PN 440 **SC** 53010
SN Methods and apparatus used in the measurement of both absolute and difference thresholds for any sensory modality.
- **R** ↓ Psychophysical Measurement 1967
- Signal Detection (Perception) 1967
- ↓ Thresholds 1967

Thresholds 1967
PN 1540 **SC** 53020
SN The minimal level (e.g., intensity) of stimulation, the minimal difference between any stimuli, or the minimal stimulus change that is perceptually detectable or to which a sensory receptor or other neuron will respond. Compare SIGNAL DETECTION (PERCEPTION).
- **UF** Differential Limen
- Limen
- **N** Auditory Thresholds 1973
- Olfactory Thresholds 1973
- Pain Thresholds 1973
- ↓ Sensory Adaptation 1967
- Vibrotactile Thresholds 1973
- ↓ Visual Thresholds 1973
- **R** ↓ Perceptual Measures 1973
- Threshold Determination 1973

Thromboses 1973
PN 68 **SC** 53040
- **B** Cardiovascular Disorders 1967
- **N** Coronary Thromboses 1973
- **R** Embolisms 1973

Thumb 1973
PN 32 **SC** 53050
- **B** Fingers (Anatomy) 1973

Thumbsucking 1973
PN 79   SC 53060
B   Habits   1967
R   ↓ Behavior Disorders   1971

Thymoleptic Drugs
Use   Tranquilizing Drugs

Thyroid Disorders 1973
PN 202   SC 53090
B   Endocrine Disorders   1973
N   Goiters   1973
     Hyperthyroidism   1973
     Hypothyroidism   1973
     Thyrotoxicosis   1973
R   ↓ Endocrine Sexual Disorders   1973
     ↓ Pituitary Disorders   1973

Thyroid Extract
Use   Thyroid Hormones

Thyroid Gland 1973
PN 118   SC 53110
B   Endocrine Glands   1973

Thyroid Hormones 1973
PN 364   SC 53120
HN   In 1997, this term replaced the discontinued term THYROID EXTRACT. In 2000, THYROID EXTRACT was removed from all records containing it, and replaced with THYROID HORMONES.
UF   Thyroid Extract
B   Hormones   1967
N   Thyroxine   1973
     Triiodothyronine   1973

Thyroid Stimulating Hormone
Use   Thyrotropin

Thyroidectomy 1973
PN 33   SC 53140
B   Endocrine Gland Surgery   1973

Thyrotoxicosis 1973
PN 35   SC 53150
B   Thyroid Disorders   1973
     Toxic Disorders   1973
R   ↓ Encephalopathies   1982
     Hyperthyroidism   1973
     Toxic Psychoses   1973

Thyrotropic Hormone
Use   Thyrotropin

Thyrotropin 1973
PN 832   SC 53170
UF   Thyroid Stimulating Hormone
     Thyrotropic Hormone
B   Neuropeptides   2003
     Pituitary Hormones   1973
R   Hypothyroidism   1973

Thyroxine 1973
PN 259   SC 53180
B   Thyroid Hormones   1973
R   Hypothyroidism   1973

Tic Doloureux
Use   Trigeminal Neuralgia

Tics 1973
PN 597   SC 53200
B   Movement Disorders   1985
     Symptoms   1967

Tigers
Use   Felids

Time 1967
PN 5640   SC 53210
SN   Continuum in which events or experiences are expressed in terms of the past, the present, and the future. For effects of time-of-day or season consider also SEASONAL VARIATIONS and BIOLOGICAL RHYTHMS or their associated terms.
N   Interresponse Time   1973
R   Future   1991
     Time Disorientation   1973
     Time Management   1994
     ↓ Time Perception   1967
     Time Perspective   1978
     Trends   1991

Time Disorientation 1973
PN 98   SC 53230
UF   Disorientation (Time)
B   Consciousness Disturbances   1973
R   ↓ Time   1967

Time Estimation 1967
PN 1131   SC 53240
SN   Estimation of duration or passage of time.
B   Estimation   1967
     Time Perception   1967
R   Time Management   1994

Time Limited Psychotherapy
Use   Brief Psychotherapy

Time Management 1994
PN 242   SC 51435
B   Management   1967
R   ↓ Learning Strategies   1991
     ↓ Self Management   1985
     Study Habits   1973
     ↓ Time   1967
     Time Estimation   1967
     Time On Task   1988
     ↓ Time Perception   1967
     Time Perspective   1978

Time On Task 1988
PN 628   SC 53244
SN   Period of active involvement in a learning or production activity.
R   ↓ Attention   1967
     ↓ Learning   1967
     Time Management   1994

Time Out 1985
PN 176   SC 53245
SN   Removal of the availability of gratification and reinforcement for any behavior following the occurrence of an undesired response. Has application in therapeutic, experimental, educational, and childrearing contexts.
B   Behavior Modification   1973
     Operant Conditioning   1967
R   Omission Training   1985

Time Perception 1967
PN 2237   SC 53250
SN   Perception of duration, simultaneity, or succession in the passage of time.
HN   Prior to the introduction of TIME PERSPECTIVE in 1978, TIME PERCEPTION was used for this concept also.
B   Perception   1967
N   Time Estimation   1967
R   Tempo   1997
     ↓ Time   1967
     Time Management   1994
     Time Perspective   1978

Time Perspective 1978
PN 1113   SC 53255
SN   Mental representation of temporal relationships or the capacity to remember events in their actual chronology. Also, one's outlook on the past, present, and/or future in relation to subjective qualities of time passage.
HN   To access references prior to 1978 use TIME PERCEPTION.
R   ↓ Perceptual Orientation   1973
     ↓ Time   1967
     Time Management   1994
     ↓ Time Perception   1967

Time Series 1985
PN 489   SC 53257
SN   A set of observational data ordered in time, typically with observations made at regular intervals.
B   Statistical Analysis   1967
R   Statistical Data   1982
     ↓ Stochastic Modeling   1973

Timers (Apparatus) 1973
PN 54   SC 53260
B   Apparatus   1967

Timidity 1973
PN 631   SC 53270
UF   Shyness
B   Personality Traits   1967

Tinnitus 1973
PN 215   SC 53280
B   Ear Disorders   1973

Tiredness
Use   Fatigue

Tissue Donation 1991
PN 322   SC 53295
SN   Donation of organs, blood, sperm, or other tissues for medical use.
UF   Blood Donation
     Organ Donation
     Sperm Donation
R   Blood Transfusion   1973
     Charitable Behavior   1973
     Neural Transplantation   1985
     Organ Transplantation   1973

Tissues (Body) 1973
PN 165   SC 53300
B   Anatomy   1967
N   Bone Marrow   1973
     ↓ Connective Tissues   1973
     ↓ Membranes   1973
     ↓ Nerve Tissues   1973
     Skin (Anatomy)   1967

Tissues (Body) — (cont'd)
- R   Histology 1973
- ↓ Muscles 1967

Toads 1973
PN 210   SC 53320
- B   Amphibia 1973
- R   Larvae 1973

Tobacco (Drug)
- Use Nicotine

Tobacco (Smokeless)
- Use Smokeless Tobacco

Tobacco Smoking 1967
PN 8862   SC 53340
- UF Cigarette Smoking
      Smoking (Tobacco)
- B   Drug Usage 1971
      Habits 1967
- R   Carcinogens 1973
      Nicotine 1973
      Nicotine Withdrawal 1997
      Prenatal Exposure 1991
      Smokeless Tobacco 1994
      Smoking Cessation 1988

Toes (Anatomy)
- Use Feet (Anatomy)

Tofranil
- Use Imipramine

Toilet Training 1973
PN 137   SC 53400
- B   Childrearing Practices 1967

Token Economy Programs 1973
PN 680   SC 53410
SN Group treatment based on operant conditioning in which elements in a patient's environment are arranged so that reinforcement is made contingent on the patient's behavior. When the desired behavior occurs, a token is given which may be exchanged for a reinforcing agent (e.g., goods or services).
- B   Contingency Management 1973
- R ↓ Psychiatric Hospital Programs 1967
      Response Cost 1997

Token Reinforcement
- Use Secondary Reinforcement

Tolerance 1973
PN 500   SC 53440
- B   Personality Traits 1967
- N   Tolerance for Ambiguity 1967
- R   Agreeableness 1997
      Openness to Experience 1997
      Social Acceptance 1967

Tolerance (Drug)
- Use Drug Tolerance

Tolerance for Ambiguity 1967
PN 469   SC 53460
SN Willingness to accept situations having conflicting or multiple interpretations or outcomes.

Tolerance for Ambiguity — (cont'd)
- UF Ambiguity (Tolerance)
- B   Tolerance 1973

Toluene 1991
PN 50   SC 53465
- B   Solvents 1982

Tomography 1988
PN 2771   SC 53470
- UF CAT Scan
      Positron Emission Tomography
- B   Medical Diagnosis 1973
      Neuroimaging 2003
- N   Magnetic Resonance Imaging 1994
- R   Computer Assisted Diagnosis 1973
- ↓ Roentgenography 1973

Tone (Frequency)
- Use Pitch (Frequency)

Tongue 1973
PN 418   SC 53490
- B   Digestive System 1967
- N   Taste Buds 1973
- R   Mouth (Anatomy) 1967
      Taste Disorders 2001

Tonic Immobility 1978
PN 366   SC 53495
SN Adaptive escape or alarm response in certain species in which the animal adopts a motionless posture as if feigning death.
- B   Motor Processes 1967
- R   Alarm Responses 1973
- ↓ Animal Defensive Behavior 1982

Tool Use 1991
PN 278   SC 53497
SN Used for human or animal populations.
- UF Animal Tool Use
- B   Motor Processes 1967
- R ↓ Animal Ethology 1967

Top Level Managers 1973
PN 1715   SC 53500
SN Executives in business or industry who are responsible for the major strategic and policy decisions.
- UF Executives
- B   Management Personnel 1973
- R   Middle Level Managers 1973

Topography 1973
PN 227   SC 53510
- B   Ecological Factors 1973

Torticollis 1973
PN 93   SC 53520
- UF Wryneck
- B   Movement Disorders 1985
      Muscular Disorders 1973

Tortoises
- Use Turtles

Torture 1988
PN 347   SC 53535
- B   Antisocial Behavior 1971
- R ↓ Aggressive Behavior 1967

Torture — (cont'd)
-     Coercion 1994
-     Persecution 1973
-     Suffering 1973
-     Victimization 1973
- ↓ Violence 1973

Totalitarianism 1973
PN 64   SC 53540
- B   Political Economic Systems 1973

Touch
- Use Tactual Perception

Touching
- Use Physical Contact

Tourette Syndrome
- Use Gilles de la Tourette Disorder

Tourism 2003
PN 97   SC 53558
HN This term was introduced in June 2003. PsycINFO records from the past 10 years were re-indexed with this term. The posting note reflects the number of records that were re-indexed.
- R   Holidays 1988
- ↓ Recreation 1967
      Traveling 1973
      Vacationing 1973

Towns 1973
PN 80   SC 53560
- B   Social Environments 1973

Toxic Disorders 1973
PN 493   OO 50570
- UF Intoxication
      Poisoning
- B   Physical Disorders 1997
- N   Acute Alcoholic Intoxication 1973
      Barbiturate Poisoning 1970
      Carbon Monoxide Poisoning 1973
- ↓ Drug Induced Congenital Disorders 1973
      Lead Poisoning 1973
      Mercury Poisoning 1973
      Narcosis 1973
      Neuroleptic Malignant Syndrome 1988
      Thyrotoxicosis 1973
      Toxic Encephalopathies 1973
      Toxic Hepatitis 1973
      Toxic Psychoses 1973
- R ↓ Alcohol Intoxication 1973
- ↓ Alcoholism 1967
- ↓ Dermatitis 1973
- ↓ Digestive System Disorders 1973
- ↓ Gastrointestinal Disorders 1973
      Hyponatremia 1997
- ↓ Liver Disorders 1973
- ↓ Mental Disorders 1967
- ↓ Neurotoxins 1982
- ↓ Toxicity 1973
      Toxicomania 1973

Toxic Encephalopathies 1973
PN 104   SC 53580
- B   Encephalopathies 1982
      Toxic Disorders 1973
- R   Acute Alcoholic Intoxication 1973
      Chronic Alcoholic Intoxication 1973
      Toxic Psychoses 1973

Toxic Hepatitis 1973
PN 12   SC 53590
- B   Hepatitis 1973
-     Toxic Disorders 1973

Toxic Psychoses 1973
PN 147   SC 53600
SN Psychotic states or conditions resulting from ingestion of toxic agents or by the presence of toxins within the body. Compare EXPERIMENTAL PSYCHOSIS.
- B   Organic Brain Syndromes 1973
-     Psychosis 1967
-     Toxic Disorders 1973
- R ↓ Alcohol Intoxication 1973
-     ↓ Alcoholic Psychosis 1973
-     Thyrotoxicosis 1973
-     Toxic Encephalopathies 1973

Toxic Waste
Use Hazardous Materials

Toxicity 1973
PN 1097   SC 53610
- N Neurotoxicity 2003
- R ↓ Drugs 1967
-     ↓ Hazardous Materials 1991
-     ↓ Neurotoxins 1982
-     Teratogens 1988
-     ↓ Toxic Disorders 1973

Toxicomania 1973
PN 16   SC 53620
- R Pica 1973
-     ↓ Toxic Disorders 1973

Toxins
Use Poisons

Toy Selection 1973
PN 207   SC 53650
- R Childhood Play Behavior 1978
-     ↓ Toys 1973

Toys 1973
PN 509   SC 53660
- N Anatomically Detailed Dolls 1991
-     Educational Toys 1973
- R Childhood Play Behavior 1978
-     Childrens Recreational Games 1973
-     Computer Games 1988
-     ↓ Games 1967
-     ↓ Recreation 1967
-     Toy Selection 1973

Trachea 1973
PN 46   SC 53680
- B Respiratory System 1973

Tracking 1967
PN 558   SC 53700
SN Following the movement of a moving stimulus or the contours (or shape) of a stationary target by means of direct physical contact or through any sensory modality. Used for human or animal populations.
- B Perceptual Motor Processes 1967
- N Rotary Pursuit 1967
-     Visual Tracking 1973
- R ↓ Attention 1967
-     ↓ Monitoring 1973
-     Motor Skills 1973

Tracking — (cont'd)
-   ↓ Perceptual Localization 1967
-   ↓ Perceptual Motor Learning 1967

Tractotomy 1973
PN 22   SC 53710
- B Neurosurgery 1973
- R ↓ Psychosurgery 1973
-     Pyramidotomy 1973

Traditionalism
Use Conservatism

Traffic Accidents (Motor)
Use Motor Traffic Accidents

Trainable Mentally Retarded
Use Moderate Mental Retardation

Training
Use Education

Training (Athletic)
Use Athletic Training

Training (Clinical Methods)
Use Clinical Methods Training

Training (Clinical Psychology Graduate)
Use Clinical Psychology Graduate Training

Training (Community Mental Health)
Use Community Mental Health Training

Training (Graduate Psychology)
Use Graduate Psychology Education

Training (Mental Health Inservice)
Use Mental Health Inservice Training

Training (Motivation)
Use Motivation Training

Training (Personnel)
Use Personnel Training

Training (Psychiatric)
Use Psychiatric Training

Training (Psychoanalytic)
Use Psychoanalytic Training

Training (Psychotherapy)
Use Psychotherapy Training

Trains (Railroad)
Use Railroad Trains

Tranquilizing Drugs 1967
PN 2290   SC 53900
- UF Antianxiety Drugs
-     Anxiety Reducing Drugs

Tranquilizing Drugs — (cont'd)
-     Anxiolytic Drugs
-     Ataractic Drugs
-     Ataraxic Drugs
-     Thymoleptic Drugs
- B Drugs 1967
- N Amitriptyline 1973
-     Benactyzine 1973
-     Doxepin 1994
-     Haloperidol 1973
-     Meprobamate 1973
-     ↓ Minor Tranquilizers 1973
-     ↓ Neuroleptic Drugs 1973
-     ↓ Phenothiazine Derivatives 1973
-     Pimozide 1973
-     Thiothixene 1973
- R ↓ Anticonvulsive Drugs 1973
-     ↓ Antiemetic Drugs 1973
-     ↓ Antihypertensive Drugs 1973
-     ↓ Benzodiazepines 1978
-     ↓ Dopamine Antagonists 1982
-     ↓ Muscle Relaxing Drugs 1973
-     ↓ Narcotic Drugs 1973
-     ↓ Sedatives 1973

Transactional Analysis 1973
PN 1059   SC 53910
SN Type of psychotherapy developed by E. Berne based on the theory that all interactions between individuals reflect the inner relationships of the "Parent," "Adult," and "Child" ego states.
- B Human Potential Movement 1982
-     Psychotherapy 1967
- R ↓ Group Psychotherapy 1967
-     ↓ Psychoanalysis 1967

Transaminases 1973
PN 38   SC 53920
- UF Aminotransferases
- B Transferases 1973

Transcranial Magnetic Stimulation 2003
PN 367   SC 53925
SN Noninvasive therapeutic technique for stimulating the brain.
HN This term was introduced in June 2003. PsycINFO records from the past 10 years were re-indexed with this term. The posting note reflects the number of records that were re-indexed.
- UF Repetitive Transcranial Magnetic Stimulation
- B Brain Stimulation 1967
-     Physical Treatment Methods 1973
- R Magnetism 1985

Transcultural Psychiatry 1973
PN 534   SC 53930
SN Comparative study of mental illness and mental health among various societies or cultures, including epidemiology and symptomatology.
- UF Comparative Psychiatry
-     Cultural Psychiatry
- B Psychiatry 1967
- R ↓ Alternative Medicine 1997
-     Cross Cultural Psychology 1997
-     ↓ Cross Cultural Treatment 1994
-     ↓ Culture Bound Syndromes 2004
-     Ethnology 1967
-     Folk Medicine 1973
-     Folk Psychology 1997
-     Myths 1967
-     Shamanism 1973
-     Taboos 1973

Transducers 1973
PN 30   SC 53940
B   Apparatus 1967

Transfer (Learning) 1967
PN 3454   SC 53950
SN Effect of previous learning on the acquisition of new material or skills as a function of the relative similarity between the prior and current learning situations. Compare GENERALIZATION (LEARNING).
B   Learning 1967
N   Negative Transfer 1973
     Positive Transfer 1973
R   ↓ Generalization (Learning) 1982

Transfer Students 1973
PN 166   SC 53955
SN Students transferring from one school or educational program to another.
B   Students 1967
R   Grade Level 1994

Transferases 1973
PN 341   SC 53960
B   Enzymes 1973
N   Transaminases 1973

Transference (Psychotherapeutic)
Use Psychotherapeutic Transference

Transformational Generative Grammar 1973
PN 113   SC 53980
SN Transformational grammar relates the deep syntactic structures of a language to the surface structures by means of transformational rules. Generative grammar represents, through abstract formulas, all and only the grammatical utterances of a language.
B   Grammar 1967
R   ↓ Syntax 1971

Transformational Leadership 2003
PN 171   SC 53985
SN A style of leadership that motivates and transforms followers to transcend their self-interests and personal goals to work for a common goal.
HN This term was introduced in June 2003. PsycINFO records from the past 10 years were re-indexed with this term. The posting note reflects the number of records that were re-indexed.
UF   Charismatic Leadership
B   Leadership 1967
R   Charisma 1988
     Leadership Style 1973
     ↓ Management 1967

Transfusion (Blood)
Use Blood Transfusion

Transgendered
Use Transsexualism

Transgenerational Patterns 1991
PN 874   SC 54005
SN Patterns of behavior (e.g., adolescent pregnancy, drug abuse, or child abuse) appearing in successive generations.
UF   Intergenerational Transmission
R   Children of Alcoholics 2003

Transgenerational Patterns — (cont'd)
   ↓ Family 1967
   ↓ Family Relations 1967
     Family Resemblance 1991
     Generation Gap 1973
     Intergenerational Relations 1988
   ↓ Parent Child Relations 1967
     Trends 1991

Transistors (Apparatus)
Use Apparatus

Transitional Objects 1985
PN 283   SC 54015
SN Psychoanalytic concept referring to any material object having a special value that serves an anxiety-reducing function. Such attachment is a normal phenomenon during transition from one phase to another in separation-individuation.
R   ↓ Childhood Development 1967
     Object Relations 1982
     Separation Individuation 1982

Translocation (Chromosome) 1973
PN 43   SC 54020
B   Chromosome Disorders 1973
R   ↓ Genetics 1967
     Mutations 1973

Transpersonal Psychology 1988
PN 429   SC 54025
SN Subdiscipline of humanistic psychology which studies higher states of consciousness and transcendental experiences.
R   Humanistic Psychology 1988

Transplants (Organ)
Use Organ Transplantation

Transportation 1973
PN 204   SC 54040
N   Air Transportation 1973
   ↓ Ground Transportation 1973
     Public Transportation 1973
   ↓ Water Transportation 1973
R   Commuting (Travel) 1985
   ↓ Transportation Accidents 1973

Transportation Accidents 1973
PN 178   SC 54050
B   Accidents 1967
N   Air Traffic Accidents 1973
     Motor Traffic Accidents 1973
R   Accident Prevention 1973
     Air Traffic Control 1973
   ↓ Aviation Safety 1973
     Highway Safety 1973
     Safety Belts 1973
   ↓ Transportation 1973

Transposition (Cognition) 1973
PN 49   SC 54060
SN Condition in learning in which subjects react to relationships between stimuli rather than to each stimulus itself.
B   Cognitive Processes 1967

Transracial Adoption
Use Interracial Adoption

Transsexualism 1973
PN 993   SC 54070
SN The urge to belong to the opposite sex that may include surgical procedures to modify the sex organs in order to appear as the opposite sex.
UF   Transgendered
B   Gender Identity 1985
     Gender Identity Disorder 1997
     Psychosexual Behavior 1967
R   Bisexuality 1973
   ↓ Homosexuality 1967
     Sex Change 1988
     Transvestism 1973

Transvestism 1973
PN 270   SC 54080
SN The act of dressing like and adopting the behavior of the opposite sex, often for sexual gratification.
B   Paraphilias 1988
     Psychosexual Behavior 1967
R   Bisexuality 1973
     Fetishism 1973
   ↓ Gender Identity Disorder 1997
   ↓ Homosexuality 1967
     Transsexualism 1973

Tranylcypromine 1973
PN 185   SC 54090
B   Antidepressant Drugs 1971
     Monoamine Oxidase Inhibitors 1973

Trauma (Emotional)
Use Emotional Trauma

Trauma (Physical)
Use Injuries

Traumatic Brain Injury 1997
PN 2308   SC 54115
SN Brain injury resulting from an accident, surgery, or other trauma.
HN Consider BRAIN DAMAGE or BRAIN DAMAGED to access references prior to 1997.
UF   Brain Injury (Traumatic)
B   Brain Damage 1967
R   ↓ Head Injuries 1973
   ↓ Neuropsychological Assessment 1982

Traumatic Neurosis 1973
PN 188   SC 54130
HN Use TRAUMATIC NEUROSIS or STRESS REACTIONS to access references to POSTTRAUMATIC STRESS DISORDER from 1973-1984.
B   Neurosis 1967
R   Posttraumatic Stress Disorder 1985

Traumatic Psychosis
Use Reactive Psychosis

Traveling 1973
PN 414   SC 54150
B   Recreation 1967
R   Commuting (Travel) 1985
     Tourism 2003
     Vacationing 1973

Trazodone 1988
PN 250   SC 54152
B   Antidepressant Drugs 1971
     Piperazines 1994

Treatment 1967

PN 26110 SC 54190
SN Conceptually broad term referring to psychological or physical measures designed to ameliorate or cure an abnormal or undesirable condition. Use a more specific term if possible.
UF Therapy
N Aftercare 1973
↓ Alternative Medicine 1997
↓ Behavior Modification 1973
Bibliotherapy 1973
↓ Cognitive Techniques 1985
↓ Creative Arts Therapy 1994
↓ Crisis Intervention Services 1973
↓ Cross Cultural Treatment 1994
↓ Health Care Services 1978
Interdisciplinary Treatment Approach 1973
Involuntary Treatment 1994
Life Sustaining Treatment 1997
Medical Treatment (General) 1973
Milieu Therapy 1988
Movement Therapy 1997
Multimodal Treatment Approach 1991
Online Therapy 2003
↓ Outpatient Treatment 1967
Pain Management 1994
Partial Hospitalization 1985
Personal Therapy 1991
↓ Physical Treatment Methods 1973
Preventive Medicine 1973
↓ Psychotherapeutic Techniques 1967
↓ Psychotherapy 1967
↓ Rehabilitation 1967
↓ Relaxation Therapy 1978
Sex Therapy 1978
Social Casework 1967
Sociotherapy 1967
Speech Therapy 1967
Treatment Guidelines 2001
R Caregivers 1988
↓ Case Management 1991
↓ Client Rights 1988
Client Transfer 1997
Client Treatment Matching 1997
↓ Clinics 1967
Cost Containment 1991
↓ Counseling 1967
Court Referrals 1994
Death Education 1982
Early Intervention 1982
Euthanasia 1973
Health Care Costs 1994
↓ Health Care Delivery 1978
Health Care Seeking Behavior 1997
↓ Intervention 2003
Life Review 1991
↓ Medical Records 1978
Mental Health Program Evaluation 1973
Patient Abuse 1991
Patient History 1973
Physical Restraint 1982
Posttreatment Followup 1973
Prescribing (Drugs) 1991
↓ Prevention 1973
Prognosis 1973
↓ Psychiatry 1967
Psychoeducation 1994
Psychosocial Readjustment 1973
Quality of Care 1988
Relapse Prevention 1994
↓ Self Help Techniques 1982
Sensory Integration 1991
Shamanism 1973
↓ Side Effects (Treatment) 1988

Treatment — (cont'd)

Spontaneous Remission 1973
Stress Management 1985
Therapeutic Alliance 1994
↓ Therapeutic Processes 1978
Therapeutic Social Clubs 1973
Therapist Selection 1994
Treatment Compliance 1982
↓ Treatment Duration 1988
Treatment Effectiveness Evaluation 1973
↓ Treatment Facilities 1973
↓ Treatment Outcomes 1982
↓ Treatment Planning 1997
↓ Treatment Resistant Disorders 1994
Treatment Termination 1982
Treatment Withholding 1988
↓ Twelve Step Programs 1997

Treatment Client Matching

Use Client Treatment Matching

Treatment Compliance 1982

PN 4853 SC 54153
SN Adherence by a patient or client to professional advice or a systematic plan of treatment.
UF Client Compliance
Medical Regimen Compliance
B Compliance 1973
R ↓ Client Attitudes 1982
Client Education 1985
Client Participation 1997
↓ Client Rights 1988
Illness Behavior 1982
Informed Consent 1985
Involuntary Treatment 1994
↓ Treatment 1967
Treatment Dropouts 1978
↓ Treatment Duration 1988
Treatment Refusal 1994
Treatment Withholding 1988

Treatment Dropouts 1978

PN 1402 SC 54155
SN Persons who drop out of treatment, or discontinuation of treatment without the consent of the person in charge of treatment or before scheduled termination. Compare TREATMENT TERMINATION.
UF Client Dropouts
Patient Dropouts
B Dropouts 1973
R Involuntary Treatment 1994
Psychotherapeutic Outcomes 1973
Treatment Compliance 1982
↓ Treatment Duration 1988
↓ Treatment Outcomes 1982
Treatment Refusal 1994
Treatment Termination 1982

Treatment Duration 1988

PN 1943 SC 54157
SN Length of hospital or institutional stay and length or number of treatment or therapy sessions. Used for any treatment modality.
UF Length of Stay
N Long Term Care 1994
R ↓ Case Management 1991
Maintenance Therapy 1997
↓ Treatment 1967
Treatment Compliance 1982
Treatment Dropouts 1978
↓ Treatment Outcomes 1982
↓ Treatment Planning 1997
Treatment Termination 1982

Treatment Effectiveness Evaluation 1973

PN 5733 SC 54160
SN Methodology or procedures for assessment of treatment success in relation to previously established goals or other criteria. Also used for formal evaluations themselves. For effectiveness of particular treatment modes, use the specific type of treatment (e.g., DRUG THERAPY). For efficacy of treatment for a particular disorder, use the specific disorder (e.g., MANIA) and the specific type of treatment.
UF Evaluation (Treatment Effectiveness)
B Evaluation 1967
R Clinical Trials 2004
Mental Health Program Evaluation 1973
Psychotherapeutic Outcomes 1973
↓ Treatment 1967
↓ Treatment Outcomes 1982

Treatment Environment

Use Therapeutic Environment

Treatment Facilities 1973

PN 509 SC 54170
N ↓ Clinics 1967
Community Mental Health Centers 1973
Halfway Houses 1973
↓ Hospitals 1967
Nursing Homes 1973
Therapeutic Camps 1978
R ↓ Crisis Intervention Services 1973
↓ Facility Admission 1988
↓ Facility Discharge 1988
↓ Facility Environment 1988
↓ Health Care Administration 1997
Institutional Schools 1978
↓ Residential Care Institutions 1973
↓ Therapeutic Environment 2001
↓ Treatment 1967

Treatment Guidelines 2001

PN 512 SC 54175
B Treatment 1967
R Client Treatment Matching 1997
↓ Professional Standards 1973
↓ Quality of Services 1997
↓ Treatment Planning 1997

Treatment Methods (Physical)

Use Physical Treatment Methods

Treatment Outcomes 1982

PN 9749 SC 54185
SN Limited to treatment results that are a function of unique or specifically-described circumstances or characteristics (e.g., race) of the clients/patients, the treatment provider, or the treatment itself. For effectiveness of particular treatment modes, use the specific type of treatment (e.g., DRUG THERAPY). For efficacy of treatment for a particular disorder, use the specific disorder (e.g., MANIA) and the specific type of treatment.
UF Outcomes (Treatment)
Therapeutic Outcomes
N Psychotherapeutic Outcomes 1973
R Client Treatment Matching 1997
Mental Health Program Evaluation 1973
Postsurgical Complications 1973
↓ Psychotherapeutic Processes 1967
Recovery (Disorders) 1973
Relapse (Disorders) 1973
Relapse Prevention 1994

Treatment Outcomes — (cont'd)
↓ Remission (Disorders) 1973
↓ Side Effects (Treatment) 1988
↓ Therapeutic Processes 1978
↓ Treatment 1967
  Treatment Dropouts 1978
↓ Treatment Duration 1988
  Treatment Effectiveness Evaluation 1973
  Treatment Termination 1982

Treatment Planning 1997
PN 1028   **SC** 54189
UF Patient Care Planning
N Discharge Planning 1994
R Aftercare 1973
↓ Case Management 1991
↓ Client Characteristics 1973
  Client Treatment Matching 1997
  Clinical Judgment (Not Diagnosis) 1973
↓ Health Care Delivery 1978
↓ Managed Care 1994
  Needs Assessment 1985
  Posttreatment Followup 1973
↓ Treatment 1967
↓ Treatment Duration 1988
  Treatment Guidelines 2001

Treatment Refusal 1994
PN 306   **SC** 54186
SN Patient or client refusal of or resistance to medical, psychological, or psychiatric treatment. Consider TREATMENT WITHHOLDING for life sustaining contexts.
UF Refusal (Treatment)
R Advance Directives 1994
  Assisted Suicide 1997
↓ Client Rights 1988
  Client Transfer 1997
  Informed Consent 1985
  Involuntary Treatment 1994
  Life Sustaining Treatment 1997
  Psychotherapeutic Resistance 1973
↓ Resistance 1997
  Treatment Compliance 1982
  Treatment Dropouts 1978
  Treatment Termination 1982
  Treatment Withholding 1988

Treatment Resistant Depression 1994
PN 552   **SC** 57440
UF Tricyclic Resistant Depression
B Major Depression 1988
  Treatment Resistant Disorders 1994
R ↓ Drug Therapy 1967

Treatment Resistant Disorders 1994
PN 936   **SC** 57445
SN Used for any disorder that is resistant to any type of psychological or medical treatment.
N Treatment Resistant Depression 1994
R ↓ Chronic Mental Illness 1997
↓ Mental Disorders 1967
↓ Physical Disorders 1997
↓ Treatment 1967

Treatment Seeking Behavior
Use Health Care Seeking Behavior

Treatment Termination 1982
PN 1112   **SC** 54187
SN Completion of medical or psychological/behavioral treatment programs. Compare TREATMENT DROPOUTS.

Treatment Termination — (cont'd)
R Client Transfer 1997
  Discharge Planning 1994
↓ Hospital Discharge 1973
  Psychiatric Hospital Discharge 1978
↓ Therapeutic Processes 1978
↓ Treatment 1967
  Treatment Dropouts 1978
↓ Treatment Duration 1988
↓ Treatment Outcomes 1982
  Treatment Refusal 1994
  Treatment Withholding 1988

Treatment Withholding 1988
PN 289   **SC** 54188
SN Limiting or restricting medical treatment for seriously ill persons. Includes do-not-resuscitate orders. Compare TREATMENT TERMINATION.
R Advance Directives 1994
  Assisted Suicide 1997
↓ Client Rights 1988
↓ Death and Dying 1967
  Euthanasia 1973
↓ Human Rights 1978
  Informed Consent 1985
  Life Sustaining Treatment 1997
↓ Treatment 1967
  Treatment Compliance 1982
  Treatment Refusal 1994
  Treatment Termination 1982

Tremor 1973
PN 344   **SC** 54200
B Movement Disorders 1985
  Symptoms 1967
R ↓ Antitremor Drugs 1973
  Parkinsonism 1994
  Parkinsons Disease 1973

Trends 1991
PN 2275   **SC** 54204
SN Used specifically for analysis of past, present, or future patterns in technology, economics, and social or developmental processes.
R ↓ Fads and Fashions 1973
  Future 1991
↓ History 1973
  Popular Culture 2003
  Social Change 1967
↓ Social Processes 1967
↓ Time 1967
  Transgenerational Patterns 1991

Triadic Therapy
Use Conjoint Therapy

Trial and Error Learning 1973
PN 76   **SC** 54210
B Learning 1967
  Learning Strategies 1991

Triazolam 1988
PN 278   **SC** 54215
UF Halcion
B Hypnotic Drugs 1973
  Sedatives 1973

Tribes 1973
PN 549   **SC** 54220
R Alaska Natives 1997
  American Indians 1967
↓ Racial and Ethnic Groups 2001

Trichotillomania 2003
PN 360   **SC** 54225
SN Excessive pulling of one's own hair.
HN In June 2003, this term replaced the discontinued term HAIR PULLING. HAIR PULLING was removed from all records containing it and replaced with TRICHOTILLOMANIA.
UF Hair Pulling
B Habits 1967
R ↓ Behavior Disorders 1971
↓ Self Destructive Behavior 1985

Tricyclic Antidepressant Drugs 1997
PN 330   **SC** 54226
B Antidepressant Drugs 1971
N Amitriptyline 1973
  Chlorimipramine 1973
  Desipramine 1973
  Doxepin 1994
  Imipramine 1973
  Maprotiline 1982
  Nortriptyline 1994
R ↓ Adrenergic Blocking Drugs 1973
↓ Lithium 1973
↓ Monoamine Oxidase Inhibitors 1973

Tricyclic Resistant Depression
Use Treatment Resistant Depression

Trifluoperazine 1973
PN 121   **SC** 54230
UF Stelazine
B Phenothiazine Derivatives 1973

Triflupromazine
Use Phenothiazine Derivatives

Trigeminal Nerve 1973
PN 225   **SC** 54250
B Cranial Nerves 1973

Trigeminal Neuralgia 1973
PN 81   **SC** 54260
UF Tic Douloureux
B Neuralgia 1973

Trigonum Cerebrale
Use Fornix

Trihexyphenidyl 1973
PN 64   **SC** 54270
B Alcohols 1967
  Amines 1973
  Antispasmodic Drugs 1973
  Antitremor Drugs 1973
  Cholinergic Blocking Drugs 1973

Triiodothyronine 1973
PN 157   **SC** 54280
B Thyroid Hormones 1973

Triplets 1973
PN 38   **SC** 54310
B Multiple Births 1973

Trisomy 1973
PN 80   **SC** 54320
B Chromosome Disorders 1973
N Trisomy 21 1973

Trisomy 21   1973
PN 67   SC 54340
B   Autosome Disorders   1973
     Trisomy   1973
R   Downs Syndrome   1967

Trochlear Nerve
Use   Cranial Nerves

Truancy   1973
PN 94   SC 54360
N   School Truancy   1973

Trucks
Use   Motor Vehicles

True False Tests
Use   Forced Choice (Testing Method)

Trust (Social Behavior)   1967
PN 1952   SC 54370
B   Prosocial Behavior   1982
R   Hope   1991

Tryptamine   1973
PN 112   SC 54380
B   Amines   1973
     Vasoconstrictor Drugs   1973

Tryptophan   1973
PN 1134   SC 54390
B   Amino Acids   1973
     Serotonin Precursors   1978
N   Hydroxytryptophan (5-)   1991

Tubal Ligation   1973
PN 51   SC 54400
B   Birth Control   1971
     Sterilization (Sex)   1973

Tuberculosis   1973
PN 159   SC 54410
B   Bacterial Disorders   1973
N   Pulmonary Tuberculosis   1973
R   Addisons Disease   1973
     ↓ Antitubercular Drugs   1973
     Lupus   1973
     ↓ Musculoskeletal Disorders   1973
     ↓ Nervous System Disorders   1967
     ↓ Skin Disorders   1973

Tubocurarine   1973
PN 15   SC 54420
B   Alkaloids   1973
     Muscle Relaxing Drugs   1973
R   Curare   1973

Tumors
Use   Neoplasms

Tunnel Vision   1973
PN 15   SC 54440
SN   Disorder characterized by severe limitation or total lack of peripheral vision.
B   Eye Disorders   1973
R   ↓ Vision   1967

Turners Syndrome   1973
PN 174   SC 54460

Turners Syndrome   —   (cont'd)
B   Hypogonadism   1973
     Neonatal Disorders   1973
     Sex Linked Hereditary Disorders   1973
     Syndromes   1973
R   Sterility   1973

Turnover
Use   Employee Turnover

Turtles   1973
PN 228   SC 54480
UF   Tortoises
B   Reptiles   1967

Tutoring   1973
PN 873   SC 54490
B   Teaching Methods   1967
N   Peer Tutoring   1973
R   Individualized Instruction   1973
     Test Coaching   1997

Tutors
Use   Teachers

Twelve Step Programs   1997
PN 216   SC 54505
UF   Gamblers Anonymous
     Narcotics Anonymous
B   Support Groups   1991
N   Alcoholics Anonymous   1973
R   ↓ Drug Rehabilitation   1973
     Group Counseling   1973
     ↓ Group Psychotherapy   1967
     ↓ Mental Health Services   1978
     ↓ Psychotherapeutic Techniques   1967
     ↓ Rehabilitation   1967
     ↓ Self Help Techniques   1982
     ↓ Treatment   1967

Twins   1967
PN 1975   SC 54510
B   Multiple Births   1973
N   Conjoined Twins   2003
     Heterozygotic Twins   1973
     Monozygotic Twins   1973
R   Family Resemblance   1991
     ↓ Genetics   1967

Tympanic Membrane
Use   Middle Ear

Type A Personality
Use   Coronary Prone Behavior

Type B Personality
Use   Coronary Prone Behavior

Type I Errors   1973
PN 345   SC 54530
B   Prediction Errors   1973
R   Statistical Power   1991

Type II Errors   1973
PN 90   SC 54540
B   Prediction Errors   1973
R   Statistical Power   1991

Typing   1991
PN 84   SC 54550
HN   Use CLERICAL SECRETARIAL SKILLS to access references from 1973-1990.
R   Clerical Secretarial Skills   1973
     Keyboards   1985
     Word Processing   1991

Typists
Use   Clerical Personnel

Typologies (General)
Use   Taxonomies

Typologies (Psychodiagnostic)
Use   Psychodiagnostic Typologies

Tyramine   1973
PN 88   SC 54580
B   Adrenergic Drugs   1973
     Sympathomimetic Amines   1973
     Vasoconstrictor Drugs   1973
R   ↓ Ergot Derivatives   1973

Tyrosine   1973
PN 429   SC 54590
B   Amino Acids   1973
N   Alpha Methylparatyrosine   1078
R   Melanin   1973

Ulcerative Colitis   1973
PN 173   SC 54620
B   Colitis   1973

Ulcers (Gastrointestinal)
Use   Gastrointestinal Ulcers

Ulnar Nerve
Use   Spinal Nerves

Ultrasound   1973
PN 364   SC 54650
SN   Sound waves with frequencies above the range of human hearing.
B   Pitch (Frequency)   1967

Uncertainty   1991
PN 1271   SC 54655
SN   May be used for uncertainty reduction processes; uncertainty in decision making, choice, or judgment; or in statistical contexts.
R   ↓ Chance (Fortune)   1973
     Chaos Theory   1997
     Choice Behavior   1967
     ↓ Decision Making   1967
     Doubt   1973
     Impression Management   1978
     ↓ Judgment   1967
     Skepticism   2004
     ↓ Statistical Analysis   1967
     Suspicion   1973

Unconditioned Reflex
Use   Reflexes

Unconditioned Responses   1973
PN 164   SC 54680
B   Classical Conditioning   1967

Unconditioned Responses — (cont'd)
    Responses 1967

Unconditioned Stimulus 1973
PN 1378   SC 54690
  UF   Stimulus (Unconditioned)
  B   Conditioning 1967
  R   ↓ Classical Conditioning 1967
       ↓ Operant Conditioning 1967
       Primary Reinforcement 1973
       ↓ Stimulation 1967

Unconscious (Personality Factor) 1967
PN 1924   SC 54700
  B   Psychoanalytic Personality Factors 1973
  R   Archetypes 1991
       Death Instinct 1988
       Free Association 1994
       Id 1973
       Mind 1001

Underachievement (Academic)
  Use Academic Underachievement

Underdeveloped Countries
  Use Developing Countries

Undergraduate Degrees
  Use Educational Degrees

Undergraduate Education 1978
PN 1366   SC 54725
  UF   College Education
  B   Higher Education 1973

Undergraduates
  Use College Students

Underprivileged
  Use Disadvantaged

Understanding
  Use Comprehension

Underwater Effects 1973
PN 209   SC 54760
  B   Environmental Effects 1973
  R   Decompression Effects 1973
       ↓ Gravitational Effects 1967

Underweight 1973
PN 71   SC 54770
  B   Body Weight 1967
       Symptoms 1967
  N   Anorexia Nervosa 1973
  R   Diets 1978
       ↓ Eating Disorders 1997
       Hyperthyroidism 1973
       ↓ Nutritional Deficiencies 1973

Undifferentiated Schizophrenia 1973
PN 105   SC 54780
  B   Schizophrenia 1967

Unemployment 1967
PN 1775   SC 54790
  B   Employment Status 1982
       Social Issues 1991

Unemployment — (cont'd)
  R   Employment History 1978
       Job Search 1985
       Job Security 1978
       ↓ Personnel 1967
       Personnel Termination 1973
       Reemployment 1991
       Retirement 1973

Unipolar Depression
  Use Major Depression

Universities
  Use Colleges

Unskilled Industrial Workers 1973
PN 92   SC 54880
SN Blue collar workers who perform unskilled labor
in an industrial setting.
  B   Blue Collar Workers 1973

Unwed Mothers 1973
PN 261   SC 54890
SN Consider also ADOLESCENT MOTHERS.
  B   Mothers 1967
  R   Never Married 1994
       Premarital Intercourse 1973
       Single Mothers 1994
       ↓ Single Parents 1978

Upper Class 1973
PN 141   SC 54900
  B   Social Class 1967

Upper Class Attitudes 1973
PN 13   SC 54910
SN Attitudes of, not toward, the upper class.
  B   Socioeconomic Class Attitudes 1973

Upper Income Level 1973
PN 78   SC 54920
  B   Income Level 1973

Upward Bound 1973
PN 49   SC 54930
SN U.S. Government educational and counseling
program for disadvantaged high school and college
students.
  B   Educational Programs 1973
       Government Programs 1973
  R   Compensatory Education 1973
       Government 1967

Upward Mobility
  Use Social Mobility

Urban Development
  Use Community Development

Urban Environments 1967
PN 7873   SC 54940
  UF   Cities
       Inner City
  B   Social Environments 1973
  N   Ghettoes 1973
  R   Community Development 1997
       Urban Planning 1973

Urban Ghettoes
  Use Ghettoes

Urban Planning 1973
PN 223   SC 54960
  B   Environmental Planning 1982
  R   ↓ Architecture 1973
       Community Development 1997
       ↓ Community Facilities 1973
       ↓ Environment 1967
       ↓ Recreation Areas 1973
       ↓ Urban Environments 1967

Urbanization 1973
PN 199   SC 54970
  B   Social Processes 1967
  R   Industrialization 1973
       Modernization 2003

Uric Acid 1973
PN 68   SC 55010
  B   Acids 1973

Urinalysis 1973
PN 263   SC 55020
  B   Medical Diagnosis 1973
  R   Drug Usage Screening 1988

Urinary Function Disorders 1973
PN 179   SC 55040
  B   Urogenital Disorders 1973
  N   Urinary Incontinence 1973
  R   ↓ Somatoform Disorders 2001

Urinary Incontinence 1973
PN 1004   SC 55050
  UF   Bedwetting
       Enuresis
       Incontinence (Urinary)
  B   Urinary Function Disorders 1973
  R   ↓ Behavior Disorders 1971
       ↓ Symptoms 1967

Urination 1967
PN 268   SC 55070
  UF   Micturition
  B   Excretion 1967
  N   Diuresis 1973
  R   ↓ Diuretics 1973

Urine 1973
PN 926   SC 55080
  B   Body Fluids 1973

Urogenital Disorders 1973
PN 286   SC 55090
  B   Physical Disorders 1997
  N   ↓ Genital Disorders 1967
       ↓ Gynecological Disorders 1973
       Kidney Diseases 1988
       ↓ Urinary Function Disorders 1973
  R   ↓ Sexual Function Disturbances 1973
       ↓ Sexually Transmitted Diseases 2003
       ↓ Somatoform Disorders 2001
       ↓ Urogenital System 1973

Urogenital System 1973
PN 69   SC 55100
  B   Anatomical Systems 1973
  N   Bladder 1973
       ↓ Female Genitalia 1973

Urogenital System — (cont'd)
    ↓ Gonads   1973
    Kidneys   1973
    ↓ Male Genitalia   1973
  R   ↓ Urogenital Disorders   1973

Usability (Systems)
  Use   Human Factors Engineering

Uterus   1973
PN   86   **SC**   55110
  B   Female Genitalia   1973
  N   Cervix   1973
  R   Placenta   1973

Utility Theory   2004
PN   7   **SC**   55113
SN   Asserts that rational choices are made based on logical analysis of the subjective value of the outcomes.
HN   This term was introduced in June 2004. PsycINFO records from the past 10 years were re-indexed with this term. The posting note reflects the number of records that were re-indexed.
  B   Theories   1967
  R   Choice Behavior   1967
    ↓ Decision Making   1967

Utilization (Health Care)
  Use   Health Care Utilization

Vacation Benefits
  Use   Employee Leave Benefits

Vacationing   1973
PN   214   **SC**   55130
  B   Recreation   1967
  R   Camping   1973
         Holidays   1988
         Summer Camps (Recreation)   1973
         Tourism   2003
         Traveling   1973

Vaccination
  Use   Immunization

Vagina   1973
PN   238   **SC**   55150
  B   Female Genitalia   1973

Vaginismus   1973
PN   89   **SC**   55160
  B   Sexual Function Disturbances   1973
  R   Dyspareunia   1973
         Frigidity   1973

Vagotomy   1973
PN   146   **SC**   55170
  B   Neurosurgery   1973

Vagus Nerve   1973
PN   288   **SC**   55180
  B   Cranial Nerves   1973
         Parasympathetic Nervous System   1973
  R   ↓ Heart   1967

Validity (Statistical)
  Use   Statistical Validity

Validity (Test)
  Use   Test Validity

Valium
  Use   Diazepam

Valproic Acid   1991
PN   562   **SC**   55215
  B   Anticonvulsive Drugs   1973

Values   1967
PN   6796   **SC**   55220
SN   Qualities, principles or behaviors considered to be morally or intrinsically valuable or desirable. Use a more specific term if possible.
  UF   Mores
  N   Ethnic Values   1973
         Personal Values   1973
         Social Values   1973
  R   ↓ Ethics   1967
         Integrity   1997
         Morality   1967
         World View   1988

Valves (Heart)
  Use   Heart Valves

Vandalism   1978
PN   114   **SC**   55235
SN   Willful or malicious destruction or defacement of public or private property.
  B   Crime   1967

Vane Kindergarten Test
  Use   Intelligence Measures

Variability (Response)
  Use   Response Variability

Variability (Stimulus)
  Use   Stimulus Variability

Variability Measurement   1973
PN   342   **SC**   55270
  B   Statistical Analysis   1967
         Statistical Measurement   1973
  N   Analysis of Covariance   1973
         Analysis of Variance   1967
         Interaction Variance   1973
         Standard Deviation   1973
  R   ↓ Central Tendency Measures   1973
         F Test   1973
         ↓ Statistical Correlation   1967

Variable Interval Reinforcement   1973
PN   752   **SC**   55280
  UF   Interval Reinforcement
  B   Reinforcement Schedules   1967

Variable Ratio Reinforcement   1973
PN   198   **SC**   55290
  UF   Ratio Reinforcement
  B   Reinforcement Schedules   1967

Variance Homogeneity
  Use   Homogeneity of Variance

Varimax Rotation   1973
PN   57   **SC**   55330
  B   Orthogonal Rotation   1973

Vascular Dementia   1997
PN   539   **SC**   55333
  B   Dementia   1985
  N   Multi Infarct Dementia   1991
  R   ↓ Cerebrovascular Disorders   1973

Vascular Disorders
  Use   Cardiovascular Disorders

Vasectomy   1973
PN   85   **SC**   55350
  B   Birth Control   1971
         Sterilization (Sex)   1973
         Surgery   1971

Vasoconstriction   1973
PN   108   **SC**   55360
  R   ↓ Blood Pressure Disorders   1973
         Epinephrine   1967

Vasoconstrictor Drugs   1973
PN   34   **SC**   55370
  UF   Pressors (Drugs)
         Vasopressor Drugs
  B   Drugs   1967
  N   ↓ Amphetamine   1967
         Angiotensin   1973
         Bufotenine   1973
         Dihydroergotamine   1973
         Ephedrine   1973
         Methamphetamine   1973
         Methoxamine   1973
         Norepinephrine   1973
         Serotonin   1973
         Tryptamine   1973
         Tyramine   1973
  R   ↓ Blood Pressure   1967
         ↓ Heart Rate Affecting Drugs   1973
         ↓ Vasodilator Drugs   1973
         Vasopressin   1973

Vasodilation   1973
PN   91   **SC**   55380
  R   ↓ Blood Pressure Disorders   1973
         Epinephrine   1967
         ↓ Muscle Relaxing Drugs   1973
         Theophylline   1973

Vasodilator Drugs   1973
PN   195   **SC**   55390
  B   Drugs   1967
  N   Nicotinic Acid   1973
         Verapamil   1991
  R   ↓ Antihypertensive Drugs   1973
         ↓ Blood Pressure   1967
         Channel Blockers   1991
         ↓ Heart Rate Affecting Drugs   1973
         ↓ Vasoconstrictor Drugs   1973

Vasopressin   1973
PN   933   **SC**   55400
  B   Neuropeptides   2003
         Pituitary Hormones   1973
  R   ↓ Vasoconstrictor Drugs   1973

Vasopressor Drugs
  Use   Vasoconstrictor Drugs

Veins (Anatomy) 1973
PN 41   SC 55420
  B   Blood Vessels 1973

Velocity 1973
PN 1339   SC 55430
  UF   Speed
  R   Vibration 1967

Venereal Diseases
  Use   Sexually Transmitted Diseases

Venlafaxine 2003
PN 313   SC 55450
HN   This term was introduced in June 2003. Psyc-INFO records from the past 10 years were re-indexed with this term. The posting note reflects the number of records that were re-indexed.
  B   Antidepressant Drugs 1971

Ventral Roots 1973
PN 29   SC 55460
  B   Spinal Cord 1973

Ventral Striatum
  Use   Basal Ganglia

Ventral Tegmental Area
  Use   Tegmentum

Ventricles (Cerebral)
  Use   Cerebral Ventricles

Ventricles (Heart)
  Use   Heart Ventricles

Ventricular Fibrillation
  Use   Fibrillation (Heart)

Verapamil 1991
PN 70   SC 55495
  B   Heart Rate Affecting Drugs 1973
        Vasodilator Drugs 1973
  R   Channel Blockers 1991

Verbal Ability 1967
PN 3250   SC 55500
  B   Cognitive Ability 1973
  R   Academic Aptitude 1973
        Language Proficiency 1988
        Metalinguistics 1994
        ↓ Oral Communication 1985
        Proofreading 1988
        ↓ Verbal Communication 1967
        ↓ Verbal Memory 1994
        Writing Skills 1985
        ↓ Written Communication 1985

Verbal Abuse 2003
PN 19   SC 55504
SN   Written or spoken words that are excessively critical, insulting, and/or intimidating.
HN   This term was introduced in June 2003. Psyc-INFO records from the past 10 years were re-indexed with this term. The posting note reflects the number of records that were re-indexed.
  B   Antisocial Behavior 1971
  R   ↓ Child Abuse 1971

Verbal Abuse — (cont'd)
        Elder Abuse 1988
        Emotional Abuse 1991
        Partner Abuse 1991
        Patient Abuse 1991
        Physical Abuse 1991

Verbal Communication 1967
PN 10643   SC 55520
SN   Communication through spoken or written language. Use narrower terms if possible.
  B   Communication 1967
  N   Articulation (Speech) 1967
        Conversation 1973
        ↓ Handwriting 1967
        Language Proficiency 1988
        ↓ Manual Communication 1978
        Narratives 1997
        ↓ Oral Communication 1985
        Pragmatics 1985
        Storytelling 1988
        ↓ Written Communication 1985
  R   ↓ Communication Skills 1973
        Discourse Analysis 1997
        ↓ Grammar 1967
        ↓ Language 1967
        ↓ Language Development 1967
        ↓ Linguistics 1973
        Metalinguistics 1994
        Neurolinguistics 1991
        ↓ Speech Processing (Mechanical) 1973
        Text Structure 1982
        Verbal Ability 1967
        ↓ Vocabulary 1967
        ↓ Vocalization 1967

Verbal Comprehension 1985
PN 1497   SC 55525
  B   Comprehension 1967
  N   Listening Comprehension 1973
        Reading Comprehension 1973
        Sentence Comprehension 1973

Verbal Conditioning
  Use   Verbal Learning

Verbal Fluency 1973
PN 1904   SC 55540
SN   Ability to produce and manipulate words in thought or speech.
  UF   Fluency
  R   Language Proficiency 1988
        ↓ Oral Communication 1985
        Speech Rate 1973

Verbal Learning 1967
PN 3846   SC 55550
SN   Acquisition, retention, and retrieval of verbal stimulus materials such as nonsense syllables, words, or sentences. Compare LANGUAGE DEVELOPMENT.
  UF   Conditioning (Verbal)
        Verbal Conditioning
  B   Learning 1967
  N   Nonsense Syllable Learning 1967
        Paired Associate Learning 1967
  R   Isolation Effect 1973
        Serial Anticipation (Learning) 1973
        ↓ Serial Learning 1967
        ↓ Verbal Memory 1994

Verbal Meaning 1973
PN 867   SC 55560

Verbal Meaning — (cont'd)
SN   Connotative or denotative meaning associated with any verbally informative unit (e.g., morpheme, word, sentence, or phrase).
  B   Meaning 1967
  N   Word Meaning 1973
  R   ↓ Figurative Language 1985
        ↓ Semantics 1967

Verbal Memory 1994
PN 1149   SC 55565
  B   Memory 1967
  N   Semantic Memory 1988
  R   ↓ Lexical Access 1988
        Lexical Decision 1988
        Verbal Ability 1967
        ↓ Verbal Learning 1967

Verbal Reinforcement 1973
PN 718   SC 55570
  B   Social Reinforcement 1967
  N   Praise 1973

Verbal Stimuli 1982
PN 1307   SC 55575
SN   Aural or visual presentation of syllables or words or nonword letter combinations.
  B   Stimulation 1967
  R   ↓ Stimulus Presentation Methods 1973

Verbal Tests 1973
PN 177   SC 55580
SN   Tests designed to assess verbal ability or in which performance depends upon verbal ability.
  B   Measurement 1967

Verbalization
  Use   Oral Communication

Verbs 1973
PN 1341   SC 55600
  B   Form Classes (Language) 1973

Verdict Determination
  Use   Adjudication

Vergence Movements
  Use   Eye Convergence

Verification (of Theories)
  Use   Theory Verification

Vernier Acuity
  Use   Visual Acuity

Vertebrates 1973
PN 265   SC 55620
  B   Animals 1967
  N   ↓ Amphibia 1973
        ↓ Birds 1967
        ↓ Fishes 1967
        ↓ Mammals 1973
        Pigs 1973
        ↓ Reptiles 1967
  R   ↓ Invertebrates 1973

Vertigo 1973
PN 210   SC 55630
  UF   Dizziness

Vertigo — (cont'd)
- B   Symptoms   1967
- R   ↓ Labyrinth Disorders   1973
-     Menieres Disease   1973
-     Syncope   1973

Vestibular Apparatus   1967
PN   760   SC   55660
SN   Major organ of equilibrium which acts as a sensory receptor that detects the position and changes in the position of the head in space.
- B   Ear (Anatomy)   1967
- N   Semicircular Canals   1973
- R   ↓ Labyrinth (Anatomy)   1973

Vestibular Nystagmus
   Use   Nystagmus

Vestibular Stimulation
   Use   Somesthetic Stimulation

Veterans (Military)
   Use   Military Veterans

Veterinary Medicine   1973
PN   80   SC   55680
- B   Medical Sciences   1967

Vibration   1967
PN   483   SC   55690
- UF   Resonance
- R   Velocity   1973

Vibrators (Apparatus)   1973
PN   20   SC   55700
- B   Apparatus   1967
- R   ↓ Stimulators (Apparatus)   1973

Vibrotactile Thresholds   1973
PN   340   SC   55710
SN   The minimal level of vibratory stimulation, the minimal difference between any such stimuli, or the minimal vibratory stimulus change that is tactually perceptible.
- B   Tactual Perception   1967
-     Thresholds   1967
- R   ↓ Perceptual Measures   1973

Vicarious Experiences   1973
PN   351   SC   55713
- UF   Reinforcement (Vicarious)
-     Vicarious Reinforcement
- B   Experiences (Events)   1973
- R   Imagination   1967
-     ↓ Reinforcement   1967

Vicarious Reinforcement
   Use   Vicarious Experiences

Victimization   1973
PN   7369   SC   55716
SN   Process or state of having been personally subjected to crime, deception, fraud, or other detrimental circumstances as a result of the deeds of others.
- B   Social Interaction   1967
- R   Bullying   2003
-     ↓ Crime   1967
-     ↓ Crime Victims   1982
-     Erotomania   1997
-     ↓ Harassment   2001

Victimization — (cont'd)
-     Hate Crimes   2003
-     ↓ Perpetrators   1988
-     Persecution   1973
-     Sexual Harassment   1985
-     Stalking   2001
-     Teasing   2003
-     Torture   1988
-     ↓ Violent Crime   2003

Video Display Terminals
   Use   Video Display Units

Video Display Units   1985
PN   640   SC   55718
SN   Electronic devices used to present information or stimulation through visual means.
HN   Use VISUAL DISPLAYS to access references from 1973-1984.
- UF   Cathode Ray Tubes
-     CRT
-     Video Display Terminals
- B   Computer Peripheral Devices   1985
-     Visual Displays   1973
- R   ↓ Television   1967
-     ↓ Visual Stimulation   1973

Video Games
   Use   Computer Games

Videotape Instruction   1973
PN   692   SC   55720
SN   Audiovisual teaching method which employs presentation of feedback as an aid to learning.
- B   Audiovisual Instruction   1973
- R   ↓ Educational Audiovisual Aids   1973

Videotape Recorders   1973
PN   115   SC   55730
SN   Device for recording on magnetic tape and having varied applications (e.g., teaching aid, analysis of research data).
- B   Tape Recorders   1973

Videotapes   1973
PN   1661   SC   55740
SN   Audiovisual tape recordings used in both noneducational and educational settings.
- B   Audiovisual Communications Media   1973

Vietnamese Cultural Groups   1997
PN   154   SC   57748
HN   Use ASIANS to access references from 1982-1996.
- B   Asians   1982
-     Southeast Asian Cultural Groups   2004

Vigilance   1967
PN   1592   SC   55750
SN   Intentional and conscious alertness characterized by a readiness to respond to environmental changes. Compare ATTENTION.
- B   Attention   1967
-     Monitoring   1973
-     Sustained Attention   1997
- R   Attention Span   1973
-     Selective Attention   1973

Vineland Social Maturity Scale   1973
PN   23   SC   55760
- B   Nonprojective Personality Measures   1973

Violence   1973
PN   9565   SC   55770
- B   Antisocial Behavior   1971
-     Conflict   1967
- N   Family Violence   1982
-     Patient Violence   1994
-     School Violence   2003
-     ↓ Violent Crime   2003
- R   Coercion   1994
-     Dangerousness   1988
-     Hate Crimes   2003
-     Nonviolence   1991
-     Partner Abuse   1991
-     Physical Abuse   1991
-     Riots   1973
-     Self Defense   1985
-     Terrorism   1982
-     Torture   1988
-     ↓ War   1967

Violent Crime   2003
PN   97   SC   55773
HN   This term was introduced in June 2003. PsycINFO records from the past 10 years were re-indexed with this term. The posting note reflects the number of records that were re-indexed.
- B   Crime   1967
-     Violence   1973
- N   Family Violence   1982
-     ↓ Homicide   1967
-     Physical Abuse   1991
-     Political Assassination   1973
-     ↓ Rape   1973
-     Terrorism   1982
- R   Arson   1985
-     ↓ Child Abuse   1971
-     Kidnapping   1988
-     ↓ Sexual Abuse   1988
-     Victimization   1973

Viral Disorders   1973
PN   474   SC   55780
- B   Infectious Disorders   1973
- N   Creutzfeldt Jakob Syndrome   1994
-     Encephalitis   1973
-     Epstein Barr Viral Disorder   1994
-     Herpes Genitalis   1988
-     Herpes Simplex   1973
-     ↓ Human Immunodeficiency Virus   1991
-     Influenza   1973
-     Measles   1973
-     Poliomyelitis   1973
-     Rubella   1973
- R   Chronic Fatigue Syndrome   1997
-     Pneumonia   1973

Virginity   1973
PN   118   SC   55810
- B   Psychosexual Behavior   1967
- R   Premarital Intercourse   1973
-     Sexual Abstinence   1973

Virtual Reality   1997
PN   812   SC   55815
- B   Computer Simulation   1973
- R   ↓ Computer Applications   1973
-     Human Machine Systems   1997

Vision   1967
PN   3621   SC   55820
- N   Linear Perspective   1982
-     ↓ Visual Perception   1967
- R   Tunnel Vision   1973

Vision — (cont'd)

    Visual Cortex 1967
    Visual Evoked Potentials 1973
    Visual Hallucinations 1973
    Visual Tracking 1973

Vision Disorders 1982

PN 3069   **SC** 55825
SN Disorders involving the visual system, including visual neural pathways.
HN The term VISUALLY HANDICAPPED was also used to represent this concept from 1967-1996, and VISUALLY DISABLED was used from 1997-2000. In 2000, VISION DISORDERS replaced the discontinued and deleted term VISUALLY DISABLED. VISUALLY DISABLED and VISUALLY HANDICAPPED were removed from all records containing them and replaced with VISION DISORDERS.
UF Visual Impairment
    Visually Handicapped
B Physical Disorders 1997
    Sense Organ Disorders 1973
N ↓ Blind 1967
    ↓ Eye Disorders 1973

Vision Disturbances (Hysterical)

Use Hysterical Vision Disturbances

Visions (Mysticism)

Use Mysticism

Visitation (Institution)

Use Institution Visitation

Visitation Rights

Use Child Visitation

Visual Acuity 1982

PN 1113   **SC** 55897
SN The ability or capacity of an observer to perceive fine detail.
HN Consider VISUAL THRESHOLDS or VISUAL DISCRIMINATION to access references prior to 1982.
UF Vernier Acuity
B Visual Perception 1967
R Pattern Discrimination 1967
    ↓ Spatial Perception 1967

Visual Attention 2004

PN 303   **SC** 58080
HN This term was introduced in June 2004. PsycINFO records from the past 10 years were re-indexed with this term. The posting note reflects the number of records that were re-indexed.
B Attention 1967
R Eye Fixation 1982
    ↓ Visual Perception 1967

Visual Contrast 1985

PN 1336   **SC** 55898
SN Perceived difference in color, brightness, or other qualities of two or more simultaneously or successively presented visual stimuli despite a lack of objective differences.
B Visual Perception 1967
N Brightness Contrast 1985
    Color Contrast 1985

Visual Cortex 1967

PN 3286   **SC** 55900
UF Cortex (Visual)
    Striate Cortex
B Occipital Lobe 1973
R ↓ Vision 1967
    Visual Receptive Fields 1982

Visual Discrimination 1967

PN 6880   **SC** 55910
SN Ability to recognize quantitative or qualitative differences between visual shapes, forms, and patterns.
HN Use VISUAL DISCRIMINATION or VISUAL THRESHOLDS to access references on visual acuity prior to 1982.
B Perceptual Discrimination 1973
    Visual Perception 1967
R Visual Search 1982
    Visual Tracking 1973

Visual Displays 1973

PN 3041   **SC** 55920
SN Presentation of visual information in the form of charts, graphs, maps, signs, symbols, or patterns.
HN Prior to 1985, used for visual devices such as cathode-ray tubes or instrument panels. From 1985, consider also VIDEO DISPLAY UNITS, INSTRUMENT CONTROLS, or GRAPHICAL DISPLAYS.
B Displays 1967
    Visual Stimulation 1973
N Video Display Units 1985
R ↓ Computer Peripheral Devices 1985
    Pictorial Stimuli 1978
    Spatial Frequency 1982
    Temporal Frequency 1985

Visual Evoked Potentials 1973

PN 3026   **SC** 55930
B Evoked Potentials 1967
R ↓ Cortical Evoked Potentials 1973
    ↓ Vision 1967

Visual Feedback 1973

PN 591   **SC** 55940
SN Return of information on specified behavioral functions or parameters by means of visual stimulation. Such stimulation may serve to regulate or control subsequent behavior, cognition, perception, or performance.
B Sensory Feedback 1973
    Visual Stimulation 1973

Visual Field 1967

PN 3505   **SC** 55950
R Eye Fixation 1982
    Fovea 1982
    Peripheral Vision 1988
    ↓ Visual Perception 1967

Visual Fixation

Use Eye Fixation

Visual Hallucinations 1973

PN 368   **SC** 55960
B Hallucinations 1967
R ↓ Vision 1967

Visual Impairment

Use Vision Disorders

Visual Masking 1973

PN 1111   **SC** 55970
SN Changes in perceptual sensitivity to a visual stimulus due to the presence of a second stimulus in close temporal proximity.
B Masking 1967
R ↓ Visual Stimulation 1973

Visual Memory 1994

PN 973   **SC** 55973
B Memory 1967
N Visuospatial Memory 1997
R Eidetic Imagery 1973
    ↓ Spatial Memory 1988
    ↓ Visual Perception 1967

Visual Neglect

Use Sensory Neglect

Visual Perception 1967

PN 19686   **SC** 55980
B Perception 1967
    Vision 1967
N Autokinetic Illusion 1967
    Binocular Vision 1967
    ↓ Brightness Perception 1973
    ↓ Color Perception 1967
    Dark Adaptation 1973
    Eye Fixation 1982
    Face Perception 1985
    Foveal Vision 1988
    Interocular Transfer 1985
    Monocular Vision 1973
    Peripheral Vision 1988
    Stereoscopic Vision 1973
    Texture Perception 1982
    Visual Acuity 1982
    ↓ Visual Contrast 1985
    Visual Discrimination 1967
    ↓ Visual Thresholds 1973
    ↓ Visuospatial Ability 1997
R ↓ Eye (Anatomy) 1967
    ↓ Eye Disorders 1973
    Lipreading 1973
    Mirror Image 1991
    Retinal Eccentricity 1991
    Visual Attention 2004
    Visual Field 1967
    ↓ Visual Memory 1994
    Visual Receptive Fields 1982
    Visual Tracking 1973

Visual Perspective

Use Linear Perspective

Visual Receptive Fields 1982

PN 679   **SC** 55985
SN Area of the retina which, when stimulated, affects a specific ganglion cell or lateral geniculate body cell, with zones in each field responding in a complementary way to various properties of visual stimuli such as color or onset/offset. Also, those zones in visual cortex which respond in a complementary way to straight-edge orientation-specific stimuli.
B Receptive Fields 1985
R Geniculate Bodies (Thalamus) 1973
    ↓ Neurons 1973
    ↓ Photoreceptors 1973
    Retinal Eccentricity 1991
    Visual Cortex 1967
    ↓ Visual Perception 1967

Visual Search   1982

PN 1975   SC 55987

SN Perceptual processes associated with detecting and/or locating specified visual targets which are usually not continuously visible. Compare VISUAL TRACKING.

R   Cognitive Discrimination   1973
   ↓ Eye Movements   1967
    Pattern Discrimination   1967
    Signal Detection (Perception)   1967
    Visual Discrimination   1967
   ↓ Visual Thresholds   1973

Visual Spatial Ability

Use   Visuospatial Ability

Visual Spatial Memory

Use   Visuospatial Memory

Visual Stimulation   1973

PN 9105   SC 55990

B   Perceptual Stimulation   1973
N   Dichoptic Stimulation   1982
   ↓ Illumination   1967
    Prismatic Stimulation   1973
    Stereoscopic Presentation   1973
    Tachistoscopic Presentation   1973
   ↓ Visual Displays   1973
    Visual Feedback   1973
R   ↓ Color   1967
    Linear Perspective   1982
    Pictorial Stimuli   1978
    Spatial Frequency   1982
    Temporal Frequency   1985
    Video Display Units   1985
    Visual Masking   1973

Visual Thresholds   1973

PN 2366   SC 56000

SN The minimal level of stimulation, the minimal difference between any stimuli, or the minimal stimulus change that is visually detectable.

UF   Luminance Threshold
    Photic Threshold
B   Thresholds   1967
    Visual Perception   1967
N   Critical Flicker Fusion Threshold   1967
R   Dark Adaptation   1973
    Light Adaptation   1982
    Luminance   1982
   ↓ Perceptual Measures   1973
    Retinal Eccentricity   1991
    Visual Search   1982

Visual Tracking   1973

PN 1464   SC 56010

SN Perceptual processes associated with following a specified visual target with the eyes along its path of movement. Usually involves a continuously visible target. Compare VISUAL SEARCH.

B   Tracking   1967
R   ↓ Vision   1967
    Visual Discrimination   1967
   ↓ Visual Perception   1967

Visualization

Use   Imagery

Visually Handicapped

Use   Vision Disorders

Visuospatial Ability   1997

PN 1025   SC 56025

UF   Visual Spatial Ability
B   Spatial Ability   1982
    Visual Perception   1967
N   Visuospatial Memory   1997

Visuospatial Memory   1997

PN 408   SC 56027

UF   Visual Spatial Memory
B   Spatial Memory   1988
    Visual Memory   1994
    Visuospatial Ability   1997

Vitamin C

Use   Ascorbic Acid

Vitamin Deficiency Disorders   1973

PN 182   SC 56040

B   Nutritional Deficiencies   1973
N   Pellagra   1973
    Wernickes Syndrome   1973
R   ↓ Vitamins   1973

Vitamin Therapy   1978

PN 313   SC 56045

B   Drug Therapy   1967
R   ↓ Vitamins   1973

Vitamins   1973

PN 598   SC 56050

N   Ascorbic Acid   1973
   ↓ Choline   1973
    Folic Acid   1973
    Nicotinamide   1973
    Nicotinic Acid   1973
R   ↓ Antioxidants   2004
    Dietary Supplements   2001
   ↓ Drugs   1967
   ↓ Vitamin Deficiency Disorders   1973
    Vitamin Therapy   1978

Vocabulary   1967

PN 2481   SC 56060

UF   Words (Vocabulary)
B   Language   1967
N   Anagrams   1973
    Antonyms   1973
    Homographs   1973
    Homonyms   1973
    Neologisms   1973
    Sight Vocabulary   1973
    Slang   1973
    Synonyms   1973
R   ↓ Semantics   1967
   ↓ Verbal Communication   1967

Vocal Cords   1973

PN 60   SC 56070

B   Larynx   1973

Vocalization   1967

PN 873   SC 56075

SN Production of sounds by means of vocal cord vibrations.

N   ↓ Animal Vocalizations   1973
    Crying   1973
    Laughter   1978
    Subvocalization   1973
   ↓ Voice   1973
R   ↓ Animal Communication   1967
   ↓ Communication   1967

Vocalization — (cont'd)

   ↓ Oral Communication   1985
    Singing   1997
   ↓ Verbal Communication   1967

Vocalization (Infant)

Use   Infant Vocalization

Vocalizations (Animal)

Use   Animal Vocalizations

Vocational Adjustment

Use   Occupational Adjustment

Vocational Aspirations

Use   Occupational Aspirations

Vocational Choice

Use   Occupational Choice

Vocational Counseling

Use   Occupational Guidance

Vocational Counselors   1973

PN 290   SC 56140

SN Persons engaged in career guidance, usually in social service, school, government agency, industrial, or employment center settings.

B   Counselors   1967
R   Mentor   1985
    Occupational Guidance   1967
    School Counselors   1973
   ↓ Social Workers   1973

Vocational Education   1973

PN 1602   SC 56150

SN Formal training in or out of school, designed to teach skills and knowledge required for occupational proficiency, especially for paraprofessional, trade, or clerical occupations.

UF   Industrial Arts Education
B   Curriculum   1967
N   Cooperative Education   1982
R   ↓ Occupations   1967

Vocational Education Teachers   1988

PN 54   SC 56155

UF   Technical Education Teachers
B   Teachers   1967

Vocational Evaluation   1991

PN 174   SC 56157

SN Assessment of vocational aptitude, job skills, and performance potential using simulated or real work experiences and measures. Used for disabled or disordered populations.

B   Evaluation   1967
    Vocational Rehabilitation   1967
R   Disability Management   1991
    Employability   1973
   ↓ Employee Skills   1973
    Work Adjustment Training   1991

Vocational Guidance

Use   Occupational Guidance

Vocational Interests

Use   Occupational Interests

Vocational Maturity 1978
PN 971   **SC** 56175
SN Ability to make age-appropriate vocational decisions and choices, usually predictive of good vocational adjustment.
UF Career Maturity
   Maturity (Vocational)
R Occupational Attitudes 1973
   Occupational Choice 1967
   Occupational Interests 1967
   Occupational Preference 1973
   ↓ Occupations 1967

Vocational Mobility
Use Occupational Mobility

Vocational Preference
Use Occupational Preference

Vocational Rehabilitation 1967
PN 3472   **SC** 56210
SN Planning and providing necessary services required for successful job placement and subsequent vocational adjustment of handicapped clients.
UF Rehabilitation (Vocational)
B Psychosocial Rehabilitation 1973
N Supported Employment 1994
   Vocational Evaluation 1991
   Work Adjustment Training 1991
R Disability Management 1991
   Rehabilitation Counseling 1978
   School to Work Transition 1994

Vocational School Students 1973
PN 378   **SC** 56220
B Students 1967

Vocational Schools
Use Technical Schools

Vocations
Use Occupations

Voice 1973
PN 1032   **SC** 56250
B Vocalization 1967
N Crying 1973
   Infant Vocalization 1973
R ↓ Communication 1967
   ↓ Oral Communication 1985
   Singing 1997

Voice Disorders
Use Dysphonia

Voles 2004
PN   **SC** 56255
HN Use RODENTS to access references from 1973 to June 2004.
B Rodents 1973

Volition 1988
PN 620   **SC** 56257
SN Process of deciding on a course of action voluntarily or without direct external influence.
UF Free Will
B Choice Behavior 1967
   ↓ Decision Making 1967
   Determinism 1997

Volition — (cont'd)
   Freedom 1978
   Self Determination 1994

Volt Meters
Use Apparatus

Volunteer Civilian Personnel
Use Volunteers

Volunteer Military Personnel 1973
PN 35   **SC** 56290
SN Persons who enter military service voluntarily.
B Military Personnel 1967
R Commissioned Officers 1973
   ↓ Enlisted Military Personnel 1973
   National Guardsmen 1973
   ROTC Students 1973
   Volunteers 2003

Volunteer Personnel
Use Volunteers

Volunteerism
Use Volunteers

Volunteers 2003
PN 1378   **SC** 56303
SN Individuals who willingly undertake a service.
HN In June 2003, this term was created to replace the discontinued terms VOLUNTEER PERSONNEL and VOLUNTEER CIVILIAN PERSONNEL. VOLUNTEER PERSONNEL and VOLUNTEER CIVILIAN PERSONNEL were removed from all records containing them and replaced with VOLUNTEERS.
UF Volunteer Civilian Personnel
   Volunteer Personnel
   Volunteerism
R ↓ Assistance (Social Behavior) 1973
   Charitable Behavior 1973
   Community Involvement 2003
   Cooperation 1967
   ↓ Prosocial Behavior 1982
   Volunteer Military Personnel 1973

Volunteers (Experiment)
Use Experimental Subjects

Vomeronasal Sense 1982
PN 163   **SC** 56327
SN Perceptual system activated by chemical stimuli which trigger vomeronasal nerve activity
R Chemoreceptors 1973
   ↓ Olfactory Perception 1967

Vomit Inducing Drugs
Use Emetic Drugs

Vomiting 1973
PN 536   **SC** 56340
UF Regurgitation
B Gastrointestinal Disorders 1973
   Symptoms 1967
R ↓ Antiemetic Drugs 1973
   ↓ Emetic Drugs 1973
   Nausea 1973
   Purging (Eating Disorders) 2003
   Rumination (Eating) 2001

Voting Behavior 1973
PN 1049   **SC** 56350
B Behavior 1967
   Political Participation 1988
   Political Processes 1973
R ↓ Political Attitudes 1973
   Political Elections 1973
   Political Issues 1973
   Political Psychology 1997

Vowels 1973
PN 1199   **SC** 56360
B Letters (Alphabet) 1973
   Phonology 1973
R ↓ Phonemes 1973
   Syllables 1973
   Words (Phonetic Units) 1967

Voyeurism 1973
PN 69   **SC** 56370
B Paraphilias 1988
R Exhibitionism 1973

Vulnerability (Disorders)
Use Susceptibility (Disorders)

Vygotsky (Lev) 1991
PN 509   **SC** 56375
SN Identifies biographical or autobiographical studies and discussions of Vygotsky's works. Sometimes spelled Vigotsky or Vygotski.
R Activity Theory 2003
   ↓ Language Development 1967
   Psycholinguistics 1967
   ↓ Psychologists 1967

Wages
Use Salaries

Wakefulness 1973
PN 1202   **SC** 56410
B Consciousness States 1971
R Sleep Wake Cycle 1985

Walk In Clinics 1973
PN 56   **SC** 56430
SN Facilities in hospitals or other community locations which typically provide immediate access to counseling and referral; are often staffed by volunteers and nondegreed counselors and focus on minority, indigent, or youthful populations.
B Clinics 1967
R ↓ Crisis Intervention Services 1973
   Psychiatric Clinics 1973

Walking 1973
PN 827   **SC** 56440
B Motor Performance 1973

Wandering Behavior 1991
PN 73   **SC** 56450
SN Aimless activity usually resulting from a confused mental state.
B Behavior 1967
   Motor Processes 1967
R Mental Confusion 1973
   Place Disorientation 1973
   ↓ Symptoms 1967

War 1967
PN 3331   **SC** 56460

War — (cont'd)
- **B** Conflict 1967
- Social Issues 1991
- **N** Nuclear War 1985
- **R** Combat Experience 1991
- Foreign Policy Making 1973
- ↓ Government Policy Making 1973
- Peace 1988
- ↓ Violence 1973

Warning Labels 1997
PN 36   SC 56464
- **B** Warnings 1997
- **R** Accident Prevention 1973
- ↓ Accidents 1967
- Consumer Protection 1973
- Hazards 1973
- ↓ Safety 1967
- ↓ Safety Devices 1973

Warning Signs
Use Warnings

Warnings 1997
PN 181   SC 56470
- **UF** Safety Warnings
- Warning Signs
- **N** Warning Labels 1997
- **R** Accident Prevention 1973
- ↓ Accidents 1967
- Consumer Protection 1973
- Hazards 1973
- ↓ Safety 1967
- ↓ Safety Devices 1973

Wasps 1982
PN 329   SC 56475
SN Any of numerous social or solitary winged hymenopterous insects.
- **B** Insects 1967
- **R** Larvae 1973

Water Deprivation 1967
PN 751   SC 56480
SN Absence of ad libitum water access. In experimental settings, water deprivation is used to achieve a definable level of motivation within the organism.
- **B** Deprivation 1967
- Stimulus Deprivation 1973
- **R** Dehydration 1988
- Thirst 1907

Water Intake 1967
PN 2093   SC 56490
SN Ingestion of water. Frequently used as an objective measure of physiological or motivational state or learning. Used for human or animal populations.
- **B** Drinking Behavior 1978
- Fluid Intake 1985
- **R** Animal Drinking Behavior 1973
- Dehydration 1988

Water Safety 1973
PN 137   SC 56500
SN Programs or activities for accident prevention in aquatic environments.
- **B** Safety 1967

Water Transportation 1973
PN 179   SC 56510
- **B** Transportation 1973
- **N** Submarines 1973

Watson (John Broadus) 1991
PN 30   SC 56515
SN Identifies biographical or autobiographical studies and discussions of Watson's works.
- **R** Behaviorism 1967
- ↓ Psychologists 1967

Weaning 1973
PN 311   SC 56520
SN Process of acclimating an infant or child to a substitute for the mother's milk. Used for human or animal populations.
- **B** Childrearing Practices 1967
- Eating Behavior 2004
- **R** Breast Feeding 1973
- Sucking 1978

Weapons 1978
PN 592   SC 56525
- **N** Firearms 2003

Weather
Use Atmospheric Conditions

Web Based Mental Health Services
Use Online Therapy

Wechsler Adult Intelligence Scale 1967
PN 1815   SC 56530
- **B** Intelligence Measures 1967

Wechsler Bellevue Intelligence Scale 1967
PN 47   SC 56540
- **B** Intelligence Measures 1967

Wechsler Intelligence Scale for Children 2001
PN 2376   SC 56551
HN In 2000, the truncated term WECHSLER INTELLIGENCE SCALE CHILDREN (which was used from 1967-2000) was deleted, removed from all records containing it, and replaced with its expanded form WECHSLER INTELLIGENCE SCALE FOR CHILDREN.
- **B** Intelligence Measures 1967

Wechsler Memory Scale 1988
PN 258   SC 56553
- **B** Neuropsychological Assessment 1982
- Retention Measures 1973

Wechsler Preschool Primary Scale 1988
PN 110   SC 56555
- **B** Intelligence Measures 1967

Weight (Body)
Use Body Weight

Weight (Statistics)
Use Statistical Weighting

Weight Control 1985
PN 1745   SC 56565
SN Deliberate regulation of one's weight through diet, exercise, or other means. Also, the relative weight change resulting from such regulation practices. Used for human populations only.
- **R** Aerobic Exercise 1988
- ↓ Body Weight 1967

Weight Control — (cont'd)
- Diets 1978
- ↓ Exercise 1973
- Food Intake 1967
- ↓ Health Behavior 1982
- Obesity (Attitudes Toward) 1997

Weight Perception 1967
PN 310   SC 56570
SN Awareness of mass or weight.
- **B** Somesthetic Perception 1967

Weightlessness 1967
PN 72   SC 56580
- **B** Gravitational Effects 1967
- **R** ↓ Somesthetic Stimulation 1973
- Spaceflight 1967

Weightlifting 1994
PN 96   SC 56585
- **B** Exercise 1973
- Recreation 1967
- Sports 1967

Welfare Services (Government) 1973
PN 1063   SC 56600
- **B** Government Programs 1973
- **R** Community Welfare Services 1973
- Government 1967
- Medicaid 1994

Well Being 1994
PN 5659   SC 56603
- **R** ↓ Adjustment 1967
- ↓ Health 1973
- Life Changes 2004
- Life Satisfaction 1985
- Lifestyle Changes 1997
- ↓ Mental Health 1967
- Positive Psychology 2003
- ↓ Quality of Life 1985

Wellness
Use Health

Wernickes Syndrome 1973
PN 126   SC 56630
SN Use APHASIA for Wernicke's aphasia.
- **B** Alcoholic Hallucinosis 1973
- Encephalopathies 1982
- Syndromes 1973
- Vitamin Deficiency Disorders 1973

Whales 1985
PN 97   SC 56665
- **B** Mammals 1973
- **N** Dolphins 1973
- Porpoises 1973

Wheelchairs
Use Mobility Aids

Whiplash 1997
PN 98   SC 56669
SN Soft tissue injury of cervical spine due to sudden hyperextension or hyperflexion or hyperrotation of neck or limbs.
- **UF** Cervical Sprain Syndrome
- **B** Spinal Cord Injuries 1973
- **R** ↓ Head Injuries 1973

Whistleblowing
Use Informants

White Betz A B Scale
Use Nonprojective Personality Measures

White Blood Cells
Use Leucocytes

White Collar Workers 1973
PN 554 **SC** 56690
SN Individuals employed in technical, professional, sales, administrative, or clerical positions.
B Business and Industrial Personnel 1967
N Accountants 1973
Clerical Personnel 1973
↓ Management Personnel 1973
Sales Personnel 1973
Secretarial Personnel 1973

White Noise 1973
PN 373 **SC** 56700
SN Noise composed of random mixture of sounds of different wavelengths.
B Auditory Stimulation 1967

White Rats
Use Rats

Whites 1982
PN 11645 **SC** 56720
HN In 1982, this term was created to replace the discontinued term CAUCASIANS. In 2000, CAUCASIANS was removed from all records and replaced with WHITES.
UF Caucasians
B Racial and Ethnic Groups 2001
N Anglos 1988
R Race (Anthropological) 1973

Wholistic Health
Use Holistic Health

Wide Range Achievement Test 1973
PN 173 **SC** 56730
B Achievement Measures 1967

Widowers 1973
PN 458 **SC** 56740
B Human Males 1973
R ↓ Family 1967
↓ Marital Status 1973
↓ Parental Absence 1973

Widows 1973
PN 925 **SC** 56750
B Human Females 1973
R ↓ Family 1967
↓ Marital Status 1973
↓ Parental Absence 1973

Wilcoxon Sign Rank Test 1973
PN 16 **SC** 56760
UF Sign Rank Test
B Nonparametric Statistical Tests 1967

Wilderness Experience 1991
PN 173 **SC** 56763

Wilderness Experience — **(cont'd)**
SN Outdoor environment and activities used to promote experiential learning or to treat and rehabilitate individuals with physical, emotional, or behavioral problems.
UF Outward Bound
R Management Training 1973
↓ Psychotherapeutic Techniques 1967
↓ Recreation 1967
↓ Rehabilitation 1967
↓ Sports 1967
Therapeutic Camps 1978

Williams Syndrome 2003
PN 171 **SC** 56764
SN A genetic disorder with onset in infancy that is characterized by supravalvular aortic stenosis, mental retardation, elfin facies, and hypercalcemia.
HN This term was introduced in June 2003. PsycINFO records from the past 10 years were re-indexed with this term. The posting note reflects the number of records that were re-indexed.
B Chromosome Disorders 1973
Genetic Disorders 1973
Syndromes 1973
R ↓ Heart Disorders 1973
↓ Mental Retardation 1967

Willpower
Use Self Control

Wilson Patterson Conservatism Scale 1973
PN 17 **SC** 56780
B Attitude Measures 1967

Wine 1973
PN 82 **SC** 56810
B Alcoholic Beverages 1973

Winnicottian Theory
Use Object Relations

Winter Depression
Use Seasonal Affective Disorder

Wisconsin Card Sorting Test 1994
PN 247 **SC** 56835
B Neuropsychological Assessment 1982

Wisdom 1994
PN 210 **SC** 56837
R ↓ Intelligence 1967
↓ Judgment 1967
↓ Knowledge Level 1978

Witchcraft 1973
PN 142 **SC** 56840
R Ethnology 1967
Faith Healing 1973
Mysticism 1967
Occultism 1978
↓ Parapsychology 1967
↓ Religious Beliefs 1973
Shamanism 1973

Withdrawal (Defense Mechanism) 1973
PN 281 **SC** 56860
SN Psychoanalytic term describing the escape from or avoidance of emotionally or psychologically painful situations.

Withdrawal (Defense Mechanism) — **(cont'd)**
B Defense Mechanisms 1967
R ↓ Separation Reactions 1997

Withdrawal (Drug)
Use Drug Withdrawal

Within Subjects Design
Use Repeated Measures

Witnesses 1985
PN 1729 **SC** 56885
SN Persons giving evidence in a court of law or observing traumatic events in a nonlegal context. Also used for analog studies of eyewitness identification performance, perception of witness credibility, and other studies of witness characteristics having legal implications.
UF Eyewitnesses
R ↓ Legal Evidence 1991
Legal Interrogation 1994
↓ Legal Testimony 1982

Wives 1973
PN 2449 **SC** 56900
B Human Females 1973
Spouses 1973

Wolves 1973
PN 143 **SC** 56910
B Canids 1997

Women
Use Human Females

Womens Liberation Movement 1973
PN 459 **SC** 56920
B Social Movements 1967
R ↓ Activism 2003
Feminism 1978

Woodcock Johnson Psychoeducational Battery 2001
PN 46
HN In 2001, the truncated term WOODCOCK JOHNSON PSYCHOED BATTERY (which was used from 1994-2000) was deleted, removed from all records containing it, and replaced with its expanded form WOODCOCK JOHNSON PSYCHOEDUCATIONAL BATTERY.
B Achievement Measures 1967
R Educational Diagnosis 1978

Word Associations 1967
PN 2013 **SC** 56930
UF Associations (Word)
R ↓ Associative Processes 1967
↓ Cognitive Processes 1967
Paired Associate Learning 1967

Word Blindness
Use Alexia

Word Deafness
Use Aphasia

Word Frequency 1973
PN 1041 **SC** 56970

Word Frequency — (cont'd)
SN Statistical probability of the occurrence of a given word in a given natural language.
R   Contextual Associations 1967

Word Meaning 1973
PN 2757   SC 56980
SN Connotative or denotative significance of a word.
B   Verbal Meaning 1973
R   Connotations 1973
     Contextual Associations 1967
     ↓ Lexical Access 1988
     Lexical Decision 1988

Word Origins
Use Etymology

Word Processing 1991
PN 204   SC 56993
SN Use of computer software to compose, edit, and produce text.
B   Computer Software 1967
     Data Processing 1967
R   Clerical Secretarial Skills 1973
     ↓ Computer Applications 1973
     ↓ Information Systems 1991
     Typing 1991

Word Recognition 1988
PN 3699   SC 56995
R   ↓ Associative Processes 1967
     Human Information Storage 1973
     Phonological Awareness 2004
     ↓ Reading Skills 1973
     ↓ Recognition (Learning) 1967
     Sight Vocabulary 1973
     Speech Perception 1967
     Words (Phonetic Units) 1967

Words (Form Classes)
Use Form Classes (Language)

Words (Phonetic Units) 1967
PN 7831   SC 57020
SN Spoken or written symbolic representation of an idea, frequently viewed as the smallest grammatically independent unit.
R   Antonyms 1973
     Consonants 1973
     Etymology 1973
     ↓ Grammar 1967
     Homographs 1973
     Homonyms 1973
     ↓ Lexical Access 1988
     Lexical Decision 1988
     Morphology (Language) 1973
     Neologisms 1973
     Rhyme 2004
     ↓ Semantics 1967
     Synonyms 1973
     Vowels 1973
     Word Recognition 1988

Words (Vocabulary)
Use Vocabulary

Work (Attitudes Toward) 1973
PN 3438   SC 57037

Work (Attitudes Toward) — (cont'd)
SN General work values. Use EMPLOYEE ATTI-TUDES for specific job situations and OCCUPA-TIONAL ATTITUDES for specific careers.
UF   Work Ethic
B   Attitudes 1967
R   ↓ Employee Attitudes 1967
     Employer Attitudes 1973
     Family Work Relationship 1997
     Job Involvement 1978
     Occupational Attitudes 1973
     ↓ Personnel 1967
     Professionalism 2003
     Workaholism 2004

Work Addiction
Use Workaholism

Work Adjustment Training 1991
PN 60   SC 57045
SN Training or programs to help disabled individuals increase work productivity, handle day to day demands of competitive employment, develop work tolerance, and to encourage interpersonal work relationships.
B   Vocational Rehabilitation 1967
R   ↓ Adjustment 1967
     Occupational Adjustment 1973
     Rehabilitation Counseling 1978
     Supported Employment 1994
     Vocational Evaluation 1991

Work at Home
Use Telecommuting

Work Environments
Use Working Conditions

Work Ethic
Use Work (Attitudes Toward)

Work Family Relationship
Use Family Work Relationship

Work Load 1982
PN 1068   SC 57055
SN Amount of work or working time expected from, assigned to, or performed by an individual.
B   Job Characteristics 1985
R   ↓ Division of Labor 1988
     Human Channel Capacity 1973
     Job Analysis 1967
     ↓ Job Performance 1967
     Work Scheduling 1973
     ↓ Working Conditions 1973

Work Related Illnesses 1994
PN 338   SC 57057
SN Includes both physical and mental illnesses, injuries, or disorders. Consider OCCUPATIONAL STRESS for work related stress.
R   Industrial Accidents 1973
     ↓ Mental Disorders 1967
     Occupational Exposure 1988
     Occupational Safety 1973
     Occupational Stress 1973
     ↓ Physical Disorders 1997
     Workers' Compensation Insurance 2003
     ↓ Working Conditions 1973

Work Rest Cycles 1973
PN 143   SC 57060
SN Strictly scheduled periods of working and resting based on observations that any increase in number of working hours beyond an optimal point diminishes production and efficiency.
B   Working Conditions 1973
R   Work Scheduling 1973
     Workaholism 2004

Work Satisfaction
Use Job Satisfaction

Work Scheduling 1973
PN 526   SC 57070
SN Individual or organizational distribution of work-load or work hours. Consider also WORKDAY SHIFTS.
UF   Flextime
     Scheduling (Work)
R   ↓ Management Methods 1973
     Work Load 1982
     Work Rest Cycles 1973

Work Stress
Use Occupational Stress

Work Study Programs
Use Educational Programs

Work Teams 2001
PN 533   SC 57077
B   Teams 1988
N   Self Managing Work Teams 2001
R   Groupware 2003
     ↓ Management 1967
     ↓ Management Methods 1973
     Organizational Structure 1967

Work Week Length 1973
PN 91   SC 57080
SN Actual number of hours or workdays an employee is required to work during a consecutive 7-day period.
B   Working Conditions 1973

Workaholism 2004
PN 56   SC 57085
SN Compulsive or excessive need to work.
HN This term was introduced in June 2004. Psyc-INFO records from the past 10 years were re-indexed with this term. The posting note reflects the number of records that were re-indexed.
UF   Work Addiction
R   ↓ Addiction 1973
     ↓ Employee Characteristics 1988
     Occupational Stress 1973
     Work (Attitudes Toward) 1973
     Work Rest Cycles 1973

Workday Shifts 1973
PN 703   SC 57090
SN Regularly scheduled daily working hours or scheduled working shifts with core hours being in morning, evening, or late night/predawn. Consider also WORK SCHEDULING.
UF   Shifts (Workday)
B   Working Conditions 1973

Workers
Use Personnel

Workers' Compensation Insurance [2003]
PN 228   **SC** 57103
SN Insurance providing medical benefits for employees injured in work-related accidents and provides continued income during disability.
HN In June 2003, this term was created to update the spelling from the discontinued term WORKMEN'S COMPENSATION INSURANCE which was removed from all records containing it, and replaced with WORKERS' COMPENSATION INSURANCE.
  UF Workmen's Compensation Insurance
  B Employee Benefits [1973]
    Employee Health Insurance [1973]
  R Disabled Personnel [1997]
    Work Related Illnesses [1994]

Workforce Diversity
Use Diversity in the Workplace

Working Alliance
Use Therapeutic Alliance

Working Conditions [1973]
PN 6758   **SC** 57120
SN Factors which contribute to the global milieu of the workplace. Includes physical environment characteristics, job content and work load, and psychosocial factors such as personnel composition, norms, attitudes, motivation, and employee services.
  UF Factory Environments
    Office Environment
    Work Environments
  B Social Environments [1973]
  N Job Enrichment [1973]
    Noise Levels (Work Areas) [1973]
    Occupational Safety [1973]
    Work Rest Cycles [1973]
    Work Week Length [1973]
    Workday Shifts [1973]
    Working Space [1973]
  R Disabled Personnel [1997]
    Family Work Relationship [1997]
    Groupware [2003]
    Human Factors Engineering [1973]
    Occupational Exposure [1988]
    Organizational Climate [1973]
    Person Environment Fit [1991]
    ↓ Personnel [1967]
    Quality of Work Life [1988]
    Telecommuting [2003]
    Work Load [1982]
    Work Related Illnesses [1994]

Working Memory
Use Short Term Memory

Working Space [1973]
PN 116   **SC** 57130
SN Physical characteristics of job setting, including such factors as amount of space, noise level, or lighting conditions.
  B Working Conditions [1973]

Working Women [1978]
PN 3191   **SC** 57135
  B Human Females [1973]
  R Dual Careers [1982]

Working Women — (cont'd)
  ↓ Employment Status [1982]
  ↓ Family [1967]
    Family Work Relationship [1997]
  ↓ Occupations [1967]
  ↓ Personnel [1967]
    Single Mothers [1994]

Workmen's Compensation Insurance
Use Workers' Compensation Insurance

Workplace Diversity
Use Diversity in the Workplace

World View [1988]
PN 1537   **SC** 57150
  UF Philosophy of Life
  R ↓ Attitudes [1967]
    Self Determination [1994]
    ↓ Values [1967]

World Wide Web (WWW)
Use Internet

Worms [1967]
PN 182   **SC** 57160
  B Invertebrates [1973]
  N Earthworms [1973]
    Planarians [1973]

Worry
Use Anxiety

Worship
Use Religious Practices

Wounds [1973]
PN 62   **SC** 57180
  B Injuries [1973]
  N Self Inflicted Wounds [1973]
  R Burns [1973]
    Electrical Injuries [1973]
    ↓ Head Injuries [1973]

Wrist [1973]
PN 148   **SC** 57190
  B Joints (Anatomy) [1973]
  R Arm (Anatomy) [1973]
    Hand (Anatomy) [1967]

Writers [1991]
PN 828   **SC** 57195
  UF Authors
  B Artists [1973]
  R Drama [1973]
    ↓ Literature [1967]

Writing (Creative)
Use Creative Writing

Writing (Cursive)
Use Cursive Writing

Writing (Handwriting)
Use Handwriting

Writing Skills [1985]
PN 2344   **SC** 57225
SN Proficiency in writing as developed through practice and influenced by ability.
  B Communication Skills [1973]
  R ↓ Literacy [1973]
    Literacy Programs [1997]
    Verbal Ability [1967]
    ↓ Written Communication [1985]

Written Communication [1985]
PN 4171   **SC** 57227
SN Expression of information in written form.
  B Verbal Communication [1967]
  N Creative Writing [1994]
  R Note Taking [1991]
    Proofreading [1988]
    Rhetoric [1991]
    Verbal Ability [1967]
    Writing Skills [1985]

Written Language [1967]
PN 1822   **SC** 57230
SN System of signs and symbols used to convey information.
  B Language [1967]
  N ↓ Alphabets [1973]
    ↓ Handwriting [1967]
    Numbers (Numerals) [1967]
    Paragraphs [1973]
    Readability [1978]
  R ↓ Legibility [1978]
    Orthography [1973]

Wryneck
Use Torticollis

X Rated Materials
Use Pornography

X Ray Diagnosis
Use Roentgenography

X Ray Therapy
Use Radiation Therapy

Xenophobia
Use Stranger Reactions

Xylocaine
Use Lidocaine

Yawning [1988]
PN 137   **SC** 57300
  B Reflexes [1971]
  R Respiration [1967]

Yoga [1973]
PN 328   **SC** 57310
  B Exercise [1973]
    Religious Practices [1973]
  R Relaxation [1973]

Yohimbine [1988]
PN 264   **SC** 57315
  B Adrenergic Blocking Drugs [1973]

Z Scores
   Use Standard Scores

Zen Buddhism [1973]
PN 163   **SC** 57370
   B   Buddhism [1973]

Zidovudine [1994]
PN 65   **SC** 57371
   UF   Azidothymidine
         AZT

Zidovudine — (cont'd)
   B   Antiviral Drugs [1994]
   R   Acquired Immune Deficiency
         Syndrome [1988]
     ↓ Human Immunodeficiency Virus [1991]

Zimeldine [1988]
PN 47   **SC** 57373
   B   Antidepressant Drugs [1971]
        Serotonin Reuptake Inhibitors [1997]

Zinc [1985]
PN 164   **SC** 57375
   B   Electrolytes [1973]
        Metallic Elements [1973]

Zoo Environment
   Use Animal Captivity

Zoology [1973]
PN 28   **SC** 57380
   B   Biology [1967]

Zulliger Z Test [1973]
PN 15   **SC** 57390
   B   Projective Personality Measures [1973]

Zungs Self Rating Depression Scale [1973]
PN 80   **SC** 57400
   B   Nonprojective Personality Measures [1973]

ROTATED ALPHABETICAL TERMS SECTION

Abandonment
Abdomen
Abdominal Wall
Abducens Nerve
Child Abduction *USE Kidnapping*
Illinois Test of Psycholinguistic **Abilities**
Ability
Ability Grouping
Ability Level
Ability Tests *USE Aptitude Measures*
Artistic **Ability**
Cognitive **Ability**
Henmon Nelson Tests of Mental Ability *USE Intelligence Measures*
Learning **Ability**
Mathematical **Ability**
Musical **Ability**
Nonverbal **Ability**
Numerical Ability *USE Mathematical Ability*
Reading **Ability**
School and College Ability Test *USE Aptitude Measures*
Spatial **Ability**
Verbal **Ability**
Visual Spatial Ability *USE Visuospatial Ability*
Visuospatial **Ability**
Ablation *USE Lesions*
Brain Ablation *USE Brain Lesions*
Abnormal Psychology
Aboriginal Populations
USE Indigenous Populations
Abortion Laws
Elective Abortion *USE Induced Abortion*
Induced **Abortion**
Spontaneous **Abortion**
Therapeutic Abortion *USE Induced Abortion*
Maslow **(Abraham** Harold)
Abreaction *USE Catharsis*
Father **Absence**
Mother **Absence**
Parental **Absence**
Employee **Absenteeism**
Absorption (Physiological)
Alcohol Abstinence *USE Sobriety*
Drug **Abstinence**
Sexual **Abstinence**
Abstraction
Abuse of Power
Abuse Reporting
Alcohol **Abuse**
Child **Abuse**
Child **Abuse** Reporting
Client Abuse *USE Patient Abuse*
Drug **Abuse**
Drug **Abuse** Liability
Drug **Abuse** Prevention
Elder **Abuse**
Emotional **Abuse**
Inhalant **Abuse**
Multidrug Abuse *USE Polydrug Abuse*
Partner **Abuse**
Patient **Abuse**
Physical **Abuse**
Polydrug **Abuse**
Psychological Abuse *USE Emotional Abuse*
Sexual **Abuse**
Solvent Abuse *USE Inhalant Abuse*
Spouse Abuse *USE Partner Abuse*
Substance Abuse *USE Drug Abuse*
Substance Abuse Prevention
USE Drug Abuse Prevention
Verbal **Abuse**
Academic Achievement
Academic Achievement Motivation
Academic Achievement Prediction
Academic Aptitude
Academic Environment
Academic Failure
Academic Grade Level *USE Grade Level*

Academic Overachievement
Academic Records *USE Student Records*
Academic Self Concept
Academic Specialization
Academic Underachievement
College **Academic** Achievement
Acalculia
Accelerated Speech *USE Speech Rate*
Acceleration Effects
Self Acceptance *USE Self Perception*
Social **Acceptance**
Lexical **Access**
Accessory Nerve *USE Cranial Nerves*
Accident Prevention
Accident Proneness
Accidents
Air Traffic **Accidents**
Automobile Accidents *USE Motor Traffic Accidents*
Cerebrovascular **Accidents**
Home **Accidents**
Industrial **Accidents**
Motor Traffic **Accidents**
Pedestrian **Accidents**
Transportation **Accidents**
Thermal **Acclimatization**
Eye Accommodation
USE Ocular Accommodation
Ocular **Accommodation**
Accomplishment *USE Achievement*
Accountability
Accountants
Certified Public Accountants *USE Accountants*
Accreditation (Education Personnel)
Educational Program **Accreditation**
Hospital **Accreditation**
School Accreditation *USE Educational Program Accreditation*
Teacher Accreditation *USE Accreditation (Education Personnel)*
Acculturation
Nucleus **Accumbens**
Acetaldehyde
Acetazolamide
Acetic Aldehyde *USE Acetaldehyde*
Acetylcholine
Acetylcholine Receptors
USE Cholinergic Receptors
Acetylcholinesterase
Acetylsalicylic Acid *USE Aspirin*
Aches *USE Pain*
Achievement
Achievement Measures
Achievement Motivation
Achievement Potential
Academic **Achievement**
Academic **Achievement** Motivation
Academic **Achievement** Prediction
College Academic **Achievement**
Mathematics **Achievement**
Need Achievement *USE Achievement Motivation*
Reading **Achievement**
Scholastic Achievement *USE Academic Achievement*
School Achievement *USE Academic Achievement*
Science **Achievement**
Stanford **Achievement** Test
Wide Range **Achievement** Test
Achilles Tendon Reflex
Achromatic Color
Acetylsalicylic Acid *USE Aspirin*
Ascorbic **Acid**
Aspartic **Acid**
Deoxyribonucleic **Acid**
Dihydroxyphenylacetic **Acid**
Folic **Acid**
Gamma Aminobutyric **Acid**
Gamma Aminobutyric **Acid** Agonists
Gamma Aminobutyric **Acid** Antagonists

Glutamic **Acid**
Homovanillic **Acid**
Hydroxyindoleacetic **Acid** (5-)
Ibotenic **Acid**
Kainic **Acid**
Lactic **Acid**
Lysergic **Acid** Diethylamide
Nicotinic **Acid**
Nicotinic Acid Amide *USE Nicotinamide*
Ribonucleic **Acid**
Uric **Acid**
Valproic **Acid**
Acids
Amino **Acids**
Fatty **Acids**
Nucleic **Acids**
Acoustic Nerve
Acoustic Reflex
Acoustic Stimuli *USE Auditory Stimulation*
Acoustics
Acquaintance Rape
Acquired Immune Deficiency Syndrome
Acrophobia
ACTH Releasing Factor
　　USE Corticotropin Releasing Factor
Acting Out
Affirmative **Action**
Active Avoidance
　　USE Avoidance Conditioning
Activism
Student **Activism**
Activist Movements *USE Activism*
Activities of Daily Living
Daily **Activities**
Extracurricular **Activities**
Activity Level
Activity Theory
Activity Therapy *USE Recreation Therapy*
Electrical **Activity**
Physical Activity *USE Motor Processes*
Self **Actualization**
Auditory **Acuity**
Hearing Acuity *USE Auditory Acuity*
Vernier Acuity *USE Visual Acuity*
Visual **Acuity**
Acupuncture
Acute Alcoholic Intoxication
Acute Paranoid Disorder
　　USE Paranoia (Psychosis)
Acute Psychosis
Acute Psychotic Episode
　　USE Acute Psychosis
Acute Schizophrenia
Acute Stress Disorder
Adaptability (Personality)
Adaptation
Dark **Adaptation**
Environmental **Adaptation**
Light **Adaptation**
Sensory **Adaptation**
Social Adaptation *USE Social Adjustment*
Kirton **Adaption** Innovation Inventory
Adaptive Behavior
Adaptive Testing
Addiction
Alcohol Addiction *USE Alcoholism*
Drug **Addiction**
Heroin **Addiction**
Hospital Addiction Syndrome
　　USE Munchausen Syndrome
Sexual **Addiction**
Work Addiction *USE Workaholism*
Addisons Disease
Food **Additives**
Adenosine
Cyclic **Adenosine** Monophosphate

ADHD *USE Attention Deficit Disorder with*
　　Hyperactivity
Gough **Adjective** Check List
Adjectives
Adjudication
Adjunctive Behavior
Adjustment
Adjustment Disorders
Emotional **Adjustment**
Marital Adjustment *USE Marital Relations*
Occupational **Adjustment**
Personal Adjustment *USE Emotional Adjustment*
Psychological Adjustment *USE Emotional Adjustment*
School **Adjustment**
Social **Adjustment**
Student Adjustment *USE School Adjustment*
Vocational Adjustment *USE Occupational Adjustment*
Work **Adjustment** Training
Adler (Alfred)
Adlerian Psychotherapy
Drug Self **Administration**
Drug **Administration** Methods
Educational **Administration**
Health Care **Administration**
Hospital **Administration**
School Administration
　　USE Educational Administration
Test **Administration**
Administrators
　　USE Management Personnel
Educational Administrators *USE School Administrators*
School **Administrators**
Facility **Admission**
Hospital **Admission**
Psychiatric Hospital **Admission**
Student **Admission** Criteria
Adolescent Attitudes
Adolescent Development
Adolescent Fathers
Adolescent Mothers
Adolescent Pregnancy
Adolescent Psychiatry
Adolescent Psychology
Adolescent Psychotherapy
Adopted Children
Adoptees
Adoption (Child)
Interracial **Adoption**
Transracial Adoption *USE Interracial Adoption*
Adoptive Parents
Adrenal Cortex Hormones
Adrenal Cortex Steroids
　　USE Corticosteroids
Adrenal Gland Disorders
Adrenal Gland Secretion
Adrenal Glands
Adrenal Medulla Hormones
Hypothalamo Pituitary **Adrenal** System
Adrenalectomy
Adrenaline *USE Epinephrine*
Adrenaline Receptors
　　USE Adrenergic Receptors
Adrenergic Blocking Drugs
Adrenergic Drugs
Adrenergic Nerves
Adrenergic Receptors
Adrenoceptors *USE Adrenergic Receptors*
Adrenocorticotropin *USE Corticotropin*
Adrenolytic Drugs *USE Adrenergic Drugs*
Adult Attitudes
Adult Children of Alcoholics
　　USE Children of Alcoholics
Adult Children *USE Adult Offspring*
Adult Day Care
Adult Development
Adult Education
Adult Learning

Adult Offspring
Leiter Adult Intelligence Scale
     USE Intelligence Measures
Wechsler **Adult** Intelligence Scale
Adultery *USE Extramarital Intercourse*
Advance Directives
Advance Organizers
Adventitious Disorders
Adventitiously Handicapped
     USE Adventitious Disorders
Adverbs
Drug Adverse Reactions
     USE Side Effects (Drug)
Advertising
Television **Advertising**
Advocacy
Child Advocacy *USE Advocacy*
Aerobic Exercise
Aerospace Personnel
Aesthetic Preferences
Aesthetics
Aetiology *USE Etiology*
CNS **Affecting** Drugs
Heart Rate **Affecting** Drugs
Affection
Affective Disorders
Affective Disturbances
     USE Affective Disorders
Affective Education
Affective Psychosis
Bipolar Affective Disorder *USE Bipolar Disorder*
Seasonal **Affective** Disorder
Afferent Pathways
Afferent Stimulation
Afferentation *USE Afferent Stimulation*
Affiliation Motivation
Need for Affiliation *USE Affiliation Motivation*
Religious **Affiliation**
Affirmative Action
African Americans *USE Blacks*
After School Programs
Aftercare
Perceptual **Aftereffect**
Afterimage
Age Differences
Age Discrimination
Age Regression (Hypnotic)
Developmental **Age** Groups
Intelligence Age *USE Mental Age*
Mental **Age**
Aged (Attitudes Toward)
Ageism
Government **Agencies**
County Agricultural Agents *USE Agricultural Extension Workers*
Insurance Agents *USE Sales Personnel*
Aggressive Behavior
Aggressive Driving Behavior
Animal **Aggressive** Behavior
Passive **Aggressive** Personality Disorder
Aggressiveness
Physical **Agility**
Aging
Aging (Attitudes Toward)
Physiological **Aging**
Paralysis Agitans *USE Parkinsons Disease*
Agitated Depression
     USE Major Depression
Agitation
Agnosia
Agonistic Behavior
     USE Aggressive Behavior
Benzodiazepine **Agonists**
Dopamine **Agonists**
GABA Agonists *USE Gamma Aminobutyric Acid Agonists*
Gamma Aminobutyric Acid **Agonists**
Narcotic **Agonists**

Opiate Agonists *USE Narcotic Agonists*
Serotonin **Agonists**
Agoraphobia
Agrammatism *USE Aphasia*
Agraphia
Agreeableness
Agricultural Extension Workers
Agricultural Workers
County Agricultural Agents
     USE Agricultural Extension Workers
School Federal Aid *USE Educational Financial Assistance*
Home Health Aides *USE Home Care Personnel*
Psychiatric **Aides**
Teacher **Aides**
AIDS (Attitudes Toward)
AIDS *USE Acquired Immune Deficiency Syndrome*
AIDS Dementia Complex
AIDS Prevention
AIDS Testing *USE HIV Testing*
Educational Audiovisual **Aids**
Hearing **Aids**
Mobility **Aids**
Optical **Aids**
Air Encephalography
     USE Pneumoencephalography
Air Force Personnel
Air Traffic Accidents
Air Traffic Control
Air Transportation
Aircraft
Aircraft Crew *USE Aerospace Personnel*
Aircraft Pilots
Airplanes *USE Aircraft*
Akathisia
Akinesia *USE Apraxia*
Alanines
Alanon *USE Alcohol Rehabilitation*
Alarm Responses
Alaska Natives
Native Alaskans *USE Alaska Natives*
Alateen *USE Alcohol Rehabilitation*
Ellis **(Albert)**
Albinism
Albino Rats *USE Rats*
Serum **Albumin**
Alcohol Abstinence *USE Sobriety*
Alcohol Abuse
Alcohol Addiction *USE Alcoholism*
Alcohol Dehydrogenases
Alcohol Drinking Attitudes
Alcohol Drinking Patterns
Alcohol Education *USE Drug Education*
Alcohol Intoxication
Alcohol Rehabilitation
Alcohol Withdrawal
Blood **Alcohol** Concentration
Ethyl Alcohol *USE Ethanol*
Fetal **Alcohol** Syndrome
Methyl Alcohol *USE Methanol*
Alcoholic Beverages
Alcoholic Hallucinosis
Alcoholic Offspring
     USE Children of Alcoholics
Alcoholic Psychosis
Acute **Alcoholic** Intoxication
Chronic **Alcoholic** Intoxication
Alcoholics Anonymous
Adult Children of Alcoholics *USE Children of Alcoholics*
Children of **Alcoholics**
Offspring of Alcoholics *USE Children of Alcoholics*
Alcoholism
Alcohols
Acetic Aldehyde *USE Acetaldehyde*
Aldolases *USE Enzymes*
Aldosterone
Alexia

Alexithymia
Adler **(Alfred)**
Algebra
Algorithms
Alienation
Alkaloids
Opium Alkaloids *USE Alkaloids*
Opium Alkaloids *USE Opiates*
Allergens *USE Antigens*
Allergic Disorders
Allergic Skin Disorders
Drug **Allergies**
Food **Allergies**
Therapeutic **Alliance**
Working Alliance *USE Therapeutic Alliance*
Alligators *USE Crocodilians*
Allocation of Resources
　　USE Resource Allocation
Resource **Allocation**
Reward **Allocation**
Allport Vernon Lindzey Study Values
　　USE Attitude Measures
Living **Alone**
Alopecia
Reading Aloud *USE Oral Reading*
Alpha Methylparatyrosine
Alpha Methyltyrosine
　　USE Alpha Methylparatyrosine
Alpha Rhythm
Initial Teaching **Alphabet**
Letters **(Alphabet)**
Alphabets
Alprazolam
Delayed **Alternation**
Language Alternation *USE Code Switching*
Spontaneous **Alternation**
Alternative Medicine
Alternative Schools
　　USE Nontraditional Education
Altitude Effects
Altruism
Aluminum
Alzheimers Disease
Dementia of Alzheimers Type *USE Alzheimers Disease*
Amantadine
Amatadine *USE Amantadine*
Amaurotic Familial Idiocy
　　USE Tay Sachs Disease
Ambidexterity *USE Handedness*
Stimulus **Ambiguity**
Tolerance for **Ambiguity**
Ambition *USE Aspirations*
Ambivalence
Amblyopia
Ambulatory Care
　　USE Outpatient Treatment
Amenorrhea
Amentia *USE Mental Retardation*
American Indians
African Americans *USE Blacks*
Asian Americans *USE Asians*
Cuban Americans *USE Hispanics*
Japanese **Americans**
Mexican **Americans**
Native Americans *USE American Indians*
Puerto Rican Americans *USE Hispanics*
Spanish Americans *USE Hispanics*
Nicotinic Acid Amide *USE Nicotinamide*
Amine Oxidase Inhibitors
Amines
Sympathomimetic **Amines**
Amino Acids
Gamma **Aminobutyric** Acid
Gamma **Aminobutyric** Acid Agonists
Gamma **Aminobutyric** Acid Antagonists
Aminotransferases *USE Transaminases*
Amitriptyline

Amnesia
Anterograde **Amnesia**
Global **Amnesia**
Retrograde **Amnesia**
Amniocentesis *USE Prenatal Diagnosis*
Amniotic Fluid
Amobarbital
Amobarbital Sodium *USE Amobarbital*
Reinforcement **Amounts**
Amphetamine
Amphetamine Sulfate *USE Amphetamine*
Amphibia
Amplifiers (Apparatus)
Response **Amplitude**
Amputation
Amygdala
Amygdaloid Body *USE Amygdala*
Amytal *USE Amobarbital*
Anabolism
Anabolites *USE Metabolites*
Anaclitic Depression
Anagram Problem Solving
Anagrams
Analeptic Drugs
Analgesia
Analgesic Drugs
Analog Computers
Miller **Analogies** Test
Analogy
Analysis
Analysis of Covariance
Analysis of Variance
Behavior **Analysis**
Causal **Analysis**
Cluster **Analysis**
Cohort **Analysis**
Confirmatory Factor Analysis *USE Factor Analysis*
Content **Analysis**
Content **Analysis** (Test)
Costs and Cost **Analysis**
Discourse **Analysis**
Dream **Analysis**
Error **Analysis**
Factor **Analysis**
Functional **Analysis**
Interaction **Analysis** (Statistics)
Item **Analysis** (Statistical)
Item **Analysis** (Test)
Job **Analysis**
Linkage Analysis *USE Genetic Linkage*
Meta **Analysis**
Multivariate **Analysis**
Path **Analysis**
Regression Analysis *USE Statistical Regression*
Risk Analysis *USE Risk Assessment*
Self **Analysis**
Statistical **Analysis**
Systems **Analysis**
Task **Analysis**
Transactional **Analysis**
Analysts *USE Psychoanalysts*
Analytic Psychology
　　USE Jungian Psychology
Analytical Psychotherapy
Neural **Analyzers**
Anankastic Personality
　　USE Obsessive Compulsive
　　Personality Disorder
Anaphylactic Shock
Anatomical Systems
Anatomically Detailed Dolls
Anatomy
Arm **(Anatomy)**
Arteries **(Anatomy)**
Back **(Anatomy)**
Capillaries **(Anatomy)**
Diaphragm **(Anatomy)**

Ear **(Anatomy)**
Elbow **(Anatomy)**
Eye **(Anatomy)**
Face **(Anatomy)**
Feet **(Anatomy)**
Fingers **(Anatomy)**
Hand **(Anatomy)**
Head **(Anatomy)**
Joints **(Anatomy)**
Labyrinth **(Anatomy)**
Leg **(Anatomy)**
Mouth **(Anatomy)**
Neck **(Anatomy)**
Palm **(Anatomy)**
Scalp **(Anatomy)**
Shoulder **(Anatomy)**
Skin **(Anatomy)**
Teeth **(Anatomy)**
Veins **(Anatomy)**
Ancestors
Androgen Antagonists *USE Antiandrogens*
Androgens
Androgyny
Anemia
Anencephaly
Anesthesia (Feeling)
Anesthesiology
Anesthetic Drugs
Ether **(Anesthetic)**
General **Anesthetics**
Local **Anesthetics**
Aneurysms
Anger
Anger Control
Anger Management *USE Anger Control*
Angina Pectoris
Angiography
Angiotensin
Cerebellopontile Angle *USE Cerebellum*
Anglos
Angst *USE Anxiety*
Anguish *USE Distress*
Anhedonia
Carbonic Anhydrase *USE Enzymes*
Animal Aggressive Behavior
Animal Assisted Therapy
Animal Behavior *USE Animal Ethology*
Animal Biological Rhythms
Animal Breeding
Animal Captivity
Animal Circadian Rhythms
Animal Coloration
Animal Communication
Animal Courtship Behavior
Animal Courtship Displays
Animal Defensive Behavior
Animal Development
Animal Distress Calls
Animal Division of Labor
Animal Domestication
Animal Dominance
Animal Drinking Behavior
Animal Emotionality
Animal Environments
Animal Escape Behavior
Animal Ethology
Animal Exploratory Behavior
Animal Feeding Behavior
Animal Foraging Behavior
Animal Grooming Behavior
Animal Hoarding Behavior
Animal Homing
Animal Human Interaction
USE Interspecies Interaction
Animal Innate Behavior
USE Instinctive Behavior

Animal Instinctive Behavior
USE Instinctive Behavior
Animal Learning
Animal Licking Behavior *USE Licking*
Animal Locomotion
Animal Mate Selection
Animal Maternal Behavior
Animal Maternal Deprivation
Animal Mating Behavior
Animal Models
Animal Motivation
Animal Navigation
USE Migratory Behavior (Animal)
Animal Nocturnal Behavior
Animal Open Field Behavior
Animal Parental Behavior
Animal Paternal Behavior
Animal Play
Animal Predatory Behavior
Animal Rearing
Animal Scent Marking
Animal Sex Differences
Animal Sexual Behavior
Animal Sexual Receptivity
Animal Social Behavior
Animal Strain Differences
Animal Tool Use *USE Tool Use*
Animal Vocalizations
Animal Welfare
Human Animal Interaction
USE Interspecies Interaction
Infants **(Animal)**
Migratory Behavior **(Animal)**
Seals **(Animal)**
Animals
Female **Animals**
Male **Animals**
Animism
Ankle
Anniversary Events
Anniversary Reactions
USE Anniversary Events
Public Service **Announcements**
Annual Leave
USE Employee Leave Benefits
Anodynes *USE Analgesic Drugs*
Anomie
Anonymity
Alcoholics **Anonymous**
Gamblers Anonymous *USE Twelve Step Programs*
Narcotics Anonymous *USE Twelve Step Programs*
Anorexia Nervosa
Anorexigenic Drugs
USE Appetite Depressing Drugs
Anosmia
Anosognosia
Anoxia
Antabuse *USE Disulfiram*
Antagonism *USE Hostility*
Androgen Antagonists *USE Antiandrogens*
Benzodiazepine **Antagonists**
CNS Depressant Drug Antagonists *USE Analeptic Drugs*
Dopamine **Antagonists**
Estrogen Antagonists *USE Antiestrogens*
GABA Antagonists
*USE Gamma Aminobutyric Acid
Antagonists*
Gamma Aminobutyric Acid **Antagonists**
Narcotic **Antagonists**
Opiate Antagonists *USE Narcotic Antagonists*
Opioid Antagonists *USE Narcotic Antagonists*
Serotonin **Antagonists**
Anterograde Amnesia
Culture **(Anthropological)**
Race **(Anthropological)**
Subculture **(Anthropological)**
Anthropologists

Anthropology
Anti Inflammatory Drugs
Antiadrenergic Drugs
   USE Sympatholytic Drugs
Antiandrogens
Antianxiety Drugs *USE Tranquilizing Drugs*
Antibiotics
Antibodies
Anticholinergic Drugs
   USE Cholinergic Blocking Drugs
Anticholinesterase Drugs
   USE Cholinesterase Inhibitors
Serial **Anticipation** (Learning)
Anticoagulant Drugs
Anticonvulsive Drugs
Antidepressant Drugs
Tricyclic **Antidepressant** Drugs
Antiemetic Drugs
Antiepileptic Drugs
   USE Anticonvulsive Drugs
Antiestrogens
Antigens
Antihistaminic Drugs
Antihypertensive Drugs
Antinauseant Drugs *USE Antiemetic Drugs*
Antineoplastic Drugs
Antioxidants
Antiparkinsonian Drugs
   USE Antitremor Drugs
Antipathy *USE Aversion*
Antipsychotic Drugs
   USE Neuroleptic Drugs
Antipyretic Drugs
   USE Anti Inflammatory Drugs
Antischizophrenic Drugs
   USE Neuroleptic Drugs
AntiSemitism
Antisocial Behavior
Antisocial Personality Disorder
Antispasmodic Drugs
Antitremor Drugs
Antitubercular Drugs
Antiviral Drugs
Antonyms
Ants
Anxiety
Anxiety Disorders
Anxiety Management
Anxiety Neurosis *USE Anxiety Disorders*
Anxiety Reducing Drugs
   USE Tranquilizing Drugs
Castration **Anxiety**
Childrens Manifest **Anxiety** Scale
Computer **Anxiety**
Death **Anxiety**
Generalized **Anxiety** Disorder
Mathematics **Anxiety**
Performance **Anxiety**
Separation **Anxiety**
Social **Anxiety**
Social Anxiety Disorder *USE Social Phobia*
Speech **Anxiety**
State Trait **Anxiety** Inventory
Taylor Manifest **Anxiety** Scale
Test **Anxiety**
Anxiolytic Drugs *USE Tranquilizing Drugs*
Anxiousness *USE Anxiety*
Aorta
Apathy
Apes *USE Primates (Nonhuman)*
Aphagia
Aphasia
Aphrodisiacs
Aplysia *USE Snails*
Apnea
Sleep **Apnea**
Apolipoproteins

Apomorphine
Apomorphine Hydrochloride
   USE Apomorphine
Apoplexy *USE Cerebrovascular Accidents*
Apparatus
Amplifiers **(Apparatus)**
Cage **Apparatus**
Experimental Apparatus *USE Apparatus*
Generators **(Apparatus)**
Incubators **(Apparatus)**
Stimulators **(Apparatus)**
Timers **(Apparatus)**
Vestibular **Apparatus**
Vibrators **(Apparatus)**
Apparent Distance
Apparent Movement
Apparent Size
Physical **Appearance**
Apperception
Childrens **Apperception** Test
Thematic **Apperception** Test
Appetite
Appetite Depressing Drugs
Appetite Disorders *USE Eating Disorders*
Job **Applicant** Attitudes
Job **Applicant** Interviews
Job **Applicant** Screening
Job **Applicants**
Computer **Applications**
Applied Psychology
Cognitive **Appraisal**
Apprehension *USE Anxiety*
Communication Apprehension *USE Speech Anxiety*
Apprenticeship
Biopsychosocial **Approach**
Interdisciplinary Treatment **Approach**
Multidisciplinary Treatment Approach *USE Interdisciplinary Treatment*
   Approach
Multimodal Treatment **Approach**
Need for **Approval**
Social **Approval**
Apraxia
Aptitude *USE Ability*
Aptitude Measures
Academic **Aptitude**
College Entrance Examination
Board Scholastic **Aptitude** Test
Differential **Aptitude** Tests
General **Aptitude** Test Battery
Mechanical **Aptitude**
Preliminary Scholastic Aptitude Test
   USE College Entrance Examination
   Board Scholastic Aptitude Test
Scholastic Aptitude *USE Academic Aptitude*
Scholastic Aptitude Test
   USE College Entrance Examination
   Board Scholastic Aptitude Test
Cerebral Aqueduct *USE Cerebral Ventricles*
Arabs
Arachnida
Arachnophobia *USE Phobias*
Archetypes
Architects
Architecture
Broca's **Area**
Preoptic **Area**
Ventral Tegmental Area *USE Tegmentum*
Noise Levels (Work **Areas)**
Poverty **Areas**
Recreation **Areas**
Arecoline
Arecoline Hydrobromide *USE Arecoline*
Arguments
Arithmetic *USE Mathematics*
Arm (Anatomy)
Army General Classification Test
Army Personnel

Physiological **Arousal**
Sexual **Arousal**
Living **Arrangements**
Cardiac Arrest *USE Heart Disorders*
Legal **Arrest**
Arrhythmias (Heart)
Arson
Art
Art Education
Art Therapy
Body Art *USE Cosmetic Techniques*
Painting **(Art)**
Photographic **Art**
Arterial Pulse
Arteries (Anatomy)
Carotid **Arteries**
Arteriosclerosis
Cerebral **Arteriosclerosis**
Arthritis
Rheumatoid **Arthritis**
Arthropoda
Articulation (Speech)
Articulation Disorders
Regression Artifact *USE Statistical Regression*
Artificial Insemination
    USE Reproductive Technology
Artificial Intelligence
Artificial Limbs *USE Prostheses*
Artificial Pacemakers
Artificial Respiration
Artistic Ability
Artists
Arts
Creative **Arts** Therapy
Industrial Arts Education *USE Vocational Education*
Language **Arts** Education
Martial **Arts**
Performing Arts *USE Arts*
Artwork *USE Art*
Asbestos *USE Hazardous Materials*
Asceticism
Ascorbic Acid
Asian Americans *USE Asians*
South East Asian Cultural Groups
    USE Southeast Asian Cultural Groups
South **Asian** Cultural Groups
Southeast **Asian** Cultural Groups
Asians
Aspartic Acid
Aspergers Syndrome
Asphyxia *USE Anoxia*
Aspiration Level
Aspirations
Career Aspirations *USE Occupational Aspirations*
Educational **Aspirations**
Occupational **Aspirations**
Vocational Aspirations *USE Occupational Aspirations*
Aspirin
Political **Assassination**
Assertiveness
Assertiveness Training
Assessment *USE Measurement*
Assessment Centers
Assessment Criteria
    USE Evaluation Criteria
Behavioral **Assessment**
Cognitive **Assessment**
Curriculum Based **Assessment**
Geriatric **Assessment**
Kaufman **Assessment** Battery for Children
Needs **Assessment**
Neuropsychological **Assessment**
Personality Assessment *USE Personality Measures*
Psychological **Assessment**
Risk **Assessment**
Self Assessment *USE Self Evaluation*
Cultural Assimilation *USE Acculturation*

Assistance (Social Behavior)
Educational Financial **Assistance**
Employee **Assistance** Programs
School Financial Assistance
    USE Educational Financial Assistance
Assisted Living
Assisted Suicide
Animal **Assisted** Therapy
Computer **Assisted** Design
Computer **Assisted** Diagnosis
Computer **Assisted** Instruction
Computer **Assisted** Testing
Paired **Associate** Learning
Free **Association**
Associationism
Contextual **Associations**
Loosening of Associations
    USE Fragmentation (Schizophrenia)
Word **Associations**
Associative Processes
Assortative Mating
Assortive Mating *USE Assortative Mating*
Asthenia
Asthenic Personality
    USE Personality Disorders
Asthma
Astrology
Astronauts
Asylums *USE Psychiatric Hospitals*
Ataractic Drugs *USE Tranquilizing Drugs*
Ataraxic Drugs *USE Tranquilizing Drugs*
Ataxia
Atheism
Atherosclerosis
Athetosis
Athletes
College **Athletes**
Athletic Participation
Athletic Performance
Athletic Training
Stereotaxic **Atlas**
Atmospheric Conditions
Atomism *USE Reductionism*
Atrial Fibrillation *USE Fibrillation (Heart)*
Cerebral **Atrophy**
Cortical Atrophy *USE Cerebral Atrophy*
Muscular **Atrophy**
Atropine
Attachment Behavior
Attachment Disorders
Reactive Attachment Disorder
    USE Attachment Disorders
Attack Behavior
Panic **Attack**
Heart Attacks *USE Heart Disorders*
Educational **Attainment** Level
Attempted Suicide
School **Attendance**
Attendants (Institutions)
Flight Attendants *USE Aerospace Personnel*
Hospital Attendants *USE Attendants (Institutions)*
Residential Care Attendants *USE Attendants (Institutions)*
Attention
Attention Deficit Disorder
Attention Deficit Disorder with Hyperactivity
Attention Span
Divided **Attention**
Selective **Attention**
Sustained **Attention**
Visual **Attention**
Stimulus **Attenuation**
Attitude Change
Attitude Formation
Attitude Measurement
Attitude Measures
Attitude Similarity
Minnesota Teacher Attitude Inventory *USE Attitude Measures*

315

Opinion Attitude and Interest Survey
    USE Attitude Measures
    Attitudes
Adolescent **Attitudes**
Adult **Attitudes**
Aged **(Attitudes** Toward)
Aging **(Attitudes** Toward)
AIDS **(Attitudes** Toward)
Alcohol Drinking **Attitudes**
Birth Control Attitudes *USE Family Planning Attitudes*
Child **Attitudes**
Childrearing **Attitudes**
Class Attitudes
    USE Socioeconomic Class Attitudes
Client **Attitudes**
Community **Attitudes**
Computer **Attitudes**
Consumer **Attitudes**
Counselor **Attitudes**
Death **Attitudes**
Disabled **(Attitudes** Toward)
Drinking Attitudes *USE Alcohol Drinking Attitudes*
Drug Usage **Attitudes**
Eating **Attitudes**
Employee **Attitudes**
Employer **Attitudes**
Environmental **Attitudes**
Family Planning **Attitudes**
Gender Role Attitudes *USE Sex Role Attitudes*
Health Personnel **Attitudes**
Health **Attitudes**
Homosexuality **(Attitudes** Toward)
Job Applicant **Attitudes**
Lower Class **Attitudes**
Marriage **Attitudes**
Mental Illness **(Attitudes** Toward)
Mental Retardation **(Attitudes** Toward)
Middle Class **Attitudes**
Obesity **(Attitudes** Toward)
Occupational **Attitudes**
Parental **Attitudes**
Patient Attitudes *USE Client Attitudes*
Physical Disabilities **(Attitudes** Toward)
Physical Illness **(Attitudes** Toward)
Political **Attitudes**
Psychologist **Attitudes**
Psychotherapist **Attitudes**
Public Attitudes *USE Public Opinion*
Race Attitudes *USE Racial and Ethnic Attitudes*
Racial and Ethnic **Attitudes**
Sensory Disabilities **(Attitudes** Toward)
Sex Role **Attitudes**
Sexual **Attitudes**
Social Class Attitudes
    USE Socioeconomic Class Attitudes
Socioeconomic Class **Attitudes**
Sports **(Attitudes** Toward)
Stereotyped **Attitudes**
Student **Attitudes**
Teacher **Attitudes**
Therapist **Attitudes**
Upper Class **Attitudes**
Work **(Attitudes** Toward)
    Attorneys
Interpersonal **Attraction**
Sexual **Attraction**
Physical **Attractiveness**
    Attribution
Experimental **Attrition**
Student **Attrition**
Atypical Paranoid Disorder
    USE Paranoia (Psychosis)
Atypical Somatoform Disorder
    USE Body Dysmorphic Disorder
Audiences
Audiogenic Seizures
Audiology

Audiometers
Audiometry
Bekesy Audiometry *USE Audiometry*
Bone Conduction **Audiometry**
Audiotapes
Audiovisual Communications Media
Audiovisual Instruction
Educational **Audiovisual** Aids
Audition *USE Auditory Perception*
Auditory Acuity
Auditory Cortex
Auditory Discrimination
Auditory Displays
Auditory Evoked Potentials
Auditory Feedback
Auditory Hallucinations
Auditory Localization
Auditory Masking
Auditory Nerve *USE Acoustic Nerve*
Auditory Neurons
Auditory Perception
Auditory Stimulation
Auditory Thresholds
Delayed **Auditory** Feedback
Drug **Augmentation**
Augmentative Communication
Aura
Intra Aural Muscle Reflex *USE Acoustic Reflex*
Aurally Handicapped
    USE Hearing Disorders
Heart **Auricles**
Auricular Fibrillation
    USE Fibrillation (Heart)
Authoritarianism
Authoritarianism Rebellion Scale
    USE Nonprojective Personality
    Measures
Parental Authoritarianism *USE Parenting Style*
Authority
Authors *USE Writers*
Autism
Autism Spectrum Disorders
    USE Pervasive Developmental
    Disorders
Early Infantile **Autism**
Autistic Children
Autistic Psychopathy
    USE Aspergers Syndrome
Autistic Thinking
Autobiographical Memory
Autobiography
Autoeroticism
Autogenic Training
Autohypnosis
Autoimmune Disorders
    USE Immunologic Disorders
Autokinetic Illusion
Automated Information Coding
Automated Information Processing
Automated Information Retrieval
Automated Information Storage
Automated Speech Recognition
Automatic Speaker Recognition
    USE Automated Speech Recognition
Automation
Automatism
Automobile Accidents
    USE Motor Traffic Accidents
Automobile Safety *USE Highway Safety*
Automobiles
Autonomic Ganglia
Autonomic Nervous System
Autonomic Nervous System Disorders
Postganglionic Autonomic Fibers *USE Autonomic Ganglia*
Preganglionic Autonomic Fibers *USE Autonomic Ganglia*
Autonomy (Government)
Autopsy

Psychological **Autopsy**
Autoregulation *USE Homeostasis*
Autoshaping
Autosome Disorders
Autosomes
Autotomy *USE Self Mutilation*
Gradepoint Average *USE Academic Achievement*
Aversion
Aversion Conditioning
Aversion Therapy
Odor Aversion Conditioning
USE Aversion Conditioning
Taste Aversion Conditioning
USE Aversion Conditioning
Aversive Stimulation
Aviation
Aviation Personnel
USE Aerospace Personnel
Aviation Safety
Aviators *USE Aircraft Pilots*
Avoidance
Avoidance Conditioning
Active Avoidance *USE Avoidance Conditioning*
Passive Avoidance *USE Avoidance Conditioning*
Avoidant Personality Disorder
Awareness
Body **Awareness**
Phonemic Awareness *USE Phonological Awareness*
Phonological **Awareness**
Axons
Azidothymidine *USE Zidovudine*
AZT *USE Zidovudine*
Type B Personality
USE Coronary Prone Behavior
White Betz A B Scale *USE Nonprojective Personality*
Measures
Babbling *USE Infant Vocalization*
Bush Babies *USE Lemurs*
Test Tube Babies *USE Reproductive Technology*
Babinski Reflex
Baboons
Babysitting *USE Child Care*
Back (Anatomy)
Back Pain
Educational **Background**
Family **Background**
Parent Educational **Background**
Backward Masking *USE Masking*
Baclofen
Bacteria *USE Microorganisms*
Bacterial Disorders
Bacterial Meningitis
Baldness *USE Alopecia*
Ballet *USE Dance*
Head **Banging**
Bannister Repertory Grid
Baptists *USE Protestants*
Barbital
Barbiturate Poisoning
Barbiturates
Bargaining
Barium
Barometric Pressure
USE Atmospheric Conditions
Baroreceptors
Epstein **Barr** Viral Disorder
Blood Brain **Barrier**
Basal Ganglia
Basal Metabolism
Basal Readers *USE Reading Materials*
Basal Skin Resistance
Nucleus **Basalis** Magnocellularis
Baseball
Case **Based** Reasoning
Computer Based Training
USE Computer Assisted Instruction
Curriculum **Based** Assessment

Evidence Based Medicine
USE Evidence Based Practice
Evidence **Based** Practice
Knowledge Based Systems *USE Expert Systems*
School **Based** Intervention
Web Based Mental Health Services
USE Online Therapy
Basic Skills Testing
USE Minimum Competency Tests
Iowa Tests of **Basic** Skills
Basketball
Bass (Fish)
Bats
Battered Child Syndrome
Battered Females
General Aptitude Test **Battery**
Halstead Reitan Neuropsychological **Battery**
Kaufman Assessment **Battery** for Children
Luria Nebraska Neuropsychological **Battery**
Woodcock Johnson
Psychoeducational **Battery**
Bayes Theorem *USE Statistical Probability*
Bayley Scales of Infant Development
Heart Beat *USE Heart Rate*
Beavers
Beck Depression Inventory
Bedwetting *USE Urinary Incontinence*
Beer
Bees
Beetles
Behavior
Behavior Analysis
Behavior Change
Behavior Contracting
Behavior Disorders
Behavior Modification
Behavior Problems
Behavior Therapy
Adaptive **Behavior**
Adjunctive **Behavior**
Aggressive Driving **Behavior**
Aggressive **Behavior**
Agonistic Behavior *USE Aggressive Behavior*
Animal Aggressive **Behavior**
Animal Courtship **Behavior**
Animal Defensive **Behavior**
Animal Drinking **Behavior**
Animal Escape **Behavior**
Animal Exploratory **Behavior**
Animal Feeding **Behavior**
Animal Foraging **Behavior**
Animal Grooming **Behavior**
Animal Hoarding **Behavior**
Animal Innate Behavior *USE Instinctive Behavior*
Animal Instinctive Behavior *USE Instinctive Behavior*
Animal Licking Behavior *USE Licking*
Animal Maternal **Behavior**
Animal Mating **Behavior**
Animal Nocturnal **Behavior**
Animal Open Field **Behavior**
Animal Parental **Behavior**
Animal Paternal **Behavior**
Animal Predatory **Behavior**
Animal Sexual **Behavior**
Animal Social **Behavior**
Animal Behavior *USE Animal Ethology*
Antisocial **Behavior**
Assistance (Social **Behavior)**
Attachment **Behavior**
Attack **Behavior**
Charitable **Behavior**
Child **Behavior** Checklist
Childhood Play **Behavior**
Choice **Behavior**
Civic Behavior *USE Community Involvement*
Classroom **Behavior**
Classroom **Behavior** Modification

Cognitive **Behavior** Therapy
Collective **Behavior**
Conservation (Ecological **Behavior)**
Consumer **Behavior**
Coping **Behavior**
Coronary Prone **Behavior**
Criminal **Behavior**
Deviant Behavior *USE Antisocial Behavior*
Disruptive Behavior *USE Behavior Problems*
Drinking **Behavior**
Driving **Behavior**
Eating **Behavior**
Exploratory **Behavior**
Fundamental Interpersonal
Relation Orientation **Behavior** Ques
Health Care Seeking **Behavior**
Health **Behavior**
Help Seeking **Behavior**
Helping Behavior *USE Assistance (Social Behavior)*
Hoarding **Behavior**
Illness **Behavior**
Instinctive **Behavior**
Migratory **Behavior** (Animal)
Modeling Behavior *USE Imitation (Learning)*
Organizational **Behavior**
Planned **Behavior**
Prosocial **Behavior**
Psychosexual **Behavior**
Rational Emotive **Behavior** Therapy
Rotational **Behavior**
Runaway **Behavior**
Self Defeating **Behavior**
Self Destructive **Behavior**
Self Injurious Behavior *USE Self Destructive Behavior*
Sexual Behavior *USE Psychosexual Behavior*
Sharing (Social **Behavior)**
Social **Behavior**
Stereotyped **Behavior**
Treatment Seeking Behavior
USE Health Care Seeking Behavior
Trust (Social **Behavior)**
Voting **Behavior**
Wandering **Behavior**
Behavioral Assessment
Behavioral Contrast
Behavioral Ecology
Behavioral Economics
Behavioral Genetics
Behavioral Health
USE Health Care Psychology
Behavioral Medicine
USE Health Care Psychology
Behavioral Sciences
Behaviorism
Well **Being**
Bekesy Audiometry *USE Audiometry*
Irrational **Beliefs**
Religious **Beliefs**
Wechsler **Bellevue** Intelligence Scale
Safety **Belts**
Seat Belts *USE Safety Belts*
Bem Sex Role Inventory
Bemegride
Benactyzine
Benadryl *USE Diphenhydramine*
Bender Gestalt Test
Employee Leave **Benefits**
Employee **Benefits**
Vacation Benefits *USE Employee Leave Benefits*
Benign Neoplasms
Benton Revised Visual Retention Test
Benzedrine *USE Amphetamine*
Benzodiazepine Agonists
Benzodiazepine Antagonists
Benzodiazepines
Bereavement *USE Grief*

Beta Blockers
USE Adrenergic Blocking Drugs
Between Groups Design
White Betz A B Scale
USE Nonprojective Personality Measures
Beverages (Nonalcoholic)
Alcoholic **Beverages**
Bias Crimes *USE Hate Crimes*
Cultural Test **Bias**
Experimenter **Bias**
Item Bias *USE Test Bias*
Response **Bias**
Test **Bias**
Biased Sampling
Bible
Bibliotherapy
Bicuculline
Spina **Bifida**
Big Five Personality Model
USE Five Factor Personality Model
Bile
Bilingual Education
Bilingualism
Double **Bind** Interaction
Receptor **Binding**
Stanford **Binet** Intelligence Scale
Binge Eating
Binocular Vision
Binomial Distribution
Bioavailability
Biochemical Markers
USE Biological Markers
Biochemistry
Biodata *USE Biographical Data*
Bioequivalence *USE Bioavailability*
Bioethics
Biofeedback
Biofeedback Training
Biographical Data
Biographical Inventories
Biography
Biological Family
Biological Markers
Biological Psychiatry
Biological Rhythms
Biological Symbiosis
Animal **Biological** Rhythms
Human **Biological** Rhythms
Biology
Cells **(Biology)**
Hybrids **(Biology)**
Mimicry **(Biology)**
Biopsy
Biopsychosocial Approach
Biopsychosocial Model
USE Biopsychosocial Approach
Biosynthesis
Bipolar Affective Disorder
USE Bipolar Disorder
Bipolar Disorder
Bipolar Mood Disorder
USE Bipolar Disorder
Biracial Children *USE Interracial Offspring*
Birds
Birth
Birth Control
Birth Control Attitudes
USE Family Planning Attitudes
Birth Injuries
Birth Order
Birth Parents *USE Biological Family*
Birth Rate
Birth Rites
Birth Trauma
Birth Weight
Diaphragms **(Birth** Control)

318

Home Birth *USE Midwifery*
Low Birth Weight *USE Birth Weight*
Premature **Birth**
Multiple **Births**
Point **Biserial** Correlation
Bisexuality
Nail **Biting**
Bitterness *USE Taste Perception*
Black Power Movement
Blackbirds
Blacks
Blacky Pictures Test
USE Projective Personality Measures
Bladder
Blame
Rotter Incomplete Sentences **Blank**
Strong Vocational Interest **Blank**
Blind
Deaf **Blind**
Color **Blindness**
Hysterical Blindness
USE Hysterical Vision Disturbances
Mind Blindness *USE Theory of Mind*
Word Blindness *USE Alexia*
Blink Reflex *USE Eyeblink Reflex*
Kohs **Block** Design Test
Beta Blockers *USE Adrenergic Blocking Drugs*
Calcium Channel Blockers *USE Channel Blockers*
Channel **Blockers**
Adrenergic **Blocking** Drugs
Cholinergic **Blocking** Drugs
Ganglion **Blocking** Drugs
Neuromuscular Blocking Drugs
USE Muscle Relaxing Drugs
Blood
Blood Alcohol Concentration
Blood and Lymphatic Disorders
Blood Brain Barrier
Blood Cells
Blood Circulation
Blood Coagulation
Blood Disorders
USE Blood and Lymphatic Disorders
Blood Donation *USE Tissue Donation*
Blood Flow
Blood Glucose *USE Blood Sugar*
Blood Groups
Blood Plasma
Blood Platelets
Blood Pressure
Blood Pressure Disorders
Blood Proteins
Blood Serum
Blood Sugar
Blood Transfusion
Blood Vessels
Blood Volume
Cerebral **Blood** Flow
Red Blood Cells *USE Erythrocytes*
White Blood Cells *USE Leucocytes*
Blue Collar Workers
College Entrance Examination **Board** Scholastic Aptitude Test
State Board Examinations
USE Professional Examinations
Boarding Schools
Boards of Education
Dementia with Lewy **Bodies**
Geniculate **Bodies** (Thalamus)
Body Art *USE Cosmetic Techniques*
Body Awareness
Body Dysmorphic Disorder
Body Fluids
Body Height
Body Image
Body Image Disturbances
Body Language
Body Rocking

Body Rotation *USE Rotational Behavior*
Body Size
Body Sway Testing
Body Temperature
Body Types *USE Somatotypes*
Body Weight
Amygdaloid Body *USE Amygdala*
Human **Body**
Lewy Body Disease
USE Dementia with Lewy Bodies
Mind Body *USE Dualism*
Out of **Body** Experiences
Pineal **Body**
Thermoregulation **(Body)**
Tissues **(Body)**
Bombesin
Bone Conduction Audiometry
Bone Disorders
Bone Marrow
Bones
Bonobos
Bonuses
Books
Borderline Mental Retardation
Borderline Personality Disorder
Borderline States
Boredom
Botany
Bottle Feeding
Culture **Bound** Syndromes
Outward Bound *USE Wilderness Experience*
Upward **Bound**
Boundaries (Psychological)
Sexual Boundary Violations
*USE Professional Client Sexual
Relations*
Bourgeois *USE Middle Class*
Bowel Disorders *USE Colon Disorders*
Irritable **Bowel** Syndrome
Shuttle Box Grids *USE Shuttle Boxes*
Shuttle Box Hurdles *USE Shuttle Boxes*
Shuttle **Boxes**
Skinner **Boxes**
Boys *USE Human Males*
Brachial Plexus *USE Spinal Nerves*
Bradycardia
Bradykinesia
Braille
Braille Instruction
Brain
Brain Ablation *USE Brain Lesions*
Brain Concussion
Brain Damage
Brain Development
USE Neural Development
Brain Disorders
Brain Lesions
Brain Mapping *USE Stereotaxic Atlas*
Brain Maps *USE Stereotaxic Atlas*
Brain Metabolism *USE Neurochemistry*
Brain Neoplasms
Brain Self Stimulation
Brain Size
Brain Stem
Brain Stimulation
Brain Weight
Blood **Brain** Barrier
Chemical **Brain** Stimulation
Decortication **(Brain)**
Electrical **Brain** Stimulation
Left **Brain**
Minimal **Brain** Disorders
Organic **Brain** Syndromes
Right **Brain**
Split Brain *USE Commissurotomy*
Traumatic **Brain** Injury
Brainstorming

Brainwashing
Brand Names
Brand Preferences
Bravery *USE Courage*
Nervous Breakdown *USE Mental Disorders*
Psychotherapeutic **Breakthrough**
Breast
Breast Cancer Screening
    USE Cancer Screening
Breast Examination
    USE Self Examination (Medical)
Breast Feeding
Breast Neoplasms
Breathing *USE Respiration*
Animal **Breeding**
Selective **Breeding**
Brief Psychotherapy
Brief Reactive Psychosis
    USE Acute Psychosis
Myers **Briggs** Type Indicator
Bright Light Therapy *USE Phototherapy*
Brightness Constancy
Brightness Contrast
Brightness Perception
Watson (John **Broadus)**
Broca's Area
Lithium Bromide *USE Bromides*
Bromides
Bromocriptine
Bronchi
Bronchial Disorders
Brothers
Spearman **Brown** Test
Bruxism
Buddhism
Zen **Buddhism**
Buddhists
Budgerigars
Budgets
Taste **Buds**
Bufotenine
Nest **Building**
Religious **Buildings**
Olfactory **Bulb**
Bulimia
Bulls *USE Cattle*
Bullying
Medial Forebrain **Bundle**
Bupropion
Caregiver **Burden**
Government Bureaucracy *USE Government*
Burnout *USE Occupational Stress*
Burns
Skinner **(Burrhus** Fredcric)
Buses *USE Motor Vehicles*
Bush Babies *USE Lemurs*
Business
Business and Industrial Personnel
Business Education
Business Management
Business Networking
    USE Professional Networking
Business Organizations
Business Students
Businessmen
    USE Business and Industrial Personnel
Buspirone
Butterflies
Butyrylperazine
    USE Phenothiazine Derivatives
Buying *USE Consumer Behavior*
Cadres *USE Social Groups*
Caffeine
Cage Apparatus
Calcium
Calcium Channel Blockers
    USE Channel Blockers

Calcium Ions
Calculators *USE Digital Computers*
Calculus
California F Scale
California Psychological Inventory
Corpus **Callosum**
Animal Distress **Calls**
Calories
Cameras
Political **Campaigns**
Camping
Concentration **Camps**
Recreational Day Camps *USE Summer Camps (Recreation)*
Summer **Camps** (Recreation)
Therapeutic **Camps**
Campuses
Ear Canal *USE External Ear*
Semicircular **Canals**
Canaries
Cancer Screening
Breast Cancer Screening *USE Cancer Screening*
Prostate Cancer Screening *USE Cancer Screening*
Skin Cancer Screening *USE Cancer Screening*
Terminal **Cancer**
Cancers *USE Neoplasms*
Political **Candidates**
Canids
Cannabinoids
Cannabis
Cannibalism
Canonical Correlation
    USE Multivariate Analysis
Human Channel **Capacity**
Capgras Syndrome
Capillaries (Anatomy)
Capital Punishment
Human **Capital**
Social **Capital**
Capitalism
Capsaicin
Animal **Captivity**
Captopril
Carbachol
Carbamazepine
Carbidopa
Carbohydrate Metabolism
Carbohydrates
Carbon
Carbon Dioxide
Carbon Monoxide
Carbon Monoxide Poisoning
Lithium **Carbonate**
Carbonic Anhydrase *USE Enzymes*
Carboxyhemoglobinemia
    USE Carbon Monoxide Poisoning
Carcinogens
Carcinomas *USE Neoplasms*
Wisconsin **Card** Sorting Test
Cardiac Arrest *USE Heart Disorders*
Cardiac Disorders *USE Heart Disorders*
Cardiac Rate *USE Heart Rate*
Cardiac Surgery *USE Heart Surgery*
Cardiography
Cardiology
Cardiotonic Drugs *USE Drugs*
Cardiovascular Disorders
Cardiovascular Reactivity
Cardiovascular System
Adult Day **Care**
Ambulatory Care *USE Outpatient Treatment*
Child Day **Care**
Child Self **Care**
Child **Care**
Child **Care** Workers
Continuity of Care *USE Continuum of Care*
Continuum of **Care**
Day **Care** Centers

Elder **Care**
Foster **Care**
Health **Care** Administration
Health **Care** Costs
Health **Care** Delivery
Health **Care** Policy
Health Care Professionals *USE Health Personnel*
Health **Care** Psychology
Health **Care** Seeking Behavior
Health **Care** Services
Health **Care** Utilization
Home **Care**
Home **Care** Personnel
Intensive **Care**
Long Term **Care**
Managed **Care**
Medical Care Costs *USE Health Care Costs*
Mental Health Care Costs *USE Health Care Costs*
Mental Health Care Policy *USE Health Care Policy*
Palliative **Care**
Patient Care Planning *USE Treatment Planning*
Prenatal **Care**
Primary Health **Care**
Quality of **Care**
Residential Care Attendants
　　　　USE Attendants (Institutions)
Residential **Care** Institutions
Respite **Care**
Self **Care** Skills
Career Aspirations
　　　　USE Occupational Aspirations
Career Change
Career Choice *USE Occupational Choice*
Career Counseling
　　　　USE Occupational Guidance
Career Development
Career Education
Career Exploration *USE Career Education*
Career Goals
　　　　USE Occupational Aspirations
Career Guidance
　　　　USE Occupational Guidance
Career Maturity *USE Vocational Maturity*
Career Preference
　　　　USE Occupational Preference
Career Transitions
　　　　USE Career Development
Careers *USE Occupations*
Dual **Careers**
Nontraditional **Careers**
Caregiver Burden
Caregivers
Family Caregivers *USE Caregivers*
Jung **(Carl)**
Rogers **(Carl)**
Carotid Arteries
Carp
Cartoons (Humor)
Case Based Reasoning
Case History *USE Patient History*
Case Management
Case Report
Social **Casework**
Caseworkers *USE Social Workers*
Social Caseworkers *USE Social Workers*
Caste System
Castration
Castration Anxiety
Male **Castration**
Cat Learning
CAT Scan *USE Tomography*
Crying **Cat** Syndrome
Catabolism
Catabolites *USE Metabolites*
Catalepsy
Catamnesis *USE Posttreatment Followup*
Cataplexy

Cataracts
Catatonia
Catatonic Schizophrenia
Catecholamines
Categorizing
　　　　USE Classification (Cognitive Process)
Catharsis
Catheterization
Cathexis
Cathode Ray Tubes
　　　　USE Video Display Units
Roman **Catholicism**
Catholics
Cats
Cattell Culture Fair Intelligence Test
　　　　USE Culture Fair Intelligence Test
Cattle
Caucasians *USE Whites*
Cauda Equina *USE Spinal Nerves*
Caudate Nucleus
Causal Analysis
Cecotrophy *USE Coprophagia*
Celebrity *USE Fame*
Celiac Plexus *USE Autonomic Ganglia*
Celibacy *USE Sexual Abstinence*
Cell Nucleus
Sickle **Cell** Disease
Single Cell Organisms *USE Microorganisms*
Cells (Biology)
Blood **Cells**
Connective Tissue **Cells**
Epithelial **Cells**
Ganglion **Cells** (Retina)
Natural Killer **Cells**
Nerve Cells *USE Neurons*
Purkinje **Cells**
Red Blood Cells *USE Erythrocytes*
Retinal Ganglion Cells *USE Ganglion Cells (Retina)*
White Blood Cells *USE Leucocytes*
Censorship
Client **Centered** Therapy
Person Centered Psychotherapy
　　　　USE Client Centered Therapy
Centering
Assessment **Centers**
Community Mental Health **Centers**
Day Care **Centers**
Growth Centers *USE Human Potential Movement*
Learning **Centers** (Educational)
Rehabilitation **Centers**
Shopping **Centers**
Suicide Prevention **Centers**
Central Nervous System
Central Nervous System Disorders
Central Nervous System Drugs
　　　　USE CNS Affecting Drugs
Central Tendency Measures
Central Vision *USE Foveal Vision*
Cerebellar Cortex *USE Cerebellum*
Cerebellar Nuclei *USE Cerebellum*
Cerebellopontile Angle *USE Cerebellum*
Cerebellum
Cerebral Aqueduct
　　　　USE Cerebral Ventricles
Cerebral Arteriosclerosis
Cerebral Atrophy
Cerebral Blood Flow
Cerebral Cortex
Cerebral Dominance
Cerebral Hemorrhage
Cerebral Ischemia
Cerebral Lesions *USE Brain Lesions*
Cerebral Palsy
Cerebral Vascular Disorders
　　　　USE Cerebrovascular Disorders
Cerebral Ventricles
Trigonum Cerebrale *USE Fornix*

Cerebrospinal Fluid
Cerebrovascular Accidents
Cerebrovascular Disorders
Certification Examinations
    USE Professional Examinations
Professional **Certification**
Certified Public Accountants
    USE Accountants
Locus **Ceruleus**
Cervical Plexus *USE Spinal Nerves*
Cervical Sprain Syndrome *USE Whiplash*
Cervix
Smoking **Cessation**
Markov **Chains**
Chance (Fortune)
Attitude **Change**
Behavior **Change**
Career **Change**
Culture **Change**
Job Change *USE Career Change*
Opinion Change *USE Attitude Change*
Organizational **Change**
Personality **Change**
Sex **Change**
Social **Change**
Stimulus **Change**
Life **Changes**
Lifestyle **Changes**
Channel Blockers
Calcium Channel Blockers *USE Channel Blockers*
Human **Channel** Capacity
Chaos Theory
Chaplains
Character *USE Personality*
Character Development
    USE Personality Development
Character Disorders
    USE Personality Disorders
Character Formation
    USE Personality Development
Client **Characteristics**
Counselor **Characteristics**
Demographic **Characteristics**
Employee **Characteristics**
Job **Characteristics**
Organizational **Characteristics**
Parental **Characteristics**
Patient Characteristics *USE Client Characteristics*
Population Characteristics
    USE Demographic Characteristics
Speech **Characteristics**
Student **Characteristics**
Teacher **Characteristics**
Therapist **Characteristics**
Charisma
Charismatic Leadership
    USE Transformational Leadership
Charitable Behavior
Cri du Chat Syndrome *USE Crying Cat Syndrome*
Cheating
Gough Adjective **Check** List
Mooney Problem **Check** List
Child Behavior **Checklist**
Symptom **Checklists**
Chemical Brain Stimulation
Chemical Elements
Chemicals
Chemistry
Chemoreceptors
Chemotherapy *USE Drug Therapy*
Chess
Chest *USE Thorax*
Chewing Tobacco
    USE Smokeless Tobacco
Chi Square Test
Optic **Chiasm**
Chicanos *USE Mexican Americans*

Chickens
Child Abduction *USE Kidnapping*
Child Abuse
Child Abuse Reporting
Child Advocacy *USE Advocacy*
Child Attitudes
Child Behavior Checklist
Child Care
Child Care Workers
Child Custody
Child Day Care
Child Discipline
Child Guidance Clinics
Child Labor
Child Maltreatment *USE Child Abuse*
Child Molestation *USE Pedophilia*
Child Neglect
Child Psychiatric Clinics
    USE Child Guidance Clinics
Child Psychiatry
Child Psychology
Child Psychotherapy
Child Self Care
Child Support
Child Visitation
Child Welfare
Adoption **(Child)**
Battered **Child** Syndrome
Father **Child** Communication
Father **Child** Relations
Mother **Child** Communication
Mother **Child** Relations
Parent **Child** Communication
Parent **Child** Relations
Childbirth *USE Birth*
Childbirth Training
Labor **(Childbirth)**
Natural **Childbirth**
Childhood Development
Childhood Memories *USE Early Memories*
Childhood Neurosis
Childhood Play Behavior
Childhood Play Development
Childhood Psychosis
Childhood Schizophrenia
Early **Childhood** Development
Childlessness
Childrearing Attitudes
Childrearing Practices
Children of Alcoholics
Adopted **Children**
Adult Children *USE Adult Offspring*
Adult Children of Alcoholics
    USE Children of Alcoholics
Autistic **Children**
Biracial Children *USE Interracial Offspring*
Foster **Children**
Grown Children *USE Adult Offspring*
Illegitimate **Children**
Kaufman Assessment Battery for **Children**
Latchkey Children *USE Child Self Care*
Only **Children**
Wechsler Intelligence Scale for **Children**
Childrens Apperception Test
Childrens Manifest Anxiety Scale
Childrens Personality Questionnaire
Childrens Recreational Games
Chimpanzees
Pygmy Chimpanzees *USE Bonobos*
Chinchillas
Chinese Cultural Groups
Chiroptera *USE Bats*
Chloral Hydrate
Chloralose *USE Hypnotic Drugs*
Chlordiazepoxide
Chloride Ions
Choline Chloride *USE Choline*

Chlorimipramine
Chlorisondamine *USE Amines*
Chloroform
Chlorophenylpiperazine *USE Piperazines*
Chlorpromazine
Chlorprothixene
Choice Behavior
Choice Shift
Career Choice *USE Occupational Choice*
Forced **Choice** (Testing Method)
Multiple **Choice** (Testing Method)
Occupational **Choice**
Vocational Choice *USE Occupational Choice*
Cholecystokinin
Cholesterol
Choline
Choline Chloride *USE Choline*
Cholinergic Blocking Drugs
Cholinergic Drugs
Cholinergic Nerves
Cholinergic Receptors
Cholinesterase
Cholinesterase Inhibitors
Cholinoceptors *USE Cholinergic Receptors*
Cholinolytic Drugs
USE Cholinergic Blocking Drugs
Cholinomimetic Drugs
Chorda Tympani Nerve *USE Facial Nerve*
Chorea
Huntingtons Chorea *USE Huntingtons Disease*
Choroid *USE Eye (Anatomy)*
Choroid Plexus *USE Cerebral Ventricles*
Christianity
Christians
Chromaticity
Chromosome Disorders
Deletion **(Chromosome)**
Sex **Chromosome** Disorders
Translocation **(Chromosome)**
Chromosomes
Sex **Chromosomes**
Chronic Alcoholic Intoxication
Chronic Fatigue Syndrome
Chronic Illness
Chronic Mental Illness
Chronic Pain
Chronic Psychosis
Chronic Schizophrenia *USE Schizophrenia*
Chronic Stress
Chronicity (Disorders)
Chunking
Churches *USE Religious Buildings*
Cichlids
Cigarette Smoking *USE Tobacco Smoking*
Cimetidine
Gyrus **Cinguli**
Animal **Circadian** Rhythms
Quality Circles *USE Participative Management*
Closed **Circuit** Television
Blood **Circulation**
Circulatory Disorders
USE Cardiovascular Disorders
Circumcision
Cirrhosis (Liver)
Citalopram
Cities *USE Urban Environments*
Citizen Participation
USE Community Involvement
Citizenship
Inner City *USE Urban Environments*
Civic Behavior
USE Community Involvement
Civil Law
Civil Rights
Civil Rights Movement
Civil Servants *USE Government Personnel*
Volunteer Civilian Personnel *USE Volunteers*

Clairvoyance
Class Attitudes
USE Socioeconomic Class Attitudes
Class Size
Lower **Class**
Lower **Class** Attitudes
Middle **Class**
Middle **Class** Attitudes
Social **Class**
Social Class Attitudes
USE Socioeconomic Class Attitudes
Socioeconomic **Class** Attitudes
Upper **Class**
Upper **Class** Attitudes
Form **Classes** (Language)
Classical Conditioning
Classical Test Theory
Classification (Cognitive Process)
Classification Systems *USE Taxonomies*
Army General **Classification** Test
International **Classification** of Diseases
Classmates
Classroom Behavior
Classroom Behavior Modification
Classroom Discipline
Classroom Environment
Classroom Instruction *USE Teaching*
Classroom Management
Classroom Teachers *USE Teachers*
Open **Classroom** Method
Classrooms
Claustrophobia
Cleft Palate
Clergy
Clerical Personnel
Clerical Secretarial Skills
Client Abuse *USE Patient Abuse*
Client Attitudes
Client Centered Therapy
Client Characteristics
Client Compliance
USE Treatment Compliance
Client Counselor Interaction
USE Psychotherapeutic Processes
Client Dropouts *USE Treatment Dropouts*
Client Education
Client Participation
Client Records
Client Rights
Client Satisfaction
Client Transfer
Client Treatment Matching
Client Violence *USE Patient Violence*
Counselor Client Interaction
USE Psychotherapeutic Processes
Professional **Client** Sexual Relations
Treatment Client Matching
USE Client Treatment Matching
Clients
Climacteric Depression
USE Involutional Depression
Climacteric Paranoia
USE Involutional Paranoid Psychosis
Organizational **Climate**
Clinical Judgment (Not Diagnosis)
Clinical Markers *USE Biological Markers*
Clinical Methods Training
Clinical Psychologists
Clinical Psychology
Clinical Psychology Graduate Training
Clinical Psychology Internship
Clinical Supervision
USE Professional Supervision
Clinical Trials
Millon **Clinical** Multiaxial Inventory
Structured **Clinical** Interview
Clinicians

Clinics
Child Guidance **Clinics**
Child Psychiatric Clinics *USE Child Guidance Clinics*
Outpatient Psychiatric Clinics *USE Psychiatric Clinics*
Psychiatric **Clinics**
Walk In **Clinics**
Cliques *USE Social Groups*
Clomipramine *USE Chlorimipramine*
Clonazepam
Clonidine
Cloning
Closed Circuit Television
Closed Head Injuries *USE Head Injuries*
Closedmindedness *USE Openmindedness*
Perceptual **Closure**
Clothing
Clozapine
Cloze Testing
School **Club** Membership
Clubs (Social Organizations)
Therapeutic Social **Clubs**
Cluster Analysis
Clustering *USE Cluster Analysis*
CNS Affecting Drugs
CNS Depressant Drug Antagonists
USE Analeptic Drugs
CNS Depressant Drugs
CNS Stimulating Drugs
Stimulants of CNS *USE CNS Stimulating Drugs*
Coaches
Test **Coaching**
Blood **Coagulation**
Coalition Formation
Coast Guard Personnel
Cobalt
Cocaine
Crack **Cocaine**
Cochlea
Cochlear Implants
Cochran Q Test
Cockroaches
Code Switching
Codeine
Codeine Sulfate *USE Codeine*
Codependency
Automated Information **Coding**
Coeds *USE College Students*
Coeducation
Pearson Product
Moment Correlation Coefficient
USE Statistical Correlation
Phi **Coefficient**
Coercion
Coffee *USE Beverages (Nonalcoholic)*
Cognition
Cognition Enhancing Drugs
USE Nootropic Drugs
Need for **Cognition**
Social **Cognition**
Transposition **(Cognition)**
Cognitions
Cognitive Ability
Cognitive Appraisal
Cognitive Assessment
Cognitive Behavior Therapy
Cognitive Complexity
Cognitive Contiguity
Cognitive Deficits
USE Cognitive Impairment
Cognitive Development
Cognitive Discrimination
Cognitive Dissonance
Cognitive Dysfunction
USE Cognitive Impairment
Cognitive Functioning *USE Cognitive Ability*
Cognitive Generalization
Cognitive Hypothesis Testing

Cognitive Impairment
Cognitive Load
USE Human Channel Capacity
Cognitive Maps
Cognitive Mediation
Cognitive Processes
Cognitive Processing Speed
Cognitive Psychology
Cognitive Rehabilitation
Cognitive Restructuring
Cognitive Science
Cognitive Style
Cognitive Techniques
Cognitive Therapy
Classification **(Cognitive** Process)
Rumination **(Cognitive** Process)
Cohabitation
Group **Cohesion**
Cohort Analysis
Coitus *USE Sexual Intercourse (Human)*
Cold Effects
Colitis
Ulcerative **Colitis**
Collaboration *USE Cooperation*
Blue **Collar** Workers
White **Collar** Workers
Data **Collection**
Collective Behavior
Collective Unconscious
College Academic Achievement
College Athletes
College Degrees
USE Educational Degrees
College Dropouts
College Education
USE Undergraduate Education
College Entrance Examination Board
Scholastic Aptitude Test
College Environment
College Graduates
College Major
USE Academic Specialization
College Students
College Teachers
Community **College** Students
Junior **College** Students
School and College Ability Test
USE Aptitude Measures
Colleges
Community **Colleges**
Junior Colleges *USE Colleges*
Inferior **Colliculus**
Superior **Colliculus**
Colon Disorders
Color
Color Blindness
Color Constancy
Color Contrast
Color Perception
Color Pyramid Test
USE Projective Personality Measures
Color Saturation
Achromatic **Color**
Eye **Color**
Stroop **Color** Word Test
Animal **Coloration**
Colostomy
Raven **Coloured** Progressive Matrices
Columbia Mental Maturity Scale
Spinal **Column**
Coma
Combat Experience
Physical **Comfort**
Commerce *USE Business*
Commercials *USE Television Advertising*
Commissioned Officers
Hippocampal Commissure *USE Fornix*

324

Commissurotomy
Commitment
Commitment (Psychiatric)
Organizational **Commitment**
Outpatient **Commitment**
Communes
Communicable Diseases
    USE Infectious Disorders
Communication
Communication Apprehension
    USE Speech Anxiety
Communication Disorders
Communication Skills
Communication Skills Training
Communication Systems
Communication Theory
Animal **Communication**
Augmentative **Communication**
Computer Mediated **Communication**
Cross Cultural **Communication**
Electronic **Communication**
Facilitated Communication
    USE Augmentative Communication
Father Child **Communication**
Intercultural Communication
    USE Cross Cultural Communication
Interethnic Communication
    USE Cross Cultural Communication
Interpersonal **Communication**
Manual **Communication**
Mother Child **Communication**
Nonverbal **Communication**
Oral **Communication**
Parent Child **Communication**
Persuasive **Communication**
Privileged **Communication**
Professional Communication
    USE Scientific Communication
Scientific **Communication**
Verbal **Communication**
Written **Communication**
Communications Media
Audiovisual **Communications** Media
Printed **Communications** Media
Communicative Competence
    USE Communication Skills
Communism
Communities
Retirement **Communities**
Community Attitudes
Community College Students
Community Colleges
Community Development
Community Facilities
Community Involvement
Community Mental Health
Community Mental Health Centers
Community Mental Health Services
Community Mental Health Training
Community Psychiatry
Community Psychology
Community Services
Community Welfare Services
Therapeutic **Community**
Commuting (Travel)
Comorbidity
Companies *USE Business Organizations*
Comparative Psychiatry
    USE Transcultural Psychiatry
Comparative Psychology
Social **Comparison**
Interpersonal **Compatibility**
Compensation (Defense Mechanism)
Workers' **Compensation** Insurance
Workmen's Compensation Insurance
    USE Workers' Compensation Insurance
Compensatory Education

Competence
Communicative Competence *USE Communication Skills*
Interpersonal Competence *USE Social Skills*
Professional **Competence**
Social Competence *USE Social Skills*
Competency to Stand Trial
Minimum **Competency** Tests
Competition
Health **Complaints**
Complementary Medicine
    USE Alternative Medicine
Sentence **Completion** Tests
AIDS Dementia **Complex**
Electra **Complex**
Oedipal **Complex**
Cognitive **Complexity**
Stimulus **Complexity**
Task **Complexity**
Compliance
Client Compliance *USE Treatment Compliance*
Medical Regimen Compliance *USE Treatment Compliance*
Treatment **Compliance**
Obstetrical **Complications**
Postsurgical **Complications**
Surgical Complications
    USE Postsurgical Complications
Comprehension
Comprehension Tests
Listening **Comprehension**
Number **Comprehension**
Reading **Comprehension**
Sentence **Comprehension**
Verbal **Comprehension**
Compressed Speech
Compulsions
Compulsive Gambling
    USE Pathological Gambling
Compulsive Neurosis
    USE Obsessive Compulsive Disorder
Compulsive Personality Disorder
    *USE Obsessive Compulsive
    Personality Disorder*
Compulsive Repetition
Obsessive **Compulsive** Disorder
Obsessive Compulsive Neurosis
    USE Obsessive Compulsive Disorder
Obsessive **Compulsive** Personality Disorder
Sexual Compulsivity *USE Sexual Addiction*
Computer Anxiety
Computer Applications
Computer Assisted Design
Computer Assisted Diagnosis
Computer Assisted Instruction
Computer Assisted Testing
Computer Attitudes
Computer Based Training
    USE Computer Assisted Instruction
Computer Conferencing
    USE Teleconferencing
Computer Games
Computer Literacy
Computer Mediated Communication
Computer Peripheral Devices
Computer Programming
Computer Programming Languages
Computer Programs
    USE Computer Software
Computer Searching
Computer Simulation
Computer Software
Computer Supported Cooperative Work
    USE Groupware
Computer Training
Human **Computer** Interaction
Human Computer Interface
    USE Human Computer Interaction
Computerized Databases *USE Databases*

Computers
Analog **Computers**
Digital **Computers**
Personal Computers *USE Microcomputers*
Concentration
Concentration Camps
Blood Alcohol **Concentration**
Concept Formation
Concept Learning *USE Concept Formation*
Concept Validity *USE Test Validity*
Academic Self **Concept**
Conservation **(Concept)**
Self **Concept**
Temporal Spatial Concept Scale *USE Intelligence Measures*
Tennessee Self **Concept** Scale
Concepts
God **Concepts**
Mathematics **(Concepts)**
Conceptual Imagery
Conceptual Tempo
Conceptualization *USE Concept Formation*
Concurrent Reinforcement Schedules
Concurrent Validity *USE Test Validity*
Brain **Concussion**
Conditioned Emotional Responses
Conditioned Fear
Conditioned Inhibition
    USE Conditioned Suppression
Conditioned Place Preference
    USE Place Conditioning
Conditioned Reflex
    USE Conditioned Responses
Conditioned Responses
Conditioned Stimulus
Conditioned Suppression
Conditioning
Aversion **Conditioning**
Avoidance **Conditioning**
Classical **Conditioning**
Escape **Conditioning**
Eyelid **Conditioning**
Fading **(Conditioning)**
Higher Order **Conditioning**
Instrumental Conditioning *USE Operant Conditioning*
Odor Aversion Conditioning *USE Aversion Conditioning*
Operant **Conditioning**
Pavlovian Conditioning *USE Classical Conditioning*
Place **Conditioning**
Respondent Conditioning *USE Classical Conditioning*
Second Order Conditioning
    USE Higher Order Conditioning
Taste Aversion Conditioning *USE Aversion Conditioning*
Verbal Conditioning *USE Verbal Learning*
Atmospheric **Conditions**
Mental Disorders due to
General Medical **Conditions**
Working **Conditions**
Condoms
Conduct Disorder
Bone **Conduction** Audiometry
Skin Conduction *USE Skin Resistance*
Cones (Eye)
Confabulation
Computer Conferencing *USE Teleconferencing*
Confession (Religion)
Legal **Confession**
Confidence Limits (Statistics)
Self **Confidence**
Confidentiality of Information
    USE Privileged Communication
Confirmatory Factor Analysis
    USE Factor Analysis
Conflict
Conflict Resolution
Family **Conflict**
Marital **Conflict**
Role **Conflicts**

Conformity (Personality)
Mental **Confusion**
Congenital Disorders
Drug Induced **Congenital** Disorders
Congenitally Handicapped
    USE Congenital Disorders
Self **Congruence**
Conjoined Twins
Conjoint Measurement
Conjoint Therapy
Connectionism
Connective Tissue Cells
Connective Tissues
Connotations
Consanguineous Marriage
Conscience
Conscientiousness
Conscious (Personality Factor)
Consciousness Disturbances
Consciousness Raising Groups
Consciousness States
Self Consciousness *USE Self Perception*
Informed **Consent**
Conservation (Concept)
Conservation (Ecological Behavior)
Conservatism
Political **Conservatism**
Wilson Patterson **Conservatism** Scale
Conservatorship *USE Guardianship*
Consistency (Measurement)
Internal Consistency *USE Test Reliability*
Response Consistency *USE Response Variability*
Consonants
Conspecifics
Brightness **Constancy**
Color **Constancy**
Perceptual **Constancy**
Size **Constancy**
Constant Time Delay
Constipation
Construct Validity *USE Test Validity*
Personal Construct Theory *USE Personality Theory*
Test **Construction**
Constructionism *USE Constructivism*
Constructivism
Consultation Liaison Psychiatry
Mental Health Consultation *USE Professional Consultation*
Professional **Consultation**
Consumer Attitudes
Consumer Behavior
Consumer Fraud *USE Fraud*
Consumer Product Design
    USE Product Design
Consumer Protection
Consumer Psychology
Consumer Research
Consumer Satisfaction
Consumer Surveys
Contact Lenses
Eye **Contact**
Physical **Contact**
Contagion
Cost **Containment**
Content Analysis
Content Analysis (Test)
Content Validity *USE Test Validity*
Dream **Content**
Emotional **Content**
Item **Content** (Test)
Thought Content *USE Cognitions*
Contextual Associations
Cognitive **Contiguity**
Contingency Management
Contingent Negative Variation
Continuing Education
Continuity of Care *USE Continuum of Care*

Continuous Reinforcement
USE Reinforcement Schedules
Continuum of Care
Contour *USE Form and Shape Perception*
Contour Perception
USE Form and Shape Perception
Contraception *USE Birth Control*
Contraceptive Devices
Oral **Contraceptives**
Behavior **Contracting**
Muscle **Contraction** Headache
Muscle **Contractions**
Psychological **Contracts**
Behavioral **Contrast**
Brightness **Contrast**
Color **Contrast**
Successive Contrast *USE Afterimage*
Visual **Contrast**
Control Groups *USE Experiment Controls*
Air Traffic **Control**
Anger **Control**
Birth **Control**
Birth Control Attitudes
USE Family Planning Attitudes
Diaphrams (Birth **Control)**
Emotional **Control**
Gun **Control** Laws
Health Locus of Control *USE Health Attitudes*
Impulse **Control** Disorders
Internal External Locus of **Control**
Locus of Control
USE Internal External Locus of Control
Population Control *USE Birth Control*
Quality **Control**
Rotter Internal External Locus of **Control** Scale
Self **Control**
Social **Control**
Stimulus **Control**
Thought Control *USE Brainwashing*
Weight **Control**
Experiment **Controls**
Instrument **Controls**
Eye **Convergence**
Convergent Thinking
USE Inductive Deductive Reasoning
Convergent Validity *USE Test Validity*
Conversation
Conversion Disorder
Conversion Hysteria
USE Conversion Disorder
Conversion Neurosis
USE Conversion Disorder
Criminal **Conviction**
Convulsions
Cooperating Teachers
Cooperation
Cooperative Education
Cooperative Learning
Cooperative Therapy *USE Cotherapy*
Computer Supported Cooperative Work *USE Groupware*
Motor **Coordination**
Perceptual Motor **Coordination**
Coping Behavior
Copper
Coprophagia
Copulation
USE Sexual Intercourse (Human)
Cranial Spinal **Cord**
Lumbar Spinal **Cord**
Spinal **Cord**
Spinal **Cord** Injuries
Vocal **Cords**
Cornea
Coronary Disorders
USE Cardiovascular Disorders
Coronary Heart Disease
USE Heart Disorders

Coronary Prone Behavior
Coronary Thromboses
Coronary Vessels *USE Arteries (Anatomy)*
Corporal Punishment *USE Punishment*
Corporations *USE Business Organizations*
Job **Corps**
Peace **Corps**
Corpus Callosum
Corpus Striatum *USE Basal Ganglia*
Correctional Institutions
Corrective Lenses *USE Optical Aids*
Personality **Correlates**
Physiological **Correlates**
Psychological Correlates *USE Psychodynamics*
Canonical Correlation *USE Multivariate Analysis*
Pearson Product Moment Correlation Coefficient
USE Statistical Correlation
Point Biserial **Correlation**
Rank Difference **Correlation**
Rank Order **Correlation**
Statistical **Correlation**
Tetrachoric **Correlation**
Adrenal **Cortex** Hormones
Adrenal Cortex Steroids *USE Corticosteroids*
Auditory **Cortex**
Cerebellar Cortex *USE Cerebellum*
Cerebral **Cortex**
Motor **Cortex**
Prefrontal **Cortex**
Somatosensory **Cortex**
Striate Cortex *USE Visual Cortex*
Visual **Cortex**
Organ of Corti *USE Cochlea*
Cortical Atrophy *USE Cerebral Atrophy*
Cortical Evoked Potentials
Corticoids *USE Corticosteroids*
Corticosteroids
Corticosterone
Corticotropin
Corticotropin Releasing Factor
Cortisol *USE Hydrocortisone*
Cortisone
Cosmetic Techniques
Cost Containment
Cost Effectiveness
USE Costs and Cost Analysis
Costs and **Cost** Analysis
Response **Cost**
Costs and Cost Analysis
Health Care **Costs**
Medical Care Costs *USE Health Care Costs*
Mental Health Care Costs *USE Health Care Costs*
Cotherapy
Counselees *USE Clients*
Counseling
Counseling Psychologists
Counseling Psychology
Career Counseling *USE Occupational Guidance*
Cross Cultural **Counseling**
Educational **Counseling**
Family Counseling *USE Family Therapy*
Genetic **Counseling**
Group **Counseling**
Guidance Counseling *USE School Counseling*
Individual Counseling *USE Individual Psychotherapy*
Internet Counseling *USE Online Therapy*
Marriage **Counseling**
Pastoral **Counseling**
Peer **Counseling**
Premarital **Counseling**
Psychotherapeutic **Counseling**
Rehabilitation **Counseling**
School **Counseling**
Vocational Counseling *USE Occupational Guidance*
Counselor Attitudes
Counselor Characteristics

Counselor Client Interaction
  USE Psychotherapeutic Processes
Counselor Education
Counselor Effectiveness
  USE Counselor Characteristics
Counselor Personality
  USE Counselor Characteristics
Counselor Role
Counselor Trainees
Client Counselor Interaction
  USE Psychotherapeutic Processes
Counselors
Rehabilitation **Counselors**
School **Counselors**
Vocational **Counselors**
Over the Counter Drugs *USE Nonprescription Drugs*
Counterconditioning
Countertransference
Countries
Developed **Countries**
Developing **Countries**
Third World Countries *USE Developing Countries*
Underdeveloped Countries *USE Developing Countries*
County Agricultural Agents
  USE Agricultural Extension Workers
Couples
Couples Therapy
Married Couples *USE Spouses*
Courage
Course Evaluation
Course Objectives
  USE Educational Objectives
Course of Illness *USE Disease Course*
Disease **Course**
Disorder Course *USE Disease Course*
Life Course *USE Life Span*
Court Ordered Treatment
  USE Court Referrals
Court Referrals
Juvenile Court *USE Adjudication*
Courts *USE Adjudication*
Animal **Courtship** Behavior
Animal **Courtship** Displays
Human **Courtship**
Cousins
Analysis of **Covariance**
Covert Sensitization
Least Preferred **Coworker** Scale
Cows *USE Cattle*
Coyotes *USE Canids*
Crabs
Crack Cocaine
Crafts
Muscle Cramps *USE Muscular Disorders*
Cranial Nerves
Cranial Spinal Cord
Craving
Crayfish
Creative Arts Therapy
Creative Writing
Creativity
Creativity Measurement
Credibility
Creutzfeldt Jakob Syndrome
Aircraft Crew *USE Aerospace Personnel*
Cri du Chat Syndrome
  USE Crying Cat Syndrome
Crib Death *USE Sudden Infant Death*
Crime
Crime Prevention
Crime Victims
Violent **Crime**
Bias Crimes *USE Hate Crimes*
Hate **Crimes**
Criminal Behavior
Criminal Conviction

Criminal Interrogation
  USE Legal Interrogation
Criminal Justice
Criminal Law
Criminal Rehabilitation
Criminal Responsibility
Criminality *USE Criminal Behavior*
Criminally Insane
  USE Mentally Ill Offenders
Criminals
Female **Criminals**
Male **Criminals**
Criminology
Crises
Family **Crises**
Organizational **Crises**
Crisis Intervention
Crisis Intervention Services
Identity **Crisis**
Assessment Criteria *USE Evaluation Criteria*
Evaluation **Criteria**
Research Diagnostic **Criteria**
Student Admission **Criteria**
Criterion Referenced Tests
Criterion Related Validity *USE Test Validity*
Critical Flicker Fusion Threshold
Critical Incident Debriefing
  USE Debriefing (Psychological)
Critical Period
Critical Scores *USE Cutting Scores*
Criticism
Self **Criticism**
Crocodilians
Cross Cultural Communication
Cross Cultural Counseling
Cross Cultural Differences
Cross Cultural Psychology
Cross Cultural Treatment
Cross Disciplinary Research
  USE Interdisciplinary Research
Crossed Eyes *USE Strabismus*
Crowding
Marlowe **Crowne** Social Desirability Scale
CRT *USE Video Display Units*
Cruelty
Crustacea
Crying
Crying Cat Syndrome
Cuban Americans *USE Hispanics*
Cued Recall
Cues
Cultism
Cultural Assimilation *USE Acculturation*
Cultural Deprivation
Cultural Differences
  USE Cross Cultural Differences
Cultural Factors *USE Sociocultural Factors*
Cultural Familial Mental Retardation
  USE Psychosocial Mental Retardation
Cultural Pluralism *USE Multiculturalism*
Cultural Psychiatry
  USE Transcultural Psychiatry
Cultural Sensitivity
Cultural Test Bias
Chinese **Cultural** Groups
Cross **Cultural** Communication
Cross **Cultural** Counseling
Cross **Cultural** Differences
Cross **Cultural** Psychology
Cross **Cultural** Treatment
Japanese **Cultural** Groups
Korean **Cultural** Groups
South Asian **Cultural** Groups
South East Asian Cultural Groups
  USE Southeast Asian Cultural Groups
Southeast Asian **Cultural** Groups
Vietnamese **Cultural** Groups

Culturally Disadvantaged
    USE Cultural Deprivation
Culture (Anthropological)
Culture Bound Syndromes
Culture Change
Culture Fair Intelligence Test
Culture Shock
Culture Specific Syndromes
    USE Culture Bound Syndromes
Cattell Culture Fair Intelligence Test
    USE Culture Fair Intelligence Test
Mass Culture *USE Popular Culture*
Organizational Culture *USE Organizational Climate*
Popular **Culture**
Curare
Curiosity
Curricular Field Experience
Curriculum
Curriculum Based Assessment
Curriculum Development
Cursive Writing
Cushings Syndrome
Child **Custody**
Joint **Custody**
Customer Satisfaction
    USE Consumer Satisfaction
Cutaneous Receptive Fields
Cutaneous Sense
Cutting Scores
Cybercounseling *USE Online Therapy*
Cybernetics
Lunar Synodic **Cycle**
Menstrual **Cycle**
Sleep Wake **Cycle**
Work Rest **Cycles**
Cyclic Adenosine Monophosphate
Cycloheximide
Cyclothymic Disorder
    USE Cyclothymic Personality
Cyclothymic Personality
Cynicism
Cysteine
Cystic Fibrosis
Cytochrome Oxidase
Cytokines
Cytology
Cytoplasm
Daily Activities
Activities of **Daily** Living
Brain **Damage**
Dance
Dance Therapy
Dangerousness
Dark Adaptation
Darwinism
Data Collection
Data Pooling *USE Meta Analysis*
Data Processing
Biographical **Data**
Statistical **Data**
Databases
Computerized Databases *USE Databases*
Online Databases *USE Databases*
Date Rape *USE Acquaintance Rape*
Social **Dating**
Daughters
Day Care Centers
Day Hospital *USE Partial Hospitalization*
Adult **Day** Care
Child **Day** Care
Recreational Day Camps
    USE Summer Camps (Recreation)
Daydreaming
DDT (Insecticide)
Deaf
Deaf Blind
Word Deafness *USE Aphasia*

Deanol *USE Antidepressant Drugs*
Death and Dying
Death Anxiety
Death Attitudes
Death Education
Death Instinct
Death Penalty *USE Capital Punishment*
Death Rate *USE Mortality Rate*
Death Rites
Crib Death *USE Sudden Infant Death*
Near **Death** Experiences
Parental **Death**
Sudden Infant **Death**
Debates
Political Debates *USE Debates*
Presidential Debates *USE Debates*
Debriefing (Experimental)
Debriefing (Psychological)
Critical Incident Debriefing *USE Debriefing (Psychological)*
Psychological Debriefing *USE Debriefing (Psychological)*
Decarboxylase Inhibitors
Decarboxylases
Memory **Decay**
Decentralization
Deception
Decerebration
Decision Making
Decision Support Systems
Decision Theory
Group **Decision** Making
Lexical **Decision**
Management **Decision** Making
Legal **Decisions**
Declarative Knowledge
Decoding *USE Human Information Storage*
Decompression Effects
Decortication (Brain)
Deductive Reasoning
    USE Inductive Deductive Reasoning
Inductive **Deductive** Reasoning
Deer
Self **Defeating** Behavior
Defecation
Defendants
Defense Mechanisms
Compensation **(Defense** Mechanism)
Displacement **(Defense** Mechanism)
Fantasy **(Defense** Mechanism)
Identification **(Defense** Mechanism)
Insanity **Defense**
Isolation **(Defense** Mechanism)
Personal Defense *USE Self Defense*
Projection **(Defense** Mechanism)
Regression **(Defense** Mechanism)
Repression **(Defense** Mechanism)
Self **Defense**
Suppression **(Defense** Mechanism)
Withdrawal **(Defense** Mechanism)
Animal **Defensive** Behavior
Defensiveness
Oppositional **Defiant** Disorder
Nutritional **Deficiencies**
Acquired Immune **Deficiency** Syndrome
Mental Deficiency *USE Mental Retardation*
Protein **Deficiency** Disorders
Vitamin **Deficiency** Disorders
Attention **Deficit** Disorder
Attention **Deficit** Disorder with Hyperactivity
Cognitive Deficits *USE Cognitive Impairment*
Deformity *USE Physical Disfigurement*
College Degrees *USE Educational Degrees*
Educational **Degrees**
Graduate Degrees *USE Educational Degrees*
Undergraduate Degrees *USE Educational Degrees*
Dehydration
Lactate **Dehydrogenase**
Dehydrogenases

Alcohol **Dehydrogenases**
Deinstitutionalization
Deja Vu *USE Consciousness States*
Delay of Gratification
Constant Time **Delay**
Language **Delay**
Reinforcement **Delay**
Delayed Alternation
Delayed Auditory Feedback
Delayed Development
Delayed Feedback
Delayed Parenthood
Delayed Reinforcement
USE Reinforcement Delay
Delayed Speech
USE Retarded Speech Development
Deletion (Chromosome)
Female **Delinquency**
Juvenile **Delinquency**
Male **Delinquency**
Sexual Delinquency *USE Promiscuity*
Delirium
Delirium Tremens
Health Care **Delivery**
Delta Rhythm
Delusions
Supply and **Demand**
Dementia
Dementia of Alzheimers Type
USE Alzheimers Disease
Dementia Paralytica *USE General Paresis*
Dementia Praecox *USE Schizophrenia*
Dementia with Lewy Bodies
AIDS **Dementia** Complex
Multi Infarct **Dementia**
Presenile **Dementia**
Senile **Dementia**
Vascular **Dementia**
Democracy
Democratic Party *USE Political Parties*
Demographic Characteristics
Demonic Possession
USE Spirit Possession
Social **Demonstrations**
Dendrites
Denial
Population Density *USE Social Density*
Social **Density**
Dental Education
Dental Students
Dental Surgery
Dental Treatment
Dentist Patient Interaction
USE Thorapeutic Processes
Dentistry
Dentists
Deoxycorticosterone
Deoxyglucose
Deoxyribonucleic Acid
Field **Dependence**
Dependency (Personality)
Drug **Dependency**
Dependent Personality Disorder
Dependent Variables
State **Dependent** Learning
Depersonalization
CNS Depressant Drug Antagonists
USE Analeptic Drugs
CNS **Depressant** Drugs
Appetite **Depressing** Drugs
Depression (Emotion)
Agitated Depression *USE Major Depression*
Anaclitic **Depression**
Beck **Depression** Inventory
Climacteric Depression *USE Involutional Depression*
Endogenous **Depression**

Involutional **Depression**
Major **Depression**
Manic Depression *USE Bipolar Disorder*
Postnatal Depression *USE Postpartum Depression*
Postpartum **Depression**
Puerperal Depression *USE Postpartum Depression*
Reactive **Depression**
Recurrent **Depression**
Spreading **Depression**
Treatment Resistant **Depression**
Tricyclic Resistant Depression
USE Treatment Resistant Depression
Unipolar Depression *USE Major Depression*
Winter Depression
USE Seasonal Affective Disorder
Zungs Self Rating **Depression** Scale
Manic Depressive Psychosis
USE Bipolar Disorder
Neurotic Depressive Reaction
USE Major Depression
Psychotic Depressive Reaction
USE Major Depression
Deprivation
Animal Maternal **Deprivation**
Cultural **Deprivation**
Food **Deprivation**
REM Dream **Deprivation**
Sensory **Deprivation**
Sleep **Deprivation**
Social **Deprivation**
Stimulus **Deprivation**
Water **Deprivation**
Depth Perception
Depth Psychology
Ergot **Derivatives**
Opium Derivatives *USE Opiates*
Phenothiazine **Derivatives**
Dermatitis
Dermatomes
USE Cutaneous Receptive Fields
Desegregation *USE Social Integration*
Eye Movement **Desensitization** Therapy
Systematic **Desensitization** Therapy
Desertion *USE Abandonment*
Between Groups **Design**
Computer Assisted **Design**
Consumer Product Design *USE Product Design*
Environmental Design *USE Environmental Planning*
Experimental **Design**
Human Machine Systems **Design**
Interior **Design**
Kohs Block **Design** Test
Man Machine Systems Design
USE Human Machine Systems Design
Product **Design**
Research Design *USE Experimental Design*
Systems **Design**
Within Subjects Design *USE Repeated Measures*
Memory for **Designs** Test
Desipramine
Edwards Social **Desirability** Scale
Marlowe Crowne Social **Desirability** Scale
Social **Desirability**
Hypoactive Sexual Desire Disorder
USE Inhibited Sexual Desire
Inhibited Sexual **Desire**
Desires *USE Motivation*
Self **Destructive** Behavior
Anatomically **Detailed** Dolls
Signal **Detection** (Perception)
Legal **Detention**
Self **Determination**
Threshold **Determination**
Verdict Determination *USE Adjudication*
Determinism
Detoxification

Kupfer Detre Self Rating Scale
  USE Nonprojective Personality
  Measures
Folie A **Deux**
Developed Countries
Developing Countries
Development
Adolescent **Development**
Adult **Development**
Animal **Development**
Bayley Scales of Infant **Development**
Brain Development *USE Neural Development*
Career **Development**
Character Development *USE Personality Development*
Childhood Play **Development**
Childhood **Development**
Cognitive **Development**
Community **Development**
Curriculum **Development**
Delayed **Development**
Early Childhood **Development**
Ego **Development**
Emotional **Development**
Group **Development**
Human **Development**
Infant **Development**
Intellectual **Development**
Language **Development**
Management Development *USE Career Development*
Moral **Development**
Motor **Development**
Neonatal **Development**
Neural **Development**
Organizational **Development**
Perceptual Motor **Development**
Perceptual **Development**
Personality **Development**
Personnel Development *USE Personnel Training*
Physical **Development**
Precocious **Development**
Prenatal **Development**
Professional **Development**
Program **Development**
Psychological Development *USE Psychogenesis*
Psychomotor **Development**
Psychosexual **Development**
Psychosocial **Development**
Reading **Development**
Retarded Speech **Development**
Rural Development
  USE Community Development
Sensorimotor Development
  USE Perceptual Motor Development
Sexual **Development**
Social Development
  USE Psychosocial Development
Speech **Development**
Urban Development
  USE Community Development
Developmental Age Groups
Developmental Differences
  USE Age Differences
Developmental Disabilities
Developmental Measures
Developmental Psychology
Developmental Stages
Frostig **Developmental** Test of Visual Perception
Pervasive **Developmental** Disorders
Prenatal **Developmental** Stages
Sex Linked **Developmental** Differences
Deviant Behavior *USE Antisocial Behavior*
Deviation IQ *USE Standard Scores*
Standard **Deviation**
Sexual Deviations *USE Paraphilias*
Computer Peripheral **Devices**
Contraceptive **Devices**
Intrauterine **Devices**

Medical Therapeutic **Devices**
Safety **Devices**
Dexamethasone
Dexamethasone Suppression Test
Dexamphetamine *USE Dextroamphetamine*
Dexedrine *USE Dextroamphetamine*
Physical **Dexterity**
Dextroamphetamine
Diabetes
Diabetes Insipidus
Diabetes Mellitus
Diacetylmorphine *USE Heroin*
Diagnosis
Diagnosis Related Groups
Clinical Judgment (Not **Diagnosis)**
Computer Assisted **Diagnosis**
Differential **Diagnosis**
Dual **Diagnosis**
Educational **Diagnosis**
Medical **Diagnosis**
Prenatal **Diagnosis**
X Ray Diagnosis *USE Roentgenography*
Diagnostic and Statistical Manual
Diagnostic Interview Schedule
Research **Diagnostic** Criteria
Dialect
Dialectics
Dialysis
Diaphragm (Anatomy)
Diaphragms (Birth Control)
Diarrhea
Diastolic Pressure
Diazepam
Dichoptic Stimulation
Dichotic Stimulation
Dieldrin *USE Insecticides*
Diencephalon
Dietary Restraint
Dietary Supplements
Lysergic Acid **Diethylamide**
Diets
Rank **Difference** Correlation
Age **Differences**
Animal Sex **Differences**
Animal Strain **Differences**
Cross Cultural **Differences**
Cultural Differences *USE Cross Cultural Differences*
Developmental Differences *USE Age Differences*
Ethnic Differences
  USE Racial and Ethnic Differences
Gender Differences *USE Human Sex Differences*
Geographical Differences *USE Regional Differences*
Human Sex **Differences**
Individual **Differences**
Racial and Ethnic **Differences**
Racial Differences
  USE Racial and Ethnic Differences
Regional **Differences**
Sex Linked Developmental **Differences**
Species **Differences**
Differential Aptitude Tests
Differential Diagnosis
Differential Limen *USE Thresholds*
Differential Personality Inventory
  USE Nonprojective Personality
  Measures
Differential Reinforcement
Semantic **Differential**
Sex Differentiation Disorders
  USE Genital Disorders
Difficulty Level (Test)
Task Difficulty *USE Task Complexity*
Test Difficulty *USE Difficulty Level (Test)*
Digestion
Digestive System
Digestive System Disorders
Digit Span Testing

Digital Computers
Dihydroergotamine
Dihydroxyphenylacetic Acid
Dihydroxytryptamine
Dilantin *USE Diphenylhydantoin*
Pupil **Dilation**
Prisoners **Dilemma** Game
Social **Dilemma**
Carbon **Dioxide**
Diphenhydramine
Diphenylhydantoin
Diphenylhydantoin Sodium
    USE Diphenylhydantoin
Diptera
Directed Discussion Method
Directed Reverie Therapy
    USE Guided Imagery
Self Directed Learning
    USE Individualized Instruction
Direction Perception
Advance **Directives**
Disabilities
Developmental **Disabilities**
Learning **Disabilities**
Multiple **Disabilities**
Physical **Disabilities** (Attitudes Toward)
Reading **Disabilities**
Sensory **Disabilities** (Attitudes Toward)
Disability Discrimination
Disability Evaluation
Disability Laws
Disability Management
Disabled (Attitudes Toward)
Disabled Personnel
Disadvantaged
Culturally Disadvantaged *USE Cultural Deprivation*
Economically Disadvantaged *USE Disadvantaged*
Socially Disadvantaged *USE Disadvantaged*
Disappointment
Disasters
Natural **Disasters**
Discharge Planning
Facility **Discharge**
Hospital **Discharge**
Psychiatric Hospital **Discharge**
Cross Disciplinary Research
    USE Interdisciplinary Research
Child **Discipline**
Classroom **Discipline**
Self **Disclosure**
Discourse Analysis
Discovery Teaching Method
Discriminant Validity *USE Test Validity*
Discrimination
Discrimination Learning
Age **Discrimination**
Auditory **Discrimination**
Cognitive **Discrimination**
Disability **Discrimination**
Distance Discrimination *USE Distance Perception*
Drug **Discrimination**
Employment **Discrimination**
Ethnic Discrimination
    USE Race and Ethnic Discrimination
Figure Ground **Discrimination**
Job Discrimination
    USE Employment Discrimination
Loudness **Discrimination**
Minority Group Discrimination
    USE Race and Ethnic Discrimination
Odor **Discrimination**
Pattern **Discrimination**
Perceptual **Discrimination**
Pitch **Discrimination**
Race and Ethnic **Discrimination**
Racial Discrimination
    USE Race and Ethnic Discrimination

Sex **Discrimination**
Size **Discrimination**
Social **Discrimination**
Spatial Discrimination *USE Spatial Perception*
Stimulus **Discrimination**
Tactual Discrimination *USE Tactual Perception*
Taste Discrimination *USE Taste Perception*
Visual **Discrimination**
Discriminative Learning
    USE Discrimination Learning
Discriminative Stimulus
    USE Conditioned Stimulus
Directed **Discussion** Method
Group **Discussion**
Nondirected **Discussion** Method
Disease Course
Disease Outbreaks *USE Epidemics*
Disease Transmission
Addisons **Disease**
Alzheimers **Disease**
Coronary Heart Disease *USE Heart Disorders*
Duchennes Disease *USE Muscular Disorders*
Huntingtons **Disease**
Lewy Body Disease *USE Dementia with Lewy Bodies*
Menieres **Disease**
Parkinsons **Disease**
Picks **Disease**
Raynauds Disease *USE Cardiovascular Disorders*
Sickle Cell **Disease**
Tay Sachs **Disease**
Communicable Diseases *USE Infectious Disorders*
International Classification of **Diseases**
Kidney **Diseases**
Neurodegenerative **Diseases**
Renal Diseases *USE Kidney Diseases*
Sexually Transmitted **Diseases**
Venereal Diseases
    USE Sexually Transmitted Diseases
Physical **Disfigurement**
Disgust
Dishonesty
Dislike *USE Aversion*
Disorder Course *USE Disease Course*
Acute Paranoid Disorder *USE Paranoia (Psychosis)*
Acute Stress **Disorder**
Antisocial Personality **Disorder**
Attention Deficit **Disorder**
Attention Deficit **Disorder** with Hyperactivity
Atypical Paranoid Disorder *USE Paranoia (Psychosis)*
Atypical Somatoform Disorder *USE Body Dysmorphic Disorder*
Avoidant Personality **Disorder**
Bipolar Affective Disorder *USE Bipolar Disorder*
Bipolar Mood Disorder *USE Bipolar Disorder*
Bipolar **Disorder**
Body Dysmorphic **Disorder**
Borderline Personality **Disorder**
Compulsive Personality Disorder *USE Obsessive Compulsive*
    Personality Disorder
Conduct **Disorder**
Conversion **Disorder**
Cyclothymic Disorder *USE Cyclothymic Personality*
Dependent Personality **Disorder**
Dissociative Identity **Disorder**
Dysthymic **Disorder**
Epstein Barr Viral **Disorder**
Explosive **Disorder**
Gender Identity **Disorder**
Generalized Anxiety **Disorder**
Gilles de la Tourette **Disorder**
Histrionic Personality **Disorder**
Hypoactive Sexual Desire Disorder *USE Inhibited Sexual Desire*
Intermittent Explosive Disorder *USE Explosive Disorder*
Narcissistic Personality **Disorder**
Obsessive Compulsive Personality **Disorder**
Obsessive Compulsive **Disorder**
Oppositional Defiant **Disorder**
Pain Disorder *USE Somatoform Pain Disorder*

Panic **Disorder**
Paranoid Personality **Disorder**
Paranoid Disorder *USE Paranoia (Psychosis)*
Passive Aggressive Personality **Disorder**
Posttraumatic Stress **Disorder**
Premenstrual Dysphoric **Disorder**
Reactive Attachment Disorder *USE Attachment Disorders*
Schizoaffective **Disorder**
Schizoid Personality **Disorder**
Schizophreniform **Disorder**
Schizotypal Personality **Disorder**
Seasonal Affective **Disorder**
Shared Paranoid Disorder *USE Folie A Deux*
Social Anxiety Disorder *USE Social Phobia*
Somatization **Disorder**
Somatoform Pain **Disorder**
Disorders
Adjustment **Disorders**
Adrenal Gland **Disorders**
Adventitious **Disorders**
Affective **Disorders**
Allergic Skin **Disorders**
Allergic **Disorders**
Anxiety **Disorders**
Appetite Disorders *USE Eating Disorders*
Articulation **Disorders**
Attachment **Disorders**
Autism Spectrum Disorders *USE Pervasive Developmental Disorders*
Autoimmune Disorders *USE Immunologic Disorders*
Autonomic Nervous System **Disorders**
Autosome **Disorders**
Bacterial **Disorders**
Behavior **Disorders**
Blood and Lymphatic **Disorders**
Blood Pressure **Disorders**
Blood Disorders
USE Blood and Lymphatic Disorders
Bone **Disorders**
Bowel Disorders *USE Colon Disorders*
Brain **Disorders**
Bronchial **Disorders**
Cardiac Disorders *USE Heart Disorders*
Cardiovascular **Disorders**
Central Nervous System **Disorders**
Cerebral Vascular Disorders *USE Cerebrovascular Disorders*
Cerebrovascular **Disorders**
Character Disorders *USE Personality Disorders*
Chromosome **Disorders**
Chronicity **(Disorders)**
Circulatory Disorders *USE Cardiovascular Disorders*
Colon **Disorders**
Communication **Disorders**
Congenital **Disorders**
Coronary Disorders *USE Cardiovascular Disorders*
Digestive System **Disorders**
Dissociative **Disorders**
Drug Induced Congenital **Disorders**
Ear **Disorders**
Eating **Disorders**
Endocrine Sexual **Disorders**
Endocrine **Disorders**
Eye **Disorders**
Factitious **Disorders**
Gastrointestinal **Disorders**
Genetic **Disorders**
Genital **Disorders**
Gynecological **Disorders**
Hearing **Disorders**
Heart **Disorders**
Hematologic Disorders
USE Blood and Lymphatic Disorders
Hepatic Disorders *USE Liver Disorders*
Hereditary Disorders *USE Genetic Disorders*
Hypophysis Disorders *USE Pituitary Disorders*
Immunologic **Disorders**
Impulse Control **Disorders**

Infectious **Disorders**
Joint **Disorders**
Karyotype Disorders *USE Chromosome Disorders*
Labyrinth **Disorders**
Language **Disorders**
Laryngeal **Disorders**
Learning **Disorders**
Lipid Metabolism **Disorders**
Liver **Disorders**
Lung **Disorders**
Lymphatic Disorders
USE Blood and Lymphatic Disorders
Male Genital **Disorders**
Memory **Disorders**
Menstrual **Disorders**
Mental **Disorders**
Mental **Disorders** due to General Medical Conditions
Metabolism **Disorders**
Minimal Brain **Disorders**
Mood Disorders *USE Affective Disorders*
Motor Disorders *USE Nervous System Disorders*
Movement **Disorders**
Muscular **Disorders**
Musculoskeletal **Disorders**
Neonatal **Disorders**
Nervous System **Disorders**
Neurological Disorders *USE Nervous System Disorders*
Neuromuscular **Disorders**
Onset **(Disorders)**
Ovary Disorders *USE Endocrine Sexual Disorders*
Parasitic **Disorders**
Parathyroid **Disorders**
Peripheral Nerve **Disorders**
Personality **Disorders**
Pervasive Developmental **Disorders**
Pharyngeal **Disorders**
Physical **Disorders**
Pituitary **Disorders**
Protein Deficiency **Disorders**
Psychiatric Disorders *USE Mental Disorders*
Psychophysiologic Disorders *USE Somatoform Disorders*
Psychosomatic Disorders *USE Somatoform Disorders*
Pulmonary Disorders *USE Lung Disorders*
Purging (Eating **Disorders)**
Recovery **(Disorders)**
Relapse **(Disorders)**
Remission **(Disorders)**
Respiratory Tract **Disorders**
Scalp Disorders *USE Skin Disorders*
Sense Organ **Disorders**
Sensory System **Disorders**
Severity **(Disorders)**
Sex Chromosome **Disorders**
Sex Differentiation Disorders *USE Genital Disorders*
Sex Linked Hereditary **Disorders**
Skeletomuscular Disorders *USE Musculoskeletal Disorders*
Skin **Disorders**
Sleep **Disorders**
Somatoform **Disorders**
Somatosensory **Disorders**
Speech **Disorders**
Subtypes **(Disorders)**
Susceptibility **(Disorders)**
Taste **Disorders**
Testes Disorders *USE Endocrine Sexual Disorders*
Thyroid **Disorders**
Toxic **Disorders**
Treatment Resistant **Disorders**
Urinary Function **Disorders**
Urogenital **Disorders**
Vascular Disorders *USE Cardiovascular Disorders*
Viral **Disorders**
Vision **Disorders**
Vitamin Deficiency **Disorders**
Voice Disorders *USE Dysphonia*
Schizophrenia **(Disorganized** Type)

Place **Disorientation**
Time **Disorientation**
Displacement (Defense Mechanism)
Video **Display** Terminals *USE Video Display Units*
Video **Display** Units
Displays
Animal Courtship **Displays**
Auditory **Displays**
Graphical **Displays**
Tactual **Displays**
Visual **Displays**
Disposition *USE Personality*
Disruptive Behavior
USE Behavior Problems
Dissatisfaction
Dissociation
Drug Dissociation
USE State Dependent Learning
Dissociative Disorders
Dissociative Identity Disorder
Dissociative Neurosis
USE Dissociative Disorders
Dissociative Patterns
USE Dissociative Disorders
Cognitive **Dissonance**
Distance Discrimination
USE Distance Perception
Distance Education
Distance Learning
USE Distance Education
Distance Perception
Apparent **Distance**
Interpersonal Distance *USE Personal Space*
Perceptual **Distortion**
Spatial **Distortion**
Distractibility
Distraction
Distress
Animal **Distress** Calls
Respiratory **Distress**
Distributed Practice
Binomial **Distribution**
Drug **Distribution**
Frequency **Distribution**
Gaussian Distribution *USE Normal Distribution*
Normal **Distribution**
Poisson Distribution *USE Skewed Distribution*
Skewed **Distribution**
Distributive Justice
Distrust *USE Suspicion*
Affective Disturbances *USE Affective Disorders*
Body Image **Disturbances**
Consciousness **Disturbances**
Fantasies (Thought **Disturbances)**
Hysterical Vision **Disturbances**
Judgment **Disturbances**
Perceptual **Disturbances**
Sexual Function **Disturbances**
Thought **Disturbances**
Emotionally **Disturbed**
Disulfiram
Diuresis
Diuretics
Diurnal Variations
USE Human Biological Rhythms
Divergent Thinking
Diversity in the Workplace
Workforce Diversity *USE Diversity in the Workplace*
Workplace Diversity *USE Diversity in the Workplace*
Divided Attention
Division of Labor
Animal **Division** of Labor
Divorce
Divorced Persons
Dizygotic Twins *USE Heterozygotic Twins*
Dizziness *USE Vertigo*
Doctors *USE Physicians*

Dogmatism
Rokeach **Dogmatism** Scale
Dogs
Seeing Eye Dogs *USE Mobility Aids*
Doll Play
Anatomically Detailed **Dolls**
Tic Douloureux *USE Trigeminal Neuralgia*
Dolphins
Domestic Service Personnel
Domestic Violence *USE Family Violence*
Animal **Domestication**
Dominance
Dominance Hierarchy
Animal **Dominance**
Cerebral **Dominance**
Eye Dominance *USE Ocular Dominance*
Genetic **Dominance**
Lateral **Dominance**
Ocular **Dominance**
Domination *USE Authoritarianism*
Blood Donation *USE Tissue Donation*
Organ Donation *USE Tissue Donation*
Sperm Donation *USE Tissue Donation*
Tissue **Donation**
DOPA
L Dopa *USE Levodopa*
DOPAC *USE Dihydroxyphenylacetic Acid*
Dopamine
Dopamine Agonists
Dopamine Antagonists
Dopamine Metabolites
Dormitories
Dorsal Horns
Dorsal Roots
Drug **Dosages**
Double Bind Interaction
Doubt
Doves
Downs Syndrome
Downsizing
Doxepin
Draftees
Drama
Drama Therapy *USE Psychodrama*
Draw A Man Test
USE Human Figures Drawing
Goodenough Harris **Draw** A Person Test
Drawing
Human Figures **Drawing**
Dream Analysis
Dream Content
Dream Interpretation *USE Dream Analysis*
Dream Recall
REM **Dream** Deprivation
Dreaming
Lucid **Dreaming**
Rapid Eye Movement Dreams *USE REM Dreams*
REM **Dreams**
DRGs *USE Diagnosis Related Groups*
Drinking Attitudes
USE Alcohol Drinking Attitudes
Drinking Behavior
Alcohol **Drinking** Attitudes
Alcohol **Drinking** Patterns
Animal **Drinking** Behavior
Problem Drinking *USE Alcohol Abuse*
Social **Drinking**
Drive *USE Motivation*
Sex **Drive**
Driver Education
Driver Safety *USE Highway Safety*
Drivers
Driving Behavior
Driving Under the Influence
Aggressive **Driving** Behavior
Drunk Driving *USE Driving Under the Influence*
Dropouts

Client Dropouts *USE Treatment Dropouts*
College **Dropouts**
Patient Dropouts *USE Treatment Dropouts*
Potential **Dropouts**
Research Dropouts *USE Experimental Attrition*
School **Dropouts**
Treatment **Dropouts**
Drosophila
Drowsiness *USE Sleep Onset*
Drug Abstinence
Drug Abuse
Drug Abuse Liability
Drug Abuse Prevention
Drug Addiction
Drug Administration Methods
Drug Adverse Reactions
USE Side Effects (Drug)
Drug Allergies
Drug Augmentation
Drug Dependency
Drug Discrimination
Drug Dissociation
USE State Dependent Learning
Drug Distribution
Drug Dosages
Drug Education
Drug Effects *USE Drugs*
Drug Induced Congenital Disorders
Drug Induced Hallucinations
Drug Interactions
Drug Laws
Drug Legalization
Drug Overdoses
Drug Potentiation *USE Drug Interactions*
Drug Rehabilitation
Drug Self Administration
Drug Sensitivity
Drug Synergism *USE Drug Interactions*
Drug Testing *USE Drug Usage Screening*
Drug Therapy
Drug Tolerance
Drug Usage
Drug Usage Attitudes
Drug Usage Screening
Drug Withdrawal
Drug Withdrawal Effects
USE Drug Withdrawal
CNS Depressant Drug Antagonists *USE Analeptic Drugs*
Intravenous **Drug** Usage
IV Drug Usage *USE Intravenous Drug Usage*
Side Effects **(Drug)**
Drugs
Adrenergic Blocking **Drugs**
Adrenergic **Drugs**
Adrenolytic Drugs *USE Adrenergic Drugs*
Analeptic **Drugs**
Analgesic **Drugs**
Anesthetic **Drugs**
Anorexigenic Drugs *USE Appetite Depressing Drugs*
Anti Inflammatory **Drugs**
Antiadrenergic Drugs *USE Sympatholytic Drugs*
Antianxiety Drugs *USE Tranquilizing Drugs*
Anticholinergic Drugs *USE Cholinergic Blocking Drugs*
Anticholinesterase Drugs *USE Cholinesterase Inhibitors*
Anticoagulant **Drugs**
Anticonvulsive **Drugs**
Antidepressant **Drugs**
Antiemetic **Drugs**
Antiepileptic Drugs *USE Anticonvulsive Drugs*
Antihistaminic **Drugs**
Antihypertensive **Drugs**
Antinauseant Drugs *USE Antiemetic Drugs*
Antineoplastic **Drugs**
Antiparkinsonian Drugs *USE Antitremor Drugs*
Antipsychotic Drugs *USE Neuroleptic Drugs*
Antipyretic Drugs *USE Anti Inflammatory Drugs*
Antischizophrenic Drugs *USE Neuroleptic Drugs*

Antispasmodic **Drugs**
Antitremor **Drugs**
Antitubercular **Drugs**
Antiviral **Drugs**
Anxiety Reducing Drugs *USE Tranquilizing Drugs*
Anxiolytic Drugs *USE Tranquilizing Drugs*
Appetite Depressing **Drugs**
Ataractic Drugs *USE Tranquilizing Drugs*
Ataraxic Drugs *USE Tranquilizing Drugs*
Cardiotonic Drugs *USE Drugs*
Central Nervous System Drugs *USE CNS Affecting Drugs*
Cholinergic Blocking **Drugs**
Cholinergic **Drugs**
Cholinolytic Drugs *USE Cholinergic Blocking Drugs*
Cholinomimetic **Drugs**
CNS Affecting **Drugs**
CNS Depressant **Drugs**
CNS Stimulating **Drugs**
Cognition Enhancing Drugs *USE Nootropic Drugs*
Emetic **Drugs**
Ganglion Blocking **Drugs**
Hallucinogenic **Drugs**
Heart Rate Affecting **Drugs**
Hypnotic **Drugs**
Memory Enhancing Drugs *USE Nootropic Drugs*
Muscarinic Drugs *USE Cholinergic Drugs*
Muscle Relaxing **Drugs**
Narcoanalytic Drugs *USE Drugs*
Narcotic **Drugs**
Neuroleptic **Drugs**
Neuromuscular Blocking Drugs *USE Muscle Relaxing Drugs*
Nonprescription **Drugs**
Nootropic **Drugs**
Over the Counter Drugs *USE Nonprescription Drugs*
Pain Relieving Drugs *USE Analgesic Drugs*
Parasympatholytic Drugs *USE Antispasmodic Drugs*
Parasympathomimetic Drugs *USE Cholinomimetic Drugs*
Prescribing **(Drugs)**
Prescription **Drugs**
Psychedelic **Drugs**
Psychoactive Drugs *USE Drugs*
Psychostimulant Drugs *USE CNS Stimulating Drugs*
Psychotomimetic **Drugs**
Psychotropic Drugs *USE Drugs*
Respiration Stimulating **Drugs**
Sleep Inducing Drugs *USE Hypnotic Drugs*
Sympatholytic **Drugs**
Sympathomimetic **Drugs**
Thymoleptic Drugs *USE Tranquilizing Drugs*
Tranquilizing **Drugs**
Tricyclic Antidepressant **Drugs**
Vasoconstrictor **Drugs**
Vasodilator **Drugs**
Vasopressor Drugs *USE Vasoconstrictor Drugs*
Vomit Inducing Drugs *USE Emetic Drugs*
Drunk Driving
USE Driving Under the Influence
Drunkenness *USE Alcohol Intoxication*
DSM
USE Diagnostic and Statistical Manual
Dual Careers
Dual Diagnosis
Dual Relationships
Dualism
Duchennes Disease
USE Muscular Disorders
Ducks
Mental Disorders **due** to General Medical Conditions
Duodenum *USE Intestines*
Response **Duration**
Stimulus **Duration**
Treatment **Duration**
Duty to Warn
Pituitary Dwarfism *USE Hypopituitarism*
Dyads
Dying *USE Death and Dying*
Dying Patients *USE Terminally Ill Patients*

Death and **Dying**
Family Dynamics *USE Family Relations*
Group **Dynamics**
Intergroup **Dynamics**
Dynorphins
Dysarthria
Dyscalculia *USE Acalculia*
Cognitive Dysfunction *USE Cognitive Impairment*
Dysfunctional Family
Dyskinesia
Tardive **Dyskinesia**
Dyslexia
Dysmenorrhea
Dysmetria *USE Ataxia*
Body **Dysmorphic** Disorder
Dysmorphophobia
USE Body Dysmorphic Disorder
Dyspareunia
Dysphagia
Dysphasia
Dysphonia
Dysphoria *USE Major Depression*
Postnatal Dysphoria *USE Postpartum Depression*
Premenstrual **Dysphoric** Disorder
Dyspnea
Dyspraxia *USE Movement Disorders*
Dysthymia *USE Dysthymic Disorder*
Dysthymic Disorder
Dystonia *USE Muscular Disorders*
Muscular **Dystrophy**
E-Therapy *USE Online Therapy*
Eagerness *USE Enthusiasm*
Ear (Anatomy)
Ear Canal *USE External Ear*
Ear Disorders
Ear Ossicles *USE Middle Ear*
External **Ear**
Inner Ear *USE Labyrinth (Anatomy)*
Middle **Ear**
Early Childhood Development
Early Experience
Early Infantile Autism
Early Intervention
Early Memories
Earthworms
South East Asian Cultural Groups
USE Southeast Asian Cultural Groups
Eating *USE Eating Behavior*
Eating Attitudes
Eating Behavior
Eating Disorders
Eating Habits *USE Eating Behavior*
Eating Patterns *USE Eating Behavior*
Binge **Eating**
Purging **(Eating** Disorders)
Rumination **(Eating)**
Retinal **Eccentricity**
Echinodermata
Echoencephalography
Echolalia
Echolocation
Eclectic Psychology
USE Theoretical Orientation
Eclectic Psychotherapy
Ecological Factors
Ecological Psychology
Conservation **(Ecological** Behavior)
Ecology
Behavioral **Ecology**
Income **(Economic)**
Political **Economic** Systems
Economically Disadvantaged
USE Disadvantaged
Economics
Behavioral **Economics**
Home **Economics**
Economy

Token **Economy** Programs
ECS Therapy
USE Electroconvulsive Shock Therapy
Eczema
Educable Mentally Retarded
USE Mild Mental Retardation
Education
Education Students
Accreditation **(Education** Personnel)
Adult **Education**
Affective **Education**
Alcohol Education *USE Drug Education*
Art **Education**
Bilingual **Education**
Boards of **Education**
Business **Education**
Career **Education**
Client **Education**
College Education *USE Undergraduate Education*
Compensatory **Education**
Continuing **Education**
Cooperative **Education**
Counselor **Education**
Death **Education**
Dental **Education**
Distance **Education**
Driver **Education**
Drug **Education**
Elementary **Education**
Environmental **Education**
Equal **Education**
Family Life **Education**
Foreign Language **Education**
Graduate Psychology **Education**
Graduate **Education**
Health **Education**
High School **Education**
Higher **Education**
Humanistic Education *USE Affective Education*
Industrial Arts Education *USE Vocational Education*
Inservice Teacher **Education**
Language Arts **Education**
Marriage and Family Education *USE Family Life Education*
Mathematics **Education**
Medical **Education**
Middle School **Education**
Multicultural **Education**
Music **Education**
Nontraditional **Education**
Nursing **Education**
Paraprofessional **Education**
Parochial School Education *USE Private School Education*
Patient Education *USE Client Education*
Physical **Education**
Preschool **Education**
Private School **Education**
Psychology **Education**
Public School **Education**
Quality of Education *USE Educational Quality*
Reading **Education**
Rehabilitation **Education**
Religious **Education**
Remedial **Education**
Same Sex **Education**
Science **Education**
Second Language Education
USE Foreign Language Education
Secondary **Education**
Sex **Education**
Single Sex Education *USE Same Sex Education*
Social Studies **Education**
Social Work **Education**
Special **Education**
Special **Education** Students
Special **Education** Teachers
Teacher **Education**

Technical Education Teachers
    USE Vocational Education Teachers
Theories of **Education**
Undergraduate **Education**
Vocational **Education**
Vocational **Education** Teachers
Educational Administration
Educational Administrators
    USE School Administrators
Educational Aspirations
Educational Attainment Level
Educational Audiovisual Aids
Educational Background
Educational Counseling
Educational Degrees
Educational Diagnosis
Educational Environment
    USE School Environment
Educational Field Trips
Educational Financial Assistance
Educational Guidance
    USE Educational Counseling
Educational Incentives
Educational Inequality
    USE Equal Education
Educational Intervention
    USE School Based Intervention
Educational Laboratories
Educational Measurement
Educational Objectives
Educational Personnel
Educational Placement
Educational Process *USE Education*
Educational Program Accreditation
Educational Program Evaluation
Educational Program Planning
Educational Programs
Educational Psychologists
Educational Psychology
Educational Quality
Educational Reform
Educational Supervision
    USE Professional Supervision
Educational Television
Educational Theory
    USE Theories of Education
Educational Therapy
Educational Toys
Grading **(Educational)**
Learning Centers **(Educational)**
Mainstreaming **(Educational)**
Motion Pictures **(Educational)**
Parent **Educational** Background
Edwards Personal Preference Schedule
Edwards Personality Inventory
Edwards Social Desirability Scale
Effect Size (Statistical)
Generation **Effect** (Learning)
Halo **Effect**
Isolation **Effect**
Primacy **Effect**
Pygmalion Effect *USE Self Fulfilling Prophecies*
Recency **Effect**
Serial Position **Effect**
Stroop **Effect**
Cost Effectiveness *USE Costs and Cost Analysis*
Counselor Effectiveness
    USE Counselor Characteristics
Organizational **Effectiveness**
Parent Effectiveness Training *USE Parent Training*
Teacher Effectiveness *USE Teacher Characteristics*
Teacher **Effectiveness** Evaluation
Therapist Effectiveness
    USE Therapist Characteristics
Treatment **Effectiveness** Evaluation
Acceleration **Effects**
Altitude **Effects**

Cold **Effects**
Decompression **Effects**
Drug Withdrawal Effects *USE Drug Withdrawal*
Drug Effects *USE Drugs*
Environmental **Effects**
Gravitational **Effects**
Heat **Effects**
Iatrogenic Effects *USE Side Effects (Treatment)*
Noise **Effects**
Practice Effects *USE Practice*
Side **Effects** (Drug)
Side **Effects** (Treatment)
Temperature **Effects**
Underwater **Effects**
Efferent Pathways
Efficacy Expectations *USE Self Efficacy*
Self **Efficacy**
Employee **Efficiency**
Effort *USE Energy Expenditure*
Egalitarianism
Ego
Ego Development
Ego Identity
Egocentrism
Egotism
Eidetic Imagery
Ejaculation *USE Male Orgasm*
Premature **Ejaculation**
Elavil *USE Amitriptyline*
Elbow (Anatomy)
Elder Abuse
Elder Care
Elected Government Officials
    USE Government Personnel
Political **Elections**
Elective Abortion *USE Induced Abortion*
Elective Mutism
Electra Complex
Electric Fishes
Electrical Activity
Electrical Brain Stimulation
Electrical Injuries
Electrical Stimulation
Skin **Electrical** Properties
Electro Oculography
Electrocardiography
Electroconvulsive Shock
Electroconvulsive Shock Therapy
Electrodermal Response
    USE Galvanic Skin Response
Electrodes
Electroencephalography
Electrolytes
Electromyography
Electronic Communication
Electronic Mail *USE Computer Mediated Communication*
Electronystagmography
Electrophysiology
Electroplethysmography
Electroretinography
Electroshock Therapy
    USE Electroconvulsive Shock Therapy
Electrosleep Treatment
Elementarism *USE Reductionism*
Elementary Education
Elementary School Students
Elementary School Teachers
Elementary Schools
Chemical **Elements**
Metallic **Elements**
Nonmetallic Elements *USE Chemical Elements*
Elephants
Ellis (Albert)
Email *USE Computer Mediated Communication*
Embarrassment

Embedded Figures Testing
Embolisms
Embryo
EMDR *USE Eye Movement Desensitization Therapy*
Emergency Services
Emetic Drugs
Nocturnal **Emission**
Positron Emission Tomography *USE Tomography*
Depression **(Emotion)**
Expressed **Emotion**
Emotional Abuse
Emotional Adjustment
Emotional Content
Emotional Control
Emotional Development
Emotional Expressiveness
USE Emotionality (Personality)
Emotional Immaturity
Emotional Inferiority
Emotional Insecurity
USE Emotional Security
Emotional Instability
Emotional Intelligence
Emotional Maladjustment
USE Emotional Adjustment
Emotional Maturity
Emotional Needs
USE Psychological Needs
Emotional Responses
Emotional Restraint *USE Emotional Control*
Emotional Security
Emotional Stability
Emotional States
Emotional Superiority
Emotional Trauma
Conditioned **Emotional** Responses
Emotionality (Personality)
Animal **Emotionality**
Emotionally Disturbed
Emotions
Rational **Emotive** Behavior Therapy
Rational Emotive Therapy
USE Rational Emotive Behavior Therapy
Empathy
Pulmonary **Emphysema**
Empirical Methods
Employability
Employee Absenteeism
Employee Assistance Programs
Employee Attitudes
Employee Benefits
Employee Characteristics
Employee Efficiency
Employee Health Insurance
Employee Interaction
Employee Leave Benefits
Employee Motivation
Employee Pension Plans
Employee Productivity
Employee Selection
USE Personnel Selection
Employee Skills
Employee Supervisor Interaction
USE Supervisor Employee Interaction
Employee Termination
USE Personnel Termination
Employee Turnover
Manager Employee Interaction
USE Supervisor Employee Interaction
Supervisor **Employee** Interaction
Employees *USE Personnel*
Employer Attitudes
Employment *USE Employment Status*
Employment Discrimination
Employment History

Employment Interviews
USE Job Applicant Interviews
Employment Processes
USE Personnel Recruitment
Employment Status
Employment Tests
Self **Employment**
Supported **Employment**
Empowerment
Empty Nest
Enabling
Enactments
Encephalitis
Encephalography
Air Encephalography
USE Pneumoencephalography
Encephalomyelitis
Encephalopathies
Toxic **Encephalopathies**
Encoding *USE Human Information Storage*
Encopresis *USE Fecal Incontinence*
Encounter Group Therapy
Encouragement
Nerve **Endings**
Endocrine Disorders
Endocrine Gland Secretion
Endocrine Gland Surgery
Endocrine Glands
Endocrine Neoplasms
Endocrine Sexual Disorders
Endocrine System
Endocrinology
Endogamous Marriage
Endogenous Depression
Endogenous Opiates
Endorphins
Endurance
Physical **Endurance**
Psychological **Endurance**
Energy Expenditure
Law **Enforcement**
Law **Enforcement** Personnel
Engineering Psychology
Genetic **Engineering**
Human Factors **Engineering**
Knowledge **Engineering**
Engineers
English as Second Language
Limited English Proficiency
USE Language Proficiency
Nonstandard **English**
Fertility **Enhancement**
Cognition Enhancing Drugs *USE Nootropic Drugs*
Memory Enhancing Drugs *USE Nootropic Drugs*
Enjoyment *USE Pleasure*
Enkephalins
Enlisted Military Personnel
Military **Enlistment**
Job **Enrichment**
School **Enrollment**
Enteropeptidase *USE Kinases*
Motion Pictures **(Entertainment)**
Enthusiasm
Entrance Examinations
College **Entrance** Examination Board Scholastic Aptitude Test
Entrapment Games
Entrepreneurship
Enuresis *USE Urinary Incontinence*
Environment
Academic **Environment**
Classroom **Environment**
College **Environment**
Educational Environment *USE School Environment*
Experimental Environment *USE Research Setting*
Facility **Environment**
Family Environment *USE Home Environment*

338

Home **Environment**
Hospital **Environment**
Learning **Environment**
Office Environment *USE Working Conditions*
Person **Environment** Fit
School **Environment**
Therapeutic **Environment**
Treatment Environment *USE Therapeutic Environment*
Zoo Environment *USE Animal Captivity*
Environmental Adaptation
Environmental Attitudes
Environmental Design
    USE Environmental Planning
Environmental Education
Environmental Effects
Environmental Planning
Environmental Psychology
Environmental Stress
Environmental Therapy
    USE Milieu Therapy
Restricted Environmental Stimulation
    USE Stimulus Deprivation
Animal **Environments**
Factory Environments *USE Working Conditions*
Female Only Environments
    USE Single Sex Environments
Male Only Environments
    USE Single Sex Environments
Rural **Environments**
Same Sex Environments
    USE Single Sex Environments
Single Sex **Environments**
Social **Environments**
Suburban **Environments**
Urban **Environments**
Work Environments *USE Working Conditions*
Envy *USE Jealousy*
Penis **Envy**
Enzyme Inhibitors
Enzymes
Ependyma *USE Cerebral Ventricles*
Ephedrine
Epidemics
Epidemiology
Epilepsy
Experimental **Epilepsy**
Grand Mal **Epilepsy**
Petit Mal **Epilepsy**
Epileptic Seizures
Epinephrine
Episcopalians *USE Protestants*
Acute Psychotic Episode *USE Acute Psychosis*
Episodic Memory
Epistemology
Epithelial Cells
Epithelium *USE Skin (Anatomy)*
Epstein Barr Viral Disorder
Equal Education
Social **Equality**
Score **Equating**
Test Equating *USE Score Equating*
Structural **Equation** Modeling
Equilibrium
Cauda Equina *USE Spinal Nerves*
Equipment *USE Apparatus*
Equity (Payment)
Equity (Social)
High School Equivalency *USE Adult Education*
Erection (Penis)
Ergonomics
    USE Human Factors Engineering
Ergot Derivatives
Erikson **(Erik)**
Erikson (Erik)
Eroticism
Erotomania
Error Analysis

Error of Measurement
Error Variance *USE Error of Measurement*
Measurement Error *USE Error of Measurement*
Standard Error of Measurement
    USE Error of Measurement
Trial and **Error** Learning
Errors
Prediction **Errors**
Refraction **Errors**
Type I **Errors**
Type II **Errors**
Erythroblastosis Fetalis
    USE Rh Incompatibility
Erythrocytes
Escape *USE Avoidance*
Escape Conditioning
Animal **Escape** Behavior
Eserine *USE Physostigmine*
Eskimos *USE Inuit*
ESL *USE English as Second Language*
Esophagus
Essay Testing
Essential Hypertension
Self **Esteem**
Esterases
Estimation
Magnitude **Estimation**
Parameter Estimation *USE Statistical Estimation*
Statistical **Estimation**
Time **Estimation**
Estradiol
Estrogen Antagonists *USE Antiestrogens*
Estrogen Replacement Therapy
    USE Hormone Therapy
Estrogens
Estrone
Estrus
Ethanal *USE Acetaldehyde*
Ethanol
Ether (Anesthetic)
Work Ethic *USE Work (Attitudes Toward)*
Ethics
Experimental **Ethics**
Medical Ethics *USE Bioethics*
Professional **Ethics**
Ethnic Differences
    USE Racial and Ethnic Differences
Ethnic Discrimination
    USE Race and Ethnic Discrimination
Ethnic Groups
    USE Racial and Ethnic Groups
Ethnic Identity
Ethnic Sensitivity *USE Cultural Sensitivity*
Ethnic Values
Race and **Ethnic** Discrimination
Racial and **Ethnic** Attitudes
Racial and **Ethnic** Differences
Racial and **Ethnic** Groups
Racial and **Ethnic** Relations
Ethnicity *USE Ethnic Identity*
Ethnocentrism
Ethnography
Ethnolinguistics
Ethnology
Animal **Ethology**
Ethyl Alcohol *USE Ethanol*
Ethylaldehyde *USE Acetaldehyde*
Etiology
Etiopathogenesis *USE Etiology*
Etymology
Eugenics
Euphoria
Eustachian Tube *USE Middle Ear*
Euthanasia
Evaluation
Evaluation Criteria
Course **Evaluation**

Disability **Evaluation**
Educational Program **Evaluation**
Forensic **Evaluation**
Mental Health Program **Evaluation**
Peer **Evaluation**
Personnel **Evaluation**
Program **Evaluation**
Psychiatric **Evaluation**
Self **Evaluation**
Teacher Effectiveness **Evaluation**
Treatment Effectiveness **Evaluation**
Vocational **Evaluation**
Evangelists
Event Related Potentials
USE Evoked Potentials
Anniversary **Events**
Experiences **(Events)**
Evidence Based Medicine
USE Evidence Based Practice
Evidence Based Practice
Legal **Evidence**
Evil
Evoked Potentials
Auditory **Evoked** Potentials
Cortical **Evoked** Potentials
Motor Evoked Potentials
USE Somatosensory Evoked Potentials
Olfactory **Evoked** Potentials
Somatosensory **Evoked** Potentials
Visual **Evoked** Potentials
Theory of **Evolution**
Evolutionary Psychology
Breast Examination
USE Self Examination (Medical)
College Entrance **Examination** Board Scholastic Aptitude
Test
Eye Examination
USE Ophthalmologic Examination
Graduate Record **Examination**
Mini Mental State **Examination**
Ophthalmologic **Examination**
Physical **Examination**
Self **Examination** (Medical)
Certification Examinations
USE Professional Examinations
Entrance **Examinations**
Licensure Examinations
USE Professional Examinations
Professional **Examinations**
State Board Examinations
USE Professional Examinations
Information Exchange *USE Communication*
Needle **Exchange** Programs
Excretion
Executive Functioning
USE Cognitive Ability
Executives *USE Top Level Managers*
Exercise
Aerobic **Exercise**
Physical Exercise *USE Exercise*
Exhaustion *USE Fatigue*
Exhibitionism
Existential Therapy
Existentialism
Exogamous Marriage
Life **Expectancy**
Expectant Fathers
Expectant Mothers
Expectant Parents
Expectations
Efficacy Expectations *USE Self Efficacy*
Experimenter **Expectations**
Parental **Expectations**
Role **Expectations**
Teacher **Expectations**
Energy **Expenditure**
Experience Level

Combat **Experience**
Curricular Field **Experience**
Early **Experience**
Job **Experience** Level
Openness to **Experience**
Therapist Experience *USE Therapist Characteristics*
Wilderness **Experience**
Experiences (Events)
First **Experiences**
Life **Experiences**
Near Death **Experiences**
Out of Body **Experiences**
Psychedelic **Experiences**
Religious **Experiences**
Vicarious **Experiences**
Experiential Learning
Experiential Psychotherapy
Experiment Controls
Experiment Volunteers
USE Experimental Subjects
Field Experiment *USE Observation Methods*
Experimental Apparatus *USE Apparatus*
Experimental Attrition
Experimental Design
Experimental Environment
USE Research Setting
Experimental Epilepsy
Experimental Ethics
Experimental Instructions
Experimental Laboratories
Experimental Methods
Experimental Neurosis
Experimental Psychologists
Experimental Psychology
Experimental Psychosis
Experimental Replication
Experimental Setting
USE Research Setting
Experimental Subjects
Debriefing **(Experimental)**
Quasi **Experimental** Methods
Sampling **(Experimental)**
Experimentation
Experimenter Bias
Experimenter Expectations
Experimenters
Expert Systems
Expert Testimony
Expertise *USE Experience Level*
Explicit Memory
Career Exploration *USE Career Education*
Exploratory Behavior
Animal **Exploratory** Behavior
Explosive Disorder
Explosive Personality
USE Explosive Disorder
Intermittent Explosive Disorder *USE Explosive Disorder*
Exposure Therapy
Fetal Exposure *USE Prenatal Exposure*
Occupational **Exposure**
Prenatal **Exposure**
Expressed Emotion
Gene **Expression**
Facial **Expressions**
Expressive Psychotherapy
Emotional Expressiveness
USE Emotionality (Personality)
School **Expulsion**
Extended Family
Agricultural **Extension** Workers
External Ear
External Rewards
Internal **External** Locus of Control
Rotter Internal **External** Locus of Control Scale
Externalization
Extinction (Learning)
Thyroid Extract *USE Thyroid Hormones*

Extracurricular Activities
Extradimensional Shift Learning
    USE Nonreversal Shift Learning
Extramarital Intercourse
Extrapyramidal Symptoms
Extrapyramidal Tracts
Extrasensory Perception
Extraversion
Extrinsic Motivation
Extrinsic Rewards *USE External Rewards*
Eye (Anatomy)
Eye Accommodation
    USE Ocular Accommodation
Eye Color
Eye Contact
Eye Convergence
Eye Disorders
Eye Dominance *USE Ocular Dominance*
Eye Examination
    USE Ophthalmologic Examination
Eye Fixation
Eye Movement Desensitization Therapy
Eye Movements
Cones **(Eye)**
Iris **(Eye)**
Lens **(Eye)**
Nonrapid Eye Movement Sleep *USE NREM Sleep*
Pupil **(Eye)**
Rapid **Eye** Movement
Rapid Eye Movement Dreams *USE REM Dreams*
Rapid Eye Movement Sleep *USE REM Sleep*
Rods **(Eye)**
Saccadic Eye Movements *USE Eye Movements*
Seeing Eye Dogs *USE Mobility Aids*
Eyeblink Reflex
Eyelid Conditioning
Crossed Eyes *USE Strabismus*
Eyewitnesses *USE Witnesses*
Eysenck Personality Inventory
F Test
California **F** Scale
Face (Anatomy)
Face Perception
Face Recognition *USE Face Perception*
Lips **(Face)**
Facial Expressions
Facial Features
Facial Muscles
Facial Nerve
Facilitated Communication
    USE Augmentative Communication
Social **Facilitation**
Community **Facilities**
Maximum Security **Facilities**
School **Facilities**
Treatment **Facilities**
Facility Admission
Facility Discharge
Facility Environment
Facility Readmission
    USE Facility Admission
Factitious Disorders
Factor Analysis
Factor Structure
ACTH Releasing Factor *USE Corticotropin Releasing Factor*
Confirmatory Factor Analysis *USE Factor Analysis*
Conscious (Personality **Factor)**
Corticotropin Releasing **Factor**
Five **Factor** Personality Model
Nerve Growth **Factor**
Unconscious (Personality **Factor)**
Factorial Validity *USE Statistical Validity*
Cultural Factors *USE Sociocultural Factors*
Ecological **Factors**
Human **Factors** Engineering
Immunologic **Factors**
Personality Factors *USE Personality Traits*

Psychoanalytic Personality **Factors**
Psychosocial **Factors**
Risk **Factors**
Sixteen Personality **Factors** Questionnaire
Sociocultural **Factors**
Thermal Factors *USE Temperature Effects*
Factory Environments
    USE Working Conditions
Factual Knowledge
    USE Declarative Knowledge
Faculty *USE Educational Personnel*
Fading (Conditioning)
Fads and Fashions
Failure
Failure to Thrive
Academic **Failure**
Fainting *USE Syncope*
Cattell Culture Fair Intelligence Test
    USE Culture Fair Intelligence Test
Culture **Fair** Intelligence Test
Fairbairnian Theory *USE Object Relations*
Fairy Tales *USE Folklore*
Faith Healing
Faking
Falls
False Memory
False Pregnancy *USE Pseudocyesis*
True False Tests
    USE Forced Choice (Testing Method)
Fame
Amaurotic Familial Idiocy *USE Tay Sachs Disease*
Cultural Familial Mental Retardation
    USE Psychosocial Mental Retardation
Familiarity
Family
Family Background
Family Caregivers *USE Caregivers*
Family Conflict
Family Counseling *USE Family Therapy*
Family Crises
Family Dynamics *USE Family Relations*
Family Environment
    USE Home Environment
Family Intervention
Family Life Education
Family Life *USE Family Relations*
Family Medicine
Family Members
Family of Origin
Family Physicians
Family Planning
Family Planning Attitudes
Family Relations
Family Resemblance
Family Size
Family Socioeconomic Level
Family Structure
Family Systems Model
    USE Family Systems Theory
Family Systems Theory
Family Therapy
Family Violence
Family Work Relationship
Biological **Family**
Dysfunctional **Family**
Extended **Family**
Interethnic **Family**
Interracial **Family**
Job Family Relationship
    USE Family Work Relationship
Marriage and Family Education
    USE Family Life Education
Natural Family *USE Biological Family*
Nuclear **Family**
Schizophrenogenic **Family**
Work Family Relationship
    USE Family Work Relationship

341

Fantasies (Thought Disturbances)
Fantasy
Fantasy (Defense Mechanism)
Guided Fantasy *USE Guided Imagery*
Sexual **Fantasy**
Migrant **Farm** Workers
Farmers *USE Agricultural Workers*
Fascism
Fads and **Fashions**
Fat Metabolism *USE Lipid Metabolism*
Fatalism
Father Absence
Father Child Communication
Father Child Relations
Fathers
Adolescent **Fathers**
Expectant **Fathers**
Single **Fathers**
Teenage Fathers *USE Adolescent Fathers*
Fatigue
Chronic **Fatigue** Syndrome
Fatty Acids
Fear
Fear of Public Speaking
    USE Speech Anxiety
Fear of Strangers *USE Stranger Reactions*
Fear of Success
Fear Survey Schedule
Conditioned **Fear**
Facial **Features**
Fecal Incontinence
School Federal Aid
    USE Educational Financial Assistance
Fee for Service
Feedback
Auditory **Feedback**
Delayed Auditory **Feedback**
Delayed **Feedback**
Sensory **Feedback**
Visual **Feedback**
Feeding Practices *USE Eating Behavior*
Animal **Feeding** Behavior
Bottle **Feeding**
Breast **Feeding**
Anesthesia **(Feeling)**
Feelings *USE Emotions*
Professional **Fees**
Feet (Anatomy)
Felids
Felonies *USE Crime*
Female Animals
Female Criminals
Female Delinquency
Female Genital Mutilation
    USE Circumcision
Female Genitalia
Female Homosexuality *USE Lesbianism*
Female Only Environments
    USE Single Sex Environments
Female Orgasm
Male **Female** Relations
Battered **Females**
Human **Females**
Femininity
Feminism
Feminist Therapy
Testicular **Feminization** Syndrome
Femoral Nerve *USE Spinal Nerves*
Fenfluramine
Fentanyl
Fertility
Fertility Enhancement
Fertilization
In Vitro Fertilization *USE Reproductive Technology*
Fetal Alcohol Syndrome
Fetal Exposure *USE Prenatal Exposure*
Erythroblastosis Fetalis *USE Rh Incompatibility*

Fetishism
Sexual Fetishism *USE Fetishism*
Fetus
Fever *USE Hyperthermia*
Hay **Fever**
Rheumatic **Fever**
Postganglionic Autonomic Fibers *USE Autonomic Ganglia*
Preganglionic Autonomic Fibers *USE Autonomic Ganglia*
Fibrillation (Heart)
Atrial Fibrillation *USE Fibrillation (Heart)*
Auricular Fibrillation *USE Fibrillation (Heart)*
Ventricular Fibrillation *USE Fibrillation (Heart)*
Fibromyalgia
Cystic **Fibrosis**
Fiction *USE Literature*
Marital Fidelity *USE Monogamy*
Field Dependence
Field Experiment
    USE Observation Methods
Field Instruction
    USE Curricular Field Experience
Animal Open **Field** Behavior
Curricular **Field** Experience
Educational **Field** Trips
Visual **Field**
Cutaneous Receptive **Fields**
Receptive **Fields**
Visual Receptive **Fields**
Fire **Fighters**
Fighting *USE Aggressive Behavior*
Figurative Language
Figure Ground Discrimination
Figures of Speech
    USE Figurative Language
Embedded **Figures** Testing
Human **Figures** Drawing
Perceptual Fill *USE Perceptual Closure*
Film Strips
Filtered Noise
Filtered Speech
Educational **Financial** Assistance
School Financial Assistance
    USE Educational Financial Assistance
Fine Motor Skill Learning
Finger Tapping
Fingers (Anatomy)
Fingerspelling
Fire Fighters
Fire Prevention
Firearms
Firesetting *USE Arson*
FIRO-B *USE Fundamental Interpersonal*
    Relation Orientation Behavior Ques
First Experiences
First Language *USE Native Language*
Bass **(Fish)**
Fishes
Electric **Fishes**
Goodness of **Fit**
Person Environment **Fit**
Physical **Fitness**
Five Factor Personality Model
Big Five Personality Model
    USE Five Factor Personality Model
Eye **Fixation**
Ocular Fixation *USE Eye Fixation*
Visual Fixation *USE Eye Fixation*
Fixed Interval Reinforcement
Fixed Ratio Reinforcement
Flashbacks *USE Hallucinations*
Flexion Reflex
Flextime *USE Work Scheduling*
Flicker Fusion Frequency
    USE Critical Flicker Fusion Threshold
Critical **Flicker** Fusion Threshold
Flies *USE Diptera*

Flight Attendants
  USE Aerospace Personnel
Flight Instrumentation
Flight Simulation
Flooding Therapy USE Implosive Therapy
Blood **Flow**
Cerebral Blood **Flow**
Fluency USE Verbal Fluency
Verbal **Fluency**
Fluid Intake
Amniotic **Fluid**
Cerebrospinal **Fluid**
Spinal Fluid USE Cerebrospinal Fluid
Body **Fluids**
Flunitrazepam
Fluoxetine
Fluphenazine
Flurazepam
Fluvoxamine
Fruit Fly USE Drosophila
Solution **Focused** Therapy
Folic Acid
Folie A Deux
Folk Medicine
Folk Psychology
Folklore
Folktales USE Folklore
Follicle Stimulating Hormone
Project **Follow** Through
Followup Studies
Posttreatment **Followup**
Food
Food Additives
Food Allergies
Food Deprivation
Food Intake
Food Preferences
Football
Animal **Foraging** Behavior
Air **Force** Personnel
Forced Choice (Testing Method)
Forebrain
Medial **Forebrain** Bundle
Foreign Language Education
Foreign Language Learning
Foreign Language Translation
Foreign Languages
Foreign Nationals
Foreign Organizations
Foreign Policy Making
Foreign Students
Foreign Study
Foreign Workers
Industrial **Foremen**
Forensic Evaluation
Forensic Psychiatry
Forensic Psychology
Forgetting
Forgiveness
Form and Shape Perception
Form Classes (Language)
Form Perception
  USE Form and Shape Perception
Attitude **Formation**
Character Formation USE Personality Development
Coalition **Formation**
Concept **Formation**
Identity **Formation**
Impression **Formation**
Reaction **Formation**
Reticular **Formation**
Test **Forms**
Theory **Formulation**
Fornix
FORTRAN USE Computer Programming
  Languages
Chance **(Fortune)**

Forward Masking USE Masking
Foster Care
Foster Children
Foster Homes USE Foster Care
Foster Parents
Fovea
Foveal Vision
Fowl USE Birds
Foxes
Fragile X Syndrome
Fragmentation (Schizophrenia)
Frail USE Health Impairments
Rod and **Frame** Test
Frankness USE Honesty
Fraternal Twins USE Heterozygotic Twins
Fraternity Membership
Fraud
Consumer Fraud USE Fraud
Skinner (Burrhus **Frederic)**
Free Association
Free Recall
Free Will USE Volition
Freedom
Frequency Distribution
Flicker Fusion Frequency
  USE Critical Flicker Fusion Threshold
Pitch **(Frequency)**
Response **Frequency**
Spatial **Frequency**
Stimulus **Frequency**
Temporal **Frequency**
Word **Frequency**
Freud (Sigmund)
Freudian Psychoanalytic School
Friendship
Frigidity
Frogs
Frontal Lobe
Frostig Developmental Test of Visual
  Perception
Fruit Fly USE Drosophila
Frustration
Rosenzweig Picture **Frustration** Study
Fugue Reaction
Self **Fulfilling** Prophecies
Fulfillment USE Satisfaction
Sexual **Function** Disturbances
Urinary **Function** Disorders
Functional Analysis
Functional Knowledge
  USE Procedural Knowledge
Functional Status USE Ability Level
Functionalism
Cognitive Functioning USE Cognitive Ability
Executive Functioning USE Cognitive Ability
Intellectual Functioning USE Cognitive Ability
Level of Functioning USE Ability Level
Fundamental Interpersonal Relation
  Orientation Behavior Ques
Religious **Fundamentalism**
Funding
Funerals USE Death Rites
Furniture
Critical Flicker **Fusion** Threshold
Flicker Fusion Frequency
  USE Critical Flicker Fusion Threshold
Future
Fuzzy Logic
Fuzzy Set Theory
GABA Agonists
  USE Gamma Aminobutyric Acid
  Agonists
GABA Antagonists
  USE Gamma Aminobutyric Acid
  Antagonists
Galanin USE Peptides
Galantamine USE Galanthamine

Galanthamine
Galvanic Skin Response
Gamblers Anonymous
    USE Twelve Step Programs
Gambling
Compulsive Gambling *USE Pathological Gambling*
Pathological **Gambling**
Game Theory
Prisoners Dilemma **Game**
Games
Childrens Recreational **Games**
Computer **Games**
Entrapment **Games**
Non Zero Sum **Games**
Simulation **Games**
Video Games *USE Computer Games*
Gamma Aminobutyric Acid
Gamma Aminobutyric Acid Agonists
Gamma Aminobutyric Acid Antagonists
Gamma Globulin
Ganglia
Autonomic **Ganglia**
Basal **Ganglia**
Spinal **Ganglia**
Ganglion Blocking Drugs
Ganglion Cells (Retina)
Retinal Ganglion Cells
    USE Ganglion Cells (Retina)
Stellate Ganglion *USE Autonomic Ganglia*
Juvenile **Gangs**
Ganser Syndrome
    USE Factitious Disorders
Generation **Gap**
Gastrointestinal Disorders
Gastrointestinal System
Gastrointestinal Ulcers
Gastropods *USE Mollusca*
Gates MacGinitie Reading Tests
Gates Reading Readiness Tests
    USE Gates MacGinitie Reading Tests
Gates Reading Test
    USE Gates MacGinitie Reading Tests
Sensory **Gating**
Gaussian Distribution
    USE Normal Distribution
Gay Liberation Movement
    USE Homosexual Liberation Movement
Gay Males *USE Male Homosexuality*
Gay Parents *USE Homosexual Parents*
Gazing *USE Eye Fixation*
Geese
Gender Differences
    USE Human Sex Differences
Gender Identity
Gender Identity Disorder
Gender Role Attitudes
    USE Sex Role Attitudes
Gender Roles *USE Sex Roles*
Gene Expression
General Anesthetics
General Aptitude Test Battery
General Health Questionnaire
General Paresis
General Practitioners
Army **General** Classification Test
Medical Treatment **(General)**
Mental Disorders due to **General** Medical Conditions
Generalization (Learning)
Cognitive **Generalization**
Response **Generalization**
Semantic **Generalization**
Stimulus **Generalization**
Generalized Anxiety Disorder
Generation Effect (Learning)
Generation Gap
Transformational **Generative** Grammar
Generativity

Generators (Apparatus)
Genes
Genetic Counseling
Genetic Disorders
Genetic Dominance
Genetic Engineering
Genetic Linkage
Genetic Recessiveness
Genetic Screening *USE Genetic Testing*
Genetic Testing
Genetics
Behavioral **Genetics**
Population **Genetics**
Geniculate Bodies (Thalamus)
Genital Disorders
Genital Herpes *USE Herpes Genitalis*
Female Genital Mutilation *USE Circumcision*
Male **Genital** Disorders
Female **Genitalia**
Male **Genitalia**
Herpes **Genitalis**
Geniuses *USE Gifted*
Genocide
Genome
Human Genome *USE Genome*
Genotypes
Genuineness *USE Sincerity*
Geographic Regions *USE Geography*
Geographical Differences
    USE Regional Differences
Geographical Mobility
Geography
Physical Geography *USE Geography*
Geomagnetism *USE Magnetism*
Geometry
Gerbils
Geriatric Assessment
Geriatric Patients
Geriatric Psychiatry
Geriatric Psychotherapy
Geriatrics
German Measles *USE Rubella*
Gerontology
Gestalt Psychology
Gestalt Therapy
Bender **Gestalt** Test
Gestation *USE Pregnancy*
Gestures
Ghettoes
Urban Ghettoes *USE Ghettoes*
Gifted
Intellectually Gifted *USE Gifted*
Gilles de la Tourette Disorder
Gipsies *USE Gypsies*
Girls *USE Human Females*
Adrenal **Gland** Disorders
Adrenal **Gland** Secretion
Endocrine **Gland** Secretion
Endocrine **Gland** Surgery
Pituitary **Gland**
Pituitary Gland Surgery *USE Hypophysectomy*
Secretion **(Gland)**
Thyroid **Gland**
Glands
Adrenal **Glands**
Endocrine **Glands**
Mammary **Glands**
Parathyroid **Glands**
Salivary **Glands**
Glaucoma
Global Amnesia
Globalization
Gamma **Globulin**
Globulins
Globus Pallidus
Glossolalia

Glossopharyngeal Nerve
    USE Cranial Nerves
Glucagon
Glucocorticoids
Glucose
Glucose Metabolism
Blood Glucose *USE Blood Sugar*
Glue Sniffing
Glutamate *USE Glutamic Acid*
Glutamic Acid
Glutamine
Glutethimide
Glycine
Glycogen
Glycoproteins *USE Globulins*
Goal Setting
Goals
Career Goals *USE Occupational Aspirations*
Organizational Goals *USE Organizational Objectives*
Goats
God Concepts
Goiters
Goldfish
Gonadotropic Hormones
Gonadotropin
    USE Gonadotropic Hormones
Gonads
Gonorrhea
Goodenough Harris Draw A Person Test
Goodness of Fit
Gorillas
Gossip
Gough Adjective Check List
Government
Government Agencies
Government Bureaucracy
    USE Government
Government Personnel
Government Policy Making
Government Programs
Autonomy **(Government)**
Elected Government Officials
    USE Government Personnel
Law **(Government)**
Welfare Services **(Government)**
Grade Level
Academic Grade Level *USE Grade Level*
Gradepoint Average
    USE Academic Achievement
Grading (Educational)
Graduate Degrees
    USE Educational Degrees
Graduate Education
Graduate Psychology Education
Graduate Record Examination
Graduate Schools
Graduate Students
Clinical Psychology **Graduate** Training
College **Graduates**
High School **Graduates**
School **Graduation**
Grammar
Grammar Schools
    USE Elementary Schools
Transformational Generative **Grammar**
Grand Mal Epilepsy
Grandchildren
Grandiosity
Grandparents
Great Grandparents *USE Ancestors*
Graphical Displays
Graphology *USE Handwriting*
Grasping
Grasshoppers
Delay of **Gratification**
Myasthenia **Gravis**
Gravitational Effects

Periaqueductal **Gray**
Great Grandparents *USE Ancestors*
Gregariousness
Bannister Repertory **Grid**
Shuttle Box Grids *USE Shuttle Boxes*
Grief
Grimaces
Nocturnal Teeth **Grinding**
Teeth Grinding *USE Bruxism*
Animal **Grooming** Behavior
Gross Motor Skill Learning
Ground Transportation
Figure **Ground** Discrimination
Grounded Theory
Group Cohesion
Group Counseling
Group Decision Making
Group Development
Group Discussion
Group Dynamics
Group Health Plans
    USE Health Maintenance
        Organizations
Group Homes
Group Instruction
Group Participation
Group Performance
Group Problem Solving
Group Psychotherapy
Group Size
Group Structure
Group Testing
Group Therapy *USE Group Psychotherapy*
Encounter **Group** Therapy
Marathon **Group** Therapy
Minority Group Discrimination
    USE Race and Ethnic Discrimination
Ability **Grouping**
Between **Groups** Design
Blood **Groups**
Chinese Cultural **Groups**
Consciousness Raising **Groups**
Control Groups *USE Experiment Controls*
Developmental Age **Groups**
Diagnosis Related **Groups**
Ethnic Groups *USE Racial and Ethnic Groups*
Japanese Cultural **Groups**
Korean Cultural **Groups**
Minority **Groups**
Racial and Ethnic **Groups**
Reference **Groups**
Religious **Groups**
Social **Groups**
South Asian Cultural **Groups**
South East Asian Cultural Groups
    USE Southeast Asian Cultural Groups
Southeast Asian Cultural **Groups**
Support **Groups**
T Groups *USE Human Relations Training*
Vietnamese Cultural **Groups**
Groupware
Grown Children *USE Adult Offspring*
Growth *USE Development*
Growth Centers
    USE Human Potential Movement
Growth Hormone Inhibitor
    USE Somatostatin
Growth Hormone *USE Somatotropin*
Nerve **Growth** Factor
Personal Growth Techniques
    USE Human Potential Movement
Physical Growth *USE Physical Development*
Guanethidine
Guanosine
Coast **Guard** Personnel
Guardianship
National **Guardsmen**

Guessing
Guest Workers *USE Foreign Workers*
Guidance Counseling
 USE School Counseling
Career Guidance *USE Occupational Guidance*
Child **Guidance** Clinics
Educational Guidance *USE Educational Counseling*
Occupational **Guidance**
School Guidance *USE School Counseling*
Vocational Guidance *USE Occupational Guidance*
Guided Fantasy *USE Guided Imagery*
Guided Imagery
Treatment **Guidelines**
Guilford Zimmerman Temperament Survey
Guilt
Guinea Pigs
Gulls *USE Sea Gulls*
Sea **Gulls**
Gun Control Laws
Guns *USE Firearms*
Gustatory Perception
 USE Taste Perception
Gymnastic Therapy
 USE Recreation Therapy
Gynecological Disorders
Gynecologists
Gynecology
Gypsies
Gyrus Cinguli
Habilitation
Habitat Selection *USE Territoriality*
Habits
Eating Habits *USE Eating Behavior*
Study **Habits**
Habituation
Hair
Hair Loss *USE Alopecia*
Hair Pulling *USE Trichotillomania*
Halcion *USE Triazolam*
Halfway Houses
Residence Halls *USE Dormitories*
Hallucinations
Auditory **Hallucinations**
Drug Induced **Hallucinations**
Hypnagogic **Hallucinations**
Visual **Hallucinations**
Hallucinogenic Drugs
Hallucinosis
Alcoholic **Hallucinosis**
Halo Effect
Haloperidol
Halstead Reitan Neuropsychological
 Battery
Hamsters
Hand (Anatomy)
Handedness
Adventitiously Handicapped *USE Adventitious Disorders*
Aurally Handicapped *USE Hearing Disorders*
Congenitally Handicapped *USE Congenital Disorders*
Multiply Handicapped *USE Multiple Disabilities*
Orthopedically Handicapped *USE Physical Disorders*
Physically Handicapped *USE Physical Disorders*
Sensorially Handicapped
 USE Sensory System Disorders
Speech Handicapped *USE Speech Disorders*
Visually Handicapped *USE Vision Disorders*
Self **Handicapping** Strategy
Handicaps *USE Disabilities*
Handicrafts *USE Crafts*
Handwriting
Handwriting Legibility
Printing **(Handwriting)**
Happiness
Haptic Perception *USE Cutaneous Sense*
Harassment
Sexual **Harassment**
Hardiness *USE Resilience (Psychological)*

Harm Reduction
Maslow (Abraham **Harold)**
Goodenough **Harris** Draw A Person Test
Hashish
Hate
Hate Crimes
Hawaii Natives
Native Hawaiians *USE Hawaii Natives*
Hay Fever
Hazardous Materials
Hazards
Head (Anatomy)
Head Banging
Head Injuries
Head Start *USE Project Head Start*
Closed Head Injuries *USE Head Injuries*
Project **Head** Start
Headache
Migraine **Headache**
Muscle Contraction **Headache**
Tension Headache
 USE Muscle Contraction Headache
Faith **Healing**
Psychic Healing *USE Faith Healing*
Health
Health Attitudes
Health Behavior
Health Care Administration
Health Care Costs
Health Care Delivery
Health Care Policy
Health Care Professionals
 USE Health Personnel
Health Care Psychology
Health Care Seeking Behavior
Health Care Services
Health Care Utilization
Health Complaints
Health Education
Health Impairments
Health Insurance
Health Knowledge
Health Locus of Control
 USE Health Attitudes
Health Maintenance Organizations
Health Personnel
Health Personnel Attitudes
Health Promotion
Health Psychology
 USE Health Care Psychology
Health Screening
Health Service Needs
Health Service Utilization
 USE Health Care Utilization
Behavioral Health *USE Health Care Psychology*
Community Mental **Health**
Community Mental **Health** Centers
Community Mental **Health** Services
Community Mental **Health** Training
Employee **Health** Insurance
General **Health** Questionnaire
Group Health Plans *USE Health Maintenance*
 Organizations
Holistic **Health**
Home Health Aides *USE Home Care Personnel*
Mental **Health**
Mental Health Care Costs *USE Health Care Costs*
Mental Health Care Policy *USE Health Care Policy*
Mental Health Consultation
 USE Professional Consultation
Mental **Health** Inservice Training
Mental **Health** Personnel
Mental Health Personnel Supply
Mental Health Program Evaluation
Mental **Health** Programs
Mental Health Service Needs
 USE Health Service Needs

Mental **Health** Services
Primary Mental **Health** Prevention
Primary **Health** Care
Public **Health**
Public **Health** Service Nurses
Public **Health** Services
Web Based Mental Health Services *USE Online Therapy*
Wholistic Health *USE Holistic Health*
Hearing Acuity *USE Auditory Acuity*
Hearing Aids
Hearing Disorders
Hearing Measures
USE Speech and Hearing Measures
Partially **Hearing** Impaired
Sensorineural Hearing Loss *USE Hearing Disorders*
Speech and **Hearing** Measures
Heart
Heart Attacks *USE Heart Disorders*
Heart Auricles
Heart Beat *USE Heart Rate*
Heart Disorders
Heart Rate
Heart Rate Affecting Drugs
Heart Surgery
Heart Transplants
USE Organ Transplantation
Heart Valves
Heart Ventricles
Arrhythmias **(Heart)**
Coronary Heart Disease *USE Heart Disorders*
Fibrillation **(Heart)**
Rapid Heart Rate *USE Tachycardia*
Heartbeat *USE Heart Rate*
Heat Effects
Hebephrenic Schizophrenia
USE Schizophrenia (Disorganized Type)
Hedonism
Body **Height**
Helicopters
Helium
Help Seeking Behavior
Self **Help** Techniques
Helping Behavior
USE Assistance (Social Behavior)
Helplessness
Learned **Helplessness**
Hematologic Disorders
USE Blood and Lymphatic Disorders
Hematoma
Hemianopia
Hemiopia *USE Hemianopia*
Hemiplegia
Hemispherectomy
Hemispheric Specialization
USE Lateral Dominance
Hemodialysis
Hemoglobin
Hemophilia
Hemorrhage
Cerebral **Hemorrhage**
Henmon Nelson Tests of Mental Ability
USE Intelligence Measures
Heparin
Hepatic Disorders *USE Liver Disorders*
Hepatitis
Toxic **Hepatitis**
Medicinal **Herbs** and Plants
Hereditary Disorders
USE Genetic Disorders
Sex Linked **Hereditary** Disorders
Heredity *USE Genetics*
Hermaphroditism
Hermeneutics
Heroin
Heroin Addiction
Herpes Genitalis

Herpes Simplex
Genital Herpes *USE Herpes Genitalis*
Heterogeneity of Variance
USE Homogeneity of Variance
Heterosexism
USE Homosexuality (Attitudes Toward)
Heterosexual Interaction
USE Male Female Relations
Heterosexuality
Heterozygotic Twins
Heuristic Modeling
Heuristics
Hexamethonium
Hexobarbital
Hibernation
Dominance **Hierarchy**
High Risk Populations
USE At Risk Populations
High School Education
High School Equivalency
USE Adult Education
High School Graduates
High School Personality Questionnaire
High School Students
High School Teachers
High Schools
Junior **High** School Students
Junior **High** School Teachers
Junior **High** Schools
Higher Education
Higher Order Conditioning
Highway Safety
Hindbrain
Hinduism
Hindus
Hippies *USE Subculture (Anthropological)*
Hippocampal Commissure *USE Fornix*
Hippocampus
Hips
Hiring *USE Personnel Selection*
Hispanics
Histamine
Histidine
Histology
History
History of Psychology
Case History *USE Patient History*
Employment **History**
Medical History *USE Patient History*
Patient **History**
Psychiatric History *USE Patient History*
Histrionic Personality Disorder
HIV *USE Human Immunodeficiency Virus*
HIV Testing
HMO *USE Health Maintenance Organizations*
Hoarding Behavior
Animal **Hoarding** Behavior
Hobbies
Hoffmanns Reflex
Holidays
Holistic Health
Holocaust
Holocaust Survivors
Holtzman Inkblot Technique
Homatropine *USE Alkaloids*
Home Accidents
Home Birth *USE Midwifery*
Home Care
Home Care Personnel
Home Economics
Home Environment
Home Health Aides
USE Home Care Personnel
Home Reared Mentally Retarded
Home Schooling
Home Visiting Programs

Return to Home *USE Empty Nest*
Work at Home *USE Telecommuting*
Homebound
Homeless
Homeless Mentally Ill
Mentally Ill Homeless *USE Homeless Mentally Ill*
Homemakers
Homemaking *USE Household Management*
Homeopathic Medicine
  USE Alternative Medicine
Homeostasis
Foster Homes *USE Foster Care*
Group **Homes**
Nursing **Homes**
Homesickness
Homework
Homicide
Serial **Homicide**
Animal **Homing**
Homogeneity of Variance
Variance Homogeneity
  USE Homogeneity of Variance
Homographs
Homonyms
Homophobia
  USE Homosexuality (Attitudes Toward)
Homosexual Liberation Movement
Homosexual Parents
Homosexuallty
Homosexuality (Attitudes Toward)
Female Homosexuality *USE Lesbianism*
Male **Homosexuality**
Homovanillic Acid
Honesty
Hope
Hopelessness
Hormone Therapy
Follicle Stimulating **Hormone**
Growth Hormone *USE Somatotropin*
Growth Hormone Inhibitor *USE Somatostatin*
Luteinizing **Hormone**
Melanocyte Stimulating **Hormone**
Parathyroid **Hormone**
Thyroid Stimulating Hormone *USE Thyrotropin*
Thyrotropic Hormone *USE Thyrotropin*
Hormones
Adrenal Cortex **Hormones**
Adrenal Medulla **Hormones**
Gonadotropic **Hormones**
Pituitary **Hormones**
Progestational **Hormones**
Sex **Hormones**
Thyroid **Hormones**
Dorsal **Horns**
Horses
Hospice
Hospital Accreditation
Hospital Addiction Syndrome
  USE Munchausen Syndrome
Hospital Administration
Hospital Admission
Hospital Attendants
  USE Attendants (Institutions)
Hospital Discharge
Hospital Environment
Hospital Programs
Hospital Psychiatric Units
  USE Psychiatric Units
Hospital Staff *USE Medical Personnel*
Day Hospital *USE Partial Hospitalization*
Psychiatric **Hospital** Admission
Psychiatric **Hospital** Discharge
Psychiatric **Hospital** Programs
Psychiatric **Hospital** Readmission
Psychiatric **Hospital** Staff
Hospitalization
Partial **Hospitalization**

Psychiatric **Hospitalization**
Hospitalized Patients
Hospitals
Mental Hospitals *USE Psychiatric Hospitals*
Psychiatric **Hospitals**
State Hospitals *USE Psychiatric Hospitals*
Hostages
Hostility
Hot Line Services
Telephone Hot Lines *USE Hot Line Services*
Household Management
Household Structure
  USE Living Arrangements
Halfway **Houses**
Housewives *USE Homemakers*
Housework *USE Household Management*
Housing
Hue
Human Animal Interaction
  USE Interspecies Interaction
Human Biological Rhythms
Human Body
Human Capital
Human Channel Capacity
Human Computer Interaction
Human Computer Interface
  USE Human Computer Interaction
Human Courtship
Human Development
Human Factors Engineering
Human Females
Human Figures Drawing
Human Genome *USE Genome*
Human Immunodeficiency Virus
Human Information Processes
  USE Cognitive Processes
Human Information Storage
Human Machine Systems
Human Machine Systems Design
Human Males
Human Mate Selection
Human Migration
Human Nature
Human Potential Movement
Human Relations Training
Human Resource Management
Human Resources
  USE Human Resource Management
Human Rights
Human Sex Differences
Animal Human Interaction
  USE Interspecies Interaction
Sexual Intercourse **(Human)**
Humanism
Humanistic Education
  USE Affective Education
Humanistic Psychology
Humanistic Psychotherapy
Humanities
Surrogate Parents **(Humans)**
Humor
Cartoons **(Humor)**
Hunger
Huntingtons Chorea
  USE Huntingtons Disease
Huntingtons Disease
Shuttle Box Hurdles *USE Shuttle Boxes*
Husbands
Hybrids (Biology)
Hydralazine
Chloral **Hydrate**
Arecoline Hydrobromide *USE Arecoline*
Scopolamine Hydrobromide *USE Scopolamine*
Hydrocephaly
Apomorphine Hydrochloride *USE Apomorphine*
Hydrocortisone
Hydrogen

Hydroxydopamine (6-)
Hydroxyindoleacetic Acid (5-)
Hydroxylase Inhibitors
Hydroxylases
Hydroxytryptophan (5-)
Hydroxyzine
Hygiene
Hyoscine *USE Scopolamine*
Hyperactivity *USE Hyperkinesis*
Attention Deficit Disorder with **Hyperactivity**
Hyperalgesia
    USE Somatosensory Disorders
Hypercholesterolemia
    USE Metabolism Disorders
Hyperesthesia
    USE Somatosensory Disorders
Hyperglycemia
Hypericum Perforatum
Hyperkinesis
Hypermedia
Hyperparathyroidism
    USE Parathyroid Disorders
Hyperphagia
Hypersexuality
Hypersomnia
Hypertension
Essential **Hypertension**
Hypertext
Hyperthermia
Hyperthyroidism
Hyperventilation
Hypesthesia
    USE Somatosensory Disorders
Hypnagogic Hallucinations
Hypnoanalysis *USE Hypnotherapy*
Hypnosis
Self Hypnosis *USE Autohypnosis*
Hypnotherapists
Hypnotherapy
Hypnotic Drugs
Hypnotic Susceptibility
Age Regression **(Hypnotic)**
Hypnotists
Hypoactive Sexual Desire Disorder
    USE Inhibited Sexual Desire
Hypochondriasis
Hypogastric Plexus
    USE Autonomic Ganglia
Hypoglossal Nerve *USE Cranial Nerves*
Hypoglycemia
Hypogonadism
Hypokinesia *USE Bradykinesia*
Hypomania
Hyponatremia
Hypoparathyroidism
    USE Parathyroid Disorders
Hypothalamo **Hypophyseal** System
Hypophysectomy
Hypophysis Disorders
    USE Pituitary Disorders
Hypopituitarism
Hypotension
Hypothalamo Hypophyseal System
Hypothalamo Pituitary Adrenal System
Hypothalamus
Hypothalamus Lesions
Hypothermia
Hypothesis Testing
Cognitive **Hypothesis** Testing
Null **Hypothesis** Testing
Hypothyroidism
Hypoxia *USE Anoxia*
Hysterectomy
Hysteria
Conversion Hysteria *USE Conversion Disorder*
Mass **Hysteria**

Hysterical Blindness
    USE Hysterical Vision Disturbances
Hysterical Paralysis
Hysterical Personality
    USE Histrionic Personality Disorder
Hysterical Vision Disturbances
Iatrogenic Effects
    USE Side Effects (Treatment)
Ibotenic Acid
ICD *USE International Classification of*
    Diseases
Iconic Memory
Id
Ideal Self *USE Self Concept*
Idealism
Ideation
Suicidal **Ideation**
Identical Twins *USE Monozygotic Twins*
Identification (Defense Mechanism)
Projective **Identification**
Identity Crisis
Identity Formation
Dissociative **Identity** Disorder
Ego **Identity**
Ethnic **Identity**
Gender **Identity**
Gender **Identity** Disorder
Professional **Identity**
Social **Identity**
Amaurotic Familial Idiocy *USE Tay Sachs Disease*
Idiot Savants *USE Savants*
Ileum *USE Intestines*
Homeless Mentally **Ill**
Mentally Ill Homeless *USE Homeless Mentally Ill*
Mentally **Ill** Offenders
Terminally **Ill** Patients
Illegitimate Children
Illinois Test of Psycholinguistic Abilities
Illiteracy *USE Literacy*
Illness Behavior
Chronic Mental **Illness**
Chronic **Illness**
Course of Illness *USE Disease Course*
Mental **Illness** (Attitudes Toward)
Mental Illness *USE Mental Disorders*
Persistent Mental Illness *USE Chronic Mental Illness*
Physical **Illness** (Attitudes Toward)
Physical Illness *USE Physical Disorders*
Work Related **Illnesses**
Illumination
Illumination Therapy *USE Phototherapy*
Autokinetic **Illusion**
Mueller Lyer **Illusion**
Illusions (Perception)
Optical Illusions *USE Illusions (Perception)*
Body **Image**
Body **Image** Disturbances
Mirror **Image**
Retinal **Image**
Self Image *USE Self Concept*
Imagery
Conceptual **Imagery**
Eidetic **Imagery**
Guided **Imagery**
Spatial **Imagery**
Onomatopoeia and Images Test
    USE Projective Personality Measures
Imagination
Imaginativeness
    USE Openness to Experience
Magnetic Resonance **Imaging**
Imipramine
Imitation (Learning)
Emotional **Immaturity**
Immersion Programs
    USE Foreign Language Education
Immigrants *USE Immigration*

349

Immigration
Social Immobility *USE Social Mobility*
Tonic Immobility
Acquired Immune Deficiency Syndrome
Immunization
Human Immunodeficiency Virus
Immunogens *USE Antigens*
Immunoglobulins
Immunologic Disorders
Immunologic Factors
Immunology
Immunopathology *USE Immunology*
Immunoreactivity
Impaired Professionals
Partially Hearing Impaired
Cognitive Impairment
Olfactory Impairment *USE Anosmia*
Visual Impairment *USE Vision Disorders*
Health Impairments
Cochlear Implants
Implicit Learning
Implicit Memory
Implosive Therapy
Impotence
Impression Formation
Impression Management
Imprinting
Improvisation
Impulse Control Disorders
Impulsiveness
Inadequate Personality
Incarceration
Incentives
Educational Incentives
Monetary Incentives
Incest
Critical Incident Debriefing
USE Debriefing (Psychological)
Incidental Learning
Income (Economic)
Income Level
Lower Income Level
Middle Income Level
Upper Income Level
Rh Incompatibility
Rotter Incomplete Sentences Blank
Fecal Incontinence
Urinary Incontinence
Incubators (Apparatus)
Independence (Personality)
Independent Living Programs
Independent Living *USE Self Care Skills*
Independent Study
USE Individualized Instruction
Independent Variables
American Indians
Myers Briggs Type Indicator
Indifference *USE Apathy*
Indigenous Populations
Individual Counseling
USE Individual Psychotherapy
Individual Differences
Individual Problem Solving
USE Problem Solving
Individual Psychology
Individual Psychotherapy
Individual Testing
Individual Therapy
USE Individual Psychotherapy
Individualism *USE Individuality*
Individuality
Individualized Instruction
Separation Individuation
Induced Abortion
Drug Induced Congenital Disorders
Drug Induced Hallucinations
Sleep Inducing Drugs *USE Hypnotic Drugs*

Vomit Inducing Drugs *USE Emetic Drugs*
Inductive Deductive Reasoning
Industrial Accidents
Industrial and Organizational Psychology
Industrial Arts Education
USE Vocational Education
Industrial Foremen
Industrial Personnel
USE Business and Industrial Personnel
Industrial Psychologists
Industrial Psychology
*USE Industrial and Organizational
Psychology*
Industrial Safety *USE Occupational Safety*
Business and Industrial Personnel
Skilled Industrial Workers
Unskilled Industrial Workers
Industrialization
Industry *USE Business*
Educational Inequality *USE Equal Education*
Infant Development
Infant Vocalization
Bayley Scales of Infant Development
Sudden Infant Death
Infanticide
Infantile Neurosis *USE Childhood Neurosis*
Infantile Paralysis *USE Poliomyelitis*
Infantile Psychosis
USE Childhood Psychosis
Early Infantile Autism
Symbiotic Infantile Psychosis
Infantilism
Infants (Animal)
Multi Infarct Dementia
Myocardial Infarctions
Infections *USE Infectious Disorders*
Infectious Disorders
Inference
Inferior Colliculus
Emotional Inferiority
Infertility
Infirmaries *USE Hospitals*
Inflammation
Anti Inflammatory Drugs
Inflection
Self Inflicted Wounds
Driving Under the Influence
Parental Influence *USE Parent Child Relations*
Interpersonal Influences
Social Influences
Influenza
Informants
Information
Information Exchange *USE Communication*
Information Processing Speed
USE Cognitive Processing Speed
Information Seeking
Information Services
Information Specialists
Information Systems
Information Theory
Automated Information Coding
Automated Information Processing
Automated Information Retrieval
Automated Information Storage
Confidentiality of Information *USE Privileged Communication*
Human Information Processes
USE Cognitive Processes
Human Information Storage
Management Information Systems
USE Information Systems
Informed Consent
Ingestion
Ingratiation *USE Impression Management*
Ingroup Outgroup
Outgroup Ingroup *USE Ingroup Outgroup*
Inhalant Abuse

Inhibited Sexual Desire
Inhibition (Personality)
Conditioned Inhibition *USE Conditioned Suppression*
Latent **Inhibition**
Prepulse **Inhibition**
Proactive **Inhibition**
Reciprocal **Inhibition** Therapy
Response **Inhibition**
Retroactive **Inhibition**
Growth Hormone Inhibitor *USE Somatostatin*
Amine Oxidase **Inhibitors**
Cholinesterase **Inhibitors**
Decarboxylase **Inhibitors**
Enzyme **Inhibitors**
Hydroxylase **Inhibitors**
Monoamine Oxidase **Inhibitors**
Serotonin Reuptake **Inhibitors**
Initial Teaching Alphabet
Initiation Rites
Initiative
Injections
Intramuscular **Injections**
Intraperitoneal **Injections**
Intravenous **Injections**
Subcutaneous **Injections**
Injuries
Birth **Injuries**
Closed Head Injuries *USE Head Injuries*
Electrical **Injuries**
Head **Injuries**
Spinal Cord **Injuries**
Self Injurious Behavior
USE Self Destructive Behavior
Traumatic Brain **Injury**
Holtzman **Inkblot** Technique
Inlaws
Animal Innate Behavior *USE Instinctive Behavior*
Inner City *USE Urban Environments*
Inner Ear *USE Labyrinth (Anatomy)*
Inner Speech *USE Self Talk*
Kirton Adaption **Innovation** Inventory
Innovativeness *USE Creativity*
Inquisitiveness *USE Curiosity*
Criminally Insane *USE Mentally Ill Offenders*
Insanity *USE Mental Disorders*
Insanity Defense
DDT **(Insecticide)**
Insecticides
Insects
Emotional Insecurity *USE Emotional Security*
Artificial Insemination *USE Reproductive Technology*
Inservice Teacher Education
Inservice Training
Mental Health **Inservice** Training
Insight
Insight (Psychotherapeutic Process)
Insight Therapy
Diabetes **Insipidus**
Insomnia
Emotional **Instability**
Death **Instinct**
Survival Instinct *USE Self Preservation*
Instinctive Behavior
Animal Instinctive Behavior
USE Instinctive Behavior
Institution Visitation
Institutional Release
Institutional Schools
Institutionalization
Institutionalized Mentally Retarded
Attendants **(Institutions)**
Correctional **Institutions**
Residential Care **Institutions**
Instruction *USE Teaching*
Audiovisual **Instruction**
Braille **Instruction**
Classroom Instruction *USE Teaching*

Computer Assisted **Instruction**
Field Instruction *USE Curricular Field Experience*
Group **Instruction**
Individualized **Instruction**
Programmed **Instruction**
Self Instruction *USE Individualized Instruction*
Televised **Instruction**
Videotape **Instruction**
Instructional Media
Instructional Objectives
USE Educational Objectives
Self **Instructional** Training
Experimental **Instructions**
Instructors *USE Teachers*
Instrument Controls
Instrumental Conditioning
USE Operant Conditioning
Instrumental Learning
USE Operant Conditioning
Instrumentality
Flight **Instrumentation**
Musical **Instruments**
Insulin
Insulin Shock Therapy
Insurance
Insurance Agents *USE Sales Personnel*
Employee Health **Insurance**
Health **Insurance**
Life **Insurance**
Workers' Compensation **Insurance**
Workmen's Compensation Insurance
USE Workers' Compensation Insurance
Intake Interview
Fluid **Intake**
Food **Intake**
Water **Intake**
Integrated Services
Intersensory Integration *USE Sensory Integration*
Racial Integration *USE Social Integration*
School **Integration**
Sensory **Integration**
Social **Integration**
Integrative Psychotherapy
Integrity
Intellectual Development
Intellectual Functioning
USE Cognitive Ability
Intellectualism
Intellectualization
Intellectually Gifted *USE Gifted*
Intelligence
Intelligence Age *USE Mental Age*
Intelligence Measures
Intelligence Quotient
Artificial **Intelligence**
Cattell Culture Fair Intelligence Test
USE Culture Fair Intelligence Test
Culture Fair **Intelligence** Test
Emotional **Intelligence**
Leiter Adult Intelligence Scale
USE Intelligence Measures
Slosson **Intelligence** Test
Stanford Binet **Intelligence** Scale
Wechsler Adult **Intelligence** Scale
Wechsler Bellevue **Intelligence** Scale
Wechsler **Intelligence** Scale for Children
Intelligent Tutoring Systems
Signal Intensity *USE Stimulus Intensity*
Stimulus **Intensity**
Intensive Care
Intention
Intentional Learning
Interaction Analysis (Statistics)
Interaction Variance
Animal Human Interaction *USE Interspecies Interaction*
Client Counselor Interaction
USE Psychotherapeutic Processes

ROTATED ALPHABETICAL TERMS SECTION

Counselor Client Interaction
USE *Psychotherapeutic Processes*
Dentist Patient Interaction *USE Therapeutic Processes*
Double Bind **Interaction**
Employee Supervisor Interaction
USE *Supervisor Employee Interaction*
Employee **Interaction**
Heterosexual Interaction *USE Male Female Relations*
Human Animal Interaction *USE Interspecies Interaction*
Human Computer **Interaction**
Interhemispheric **Interaction**
Interpersonal **Interaction**
Interspecies **Interaction**
Manager Employee Interaction
USE *Supervisor Employee Interaction*
Nurse Patient Interaction *USE Therapeutic Processes*
Patient Therapist Interaction
USE *Psychotherapeutic Processes*
Physician Patient Interaction *USE Therapeutic Processes*
Social **Interaction**
Supervisor Employee **Interaction**
Teacher Student **Interaction**
Therapist Patient Interaction
USE *Psychotherapeutic Processes*
Symbolic **Interactionism**
Drug **Interactions**
Interagency Services
USE *Integrated Services*
Extramarital **Intercourse**
Premarital **Intercourse**
Sexual **Intercourse** (Human)
Intercultural Communication
USE *Cross Cultural Communication*
Interdisciplinary Research
Interdisciplinary Treatment Approach
Interest Inventories
Interest Patterns *USE Interests*
Kuder Occupational **Interest** Survey
Occupational **Interest** Measures
Opinion Attitude and Interest Survey *USE Attitude Measures*
Strong Vocational **Interest** Blank
Interests
Occupational **Interests**
Vocational Interests *USE Occupational Interests*
Interethnic Communication
USE *Cross Cultural Communication*
Interethnic Family
Interethnic Marriage
USE *Exogamous Marriage*
Human Computer Interface *USE Human Computer Interaction*
Interfaith Marriage
Interference (Learning)
Interferons
Intergenerational Relations
Intergenerational Transmission
USE *Transgenerational Patterns*
Intergroup Dynamics
Interhemispheric Interaction
Interhemispheric Transfer
USE *Interhemispheric Interaction*
Interior Design
Interleukins
Intermarriage *USE Exogamous Marriage*
Intermediate School Students
Intermittent Explosive Disorder
USE *Explosive Disorder*
Intermittent Reinforcement
USE *Reinforcement Schedules*
Internal Consistency *USE Test Reliability*
Internal External Locus of Control
Internal Rewards
Rotter **Internal** External Locus of Control Scale
Internalization
International Classification of Diseases
International Organizations
International Relations
Internet

Internet Counseling *USE Online Therapy*
Internists
Clinical Psychology **Internship**
Medical **Internship**
Teaching Internship *USE Student Teaching*
Interobserver Reliability
USE *Interrater Reliability*
Interocular Transfer
Interpersonal Attraction
Interpersonal Communication
Interpersonal Compatibility
Interpersonal Competence
USE *Social Skills*
Interpersonal Distance
USE *Personal Space*
Interpersonal Influences
Interpersonal Interaction
Interpersonal Perception
USE *Social Perception*
Interpersonal Psychotherapy
Interpersonal Relationship Satisfaction
USE *Relationship Satisfaction*
Interpersonal Relationships
Fundamental **Interpersonal** Relation Orientation
Behavior Ques
Listening **(Interpersonal)**
Dream Interpretation *USE Dream Analysis*
Psychoanalytic **Interpretation**
Psychological Interpretation
USE *Theoretical Interpretation*
Test **Interpretation**
Theoretical **Interpretation**
Interracial Adoption
Interracial Family
Interracial Marriage
Interracial Offspring
Interrater Reliability
Interresponse Time
Criminal Interrogation *USE Legal Interrogation*
Legal **Interrogation**
Police Interrogation *USE Legal Interrogation*
Intersensory Integration
USE *Sensory Integration*
Intersensory Processes
Intersexuality *USE Hermaphroditism*
Interspecies Interaction
Interstimulus Interval
Intertrial Interval
Interval Reinforcement
USE *Fixed Interval Reinforcement*
Interval Reinforcement
USE *Variable Interval Reinforcement*
Fixed **Interval** Reinforcement
Interstimulus **Interval**
Intertrial **Interval**
Variable **Interval** Reinforcement
Stimulus **Intervals**
Intervention
Crisis **Intervention**
Crisis **Intervention** Services
Early **Intervention**
Educational Intervention *USE School Based Intervention*
Family **Intervention**
School Based **Intervention**
Interview Schedules
Diagnostic **Interview** Schedule
Intake **Interview**
Psychodiagnostic **Interview**
Structured Clinical **Interview**
Interviewers
Interviewing
Interviews
Employment Interviews *USE Job Applicant Interviews*
Job Applicant **Interviews**
Intestines
Intimacy
Intoxication *USE Toxic Disorders*

Acute Alcoholic **Intoxication**
Alcohol **Intoxication**
Chronic Alcoholic **Intoxication**
Intra Aural Muscle Reflex
USE Acoustic Reflex
Intracranial Self Stimulation
USE Brain Self Stimulation
Intramuscular Injections
Intraperitoneal Injections
Intrauterine Devices
Intravenous Drug Usage
Intravenous Injections
Intrinsic Motivation
Intrinsic Rewards *USE Internal Rewards*
Introjection
Introspection
Introversion
Intuition
Inuit
Inventories
Biographical **Inventories**
Interest **Inventories**
Beck Depression **Inventory**
Bem Sex Role **Inventory**
California Psychological **Inventory**
Differential Personality Inventory *USE Nonprojective Personality Measures*
Edwards Personality **Inventory**
Eysenck Personality **Inventory**
Kirton Adaption Innovation **Inventory**
Millon Clinical Multiaxial **Inventory**
Minnesota Multiphasic Personality **Inventory**
Minnesota Teacher Attitude Inventory *USE Attitude Measures*
NEO Personality **Inventory**
Personal Orientation **Inventory**
Psychological Screening **Inventory**
State Trait Anxiety **Inventory**
Invertebrates
Investigation *USE Experimentation*
Maternal Investment *USE Parental Investment*
Parental **Investment**
Paternal Investment *USE Parental Investment*
Involuntary Treatment
Involutional Depression
Involutional Paranoid Psychosis
Involvement
Community **Involvement**
Job **Involvement**
Political Involvement *USE Political Participation*
Ions *USE Electrolytes*
Calcium **Ions**
Chloride **Ions**
Magnesium **Ions**
Potassium **Ions**
Sodium **Ions**
Iowa Tests of Basic Skills
Iproniazid
Deviation IQ *USE Standard Scores*
Iris (Eye)
Iron
Irradiation *USE Radiation*
Laser **Irradiation**
Irrational Beliefs
Irritability
Irritable Bowel Syndrome
Ischemia
Cerebral **Ischemia**
Islam
Pacific **Islanders**
Isocarboxazid
Isoenzymes *USE Isozymes*
Isolation (Defense Mechanism)
Isolation Effect
Social **Isolation**
Isoniazid
Isoproterenol
Isozymes

Political **Issues**
Social **Issues**
Itching *USE Pruritus*
Item Analysis (Statistical)
Item Analysis (Test)
Item Bias *USE Test Bias*
Item Content (Test)
Item Response Theory
Test **Items**
IV Drug Usage
USE Intravenous Drug Usage
Pavlov **(Ivan)**
Jails *USE Prisons*
Creutzfeldt **Jakob** Syndrome
James (William)
Japanese Americans
Japanese Cultural Groups
Jaundice
Jaw
Jealousy
Piaget **(Jean)**
Jews
Job Analysis
Job Applicant Attitudes
Job Applicant Interviews
Job Applicant Screening
Job Applicants
Job Change *USE Career Change*
Job Characteristics
Job Corps
Job Discrimination
USE Employment Discrimination
Job Enrichment
Job Experience Level
Job Family Relationship
USE Family Work Relationship
Job Involvement
Job Knowledge
Job Mobility *USE Occupational Mobility*
Job Performance
Job Promotion *USE Personnel Promotion*
Job Reentry *USE Reemployment*
Job Satisfaction
Job Search
Job Security
Job Selection *USE Occupational Choice*
Job Status *USE Occupational Status*
Job Stress *USE Occupational Stress*
Job Training *USE Personnel Training*
On the **Job** Training
Jobs *USE Occupations*
Saint John's Wort *USE Hypericum Perforatum*
St. John's Wort *USE Hypericum Perforatum*
Watson **(John** Broadus)
Woodcock **Johnson** Psychoeducational Battery
Joint Custody
Joint Disorders
Temporomandibular Joint Syndrome
USE Musculoskeletal Disorders
Joints (Anatomy)
Jokes
Journalists
Joy *USE Happiness*
Judaism
Judges
Judgment
Judgment Disturbances
Clinical **Judgment** (Not Diagnosis)
Probability **Judgment**
Judo
Jumping
Jung (Carl)
Jungian Psychology
Jungian Psychotherapy
USE Analytical Psychotherapy
Junior College Students
Junior Colleges *USE Colleges*

Junior High School Students	**Labor** Management Relations
Junior High School Teachers	Labor Relations
Junior High Schools	*USE Labor Management Relations*
Juries	**Labor** Union Members
Jury Selection	**Labor** Unions
Justice	Animal Division of **Labor**
Criminal **Justice**	Child **Labor**
Distributive **Justice**	Division of **Labor**
Juvenile **Justice**	Educational **Laboratories**
Procedural **Justice**	Experimental **Laboratories**
Juvenile Court *USE Adjudication*	Language **Laboratories**
Juvenile Delinquency	**Labyrinth** (Anatomy)
Juvenile Gangs	**Labyrinth** Disorders
Juvenile Justice	**Lactate** Dehydrogenase
Kainic Acid	Sodium Lactate *USE Lactic Acid*
Kangaroos	**Lactation**
Karate *USE Martial Arts*	**Lactic** Acid
Karyotype Disorders	Response Lag *USE Reaction Time*
USE Chromosome Disorders	**Language**
Kaufman Assessment Battery for Children	Language Alternation *USE Code Switching*
Ketamine	**Language** Arts Education
Keyboards	**Language** Delay
Keypunch Operators	**Language** Development
USE Clerical Personnel	**Language** Disorders
Kibbutz	**Language** Laboratories
Kidnapping	**Language** Proficiency
Kidney Diseases	Body **Language**
Kidney Transplants	English as Second **Language**
USE Organ Transplantation	Figurative **Language**
Kidneys	First Language *USE Native Language*
Natural **Killer** Cells	Foreign **Language** Education
Mercy Killing *USE Euthanasia*	Foreign **Language** Learning
Mouse Killing *USE Muricide*	Foreign **Language** Translation
Kinases	Form Classes **(Language)**
Kindergarten Students	Morphology **(Language)**
Vane Kindergarten Test	Native **Language**
USE Intelligence Measures	Second Language Education
Kindergartens	*USE Foreign Language Education*
Kindling	Sign **Language**
Kinesics *USE Body Language*	Written **Language**
Kinesthetic Perception	Computer Programming **Languages**
Kinship	Foreign **Languages**
Kinship Recognition	**Larvae**
Kinship Structure	**Laryngeal** Disorders
Kirton Adaption Innovation Inventory	**Larynx**
Kleine Levin Syndrome	**Laser** Irradiation
Kleptomania	Latchkey Children *USE Child Self Care*
Klinefelters Syndrome	Response **Latency**
Knee	Lateness *USE Tardiness*
Knowledge Based Systems	**Latent** Inhibition
USE Expert Systems	**Latent** Learning
Knowledge Engineering	Latent Trait Theory
Knowledge Level	*USE Item Response Theory*
Knowledge of Results	**Lateral** Dominance
Declarative **Knowledge**	Latinos/Latinas *USE Hispanics*
Factual Knowledge *USE Declarative Knowledge*	**Laughter**
Functional Knowledge *USE Procedural Knowledge*	**Law** (Government)
Health **Knowledge**	**Law** Enforcement
Job **Knowledge**	**Law** Enforcement Personnel
Practical Knowledge *USE Procedural Knowledge*	**Law** Students
Procedural **Knowledge**	Civil **Law**
Kohlberg (Lawrence)	Criminal **Law**
Kohs Block Design Test	Kohlberg **(Lawrence)**
Kolmogorov Smirnov Test	**Laws**
Korean Cultural Groups	Abortion **Laws**
Koro	Disability **Laws**
Korsakoffs Psychosis	Drug **Laws**
Kuder Occupational Interest Survey	Gun Control **Laws**
Kuder Preference Record	Marijuana **Laws**
Kupfer Detre Self Rating Scale	Lawsuits *USE Litigation*
USE Nonprojective Personality	Lawyers *USE Attorneys*
Measures	**Lay** Religious Personnel
Kwashiorkor	**Lead** (Metal)
L Dopa *USE Levodopa*	**Lead** Poisoning
Labeling	**Leadership**
Warning **Labels**	**Leadership** Qualities
Labor (Childbirth)	**Leadership** Style

Charismatic Leadership
  USE Transformational Leadership
Transformational **Leadership**
  Learned Helplessness
Slow Learners
  USE Borderline Mental Retardation
  Learning
  Learning Ability
  Learning Centers (Educational)
  Learning Disabilities
  Learning Disorders
  Learning Environment
Learning Organizations
  USE Organizational Learning
  Learning Rate
  Learning Schedules
  Learning Strategies
Learning Style *USE Cognitive Style*
  Learning Theory
Adult **Learning**
Animal **Learning**
Cat **Learning**
Concept Learning *USE Concept Formation*
Cooperative **Learning**
Discrimination **Learning**
Discriminative Learning *USE Discrimination Learning*
Distance Learning *USE Distance Education*
Experiential **Learning**
Extinction **(Learning)**
Extradimensional Shift Learning *USE Nonreversal Shift Learning*
Fine Motor Skill **Learning**
Foreign Language **Learning**
Generalization **(Learning)**
Generation Effect **(Learning)**
Gross Motor Skill **Learning**
Imitation **(Learning)**
Implicit **Learning**
Incidental **Learning**
Instrumental Learning *USE Operant Conditioning*
Intentional **Learning**
Interference **(Learning)**
Latent **Learning**
Machine **Learning**
Mastery **Learning**
Maze **Learning**
Mnemonic **Learning**
Motor Skill Learning *USE Perceptual Motor Learning*
Nonreversal Shift **Learning**
Nonsense Syllable **Learning**
Nonverbal **Learning**
Observational **Learning**
Organizational **Learning**
Paired Associate **Learning**
Perceptual Motor **Learning**
Probability **Learning**
Rat **Learning**
Recall **(Learning)**
Recognition **(Learning)**
Reconstruction **(Learning)**
Reversal Shift **Learning**
Rote **Learning**
Rule Learning *USE Cognitive Hypothesis Testing*
School **Learning**
Self Directed Learning *USE Individualized Instruction*
Self Regulated **Learning**
Sequential **Learning**
Serial Anticipation **(Learning)**
Serial **Learning**
Skill **Learning**
Social **Learning**
Spatial **Learning**
Spontaneous Recovery **(Learning)**
State Dependent **Learning**
Transfer **(Learning)**
Trial and Error **Learning**
Verbal **Learning**
  Least Preferred Coworker Scale

  Least Squares
Annual Leave *USE Employee Leave Benefits*
Employee **Leave** Benefits
Sick Leave *USE Employee Leave Benefits*
School **Leavers**
  Lecithin
  Lecture Method
  Left Brain
  Leg (Anatomy)
  Legal Arrest
  Legal Confession
  Legal Decisions
  Legal Detention
  Legal Evidence
  Legal Interrogation
  Legal Personnel
  Legal Processes
Legal Psychology
  USE Forensic Psychology
  Legal Testimony
Drug **Legalization**
Marijuana **Legalization**
  Legibility
Handwriting **Legibility**
  Legislative Processes
  Leisure Time
Leiter Adult Intelligence Scale
  USE Intelligence Measures
  Lemniscal System
  Lemurs
Length of Stay *USE Treatment Duration*
Work Week **Length**
  Lens (Eye)
Contact **Lenses**
Corrective Lenses *USE Optical Aids*
  Leptin
Lesbian Parents *USE Homosexual Parents*
  Lesbianism
  Lesions
Brain **Lesions**
Cerebral Lesions *USE Brain Lesions*
Hypothalamus **Lesions**
Neural **Lesions**
Subcortical Lesions *USE Brain Lesions*
  Lesson Plans
  Letters (Alphabet)
  Leucine
  Leucocytes
  Leukemias
Leukocytes *USE Leucocytes*
Leukotomy *USE Psychosurgery*
Vygotsky **(Lev)**
Level of Functioning *USE Ability Level*
Ability **Level**
Academic Grade Level *USE Grade Level*
Activity **Level**
Aspiration **Level**
Difficulty **Level** (Test)
Educational Attainment **Level**
Experience **Level**
Family Socioeconomic **Level**
Grade **Level**
Income **Level**
Job Experience **Level**
Knowledge **Level**
Lower Income **Level**
Middle Income **Level**
Middle **Level** Managers
Sound Pressure Level *USE Loudness*
Top **Level** Managers
Upper Income **Level**
Noise **Levels** (Work Areas)
Kleine **Levin** Syndrome
  Levodopa
Lewy Body Disease
  USE Dementia with Lewy Bodies
Dementia with **Lewy** Bodies

Lexical Access
Lexical Decision
Drug Abuse **Liability**
Professional **Liability**
Consultation **Liaison** Psychiatry
Liberalism
Political **Liberalism**
Gay Liberation Movement
    USE Homosexual Liberation Movement
Homosexual **Liberation** Movement
Womens **Liberation** Movement
Libido
Librarians
Libraries
School **Libraries**
Librium *USE Chlordiazepoxide*
Professional **Licensing**
Licensure Examinations
    USE Professional Examinations
Licking
Animal Licking Behavior *USE Licking*
Lidocaine
Life Changes
Life Course *USE Life Span*
Life Expectancy
Life Experiences
Life Insurance
Life Review
Life Satisfaction
Life Span
Life Sustaining Treatment
Life Transitions *USE Life Changes*
Family Life *USE Family Relations*
Family **Life** Education
Philosophy of Life *USE World View*
Quality of Work **Life**
Quality of **Life**
Lifesaving *USE Artificial Respiration*
Lifestyle
Lifestyle Changes
Tubal **Ligation**
Light *USE Illumination*
Light Adaptation
Light Refraction
Light Therapy *USE Phototherapy*
Bright Light Therapy *USE Phototherapy*
Likability
Maximum **Likelihood**
Likert Scales
Liking *USE Affection*
Limbic System
Artificial Limbs *USE Prostheses*
Phantom **Limbs**
Limen *USE Thresholds*
Differential Limen *USE Thresholds*
Limited English Proficiency
    USE Language Proficiency
Time Limited Psychotherapy
    USE Brief Psychotherapy
Confidence **Limits** (Statistics)
Allport Vernon Lindzey Study Values
    USE Attitude Measures
Hot **Line** Services
Linear Perspective
Linear Regression
Telephone Hot Lines *USE Hot Line Services*
Linguistics
Linkage Analysis *USE Genetic Linkage*
Genetic **Linkage**
Sex **Linked** Developmental Differences
Sex **Linked** Hereditary Disorders
Lions *USE Felids*
Lipid Metabolism
Lipid Metabolism Disorders
Lipids
Lipoproteins
Lipreading

Lips (Face)
Liquor
Gough Adjective Check **List**
Mooney Problem Check **List**
Listening (Interpersonal)
Listening *USE Auditory Perception*
Listening Comprehension
Literacy
Literacy Programs
Computer **Literacy**
Literature
Literature Review
Religious **Literature**
Lithium
Lithium Bromide *USE Bromides*
Lithium Carbonate
Litigation
Litter Size
Liver
Liver Disorders
Cirrhosis **(Liver)**
Living Alone
Living Arrangements
Living Wills *USE Advance Directives*
Activities of Daily **Living**
Assisted **Living**
Independent Living *USE Self Care Skills*
Independent **Living** Programs
Lizards
Cognitive Load *USE Human Channel Capacity*
Mental Load *USE Human Channel Capacity*
Work **Load**
Social **Loafing**
Frontal **Lobe**
Occipital **Lobe**
Optic **Lobe**
Parietal **Lobe**
Temporal **Lobe**
Lobectomy *USE Psychosurgery*
Lobotomy *USE Psychosurgery*
Local Anesthetics
Auditory **Localization**
Perceptual **Localization**
Sound Localization *USE Auditory Localization*
Quantitative Trait **Loci**
Animal **Locomotion**
Locus Ceruleus
Locus of Control
    USE Internal External Locus of Control
Health Locus of Control *USE Health Attitudes*
Internal External **Locus** of Control
Rotter Internal External **Locus** of Control Scale
Logic (Philosophy)
Fuzzy **Logic**
Logical Thinking
Logistic Models
    USE Item Response Theory
Logistic Regression
Logotherapy
Loneliness
Long Term Care
Long Term Memory
Long Term Potentiation
    USE Postactivation Potentials
Longevity *USE Life Expectancy*
Longitudinal Studies
Loosening of Associations
    USE Fragmentation (Schizophrenia)
Lorazepam
Hair Loss *USE Alopecia*
Sensorineural Hearing Loss *USE Hearing Disorders*
Loudness
Loudness Discrimination
Loudness Perception
Love
Low Birth Weight *USE Birth Weight*
Lower Class

Lower Class Attitudes
Lower Income Level
Loxapine
Loyalty
Lucid Dreaming
Luck *USE Chance (Fortune)*
Lumbar Spinal Cord
Lumbrosacral Plexus *USE Spinal Nerves*
Luminance
Luminance Threshold
    USE Brightness Perception
Luminance Threshold
    USE Visual Thresholds
Lunar Synodic Cycle
Lung
Lung Disorders
Lupus
Luria Nebraska Neuropsychological Battery
Luteinizing Hormone
Lutherans *USE Protestants*
Mueller **Lyer** Illusion
Lying *USE Deception*
Lymphatic Disorders
    USE Blood and Lymphatic Disorders
Blood and **Lymphatic** Disorders
Lymphocytes
Lysergic Acid Diethylamide
Gates **MacGinitie** Reading Tests
Machiavellianism
Machine Learning
Human **Machine** Systems
Human **Machine** Systems Design
Man Machine Systems Design
    USE Human Machine Systems Design
Man Machine Systems
    USE Human Machine Systems
Teaching **Machines**
Magazines
Magical Thinking
Magnesium
Magnesium Ions
Magnet Schools
    USE Nontraditional Education
Magnetic Resonance Imaging
Repetitive Transcranial Magnetic Stimulation
    USE Transcranial Magnetic Stimulation
Transcranial **Magnetic** Stimulation
Magnetism
Magnetoencephalography
Magnitude Estimation
Nucleus Basalis **Magnocellularis**
Maids *USE Domestic Service Personnel*
Mail Surveys
Electronic Mail *USE Computer Mediated*
    Communication
Mainstreaming
Mainstreaming (Educational)
Maintenance Therapy
Health **Maintenance** Organizations
Methadone **Maintenance**
Major Depression
Major Tranquilizers *USE Neuroleptic Drugs*
College Major *USE Academic Specialization*
Decision **Making**
Foreign Policy **Making**
Government Policy **Making**
Group Decision **Making**
Management Decision **Making**
Organizational Policy Making *USE Policy Making*
Policy **Making**
Grand **Mal** Epilepsy
Petit **Mal** Epilepsy
Emotional Maladjustment *USE Emotional Adjustment*
Social Maladjustment *USE Social Adjustment*
Malaria
Male Animals
Male Castration

Male Criminals
Male Delinquency
Male Female Relations
Male Genital Disorders
Male Genitalia
Male Homosexuality
Male Only Environments
    USE Single Sex Environments
Male Orgasm
Gay Males *USE Male Homosexuality*
Human **Males**
Malignant Neoplasms *USE Neoplasms*
Neuroleptic **Malignant** Syndrome
Malingering
Malnutrition *USE Nutritional Deficiencies*
Malpractice *USE Professional Liability*
Child Maltreatment *USE Child Abuse*
Mammals
Mammary Glands
Mammary Neoplasms
    USE Breast Neoplasms
Mammography
Man Machine Systems Design
    USE Human Machine Systems Design
Man Machine Systems
    USE Human Machine Systems
Draw A Man Test *USE Human Figures Drawing*
Managed Care
Management
Management Decision Making
Management Development
    USE Career Development
Management Information Systems
    USE Information Systems
Management Methods
Management Personnel
Management Planning
Management Training
Anger Management *USE Anger Control*
Anxiety **Management**
Business **Management**
Case **Management**
Classroom **Management**
Contingency **Management**
Disability **Management**
Household **Management**
Human Resource **Management**
Impression **Management**
Labor **Management** Relations
Pain **Management**
Participative **Management**
Personnel Management
    USE Human Resource Management
Risk **Management**
Self **Management**
Stress **Management**
Time **Management**
Manager Employee Interaction
    USE Supervisor Employee Interaction
Middle Level **Managers**
Top Level **Managers**
Self **Managing** Work Teams
Mandibula *USE Jaw*
Mania
Manic Depression *USE Bipolar Disorder*
Manic Depressive Psychosis
    USE Bipolar Disorder
Childrens **Manifest** Anxiety Scale
Taylor **Manifest** Anxiety Scale
Mann Whitney U Test
Mannerisms *USE Habits*
Manpower *USE Personnel Supply*
Mantis
Praying Mantis *USE Mantis*
Manual Communication
Diagnostic and Statistical **Manual**
Manufacturing *USE Business*

Maori *USE Indigenous Populations*
Brain Mapping *USE Stereotaxic Atlas*
Maprotiline
Brain Maps *USE Stereotaxic Atlas*
Cognitive **Maps**
Tactual Maps *USE Mobility Aids*
Marathon Group Therapy
Marihuana *USE Marijuana*
Marijuana
Marijuana Laws
Marijuana Legalization
Marijuana Usage
Marine Personnel
Marital Adjustment *USE Marital Relations*
Marital Conflict
Marital Fidelity *USE Monogamy*
Marital Relations
Marital Satisfaction
Marital Separation
Marital Status
Marital Therapy *USE Marriage Counseling*
Biochemical Markers *USE Biological Markers*
Biological **Markers**
Clinical Markers *USE Biological Markers*
Marketing
Animal Scent **Marking**
Markov Chains
Marlowe Crowne Social Desirability Scale
Marriage
Marriage and Family Education
USE Family Life Education
Marriage Attitudes
Marriage Counseling
Marriage Rites
Marriage Therapy
USE Marriage Counseling
Consanguineous **Marriage**
Endogamous **Marriage**
Exogamous **Marriage**
Interethnic Marriage *USE Exogamous Marriage*
Interfaith **Marriage**
Interracial **Marriage**
Miscegenous Marriage *USE Interracial Marriage*
Married Couples *USE Spouses*
Never **Married**
Bone **Marrow**
Marsupials
Martial Arts
Marxism *USE Communism*
Masculinity
Masking
Auditory **Masking**
Backward Masking *USE Masking*
Forward Masking *USE Masking*
Visual **Masking**
Maslow (Abraham Harold)
Masochism
Sexual **Masochism**
Masochistic Personality
Mass Culture *USE Popular Culture*
Mass Hysteria
Mass Media
Massage
Massed Practice
Mastectomy
Mastery Learning
Mastery Tests
USE Criterion Referenced Tests
Masticatory Muscles
Masturbation
Matching Test *USE Matching to Sample*
Matching to Sample
Client Treatment **Matching**
Patient Treatment Matching *USE Client Treatment Matching*
Treatment Client Matching *USE Client Treatment Matching*
Mate Selection *USE Animal Mate Selection*

Mate Selection
USE Human Mate Selection
Mate Swapping
USE Extramarital Intercourse
Animal **Mate** Selection
Human **Mate** Selection
Materialism
Hazardous **Materials**
Reading **Materials**
X Rated Materials *USE Pornography*
Maternal Investment
USE Parental Investment
Animal **Maternal** Behavior
Animal **Maternal** Deprivation
Mathematical Ability
Mathematical Modeling
Mathematical Psychology
Mathematicians
Mathematics
Mathematics (Concepts)
Mathematics Achievement
Mathematics Anxiety
Mathematics Education
Animal **Mating** Behavior
Assortative **Mating**
Assortive Mating *USE Assortative Mating*
Matriarchy
Raven Coloured Progressive **Matrices**
Raven Progressive **Matrices**
Matriculation *USE School Enrollment*
Maturation *USE Human Development*
Career Maturity *USE Vocational Maturity*
Columbia Mental **Maturity** Scale
Emotional **Maturity**
Physical **Maturity**
Vineland Social **Maturity** Scale
Vocational **Maturity**
Maxilla *USE Jaw*
Maximum Likelihood
Maximum Security Facilities
Maze Learning
Maze Pathways
Porteus **Maze** Test
Mazes
T **Mazes**
MCPP *USE Piperazines*
MDMA
USE Methylenedioxymethamphetamine
Mealtimes
Mean
Meaning
Nonverbal **Meaning**
Verbal **Meaning**
Word **Meaning**
Meaningfulness
Measles
German Measles *USE Rubella*
Measurement
Measurement Error
USE Error of Measurement
Attitude **Measurement**
Conjoint **Measurement**
Consistency **(Measurement)**
Creativity **Measurement**
Educational **Measurement**
Error of **Measurement**
Pain **Measurement**
Predictability **(Measurement)**
Profiles **(Measurement)**
Psychophysical **Measurement**
Standard Error of Measurement *USE Error of Measurement*
Statistical **Measurement**
Variability **Measurement**
Achievement **Measures**
Aptitude **Measures**
Attitude **Measures**
Central Tendency **Measures**

ROTATED ALPHABETICAL TERMS SECTION

Developmental **Measures**
Hearing Measures
  USE Speech and Hearing Measures
Intelligence **Measures**
Nonprojective Personality **Measures**
Occupational Interest **Measures**
Perceptual Motor Measures *USE Sensorimotor Measures*
Perceptual **Measures**
Personality **Measures**
Preference **Measures**
Projective Personality **Measures**
Reading **Measures**
Repeated **Measures**
Retention **Measures**
Sensorimotor **Measures**
Speech and Hearing **Measures**
Speech Measures
  USE Speech and Hearing Measures
Mecamylamine
Mechanical Aptitude
Speech Processing **(Mechanical)**
Compensation (Defense **Mechanism)**
Displacement (Defense **Mechanism)**
Fantasy (Defense **Mechanism)**
Identification (Defense **Mechanism)**
Isolation (Defense **Mechanism)**
Projection (Defense **Mechanism)**
Regression (Defense **Mechanism)**
Repression (Defense **Mechanism)**
Suppression (Defense **Mechanism)**
Withdrawal (Defense **Mechanism)**
Defense **Mechanisms**
Mechanoreceptors
Audiovisual Communications **Media**
Communications **Media**
Instructional **Media**
Mass **Media**
News **Media**
Printed Communications **Media**
Telecommunications **Media**
Medial Forebrain Bundle
Median
Median Nerve *USE Spinal Nerves*
Mediated Responses
Computer **Mediated** Communication
Mediation
Cognitive **Mediation**
Medicaid
Medical Care Costs
  USE Health Care Costs
Medical Diagnosis
Medical Education
Medical Ethics *USE Bioethics*
Medical History *USE Patient History*
Medical Internship
Medical Model
Medical Patients
Medical Personnel
Medical Personnel Supply
Medical Psychology
Medical Records
Medical Regimen Compliance
  USE Treatment Compliance
Medical Residency
Medical Sciences
Medical Students
Medical Therapeutic Devices
Medical Treatment (General)
Mental Disorders due to General **Medical** Conditions
Military **Medical** Personnel
Self Examination **(Medical)**
Medicare
Medication *USE Drug Therapy*
Self **Medication**
Medicinal Herbs and Plants
Alternative **Medicine**
Behavioral Medicine *USE Health Care Psychology*

Complementary Medicine *USE Alternative Medicine*
Evidence Based Medicine *USE Evidence Based Practice*
Family **Medicine**
Folk **Medicine**
Homeopathic Medicine *USE Alternative Medicine*
Osteopathic **Medicine**
Preventive **Medicine**
Psychosomatic **Medicine**
Veterinary **Medicine**
Medics *USE Paramedical Personnel*
Meditation
Medulla Oblongata
Adrenal **Medulla** Hormones
Melancholia *USE Major Depression*
Melancholy *USE Sadness*
Melanin
Melanocyte Stimulating Hormone
Melanotropin
  USE Melanocyte Stimulating Hormone
Melatonin
Mellaril *USE Thioridazine*
Diabetes **Mellitus**
Family **Members**
Labor Union **Members**
Fraternity **Membership**
School Club **Membership**
Sorority **Membership**
Nictitating **Membrane**
Tympanic Membrane *USE Middle Ear*
Membranes
Childhood Memories *USE Early Memories*
Early **Memories**
Memory
Memory Decay
Memory Disorders
Memory Enhancing Drugs
  USE Nootropic Drugs
Memory for Designs Test
Memory Trace
Memory Training
Autobiographical **Memory**
Episodic **Memory**
Explicit **Memory**
False **Memory**
Iconic **Memory**
Implicit **Memory**
Long Term **Memory**
Photographic Memory *USE Eidetic Imagery*
Repressed **Memory**
Semantic **Memory**
Short Term **Memory**
Spatial **Memory**
Verbal **Memory**
Visual Spatial Memory *USE Visuospatial Memory*
Visual **Memory**
Visuospatial **Memory**
Wechsler **Memory** Scale
Working Memory *USE Short Term Memory*
Men *USE Human Males*
Menarche
Menieres Disease
Meninges
Meningitis
Bacterial **Meningitis**
Meningomyelocele *USE Spina Bifida*
Menopause
Menstrual Cycle
Menstrual Disorders
Menstruation
Mental Age
Mental Confusion
Mental Deficiency *USE Mental Retardation*
Mental Disorders
Mental Disorders due to General Medical Conditions
Mental Health

359

Mental Health Care Costs
    USE Health Care Costs
Mental Health Care Policy
    USE Health Care Policy
Mental Health Consultation
    USE Professional Consultation
Mental Health Inservice Training
Mental Health Personnel
Mental Health Personnel Supply
Mental Health Program Evaluation
Mental Health Programs
Mental Health Service Needs
    USE Health Service Needs
Mental Health Services
Mental Hospitals *USE Psychiatric Hospitals*
Mental Illness (Attitudes Toward)
Mental Illness *USE Mental Disorders*
Mental Load
    USE Human Channel Capacity
Mental Models
Mental Retardation
Mental Retardation (Attitudes Toward)
Mental Rotation
Borderline **Mental** Retardation
Chronic **Mental** Illness
Columbia **Mental** Maturity Scale
Community **Mental** Health
Community **Mental** Health Centers
Community **Mental** Health Services
Community **Mental** Health Training
Cultural Familial Mental Retardation
    USE Psychosocial Mental Retardation
Henmon Nelson Tests of Mental Ability *USE Intelligence Measures*
Mild **Mental** Retardation
Mini **Mental** State Examination
Moderate **Mental** Retardation
Persistent Mental Illness *USE Chronic Mental Illness*
Primary **Mental** Health Prevention
Profound **Mental** Retardation
Psychosocial **Mental** Retardation
Severe **Mental** Retardation
Web Based Mental Health Services
    USE Online Therapy
Mentally Ill Homeless
    USE Homeless Mentally Ill
Mentally Ill Offenders
Educable Mentally Retarded
    USE Mild Mental Retardation
Home Reared **Mentally** Retarded
Homeless **Mentally** Ill
Institutionalized **Mentally** Retarded
Trainable Mentally Retarded
    USE Moderate Mental Retardation
Mentor
Meperidine
Mephenesin *USE Muscle Relaxing Drugs*
Meprobamate
Mercury (Metal)
Mercury Poisoning
Mercy Killing *USE Euthanasia*
Organizational **Merger**
Mescaline
Mesencephalon
Mesoridazine
Messages
Meta Analysis
Metabolic Rates
Metabolism
Metabolism Disorders
Basal **Metabolism**
Brain Metabolism *USE Neurochemistry*
Carbohydrate **Metabolism**
Fat Metabolism *USE Lipid Metabolism*
Glucose **Metabolism**
Lipid **Metabolism**
Lipid **Metabolism** Disorders
Protein **Metabolism**

Metabolites
Dopamine **Metabolites**
Norepinephrine **Metabolites**
Serotonin **Metabolites**
Metacognition
Lead **(Metal)**
Mercury **(Metal)**
Metalinguistics
Metallic Elements
Metals
Metamemory *USE Metacognition*
Metaphor
Metaphysics
Metapsychology
Volt Meters *USE Apparatus*
Methadone
Methadone Maintenance
Methamphetamine
Methanol
Methaqualone
Methedrine *USE Methamphetamine*
Methionine
Directed Discussion **Method**
Discovery Teaching **Method**
Forced Choice (Testing **Method)**
Lecture **Method**
Montessori **Method**
Multiple Choice (Testing **Method)**
Nondirected Discussion **Method**
Open Classroom **Method**
Rhythm **Method**
Team Teaching **Method**
Methodists *USE Protestants*
Methodology
Clinical **Methods** Training
Drug Administration **Methods**
Empirical **Methods**
Experimental **Methods**
Management **Methods**
Observation **Methods**
Physical Treatment **Methods**
Psychotherapeutic Methods
    USE Psychotherapeutic Techniques
Qualitative Methods *USE Qualitative Research*
Quantitative **Methods**
Quasi Experimental **Methods**
Research Methods *USE Methodology*
Scientific Methods *USE Experimental Methods*
Stimulus Presentation **Methods**
Teaching **Methods**
Testing **Methods**
Methohexital
Methoxamine
Methoxyhydroxyphenylglycol (3,4)
Methyl Alcohol *USE Methanol*
Methylatropine *USE Atropine*
Methyldiphenylhydramine
    USE Orphenadrine
Methyldopa
Methylenedioxymethamphetamine
Methylmorphine *USE Codeine*
Alpha **Methylparatyrosine**
Methylphenidate
Methylphenyltetrahydropyridine
Alpha Methyltyrosine
    USE Alpha Methylparatyrosine
Methysergide *USE Serotonin Antagonists*
Metrazole *USE Pentylenetetrazol*
Metronomes
Metropolitan Readiness Tests
Mexican Americans
MHPG
    USE Methoxyhydroxyphenylglycol (3,4)
Mianserin
Mice
Microcephaly
Microcomputers

Microcounseling
Microorganisms
Microscopes
Micturition *USE Urination*
Midazolam
Midbrain *USE Mesencephalon*
Middle Class
Middle Class Attitudes
Middle Ear
Middle Income Level
Middle Level Managers
Middle School Education
Middle School Students
Middle School Teachers
Middle Schools
Midwifery
Migraine Headache
Migrant Farm Workers
Human **Migration**
Migratory Behavior (Animal)
Mild Mental Retardation
Milieu Therapy
Militancy
Military Enlistment
Military Medical Personnel
Military Officers
    USE Commissioned Officers
Military Personnel
Military Psychologists
Military Psychology
Military Recruitment
Military Schools
Military Training
Military Veterans
Enlisted **Military** Personnel
Volunteer **Military** Personnel
Miller Analogies Test
Millon Clinical Multiaxial Inventory
Mimicry (Biology)
Mind
Mind Blindness *USE Theory of Mind*
Mind Body *USE Dualism*
Theory of **Mind**
Mini Mental State Examination
Minimal Brain Disorders
Minimum Competency Tests
Ministers (Religion)
Minks
Minnesota Multiphasic Personality
    Inventory
Minnesota Teacher Attitude Inventory
    USE Attitude Measures
Minor Tranquilizers
Minority Group Discrimination
    USE Race and Ethnic Discrimination
Minority Groups
Mirror Image
Mirroring
Misanthropy
Misarticulation *USE Articulation Disorders*
Misbehavior *USE Behavior Problems*
Miscarriage *USE Spontaneous Abortion*
Miscegenous Marriage
    USE Interracial Marriage
Misconduct *USE Behavior Problems*
Misdemeanors *USE Crime*
Misdiagnosis
Misogyny *USE Misanthropy*
Missionaries
Mistakes *USE Errors*
MMPI *USE Minnesota Multiphasic*
    Personality Inventory
Mnemonic Learning
Mobility Aids
Geographical **Mobility**
Job Mobility *USE Occupational Mobility*
Occupational **Mobility**

Physical **Mobility**
Social **Mobility**
Upward Mobility *USE Social Mobility*
Vocational Mobility *USE Occupational Mobility*
Moclobemide
Big Five Personality Model *USE Five Factor Personality Model*
Biopsychosocial Model *USE Biopsychosocial Approach*
Family Systems Model *USE Family Systems Theory*
Five Factor Personality **Model**
Medical **Model**
Rasch Model *USE Item Response Theory*
Modeling *USE Simulation*
Modeling Behavior
    USE Imitation (Learning)
Heuristic **Modeling**
Mathematical **Modeling**
Stochastic **Modeling**
Structural Equation **Modeling**
Models
Animal **Models**
Logistic Models *USE Item Response Theory*
Mental **Models**
Role **Models**
Moderate Mental Retardation
Modernization
Behavior **Modification**
Classroom Behavior **Modification**
Child Molestation *USE Pedophilia*
Molindone
Mollusca
Pearson Product Moment Correlation Coefficient
    USE Statistical Correlation
Monetary Incentives
Monetary Rewards
Money
Mongolism *USE Downs Syndrome*
Monitoring
Self **Monitoring**
Self **Monitoring** (Personality)
Sleep Monitoring *USE Polysomnography*
Source **Monitoring**
Monkeys
Monoamine Oxidase Inhibitors
Monoamine Oxidases
Monocular Vision
Monogamy
Monolingualism
Cyclic Adenosine **Monophosphate**
Monotony
Carbon **Monoxide**
Carbon **Monoxide** Poisoning
Monozygotic Twins
Montessori Method
Mood Disorders *USE Affective Disorders*
Bipolar Mood Disorder *USE Bipolar Disorder*
Moodiness
Moods *USE Emotional States*
Mooney Problem Check List
Moral Development
Morale
Morality
Morals *USE Morality*
Mores *USE Values*
Morita Therapy
Morphemes
Morphine
Morphology
Morphology (Language)
Mortality *USE Death and Dying*
Mortality Rate
Mosaicism *USE Chromosome Disorders*
Moslems *USE Muslims*
Mother Absence
Mother Child Communication
Mother Child Relations
Mothers
Adolescent **Mothers**

Expectant **Mothers**
Schizophrenogenic **Mothers**
Single **Mothers**
Teenage Mothers *USE Adolescent Mothers*
Unwed **Mothers**
Moths
Motion Parallax
Motion Perception
Motion Pictures
Motion Pictures (Educational)
Motion Pictures (Entertainment)
Motion Sickness
Motivation
Motivation Training
Academic Achievement **Motivation**
Achievement **Motivation**
Affiliation **Motivation**
Animal **Motivation**
Employee **Motivation**
Extrinsic **Motivation**
Intrinsic **Motivation**
Motor Coordination
Motor Cortex
Motor Development
Motor Disorders
    USE Nervous System Disorders
Motor Evoked Potentials
    USE Somatosensory Evoked Potentials
Motor Neurons
Motor Pathways *USE Efferent Pathways*
Motor Performance
Motor Processes
Motor Skill Learning
    USE Perceptual Motor Learning
Motor Skills
Motor Traffic Accidents
Motor Vehicles
Fine **Motor** Skill Learning
Gross **Motor** Skill Learning
Perceptual **Motor** Coordination
Perceptual **Motor** Development
Perceptual **Motor** Learning
Perceptual Motor Measures
    USE Sensorimotor Measures
Perceptual **Motor** Processes
Motorcycles *USE Motor Vehicles*
Mourning *USE Grief*
Mouse Killing *USE Muricide*
Mouth (Anatomy)
Movement Disorders
Movement Perception
    USE Motion Perception
Movement Therapy
Apparent **Movement**
Black Power **Movement**
Civil Rights **Movement**
Eye **Movement** Desensilization Therapy
Gay Liberation Movement
    USE Homosexual Liberation Movement
Homosexual Liberation **Movement**
Human Potential **Movement**
Nonrapid Eye Movement Sleep *USE NREM Sleep*
Rapid Eye **Movement**
Rapid Eye Movement Dreams *USE REM Dreams*
Rapid Eye Movement Sleep *USE REM Sleep*
Stroboscopic Movement *USE Apparent Movement*
Womens Liberation **Movement**
Activist Movements *USE Activism*
Eye **Movements**
Radical **Movements**
Saccadic Eye Movements *USE Eye Movements*
Social **Movements**
Vergence Movements *USE Eye Convergence*
Movies
    USE Motion Pictures (Entertainment)
MPTP *USE Methylphenyltetrahydropyridine*
MRI *USE Magnetic Resonance Imaging*

Nasal **Mucosa**
Olfactory **Mucosa**
Mucus
Mueller Lyer Illusion
Multi Infarct Dementia
Millon Clinical **Multiaxial** Inventory
Multicultural Education
Multiculturalism
Multidimensional Scaling
Multidisciplinary Research
    USE Interdisciplinary Research
Multidisciplinary Treatment Approach
    USE Interdisciplinary Treatment
    Approach
Multidrug Abuse *USE Polydrug Abuse*
Multilingualism
Multimodal Treatment Approach
Minnesota **Multiphasic** Personality Inventory
Multiple Births
Multiple Choice (Testing Method)
Multiple Disabilities
Multiple Personality
    USE Dissociative Identity Disorder
Multiple Regression
Multiple Sclerosis
Multiple Therapy *USE Cotherapy*
Multiply Handicapped
    USE Multiple Disabilities
Multivariate Analysis
Munchausen Syndrome
Munchausen Syndrome by Proxy
Murder *USE Homicide*
Serial Murder *USE Serial Homicide*
Muricide
Muscarinic Drugs *USE Cholinergic Drugs*
Muscarinic Receptors
    USE Cholinergic Receptors
Muscimol
Muscle Contraction Headache
Muscle Contractions
Muscle Cramps *USE Muscular Disorders*
Muscle Relaxation
Muscle Relaxation Therapy
    USE Relaxation Therapy
Muscle Relaxing Drugs
Muscle Spasms
Muscle Tone
Intra Aural Muscle Reflex *USE Acoustic Reflex*
Muscles
Facial **Muscles**
Masticatory **Muscles**
Oculomotor **Muscles**
Muscular Atrophy
Muscular Disorders
Muscular Dystrophy
Musculocutaneous Nerve
    USE Spinal Nerves
Musculoskeletal Disorders
Musculoskeletal System
Music
Music Education
Music Perception
Music Therapy
Rock **Music**
Musical Ability
Musical Instruments
Musicians
Muslims
Mutations
Female Genital Mutilation *USE Circumcision*
Self **Mutilation**
Mutism
Elective **Mutism**
Selective Mutism *USE Elective Mutism*
Mutual Storytelling Technique
Myasthenia
Myasthenia Gravis

Myelin Sheath
Myelitis
Myelomeningocele *USE Spina Bifida*
Myenteric Plexus *USE Autonomic Ganglia*
Myers Briggs Type Indicator
Myocardial Infarctions
Myocardium
Myoclonia
Myofascial Pain
Myopia
Myotonia
Mysticism
Myths
Myxedema *USE Hypothyroidism*
N-Methyl-D-Aspartate
Nabilone *USE Cannabinoids*
NAch *USE Achievement Motivation*
Nail Biting
Nalorphine
Naloxone
Naltrexone
Names
Brand **Names**
Naming
Napping
Narcissism
Narcissistic Personality Disorder
Narcoanalysis
Narcoanalytic Drugs *USE Drugs*
Narcolepsy
Narcosis
Narcotic Agonists
Narcotic Antagonists
Narcotic Drugs
Narcotics Anonymous
    USE Twelve Step Programs
Narratives
Nasal Mucosa
National Guardsmen
Nationalism
Foreign **Nationals**
Native Alaskans *USE Alaska Natives*
Native Americans *USE American Indians*
Native Hawaiians *USE Hawaii Natives*
Native Language
Natives *USE Indigenous Populations*
Alaska **Natives**
Hawaii **Natives**
Natural Childbirth
Natural Disasters
Natural Family *USE Biological Family*
Natural Killer Cells
Natural Selection
Naturalistic Observation
    USE Observation Methods
Nature Nurture
Human **Nature**
Nausea
Animal Navigation
    USE Migratory Behavior (Animal)
Navy Personnel
Nazism *USE Fascism*
Near Death Experiences
Nearsightedness *USE Myopia*
Luria **Nebraska** Neuropsychological Battery
Neck (Anatomy)
Need Achievement
    USE Achievement Motivation
Need for Affiliation
    USE Affiliation Motivation
Need for Approval
Need for Cognition
Need Satisfaction
Needle Exchange Programs
Needle Sharing
Needs
Needs Assessment

Emotional Needs *USE Psychological Needs*
Health Service **Needs**
Mental Health Service Needs *USE Health Service Needs*
Psychological **Needs**
Special **Needs**
Nefazodone
Negative and Positive Symptoms
    USE Positive and Negative Symptoms
Negative Reinforcement
Negative Therapeutic Reaction
Negative Transfer
Contingent **Negative** Variation
Positive and **Negative** Symptoms
Negativism
Child **Neglect**
Perceptual Neglect *USE Sensory Neglect*
Sensory **Neglect**
Spatial Neglect *USE Sensory Neglect*
Visual Neglect *USE Sensory Neglect*
Negotiation
Negroes *USE Blacks*
Neighborhoods
Henmon Nelson Tests of Mental Ability
    USE Intelligence Measures
Nembutal *USE Pentobarbital*
NEO Personality Inventory
NeoFreudian School
    USE Neopsychoanalytic School
Neologisms
Neonatal Development
Neonatal Disorders
Neonatal Period
Neonaticide *USE Infanticide*
Neophobia
Neoplasms
Benign **Neoplasms**
Brain **Neoplasms**
Breast **Neoplasms**
Endocrine **Neoplasms**
Malignant Neoplasms *USE Neoplasms*
Mammary Neoplasms *USE Breast Neoplasms*
Nervous System **Neoplasms**
Neopsychoanalytic School
Neostigmine
Neostriatum *USE Striatum*
Nerve Cells *USE Neurons*
Nerve Endings
Nerve Growth Factor
Nerve Tissues
Abducens **Nerve**
Accessory Nerve *USE Cranial Nerves*
Acoustic **Nerve**
Auditory Nerve *USE Acoustic Nerve*
Chorda Tympani Nerve *USE Facial Nerve*
Facial **Nerve**
Femoral Nerve *USE Spinal Nerves*
Glossopharyngeal Nerve *USE Cranial Nerves*
Hypoglossal Nerve *USE Cranial Nerves*
Median Nerve *USE Spinal Nerves*
Musculocutaneous Nerve *USE Spinal Nerves*
Obturator Nerve *USE Spinal Nerves*
Oculomotor Nerve *USE Cranial Nerves*
Olfactory **Nerve**
Optic **Nerve**
Peripheral **Nerve** Disorders
Phrenic Nerve *USE Spinal Nerves*
Radial Nerve *USE Spinal Nerves*
Sciatic Nerve *USE Spinal Nerves*
Trigeminal **Nerve**
Trochlear Nerve *USE Cranial Nerves*
Ulnar Nerve *USE Spinal Nerves*
Vagus **Nerve**
Adrenergic **Nerves**
Cholinergic **Nerves**
Cranial **Nerves**
Spinal **Nerves**
Thoracic Nerves *USE Spinal Nerves*

Anorexia **Nervosa**
Nervous Breakdown *USE Mental Disorders*
Nervous System
Nervous System Disorders
Nervous System Neoplasms
Nervous System Plasticity
    USE Neural Plasticity
Autonomic **Nervous** System
Autonomic **Nervous** System Disorders
Central **Nervous** System
Central **Nervous** System Disorders
Central Nervous System Drugs
    USE CNS Affecting Drugs
Parasympathetic **Nervous** System
Peripheral **Nervous** System
Sclerosis **(Nervous** System)
Sympathetic **Nervous** System
Nervousness
Nest Building
Empty **Nest**
Business Networking *USE Professional Networking*
Professional **Networking**
Neural **Networks**
Social Support Networks *USE Social Support*
Social **Networks**
Neural Analyzers
Neural Development
Neural Lesions
Neural Networks
Neural Pathways
Neural Plasticity
Neural Receptors
Neural Regeneration
    USE Neural Development
Neural Transmission
    USE Neurotransmission
Neural Transplantation
Neuralgia
Trigeminal **Neuralgia**
Neurasthenic Neurosis
Neuroanatomy
Neurobiology
Neurochemistry
Neurodegenerative Diseases
Neurodermatitis
Neuroendocrinology
Neuroimaging
Neuroinfections *USE Infectious Disorders*
Neuroinfections
    USE Nervous System Disorders
Neurokinins
Neuroleptic Drugs
Neuroleptic Malignant Syndrome
Neurolinguistic Programming
Neurolinguistics
Neurological Disorders
    USE Nervous System Disorders
Neurologists
Neurology
Neuromuscular Blocking Drugs
    USE Muscle Relaxing Drugs
Neuromuscular Disorders
Neurons
Auditory **Neurons**
Motor **Neurons**
Sensory **Neurons**
Neuropathologists *USE Neurologists*
Neuropathology
Neuropathy
    USE Nervous System Disorders
Neuropeptide Y
Neuropeptides
Neurophysiology
Neuropsychiatrists *USE Psychiatrists*
Neuropsychiatry
Neuropsychological Assessment
Neuropsychological Rehabilitation

Halstead Reitan **Neuropsychological** Battery
Luria Nebraska **Neuropsychological** Battery
Neuropsychology
Neurosciences
Neurosis
Anxiety Neurosis *USE Anxiety Disorders*
Childhood **Neurosis**
Compulsive Neurosis
    USE Obsessive Compulsive Disorder
Conversion Neurosis *USE Conversion Disorder*
Dissociative Neurosis *USE Dissociative Disorders*
Experimental **Neurosis**
Infantile Neurosis *USE Childhood Neurosis*
Neurasthenic **Neurosis**
Obsessive Compulsive Neurosis
    USE Obsessive Compulsive Disorder
Obsessive Neurosis
    USE Obsessive Compulsive Disorder
Occupational **Neurosis**
Phobic Neurosis *USE Phobias*
Traumatic **Neurosis**
Neurosurgeons *USE Surgeons*
Neurosurgery
Neurosyphilis
Neurotensin
Neurotic Depressive Reaction
    USE Major Depression
Neuroticism
Neurotoxicity
Neurotoxins
Neurotransmission
Neurotransmitters
Psychotherapeutic **Neutrality**
Never Married
News Media
Professional Newsletters *USE Scientific Communication*
Newspapers
Niacin *USE Nicotinic Acid*
Niacinamide *USE Nicotinamide*
Nialamide
Nicotinamide
Nicotine
Nicotine Withdrawal
Nicotinic Acid
Nicotinic Acid Amide *USE Nicotinamide*
Nicotinic Receptors
    USE Cholinergic Receptors
Nictitating Membrane
Night Terrors *USE Sleep Disorders*
Nightmares
Substantia **Nigra**
Nihilism
Nitrazepam
Nitric Oxide
Nitrogen
NMDA *USE N-Methyl-D-Aspartate*
Nociception *USE Pain Perception*
Nociceptors
Nocturnal Emission
Nocturnal Teeth Grinding
Animal **Nocturnal** Behavior
Noise Effects
Noise Levels (Work Areas)
Filtered **Noise**
White **Noise**
Nomifensine
Non Zero Sum Games
Beverages **(Nonalcoholic)**
Noncommissioned Officers
Nonconformity (Personality)
Noncontingent Reinforcement
Nondirected Discussion Method
Nondirective Therapy
    USE Client Centered Therapy
Nongraded Schools
Primates **(Nonhuman)**
Nonlinear Regression

Nonmetallic Elements
    USE Chemical Elements
Nonparametric Statistical Tests
Nonprescription Drugs
Nonprofessional Personnel
Nonprofit Organizations
Nonprojective Personality Measures
Nonrapid Eye Movement Sleep
    USE NREM Sleep
Rites **(Nonreligious)**
NonREM Sleep *USE NREM Sleep*
Nonreversal Shift Learning
Nonsense Syllable Learning
Nonstandard English
Nontraditional Careers
Nontraditional Education
Nonverbal Ability
Nonverbal Communication
Nonverbal Learning
Nonverbal Meaning
Nonverbal Reinforcement
Nonviolence
Nootropic Drugs
Noradrenaline *USE Norepinephrine*
Norepinephrine
Norepinephrine Metabolites
Normal Distribution
Test Normalization *USE Test Standardization*
Social **Norms**
Statistical **Norms**
Test **Norms**
Nortriptyline
Norway Rats
Nose
Note Taking
Nouns
Novel Stimuli *USE Stimulus Novelty*
Novelty Seeking *USE Sensation Seeking*
Stimulus **Novelty**
Novocaine *USE Procaine*
NREM Sleep
Nuclear Family
Nuclear Technology
Nuclear War
Cerebellar Nuclei *USE Cerebellum*
Raphe **Nuclei**
Septal **Nuclei**
Thalamic **Nuclei**
Nucleic Acids
Nucleotides
Nucleus Accumbens
Nucleus Basalis Magnocellularis
Caudate **Nucleus**
Cell **Nucleus**
Red Nucleus *USE Mesencephalon*
Nudity
Null Hypothesis Testing
Number Comprehension
Number Systems
Numbers (Numerals)
Numbers **(Numerals)**
Numerical Ability *USE Mathematical Ability*
Numerosity Perception
Nuns
Nurse Patient Interaction
    USE Therapeutic Processes
Nursery School Students
Nursery Schools
Nurses
Psychiatric **Nurses**
Public Health Service **Nurses**
School **Nurses**
Nursing
Nursing Education
Nursing Homes
Nursing Students
Nurturance

Nature **Nurture**
Nutrition
Nutritional Deficiencies
Nutritional Supplements
    USE Dietary Supplements
Nymphomania *USE Hypersexuality*
Nystagmus
Optokinetic Nystagmus *USE Nystagmus*
Vestibular Nystagmus *USE Nystagmus*
Obedience
Obesity
Obesity (Attitudes Toward)
Object Permanence
Object Recognition
Object Relations
Objective Referenced Tests
    USE Criterion Referenced Tests
Objectives *USE Goals*
Course Objectives *USE Educational Objectives*
Educational **Objectives**
Instructional Objectives *USE Educational Objectives*
Organizational **Objectives**
Objectivity
Transitional **Objects**
Oblique Rotation
Medulla **Oblongata**
Obscenity
Observation Methods
Naturalistic Observation *USE Observation Methods*
Self Observation *USE Self Monitoring*
Observational Learning
Observers
Obsessions
Obsessive Compulsive Disorder
Obsessive Compulsive Neurosis
    USE Obsessive Compulsive Disorder
Obsessive Compulsive Personality
Disorder
Obsessive Neurosis
    USE Obsessive Compulsive Disorder
Obstetrical Complications
Obstetricians
Obstetrics
Obturator Nerve *USE Spinal Nerves*
Occipital Lobe
Occultism
Parental **Occupation**
Occupational Adjustment
Occupational Aspirations
Occupational Attitudes
Occupational Choice
Occupational Exposure
Occupational Guidance
Occupational Interest Measures
Occupational Interests
Occupational Mobility
Occupational Neurosis
Occupational Preference
Occupational Safety
Occupational Status
Occupational Stress
Occupational Success
Occupational Success Prediction
Occupational Tenure
Occupational Therapists
Occupational Therapy
Kuder **Occupational** Interest Survey
Occupations
Religious Occupations *USE Religious Personnel*
Octopus
Ocular Accommodation
Ocular Dominance
Ocular Fixation *USE Eye Fixation*
Electro **Oculography**
Oculomotor Muscles
Oculomotor Nerve *USE Cranial Nerves*

Oculomotor Response
    USE Eye Movements
Odor Aversion Conditioning
    USE Aversion Conditioning
Odor Discrimination
Oedipal Complex
Mentally Ill **Offenders**
Sex **Offenses**
Office Environment
    USE Working Conditions
Commissioned **Officers**
Military Officers *USE Commissioned Officers*
Noncommissioned **Officers**
Parole **Officers**
Probation **Officers**
Elected Government Officials *USE Government Personnel*
Stimulus **Offset**
Offspring
Offspring of Alcoholics
    USE Children of Alcoholics
Adult **Offspring**
Alcoholic Offspring *USE Children of Alcoholics*
Interracial **Offspring**
Olanzapine
Olfactory Bulb
Olfactory Evoked Potentials
Olfactory Impairment *USE Anosmia*
Olfactory Mucosa
Olfactory Nerve
Olfactory Perception
Olfactory Stimulation
Olfactory Thresholds
Oligophrenia *USE Mental Retardation*
Omission Training
Omnipotence
Online Databases *USE Databases*
Online Searching
    USE Computer Searching
Online Therapy
Only Children
Female Only Environments
    USE Single Sex Environments
Male Only Environments
    USE Single Sex Environments
Onomatopoeia and Images Test
    USE Projective Personality Measures
Onset (Disorders)
Sleep **Onset**
Stimulus **Onset**
Ontogeny *USE Development*
Open Classroom Method
Open Universities
    USE Nontraditional Education
Animal **Open** Field Behavior
Openmindedness
Openness to Experience
Operant Conditioning
Keypunch Operators *USE Clerical Personnel*
Ophidiophobia
Ophthalmologic Examination
Ophthalmology
Opiate Agonists *USE Narcotic Agonists*
Opiate Antagonists
    USE Narcotic Antagonists
Opiates
Endogenous **Opiates**
Opinion Attitude and Interest Survey
    USE Attitude Measures
Opinion Change *USE Attitude Change*
Opinion Questionnaires
    USE Attitude Measures
Opinion Surveys *USE Attitude Measures*
Public **Opinion**
Opinions *USE Attitudes*
Opioid Antagonists
    USE Narcotic Antagonists
Opioids *USE Opiates*

Opium Alkaloids *USE Alkaloids*
Opium Alkaloids *USE Opiates*
Opium Derivatives *USE Opiates*
Opossums
Oppositional Defiant Disorder
Optic Chiasm
Optic Lobe
Optic Nerve
Optic Tract
Optical Aids
Optical Illusions *USE Illusions (Perception)*
Optimism
Optokinetic Nystagmus *USE Nystagmus*
Optometrists
Optometry
Oral Communication
Oral Contraceptives
Oral Reading
Birth **Order**
Higher **Order** Conditioning
Pecking Order *USE Animal Dominance*
Rank **Order** Correlation
Second Order Conditioning
    USE Higher Order Conditioning
Court Ordered Treatment *USE Court Referrals*
Organ Donation *USE Tissue Donation*
Organ of Corti *USE Cochlea*
Organ Transplantation
Sense **Organ** Disorders
Organic Brain Syndromes
Organic Therapies
    USE Physical Treatment Methods
Single Cell Organisms *USE Microorganisms*
School Organization
    USE Educational Administration
Spatial **Organization**
Organizational Behavior
Organizational Change
Organizational Characteristics
Organizational Climate
Organizational Commitment
Organizational Crises
Organizational Culture
    USE Organizational Climate
Organizational Development
Organizational Effectiveness
Organizational Goals
    USE Organizational Objectives
Organizational Learning
Organizational Merger
Organizational Objectives
Organizational Performance
    USE Organizational Effectiveness
Organizational Policy Making
    USE Policy Making
Organizational Psychology
    USE Industrial and Organizational
    Psychology
Organizational Structure
Industrial and **Organizational** Psychology
Organizations
Business **Organizations**
Clubs (Social **Organizations)**
Foreign **Organizations**
Health Maintenance **Organizations**
International **Organizations**
Learning Organizations *USE Organizational Learning*
Nonprofit **Organizations**
Professional **Organizations**
Religious **Organizations**
Advance **Organizers**
Sense **Organs**
Orgasm
Female **Orgasm**
Male **Orgasm**
Fundamental Interpersonal Relation **Orientation** Behavior Ques
Perceptual **Orientation**

Personal **Orientation** Inventory
Professional Orientation *USE Theoretical Orientation*
Sexual **Orientation**
Spatial **Orientation** (Perception)
Theoretical **Orientation**
Psychoanalytically Oriented Psychotherapy
    USE Psychodynamic Psychotherapy
Orienting Reflex
Orienting Responses
Family of **Origin**
Originality *USE Creativity*
Word Origins *USE Etymology*
Orphanages
Orphans
Orphenadrine
Orthogonal Rotation
Orthography
Orthopedically Handicapped
    USE Physical Disorders
Orthopsychiatry
Oscilloscopes
Ear Ossicles *USE Middle Ear*
Osteopathic Medicine
Osteopathy *USE Osteopathic Medicine*
Osteoporosis
Significant **Others**
Otosclerosis *USE Ear Disorders*
Out of Body Experiences
Acting **Out**
Time **Out**
Disease Outbreaks *USE Epidemics*
Psychotherapeutic **Outcomes**
Therapeutic Outcomes *USE Treatment Outcomes*
Treatment **Outcomes**
Outgroup Ingroup *USE Ingroup Outgroup*
Ingroup **Outgroup**
Outpatient Commitment
Outpatient Psychiatric Clinics
    USE Psychiatric Clinics
Outpatient Treatment
Outpatients
Outreach Programs
Outward Bound
    USE Wilderness Experience
Ovariectomy
Ovaries
Ovary Disorders
    USE Endocrine Sexual Disorders
Over the Counter Drugs
    USE Nonprescription Drugs
Academic **Overachievement**
Overcorrection
Drug **Overdoses**
Overlearning
Overpopulation
Structured Overview *USE Advance Organizers*
Overweight *USE Obesity*
Ovulation
Owls
Ownership
Oxazepam
Amine **Oxidase** Inhibitors
Cytochrome **Oxidase**
Monoamine **Oxidase** Inhibitors
Oxidases
Monoamine **Oxidases**
Nitric **Oxide**
Oxidopamine *USE Hydroxydopamine (6-)*
Oxilapine *USE Loxapine*
Oxygen
Oxygenation
Oxytocin
Artificial **Pacemakers**
Pacific Islanders
Pacifism
Pain

Pain Disorder
    USE Somatoform Pain Disorder
Pain Management
Pain Measurement
Pain Perception
Pain Receptors *USE Nociceptors*
Pain Relieving Drugs *USE Analgesic Drugs*
Pain Thresholds
Back **Pain**
Chronic **Pain**
Myofascial **Pain**
Psychogenic Pain *USE Somatoform Pain Disorder*
Somatoform **Pain** Disorder
Painting (Art)
Paired Associate Learning
Cleft **Palate**
Palestinians *USE Arabs*
Palliative Care
Globus **Pallidus**
Palm (Anatomy)
Palsy *USE Paralysis*
Cerebral **Palsy**
Progressive Supranuclear **Palsy**
Pancreas
Pancreozymin *USE Cholecystokinin*
Panic
Panic Attack
Panic Disorder
Pantherine *USE Muscimol*
Papaverine
Parachlorophenylalanine
Paradigmatic Techniques
    USE Paradoxical Techniques
Paradoxical Sleep *USE REM Sleep*
Paradoxical Techniques
Paragraphs
Paraldehyde *USE Anticonvulsive Drugs*
Paralegal Personnel *USE Legal Personnel*
Motion **Parallax**
Paralysis
Paralysis Agitans *USE Parkinsons Disease*
Hysterical **Paralysis**
Infantile Paralysis *USE Poliomyelitis*
Dementia Paralytica *USE General Paresis*
Paramedical Personnel
Paramedical Sciences
Parameter Estimation
    USE Statistical Estimation
Response **Parameters**
Statistical Sample **Parameters**
Stimulus **Parameters**
Parametric Statistical Tests
Paranoia
Paranoia (Psychosis)
Climacteric Paranoia
    USE Involutional Paranoid Psychosis
Paranoid Disorder
    USE Paranoia (Psychosis)
Paranoid Personality Disorder
Paranoid Schizophrenia
Acute Paranoid Disorder
    USE Paranoia (Psychosis)
Atypical Paranoid Disorder
    USE Paranoia (Psychosis)
Involutional **Paranoid** Psychosis
Shared Paranoid Disorder *USE Folie A Deux*
Paraphilias
Paraplegia
Paraprofessional Education
Paraprofessional Personnel
Parapsychological Phenomena
Parapsychology
Parasitic Disorders
Parasitism *USE Biological Symbiosis*
Parasuicide *USE Attempted Suicide*
Parasympathetic Nervous System

367

Parasympatholytic Drugs
    USE Antispasmodic Drugs
Parasympathomimetic Drugs
    USE Cholinomimetic Drugs
Parathion
Parathyroid Disorders
Parathyroid Glands
Parathyroid Hormone
Parent Child Communication
Parent Child Relations
Parent Educational Background
Parent Effectiveness Training
    USE Parent Training
Parent School Relationship
Parent Training
Parental Absence
Parental Attitudes
Parental Authoritarianism
    USE Parenting Style
Parental Characteristics
Parental Death
Parental Expectations
Parental Influence
    USE Parent Child Relations
Parental Investment
Parental Occupation
Parental Permissiveness
Parental Role
Animal **Parental** Behavior
Parenthood Status
Delayed **Parenthood**
Parenting Skills
Parenting Style
Parents
Adoptive **Parents**
Birth Parents *USE Biological Family*
Expectant **Parents**
Foster **Parents**
Gay Parents *USE Homosexual Parents*
Homosexual **Parents**
Lesbian Parents *USE Homosexual Parents*
Single **Parents**
Surrogate **Parents** (Humans)
General **Paresis**
Paresthesia *USE Somatosensory Disorders*
Pargyline
Parietal Lobe
Parkinsonism
Parkinsons Disease
Parochial School Education
    USE Private School Education
Parole
Parole Officers
Parolees *USE Parole*
Paroxetlne
Paroxysmal Sleep *USE Narcolepsy*
Partial Hospitalization
Partial Reinforcement
    USE Reinforcement Schedules
Partially Hearing Impaired
Partially Sighted
Participation
Athletic **Participation**
Citizen Participation *USE Community Involvement*
Client **Participation**
Group **Participation**
Patient Participation *USE Client Participation*
Political **Participation**
Participative Management
Political **Parties**
Partner Abuse
Sexual **Partners**
Parturition *USE Birth*
Democratic Party *USE Political Parties*
Republican Party *USE Political Parties*
Rites of **Passage**
Passive Aggressive Personality Disorder

Passive Avoidance
    USE Avoidance Conditioning
Passiveness
Pastoral Counseling
Pastors *USE Ministers (Religion)*
Paternal Investment
    USE Parental Investment
Animal **Paternal** Behavior
Path Analysis
Pathogenesis *USE Etiology*
Pathological Gambling
Pathologists
Pathology
Afferent **Pathways**
Efferent **Pathways**
Maze **Pathways**
Motor Pathways *USE Efferent Pathways*
Neural **Pathways**
Sensory Pathways *USE Afferent Pathways*
Patient Abuse
Patient Attitudes *USE Client Attitudes*
Patient Care Planning
    USE Treatment Planning
Patient Characteristics
    USE Client Characteristics
Patient Dropouts *USE Treatment Dropouts*
Patient Education *USE Client Education*
Patient History
Patient Participation
    USE Client Participation
Patient Records *USE Client Records*
Patient Rights *USE Client Rights*
Patient Satisfaction *USE Client Satisfaction*
Patient Seclusion
Patient Selection
Patient Therapist Interaction
    USE Psychotherapeutic Processes
Patient Therapist Sexual Relations
    USE Professional Client Sexual
    Relations
Patient Transfer *USE Client Transfer*
Patient Treatment Matching
    USE Client Treatment Matching
Patient Violence
Dentist Patient Interaction
    USE Therapeutic Processes
Nurse Patient Interaction
    USE Therapeutic Processes
Physician Patient Interaction
    USE Therapeutic Processes
Therapist Patient Interaction
    USE Psychotherapeutic Processes
Therapist Patient Sexual Relations
    USE Professional Client Sexual
    Relations
Patients
Dying Patients *USE Terminally Ill Patients*
Geriatric **Patients**
Hospitalized **Patients**
Medical **Patients**
Psychiatric **Patients**
Surgical **Patients**
Terminally Ill **Patients**
Patriarchy
Pattern Discrimination
Stimulus Pattern *USE Stimulus Variability*
Alcohol Drinking **Patterns**
Dissociative Patterns *USE Dissociative Disorders*
Eating Patterns *USE Eating Behavior*
Interest Patterns *USE Interests*
Transgenerational **Patterns**
Wilson **Patterson** Conservatism Scale
Speech **Pauses**
Pavlov (Ivan)
Pavlovian Conditioning
    USE Classical Conditioning
Pay *USE Salaries*

368

Equity **(Payment)**
PCP *USE Phencyclidine*
Peabody Picture Vocabulary Test
Peace
Peace Corps
Pearson Product Moment Correlation
    Coefficient *USE Statistical Correlation*
Pecking Order *USE Animal Dominance*
Angina **Pectoris**
Pedagogy *USE Teaching*
Pederasty *USE Pedophilia*
Pedestrian Accidents
Pedestrians
Pediatricians
Pediatrics
Pedophilia
Peer Counseling
Peer Evaluation
Peer Pressure
Peer Relations
Peer Review *USE Peer Evaluation*
Peer Tutoring
Peers
Pellagra
Pemoline
Death Penalty *USE Capital Punishment*
Penguins
Penicillins
Penis
Penis Envy
Erection **(Penis)**
Penitentiaries *USE Prisons*
Penology
Employee **Pension** Plans
Pentazocine
Pentobarbital
Sodium Pentobarbital *USE Pentobarbital*
Pentothal *USE Thiopental*
Pentylenetetrazol
Pentylenetetrazole *USE Pentylenetetrazol*
Peptic Ulcers *USE Gastrointestinal Ulcers*
Peptides
Perception
Auditory **Perception**
Brightness **Perception**
Color **Perception**
Contour Perception
    USE Form and Shape Perception
Depth **Perception**
Direction **Perception**
Distance **Perception**
Extrasensory **Perception**
Face **Perception**
Form and Shape **Perception**
Form Perception
    USE Form and Shape Perception
Frostig Developmental
Test of Visual **Perception**
Gustatory Perception *USE Taste Perception*
Haptic Perception *USE Cutaneous Sense*
Illusions **(Perception)**
Interpersonal Perception *USE Social Perception*
Kinesthetic **Perception**
Loudness **Perception**
Motion **Perception**
Movement Perception *USE Motion Perception*
Music **Perception**
Numerosity **Perception**
Olfactory **Perception**
Pain **Perception**
Pitch **Perception**
Risk **Perception**
Role **Perception**
Self **Perception**
Shape Perception
    USE Form and Shape Perception
Signal Detection **(Perception)**

Smell Perception *USE Olfactory Perception*
Social **Perception**
Somesthetic **Perception**
Spatial Orientation **(Perception)**
Spatial **Perception**
Speech **Perception**
Subliminal **Perception**
Tactual **Perception**
Taste **Perception**
Temperature **Perception**
Texture **Perception**
Time **Perception**
Visual **Perception**
Weight **Perception**
Perceptiveness (Personality)
Perceptual Aftereffect
Perceptual Closure
Perceptual Constancy
Perceptual Development
Perceptual Discrimination
Perceptual Distortion
Perceptual Disturbances
Perceptual Fill *USE Perceptual Closure*
Perceptual Localization
Perceptual Measures
Perceptual Motor Coordination
Perceptual Motor Development
Perceptual Motor Learning
Perceptual Motor Measures
    USE Sensorimotor Measures
Perceptual Motor Processes
Perceptual Neglect *USE Sensory Neglect*
Perceptual Orientation
Perceptual Stimulation
Perceptual Style
Perfectionism
Hypericum **Perforatum**
Performance
Performance Anxiety
Performance Tests
Athletic **Performance**
Group **Performance**
Job **Performance**
Motor **Performance**
Organizational Performance
    USE Organizational Effectiveness
Sport Performance *USE Athletic Performance*
Performing Arts *USE Arts*
Periaqueductal Gray
Perinatal Period
Critical **Period**
Neonatal **Period**
Perinatal **Period**
Postnatal **Period**
Peripheral Nerve Disorders
Peripheral Nervous System
Peripheral Vision
Computer **Peripheral** Devices
Object **Permanence**
Parental **Permissiveness**
Perpetrators
Perphenazine
Persecution
Perseverance *USE Persistence*
Perseveration
Persistence
Persistent Mental Illness
    USE Chronic Mental Illness
Person Centered Psychotherapy
    USE Client Centered Therapy
Person Environment Fit
Goodenough Harris Draw A **Person** Test
Personal Adjustment
    USE Emotional Adjustment
Personal Computers *USE Microcomputers*
Personal Construct Theory
    USE Personality Theory

Personal Defense *USE Self Defense*
Personal Growth Techniques
    USE Human Potential Movement
Personal Orientation Inventory
Personal Relationships
    USE Interpersonal Relationships
Personal Space
Personal Therapy
Personal Values
Edwards **Personal** Preference Schedule
Personality
Personality Assessment
    USE Personality Measures
Personality Change
Personality Correlates
Personality Development
Personality Disorders
Personality Factors *USE Personality Traits*
Personality Measures
Personality Processes
Personality Tests
    USE Personality Measures
Personality Theory
Personality Traits
Adaptability **(Personality)**
Anankastic Personality *USE Obsessive Compulsive*
    Personality Disorder
Antisocial **Personality** Disorder
Asthenic Personality *USE Personality Disorders*
Avoidant **Personality** Disorder
Big Five Personality Model
    USE Five Factor Personality Model
Borderline **Personality** Disorder
Childrens **Personality** Questionnaire
Compulsive Personality Disorder
    USE Obsessive Compulsive
    Personality Disorder
Conformity **(Personality)**
Conscious **(Personality** Factor)
Counselor Personality *USE Counselor Characteristics*
Cyclothymic **Personality**
Dependency **(Personality)**
Dependent **Personality** Disorder
Differential Personality Inventory
    USE Nonprojective Personality
    Measures
Edwards **Personality** Inventory
Emotionality **(Personality)**
Explosive Personality *USE Explosive Disorder*
Eysenck **Personality** Inventory
Five Factor **Personality** Model
High School **Personality** Questionnaire
Histrionic **Personality** Disorder
Hysterical Personality
    USE Histrionic Personality Disorder
Inadequate **Personality**
Independence **(Personality)**
Inhibition **(Personality)**
Masochistic **Personality**
Minnesota Multiphasic **Personality** Inventory
Multiple Personality
    USE Dissociative Identity Disorder
Narcissistic **Personality** Disorder
NEO **Personality** Inventory
Nonconformity **(Personality)**
Nonprojective **Personality** Measures
Obsessive Compulsive **Personality** Disorder
Paranoid **Personality** Disorder
Passive Aggressive **Personality** Disorder
Perceptiveness **(Personality)**
Projective **Personality** Measures
Psychoanalytic **Personality** Factors
Rigidity **(Personality)**
Sadomasochistic **Personality**
Schizoid **Personality** Disorder
Schizotypal **Personality** Disorder
Self Monitoring **(Personality)**

Sensitivity **(Personality)**
Sixteen **Personality** Factors Questionnaire
Split Personality
    USE Dissociative Identity Disorder
Teacher **Personality**
Therapist Personality *USE Therapist Characteristics*
Type A Personality *USE Coronary Prone Behavior*
Type B Personality *USE Coronary Prone Behavior*
Unconscious **(Personality** Factor)
Personnel
Personnel Development
    USE Personnel Training
Personnel Evaluation
Personnel Management
    USE Human Resource Management
Personnel Placement
Personnel Promotion
Personnel Recruitment
Personnel Selection
Personnel Supply
Personnel Termination
Personnel Training
Personnel Turnover
    USE Employee Turnover
Accreditation (Education **Personnel)**
Aerospace **Personnel**
Air Force **Personnel**
Army **Personnel**
Aviation Personnel *USE Aerospace Personnel*
Business and Industrial **Personnel**
Clerical **Personnel**
Coast Guard **Personnel**
Disabled **Personnel**
Domestic Service **Personnel**
Educational **Personnel**
Enlisted Military **Personnel**
Government **Personnel**
Health **Personnel**
Health **Personnel** Attitudes
Home Care **Personnel**
Industrial Personnel
    USE Business and Industrial Personnel
Law Enforcement **Personnel**
Lay Religious **Personnel**
Legal **Personnel**
Management **Personnel**
Marine **Personnel**
Medical **Personnel**
Medical **Personnel** Supply
Mental Health **Personnel**
Mental Health **Personnel** Supply
Military Medical **Personnel**
Military **Personnel**
Navy **Personnel**
Nonprofessional **Personnel**
Paralegal Personnel *USE Legal Personnel*
Paramedical **Personnel**
Paraprofessional **Personnel**
Police **Personnel**
Prison **Personnel**
Professional **Personnel**
Religious **Personnel**
Sales **Personnel**
Secretarial **Personnel**
Service **Personnel**
Student **Personnel** Services
Technical Service **Personnel**
Technical **Personnel**
Volunteer Civilian Personnel *USE Volunteers*
Volunteer Military **Personnel**
Volunteer Personnel *USE Volunteers*
Divorced **Persons**
Single **Persons**
Perspective Taking *USE Role Taking*
Linear **Perspective**
Time **Perspective**
Visual Perspective *USE Linear Perspective*

Perspiration *USE Sweat*
Persuasion Therapy
Persuasive Communication
Pervasive Developmental Disorders
Pessimism
Pesticides *USE Insecticides*
Pet Therapy *USE Animal Assisted Therapy*
Petit Mal Epilepsy
Pets
Peyote
Phantom Limbs
Pharmacists
Pharmacology
Pharmacotherapy *USE Drug Therapy*
Pharyngeal Disorders
Pharynx
Phenaglycodol *USE Sedatives*
Phencyclidine
Phenelzine
Phenethylamines
Pheniprazine
Phenmetrazine
Phenobarbital
Parapsychological **Phenomena**
Phenomenology
Phenothiazine Derivatives
Phenotypes
Phenoxybenzamine
Phenylalanine
Phenylethylamines *USE Phenethylamines*
Phenylketonuria
Phenytoin *USE Diphenylhydantoin*
Pheromones
Phi Coefficient
Philosophies
Philosophy of Life *USE World View*
Logic **(Philosophy)**
Positivism **(Philosophy)**
Realism **(Philosophy)**
School **Phobia**
Snake Phobia *USE Ophidiophobia*
Social **Phobia**
Spider Phobia *USE Phobias*
Phobias
Phobic Neurosis *USE Phobias*
Phonemes
Phonemic Awareness
    USE Phonological Awareness
Words **(Phonetic Units)**
Phonetics
Phonics
Phonological Awareness
Phonology
Phosphatases
Phosphatides
Phospholipids *USE Phosphatides*
Phosphorus
Phosphorylases
Photic Threshold *USE Illumination*
Photic Threshold *USE Visual Thresholds*
Photographic Art
Photographic Memory
    USE Eidetic Imagery
Photographs
Photopic Stimulation
Photoreceptors
Phototherapy
Phrases
Phrenic Nerve *USE Spinal Nerves*
Phylogenesis
Physical Abuse
Physical Activity *USE Motor Processes*
Physical Agility
Physical Appearance
Physical Attractiveness
Physical Comfort
Physical Contact

Physical Development
Physical Dexterity
Physical Disabilities (Attitudes Toward)
Physical Disfigurement
Physical Disorders
Physical Education
Physical Endurance
Physical Examination
Physical Exercise *USE Exercise*
Physical Fitness
Physical Geography *USE Geography*
Physical Growth
    USE Physical Development
Physical Illness (Attitudes Toward)
Physical Illness *USE Physical Disorders*
Physical Maturity
Physical Mobility
Physical Restraint
Physical Strength
Physical Therapists
Physical Therapy
Physical Trauma *USE Injuries*
Physical Treatment Methods
Physically Handicapped
    USE Physical Disorders
Physician Patient Interaction
    USE Therapeutic Processes
Physicians
Family **Physicians**
Physicists
Physics
Physiological Aging
Physiological Arousal
Physiological Correlates
Physiological Psychology
Physiological Stress
Absorption **(Physiological)**
Physiology
Physiotherapy *USE Physical Therapy*
Physique
Physostigmine
Piaget (Jean)
Piagetian Tasks
Piano *USE Musical Instruments*
Pica
Picketing *USE Social Demonstrations*
Picks Disease
Picrotoxin
Pictorial Stimuli
Peabody **Picture** Vocabulary Test
Rosenzweig **Picture** Frustration Study
Blacky Pictures Test
    USE Projective Personality Measures
Motion **Pictures**
Motion **Pictures** (Educational)
Motion **Pictures** (Entertainment)
Piercings *USE Cosmetic Techniques*
Pigeons
Pigments
Pigs
Guinea **Pigs**
Pilocarpine
Aircraft **Pilots**
Pimozide
Pineal Body
Pinealectomy
Piperazines
Pipradrol
Piracetam
Pitch (Frequency)
Pitch Discrimination
Pitch Perception
Speech **Pitch**
Pituitary Disorders
Pituitary Dwarfism *USE Hypopituitarism*
Pituitary Gland

Pituitary Gland Surgery
    USE Hypophysectomy
Pituitary Hormones
Hypothalamo **Pituitary** Adrenal System
Place Conditioning
Place Disorientation
Conditioned Place Preference *USE Place Conditioning*
Placebo
Educational **Placement**
Personnel **Placement**
Placenta
Planarians
Planned Behavior
Discharge **Planning**
Educational Program **Planning**
Environmental **Planning**
Family **Planning**
Family **Planning** Attitudes
Management **Planning**
Patient Care Planning *USE Treatment Planning*
Program Planning *USE Program Development*
Treatment **Planning**
Urban **Planning**
Employee Pension **Plans**
Group Health Plans *USE Health Maintenance*
    Organizations
Lesson **Plans**
Medicinal Herbs and **Plants**
Blood **Plasma**
Plastic Surgery
Nervous System Plasticity *USE Neural Plasticity*
Neural **Plasticity**
Blood **Platelets**
Play *USE Recreation*
Play Therapy
Animal **Play**
Childhood **Play** Behavior
Childhood **Play** Development
Doll **Play**
Playgrounds
Role **Playing**
Stage Plays *USE Theatre*
Pleasure
Plethysmography
Brachial Plexus *USE Spinal Nerves*
Celiac Plexus *USE Autonomic Ganglia*
Cervical Plexus *USE Spinal Nerves*
Choroid Plexus *USE Cerebral Ventricles*
Hypogastric Plexus *USE Autonomic Ganglia*
Lumbrosacral Plexus *USE Spinal Nerves*
Myenteric Plexus *USE Autonomic Ganglia*
Submucous Plexus *USE Autonomic Ganglia*
Cultural Pluralism *USE Multiculturalism*
PMS *USE Premenstrual Syndrome*
Pneumoencephalography
Pneumonia
Poetry
Poetry Therapy
Point Biserial Correlation
Poisoning *USE Toxic Disorders*
Barbiturate **Poisoning**
Carbon Monoxide **Poisoning**
Lead **Poisoning**
Mercury **Poisoning**
Poisons
Poisson Distribution
    USE Skewed Distribution
Police Interrogation
    USE Legal Interrogation
Police Personnel
Policy Making
Foreign **Policy** Making
Government **Policy** Making
Health Care **Policy**
Mental Health Care Policy *USE Health Care Policy*
Organizational Policy Making *USE Policy Making*
Public Policy *USE Government Policy Making*

Poliomyelitis
Political Assassination
Political Attitudes
Political Campaigns
Political Candidates
Political Conservatism
Political Debates *USE Debates*
Political Economic Systems
Political Elections
Political Involvement
    USE Political Participation
Political Issues
Political Liberalism
Political Participation
Political Parties
Political Processes
Political Psychology
Political Radicalism
Political Refugees *USE Refugees*
Political Revolution
Political Socialization
Politicians
Politics
Pollution
Polydipsia
Polydrug Abuse
Polygamy
Polygraphs
Polymorphism
Polyphagia *USE Hyperphagia*
Polypharmacy
Polysomnography
Pons
Data Pooling *USE Meta Analysis*
Popular Culture
Popularity
Population
Population (Statistics)
Population Characteristics
    USE Demographic Characteristics
Population Control *USE Birth Control*
Population Density *USE Social Density*
Population Genetics
Population Shifts *USE Human Migration*
Aboriginal Populations *USE Indigenous Populations*
At Risk **Populations**
High Risk Populations *USE At Risk Populations*
Indigenous **Populations**
Risk Populations *USE At Risk Populations*
Pornography
Porphyria
Porpoises
Porteus Maze Test
Serial **Position** Effect
Positive and Negative Symptoms
Positive Psychology
Positive Reinforcement
Positive Transfer
Negative and Positive Symptoms
    USE Positive and Negative Symptoms
Positivism
Positivism (Philosophy)
Positron Emission Tomography
    USE Tomography
Possession *USE Ownership*
Demonic Possession *USE Spirit Possession*
Spirit **Possession**
Postactivation Potentials
Postganglionic Autonomic Fibers
    USE Autonomic Ganglia
Postgraduate Students
Postgraduate Training
Posthypnotic Suggestions
Postmodernism
Postnatal Depression
    USE Postpartum Depression

Postnatal Dysphoria
    USE Postpartum Depression
Postnatal Period
Postpartum Depression
Postpartum Psychosis
Postsurgical Complications
Posttesting
Posttraumatic Stress Disorder
Posttreatment Followup
Posture
Threat **Postures**
Potassium
Potassium Ions
Potential Dropouts
Achievement **Potential**
Human **Potential** Movement
Readiness Potential
    USE Contingent Negative Variation
Skin **Potential**
Auditory Evoked **Potentials**
Cortical Evoked **Potentials**
Event Related Potentials *USE Evoked Potentials*
Evoked **Potentials**
Motor Evoked Potentials
    USE Somatosensory Evoked Potentials
Olfactory Evoked **Potentials**
Postactivation **Potentials**
Somatosensory Evoked **Potentials**
Visual Evoked **Potentials**
Drug Potentiation *USE Drug Interactions*
Long Term Potentiation *USE Postactivation Potentials*
Short Term Potentiation *USE Postactivation Potentials*
Poverty
Poverty Areas
Power
Abuse of **Power**
Black **Power** Movement
Statistical **Power**
Practical Knowledge
    USE Procedural Knowledge
Practice
Practice Effects *USE Practice*
Distributed **Practice**
Evidence Based **Practice**
Massed **Practice**
Private **Practice**
Childrearing **Practices**
Feeding Practices *USE Eating Behavior*
Religious **Practices**
Practicum Supervision
General **Practitioners**
Prader Willi Syndrome
Dementia Praecox *USE Schizophrenia*
Pragmatics
Pragmatism
Praise
Prayer
Praying Mantis *USE Mantis*
Precocious Development
Precognition
Preconditioning
Sensory Preconditioning *USE Preconditioning*
Serotonin **Precursors**
Animal **Predatory** Behavior
Predelinquent Youth
Predictability (Measurement)
Prediction
Prediction Errors
Academic Achievement **Prediction**
Occupational Success **Prediction**
Predictive Validity *USE Statistical Validity*
Predisposition
Prednisolone
Preference Measures
Career Preference *USE Occupational Preference*
Conditioned Place Preference *USE Place Conditioning*
Edwards Personal **Preference** Schedule

Kuder **Preference** Record
Occupational **Preference**
Vocational Preference *USE Occupational Preference*
Preferences
Aesthetic **Preferences**
Brand **Preferences**
Food **Preferences**
Preferred Rewards
Least **Preferred** Coworker Scale
Prefrontal Cortex
Preganglionic Autonomic Fibers
    USE Autonomic Ganglia
Pregnancy
Adolescent **Pregnancy**
False Pregnancy *USE Pseudocyesis*
Teenage Pregnancy *USE Adolescent Pregnancy*
Prejudice
Religious **Prejudices**
Preliminary Scholastic Aptitude Test
    USE College Entrance Examination
    Board Scholastic Aptitude Test
Premarital Counseling
Premarital Intercourse
Premature Birth
Premature Ejaculation
Premenstrual Dysphoric Disorder
Premenstrual Syndrome
Premenstrual Tension
    USE Premenstrual Syndrome
Premorbidity
Prenatal Care
Prenatal Development
Prenatal Developmental Stages
Prenatal Diagnosis
Prenatal Exposure
Preoptic Area
Prepulse Inhibition
Presbyterians *USE Protestants*
Preschool Education
Preschool Students
Preschool Teachers
Wechsler **Preschool** Primary Scale
Prescribing (Drugs)
Prescription Drugs
Symptom Prescription *USE Paradoxical Techniques*
Presenile Dementia
Stereoscopic **Presentation**
Stimulus **Presentation** Methods
Tachistoscopic **Presentation**
Self **Preservation**
Preservice Teachers
Presidential Debates *USE Debates*
Pressoreceptors *USE Baroreceptors*
Pressure Sensation
Barometric Pressure *USE Atmospheric Conditions*
Blood **Pressure**
Blood **Pressure** Disorders
Diastolic **Pressure**
Peer **Pressure**
Sound Pressure Level *USE Loudness*
Systolic **Pressure**
Pretesting
Prevention
Accident **Prevention**
AIDS **Prevention**
Crime **Prevention**
Drug Abuse **Prevention**
Fire **Prevention**
Primary Mental Health **Prevention**
Relapse **Prevention**
Substance Abuse Prevention *USE Drug Abuse Prevention*
Suicide **Prevention**
Suicide **Prevention** Centers
Preventive Medicine
Price *USE Costs and Cost Analysis*
Pride
Priests

Primacy Effect
Primal Therapy
Primary Health Care
Primary Mental Health Prevention
Primary Reinforcement
Primary School Students
Primary Schools *USE Elementary Schools*
Wechsler Preschool **Primary** Scale
Primates (Nonhuman)
Primidone
Priming
Semantic **Priming**
Primipara
School **Principals**
Printed Communications Media
Printing (Handwriting)
Prismatic Stimulation
Prison Personnel
Prisoners
Prisoners Dilemma Game
Prisoners of War
Prisons
Privacy
Private Practice
Private School Education
Private Sector
Privileged Communication
Proactive Inhibition
Probability
Probability Judgment
Probability Learning
Response **Probability**
Statistical **Probability**
Probation
Probation Officers
Probenecid
Problem Drinking *USE Alcohol Abuse*
Problem Solving
Anagram **Problem** Solving
Group **Problem** Solving
Individual Problem Solving *USE Problem Solving*
Mooney **Problem** Check List
Behavior **Problems**
Social Problems *USE Social Issues*
Procaine
Procedural Justice
Procedural Knowledge
Process Psychosis
Process Schizophrenia
    USE Process Psychosis
Process Schizophrenia *USE Schizophrenia*
Classification (Cognitive **Process)**
Educational Process *USE Education*
Insight (Psychotherapeutic **Process)**
Rumination (Cognitive **Process)**
Associative **Processes**
Cognitive **Processes**
Employment Processes *USE Personnel Recruitment*
Human Information Processes *USE Cognitive Processes*
Intersensory **Processes**
Legal **Processes**
Legislative **Processes**
Motor **Processes**
Perceptual Motor **Processes**
Personality **Processes**
Political **Processes**
Psychomotor Processes
    USE Perceptual Motor Processes
Psychotherapeutic **Processes**
Sensorimotor Processes
    USE Perceptual Motor Processes
Social **Processes**
Therapeutic **Processes**
Automated Information **Processing**
Cognitive **Processing** Speed
Data **Processing**

Information Processing Speed
    USE Cognitive Processing Speed
Speech **Processing** (Mechanical)
Word **Processing**
Prochlorperazine
Procrastination
Prodrome
Product Design
Consumer Product Design *USE Product Design*
Pearson Product Moment Correlation Coefficient
    USE Statistical Correlation
Employee **Productivity**
Profanity
Professional Certification
Professional Client Sexual Relations
Professional Communication
    USE Scientific Communication
Professional Competence
Professional Consultation
Professional Development
Professional Ethics
Professional Examinations
Professional Fees
Professional Identity
Professional Liability
Professional Licensing
Professional Networking
Professional Newsletters
    USE Scientific Communication
Professional Organizations
Professional Orientation
    USE Theoretical Orientation
Professional Personnel
Professional Referral
Professional Specialization
Professional Standards
Professional Supervision
Professionalism
Health Care Professionals *USE Health Personnel*
Impaired **Professionals**
Professors *USE College Teachers*
Language **Proficiency**
Limited English Proficiency *USE Language Proficiency*
Profiles (Measurement)
Profound Mental Retardation
Progestational Hormones
Progesterone
Progestins *USE Progestational Hormones*
Prognosis
Program Development
Program Evaluation
Program Planning
    USE Program Development
Educational **Program** Accreditation
Educational **Program** Evaluation
Educational **Program** Planning
Mental Health **Program** Evaluation
Programmed Instruction
Programmed Textbooks
Computer **Programming**
Computer **Programming** Languages
Neurolinguistic **Programming**
After School **Programs**
Computer Programs *USE Computer Software*
Educational **Programs**
Employee Assistance **Programs**
Government **Programs**
Home Visiting **Programs**
Hospital **Programs**
Immersion Programs
    USE Foreign Language Education
Independent Living **Programs**
Literacy **Programs**
Mental Health **Programs**
Needle Exchange **Programs**
Outreach **Programs**
Psychiatric Hospital **Programs**

Social **Programs**
Token Economy **Programs**
Twelve Step **Programs**
Work Study Programs *USE Educational Programs*
Progressive Relaxation Therapy
Progressive Supranuclear Palsy
Raven Coloured **Progressive** Matrices
Raven **Progressive** Matrices
Project Follow Through
Project Head Start
Projection (Defense Mechanism)
Projective Identification
Projective Personality Measures
Projective Techniques
Projective Testing Technique
Projective Tests *USE Projective Techniques*
Prolactin
Proline
Prolixin *USE Fluphenazine*
Promazine
Promethazine
Promiscuity
Health **Promotion**
Job Promotion *USE Personnel Promotion*
Personnel **Promotion**
Prompting
Coronary **Prone** Behavior
Accident **Proneness**
Pronouns
Pronunciation
Proofreading
Propaganda
Skin Electrical **Properties**
Property *USE Ownership*
Self Fulfilling **Prophecies**
Propranolol
Proprioceptors
Prose
Prosencephalon *USE Forebrain*
Prostigmine *USE Neostigmine*
Prosocial Behavior
Prosody
Prosopagnosia
Prospective Studies
Prostaglandins
Prostate
Prostate Cancer Screening
   USE Cancer Screening
Prostheses
Prostitution
Consumer **Protection**
Protective Services
Protein Deficiency Disorders
Protein Metabolism
Protein Sensitization
   USE Anaphylactic Shock
Proteinases
Proteins
Blood **Proteins**
Student Protest *USE Student Activism*
Protestantism
Protestants
Protozoa
Munchausen Syndrome by **Proxy**
Prozac *USE Fluoxetine*
Pruritus
Pseudocyesis
Pseudodementia
Pseudohermaphroditism
   USE Hermaphroditism
Pseudomemory *USE False Memory*
Pseudopregnancy *USE Pseudocyesis*
Pseudopsychopathic Schizophrenia
   USE Schizophrenia
Psilocybin
Psyche *USE Mind*
Psychedelic Drugs

Psychedelic Experiences
Psychiatric Aides
Psychiatric Clinics
Psychiatric Disorders
   USE Mental Disorders
Psychiatric Evaluation
Psychiatric History *USE Patient History*
Psychiatric Hospital Admission
Psychiatric Hospital Discharge
Psychiatric Hospital Programs
Psychiatric Hospital Readmission
Psychiatric Hospital Staff
Psychiatric Hospitalization
Psychiatric Hospitals
Psychiatric Nurses
Psychiatric Patients
Psychiatric Report
   USE Psychological Report
Psychiatric Residency
   USE Medical Residency
Psychiatric Residency
   USE Psychiatric Training
Psychiatric Social Workers
Psychiatric Symptoms
Psychiatric Training
Psychiatric Units
Child Psychiatric Clinics
   USE Child Guidance Clinics
Commitment **(Psychiatric)**
Hospital Psychiatric Units *USE Psychiatric Units*
Outpatient Psychiatric Clinics *USE Psychiatric Clinics*
Psychiatrists
Psychiatry
Adolescent **Psychiatry**
Biological **Psychiatry**
Child **Psychiatry**
Community **Psychiatry**
Comparative Psychiatry *USE Transcultural Psychiatry*
Consultation Liaison **Psychiatry**
Cultural Psychiatry *USE Transcultural Psychiatry*
Forensic **Psychiatry**
Geriatric **Psychiatry**
Social **Psychiatry**
Transcultural **Psychiatry**
Psychic Healing *USE Faith Healing*
Psychoactive Drugs *USE Drugs*
Psychoanalysis
Psychoanalysts
Psychoanalytic Interpretation
Psychoanalytic Personality Factors
Psychoanalytic Theory
Psychoanalytic Therapy
   USE Psychoanalysis
Psychoanalytic Training
Freudian **Psychoanalytic** School
Psychoanalytically Oriented Psychotherapy
   USE Psychodynamic Psychotherapy
Psychobiology
Psychodiagnosis
Psychodiagnostic Interview
Psychodiagnostic Typologies
Psychodrama
Psychodynamic Psychotherapy
Psychodynamics
Psychoeducation
Woodcock Johnson **Psychoeducational** Battery
Psychogalvanic Reflex
   USE Galvanic Skin Response
Psychogenesis
Psychogenic Pain
   USE Somatoform Pain Disorder
Psychohistory
Psychoimmunology
   USE Psychoneuroimmunology
Psychokinesis
Illinois Test of **Psycholinguistic** Abilities
Psycholinguistics

Psychological Abuse
    USE Emotional Abuse
Psychological Adjustment
    USE Emotional Adjustment
Psychological Assessment
Psychological Autopsy
Psychological Contracts
Psychological Correlates
    USE Psychodynamics
Psychological Debriefing
    USE Debriefing (Psychological)
Psychological Development
    USE Psychogenesis
Psychological Endurance
Psychological Interpretation
    USE Theoretical Interpretation
Psychological Needs
Psychological Reactance
Psychological Report
Psychological Screening Inventory
Psychological Stress
Psychological Terminology
Psychological Testing *USE Psychometrics*
Psychological Theories
Boundaries **(Psychological)**
California **Psychological** Inventory
Debriefing **(Psychological)**
Resilience **(Psychological)**
Psychologist Attitudes
Psychologists
Clinical **Psychologists**
Counseling **Psychologists**
Educational **Psychologists**
Experimental **Psychologists**
Industrial **Psychologists**
Military **Psychologists**
School **Psychologists**
Social **Psychologists**
Psychology
Psychology Education
Abnormal **Psychology**
Adolescent **Psychology**
Analytic Psychology *USE Jungian Psychology*
Applied **Psychology**
Child **Psychology**
Clinical **Psychology**
Clinical **Psychology** Graduate Training
Clinical **Psychology** Internship
Cognitive **(Psychology)**
Community **Psychology**
Comparative **Psychology**
Consumer **Psychology**
Counseling **Psychology**
Cross Cultural **Psychology**
Depth **Psychology**
Developmental **Psychology**
Eclectic Psychology *USE Theoretical Orientation*
Ecological **Psychology**
Educational **Psychology**
Engineering **Psychology**
Environmental **Psychology**
Evolutionary **Psychology**
Experimental **Psychology**
Folk **Psychology**
Forensic **Psychology**
Gestalt **Psychology**
Graduate **Psychology** Education
Health Care **Psychology**
Health Psychology *USE Health Care Psychology*
History of **Psychology**
Humanistic **Psychology**
Individual **Psychology**
Industrial and Organizational **Psychology**
Industrial Psychology
    USE Industrial and Organizational
    Psychology
Jungian **Psychology**

Legal Psychology *USE Forensic Psychology*
Mathematical **Psychology**
Medical **Psychology**
Military **Psychology**
Organizational Psychology
    USE Industrial and Organizational
    Psychology
Physiological **Psychology**
Political **Psychology**
Positive **Psychology**
School **Psychology**
Self **Psychology**
Social **Psychology**
Sport **Psychology**
Transpersonal **Psychology**
Psychometrics
Psychomotor Development
Psychomotor Processes
    USE Perceptual Motor Processes
Psychoneuroimmunology
Psychoneurosis *USE Neurosis*
Psychopath
    USE Antisocial Personality Disorder
Psychopathology
Psychopathy
    USE Antisocial Personality Disorder
Autistic Psychopathy *USE Aspergers Syndrome*
Psychopharmacology
Psychophysical Measurement
Psychophysics
Psychophysiologic Disorders
    USE Somatoform Disorders
Psychophysiology
Toxic **Psychoses**
Psychosexual Behavior
Psychosexual Development
Psychosis
Acute **Psychosis**
Affective **Psychosis**
Alcoholic **Psychosis**
Brief Reactive Psychosis *USE Acute Psychosis*
Childhood **Psychosis**
Chronic **Psychosis**
Experimental **Psychosis**
Infantile Psychosis *USE Childhood Psychosis*
Involutional Paranoid **Psychosis**
Korsakoffs **Psychosis**
Manic Depressive Psychosis *USE Bipolar Disorder*
Paranoia **(Psychosis)**
Postpartum **Psychosis**
Process **Psychosis**
Puerperal Psychosis *USE Postpartum Psychosis*
Reactive **Psychosis**
Senile **Psychosis**
Symbiotic Infantile **Psychosis**
Traumatic Psychosis *USE Reactive Psychosis*
Psychosocial Development
Psychosocial Factors
Psychosocial Mental Retardation
Psychosocial Readjustment
Psychosocial Rehabilitation
Psychosocial Resocialization
    USE Psychosocial Readjustment
Psychosomatic Disorders
    USE Somatoform Disorders
Psychosomatic Medicine
Psychostimulant Drugs
    USE CNS Stimulating Drugs
Psychosurgery
Psychotherapeutic Breakthrough
Psychotherapeutic Counseling
Psychotherapeutic Methods
    USE Psychotherapeutic Techniques
Psychotherapeutic Neutrality
Psychotherapeutic Outcomes
Psychotherapeutic Processes
Psychotherapeutic Resistance

ROTATED ALPHABETICAL TERMS SECTION

Psychotherapeutic Techniques
Psychotherapeutic Transference
Insight **(Psychotherapeutic** Process)
Psychotherapist Attitudes
Psychotherapist Trainees
    USE Therapist Trainees
Psychotherapists
Psychotherapy
Psychotherapy Training
Adlerian **Psychotherapy**
Adolescent **Psychotherapy**
Analytical **Psychotherapy**
Brief **Psychotherapy**
Child **Psychotherapy**
Eclectic **Psychotherapy**
Experiential **Psychotherapy**
Expressive **Psychotherapy**
Geriatric **Psychotherapy**
Group **Psychotherapy**
Humanistic **Psychotherapy**
Individual **Psychotherapy**
Integrative **Psychotherapy**
Interpersonal **Psychotherapy**
Jungian Psychotherapy
    USE Analytical Psychotherapy
Person Centered Psychotherapy
    USE Client Centered Therapy
Psychoanalytically Oriented Psychotherapy
    USE Psychodynamic Psychotherapy
Psychodynamic **Psychotherapy**
Reconstructive Psychotherapy *USE Psychotherapy*
Short Term Psychotherapy *USE Brief Psychotherapy*
Supportive **Psychotherapy**
Time Limited Psychotherapy *USE Brief Psychotherapy*
Psychotic Depressive Reaction
    USE Major Depression
Psychotic Symptoms
    USE Psychiatric Symptoms
Acute Psychotic Episode *USE Acute Psychosis*
Psychoticism
Psychotomimetic Drugs
Psychotropic Drugs *USE Drugs*
PTA *USE Parent School Relationship*
Puberty
Pubescence *USE Sexual Development*
Public Attitudes *USE Public Opinion*
Public Health
Public Health Service Nurses
Public Health Services
Public Opinion
Public Policy
    USE Government Policy Making
Public Relations
Public School Education
Public Sector
Public Service Announcements
Public Speaking
Public Transportation
Public Welfare Services
    USE Community Welfare Services
Certified Public Accountants *USE Accountants*
Fear of Public Speaking *USE Speech Anxiety*
Puerperal Depression
    USE Postpartum Depression
Puerperal Psychosis
    USE Postpartum Psychosis
Puerto Rican Americans *USE Hispanics*
Hair Pulling *USE Trichotillomania*
Pulmonary Disorders *USE Lung Disorders*
Pulmonary Emphysema
Pulmonary Tuberculosis
Arterial **Pulse**
Punishment
Capital **Punishment**
Corporal Punishment *USE Punishment*
Pupil (Eye)
Pupil Dilation

Purging (Eating Disorders)
Purkinje Cells
Puromycin
Rotary **Pursuit**
Putamen
Pygmalion Effect
    USE Self Fulfilling Prophecies
Pygmy Chimpanzees *USE Bonobos*
Color Pyramid Test
    USE Projective Personality Measures
Pyramidal Tracts
Pyramidotomy
Pyromania
Q Sort Testing Technique
Q Test *USE Cochran Q Test*
Cochran **Q** Test
Quaalude *USE Methaqualone*
Quadriplegia
Quails
Qualitative Methods
    USE Qualitative Research
Qualitative Research
Leadership **Qualities**
Quality Circles
    USE Participative Management
Quality Control
Quality of Care
Quality of Education
    USE Educational Quality
Quality of Life
Quality of Services
Quality of Work Life
Educational **Quality**
Relationship **Quality**
Service Quality *USE Quality of Services*
Quantitative Methods
Quantitative Research
    USE Quantitative Methods
Quantitative Trait Loci
Quasi Experimental Methods
Fundamental Interpersonal Relation
Orientation Behavior **Ques**
Questioning
Childrens Personality **Questionnaire**
General Health **Questionnaire**
High School Personality **Questionnaire**
Sixteen Personality Factors **Questionnaire**
Questionnaires
Opinion Questionnaires *USE Attitude Measures*
Quetiapine
Quinidine *USE Alkaloids*
Quinine
Quinpirole
Intelligence **Quotient**
Rabbis
Rabbits
Race (Anthropological)
Race and Ethnic Discrimination
Race Attitudes
    USE Racial and Ethnic Attitudes
Race Relations
    USE Racial and Ethnic Relations
Racial and Ethnic Attitudes
Racial and Ethnic Differences
Racial and Ethnic Groups
Racial and Ethnic Relations
Racial Differences
    USE Racial and Ethnic Differences
Racial Discrimination
    USE Race and Ethnic Discrimination
Racial Integration *USE Social Integration*
Racism
Radial Nerve *USE Spinal Nerves*
Radiation
Radiation Therapy
Radical Movements
Political **Radicalism**

377

Radio
Radiography *USE Roentgenography*
Radiology
Rage *USE Anger*
Road Rage *USE Aggressive Driving Behavior*
Railroad Trains
Consciousness **Raising** Groups
Random Sampling
Wide **Range** Achievement Test
Rank Difference Correlation
Rank Order Correlation
Sign Rank Test *USE Wilcoxon Sign Rank Test*
Wilcoxon Sign **Rank** Test
Rape
Acquaintance **Rape**
Date Rape *USE Acquaintance Rape*
Raphe Nuclei
Rapid Eye Movement
Rapid Eye Movement Dreams
USE REM Dreams
Rapid Eye Movement Sleep
USE REM Sleep
Rapid Heart Rate *USE Tachycardia*
Rapport *USE Interpersonal Interaction*
Rasch Model *USE Item Response Theory*
Rat Learning
Birth **Rate**
Cardiac Rate *USE Heart Rate*
Death Rate *USE Mortality Rate*
Heart **Rate**
Heart **Rate** Affecting Drugs
Learning **Rate**
Mortality **Rate**
Rapid Heart Rate *USE Tachycardia*
Response Rate *USE Response Frequency*
Speech **Rate**
X Rated Materials *USE Pornography*
Metabolic **Rates**
Rating
Rating Scales
Kupfer Detre Self Rating Scale *USE Nonprojective*
Personality Measures
Zungs Self **Rating** Depression Scale
Ratio Reinforcement
USE Fixed Ratio Reinforcement
Ratio Reinforcement
USE Variable Ratio Reinforcement
Fixed **Ratio** Reinforcement
Variable **Ratio** Reinforcement
Ratiocination *USE Logical Thinking*
Rational Emotive Behavior Therapy
Rational Emotive Therapy *USE Rational*
Emotive Behavior Therapy
Rationalization
Rats
Albino Rats *USE Rats*
Norway **Rats**
White Rats *USE Rats*
Rauwolfia *USE Alkaloids*
Raven Coloured Progressive Matrices
Raven Progressive Matrices
Cathode Ray Tubes *USE Video Display Units*
X Ray Diagnosis *USE Roentgenography*
X Ray Therapy *USE Radiation Therapy*
Raynauds Disease
USE Cardiovascular Disorders
RDC *USE Research Diagnostic Criteria*
Reactance *USE Psychological Reactance*
Psychological **Reactance**
Reaction Formation
Reaction Time
Fugue **Reaction**
Negative Therapeutic **Reaction**
Neurotic Depressive Reaction *USE Major Depression*
Psychotic Depressive Reaction *USE Major Depression*
Anniversary Reactions *USE Anniversary Events*
Drug Adverse Reactions *USE Side Effects (Drug)*

Separation **Reactions**
Stranger **Reactions**
Stress **Reactions**
Reactive Attachment Disorder
USE Attachment Disorders
Reactive Depression
Reactive Psychosis
Reactive Schizophrenia
USE Reactive Psychosis
Reactive Schizophrenia
USE Schizophrenia
Brief Reactive Psychosis *USE Acute Psychosis*
Cardiovascular **Reactivity**
Readability
Readaptation *USE Adaptation*
Basal Readers *USE Reading Materials*
Readiness Potential
USE Contingent Negative Variation
Gates Reading Readiness Tests
USE Gates MacGinitie Reading Tests
Metropolitan **Readiness** Tests
Reading **Readiness**
School **Readiness**
Reading
Reading Ability
Reading Achievement
Reading Aloud *USE Oral Reading*
Reading Comprehension
Reading Development
Reading Disabilities
Reading Education
Reading Materials
Reading Measures
Reading Readiness
Reading Skills
Reading Speed
Gates MacGinitie **Reading** Tests
Gates Reading Readiness Tests
USE Gates MacGinitie Reading Tests
Gates Reading Test
USE Gates MacGinitie Reading Tests
Oral **Reading**
Remedial **Reading**
Silent **Reading**
Psychosocial **Readjustment**
Facility Readmission *USE Facility Admission*
Psychiatric Hospital **Readmission**
Realism (Philosophy)
Reality
Reality Testing
Reality Therapy
Virtual **Reality**
Self Realization *USE Self Actualization*
Home **Reared** Mentally Retarded
Animal **Rearing**
Reasoning
Case Based **Reasoning**
Deductive Reasoning
USE Inductive Deductive Reasoning
Inductive Deductive **Reasoning**
Syllogistic Reasoning
USE Inductive Deductive Reasoning
Sexual Reassignment *USE Sex Change*
Authoritarianism Rebellion Scale *USE Nonprojective*
Personality Measures
Rebelliousness
Recall (Learning)
Cued **Recall**
Dream **Recall**
Free **Recall**
Serial **Recall**
Recency Effect
Receptive Fields
Cutaneous **Receptive** Fields
Visual **Receptive** Fields
Animal Sexual **Receptivity**
Receptor Binding

Acetylcholine Receptors *USE Cholinergic Receptors*
Adrenaline Receptors *USE Adrenergic Receptors*
Adrenergic **Receptors**
Cholinergic **Receptors**
Muscarinic Receptors *USE Cholinergic Receptors*
Neural **Receptors**
Nicotinic Receptors *USE Cholinergic Receptors*
Pain Receptors *USE Nociceptors*
Genetic **Recessiveness**
Recidivism
Reciprocal Inhibition Therapy
Reciprocity
Recognition (Learning)
Automated Speech **Recognition**
Automatic Speaker Recognition
    USE Automated Speech Recognition
Face Recognition *USE Face Perception*
Kinship **Recognition**
Object **Recognition**
Sex **Recognition**
Species **Recognition**
Word **Recognition**
Reconstruction (Learning)
Reconstructive Psychotherapy
    USE Psychotherapy
Graduate **Record** Examination
Kuder Preference **Record**
Tape **Recorders**
Videotape **Recorders**
Academic Records *USE Student Records*
Client **Records**
Medical **Records**
Patient Records *USE Client Records*
Student **Records**
Recovery (Disorders)
Spontaneous **Recovery** (Learning)
Recreation
Recreation Areas
Recreation Therapy
Summer Camps **(Recreation)**
Recreational Day Camps
    USE Summer Camps (Recreation)
Childrens **Recreational** Games
Military **Recruitment**
Personnel **Recruitment**
Teacher **Recruitment**
Recurrent Depression
Recycling *USE Conservation*
    (Ecological Behavior)
Red Blood Cells *USE Erythrocytes*
Red Nucleus *USE Mesencephalon*
Anxiety Reducing Drugs *USE Tranquilizing Drugs*
Harm **Reduction**
Reductionism
Reemployment
Reenactments *USE Enactments*
Reentry Students
Job Reentry *USE Reemployment*
Reference Groups
Self **Reference**
Criterion **Referenced** Tests
Objective Referenced Tests
    USE Criterion Referenced Tests
Professional **Referral**
Self **Referral**
Court **Referrals**
Reflectiveness
Achilles Tendon **Reflex**
Acoustic **Reflex**
Babinski **Reflex**
Blink Reflex *USE Eyeblink Reflex*
Conditioned Reflex *USE Conditioned Responses*
Eyeblink **Reflex**
Flexion **Reflex**
Hoffmanns **Reflex**
Intra Aural Muscle Reflex *USE Acoustic Reflex*
Orienting **Reflex**

Psychogalvanic Reflex *USE Galvanic Skin Response*
Stapedius Reflex *USE Acoustic Reflex*
Startle **Reflex**
Unconditioned Reflex *USE Reflexes*
Reflexes
Educational **Reform**
Reformatories
Refraction Errors
Light **Refraction**
Reframing *USE Paradoxical Techniques*
Refugees
Political Refugees *USE Refugees*
School **Refusal**
Treatment **Refusal**
Neural Regeneration *USE Neural Development*
Medical Regimen Compliance
    USE Treatment Compliance
Regional Differences
Geographic Regions *USE Geography*
Regression (Defense Mechanism)
Regression Analysis
    USE Statistical Regression
Regression Artifact
    USE Statistical Regression
Age **Regression** (Hypnotic)
Linear **Regression**
Logistic **Regression**
Multiple **Regression**
Nonlinear **Regression**
Statistical **Regression**
Self **Regulated** Learning
Self **Regulation**
Regurgitation *USE Vomiting*
Rehabilitation
Rehabilitation Centers
Rehabilitation Counseling
Rehabilitation Counselors
Rehabilitation Education
Alcohol **Rehabilitation**
Cognitive **Rehabilitation**
Criminal **Rehabilitation**
Drug **Rehabilitation**
Neuropsychological **Rehabilitation**
Psychosocial **Rehabilitation**
Vocational **Rehabilitation**
Rehearsal *USE Practice*
Reinforcement
Reinforcement Amounts
Reinforcement Delay
Reinforcement Schedules
Concurrent **Reinforcement** Schedules
Continuous Reinforcement
    USE Reinforcement Schedules
Delayed Reinforcement *USE Reinforcement Delay*
Differential **Reinforcement**
Fixed Interval **Reinforcement**
Fixed Ratio **Reinforcement**
Intermittent Reinforcement
    USE Reinforcement Schedules
Interval Reinforcement
    USE Fixed Interval Reinforcement
Interval Reinforcement
    USE Variable Interval Reinforcement
Negative **Reinforcement**
Noncontingent **Reinforcement**
Nonverbal **Reinforcement**
Partial Reinforcement
    USE Reinforcement Schedules
Positive **Reinforcement**
Primary **Reinforcement**
Ratio Reinforcement
    USE Fixed Ratio Reinforcement
Ratio Reinforcement
    USE Variable Ratio Reinforcement
Secondary **Reinforcement**
Self **Reinforcement**
Social **Reinforcement**

Token Reinforcement
USE Secondary Reinforcement
Variable Interval **Reinforcement**
Variable Ratio **Reinforcement**
Verbal **Reinforcement**
Vicarious Reinforcement *USE Vicarious Experiences*
Reinnervation *USE Neural Development*
Halstead **Reitan** Neuropsychological Battery
Social Rejection *USE Social Acceptance*
Relapse (Disorders)
Relapse Prevention
Criterion Related Validity *USE Test Validity*
Diagnosis **Related** Groups
Event Related Potentials *USE Evoked Potentials*
Work **Related** Illnesses
Fundamental Interpersonal **Relation** Orientation Behavior Ques
Family **Relations**
Father Child **Relations**
Human **Relations** Training
Intergenerational **Relations**
International **Relations**
Labor Management **Relations**
Labor Relations
USE Labor Management Relations
Male Female **Relations**
Marital **Relations**
Mother Child **Relations**
Object **Relations**
Parent Child **Relations**
Patient Therapist Sexual Relations *USE Professional Client*
Sexual Relations
Peer **Relations**
Professional Client Sexual **Relations**
Public **Relations**
Race Relations *USE Racial and Ethnic Relations*
Racial and Ethnic **Relations**
Sibling **Relations**
Therapist Patient Sexual Relations *USE Professional Client*
Sexual Relations
Relationship Quality
Relationship Satisfaction
Relationship Termination
Relationship Therapy
Family Work **Relationship**
Interpersonal Relationship Satisfaction
USE Relationship Satisfaction
Job Family Relationship *USE Family Work Relationship*
Parent School **Relationship**
Work Family Relationship *USE Family Work Relationship*
Dual **Relationships**
Interpersonal **Relationships**
Personal Relationships
USE Interpersonal Relationships
Relativism
Relaxation
Relaxation Therapy
Muscle **Relaxation**
Muscle Relaxation Therapy
USE Relaxation Therapy
Progressive **Relaxation** Therapy
Muscle **Relaxing** Drugs
Relearning
Institutional **Release**
ACTH Releasing Factor
USE Corticotropin Releasing Factor
Corticotropin **Releasing** Factor
Interobserver Reliability *USE Interrater Reliability*
Interrater **Reliability**
Statistical **Reliability**
Test **Reliability**
Pain Relieving Drugs *USE Analgesic Drugs*
Religion
Confession **(Religion)**
Ministers **(Religion)**
Religiosity
Religious Affiliation
Religious Beliefs

Religious Buildings
Religious Education
Religious Experiences
Religious Fundamentalism
Religious Groups
Religious Literature
Religious Occupations
USE Religious Personnel
Religious Organizations
Religious Personnel
Religious Practices
Religious Prejudices
Lay **Religious** Personnel
REM *USE Rapid Eye Movement*
REM Dream Deprivation
REM Dreams
REM Sleep
Remarriage
Remedial Education
Remedial Reading
Remembering *USE Retention*
Reminiscence
Remission (Disorders)
Spontaneous **Remission**
Symptom **Remission**
Renal Diseases *USE Kidney Diseases*
Renal Transplantation
USE Organ Transplantation
Repairmen
USE Technical Service Personnel
Repeated Measures
Bannister **Repertory** Grid
Compulsive **Repetition**
Repetitive Transcranial Magnetic
Stimulation *USE Transcranial*
Magnetic Stimulation
Estrogen Replacement Therapy
USE Hormone Therapy
Experimental **Replication**
Case **Report**
Psychiatric Report *USE Psychological Report*
Psychological **Report**
Self **Report**
Abuse **Reporting**
Child Abuse **Reporting**
Repressed Memory
Repression (Defense Mechanism)
Repression Sensitization
Repression Sensitization Scale
Sensitization Repression *USE Repression Sensitization*
Sexual **Reproduction**
Reproductive Technology
Reptiles
Republican Party *USE Political Parties*
Reputation
Research *USE Experimentation*
Research Design
USE Experimental Design
Research Diagnostic Criteria
Research Dropouts
USE Experimental Attrition
Research Methods *USE Methodology*
Research Setting
Research Subjects
USE Experimental Subjects
Consumer **Research**
Cross Disciplinary Research *USE Interdisciplinary Research*
Interdisciplinary **Research**
Multidisciplinary Research *USE Interdisciplinary Research*
Qualitative **Research**
Quantitative Research *USE Quantitative Methods*
Family **Resemblance**
Resentment *USE Hostility*
Reserpine
Residence Halls *USE Dormitories*
Medical **Residency**
Psychiatric Residency *USE Medical Residency*

380

Psychiatric Residency *USE Psychiatric Training*
Residential Care Attendants
    USE Attendants (Institutions)
Residential Care Institutions
Resilience (Psychological)
Resistance
Basal Skin **Resistance**
Psychotherapeutic **Resistance**
Skin **Resistance**
Treatment **Resistant** Depression
Treatment **Resistant** Disorders
Tricyclic Resistant Depression
    USE Treatment Resistant Depression
Psychosocial Resocialization
    USE Psychosocial Readjustment
Conflict **Resolution**
Resonance *USE Vibration*
Magnetic **Resonance** Imaging
Resource Allocation
Resource Teachers
Human **Resource** Management
Allocation of Resources *USE Resource Allocation*
Human Resources
    USE Human Resource Management
Self Respect *USE Self Esteem*
Respiration
Respiration Stimulating Drugs
Artificial **Respiration**
Respiratory Distress
Respiratory System
Respiratory Tract Disorders
Respite Care
Respondent Conditioning
    USE Classical Conditioning
Response Amplitude
Response Bias
Response Consistency
    USE Response Variability
Response Cost
Response Duration
Response Frequency
Response Generalization
Response Inhibition
Response Lag *USE Reaction Time*
Response Latency
Response Parameters
Response Probability
Response Rate *USE Response Frequency*
Response Set
Response Speed *USE Reaction Time*
Response Time *USE Reaction Time*
Response Variability
Electrodermal Response *USE Galvanic Skin Response*
Galvanic Skin **Response**
Item **Response** Theory
Oculomotor Response *USE Eye Movements*
Responses
Alarm **Responses**
Conditioned Emotional **Responses**
Conditioned **Responses**
Emotional **Responses**
Mediated **Responses**
Orienting **Responses**
Unconditioned **Responses**
Responsibility
Criminal **Responsibility**
Work **Rest** Cycles
Restlessness
Dietary **Restraint**
Emotional Restraint *USE Emotional Control*
Physical **Restraint**
Restricted Environmental Stimulation
    USE Stimulus Deprivation
Cognitive **Restructuring**
Knowledge of **Results**
Retail Stores *USE Retailing*
Retailing

Retaliation
Borderline Mental **Retardation**
Cultural Familial Mental Retardation
    USE Psychosocial Mental Retardation
Mental **Retardation**
Mental **Retardation** (Attitudes Toward)
Mild Mental **Retardation**
Moderate Mental **Retardation**
Profound Mental **Retardation**
Psychosocial Mental **Retardation**
Severe Mental **Retardation**
Retarded Speech Development
Educable Mentally Retarded *USE Mild Mental Retardation*
Home Reared Mentally **Retarded**
Institutionalized Mentally **Retarded**
Trainable Mentally Retarded
    USE Moderate Mental Retardation
Retention
Retention Measures
Benton Revised Visual **Retention** Test
School **Retention**
Reticular Formation
Retina
Ganglion Cells **(Retina)**
Retinal Eccentricity
Retinal Ganglion Cells
    USE Ganglion Cells (Retina)
Retinal Image
Retinal Vessels *USE Arteries (Anatomy)*
Retirement
Retirement Communities
Automated Information **Retrieval**
Retroactive Inhibition
Retrograde Amnesia
Retrospective Studies
Rett Syndrome
Return to Home *USE Empty Nest*
Return to Work *USE Reemployment*
Serotonin **Reuptake** Inhibitors
Revenge *USE Retaliation*
Directed Reverie Therapy *USE Guided Imagery*
Reversal Shift Learning
Life **Review**
Literature **Review**
Peer Review *USE Peer Evaluation*
Benton **Revised** Visual Retention Test
Political **Revolution**
Reward Allocation
Rewards
External **Rewards**
Extrinsic Rewards *USE External Rewards*
Internal **Rewards**
Intrinsic Rewards *USE Internal Rewards*
Monetary **Rewards**
Preferred **Rewards**
Rh Incompatibility
Rheoencephalography
Rhetoric
Rheumatic Fever
Rheumatism *USE Arthritis*
Rheumatoid Arthritis
Spearman Rho *USE Rank Difference Correlation*
Rhodopsin
Rhombencephalon *USE Hindbrain*
Rhyme
Rhythm
Rhythm Method
Alpha **Rhythm**
Delta **Rhythm**
Speech **Rhythm**
Theta **Rhythm**
Animal Biological **Rhythms**
Animal Circadian **Rhythms**
Biological **Rhythms**
Human Biological **Rhythms**
Ribonucleic Acid
Puerto Rican Americans *USE Hispanics*

Right Brain
Right to Treatment
Civil Rights
Civil Rights Movement
Client Rights
Human Rights
Patient Rights *USE Client Rights*
Visitation Rights *USE Child Visitation*
Rigidity (Personality)
Riots
Risk Analysis *USE Risk Assessment*
Risk Assessment
Risk Factors
Risk Management
Risk Perception
Risk Populations *USE At Risk Populations*
Risk Taking
At Risk Populations
High Risk Populations *USE At Risk Populations*
Sexual Risk Taking
Risky Shift *USE Choice Shift*
Risperidone
Ritalin *USE Methylphenidate*
Ritanserin
Rites (Nonreligious)
Rites of Passage
Birth Rites
Death Rites
Initiation Rites
Marriage Rites
Rivalry
Road Rage
USE Aggressive Driving Behavior
Robbery *USE Theft*
Robins
Robotics
Rock Music
Body Rocking
Rod and Frame Test
Rodents
Rods (Eye)
Roentgenography
Rogerian Therapy
USE Client Centered Therapy
Rogers (Carl)
Rohypnol *USE Flunitrazepam*
Rokeach Dogmatism Scale
Role Conflicts
Role Expectations
Role Models
Role Perception
Role Playing
Role Satisfaction
Role Strain *USE Role Conflicts*
Role Taking
Bem Sex Role Inventory
Counselor Role
Gender Role Attitudes *USE Sex Role Attitudes*
Parental Role
Sex Role Attitudes
Sex Role Stereotyping *USE Sex Role Attitudes*
Therapist Role
Roles
Gender Roles *USE Sex Roles*
Sex Roles
Roman Catholicism
Romance
Roommates
Dorsal Roots
Ventral Roots
Rorschach Test
Rosenzweig Picture Frustration Study
Rotary Pursuit
Body Rotation *USE Rotational Behavior*
Mental Rotation
Oblique Rotation
Orthogonal Rotation

Statistical Rotation
Varimax Rotation
Rotational Behavior
ROTC Students
Rote Learning
Rotter Incomplete Sentences Blank
Rotter Internal External Locus of Control Scale
Rubella
Rule Learning
USE Cognitive Hypothesis Testing
Rumination (Cognitive Process)
Rumination (Eating)
Rumors *USE Gossip*
Runaway Behavior
Running
Rural Development
USE Community Development
Rural Environments
Saccadic Eye Movements
USE Eye Movements
Saccharin
Tay Sachs Disease
SAD *USE Seasonal Affective Disorder*
Sadism
Sexual Sadism
Sadness
Sadomasochism
Sadomasochistic Personality
Safe Sex
Safety
Safety Belts
Safety Devices
Safety Warnings *USE Warnings*
Automobile Safety *USE Highway Safety*
Aviation Safety
Driver Safety *USE Highway Safety*
Highway Safety
Industrial Safety *USE Occupational Safety*
Occupational Safety
Water Safety
Saint John's Wort
USE Hypericum Perforatum
Salamanders
Salaries
Sales Personnel
Stimulus Salience
Saliva
Salivary Glands
Salivation
Salmon
Saltiness *USE Taste Perception*
Same Sex Education
Same Sex Environments
USE Single Sex Environments
Sample Size
Matching to Sample
Statistical Sample Parameters
Statistical Samples
Sampling (Experimental)
Biased Sampling
Random Sampling
Sanatoriums
Sarcomas *USE Neoplasms*
SAT *USE College Entrance Examination Board Scholastic Aptitude Test*
Satiation
Satisfaction
Client Satisfaction
Consumer Satisfaction
Customer Satisfaction *USE Consumer Satisfaction*
Interpersonal Relationship Satisfaction *USE Relationship Satisfaction*
Job Satisfaction
Life Satisfaction
Marital Satisfaction
Need Satisfaction
Patient Satisfaction *USE Client Satisfaction*

Relationship **Satisfaction**
Role **Satisfaction**
Sexual **Satisfaction**
Work Satisfaction *USE Job Satisfaction*
Color **Saturation**
Savants
Idiot Savants *USE Savants*
Authoritarianism Rebellion Scale *USE Nonprojective Personality Measures*
California F **Scale**
Childrens Manifest Anxiety **Scale**
Columbia Mental Maturity **Scale**
Edwards Social Desirability **Scale**
Kupfer Detre Self Rating Scale *USE Nonprojective Personality Measures*
Least Preferred Coworker **Scale**
Leiter Adult Intelligence Scale *USE Intelligence Measures*
Marlowe Crowne Social Desirability **Scale**
Repression Sensitization **Scale**
Rokeach Dogmatism **Scale**
Rotter Internal External Locus of Control **Scale**
Sensation Seeking **Scale**
Stanford Binet Intelligence **Scale**
Taylor Manifest Anxiety **Scale**
Temporal Spatial Concept Scale *USE Intelligence Measures*
Tennessee Self Concept **Scale**
Vineland Social Maturity **Scale**
Wechsler Adult Intelligence **Scale**
Wechsler Bellevue Intelligence **Scale**
Wechsler Intelligence **Scale** for Children
Wechsler Memory **Scale**
Wechsler Preschool Primary **Scale**
White Betz A B Scale *USE Nonprojective Personality Measures*
Wilson Patterson Conservatism **Scale**
Zungs Self Rating Depression **Scale**
Bayley **Scales** of Infant Development
Likert **Scales**
Rating **Scales**
Scaling (Testing)
Multidimensional **Scaling**
Scalp (Anatomy)
Scalp Disorders *USE Skin Disorders*
CAT Scan *USE Tomography*
Animal **Scent** Marking
Diagnostic Interview **Schedule**
Edwards Personal Preference **Schedule**
Fear Survey **Schedule**
Concurrent Reinforcement **Schedules**
Interview **Schedules**
Learning **Schedules**
Reinforcement **Schedules**
Work **Scheduling**
Schema
Schizoaffective Disorder
Schizoid Personality Disorder
Schizophrenia
Schizophrenia (Disorganized Type)
Acute **Schizophrenia**
Catatonic **Schizophrenia**
Childhood **Schizophrenia**
Chronic Schizophrenia *USE Schizophrenia*
Fragmentation **(Schizophrenia)**
Hebephrenic Schizophrenia *USE Schizophrenia (Disorganized Type)*
Paranoid **Schizophrenia**
Process Schizophrenia *USE Process Psychosis*
Process Schizophrenia *USE Schizophrenia*
Pseudopsychopathic Schizophrenia *USE Schizophrenia*
Reactive Schizophrenia *USE Reactive Psychosis*
Reactive Schizophrenia *USE Schizophrenia*
Simple Schizophrenia *USE Schizophrenia*
Undifferentiated **Schizophrenia**
Schizophreniform Disorder
Schizophrenogenic Family
Schizophrenogenic Mothers

Schizotypal Personality Disorder
Scholarships
USE Educational Financial Assistance
Scholastic Achievement
USE Academic Achievement
Scholastic Aptitude Test
USE College Entrance Examination Board Scholastic Aptitude Test
Scholastic Aptitude
USE Academic Aptitude
College Entrance Examination Board **Scholastic** Aptitude Test
Preliminary Scholastic Aptitude Test
USE College Entrance Examination Board Scholastic Aptitude Test
School Accreditation
USE Educational Program Accreditation
School Achievement
USE Academic Achievement
School Adjustment
School Administration
USE Educational Administration
School Administrators
School and College Ability Test
USE Aptitude Measures
School Attendance
School Based Intervention
School Club Membership
School Counseling
School Counselors
School Dropouts
School Enrollment
School Environment
School Expulsion
School Facilities
School Federal Aid
USE Educational Financial Assistance
School Financial Assistance
USE Educational Financial Assistance
School Graduation
School Guidance *USE School Counseling*
School Integration
School Learning
School Leavers
School Libraries
School Nurses
School Organization
USE Educational Administration
School Phobia
School Principals
School Psychologists
School Psychology
School Readiness
School Refusal
School Retention
School Superintendents
School Suspension
School to Work Transition
School Transition
School Truancy
School Violence
After **School** Programs
Elementary **School** Students
Elementary **School** Teachers
Freudian Psychoanalytic **School**
High **School** Education
High School Equivalency *USE Adult Education*
High **School** Graduates
High **School** Personality Questionnaire
High **School** Students
High **School** Teachers
Intermediate **School** Students
Junior High **School** Students
Junior High **School** Teachers
Middle **School** Education
Middle **School** Students

Middle **School** Teachers
NeoFreudian School *USE Neopsychoanalytic School*
Neopsychoanalytic **School**
Nursery **School** Students
Parent **School** Relationship
Parochial School Education
    USE Private School Education
Primary **School** Students
Private **School** Education
Public **School** Education
Vocational **School** Students
Home **Schooling**
Schools
Alternative Schools *USE Nontraditional Education*
Boarding **Schools**
Elementary **Schools**
Graduate **Schools**
Grammar Schools *USE Elementary Schools*
High **Schools**
Institutional **Schools**
Junior High **Schools**
Magnet Schools *USE Nontraditional Education*
Middle **Schools**
Military **Schools**
Nongraded **Schools**
Nursery **Schools**
Primary Schools *USE Elementary Schools*
Technical **Schools**
Vocational Schools *USE Technical Schools*
Sciatic Nerve *USE Spinal Nerves*
SCID *USE Structured Clinical Interview*
Science Achievement
Science Education
Cognitive **Science**
Sciences
Behavioral **Sciences**
Medical **Sciences**
Paramedical **Sciences**
Social **Sciences**
Scientific Communication
Scientific Methods
    USE Experimental Methods
Scientists
Sclera *USE Eye (Anatomy)*
Sclerosis (Nervous System)
Multiple **Sclerosis**
Scopolamine
Scopolamine Hydrobromide
    USE Scopolamine
Score Equating
Critical Scores *USE Cutting Scores*
Cutting **Scores**
Standard **Scores**
Test **Scores**
Z Scores *USE Standard Scores*
Scoring (Testing)
Scotopic Stimulation
Scratching
Screening
Screening Tests
Breast Cancer Screening *USE Cancer Screening*
Cancer **Screening**
Drug Usage **Screening**
Genetic Screening *USE Genetic Testing*
Health **Screening**
Job Applicant **Screening**
Prostate Cancer Screening *USE Cancer Screening*
Psychological **Screening** Inventory
Skin Cancer Screening *USE Cancer Screening*
Scripts *USE Schema*
Sculpturing
Sea Gulls
Seals (Animal)
Job **Search**
Visual **Search**
Computer **Searching**
Online Searching *USE Computer Searching*

Seasonal Affective Disorder
Seasonal Variations
Seat Belts *USE Safety Belts*
Patient **Seclusion**
Secobarbital
Seconal *USE Secobarbital*
Second Language Education
    USE Foreign Language Education
Second Order Conditioning
    USE Higher Order Conditioning
English as **Second** Language
Secondary Education
Secondary Reinforcement
Secrecy
Secretarial Personnel
Secretarial Skills
    USE Clerical Secretarial Skills
Clerical **Secretarial** Skills
Secretion (Gland)
Adrenal Gland **Secretion**
Endocrine Gland **Secretion**
Private **Sector**
Public **Sector**
Emotional **Security**
Job **Security**
Maximum **Security** Facilities
Social **Security**
Sedatives
Seduction
Seeing Eye Dogs *USE Mobility Aids*
Health Care **Seeking** Behavior
Help **Seeking** Behavior
Information **Seeking**
Novelty Seeking *USE Sensation Seeking*
Sensation **Seeking**
Sensation **Seeking** Scale
Treatment Seeking Behavior
    USE Health Care Seeking Behavior
Seizures *USE Convulsions*
Audiogenic **Seizures**
Epileptic **Seizures**
Selection Tests
Animal Mate **Selection**
Employee Selection *USE Personnel Selection*
Habitat Selection *USE Territoriality*
Human Mate **Selection**
Job Selection *USE Occupational Choice*
Jury **Selection**
Mate Selection *USE Animal Mate Selection*
Mate Selection *USE Human Mate Selection*
Natural **Selection**
Patient **Selection**
Personnel **Selection**
Therapist **Selection**
Toy **Selection**
Selective Attention
Selective Breeding
Selective Mutism *USE Elective Mutism*
Self Acceptance *USE Self Perception*
Self Actualization
Self Analysis
Self Assessment *USE Self Evaluation*
Self Care Skills
Self Concept
Self Confidence
Self Congruence
Self Consciousness *USE Self Perception*
Self Control
Self Criticism
Self Defeating Behavior
Self Defense
Self Destructive Behavior
Self Determination
Self Directed Learning
    USE Individualized Instruction
Self Disclosure
Self Efficacy

Self Employment
Self Esteem
Self Evaluation
Self Examination (Medical)
Self Fulfilling Prophecies
Self Handicapping Strategy
Self Help Techniques
Self Hypnosis *USE Autohypnosis*
Self Image *USE Self Concept*
Self Inflicted Wounds
Self Injurious Behavior
    USE Self Destructive Behavior
Self Instruction
    USE Individualized Instruction
Self Instructional Training
Self Management
Self Managing Work Teams
Self Medication
Self Monitoring
Self Monitoring (Personality)
Self Mutilation
Self Observation *USE Self Monitoring*
Self Perception
Self Preservation
Self Psychology
Self Realization *USE Self Actualization*
Self Reference
Self Referral
Self Regulated Learning
Self Regulation
Self Reinforcement
Self Report
Self Respect *USE Self Esteem*
Self Stimulation
Self Talk
Academic **Self** Concept
Brain **Self** Stimulation
Child **Self** Care
Drug **Self** Administration
Ideal Self *USE Self Concept*
Intracranial Self Stimulation *USE Brain Self Stimulation*
Kupfer Detre Self Rating Scale *USE Nonprojective*
    Personality Measures
Tennessee **Self** Concept Scale
Zungs **Self** Rating Depression Scale
Selfishness
Semantic Differential
Semantic Generalization
Semantic Memory
Semantic Priming
Semantics
Semicircular Canals
Seminarians
Seminaries
Semiotics
Senile Dementia
Senile Psychosis
Sensation *USE Perception*
Sensation Seeking
Sensation Seeking Scale
Pressure **Sensation**
Sense Organ Disorders
Sense Organs
Cutaneous **Sense**
Vomeronasal **Sense**
Sensitivity (Personality)
Sensitivity Training
Cultural **Sensitivity**
Drug **Sensitivity**
Ethnic Sensitivity *USE Cultural Sensitivity*
Spectral Sensitivity *USE Color Perception*
Sensitization Repression
    USE Repression Sensitization
Covert **Sensitization**
Protein Sensitization *USE Anaphylactic Shock*
Repression **Sensitization**
Repression **Sensitization** Scale

Sensorially Handicapped
    USE Sensory System Disorders
Sensorimotor Development
    USE Perceptual Motor Development
Sensorimotor Measures
Sensorimotor Processes
    USE Perceptual Motor Processes
Sensorineural Hearing Loss
    USE Hearing Disorders
Sensory Adaptation
Sensory Deprivation
Sensory Disabilities (Attitudes Toward)
Sensory Feedback
Sensory Gating
Sensory Integration
Sensory Neglect
Sensory Neurons
Sensory Pathways *USE Afferent Pathways*
Sensory Preconditioning
    USE Preconditioning
Sensory System Disorders
Sentence Completion Tests
Sentence Comprehension
Sentence Structure
Sentences
Rotter Incomplete **Sentences** Blank
Sentencing *USE Adjudication*
Separation Anxiety
Separation Individuation
Separation Reactions
Marital **Separation**
Septal Nuclei
Septum *USE Septal Nuclei*
Sequential Learning
Serial Anticipation (Learning)
Serial Homicide
Serial Learning
Serial Murder *USE Serial Homicide*
Serial Position Effect
Serial Recall
Time **Series**
Seriousness
Serotonin
Serotonin Agonists
Serotonin Antagonists
Serotonin Metabolites
Serotonin Precursors
Serotonin Reuptake Inhibitors
Serpasil *USE Reserpine*
Sertraline
Serum Albumin
Blood **Serum**
Civil Servants *USE Government Personnel*
Service Personnel
Service Quality *USE Quality of Services*
Domestic **Service** Personnel
Fee for **Service**
Health **Service** Needs
Health Service Utilization
    USE Health Care Utilization
Mental Health Service Needs *USE Health Service Needs*
Public Health **Service** Nurses
Public **Service** Announcements
Technical **Service** Personnel
Servicemen *USE Military Personnel*
Community Mental Health **Services**
Community Welfare **Services**
Community **Services**
Crisis Intervention **Services**
Emergency **Services**
Health Care **Services**
Hot Line **Services**
Information **Services**
Integrated **Services**
Interagency Services *USE Integrated Services*
Mental Health **Services**
Protective **Services**

Public Health **Services**
Public Welfare Services *USE Community Welfare Services*
Quality of **Services**
Social **Services**
Student Personnel **Services**
Web Based Mental Health Services *USE Online Therapy*
Welfare **Services** (Government)
Fuzzy **Set** Theory
Response **Set**
Experimental Setting *USE Research Setting*
Goal **Setting**
Research **Setting**
Severe Mental Retardation
Severity (Disorders)
Sex
Sex Change
Sex Chromosome Disorders
Sex Chromosomes
Sex Differentiation Disorders
    USE Genital Disorders
Sex Discrimination
Sex Drive
Sex Education
Sex Hormones
Sex Linked Developmental Differences
Sex Linked Hereditary Disorders
Sex Offenses
Sex Recognition
Sex Role Attitudes
Sex Role Stereotyping
    USE Sex Role Attitudes
Sex Roles
Sex Therapy
Animal **Sex** Differences
Bem **Sex** Role Inventory
Human **Sex** Differences
Safe **Sex**
Same **Sex** Education
Same Sex Environments
    USE Single Sex Environments
Single Sex Education *USE Same Sex Education*
Single **Sex** Environments
Sterilization **(Sex)**
Sexism
Sexual Abstinence
Sexual Abuse
Sexual Addiction
Sexual Arousal
Sexual Attitudes
Sexual Attraction
Sexual Behavior
    USE Psychosexual Behavior
Sexual Boundary Violations
    USE Professional Client Sexual
    Relations
Sexual Compulsivity *USE Sexual Addiction*
Sexual Delinquency *USE Promiscuity*
Sexual Development
Sexual Deviations *USE Paraphilias*
Sexual Fantasy
Sexual Fetishism *USE Fetishism*
Sexual Function Disturbances
Sexual Harassment
Sexual Intercourse (Human)
Sexual Masochism
Sexual Orientation
Sexual Partners
Sexual Reassignment *USE Sex Change*
Sexual Reproduction
Sexual Risk Taking
Sexual Sadism
Sexual Satisfaction
Animal **Sexual** Behavior
Animal **Sexual** Receptivity
Endocrine **Sexual** Disorders
Hypoactive Sexual Desire Disorder
    USE Inhibited Sexual Desire

Inhibited **Sexual** Desire
Patient Therapist Sexual Relations
    USE Professional Client Sexual
    Relations
Professional Client **Sexual** Relations
Therapist Patient Sexual Relations
    USE Professional Client Sexual
    Relations
Sexuality
Sexually Transmitted Diseases
Shamanism
Shame
Shape Perception
    USE Form and Shape Perception
Form and **Shape** Perception
Shared Paranoid Disorder
    USE Folie A Deux
Sharing (Social Behavior)
Needle **Sharing**
Myelin **Sheath**
Sheep
Sheltered Workshops
Shelters
Choice **Shift**
Extradimensional Shift Learning
    USE Nonreversal Shift Learning
Nonreversal **Shift** Learning
Reversal **Shift** Learning
Risky Shift *USE Choice Shift*
Population Shifts *USE Human Migration*
Workday **Shifts**
Shock
Shock Therapy
Shock Units
Anaphylactic **Shock**
Culture **Shock**
Electroconvulsive **Shock**
Electroconvulsive **Shock** Therapy
Insulin **Shock** Therapy
Shoplifting
Shopping
Shopping Centers
Short Term Memory
Short Term Potentiation
    USE Postactivation Potentials
Short Term Psychotherapy
    USE Brief Psychotherapy
Shoulder (Anatomy)
Shuttle Box Grids *USE Shuttle Boxes*
Shuttle Box Hurdles *USE Shuttle Boxes*
Shuttle Boxes
Shyness *USE Timidity*
Siamese Twins *USE Conjoined Twins*
Sibling Relations
Siblings
Sick Leave *USE Employee Leave Benefits*
Sickle Cell Disease
Motion **Sickness**
Side Effects (Drug)
Side Effects (Treatment)
Sight Vocabulary
Partially **Sighted**
Freud **(Sigmund)**
Sign Language
Sign Rank Test
    USE Wilcoxon Sign Rank Test
Sign Test
Wilcoxon **Sign** Rank Test
Signal Detection (Perception)
Signal Intensity *USE Stimulus Intensity*
Statistical **Significance**
Significant Others
Warning Signs *USE Warnings*
Sikhism
Sikhs
Silence
Silent Reading

Attitude **Similarity**
Stimulus **Similarity**
Simile *USE Figurative Language*
Simple Schizophrenia *USE Schizophrenia*
Herpes **Simplex**
Simulation
Simulation Games
Computer **Simulation**
Flight **Simulation**
Simulators *USE Simulation*
Sin
Sincerity
Singing
Single Cell Organisms
    USE Microorganisms
Single Fathers
Single Mothers
Single Parents
Single Persons
Single Sex Education
    USE Same Sex Education
Single Sex Environments
Sisters
Sixteen Personality Factors Questionnaire
Size
Size Constancy
Size Discrimination
Apparent **Size**
Body **Size**
Brain **Size**
Class **Size**
Effect **Size** (Statistical)
Family **Size**
Group **Size**
Litter **Size**
Sample **Size**
Skeletomuscular Disorders
    USE Musculoskeletal Disorders
Skepticism
Skewed Distribution
Skill Learning
Fine Motor **Skill** Learning
Gross Motor **Skill** Learning
Motor Skill Learning
    USE Perceptual Motor Learning
Skilled Industrial Workers
Skills *USE Ability*
Basic Skills Testing
    USE Minimum Competency Tests
Clerical Secretarial **Skills**
Communication **Skills**
Communication **Skills** Training
Employee **Skills**
Iowa Tests of Basic **Skills**
Motor **Skills**
Parenting **Skills**
Reading **Skills**
Secretarial Skills *USE Clerical Secretarial Skills*
Self Care **Skills**
Social **Skills**
Social **Skills** Training
Study Skills *USE Study Habits*
Writing **Skills**
Skin (Anatomy)
Skin Cancer Screening
    USE Cancer Screening
Skin Conduction *USE Skin Resistance*
Skin Disorders
Skin Electrical Properties
Skin Potential
Skin Resistance
Skin Temperature
Allergic **Skin** Disorders
Basal **Skin** Resistance
Galvanic **Skin** Response
Skinner (Burrhus Frederic)
Skinner Boxes

Skull
Slang
Sleep
Sleep Apnea
Sleep Deprivation
Sleep Disorders
Sleep Inducing Drugs *USE Hypnotic Drugs*
Sleep Monitoring *USE Polysomnography*
Sleep Onset
Sleep Talking
Sleep Treatment
Sleep Wake Cycle
Nonrapid Eye Movement Sleep *USE NREM Sleep*
NonREM Sleep *USE NREM Sleep*
NREM **Sleep**
Paradoxical Sleep *USE REM Sleep*
Paroxysmal Sleep *USE Narcolepsy*
Rapid Eye Movement Sleep *USE REM Sleep*
REM **Sleep**
Slow Wave Sleep *USE NREM Sleep*
Sleeplessness *USE Insomnia*
Sleepwalking
Slosson Intelligence Test
Slow Learners
    USE Borderline Mental Retardation
Slow Wave Sleep *USE NREM Sleep*
Slums *USE Poverty Areas*
Smell Perception *USE Olfactory Perception*
Smiles
Kolmogorov **Smirnov** Test
Smokeless Tobacco
Smoking Cessation
Cigarette Smoking *USE Tobacco Smoking*
Tobacco **Smoking**
Snails
Snake Phobia *USE Ophidiophobia*
Snakes
Glue **Sniffing**
Snuff *USE Smokeless Tobacco*
Sobriety
Soccer
Sociability
Social Acceptance
Social Adaptation *USE Social Adjustment*
Social Adjustment
Social Anxiety
Social Anxiety Disorder *USE Social Phobia*
Social Approval
Social Behavior
Social Capital
Social Casework
Social Caseworkers *USE Social Workers*
Social Change
Social Class
Social Class Attitudes
    USE Socioeconomic Class Attitudes
Social Cognition
Social Comparison
Social Competence *USE Social Skills*
Social Control
Social Dating
Social Demonstrations
Social Density
Social Deprivation
Social Desirability
Social Development
    USE Psychosocial Development
Social Dilemma
Social Discrimination
Social Drinking
Social Environments
Social Equality
Social Facilitation
Social Groups
Social Identity
Social Immobility *USE Social Mobility*
Social Influences

Social Integration
Social Interaction
Social Isolation
Social Issues
Social Learning
Social Loafing
Social Maladjustment
    USE Social Adjustment
Social Mobility
Social Movements
Social Networks
Social Norms
Social Perception
Social Phobia
Social Problems *USE Social Issues*
Social Processes
Social Programs
Social Psychiatry
Social Psychologists
Social Psychology
Social Reinforcement
Social Rejection *USE Social Acceptance*
Social Sciences
Social Security
Social Services
Social Skills
Social Skills Training
Social Stigma *USE Stigma*
Social Stress
Social Structure
Social Studies Education
Social Support
Social Support Networks
    USE Social Support
Social Values
Social Work Education
Social Work *USE Social Casework*
Social Workers
Animal Social Behavior
Assistance (Social Behavior)
Clubs (Social Organizations)
Edwards Social Desirability Scale
Equity (Social)
Marlowe Crowne Social Desirability Scale
Psychiatric Social Workers
Sharing (Social Behavior)
Therapeutic Social Clubs
Trust (Social Behavior)
Vineland Social Maturity Scale
Socialism
Socialization
Political Socialization
Socially Disadvantaged
    USE Disadvantaged
Society
Sociobiology
Sociocultural Factors
Socioeconomic Class Attitudes
Socioeconomic Status
Family Socioeconomic Level
Socioenvironmental Therapy
    USE Milieu Therapy
Sociograms
Sociolinguistics
Sociologists
Sociology
Sociometric Tests
Sociometry
Sociopath
    USE Antisocial Personality Disorder
Sociopathology *USE Antisocial Behavior*
Sociotherapy
Sodium
Sodium Ions
Sodium Lactate *USE Lactic Acid*
Sodium Pentobarbital *USE Pentobarbital*
Amobarbital Sodium *USE Amobarbital*

Diphenylhydantoin Sodium *USE Diphenylhydantoin*
Computer Software
Solution Focused Therapy
Solvent Abuse *USE Inhalant Abuse*
Solvents
Anagram Problem Solving
Group Problem Solving
Individual Problem Solving *USE Problem Solving*
Problem Solving
Somatization
Somatization Disorder
Somatoform Disorders
Somatoform Pain Disorder
Atypical Somatoform Disorder
    USE Body Dysmorphic Disorder
Somatosensory Cortex
Somatosensory Disorders
Somatosensory Evoked Potentials
Somatostatin
Somatotropin
Somatotypes
Somesthetic Perception
Somesthetic Stimulation
Somnambulism *USE Sleepwalking*
Sonar
Songs *USE Music*
Sons
Sorority Membership
Q Sort Testing Technique
Wisconsin Card Sorting Test
Soul
Sound *USE Auditory Stimulation*
Sound Localization
    USE Auditory Localization
Sound Pressure Level *USE Loudness*
Sound Waves *USE Acoustics*
Source Monitoring
Sourness *USE Taste Perception*
South Asian Cultural Groups
South East Asian Cultural Groups
    USE Southeast Asian Cultural Groups
Southeast Asian Cultural Groups
Personal Space
Working Space
Spacecraft
Spaceflight
Attention Span
Digit Span Testing
Life Span
Spanish Americans *USE Hispanics*
Spasms
Muscle Spasms
Spatial Ability
Spatial Discrimination
    USE Spatial Perception
Spatial Distortion
Spatial Frequency
Spatial Imagery
Spatial Learning
Spatial Memory
Spatial Neglect *USE Sensory Neglect*
Spatial Organization
Spatial Orientation (Perception)
Spatial Perception
Temporal Spatial Concept Scale
    USE Intelligence Measures
Visual Spatial Ability *USE Visuospatial Ability*
Visual Spatial Memory *USE Visuospatial Memory*
Automatic Speaker Recognition
    USE Automated Speech Recognition
Fear of Public Speaking *USE Speech Anxiety*
Public Speaking
Spearman Brown Test
Spearman Rho
    USE Rank Difference Correlation
Special Education
Special Education Students

Special Education Teachers
Special Needs
Information **Specialists**
Academic **Specialization**
Hemispheric Specialization *USE Lateral Dominance*
Professional **Specialization**
Species Differences
Species Recognition
Culture Specific Syndromes
    USE Culture Bound Syndromes
Sports **Spectators**
Spectral Sensitivity *USE Color Perception*
Autism Spectrum Disorders *USE Pervasive*
    Developmental Disorders
Speech *USE Oral Communication*
Speech and Hearing Measures
Speech Anxiety
Speech Characteristics
Speech Development
Speech Disorders
Speech Handicapped
    USE Speech Disorders
Speech Measures
    USE Speech and Hearing Measures
Speech Pauses
Speech Perception
Speech Pitch
Speech Processing (Mechanical)
Speech Rate
Speech Rhythm
Speech Therapists
Speech Therapy
Accelerated Speech *USE Speech Rate*
Articulation **(Speech)**
Automated **Speech** Recognition
Compressed **Speech**
Delayed Speech
    USE Retarded Speech Development
Figures of Speech *USE Figurative Language*
Filtered **Speech**
Inner Speech *USE Self Talk*
Retarded **Speech** Development
Synthetic **Speech**
Speechreading *USE Lipreading*
Speed *USE Velocity*
Cognitive Processing **Speed**
Information Processing Speed *USE Cognitive Processing Speed*
Reading **Speed**
Response Speed *USE Reaction Time*
Spelling
Sperm
Sperm Donation *USE Tissue Donation*
Spider Phobia *USE Phobias*
Spiders *USE Arachnida*
Spina Bifida
Spinal Column
Spinal Cord
Spinal Cord Injuries
Spinal Fluid *USE Cerebrospinal Fluid*
Spinal Ganglia
Spinal Nerves
Cranial **Spinal** Cord
Lumbar **Spinal** Cord
Spinothalamic Tracts
Spiperone *USE Spiroperidol*
Spirit Possession
Spirituality
Spiroperidol
Spleen
Split Brain *USE Commissurotomy*
Split Personality
    USE Dissociative Identity Disorder
Spontaneous Abortion
Spontaneous Alternation
Spontaneous Recovery (Learning)
Spontaneous Remission

Sport Performance
    USE Athletic Performance
Sport Psychology
Sport Training *USE Athletic Training*
Sports
Sports (Attitudes Toward)
Sports Spectators
Sportsmanship
    USE Sports (Attitudes Toward)
Sportspersonship
    USE Sports (Attitudes Toward)
Spouse Abuse *USE Partner Abuse*
Spouses
Cervical Sprain Syndrome *USE Whiplash*
Spreading Depression
Chi **Square** Test
Least **Squares**
Squirrels
St. John's Wort *USE Hypericum Perforatum*
Emotional **Stability**
Hospital Staff *USE Medical Personnel*
Psychiatric Hospital **Staff**
Stage Plays *USE Theatre*
Developmental **Stages**
Prenatal Developmental **Stages**
Stalking
Stammering *USE Stuttering*
Competency to **Stand** Trial
Standard Deviation
Standard Error of Measurement
    USE Error of Measurement
Standard Scores
Test **Standardization**
Standardized Tests
Professional **Standards**
Stanford Achievement Test
Stanford Binet Intelligence Scale
Stanines *USE Standard Scores*
Stapedius Reflex *USE Acoustic Reflex*
Starfish *USE Echinodermata*
Head Start *USE Project Head Start*
Project Head **Start**
Startle Reflex
Starvation
State Board Examinations
    USE Professional Examinations
State Dependent Learning
State Hospitals *USE Psychiatric Hospitals*
State Trait Anxiety Inventory
Mini Mental **State** Examination
Borderline **States**
Consciousness **States**
Emotional **States**
Statistical Analysis
Statistical Correlation
Statistical Data
Statistical Estimation
Statistical Measurement
Statistical Norms
Statistical Power
Statistical Probability
Statistical Regression
Statistical Reliability
Statistical Rotation
Statistical Sample Parameters
Statistical Samples
Statistical Significance
Statistical Tables
Statistical Tests
Statistical Validity
Statistical Variables
Statistical Weighting
Diagnostic and **Statistical** Manual
Effect Size **(Statistical)**
Item Analysis **(Statistical)**
Nonparametric **Statistical** Tests
Parametric **Statistical** Tests

Statistics
Confidence Limits **(Statistics)**
Interaction Analysis **(Statistics)**
Population **(Statistics)**
Status
Employment **Status**
Functional Status *USE Ability Level*
Job Status *USE Occupational Status*
Marital **Status**
Occupational **Status**
Parenthood **Status**
Socioeconomic **Status**
Length of Stay *USE Treatment Duration*
Stealing *USE Theft*
Stelazine *USE Trifluoperazine*
Stellate Ganglion *USE Autonomic Ganglia*
Brain **Stem**
Twelve **Step** Programs
Stepchildren
Stepfamily
Stepparents
Stereopsis *USE Stereoscopic Vision*
Stereoscopic Presentation
Stereoscopic Vision
Stereotaxic Atlas
Stereotaxic Techniques
Stereotyped Attitudes
Stereotyped Behavior
Stereotyping *USE Stereotyped Attitudes*
Sex Role Stereotyping *USE Sex Role Attitudes*
Sterility
Sterilization (Sex)
Steroids
Adrenal Cortex Steroids *USE Corticosteroids*
Sticklebacks
Stigma
Social Stigma *USE Stigma*
Stimulants of CNS
USE CNS Stimulating Drugs
CNS **Stimulating** Drugs
Follicle **Stimulating** Hormone
Melanocyte **Stimulating** Hormone
Respiration **Stimulating** Drugs
Thyroid Stimulating Hormone *USE Thyrotropin*
Stimulation
Afferent **Stimulation**
Auditory **Stimulation**
Aversive **Stimulation**
Brain Self **Stimulation**
Brain **Stimulation**
Chemical Brain **Stimulation**
Dichoptic **Stimulation**
Dichotic **Stimulation**
Electrical Brain **Stimulation**
Electrical **Stimulation**
Intracranial Self Stimulation *USE Brain Self Stimulation*
Olfactory **Stimulation**
Perceptual **Stimulation**
Photopic **Stimulation**
Prismatic **Stimulation**
Repetitive Transcranial Magnetic Stimulation
USE Transcranial Magnetic Stimulation
Restricted Environmental Stimulation *USE Stimulus Deprivation*
Scotopic **Stimulation**
Self **Stimulation**
Somesthetic **Stimulation**
Subliminal **Stimulation**
Tactual **Stimulation**
Taste **Stimulation**
Transcranial Magnetic **Stimulation**
Vestibular Stimulation *USE Somesthetic Stimulation*
Visual **Stimulation**
Stimulators (Apparatus)
Acoustic Stimuli *USE Auditory Stimulation*
Novel Stimuli *USE Stimulus Novelty*
Pictorial **Stimuli**
Verbal **Stimuli**

Stimulus Ambiguity
Stimulus Attenuation
Stimulus Change
Stimulus Complexity
Stimulus Control
Stimulus Deprivation
Stimulus Discrimination
Stimulus Duration
Stimulus Frequency
Stimulus Generalization
Stimulus Intensity
Stimulus Intervals
Stimulus Novelty
Stimulus Offset
Stimulus Onset
Stimulus Parameters
Stimulus Pattern *USE Stimulus Variability*
Stimulus Presentation Methods
Stimulus Salience
Stimulus Similarity
Stimulus Variability
Conditioned **Stimulus**
Discriminative Stimulus *USE Conditioned Stimulus*
Unconditioned **Stimulus**
Stipends
USE Educational Financial Assistance
Stochastic Modeling
Stomach
Automated Information **Storage**
Human Information **Storage**
Retail Stores *USE Retailing*
Storytelling
Storytelling Technique
USE Mutual Storytelling Technique
Mutual **Storytelling** Technique
Strabismus
Animal **Strain** Differences
Role Strain *USE Role Conflicts*
Stranger Reactions
Fear of Strangers *USE Stranger Reactions*
Strategies
Learning **Strategies**
Self Handicapping **Strategy**
Physical **Strength**
Stress
Stress Management
Stress Reactions
Acute **Stress** Disorder
Chronic **Stress**
Environmental **Stress**
Job Stress *USE Occupational Stress*
Occupational **Stress**
Physiological **Stress**
Posttraumatic **Stress** Disorder
Psychological **Stress**
Social **Stress**
Work Stress *USE Occupational Stress*
Striate Cortex *USE Visual Cortex*
Striatum
Corpus Striatum *USE Basal Ganglia*
Ventral Striatum *USE Basal Ganglia*
Strikes
Film **Strips**
Stroboscopic Movement
USE Apparent Movement
Strong Vocational Interest Blank
Stroop Color Word Test
Stroop Effect
Structural Equation Modeling
Structuralism
Factor **Structure**
Family **Structure**
Group **Structure**
Household Structure *USE Living Arrangements*
Kinship **Structure**
Organizational **Structure**
Sentence **Structure**

Social **Structure**
Text **Structure**
Structured Clinical Interview
Structured Overview
    USE Advance Organizers
Strychnine
Student Activism
Student Adjustment
    USE School Adjustment
Student Admission Criteria
Student Attitudes
Student Attrition
Student Characteristics
Student Personnel Services
Student Protest *USE Student Activism*
Student Records
Student Teachers
Student Teaching
Teacher **Student** Interaction
Students
Students T Test *USE T Test*
Business **Students**
College **Students**
Community College **Students**
Dental **Students**
Education **Students**
Elementary School **Students**
Foreign **Students**
Graduate **Students**
High School **Students**
Intermediate School **Students**
Junior College **Students**
Junior High School **Students**
Kindergarten **Students**
Law **Students**
Medical **Students**
Middle School **Students**
Nursery School **Students**
Nursing **Students**
Postgraduate **Students**
Preschool **Students**
Primary School **Students**
Reentry **Students**
ROTC **Students**
Special Education **Students**
Transfer **Students**
Vocational School **Students**
Followup **Studies**
Longitudinal **Studies**
Prospective **Studies**
Retrospective **Studies**
Social **Studies** Education
Study Habits
Study Skills *USE Study Habits*
Allport Vernon Lindzey Study Values *USE Attitude Measures*
Foreign **Study**
Independent Study *USE Individualized Instruction*
Rosenzweig Picture Frustration **Study**
Work Study Programs
    USE Educational Programs
Stuttering
Cognitive **Style**
Leadership **Style**
Learning Style *USE Cognitive Style*
Parenting **Style**
Perceptual **Style**
Subconscious
Subcortical Lesions *USE Brain Lesions*
Subculture (Anthropological)
Subcutaneous Injections
Subjectivity
Experimental **Subjects**
Research Subjects *USE Experimental Subjects*
Within Subjects Design *USE Repeated Measures*
Sublimation
Subliminal Perception
Subliminal Stimulation

Submarines
Submissiveness *USE Obedience*
Submucous Plexus
    USE Autonomic Ganglia
Substance Abuse Prevention
    USE Drug Abuse Prevention
Substance Abuse *USE Drug Abuse*
Substance P
Substantia Nigra
Subtests
Subtypes (Disorders)
Suburban Environments
Subvocalization
Success *USE Achievement*
Fear of **Success**
Occupational **Success**
Occupational **Success** Prediction
Successive Contrast *USE Afterimage*
Succinylcholine
Sucking
Sudden Infant Death
Suffering
Suffocation *USE Anoxia*
Blood **Sugar**
Sugars
Suggestibility
Posthypnotic **Suggestions**
Suicidal Ideation
Suicide
Suicide Prevention
Suicide Prevention Centers
Assisted **Suicide**
Attempted **Suicide**
Amphetamine Sulfate *USE Amphetamine*
Codeine Sulfate *USE Codeine*
Sulpiride
Non Zero **Sum** Games
Summer Campo (Recreation)
Superego
School **Superintendents**
Superior Colliculus
Emotional **Superiority**
Superstitions
Supervising Teachers
    USE Cooperating Teachers
Clinical Supervision *USE Professional Supervision*
Educational Supervision *USE Professional Supervision*
Practicum **Supervision**
Professional **Supervision**
Supervisor Employee Interaction
Employee Supervisor Interaction
    USE Supervisor Employee Interaction
Supervisors *USE Management Personnel*
Dietary **Supplements**
Nutritional Supplements *USE Dietary Supplements*
Supply and Demand
Medical Personnel **Supply**
Mental Health Personnel **Supply**
Personnel **Supply**
Support Groups
Child **Support**
Decision **Support** Systems
Social **Support**
Social Support Networks *USE Social Support*
Supported Employment
Computer Supported Cooperative Work
    USE Groupware
Supportive Psychotherapy
Suppression (Defense Mechanism)
Conditioned **Suppression**
Dexamethasone **Suppression** Test
Thought **Suppression**
Progressive **Supranuclear** Palsy
Surgeons
Surgery
Cardiac Surgery *USE Heart Surgery*
Dental **Surgery**

Endocrine Gland **Surgery**
Heart **Surgery**
Pituitary Gland Surgery *USE Hypophysectomy*
Plastic **Surgery**
Surgical Complications
    USE Postsurgical Complications
Surgical Patients
Surrogate Parents (Humans)
Fear **Survey** Schedule
Guilford Zimmerman Temperament **Survey**
Kuder Occupational Interest **Survey**
Opinion Attitude and Interest Survey *USE Attitude Measures*
Surveys
Consumer **Surveys**
Mail **Surveys**
Opinion Surveys *USE Attitude Measures*
Telephone **Surveys**
Survival Instinct *USE Self Preservation*
Survivors
Holocaust **Survivors**
Susceptibility (Disorders)
Hypnotic **Susceptibility**
School **Suspension**
Suspicion
Sustained Attention
Life **Sustaining** Treatment
Swallowing
Mate Swapping *USE Extramarital Intercourse*
Body **Sway** Testing
Sweat
Sweating
Sweetness *USE Taste Perception*
Swimming
Code **Switching**
Nonsense **Syllable** Learning
Syllables
Syllogistic Reasoning
    USE Inductive Deductive Reasoning
Biological **Symbiosis**
Symbiotic Infantile Psychosis
Symbolic Interactionism
Symbolism
Sympathectomy
Sympathetic Nervous System
Sympatholytic Drugs
Sympathomimetic Amines
Sympathomimetic Drugs
Sympathy
Symptom Checklists
Symptom Prescription
    USE Paradoxical Techniques
Symptom Remission
Symptoms
Extrapyramidal **Symptoms**
Negative and Positive Symptoms
    USE Positive and Negative Symptoms
Positive and Negative **Symptoms**
Psychiatric **Symptoms**
Psychotic Symptoms *USE Psychiatric Symptoms*
Synapses
Synaptic Transmission
    USE Neurotransmission
Syncope
Acquired Immune Deficiency **Syndrome**
Aspergers **Syndrome**
Battered Child **Syndrome**
Capgras **Syndrome**
Cervical Sprain Syndrome *USE Whiplash*
Chronic Fatigue **Syndrome**
Creutzfeldt Jakob **Syndrome**
Cri du Chat Syndrome *USE Crying Cat Syndrome*
Crying Cat **Syndrome**
Cushings **Syndrome**
Downs **Syndrome**
Fetal Alcohol **Syndrome**
Fragile X **Syndrome**
Ganser Syndrome *USE Factitious Disorders*

Hospital Addiction Syndrome *USE Munchausen Syndrome*
Irritable Bowel **Syndrome**
Kleine Levin **Syndrome**
Klinefelters **Syndrome**
Munchausen **Syndrome**
Munchausen **Syndrome** by Proxy
Neuroleptic Malignant **Syndrome**
Prader Willi **Syndrome**
Premenstrual **Syndrome**
Rett **Syndrome**
Temporomandibular Joint Syndrome *USE Musculoskeletal Disorders*
Testicular Feminization **Syndrome**
Tourette Syndrome
    USE Gilles de la Tourette Disorder
Turners **Syndrome**
Wernickes **Syndrome**
Williams **Syndrome**
Syndromes
Culture Bound **Syndromes**
Culture Specific Syndromes *USE Culture Bound Syndromes*
Organic Brain **Syndromes**
Drug Synergism *USE Drug Interactions*
Synesthesia
Lunar **Synodic** Cycle
Synonyms
Syntax
Synthetic Speech
Syphilis
Autonomic Nervous **System**
Autonomic Nervous **System** Disorders
Cardiovascular **System**
Caste **System**
Central Nervous **System**
Central Nervous **System** Disorders
Central Nervous System Drugs *USE CNS Affecting Drugs*
Digestive **System**
Digestive **System** Disorders
Endocrine **System**
Gastrointestinal **System**
Hypothalamo Hypophyseal **System**
Hypothalamo Pituitary Adrenal **System**
Lemniscal **System**
Limbic **System**
Musculoskeletal **System**
Nervous **System**
Nervous **System** Disorders
Nervous **System** Neoplasms
Nervous System Plasticity *USE Neural Plasticity*
Parasympathetic Nervous **System**
Peripheral Nervous **System**
Respiratory **System**
Sclerosis (Nervous **System**)
Sensory **System** Disorders
Sympathetic Nervous **System**
Urogenital **System**
Systematic Desensitization Therapy
Systems
Systems Analysis
Systems Design
Systems Theory
Anatomical **Systems**
Classification Systems *USE Taxonomies*
Communication **Systems**
Decision Support **Systems**
Expert **Systems**
Family Systems Model
    USE Family Systems Theory
Family **Systems** Theory
Human Machine **Systems**
Human Machine **Systems** Design
Information **Systems**
Intelligent Tutoring **Systems**
Knowledge Based Systems *USE Expert Systems*
Man Machine Systems *USE Human Machine Systems*
Man Machine Systems Design
    USE Human Machine Systems Design
Management Information Systems *USE Information Systems*

ROTATED ALPHABETICAL TERMS SECTION

Number **Systems**
Political Economic **Systems**
Telephone **Systems**
Systolic Pressure
Szondi Test
T Groups *USE Human Relations Training*
T Mazes
T Test
Students **T** Test *USE T Test*
Statistical **Tables**
Taboos
Tachistoscopes
Tachistoscopic Presentation
Tachycardia
Tactual Discrimination
USE Tactual Perception
Tactual Displays
Tactual Maps *USE Mobility Aids*
Tactual Perception
Tactual Stimulation
Tailored Testing *USE Adaptive Testing*
Note **Taking**
Perspective Taking *USE Role Taking*
Risk **Taking**
Role **Taking**
Sexual Risk **Taking**
Test **Taking**
Talent *USE Ability*
Talented *USE Gifted*
Fairy Tales *USF Folklore*
Self **Talk**
Sleep **Talking**
Tantrums
Tape Recorders
Finger **Tapping**
Tardiness
Tardive Dyskinesia
Task Analysis
Task Complexity
Task Difficulty *USE Task Complexity*
Time On **Task**
Piagetian **Tasks**
Taste Aversion Conditioning
USE Aversion Conditioning
Taste Buds
Taste Discrimination *USE Taste Perception*
Taste Disorders
Taste Perception
Taste Stimulation
Tattoos *USE Cosmetic Techniques*
Taurine
Taxation
Taxonomies
Tay Sachs Disease
Taylor Manifest Anxiety Scale
Tea *USE Beverages (Nonalcoholic)*
Teacher Accreditation *USE Accreditation*
(Education Personnel)
Teacher Aides
Teacher Attitudes
Teacher Characteristics
Teacher Education
Teacher Effectiveness Evaluation
Teacher Effectiveness
USE Teacher Characteristics
Teacher Expectations
Teacher Personality
Teacher Recruitment
Teacher Student Interaction
Teacher Tenure
Teacher Training *USE Teacher Education*
Inservice **Teacher** Education
Minnesota **Teacher** Attitude Inventory
USE Attitude Measures
Teachers
Classroom Teachers *USE Teachers*
College **Teachers**

Cooperating **Teachers**
Elementary School **Teachers**
High School **Teachers**
Junior High School **Teachers**
Middle School **Teachers**
Preschool **Teachers**
Preservice **Teachers**
Resource **Teachers**
Special Education **Teachers**
Student **Teachers**
Supervising Teachers *USE Cooperating Teachers*
Technical Education Teachers
USE Vocational Education Teachers
Vocational Education **Teachers**
Teaching
Teaching Internship *USE Student Teaching*
Teaching Machines
Teaching Methods
Discovery **Teaching** Method
Initial **Teaching** Alphabet
Student **Teaching**
Team **Teaching** Method
Team Teaching Method
Teams
Self Managing Work **Teams**
Work **Teams**
Teasing
Technical Education Teachers
USE Vocational Education Teachers
Technical Personnel
Technical Schools
Technical Service Personnel
Holtzman Inkblot **Technique**
Mutual Storytelling **Technique**
Projective Testing **Technique**
Q Sort Testing **Technique**
Storytelling Technique
USF Mutual Storytelling Technique
Cognitive **Techniques**
Cosmetic **Techniques**
Paradigmatic Techniques *USE Paradoxical Techniques*
Paradoxical **Techniques**
Personal Growth Techniques
USE Human Potential Movement
Projective **Techniques**
Psychotherapeutic **Techniques**
Self Help **Techniques**
Stereotaxic **Techniques**
Technology
Nuclear **Technology**
Reproductive **Technology**
Teenage Fathers *USE Adolescent Fathers*
Teenage Mothers *USE Adolescent Mothers*
Teenage Pregnancy
USE Adolescent Pregnancy
Teeth (Anatomy)
Teeth Grinding *USE Bruxism*
Nocturnal **Teeth** Grinding
Ventral Tegmental Area *USE Tegmentum*
Tegmentum
Telecommunications Media
Telecommuting
Teleconferencing
Telehealth *USE Telemedicine*
Telekinesis *USE Psychokinesis*
Telemedicine
Telemetry
Telencephalon
Telepathy
Telephone Hot Lines
USE Hot Line Services
Telephone Surveys
Telephone Systems
Teletherapy *USE Online Therapy*
Televised Instruction
Television
Television Advertising

Television Viewing
Closed Circuit **Television**
Educational **Television**
Temperament *USE Personality*
Guilford Zimmerman **Temperament** Survey
Temperature Effects
Temperature Perception
Body **Temperature**
Skin **Temperature**
Tempo
Conceptual **Tempo**
Temporal Frequency
Temporal Lobe
Temporal Spatial Concept Scale
    USE Intelligence Measures
Temporomandibular Joint Syndrome
    USE Musculoskeletal Disorders
Temptation
Central **Tendency** Measures
Achilles **Tendon** Reflex
Tendons
Tennessee Self Concept Scale
Tennis
Tension Headache
    USE Muscle Contraction Headache
Premenstrual Tension *USE Premenstrual Syndrome*
Occupational **Tenure**
Teacher **Tenure**
Teratogens
Long **Term** Care
Long **Term** Memory
Long Term Potentiation
    USE Postactivation Potentials
Short **Term** Memory
Short Term Potentiation
    USE Postactivation Potentials
Short Term Psychotherapy
    USE Brief Psychotherapy
Terminal Cancer
Terminally Ill Patients
Video Display Terminals *USE Video Display Units*
Employee Termination *USE Personnel Termination*
Personnel **Termination**
Relationship **Termination**
Treatment **Termination**
Terminology
Psychological **Terminology**
Territoriality
Terrorism
Night Terrors *USE Sleep Disorders*
Test Administration
Test Anxiety
Test Bias
Test Coaching
Test Construction
Test Difficulty *USE Difficulty Level (Test)*
Test Equating *USE Score Equating*
Test Forms
Test Interpretation
Test Items
Test Normalization
    USE Test Standardization
Test Norms
Test Reliability
Test Scores
Test Standardization
Test Taking
Test Tube Babies
    USE Reproductive Technology
Test Validity
Army General Classification **Test**
Bender Gestalt **Test**
Benton Revised Visual Retention **Test**
Blacky Pictures Test *USE Projective Personality Measures*
Cattell Culture Fair Intelligence Test *USE Culture Fair Intelligence Test*
Chi Square **Test**
Childrens Apperception **Test**

Classical **Test** Theory
Cochran Q **Test**
College Entrance Examination
Board Scholastic Aptitude **Test**
Color Pyramid Test *USE Projective Personality Measures*
Content Analysis **(Test)**
Cultural **Test** Bias
Culture Fair Intelligence **Test**
Dexamethasone Suppression **Test**
Difficulty Level **(Test)**
Draw A Man Test *USE Human Figures Drawing*
F **Test**
Frostig Developmental **Test** of Visual Perception
Gates Reading Test *USE Gates MacGinitie Reading Tests*
General Aptitude **Test** Battery
Goodenough Harris Draw A Person **Test**
Illinois **Test** of Psycholinguistic Abilities
Item Analysis **(Test)**
Item Content **(Test)**
Kohs Block Design **Test**
Kolmogorov Smirnov **Test**
Mann Whitney U **Test**
Matching Test *USE Matching to Sample*
Memory for Designs **Test**
Miller Analogies **Test**
Onomatopoeia and Images Test *USE Projective Personality Measures*
Peabody Picture Vocabulary **Test**
Porteus Maze **Test**
Preliminary Scholastic Aptitude Test *USE College Entrance Examination*
    Board Scholastic Aptitude Test
Q Test *USE Cochran Q Test*
Rod and Frame **Test**
Rorschach **Test**
Scholastic Aptitude Test *USE College Entrance Examination*
    Board Scholastic Aptitude Test
School and College Ability Test *USE Aptitude Measures*
Sign Rank Test *USE Wilcoxon Sign Rank Test*
Sign **Test**
Slosson Intelligence **Test**
Spearman Brown **Test**
Stanford Achievement **Test**
Stroop Color Word **Test**
Students T Test *USE T Test*
Szondi **Test**
T **Test**
Thematic Apperception **Test**
Vane Kindergarten Test *USE Intelligence Measures*
Wide Range Achievement **Test**
Wilcoxon Sign Rank **Test**
Wisconsin Card Sorting **Test**
Zulliger Z **Test**
Testes
Testes Disorders
    USE Endocrine Sexual Disorders
Testicular Feminization Syndrome
Expert **Testimony**
Legal **Testimony**
Testing
Testing Methods
Adaptive **Testing**
AIDS Testing *USE HIV Testing*
Basic Skills Testing *USE Minimum Competency Tests*
Body Sway **Testing**
Cloze **Testing**
Cognitive Hypothesis **Testing**
Computer Assisted **Testing**
Digit Span **Testing**
Drug Testing *USE Drug Usage Screening*
Embedded Figures **Testing**
Essay **Testing**
Forced Choice **(Testing** Method)
Genetic **Testing**
Group **Testing**
HIV **Testing**
Hypothesis **Testing**
Individual **Testing**
Multiple Choice **(Testing** Method)

Null Hypothesis **Testing**
Projective **Testing** Technique
Psychological Testing *USE Psychometrics*
Q Sort **Testing** Technique
Reality **Testing**
Scaling **(Testing)**
Scoring **(Testing)**
Tailored Testing *USE Adaptive Testing*
Testosterone
Tests *USE Measurement*
Ability Tests *USE Aptitude Measures*
Comprehension **Tests**
Criterion Referenced **Tests**
Differential Aptitude **Tests**
Employment **Tests**
Gates MacGinitie Reading **Tests**
Gates Reading Readiness Tests *USE Gates MacGinitie Reading Tests*
Henmon Nelson Tests of Mental Ability
USE Intelligence Measures
Iowa **Tests** of Basic Skills
Mastery Tests *USE Criterion Referenced Tests*
Metropolitan Readiness **Tests**
Minimum Competency **Tests**
Nonparametric Statistical **Tests**
Objective Referenced Tests *USE Criterion Referenced Tests*
Parametric Statistical **Tests**
Performance **Tests**
Personality Tests *USE Personality Measures*
Projective Tests *USE Projective Techniques*
Screening **Tests**
Selection **Tests**
Sentence Completion **Tests**
Sociometric **Tests**
Standardized **Tests**
Statistical **Tests**
True False Tests *USE Forced Choice (Testing Method)*
Verbal **Tests**
Testwiseness
Tetrabenazine
Tetrachoric Correlation
Tetrahydrocannabinol
Text Structure
Textbooks
Programmed **Textbooks**
Texture Perception
Thalamic Nuclei
Thalamotomy
Thalamus
Geniculate Bodies **(Thalamus)**
Thalidomide
Thanatology *USE Death Education*
Thanatos *USE Death Instinct*
Theatre
Theft
Thematic Apperception Test
Theology
Theophylline
Bayes Theorem *USE Statistical Probability*
Theoretical Interpretation
Theoretical Orientation
Theories
Theories of Education
Psychological **Theories**
Theory Formulation
Theory of Evolution
Theory of Mind
Theory Verification
Activity **Theory**
Chaos **Theory**
Classical Test **Theory**
Communication **Theory**
Decision **Theory**
Educational Theory *USE Theories of Education*
Fairbairnian Theory *USE Object Relations*
Family Systems **Theory**
Fuzzy Set **Theory**
Game **Theory**

Grounded **Theory**
Information **Theory**
Item Response **Theory**
Latent Trait Theory *USE Item Response Theory*
Learning **Theory**
Personal Construct Theory *USE Personality Theory*
Personality **Theory**
Psychoanalytic **Theory**
Systems **Theory**
Utility **Theory**
Winnicottian Theory *USE Object Relations*
Therapeutic Abortion
USE Induced Abortion
Therapeutic Alliance
Therapeutic Camps
Therapeutic Community
Therapeutic Environment
Therapeutic Outcomes
USE Treatment Outcomes
Therapeutic Processes
Therapeutic Social Clubs
Medical **Therapeutic** Devices
Negative **Therapeutic** Reaction
Organic Therapies
USE Physical Treatment Methods
Therapist Attitudes
Therapist Characteristics
Therapist Effectiveness
USE Therapist Characteristics
Therapist Experience
USE Therapist Characteristics
Therapist Patient Interaction
USE Psychotherapeutic Processes
Therapist Patient Sexual Relations
USE Professional Client Sexual Relations
Therapist Personality
USE Therapist Characteristics
Therapist Role
Therapist Selection
Therapist Trainees
Patient Therapist Interaction
USE Psychotherapeutic Processes
Patient Therapist Sexual Relations
USE Professional Client Sexual Relations
Therapists
Occupational **Therapists**
Physical **Therapists**
Speech **Therapists**
Therapy *USE Treatment*
Activity Therapy *USE Recreation Therapy*
Animal Assisted **Therapy**
Art **Therapy**
Aversion **Therapy**
Behavior **Therapy**
Bright Light Therapy *USE Phototherapy*
Client Centered **Therapy**
Cognitive Behavior **Therapy**
Cognitive **Therapy**
Conjoint **Therapy**
Cooperative Therapy *USE Cotherapy*
Couples **Therapy**
Creative Arts **Therapy**
Dance **Therapy**
Directed Reverie Therapy *USE Guided Imagery*
Drama Therapy *USE Psychodrama*
Drug **Therapy**
ECS Therapy
USE Electroconvulsive Shock Therapy
Educational **Therapy**
Electroconvulsive Shock **Therapy**
Electroshock Therapy
USE Electroconvulsive Shock Therapy
Encounter Group **Therapy**
Environmental Therapy *USE Milieu Therapy*
Estrogen Replacement Therapy *USE Hormone Therapy*

395

Existential **Therapy**
Exposure **Therapy**
Eye Movement Desensitization **Therapy**
Family **Therapy**
Feminist **Therapy**
Flooding Therapy *USE Implosive Therapy*
Gestalt **Therapy**
Group Therapy *USE Group Psychotherapy*
Gymnastic Therapy *USE Recreation Therapy*
Hormone **Therapy**
Illumination Therapy *USE Phototherapy*
Implosive **Therapy**
Individual Therapy *USE Individual Psychotherapy*
Insight **Therapy**
Insulin Shock **Therapy**
Light Therapy *USE Phototherapy*
Maintenance **Therapy**
Marathon Group **Therapy**
Marital Therapy *USE Marriage Counseling*
Marriage Therapy *USE Marriage Counseling*
Milieu **Therapy**
Morita **Therapy**
Movement **Therapy**
Multiple Therapy *USE Cotherapy*
Muscle Relaxation Therapy *USE Relaxation Therapy*
Music **Therapy**
Nondirective Therapy *USE Client Centered Therapy*
Occupational **Therapy**
Online **Therapy**
Personal **Therapy**
Persuasion **Therapy**
Pet Therapy *USE Animal Assisted Therapy*
Physical **Therapy**
Play **Therapy**
Poetry **Therapy**
Primal **Therapy**
Progressive Relaxation **Therapy**
Psychoanalytic Therapy *USE Psychoanalysis*
Radiation **Therapy**
Rational Emotive Behavior **Therapy**
Rational Emotive Therapy *USE Rational Emotive Behavior Therapy*
Reality **Therapy**
Reciprocal Inhibition **Therapy**
Recreation **Therapy**
Relationship **Therapy**
Relaxation **Therapy**
Rogerian Therapy *USE Client Centered Therapy*
Sex **Therapy**
Shock **Therapy**
Socioenvironmental Therapy *USE Milieu Therapy*
Solution Focused **Therapy**
Speech **Therapy**
Systematic Desensitization **Therapy**
Triadic Therapy *USE Conjoint Therapy*
Vitamin **Therapy**
X Ray Therapy *USE Radiation Therapy*
Thermal Acclimatization
Thermal Factors *USE Temperature Effects*
Thermoreceptors
Thermoregulation (Body)
Theta Rhythm
Thigh
Thinking
Autistic **Thinking**
Convergent Thinking
USE Inductive Deductive Reasoning
Divergent **Thinking**
Logical **Thinking**
Magical **Thinking**
Thiopental
Thioridazine
Thiothixene
Third World Countries
USE Developing Countries
Thirst
Thoracic Nerves *USE Spinal Nerves*

Thorax
Thorazine *USE Chlorpromazine*
Thought Content *USE Cognitions*
Thought Control *USE Brainwashing*
Thought Disturbances
Thought Suppression
Fantasies **(Thought** Disturbances)
Threat
Threat Postures
Threshold Determination
Critical Flicker Fusion **Threshold**
Luminance Threshold *USE Brightness Perception*
Luminance Threshold *USE Visual Thresholds*
Photic Threshold *USE Illumination*
Photic Threshold *USE Visual Thresholds*
Thresholds
Auditory **Thresholds**
Olfactory **Thresholds**
Pain **Thresholds**
Vibrotactile **Thresholds**
Visual **Thresholds**
Failure to **Thrive**
Thromboses
Coronary **Thromboses**
Project Follow **Through**
Thumb
Thumbsucking
Thymoleptic Drugs
USE Tranquilizing Drugs
Thyroid Disorders
Thyroid Extract *USE Thyroid Hormones*
Thyroid Gland
Thyroid Hormones
Thyroid Stimulating Hormone
USE Thyrotropin
Thyroidectomy
Thyrotoxicosis
Thyrotropic Hormone *USE Thyrotropin*
Thyrotropin
Thyroxine
Tic Doloureux *USE Trigeminal Neuralgia*
Tics
Tigers *USE Felids*
Time
Time Disorientation
Time Estimation
Time Limited Psychotherapy
USE Brief Psychotherapy
Time Management
Time On Task
Time Out
Time Perception
Time Perspective
Time Series
Constant **Time** Delay
Interresponse **Time**
Leisure **Time**
Reaction **Time**
Response Time *USE Reaction Time*
Timers (Apparatus)
Timidity
Tinnitus
Tiredness *USE Fatigue*
Tissue Donation
Connective **Tissue** Cells
Tissues (Body)
Connective **Tissues**
Nerve **Tissues**
Toads
Tobacco Smoking
Chewing Tobacco *USE Smokeless Tobacco*
Smokeless **Tobacco**
Tofranil *USE Imipramine*
Toilet Training
Token Economy Programs
Token Reinforcement
USE Secondary Reinforcement

Tolerance
Tolerance for Ambiguity
Drug Tolerance
Toluene
Tomography
Positron Emission Tomography *USE Tomography*
Muscle Tone
Tongue
Tonic Immobility
Tool Use
Animal Tool Use *USE Tool Use*
Top Level Managers
Topography
Torticollis
Tortoises *USE Turtles*
Torture
Totalitarianism
Touch *USE Tactual Perception*
Touching *USE Physical Contact*
Tourette Syndrome
    USE Gilles de la Tourette Disorder
Gilles de la Tourette Disorder
Tourism
Aged (Attitudes Toward)
Aging (Attitudes Toward)
AIDS (Attitudes Toward)
Disabled (Attitudes Toward)
Homosexuality (Attitudes Toward)
Mental Illness (Attitudes Toward)
Mental Retardation (Attitudes Toward)
Obesity (Attitudes Toward)
Physical Disabilities (Attitudes Toward)
Physical Illness (Attitudes Toward)
Sensory Disabilities (Attitudes Toward)
Sports (Attitudes Toward)
Work (Attitudes Toward)
Towns
Toxic Disorders
Toxic Encephalopathies
Toxic Hepatitis
Toxic Psychoses
Toxic Waste *USE Hazardous Materials*
Toxicity
Toxicomania
Toxins *USE Poisons*
Toy Selection
Toys
Educational Toys
Memory Trace
Trachea
Tracking
Visual Tracking
Optic Tract
Respiratory Tract Disorders
Tractotomy
Extrapyramidal Tracts
Pyramidal Tracts
Spinothalamic Tracts
Traditionalism *USE Conservatism*
Air Traffic Accidents
Air Traffic Control
Motor Traffic Accidents
Trainable Mentally Retarded
    USE Moderate Mental Retardation
Counselor Trainees
Psychotherapist Trainees *USE Therapist Trainees*
Therapist Trainees
Training *USE Education*
Assertiveness Training
Athletic Training
Autogenic Training
Biofeedback Training
Childbirth Training
Clinical Methods Training
Clinical Psychology Graduate Training
Communication Skills Training
Community Mental Health Training

Computer Based Training *USE Computer Assisted Instruction*
Computer Training
Human Relations Training
Inservice Training
Job Training *USE Personnel Training*
Management Training
Memory Training
Mental Health Inservice Training
Military Training
Motivation Training
Omission Training
On the Job Training
Parent Effectiveness Training *USE Parent Training*
Parent Training
Personnel Training
Postgraduate Training
Psychiatric Training
Psychoanalytic Training
Psychotherapy Training
Self Instructional Training
Sensitivity Training
Social Skills Training
Sport Training *USE Athletic Training*
Teacher Training *USE Teacher Education*
Toilet Training
Work Adjustment Training
Railroad Trains
Latent Trait Theory *USE Item Response Theory*
Quantitative Trait Loci
State Trait Anxiety Inventory
Personality Traits
Major Tranquilizers *USE Neuroleptic Drugs*
Minor Tranquilizers
Tranquilizing Drugs
Transactional Analysis
Transaminases
Transcranial Magnetic Stimulation
Repetitive Transcranial Magnetic Stimulation
    USE Transcranial Magnetic Stimulation
Transcultural Psychiatry
Transducers
Transfer (Learning)
Transfer Students
Client Transfer
Interhemispheric Transfer *USE Interhemispheric Interaction*
Interocular Transfer
Negative Transfer
Patient Transfer *USE Client Transfer*
Positive Transfer
Transferases
Psychotherapeutic Transference
Transformational Generative Grammar
Transformational Leadership
Blood Transfusion
Transgendered *USE Transsexualism*
Transgenerational Patterns
School to Work Transition
School Transition
Transitional Objects
Career Transitions *USE Career Development*
Life Transitions *USE Life Changes*
Foreign Language Translation
Translocation (Chromosome)
Disease Transmission
Intergenerational Transmission
    USE Transgenerational Patterns
Neural Transmission *USE Neurotransmission*
Synaptic Transmission *USE Neurotransmission*
Sexually Transmitted Diseases
Transpersonal Psychology
Neural Transplantation
Organ Transplantation
Renal Transplantation *USE Organ Transplantation*
Heart Transplants *USE Organ Transplantation*
Kidney Transplants *USE Organ Transplantation*
Transportation
Transportation Accidents

Air **Transportation**
Ground **Transportation**
Public **Transportation**
Water **Transportation**
Transposition (Cognition)
Transracial Adoption
    USE Interracial Adoption
Transsexualism
Transvestism
Tranylcypromine
Birth **Trauma**
Emotional **Trauma**
Physical Trauma *USE Injuries*
Traumatic Brain Injury
Traumatic Neurosis
Traumatic Psychosis
    USE Reactive Psychosis
Commuting **(Travel)**
Traveling
Trazodone
Treatment
Treatment Client Matching
    USE Client Treatment Matching
Treatment Compliance
Treatment Dropouts
Treatment Duration
Treatment Effectiveness Evaluation
Treatment Environment
    USE Therapeutic Environment
Treatment Facilities
Treatment Guidelines
Treatment Outcomes
Treatment Planning
Treatment Refusal
Treatment Resistant Depression
Treatment Resistant Disorders
Treatment Seeking Behavior
    USE Health Care Seeking Behavior
Treatment Termination
Treatment Withholding
Client **Treatment** Matching
Court Ordered Treatment *USE Court Referrals*
Cross Cultural **Treatment**
Dental **Treatment**
Electrosleep **Treatment**
Interdisciplinary **Treatment** Approach
Involuntary **Treatment**
Life Sustaining **Treatment**
Medical **Treatment** (General)
Multidisciplinary Treatment Approach *USE Interdisciplinary*
    Treatment Approach
Multimodal **Treatment** Approach
Outpatient **Treatment**
Patient Treatment Matching
    USE Client Treatment Matching
Physical **Treatment** Methods
Right to **Treatment**
Side Effects **(Treatment)**
Sleep **Treatment**
Delirium **Tremens**
Tremor
Trends
Triadic Therapy *USE Conjoint Therapy*
Trial and Error Learning
Competency to Stand **Trial**
Clinical **Trials**
Triazolam
Tribes
Trichotillomania
Tricyclic Antidepressant Drugs
Tricyclic Resistant Depression
    USE Treatment Resistant Depression
Trifluoperazine
Triflupromazine
    USE Phenothiazine Derivatives
Trigeminal Nerve
Trigeminal Neuralgia

Trigonum Cerebrale *USE Fornix*
Trihexyphenidyl
Triiodothyronine
Triplets
Educational Field **Trips**
Trisomy
Trisomy 21
Trochlear Nerve *USE Cranial Nerves*
Truancy
School **Truancy**
Trucks *USE Motor Vehicles*
True False Tests
    USE Forced Choice (Testing Method)
Trust (Social Behavior)
Tryptamine
Tryptophan
Tubal Ligation
Eustachian Tube *USE Middle Ear*
Test Tube Babies *USE Reproductive Technology*
Tuberculosis
Pulmonary **Tuberculosis**
Cathode Ray Tubes *USE Video Display Units*
Tubocurarine
Tumors *USE Neoplasms*
Tunnel Vision
Turners Syndrome
Turnover *USE Employee Turnover*
Employee **Turnover**
Personnel Turnover *USE Employee Turnover*
Turtles
Tutoring
Intelligent **Tutoring** Systems
Peer **Tutoring**
Tutors *USE Teachers*
Twelve Step Programs
Twins
Conjoined **Twins**
Dizygotic Twins *USE Heterozygotic Twins*
Fraternal Twins *USE Heterozygotic Twins*
Heterozygotic **Twins**
Identical Twins *USE Monozygotic Twins*
Monozygotic **Twins**
Siamese Twins *USE Conjoined Twins*
Chorda Tympani Nerve *USE Facial Nerve*
Tympanic Membrane *USE Middle Ear*
Type A Personality
    USE Coronary Prone Behavior
Type B Personality
    USE Coronary Prone Behavior
Type I Errors
Type II Errors
Dementia of Alzheimers Type *USE Alzheimers Disease*
Myers Briggs **Type** Indicator
Schizophrenia (Disorganized **Type)**
Body Types *USE Somatotypes*
Typing
Typists *USE Clerical Personnel*
Psychodiagnostic **Typologies**
Tyramine
Tyrosine
Mann Whitney **U** Test
Ulcerative Colitis
Gastrointestinal **Ulcers**
Peptic Ulcers *USE Gastrointestinal Ulcers*
Ulnar Nerve *USE Spinal Nerves*
Ultrasound
Uncertainty
Unconditioned Reflex *USE Reflexes*
Unconditioned Responses
Unconditioned Stimulus
Unconscious (Personality Factor)
Collective **Unconscious**
Driving **Under** the Influence
Academic **Underachievement**
Underdeveloped Countries
    USE Developing Countries

Undergraduate Degrees
  USE Educational Degrees
Undergraduate Education
Undergraduates *USE College Students*
Underprivileged *USE Disadvantaged*
Understanding *USE Comprehension*
Underwater Effects
Underweight
Undifferentiated Schizophrenia
Unemployment
Labor **Union** Members
Labor **Unions**
Unipolar Depression
  USE Major Depression
Hospital Psychiatric Units *USE Psychiatric Units*
Psychiatric **Units**
Shock **Units**
Video Display **Units**
Words (Phonetic **Units)**
Universities *USE Colleges*
Open Universities *USE Nontraditional Education*
Unskilled Industrial Workers
Unwed Mothers
Upper Class
Upper Class Attitudes
Upper Income Level
Upward Bound
Upward Mobility *USE Social Mobility*
Urban Development
  USE Community Development
Urban Environments
Urban Ghettoes *USE Ghettoes*
Urban Planning
Urbanization
Uric Acid
Urinalysis
Urinary Function Disorders
Urinary Incontinence
Urination
Urine
Urogenital Disorders
Urogenital System
Drug **Usage**
Drug **Usage** Attitudes
Drug **Usage** Screening
Intravenous Drug **Usage**
IV Drug Usage *USE Intravenous Drug Usage*
Marijuana **Usage**
Animal Tool Use *USE Tool Use*
Tool **Use**
Uterus
Utility Theory
Health Care **Utilization**
Health Service Utilization *USE Health Care Utilization*
Vacation Benefits
  USE Employee Leave Benefits
Vacationing
Vaccination *USE Immunization*
Vagina
Vaginismus
Vagotomy
Vagus Nerve
Concept Validity *USE Test Validity*
Concurrent Validity *USE Test Validity*
Construct Validity *USE Test Validity*
Content Validity *USE Test Validity*
Convergent Validity *USE Test Validity*
Criterion Related Validity *USE Test Validity*
Discriminant Validity *USE Test Validity*
Factorial Validity *USE Statistical Validity*
Predictive Validity *USE Statistical Validity*
Statistical **Validity**
Test **Validity**
Valium *USE Diazepam*
Valproic Acid
Values
Allport Vernon Lindzey Study Values *USE Attitude Measures*

Ethnic **Values**
Personal **Values**
Social **Values**
Heart **Valves**
Vandalism
Vane Kindergarten Test
  USE Intelligence Measures
Variability Measurement
Response **Variability**
Stimulus **Variability**
Variable Interval Reinforcement
Variable Ratio Reinforcement
Dependent **Variables**
Independent **Variables**
Statistical **Variables**
Variance Homogeneity
  USE Homogeneity of Variance
Analysis of **Variance**
Error Variance *USE Error of Measurement*
Heterogeneity of Variance *USE Homogeneity of Variance*
Homogeneity of **Variance**
Interaction **Variance**
Contingent Negative **Variation**
Diurnal Variations *USE Human Biological Rhythms*
Seasonal **Variations**
Varimax Rotation
Vascular Dementia
Vascular Disorders
  USE Cardiovascular Disorders
Cerebral Vascular Disorders
  USE Cerebrovascular Disorders
Vasectomy
Vasoconstriction
Vasoconstrictor Drugs
Vasodilation
Vasodilator Drugs
Vasopressin
Vasopressor Drugs
  USE Vasoconstrictor Drugs
Motor **Vehicles**
Veins (Anatomy)
Velocity
Venereal Diseases
  USE Sexually Transmitted Diseases
Venlafaxine
Ventral Roots
Ventral Striatum *USE Basal Ganglia*
Ventral Tegmental Area *USE Tegmentum*
Cerebral **Ventricles**
Heart **Ventricles**
Ventricular Fibrillation
  USE Fibrillation (Heart)
Verapamil
Verbal Ability
Verbal Abuse
Verbal Communication
Verbal Comprehension
Verbal Conditioning *USE Verbal Learning*
Verbal Fluency
Verbal Learning
Verbal Meaning
Verbal Memory
Verbal Reinforcement
Verbal Stimuli
Verbal Tests
Verbalization *USE Oral Communication*
Verbs
Verdict Determination *USE Adjudication*
Vergence Movements
  USE Eye Convergence
Theory **Verification**
Vernier Acuity *USE Visual Acuity*
Allport Vernon Lindzey Study Values
  USE Attitude Measures
Vertebrates
Vertigo
Blood **Vessels**

Coronary Vessels *USE Arteries (Anatomy)*
Retinal Vessels *USE Arteries (Anatomy)*
Vestibular Apparatus
Vestibular Nystagmus *USE Nystagmus*
Vestibular Stimulation
    USE Somesthetic Stimulation
Military **Veterans**
Veterinary Medicine
Vibration
Vibrators (Apparatus)
Vibrotactile Thresholds
Vicarious Experiences
Vicarious Reinforcement
    USE Vicarious Experiences
Victimization
Crime **Victims**
Video Display Terminals
    USE Video Display Units
Video Display Units
Video Games *USE Computer Games*
Videotape Instruction
Videotape Recorders
Videotapes
Vietnamese Cultural Groups
World **View**
Television **Viewing**
Vigilance
Vineland Social Maturity Scale
Sexual Boundary Violations *USE Professional Client*
    Sexual Relations
Violence
Client Violence *USE Patient Violence*
Domestic Violence *USE Family Violence*
Family **Violence**
Patient **Violence**
School **Violence**
Violent Crime
Viral Disorders
Epstein Barr **Viral** Disorder
Virginity
Virtual Reality
Human Immunodeficiency **Virus**
Vision
Vision Disorders
Binocular **Vision**
Central Vision *USE Foveal Vision*
Foveal **Vision**
Hysterical **Vision** Disturbances
Monocular **Vision**
Peripheral **Vision**
Stereoscopic **Vision**
Tunnel **Vision**
Visitation Rights *USE Child Visitation*
Child **Visitation**
Institution **Visitation**
Home **Visiting** Programs
Visual Acuity
Visual Attention
Visual Contrast
Visual Cortex
Visual Discrimination
Visual Displays
Visual Evoked Potentials
Visual Feedback
Visual Field
Visual Fixation *USE Eye Fixation*
Visual Hallucinations
Visual Impairment *USE Vision Disorders*
Visual Masking
Visual Memory
Visual Neglect *USE Sensory Neglect*
Visual Perception
Visual Perspective *USE Linear Perspective*
Visual Receptive Fields
Visual Search
Visual Spatial Ability
    USE Visuospatial Ability

Visual Spatial Memory
    USE Visuospatial Memory
Visual Stimulation
Visual Thresholds
Visual Tracking
Benton Revised **Visual** Retention Test
Frostig Developmental Test of **Visual** Perception
Visualization *USE Imagery*
Visually Handicapped
    USE Vision Disorders
Visuospatial Ability
Visuospatial Memory
Vitamin C *USE Ascorbic Acid*
Vitamin Deficiency Disorders
Vitamin Therapy
Vitamins
In Vitro Fertilization
    USE Reproductive Technology
Vocabulary
Peabody Picture **Vocabulary** Test
Sight **Vocabulary**
Vocal Cords
Vocalization
Infant **Vocalization**
Animal **Vocalizations**
Vocational Adjustment
    USE Occupational Adjustment
Vocational Aspirations
    USE Occupational Aspirations
Vocational Choice
    USE Occupational Choice
Vocational Counseling
    USE Occupational Guidance
Vocational Counselors
Vocational Education
Vocational Education Teachers
Vocational Evaluation
Vocational Guidance
    USE Occupational Guidance
Vocational Interests
    USE Occupational Interests
Vocational Maturity
Vocational Mobility
    USE Occupational Mobility
Vocational Preference
    USE Occupational Preference
Vocational Rehabilitation
Vocational School Students
Vocational Schools *USE Technical Schools*
Strong **Vocational** Interest Blank
Vocations *USE Occupations*
Voice
Voice Disorders *USE Dysphonia*
Voles
Volition
Volt Meters *USE Apparatus*
Blood **Volume**
Volunteer Civilian Personnel
    USE Volunteers
Volunteer Military Personnel
Volunteer Personnel *USE Volunteers*
Volunteerism *USE Volunteers*
Volunteers
Experiment Volunteers *USE Experimental Subjects*
Vomeronasal Sense
Vomit Inducing Drugs *USE Emetic Drugs*
Vomiting
Voting Behavior
Vowels
Voyeurism
Deja Vu *USE Consciousness States*
Vygotsky (Lev)
Wages *USE Salaries*
Sleep **Wake** Cycle
Wakefulness
Walk In Clinics
Walking

Abdominal **Wall**
Wandering Behavior
War
Nuclear **War**
Prisoners of **War**
Duty to **Warn**
Warning Labels
Warning Signs *USE Warnings*
Warnings
Safety Warnings *USE Warnings*
Wasps
Toxic Waste *USE Hazardous Materials*
Water Deprivation
Water Intake
Water Safety
Water Transportation
Watson (John Broadus)
Slow Wave Sleep *USE NREM Sleep*
Sound Waves *USE Acoustics*
Weaning
Weapons
Weather *USE Atmospheric Conditions*
Web Based Mental Health Services
    USE Online Therapy
Wechsler Adult Intelligence Scale
Wechsler Bellevue Intelligence Scale
Wechsler Intelligence Scale for Children
Wechsler Memory Scale
Wechsler Preschool Primary Scale
Work **Week** Length
Weight Control
Weight Perception
Birth **Weight**
Body **Weight**
Brain **Weight**
Low Birth Weight *USE Birth Weight*
Statistical **Weighting**
Weightlessness
Weightlifting
Welfare Services (Government)
Animal **Welfare**
Child **Welfare**
Community **Welfare** Services
Public Welfare Services
    USE Community Welfare Services
Well Being
Wellness *USE Health*
Wernickes Syndrome
Whales
Wheelchairs *USE Mobility Aids*
Whiplash
Whistleblowing *USE Informants*
White Betz A B Scale
    USE Nonprojective Personality
    Measures
White Blood Cells *USE Leucocytes*
White Collar Workers
White Noise
White Rats *USE Rats*
Whites
Mann **Whitney** U Test
Wholistic Health *USE Holistic Health*
Wide Range Achievement Test
Widowers
Widows
Wilcoxon Sign Rank Test
Wilderness Experience
Free Will *USE Volition*
Prader **Willi** Syndrome
James **(William)**
Williams Syndrome
Willpower *USE Self Control*
Living Wills *USE Advance Directives*
Wilson Patterson Conservatism Scale
Wine
Winnicottian Theory *USE Object Relations*

Winter Depression
    USE Seasonal Affective Disorder
Wisconsin Card Sorting Test
Wisdom
Witchcraft
Attention Deficit Disorder **with** Hyperactivity
Dementia **with** Lewy Bodies
Withdrawal (Defense Mechanism)
Alcohol **Withdrawal**
Drug **Withdrawal**
Drug Withdrawal Effects *USE Drug Withdrawal*
Nicotine **Withdrawal**
Treatment **Withholding**
Within Subjects Design
    USE Repeated Measures
Witnesses
Wives
Wolves
Women *USE Human Females*
Working **Women**
Womens Liberation Movement
Woodcock Johnson Psychoeducational
    Battery
Word Associations
Word Blindness *USE Alexia*
Word Deafness *USE Aphasia*
Word Frequency
Word Meaning
Word Origins *USE Etymology*
Word Processing
Word Recognition
Stroop Color **Word** Test
Words (Phonetic Units)
Work (Attitudes Toward)
Work Addiction *USE Workaholism*
Work Adjustment Training
Work at Home *USE Telecommuting*
Work Environments
    USE Working Conditions
Work Ethic *USE Work (Attitudes Toward)*
Work Family Relationship
    USE Family Work Relationship
Work Load
Work Related Illnesses
Work Rest Cycles
Work Satisfaction *USE Job Satisfaction*
Work Scheduling
Work Stress *USE Occupational Stress*
Work Study Programs
    USE Educational Programs
Work Teams
Work Week Length
Computer Supported Cooperative Work *USE Groupware*
Family **Work** Relationship
Noise Levels **(Work** Areas)
Quality of **Work** Life
Return to Work *USE Reemployment*
School to **Work** Transition
Self Managing **Work** Teams
Social Work *USE Social Casework*
Social **Work** Education
Workaholism
Workday Shifts
Workers' Compensation Insurance
Workers *USE Personnel*
Agricultural Extension **Workers**
Agricultural **Workers**
Blue Collar **Workers**
Child Care **Workers**
Foreign **Workers**
Guest Workers *USE Foreign Workers*
Migrant Farm **Workers**
Psychiatric Social **Workers**
Skilled Industrial **Workers**
Social **Workers**
Unskilled Industrial **Workers**
White Collar **Workers**

ROTATED ALPHABETICAL TERMS SECTION

Workforce Diversity
USE Diversity in the Workplace
Working Alliance *USE Therapeutic Alliance*
Working Conditions
Working Memory *USE Short Term Memory*
Working Space
Working Women
Workmen's Compensation Insurance
USE Workers' Compensation Insurance
Workplace Diversity
USE Diversity in the Workplace
Diversity in the **Workplace**
Sheltered **Workshops**
World View
Third World Countries
USE Developing Countries
Worms
Worry *USE Anxiety*
Worship *USE Religious Practices*
Saint John's Wort *USE Hypericum Perforatum*
St. John's Wort *USE Hypericum Perforatum*
Wounds
Self Inflicted **Wounds**
Wrist
Writers
Writing Skills
Creative **Writing**

Cursive **Writing**
Written Communication
Written Language
Wryneck *USE Torticollis*
X Rated Materials *USE Pornography*
X Ray Diagnosis *USE Roentgenography*
X Ray Therapy *USE Radiation Therapy*
Fragile **X** Syndrome
Xenophobia *USE Stranger Reactions*
Xylocaine *USE Lidocaine*
Yawning
Yoga
Yohimbine
Predelinquent **Youth**
Z Scores *USE Standard Scores*
Zulliger **Z** Test
Zen Buddhism
Non **Zero** Sum Games
Zidovudine
Zimeldine
Guilford **Zimmerman** Temperament Survey
Zinc
Zoo Environment *USE Animal Captivity*
Zoology
Zulliger Z Test
Zungs Self Rating Depression Scale

TERM CLUSTERS SECTION

Term Cluster/Subcluster Subject Areas

Computers Cluster
Computer Applications
Computer Automation
Computers & Communication
Computers & Media
Education & Training
Equipment
Human Machine Systems & Engineering
Information

Disorders Cluster
Antisocial Behavior & Behavior Disorders
Diagnosis
Disorder Characteristics
Learning Disorders & Mental Retardation
Physical & Psychosomatic Disorders
Psychological Disorders
Speech & Language Disorders
Symptomatology

Educational Cluster
Academic Learning & Achievement
Curricula
Educational Personnel & Administration
Educational Testing & Counseling
Schools & Institutions
Special Education
Student Characteristics & Academic
   Environment
Student Populations
Teaching & Teaching Methods

Legal Cluster
Adjudication
Criminal Groups
Criminal Offenses
Criminal Rehabilitation
Laws
Legal Issues
Legal Personnel
Legal Processes

Neuropsychology & Neurology Cluster
Assessment & Diagnosis
Electrophysiology
Neuroanatomy
Neurological Disorders
Neurological Intervention
Neurosciences
Neurotransmitters & Neuroregulators

Occupational & Employment Cluster
Career Areas
Employee, Occupational & Job
   Characteristics
Occupational Groups
Organizations & Organizational Behavior
Personnel Management & Professional
   Personnel Issues

Statistical Cluster
Design, Analysis & Interpretation
Statistical Reliability & Validity
Statistical Theory & Experimental

Tests & Testing Cluster
Academic Achievement & Aptitude Measures
Attitude & Interest Measures
Developmental Measures
Intelligence Measures
Neuropsychological Measures
Nonprojective Personality Measures
Perceptual Measures
Projective Personality Measures
Testing
Testing Methods

Treatment Cluster
Alternative Therapies
Behavior Modification & Therapy
Counseling
Hospitalization & Institutionalization
Medical & Physical Treatment
Psychotherapy
Rehabilitation
Treatment (General)
Treatment Facilities

404

COMPUTERS CLUSTER

- Computer Applications
- Computer Automation
- Computers & Communication
- Computers & Media
- Education & Training
- Equipment
- Human Machine Systems & Engineering
- Information

Computer Applications

Algorithms
Artificial Intelligence
Audiovisual Communications Media
Automated Information Coding
Automated Information Processing
Automated Information Retrieval
Automated Information Storage
Automated Speech Recognition
Computer Applications
Computer Assisted Design
Computer Assisted Diagnosis
Computer Assisted Instruction
Computer Assisted Testing
Computer Games
Computer Programming
Computer Programming Languages
Computer Searching
Computer Simulation
Computer Software
Cybernetics
Data Processing
Databases
Decision Support Systems
Electronic Communication
Error Analysis
Expert Systems
Groupware
Hypermedia
Hypertext
Information Systems
Internet
Neural Networks
Online Therapy
Word Processing

Computer Automation

Artificial Intelligence
Automated Information Coding
Automated Information Processing
Automated Information Retrieval
Automated Information Storage
Automated Speech Recognition
Automation
Computer Assisted Design
Computer Assisted Diagnosis

Computer Assisted Instruction
Computer Assisted Testing
Cybernetics
Decision Support Systems
Human Machine Systems
Neural Networks
Robotics

Computers & Communication

Audiovisual Communications Media
Communication Systems
Communication Theory
Communications Media
Computer Mediated Communication
Electronic Communication
Groupware
Hot Line Services
Hypermedia
Hypertext
Internet
Mass Media
Scientific Communication
Telecommunications Media
Television Advertising

Computers & Media

Audiovisual Communications Media
Communications Media
Computer Software
Databases
Electronic Communication
Hot Line Services
Hypermedia
Hypertext
Information Services
Information Systems
Internet
Mass Media
News Media
Telecommunications Media
Televised Instruction

Education & Training

Computer Assisted Instruction
Computer Assisted Testing
Computer Literacy
Computer Training
Educational Television
Teaching Machines
Televised Instruction

Equipment

Analog Computers
Apparatus
Computer Peripheral Devices
Digital Computers
Human Computer Interaction
Keyboards
Microcomputers

Robotics
Video Display Units
Visual Displays

Human Machine Systems & Engineering

Automated Speech Recognition
Computer Peripheral Devices
Decision Support Systems
Human Computer Interaction
Human Factors Engineering
Human Machine Systems
Human Machine Systems Design
Instrument Controls
Intelligent Tutoring Systems
Knowledge Engineering
Person Environment Fit
Systems Design
Teaching Machines
Virtual Reality

Information

Automated Information Coding
Automated Information Processing
Automated Information Retrieval
Automated Information Storage
Communication Theory
Communications Media
Computer Searching
Data Collection
Data Processing
Databases
Expert Systems
Hot Line Services
Hypermedia
Hypertext
Information
Information Seeking
Information Services
Information Specialists
Information Systems
Information Theory
Internet
Mass Media
Telecommunications Media

DISORDERS CLUSTER

- Antisocial Behavior & Behavior Disorders
- Diagnosis
- Disorder Characteristics
- Learning Disorders & Mental Retardation
- Physical & Psychosomatic Disorders
- Psychological Disorders
- Speech & Language Disorders
- Symptomatology

Consult Relationship Section for more information

Antisocial Behavior & Behavior Disorders

Abuse of Power
Acquaintance Rape
Acute Alcoholic Intoxication
Addiction
Aggressive Driving Behavior
Alcohol Abuse
Alcoholism
Antisocial Behavior
Antisocial Personality
Arson
Attachment Disorders
Attempted Suicide
Attention Deficit Disorder
Attention Deficit Disorder with
    Hyperactivity
Battered Child Syndrome
Battered Females
Behavior Disorders
Behavior Problems
Bullying
Child Abuse
Child Neglect
Chronic Alcoholic Intoxication
Conduct Disorder
Crime
Criminal Behavior
Criminals
Cruelty
Driving Under the Influence
Drug Abuse
Drug Addiction
Drug Dependency
Drug Distribution
Elder Abuse
Emotional Abuse
Erotomania
Exhibitionism
Family Violence
Female Criminals
Female Delinquency
Fetishism
Genocide
Glue Sniffing
Harassment
Hate Crimes
Heroin Addiction
Homicide
Impulse Control Disorders
Incest
Infanticide
Inhalant Abuse
Intravenous Drug Usage
Juvenile Delinquency
Juvenile Gangs
Kidnapping
Kleptomania

Male Criminals
Male Delinquency
Masochism
Mentally Ill Offenders
Oppositional Defiant Disorder
Paraphilias
Partner Abuse
Pathological Gambling
Patient Abuse
Patient Violence
Pedophilia
Perpetrators
Persecution
Physical Abuse
Polydrug Abuse
Pyromania
Rape
Recidivism
Runaway Behavior
Sadism
Sadomasochism
Sadomasochistic Personality
School Truancy
School Violence
Self Destructive Behavior
Self Mutilation
Serial Homicide
Sex Offenses
Sexual Abuse
Sexual Addiction
Sexual Harassment
Sexual Masochism
Sexual Sadism
Shoplifting
Stalking
Suicidal Ideation
Suicide
Tantrums
Terrorism
Theft
Torture
Transvestism
Truancy
Vandalism
Verbal Abuse
Victimization
Violence
Violent Crime
Voyeurism

Diagnosis

Anatomically Detailed Dolls
Angiography
Biological Markers
Biopsy
Cancer Screening
Cardiography
Clinical Judgment (Not Diagnosis)

Cognitive Assessment
Computer Assisted Diagnosis
Dexamethasone Suppression Test
Diagnosis
Diagnosis Related Groups
Diagnostic and Statistical Manual
Diagnostic Interview Schedule
Disease Transmission
Differential Diagnosis
Drug Usage Screening
Dual Diagnosis
Echoencephalography
Electro Oculography
Electrocardiography
Electroencephalography
Electromyography
Electronystagmography
Electroplethysmography
Electroretinography
Encephalography
General Health Questionnaire
Genetic Testing
Geriatric Assessment
Health Screening
HIV Testing
Intake Interview
International Classification of Diseases
Magnetic Resonance Imaging
Mammography
Medical Diagnosis
Medical Model
Misdiagnosis
Needs Assessment
Neuroimaging
Neuropsychological Assessment
Ophthalmologic Examination
Pain Measurement
Physical Examination
Plethysmography
Pneumoencephalography
Polysomnography
Prenatal Diagnosis
Psychiatric Evaluation
Psychodiagnosis
Psychodiagnostic Interview
Psychodiagnostic Typologies
Psychological Assessment
Research Diagnostic Criteria
Rheoencephalography
Roentgenography
Screening
Structured Clinical Interview
Subtypes (Disorders)
Symptom Checklists
Tomography
Urinalysis

Consult Relationship Section for more information

Disorder Characteristics

At Risk Populations
Chronicity (Disorders)
Client Attitudes
Client Characteristics
Comorbidity
Diagnosis
Disease Course
Disease Transmission
Dual Diagnosis
Epidemics
Epidemiology
Etiology
Health Complaints
Illness Behavior
Mortality Rate
Onset (Disorders)
Patient History
Positive and Negative Symptoms
Predisposition
Premorbidity
Prodrome
Prognosis
Psychiatric Symptoms
Purging (Eating Disorders)
Recovery (Disorders)
Relapse (Disorders)
Remission (Disorders)
Risk Factors
Seasonal Variations
Severity (Disorders)
Spontaneous Remission
Subtypes (Disorders)
Susceptibility (Disorders)
Symptom Remission
Symptoms
Treatment Resistant Disorders

Learning Disorders & Mental Retardation

Acalculia
Agnosia
Agraphia
Alexia
Anencephaly
Attention Deficit Disorder
Attention Deficit Disorder with
    Hyperactivity
Autism
Borderline Mental Retardation
Cognitive Impairment
Crying Cat Syndrome
Downs Syndrome
Dyslexia
Dysphasia
Home Reared Mentally Retarded
Hyperkinesis
Institutionalized Mentally Retarded

Learning Disabilities
Learning Disorders
Mental Retardation
Mental Retardation (Attitudes Toward)
Microcephaly
Mild Mental Retardation
Moderate Mental Retardation
Profound Mental Retardation
Psychosocial Mental Retardation
Reading Disabilities
Rett Syndrome
Savants
Severe Mental Retardation
Tay Sachs Disease
Trisomy
Trisomy 21
Williams Syndrome

Physical & Psychosomatic Disorders

Acalculia
Acquired Immune Deficiency Syndrome
Addisons Disease
Adrenal Gland Disorders
Adventitious Disorders
Agnosia
Agraphia
AIDS (Attitudes Toward)
AIDS Dementia Complex
Albinism
Allergic Disorders
Allergic Skin Disorders
Alopecia
Alzheimers Disease
Amblyopia
Amenorrhea
Amnesia
Anaphylactic Shock
Anemia
Anencephaly
Aneurysms
Angina Pectoris
Anorexia Nervosa
Anosmia
Anosognosia
Anterograde Amnesia
Aphagia
Aphasia
Apnea
Apraxia
Arrhythmias (Heart)
Arteriosclerosis
Arthritis
Asthenia
Asthma
Ataxia
Atherosclerosis
Athetosis

Audiogenic Seizures
Autonomic Nervous System Disorders
Autosome Disorders
Back Pain
Bacterial Disorders
Bacterial Meningitis
Barbiturate Poisoning
Benign Neoplasms
Birth Injuries
Blind
Blood and Lymphatic Disorders
Blood Pressure Disorders
Body Dysmorphic Disorder
Bone Disorders
Bradycardia
Bradykinesia
Brain Concussion
Brain Damage
Brain Disorders
Brain Neoplasms
Breast Neoplasms
Bronchial Disorders
Bruxism
Bulimia
Burns
Carbon Monoxide Poisoning
Cardiovascular Disorders
Catabolism
Catalepsy
Cataplexy
Cataracts
Central Nervous System Disorders
Cerebral Arteriosclerosis
Cerebral Hemorrhage
Cerebral Ischemia
Cerebral Palsy
Cerebrovascular Accidents
Cerebrovascular Disorders
Chorea
Chromosome Disorders
Chronic Fatigue Syndrome
Chronic Illness
Chronic Pain
Chronic Stress
Cirrhosis (Liver)
Cleft Palate
Cognitive Impairment
Colitis
Colon Disorders
Color Blindness
Congenital Disorders
Constipation
Conversion Disorder
Convulsions
Coronary Prone Behavior
Coronary Thromboses
Creutzfeldt Jakob Syndrome
Crying Cat Syndrome
Culture Bound Syndromes

Consult Relationship Section for more information

Physical & Psychosomatic Disorders — (cont'd)

Cushings Syndrome
Cystic Fibrosis
Deaf
Deaf Blind
Delirium Tremens
Dementia
Dementia with Lewy Bodies
Dermatitis
Developmental Disabilities
Diabetes
Diabetes Insipidus
Diabetes Mellitus
Diarrhea
Digestive System Disorders
Disabilities
Disabled (Attitudes Toward)
Disorders
Downs Syndrome
Drug Allergies
Drug Induced Congenital Disorders
Drug Induced Hallucinations
Dysarthria
Dyskinesia
Dysmenorrhea
Dyspareunia
Dysphagia
Dysphasia
Dyspnea
Ear Disorders
Eating Disorders
Eczema
Electrical Injuries
Embolisms
Encephalitis
Encephalomyelitis
Encephalopathies
Endocrine Disorders
Endocrine Neoplasms
Endocrine Sexual Disorders
Epilepsy
Epileptic Seizures
Epstein Barr Viral Disorder
Essential Hypertension
Eye Disorders
Failure to Thrive
Fecal Incontinence
Fetal Alcohol Syndrome
Fibrillation (Heart)
Fibromyalgia
Food Allergies
Fragile X Syndrome
Frigidity
Gastrointestinal Disorders
Gastrointestinal Ulcers
General Paresis
Genetic Disorders

Genital Disorders
Gilles de la Tourette Disorder
Glaucoma
Global Amnesia
Goiters
Gonorrhea
Grand Mal Epilepsy
Gynecological Disorders
Hay Fever
Head Injuries
Headache
Health Impairments
Hearing Disorders
Heart Disorders
Hematoma
Hemianopia
Hemiplegia
Hemophilia
Hemorrhage
Hepatitis
Hermaphroditism
Herpes Genitalis
Herpes Simplex
Human Immunodeficiency Virus
Huntingtons Disease
Hydrocephaly
Hyperglycemia
Hyperkinesis
Hyperphagia
Hypersexuality
Hypersomnia
Hypertension
Hyperthyroidism
Hypochondriasis
Hypoglycemia
Hypogonadism
Hyponatremia
Hypopituitarism
Hypotension
Hypothyroidism
Hysterical Paralysis
Hysterical Vision Disturbances
Immunologic Disorders
Impotence
Infectious Disorders
Infertility
Influenza
Injuries
Insomnia
Irritable Bowel Syndrome
Ischemia
Jaundice
Joint Disorders
Kidney Diseases
Kleine Levin Syndrome
Klinefelters Syndrome
Korsakoffs Psychosis
Kwashiorkor
Labyrinth Disorders

Laryngeal Disorders
Lead Poisoning
Leukemias
Lipid Metabolism Disorders
Liver Disorders
Lung Disorders
Lupus
Malaria
Male Genital Disorders
Measles
Memory Disorders
Menieres Disease
Meningitis
Menstrual Disorders
Mercury Poisoning
Metabolism Disorders
Microcephaly
Migraine Headache
Minimal Brain Disorders
Motion Sickness
Movement Disorders
Multi Infarct Dementia
Multiple Disabilities
Multiple Sclerosis
Munchausen Syndrome
Munchausen Syndrome by Proxy
Muscle Contraction Headache
Muscle Spasms
Muscular Atrophy
Muscular Disorders
Muscular Dystrophy
Musculoskeletal Disorders
Myasthenia
Myasthenia Gravis
Myelitis
Myocardial Infarctions
Myoclonia
Myofascial Pain
Myopia
Myotonia
Narcolepsy
Narcosis
Neonatal Disorders
Neoplasms
Nervous System Disorders
Nervous System Neoplasms
Neuralgia
Neurasthenic Neurosis
Neurodegenerative Diseases
Neurodermatitis
Neuroleptic Malignant Syndrome
Neuromuscular Disorders
Neurosyphilis
Nocturnal Teeth Grinding
Nutritional Deficiencies
Nystagmus
Obesity
Obesity (Attitudes Toward)
Obstetrical Complications

Consult Relationship Section for more information

Physical & Psychosomatic Disorders — (cont'd)

Organic Brain Syndromes
Osteoporosis
Pain
Paralysis
Paraplegia
Parasitic Disorders
Parathyroid Disorders
Parkinsonism
Parkinsons Disease
Partially Hearing Impaired
Partially Sighted
Pellagra
Perceptual Disturbances
Peripheral Nerve Disorders
Petit Mal Epilepsy
Phantom Limbs
Pharyngeal Disorders
Phenylketonuria
Physical Disabilities (Attitudes Toward)
Physical Disfigurement
Physical Disorders
Physical Illness (Attitudes Toward)
Pica
Picks Disease
Pituitary Disorders
Pneumonia
Poliomyelitis
Porphyria
Prader Willi Syndrome
Premature Ejaculation
Premenstrual Dysphoric Disorder
Premenstrual Syndrome
Presenile Dementia
Progressive Supranuclear Palsy
Prosopagnosia
Protein Deficiency Disorders
Pruritus
Pseudocyesis
Pseudodementia
Pulmonary Emphysema
Pulmonary Tuberculosis
Quadriplegia
Refraction Errors
Respiratory Distress
Respiratory Tract Disorders
Retrograde Amnesia
Rett Syndrome
Rheumatic Fever
Rheumatoid Arthritis
Rubella
Sclerosis (Nervous System)
Self Inflicted Wounds
Senile Dementia
Senile Psychosis
Sense Organ Disorders
Sensory Disabilities (Attitudes Toward)

Sensory System Disorders
Sex Chromosome Disorders
Sex Linked Hereditary Disorders
Sexual Function Disturbances
Sexually Transmitted Diseases
Sickle Cell Disease
Skin Disorders
Sleep Apnea
Sleep Disorders
Somatization
Somatoform Disorders
Somatoform Pain Disorder
Somatosensory Disorders
Spasms
Spina Bifida
Spinal Cord Injuries
Sterility
Strabismus
Sudden Infant Death
Syncope
Syndromes
Synesthesia
Syphilis
Tachycardia
Tardive Dyskinesia
Taste Disorders
Tay Sachs Disease
Terminal Cancer
Terminally Ill Patients
Testicular Feminization Syndrome
Thrombosis
Thyroid Disorders
Thyrotoxicosis
Tics
Tinnitus
Torticollis
Toxic Disorders
Toxic Encephalopathies
Toxic Hepatitis
Toxic Psychoses
Toxicomania
Traumatic Brain Injury
Tremor
Trichotillomania
Trigeminal Neuralgia
Trisomy 21
Tuberculosis
Tunnel Vision
Turners Syndrome
Ulcerative Colitis
Urinary Function Disorders
Urinary Incontinence
Urogenital Disorders
Vaginismus
Vascular Dementia
Viral Disorders
Vision Disorders
Vitamin Deficiency Disorders
Vomiting

Wernickes Syndrome
Whiplash
Williams Syndrome
Work Related Illnesses
Wounds

Psychological Disorders

Acrophobia
Acute Psychosis
Acute Schizophrenia
Acute Stress Disorder
Adjustment Disorders
Affective Disorders
Affective Psychosis
Agoraphobia
AIDS Dementia Complex
Alcoholic Hallucinosis
Alcoholic Psychosis
Alexithymia
Alzheimers Disease
Amnesia
Anaclitic Depression
Anorexia Nervosa
Antisocial Personality Disorder
Anxiety Disorders
Aspergers Syndrome
Auditory Hallucinations
Autism
Autistic Children
Avoidant Personality Disorder
Bipolar Disorder
Body Dysmorphic Disorder
Body Image Disturbances
Borderline Personality Disorder
Borderline States
Bulimia
Capgras Syndrome
Castration Anxiety
Catatonic Schizophrenia
Childhood Neurosis
Childhood Psychosis
Childhood Schizophrenia
Chronic Mental Illness
Chronic Psychosis
Chronic Stress
Claustrophobia
Compulsive Repetition
Confabulation
Consciousness Disturbances
Coprophagia
Creutzfeldt Jakob Syndrome
Culture Bound Syndromes
Cyclothymic Personality
Death Anxiety
Delirium Tremens
Delusions
Dementia
Dementia with Lewy Bodies

Consult Relationship Section for more information

Psychological Disorders — (cont'd)

Dependent Personality Disorder
Depersonalization
Depression (Emotion)
Dissociative Disorders
Dissociative Identity Disorder
Dysfunctional Family
Dysthymic Disorder
Early Infantile Autism
Eating Disorders
Elective Mutism
Electra Complex
Emotionally Disturbed
Endogenous Depression
Erotomania
Explosive Disorder
Factitious Disorders
Fantasies (Thought Disturbances)
Fetal Alcohol Syndrome
Folie A Deux
Fragmentation (Schizophrenia)
Fugue Reaction
Gender Identity Disorder
General Anxiety Disorder
Global Amnesia
Hallucinations
Hallucinosis
Histrionic Personality Disorder
Homeless Mentally Ill
Hypnagogic Hallucinations
Hypomania
Hysteria
Impulse Control Disorders
Inadequate Personality
Infantilism
Inhibited Sexual Desire
Involutional Depression
Involutional Paranoid Psychosis
Judgment Disturbances
Koro
Korsakoffs Psychosis
Magical Thinking
Major Depression
Malingering
Mania
Masochistic Personality
Mass Hysteria
Memory Disorders
Mental Disorders
Mental Disorders due to General
    Medical Conditions
Mental Illness (Attitudes Toward)
Mentally Ill Offenders
Multi Infarct Dementia
Munchausen Syndrome
Munchausen Syndrome by Proxy
Narcissistic Personality Disorder

Neurosis
Obsessive Compulsive Disorder
Obsessive Compulsive Personality
    Disorder
Occupational Neurosis
Oedipal Complex
Ophidiophobia
Organic Brain Syndromes
Panic Disorder
Paranoia (Psychosis)
Paranoid Personality Disorder
Paranoid Schizophrenia
Paraphilias
Passive Aggressive Personality
    Disorder
Personality Disorders
Pervasive Developmental Disorders
Phobias
Pica
Picks Disease
Postpartum Depression
Postpartum Psychosis
Posttraumatic Stress Disorder
Presenile Dementia
Process Psychosis
Pseudodementia
Psychosis
Reactive Depression
Reactive Psychosis
Recurrent Depression
Sadomasochistic Personality
Schizoaffective Disorder
Schizoid Personality Disorder
Schizophrenia
Schizophrenia (Disorganized Type)
Schizophreniform Disorder
Schizophrenogenic Family
Schizophrenogenic Mothers
Schizotypal Personality Disorder
School Phobia
Seasonal Affective Disorder
Self Defeating Behavior
Self Destructive Behavior
Self Mutilation
Senile Dementia
Senile Psychosis
Separation Anxiety
Sexual Addiction
Social Anxiety
Social Phobia
Speech Anxiety
Stress Reactions
Symbiotic Infantile Psychosis
Syndromes
Thought Disturbances
Toxic Psychoses
Traumatic Neurosis
Treatment Resistant Depression
Undifferentiated Schizophrenia

Vascular Dementia
Visual Hallucinations
Work Related Illnesses

Speech & Language Disorders

Acalculia
Agnosia
Agraphia
Alexia
Anosognosia
Aphasia
Articulation Disorders
Communication Disorders
Dysarthria
Dyslexia
Dysphasia
Dysphonia
Echolalia
Elective Mutism
Glossolalia
Language Delay
Language Disorders
Mutism
Prosopagnosia
Reading Disabilities
Retarded Speech Development
Speech Disorders
Stuttering

Symptomatology

Acting Out
Agitation
Akathisia
Amnesia
Anhedonia
Anoxia
Anxiety
Aphagia
Apnea
Apraxia
Asthenia
Ataxia
Automatism
Back Pain
Behavior Change
Binge Eating
Body Rocking
Bruxism
Catalepsy
Catatonia
Chronic Pain
Chronic Stress
Cognitive Impairment
Coma
Constipation
Convulsions
Craving
Delirium

Consult Relationship Section for more information

Symptomatology — (cont'd)

Depersonalization
Diarrhea
Dissociation
Distractibility
Drug Withdrawal
Dyskinesia
Dysphagia
Dyspnea
Extrapyramidal Symptoms
Falls
Fatigue
Fecal Incontinence
Head Banging
Headache
Health Complaints
Hematoma
Hemorrhage
Hoarding Behavior
Hyperglycemia
Hypersomnia
Hypertension
Hyperthermia
Hyperventilation
Hypoglycemia
Hyponatremia
Hypotension
Hypothermia
Inflammation
Insomnia
Mental Confusion
Muscle Spasms
Nail Biting
Nausea
Neurotoxicity
Nicotine Withdrawal
Nocturnal Teeth Grinding
Pain
Panic Attack
Parkinsonism
Personality Change
Physiological Correlates
Place Disorientation
Positive and Negative Symptoms
Prodrome
Pruritus
Psychiatric Symptoms
Purging (Eating Disorders)
Respiratory Distress
Restlessness
Scratching
Self Destructive Behavior
Shock
Somatization
Spasms
Symptom Checklists
Symptom Remission
Symptoms

Syncope
Tics
Time Disorientation
Tremor
Urinary Incontinence
Vertigo
Vomiting
Wandering Behavior

EDUCATIONAL CLUSTER

- Academic Learning & Achievement
- Curricula
- Educational Personnel & Administration
- Educational Testing & Counseling
- Schools & Institutions
- Special Education
- Student Characteristics & Academic Environment
- Student Populations
- Teaching & Teaching Methods

Academic Learning & Achievement

Academic Achievement
Academic Achievement Motivation
Academic Achievement Prediction
Academic Aptitude
Academic Failure
Academic Overachievement
Academic Self Concept
Academic Specialization
Academic Underachievement
Adult Learning
College Academic Achievement
Cooperative Learning
Discrimination Learning
Educational Attainment Level
Experiential Learning
Foreign Language Learning
Generalization (Learning)
Grade Level
Incidental Learning
Intentional Learning
Interference (Learning)
Latent Learning
Learning
Learning Ability
Learning Environment
Learning Rate
Learning Schedules
Learning Strategies
Learning Theory
Literacy
Mastery Learning
Mathematics Achievement
Metacognition

Mnemonic Learning
Nonsense Syllable Learning
Nonverbal Learning
Note Taking
Observational Learning
Overlearning
Paired Associate Learning
Perceptual Motor Learning
Phonological Awareness
Probability Learning
Reading Achievement
Reading Readiness
Reading Skills
Reading Speed
Recall (Learning)
Recognition (Learning)
Reconstruction (Learning)
Relearning
Retention
Rote Learning
School Graduation
School Learning
School Retention
Science Achievement
Self Regulated Learning
Sequential Learning
Serial Anticipation (Learning)
Serial Learning
Skill Learning
Social Learning
Spatial Learning
State Dependent Learning
Time On Task
Transfer (Learning)
Trial and Error Learning
Verbal Learning
Writing Skills

Curricula

Adult Education
Affective Education
After School Programs
Algebra
Apprenticeship
Art Education
Bilingual Education
Braille Instruction
Business Education
Calculus
Career Education
Clinical Methods Training
Clinical Psychology Graduate Training
Clinical Psychology Internship
Community Mental Health Training
Compensatory Education
Computer Training
Continuing Education
Cooperative Education

Consult Relationship Section for more information

Curricula — (cont'd)

Counselor Education
Curriculum
Curriculum Development
Death Education
Dental Education
Distance Education
Driver Education
Drug Education
Education
Educational Program Accreditation
Educational Program Planning
Educational Programs
Elementary Education
English as Second Language
Environmental Education
Equal Education
Extracurricular Activities
Family Life Education
Foreign Language Education
Foreign Study
Geometry
Graduate Education
Graduate Psychology Education
Health Education
High School Education
Higher Education
Home Economics
Home Schooling
Humanities
Inservice Teacher Education
Inservice Training
Language Arts Education
Literacy Programs
Management Training
Mathematics Education
Medical Education
Medical Internship
Medical Residency
Mental Health Inservice Training
Middle School Education
Military Training
Multicultural Education
Music Education
Nontraditional Education
Nursing Education
On the Job Training
Paraprofessional Education
Parent Training
Personnel Training
Phonics
Physical Education
Postgraduate Training
Preschool Education
Private School Education
Project Follow Through
Project Head Start
Psychiatric Training

Psychoanalytic Training
Psychology Education
Psychotherapy Training
Public School Education
Reading Education
Rehabilitation Education
Religious Education
Remedial Education
Remedial Reading
Same Sex Education
Science Education
Secondary Education
Sex Education
Social Studies Education
Social Work Education
Special Education
Spelling
Sports
Student Teaching
Teacher Education
Undergraduate Education
Upward Bound
Vocational Education

Educational Personnel & Administration

Accreditation (Education Personnel)
Boards of Education
Budgets
College Teachers
Cooperating Teachers
Educational Administration
Educational Personnel
Educational Program Accreditation
Educational Psychologists
Educational Quality
Educational Reform
Elementary School Teachers
High School Teachers
Junior High School Teachers
Librarians
Middle School Teachers
Parent School Relationship
Preschool Teachers
Preservice Teachers
Resource Teachers
School Administrators
School Counselors
School Nurses
School Principals
School Psychologists
School Superintendents
Special Education Teachers
Speech Therapists
Student Teachers
Teacher Aides
Teacher Attitudes
Teacher Characteristics

Teacher Education
Teacher Effectiveness Evaluation
Teacher Expectations
Teacher Personality
Teacher Recruitment
Teacher Student Interaction
Teacher Tenure
Teachers
Vocational Counselors
Vocational Education Teachers

Educational Testing & Counseling

Achievement Measures
Adaptive Testing
Aptitude Measures
College Entrance Examination Board
    Scholastic Aptitude Test
Computer Assisted Testing
Course Evaluation
Criterion Referenced Tests
Cultural Test Bias
Curriculum Based Assessment
Educational Counseling
Educational Diagnosis
Educational Financial Assistance
Educational Measurement
Educational Placement
Educational Program Evaluation
Educational Psychology
Educational Therapy
Entrance Examinations
Essay Testing
Grading (Educational)
Graduate Record Examination
Group Testing
Minimum Competency Tests
Posttesting
School Based Intervention
School Counseling
School Psychology
Student Admission Criteria
Student Personnel Services
Student Records
Teacher Effectiveness Evaluation
Test Coaching
Test Taking
Testing
Testing Methods
Testwiseness
Woodcock Johnson Psychoeducational
    Battery

Schools & Institutions

Boarding Schools
Campuses
Classrooms
Colleges
Community Colleges

Consult Relationship Section for more information

Schools & Institutions — (cont'd)

Dormitories
Educational Laboratories
Elementary Schools
Graduate Schools
High Schools
Institutional Schools
Junior High Schools
Kindergartens
Learning Centers (Educational)
Middle Schools
Military Schools
Nongraded Schools
Nursery Schools
School Facilities
School Libraries
Schools
Seminaries
Technical Schools

Special Education

Acalculia
Agnosia
Agraphia
Alexia
Anencephaly
Aphasia
Apraxia
Articulation Disorders
Aspergers Syndrome
Ataxia
Attention Deficit Disorder
Attention Deficit Disorder with
 Hyperactivity
Augmentative Communication
Autism
Autistic Children
Behavior Disorders
Behavior Modification
Behavior Problems
Blind
Borderline Mental Retardation
Braille Instruction
Classroom Behavior Modification
Cleft Palate
Communication Disorders
Communication Skills Training
Compensatory Education
Crying Cat Syndrome
Deaf
Deaf Blind
Delayed Development
Developmental Disabilities
Downs Syndrome
Dysarthria
Dyskinesia
Dyslexia
Dysphasia

Dysphonia
Ear Disorders
Early Infantile Autism
Early Intervention
Echolalia
Educational Placement
Educational Therapy
Emotionally Disturbed
Gifted
Hearing Disorders
Home Reared Mentally Retarded
Hyperkinesis
Institutionalized Mentally Retarded
Language Delay
Language Disorders
Learning Disabilities
Learning Disorders
Literacy Programs
Mainstreaming
Mainstreaming (Educational)
Memory Disorders
Mental Retardation
Microcephaly
Mild Mental Retardation
Minimal Brain Disorders
Moderate Mental Retardation
Mutism
Partially Hearing Impaired
Perceptual Disturbances
Pervasive Developmental Disorders
Profound Mental Retardation
Psychosocial Mental Retardation
Reading Disabilities
Remedial Education
Remedial Reading
Retarded Speech Development
Rett Syndrome
Savants
School Based Intervention
Severe Mental Retardation
Social Skills Training
Special Education
Special Education Students
Special Needs
Speech Disorders
Speech Therapy
Stuttering
Tay Sachs Disease
Vision Disorders

Student Characteristics & Academic Environment

Ability Level
Academic Achievement
Academic Achievement Motivation
Academic Aptitude
Academic Environment
Academic Failure

Academic Overachievement
Academic Self Concept
Academic Specialization
Academic Underachievement
Artistic Ability
Athletic Participation
Bullying
Class Size
Classroom Behavior
Classroom Environment
Classroom Management
Classrooms
Coeducation
Cognitive Ability
College Academic Achievement
College Environment
Computer Anxiety
Computer Literacy
Declarative Knowledge
Educational Aspirations
Educational Attainment Level
Educational Background
Educational Degrees
Educational Incentives
Educational Objectives
Fraternity Membership
Grade Level
Learning Ability
Learning Environment
Literacy
Mathematical Ability
Mathematics Anxiety
Musical Ability
Native Language
Nonverbal Ability
Performance Anxiety
Phonological Awareness
Procedural Knowledge
Reading Ability
Reading Comprehension
Reading Skills
Same Sex Education
School Adjustment
School Attendance
School Club Membership
School Enrollment
School Environment
School Expulsion
School Graduation
School Integration
School Phobia
School Readiness
School Refusal
School Retention
School Suspension
School to Work Transition
School Transition
School Truancy
School Violence

Consult Relationship Section for more information

Student Characteristics & Academic Environment — (cont'd)

Social Loafing
Sorority Membership
Special Needs
Speech Anxiety
Student Activism
Student Attitudes
Student Attrition
Student Characteristics
Student Records
Study Habits
Tardiness
Teacher Student Interaction
Test Anxiety
Truancy
Verbal Ability
Writing Skills

Student Populations

Business Students
Classmates
College Athletes
College Dropouts
College Graduates
College Students
Community College Students
Counselor Trainees
Dental Students
Dropouts
Education Students
Elementary School Students
Foreign Students
Gifted
Graduate Students
High School Graduates
High School Students
Intermediate School Students
Junior College Students
Junior High School Students
Kindergarten Students
Law Students
Medical Students
Middle School Students
Nursery School Students
Nursing Students
Postgraduate Students
Potential Dropouts
Preschool Students
Preservice Teachers
Primary School Students
Reentry Students
ROTC Students
School Dropouts
School Leavers
Seminarians
Special Education Students

Student Teachers
Students
Therapist Trainees
Transfer Students
Vocational School Students

Teaching & Teaching Methods

Ability Grouping
Advance Organizers
Apprenticeship
Audiovisual Instruction
Braille Instruction
Classroom Behavior Modification
Classroom Discipline
Classroom Management
Computer Assisted Instruction
Constant Time Delay
Cooperative Learning
Curricular Field Experience
Directed Discussion Method
Discovery Teaching Method
Distance Education
Education
Educational Audiovisual Aids
Educational Field Trips
Educational Incentives
Educational Laboratories
Educational Objectives
Educational Programs
Educational Television
Educational Toys
Experiential Learning
Feedback
Film Strips
Group Discussion
Group Instruction
Home Schooling
Homework
Individualized Instruction
Initial Teaching Alphabet
Instructional Media
Language Laboratories
Learning Strategies
Lecture Method
Lesson Plans
Montessori Method
Motion Pictures (Educational)
Nondirected Discussion Method
On the Job Training
Open Classroom Method
Peer Tutoring
Programmed Instruction
Programmed Textbooks
Prompting
Psychoeducation
Reading Materials
Remedial Reading
School Learning

Self Instructional Training
Sight Vocabulary
Silent Reading
Student Teaching
Teaching
Teaching Machines
Teaching Methods
Team Teaching Method
Televised Instruction
Textbooks
Theories of Education
Tutoring
Videotape Instruction

LEGAL CLUSTER

- Adjudication
- Criminal Groups
- Criminal Offenses
- Criminal Rehabilitation
- Laws
- Legal Issues
- Legal Personnel
- Legal Processes

Adjudication

Adjudication
Capital Punishment
Commitment (Psychiatric)
Competency to Stand Trial
Court Referrals
Crime
Crime Victims
Criminal Conviction
Criminal Justice
Criminal Responsibility
Defendants
Expert Testimony
Forensic Evaluation
Informants
Informed Consent
Insanity Defense
Juries
Jury Selection
Justice
Juvenile Justice
Law Enforcement
Legal Arrest
Legal Decisions
Legal Detention
Legal Evidence
Legal Interrogation
Legal Processes
Legal Testimony
Litigation
Parole
Perpetrators
Polygraphs

Consult Relationship Section for more information

Adjudication — (cont'd)

Probation
Protective Services
Witnesses

Criminal Groups

Criminals
Defendants
Female Criminals
Female Delinquency
Juvenile Delinquency
Juvenile Gangs
Male Criminals
Male Delinquency
Mentally Ill Offenders
Perpetrators
Predelinquent Youth
Prisoners

Criminal Offenses

Abandonment
Acquaintance Rape
Age Discrimination
Arson
Assisted Suicide
Battered Child Syndrome
Battered Females
Child Abuse
Child Neglect
Crime
Criminal Behavior
Disability Discrimination
Driving Under The Influence
Drug Distribution
Elder Abuse
Employment Discrimination
Family Violence
Fraud
Gambling
Genocide
Harassment
Hate Crimes
Homicide
Incest
Infanticide
Kidnapping
Kleptomania
Partner Abuse
Pathological Gambling
Patient Abuse
Pedophilia
Persecution
Physical Abuse
Political Assassination
Pornography
Prostitution
Race and Ethnic Discrimination

Rape
Runaway Behavior
School Violence
Serial Homicide
Sex Discrimination
Sex Offenses
Sexual Abuse
Sexual Harassment
Shoplifting
Social Discrimination
Stalking
Terrorism
Theft
Torture
Vandalism
Victimization
Violent Crime

Criminal Rehabilitation

Correctional Institutions
Criminal Rehabilitation
Criminology
Forensic Psychiatry
Forensic Psychology
Incarceration
Institutional Release
Institutional Schools
Institutionalization
Maximum Security Facilities
Parole
Penology
Prisons
Probation
Recidivism
Reformatories

Laws

Abortion Laws
Abuse Reporting
Affirmative Action
Child Abuse Reporting
Child Labor
Civil Law
Criminal Law
Disability Laws
Drug Laws
Equal Education
Government Policy Making
Gun Control Laws
Health Care Policy
Law (Government)
Laws
Legal Decisions
Legislative Processes
Marijuana Laws
Medicare
Social Security
Taxation

Legal Issues

Affirmative Action
Age Discrimination
Assisted Suicide
Capital Punishment
Censorship
Child Care
Child Welfare
Civil Rights
Crime Prevention
Criminal Justice
Criminal Responsibility
Dangerousness
Disability Discrimination
Drug Legalization
Drug Usage Screening
Duty to Warn
Employment Discrimination
Equal Education
Eugenics
Euthanasia
HIV Testing
Human Rights
Informed Consent
Life Sustaining Treatment
Marijuana Legalization
Morality
Political Revolution
Privileged Communication
Professional Client Sexual Relations
Professional Liability
Race and Ethnic Discrimination
Refugees
Right to Treatment
Riots
Safety Belts
Safety Devices
School Integration
School Truancy
Self Defense
Sex Discrimination
Social Discrimination
Social Equality
Social Integration
Surrogate Parents (Humans)
Treatment Withholding
Victimization
Warning Labels

Legal Personnel

Attorneys
Judges
Juries
Law Enforcement Personnel
Law Students
Legal Personnel
Parole Officers
Police Personnel

Consult Relationship Section for more information

Legal Personnel — (cont'd)

Prison Personnel
Probation Officers

Legal Processes

Abuse Reporting
Adoption (Child)
Advance Directives
Advocacy
Autopsy
Censorship
Child Abuse Reporting
Child Custody
Child Support
Child Visitation
Child Welfare
Citizenship
Civil Rights
Client Rights
Commitment (Psychiatric)
Conflict Resolution
Consumer Protection
Court Referrals
Crime Prevention
Criminology
Divorce
Drug Legalization
Forensic Evaluation
Forensic Psychiatry
Forensic Psychology
Foster Care
Guardianship
Immigration
Interracial Adoption
Involuntary Treatment
Joint Custody
Juvenile Justice
Labor Management Relations
Labor Union Members
Labor Unions
Legal Confession
Legal Processes
Litigation
Marijuana Legalization
Marital Separation
Mediation
Organizational Merger
Outpatient Commitment
Professional Licensing
Protective Services
Psychiatric Evaluation
School Integration
Social Integration
Strikes

NEUROPSYCHOLOGY & NEUROLOGY CLUSTER

- Assessment & Diagnosis
- Electrophysiology
- Neuroanatomy
- Neurological Disorders
- Neurological Intervention
- Neurosciences
- Neurotransmitters & Neuroregulators

Assessment & Diagnosis

Bender Gestalt Test
Echoencephalography
Electroencephalography
Halstead Reitan Neuropsychological Battery
Luria Nebraska Neuropsychological Battery
Magnetic Resonance Imaging
Magnetoencephalography
Memory for Designs Test
Mini Mental State Examination
Neuroimaging
Neuropsychological Assessment
Pneumoencephalography
Polysomnography
Rheoencephalography
Wechsler Memory Scale
Wisconsin Card Sorting Test

Electrophysiology

Alpha Rhythm
Auditory Evoked Potentials
Basal Skin Resistance
Contingent Negative Variation
Cortical Evoked Potentials
Delta Rhythm
Electrical Activity
Electrical Brain Stimulation
Electroencephalography
Electrophysiology
Evoked Potentials
Galvanic Skin Response
Kindling
Magnetoencephalography
Olfactory Evoked Potentials
Polysomnography
Postactivation Potentials
Skin Electrical Properties
Skin Potential
Skin Resistance
Somatosensory Evoked Potentials
Theta Rhythm
Visual Evoked Potentials

Neuroanatomy

Abducens Nerve
Acoustic Nerve
Adrenergic Nerves
Adrenergic Receptors
Afferent Pathways
Amygdala
Auditory Cortex
Auditory Neurons
Autonomic Ganglia
Autonomic Nervous System
Axons
Baroreceptors
Basal Ganglia
Blood Brain Barrier
Brain
Brain Size
Brain Stem
Brain Weight
Broca's Area
Caudate Nucleus
Central Nervous System
Cerebellum
Cerebral Blood Flow
Cerebral Cortex
Cerebral Dominance
Cerebral Ventricles
Cerebrospinal Fluid
Chemoreceptors
Cholinergic Nerves
Cholinergic Receptors
Cones (Eye)
Corpus Callosum
Cranial Spinal Cord
Cutaneous Receptive Fields
Cutaneous Sense
Dendrites
Diencephalon
Dorsal Horns
Dorsal Roots
Efferent Pathways
Extrapyramidal Tracts
Facial Nerve
Forebrain
Fornix
Fovea
Frontal Lobe
Ganglia
Ganglion Cells (Retina)
Geniculate Bodies (Thalamus)
Globus Pallidus
Gyrus Cinguli
Hindbrain
Hippocampus
Hypothalamo Hypophyseal System
Hypothalamo Pituitary Adrenal System
Hypothalamus
Inferior Colliculus

Consult Relationship Section for more information

Neuroanatomy — (cont'd)

Interhemispheric Interaction
Lateral Dominance
Left Brain
Lemniscal System
Limbic System
Locus Ceruleus
Lumbar Spinal Cord
Mechanoreceptors
Medial Forebrain Bundle
Medulla Oblongata
Meninges
Mesencephalon
Motor Cortex
Motor Neurons
Myelin Sheath
Nerve Endings
Nerve Growth Factor
Nerve Tissues
Nervous System
Neural Analyzers
Neural Development
Neural Pathways
Neural Plasticity
Neural Receptors
Neurons
Nociceptors
Nucleus Basalis Magnocellularis
Occipital Lobe
Ocular Dominance
Olfactory Bulb
Olfactory Nerve
Optic Chiasm
Optic Lobe
Optic Nerve
Optic Tract
Parasympathetic Nervous System
Parietal Lobe
Periaqueductal Gray
Peripheral Nervous System
Photoreceptors
Pons
Preoptic Area
Proprioceptors
Purkinje Cells
Putamen
Pyramidal Tracts
Raphe Nuclei
Receptive Fields
Receptor Binding
Reticular Formation
Retina
Right Brain
Rods (Eye)
Sense Organs
Sensory Neurons
Septal Nuclei
Somatosensory Cortex

Spinal Column
Spinal Cord
Spinal Ganglia
Spinothalamic Tracts
Striatum
Substantia Nigra
Sympathetic Nervous System
Tegmentum
Telencephalon
Thalamic Nuclei
Thalamus
Trigeminal Nerve
Vagus Nerve
Ventral Roots
Visual Cortex

Neurological Disorders

Acalculia
Agnosia
Agraphia
AIDS Dementia Complex
Alcoholic Hallucinosis
Alcoholic Psychosis
Alexia
Alzheimers Disease
Anencephaly
Anosognosia
Anoxia
Anterograde Amnesia
Aphasia
Apraxia
Ataxia
Athetosis
Audiogenic Seizures
Autonomic Nervous System Disorders
Back Pain
Bacterial Meningitis
Bradykinesia
Brain Concussion
Brain Damage
Brain Disorders
Brain Neoplasms
Catalepsy
Cataplexy
Central Nervous System Disorders
Cerebral Arteriosclerosis
Cerebral Atrophy
Cerebral Hemorrhage
Cerebral Ischemia
Cerebral Palsy
Cerebrovascular Accidents
Cerebrovascular Disorders
Chorea
Chronic Pain
Cognitive Impairment
Coma
Convulsions
Creutzfeldt Jakob Syndrome

Delirium Tremens
Dementia
Dementia with Lewy Bodies
Dysarthria
Dyskinesia
Dyslexia
Dysphasia
Dysphonia
Encephalitis
Encephalomyelitis
Encephalopathies
Epilepsy
Epileptic Seizures
Extrapyramidal Symptoms
General Paresis
Gilles de la Tourette Disorder
Global Amnesia
Grand Mal Epilepsy
Head Injuries
Headache
Hemianopia
Hemiplegia
Huntingtons Disease
Hydrocephaly
Hyperkinesis
Korsakoffs Psychosis
Memory Disorders
Meningitis
Microcephaly
Migraine Headache
Minimal Brain Disorders
Movement Disorders
Multi Infarct Dementia
Multiple Sclerosis
Muscle Contraction Headache
Muscular Dystrophy
Myasthenia Gravis
Myelitis
Myoclonia
Myofascial Pain
Narcolepsy
Nervous System Disorders
Nervous System Neoplasms
Neuralgia
Neurodegenerative Diseases
Neuroleptic Malignant Syndrome
Neuromuscular Disorders
Neuropathology
Neurosyphilis
Organic Brain Syndromes
Pain
Paralysis
Paraplegia
Parkinsons Disease
Peripheral Nerve Disorders
Petit Mal Epilepsy
Picks Disease
Poliomyelitis
Presenile Dementia

Consult Relationship Section for more information

Neurological Disorders — (cont'd)

Progressive Supranuclear Palsy
Prosopagnosia
Quadriplegia
Sclerosis (Nervous System)
Senile Dementia
Senile Psychosis
Spasms
Spinal Cord Injuries
Synesthesia
Tardive Dyskinesia
Tics
Torticollis
Toxic Encephalopathies
Traumatic Brain Injury
Tremor
Trigeminal Neuralgia
Vascular Dementia
Wernickes Syndrome
Williams Syndrome

Neurological Intervention

Afferent Stimulation
Brain Lesions
Brain Self Stimulation
Brain Stimulation
Chemical Brain Stimulation
Commissurotomy
Decerebration
Decortication (Brain)
Electrical Brain Stimulation
Hemispherectomy
Hypothalamus Lesions
Kindling
Neural Lesions
Neural Transplantation
Neurosurgery
Psychosurgery
Pyramidotomy
Stereotaxic Techniques
Sympathectomy
Thalamotomy
Tractotomy
Vagotomy

Neurosciences

Neural Networks
Neuroanatomy
Neurobiology
Neurochemistry
Neuroendocrinology
Neurolinguistics
Neurology
Neuropathology
Neurophysiology
Neuropsychiatry
Neuropsychology

Neurosciences
Neurosurgery
Psychoneuroimmunology
Psychopharmacology
Psychosurgery

Neurotransmitters & Neuroregulators

Acetylcholine
Acetylcholinesterase
Adenosine
Alanines
Amino Acids
Angiotensin
Aspartic Acid
Bombesin
Catecholamines
Cholecystokinin
Choline
Cholinesterase
Dihydroxyphenylacetic Acid
Dihydroxytryptamine
Dopamine
Dopamine Metabolites
Dynorphins
Endogenous Opiates
Endorphins
Enkephalins
Epinephrine
Gamma Aminobutyric Acid
Glutamic Acid
Glycine
Histamine
Homovanillic Acid
Hydroxydopamine (6-)
Hydroxyindoleacetic Acid (5-)
Ibotenic Acid
Kainic Acid
Leptin
Melanocyte Stimulating Hormone
Methoxyhydroxyphenylglycol (3,4)
Monoamine Oxidases
Neurokinins
Neuropeptide Y
Neuropeptides
Neurotensin
Neurotoxicity
Neurotoxins
Neurotransmission
Neurotransmitters
Nitric Oxide
Norepinephrine
Norepinephrine Metabolites
Oxytocin
Peptides
Phenethylamines
Serotonin
Serotonin Metabolites

Somatostatin
Substance P
Taurine
Tryptamine
Tyramine

OCCUPATIONAL & EMPLOYMENT CLUSTER

- Career Areas
- Employee, Occupational & Job Characteristics
- Occupational Groups
- Organizations & Organizational Behavior
- Personnel Management & Professional Personnel Issues

Career Areas

Advertising
Air Traffic Control
Behavioral Sciences
Business
Business Management
Child Care
Child Day Care
Community Psychology
Computer Programming
Consultation Liaison Psychiatry
Counseling
Cross Cultural Psychology
Data Processing
Education
Educational Administration
Educational Psychology
Entrepreneurship
Experimental Psychology
Family Therapy
Forensic Psychiatry
Forensic Psychology
Geriatric Psychiatry
Gynecology
Health Care Administration
Health Promotion
Human Factors Engineering
Hypnotherapy
Industrial and Organizational Psychology
Job Corps
Law Enforcement
Marketing
Marriage Counseling
News Media
Nontraditional Careers
Nursing
Obstetrics
Occupational Therapy
Optometry
Paramedical Sciences

Consult Relationship Section for more information

Career Areas — (cont'd)

Pathology
Peace Corps
Pediatrics
Physical Therapy
Politics
Product Design
Psychiatry
Psychology
Psychotherapy
Public Relations
Rehabilitation
Rehabilitation Counseling
Retailing
School Psychology
Sciences
Self Employment
Social Casework
Social Psychology
Speech Therapy
Sports
Surgery
Teaching
Veterinary Medicine
Vocational Rehabilitation
Zoology

Employee, Occupational, & Job Characteristics

Bonuses
Career Change
Child Labor
Clerical Secretarial Skills
Disabled Personnel
Diversity in the Workplace
Division of Labor
Dual Careers
Employability
Employee Absenteeism
Employee Attitudes
Employee Benefits
Employee Characteristics
Employee Efficiency
Employee Health Insurance
Employee Interaction
Employee Leave Benefits
Employee Motivation
Employee Pension Plans
Employee Productivity
Employee Skills
Employee Turnover
Employment History
Employment Status
Family Work Relationship
Health Personnel Attitudes
Impaired Professionals
Income Level
Industrial Accidents

Job Applicant Attitudes
Job Characteristics
Job Enrichment
Job Experience Level
Job Involvement
Job Knowledge
Job Performance
Job Satisfaction
Job Search
Job Security
Labor Union Members
Leadership Qualities
Mentor
Noise Levels (Work Areas)
Occupational Adjustment
Occupational Aspirations
Occupational Attitudes
Occupational Choice
Occupational Exposure
Occupational Interests
Occupational Mobility
Occupational Neurosis
Occupational Preference
Occupational Safety
Occupational Status
Occupational Stress
Occupational Success
Occupational Tenure
Organizational Characteristics
Organizational Climate
Organizational Commitment
Organizational Learning
Private Practice
Procedural Justice
Professional Competence
Professional Identity
Professional Networking
Professional Specialization
Professionalism
Psychological Contracts
Quality of Work Life
Reemployment
Retirement
Salaries
Social Loafing
School to Work Transition
Supervisor Employee Interaction
Tardiness
Telecommuting
Typing
Unemployment
Vocational Maturity
Work (Attitudes Toward)
Work Adjustment Training
Work Load
Work Related Illnesses
Work Rest Cycles
Work Scheduling
Work Week Length

Workaholism
Workday Shifts
Working Conditions
Working Space
Working Women

Occupational Groups

Accountants
Aerospace Personnel
Agricultural Extension Workers
Agricultural Workers
Air Force Personnel
Aircraft Pilots
Anthropologists
Apprenticeship
Architects
Army Personnel
Artists
Astronauts
Athletes
Attendants (Institutions)
Attorneys
Blue Collar Workers
Business and Industrial Personnel
Chaplains
Child Care Workers
Clergy
Clerical Personnel
Clinical Psychologists
Clinicians
Coaches
Coast Guard Personnel
College Teachers
Commissioned Officers
Cooperating Teachers
Counseling Psychologists
Counselor Trainees
Counselors
Dentists
Disabled Personnel
Domestic Service Personnel
Draftees
Educational Personnel
Educational Psychologists
Elementary School Teachers
Engineers
Enlisted Military Personnel
Evangelists
Experimental Psychologists
Family Physicians
Fire Fighters
Foreign Workers
General Practitioners
Government Personnel
Gynecologists
Health Personnel
High School Teachers
Home Care Personnel

Consult Relationship Section for more information

Occupational Groups — (cont'd)

Hypnotherapists
Hypnotists
Industrial Foremen
Industrial Psychologists
Information Specialists
Internists
Interviewers
Job Applicants
Journalists
Judges
Junior High School Teachers
Labor Union Members
Law Enforcement Personnel
Lay Religious Personnel
Legal Personnel
Librarians
Management Personnel
Marine Personnel
Mathematicians
Medical Personnel
Mental Health Personnel
Mentor
Middle Level Managers
Migrant Farm Workers
Military Medical Personnel
Military Personnel
Military Psychologists
Ministers (Religion)
Missionaries
Musicians
National Guardsmen
Navy Personnel
Neurologists
Noncommissioned Officers
Nonprofessional Personnel
Nuns
Nurses
Obstetricians
Occupational Therapists
Occupations
Optometrists
Paramedical Personnel
Paraprofessional Personnel
Parole Officers
Pathologists
Pediatricians
Personnel
Pharmacists
Physical Therapists
Physicians
Physicists
Police Personnel
Politicians
Preschool Teachers
Preservice Teachers
Priests
Prison Personnel

Probation Officers
Professional Personnel
Psychiatric Aides
Psychiatric Hospital Staff
Psychiatric Nurses
Psychiatric Social Workers
Psychiatrists
Psychoanalysts
Psychologists
Psychotherapists
Public Health Service Nurses
Rabbis
Rehabilitation Counselors
Religious Personnel
Resource Teachers
Sales Personnel
School Administrators
School Counselors
School Nurses
School Principals
School Psychologists
School Superintendents
Scientists
Secretarial Personnel
Seminarians
Service Personnel
Skilled Industrial Workers
Social Psychologists
Social Workers
Sociologists
Special Education Teachers
Speech Therapists
Student Teachers
Surgeons
Teacher Aides
Teachers
Technical Personnel
Technical Service Personnel
Therapist Trainees
Therapists
Top Level Managers
Unskilled Industrial Workers
Vocational Counselors
Vocational Education Teachers
Volunteer Military Personnel
Volunteers
White Collar Workers
Working Women
Writers

Organizations & Organizational Behavior

Business Organizations
Decentralization
Diversity in the Workplace
Division of Labor
Downsizing
Entrepreneurship

Foreign Organizations
Globalization
Government Agencies
Government Policy Making
Health Care Policy
Health Maintenance Organizations
International Organizations
Labor Unions
Nonprofit Organizations
Organizational Behavior
Organizational Change
Organizational Characteristics
Organizational Climate
Organizational Commitment
Organizational Crises
Organizational Development
Organizational Effectiveness
Organizational Learning
Organizational Merger
Organizational Objectives
Organizational Structure
Organizations
Policy Making
Professional Organizations
Professional Networking
Religious Organizations
Self Managing Work Teams
Teams
Work Teams

Personnel Management & Professional Personnel Issues

Affirmative Action
Age Discrimination
Assessment Centers
Bonuses
Budgets
Career Development
Career Education
Conflict Resolution
Disability Discrimination
Disability Evaluation
Disability Management
Distributive Justice
Diversity in the Workplace
Downsizing
Employee Assistance Programs
Employee Attitudes
Employee Benefits
Employee Health Insurance
Employee Leave Benefits
Employee Pension Plans
Employee Turnover
Employer Attitudes
Employment Discrimination
Employment Tests
Entrepreneurship
Human Capital
Human Resource Management

Consult Relationship Section for more information

Personnel Management & Professional Personnel Issues — (cont'd)

Inservice Training
Job Analysis
Job Applicant Interviews
Job Applicant Screening
Job Enrichment
Job Search
Labor Management Relations
Leadership
Leadership Qualities
Leadership Style
Management
Management Decision Making
Management Methods
Management Personnel
Management Planning
Management Training
Mediation
Medical Personnel Supply
Mental Health Inservice Training
Mental Health Personnel Supply
Middle Level Managers
Military Recruitment
Military Training
Negotiation
Occupational Guidance
Occupational Success Prediction
On the Job Training
Organizational Learning
Participative Management
Personnel Evaluation
Personnel Placement
Personnel Promotion
Personnel Recruitment
Personnel Selection
Personnel Supply
Personnel Termination
Personnel Training
Policy Making
Private Practice
Procedural Justice
Professional Certification
Professional Consultation
Professional Development
Professional Ethics
Professional Examinations
Professional Fees
Professional Identity
Professional Liability
Professional Licensing
Professional Referral
Professional Specialization
Professional Standards
Professional Supervision
Professionalism
Psychological Contracts
Quality Control
Race and Ethnic Discrimination

Reemployment
Retirement
Salaries
Sex Discrimination
Sexual Harassment
Social Security
Stress Management
Strikes
Supervisor Employee Interaction
Supported Employment
Tardiness
Teacher Recruitment
Telecommuting
Top Level Managers
Transformational Leadership
Unemployment
Vocational Evaluation
Workers' Compensation Insurance

STATISTICAL CLUSTER

- Design, Analysis & Interpretation
- Statistical Reliability & Validity
- Statistical Theory & Experimentation

Design, Analysis, & Interpretation

Algorithms
Analysis of Covariance
Analysis of Variance
Between Groups Design
Causal Analysis
Central Tendency Measures
Chi Square Test
Cluster Analysis
Cochran Q Test
Cohort Analysis
Content Analysis
Content Analysis (Test)
Decision Theory
Error Analysis
Error of Measurement
Evaluation Criteria
Experimental Design
F Test
Factor Analysis
Factor Structure
Fuzzy Set Theory
Goodness of Fit
Heuristic Modeling
Homogeneity of Variance
Interaction Analysis (Statistics)
Interaction Variance
Item Analysis (Statistical)
Item Analysis (Test)
Item Response Theory
Kolmogorov Smirnov Test
Least Squares
Linear Regression
Logistic Regression
Mann Whitney U Test

Markov Chains
Mathematical Modeling
Maximum Likelihood
Mean
Median
Meta Analysis
Multidimensional Scaling
Multiple Regression
Multivariate Analysis
Nonlinear Regression
Nonparametric Statistical Tests
Oblique Rotation
Orthogonal Rotation
Parametric Statistical Tests
Path Analysis
Phi Coefficient
Point Biserial Correlation
Probability
Q Sort Testing Technique
Rank Difference Correlation
Rank Order Correlation
Repeated Measures
Scaling (Testing)
Score Equating
Scoring (Testing)
Sign Test
Spearman Brown Test
Standard Deviation
Standard Scores
Statistical Analysis
Statistical Correlation
Statistical Data
Statistical Estimation
Statistical Measurement
Statistical Norms
Statistical Probability
Statistical Regression
Statistical Reliability
Statistical Rotation
Statistical Significance
Statistical Tables
Statistical Tests
Statistical Validity
Statistical Variables
Statistical Weighting
Stochastic Modeling
Structural Equation Modeling
T Test
Tetrachoric Correlation
Time Series
Variability Measurement
Varimax Rotation
Wilcoxon Sign Rank Test
Zulliger Z Test

Statistical Reliability & Validity

Content Analysis
Content Analysis (Test)
Error Analysis
Error of Measurement

Consult Relationship Section for more information

Statistical Reliability & Validity — (cont'd)

Interrater Reliability
Item Analysis (Statistical)
Item Content (Test)
Statistical Power
Statistical Reliability
Statistical Validity
Test Reliability
Test Validity

Statistical Theory & Experimentation

Biased Sampling
Binomial Distribution
Chaos Theory
Classical Test Theory
Confidence Limits (Statistics)
Conjoint Measurement
Consistency (Measurement)
Cutting Scores
Data Collection
Data Processing
Dependent Variables
Effect Size (Statistical)
Empirical Methods
Experiment Controls
Experimental Design
Experimental Replication
Experimental Subjects
Experimentation
Experimenter Bias
Followup Studies
Frequency Distribution
Fuzzy Set Theory
Halo Effect
Independent Variables
Knowledge of Results
Longitudinal Studies
Maximum Likelihood
Methodology
Normal Distribution
Null Hypothesis Testing
Population (Statistics)
Prediction Errors
Prospective Studies
Qualitative Research
Quantitative Methods
Quasi Experimental Methods
Random Sampling
Research Setting
Retrospective Studies
Sample Size
Sampling (Experimental)
Skewed Distribution
Statistical Data
Statistical Sample Parameters
Statistical Samples
Statistical Significance

Statistical Tables
Statistical Variables
Statistics
Type I Errors
Type II Errors

TESTS & TESTING CLUSTER

- Academic Achievement & Aptitude Measures
- Attitude & Interest Measures
- Developmental Measures
- Intelligence Measures
- Neuropsychological Measures
- Nonprojective Personality Measures
- Perceptual Measures
- Projective Personality Measures
- Testing
- Testing Methods

Academic Achievement & Aptitude Measures

Achievement Measures
Aptitude Measures
Army General Classification Test
College Entrance Examination Board Scholastic Aptitude Test
Comprehension Tests
Curriculum Based Assessment
Differential Aptitude Tests
Educational Measurement
Entrance Examinations
Gates MacGinitie Reading Tests
General Aptitude Test Battery
Graduate Record Examination
Iowa Tests of Basic Skills
Metropolitan Readiness Tests
Minimum Competency Tests
Professional Examinations
Reading Measures
Retention Measures
Stanford Achievement Test
Verbal Tests
Wide Range Achievement Test
Woodcock Johnson Psychoeducational Battery

Attitude & Interest Measures

Attitude Measurement
Attitude Measures
Consumer Surveys
Interest Inventories
Kuder Occupational Interest Survey
Kuder Preference Record
Least Preferred Coworker Scale
Occupational Interest Measures
Preference Measures
Strong Vocational Interest Blank

Wilson Patterson Conservatism Scale

Developmental Measures

Bayley Scales of Infant Development
Developmental Measures

Intelligence Measures

Benton Revised Visual Retention Test
Cognitive Assessment
Columbia Mental Maturity Scale
Creativity Measurement
Culture Fair Intelligence Test
Frostig Developmental Test of Visual Perception
Goodenough Harris Draw A Person Test
Illinois Test of Psycholinguistic Abilities
Intelligence Measures
Kaufman Assessment Battery for Children
Kohs Block Design Test
Miller Analogies Test
Peabody Picture Vocabulary Test
Porteus Maze Test
Raven Coloured Progressive Matrices
Raven Progressive Matrices
Slosson Intelligence Test
Stanford Binet Intelligence Scale
Verbal Tests
Wechsler Adult Intelligence Scale
Wechsler Bellevue Intelligence Scale
Wechsler Intelligence Scale for Children
Wechsler Memory Scale
Wechsler Preschool Primary Scale

Neuropsychological Measures

Bender Gestalt Test
Benton Revised Visual Retention Test
Body Sway Testing
Halstead Reitan Neuropsychological Battery
Luria Nebraska Neuropsychological Battery
Memory for Designs Test
Mini Mental State Examination
Neuropsychological Assessment
Wechsler Memory Scale
Wisconsin Card Sorting Test

Nonprojective Personality Measures

Bannister Repertory Grid
Beck Depression Inventory
Bem Sex Role Inventory
California F Scale
California Psychological Inventory
Child Behavior Checklist

Consult Relationship Section for more information

Nonprojective Personality Measures — (cont'd)

Childrens Manifest Anxiety Scale
Childrens Personality Questionnaire
Edwards Personal Preference Schedule
Edwards Personality Inventory
Edwards Social Desirability Scale
Embedded Figures Testing
Eysenck Personality Inventory
Fear Survey Schedule
Fundamental Interpersonal Relation
    Orientation Behavior Ques
General Health Questionnaire
Gough Adjective Check List
Guilford Zimmerman Temperament
    Survey
High School Personality Questionnaire
Kirton Adaption Innovation Inventory
Marlowe Crowne Social Desirability
    Scale
Memory for Designs Test
Millon Clinical Multiaxial Inventory
Minnesota Multiphasic Personality
    Inventory
Mooney Problem Check List
Myers Briggs Type Indicator
NEO Personality Inventory
Nonprojective Personality Measures
Personal Orientation Inventory
Personality Measures
Psychological Screening Inventory
Repression Sensitization Scale
Rod and Frame Test
Rokeach Dogmatism Scale
Rotter Internal External Locus of
    Control Scale
Sensation Seeking Scale
Sixteen Personality Factors
    Questionnaire
State Trait Anxiety Inventory
Taylor Manifest Anxiety Scale
Tennessee Self Concept Scale
Vineland Social Maturity Scale
Zungs Self Rating Depression Scale

Perceptual Measures

Audiometry
Bone Conduction Audiometry
Pain Measurement
Perceptual Measures
Psychophysical Measurement
Rod and Frame Test
Sensorimotor Measures
Speech and Hearing Measures
Stroop Color Word Test
Projective Personality Measures
Bender Gestalt Test
Childrens Apperception Test

Holtzman Inkblot Technique
Human Figures Drawing
Personality Measures
Projective Personality Measures
Projective Techniques
Projective Testing Technique
Rorschach Test
Rosenzweig Picture Frustration Study
Rotter Incomplete Sentences Blank
Sentence Completion Tests
Szondi Test
Thematic Apperception Test
Zulliger Z Test

Testing

Consistency (Measurement)
Content Analysis (Test)
Cultural Test Bias
Cutting Scores
Difficulty Level (Test)
Employment Tests
Evaluation Criteria
Factor Analysis
Factor Structure
Foreign Language Translation
Interview Schedules
Inventories
Item Analysis (Test)
Item Content (Test)
Item Response Theory
Measurement
Performance Tests
Piagetian Tasks
Profiles (Measurement)
Psychometrics
Rating Scales
Score Equating
Scoring (Testing)
Screening Tests
Selection Tests
Semantic Differential
Sociometric Tests
Sociometry
Standard Scores
Standardized Tests
Statistical Validity
Statistical Weighting
Subtests
Test Administration
Test Anxiety
Test Bias
Test Construction
Test Forms
Test Interpretation
Test Items
Test Norms
Test Reliability
Test Scores

Test Standardization
Test Taking
Testing
Testwiseness

Testing Methods

Adaptive Testing
Behavioral Assessment
Biographical Inventories
Body Sway Testing
Clinical Trials
Cloze Testing
Cognitive Assessment
Computer Assisted Testing
Consumer Surveys
Criterion Referenced Tests
Digit Span Testing
Essay Testing
Forced Choice (Testing Method)
Group Testing
Individual Testing
Interview Schedules
Inventories
Likert Scales
Mail Surveys
Matching to Sample
Multidimensional Scaling
Multiple Choice (Testing Method)
Neuropsychological Assessment
Performance Tests
Posttesting
Pretesting
Psychological Assessment
Q Sort Testing Technique
Questionnaires
Rating Scales
Scaling (Testing)
Screening
Screening Tests
Standardized Tests
Surveys
Symptom Checklists
Telephone Surveys
Testing Methods
Verbal Tests

TREATMENT CLUSTER

- Alternative Therapies
- Behavior Modification & Therapy
- Counseling
- Hospitalization & Institutionalization
- Medical & Physical Treatment
- Psychotherapy
- Rehabilitation
- Treatment (General)
- Treatment Facilities

Consult Relationship Section for more information

Alternative Therapies

Acupuncture
Aerobic Exercise
Alternative Medicine
Animal Assisted Therapy
Art Therapy
Autohypnosis
Biofeedback Training
Communication Skills Training
Consciousness Raising Groups
Creative Arts Therapy
Dance Therapy
Dietary Supplements
Encounter Group Therapy
Eye Movement Desensitization Therapy
Faith Healing
Folk Medicine
Guided Imagery
Holistic Health
Human Relations Training
Hypericum Perforatum
Hypnosis
Hypnotherapy
Imagery
Massage
Medicinal Herbs and Plants
Meditation
Milieu Therapy
Morita Therapy
Motivation Training
Movement Therapy
Music Therapy
Narcoanalysis
Online Therapy
Osteopathic Medicine
Pain Management
Phototherapy
Poetry Therapy
Recreation Therapy
Relaxation Therapy
Role Playing
Self Medication
Sensitivity Training
Sex Therapy
Sleep Treatment
Social Skills Training
Sociotherapy
Stress Management
Support Groups
Therapeutic Camps
Therapeutic Social Clubs
Wilderness Experience

Behavior Modification & Therapy

Anger Control
Anxiety Management
Assertiveness Training
Aversion Therapy

Behavior Contracting
Behavior Modification
Behavior Therapy
Biofeedback Training
Cognitive Behavior Therapy
Cognitive Restructuring
Cognitive Techniques
Cognitive Therapy
Conditioning
Contingency Management
Counterconditioning
Covert Sensitization
Differential Reinforcement
Exposure Therapy
Fading (Conditioning)
Functional Analysis
Harm Reduction
Implosive Therapy
Omission Training
Operant Conditioning
Overcorrection
Paradoxical Techniques
Progressive Relaxation Therapy
Rational Emotive Behavior Therapy
Reciprocal Inhibition Therapy
Relaxation Therapy
Response Cost
Self Help Techniques
Self Management
Self Monitoring
Stress Management
Systematic Desensitization Therapy
Time Out
Token Economy Programs

Counseling

AIDS Prevention
Counseling
Counseling Psychology
Couples Therapy
Crisis Intervention
Crisis Intervention Services
Cross Cultural Counseling
Debriefing (Psychological)
Drug Abuse Prevention
Family Intervention
Family Planning
Feminist Therapy
Genetic Counseling
Group Counseling
Health Promotion
Hot Line Services
Marriage Counseling
Microcounseling
Online Therapy
Pastoral Counseling
Peer Counseling
Premarital Counseling

Psychotherapeutic Counseling
Rehabilitation Counseling
Social Casework
Suicide Prevention
Suicide Prevention Centers

Hospitalization & Institutionalization

Aftercare
Client Transfer
Commitment (Psychiatric)
Continuum of Care
Deinstitutionalization
Discharge Planning
Emergency Services
Facility Admission
Facility Discharge
Hospice
Hospital Admission
Hospital Discharge
Hospital Environment
Hospital Programs
Hospitalization
Hospitalized Patients
Hospitals
Institution Visitation
Institutional Release
Institutionalization
Intensive Care
Outpatient Commitment
Outpatient Treatment
Outpatients
Partial Hospitalization
Patient Seclusion
Psychiatric Hospital Admission
Psychiatric Hospital Discharge
Psychiatric Hospital Programs
Psychiatric Hospital Readmission
Psychiatric Hospitalization
Psychiatric Units
Sanatoriums
Therapeutic Community

Medical & Physical Treatment

Acupuncture
Adolescent Psychiatry
Adrenalectomy
Amputation
Artificial Pacemakers
Artificial Respiration
Biological Psychiatry
Biopsy
Blood Transfusion
Castration
Catheterization
Child Psychiatry
Circumcision
Cochlear Implants

Consult Relationship Section for more information

Medical & Physical Treatment — (cont'd)

Colostomy
Commissurotomy
Community Psychiatry
Dental Surgery
Dental Treatment
Dialysis
Drug Augmentation
Drug Self Administration
Drug Therapy
Electroconvulsive Shock Therapy
Electrosleep Treatment
Endocrine Gland Surgery
Evidence Based Practice
Family Medicine
Fertility Enhancement
Geriatric Psychiatry
Health Care Services
Health Maintenance Organizations
Heart Surgery
Hemispherectomy
Hemodialysis
Hormone Therapy
Hypophysectomy
Hysterectomy
Immunization
Induced Abortion
Insulin Shock Therapy
Intensive Care
Laser Irradiation
Male Castration
Massage
Mastectomy
Medical Therapeutic Devices
Medical Treatment (General)
Mobility Aids
Movement Therapy
Narcoanalysis
Neural Transplantation
Neurosurgery
Organ Transplantation
Orthopsychiatry
Ovariectomy
Pain Management
Phototherapy
Physical Therapy
Physical Treatment Methods
Pinealectomy
Plastic Surgery
Polypharmacy
Postsurgical Complications
Prenatal Care
Prescribing (Drugs)
Prescription Drugs
Preventive Medicine
Primary Health Care
Prostheses
Psychiatric Patients
Psychiatry

Psychosomatic Medicine
Psychosurgery
Public Health Services
Pyramidotomy
Radiation Therapy
Self Medication
Sex Change
Shock Therapy
Sleep Treatment
Stereotaxic Techniques
Surgery
Surgical Patients
Sympathectomy
Telemedicine
Thalamotomy
Thyroidectomy
Tractotomy
Transcranial Magnetic Stimulation
Tubal Ligation
Vagotomy
Vasectomy
Vitamin Therapy

Psychotherapy

Adlerian Psychotherapy
Adolescent Psychotherapy
Age Regression (Hypnotic)
Analytical Psychotherapy
Autogenic Training
Bibliotherapy
Brief Psychotherapy
Centering
Child Psychotherapy
Client Centered Therapy
Cognitive Behavior Therapy
Cognitive Restructuring
Cognitive Techniques
Cognitive Therapy
Conjoint Therapy
Consultation Liaison Psychiatry
Cotherapy
Countertransference
Couples Therapy
Crisis Intervention
Debriefing (Psychological)
Dream Analysis
Eclectic Psychotherapy
Enactments
Encounter Group Therapy
Existential Therapy
Experiential Psychotherapy
Expressive Psychotherapy
Family Therapy
Feminist Therapy
Free Association
Geriatric Psychotherapy
Gestalt Therapy
Group Psychotherapy
Guided Imagery
Humanistic Psychotherapy

Hypnotherapy
Individual Psychotherapy
Insight (Psychotherapeutic Process)
Insight Therapy
Integrative Psychotherapy
Interpersonal Psychotherapy
Logotherapy
Marathon Group Therapy
Marriage Counseling
Mirroring
Morita Therapy
Mutual Storytelling Technique
Negative Therapeutic Reaction
Online Therapy
Paradoxical Techniques
Personal Therapy
Persuasion Therapy
Play Therapy
Primal Therapy
Psychoanalysis
Psychodrama
Psychodynamic Psychotherapy
Psychotherapeutic Breakthrough
Psychotherapeutic Counseling
Psychotherapeutic Neutrality
Psychotherapeutic Outcomes
Psychotherapeutic Processes
Psychotherapeutic Resistance
Psychotherapeutic Techniques
Psychotherapeutic Transference
Psychotherapy
Rational Emotive Behavior Therapy
Reality Therapy
Relationship Therapy
Self Analysis
Solution Focused Therapy
Supportive Psychotherapy
Therapeutic Alliance
Therapeutic Community
Therapist Selection
Transactional Analysis

Rehabilitation

Activities of Daily Living
Adaptive Behavior
Aftercare
Alcohol Rehabilitation
Alcoholics Anonymous
Assisted Living
Augmentative Communication
Cochlear Implants
Cognitive Rehabilitation
Criminal Rehabilitation
Detoxification
Disability Management
Drug Rehabilitation
Habilitation
Halfway Houses
Harm Reduction
Independent Living Programs

Consult Relationship Section for more information

Rehabilitation — (cont'd)

Mainstreaming
Maintenance Therapy
Memory Training
Methadone Maintenance
Needle Exchange Programs
Neuropsychological Rehabilitation
Occupational Therapy
Physical Therapy
Prostheses
Psychosocial Rehabilitation
Rehabilitation
Rehabilitation Centers
Rehabilitation Counseling
Self Care Skills
Sheltered Workshops
Smoking Cessation
Speech Therapy
Support Groups
Therapeutic Community
Therapeutic Social Clubs
Twelve Step Programs
Vocational Evaluation
Vocational Rehabilitation
Wilderness Experience
Work Adjustment Training

Treatment (General)

Adolescent Psychiatry
Adult Day Care
Advance Directives
AIDS Prevention
Assisted Suicide
Biological Psychiatry
Biopsychosocial Approach
Caregiver Burden
Caregivers
Case Management
Child Psychiatry
Child Psychology
Childbirth Training
Client Education
Client Participation
Client Records
Client Rights
Client Transfer
Client Treatment Matching
Clinical Psychology
Community Psychiatry
Continuum of Care
Cross Cultural Treatment
Discharge Planning
Drug Abuse Prevention
Drug Education
Early Intervention
Elder Care
Euthanasia
Evidence Based Practice
Family Intervention

Fee for Service
Geriatric Patients
Geriatric Psychiatry
Health Care Costs
Health Care Delivery
Health Care Policy
Health Care Psychology
Health Care Seeking Behavior
Health Care Services
Health Care Utilization
Health Education
Health Insurance
Health Promotion
Health Service Needs
Help Seeking Behavior
Holistic Health
Home Visiting Programs
Hospice
Informed Consent
Integrated Services
Interdisciplinary Treatment Approach
Intervention
Involuntary Treatment
Life Sustaining Treatment
Long Term Care
Maintenance Therapy
Managed Care
Medicaid
Medical Patients
Medical Psychology
Medical Records
Medical Treatment (General)
Medicare
Multimodal Treatment Approach
Nonprescription Drugs
Online Therapy
Optical Aids
Orthopsychiatry
Osteopathic Medicine
Outreach Programs
Palliative Care
Patient Abuse
Patient History
Patient Selection
Patients
Physical Examination
Posttreatment Followup
Prescribing (Drugs)
Prescription Drugs
Primary Mental Health Prevention
Private Practice
Psychiatric Patients
Psychiatry
Psychoeducation
Quality of Care
Quality of Services
Relapse Prevention
Respite Care
Right to Treatment
Self Examination (Medical)
Self Medication

Self Referral
Sex Education
Side Effects (Treatment)
Social Psychiatry
Social Services
Surgical Patients
Telemedicine
Therapeutic Alliance
Therapeutic Processes
Treatment
Treatment Compliance
Treatment Dropouts
Treatment Duration
Treatment Effectiveness Evaluation
Treatment Guidelines
Treatment Outcomes
Treatment Planning
Treatment Refusal
Treatment Termination
Treatment Withholding

Treatment Facilities

Adult Day Care
Assisted Living
Child Guidance Clinics
Clinics
Community Facilities
Community Mental Health Centers
Community Mental Health Services
Day Care Centers
Facility Environment
Group Homes
Halfway Houses
Health Care Services
Health Maintenance Organizations
Home Care
Hospital Environment
Hospitals
Institutional Schools
Intensive Care
Maximum Security Facilities
Mental Health Programs
Mental Health Services
Nursing Homes
Orphanages
Psychiatric Clinics
Psychiatric Hospitals
Psychiatric Units
Public Health Services
Rehabilitation Centers
Residential Care Institutions
Sanatoriums
Shelters
Social Services
Suicide Prevention Centers
Therapeutic Camps
Therapeutic Community
Therapeutic Environment
Treatment Facilities
Walk In Clinics

Consult Relationship Section for more information